MW01234109

NATIVE AMERICANS INFORMATION DIRECTORY

ISSN 1063-9632

NATIVE AMERICANS INFORMATION DIRECTORY

2nd Edition

A Guide to Organizations, Agencies, Institutions, Programs, Publications, Services, and Other Resources Concerned with the Indigenous Peoples of the United States and Canada, including:

- American Indians
- Alaska Natives
- Native Hawaiians
- Aboriginal Canadians

Kenneth Estell, Editor

GALE

DETROIT · LONDON

Kenneth Estell, *Senior Editor*
Sharon Malinowski, *Contributing Editor*
Ashyia N. Henderson & David G. Oblender, *Associate Editors*
Linda S. Hubbard, *Managing Editor, Multicultural Team*

Victoria B. Cariappa, *Research Manager*
Barbara McNeil, *Research Specialist*

Mary Beth Trimper, *Production Director*
Deborah Milliken, *Production Assistant*
Evi Seoud, *Assistant Production Manager*

Cynthia D. Baldwin, *Product Design Manager*
Barbara Yarrow, *Graphic Services Manager*
Gary Leach, *Macintosh Artist*

Eleanor Allison, *Manager, Data Entry Services*
Janine Whitney, *Data Entry Coordinator*
Civie Ann Green & Beverly Jendrowski, *Senior Data Entry Associates*
Cynthia A. Jones & Nancy K. Sheridan, *Data Entry Associates*

Theresa Rocklin, *Manager, Technical Support Services*
Flavio Bezerra, *Programmer/Analyst*

Copyright © 1998
Gale Research
835 Penobscot Bldg.
Detroit, MI 48226-4094

ISBN 0-8103-9116-3

Printed in the United States of America

CONTENTS

INTRODUCTION..vii

USER'S GUIDE... ix

NATIVE AMERICANS INFORMATION DIRECTORY

American Indians
Tribal Communities 1
National Organizations.. 17
Regional, State/Provincial & Local Organizations 24
Federal Government Agencies 30
Federal Domestic Assistance Programs 31
State/Provincial & Local Government Agencies 35
Library Collections... 37
Museums & Other Cultural Facilities... 59
Research Centers 71
Education Programs and Services.. 76
Studies Programs... 87
Scholarships, Fellowships & Loans 90
Awards, Honors & Prizes 97
Publishers 99
Print & Broadcast Media 107
Videos 117
Internet & Online Databases 148

Alaska Natives (Including Indians, Eskimos, and Aleuts)
Tribal Communities 151
National Organizations...160
Regional, State/Provincial & Local Organizations 160
Federal Government Agencies 161
Federal Domestic Assistance Programs..161
State/Provincial & Local Government Agencies 164
Library Collections..164
Museums & Other Cultural Facilities...165
Research Centers 166
Education Programs and Services..167
Studies Programs...168
Scholarships, Fellowships & Loans 168
Awards, Honors & Prizes 169
Publishers 170
Print & Broadcast Media 170
Videos 172
Internet & Online Databases..175

Native Hawaiians (Including descendents of aboriginal inhabitants of the Hawaiian Islands)
National Organizations...177
Regional, State/Provincial & Local Organizations 178
Federal Domestic Assistance Programs..178
State/Provincial & Local Government Agencies 179
Library Collections..179

Museums & Other Cultural Facilities..181
Education Programs and Services...182
Studies Programs...182
Publishers 182
Print & Broadcast Media 184
Internet & Online Databases 184

Aboriginal Canadians (Including Indians, Inuits, and Metis)
Tribal Communities 187
National Organizations..206
Federal Government Agencies 207
State/Provincial & Local Government Agencies 208
Library Collections..209
Museums & Other Cultural Facilities...209
Research Centers 210
Education Programs and Services..212
Studies Programs..212
Scholarships, Fellowships & Loans 212
Awards, Honors & Prizes 213
Publishers 213
Print & Broadcast Media 214
Videos 217
Internet & Online Databases 219

General Resources
National Organizations...221
Regional, State/Provincial & Local Organizations 238
Federal Government Agencies 256
Federal Domestic Assistance Programs..263
State/Provincial & Local Government Agencies 275
Library Collections...288
Research Centers 288
Scholarships, Fellowships & Loans 289
Awards, Honors & Prizes 297
Publishers 298
Print & Broadcast Media 301
Videos 305
Internet & Online Databases..307
Master Name and Keyword Index..313

INTRODUCTION

The more than 2 million descendents of aboriginal inhabitants of North America living in the United States and Canada share a rich and diverse heritage. *Native Americans Information Directory,* a comprehensive guide to resources on and for Native North Americans, helps to facilitate social, cultural, economic, technical, and information exchange among these groups and the many students, tourists, journalists, and researchers interested in them.

This updated edition lists more than 4,400 resources, including:

• Tribal and Native Communities
        • Nonprofit Associations

• Cultural Organizations and Facilities

• Library Collections

• Research Centers

• Scholarships and Awards

• Federal, State/Provincial, and Local Government Agencies

• Publishers

• Print and Broadcast Media

• Videos

• Internet and Online Databases

Covers the Indigenous Peoples of the United States and Canada

Native Americans Information Directory's coverage encompasses native groups whose origins are in the aboriginal peoples of the United States and Canada, including:

American Indians

Alaska Natives (Indians, Eskimos, and Aleuts)

Native Hawaiians (Descendants of aboriginal inhabitants of the Hawaiian Islands)

Aboriginal Canadians (Indians, Inuits, and Metis)

Features of This Edition

Completely Updated—Entries listed in previous edition have been thoroughly updated using the most recent data information available.

Expanded Coverage—This revised edition features new resources and contacts including Internet and online databases, as well as awards, honors, and prizes.

Full Contact Information—Entries include complete contact information, including organization or publication name, address, phone number, and fax and toll-free numbers when available.

Arrangement, Content, and Indexing

Native Americans Information Directory consists of **descriptive listings** and a **Master Name and Keyword Index.**

The **descriptive listings** are organized into five sections, as listed on the "Contents" page. Each section contains up to 17 categories of information sources. Listings typically provide contact information and descriptive data. The **Master Name and Keyword Index** provides one-stop access to all organizations, agencies, programs, publications, and other significant details mentioned within the descriptive listings.

For more information on the content, arrangement, and indexing consult the "User's Guide."

Method of Compilation

Native Americans Information Directory is compiled from a variety of sources. Information was carefully selected from other Gale Research directories, government publications, and lists supplied by other organizations. Telephone research was conducted, in conjunction with secondary source research, to verify contact information.

For specific sources for each type of information consult the "User's Guide."

Comments and Suggestions Welcome

Native Americans Information Directory
835 Penobscot Bldg.
Detroit, MI 48226-4094
Phone: (313)961-2242
Toll-free: 800-347-GALE
Fax: (313) 961-6815

USER'S GUIDE

Native Americans Information Directory consists of :

- Descriptive Listings
- Master Name and Keyword Index

The Descriptive Listings are organized into five sections:

American Indians
Alaska Natives
Aboriginal Canadians
Native Hawaiians
General Resources

The first four sections contain information resources targeted specifically to each group of native peoples; the final section covers resources addressing the needs and concerns of Native North Americans in general.

Each section contains up to 17 categories of information sources, as described below. Entries within each section are grouped by category, then listed alphabetically either by name or title, state or province. Categories appear in the order listed. Entries are numbered sequentially.

1. Tribal Communities

- **Scope:** More than 1100 tribes, bands, and tribal communities in the United States and Canada.
- **Entries include:** Name, address, telephone number, fax and toll-free numbers when available.
- **Arrangement:** Alphabetical by state or province, then alphabetical by city names within state or province.
- **Source:** Original research by editorial staff.
- **Indexed by:** Organization name and significant keywords.

2. National Organizations

- **Scope:** More than 200 nonprofit membership organizations, including social, philanthropic, professional, and business groups concerned with Native American affairs.
- **Entries include:** Organization name, address, telephone number, fax and toll-free numbers when available, name of contact, and a brief description of the organization's purpose and activities.
- **Arrangement:** Alphabetical by organization name.
- **Source:** *Encyclopedia of Associations: National Organizations of the U.S.,* 33rd Edition (published by Gale Research).
- **Indexed by:** Organization name and significant keywords.

3. Regional, State/Provincial and Local Organizations

• **Scope:** More than 400 regional, state/provincial, and local organizations and chapters of selected national organizations, including social, philanthropic, professional, and business groups concerned with Native American affairs.

• **Entries include:** Organization name, address, telephone number, fax and toll-free numbers when available, and name of contact. (For more information on local chapters of national organizations contact the national office listed in Chapter 1.)
• **Arrangement:** Alphabetical by state or province, then alphabetical by city names within state or province.
• **Source:** *Encyclopedia of Associations: Regional, State, and Local Organizations,* 7th Edition (published by Gale Research) and original research by editorial staff.
• **Indexed by:** Organization name and significant keywords.

4. Federal Government Agencies

• **Scope:** 180 units of the federal government in the United States and Canada concerned specifically with Native North Americans or with such issues as civil rights, equal employment opportunity, and other areas of interest to Native Americans.
• **Entries include:** Sponsoring agency and sub-unit name, address, telephone number, fax and toll-free numbers when available, and contact person.
• **Arrangement:** Alphabetical by agency name.
• **Source:** Original research by editorial staff.
• **Indexed by:** Sponsoring agency name and significant keywords.

5. Federal Domestic Assistance Programs

• **Scope:** More than 120 U.S. federally funded programs offering such benefits as business assistance, civil rights assistance, and education.
• **Entries include:** Sponsoring agency and sub-unit name, program name, address, telephone number, fax and toll-free numbers when available, and a brief description of program.
• **Arrangement:** Alphabetical by agency name.
• **Source:** *Catalog of Federal Domestic Assistance.*
• **Indexed by:** Sponsoring agency name, program name, and significant keywords.

6. State/Provincial, and Local Government Agencies

• **Scope:** More than 260 state/provincial and local agencies concerned specifically with Native North Americans or with such issues as civil rights, housing, business development, and education.
• **Entries include:** Sponsoring agency and sub-unit name, address, telephone number, fax and toll-free numbers when available, and contact person.
• **Arrangement:** Alphabetical by state or province, then alphabetical by agency names within state or province.
• **Source:** Original research by editorial staff.
• **Indexed by:** Sponsoring agency name and significant keywords.

7. Library Collections

• **Scope:** 260 libraries with special collections of interest to Native North Americans.
• **Entries include:** Institution name, address, telephone number, fax and toll-free numbers when available, name of contact, and a brief description of the institution's purpose and activities.
• **Arrangement:** Alphabetical by institution name.
• **Source:** *Directory of Special Libraries and Information Centers,* 22nd Edition (published by Gale Research).
• **Indexed by:** Institution name and significant keywords.

8. Museums and Other Cultural Facilities

- **Scope:** More than 240 museums, galleries, and other cultural facilities in the United States and Canada.
- **Entries include:** Organization name, address, telephone number, fax and toll-free numbers when available, and name of contact. Some entries also include a brief description.
- **Arrangement:** Alphabetical by state or province with organizations listed alphabetically within states/province.
- **Source:** Original research by the editorial staff.
- **Indexed by:** Organization name and significant keywords.

9. Research Centers

- **Scope:** 75 university-related and nonprofit organization research centers covering topics of concern to Native North Americans.
- **Entries include:** Institution name, address, telephone number, fax and toll-free numbers when available, name of contact, and a brief description of the institution's purpose and activities.
- **Arrangement:** Alphabetical by institution name.
- **Source:** *Research Centers Directory,* 23rd Edition (published by Gale Research).
- **Indexed by:** Institution name and significant keywords.

10. Educational Programs and Services

- **Scope:** More than 300 educational institutions and programs operated by and for Native North Americans.
- **Entries include:** Institution name, address, telephone number, and fax and toll-free numbers when available.
- **Arrangement:** Alphabetical by state or province within the following three categories: Head Start Programs; Schools; and Community Colleges.
- **Source:** Original research by editorial staff.
- **Indexed by:** Institution name.

11. Studies Programs

- **Scope:** More 80 colleges and universities that offer Native studies programs.
- **Entries include:** Institution name, address, telephone number, and fax and toll-free numbers when available.
- **Arrangement:** Alphabetical by institution name within the following three categories: Two-Year Programs; Four-Year Programs; and Graduate Programs.
- **Source:** Original research by editorial staff.
- **Indexed by:** Institution name.

12. Scholarships, Fellowships, and Loans

- **Scope:** 100 scholarships, fellowships, and loans available to Native North American undergraduate, graduate, and professional school students.
- **Entries include:** Sponsoring organization name, address, telephone number, fax and toll-free numbers when available, and brief description of award.
- **Arrangement:** Alphabetical by award name.
- **Source:** *Scholarships, Fellowships, and Loans,* 1998 Edition (published by Gale Research)
- **Indexed by:** Award name.

13. Awards, Honors, and Prizes

- **Scope:** 20 awards bestowed by government, civic, professional, and business groups.
- **Entries include:** Sponsoring organization name, address, telephone number, fax and toll-free numbers when available, and brief description of award.
- **Arrangement:** Alphabetical by award name.
- **Source:** *Awards, Honors, and Prizes,* 14th Edition (published by Gale Research)
- **Indexed by:** Award name.

14. Publishers

- **Scope:** 210 publishers of books on Native or multicultural issues.
- **Entries include:** Publisher name, address, telephone number, fax and toll-free numbers when available, and a brief description of the publishing program.
- **Arrangement:** Alphabetical by publisher name.
- **Source:** *Publishers Directory,* 19th Edition (published by Gale Research).
- **Indexed by:** Publisher name.

15. Print and Broadcast Media

- **Scope:** 200 newspapers, periodicals, newsletters, and directories with a significant focus on Native North American or minority issues; and radio stations with Native ownership or programming targeted at the Native North American community.
- **Entries include:** Publication title and publisher name or station call letters, address, telephone number, fax and toll-free numbers when available, and a brief description of the publication of station frequency and programming information.
- **Arrangement:** Alphabetical by publication title within five subcategories: (1) Directories, (2) Journals and Magazines, (3) Newsletters, (4) Newspapers, (5) Radio Stations.
- **Source:** *Gale Directory of Publications and Broadcast Media,* 131st Edition, *Newsletters in Print,* 10th Edition, *Directories in Print,* 15th Edition (all published by Gale Research).
- **Indexed by:** Publication title or radio station call letters and significant keywords.

16. Videos

- **Scope:** More than 500 educational and general interest videos on Native North American history and culture.
- **Entries include:** Video title, distributor name, address, telephone number, fax and toll-free numbers when available, program description, release date, run time, format, and acquisition availability.
- **Arrangement:** Alphabetical by video title.
- **Source:** *Video Source Book,* 20th Edition (published by Gale Research).
- **Indexed by:** Video title and significant keywords.

17. Internet and Online Databases

- **Scope:** 60 databases available via the Internet and through online service providers.
- **Entries include:** Database name, host name, address, and telephone number when available; URL, Gopher, or FTP address; description of databases; updating frequency; and fees.
- **Arrangement:** Alphabetical by database name.
- **Source:** *Gale Guide to Internet Database,* 1998 Edition, *Gale Directory of Databases,* 1998 Edition
- **Indexed by:** Database name and significant keywords.

Master Name and Keyword Index

The Master Name and Subject Index provides access to all entries included in Native *Americans Information Directory,* as well as organization names that appear within entry text.

Index references are to book entry numbers rather than page numbers. Entry numbers appear in the index in boldface type if the reference is to the name used at the top of the entry and in lightface if the reference is to a name included in the text.

If several entries have the same parent organization, as is the case with many government agencies, related units are indexed under the parent organization. The names of all federal government agencies are indexed under "U.S." The terms "Indian," "Native American," and "Aboriginal Canadian" have not been used as keywords, since these terms cover all entries in the book.

NATIVE AMERICANS INFORMATION DIRECTORY

American Indians

Tribal Communities

Alabama

★1★
Poarch Band of Creek Indians
5811 Jack Springs Rd.   Ph: (334)368-9136
Atmore, AL 36502   Fax: (334)368-4502
BIA Area Office: Eastern. **BIA Agency:** Choctaw.

Arizona

★2★
Camp Verde Yavapai-Apache
PO Box 1188
Camp Verde, AZ   Ph: (520)567-3649

★3★
Yavapai-Apache Community Council
PO Box 1188
Camp Verde, AZ 86322   Ph: (602)567-3649
BIA Area Office: Phoenix. **BIA Agency:** Truxton Canon.

★4★
Fort McDowell Mohave-Apache
PO Box 17779
Fountain Hills, AZ 85268   Ph: (520)990-0995

★5★
Mohave-Apache Community Council (Fort McDowell)
PO Box 17779   Ph: (602)837-5121
Fountain Hills, AZ 85268   Fax: (602)837-1630
BIA Area Office: Phoenix. **BIA Agency:** Salt River.

★6★
Kaibab Paiute Tribe
Tribal Affairs Bldg.
HC65 Box 2   Ph: (520)643-7245
Fredonia, AZ 86022   Fax: (520)643-7260
BIA Area Office: Phoenix. **BIA Agency:** So. Paiute.

★7★
Hopi Tribal Council
PO Box 123   Ph: (520)734-2441
Kykotsmovi, AZ 86039   Fax: (520)734-2435
BIA Area Office: Phoenix. **BIA Agency:** Hopi.

★8★
Ak Chin Indian Community
Rte. 2, Box 27
Maricopa, AZ 85239   Ph: (520)568-2227
BIA Area Office: Phoenix. **BIA Agency:** Pima.

★9★
Colorado River Tribal Council
Rte. 1, Box 23-B   Ph: (520)669-9211
Parker, AZ 85344   Fax: (520)669-5675
BIA Area Office: Phoenix. **BIA Agency:** Colorado River.

★10★
Hualapai Tribal Council
PO Box 168
Peach Springs, AZ 86434   Ph: (520)769-2216
BIA Area Office: Phoenix. **BIA Agency:** Truxton Canon.

★11★
Yavapai-Prescott Tribe
PO Box 348   Ph: (520)445-8790
Prescott, AZ 86301-2038   Fax: (520)778-9445
BIA Area Office: Phoenix. **BIA Agency:** Truxton Canon.

★12★
Gila River Indian Community
PO Box 97   Ph: (520)562-3311
Sacaton, AZ 85247   Fax: (520)562-3422
BIA Area Office: Phoenix.

★13★
San Carlos Apache Tribe
PO Box 0   Ph: (520)475-2361
San Carlos, AZ 85550   Fax: (520)475-2566
BIA Area Office: Phoenix. **BIA Agency:** San Carlos.

★14★
Salt River Pima-Maricopa Indian Community
Rte. 1, Box 21   Ph: (520)941-7277
Scottsdale, AZ 85256   Fax: (520)945-3698
BIA Area Office: Phoenix. **BIA Agency:** Salt River.

★15★
Tohono O'Odham Nation
PO Box 837
Sells, AZ 85634   Ph: (520)383-2221
BIA Area Office: Phoenix. **BIA Agency:** Papago.

★16★
Cocopah Tribe
15th and Ave. G   Ph: (520)627-2102
Somerton, AZ 85350   Fax: (520)627-3173
BIA Area Office: Phoenix. **BIA Agency:** Ft. Yuma.

★17★
Havasupai Tribe
PO Box 10   Ph: (520)448-2961
Supai, AZ 86435   Fax: (520)448-2551
BIA Area Office: Phoenix. **BIA Agency:** Truxton Conon.

★18★
San Juan Southern Paiute Tribe
PO Box 2656
Tuba City, AZ 86045   Ph: (520)283-4583
BIA Area Office: Phoenix. **BIA Agency:** So. Paiute.

★19★
Pascua Yaqui Tribe
7474 S. Camino de Oeste   Ph: (520)883-5000
Tucson, AZ 85746   Fax: (520)883-5014
BIA Area Office: Phoenix. **BIA Agency:** Salt River.

★20★
White Mountain Apache Tribe
PO Box 700   Ph: (520)338-4346
Whiteriver, AZ 85941   Fax: (520)338-4778
BIA Area Office: Phoenix. **BIA Agency:** Ft. Apache.

★21★
Navajo Nation
PO Box 9000   Ph: (520)871-4941
Window Rock, AZ 86515   Fax: (520)871-4025
BIA Area Office: Navajo. **BIA Agency:** Navajo.

★22★
Quechan Tribe (Fort Yuma)
PO Box 11352
Yuma, AZ 85364   Ph: (619)572-0213
BIA Area Office: Phoenix. **BIA Agency:** Ft. Yuma.

──────── **California** ────────

★23★
Cuyapaipe Band of Mission Indians
2271 Alpine Blvd.
Alpine, CA 91901   Ph: (619)455-6315
BIA Area Office: Sacramento. **BIA Agency:** So. Calif.

★24★
Sycuan Tribe
PO Box 520
Alpine, CA 92001   Ph: (619)445-2613
BIA Area Office: Sacramento. **BIA Agency:** So. Calif.

★25★
Viejas Tribe
PO Box 908
Alpine, CA 92001   Ph: (619)445-3810
BIA Area Office: Sacramento. **BIA Agency:** So. Calif.

★26★
Alturas Rancheria
PO Box 1035
Alturas, CA 96101   Ph: (916)233-5571
BIA Area Office: Sacramento. **BIA Agency:** No. Calif.

★27★
Cahuilla Band of Mission Indians
PO Box 391760
Anza, CA 92539-1760   Ph: (909)763-5549
BIA Area Office: Sacramento. **BIA Agency:** So. Calif.

★28★
Ramona Band of Cahuilla Indians
3940 Cary Rd.
Anza, CA 92539   Ph: (909)763-0371
BIA Area Office: Sacramento. **BIA Agency:** So. Calif.

★29★
Big Sandy Rancheria
PO Box 337
Auberry, CA 93602   Ph: (209)855-4003
BIA Area Office: Sacramento. **BIA Agency:** Cent. Calif.

★30★
Augustine Band of Mission Indians
1185 Hargrave St.
Banning, CA 92220   Ph: (909)922-9727

★31★
Morongo Band of Mission Indians
11581 Potrero Rd.   Ph: (909)849-4697
Banning, CA 92220   Fax: (909)849-4698
BIA Area Office: Sacramento. **BIA Agency:** So. Calif.

★32★
Benton Paiute Reservation
Star Rte. 4, Box 56-A
Benton, CA 93512   Ph: (619)933-2321
BIA Area Office: Sacramento. **BIA Agency:** Cent. Calif.

★33★
Big Bend Rancheria
PO Box 255
Big Bend, CA 96001   Ph: (916)337-6605

★34★
Big Pine Reservation
PO Box 700   Ph: (619)938-2003
Big Pine, CA 93513   Fax: (619)938-2942
BIA Area Office: Sacramento. **BIA Agency:** Cent. Calif.

★35★
Bishop Reservation Tribe
PO Box 548   Ph: (619)873-3584
Bishop, CA 93515   Fax: (619)873-4143
BIA Area Office: Sacramento. **BIA Agency:** Cent. Calif.

★36★
Blue Lake Rancheria
PO Box 428
Blue Lake, CA 95525   Ph: (707)668-5101
BIA Area Office: Sacramento. **BIA Agency:** No. Calif.

★37★
Manzanita General Council
PO Box 1302
Boulevard, CA 91905   Ph: (619)766-4930
BIA Area Office: Sacramento. **BIA Agency:** So. Calif.

★38★
Bridgeport Indian Colony
PO Box 37
Bridgeport, CA 93517   Ph: (619)932-7083
BIA Area Office: Sacramento. **BIA Agency:** Cent. Calif.

★39★
Rumsey Rancheria
PO Box 18
Brooks, CA 95606   Ph: (916)796-3400
BIA Area Office: Sacramento. **BIA Agency:** Cent. Calif.

★40★
Pit River Tribe
PO Drawer 1570
Burney, CA 96013   Ph: (916)335-5421
BIA Area Office: Sacramento. **BIA Agency:** No. Calif.

★41★
Campo Band of Mission Indians
1779 Campo Truck Trail   Ph: (909)276-6624
Campo, CA 91606   Fax: (909)276-6641
BIA Area Office: Sacramento. **BIA Agency:** So. Calif.

★42★
Cedarville Rancheria
PO Box 126
Cedarville, CA 96104   Ph: (916)233-2439
BIA Area Office: Sacramento. **BIA Agency:** No. Calif.

★43★
Mechoopda Maidu Indian Tribe of Chico Rancheria
3006 Esplanada St., Ste. H & I   Ph: (916)899-8922
Chico, CA 95973   Fax: (916)899-8517

★44★
Cortina Rancheria
PO Box 7470
Citrus Heights, CA 95621-7470   Ph: (916)726-7118
BIA Area Office: Sacramento. **BIA Agency:** Cent. Calif.

★45★
Elem Indian Colony of Pomo Indians
PO Box 618
Clearlake Oaks, CA 95423   Ph: (707)998-2549
BIA Area Office: Sacramento. **BIA Agency:** Cent. Calif.

★46★
North Fork Band of Mono Indians
133 Sierra
Clovis, CA 93612   Ph: (209)299-3729

★47★
Picayune Rancheria
PO Box 269   Ph: (209)683-6633
Coarsegold, CA 93614   Fax: (209)683-0599
BIA Area Office: Sacramento. **BIA Agency:** Cent. Calif.

★48★
Antelope Valley Paiute Tribe
Camp Antelope #11
Coleville, CA 96107   Ph: (916)495-2801

★49★
Colusa Rancheria
PO Box 8
Colusa, CA 95932   Ph: (916)458-8231
BIA Area Office: Sacramento. **BIA Agency:** Cent. Calif.

★50★
Round Valley Reservation
PO Box 448
Covelo, CA 95428   Ph: (707)983-6126
BIA Area Office: Sacramento. **BIA Agency:** Cent. Calif.

★51★
Elk Valley Rancheria
PO Box 1042
375 Wyentae St.   Ph: (707)464-4680
Crescent City, CA 95531   Fax: (707)464-4519
BIA Area Office: Sacramento. **BIA Agency:** No. Calif.

★52★
Timbisha-Sha Western Shoshone Tribe
PO Box 206   Ph: (619)786-2374
Death Valley, CA 92328   Fax: (619)786-2375
BIA Area Office: Sacramento. **BIA Agency:** Cent. Calif.

★53★
Dunlap Band of Mono Indians
PO Box 344
Dunlap, CA 93621

★54★
Grindstone Rancheria
PO Box 63   Ph: (916)566-7121
Elk Creek, CA 95939   Fax: (916)566-7510
BIA Area Office: Sacramento. **BIA Agency:** Cent. Calif.

★55★
Quartz Valley Reservation
PO Box 737   Ph: (916)467-3307
Etna, CA 96027   Fax: (916)467-3466
BIA Area Office: Sacramento. **BIA Agency:** No. Calif.

★56★
Bear River Band of Rohnerville Rancheria
PO Box 108   Ph: (707)443-6150
Eureka, CA 95502   Fax: (707)442-6403

★57★
Chilula Tribe
PO Box 724
Eureka, CA 95502

★58★
Rohnerville Rancheria
PO Box 3443
Eureka, CA 99501   Ph: (707)442-3931
BIA Area Office: Sacramento. **BIA Agency:** No. Calif.

★59★
Yurok Tribe
517 3rd St., Ste. 18   Ph: (707)444-0433
Eureka, CA 95501   Free: 800-848-8765
BIA Area Office: Sacramento. **BIA Agency:** No. Calif.

★60★
Fort Bidwell Reservation
PO Box 127
Fort Bidwell, CA 96112   Ph: (916)279-6310
BIA Area Office: Sacramento. **BIA Agency:** No. Calif.

★61★
Table Mountain Rancheria
PO Box 243
Friant, CA 93626   Ph: (209)849-4823
BIA Area Office: Sacramento. **BIA Agency:** Cent. Calif.

★62★
Dry Creek Rancheria
PO. Box 607
Geyserville, CA 95441   Ph: (707)857-3045
BIA Area Office: Sacramento. **BIA Agency:** Cent. Calif.

★63★
Greenville Rancheria
Box 237   Ph: (916)528-9000
Greenville, CA 95947   Fax: (916)528-9002
BIA Area Office: Sacramento. **BIA Agency:** Cent. Calif.

★64★
Karuk Tribe of California
PO Box 1016
Happy Camp, CA 96039   Ph: (916)493-5305
BIA Area Office: Sacramento. **BIA Agency:** No. Calif.

★65★
Chemehuevi Tribe
PO Box 1976   Ph: (619)858-4531
Havasu Lake, CA 92363   Fax: (619)858-5400
BIA Area Office: Phoenix. **BIA Agency:** Colorado River.

★66★
Santa Rosa Reservation
325 N. Western Ave.
Hemet, CA 92343   Ph: (714)925-7190
BIA Area Office: Sacramento. **BIA Agency:** So. Calif.

★67★
San Manuel Tribe
2439 N. Victoria Ave.
Highland, CA 92346   Ph: (714)862-2439
BIA Area Office: Sacramento. **BIA Agency:** So. Calif.

★68★
Indian Canyon Nation of Costanoan People
PO Box 28
Hollister, CA 95024-0028   Ph: (408)637-4238

★69★
Hoopa Valley Indian Reservation
PO Box 1348
Hoopa, CA 95546   Ph: (916)625-4211
BIA Area Office: Sacramento. **BIA Agency:** No. Calif.

★70★
Hopland Reservation
PO Box 610   Ph: (707)744-1647
Hopland, CA 95449   Fax: (707)744-1506
BIA Area Office: Sacramento. **BIA Agency:** Cent. Calif.

★71★
Fort Independence Reservation
PO Box 67
Independence, CA 93526   Ph: (619)878-2126
BIA Area Office: Sacramento. **BIA Agency:** Cent. Calif.

★72★
Cabazon Indians of California
84-245 Indio Springs Dr.   Ph: (619)342-2593
Indio, CA 92201   Fax: (619)342-7886
BIA Area Office: Sacramento. **BIA Agency:** So. Calif.

★73★
Buena Vista Rancheria
4650 Coalmine Rd.   Ph: (916)392-5003
Ione, CA 95640   Fax: (916)424-1077
BIA Area Office: Sacramento. **BIA Agency:** Cent. Calif.

★74★
Jackson Rancheria
PO Box 429
16070 Miwak Dr.   Ph: (209)223-1935
Jackson, CA 95642   Fax: (209)223-5366
BIA Area Office: Sacramento. **BIA Agency:** Cent. Calif.

★75★
Chicken Ranch Rancheria
PO Box 1699
Jamestown, CA 95327   Ph: (209)984-4806
BIA Area Office: Sacramento. **BIA Agency:** Cent. Calif.

★76★
Jamul Band of Mission Indians
PO Box 612
Jamul, CA 92035   Ph: (614)669-4785
BIA Area Office: Sacramento. **BIA Agency:** So. Calif.

★77★
Kern Valley Indian Community
PO Box 168
Kernville, CA 93238   Ph: (619)376-4240

★78★
Salinan Nation
PO Box 403
King City, CA 93930   Ph: (916)458-4551

★79★
Coast Indian Community of the Resighini Rancheria
PO Box 529   Ph: (707)484-2431
Klamath, CA 95548   Fax: (707)484-2431
BIA Area Office: Sacramento. **BIA Agency:** No. Calif.

★80★
Big Valley Rancheria
PO Box 955   Ph: (707)263-3924
Lakeport, CA 95453   Fax: (707)263-3977
BIA Area Office: Sacramento. **BIA Agency:** Cent. Calif.

★81★
Barona Rancheria
1095 Barona Rd.   Ph: (619)443-6612
Lakeside, CA 92040   Fax: (619)443-6613
BIA Area Office: Sacramento. **BIA Agency:** So. Calif.

★82★
La Posta Band
1064 Barona Rd.
Lakeside, CA 92040   Ph: (619)561-2924
BIA Area Office: Sacramento. **BIA Agency:** So. Calif.

★83★
Laytonville Rancheria
PO Box 1239   Ph: (707)984-6197
Laytonville, CA 95454   Fax: (707)984-6201
BIA Area Office: Sacramento. **BIA Agency:** Cent. Calif.

★84★
Mono Lake Indian Community
PO Box 237
Lee Vining, CA 93541   Ph: (619)647-6471

★85★
Santa Rosa Rancheria
16835 Alkali Dr.   Ph: (209)924-1278
Lemoore, CA 93245   Fax: (209)924-8949
BIA Area Office: Sacramento. **BIA Agency:** Cent. Calif.

★86★
Table Bluff Rancheria
PO Box 519   Ph: (707)733-5583
Loleta, CA 95551   Fax: (707)733-5601
BIA Area Office: Sacramento. **BIA Agency:** No. Calif.

★87★
Coastal Band of Chumash
4093 Draco Dr.
Lompoc, CA 93436   Ph: (805)733-9002

★88★
Lone Pine Reservation
Star Rte. 1-1101 S. Main St.
Lone Pine, CA 93545   Ph: (619)876-5414
BIA Area Office: Sacramento. **BIA Agency:** Cent. Calif.

★89★
Chukchansi Yokotch of Mariposa
4962 Watt Rd.
Mariposa, CA 95538

★90★
Woodfords Community Council
96 Washoe Blvd.
Markleeville, CA 96120   Ph: (916)694-2170
BIA Area Office: Phoenix. **BIA Agency:** W. Nevada.

★91★
Middletown Rancheria
PO Box 1035   Ph: (707)987-3670
Middletown, CA 95461   Fax: (707)987-9015
BIA Area Office: Sacramento. **BIA Agency:** Cent. Calif.

★92★
Coastanoan Band of Carmel Mission Indians
PO Box 1657
Monrovia, CA 91016

★93★
Fort Mohave Tribe
500 Merriman Ave.
Needles, CA 92363   Ph: (619)326-4591
BIA Area Office: Phoenix. **BIA Agency:** Colorado River.

★94★
Robinson Rancheria
PO Box 1119   Ph: (707)275-0527
Nice, CA 95464   Fax: (707)275-9132
BIA Area Office: Sacramento. **BIA Agency:** Cent. Calif.

★95★
Berry Creek Rancheria
1779 Mitchell Ave.
Oroville, CA 95966   Ph: (916)534-3859
BIA Area Office: Sacramento. **BIA Agency:** No. Calif.

★96★
Mooretown Rancheria
PO Box 1842   Ph: (916)533-3625
Oroville, CA 95965   Fax: (916)533-3680
BIA Area Office: Sacramento. **BIA Agency:** Cent. Calif.

★97★
Pala Band of Mission Indians
PO Box 43   Ph: (619)742-3784
Pala, CA 92059   Fax: (619)742-1411
BIA Area Office: Sacramento. **BIA Agency:** So. Calif.

★98★
Agua Caliente Tribe
960 E. Tahquitz Way, No. 106
Palm Springs, CA 92262   Ph: (619)325-5673
BIA Area Office: Sacramento. **BIA Agency:** Palm Springs.

★99★
Twenty Nine Palms
58 S. El Ceilo, Apt. 2
Palm Springs, CA 92262   Ph: (619)322-1914
BIA Area Office: Sacramento. **BIA Agency:** So. Calif.

★100★
Pauma Band of Mission Indians
PO Box 86   Ph: (619)742-1289
Pauma Valley, CA 92061   Fax: (619)742-3422
BIA Area Office: Sacramento. **BIA Agency:** So. Calif.

★101★
Manchester/Point Arena Rancheria
PO Box 623
Point Arena, CA 95468   Ph: (707)882-2788
BIA Area Office: Sacramento. **BIA Agency:** Cent. Calif.

★102★
Tule River Reservation
PO Box 589   Ph: (209)781-4271
Porterville, CA 93257   Fax: (209)781-4610
BIA Area Office: Sacramento. **BIA Agency:** Cent. Calif.

★103★
Redding Rancheria
2200 Rancheria Rd.   Ph: (916)225-8979
Redding, CA 96001   Fax: (916)241-1879
BIA Area Office: Sacramento. **BIA Agency:** No. Calif.

★104★
Coyote Valley Reservation
PO Box 39   Ph: (707)485-9723
Redwood Valley, CA 95470-0039   Fax: (707)468-5615
BIA Area Office: Sacramento. **BIA Agency:** Cent. Calif.

★105★
Redwood Valley Rancheria
PO Box 499
Redwood Valley, CA 95470   Ph: (707)485-0361
BIA Area Office: Sacramento. **BIA Agency:** Cent. Calif.

★106★
Upper Lake Rancheria
PO Box 20272
Sacramento, CA 95820   Ph: (916)371-5637
BIA Area Office: Sacramento. **BIA Agency:** Cent. Calif.

★107★
North Fork Rancheria
3027 Clement St., No. 2   Ph: (209)877-2461
San Francisco, CA 94121   Fax: (209)877-2467
BIA Area Office: Sacramento. **BIA Agency:** Cent. Calif.

★108★
Soboba
PO Box 562
San Jacinto, CA 92383   Ph: (714)654-2765
BIA Area Office: Sacramento. **BIA Agency:** So. Calif.

★109★
Muwekma Ohlone Tribe
226 Airport Parkway, Ste. 630
San Jose, CA 95110-1029   Ph: (408)441-6473

★110★
Juaneno Band of Mission Indians 84-A
31877 Del Obispo, Ste. 106-A   Ph: (714)488-3484
San Juan Capistrano, CA 92675   Fax: (714)488-3294

★111★
Juaneno Band of Mission Indians 84-B
PO Box 25628   Ph: (714)841-0441
Santa Ana, CA 92799   Fax: (714)848-2951

★112★
Santa Ynez Tribe
PO Box 517
Santa Ynez, CA 93460   Ph: (805)688-7997
BIA Area Office: Sacramento. **BIA Agency:** So. Calif.

★113★
Inaja and Cosmit Band of Mission Indians
PO Box 491
Santa Ysabel, CA 92070   Ph: (619)765-1993
BIA Area Office: Sacramento. **BIA Agency:** So. Calif.

★114★
Mesa Grande Band of Mission Indians
PO Box 270
Santa Ysabel, CA 92070   Ph: (619)282-9650
BIA Area Office: Sacramento. **BIA Agency:** So. Calif.

★115★
Santa Ysabel Tribe
PO Box 126
Santa Ysabel, CA 92070   Ph: (619)765-0845
BIA Area Office: Sacramento. **BIA Agency:** So. Calif.

★116★
Shingle Springs Rancheria
PO Box 1340
Shingle Springs, CA 95682   Ph: (916)391-7822
BIA Area Office: Sacramento. **BIA Agency:** Cent. Calif.

★117★
Smith River Rancheria
250 N. Indian Rd.   Ph: (707)487-9255
Smith River, CA 95567-9525   Fax: (707)487-0930
BIA Area Office: Sacramento. **BIA Agency:** No. Calif.

★118★
Cloverdale Rancheria
4555 Redwood Hwy.
South Petaluma, CA 95424   Ph: (707)894-9377
BIA Area Office: Sacramento. **BIA Agency:** Cent. Calif.

★119★
Esselen Nation
PO Box 7383
Spreckels, CA 93962

★120★
Stewarts Point Rancheria
PO Box 54
Stewarts Point, CA 95480   Ph: (707)795-2594
BIA Area Office: Sacramento. **BIA Agency:** Cent. Calif.

★121★
Susanville Rancheria
PO Drawer U
Susanville, CA 96130   Ph: (916)257-6264
BIA Area Office: Sacramento. **BIA Agency:** No. Calif.

★122★
Winnemucca Colony
C/O 420 Pardde
Susanville, CA 96130   Ph: (916)257-7093
BIA Area Office: Phoenix. **BIA Agency:** W. Nevada.

★123★
Pechanga Band of Mission Indians
PO Box 1477   Ph: (919)676-2768
Temecula, CA 92390   Fax: (909)695-1778
BIA Area Office: Sacramento. **BIA Agency:** So. Calif.

★124★
Torres-Martinez Tribe
66-725 Martinez Rd.
Thermal, CA 92274   Ph: (619)397-0300
BIA Area Office: Sacramento. **BIA Agency:** So. Calif.

★125★
Cold Springs Rancheria
PO Box 209   Ph: (209)855-5043
Tollhouse, CA 93667   Fax: (209)855-8359
BIA Area Office: Sacramento. **BIA Agency:** Cent. Calif.

★126★
Big Lagoon Rancheria
PO Drawer 3060   Ph: (707)826-2079
Trinidad, CA 95570   Fax: (707)826-1737
BIA Area Office: Sacramento. **BIA Agency:** No. Calif.

★127★
Trinidad Rancheria
PO Box 589
Trinidad, CA 95570   Ph: (707)677-0211
BIA Area Office: Sacramento. **BIA Agency:** No. Calif.

★128★
Tuolumne Rancheria
PO Box 696
Tuolumne, CA 94379   Ph: (209)928-3475
BIA Area Office: Sacramento. **BIA Agency:** Cent. Calif.

★129★
Pinoleville Rancheria
367 N. State St., Ste. 204
Ukiah, CA 95482   Ph: (707)463-1454
BIA Area Office: Sacramento. **BIA Agency:** Cent. Calif.

★130★
Potter Valley Rancheria
755 B. El Rio St.
Ukiah, CA 95482   Ph: (707)468-7494
BIA Area Office: Sacramento. **BIA Agency:** Cent. Calif.

★131★
Sherwood Valley Rancheria
2141 S. State St.
Ukiah, CA 95482   Ph: (707)468-1337
BIA Area Office: Sacramento. **BIA Agency:** Cent. Calif.

★132★
La Jolla Band
Star Rte., Box 158   Ph: (619)742-3771
Valley Center, CA 92082   Fax: (619)742-3772
BIA Area Office: Sacramento. **BIA Agency:** So. Calif.

★133★
Rincon Band of Mission Indians
PO Box 68   Ph: (619)749-1051
Valley Center, CA 92083   Fax: (619)749-8901
BIA Area Office: Sacramento. **BIA Agency:** So. Calif.

★134★
San Pasqual Tribe
PO Box 365
Valley Center, CA 92082   Ph: (619)749-3200
BIA Area Office: Sacramento. **BIA Agency:** So. Calif.

★135★
Los Coyotes Band of Mission Indians
PO Box 249   Ph: (619)782-3269
Warner Springs, CA 92086   Fax: (619)782-2701
BIA Area Office: Sacramento. **BIA Agency:** So. Calif.

★136★
Paskenta Band of Nomlaki Indians
PO Box 988
Williams, CA 95987   Ph: (619)742-1289

★137★
Amah Mutsum Band of Mission Indians
789 Canada Rd.
Woodside, CA 94062   Ph: (415)851-7747

──────────── **Colorado** ────────────

★138★
Southern Ute Tribe
PO Box 737
Ignacio, CO 81137   Ph: (970)563-0100
BIA Area Office: Albuquerque. **BIA Agency:** Southern Ute.

★139★
Ute Mountain Ute
General Delivery
Towaoc, CO 81344   Ph: (970)565-3751
BIA Area Office: Albuquerque. **BIA Agency:** Ute Mountain.

──────────── **Connecticut** ────────────

★140★
Mashantucket Pequot Nation
PO Box 2060
Indian Town Rd.   Ph: (860)536-2681
Ledyard, CT 06339-2060   Fax: (860)536-3412

★141★
Mashantucket Pequot Tribe
PO Box 160   Ph: (203)536-2681
Ledyard, CT 06339   Fax: (203)572-0421
BIA Area Office: Eastern. **BIA Agency:** Eastern.

★142★
Paucatuck Eastern Pequot Tribe
935 Lantern Hill Rd.
Ledyard, CT 06339   Ph: (203)572-2953

★143★
Schaghticoke Indian Tribe
626 Washington Rd.
Woodbury, CT 06798   Ph: (203)263-0439

──────────── **Florida** ────────────

★144★
Seminole Tribe of Florida
6300 Stirling Rd.   Ph: (954)966-6300
Hollywood, FL 33024   Fax: (954)967-3486
BIA Area Office: Eastern. **BIA Agency:** Seminole.

★145★
Miccosukee Tribe of Florida
PO Box 440021, Tamiami Sta.   Ph: (305)223-8380
Miami, FL 33144   Fax: (305)223-1011
BIA Area Office: Eastern. **BIA Agency:** Eastern.

──────────── **Idaho** ────────────

★146★
Northwestern Band of Shoshone Nation
PO Box 637   Ph: (208)745-7401
Blackfoot, ID 99924   Fax: (208)785-2206
BIA Area Office: Portland. **BIA Agency:** Ft. Hall.

★147★
Kootenai Tribe
PO Box 1269   Ph: (208)267-3519
Bonners Ferry, ID 83805   Fax: (208)267-2762
BIA Area Office: Portland. **BIA Agency:** No. Idaho.

★148★
Fort Hall Community
PO Box 306   Ph: (208)238-3700
Fort Hall, ID 83203   Fax: (208)237-0796
BIA Area Office: Portland. **BIA Agency:** Ft. Hall.

★149★
Nez Perce Tribal Executive Committee
PO Box 305   Ph: (208)843-2253
Lapwai, ID 83540   Fax: (208)843-2036
BIA Area Office: Portland. **BIA Agency:** No. Idaho.

★150★
Coeur D'Alene Tribe
Plummer, ID 83851-9704   Ph: (208)686-1800
                                   Fax: (208)686-1182
BIA Area Office: Portland. **BIA Agency:** No. Idaho.

──────────── **Indiana** ────────────

★151★
Miami Nation of Indians
PO Box 41
Peru, IN 46970   Ph: (765)473-9631

──────────── **Kansas** ────────────

★152★
Kickapoo Tribe of Kansas
PO Box 271   Ph: (913)486-2131
Horton, KS 66349-0271   Fax: (913)486-2801
BIA Area Office: Anadarko. **BIA Agency:** Horton.

★153★
Prairie Band Potawatomi Tribe
14880 K Rd.   Ph: (913)966-2255
Mayetta, KS 66539   Fax: (913)966-2144
BIA Area Office: Anadarko. **BIA Agency:** Horton.

★154★
Sac and Fox Tribe
RR 1, Box 60   Ph: (913)742-7471
Reserve, KS 66434   Fax: (913)742-3785
BIA Area Office: Anadarko. **BIA Agency:** Horton.

★155★
Iowa Tribe of Kansas and Nebraska
Rte.1, Box 58A   Ph: (913)595-3258
White Cloud, KS 66094-9624   Fax: (913)595-6610
BIA Area Office: Anadarko. **BIA Agency:** Horton.

Louisiana

★156★
Chitimacha Tribe of Louisiana
PO Box 661   Ph: (318)923-7215
Charenton, LA 70523-0661   Fax: (318)923-6848
BIA Area Office: Eastern. **BIA Agency:** Eastern.

★157★
Coushatta Tribe of Louisiana
PO Box 818   Ph: (318)584-2261
Elton, LA 70532   Fax: (318)584-2998
BIA Area Office: Eastern. **BIA Agency:** Eastern.

★158★
Jena Band of Choctaw Indians
PO Drawer 1367   Ph: (318)992-2717
Jena, LA 71342   Fax: (318)992-8244

★159★
Tunica-Biloxi Tribe of Louisiana
PO Box 311   Ph: (318)253-9767
Marksville, LA 71351   Fax: (318)253-9791
BIA Area Office: Eastern. **BIA Agency:** Eastern.

Maine

★160★
Houlton Band of Maliseet Indians
RR3, Box 450   Ph: (207)532-4273
Houlton, ME 04730-9514   Fax: (207)532-2660
BIA Area Office: Eastern. **BIA Agency:** Eastern.

★161★
Penobscot Indian Nation
6 River Road Indian Island Reservation   Ph: (207)827-7776
Old Town, ME 04468   Fax: (207)827-6042
BIA Area Office: Eastern. **BIA Agency:** Eastern.

★162★
Passamaquoddy Tribe
PO Box 343   Ph: (207)853-2600
Perry, ME 04667   Fax: (207)853-6039
BIA Area Office: Eastern. **BIA Agency:** Eastern.

★163★
Aroostook Band of Micmacs
521-D Mani St.
PO Box 772   Ph: (207)764-1972
Presque Isle, ME 04769   Fax: (207)764-7667

★164★
Passamaquoddy Tribe of Maine
Indian Township Reservation
PO Box 301   Ph: (207)796-2301
Princeton, ME 04668   Fax: (207)796-5256
BIA Area Office: Eastern. **BIA Agency:** Eastern.

Massachusetts

★165★
Wampanoag Tribe of Gay Head
20 Black Brook Rd.   Ph: (508)645-9265
Gay Head, MA 02535-9701   Fax: (508)645-3790
BIA Area Office: Eastern. **BIA Agency:** Eastern.

★166★
Mashpee Wampanoag Tribe
PO Box 1048
Mashpee, MA 02649   Ph: (508)477-0208

★167★
Quinsigamond Band of the Nipmucs
630 Pleasant St.
Worcester, MA 01602   Free: 800-584-6040

Michigan

★168★
Keweenaw Bay Tribe
Center Bldg.
Rte.1, Box 45   Ph: (906)353-6623
Baraga, MI 49908   Fax: (906)353-7450
BIA Area Office: Minneapolis. **BIA Agency:** Michigan.

★169★
Pokagon Band of Potawatomi Indians
PO Box 180
901 Spruce St.
Dowagiac, MI 36502   Ph: (616)782-8998

★170★
Little River Band of Ottawa Indians
409 Water St.
Manistee, MI 49770   Ph: (616)723-8288

★171★
Saginaw Chippewa Tribe
7070 E. Broadway Rd.   Ph: (517)772-5700
Mt. Pleasant, MI 48858   Fax: (517)772-3508
BIA Area Office: Minneapolis. **BIA Agency:** Michigan.

★172★
Sault Ste. Marie Chippewa Tribe
206 Greenough St.   Ph: (906)635-6050
Sault Ste. Marie, MI 49783   Fax: (906)635-0741
BIA Area Office: Minneapolis. **BIA Agency:** Michigan.

★173★
Grand Traverse Tribal Council
Peshawbestown Community Center
2605 NW Bayshore Dr.   Ph: (616)271-3538
Suttons Bay, MI 49682   Fax: (616)271-4230
BIA Area Office: Minneapolis. **BIA Agency:** Michigan.

★174★
Lac Vieux Desert Band of Lake Superior Chippewa Indians of Michigan
PO Box 249 Choate Rd.   Ph: (906)358-4577
Watersmeet, MI 49969   Fax: (906)358-4785
BIA Area Office: Minneapolis. **BIA Agency:** Michigan.

★175★
Hannahville Indian Community
N14911 Hannahville Blvd. Rd.   Ph: (906)466-2342
Wilson, MI 49896-9728   Fax: (906)466-2933
BIA Area Office: Minneapolis. **BIA Agency:** Michigan.

Minnesota

★176★
Leech Lake Reservation (Chippewa)
Rte.3, Box 100   Ph: (218)335-2207
Cass Lake, MN 56633   Fax: (218)335-8309
BIA Area Office: Minneapolis. **BIA Agency:** Minnesota.

★177★
Minnesota Chippewa Tribal Executive Committee
Box 217C   Ph: (218)335-8581
Cass Lake, MN 56633   Fax: (218)335-6562
BIA Area Office: Minneapolis. **BIA Agency:** Minnesota.

★178★
Fond du Lac (Chippewa)
105 University Rd.   Ph: (218)879-4593
Cloquet, MN 55720   Fax: (218)897-4164
BIA Area Office: Minneapolis. **BIA Agency:** Minnesota.

★179★
Grand Portage Reservation Business Committee
(Chippewa)
PO Box 428   Ph: (218)475-2279
Grand Portage, MN 55605   Fax: (218)475-2284
BIA Area Office: Minneapolis. **BIA Agency:** Minnesota.

★180★
Upper Sioux Community
PO Box 147
Granite Falls, MN 56241   Ph: (612)564-4504
BIA Area Office: Minneapolis. **BIA Agency:** MN/Sioux.

★181★
Sandy Lake Band of Ojibwe
HCR 3, Box 562-7
Mc Gregor, MN 55760   Ph: (218)839-3504

★182★
Lower Sioux Mdewakanton Community
RR 1, Box 308
Morton, MN 56270   Ph: (507)697-6185
BIA Area Office: Minneapolis. **BIA Agency:** Minn./Sioux.

★183★
Mille Lacs Reservation Business Committee
(Chippewa)
HRC 67, Box 194   Ph: (612)532-4181
Onamia, MN 56359   Fax: (612)532-4209
BIA Area Office: Minneapolis. **BIA Agency:** Minnesota.

★184★
Shakopee Mdewakanton Sioux
2330 Sioux Tr., NW   Ph: (612)445-8900
Prior Lake, MN 55372   Fax: (612)445-5906
BIA Area Office: Minneapolis. **BIA Agency:** MN/Sioux.

★185★
Red Lake Band of Chippewa Indians of Minnesota
PO Box 550   Ph: (218)679-3341
Redlake, MN 56671   Fax: (218)679-3378
BIA Area Office: Minneapolis. **BIA Agency:** Red Lake.

★186★
Prairie Island Community (Minnesota Mdewakanton
Sioux)
1158 Island Blvd.   Ph: (612)388-2554
Welch, MN 55089   Fax: (612)388-1576
BIA Area Office: Minneapolis. **BIA Agency:** Minn./Sioux.

★187★
White Earth (Chippewa)
PO Box 418   Ph: (218)983-3285
White Earth, MN 56591   Fax: (218)983-3641
BIA Area Office: Minneapolis. **BIA Agency:** Minnesota.

Mississippi

★188★
Mississippi Band of Choctaw Indians
PO Box 6010   Ph: (601)656-5251
Philadelphia, MS 39350   Fax: (601)656-1992
BIA Area Office: Eastern. **BIA Agency:** Choctaw.

Missouri

★189★
Eastern Shawnee Tribe of Oklahoma
PO Box 350
Seneca, MO 64865   Ph: (918)666-2435
BIA Area Office: Muskogee. **BIA Agency:** Miami.

Montana

★190★
Chippewa-Cree Business Committee
Rocky Boy Rte.
PO Box 544   Ph: (406)395-4282
Box Elder, MT 59521   Fax: (406)395-4497
BIA Area Office: Billings. **BIA Agency:** Rocky Boy's.

★191★
Blackfeet Tribal Business Council
PO Box 850   Ph: (406)338-7276
Browning, MT 59417   Fax: (406)338-7530
BIA Area Office: Billings. **BIA Agency:** Blackfeet.

★192★
Crow Tribe
Box 159   Ph: (406)638-2601
Crow Agency, MT 59022   Fax: (406)638-7283
BIA Area Office: Billings. **BIA Agency:** Crow.

★193★
Fort Belknap Indian Community
RR1, Box 66   Ph: (406)353-2205
Harlem, MT 59526   Fax: (406)353-2797
BIA Area Office: Billings. **BIA Agency:** Ft. Belknap.

★194★
Northern Cheyenne Tribe
PO Box 128   Ph: (406)477-8284
Lame Deer, MT 59043   Fax: (406)477-6210
BIA Area Office: Billings. **BIA Agency:** No. Cheyenne.

★195★
Confederated Salish and Kootenai Tribal Council
Tribal Council
Box 278   Ph: (406)675-2700
Pablo, MT 59855   Fax: (406)675-2806
BIA Area Office: Portland. **BIA Agency:** Flathead.

★196★
Fort Peck Tribal Council
PO Box 1027   Ph: (406)768-5155
Poplar, MT 59255   Fax: (406)768-5478
BIA Area Office: Billings. **BIA Agency:** Ft. Peck.

Nebraska

★197★
Omaha Tribe
PO Box 368   Ph: (402)837-5391
Macy, NE 68039   Fax: (402)837-5308
BIA Area Office: Aberdeen. **BIA Agency:** Winnebago.

★198★
Ponca Creek Tribe of Nebraska
PO Box 288   Ph: (402)857-3391
Niobra, NE 66760   Fax: (402)857-3736
BIA Area Office: Aberdeen.

★199★
Santee Sioux Tribe
Rte. 2   Ph: (402)857-3302
Niobrara, NE 68760   Fax: (402)857-3307
BIA Area Office: Aberdeen. **BIA Agency:** Winnebago.

★200★
Winnebago Tribe
Winnebago, NE 68071   Ph: (402)878-2272
       Fax: (402)878-2963
BIA Area Office: Aberdeen. **BIA Agency:** Winnebago.

Nevada

★201★
Yomba Shoshone Tribe
HC 61 Box 6275   Ph: (702)964-2463
Austin, NV 89310   Fax: (702)964-2443
BIA Area Office: Phoenix. **BIA Agency:** W. Nevada.

★202★
Battle Mountain Band
35 Mountain View Dr., No. 138-13   Ph: (702)635-2004
Battle Mountain, NV 89820   Fax: (702)635-8016
BIA Area Office: Phoenix. **BIA Agency:** Ea. Nevada.

★203★
Carson Colony
331 Paiute St.
Carson City, NV 89703   Ph: (702)883-6431
BIA Area Office: Phoenix. **BIA Agency:** W. Nevada.

★204★
Duckwater Shoshone Tribe of the Duckwater
   Reservation
PO Box 140068   Ph: (702)863-0227
Duckwater, NV 89314   Fax: (702)863-0301
BIA Area Office: Phoenix. **BIA Agency:** Ea. Nevada.

★205★
Elko Band of The Te-Moak Tribe of Western
   Shoshone Indians
PO Box 748   Ph: (702)738-8889
Elko, NV 89801   Fax: (702)753-5439
BIA Area Office: Phoenix. **BIA Agency:** Ea. Nevada.

★206★
Te-Moak Tribe of Western Shoshone Indians
525 Sunset St.   Ph: (702)738-9251
Elko, NV 89801   Fax: (702)738-2345

★207★
Ely Colony Council
16 Shoshone Circle
Ely, NV 89301   Ph: (702)289-3013
BIA Area Office: Phoenix. **BIA Agency:** Ea. Nevada.

★208★
Fallon Business Paiute-Shoshone Tribe
8955 Mission Rd.   Ph: (702)423-6075
Fallon, NV 89406   Fax: (702)423-5202
BIA Area Office: Phoenix. **BIA Agency:** W. Nevada.

★209★
Dresslerville Colony of the Washoe Tribe of Nevada
   and California
919 Hwy 395 South   Ph: (702)265-4191
Gardnerville, NV 89410   Fax: (702)265-6240
BIA Area Office: Phoenix. **BIA Agency:** W. Nevada.

★210★
Las Vegas Paiute Tribe
1 Paiute Dr.   Ph: (702)386-3926
Las Vegas, NV 89106   Fax: (702)383-4019
BIA Area Office: Phoenix. **BIA Agency:** So. Paiute.

★211★
South Fork Band of the Te-Moak Tribe of Western
   Shoshone Indians
Box B-13   Ph: (702)744-4273
Lee, NV 89829   Fax: (702)744-4523
BIA Area Office: Phoenix. **BIA Agency:** Ea. Nevada.

★212★
Lovelock Paiute Tribe
Box 878   Ph: (702)273-7861
Lovelock, NV 89419   Fax: (702)273-7030
BIA Area Office: Phoenix. **BIA Agency:** W. Nevada.

★213★
Fort McDermitt Paiute and Shoshone Tribe
PO Box 457   Ph: (702)532-8259
McDermitt, NV 89421   Fax: (702)532-8263
BIA Area Office: Phoenix. **BIA Agency:** W. Nevada.

★214★
Moapa Paiute Band of the Moapa Indian Reservation
PO Box 340   Ph: (702)865-2787
Moapa, NV 89025-0340   Fax: (702)865-2875
BIA Area Office: Phoenix. **BIA Agency:** So. Paiute F.S.

★215★
Pyramid Lake Paiute Tribe
PO Box 256   Ph: (702)574-0140
Nixon, NV 89424-7401   Fax: (702)574-1008
BIA Area Office: Phoenix. **BIA Agency:** W. Nevada.

★216★
Shoshone Paiute Business Council
PO Box 219   Ph: (702)757-3161
Owyhee, NV 89832   Fax: (702)757-2219
BIA Area Office: Phoenix. **BIA Agency:** So. Paiute.

★217★
Reno-Sparks Indian Colony
98 Colony Rd.   Ph: (702)329-2936
Reno, NV 89502   Fax: (702)329-8710
BIA Area Office: Phoenix. **BIA Agency:** W. Nevada.

★218★
Walker River Paiute Tribe
PO Box 220   Ph: (702)773-2306
Schurz, NV 89427   Fax: (702)773-2585
BIA Area Office: Phoenix. **BIA Agency:** W. Nevada.

★219★
**Wells Band of the Te-Moak Tribe of Western
  Shoshone Indians**
PO Box 809
Wells, NV 89835   Ph: (702)752-3045
BIA Area Office: Phoenix. **BIA Agency:** Ea. Nevada.

★220★
Summit Lake Paiute Tribe
510 Melarkey No. 11   Ph: (702)623-5151
Winnemucca, NV 89445   Fax: (702)623-0558
BIA Area Office: Phoenix. **BIA Agency:** W. Nevada.

★221★
Yerington Paiute Tribe
171 Campbell Ln.   Ph: (702)463-3301
Yerington, NV 89447   Fax: (702)463-2416
BIA Area Office: Phoenix. **BIA Agency:** W. Nevada.

─────────── **New Hampshire** ───────────

★222★
Abenaki Tribe of New Hampshire
1001 Elm St.
Manchester, NH 03101   Ph: (603)644-4555

─────────── **New Jersey** ───────────

★223★
Powhatan Renape Nation
Rankokus Indian Reservation
PO Box 225
Rancocas, NJ 08073   Ph: (609)261-4747

─────────── **New Mexico** ───────────

★224★
Sandia Pueblo
PO Box 6008
Bernalillo, NM 87004   Ph: (505)867-3317
BIA Area Office: Albuquerque. **BIA Agency:** So. Pueblos.

★225★
Santa Ana Pueblo
PO Box 37
Bernalillo, NM 87004   Ph: (505)867-3301
BIA Area Office: Albuquerque. **BIA Agency:** So. Pueblos.

★226★
Cochiti Pueblo
PO Box 70
Cochiti Pueblo, NM 87041   Ph: (505)465-2244
BIA Area Office: Albuquerque. **BIA Agency:** So. Pueblos.

★227★
Jicarilla Apache Tribe
PO Box 507
Dulce, NM 87528   Ph: (505)759-3242
BIA Area Office: Albuquerque. **BIA Agency:** Jicarilla.

★228★
Santa Clara Pueblo
PO Box 580
Espanola, NM 87532   Ph: (505)753-7326
BIA Area Office: Albuquerque. **BIA Agency:** No. Pueblos.

★229★
Isleta Pueblo
PO Box 317
Isleta, NM 87022   Ph: (505)869-3111
BIA Area Office: Albuquerque. **BIA Agency:** So. Pueblos.

★230★
Jemez Pueblo
PO Box 78
Jemez Pueblo, NM 87024   Ph: (505)834-7359
BIA Area Office: Albuquerque. **BIA Agency:** So. Pueblos.

★231★
Laguna Pueblo
PO Box 194
Laguna, NM 87026   Ph: (505)552-6654
BIA Area Office: Albuquerque. **BIA Agency:** Laguna.

★232★
Mescalero Apache Tribe
PO Box 176
Mescalero, NM 87340   Ph: (505)671-4495
BIA Area Office: Albuquerque. **BIA Agency:** Mescalero.

★233★
Picuris Pueblo
PO Box 127
Penasco, NM 87553   Ph: (505)587-2519
BIA Area Office: Albuquerque. **BIA Agency:** No. Pueblos.

★234★
Acoma Pueblo
PO Box 309
Pueblo of Acoma, NM 87034   Ph: (505)552-6604
BIA Area Office: Albuquerque. **BIA Agency:** So. Pueblos.

★235★
Ramah Navajo Chapter
Rte. 2, Box 13   Ph: (505)775-3342
Ramah, NM 87321   Fax: (505)775-3538
BIA Area Office: Alburque. **BIA Agency:** Ramah/Navajo.

★236★
San Felipe Pueblo
PO Box A
San Felipe Pueblo, NM 87001   Ph: (505)687-3381
BIA Area Office: Albuquerque. **BIA Agency:** So. Pueblos.

★237★
San Juan Pueblo
PO Box 1099
San Juan Pueblo, NM 87566   Ph: (505)852-4400
BIA Area Office: Albuquerque. **BIA Agency:** No. Pueblos.

★238★
Zia Pueblo
General Delivery
San Ysidro, NM 87053   Ph: (505)867-3304
BIA Area Office: Albuquerque. **BIA Agency:** So. Pueblos.

★239★
Nambe Pueblo
Rte. 1, Box 117-BB
Santa Fe, NM 85501   Ph: (505)455-7752
BIA Area Office: Albuquerque. **BIA Agency:** No. Pueblos.

★240★
Pojoaque Pueblo
Rte. 11, Box 71
Santa Fe, NM 87501   Ph: (505)455-2278
BIA Area Office: Albuquerque. **BIA Agency:** No. Pueblos.

★241★
San Ildefonso Pueblo
Rte. 5, Box 315-A
Santa Fe, NM 87501   Ph: (505)455-2273
BIA Area Office: Albuquerque. **BIA Agency:** No. Pueblos.

★242★
Tesuque Pueblo
Rte. 11, Box 1
Santa Fe, NM 87501   Ph: (505)983-2667
BIA Area Office: Albuquerque. **BIA Agency:** No. Pueblos.

★243★
Santo Domingo Pueblo
PO Box 99
Santo Domingo Pueblo, NM 87052   Ph: (505)465-2214
BIA Area Office: Albuquerque. **BIA Agency:** So. Pueblos.

★244★
Taos Pueblo
PO Box 1846   Ph: (505)758-9626
Taos, NM 87571   Fax: (505)758-8831
BIA Area Office: Albuquerque. **BIA Agency:** No. Pueblos.

★245★
Zuni Pueblo
PO Box 339
Zuni, NM 87327   Ph: (505)782-4481
BIA Area Office: Albuquerque. **BIA Agency:** Zuni.

──────────── **New York** ────────────

★246★
Tonawanda Tribe
7027 Meadville Rd.   Ph: (716)542-4244
Basom, NY 14013   Fax: (716)542-9692
BIA Area Office: Eastern. **BIA Agency:** NY Liaison Office.

★247★
Oneida Indian Nation of New York
101 Canal St.   Ph: (315)361-6300
Canastota, NY 13032   Fax: (315)361-6333
BIA Area Office: Eastern. **BIA Agency:** NY Liaison Office.

★248★
St. Regis Band of Mohawk Indians
RR1, Box 8A   Ph: (518)358-2272
Hogansburg, NY 13655   Fax: (518)358-3203
BIA Area Office: Eastern. **BIA Agency:** NY Liaison Office.

★249★
Tuscarora Tribe
5616 Walmore Rd.
Lewiston, NY 14092   Ph: (716)297-9279
BIA Area Office: Eastern. **BIA Agency:** NY Liaison Office.

★250★
Onondaga Nation
RR1, Box 270A
Nedrow, NY 13120   Ph: (315)469-8507
BIA Area Office: Eastern. **BIA Agency:** NY Liaison Office.

★251★
Seneca Nation of Indians
G.R. Plummer Bldg.
PO Box 231   Ph: (716)945-1790
Salamanca, NY 14779   Fax: (716)945-3917
BIA Area Office: Eastern. **BIA Agency:** NY Liaison Office.

★252★
Cayuga Indian Nation
PO Box 11   Ph: (716)532-4847
Versailles, NY 14168   Fax: (716)532-5417
BIA Area Office: Eastern. **BIA Agency:** NY Liaison Office.

──────────── **North Carolina** ────────────

★253★
Eastern Band of Cherokee
PO Box 455   Ph: (704)497-2771
Cherokee, NC 28719   Fax: (704)497-2952
BIA Area Office: Eastern. **BIA Agency:** Cherokee.

★254★
Haliwa-Saponi Tribe
PO Box 99   Ph: (919)586-4017
Hollister, NC 27844   Fax: (919)586-3918

★255★
Occaneechi Band of the Saponi Nation
PO Box 356
Mebane, NC 27302   Ph: (919)304-3723

★256★
Meherrin Indian Tribe
PO Box 508   Ph: (919)358-4375
Winton, NC 27986   Fax: (919)358-1472

──────────── **North Dakota** ────────────

★257★
Turtle Mountain Tribe
Belcourt, ND 58316   Ph: (701)477-6451
                                        Fax: (701)477-6835
BIA Area Office: Aberdeen. **BIA Agency:** Turtle Mt.

★258★
Devils Lake Sioux Tribe
Sioux Community Center   Ph: (701)766-4545
Fort Totten, ND 58335   Fax: (701)766-4854
BIA Area Office: Aberdeen. **BIA Agency:** Fort Totten.

★259★
Standing Rock Sioux Tribe
Fort Yates, ND 59538   Ph: (701)854-7231
                                        Fax: (701)854-7299
BIA Area Office: Aberdeen. **BIA Agency:** Standing Rock.

★260★
Three Affiliated Tribes Business Council
PO Box 220   Ph: (701)627-4781
New Town, ND 58763   Fax: (701)627-3805
BIA Area Office: Aberdeen. **BIA Agency:** Ft. Berthold.

Oklahoma

★261★
Chickasaw Nation of Oklahoma
PO Box 1548   Ph: (405)436-2603
Ada, OK 74821-1548   Fax: (405)436-4287
BIA Area Office: Muskogee. **BIA Agency:** Chickasaw.

★262★
Apache Business Committee
PO Box 1220   Ph: (405)247-9493
Anadarko, OK 73005-1220   Fax: (405)247-3153
BIA Area Office: Anadarko. **BIA Agency:** Anadarko.

★263★
Delaware Tribe of Western Oklahoma
PO Box 825   Ph: (405)247-2448
Anadarko, OK 73005-0825   Fax: (405)247-9393
BIA Area Office: Anadarko. **BIA Agency:** Anadarko.

★264★
Wichita Tribe
PO Box 729   Ph: (405)247-2425
Anadarko, OK 73005-0729   Fax: (405)247-2430
BIA Area Office: Anadarko. **BIA Agency:** Anadarko.

★265★
Fort Sill Apache Tribe
Rte. 2, Box 121   Ph: (405)588-2298
Apache, OK 73006-9644   Fax: (405)588-3133
BIA Area Office: Anadarko. **BIA Agency:** Anadarko.

★266★
Delaware Tribe of Eastern Oklahoma
108 S. Seneca   Ph: (918)336-5272
Bartlesville, OK 74003-3834   Fax: (918)336-5513

★267★
Caddo Tribe
PO Box 487   Ph: (405)656-2344
Binger, OK 73009-0487   Fax: (405)656-2892
BIA Area Office: Anadarko. **BIA Agency:** Anadarko.

★268★
Kiowa Tribe
PO Box 369   Ph: (405)654-2300
Carnegie, OK 73015-0369   Fax: (405)654-2488
BIA Area Office: Anadarko. **BIA Agency:** Anadarko.

★269★
Cheyenne-Arapaho Tribe
PO Box 38   Ph: (405)262-0345
Concho, OK 73022-0038   Fax: (405)262-7510
BIA Area Office: Anadarko. **BIA Agency:** Concho.

★270★
Choctaw Nation of Oklahoma
16th and Locust St.
PO Drawer 1210   Ph: (405)924-8280
Durant, OK 74702-1210   Fax: (405)924-1100
BIA Area Office: Muskogee. **BIA Agency:** Talhina.

★271★
Alabama-Quassarte Tribal Town
PO Box 537   Ph: (918)652-8708
Henryetta, OK 74437-0537   Fax: (918)652-8708
BIA Area Office: Muskogee. **BIA Agency:** Okmulgee.

★272★
Kaw Tribe of Oklahoma
Drawer 50   Ph: (405)269-2552
Kaw City, OK 74641-0050   Fax: (405)269-2301
BIA Area Office: Anadarko. **BIA Agency:** Pawnee.

★273★
Comanche Tribe
HC 32, Box 1720   Ph: (405)492-4988
Lawton, OK 73502-0908   Fax: (405)492-4981
BIA Area Office: Anadarko. **BIA Agency:** Anadarko.

★274★
Kickapoo Tribe of Oklahoma
PO Box 70   Ph: (405)964-2075
McLoud, OK 74951-0070   Fax: (405)964-2745
BIA Area Office: Anadarko. **BIA Agency:** Shawnee.

★275★
Miami Tribe of Oklahoma
PO Box 1326   Ph: (918)542-1445
Miami, OK 74355-1326   Fax: (918)542-1445
BIA Area Office: Muskogee. **BIA Agency:** Miami.

★276★
Ottawa Tribe of Oklahoma
PO Box 110   Ph: (918)540-1536
Miami, OK 74355-0110   Fax: (918)542-3214
BIA Area Office: Muskogee. **BIA Agency:** Miami.

★277★
Peoria Indian Tribe of Oklahoma
PO Box 1527   Ph: (918)540-2535
Miami, OK 74355-1527   Fax: (918)540-2538
BIA Area Office: Muskogee. **BIA Agency:** Miami.

★278★
Seneca-Cayuga Tribe
PO Box 1283   Ph: (918)542-6609
Miami, OK 74355-1283   Fax: (918)542-3684
BIA Area Office: Muskogee. **BIA Agency:** Miami.

★279★
Thlopthlocco Tribal Town
Box 706   Ph: (918)623-2620
Okemah, OK 74859-0706   Fax: (918)623-0419
BIA Area Office: Muskogee. **BIA Agency:** Okmulgee.

★280★
Muscogee Creek Nation
PO Box 580   Ph: (918)756-8700
Okmulgee, OK 74447-0580   Fax: (918)758-1434

★281★
Osage Nation of Oklahoma
627 Grandview Ave.   Ph: (918)287-1128
Pawhuska, OK 74056-4201   Fax: (918)287-1259
BIA Area Office: Muskogee. **BIA Agency:** Osage.

★282★
Pawnee Tribe
PO Box 470   Ph: (918)762-3624
Pawnee, OK 74058-0470   Fax: (918)762-2389
BIA Area Office: Anadarko. **BIA Agency:** Pawnee.

★283★
Iowa Tribe of Oklahoma
RR1, Box 721
PO Box 190   Ph: (405)547-2403
Perkins, OK 74059-9599   Fax: (405)547-5294
BIA Area Office: Anadarko. **BIA Agency:** Shawnee.

★284★
Ponca Tribe
PO Box 2, White Eagle   Ph: (405)762-8104
Ponca City, OK 74601-8308   Fax: (405)762-7236
BIA Area Office: Anadarko. **BIA Agency:** Pawnee.

★285★
Quapaw Tribe
PO Box 765   Ph: (918)542-1853
Quapaw, OK 74363-0765   Fax: (918)542-4694
BIA Area Office: Muskogee. **BIA Agency:** Miami.

★286★
Otoe-Missouria Tribe
PO Box 68   Ph: (405)723-4434
Red Rock, OK 74651-0068   Fax: (405)723-4273
BIA Area Office: Anadarko. **BIA Agency:** Pawnee.

★287★
Absentee-Shawnee Tribe
2025 S. Gordon Cooper Dr.   Ph: (405)275-4030
Shawnee, OK 74801-8639   Fax: (405)275-1922
BIA Area Office: Anadarko. **BIA Agency:** Shawnee.

★288★
Citizen Band of Potawatami
Route 5, Box 151
1901 S. Gordon Cooper Dr.   Ph: (405)275-3125
Shawnee, OK 74801-0151   Fax: (405)275-0198
BIA Area Office: Anadarko. **BIA Agency:** Shawnee.

★289★
Sac and Fox
Rte. 2, Box 246
Stroud, OK 74079-9636   Ph: (918)968-3526
BIA Area Office: Anadarko. **BIA Agency:** Shawnee.

★290★
Cherokee Nation of Oklahoma
PO Box 948   Ph: (918)456-0671
Tahlequah, OK 74465   Fax: (918)456-6485
BIA Area Office: Muskogee. **BIA Agency:** Tahlequah.

★291★
Tonkawa Tribe
PO Box 70   Ph: (405)628-2561
Tonkawa, OK 74653-0070   Fax: (405)628-3375
BIA Area Office: Anadarko. **BIA Agency:** Pawnee.

★292★
Kialegee Tribal Town
318 S. Washita
PO Box 332   Ph: (405)452-3262
Wetumka, OK 74883-0332   Fax: (405)452-3413
BIA Area Office: Muskogee. **BIA Agency:** Okmulgee.

★293★
Seminole Nation
PO Box 1498   Ph: (405)257-6287
Wewoka, OK 74884-1498   Fax: (405)257-6205
BIA Area Office: Muskogee. **BIA Agency:** Wewoka.

★294★
Wyandotte
PO Box 250   Ph: (918)678-2297
Wyandotte, OK 74370-0250   Fax: (918)678-2944
BIA Area Office: Muskogee. **BIA Agency:** Miami.

Oregon

★295★
Burns-Paiute Tribe
PO Box 71, 100 Pasigo St.   Ph: (503)573-2088
Burns, OR 97720-9303   Fax: (503)573-2323
BIA Area Office: Portland. **BIA Agency:** Warm Springs.

★296★
Klamath General Council
Box 436   Ph: (503)783-2219
Chiloquin, OR 97624   Fax: (503)783-2029
BIA Area Office: Portland. **BIA Agency:** Warm Springs.

★297★
Confederated Tribes of Coos, Lower Umpqua, and Suislaw Indians
455 N. 4th St.   Ph: (503)267-5454
Coos Bay, OR 97420   Fax: (503)269-1647
BIA Area Office: Portland. **BIA Agency:** Siletz.

★298★
Coquille Indian Tribe
PO Box 1435
250 Hull St.
Coos Bay, OR 97420   Ph: (503)267-4587
BIA Area Office: Portland. **BIA Agency:** Siletz.

★299★
Confederated Tribes of the Grande Ronde Tribe
PO Box 38
9615 Grand Ronde Rd.   Ph: (503)879-5211
Grande Ronde, OR 97347   Fax: (503)879-5964
BIA Area Office: Portland. **BIA Agency:** Siletz.

★300★
Confederated Tribes of the Umatilla Indian Reservation
PO Box 638
Pendleton, OR 97801   Ph: (541)276-3165

★301★
Cow Creek Band of Umpqua Indians
2400 Stewart Pkwy, Ste. 300   Ph: (503)672-9405
Roseburg, OR 97470-2027   Fax: (503)673-0432
BIA Area Office: Portland. **BIA Agency:** Siletz.

★302★
Siletz Tribe
PO Box 549   Ph: (503)444-2532
Siletz, OR 97380   Fax: (503)444-2307
BIA Area Office: Portland. **BIA Agency:** Siletz.

★303★
Confederated Tribes of the Warm Springs Reservation
PO Box C
Warm Springs, OR 97761   Ph: (503)553-1161

Rhode Island

★304★
Pokanoket Tribe
400 Metacom Ave.   Ph: (401)253-7600
Bristol, RI 02809   Fax: (401)253-5890

★305★
Narragansett Indian Tribe
PO Box 268   Ph: (401)364-1100
Charleston, RI 02913   Fax: (401)364-1104
BIA Area Office: Eastern. **BIA Agency:** Eastern.

South Carolina

★306★
Chicora Siouan (Chicora Shakori) Indian People
PO Box 232
Andrews, SC 29510

★307★
Catawba Indian Nation
PO Box 188
Catawba, SC 29704
Ph: (803)366-4792
Fax: (803)366-9150

South Dakota

★308★
Cheyenne River Sioux Tribe
PO Box 590
Eagle Butte, SD 57625
Ph: (605)964-6611
Fax: (605)964-4060
BIA Area Office: Aberdeen. **BIA Agency:** Cheyenne River.

★309★
Flandreau Santee Sioux
PO Box 283
Flandreau, SD 57028
Ph: (605)997-3891
BIA Area Office: Aberdeen. **BIA Agency:** Aberdeen.

★310★
Crow Creek Sioux Tribe
PO Box 658
Fort Thompson, SD 57339
Ph: (605)245-2221
Fax: (605)245-2470
BIA Area Office: Aberdeen. **BIA Agency:** Crow Creek

★311★
Lower Brule Sioux Tribe
PO Box 187
Lower Brule, SD 57548
Ph: (605)473-5561
Fax: (605)473-5491
BIA Area Office: Aberdeen.

★312★
Yankton Sioux Tribe
Box 248
Marty, SD 57361
Ph: (605)384-3641
Fax: (605)384-5706
BIA Area Office: Aberdeen. **BIA Agency:** Yankton.

★313★
Oglala Sioux Tribe
Pine Ridge, SD 57770
Ph: (605)867-5871
BIA Area Office: Aberdeen. **BIA Agency:** Pine Ridge.

★314★
Rosebud Sioux Tribe
Rosebud, SD 57570
Ph: (605)747-2381
Fax: (605)747-2243
BIA Area Office: Aberdeen. **BIA Agency:** Rosebud.

★315★
Sisseton-Wahpeton Sioux Tribe
Agency Village
Rte. 2
Sisseton, SD 57262
Ph: (605)698-3911
Fax: (605)698-3708
BIA Area Office: Aberdeen. **BIA Agency:** Sisseton.

Tennessee

★316★
Kwatani Mission of Chickamuga Cherokee Mark Norman Ugaku Gigege
2624 Forest Rd.
Chattanooga, TN 37406
Ph: (615)842-2823

★317★
Free Cherokee Tennessee River Band Chickamauga
158 Pleasant View Rd
Jasper, TN 37347
Ph: (615)942-5406

Texas

★318★
Kickapoo Tribe of Texas
PO Box 972
Eagle Pass, TX 78853
Ph: (830)773-2105
Fax: (830)757-9228
BIA Area Office: Anadarko. **BIA Agency:** Anadarko Area.

★319★
Ysleta del Sur Pueblo
PO Box 17579
El Paso, TX 79917
Ph: (915)859-7913
Fax: (915)859-2988
BIA Area Office: Albuquerque. **BIA Agency:** So. Pueblos.

★320★
Alabama-Coushatta Tribe of Texas
Rte. 3, Box 640
Livingston, TX 77351
Ph: (409)563-4391
Fax: (409)363-4397
BIA Area Office: Anadarko. **BIA Agency:** Anadarko.

Utah

★321★
Paiute Indian Tribe of Utah
600 N. 100 E. Paiute Dr.
Cedar City, UT 84720
Ph: (801)586-1111
BIA Area Office: Phoenix. **BIA Agency:** So. Paiute F.S.

★322★
Skull Valley Tribe
PO Box 130
Fort Duchesne, UT 84026
Ph: (801)722-2406
Fax: (801)722-2374
BIA Area Office: Phoenix. **BIA Agency:** Unitah and Ouray.

★323★
Unitah and Ouray Tribe
PO Box 190
Fort Duchesne, UT 84026
Ph: (801)722-5141
BIA Area Office: Phoenix. **BIA Agency:** Unitah and Ouray.

★324★
Goshute Business Council
PO Box 6104
Ibapah, UT 87034
Ph: (801)234-1138
Fax: (801)234-1136
BIA Area Office: Phoenix. **BIA Agency:** Ea. Nevada.

Vermont

★325★
Abenaki Tribe of Vermont
PO Box 276
Swanton, VT 05488
Ph: (802)868-2559

Virginia

★326★
Ani-Stohini/Unami Nation
PO Box 979
Fries, VA 24330   Ph: (540)744-3640

Washington

★327★
Stillaquamish Tribe
2439 Stoluckquamish Ln.   Ph: (206)652-7362
Arlington, WA 98223   Fax: (206)435-2204

★328★
Muckleshoot Tribe
39015 172nd St., SE   Ph: (206)939-3311
Auburn, WA 98002   Fax: (206)939-5311
BIA Area Office: Portland. **BIA Agency:** Puget Sound.

★329★
Lummi Business Council
2616 Kwina Rd.   Ph: (206)734-8180
Bellingham, WA 98226-9298   Fax: (206)384-4737
BIA Area Office: Portland. **BIA Agency:** Puget Sound.

★330★
Sauk-Suiattle Tribe
5318 Chief Brown Ln.   Ph: (206)435-8366
Darrington, WA 98241   Fax: (206)436-1511
BIA Area Office: Portland. **BIA Agency:** Puget Sound.

★331★
Nooksack Tribe
PO Box 157   Ph: (360)592-5176
Deming, WA 98244   Fax: (360)592-5753
BIA Area Office: Portland. **BIA Agency:** Puget Sound.

★332★
Hoh Tribe
HC 80, Box 917   Ph: (360)374-6582
Forks, WA 98331   Fax: (360)374-6549
BIA Area Office: Portland. **BIA Agency:** Olympic Peninsula.

★333★
Port Gamble S'Klallam Tribe
31912 Little Boston Rd., NE
PO Box 280   Ph: (360)297-2646
Kingston, WA 98346   Fax: (360)287-3413
BIA Area Office: Portland. **BIA Agency:** Puget Sound.

★334★
Swinomish Tribe
PO Box 817   Ph: (360)466-3163
La Conner, WA 98257   Fax: (360)466-4047
BIA Area Office: Portland. **BIA Agency:** Puget Sound.

★335★
Quileute Tribe
PO Box 279   Ph: (360)374-6163
LaPush, WA 98537-0189   Fax: (360)374-8250
BIA Area Office: Portland. **BIA Agency:** Olympic Peninsula.

★336★
Tulalip Tribe
6700 Totem Beach Rd.
Marysville, WA 98271   Ph: (360)651-4000
BIA Area Office: Portland. **BIA Agency:** Puget Sound.

★337★
Makah Tribe
PO Box 115   Ph: (360)645-2205
Neah Bay, WA 98357   Fax: (360)645-2323
BIA Area Office: Portland. **BIA Agency:** Olympic Peninsula.

★338★
Colville Business Council
PO Box 150   Ph: (509)634-4711
Nespelem, WA 99155   Fax: (509)634-4116
BIA Area Office: Portland. **BIA Agency:** Colville.

★339★
Chehalis Business Council
PO Box 536   Ph: (360)273-5911
Oakville, WA 98568   Fax: (360)273-5914
BIA Area Office: Portland. **BIA Agency:** Olympic Peninsula.

★340★
Nisqually Tribe
4820 She-Nah-Num Dr., SE   Ph: (360)456-5221
Olympia, WA 98503   Fax: (360)438-2375
BIA Area Office: Portland. **BIA Agency:** Puget Sound.

★341★
Lower Elwha Community Council
1666 Lower Elwha Rd.   Ph: (360)452-8471
Port Angeles, WA 98362   Fax: (360)452-4848
BIA Area Office: Portland. **BIA Agency:** Olympic Peninsula.

★342★
Upper Skagit Tribe
2284 Community Plaza   Ph: (360)856-5501
Sedro Woolley, WA 98284   Fax: (360)856-2712
BIA Area Office: Portland. **BIA Agency:** Puget Sound.

★343★
Jamestown Band of S'Klallam Indians
1033 Old Blyn Hwy.   Ph: (360)683-1109
Sequim, WA 98382   Fax: (360)683-4366
BIA Area Office: Portland. **BIA Agency:** Olympic Peninsula.

★344★
Skokomish Tribe
N 80 Tribal Center Rd.   Ph: (360)426-4232
Shelton, WA 98584   Fax: (360)877-5148
BIA Area Office: Portland. **BIA Agency:** Olympic Peninsula.

★345★
Squaxin Island Tribe
W 81, Hwy 108   Ph: (360)426-9781
Shelton, WA 98584   Fax: (360)426-3971
BIA Area Office: Portland. **BIA Agency:** Olympic Peninsula.

★346★
Suquamish Tribe (Port Madison)
PO Box 498   Ph: (360)598-3311
Suquamish, WA 98392   Fax: (360)598-4666
BIA Area Office: Portland. **BIA Agency:** Puget Sound.

★347★
Puyallup Tribe
2002 E. 28th St.   Ph: (360)597-6200
Tacoma, WA 98404   Fax: (360)848-7341
BIA Area Office: Portland. **BIA Agency:** Puget Sound.

★348★
Quinault Indian Nation
PO Box 189   Ph: (360)276-8211
Taholah, WA 98587   Fax: (360)276-4682
BIA Area Office: Portland. **BIA Agency:** Olympic Peninsula.

★349★
Shoalwater Tribe
PO Box 130   Ph: (360)267-6766
Tokeland, WA 98590   Fax: (360)267-6778
BIA Area Office: Portland. **BIA Agency:** Olympic Peninsula.

★350★
Yakima Tribe
PO Box 151   Ph: (509)865-5121
Toppenish, WA 98948   Fax: (509)865-5528
BIA Area Office: Portland. **BIA Agency:** Yakima.

★351★
Kalispel Business Committee
Box 39   Ph: (509)445-1147
Usk, WA 99180   Fax: (509)455-1705
BIA Area Office: Portland. **BIA Agency:** Spokane.

★352★
Spokane Tribe
PO Box 100
Wellpinit, WA 99040   Ph: (509)258-4581
BIA Area Office: Portland. **BIA Agency:** Spokane.

───────── **Wisconsin** ─────────

★353★
Red Cliff Tribe
PO Box 529   Ph: (715)779-3700
Bayfield, WI 54814   Fax: (715)779-3151
BIA Area Office: Minneapolis. **BIA Agency:** Great Lakes.

★354★
Stockbridge-Munsee Tribe
Rte. 1   Ph: (715)793-4111
Bowler, WI 54416   Fax: (715)793-4299
BIA Area Office: Minneapolis. **BIA Agency:** Great Lakes.

★355★
Forest County Potawatomi Executive Council
PO Box 346   Ph: (715)478-2903
Crandon, WI 54520   Fax: (715)478-5280
BIA Area Office: Minneapolis. **BIA Agency:** Great Lakes.

★356★
Sokaogon Chippewa Tribe
Rte. 1, Box 328   Ph: (715)478-2604
Crandon, WI 54520   Fax: (715)478-5275
BIA Area Office: Minneapolis. **BIA Agency:** Great Lakes.

★357★
Lac Courte Oreilles Tribe
Rte. 2, Box 2700   Ph: (715)634-8934
Hayward, WI 54843   Fax: (715)634-4797
BIA Area Office: Minneapolis. **BIA Agency:** Great Lakes.

★358★
St. Croix Tribe
PO Box 287   Ph: (715)349-2195
Hertel, WI 54845   Fax: (715)349-5768
BIA Area Office: Minneapolis. **BIA Agency:** Great Lakes.

★359★
Menominee Indian Tribe of Wisconsin
PO Box 397   Ph: (715)799-5100
Keshena, WI 54135   Fax: (715)799-3802
BIA Area Office: Minneapolis. **BIA Agency:** Menominee.

★360★
Lac du Flambeau Tribe
PO Box 67   Ph: (715)588-3303
Lac du Flambeau, WI 54538   Fax: (715)588-7930
BIA Area Office: Minneapolis. **BIA Agency:** Great Lakes.

★361★
Bad River Tribe
PO Box 39   Ph: (715)682-7111
Odanah, WI 54861   Fax: (715)682-7118
BIA Area Office: Minneapolis. **BIA Agency:** Great Lakes.

★362★
Oneida Tribe
PO Box 365   Ph: (414)869-1260
Oneida, WI 54155-0365   Fax: (414)869-2194
BIA Area Office: Minneapolis. **BIA Agency:** Great Lakes.

★363★
Ho-Chunk Nation
PO Box 311
Tomah, WI 54660   Ph: (608)372-4147

───────── **Wyoming** ─────────

★364★
Arapahoe Business Council
PO Box 217   Ph: (307)332-6120
Fort Washakie, WY 82514   Fax: (307)332-7543
BIA Area Office: Billings. **BIA Agency:** Wind River.

★365★
Shoshone Business Council
PO Box 538   Ph: (307)332-3532
Fort Washakie, WY 82514   Fax: (307)332-3055
BIA Area Office: Billings. **BIA Agency:** Wind River.

National Organizations

★366★
Aboriginal Research Club
Dearborn Historical Museum
915 S. Brady Rd.
Dearborn, MI 48124

Description: Professional and amateur archaeologists, historians, and ethnologists interested in the archaeology of Michigan, historical studies of the Great Lakes region, and Indians of the area. Maintains small library. **Founded:** 1940. **Members:** 30.

★367★
All Indian Pueblo Council
PO Box 3256
Albuquerque, NM 87190   Ph: (505)881-1992

Description: Indian tribes. Serves as advocate on behalf of 19 Pueblo Indian tribes on education, health, social, and economic issues; lobbies on those issues before state and national legislatures. Activities are centered in New Mexico. Operates boarding school, Indian Pueblo Cultural Center, museum, and theater in Albuquerque, NM. Maintains Business Development Center. Offers placement service and charitable program; conducts children's services. **Founded:** 1598. **Members:** 19. **Publications:** Governors 19 Indian Pueblos; Directory, annual; Brochure; Pamphlet.

★368★
American Indian Arts Council
725 Preston Forest Shopping Center, Ste.
B
Dallas, TX 75230   Ph: (214)891-9640
Description: Promotes American Indian visual and performing arts. Preserves the art, history, and culture of American Indians. Maintains speakers bureau, Cultural Presenters Program. Conducts cultural programs such as annual American Indian Art Festival and Market. **Founded:** 1989. **Members:** 175. **State Groups:** 1. **Local Groups:** 1.

★369★
American Indian College Fund
21 W 68th St., Ste. 1F
New York, NY 10023   Ph: (212)787-6312
Description: Aims to provide Native American students "with the economic tools needed to survive in modern America and to ensure the preservation of their very cultures."

★370★
American Indian Culture Research Center
Box 98
Blue Cloud Abbey
Marvin, SD 57251-0098   Ph: (605)432-5528
Description: Corporation that supports Indian leaders and Indian educators in their ambitions for rebuilding the Indian community. Aids in teaching the non-Indian public about the culture and philosophy of the Indian. Serves as a resource for guidance and funding in Indian selfhelp programs. Has compiled an oral history and a photographic collection. Conducts workshops and seminars; compiles statistics. Maintains speakers' bureau, and small museum. **Founded:** 1967.

★371★
American Indian Development Association
PO Box 2793
Bellingham, WA 98227
Description: Purposes are to: assist American Indians and Indian organizations in developing resources in harmony with their culture; provide technical assistance, land energy, and water resource evaluation, and program development and funding assistance in both private and federal sectors. AIDA is currently unable to respond to new inquiries for assistance, and is involved with current projects only on a volunteer basis. **Founded:** 1973.

★372★
American Indian Graduate Center
4520 Montgomery Blvd. NE, Ste. 1-B
Albuquerque, NM 87109   Ph: (505)881-4584
Description: Provides scholarship and fellowship assistance for Native American or Alaskan students from federally recognized tribes at the graduate and professional school levels. Encourages colleges and universities to cooperate with financial assistance for those Indian students receiving its grants. **Founded:** 1969. **Publications:** American Indian Graduate Record; Newsletter, semiannual. **Formerly:** (1989) American Indian Scholarships.

★373★
American Indian Health Care Association
1550 Larimer St., No. 225
Denver, CO 80202-1602
Description: Urban Indian health programs; staff and support persons from member programs and other concerned persons. Develops and assists in the implementation of improved management techniques for urban Indian health care centers including quality community education programs and quality health care delivery systems responsive to community needs. Provides training, technical assistance, health care delivery management, research, and evaluation for Indian health programs and organizations. Compiles statistics on health services provided by programs of clinical, and fiscal training and information exchange; maintains speakers' bureau. **Founded:** 1975. **Members:** 35. **Regional Groups:** 9. **State Groups:** 22. **Local Groups:** 35. **Publications:** Health Promotion and Disease Prevention

Bibliography; Native AIDS Briefs Newsletter, quarterly; Summary Program Publication, annual; Brochures; Monographs; Reports.

★374★
American Indian Heritage Foundation
6051 Arlington Blvd.
Falls Church, VA 22044   Ph: (202)463-4267
Description: Informs and educates non-Indians concerning the culture and heritage of the American Indian. Seeks to respond to the spiritual and physical needs of American Indians and to inspire Indian youth. Sponsors food and clothing distribution program. Presents cultural concerts for children. Operates speakers' bureau and museum. Sponsors American Indian Heritage Month and Seminars; also sponsors annual National Indian Awards Night, Miss Indian U.S.A. Scholarship Pageant, and annual children's show. **Founded:** 1973. **Members:** 16000. **Publications:** Pathfinder Newsletter; Newsletter, periodic; Brochure. **Also Known As:** Native American Heritage Foundation.

★375★
American Indian Higher Education Consortium
121 Oronoco St.
Alexandria, VA 22314   Ph: (703)838-0400
Description: Promotes the improvement of post-secondary and higher education facilities for American Indian, Eskimo, and Alaskan Natives. Sponsors tribal colleges located on or near Indian reservations. Conducts training programs for administrators, teachers, and support staffs. Establishes information centers for the dissemination of information. Encourages the continued development of language, culture, and traditions of the American Indian, Eskimo, and Alaskan Natives. **Founded:** 1972. **Members:** 30. **Publications:** Tribal College: Journal of American Indian Education; Journal, quarterly.

★376★
American Indian Historical Society
1493 Masonic Ave.
San Francisco, CA 94117   Ph: (415)626-5235
Description: American Indians, tribal groups, and others supporting the society's educational and cultural programs. Sponsors classes, forums, and lectures on the history of American Indians. Programs include: evaluation and correction of textbooks as they depict the role of the Indian in American history; preparation of materials supporting rights of the Indian. Founded the Indian Historian Press to publish educational books and periodicals for the general reader and the educational community. Maintains library. **Founded:** 1964. **Members:** 1962. **Publications:** The Indian Historian, annual; Wassaja, periodic.

★377★
American Indian Institute
555 Constitution Ave., Ste. 237
Norman, OK 73072-7820   Ph: (405)325-4127
Description: Promotes American Indian education and research, training and career development opportunities, perpetuation of tribal cultures, traditions, and histories, and development of human and natural resources. Works to bring together representatives of North American Indian tribes and bands to provide leadership and strategies for dealing with social and human problems. Provides training to child welfare, school, mental health, and other professional personnel. Conducts research and educational programs in substance abuse prevention, cultural resource identification, and leadership training. Develops cultural curriculum and multicultural training programs. Designs and develops seminars and workshops. Provides on-site consultation and technical assistance. **Founded:** 1951. **Publications:** Child Abuse and Neglect Conference Proceedings; Proceedings, annual; Mental Health Conference Proceedings; Proceedings, annual.

★378★
American Indian Liberation Crusade
4009 S. Halldale Ave.
Los Angeles, CA 90062-1851   Ph: (213)299-1810
Description: Presents radio broadcasts (the American Indian Hour) publicizing the physical and spiritual needs of American Indians and appeals for funds. Supports missionaries on American Indian fields; sponsors summer Bible camps, Bible schools for children, and other

charitable programs; provides emergency relief. **Founded:** 1952. **Members:** 4000. **Regional Groups:** 1. **Publications:** Indian Crusader; Newsletter, quarterly.

★379★
American Indian Lore Association
960 Walhonding Ave.
Logan, OH 43138   Ph: (614)385-7136
Description: Students and patrons of the Indian arts, crafts, and history. **Founded:** 1957.

★380★
American Indian Movement
2717 Mission St., Rm. 303
San Francisco, CA 94110   Ph: (415)552-1992
Description: Primary objective is to encourage self-determination among American Indians and to establish international recognition of American Indian treaty rights. Membership limited to American Indians. Founded Heart of the Earth Survival School, which enrolls 600 students in preschool to adult programs. Maintains historical archives. Offers charitable, educational, and children's services; maintains speakers' bureau; conducts research; compiles statistics. **Founded:** 1968. **Members:** 5000. **Publications:** Survival News, quarterly.

★381★
American Indian Refugees
Description: Descendants of American Indian refugees; Indians who are nonreservation and nontribal. To acquire land for a "tribal-communal" way of life and to revive the traditional Indian attachment with the land as a vital part of Indian existence. Attempts to help Indians gain economic self-sustenance by encouraging self-confidence, control over their own affairs, and total control over their potential. Develops Indian talent by providing special education for those showing specific talents. Programs include an agricultural project in improvement of livestock, an educational program in socialism of Indians, and a program on prevention of cruelty to children and concern for animals. Sponsors competitions in the areas of agriculture and animal husbandry. Maintains 300 volume library. **Founded:** 1974. **Members:** 3. **Publications:** Smoke Signal Express, annual. **Formerly:** (1980) True People of the Western Hemisphere.

★382★
American Indian Registry for the Performing Arts
1717 N. Highland, Ste. 614
Los Angeles, CA 90028   Ph: (213)962-6594
Description: American Indian performers (172) and technical personnel in the entertainment field (43). Objective is to establish and develop a registry of American Indians seeking employment in the entertainment industry. Promotes participation by American Indians in the entertainment industry; opposes stereotypical portrayals of American Indians. Disseminates information to members on subjects pertaining to the industry and other fields. Conducts performance and technical skills training courses to enhance members' talents and marketability. Offers casting assistance. Assists in development of Tribal Film Commissions. Sponsors seminars and workshops. **Founded:** 1983. **Members:** 215. **Publications:** AIRPA Newsletter, monthly; American Indian Talent Directory, annual; Entertainment Guide to American Indian Productions.

★383★
American Indian Ritual Object Repatriation Foundation
463 E. 57th St.
New York, NY 10022-3003   Ph: (212)980-9441
Description: Intercultural partnership assisting in the return of sacred ritual material to American Indian nations. Conduits ritual objects from the private sector back to their Nation of origin. Offers speakers and educational programs to make the public aware of the importance of repatriation materials. Conducts research for tribes, museums, and private collectors. **Founded:** 1992. **Publications:** Mending the Circle: A Native American Repatriation Guide; News and Notes; Newsletter, semiannual.

★384★
American Indian Science and Education Center
1085 14th St., Ste. 1506
Boulder, CO 80302   Ph: (303)492-8658
Description: Provides training and educational opportunities to American Indian college students and tribal leaders. Sponsors internships nationwide and specially designed workshops. Conducts research and community-affiliated programs for people interested in health, natural resources, and other areas of need in Indian country. Sponsors competitive scholarships for outstanding American Indian college students. Maintains library of 1500 volumes on Indian-related issues and education. **Founded:** 1960. **Publications:** Journal, biennial. **Formerly:** (1980) United Scholarship Service for American Indian Students; (1988) National Center for American Indian Alternative Education.

★385★
American Indian Science and Engineering Society (AISES)
5661 Airport Blvd.
Boulder, CO 80301-2339   Ph: (303)939-0023
Description: American Indian and non-Indian students and professionals in science, technology, and engineering fields; corporations representing energy, mining, aerospace, electronic, and computer fields. Seeks to motivate and encourage students to pursue undergraduate and graduate studies in science, engineering, and technology. Sponsors science fairs in grade schools, teacher training workshops, summer math/science sessions for 8th-12th graders, professional chapters, and student chapters in colleges. Offers scholarships. Adult members serve as role models, advisers, and mentors for students. Operates placement service. **Founded:** 1977. **Members:** 2700. **Local Groups:** 140. **Publications:** AISES Books and Merchandise Catalog, annual; AISES Education Newsletter, quarterly; Indian Biographies; Winds of Change Magazine, quarterly; Annual Report.

★386★
American Indian Summer Seminar
Department of Anthropology
PO Box 872402
Tempe, AZ 85287-2402   Ph: (602)965-6213
Description: Provides technical training and assistance to language renewal programs for Native Americans. Develops teaching materials and techniques for linguistics education. Conducts research programs. **Founded:** 1989.

★387★
ARROW
1000 Connecticut Ave. NW, Ste. 1204   Ph: (202)296-0685
Washington, DC 20036   Free: (888)ARR-OW10
Description: Dedicated to the advancement of the American Indian. Seeks to help the American Indian achieve a better educational, cultural, and economic standard and provide needy individuals with health care. Works to improve tribal law and justice. Provides programs on drug and child abuse prevention. Offers direct aid and scholarships for graduate students. **Founded:** 1949. **Publications:** Adolescence - A Tough Time for Indian Youth Handbook; Americans for the Restitution and Righting of Old Wrongs, annual; Positive Self Esteem Can Protect Native American Youth Handbook; Protecting Youth From Alcohol and Substance Abuse: What Can We Do? Handbook; Strong Identity Can Protect Native American Youth Handbook. **Also Known As:** Americans for Restitution and Righting of Old Wrongs. **Formerly:** (1949) National Congress of American Indian Fund.

★388★
Association on American Indian Affairs
PO Box 268
Tekakwitha Complex Agency Rd. 7
Sisseton, SD 57262   Ph: (605)698-3998
Description: Provides legal and technical assistance to Indian tribes throughout the U.S. in health, education, economic development, resource utilization, family defense, and the administration of justice. Maintains American Indian Fund. **Founded:** 1923. **Members:** 40,000. **Publications:** Indian Affairs; Newsletter.

★389★
Blessed Kateri Tekakwitha League
Auriesville, NY 12016   Ph: (518)853-3153
Description: Promotes the knowledge and love of Blessed Kateri Tekakwitha and advocates her canonization. Kateri Tekakwitha (1656-80), also known as Lily of the Mohawks, was an American Indian who was instructed and baptized by Jesuits, lived a life of sanctity, and was made Venerable in 1943 by the Roman Catholic church and Blessed by Pope John Paul II on June 22, 1980. Conducts special religious services and programs and makes available cassette tapes, statues, medals, books, chaplets, prints, decals, song records, and other articles honoring Kateri. Distributes novena prayers and prayers for Kateri's canonization; maintains charitable program; operates museum. Plans to conduct research and educational programs. **Founded:** 1949. **Members:** 39. **Publications:** Lily of the Mohawks; Newspaper, quarterly; Pamphlets.

★390★
Cherokee National Historical Society
PO Box 515
Tahlequah, OK 74465   Ph: (918)456-6007
Description: Persons and organizations interested in preserving the history and tradition of the Cherokee Indian Nation. Seeks to interest the public in Cherokee history. Plans to mark locations of historic significance to the Cherokees, including graves of officials and other prominent persons of the Nation. Sponsors educational, charitable, and benevolent activities for Cherokees and their descendants. Operates Cherokee Heritage Center, which includes the Cherokee National Museum, and Cherokee Arboretum and Herb Garden (including trees and plants used traditionally by Cherokees for food, fiber, and medicines). Maintains a "living" Indian Village, circa 1700-50 and a Rural Cherokee Museum Village, circa 1875-90; annually presents The Trail of Tears, an outdoor epic symphonic drama relating to Cherokee history in the southern highlands and the Southwest. Maintains Cherokee Hall of Fame for persons of Cherokee descent who have made distinguished contributions to the nation; also maintains the Ho-Chee-Nee Trail of Tears Memorial Chapel. Plans to restore a number of both pre- and post-Civil War historic Cherokee Nation buildings in the area of the old Cherokee Nation in the Southwest. **Founded:** 1963. **Members:** 900. **Publications:** The Columns Newsletter; Trail of Tears Drama Program, annual.

★391★
Cook Inlet Native Association
1569 S. Bragaw, Ste. 200
Anchorage, AK 99508   Ph: (907)337-1800
Description: Alaskan natives and American Indians dedicated to nurturing pride in the heritage and traditions of the Alaska native and preserving the customs, folklore, and art of the people. Promotes the potentials, opportunities, and physical, economic, and social well-being of Alaskan natives and American Indians. Offers training programs for word processors, clerical workers, bank tellers, and job-seeking techniques. Sponsors competitions; bestows awards; contributes to charitable programs. Maintains museum; compiles statistics. **Founded:** 1964. **Members:** 1, 472. **Publications:** Trail Blazer Newsletter, quarterly.

★392★
Council for Indian Education
1240 Burlington Ave.
Billings, MT 59102   Ph: (406)652-7598
Description: Individuals interested in improving and securing higher standards of education for American Indian children. Promotes quality children's literature on authentic Indian culture. Publishes books about American Indian life, past and present, for use in reading programs. Conducts in-service education of teachers working on Indian reservations. **Founded:** 1970. **Members:** 100; Books. **Formerly:** (1982) Montana Council for Indian Education.

★393★
Crazy Horse Memorial Foundation
The Black Hills
Ave. of the Chiefs
Crazy Horse, SD 57730-9506   Ph: (605)673-4681
Description: Seeks completion of the memorial to North American Indians begun by sculptor Korczak Ziolkowski (1908-82). (This memorial is to be a statue, 563 feet high and 641 feet long, depicting the Sioux leader Crazy Horse astride his pony and pointing to the lands of his people. Ziolkowki's wife and children are continuing work on the statue, which is being carved from Thunderhead Mountain in South Dakota.) Maintains museum of art and artifacts of Indian tribes from many areas of the United States, a museum-studio of American and European antiques, art objects, marble, bronze, and mahogany sculpture. Plans to establish a university and medical center for Native Americans. **Founded:** 1948. **Members:** 23. **Publications:** Crazy Horse and Korczak; Crazy Horse Memorial 40th Anniversary Booklet; Booklet; Crazy Horse Progress; Newsletter, quarterly; Korczak, Sage of Sitting Bull's Bones; Korczak: Storyteller in Stone.

★394★
Creek Indian Memorial Association
Creek Council House Museum
Town Sq.
Okmulgee, OK 74447   Ph: (918)756-2324
Description: Operates museum of Creek Indian culture containing displays of Indian artifacts, archaeology artifacts, Indian murals, and paintings. Conducts fundraising activities. Provides educational programs. **Founded:** 1923. **Members:** 113. **Publications:** Booklets; Brochures. **Formerly:** (1923) Indian Historical Society.

★395★
Dakota Women of All Red Nations
c/o Lorelei DeCora
PO Box 423
Rosebud, SD 57570
Description: Grass roots organization of American Indian women seeking to advance the Native American movement. Is establishing local chapters to work on issues of concern such as sterilization abuse and women's health, adoption and foster-care abuse, community education, political imprisonment, legal and juvenile justice problems, and problems caused by energy resource development by multinational corporations on Indian land. Supports leadership roles for American Indian women. **Founded:** 1978. **Formerly:** (1985) Women of All Red Nations.

★396★
Five Civilized Tribes Foundation
c/o Chickasaw Nation
PO Box 1548
Ada, OK 74820   Ph: (405)436-2603
Description: The Cherokee, Choctaw, Chickasaw, Creek, and Seminole Indian Nations of Oklahoma. FCTF is a grant-funded organization which provides coordination to tribal activities and programs, including social programs, industrial development, and administrative activities. Provides representation for the five tribes at the national level. Presently inactive. **Founded:** 1974. **Members:** 5. **Regional Groups:** 3. **State Groups:** 9.

★397★
Indian Rights Association
PO Box 970
Horsham, PA 19044-0970
Description: Individuals interested in protection of the legal and human rights of American Indians and promotion of their welfare. Maintains first-hand knowledge of conditions in Indian communities; keeps in touch with governmental Indian affairs; monitors and reports on judicial and legislative activities involving Indian concerns; acts as a clearinghouse for appeals of all sorts for aid to Indians and for information on all phases of Indian affairs. Sponsors prominent artists and speakers in programs introducing local communities to Native American cultures. **Founded:** 1882. **Members:** 300. **Publications:** Indian Truth, bimonthly; Pamphlets.

★398★
Indian Youth of America
609 Badgerow Bldg.
PO Box 2786
Sioux City, IA 51106   Ph: (712)252-3230
Description: Native American organization dedicated to improving the lives of Indian children. Works to provide opportunities and experiences that will aid Indian youth in their educational, career, cultural, and personal growth. Maintains an Indian Child Welfare Program, which attempts to prevent the distressful effects brought on by the breakup of Indian families. Goals of the program are: to inform families, social service agencies, and courts about the rights of Indian people under the Indian Child Welfare Act; to provide referral services to social service agencies in locating tribes and suitable placement for Indian children; to counsel Indian children and their parents and recruit Indian foster homes for Indian children. Sponsors a summer camp program, an after school Indian youth program, and an annual Christmas party for Indian children. Maintains resource center. **Founded:** 1978. **Members:** 7. **Publications:** Brochure.

★399★
Indians Into Medicine
University of North Dakota
School of Medicine and Health Services
PO Box 9037
Grand Forks, ND 58202-9037   Ph: (701)777-3037
Description: Support program for American Indian students. Seeks to: increase the awareness of and interest in healthcare professions among young American Indians; recruit and enroll American Indians in healthcare education programs; place American health professionals in service to Indian communities. Coordinates financial and personal support for students in healthcare curricula. Provides referral and counseling services. Maintains 2000 volume library. Provides summer enrichment sessions at the junior high, high school and pre-medical levels. **Founded:** 1973. **Publications:** Serpent, Staff and Drum Newsletter, quarterly.

★400★
Institute of American Indian Arts
PO Box 20007
Santa Fe, NM 87504   Ph: (505)988-6463
Description: Federally chartered private institution. Offers learning opportunities in the arts and crafts to Native American youth (Indian, Eskimo, or Aleut). Emphasis is placed upon Indian traditions as the basis for creative expression in fine arts including painting, sculpture, museum studies, creative writing, printmaking, photography, communications, design, and dance, as well as training in metal crafts, jewelry, ceramics, textiles, and various traditional crafts. Students are encouraged to identify with their heritage and to be aware of themselves as members of a race rich in architecture, the fine arts, music, pageantry, and the humanities. All programs are based on elements of the Native American cultural heritage that emphasize differences between Native American and non-Native American cultures. Sponsors Indian arts-oriented junior college offering Associate of Fine Arts degrees in various fields as well as seminars, an exhibition program, and traveling exhibits. Maintains extensive library, museum, and biographical archives. Provides placement service. **Founded:** 1962. **Publications:** Faculty Handbook, annual; School Catalog, annual. **Formerly:** (1962) Sante Fe Indian School.

★401★
Institute for American Indian Studies
38 Curtis Rd.
PO Box 1260
Washington, CT 06793-0260   Ph: (860)868-0518
Description: Individuals, families, libraries, and institutions. To discover, preserve, and interpret information about Native Americans of the northeastern woodlands area of the U.S., including their migration, survival patterns, cultural changes, and beliefs; to enhance appreciation for their cultures and achievements. Conducts archaeological surveys and excavations. Provides indoor and outdoor exhibits covering 12,000 years of North American prehistory, history, and contemporary native themes. Maintains quarter-mile Quinnetukut Habitat Trail and Indian Encampment with three wigwams and a longhouse; conducts field trips. Sponsors

archaeological training sessions, teacher workshops, craft workshops, summer youth programs, and film festivals. Maintains speakers' bureau and museum center for the study of the past and present. Conducts research programs. **Founded:** 1971. **Members:** 1350. **Publications:** Calendars for Press, 3/year; Netop Newsletter, bimonthly; Brochures; Catalogs; Pamphlets. **Formerly:** (1975) Shepaug Valley Archaeological Society; (1992) American Indian Archaeological Institute.

★402★
Institute for the Development of Indian Law
c/o K. Kirke Kickingbird
Oklahoma City University
School of Law
2501 N. Blackwelder
Oklahoma City, OK 73106
Description: Public interest law firm that functions as a research training center on federal Indian law. The institute places special emphasis on three areas: Indian sovereignty; encouragement of Indian self-confidence and self-government; clarification of historical and legal foundations of modern Indian rights. Activities include: research and analysis; training and technical assistance; dissemination of educational materials relating to federal Indian law, Indian Treaties, curriculum and community development, and other subjects. Conducts educational programs for Indians and non-Indians. Holds seminars on federal Indian law, taxation, and the role of Indians in the development of the U.S. constitution. **Founded:** 1971.

★403★
Institute for the Study of Traditional American Indian Arts
PO Box 66124
Portland, OR 97290   Ph: (503)233-8131
Description: Native American artists and craftspeople, anthropologists, museum personnel, researchers, and collectors of Native American art. Promotes traditional Native American arts through publications, lectures, and seminars. Conducts research. **Founded:** 1982. **Publications:** American Indian Basketry and Other Native Arts Magazine, quarterly.

★404★
Inter-Tribal Indian Ceremonial Association
Box 1
Church Rock, NM 87311   Ph: (505)863-3896
Description: An official agency of the state of New Mexico. Members are Indian people, businessmen, dealers in Indian arts and crafts, and individuals interested in the annual Inter-Tribal Indian Ceremonial sponsored by the association each summer "to extol virtues and beauty of traditional Indian culture." The six-day program includes Indian dances, sports, arts and crafts, rituals, and a rodeo. Conducts correspondence and other activities in connection with legislation affecting Indian arts and crafts. Conducts specialized education and children's services; provides educational materials on Indian crafts; produces color slides of Indian ceremonies. Maintains Red Rock Park as a museum. Plans to operate hall of fame. **Founded:** 1921. **Members:** 350. **Publications:** A Measure of Excellence; Book.

★405★
Morning Star Institute
403 10th St. SE
Washington, DC 20003   Ph: (202)547-5531
Description: Supports the traditional and cultural beliefs of Native Americans. Promotes Native American arts. Maintains speakers' bureau; conducts research and educational programs. **Founded:** 1984; Bulletin, periodic.

★406★
National Association of Investment Companies
1111 14th St. NW, Ste. 700
Washington, DC 20005   Ph: (202)289-4336
Description: Aims to: represent the minority small business investment company industry in the public sector; provide industry education; develop research material on the activities of the industry; promote the growth of minority-owned small businesses by informing the public of their contribution to the vitality of the nation's

economy; collect and disseminate relevant business and trade information to members; facilitate the exchange of new ideas and financing strategies; assist organizing groups attempting to form or acquire minority enterprise small business investment companies; provide management and technical assistance to members; monitor regulatory agency actions. Conducts three professional seminars; sponsors research; compiles statistics. **Founded:** 1971. **Members:** 150. **Publications:** NAIC Membership Directory, annual; National Association of Investment Companies–Perspective Newsletter, monthly; Bibliographies; Handbooks. **Formerly:** (1987) American Association of Minority Enterprise Small Business Investment Companies.

★407★
National Association for Native American Children of Alcoholics

1402 Third Ave., No. 1110   Ph: (206)467-7686
Seattle, WA 98101   Free: 800-322-5601

Description: Native and non-native individuals and organizations. Promotes awareness of the needs of Native American children of alcoholics. Develops educational and support programs for Native American communities; conducts programs to educate local and national policymakers and thereby influence social change and encourage healthy community development. **Founded:** 1988. **Members:** 6,000. **Regional Groups:** 13. **Publications:** From Nightmareto Vision: A Training Manual for Native American Adult Children of Alcoholics; The Healing Journey: Hope for Children of Alcoholics; Video; Healing Our Hearts Newsletter, quarterly; Respect Handbook: A Guide for Helping Native American Children of Alcoholics.

★408★
National Center for American Indian and Alaska Native Mental Health Research

Psychiatry Department
Campus Box A011-13,
4455 E. 12th Ave.   Ph: (303)315-9232
Denver, CO 80220   Free: 800-444-6472

Description: Faculty, staff, and research associates in the mental health field. Conducts and supports research on management, prevention, and investigation of mental illness among Native Americans and Alaska Natives. Assists organizations in conducting and implementing mental health research. Disseminates information and statistics to public. **Founded:** 1987. **Publications:** Behavioral Health Issues Among American Indians and Alaska Natives: Explorations on the Frontiers of the Biobehavioral Sciencesling From the Rim: Suicidal Behavior Among American Indian and Alaska Native Adolescents Monograph; Journal of the National Center for American Indian and Alaska Native Mental Health Research Journal, 3/year; Mental Health Programs for American Indians: Their Logic, Structure and Function Monograph; New Directions in Prevention Among American Indian and Alaska Native Communities Monograph; The People Who Give More: Health and Mental Health Among the Contemporary Puyallup Indian Tribal Community Monograph.

★409★
National Center for American Indian Enterprise Development

1200 New Hampshire Ave. NW, Ste. 445   Ph: (202)545-1298
Mesa, AZ 85236   Free: 800-462-2433

Description: Promotes business and economic development among American Indians and tribes. Offers business training services to American Indians who own or plan to start businesses in fields including manufacturing, service, construction, retailing, and wholesaling. Assists Indians and tribes in: developing management abilities; assessing operating costs; preparing finance proposals; obtaining financing, bonding, and insurance; controlling the business through effective accounting and information systems; negotiating contracts, leases, and purchases; planning for future business growth. Provides services such as feasibility studies, site/location analysis, loan packaging, and promotion and fundraising campaigns. Sponsors Management Institute: Training for Indian Managers; conducts youth entrepreneurship programs. Operates the UIDA Group Inc., a development company. **Founded:** 1969. **Regional Groups:** 3. **Publications:** Directory of American Indian Businesses; Directory, annual; Indian Business and

Management, quarterly. **Formerly:** (1989) United Indian Development Association.

★410★
National Coalition for Indian Education

PO Box 91345
Albuquerque, NM 87199-1345   Ph: (505)266-6510

Description: Native American educators and others. Promotes excellence in Native American education. Conducts research activities. Offers informational services, training, and technical assistance. Maintains speakers' bureau and placement service. **Founded:** 1987. **Members:** 600. **State Groups:** 6. **Publications:** The Indian Dropout - An Annotated Bibliography; Bibliography; NCIE Newsletter, 3/year. **Formerly:** (1994) Coalition for Indian Education.

★411★
National Congress of American Indians

2010 Massachusetts Ave. NW, 2nd Fl.
Washington, DC 20036   Ph: (202)466-7767

Description: Tribes representing 800,000 Indians (185) and individuals (2500). Seeks to: protect, conserve, and develop Indian natural and human resources; serve legislative interests of Indian tribes; improve health, education, and economic conditions. Administers NCAI Fund for educational and charitable purposes. Conducts research on Indian problems as a service to Indian tribes. Compiles statistics. NCAI claims to be the oldest and largest national Indian organization advocating the interests of American Indians and Alaskan Natives. **Founded:** 1944. **Members:** 2,685. **Publications:** Sentinel Bulletin, periodic.

★412★
National Indian Athletic Association

Description: Organizes, coordinates and sponsors athletic, artistic and cultural events at local, state, regional, and national levels. Compiles statistics. **Founded:** 1973. **Members:** 6,000. **Formerly:** (1982) National Indian Activities Association.

★413★
National Indian Council on Aging

10501 Montgomery Blvd. NE, Ste. 210
Albuquerque, NM 87111   Ph: (505)292-2001

Description: Native Americans. Seeks to bring about improved, comprehensive services to the Indian and Alaska native elderly. Objectives are to act as a focal point for the articulation of the needs of the Indian elderly; to disseminate information on Indian aging programs; to provide technical assistance and training opportunities to tribal organizations in the development of their programs. Conducts research on the needs of Indian elderly. **Founded:** 1976. **Members:** 1,037. **Publications:** Elder Voices Newsletter, quarterly; Mapping Indian Elders; Reports; Monographs; Proceedings.

★414★
National Indian Counselors Association

University of Nebraska at Lincoln
220 Administration - M.C.A.
Lincoln, NE 68588-0498   Ph: (402)472-2027

Description: Native American counselors concerned with improving the counseling of Native Americans. Exchanges ideas, identifies problems, and promotes educational and counseling growth and leadership. Makes recommendations for improved policies in educating Native Americans. Conducts networking among Native American counselors. **Founded:** 1980. **Members:** 100. **Publications:** NICA Newsletter, periodic.

★415★
National Indian Education Association

121 Oronoco St.
Alexandria, VA 22314   Ph: (703)838-2870

Description: American Indians; associate members are non-Indians. Advocates educational programs to improve the social and economic well-being of American Indians and Alaskan natives. Represents diversity of geographic and tribal backgrounds. Focuses on exchange of ideas, techniques, and research methods among the participants in Indian/native education. **Founded:** 1970.

Members: 2,000. **Publications:** Indian Education Newsletter, quarterly.

★416★
National Indian Festival Association
PO Box 3492
Albany, GA 31706   Ph: (912)436-1625
Description: Seeks to broaden the public's knowledge of Native American culture and to educate them about the differences among these cultures. Is in the process of building a cultural center and a Native American village in Georgia. **Publications:** none. **Founded:** 1992.

★417★
National Indian Training and Research Center
2121 S. Mill Ave., Ste. 216
Tempe, AZ 85282   Ph: (602)967-9484
Description: To involve American Indians in leadership and professional roles in training and research projects for the social and economic betterment of Indian people. Believes that American Indians must have a free hand in determining their destiny and identity; therefore the planning and implementation of programs must be done primarily by Indians. Seeks to orient and train professionals working with American Indians so that they might better understand and appreciate the American Indian's life and culture. Conducts model and demonstration training programs to develop methodologies, curricula, and educational materials that provide the American Indian with a more meaningful and relevant education. Sponsors research and development for prototype programs and to increase information and knowledge about the American Indian, specifically in the field of education. Provides services in evaluation, program development, proposal writing, surveys, technical assistance, and training. Maintains 1000 volume library. **Founded:** 1969. **Publications:** Introducing Public School Finance to Native Americans.

★418★
National Indian Youth Council
318 Elm St. SE
Albuquerque, NM 87102   Ph: (505)247-2251
Description: Aims to protect Indian natural resources; protect Indian religious freedom and other tribal and individual civil liberties; protect and enhance treaty rights and federal government's trust relationship and responsibilities; improve Indian health and education; preserve the Indian family unit and community. Operates educational and employment programs and sponsors action-related research projects. Compiles statistics on the Indian electorate. **Founded:** 1961. **Members:** 12,000. **Publications:** Americans Before Columbus Newsletter, quarterly.

★419★
National Native American AIDS Prevention
134 Linden St.
Oakland, CA 94607   Ph: (510)444-2051
Description: Network of concerned Native people. Works to stop the spread of HIV and related diseases, including sexually transmitted disease and tuberculosis, among American Indians, Alaska Natives, and Native Hawaiians by improving their health status through empowerment and self determination. Serves as a resource to Native communities and to support community efforts by providing education and information services, thereby ehancing the physical, spiritual, and economic health of Native people. Sponsors educational programs. Maintains speakers' bureau. Compiles statistics. **Founded:** 1987. **Publications:** Season; Newsletter, quarterly

★420★
Native American Public Broadcasting Consortium
1800 N 33rd St.
PO Box 83111
Lincoln, NE 68583-3111   Free: 800-835-7087
Description: Provides support to independent Native American radio and television producers.

★421★
Native American Sports Council
PO Box 38249
Colorado Springs, CO 80937-8249
Description: Aims to work with tribal communities to develop culturally appropriate sports and wellness programs. Assists Native American Olympic hopefuls.

★422★
Native Voices Public Television
Montana State University
VCB, Rm. 222   Ph: (406)994-6218
Bozeman, MT 59717   Fax: (406)994-6545
Description: Supports film and television work of Native Americans; promotes the distribution of film and television programs; provides professional training.

★423★
Navajo Area School Board Association
PO Box 3719
Window Rock, AZ 86515-0578   Ph: (520)871-5225
Description: Elected school board members of Navajo communities authorized by the Navajo National Council to promote and advocate for quality education for the Navajo population. Provides training and technical services for school governance, improvement, and student achievement goals. Maintains speakers' bureau; bestows awards; compiles statistics. **Founded:** 1969. **Members:** 275. **Local Groups:** 54. **Publications:** NASBA News Newsletter, monthly.

★424★
Running Strong for American Indian Youth
8815 Telegraph Rd.
Lorton, VA 22079   Ph: (703)550-2123
Description: Works to help American Indian people meet daily survival needs while creating opportunities for self-sufficiency. Conducts housing, water resource development, domestic violence, organic farming and health care programs. Acts as a resource to preserve and promote Indian culture and values. Offers cultural and language preservation programs. Provides fetal alcohol syndrome education. Conducts athletic and recreational activities. Distributes grants nationwide to support infrastructural and cultural endeavors of grassroots American Indian. **Founded:** 1990 Annual Report:, American Indian Youth- Running Strong Newsletter, quarterly

★425★
Seventh Generation Fund for Indian Development
PO Box 4569
Arcata, CA 95521   Ph: (707)825-7640
Description: Indian tribes and organizations. Provides seed grants and technical assistance in order to increase self-reliance in Indian communities and decrease government dependency. Aims to: reclaim and live on aboriginal lands; protect tribal lands and natural resources; redevelop self-sufficient communities through food production, appropriate technologies, and alternative energy use; restore traditional indigenous forms of political organization or to modify existing governments along traditional lines. Supports and promotes the spiritual, cultural, and physical well-being of the Native family. Reports on such subjects as Native American rights, Indian family life, and judicial issues and cases affecting American Indians. Maintains small library on appropriate technologies, fundraising, and resource materials. The fund's title is drawn from the Hau de no sau nee (Six Nations) principle of considering the impact upon the seventh generation in the decision-making process. **Founded:** 1977; Annual Report. **Formerly:** (1984) Tribal Sovereignty Program.

★426★
Society for Advancement of Chicanos and Native Americans in Science
1156 High St.
Santa Cruz, CA 95064   Ph: (408)459-4272
Description: College professors, science professionals, undergraduate and graduate science students, and high school science teachers. Seeks to increase the participation of Latinos and

Native Americans in the sciences. **Founded:** 1973. **Members:** 800. **Publications:** SACNAS Journal, quarterly.

★427★
Survival of American Indians Association
7803-A Samurai Dr. SE
Olympia, WA 98503

Description: Indians and interested individuals. Provides public education on Indian rights and tribal government reform action. Supports independent Indian education institutions. Maintains speakers' bureau. **Founded:** 1964. **Members:** 500. **Regional Groups:** 3. **Publications:** The Renegade: A Strategy Journal of Indian Opinion Journal, periodic.

★428★
Tiyospaya American Indian Student Organization
33 4th Stn., No. 202   Ph: (813)823-3534
St. Petersburg, FL 33701   Free: 800-682-7220

Description: Native American student support and indigenous rights organization. Works to assist Indian college students in improving their graduation/retention rates. Provides substance abuse/prevention programs and American Indian parent/teacher associations. Acts as an indigenous rights group; firmly believes in treaty rights and sovereignty; will respond to any violation of indigenous peoples treaty, civil, or human rights. **Founded:** 1986. **Members:** 210. **Regional Groups:** 3. **State Groups:** 13. **Publications:** FIA Newsletter, bimonthly; TAISO News, periodic.

★429★
United South and Eastern Tribes
711 Stewarts Ferry Pike S-100
Nashville, TN 37214

Description: Alliance of 23 Indian tribes: Alabama-Coushatta Tribe of Texas; Aroostook Band of Mic Macs; Eastern Band of Cherokee Indians; Chitimacha Tribe of Louisiana; Mississippi Band of Choctaw Indians; Coushatta Tribe of Louisiana; Poarch Band of Creek Indians; Houlton Band of Maliseet Indians; Mashantucket Pequot Indians of Connecticut; Miccosukee Tribe of Indians; Narrangansett Indian Tribe; Passamaquoddy Tribe-Indian Township; Passamaquoddy Tribe-Pleasant Point; Penobscot Indian Nation; St. Regis Mohawk; Seminole Tribe of Florida; Seneca Nation of Indians; Tunica-Biloxi Tribe of Louisiana; Wampanoag Tribal Council of Gay Head; Oneida Nation of New York; Catawba Indian Nation; Jena Band of Choctaw Indians; and the Mohegan Tribe of Conneticut. Promotes "strength in unity" of American Indian tribes and assists tribes in dealing with relevant issues. Fosters better understanding with other races. **Publications:** none. **Founded:** 1969. **Members:** 23. **Formerly:** (1978) United Southeastern Tribes.

Regional, State/Provincial, & Local Organizations

Alabama

★430★
Chickamogee Cherokees of the Southeastern U.S.
1010 Gilliland Rol
Altoona, AL 35952-9724
Chief Charles R. Smith, Exec. Officer.

Alaska

★431★
Tanana Chiefs Conference
122 1st Ave.
Fairbanks, AK 99701
Gina Deluchi, Contact.

★432★
Ketchikan Indian Corporation
429 Deermont Ave.   Ph: (907)252-5158
Ketchikan, AK 99901   Free: 800-252-5158
     Fax: (907)247-0429

Description: Provides social service programs for native Alaskan Indians.

Arizona

★433★
Native Americans for Community Action
Administrative Office
2717 N. Steves Blvd., Ste. 11   Ph: (520)526-2968
Flagstaff, AZ 86004   Fax: (520)526-0708
Joanne Stucjus, Acting Exec.Dir.

Description: Promotes improved health and human services for Native Americans residing off-reservation in Coconino County, AZ. **Affiliated With:** American Indian Health Care Association.

★434★
Navajo Area Grant School Association
PO Box 609
Flagstaff, AZ 86002-0609

★435★
Phoenix Indian Center
2601 N. 3rd St., Ste. 100   Ph: (602)263-1017
Phoenix, AZ 85004   Fax: (602)263-7822
William Thorne Jr., Exec.Dir.

Description: Native Americans. Provides service programs and opportunities in urban environments for Indians. Conducts charitable events. **Publications:** none.

★436★
Southwest Indian Substance Abuse Counselor Certification
636 N 3rd Ave.
Phoenix, AZ 85003-1523

★437★
Apache Survival Coalition
PO Box 11814
Tucson, AZ 85734-1814
Ola Cassadore Davis, Contact.

★438★
Traditional Indian Alliance
2925 S. 12th Ave.   Ph: (602)882-0555
Tucson, AZ 85713   Fax: (602)623-6529
Corrine Jymm, Exec. Dir.

Description: Promotes improved urban Indian healthcare. **Affiliated With:** American Indian Health Care Association.

★439★
United Traditional Indian Council of Arizona
22305 W. Dove Valley Rd.
Wittmann, AZ 85361-9681

California

★440★
Resources for Indian Student Education
109 North St.
Alturas, CA 96101

★441★
American Indian Council of Central California
2441 G St.   Ph: (805)327-2207
Bakersfield, CA 93301   Fax: (805)327-4533
Shirley Mantaghi, Dir.
Description: Promotes improved urban Indian healthcare.
Affiliated With: American Indian Health Care Association.

★442★
American Indian Council of Mariposa County
PO Box 1200
Mariposa, CA 95338-1200

★443★
National Native American AIDS Prevention Center
3515 Grand Ave., Ste. 100
Oakland, CA 94610

★444★
Inter-Tribal Council of California
2755 Cottage Way Ste 14   Ph: (916)447-2003
Sacramento, CA 95825-1221 Fax: (916)447-6949
Toni Candelaria, Exec.Dir.
Description: Indian tribes and organizations. To advance the economic, educational, cultural, legal, and social status of California Indians. Sponsors ITCC theater. **Convention/Meeting:** none.

★445★
Sacramento Urban Indian Health Project
2020 J St.   Ph: (916)441-0918
Sacramento, CA 95818   Fax: (916)441-1261
Description: Promotes improved urban Indian healthcare.
Affiliated With: American Indian Health Care Association.

★446★
San Diego American Indian Health
2561 1st Ave.   Ph: (619)234-2158
San Diego, CA 92103   Fax: (619)234-0206
Edna Kidwell, Chm.
Description: To improve the health of Native Americans by providing culturally appropriate services to Native Americans, especially medical and dental care, outreach services, and AIDS education and prevention programs.

★447★
Native American Indian Inter-Tribal Association of Venutra County
PO Box 6459
Ventura, CA 93006-6459

Colorado

★448★
Southern Ute Indian Cultural Center
PO Box 737   Ph: (970)563-9583
Ignacio, CO 81137-0737   Fax: (970)563-4641
Helen Hoskins, Dir.

Connecticut

★449★
Algonquian Confederacy Quinnipiac Tribal Council
1044 Chapel St., Ste. 602
New Haven, CT 06510-2437

District of Columbia

★450★
United South and Eastern Tribes Gaming Association
400 N Capitol St. NW, Ste. 585
Washington, DC 20001-1590

Florida

★451★
Native American Traditions Ideas and Values Educational Society
PO Box 411
Orange Park, FL 32067-0411

★452★
American Indian Center of Central Florida
PO Box 680725
Orlando, FL 32868-0725

★453★
Talako Indian Dancers Family Club
6515 Vineland Rd.
Orlando, FL 32819   Ph: (407)352-1163
William C. Prentiss, Contact
Description: Native American families dedicated to sharing their culture with the community at large. Conducts youth programs.

★454★
Northwestern Florida Creek Indian Council
3300 N. Pace Blvd.
Pensacola, FL 32505   Ph: (904)432-9639
Darrell W. Williams, Chairperson
Description: Creek Indians seeking to provide services and further Indian movement. Conducts dance and craft competitions. Sponsors Native American Pow Wows festival.

Georgia

★455★
Native American Preservation Association of Georgia
PO Box 565
Rome, GA 30162   Ph: (706)777-1710
Brenda Bradshaw, Exec.Chm.
Description: Works to preserve and teach native American arts and crafts, history, and culture.

Idaho

★456★
Native American Coalition of Boise
PO Box 312
Boise, ID 83701-0312
Description: Navtive Americans in Boise, ID.

★457★
Latah-Nez Perce Voices for Human Rights
PO Box 8862
Moscow, ID 83843-1362

Illinois

★458★
Club of Indian Women
PO Box 72
Westmont, IL 60559   Ph: (708)850-9667
Mrs. Manju Gupta, Exec. Officer
Description: Social organization. Helps needy women.

Indiana

★459★
Children of the Bear Indian Council
204 E. Florida St., Ste. A
Evansville, IN 47711-4612   Ph: (812)423-7567
Gladys Schaefer, Pres.
Description: Supplies food and clothing to Indians locally and on reservations. Participates in Indian affairs and issues.

★460★
Native American Legal Defense Association
28 S Center St.
Flora, IN 46929-1314

★461★
Native American Preservation Society
6188 W Old U.S. 40
Knightstown, IN 46148-0000
Amelia Knight Wyatt, Contact.

Kansas

★462★
Kansas Institute for African-American and Native-American Family History
5757 Rowland St.
Kansas City, KS 66104-2843

★463★
Shawnee County Allied Tribes
810 SW Warren
Topeka, KS 66606-1881

Louisiana

★464★
Friends of Caddo Adais Indian
PO Box 5926
Shreveport, LA 71135-5926

★465★
Helping Our People Endure
1080 Dalzell
Shreveport, LA 71104-2050   Ph: (318)686-1008
Fax: (318)686-1051
Milton Houston, Exec.Dir.

★466★
Choctaw-Apache Community of Ebarb
PO Box 858
Zwolle, LA 71486-0858
Tommy W. Bolton, Contact.

Maine

★467★
Native American Appreciation Day
PO Box 280
East Lebanon, ME 04027-0280
F. Scottie Wilcox, Contact.

★468★
Native American Inter-Tribal Foundation
RR 1, Box 1749
Wells, ME 04090-9768

Massachusetts

★469★
Woods People Intertribal Native American Village
492 Winchendon Rd.
Ashburnham, MA 01430-1229

★470★
Boston Indian Council
105 S. Huntington Ave.
Boston, MA 02130   Ph: (617)232-0343
Bruce Oats, Exec.Dir.
Description: Native Americans in east central Massachusetts. Assists native Americans in transition from reservation to metropolitan environments and provides socioeconomic support.

★471★
North American Indian Center of Boston
105 S. Huntington Ave.   Ph: (617)232-0343
Jamaica Plain, MA 02130   Fax: (617)232-3863
Clifford Fox, Exec.Dir.
Description: Promotes improved urban Indian healthcare.
Affiliated With: American Indian Health Care Association.

★472★
Mashpee Wampanoag Indian Tribal Council
PO Box 1048
Mashpee, MA 02649   Ph: (508)477-0208
Joan A. Tavares, Pres.
Description: Promotes social services for Native Americans.

★473★
Inter-Tribal Council of Tolba Menahan
44 Sycamore St.
Somerville, MA 02143-1226
Margaret Clingan, Contact.

Michigan

★474★
North American Indian Association
22720 Plymouth Rd.   Ph: (313)535-2966
Detroit, MI 48239   Fax: (313)535-8060
Janis A. Fairbanks, Exec.Dir.
Description: Individuals of at least one-quarter North American Indian blood and their families. Membership centered in the Detroit, MI, area; open to natives and non-natives. Objectives are to: establish a meeting center for North American Indians; preserve and promote Indian culture; assist Indians in obtaining higher education; help each other in time of need; work for the betterment of all Indians. Provides employment and training programs, adult counseling services, and children's services. Operates Native American Gallery. Offers speakers' bureau.

★475★
American Indian Community Leadership Council
5315 Ravenswood Rd.   Ph: (810)984-3101
Kimball, MI 48074   Fax: (810)984-6606
Sharon L. Kota, Chwm.
Description: Works to expand programming money and services to Title IX Indian Education programs statewide.

★476★
Inter-Tribal Council of Michigan
405 E. Easterday
Sault Ste. Marie, MI 49783   Ph: (906)632-6896
Sharon L. Teeple, Exec.Dir.
Description: The Bay Mills Indian community, Hannahville, Keweenaw Bay, Lac Vieux Desert Indian community, Saginaw Chippewa, and Sault Ste. Marie tribes. Encourages activities intended to improve the economic and social structures of each community it serves. **Publications:** none.

★477★
Native American Business Council of Michigan
PO Box 861
Warren, MI 48090-0861
Nancy Ragsdale, Contact
Description: Promotes Native American business development.

Minnesota

★478★
Indian Health Board of Minneapolis
1315 E. 24th St.
Minneapolis, MN 55404   Ph: (612)721-9800
Norine Smith, Dir.

★479★
Native American Center of Southeastern Minnesota
Broadway Hall, No. 8, Lower Level
102 S. Broadway
Rochester, MN 55904   Ph: (507)281-4772
Nakoma Volkman, Exec. Officer
Description: Cultural organization striving to educate the community about native Americans.

★480★
Thunder Spirit Lodge
565 Kent St.
St. Paul, MN 55103-1918

Montana

★481★
North American Indian Alliance
100 E. Galena   Ph: (406)723-4361
Butte, MT 59701   Fax: (406)782-7435
Lloyd Barron, Dir.
Description: Promotes improved urban Indian healthcare.
Affiliated With: American Indian Health Care Association.

★482★
Native American Center
700 10th St., S.
PO Box 2612
Great Falls, MT 59403   Ph: (406)761-3165
Charles Walking Child, Chair
Description: Native Americans in Cascade County, MT. Promotes the social well-being of the native American population. Provides medical and human services. **Publications:** none.

★483★
Helena Indian Alliance
436 N. Jackson
Helena, MT 59601   Ph: (406)442-9244
Frances Belgarde, Dir.
Description: Promotes improved urban Indian healthcare.
Affiliated With: American Indian Health Care Association.

★484★
Missoula Indian Center
2300 Regent St., Ste. A   Ph: (406)329-3373
Missoula, MT 59801-7502   Fax: (406)329-3398
Bill Walls, Dir.
Description: Promotes improved urban Indian healthcare.
Affiliated With: American Indian Health Care Association.

Nebraska

★485★
Mid-Winter Pow-Wow and Cultural Non Profit Society
200 S Chestnut
Kimball, NE 69145-1220

★486★
Nebraska Urban Indian Health Coalition
1935 Q St.   Ph: (402)434-7177
Lincoln, NE 68503-3640   Fax: (402)434-7180
Donna Polk, Dir.
Description: Promotes improved urban Indian healthcare.
Affiliated With: American Indian Health Care Association.

New Hampshire

★487★
Friends of the Oglala Lakota
Box 497
Dublin, NH 03444-0497
Nancy Good Cayford.

★488★
Abenaki Indian Center
381 Chestnut St.
Manchester, NH 03101   Ph: (603)644-4555

New Mexico

★489★
Indigenous Communications Association
948 Sage St.
Grants, NM 87020-2932

★490★
Southwestern Association on Indian Affairs
509 Camino de Los Marquez, Ste. 1
Santa Fe, 87501   Ph: (505)983-5220

★491★
Zuni Cultural Arts Council
Drawer F
Zuni, NM 87327   Ph: (505)782-2869

New York

★492★
American Indian Community House
708 Broadway, 8th Fl.   Ph: (212)598-0100
New York, NY 10003   Fax: (212)598-4909
Description: American Indians in the New York City metropolitan
area. To foster intercultural relationships by advocating for the
teaching of Native American culture and history via speakers bureau
resource files and various cultural venues. Works to upgrade the
economic self sufficiency of Native Americans. Sponsors
employment and training programs, alcoholism/substance abuse
counseling, HIV prevention education, and case management, and
health care referral and education. Maintains art gallery, gift shop
and performing arts programs.

★493★
American Indians of All Nations
24 Pauline Circle
Rochester, NY 14623   Ph: (716)359-2858
Barbara Bethmann-Mahooty, Chairperson

★494★
**Native American Resource Center Elementary-
    Secondary Native American Student Cultural
    Program**
494 Averill Ave.   Ph: (716)262-8966
Rochester, NY 14607   Fax: (716)262-8937
Description: Provides after-school cultural education program for
Native American students in the Rochester city school district.

North Carolina

★495★
American Indian Cultural Society of North Florida
6919 Windy Rush Rd.
Charlotte, NC 28266

Ohio

★496★
Lake Erie Native American Council
PO Box 620054
Cleveland, OH 44102-9054

★497★
Ohio Center for Native American Affairs
203 E. Broad St.   Ph: (614)228-0460
Columbus, OH 43215-3701   Fax: (614)228-0484
Kenneth D. Irwin Sr., CEO

★498★
American Indian Education Center
5075 E 86th St.
Garfield Heights, OH 44125-2024
Robert Roche, Contact.

★499★
Native American Cultural Exchange Committee
2512 Aspinwall NE
Warren, OH 44483-2502

★500★
Lakota Foundation
PO Box 0446
West Chester, OH 45071-0446

★501★
Azurite Cherokee Cultural Center
427 R04 Pence Rd.
West Union, OH 45693-0000

★502★
Lower Eastern Ohio Mekoce Shawnee
2902 St. Rte. 22 W
Wilmington, OH 45177-0000
Carrie Sharp, Contact.

Oklahoma

★503★
American Indian Language Center
PO Box 247
Eufaula, OK 74432-0247

★504★
Ponca He-Thush-Ka Society
Rte. 6, Box 769C
Guthrie, OK 73044-9151

★505★
Ki He Kah Steh of Skiatook Oklahoma
PO Box 231
Skiatook, OK 74070-0231

★506★
National Indian Adult Education Association
Rte. 6, Box 81
Tahlequah, OK 74464-9611

★507★
Tulsa Indian Club
PO Box 722
Tulsa, OK 74101   Ph: (918)835-8699
Description: Seeks to perpetuate Indian culture, traditions, and
heritage. Sponsors annual "Tulsa Powwow." Conducts charitable
activities. **Publications:** none.

★508★
Plains Indians and Pioneers Museum Foundation
2009 Williams Ave.
PO Box 1167
Woodward, OK 73082   Ph: (405)256-6136
Louise B. James, Dir.
Description: Collects, preserves, and interprets historical articles
from the northwestern OK area.

Oregon

★509★
American Indian Association of Portland
722 N Killingsworth St.
Portland, OR 97217-2333

★510★
National Indian Athletic Association
4084 Ibex St. NE
Salem, OR 97305-2131

Pennsylvania

★511★
Pennsylvania Association of Native Americans
200 N Third St., Ste. 1100
Harrisburg, PA 17101-1518
Russell Simms, Contact.

★512★
Council of Three Rivers American Indian Center
200 Charles St.   Ph: (412)782-4457
Pittsburgh, PA 15238   Fax: (412)767-4808
Russell Simms, Exec.Dir.
Description: Provides educational, employment, and social service to American Indians in Pennsylvania and West Virginia.

─────────── **South Dakota** ───────────

★513★
Lakota Oyate Akicita Okolaciye
PO Box 1167
Eagle Butte, SD 57625-1167

★514★
Native American Expressions
PO Box 1000
Ft. Pierre, SD 57532-1000

★515★
Northern Plains Native American Chemical Dependency Association
PO Box 1153
Rapid City, SD 57709-1153
Description: individuals interested in reducing the rate of chemical dependency among native Americans in the northern plains of South Dakota.

★516★
United Sioux Tribes of South Dakota Development Corporation
919 Main St., Ste. 114
Rapid City, SD 57701-2686   Ph: (605)343-1100
Description: Promotes employment opportunities for Native Americans. Offers job training services.

─────────── **Tennessee** ───────────

★517★
Chattanooga Inter-Tribal Association at UTC
PO Box 1063
Chattanooga, TN 37401-1063

★518★
East Tennessee Indian League
PO Box 6253   Ph: (423)475-9386
Knoxville, TN 37914-0253   Fax: (423)475-9386
Description: Promotes American Indian heritage through educational and cultural activities. Sponsors an annual powwow and school and scouting programs.

★519★
United South and Eastern Tribes
1101 Kermit Dr., Ste. 302   Ph: (615)361-8700
Nashville, TN 37217   Fax: (615)366-8927
Lionel John, Exec.Dir.
Description: Alliance of Indian tribes: the Cherokees of North Carolina, the Choctaws of Mississippi, the Seminoles and Miccosukees of Florida, the Senecas, Oneidas, and Mohawks of New York, the Chitimacha, Coushatta, and Tunica-Biloxi of Louisiana, the Penobscot, Passamaquoddy, Micmacs, and Maliseets of Maine, Poarch Band of Creek Indians of Alabama, Narragansett of Rhode Island, Coushatta of Texas, Wampanogas of Massachusetts, and Pequot of Connecticut. United to "lift the yoke of poverty from our people" and promote better understanding with other races. Promotes stength in unity of tribes in dealing with the federal government. **Publications:** none.

─────────── **Texas** ───────────

★520★
American Indian Resource and Education Coalition, Austin Chapter
PO Box 3585
Austin, TX 78764   Ph: (512)444-6451
Diana Ramos, Pres.

★521★
Native American Student Organization, Austin Chapter
1616 Royal Crest Dr., No. 29
Austin, TX 78741   Ph: (512)441-8119
Tina Sanders, Leader.

★522★
Texas Indian Bar Association
PO Box 12911
Austin, TX 78711-2911
Description: Attorneys in good standing. Seeks to improve the administration of civil and criminal justice, and the availability of legal services to the public.

★523★
Native American Inter-Tribal Association of Texas
PO Box 71596
Corpus Christi, TX 78467-1596   Ph: (512)854-3411
Tony Torres, Pres.
Description: Native Americans in Texas. Sponsors festival and competitions; conducts charitable activities.

★524★
Dallas/Ft. Worth Intertribal Association
PO Box 4387
Dallas, TX 75208-0387
Frank Tongkemha, Exec. Officer.

★525★
American Indians in Texas
1130 Mission Rd.
San Antonio, TX 78210-4522

─────────── **Virginia** ───────────

★526★
United Indians of Virginia
8620 Varina Rd.
Richmond, VA 23231-8246
Raymond S. Adams, Contact.

─────────── **Washington** ───────────

★527★
United Indians of All Tribes Foundation
Daybreak Star Arts Center
Discovery Park
PO Box 99100   Ph: (206)285-4425
Seattle, WA 98199   Fax: (206)282-3640
Bernie Whitebear, Exec.Dir.
Description: Promotes the interests of Native Americans. Helps to develop and expand Native American economic self-sufficiency, education, arts, adult career education, and employment assistance. Operates Daybreak Star Press. Conducts rotating art exhibits. **Affiliated With:** National Congress of American Indians.

—————— **Wyoming** ——————

★528★
Native American War Dead Memorial
PO Box 1145
Lander, WY 82520-1145

Federal Government Agencies

★529★
U.S. Congress
U.S. House of Representatives
Congressional Native American Caucus
1023 Longworth House Office Bldg.
Washington, DC 20515   Ph: (202)225-2190
Katharine Mottley, Legislative Dir.

★530★
U.S. Department of Education
Office of the Assistant Secretary for Elementary and Secondary Education
Office of Indian Education
Portals Bldg.
1250 Maryland Ave. SW
Washington, DC 20202   Ph: (202)260-3774
Sandra Spaulding, Dir.

★531★
U.S. Department of Health and Human Services
Administration for Children and Families
Administration for Native Americans
Hubert H. Humphrey Bldg.
200 Independence Ave. SW
Washington, DC 20201   Ph: (220)690-7776
Gary N. Kimble, Commissioner

★532★
U.S. Department of Health and Human Services
Office of the General Counsel
Public Health Division
Office of the Indian Health Service Bureau Chief
Parklawn Bldg.
5600 Fishers Lane
Rockville, MD 20201   Ph: (301)443-7126
Duke McCloud, Bureau Chief

★533★
U.S. Department of Health and Human Services
Office of Public Health and Science
Indian Health Service
Parklawn Bldg.
5600 Fishers Lane
Rockville, MD 20857   Ph: (301)443-1083
Michael H. Trujillo, Dir.

★534★
U.S. Department of Health and Human Services
Office of Public Health and Science
Indian Health Service
Office of Tribal Self-Governance
Parklawn Bldg.
5600 Fishers Lane
Rockville, MD 20857   Ph: (301)443-7821
Paula Williams, Dir.

★535★
U.S. Department of Health and Human Services
Office of Public Health and Science
Indian Health Services
Office of Tribal Activities
Parklawn Bldg.
5600 Fishers Lane
Rockville, MD 20857   Ph: (301)443-1104
Douglas P. Black, Assoc. Dir.

★536★
U.S. Department of Housing and Urban Development
Assistant Secretary for Public and Indian Housing Department
Office of Native American Programs
451 Seventh St., SW
Washington, DC 20410   Ph: (202)675-1600
Dominic A. Nessi, Deputy Asst. Sec.

★537★
U.S. Department of Housing and Urban Development
Assistant Secretary for Public and Indian Housing Department
Office of Public and Indian Housing Comptroller
451 Seventh St., SW
Washington, DC 20410   Ph: (202)708-0099
Barbara L. Burkhalter, Comptroller

★538★
U.S. Department of the Interior
Board of Indian Appeals
Ballston Tower #3
4015 Wilson Blvd.
Arlington, VA 22203   Ph: (703)235-3816
Kathryn A. Lynn, Chief Administrative Judge

★539★
U.S. Department of the Interior
Bureau of Indian Affairs
Indian Gaming Management Staff
1849 C St., NW
Washington, DC 20240   Ph: (202)219-4066
George Skibine, Dir.

★540★
U.S. Department of the Interior
Bureau of Indian Affairs
Office of American Indian Trust
1849 C St., NW
Washington, DC 20240   Ph: (202)208-3338
Elizabeth Homer, Dir.

★541★
U.S. Department of the Interior
Bureau of Indian Affairs
Office of Indian Education Programs
1849 C St., NW   Ph: (202)208-6123
Washington, DC 20240   Fax: (202)208-3312
Joann Sebastian Morris, Dir.

★542★
U.S. Department of the Interior
Bureau of Indian Affairs
Office of Tribal Services
1849 C St., NW
Washington, DC 20240   Ph: (202)208-3463
Deborah Maddox, Dir.

★543★
U.S. Department of the Interior
Bureau of Indian Affairs
Office of Trust Responsibilities
1849 C St., NW
Washington, DC 20240
Terry Virden, Dir.
Ph: (202)208-5831
Fax: (202)219-1255

★544★
U.S. Department of the Interior
Office of the Solicitor
Indian Affairs Division
1849 C St., NW
Washington, DC 20240
Robert T. Anderson
Ph: (202)208-3401
Fax: (202)219-1791

★545★
U.S. Department of Justice
Office of Justice Programs
American Indian and Alaska Native Program
Indiana Bldg.
633 Indiana Ave., NW
Washington, DC 20530
Norena Henry, Dir.
Ph: (202)616-9053

★546★
U.S. Indian Arts and Crafts Board
1849 C St., NW
Washington, DC 20240
Geoffrey E. Stamm, Dir.
Ph: (202)208-3773

★547★
U.S. National Indian Gaming Commission
1441 L St., NW
Washington, DC 20005
Harold Montau, Chm.
Ph: (202)632-7003
Fax: (202)632-7066

★548★
U.S. Small Business Administration
Office of Native American Affairs
409 Third St., SW
Washington, DC 20416
Quanah C. Stamps, Asst. Admin.
Ph: (202)205-7364

★549★
U.S. Smithsonian Institution
Center for Museum Studies
American Indian Museum Studies Program
Arts and Industries Bldg.
900 Jefferson Dr., SW
Washington, DC 20560
Karen Cooper, Mgr.
Ph: (202)357-4456

Federal Domestic Assistance Programs

★550★
U.S. Department of Agriculture
Cooperative State Research, Education and Extension Service
Tribal Colleges Education Equity Grants
Higher Education Programs
Rm. 3433-S
Washington, DC 20250
Ph: (202)720-1973
Catalog Number: 10.221 **Objectives:** To enhance educational opportunities at the 29 Tribal Colleges designated as the 1994 Land-Grant Institutions by strengthening their teaching programs in the food and agricultural sciences in targeted need areas. **Applicant Eligibility:** Bay Mills Community College, Blackfeet Community College, Cheyenne River Community College, D-Q

University, Dullknife Memorial College, Fond Du Lac Community College, Fort Belknap Community College, Fort Berthold Community College, Fort Peck Community College, LacCourte Orielles Ojibwa Community College, Little Big Horn Community College, Little Hoop Community College, Nebraska Indian Community College, Northwest Indian College, Oglala Lakota College, Salish Kootenai College, Sinte Gleska University, Sisseton Wahpeton Community College, Standing Rock College, Stonechild Community College, Turtle Mountain Community College, Navajo Community College, United Tribes Technical College, Southwest Indian Polytechnic Institute, Institute of American Indian and Alaska Native Culture and Arts Development, Crownpoint Institute of Technology, Haskell Indian Junior College, Leech Lake Tribal College, and College of the Monoamine Nation. **Types of Assistance:** Formula Grants. **Beneficiary Eligibility:** The 1994 Institutions-Bay Mills Community College, Blackfeet Community College, Cheyenne River Community College, D-Q University, dullknife Memorial College, Fond Du Lac Community College, Fort Belknap Community College, Fort Berthold Community College, Fort Peck Community College, LacCourte Orielles Ojibwa Community College, Little Big Horn Community College, Little Hoop Community College, Nebraska Indian Community College, Northwest Indian College, Oglala Lakota College, Salish Kootenai College, Sinte Gleska University, Sisseton Wahpeton Community College, Standing Rock College, Stonechild Community College, Turtle Mountain Community College, Navajo Community College, United Tribes Technical College, Southwest Indian Polytechnic Institute, Institute of America Indian and Alaska Native Culture and Arts Development, Crownpoint Institute of Technology, Haskell Indian Junior College, Leech Lake Tribal College, and College of the Monoamine Nation.

★551★
U.S. Department of Agriculture
Farm Service Agency
Indian Tribes and Tribal Corporation Loans
Loan Marketing Division
AG Box 0522
Washington, DC 20250
Ph: (202)720-1632
Catalog Number: 10.421. **Objectives:** To enable federally recognized Indian tribes and tribal corporations to acquire land within tribal reservations and Alaskan communities. **Applicant Eligibility:** Limited to any Indian tribe recognized by the Secretary of the Interior or tribal corporation established pursuant to the Indian Reorganization Act which does not have adequate uncommitted funds to acquire lands within the tribe's reservation or in a community in Alaska incorporated by the Secretary of the Interior pursuant to the Indian Reorganization Act. Must be unable to obtain sufficient credit elsewhere at reasonable rates and terms and must be able to show reasonable prospects of success as determined by an acceptable repayment plan and a satisfactory management plan for the land being acquired. **Types of Assistance:** Direct Loans; Guaranteed/Insured Loans. **Beneficiary Eligibility:** American Indian Tribe or tribal corporation recognized by the Secretary of the Interior.

★552★
U.S. Department of Commerce
Minority Business Development Agency
American Indian Program
Office of Strategic Planning & Operations
14th & Constitution Ave. NW, Rm. 5087
Washington, DC 20230
Ph: (202)482-3237
Catalog Number: 11.801. **Objectives:** To provide business development service to American Indians interested in entering, expanding, or improving their efforts in the marketplace. To help American Indian business development centers and American Indian business consultants to provide a wide range of services to American Indian clients, from initial consultation to the identification and resolution of specific business problems. **Applicant Eligibility:** MBDA selects applicants of American Indian origin only. Eligible applicants of American Indian origin may include individuals, nonprofit firms, and American Indian tribes. **Types of Assistance:** Project Grants (Cooperative Agreements). **Beneficiary Eligibility:** American Indians will benefit. Award recipients must provide assistance to American Indians interested in starting a business.

★553★
U.S. Department of Education
Office of Elementary and Secondary Education
Indian Education —Grants to Local Educational Agencies
Office of Indian Education
60 0 Independence Ave., SW
Washington, DC 20202   Ph: (202)260-1441
Catalog Number: 84.060. **Objectives:** Support local educational agencies in their efforts to reform elementary and secondary school programs that serve Indian students in order to ensure that programs are based on challenging state content standards and student performance standards that are used for all students, and are designed to assist Indian students meet those standards in reaching the National Education goals. **Applicant Eligibility:** Local educational agencies (LEAs) that enroll at least 10 Indian children or in which Indians constitute at least 50 percent of the total enrollment. These requirements do not apply to LEAs serving Indian children in Alaska, California, and Oklahoma or located on, or in proximity to, an Indian reservation. **Types of Assistance:** Formula Grants; Project Grants. **Beneficiary Eligibility:** Eligible Indian children enrolled in eligible local educational agencies, tribal schools, and BIA schools.

★554★
U.S. Department of Education
Office of Vocational and Adult Education
Vocational Education—Indian Setaside
Division of National Programs
600 Independence Ave., SW
Washington, DC 20202-7242   Ph: (202)205-5680
Catalog Number: 84.101. **Objectives:** To make grants to or enter contracts with Indian tribes or tribal organizations and to organizations primarily serving and representing Hawaiian Natives to plan, conduct, and administer programs or portions of programs authorized by and consistent with the Carl D. Perkins Vocational Education Act. **Applicant Eligibility:** A tribal organization or an Indian tribe eligible to contract with the Secretary of the Interior for the administration of programs under the Indian Self-Determination and Education Assistance Act of 1975 or under the Act of April 16, 1934. **Types of Assistance:** Project Grants (Cooperative Agreements); Project Grants (Contracts). **Beneficiary Eligibility:** Federally recognized Indian tribes and Hawaiian Natives will benefit.

★555★
U.S. Department of Health and Human Services
Administration on Aging
American Indian, Alaskan Native, & Native Hawaiian Programs
Special Programs for the Aging, Title VI—Part B Grants to Native Hawaiians
330 Independence Ave. SW
Washington, DC 20201   Ph: (202)619-2957
Catalog Number: 93.655. **Objectives:** To promote the delivery of supportive services, including nutrition services to older Indians, Alaskan Natives, and Native Hawaiians. Services are comparable to services provided under Title III of the Older Americans Act of 1965, as amended. **Applicant Eligibility:** Includes public or nonprofit organizations which serve Native Hawaiian Elders, which represent at least 50 Indians or Hawaiians 60 years of age or older. Applicants must document that they have or will have the ability to deliver social and nutrition services. **Types of Assistance:** Project grants. **Beneficiary Eligibility:** Indians or Native Hawaiians who are 60 years of age and older, and in the case of nutrition, their spouses.

★556★
U.S. Department of Health and Human Services
Administration for Children and Families
Tribal Work Grants (Grants for Indian Tribes that Received JOBS Funds)
Office of the Director
Office of Family Assistance
Aerospace Bldg., 5th Fl.
370 L'Enfant Promenade, SW
Washington, DC 20447   Ph: (202)401-9275
Catalog Number: 93.594 **Objectives:** To allow Tribes to operate a program to make work activities available to members of the Indian tribe. **Applicant Eligibility:** An Indian tribe or Alaska Native organization that conducted a Job Opportunities and Basic Skills Training program in fiscal year 1995. **Types of Assistance:** Formula Grants. **Beneficiary Eligibility:** Members of the Indian tribe or Alaska Native organization.

★557★
U.S. Department of Health and Human Services
Indian Health Service
Health Management Development Program
Division of Acquisitions and Grants
  Operations
2300 Twinbrook Pkwy., Ste. 100
Rockville, MD 20857   Ph: (301)443-5204
Catalog Number: 93.228. **Objectives:** To improve the quality of the health of American Indians and Native Alaskans by providing a full range of curative, preventive and rehabilitative health services; and to increase the capability of American Indians and Native Alaskans to assume operation of all or part of an existing Indian Health Service direct-operated health care program. **Applicant Eligibility:** Federally-recognized tribes and tribal organizations. **Types of Assistance:** Project Grants. **Beneficiary Eligibility:** Individuals who are members of an eligible applicant tribe, band, group, or village and who may be regarded as within the scope of the Indian health and medical service program and who are regarded as an Indian by the community in which he lives as evidenced by such factors as tribal membership, enrollment, residence on tax exempt land, ownership of restricted property, active participation in tribal affairs or other relevant factors in keeping with general Bureau of Indian Affairs practices in the jurisdiction.

★558★
U.S. Department of Health and Human Services
Indian Health Service
Health Professions Preparatory Scholarship Program for Indians
12300 Twinbrook Pkwy., Ste. 100
Rockville, MD 20852   Ph: (301)443-0243
Wes Picciotti, Contact
Catalog Number: 93.971. **Objectives:** To make scholarships to American Indians and Alaska Natives for the purpose of completing compensatory pre-professional education to enable the recipient to qualify for enrollment or re-enrollment in a health professions school. **Applicant Eligibility:** Scholarship awards are made to individuals of American Indian or Native Alaskan descent, who have successfully completed high school education or high school equivalency and who have been accepted for enrollment in a compensatory, pre-professional general education course or curriculum. **Types of Assistance:** Project Grants. **Beneficiary Eligibility:** Individuals of American Indian or Native Alaskan descent.

★559★
U.S. Department of Health and Human Services
Indian Health Service
Health Professions Scholarship Program
12300 Twinbrook Pkwy., Ste. 100
Rockville, MD 20852   Ph: (301)443-0243
Catalog Number: 93.972. **Objectives:** To promote service delivery improvement through research studies, and application of knowledge. **Applicant Eligibility:** Individuals of American Indian or Native Alaskan descent are given priority. Applicants for new awards: (1) must be accepted by an accredited U.S. educational institution for a full-time course of study leading to a degree in medicine, osteopathy, dentistry, or other participating health profession which is deemed necessary by the Indian Health Service; (2) be eligible for or hold an appointment as a Commissioned Officer in the Regular or Reserve Corps of the Public Health Service; or (3) be eligible for civilian service in the Indian Health Service. **Types of Assistance:** Project Grants.

★560★
U.S. Department of Health and Human Services
Indian Health Service
Indian Health Service Loan Repayment
12300 Twinbrook Pkwy., Ste. 100
Rockville, MD 20852   Ph: (301)443-3369

Catalog Number: 93.164. **Objectives:** To insure that the Indian Health Service (IHS) has an adequate supply of trained health professionals for Indian health program facilities by providing for the repayment of educational loans for participants who agree (by written contract) to serve an applicable period of time at a facility IHS has designated as a loan repayment priority site or in a designated specialty at a site with an appropriate position. **Applicant Eligibility:** Eligible individuals must be enrolled: (1) in a course of study or program in an accredited institution, as determined by the Secretary, within any State and be scheduled to complete such course of study in the same year such as individual applied to participate in such programs; (2) in an approved graduate training program in a health profession; (3) have a dgree in the health profession and a license to practice a health profession; (4) be eligible for, or hold, an appointment as a commissioned officer in the Regular or Reserve Corps of the Public Health Service (PHS); (5) be eligible for selection for civilian service in the Regular or Reserve Corps of the PHS; (6) meet the professional standards for civil service employment in the IHS; (7) be employed with an Indian health program funded under Public Law 93-638, Indian Self-Determination, Title V of Public Law 94-437 and its amendments or the Buy Indian Act (25 U.S.C. 47); (8) submit an application to participate in the IHS Loan Repayment Program; and (9) sign and submit to the Secretary for Health and Human Services at the time of such application, a written contract agreeing to accept loan repayment of health professions educational loans and to serve for an applicable period of service at loan repayment priority site as determined by the Secretary. The term "State" is defined in Section 331 (i)(4) of the PHS Act. **Types of Assistance:** Project Grants. **Beneficiary Eligibility:** Health professionals who have Government (Federal, State, local) and commercial unpaid educational loans will benefit from this program.

★561★
U.S. Department of Health and Human Services
Indian Health Service
Indian Health Service Research
12300 Twinbrook Pkwy., Ste. 100
Rockville, MD 20852   Ph: (301)443-5204

Catalog Number: 93.905. **Objectives:** To conduct research and developmental activities in areas of Indian health care which further the performance of health responsibilities of the Indian Health Service. **Applicant Eligibility:** There are two groups of eligible applicants: (1) Federally recognized Indian tribes and tribal organizations which are contracting with the Indian Health Service under the authority of the Indian Self-Determination and Education Assistance Act; and (2) Indian Health Service components, including Service units and area offices. /TYP Direct payment for specified use. **Beneficiary Eligibility:** American Indian Tribes and Alaska Natives.

★562★
U.S. Department of Health and Human Services
Indian Health Services
Health Professions Recruitment Program for Indians
12300 Twinbrook Pkwy., Ste. 100
Rockville, MD 20852   Ph: (301)443-5204

Catalog Number: 93.970. **Objectives:** (1) To identify American Indians and Alaska Natives with a potential for education or training in the health professions, and to encourage and assist them to enroll in health or allied health professional schools (2) to increaase the number of nurses, nurse midwives, nurse practitioners and nurse anesthetists who deliver health care services to American Indians and Alaska Natives; and (3) to place health professional residents for short-term assignments at Indian Health Service facilities as a recruitment aid. **Applicant Eligibility:** Public or private nonprofit health or educational entities or Indian tribes or tribal organizations as specifically provided in legislative authority. **Types of Assistance:** Project Grants. **Beneficiary Eligibility:** Preference is given to applicants in the following order of priority: (1) Indian tribes; (2) tribal organizations; (3) urban Indian organizations and other Indian health organizations; or (4) other public or nonprofit health or educational entities.

★563★
U.S. Department of Health and Human Services
Indian Health Services
Research and Demonstration Projects for Indian Health
Division of Acquisition and Grants
  Operations
12300 Twinbrook Pkwy., Ste. 100
Rockville, MD 20852   Ph: (301)443-5204

Catalog Number: 93.933. **Objectives:** To promote improved health care among American Indians and Alaska Natives through research studies, and demonstration projects. **Applicant Eligibility:** Federally recognized Indian tribes; tribal organizations; nonprofit intertribal organizations; nonprofit urban Indian organizations contracting with the Indian Health Service under Title V of the Indian Health Care Improvement Act; public or private nonprofit health and education entities; and State and local government health agencies. **Types of Assistance:** Project Grants. **Beneficiary Eligibility:** American Indians/Alaska Natives will be the ultimate beneficiaries of the funded projects either directly or indirectly depending upon the nature of the project. For example, those individuals who participate in research studies and receive services will be direct beneficiaries while those impacted by policy changes resulting from analyses of Indian health care issues will be indirect beneficiaries.

★564★
U.S. Department of Housing and Urban Development
Public and Indian Housing
Washington, DC 20410   Ph: (202)708-0950

Catalog Number: 14.850. **Objectives:** To provide and operate cost-effective, decent, safe and sanitary dwellings for lower income families through an authorized local Public Housing Agency (PHA) or Indian Housing Authority (IHA). **Applicant Eligibility:** Public Housing Agencies and Indian Housing Authorities established in accordance with State or Tribal law are eligible. Other lower income individuals may be served under certain limited cirumstances. **Types of Assistance:** Direct payments for specified use. **Beneficiary Eligibility:** Lower income families composed of citizens or eligible immigrants. "Families" include individuals who are 62 years old or older, disabled , or handicapped, or the remaining member of a tenant family.

★565★
U.S. Department of Housing and Urban Development
Public and Indian Housing—Comprehensive Improvement Assistance Program
Washington, DC 20413   Ph: (202)708-0950

Catalog Number: 14.852. **Objectives:** To provide capital funds to improve the physical condition and upgrade the management and operation of existing Public and Indian Housing projects to assure that they continue to be available to serve low-income families. **Applicant Eligibility:** Public Housing Agencies (PHAs) and Indian Housing Authorities (IHAs) operating PHA/IHA owned low income housing projects under an existing Annual Contributions Contract (ACC) with fewer than 250 units. **Types of Assistance:** Project Grants. **Beneficiary Eligibility:** The tenants of the modernized project are the ultimate beneficiaries.

★566★
U.S. Department of the Interior
Bureau of Indian Affairs
Higher Education Grant Program
Office of Indian Educational Programs
1849 C St., NW
MS3512 - MIB
Washington, DC 20245   Ph: (202)219-1127

Catalog Number: 15.114. **Objectives:** To provide finanical aid to eligible Indian students to enable them to attended accredited institutions of higher education. **Applicant Eligibility:** Must be a member of an Indian tribe or Alaska Native Village being served by the Bureau, be enrolled or accepted for enrollment in an accredited college, and have financial need as determined by the institution's financial aid office. **Types of Assistance:** Project Grants. **Beneficiary Eligibility:** Same as applicant eligibility.

★567★
U.S. Department of the Interior
Bureau of Indian Affairs
Indian Child Welfare Act—Title II Grants
Office of Tribal Services
1847 C St. NW
MS 4603 MIB
Washington, DC 20245   Ph: (202)208-2721

Catalog Number: 15.144. **Objectives:** To promote the stability and security of Indian tribes and families by the establishment of minimum Federal standards for the removal of Indian children from their families and the placment of such children in foster or adoptive homes and providing assistance to Indian tribes in the oepration of child and family service programs. **Applicant Eligibility:** Federally recognized Indian Tribal governments. **Types of Assistance:** Project Grants. **Beneficiary Eligibility:** American Indian children and families.

★568★
U.S. Department of the Interior
Bureau of Indian Affairs
Indian Education—Assistance to Schools
Office of Indian Educational Programs
1847 C St. NW
Washington, DC 20240   Ph: (202)211-1127

Catalog Number: 15.130. **Objectives:** To provide supplemental education programs for eligible Indian students attending public schools. **Applicant Eligibility:** Tribal organizations, Indian Corporations, school districts or States which have eligible Indian children attending public school districts and have established Indian Education Committees to approve supplementary programs beneficial to Indian students. **Types of Assistance:** Direct Payments for Specified Use. **Beneficiary Eligibility:** Children who are enrolled members of a federally recognized Indian tribe or are at least one-fourth degree of Indian blood descent, who are between the age of 3 and grade 12. Priority is given to those residing on or near Indian reservations.

★569★
U.S. Department of the Interior
Bureau of Indian Affairs
Indian Employment Assistance
Office of Economic Development
1849 C St. NW
MS 2061 M1B
Washington, DC 20240   Ph: (202)208-2570

Catalog Number: 15.108. **Objectives:** To provide eligible American Indians vocational training and employment opportunities. **Applicant Eligibility:** Federally recognized Indian tribal governments and Native American organizations authorized by Indian tribal governments may apply to administer the program. Individual American Indian applicants must be a member of a federally recognized Indian tribe, be in need of financial assistance, and reside on or near an Indian reservation under the jurisdiction of the Bureau of Indian Affairs. **Types of Assistance:** Direct Payment for Specified Use. **Beneficiary Eligibility:** Members of federally recognized Indian tribes who are unemployed, underemployed, or in need of training to obtain reasonable and satisfactory employment.

★570★
U.S. Department of the Interior
Bureau of Indian Affairs
Indian Housing Assistance
Office of Tribal Services
1847 C St., NW
Washington, DC 20240   Ph: (202)208-2721

Catalog Number: 15.141. **Objectives:** To use the Indian Housing Improvement Program (HIP) and Bureau of Indian Affairs resources to substantially eliminate substandard Indian housing. This effort is combined with the Department of Health and Human Services. **Applicant Eligibility:** Federally recognized Indian tribal governments and tribal organizations to adminster the program who have needs identified in the most current tribal housing inventory. Individual Indians in need of housing assistance who are unable to obtain assistance from any other source and meet the eligibility criteria of the Housing Improvement Program (HIP) regulations.

Types of Assistance: Project Grants (Contracts); Dissemination of Techinical Information. **Beneficiary Eligibility:** Same as applicant eligibility.

★571★
U.S. Department of the Interio r
Bureau of Indian Affairs
Indian Loans—Economic Development
Office of Economic Development
1849 C St. NW, MS 2061
Washington, DC 20240   Ph: (202)208-5324

Catalog Number: 15.124. **Objectives:** To provide assistance to federally recognized Indian tribal governments, and individual America Indians in obtaining financing from private sources to promote business development initiatives on or near federally recognized Indian reservations. **Applicant Eligibility:** Federally recognized Indian tribal governments, Native American organizations authorized by Indian tribal governments, and individual American Indians. **Types of Assistance:** Direct Loans; Guaranteed/Insured Loans; Provisions of Specialized Services. **Beneficiary Eligibility:** Same as applicant eligibility.

★572★
U.S. Department of the Interior
Bureau of Indian Affairs
Indian Social Services—Child Welfare Assistance
Office of Tribal Services
1849 C St., NW
Washington, DC 20240   Ph: (202)208-2721

Catalog Number: 15.103. **Objectives:** To provide foster home care and appropriate institutional (non-medical) care for dependent, neglected, and handicapped Indian children in need of protection residing on or near reservations, including those children living in Bureau of Indian Affairs service area jurisdictions in Alaska and Oklahoma, when these services are not available from State or local public agencies. **Applicant Eligibility:** Dependent, neglected, and handicapped Indian children in need of protection whose families live on or near Indian reservations or in jurisdictions under the Bureau of Indian Affairs in Alaska and Oklahoma, and who are not eligible for similar Federal, State, or county funded programs. Applications may be made by a parent, guardian or person having custody of the child, or by court referral. **Types of Assistance:** Direct Payments for Specified Use. **Beneficiary Eligibility:** Members of federally recognized Indian tribes.

★573★
U.S. Department of the Interior
Bureau of Indian Affairs
Indian Social Services—General Assistance
Office of Tribal Services
Division of Social Services
1849 C St., NW
MS 4603 MIB
Washington, DC 20245   Ph: (202)208-2721

Catalog Number: 15.113. **Objectives:** To provide financial assistance for basic needs of needy eligible Indians who reside on or near reservations, including those Indians living under the Bureau of Indian Affairs service area jurisdictions, when such assistance is not available from state or local public agencies. **Applicant Eligibility:** Members of federally recognized Indian Tribes, residing on or near a federally recognized Indian reservation in need of financial assistance. **Types of Assistance:** Unrestricted Direct Payments. **Beneficiary Eligibility:** Members of federally recognized Indian tribes.

★574★
U.S. Department of the Interior
Bureau of Indian Affairs
Navajo-Hopi Indian Settlement Program
Office of Trust Responsibilities
1849 C St., NW
MS-4510 MIB
Washington, DC 20240   Ph: (202)208-3598

Catalog Number: 15.057 **Objectives:** To implement those provisions of the Navajo-Hopi Settlement Act of 1974, as amended, which are assigned to the Department of the Interior; and to institute conservation practices and methods to restore the grazing potential of rangelands lying within the former Navajo/Hopi Joint Use Area. **Applicant Eligibility:** Federally Recognized Indian Tribal Governments of the Navajo and Hopi Tribes and Native American Organizations authorized by either Tribe. **Types of Assistance:** Direct Payments for Specified Use. **Beneficiary Eligibility:** Federally Recognized Indian Tribal Governments of the Navajo and Hopi Tribes and individual members of both Tribes.

★575★
U.S. Department of the Interior
Indian Arts and Crafts Development
Indian Arts and Crafts Board
Main Interior Bldg., Rm. 4004
Washington, DC 20240   Ph: (202)208-3773
Catalog Number: 15.850. **Objectives:** To encourage and promote the development of American Indian arts and crafts. **Applicant Eligibility:** American Indian and Alaska Native individuals and organizations, federally recognized Indian tribal governments, State and local governments, and nonprofit organizations. **Types of Assistance:** Use of Property, Facilities, and Equipment; Advisory Services and Counseling; Investigation of Complaints. **Beneficiary Eligibility:** Same as applicant eligibility.

★576★
U.S. Department of Justice
Office for Victims of Crime
Office of Justice Programs
Children's Justice Act for Native American Indian
  Tribes
633 Indiana Ave. NW
Washington, DC 20531   Ph: (202)616-3578
Catalog Number: 16.583. **Objectives:** Fifteen percent of the first $10 million of funds from the Crime Victims Fund that are transferred to the Department of Health and Human Services as part of the Children's Justice Act are to be statutorily reserved by the Office for Victims of Crime (OVC) to make grants for the purpose of assisting Native American Indian tribes in developing, establishing, and operating programs designed to improve the handling of child abuse cases, particularly cases of child sexual abuse, in a manner which limits additional trauma to the child victim and improves the investigation and prosecution of cases of child abuse. **Applicant Eligibility:** Federally recognized Indian tribal governments and nonprofit organizations that provide services to Native Americans. Specific criteria will vary depending on the grant. **Types of Assistance:** Project Grants; Direct Payments for Specified Use. **Beneficiary Eligibility:** Native American youth who are victims of child abuse and/or child sexual abuse.

★577★
U.S. Department of Labor
Employment and Training Administration
Native American Employment and Training Programs
Division of Indian and Native American
  Programs
200 Constitution Ave., NW, Rm. N4641
Washington, DC 20210   Ph: (202)219-8502
Catalog Number: 17.251. **Objectives:** To afford job training to Native Americans facing serious barriers to employment, who are in special need of such training to obtain productive employment. To reduce the economic disadvantages among Indians and others of Native American descent and to advance the economic and social development of such people. **Applicant Eligibility:** Indian tribes, bands or groups, Alaska Native villages or groups, and Hawaiian Native communities meeting the eligibility criteria, public bodies or private nonprofit agencies selected by the Secretary. Tribes, bands and groups may also form consortia in order to qualify for designation as a grantee. An independently eligible grantee shall be an Indian or Native American entity which has: (1) An identifiable Native American resident population of at least 1,000 individuals (for new grantees) within its designated service area, and (2) the capability to administer Indian and Native American employment and training programs. **Types of Assistance:** Formula Grants. **Beneficiary Eligibility:** Members of State or federally recognized Indian tribes, bands and other individuals of Native American descent, such as, but not limited to, the Kalamaths in Oregon, Micmac and Miliseet in Maine, the Lumbees in North Carolina and

South Carolina, Indians variously descibed as terminated or landless, Eskimos and Aleuts in Alaska, and Hawaiian Natives. ("Hawaiian Native" means an individual any of whose ancestors were natives prior to 1778 of the area which now comprises the State of Hawaii.) Applicants must also be economically disadvantaged, unemployed, or underemployed. A Native American grantee may apply in some cases enroll participants who are not economically disadvantaged, unemployed, or underemployed in upgrading and retraining programs.

State/Provincial & Local Government Agencies

Alabama

★578★
Alabama Attorney General
Civil Rights Division
11 S Union St.   Ph: (334)242-7300
Montgomery, AL 36130   Fax: (334)242-7458

Arizona

★579★
Arizona Attorney General
Civil Rights Section
1275 W Washington   Ph: (602)542-4266
Phoenix, AZ 85007   Fax: (602)542-4085

California

★580★
California Health Services Department
Civil Rights Office
714 P St., Rm. 1253   Ph: (916)657-1411
Sacramento, CA 95814   Fax: (916)657-1156

★581★
California Native American Heritage Commission
915 Capitol Mall, Rm 364   Ph: (916)653-4082
Sacramento, CA 95814   Fax: (916)657-5390
Larry Myers, Exec. Sec

Colorado

★582★
Colorado Local Affairs Department
Minority Business Office
1313 Sherman St., Rm. 323   Ph: (303)866-4014
Denver, CO 80203   Fax: (303)866-2251

★583★
Colorado Regulatory Agencies Department
Civil Rights Division
1560 Broadway, Ste. 1550   Ph: (303)894-2997
Denver, CO 80202   Fax: (303)894-7885

——— Delaware ———

★584★
Delaware State Department
Human Relations Division
Carvel State Office Bldg.
820 N French St.   Ph: (302)577-3485
Wilmington, DE 19801   Fax: (302)739-3811

★585★
Delaware Transportation Department
Equal Employment Opportunity and Civil Rights
  Office
Transportation Administration Bldg.
PO Box 778   Ph: (302)739-4371
Dover, DE 19903-0778   Fax: (302)739-4329
John Mathis, EEO & Civil Rights Off.

——— Kansas ———

★586★
Kansas Commerce and Housing Department
Minority Business Office
700 SW Harrison St., Ste. 1300   Ph: (913)296-5298
Topeka, KS 66603-3712   Fax: (913)296-5055

★587★
Kansas Human Resources Department
Equal Employment Opportunity Office
401 SW Topeka Blvd.   Ph: (913)296-2667
Topeka, KS 66603-3182   Fax: (913)296-0179

——— Michigan ———

★588★
Michigan Indian Affairs Commission
201 Washington Sq., 7th Fl.   Ph: (517)373-0654
Lansing, MI 48913   Fax: (517)373-1649

——— Minnesota ———

★589★
Minnesota Indian Affairs Council
1819 Bmidji Ave.   Ph: (218)755-3825
Bemidji, MN 56601   Fax: (218)755-3739
Joseph Day, Exec. Dir.

——— New Mexico ———

★590★
Albuquerque Family and Community Services Office
Human Rights Section
PO Box 1293
Albuquerque, NM 87103   Ph: (505)924-2980
Frank Miranda

★591★
New Mexico Indian Affairs Office
La Villa Bldg.
228 E. Palace Ave.   Ph: (505)827-6440
Santa Fe, NM 87501   Fax: (505)827-6445
Regis Pecos, Exec. Dir.

——— New York ———

★592★
Albany Equal Employment Opportunity and Fair
  Housing Office
City Hall
Albany, NY 12207   Ph: (518)434-5280
Angela Dixon

——— North Dakota ———

★593★
North Dakota Public Instruction Department
Indian Education Division
600 E. Boulevard Ave.   Ph: (701)328-2720
Bismarck, ND 58505-0440   Fax: (701)328-2461

——— Oklahoma ———

★594★
Oklahoma Indian Affairs Commission
4545 N. Lincoln Blvd., Ste. 282   Ph: (405)521-3828
Oklahoma City, OK 73105   Fax: (405)521-0902
Barbara Warner, Exec. Dir.

★595★
Oklahoma School Improvement and Standards
Indian Education Office
2500 N. Lincoln Blvd.   Ph: (405)521-3311
Oklahoma City, OK 73105   Fax: (405)521-2971

——— South Dakota ———

★596★
South Dakota Office of the Governor
Indian Affairs Office
Public Safety Bldg., 3rd Fl.   Ph: (605)773-3415
Pierre, SD 57501   Fax: (605)773-4711
Webster Two Hawk, Commissioner

——— Tennessee ———

★597★
Chattanooga Equal Employment Opportunity and
  Better Housing Office
City Hall
100 E. 11th St.   Ph: (423)757-5277
Chattanooga, TN 37402   Fax: (423)757-0005
Moses Freeman, Dir.

——— Utah ———

★598★
Utah Community and Economic Development
  Department
Indian Affairs Division
324 S. State St., Ste. 500   Ph: (801)538-8700
Salt Lake City, UT 84111   Fax: (801)538-8888

Library Collections

★599★
Akwesasne Library Cultural Center
RR 1, Box 14C
Hogansburg, NY 13655
Carol White, Dir.
Ph: (518)358-2240
Fax: (518)358-2649

Founded: 1971. **Special Collections:** American Indian collection (1900 items). **Holdings:** AV programs; pamphlets. **Subscriptions:** 35 serials.

★600★
Allen County Historical Society
Elizabeth M. MacDonell Memorial Library
620 W. Market St.
Lima, OH 45801-4604
Anna B. Selfridge, Cur., Archv. & Mss.
Ph: (419)222-9426
Fax: (419)222-0649

Founded: 1908. **Subjects:** Local history and genealogy, Ohio history, railroading, American Indian. **Special Collections:** John H. Keller Railroad Collection; Interurban and Street Railway Collection; Lima Locomotive Works Collection; Railroad Labor History Collection (30 cubic feet). **Holdings:** 8271 books; 585 bound periodical volumes; Lima, Ohio newspapers, 1840s to present; Lima directories, 1876 to present; 1938 reels of microfilm of newspapers and census records. **Subscriptions:** 40 journals and other serials.

★601★
Amarillo Public Library
Local History Collection
413 E 4th
Box 2171
Amarillo, TX 79189-2171
Mary Kay Snell, Dir., Lib.Svc.
Ph: (806)378-3054
Fax: (806)378-4245

Subjects: Southwestern history, Indian tribes and customs, religion. **Special Collections:** Bush/FitzSimon Collection of Books on the Southwest; John LMcCarty Papers (4030). **Holdings:** 5078 books; 765 unbound periodicals; 219 maps.

★602★
American Indian Bible College
Dorothy Cummings Memorial Library
10020 N15th Ave.
Phoenix, AZ 85021-2199
John S. Rose, Dir.
Ph: (602)944-3335

Subjects: Biblical studies, Native Americans. **Holdings:** 14,500 books; 625 microfiche; 780 audio cassettes. **Subscriptions:** 110 journals and other serials; 5 newspapers.

★603★
American Indian Center of Santa Clara Valley, Inc.
Indian Center Library
919 The Alameda
San Jose, CA 95126-3135
Ph: (408)971-0772

Founded: 1972 **Subjects:** American Indian. **Special Collections:** American Indian newspapers and language tapes. **Holdings:** 4500 books; 60 bound periodical volumes; phonograph records; films; book and audiovisual teaching materials for and about Native Americans; pamphlets; government documents; maps; charts; pictures; publications from Indian reservations. **Subscriptions:** 27 journals and other serials; 10 newspapers.

★604★
American Indian Research Project
South Dakota Oral History Center
Library
12 Dakota Hall
University of South Dakota
414 E. Clark St.
Vermillion, SD 57069
Leonard R. Bruguier, Dir.
Ph: (605)677-5209
Fax: (605)677-6525

Founded: 1966 **Subjects:** South Dakota and Indian history. **Special Collections:** Jurrens Collection of Native American music (36 tapes); Ella C. Deloria Collection; American Indian Research Archives; South Dakota Oral History Collection (audio- and reel-to-reel tapes). **Holdings:** 5000 audiotapes.

★605★
American Philosophical Society
Library
105 S. Fifth St.
Philadelphia, PA 19106-3386
Dr. Edward C. Carter II, Libn.
Ph: (215)440-3400
Fax: (215)440-3423

Founded: 1743. **Subjects:** History of American science including important European background material; Americana (early imprints, travels). **Special Collections:** Papers of Benjamin Franklin, Charles Darwin, Charles Willson Peale; Lewis and Clark Journals; American Indian linguistics; Thomas Paine; Simon Flexner; genetics; Stephen Girard papers; Franz Boas Collection; Society's archives (history of American science); history of quantum physics. **Holdings:** 200,000 volumes; 6.5 million manuscripts; microfilm; maps; prints, especially of Philadelphia and Frankliniana. **Subscriptions:** 950 journals and other serials.

★606★
Angel Mounds State Historic Site
Library
8215 Pollack Ave.
Evansville, IN 47715
Mary Alexander, Cur.
Ph: (812)853-3956
Fax: (812)853-6271

Subjects: Native Americans, Mississippian Indians, nature, Indiana history. **Holdings:** 200 books. **Subscriptions:** 4 journals and other serials.

★607★
Arizona Historical Society
Library/Archives
949 E 2nd St.
Tucson, AZ 85719
Ph: (520)617-1157
Fax: (520)628-5695

Founded: 1884 **Subjects:** Southwestern Americana - Arizona territorial and state government, mining, Mexican history, Spanish North American colonial history, military history, ranching, Southwestern Indians. **Special Collections:** Charles B. Gatewood military collection; Byron Cummings ethnological and archaeological collection; Frederick S Dellenbaugh Colorado River collection; Aguiar Collection of early 19th century Mexican documents; Carl Hayden biographical files of 1854-1864 Arizonans; Will C Barnes ranching and forestry papers. **Holdings:** 50,000 books; 5000 bound periodical volumes; 10,000 pamphlets; 5000 maps; 250,000 photographs; 1000 manuscripts; 750 linear feet of documents. **Subscriptions:** 39 journals and other serials; 33 newspapers.

★608★
Arizona State Parks
Homolovi Ruins State Park Library
HCR63 Box 5
Winslow, AZ 86047-9803
Karen Berggren, Pk.Mgr.
Ph: (520)289-4106
Fax: (520)289-2021

Founded: 1987 **Subjects:** Anasazi culture; prehistory of Southwestern United States; Hopi, Navajo, and other Northern Arizona Indian cultures; cultural and natural history of Northern Arizona. **Special Collections:** Development and archaeological documents of Homolovi Ruins State Park. **Holdings:** 1500 books; 100 other cataloged items; teachers kit. **Subscriptions:** 5 journals and other serials; 4 newspapers.

★609★
Arkansas State University Museum
Library/Archives
Box 490
State University, AR 72467
Ph: (501)972-2074
Fax: (501)972-2793

Founded: 1936 **Subjects:** History - Indian, American military, Arkansas, United States, European; old textbooks; religion; children's rare books; minerals and fossils. **Special Collections:** Rare newspapers, 1750-1960 (1500); sheet music, 1840-1950 (1050 pieces); Sharp County, Arkansas Courthouse Ledgers. **Holdings:** 5000 books; 6500 other cataloged items. **Subscriptions:** 3 journals and other serials.

★610★
Augustana College
Center for Western Studies
PO Box 727   Ph: (605)336-4007
Sioux Falls, SD 57197   Fax: (605)336-4999
Arthur R. Huseboe, Exec.Dir.

Founded: 1970 **Subjects:** Upper Great Plains history and literature, American literature, Plains Indians history, South Dakota history, Sioux Falls history. **Special Collections:** Episcopal Diocese of South Dakota Archives; United Church of Christ, South Dakota Conference Archives (including Stephen Riggs papers); Augustana College Archives; Goertz Germans from Russia Collection. **Holdings:** 35,000 books and bound periodical volumes; 4000 linear feet of manuscript, photograph, and artifact collections. **Subscriptions:** 10 journals.

★611★
B. Robinson Department of Special Collections
Chester Fritz Library
Box 9000   Ph: (701)777-4625
Grand Forks, ND 58202-9000   Fax: (701)777-3319
Sandra Slater, Hd.Archv. & Spec.Coll.

Founded: 1963 **Subjects:** History - North and South Dakota, Northern Great Plains, Plains Indian, environmental; agrarian radicalism; Nonpartisan League (North Dakota); genealogy; oral history; ethnic heritage and family history (North Dakota); Norwegian local history. **Special Collections:** North Dakota Book Collection (20,697 volumes); Fred G. Aandahl Book Collection (1537 volumes); Family History/Genealogy Collection (4187 volumes); North Dakota State Documents (6002); university archives (2643 linear feet); Orin G. Libby Manuscript Collection (11,734 linear feet). **Holdings:** 34,757 books; 14,377 linear feet of manuscript material; 4317 reels of microfilm; 48,092 photographs; 3954 AV items; 6989 theses and dissertations. **Subscriptions:** 71 journals and other serials; 4 newspapers.

★612★
Bacone College
Library
Special Collections
2299 Old Bacone Rd.
Muskogee, OK 74403   Ph: (918)683-4581
Frances A. Donelson, Libn.

Founded: 1880 **Subjects:** North American Indians, nursing, radiologic technology, religion. **Holdings:** 31,000 books; 4746 bound periodical volumes; 10 drawers of microfiche; 2 cabinets of microfilm; 20 video cassettes. **Subscriptions:** 150 journals and other serials; 17 newspapers.

★613★
Bishop Baraga Association
Archives
444 S4th St.
Box 550   Ph: (906)225-1141
Marquette, MI 49855   Fax: (906)225-0437
Elizabeth Delene

Founded: 1930 **Subjects:** Bishop Frederic Baraga, Native Americans, Catholic Church, United States history. **Special Collections:** Baraga Collection (books, diaries, letters, 1830-1868); microfilm of the Office of Indian Affairs, early 1800s. **Holdings:** 1003 books; microfilm.

★614★
Bitter Root Valley Historical Society
Ravalli County Museum
Miles Romney Memorial Library
Old Court House
205 Bedford Ave.   Ph: (406)363-3338
Hamilton, MT 59840   Fax: (406)363-3338
Helen Ann Bibler, Dir.

Founded: 1979 **Subjects:** Pioneer and Native American history. **Special Collections:** Native American Collection; Granville Stuart Collection; Western News Files, 1890-1977; Ravalli Republican Files, 1899 to present; Northwest Tribune Files, 1906-1950; Stevensville Register Files, 1906-1914; western history (two private libraries). **Holdings:** 500 books. **Subscriptions:** 3 newspapers.

★615★
Black Hills State University
E.Y. Berry Library-Learning Center
Special Collections
1200 University   Ph: (605)642-6361
Spearfish, SD 57799-9548   Fax: (605)642-6298
Colleen Kirby, Spec.Coll.Libn.

Founded: 1925 **Subjects:** Local and regional history, biography, Dakota Indians, western industry, transportation, North American Indians. **Special Collections:** E.Y. Berry Collection (manuscripts, photographs, color slides, tape recordings, and films, all dealing with his 20 years of service in the U.S. House of Representatives, 1951-1971); Black Hills State University Archives; Leland D. Case Library for Western Historical Studies; Library of American Civilization (microfiche); Wagner-Camp Collection (microcard); Cox Library (microfilm). **Holdings:** 12,607 volumes; 949 manuscript boxes; 54 VF drawers; 85 drawers of maps and photographs; 12,888 titles on 14,548 microforms. **Subscriptions:** 60 journals and other serials; 7 newspapers.

★616★
Blue Cloud Abbey
Library
PO Box 98   Ph: (605)432-5528
Marvin, SD 57251-0098   Fax: (605)432-4754
Rev. Odilo Burkhardt, O.S.B.

Founded: 1954 **Subjects:** Scripture, monastic theology, patristics, church history, general theology, Indian history. **Special Collections:** Bureau of American Ethnology publications (complete set). **Holdings:** 50,000 books; 600 bound periodical volumes. **Subscriptions:** 150 journals and other serials; 20 newspapers.

★617★
Bowers Museum of Cultural Art
Research Library
2002 N. Main St.   Ph: (714)567-3652
Santa Ana, CA 92706   Fax: (714)567-3652
Jacqueline Bryant, Cur.Res.

Founded: 1936 **Subjects:** Art and culture - Native American, Pre-Columbian, African, Oceanic, and Asian; Orange County and California history. **Holdings:** 7000 books and ephemera; 75,000 objects; slides; films; videotapes. **Subscriptions:** 20 journals and other serials; 10 newspapers.

★618★
Bridgeton Public Library
Special Collections
150 E. Commerce St.   Ph: (609)451-2620
Bridgeton, NJ 08302-2684   Fax: (609)455-1049
Gail S. Robinson, Lib.Dir.

Founded: 1811 **Subjects:** Cumberland County history, local genealogy, Woodland Indians. **Holdings:** 2000 volumes, including newspapers, 1881 to present, bound and on microfilm; 20,000 Indian artifacts, 10,000 B.C to circa 1700 A.D., collected within a 30-mile radius of the Library. **Subscriptions:** 105 journals and other serials; 7 newspapers.

★619★
Brooklyn Museum
Art Reference Library
200 Eastern Pkwy.   Ph: (718)638-5000
Brooklyn, NY 11238   Fax: (718)638-3731
Deirdre E. Lawrence, Prin.Libn.

Founded: 1823 **Subjects:** American and European painting and sculpture; decorative arts; art - African, Oceanic, Native American; prints and drawings; Asian art; costumes and textiles. **Special Collections:** American fashion sketches, 1900-1950; museum archives. **Holdings:** 170,000 books and exhibition catalogs; 25,000 bound periodical volumes; 100 VF drawers of ephemeral materials; museum archival materials. **Subscriptions:** 400 journals and other serials.

★620★
Brown and Bain, P.A.
Library
2901 N. Central   Ph: (602)351-8039
Phoenix, AZ 85001-0400   Fax: (602)351-8516
Ellen Hepner, Law Libn.

Subjects: Law. **Special Collections:** Antitrust law; American Indian law; computer/technology law; trade secrets. **Holdings:** 50,000 volumes. **Subscriptions:** 300 journals and other serials.

★621★
Buffalo Bill Historical Center
McCracken Research Library
Box 1000   Ph: (307)578-4059
Cody, WY 82414   Fax: (307)587-5714
Nathan E. Bender, Cur.

Founded: 1980 **Subjects:** Western American history and art, Plains Indian studies, firearms technology and history, natural sciences of the Greater Yellowstone/Big Horn Basin Region. **Special Collections:** William F. Cody Collection; Valley Ranch manuscript collection; Charles Belden Photo Collection; Mercaldo Photo Archives of Western subjects; photographs of noted Indians, military leaders, Indian campaigns; Winchester Repeating Arms Company archives; Yellowstone National Park (200 volumes; maps, stereoviews, and other nonbook items); Frederic Remington Illustrations (200 books; clippings; ephemera; reference photographs); Frank Tenney Johnson Archives; Joseph H Sharp Archives; W.H.D. Koerner Studio Archives; I.H. Larom Dude Ranch Collection; Don Russell Collection; Victor Alexander Saddle Catalog Collection. **Holdings:** 15,000 volumes; 30 volumes of press clippings; motion picture films; archival film footage 616 reels of microfilm and 7000 books in the Yale Western Americana microfilm collection; 4000 slides; vertical files of gallery, museum, artist files, subject files; 2000 audiocassettes; 300 videocassettes. **Subscriptions:** 40 journals and other serials.

★622★
The Cayuga Museum
Library
203 Genesee St.
Auburn, NY 13021   Ph: (315)253-8051

Founded: 1936 **Subjects:** Central New York Indian and Cayuga County history, early sound motion pictures. **Special Collections:** General John S. Clark Collection of Indian history; Auburn Theological Seminary; Civil War; Case Film Research Laboratory materials; Cayuga County Historical Society collections and archives (1876-1973). **Holdings:** 3000 books; bound periodical volumes.

★623★
Center for Religion, Ethics and Social Policy
Durland Alternatives Library
127 Anabel Taylor Hall
Cornell University   Ph: (607)255-6486
Ithaca, NY 14853   Fax: (607)255-9985
Lynn Andersen, Libn.

Founded: 1974 **Subjects:** Afro-America, alternative education, farming & organic gardening, gay & lesbian issues, holistic health, international issues, Native America, disarmament, empowerment, environmental issues, human rights, new age movement, psychology, sexuality, gender, spirituality, women's studies. **Special Collections:** Eco-justice, environment, peace movement, Native Americans, counter-culture. **Holdings:** 7000 books; 900 audiotapes; 400 videotapes. **Subscriptions:** 320 journals and other serials.

★624★
Central Michigan University
Clarke Historical Library
Mt. Pleasant, MI 48859   Ph: (517)774-3352
                                         Fax: (517)774-2179
Frank Boles, Dir.

Founded: 1955 **Subjects:** Michigan, Old Northwest Territory, early travel in the Midwest, Afro-Americana, Native Americans, children's literature, angling. **Special Collections:** Lucile Clarke Memorial Children's Library (6768 volumes); Wilbert Wright Collection Afro-

Americana (5000 volumes); Reed T Draper Angling Collection (1261 volumes); Presidential Campaign Biography Collection (778 volumes); university archives. **Holdings:** 60,000 books; 1440 maps; 3274 manuscripts; 1100 broadsides; 26,400 photographs; 8072 microforms; 3564 pieces of sheet music; 900 newspapers; 12,000 pieces of ephemera; 50 tape recordings; 100 phonograph records. **Subscriptions:** 103 journals and other serials.

★625★
Cherokee National Historical Society, Inc.
Cherokee National Archives
Box 515
TSA-LA-GI   Ph: (918)456-6007
Tahlequah, OK 74465   Fax: (918)456-6165
Tom Mooney, Archv.

Founded: 1963 **Subjects:** Cherokee history. **Special Collections:** W.W. Keeler (Principal Chief of Cherokees) papers; Cherokee National Executive Committee minutes, 1948 (origin) to 1970 (disbandment); Cherokee Nation papers, 1969-1975; Earl Boyd Pierce (Counsel General of the Cherokee Nation) papers, 1928-1983; manuscript collections. **Holdings:** 3000 books; 500 bound periodical volumes; 147 reels of microfilm; 5 VF drawers of pamphlets; 7 VF drawers of papers and committee minutes. **Subscriptions:** 20 journals and other serials.

★626★
Chickasaw Council House Library
Court House Square
Box 717
Tishomingo, OK 73460   Ph: (405)371-3351

Founded: 1970 **Subjects:** Chickasaw Indian history, biographies, and statistics. **Special Collections:** Oklahoma Chronicles - Chickasaw Constitution and law books. **Holdings:** 50 maps; county and Chickasaw Nation records; 250 reels of microfilm; county newspapers on microfilm; indexes to 5 civilized tribes; pamphlets; Dawes Roll, application on Chickasaw and Choctaw; 1900-1920 census. **Subscriptions:** 6 journals and other serials.

★627★
Children's Museum of Indianapolis
Rauh Memorial Library
3000 N. Meridian St.
Box 3000   Ph: (317)924-5431
Indianapolis, IN 46208   Fax: (317)921-4019
Gregg Jackson, Libn./Archv.

Founded: 1975 **Subjects:** American history, American Indians, antiques, folk art, Indiana history, dolls, toys, museum studies, science, world cultures, education theory. **Special Collections:** Children's books (300). **Holdings:** 6000 books; 200 bound periodical volumes; 500 vertical file materials. **Subscriptions:** 65 journals and other serials.

★628★
Children's Museum
Resource Center
300 Congress St.   Ph: (617)426-6500
Boston, MA 02210   Fax: (617)426-1944

Founded: 1913 **Subjects:** Multicultural education, Native Americans, African Americans, Asian Americans, East Asia, natural and physical sciences, special needs, museum studies, museum education. **Special Collections:** Curriculum and display kits developed by museum staff. **Holdings:** 10,000 books. **Subscriptions:** 60 journals and other serials.

★629★
Colorado River Indian Tribes
Public Library and Archives
Rte. 1, Box 23-B   Ph: (602)669-9211
Parker, AZ 85344   Fax: (602)669-8262

Founded: 1958 **Subjects:** Native American publications, Arizona. **Holdings:** 20,000 books; 2000 archives; 200 reels of microfilm; 248 videotapes. **Subscriptions:** 7 journals and other serials; 7 newspapers.

★630★
Colorado Springs Fine Arts Center
Reference Library and Taylor Museum Library
30 W. Dale St.   Ph: (719)634-5581
Colorado Springs, CO 80903   Fax: (719)634-0570
Roderick Dew, Libn.

Founded: 1936 **Subjects:** Art history, drawing, painting, sculpture, folk art, graphic arts, anthropology of the Southwest, museums and private collections. **Special Collections:** Santos; Indians of the Southwest; Latin American folk and Colonial art. **Holdings:** 30,000 books; 950 bound periodical volumes; 12 shelves of biographical files; 20 shelves of museum publications. **Subscriptions:** 30 journals and other serials.

★631★
Cook College and Theological School
Mary Mildred McCarthy Library
708 S. Lindon Ln.   Ph: (602)968-9354
Tempe, AZ 85281   Fax: (602)968-9357
Mark Thomas, Dir.Lib.Svcs.

Subjects: Religion, Native Americans. **Special Collections:** Indian Collection (1500 books); archives. **Holdings:** 14,000 books; 8 VF drawers. **Subscriptions:** 45 journals and other serials.

★632★
County of Los Angeles Public Library
American Indian Resource Center
Huntington Park Library
6518 Miles Ave.   Ph: (213)583-1461
Huntington Park, CA 90255   Fax: (213)587-2061

Founded: 1979 **Subjects:** Indians of North America, including Southwest, Plains, Woodlands, and California Indians - history, tribal cultural histories, fine arts, religion, literature, laws and treaties. **Special Collections:** Federal Census Records (1880-1940); Current Events Files (700 subject headings; 12 VF drawers); Information and Referral File. **Holdings:** 8000 books; 60 16mm films; 65 titles in microform; 110 videotapes; 400 audiocassettes and CD-ROMs; 300 federal and state documents. **Subscriptions:** 45 periodical titles.

★633★
Cranford Historical Society
Museum Library
38 Springfield Ave.
Cranford, NJ 07016   Ph: (908)276-0082
Joanne Westcott

Founded: 1927 **Subjects:** Local history, Indian artifacts, paintings. **Special Collections:** Harrison Huster Indian Collection; Victorian Parlor; early agricultural and household implements; Canton export china. **Holdings:** Books; pictures; clippings; articles; maps; oral history tapes; scrapbooks. **Subscriptions:** 6 journals and other serials.

★634★
Crazy Horse Memorial
Library
University of North America
Ave. of the Chiefs   Ph: (605)673-4681
Crazy Horse, SD 57730-9998   Fax: (605)673-2185
Jessie Y. Sundstrom, Libn.

Founded: 1947 **Subjects:** American Indians, art. **Holdings:** 14,000 books. **Subscriptions:** 14 journals and other serials; 6 newspapers.

★635★
Creek Indian Memorial Association
Creek Council House Museum
Library
Town Square
106 W6th St.
Okmulgee, OK 74447   Ph: (918)756-2324
Cindy Hale

Founded: 1930 **Subjects:** Oklahoma history, Creek Indian history and culture; Native American history and culture. **Holdings:** 200 books; 60 bound periodical volumes; 2 VF drawers of clippings and biography notes. **Subscriptions:** 10 journals and other serials; 2 newspapers.

★636★
Detroit Public Library
History and Travel Department
5201 Woodward Ave.
Detroit, MI 48202   Ph: (313)833-1445
James Tong, Mgr.

Founded: 1949 **Subjects:** Political and social history, archeology, Indians, geography, travel, biography. **Special Collections:** Map Collection (254,600 sheet maps; 4368 atlases). **Holdings:** 209,000 volumes; 92 VF drawers of travel pamphlets; 10 VF drawers of map publishers catalogs; 44 VF drawers; 48 Biography clippings. **Subscriptions:** 365 journals and other serials.

★637★
Douglas County Museum
Lavola Bakken Memorial Library
123 Museum Dr.   Ph: (541)957-7007
Roseburg, OR 97470   Fax: (541)440-4506
Frederick R. Reenstjerna, Res.Libn.

Founded: 1969 **Subjects:** Douglas County history, Umpqua Indians, logging, sawmills and grist mills, marine history, mining, development of area towns, railroads, agriculture. **Special Collections:** Herbarium collection of Douglas County; photography collection (20,000 photographic prints copied from glass-plate negatives, albums, or original prints). **Holdings:** 2500 books; 350 files of letters, diaries, manuscripts, census, cemetery records; 400 oral histories; 175 genealogies. **Subscriptions:** 30 journals and other serials.

★638★
Dull Knife Memorial College
Dr. John Woodenlegs Memorial Library
Box 98   Ph: (406)477-8293
Lame Deer, MT 59043-0098   Fax: (406)477-6575
Sally Schmidt, Lib.Dir.

Founded: 1979 **Subjects:** Cheyenne history, sociology, psychology, human services. **Special Collections:** Cheyenne Collection (25 oral histories). **Holdings:** 10,000 books; CD-ROMs. **Subscriptions:** 120 journals and other serials; 8 newspapers.

★639★
Earlham College
Friends Collection
Lilly Library   Ph: (765)983-1511
Richmond, IN 47374   Fax: (765)983-1304
Thomas D. Hamm, Archv. & Cur.

Founded: 1847 **Subjects:** Society of Friends (Quakers); Earlham College. **Special Collections:** Indian Affairs; collections of Chas F. Coffin, Allen Jay, Barnabas C. Hobbs, Thomas E. Jones, David M. Edwards, William C. Dennis, Landrum Bolling, Elbert Russell, Marcus Mote, Clifford Crump, Esther Griffin White, Harlow Lindley; Earlham College Historical Collection; Willard Heiss; Homer L. Morris; Eli & Mahalah Jay; Joseph Moore; Indiana Yearly Meeting of Friends; Pusey Grave; Walter C. Woodward; Errol T. Elliott; Levi Coffin; D. Elton Trueblood; Western Yearly Meeting of Friends. **Holdings:** 12,000 books; 550 bound periodical volumes; 5000 pamphlets, manuscripts, photographs; 100 volumes of printed and bound theses; 250 audiocassettes; 1300 volumes of Quaker genealogy. **Subscriptions:** 70 journals and other serials.

★640★
East Tennessee Discovery Center
Library
PO Box 6204   Ph: (423)637-1192
Knoxville, TN 37914-0204   Fax: (423)521-7473
Susan Elder, Dir.

Founded: 1976 **Subjects:** Science, nature, history and culture, technology, arts and crafts. **Special Collections:** Old tools (200); dolls (300); costumes (25); fossils (300); rocks and minerals (5000); Indian artifacts (100); man-made artifacts (20,000); shells (5000); stuffed animals (300); charts (300). **Holdings:** 1200 books; 200 manuscripts; 15,000 slides; 300 pamphlets; 2500 postcards; 10 VF drawers; 32 videotapes; 10 compact discs; 1 laser disc. **Subscriptions:** 30 journals and other serials.

★641★
ERIC Clearinghouse on Rural Education and Small Schools
Appalachia Educational Laboratory
1031 Quarrier St.
Box 1348
Charleston, WV 25325
Craig B. Howley, Dir.
Founded: 1966 **Subjects:** Education - rural, small schools, Mexican American, American Indian, Alaska Native, migrant, outdoor. **Special Collections:** Sher Rural Education Collection. **Holdings:** 450,000 documents on ERIC microfiche. **Subscriptions:** 55 journals and other serials.

★642★
Field Museum
Webber Resource Center: Native Cultures of the Americas
Roosevelt Rd. & Lakeshore Dr.   Ph: (312)922-9410
Chicago, IL 60605-2496   Fax: (312)922-6483
Mara Cosillo, Rsrc.Ctr.Mgr.
Founded: 1987 **Subjects:** Native North and South American culture and history; archaeology; contemporary Native American issues. **Special Collections:** Department of Anthropology archival photograph collection (6 albums); artifacts. **Holdings:** 1000 books; 35 periodical titles; 103 videotapes; 30 audiotapes; 50 maps; 200 teacher resources; activity boxes. **Subscriptions:** 10 newspapers.

★643★
Fillmore County Historical Society
Historical Center
R.R1
Box 81 D
Fountain, MN 55935
Founded: 1934 **Subjects:** History - Southeastern Minnesota, Southeastern Minnesota immigrants, agrarian history, agrarian machinery, Native American, rural lifestyles. **Special Collections:** Matthew Bue Photography Collection (50,000 original glass negatives and photographs documenting life in Southeastern Minnesota, 1915-1950); Senator M Anderson Collection (notes and documents on Minnesota government, 1927-1963). **Holdings:** 3700 books; 2200 bound periodical volumes; 1100 documents; 2800 nonbook items; 67 manuscripts. **Subscriptions:** 5 newspapers.

★644★
Five Civilized Tribes Museum and Center for Study of Indian Territory
Library
Agency Hill on Honor Heights Dr.   Ph: (918)683-1701
Muskogee, OK 74401   Fax: (918)683-3070
Founded: 1966 **Subjects:** Cherokee, Choctaw, Creek, Chickasaw, and Seminole Indians - history, current history, fiction, non-fiction, Indian territory history. **Holdings:** 500 books.

★645★
Flint Institute of Arts
Library
1120 E. Kearsley St.   Ph: (810)234-1695
Flint, MI 48503   Fax: (810)234-1692
Founded: 1969 **Subjects:** Art - North American Indian, African, decorative, Oriental, contemporary; glass paperweights; painting; sculpture; photography. **Holdings:** 4500 books; catalogs of museums' collections; exhibition catalogs; prints; drawings. **Subscriptions:** 19 journals and other serials.

★646★
Fort Lewis College
Center of Southwest Studies
1000 Rim Dr.   Ph: (970)247-7456
Durango, CO 81301-3999   Fax: (970)247-7422
Dr. Duane Smith, Dir.
Founded: 1964 **Subjects:** Southwestern U.S. history, American Indians, railroads, mining, energy, water. **Special Collections:** Spanish exploration and colonization; Indians of the Southwest; records of geological surveys; mining; military; newspapers; narrow gauge railroads; politics and government. **Holdings:** 15,000 books; 600 bound periodical volumes; 7000 reels of microfilm; 800 maps; 35,000 photographs; 8000 artifacts; 600 oral histories; manuscripts; college archives; personal papers; artifacts. **Subscriptions:** 26 journals and other serials.

★647★
Fort Verde State Park
Library
PO Box 397   Ph: (520)567-3275
Camp Verde, AZ 86322   Fax: (520)567-4036
Founded: 1970 **Subjects:** U.S. Indian Wars history, Arizona history. **Special Collections:** Ft. Verde historical collection; military collection. **Holdings:** 200 books; 54 reels of microfilm; files. **Subscriptions:** 3 journals and other serials.

★648★
The Frank Phillips Foundation, Inc.
Woolaroc Museum
Library
Rte3, Box 2100   Ph: (918)336-0307
Bartlesville, OK 74003   Fax: (918)336-0084
Founded: 1929 **Subjects:** Native American culture, western art, early Americana, weaponry, natural history, history. **Holdings:** 1000 books. **Subscriptions:** 15 journals and other serials.

★649★
Fresno County Free Library
Special Collections
2420 Mariposa St.   Ph: (209)488-3195
Fresno, CA 93721   Fax: (209)488-1971
Founded: 1910 **Subjects:** Fresno County - local history, architecture; American Indians - Mono, Miwok, Yokut. **Special Collections:** William Saroyan Collection (1550 books, 432 periodicals, 4 linear feet of manuscripts, photographs); Leo Politi Collection; architectural photographs; Local History Collection (15 linear feet of oral history manuscripts, vertical files of ephemera, biographical sketches, broadsides, maps, pamphlets); Ta-Kwa-Teu-Nee-Ya-Y Collection (200 books); South East Asian Acculturation Collection (300 books); Nell Strother Mother Goose and Nursery Rhyme Collection (200 books, 1900 to present). **Holdings:** 122 bound periodical volumes; 15 linear feet of archival materials; 15,000 microfiche; Fresno newspapers on microfilm (1860 to present). **Subscriptions:** 4 journals and other serials; 5 newspapers.

★650★
Frontier Gateway Museum
Library
Belle Prairie Frontage Rd.
Box 1181
Glendive, MT 59330   Ph: (406)365-8168
Subjects: Homesteading in Montana, Indians of eastern Montana, prehistoric fossils, ranching, rural education, early businesses. **Special Collections:** Senator George McCone collection (40 items); M.E. Sutton Memorial Indian display (156 items); fossil collection. **Holdings:** 510 books; 310 unbound research items; 194 maps; 7 VF drawers of pictures; 20 VF drawers of clippings.

★651★
Fruitlands Museums
Library
102 Prospect Hill Rd.   Ph: (508)456-3924
Harvard, MA 01451   Fax: (508)456-9393
Michael Volmar, Cur.

Founded: 1914 **Subjects:** American Indians, 19th century American paintings, Transcendentalism, Shaker history. **Special Collections:** Shaker and Transcendentalist manuscripts. **Holdings:** 2000 books, bound periodical volumes, and manuscripts; 200 unbound reports. **Subscriptions:** 25 journals and other serials.

★652★
Hartwick College
Stevens-German Library
Special Collections
Oneonta, NY 13820   Ph: (607)431-4440
    Fax: (607)431-4457

Founded: 1928 **Subjects:** Indians of North America, especially Eastern Woodland Indians. **Special Collections:** Yager Collection of Rare Books; Congressman James Hanley papers concerned with Native Americans (2 cubic feet); Hatrwick Seminary records (40 cubic feet); Judge William Cooper papers (15 cubic feet); Willard E. Yager Manuscript Collection (15 cubic feet); John Christopher Hartwick Library (290 titles). **Holdings:** 6200 books; 200 bound periodical volumes; 200 folders of clippings; 1000 reels of microfilm; 3000 microfiche. **Subscriptions:** 1202 journals and other serials; 17 newspapers.

★653★
Heard Museum
Library and Archives
22 E. Monte Vista Rd.   Ph: (602)252-8840
Phoenix, AZ 85004-1480   Fax: (602)252-9757
Mario Nick Klimiades, Lib. & Archv.Mgr.

Founded: 1929 **Subjects:** American Indians, Native American art, ethnology, material culture, archeology, traditional art, Southwest travel, history, and exploration. **Special Collections:** Native American Artists Resource Center (information on 17,000 Native American artists); Fred Harvey Company papers and photographs; R. Brownell McGrew Collection; Barry M Goldwater Collection; Jeanne Snodgrass King Collection, Atlatl Collection. **Holdings:** 26,000 books; 2967 bound periodical volumes; 450 films and videotapes; 50,000 photographs; 20,000 slides; pamphlet file; clippings; museum archives; sound recordings; manuscripts. **Subscriptions:** 240 journals and other serials.

★654★
The Heritage Center
Library
Red Cloud Indian School   Ph: (605)867-5491
Pine Ridge, SD 57770   Fax: (605)867-1291

Founded: 1983 **Subjects:** Native American art, Lakota culture. **Special Collections:** Pine Ridge Oglala Sioux collection (photographs). **Holdings:** 2500 books. **Subscriptions:** 13 journals and other serials.

★655★
Hoard Historical Museum
Library
407 Merchant Ave.
Fort Atkinson, WI 53538   Ph: (414)563-7769

Founded: 1933 **Subjects:** Black Hawk War, 1800-1840; local Indians and history; birds; quilts; furniture. **Special Collections:** Rare books on Abraham Lincoln, the Civil War, Black Hawk War, local history, and regional birds; Indian artifacts, 7000 B.C. to present; National Dairy Shrine Museum. **Holdings:** 5108 books; 4813 local pictures. **Subscriptions:** 2 journals and other serials; 1 newspaper.

★656★
Huntington Free Library
National Museum of the American Indian
Library
9 Westchester Sq.   Ph: (718)829-7770
Bronx, NY 10461   Fax: (718)829-4875
Mary B. Davis, Libn.

Founded: 1930 **Subjects:** Archeology and ethnology of Indians of the Western Hemisphere; linguistics; anthropology; history; current affairs. **Special Collections:** American Indian newspapers. **Holdings:** 25,000 volumes; 140 VF drawers; 50 manuscripts. **Subscriptions:** 250 journals and other serials; 50 Indian newspapers.

★657★
Illinois State Historical Library
Old State Capitol   Ph: (217)524-6358
Springfield, IL 62701-1507   Fax: (217)785-6250

Founded: 1889 **Subjects:** Illinois history, Lincolniana, Civil War history, Midwest Americana, Mormon history, Indian history, genealogy. **Special Collections:** Abraham Lincoln Collection (1425 manuscripts; 10,000 books and pamphlets); Picture and Print Collection (350,000). **Holdings:** 172,000 volumes; 10.1 million manuscripts; 76,000 reels of newspapers on microfilm; 3000 maps; 4000 broadsides. **Subscriptions:** 600 journals and other serials; 300 newspapers.

★658★
Indian and Colonial Research Center, Inc.
Eva Butler Library
Box 525
Old Mystic, CT 06372   Ph: (860)536-9771

Founded: 1965 **Subjects:** Indians, genealogy, colonial history. **Special Collections:** Elmer Waite collection of glass plate negatives of the area; rare American school books, 1700-1850 (300). **Holdings:** 2000 books; 954 manuscripts; 90 maps and atlases; 2000 early American notebooks; 69 boxes of bulletins and pamphlets; 2000 photographs. **Subscriptions:** 2 journals and other serials.

★659★
Indian Museum of the Carolinas
Library
607 Turnpike Rd.
Laurinburg, NC 28352   Ph: (910)276-5880
Margaret Houston, Musm.Dir.

Founded: 1972 **Subjects:** American archeology, American Indians. **Holdings:** 200 books; 100 reports.

★660★
Indian Temple Mound Museum
Library
139 Miracle Strip Pkwy.
PO Box 4009
Fort Walton Beach, FL 32549   Ph: (850)833-9595

Founded: 1970 **Subjects:** Archaeology and prehistoric people, anthropology, Native Americans, museum management, archaeological sites, Florida history. **Holdings:** 3500 books; 500 bound periodical volumes; 3000 slides and photographs.

★661★
Institute of American Indian Arts
Library
Box 20007   Ph: (505)988-6423
Santa Fe, NM 87504   Fax: (505)986-5509
Allen D. Schwartz, Dirof Libs.

Founded: 1962 **Subjects:** American Indian culture, history and technique of American Indian fine arts. **Special Collections:** Exhibition catalogs. **Holdings:** 14,000 books; 8 file drawers of archival materials; 9000 art slides; 4000 Indian slides; 24 file drawers of art catalogs; 27,826 Smithsonian Indian photographs; 8 file drawers of Indian newspapers; 500 videos; Indian newspapers. **Subscriptions:** 200 journals and other serials.

★662★
Institute for American Indian Studies
Library
38 Curtis Rd.
Box 1260
Washington, CT 06793-0260   Ph: (860)868-0518
Subjects: Prehistoric and historic American Indian archeology; American Indian literature, history, crafts; ethnobotany. **Holdings:** 2000 books.

★663★
Iroquois Indian Museum
Library
PO Box 7   Ph: (518)296-8949
Howes Cave, NY 12092   Fax: (518)296-8955
Founded: 1981 **Subjects:** Iroquois Indians, Native American art, archeology. **Holdings:** 1500 books; 500 archival items; 12,000 slides and photographs. **Subscriptions:** 5 journals and other serials; 3 newspapers.

★664★
J.B. Speed Art Museum
Library
2035 S3rd St.   Ph: (502)636-2893
Louisville, KY 40208   Fax: (502)636-2899
Founded: 1927 **Subjects:** Art, decorative arts, architecture, archeology, film, photography. **Special Collections:** J.B. Speed's Lincoln Collection; Weygold Indian collection. **Holdings:** 16,613 books and bound periodical volumes; 54 VF drawers. **Subscriptions:** 59 journals and other serials.

★665★
Jesuit Oregon Province
Archives
Foley Center, Gonzaga University
E502 Boone Ave.   Ph: (509)328-4220
Spokane, WA 99258   Fax: (509)324-5904
Founded: 1931 **Subjects:** History - Northwest Church, Alaska Church and missions, Doukhobor, local; Alaskan and Indian languages. **Special Collections:** Joset Papers; Cataldo Papers; Crimont Papers; Neil Byrne Papers; Peter Prando Papers; Jesuit Mission Papers; Indian Languages Collection. **Holdings:** 3600 books; 800 bound periodical volumes; 123,000 manuscripts; 45,000 photographs. **Subscriptions:** 35 journals and other serials; 18 newspapers.

★666★
John Carter Brown Library
Box 1894   Ph: (401)863-2725
Providence, RI 02912   Fax: (401)863-3477
Norman Fiering, Dir./Libn.
Founded: 1846 **Subjects:** Discovery and exploration of North and South America to 1830; comparative colonization of the Americas, including Spain, Portugal, England, France, and Holland; impact of the new world on the old world, 1493-1800; history - maritime, science, printing. **Special Collections:** Braziliana; Caribbeana; maritime history; American Indian linguistics (books; manuscripts); history of cartography (2000 books); American Revolution (15,000 items); Arnold-Green papers (132 linear feet); Bartlett papers (15 linear feet); Brown papers (681 linear feet); History of printing in the Americas (through 1830). **Holdings:** 60,000 volumes; 3000 bound periodical volumes; 1200 maps; 350 bound volumes of codices; 36 linear feet of manuscripts. **Subscriptions:** 35 journals and other serials.

★667★
Joslyn Art Museum
Art Reference Library
2200 Dodge St.   Ph: (402)342-3300
Omaha, NE 68102   Fax: (402)342-2376
Kathryn L. Corcoran
Founded: 1931 **Subjects:** American and European art, with emphasis on 19th and 20th centuries; Western and Native American art and history. **Special Collections:** Joslyn Museum history files. **Holdings:** 27,000 books; 3000 bound periodical volumes; 100 VF drawers on artists and museums; 500 bound bulletins and Annual reports; 20,000 slides. **Subscriptions:** 100 journals and other serials.

★668★
Kankakee County Historical Society
Musuem
801 S8th Ave.
Kankakee, IL 60901   Ph: (815)932-5279
Founded: 1906 **Subjects:** County and state history, Civil War. **Special Collections:** Indian artifact collection; photograph collection (8500); French-Canadian artifacts; 75 plaster studies of the sculptor George Grey Barnard; the one-room Taylor School (1904-1954); large stone house (1854) that Gov. Len Small was born. **Holdings:** 4000 books; genealogies; city directories; manuscripts; documents; clippings; Civil War volumes. **Subscriptions:** 3 journals and other serials; 2 newspapers.

★669★
Kansas Heritage Center
Library
Box 1207   Ph: (316)227-1616
Dodge City, KS 67801-1207   Fax: (913)227-1695
Founded: 1966 **Subjects:** Frontier and pioneer life, Kansas, the West, Sante Fe Trail, Indians of North America, cowboys, cattle trade, agricultural history, folklore. **Special Collections:** Historical society journals from the states of Kansas (1881 to present), Missouri (1906 to present), Colorado (1923-1980), New Mexico (1928 to present), Montana (1954 to present), and Oklahoma (1921-1985). **Holdings:** 6000 volumes; VF drawers (Kansas and Dodge City); microfilm; audio cassettes phonograph records; 16mm films; videotapes; teaching kits. **Subscriptions:** 6 journals and other serials.

★670★
Kansas State Historical Society
Library & Archives Division
Center for Historical Research
6425 SW 6th St.   Ph: (913)272-8681
Topeka, KS 66615-1099   Fax: (913)272-8682
Patricia A. Michaelis, D iv.Dir.
Founded: 1875 **Subjects:** Kansas history, local history of other states, genealogy, American Indians, the West, American biography, Civil War. **Special Collections:** Kansas (23,000 books; 135,000 pamphlets); genealogy and local history (21,000 books; 9000 pamphlets); American Indians and the West (5800 books; 2200 pamphlets). **Holdings:** 28,466 cubic ft. of state and local government archives; 7763 cubic ft. of manuscripts; 480,000 photographs; 6575 films, videotapes, and audiotapes; 25,000 maps, blueprints, and drawings; 75,000 reels of microfilm. **Subscriptions:** 640 journals and other serials; 356 newspapers.

★671★
Kansas State University
Farrell Library
Minority Resource Research Center
Manhattan, KS 66506   Ph: (913)532-7453
                            Fax: (913)532-6144
Founded: 1971 **Subjects:** African-American history and literature, American ethnic studies, Kansas minority groups, Native American archeology, 20th century Native American sociology, Chicano studies. **Special Collections:** American Ethnic Studies (100 titles); Kansas State Minority Programs (125 titles). **Holdings:** 5000 volumes; 147 microfiche; 388 reels of microfilm; 15 VF drawers of reports; 4 VF drawers of archives; 732 AV programs. **Subscriptions:** 75 journals and other serials; 22 newspapers.

★672★
Kendall College
Library
Special Collections
2408 Orrington Ave.   Ph: (847)866-1322
Evanston, IL 60201   Fax: (847)866-1320
Iva M. Freeman, Dir.
Founded: 1934. **Special Collections:** Native American Collection (Indian museum); Culinary Collection. **Holdings:** 30,000 books. **Subscriptions:** 190 journals and other serials; 10 newspapers.

★673★
Kendall College
Mitchell Indian Museum
Library
2408 Orrington Ave.   Ph: (847)866-1395
Evanston, IL 60201   Fax: (847)866-1320
Founded: 1977 **Subjects:** Native Americans - history, anthropology, art, literature, ethnography. **Special Collections:** Jesuit relations; Bureau of Ethnology reports. **Holdings:** 2000 books; 110 AV programs. **Subscriptions:** 5 journals and other serials; 2 newspapers.

★674★
Klamath County Museum
Research Library
1451 Main St.   Ph: (541)883-4208
Klamath Falls, OR 97601   Fax: (503)884-0666
Founded: 1954 **Subjects:** Oregon and local history, Modoc and Klamath Indians, Modoc Indian War. **Special Collections:** Modoc Indian War collection; oral history collection. **Holdings:** 1650 books; photo/document archives; microfilm. **Subscriptions:** 5 journals and other serials.

★675★
Koshare Indian Museum
Koshare Indian Library
115 W18th St.
PO Box 580   Ph: (719)384-4411
La Junta, CO 81050   Fax: (719)384-8836
Founded: 1933 **Subjects:** Native Americans; Western United States. **Special Collections:** Koshare collection. **Holdings:** 10,000 books. **Subscriptions:** 15 journals and other serials.

★676★
Lake Superior State University
Kenneth J. Shouldice Library
Michigan & Marine Collections
906 Ryan   Ph: (906)635-2402
Sault Ste. Marie, MI 49783   Fax: (906)635-2193
Dr. Frederick A. Michels, Dir.
Founded: 1946 **Subjects:** History of Michigan's Upper Peninsula; Indians of Michigan's Upper Peninsula; local history of Sault Ste. Marie, Michigan. **Special Collections:** Special editions and sources of Longfellow's "Hiawatha"; Marine-Laker Collection. **Holdings:** 1400 books; Sault Evening News on microfilm; 10 VF drawers of pamphlets concerned with local and area history. **Subscriptions:** 10 journals and other serials.

★677★
Leeward Community College Library
Special Collections
96-045 Ala Ike   Ph: (808)455-0379
Pearl City, HI 96782   Fax: (808)453-6729
Founded: 1968 **Subjects:** Asia, Asian Americans. **Special Collections:** Hawaiian/Pacific Collection; selected regional federal government depository.

★678★
Lehigh County Historical Society
Scott Andrew Trexler II Memorial Library
Old Court House
5th & Hamilton Sts.
Box 1548   Ph: (610)435-1072
Allentown, PA 18105   Fax: (610)435-9812
Founded: 1904 **Subjects:** Pennsylvania and Lehigh County history, genealogy. **Special Collections:** Allentown Newspapers, 1810-1916; family genealogies; photographs; Civil War; Allentown imprints; native Indians. **Holdings:** 1000 books; 200 newspaper volumes; 2000 pamphlets; 50,000 photographs and negatives; 200 manuscripts, archives, records of local families and businesses; deeds; maps; church records. **Subscriptions:** 12 journals and other serials.

★679★
Los Angeles Public Library
History and Genealogy Department
630 W5th St.
Los Angeles, CA 90071
Founded: 1872 **Subjects:** History, travel, biography, Californiana, genealogy, local history, heraldry, newspapers. **Special Collections:** Genealogy (38,000 volumes); Californiana (20,000 items); maps and atlases; American Indians; World Wars I and II; travel; photograph collection; Herald Examiner Newspaper and Photograph Morgues. **Holdings:** 268,000 volumes; 91,000 maps; 2.7 million photographs; 800 historical specimen newspapers; 25,000 reels of microfilm of newspapers; U.S. city directories; census records. **Subscriptions:** 1300 journals and other serials; 50 newspapers.

★680★
Lutheran Bible Institute of Seattle
Library
Providence Heights
4221 228th Ave. SE   Ph: (206)392-0400
Issaquah, WA 98027   Fax: (206)392-0404
Founded: 1960 **Subjects:** Bible; theology - doctrinal, moral, pastoral, devotional; religion and philosophy; Christian church; missions; psychology; social sciences; Christian education; youth work; gerontology; Pacific Northwest Indians. **Holdings:** 30,000 books; 143 bound periodical volumes; 550 books on microfilm; 465 audio cassettes; 200 videotapes; 27 kits; 12 VF drawers. **Subscriptions:** 216 journals and other serials.

★681★
Malki Museum, Inc.
Archives
11-795 Fields Rd.
Morongo Indian Reservation
Banning, CA 92220   Ph: (909)849-7289
Founded: 1965 **Subjects:** Indians of southern California. **Special Collections:** Indian basketry, artifacts. **Holdings:** Manuscripts; photographs; oral history tapes; field notes from various anthropologists including John Peabody Harrington.

★682★
Marathon County Historical Museum
Library
403 McIndoe St.   Ph: (715)848-0378
Wausau, WI 54403   Fax: (715)848-0576
Founded: 1952 **Subjects:** State and county history, antiques, logging, Indian lore. **Special Collections:** Books published by Van Vechten and Ellis at the Philosopher Press in Wausau (20 volumes); John DMylrea Journals (15); James Colby photographs (6000 glass negatives) and postcards; D.CEverest personal papers. **Holdings:** 6000 books; 6000 maps and photographs; 80 manuscripts; 26 VF drawers of clippings. **Subscriptions:** 20 journals and other serials.

★683★
Marin Museum of the American Indian
Library
Box 864
Novato, CA 94948   Ph: (415)897-4064
Subjects: Indians of the San Francisco Bay area, California, and North America; ethnobotany; Native American arts; anthropology. **Holdings:** Figures not available.

★684★
Marquette University Libraries
Department of Special Collections and University
Archives
1415 W. Wisconsin Ave.
PO Box 3141
Milwaukee, WI 53201-3141   Ph: (414)288-7256
Founded: 1961 **Subjects:** Catholic social thought and action, Catholic Indian ministry, Marquette University history, recent U.S. political history, Catholic religious formation and vocation ministries. **Special Collections:** National Catholic Conference for Interracial Justice Collection, 1956 to present (154 feet); Project Equality, Inc. Collection, 1971 to present (40 feet); Sr. Margaret Ellen Traxler Papers, 1950 to present (20 feet); National Coalition of American Nuns Collection, 1969 to present (12 feet); Sister Formation Conference/Religious Formation Conference Archives, 1954 to present (53 feet); Clement J. Zablocki Papers, 1945-1983 (500 feet, unprocessed); Madonna Center (Chicago) Records, 1865-1967 (8 feet); Council on Urban Life (Milwaukee) Records, 1965-1980 (39 feet); Women's Ordination Conference Records, 1975 to present (33 feet); FBI investigation and surveillance records (photocopies), 1919-1984 (50 feet); Dorothy Day - Catholic Worker Collection, 1933 to present (150 feet); Catholic Association for International Peace Archives, 1926-1970 (22 feet); Monsignor Luigi G. Ligutti Papers, 1915-1984 (58 feet); Brother Leo V. Ryan Papers, 1956 to present (42 feet); New Ways Ministry Records, 1965 to present (26 feet); National Sisters Vocation Conference Archives, 1967 to present (16 feet); Joseph R. McCarthy Papers, 1930-1957 (142 feet); Charles J. Kersten papers, 1946-1971 (21 feet); Donald T. McNeill Collection, 1933-1968 (67 feet); Citizens for Educational Freedom Records, 1959 to present (20 feet); Sociology of Religion Collections, 1938 to present (62 feet); H. Herman Rauch Labor Arbitration Case Files, 1939-1978 (42 feet); John Ronald Reuel Tolkien Collection, 1930 to present (40 feet); Elizabeth Whitcomb Houghton Collection, 1900-1945 (letters and manuscripts of American and British authors; 3 feet); Joyce Kilmer/Campion College Collection, 1908-1975 (5 feet); Karl J. Priebe Papers, 1900-1978 (14 feet); National Catholic Rural Life Conference Archives, 1923 to present (98 feet); Justice and Peace Center (Milwaukee) Archives, 1970-1982 (20 feet); National Interfaith Coalition on Aging Archives, 1971-1991 (35 feet); Bureau of Catholic Indian Missions Records, 1848 to present (495 feet); Holy Rosary Mission Records, 1868 to present (57 feet); St. Francis Mission Records, 1878 to present (35 feet); Siggenauk Center Records, 1974-1989 (2.4 feet); Kisemanito Center Collection, 1976-1987 (4.6 feet); Sacred Heart Franciscan Indian Mission Records, 1829-1981 (5 feet); Tekakwitha Conference Records, 1939 to present (15 feet). **Holdings:** 11,110 volumes; 3000 bound periodical volumes; 9450 cubic feet of archives and manuscripts; 450 reels of microfilm; 4000 cubic feet of manuscript collections relating primarily to Catholic social action and Catholic relationships with Native Americans1865 to present; 5250 cubic feet of Marquette University Archives, 1881 to present; 620 cubic feet of Catholic Indian mission records, 1848 to present. **Subscriptions:** 45 journals and other serials; 20 newspapers.

★685★
Martin County Historical Society, Inc.
Pioneer Museum
Library
304 E. Blue Earth Ave.
Fairmont, MN 56031   Ph: (507)235-5178
Founded: 1929 **Subjects:** American Indian, Civil War, Minnesota history. **Special Collections:** Local newspaper file, 1874 to present (bound volumes of city and county papers). **Holdings:** 612 bound periodical volumes; 476 reels of microfilm of Martin County newspapers. **Subscriptions:** 3 newspapers.

★686★
Metropolitan Museum of Art
Department of the Arts of Africa, Oceania, and the
Americas
Photograph Study Collection
1000 Fifth Ave.   Ph: (212)650-2823
New York, NY 10028   Fax: (212)472-2872
Founded: 1957 **Subjects:** Traditional arts and culture - Africa, Oceania, Native American, Precolumbian. **Special Collections:** Paul Gebauer Collection (Cameroon, Africa; photographs and archives); Frederick Peterson Collection (Mexican art; photographs and archives); Paul Fejos Collection (Peru, Indonesia; photographs and archives); Museum of Primitive Art (archives). **Holdings:** 120,000 photographs.

★687★
Metropolitan Museum of Art
Robert Goldwater Library
1000 Fifth Ave.   Ph: (212)570-3707
New York, NY 10028-0198   Fax: (212)570-3879
Ross Day, Assoc.Musm.Libn.
Founded: 1957 **Subjects:** Archeology; art - African, Latin American, Indians of North America, Oceania. **Holdings:** 35,000 volumes. **Subscriptions:** 150 journals and other serials.

★688★
Mid-America All Indian Center
Library
650 N Seneca   Ph: (316)262-5221
Wichita, KS 67203   Fax: (316)262-4216
Jerrlea Dunn, Ch
Founded: 1976 **Subjects:** Native Americans - history, art, culture. **Special Collections:** Blackbear Bosin Collection of publications and personal papers. **Holdings:** 3000 books; 200 bound periodical volumes; 7 reports. **Subscriptions:** 3 journals and other serials; 2 newspapers.

★689★
Minneapolis Public Library
Special Collections Department
300 Nicollet Mall
Minneapolis, MN 55401-1992   Ph: (612)630-6350
Founded: 1987. **Special Collections:** Minneapolis Athenaeum Collections (North American Indians, Spencer Natural History, Early American Exploration and Travel, Heffelfinger Aesop's and Others' Fables, History of Books and Printing; 5000 volumes); Minneapolis Collection (city of Minneapolis; 3600 volumes; 10,000 photographs; 150 archival collections; pictures; maps; VF materials); Kittleson World War II Collection (World War II - military and naval operations, social and economic aspects, personal narratives, anti-Semitism and the Holocaust; 8200 books; 400 pamphlets; 14 volumes of scrapbooks; 3 VF drawers of clippings; 2000 posters; 400 unbound periodicals; 1500 leaflets and pictures; Huttner Abolition and Anti-Slavery Collection (Abolitionist movement, slavery, black writers and reformers of the 19th -century; 610 books; 50 letters and documents; 250 pamphlets, broadsides, newspapers); 19th-Century American Studies Collection (materials by and about 19th-century American writers, antislavery movement, New England descriptive and historical writings; Truman Nelson letters; John Greenleaf Whittier-Evelina Bray Downey correspondence; manuscript "Ode to France," James Russell Lowell; 4600 books; 200 bound periodical volumes; 150 pamphlets; 150 autograph letters; 150 pictures; 250 unbound periodicals, pamphlets, newspapers; 1 VF drawer of clippings; Hoag Mark Twain Collection (280 books and pamphlets). **Subscriptions:** 24 journals and other serials.

★690★
Minnesota Historical Society
Fort Snelling Branch Library
Fort Snelling History Center   Ph: (612)726-1171
St. Paul, MN 55111   Fax: (612)725-2429
Founded: 1970 **Subjects:** History - Minnesota, regional, military; American Indians; American and regional archeology; 19th century America. **Holdings:** 6000 volumes; 1500 other cataloged items. **Subscriptions:** 5 journals and other serials.

★691★
Minnesota Historical Society
Library & Archives
345 Kellogg Blvd. W.   Ph: (612)296-2143
St. Paul, MN 55102-1906   Fax: (612)297-7436

Founded: 1849 **Subjects:** Minnesota and Upper Midwest: genealogy, Scandinavians in North America, ethnic groups, transportation, agriculture, arts, commerce, family life, industry, Indians, political life. **Special Collections:** Minnesota newspapers, 1849 to present; Minnesota State Archives (45,000 cubic feet); Hubert H. Humphrey Photograph Collection (25,000) and papers; Norton & Peel Commercial Photograph Collection (75,000); St. Paul and Minneapolis newspaper negatives (1 million); Great Northern and Northern Pacific railroad records. **Holdings:** 500,000 monographs, government documents, and microform volumes; 100 VF drawers; 500,000 photographs; 35,000 maps; 1300 atlases; 4.5 million issues of 3000 titles of newspaper volumes; 37,000 cubic feet of manuscripts; 45,000 cubic feet of Minnesota government records. **Subscriptions:** 3000 journals and other serials; 436 newspapers.

★692★
Minot State University
Gordon B. Olson Library
500 University Ave. W.   Ph: (701)858-3200
Minot, ND 58707   Fax: (701)858-3581
Larry Greenwood, Dir.

Founded: 1913. **Special Collections:** North Dakota Collection; Indians of the North Central States; North Dakota government documents; U.S. government documents selective depository. **Holdings:** 122,278 documents. **Subscriptions:** 929 journals and other serials; 30 newspapers.

★693★
Missouri Historical Society
Archives
Library and Collections Center
PO Box 11940
St. Louis, MO 63112-0040   Ph: (314)746-5410
                     Fax: (314)746-4548
Chuck Hill, Archv.

Founded: 1866 **Subjects:** St. Louis history and culture, Missouri, Mississippi Valley, American West. **Special Collections:** Papers, journals, field notes of William Clark from his expedition with Meriwether Lewis; Louisiana Territory documents; papers of Thomas Jefferson; French and Spanish colonial administration; western exploration; North American Plains Indians; French settlement; German immigrants; Mexican and Civil Wars; business and commerce in the Missouri area; Women's Suffrage Movement; William Torrey Harris (founder of the St. Louis Philosophical Society); Charles Lindbergh; Russian Revolution; American fur trade; St. Louis Architecture. **Holdings:** 6000 linear feet of archival materials.

★694★
Missouri Historical Society
Library
PO Box 11940
St. Louis, MO 63112-0040   Ph: (314)746-4500

Founded: 1866 **Subjects:** History - St. Louis, Missouri, Western United States, Missouri and Mississippi Rivers; fur trade; biography; genealogy; theater; Thomas Jefferson; early Mississippi travel; steamboats; Lewis and Clark expedition; American Indians. **Special Collections:** Western Americana; maps; music collection; theater collection; scrapbook collection; 1904 World's Fair; Missouri Gazette newspaper (complete file). **Holdings:** 75,000 book, pamphlet, and periodical titles; 2000 bound newspaper volumes; 2500 maps. **Subscriptions:** 503 journals and other serials.

★695★
Monroe County Library System
General George Armstrong Custer Collection
Dorsch Memorial Library
18 E First St.   Ph: (313)241-5277
Monroe, MI 48161   Fax: (313)242-9037

Founded: 1977 **Subjects:** General George A. Custer, Battle of Little Big Horn, American Indians, Indian wars, the West, Civil War.

Special Collections: Custer Collection; Dr. Lawrence A. Frost Collection of Custeriana. **Holdings:** 4000 books; 18 bound periodical volumes; 1600 unbound periodicals; 163 newspapers; 110 books on microfilm; 5380 slides; 35 maps; 100 pictures; 150 pamphlets; 23 original manuscripts; 35 AV programs; 170 microfiche; 60 cassettes. **Subscriptions:** 4 journals and other serials.

★696★
Montana Historical Society
Library/Archives
225 N. Roberts
PO Box 201201   Ph: (406)444-2681
Helena, MT 59620   Fax: (406)444-2696
Robert M. C lark, Hd.Lib. & Archv.Div.

Founded: 1865 **Subjects:** Lewis and Clark Expedition; George Armstrong Custer; Charles M. Russell; military history of the Montana Indians; Montana biography/genealogy; mining; cattle and range; homesteading. **Special Collections:** T.C. Power papers; Senator Lee Metcalf papers; Thomas Teakle Collection of books and L.A. Huffman photographs on western cattle and range subjects (2300 books and periodicals; 1100 photographs); F.J and Jack Ellis Haynes Northern Pacific Railroad and Yellowstone National Park Photograph Collection; Anaconda Copper Mining Company papers; state government archives (5500 cubic feet). **Holdings:** 50,000 books; 5000 bound periodical volumes; 50,000 state publications; 6500 cubic feet of private papers; 200,000 photographs; 14,000 reels of microfilm of Montana and other newspapers; 16,000 maps; 4000 broadsides and ephemera; 1500 oral history interviews. **Subscriptions:** 300 journals and other serials; newspapers.

★697★
Montana State University - Libraries
Merrill G. Burlingame Special Collections/Archives
Bozeman, MT 59717-3320   Ph: (406)994-4242
                     Fax: (406)994-2851

Founded: 1953 **Subjects:** Montana history, Yellowstone National Park, Senator Burton K. Wheeler, Montana Native Americans, Montana agriculture, James Williard Schultz, Montana State University, Montana architecture **Special Collections:** Haynes Collection; M.L. Wilson Agricultural History Collection; Leggat-Donahoe Northwest Collection; Abraham Lincoln Collection; Montana Architectural Drawings Collection; Montana WPA files; Burton K. Wheeler Collection. **Holdings:** 31,903 volumes; 953 reels of microfilm; 311 microfiche; 1615 aperture cards; 1654 manuscripts; 11,005 cubic feet of University records; 10,000 photographs on Montana agriculture and Montana State University. **Subscriptions:** 14 journals and other serials.

★698★
Montclair Art Museum
Le Brun Library
3 S. Mountain Ave.   Ph: (973)746-5555
Montclair, NJ 07042-1747   Fax: (973)746-9118

Founded: 1916 **Subjects:** American and American Indian art. **Special Collections:** Bookplates collection (7000). **Holdings:** 13,000 books; 3500 bound periodical volumes; museum bulletins and catalogs of exhibitions; posters; 125 VF drawers of clippings, pictures, pamphlets; 17,000 slides; 50 tapes of museum programs and lectures. **Subscriptions:** 50 journals and other serials.

★699★
Museum of the Cherokee Indian
Archives
US 441 North-Drama Rd.
Box 1599   Ph: (704)497-3481
Cherokee, NC 28719   Fax: (704)497-4985

Founded: 1976 **Subjects:** Cherokee history. **Special Collections:** A Guide to Cherokee Documents in Foreign Archives (microfilm). **Holdings:** 15,000 books; manuscripts.

★700★
The Museum of Mobile
Museum Reference Library
355 Government St.   Ph: (334)434-7569
Mobile, AL 36602   Fax: (334)434-7686
Founded: 1964 **Subjects:** Mobile and Gulf Coast history, Civil War, American art, Indian culture, fire service. **Special Collections:** Julian Lee Rayford Folklore Collection; Mary Fenollosa Collection; negatives (6000); riverboat waybills (250 items). **Holdings:** 3000 books; 50 bound periodical volumes; 200 pamphlets; 300 historic newspapers; 300 Volunteer Fire Company records; 1400 colonial and Confederate manuscript documents; 2000 historic mercantile invoices. **Subscriptions:** 12 journals and other serials.

★701★
Museum of New Mexico
Photo Archives
Box 2087   Ph: (505)827-6472
Santa Fe, NM 87504   Fax: (505)827-6527
Founded: 1909 **Subjects:** History of New Mexico and the West, Indians, anthropology, archeology, ethnology, mining, railroading, agriculture, Latin America, Oceania, Australia, China, Japan, India, Philippines, Middle East. **Special Collections:** History of photography; photographs by William Henry Jackson, Ben Wittick, John K. Hillers, Edward S. Curtis, T. Harmon Parkhurst, J.R. Riddle, H.F. Robinson, Henry D. Tefft, Ralph H. Anderson, Nathaniel Frucht, J.C. Burge, Ferenz Fedor, Wyatt Davis, George L. Beam George C. Bennett, H.H. Bennett, Wesley Bradfield, Charles F. Lummis, Tyler Dingee, Philip E. Harroun, Harold Kellogg, Royal A. Prentice, Henry A. Schmidt, J.S.Wooley, Jesse L. Nusbaum, D.B. Chase, Timothy O'Sullivan, Nicholas Brown, Emerson APlunkett, Edward A. Kemp, Christian G. Kaadt, James N. Furlong, Kilburn Bros., George T. Miller, William H. brown, Edward A. Troutman, A. Frank Randall, Aaron B. Craycraft, O.C. Hinman, W.E. Hook, Matilda Coxe Stevenson, Carlos Vierra, C.B. Waite, Augustin V Casasola, George W. James, B.H. Gurnsey, Keystone View Co., Joseph E. Smith; international publications. **Holdings:** 2500 volumes; 350,000 photographic prints; 175,000 negatives; 75,000 color transparencies (35mm and 4x5); black/white photographs (35mm and 11x14); film and glass negatives; postcards; stereographs; photographs of artwork and graphics; photographs of collection objects in Palace of the Governors, Fine Arts Museum, Museum of Indian Arts and Culture, Museum of International Folk Art. **Subscriptions:** 25 journals and other serials.

★702★
Museum of Northern Arizona
Harold S. Colton Memorial Library
3101 N Fort Valley Rd.   Ph: (520)774-5212
Flagstaff, AZ 86001   Fax: (520)779-1527
Founded: 1928 **Subjects:** American Southwest - archeology, geology, paleontology, ethnology, natural history, history, art. **Special Collections:** Southwestern archeology; Navajo and Hopi Indians; geology of the Colorado Plate au. **Holdings:** 24,000 books; 400 periodical titles; 26,500 pamphlets; map and manuscript collections. **Subscriptions:** 75 journals and other serials; 2 newspapers.

★703★
Muskegon County Museum
Archives
430 W. Clay Ave.   Ph: (616)722-0278
Muskegon, MI 49440   Fax: (616)728-4119
Founded: 1937 **Subjects:** Muskegon County history, Woodland Indians, lumbering, natural history, Michigan history, museum operations, maritime history. **Special Collections:** Charles Yates Collection of Historical Photographs of Muskegon (2000 photographs; corresponding newspaper articles and manuscripts); Willard Gebhart collection of landscape design. **Holdings:** 2000 books; 9000 photographs; 2000 postcards. **Subscriptions:** 15 journals and other serials; 2 newspapers.

★704★
Native American Educational Service Inc.
Central Library and Resource Center
2838 W. Peterson   Ph: (773)761-5000
Chicago, IL 60659   Fax: (773)761-3808
Founded: 1970 **Subjects:** Indian community development, education, human services, history, culture and religion, government and Indian law, economic development. **Special Collections:** Sol Tax Collection; Armin Beck Special Collectionl; LaDonna Harris Collection. **Holdings:** 6000 books; 500 pamphlets; 1000 articles; studies; papers; 37 linear feet archives. **Subscriptions:** 10 journals and other serials; 5 newspapers.

★705★
Native American Indian Center of Central Ohio
Library
PO Box 07705   Ph: (614)443-6120
Columbus, OH 43207   Fax: (614)443-2651
Founded: 1989 **Subjects:** Native Americans - history, culture, stories, arts and crafts. **Holdings:** 400 books; 6 reports. **Subscriptions:** 4 journals and other serials; 3 newspapers.

★706★
Native American Public Telecommunications
Library
PO Box 83111   Ph: (402)472-3522
Lincoln, NE 68501   Fax: (402)472-8675
Founded: 1977. **Special Collections:** Native American video programs (171 titles); Spirits of the Present (audio program series)

★707★
Native American Rights Fund
National Indian Law Library
1522 Broadway   Ph: (303)447-8760
Boulder, CO 80302-6296   Fax: (303)443-7776
Founded: 1972 **Subjects:** Federal Indian law, U.S. government-Indian relations, Indians. **Special Collections:** Indian Legal Materials and Resources (10,000). **Holdings:** 7500 books; 35 bound periodical volumes. **Subscriptions:** 77 journals and other serials; 101 newspapers.

★708★
Navajo Nation Library System
PO Box 9040   Ph: (520)871-6376
Window Rock, AZ 86515   Fax: (520)871-7304
Irving Nelson, Mgr.
Founded: 1941 **Subjects:** Navajos, Indians of the Southwest, Indians of North America, archeology, Arizona history. **Special Collections:** Navajo History; Native American Research Library; J.L. Correll Collection (30 filing cabinets); Navajo Times (80 acid-free boxes). **Holdings:** 22,000 books; 1000 manuscripts; 60 films; 250 tape recordings; microfilm; CD-ROMs. **Subscriptions:** 80 journals and other serials.

★709★
Nebraska State Historical Society
John G. Neihardt State Historic Site
Research Library
Elm and Washington Sts.
Box 344
Bancroft, NE 68004   Ph: (402)648-3388
Founded: 1976 **Subjects:** John G. Neihardt; American Indian culture and religion; Missouri River; fur trade; Nebraska and Plains history. **Special Collections:** First editions, essays, and reviews of works by John Neihardt (2 VF drawer); John Neihardt's Correspondence (3 VF drawers); Bancroft Blade, June 21, 1904 to August 9, 1907 (2 reels of microfilm). **Holdings:** 202 books; 74 bound periodical volumes; 100 audiotapes and transcripts; 1 VF drawer of pamphlets and photographs; 3 dissertations; clipping files.

★710★
Nebraska State Historical Society
Library
Box 304
Crawford, NE 69339   Ph: (308)665-2852
Founded: 1970 **Subjects:** Nebraska history. **Holdings:** Fort Robinson records on microfilm; Red Cloud and Spotted Tail Agency records; diaries and interview manuscripts; newspapers of Crawford and Chadron, Nebraska.

★711★
Nelson-Atkins Museum of Art
Slide Library
4525 Oak St.
Kansas City, MO 64111-1873   Ph: (816)751-1214
Yuming Sun, Slide Libn.
Founded: 1933 **Subjects:** Oriental, Occidental, and Native art architecture, sculpture, bronzes, painting, ceramics, decorative arts, furniture, textiles. **Holdings:** 80,847 slides.

★712★
Nevada Historical Society
Library
1650 N. Virginia St.   Ph: (702)688-1190
Reno, NV 89503-1799   Fax: (702)688-2917
Founded: 1904 **Subjects:** Nevada history, mining, Indians, agriculture, water, gambling, transportation and communication. **Holdings:** 40,000 books; 5000 bound periodical volumes; 3200 manuscript collections; 7500 reels of microfilm; 300,000 photographs; 55,000 maps; government documents. **Subscriptions:** 260 journals and other serials.

★713★
Newberry Library
60 W. Walton St.   Ph: (312)943-9090
Chicago, IL 60610   Fax: (312)255-3513
Charles T. Cullen, Pres. & Libn.
Founded: 1887 **Subjects:** European, English, and American history and literature; local and family history; church history; Italian Renaissance; expansion of Europe; philology; bibliography; history and theory of music; history of cartography. **Special Collections:** History of Printing; Western Americana; American Indian; Midwest manuscripts; Sherwood Anderson; music; Melville Collection; railroad archives. **Holdings:** 1.4 million volumes; 5 million manuscripts; 225,000 microforms; 150,000 pieces of sheet music and scores. **Subscriptions:** 1500 journals and other serials.

★714★
Northeastern Oklahoma State University
John Vaughan Library/LRC
Special Collections and Archives
Tahlequah, OK 74464   Ph: (918)456-5511
     Fax: (918)458-2197
Founded: 1909. **Special Collections:** Cherokee Indian Collection (589 volumes); E. Edmondson Papers (240 boxes); Government Document Depository (332,000). **Holdings:** 10,088 books; 595 bound periodical volumes; 5172 microfiche; 1852 reels of microfilm. **Subscriptions:** 26 journals and other serials; 31 newspapers.

★715★
Northern Arizona University
Cline Library
Special Collections and Archives Department
Box 6022   Ph: (520)523-5551
Flagstaff, AZ 86011-6022   Fax: (602)523-3770
Founded: 1966 **Subjects:** Arizona, Southwestern U.S., Colorado River and Plateau, Grand Canyon, Navajo and Hopi Indians. **Special Collections:** Emery Kolb's early motion picture film and photographs of the Grand Canyon, 1911-1924 (75 reels, primarily 35mm; videotapes; 250,000 prints); Pioneer Museum, Arizona Historical Society Archives and photograph repository; United Verde (Jerome) Mining Collection; Alexander and Dorothea Leighton Collection, 1940 (Navajo field materials in anthropology); Arizona Woolgrowers Association Archives; Arizona Lumber and Timber Company Archives; Arizona AFL-CIO Labor Union Archives; First

National Bank of Arizona Archives; Apachean Language Collection, including Chiricahua dialects (over 300 cassettes); Northern Arizona University Archives; F red Harvey Collection (hotels and restaurants of the Southwest); Colorado River Collection; Stuart Young Collection (early archeologist in four corners area, 1908-1909; photographs); Malcolm (Byron) Cummings Collection (Rainbow Bridge); Gladwell (Toney) Richardson Collection (western pulp fiction writer; photographs; research files); Zane Grey book and manuscript collection; Georgie White Clark Colorado River Runner Collection; A.F. Whiting Collection (ethnobotany field notes). **Holdings:** 33,000 books; 3189 bound periodical volumes; 2334 linear feet of manuscripts, records, and archival materials; 3500 pamphlets; 750 oral history tapes; 700,000 photographs; 4344 reels of microfilm; 3545 regional historical maps. **Subscriptions:** 300 journals and other serials; 26 newspapers.

★716★
Northern Indiana Historical Society
Library
808 W. Washington   Ph: (219)235-9664
South Bend, IN 46601   Fax: (219)235-9059
Founded: 1867 **Subjects:** Native American history and language; Indiana history; French, Indian, English, and American occupations of Saint Joseph River Valley region; All-American Girls Professional Baseball League; pioneer life; Schuyler Colfax. **Special Collections:** Oliver Chilled Plow Co. Records; Oliver Family personal papers, diaries, photographs. **Holdings:** 7500 books; 1500 pamphlets; 10,000 photographs; bound newspapers, 1831-1964; 300 boxes of archival manuscripts, dissertations, documents; clipping files; oral history tapes; videotapes. **Subscriptions:** 25 journals and other serials.

★717★
Northwestern Oklahoma State University
Library
Alva, OK 73717   Ph: (405)327-1700
     Fax: (405)327-8501
Founded: 1897 **Subjects:** Education, arts and sciences, Oklahoma and local history, library science. **Special Collections:** William J. Mellor Collection of Indian artifacts, paintings, sculpture, stereoptican and slides, rare books (1000 items); Children's Literature Collection. **Holdings:** 105,000 volumes; 125,000 government publications; 325,000 items on microfiche. **Subscriptions:** 1405 journals and other serials; 20 newspapers.

★718★
Oakland Public Library
American Indian Library Collection
Dimond Branch Library
3565 Fruitvale Ave.
Oakland, CA 94602   Ph: (510)482-7823
Founded: 1979 **Subjects:** Native Americans - literature, culture, history. **Holdings:** 1000 books. **Subscriptions:** 10 journals and other serials.

★719★
Oglala Lakota College
Library
PO Box 310   Ph: (605)455-2321
Kyle, SD 57752   Fax: (605)455-2787
Subjects: American Indians, history, social science, applied science. **Special Collections:** American Indian collection (5000 volumes). **Holdings:** 20,000 books. **Subscriptions:** 180 journals and other serials; 15 newspapers.

★720★
Oklahoma Historical Society
Archives and Manuscript Division
Historical Bldg.   Ph: (405)522-5209
Oklahoma City, OK 73105   Fax: (405)521-2492
Founded: 1893 **Subjects:** Oklahoma and Indian territories, Indian tribes of Oklahoma, pioneer life, missionaries, territorial court records, explorers. **Special Collections:** Records from all state Indian agencies, except Osage Agency (3.5 million document pages; 6000 volumes); Dawes Commission Records (48 cubic feet; 242 bound volumes); Indian-Pioneer History (interviews; 112

volumes); Whipple Collection (8 cubic feet); Joseph Thoburn Collection (20 cubic feet). **Holdings:** 2900 reels of microfilm of Indian and Oklahoma affairs; 390,000 historical photographs; 29,000 reels of microfilm of newspapers; 4500 oral history tapes. **Subscriptions:** 10 journals and other serials.

★721★
Oklahoma Historical Society
Division of Library Resources
2100 N. Lincoln Blvd.   Ph: (405)521-2491
Oklahoma City, OK 73105   Fax: (405)521-2492

Founded: 1893 **Subjects:** Oklahoma and American Indian history, American west, Oklahoma genealogy. **Holdings:** 62,593 books; 10,600 reels of microfilm of U.S. Census, 1790-1920; 25,000 reels of microfilm of Oklahoma newspapers, 1893 to present. **Subscriptions:** 300 journals and other serials; 280 newspapers.

★722★
Oklahoma Historical Society
Museum of the Western Prairie
Bernice Ford Price Reference Library
1100 Memorial Dr.
Box 574
Altus, OK 73522-0574   Ph: (405)482-1044

Founded: 1982 **Subjects:** History of southwest Oklahoma, pioneer families, Plains Indians, cowboys, early settlers. **Special Collections:** Long Collection (Indians of southwest); Dr. E.E. Dale History Collection; first editions of Oklahoma University Press. **Holdings:** 1500 books; 100 bound periodical volumes; documents; oral history tapes; archival collections; photographs. **Subscriptions:** 18 journals and other serials.

★723★
Oklahoma School for the Blind
Parkview Library
3300 Gibson St.   Ph: (918)682-6641
Muskogee, OK 74403-0309   Fax: (918)682-1651
Shonda Konemann, Lib.-Media Spec.

Founded: 1997 **Subjects:** Books in Braille and talking books; large print books; Braille and large print magazines. **Special Collections:** Education of the blind; Oklahoma history and Indian cultures of Oklahoma. **Holdings:** 8013 titles; 350 videos; 4000 cassettes; records; disks. **Subscriptions:** 81 journals and other serials.

★724★
Palomar Community College
Library
Special Collections
1140 W. Mission Rd.   Ph: (760)744-1150
San Marcos, CA 92069-1487   Fax: (760)761-3500
George Mozes, Dir., Lib./Media Ctr.

Founded: 1946. **Special Collections:** Fine arts (15,500 volumes); American Indian (3400 volumes); Iceland (200 volumes); World War I poster collection. **Holdings:** 100,000 books. **Subscriptions:** 980 journals and other serials; 21 newspapers.

★725★
Panhandle-Plains Historical Museum
Research Center
WTAMU, Box 967   Ph: (806)656-2260
Canyon, TX 79016   Fax: (806)656-2250

Founded: 1932 **Subjects:** Texas and Southwest history; ranching; Indians of the Great Plains; archeology of Texas Panhandle; ethnology; clothing and textiles; fine arts; antiques; museum science. **Special Collections:** Interviews with early settlers and other citizens collected over a period of 63 years; Bob Wills Memorial Archive of Popular Music, 1915 to present (5000 phonograph records); Southwest regional architectural drawings, 1978 to present (microfilm). **Holdings:** 16,000 books; 13,000 cubic feet of manuscripts; 20 VF drawers of pamphlets; 800 maps; 1600 reels of microfilm; 45 cubic feet of manufacturers' trade literature; 300,000 historic photographs. **Subscriptions:** 250 journals and other serials; 12 newspapers.

★726★
Parmly Billings Library
Montana Room
510 N. Broadway   Ph: (406)657-8258
Billings, MT 59101   Fax: (406)657-8293

Special Collections: Local histories (100); city archives (75 archival materials). **Holdings:** 7000 books; 100 bound periodical volumes; 120 filing drawers. **Subscriptions:** 12 journals and other serials; 6 newspapers.

★727★
Pawnee Indian Village State Historic Site
Library
Rte1
PO Box 475   Ph: (785)361-2255
Republic, KS 66964   Fax: (785)361-2255

Founded: 1968 **Subjects:** Pawnee Indians, north central Kansas, Plains Indians. **Special Collections:** The Pawnee tribe in Kansas and Nebraska. **Holdings:** Books; reports; microfilm; maps.

★728★
Philbrook Museum of Art
Chapman Library
Box 52510   Ph: (918)748-5306
Tulsa, OK 74152-0510   Fax: (918)743-4230

Founded: 1939 **Subjects:** Art. **Special Collections:** Roberta Campbell Lawson Indian Library (1105 volumes). **Holdings:** 12,000 books; 7000 bound periodical volumes; 196 VF drawers; 450 linear feet of archival materials. **Subscriptions:** 143 journals and other serials.

★729★
Phoenix Indian Medical Center
Library
4212 N 16th St.   Ph: (602)263-1200
Phoenix, AZ 85016   Fax: (602)263-1577

Founded: 1965 **Subjects:** Medicine, nursing, dentistry. **Special Collections:** Indian history; Indian health. **Holdings:** 1800 books; 2000 bound periodical volumes; 3000 unbound journals; 5 VF drawers of pamphlets and reprints. **Subscriptions:** 180 journals and other serials.

★730★
Phoenix Public Library
Arizona Room
1221 N Central
Phoenix, AZ 85004   Ph: (602)262-4636

Subjects: Phoenix and Arizona history, Southwestern Indians, Southwestern water and land use, Mexican Americans, Southwestern art. **Special Collections:** James Harvey McClintock papers, 1864-1934. **Holdings:** 22,000 books; 250 bound periodical volumes; Phoenix municipal records; Arizona Republic clipping file, 1977-1990. **Subscriptions:** 45 journals and other serials.

★731★
Ponca City Cultural Center and Museums
Library
1000 E Grand Ave.
Ponca City, OK 74601   Ph: (405)767-0427

Founded: 1938 **Subjects:** American Indian, anthropology, archeology, American cowboy, museology. **Special Collections:** Personal letters and photographs of Bryant Baker, sculptor of the Pioneer Woman; Ponca Indian music (tape recordings). **Holdings:** 200 books; 15 bound periodical volumes; VF drawers of unbound reports, clippings, pamphlets, dissertations, documents. **Subscriptions:** 15 journals and other serials.

★732★
Portland Art Museum
Rex Arragon Library
1219 SW Park   Ph: (503)226-2811
Portland, OR 97205-2486   Fax: (503)226-4842

Founded: 1892 **Subjects:** Art. **Special Collections:** Art of Indian tribes of the Pacific Northwest; Oriental art, especially Japanese prints; English silver books; Northwest Artists Archives. **Holdings:**

22,442 books; 1100 bound periodical volumes; 365 pamphlet cases of catalogs relating to artists, movements, and exhibitions; 175 pamphlet cases of museum reports and bulletins; 71,500 slides. **Subscriptions:** 84 journals and other serials.

★733★
Red Clay State Historical Park
Library
1140 Red Clay Park Rd., SW
Cleveland, TN 37311   Ph: (423)478-0339
MsLois I. Osborne, Pk.Mgr

Founded: 1979 **Subjects:** Cherokee history, Native Americans, Cherokee genealogy, environment. **Holdings:** 800 books. **Subscriptions:** 1 journal; 2 newspapers.

★734★
Rochester Museum and Science Center
Library
657 East Ave.   Ph: (716)271-4320
Rochester, NY 14607   Fax: (716)271-5935

Founded: 1914 **Subjects:** Natural sciences, anthropology, local history, American Indians, antiques, archeology, costume, technology, museology. **Special Collections:** Albert Stone Collection of local photographs, 1904-1934 (15,000); slide library; museum bulletins; archival material and ephemera. **Holdings:** 26,000 volumes; museum bulletins; archival material and ephemera. **Subscriptions:** 60 journals and other serials.

★735★
Roswell Museum and Art Center
Research Library
100 W11th St.   Ph: (505)624-6744
Roswell, NM 88201   Fax: (505)624-6765

Founded: 1937 **Subjects:** Art - contemporary, Native American, Spanish Colonial, Western United States; rocketry; archeology. **Special Collections:** Robert H. Goddard Archives & Collections (36 volumes). **Holdings:** 7500 books; 3600 bound periodical volumes; 7000 color slides. **Subscriptions:** 75 journals and other serials.

★736★
Rowan University of New Jersey
Rowan University Library
Stewart Room
201 Mullica Hill Rd.   Ph: (609)256-4967
Glassboro, NJ 08028-1701   Fax: (609)256-4924

Founded: 1948 **Subjects:** New Jersey history, early religious history, genealogy, Indians of North America, Revolutionary War, War of 1812, Grinnell Arctic expedition. **Special Collections:** Family papers: Howell, Inskeep, Haines, Lippincott; Frank H Stewart Collection (8000 volumes); Charles A Wolverton Papers (10 boxes); Summit Conference Papers (4 boxes); Satterthwaite Genealogical Collection (24 VF drawers). **Holdings:** 16,300 books; 422 bound periodical volumes; 5000 manuscripts; 13 VF drawers of college archives; 4200 volumes of masters' theses; rare books; deeds; surveys; marriage licenses; acts of assembly. **Subscriptions:** 28 journals and other serials.

★737★
Sac and Fox National Public Library
Rte2, Box 246   Ph: (918)968-3526
Stroud, OK 74079   Fax: (918)968-4837
Judith A. Walkingstick, Lib.Dir

Founded: 1987 **Subjects:** American Indians, Sac and Fox history and culture, biography. **Special Collections:** Sac and Fox Photography Collection (1000); Sac and Fox Document Collection (250); Sac and Fox Oral History Collection (36 interviews). **Holdings:** 4000 books; 100 reports; 2000 archives; 46 reels of microfilm. **Subscriptions:** 2 journals and other serials; 32 newspapers.

★738★
St. Joseph Museum
Library
1100 Charles
PO Box 128   Ph: (816)232-8471
St. Joseph, MO 64502-0128   Fax: (816)232-8482

Founded: 1927 **Subjects:** Local and area history, Western movement, ethnology, natural history. **Special Collections:** American Indian Collection; Civil War period local history collection; Pony Express; bird, mammal, and fish exhibits. **Holdings:** 7000 volumes. **Subscriptions:** 40 journals and other serials.

★739★
Samford University
Harwell Goodwin Davis Library
Special Collections
800 Lakeshore Dr.   Ph: (205)870-2749
Birmingham, AL 35229   Fax: (205)870-2642

Founded: 1957 **Subjects:** Alabama history, literature, and imprints; Early Southeast - Indians, travel, law; genealogical source records; Southern Reconstruction; Irish history and genealogy. **Special Collections:** William H. Brantley Collection (books; 19th and 20th century manuscripts; 18th and 19th century maps); Albert E. Casey Collection (books; manuscripts; periodicals; maps of Ireland); Douglas C. McMurtrie Collection; John Ruskin Collection; John Masefield Collection; Alfred Tennyson Collection; Lafcadio Hearn Collection. **Holdings:** 25,653 books; 2562 bound periodical volumes; 806 microcards; 349 phonograph records; 2725 maps; 1477 linear feet of manuscripts; 7739 reels of microfilm; 7828 prints and photographs; 3113 microfiche; 150 oral histories; 37 atlases; 1 globe; 60 relief models. **Subscriptions:** 330 journals and other serials.

★740★
San Diego Museum of Man
Scientific Library
Balboa Park
1350 El Prado   Ph: (619)239-2001
San Diego, CA 92101   Fax: (619)239-2749

Founded: 1916 **Subjects:** Anthropology, pre-Columbian art, Indians of the Americas, archeology, ethnology, physical anthropology. **Special Collections:** North American Indians. **Holdings:** 8000 books; 8000 bound periodical volumes; 51 archival manuscripts. **Subscriptions:** 300 journals and other serials.

★741★
San Diego Public Library
Special Collections
Wangenheim Room
820 E St.   Ph: (619)236-5807
San Diego, CA 92101-6478   Fax: (619)236-5811

Founded: 1954 **Subjects:** History of printing and the development of the book with specimens ranging from cuneiform tablets to contemporary fine printing; illustrated books; incunabula; fine book bindings. **Special Collections:** Dime novels (769 items); bookplates (6000); fore-edge paintings (185 volumes); works of Kate Greenaway (65 volumes); works of John Ruskin (250 volumes); Curtis' North American Indians (20 volumes and 20 portfolios of photographs); Monumenta Scenica (12 portfolios); Grayson's Birds of the Pacific Slope (158 plates). **Holdings:** 8882 books; selected antiquarian book dealers' catalogs; periodicals; manuscripts; autographs; artifacts. **Subscriptions:** 6 journals and other serials.

★742★
Sara Hightower - Regional Library
Special Collections
205 Riverside Pkwy.   Ph: (706)236-4607
Rome, GA 30161   Fax: (706)236-4605
Sandra Broome, Cur.

Founded: 1911 **Subjects:** Cherokee Indians, Georgia and local history, genealogy, Southern history, Civil War. **Special Collections:** J.F. Brooks Cherokeeana Collection (401 books); Ellen Louise Axson Wilson Collection; John L Harris Papers (3 VF drawers); George M. Battey, III, Papers (5 VF drawers); Civil War collection; Yancey Lipscomb Collection (4 VF Drawers); Rome

News-Tribune Resource Collection. **Holdings:** 14,000 books; 64 VF drawers; 350 maps; 8000 microforms; 600 unbound periodicals. **Subscriptions:** 71 journals and other serials.

★743★
School of American Research
Library
Box 2188   Ph: (505)982-3583
Santa Fe, NM 87504-2188   Fax: (505)989-9809
Jane P. Gillentine, Libn.

Subjects: Anthropology, archeology, ethnology, Southwest Indian arts. **Holdings:** 6000 books; 300 bound periodical volumes. **Subscriptions:** 50 journals and other serials.

★744★
School Sisters of Saint Francis
Archives
Milwaukee, WI 53215   Ph: (414)384-4105
                                        Fax: (414)645-7198

Founded: 1974 **Subjects:** School Sisters of St. Francis. **Special Collections:** Sister Theophane Hytrek collection of music (6 cubic feet); Gros Ventre Native Americans of Montana collection (1 cubic foot); official records of the School Sisters of St. Francis; personal records of members; ministry of members. **Holdings:** 960 books; 1030 cubic feet of archival material; 131 reels of microfilm. **Subscriptions:** 3 journals and other serials.

★745★
Seminole Tribe of Florida
Seminole Tribal Library System
Rt6, Box 668   Ph: (941)763-4236
Okeechobee, FL 34974   Fax: (941)763-0679

Founded: 1976 **Subjects:** Native Americans, Seminole Indians, Florida. **Special Collections:** Vertical file of Seminole articles, dissertations, and theses; Muskogee language materials. **Holdings:** 24,182 books; 2,067 microfiche. **Subscriptions:** 161 journals and other serials; 8 newspapers.

★746★
Seneca Nation Library
1490 Rte 438   Ph: (716)532-9449
Irving, NY 14081   Fax: (716)532-6115
Ann John, Dir.

Founded: 1979. **Special Collections:** Native American collection. **Holdings:** 18,500 books; 600 bound periodical volumes; 176 microfiche and microfilm. **Subscriptions:** 5 newspapers.

★747★
Seton Memorial Library
Philmont Scout Ranch
Cimarron, NM 87714   Ph: (505)376-2281

Founded: 1967 **Subjects:** Books written by Ernest T. Seton, Boy Scouts, Southwest, natural history, Indian Art, Bureau of American Ethnology. **Special Collections:** Ernest T. Seton Collection (200 volumes; 7 VF drawers of manuscripts and correspondence). **Holdings:** 6000 books; 250 bound periodical volumes; 2000 photographs; local archeology reports (2 VF drawers). **Subscriptions:** 11 journals and other serials.

★748★
Sharlot Hall/Prescott Historical Societies
Library/Archives
415 W. Gurley St.   Ph: (520)445-3122
Prescott, AZ 86301   Fax: (520)776-9053

Founded: 1929 **Subjects:** Anglo and Indian history of the Southwest, especially Arizona; Arizona history and mining. **Special Collections:** Sharlot Hall Collection (7 cubic feet); cowboy folklore and music collection (100 cassette tapes). **Holdings:** 9000 volumes; 200 linear feet of uncataloged items; 200 oral history/folklore tapes; photographs; manuscripts; diaries; artifacts; letters. **Subscriptions:** 13 journals and other serials.

★749★
Siouxland Heritage Museums
Library
200 W6th St.   Ph: (605)367-7097
Sioux Falls, SD 57104   Fax: (605)367-4210

Founded: 1926 **Subjects:** South Dakota history; U.S. history - silver question; 19th century works on ethnology and natural science; Indians. **Special Collections:** Arthur C. Phillips Collection; Northern League Baseball records (4 linear feet); library and private papers of U.S. Senator R.F. Pettigrew (1000 volumes); South Dakota history (1500 items). **Holdings:** 9000 books; 200 bound periodical volumes; 100 maps; 150 linear feet of manuscripts; 10,000 photographs. **Subscriptions:** 10 journals and other serials.

★750★
Skagit County Historical Museum
Historical Reference Library
501 S4th St.
PO Box 818
La Conner, WA 98257   Ph: (360)452-4501

Founded: 1959 **Subjects:** Skagit County - history, statistics, demographics, industry, social, economic, community life, transportation; pioneer family genealogies; local Indian histories. **Special Collections:** Diaries of Grant Sisson, W.J. Cornelius, Arthur Champenois, and others, 1844-1964; Darius Kinsey Photographs. **Holdings:** 1500 books; 308 bound periodical volumes; 10,000 photographs; 700 newspapers; 700 business documents; 200 letters; 200 district school accounts/records; 100 maps; 700 clippings and clipping scrapbooks; 300 programs/announcements; 80 pioneer diaries; 220 oral history tapes with transcripts; American popular music, 1866-1954; local newspapers, 1900 to present. **Subscriptions:** 4 journals and other serials; 7 newspapers.

★751★
The Smoki Museum, Inc.
Library
PO Box 10224
Prescott, AZ 86304   Ph: (520)445-1230

Founded: 1935 **Subjects:** North and South American Indian ceremonials and dances, southwestern Native American ethnology and archeology. **Special Collections:** B of A.E Annuals; B of A.E Bulletins (incomplete). **Holdings:** 600 volumes. **Subscriptions:** 2 journals and other serials.

★752★
Southern Utah University
Gerald R. Sherratt Library
Special Collections Department
351 WCenter St.   Ph: (801)586-7945
Cedar City, UT 84720   Fax: (801)586-7934

Founded: 1962 **Subjects:** Southern Paiute Indian history, local history, University archives, Shakespeare. **Special Collections:** William Rees Palmer Western History Collection; Document Collection (various donors); John Laurence Seymour Collection (music, theater, humanities); Howard Smith Collection; Orien Dalley Music Collection; Homer Jones Photo Collection. **Holdings:** 7000 volumes; 925 oral history tapes; 457 phonograph records; 1445 linear feet of manuscript collections; 51,000 photographs and negatives; 804 linear feet of archives; 1743 maps.

★753★
Southwest Museum
Braun Research Library
PO Box 41558   Ph: (213)221-2164
Los Angeles, CA 90041-0558   Fax: (213)224-8223

Founded: 1907 **Subjects:** Anthropology, Native American studies, western history. **Special Collections:** Munk Library of Arizoniana; Hector Alliott Memorial Library of Archaeology; Charles FLummis Collection; George Wharton James Collection; papers of Frank Hamilton Cushing, John Charles Fremont, George Bird Grinnell, Frederick Webb Hodge, Charles FLummis; rare Western American imprints; children's books. **Holdings:** 50,000 volumes; 100,000 pamphlets and ephemera; 140,000 photographs; 900 linear feet of manuscripts; 1400 sound recordings; government publications;

2300 maps; VF drawers. **Subscriptions:** 200 journals and other serials.

★754★
State Historical Society of Iowa
Library/Archives
402 Iowa Ave.   Ph: (319)335-3916
Iowa City, IA 52240-1806   Fax: (319)335-3935
Shaner Magalhaes, Bureau Chf.

Founded: 1857 **Subjects:** History - Iowa, the frontier, agriculture, railroad, women, education in Iowa, Indians of the region; genealogy. **Special Collections:** Robert Lucas papers; Jonathan P. Dolliver papers; Gilbert Haugen papers; Cyrus Carpenter papers; Huftalen/Gillespie diaries; Mather-Bush papers; Labor Collection; Iowa industry house organs; historical Iowa photographs (1 million images); historical Iowa maps (3000). **Holdings:** 140,000 books; 12,000 bound periodical volumes; 16,000 pamphlets; 24,000 reels of microfilm; 10,000 bound newspapers; 25 VF drawers of newspaper clippings; 1800 oral history interviews; 4000 linear feet of manuscripts. **Subscriptions:** 575 serials, 65 newspapers.

★755★
State Historical Society of Wisconsin
Library
816 State St.   Ph: (608)264-6534
Madison, WI 53706-1482   Fax: (608)264-6520
JKevin Graffagnino, Dir.

Founded: 1846 **Subjects:** History - American, Canadian, Wisconsin, local, labor; radical/reform movements and groups in the U.S. and Canada; ethnic and minority groups in North America; genealogy; women's history; military history; religious history. **Special Collections:** African American History Collection (newspapers; periodicals); Native American History Collection (12,000 items; government documents; Native American publications); Women's Collection (pamphlets; periodicals; newspapers; publications of Phyllis Wheatley, Lydia Child, Harriet Jacobs, Jane Addams, Susan BAnthony, Carrie Chapman Catt, Emma Goldman, etc.). **Holdings:** 1.6 million books and bound periodical volumes; 100,000 cubic feet of archives; 1.5 million microfiche and reels of microfilm. **Subscriptions:** 8500 periodicals; 500 newspapers.

★756★
Sunset Trading Post-Old West Museum
Library
Rte1
Sunset, TX 76270

Founded: 1960 **Subjects:** Barbed wire, frontier, American Indian, cowboys and cattlemen, Civil War, Western painting, county history, guns and knives. **Special Collections:** Barbed Wire. **Holdings:** 2500 books; 200 pamphlets; clippings; drawings; Indian artifacts; Bronzes of the West by Jack Glover; unpublished stories; pictures; negatives.

★757★
Thomas Gilcrease Institute of American History and Art
Library
1400 Gilcrease Museum Rd.   Ph: (918)596-2700
Tulsa, OK 74127   Fax: (918)596-2770

Founded: 1955 **Subjects:** History - Colonial, Western, Spanish Southwest, Indian. **Special Collections:** Hispanic documents, 1500-1800; John Ross papers (Chief of Cherokees); Peter P. Pitchlynn papers (Chief of Choctaws); Grant Foreman Collection. **Holdings:** 50,000 books; 50 VF drawers of historic photographs and manuscripts; broadsides; maps; photostats. **Subscriptions:** 10 journals and other serials.

★758★
Tohono Chul Park
Library
7366 Paseo del Norte   Ph: (520)742-6455
Tucson, AZ 85704   Fax: (520)797-1213

Founded: 1985 **Subjects:** Arid regions, ethnobotany, American Southwest, Native Americans, ecology. **Holdings:** 700 books.

★759★
Totem Heritage Center
c/o 629 Dock St.   Ph: (907)225-5900
Ketchikan, AK 99901   Fax: (907)225-5602

Founded: 1976 **Subjects:** Northwest Coast Indian art, culture, and history. **Special Collections:** Northwest Coast totem poles (31). **Holdings:** 300 books; 150 bound periodical volumes; 50 manuscripts. **Subscriptions:** 3 journals and other serials.

★760★
Trinity College
Watkinson Library
300 Summit St.   Ph: (860)297-2268
Hartford, CT 06106   Fax: (860)297-2251
DrJeffrey H. Kaimowitz, Cur. & Ornithology Cur.

Founded: 1857 **Subjects:** Americana (especially 19th century), American Indians, black history, U.S. Civil War, British history and topography, folklore, witchcraft, graphic arts, history of printing, natural history, philology (especially American Indian languages), early voyages and travels, maritime history. **Special Collections:** Incunabula and 16th century imprints (especially Trumbull-Prime Collection of illustrated books); private press books (especially Ashendene Press); English and American first editions (especially Frost, E.A. Robinson, Walter Scott); 18th and 19th century English and American periodicals; ornithology (6000 volumes); Barnard Collection of early American school books (7000 volumes); manuscripts of Charles Dudley Warner, Samuel Clemens (Mark Twain Memorial deposit collection), Frost, E.A. Robinson, Walter Scott, Henry Barnard, Ely Halperine-Kaminsky, Sibour Family, Nathan Allen, James Hammond Trumbull, Odell Shepard, Nathan Allen Watkinson Family, Hartford families, Monday Evening Club papers, and other historical and literary figures; American music, including jazz and blues and 18th and 19th century religious and secular works in printed and manuscript form, 1100 song sheets, and 26,000 pieces of sheet music; Trinity College Archives. **Holdings:** 165,000 books and bound periodical volumes; atlases; 500 maps; printed ephemera including 100 indexed scrapbooks, advertisements, fashion plates, music and theater programs, and valentines. **Subscriptions:** 40 journals and other serials.

★761★
U.S. Department of the Interior
Bureau of Indian Affairs
Southwestern Indian Polytechnic Institute
Library
9169 Coors Blvd., NW
Box 10146
Albuquerque, NM 87184   Ph: (505)897-5352

Founded: 1972 **Subjects:** Vocational-technical curriculum, American Indians, recreational reading. **Special Collections:** American Indian Collection (2240 volumes; 120 newspapers and newsletters). **Holdings:** 28,000 books; 150 bound periodical volumes; 100 audio cassettes; 350 video cassettes; 16mm films. **Subscriptions:** 100 journals and other serials; 35 newspapers.

★762★
U.S. Department of the Interior
Indian Arts and Crafts Board
1849 C St., Rm. 4004-MIB
Washington, DC 20240   Ph: (202)208-3773

Founded: 1935. **Subjects:** Contemporary Native American arts and crafts.

★763★
U.S. Department of the Interior
Law Branch Library
1849 C St., NW, Rm. 7139   Ph: (202)208-4571
Washington, DC 20240   Fax: (202)219-1434

Founded: 1975. **Subjects:** Law - public land, Indian, natural resources, administrative, environmental. **Special Collections:** Pre-Federal Register regulations of the Department of the Interior (1000 pieces); Native American Legal Materials (500 microfiche). **Holdings:** 30,000 books; 2000 bound periodical volumes; 10,000 microfiche; 1000 reels of microfilm; 3000 microfiche of Indian Claims Commission materials; 10 reels of microfilm of executive orders;

1000 microfiche of Council of State Governments publications; 700 legislative histories. **Subscriptions:** 801 journals and other serials.

★764★
U.S. Department of the Interior
National Park Service
Canyon De Chelly National Monument
Library
PO Box 588   Ph: (520)674-5518
Chinle, AZ 86503   Fax: (520)672-5507
Founded: 1931 **Subjects:** Southwest archeology, southwest history, American Indian culture. **Special Collections:** Archival materials related to the prehistory and history of Canyon de Chelly. **Holdings:** 300 books; 25 reports.

★765★
U.S. Department of the Interior
National Park Service
De Soto National Memorial
Library
75th St., NW   Ph: (941)792-0458
Bradenton, FL 34209-9656   Fax: (941)792-5094
Founded: 1968 **Subjects:** Spanish exploration; general exploration; American, Florida, and natural history; Florida Indian cultures. **Holdings:** 1128 volumes. **Subscriptions:** 5 journals and other serials; 2 newspapers.

★766★
U.S. Department of the Interior
National Park Service
Fort Laramie National Historic Site
Library
HC 72, Box 389   Ph: (307)837-2221
Fort Laramie, WY 82212   Fax: (307)837-2120
Founded: 1955 **Subjects:** Frontier military history, Western history, Oregon-California-Mormon trails, Plains Indians. **Holdings:** 3500 books; 200 reels of microfilm.

★767★
U.S. Department of the Interior
National Park Service
Fort Larned National Historic Site
Library
Rte3   Ph: (316)285-6911
Larned, KS 67550-9733   Fax: (316)285-3571
Founded: 1966 **Subjects:** Fort Larned, 1859-1878; Plains Indians; Santa Fe Trail; military history; Indian Wars, 1848-1890; museum conservation and preservation. **Special Collections:** Technical products information, including manufacturers' catalogs, directories, building codes, and basic design/construction reference materials, standards, and specifications. **Holdings:** 775 books; 110 reels of microfilm; 10 binders of national archives. **Subscriptions:** 10 journals and other serials.

★768★
U.S. Department of the Interior
National Park Service
Glacier National Park
George C. Ruhle Library
West Glacier, MT 59936   Ph: (406)888-7932
                                    Fax: (406)888-7808
Founded: 1975 **Subjects:** Glacier Park history, environment, geology, glaciology, mammals, Plains Indians. **Special Collections:** Schultz books on the Plains Indians. **Holdings:** 13,000 books; 3000 reprints; 10,000 museum specimens. **Subscriptions:** 27 journals and other serials; 6 newspapers.

★769★
U.S. Department of the Interior
National Park Service
Grand Portage National Monument
Library
PO Box 668   Ph: (218)387-2788
Grand Marais, MN 55604   Fax: (218)387-2790
Subjects: American-Canadian fur trade, Chippewa Indian culture, Canadian-Minnesota exploration and history. **Special Collections:** Wisconsin Historical Collection (21 volumes); journals of the Hudson's Bay Company (24 volumes); works of Samuel De Champlain (6 volumes). **Holdings:** 900 books; 100 bound periodical volumes. **Subscriptions:** 2 journals and other serials.

★770★
U.S. Department of the Interior
National Park Service
Hopewell Culture National Historical Park
Library
16062 State Rte. 104   Ph: (614)774-1125
Chillicothe, OH 45601   Fax: (614)774-1140
Founded: 1943 **Subjects:** Archeology, Hopewell and other prehistoric Indian cultures of Ohio, environment and environmental education, Ohio history. **Special Collections:** Reports of archeological research on Hopewell and Adena cultures conducted at park; Hopewell Archeological Conference papers, 1978. **Holdings:** 1800 books; 50 magazines, reports, unbound articles. **Subscriptions:** 8 journals and other serials.

★771★
U.S. Department of the Interior
National Park Service
Intermountain Cultural Resource Center
Library
PO Box 728   Ph: (505)988-6840
Santa Fe, NM 87504-0728   Fax: (505)988-6876
Founded: 1935 **Subjects:** Southwestern archeology, Indians of the Southwest, Western U.S. history, natural history, history of the National Park Service, resource management. **Special Collections:** National Park Service publications and reports (3000); unpublished manuscripts on Southwest archeology. **Holdings:** 30,000 books; 500 unbound periodical volumes; 300 videotapes; 3000 manuscripts; 800 prints and negatives; 6000 slides; 150 maps. **Subscriptions:** 25 journals and other serials.

★772★
U.S. Department of the Interior
National Park Service
Jefferson National Expansion Memorial
Library and Archives
Old Courthouse, 2nd Fl.
11 N Fourth St.   Ph: (314)425-4468
St. Louis, MO 63102   Fax: (314)425-4570
Subjects: Jefferson National Expansion Memorial, Gateway Arch, exploration of American West. **Special Collections:** Grace Lewis Miller Book Collection; Lewis and Clark Book Collection; Office of the Superintendent, Central Files, 1935-1968; U.S. Territorial Expansion Memorial Commission Records, 1933-1975; Jefferson National Expansion Memorial Association Records, 1930-1975; Museum of Westward Expansion Exhibit Planning Records, 1959-1965 and 1972-1976; Fur Trade Illustration Project, 1945-1948; Mechanics Institute of St. Louis Records, 1830-1894; St. Louis Recorded Archives Transcription Project, Transcriptions and Indexes, 1938-1940; Grace Lewis Miller Papers; Jefferson National Expansion Memorial Research Reports; Jefferson National Expansion Memorial Newspaper Clippings. **Holdings:** Books; audiocassettes; videocassettes; pamphlets; brochures. **Subscriptions:** 104 journals and other serials; 2 newspapers.

★773★
U.S. Department of the Interior
National Park Service
Little Bighorn Battlefield National Monument
White Swan Library
Box 39   Ph: (406)638-2622
Crow Agency, MT 59022-0039   Fax: (406)638-2623
Founded: 1952 **Subjects:** Battle of Little Big Horn, George Custer, Western history, Indian wars. **Special Collections:** Elizabeth B. Custer Correspondence Collection; Walter M. Camp papers. **Holdings:** 3000 books; 500 bound periodical volumes; 24,000 artifacts, relics, and correspondences; 19 reels of microfilm; rare book and manuscript collection. **Subscriptions:** 8 journals and other serials.

★774★
U.S. Department of the Interior
National Park Service
Natchez Trace Parkway
Library & Visitor Center
2680 Natcher Trace Pkwy.   Ph: (601)680-4025
Tupelo, MS 38801   Fax: (601)680-4033
Founded: 1963 **Subjects:** History, natural history, national parks. **Special Collections:** Papers and letters related to Choctaw and Chickasaw Indians (200 items). **Holdings:** 2300 books; 200 bound periodical volumes; 1000 color slides; 10,000 negatives. **Subscriptions:** 10 journals and other serials.

★775★
U.S. Department of the Interior
National Park Service
Navajo National Monument
Library
HC 71, Box 3   Ph: (520)672-2366
Tonalea, AZ 86044-9704   Fax: (520)672-2345
Founded: 1965 **Subjects:** Southwest archeology, Navajo culture, southwest biology, Hopi culture. **Special Collections:** Southwest archeological rare books; plant collection specimens. **Holdings:** 1300 books. **Subscriptions:** 8 journals and other serials.

★776★
U.S. Department of the Interior
National Park Service
Ocmulgee National Monument Library
1207 Emery Hwy.   Ph: (912)752-8257
Macon, GA 31201   Fax: (912)752-8259
Sylvia Flowers, Cultural Rsrc.Spec.
Founded: 1936 **Subjects:** American archeology, American ethnology, Native American studies. **Special Collections:** Administrative History of Ocmulgee National Monument (assorted papers). **Holdings:** 5000 books; 300 bound periodical volumes; 100 reports; 50 archival items. **Subscriptions:** 3 journals and other serials; 2 newspapers

★777★
U.S. Department of the Interior
National Park Service
Olympic National Park
Visitor Center - Library
600 E. Park Ave.
Port Angeles, WA 98363   Ph: (360)452-4501
Henry C. Warren, Chf.Pk. Naturalist
Founded: 1938 **Subjects:** Natural history, Northwest Coast Indians, Olympic National Park. **Special Collections:** Manuscript material and reports relating to exploration and settlement of the Olympic Peninsula; correspondence, memoranda, reports, and photographs relating to the establishment and administration of Olympic National Park. **Holdings:** 2000 books; 6 VF drawers of clippings and articles relating to natural and human history of Olympic National Park. **Subscriptions:** 1 journals and other serials.

★778★
U.S. Department of the Interior
National Park Service
Pipestone National Monument
Library & Archives
Box 727   Ph: (507)825-5464
Pipestone, MN 56164   Fax: (507)825-5466
Special Collections: Publications relating to ceremonial pipes and Indian smoking customs. **Holdings:** 900 volumes; manuscripts; reports; clippings; microfilm; photographs; slides. **Subscriptions:** 12 journals and other serials; 2 newspapers.

★779★
U.S. Department of the Interior
National Park Service
Point Reyes National Seashore
Library
Point Reyes Station, CA 94956
Founded: 1963 **Subjects:** Natural history, Native Americans (Coast Miwok), environmental education, geology, California history, sea life, mammals, botany, National Park Service. **Holdings:** 2500 books; 2075 bound periodical volumes; 425 other cataloged items; reports.

★780★
U.S. Department of the Interior
National Park Service
Scotts Bluff National Monument
Library
Box 27   Ph: (308)436-4340
Gering, NE 69341   Fax: (308)436-7611
Founded: 1935 **Subjects:** Native Americans, Westward movement, Oregon Trail, natural history, park policy. **Holdings:** 3000 books and periodicals. **Subscriptions:** 4 journals and other serials.

★781★
U.S. Department of the Interior
National Park Service
Sitka National Historical Park
Library
Box 738   Ph: (907)747-6281
Sitka, AK 99835   Fax: (907)747-5938
Founded: 1965 **Subjects:** Pacific Northwest Coast Indians, Native Art, ethnology, archeology, Southeast Alaska history, natural history, Russian American history. **Special Collections:** Park archives; Old Kasaan National Monument. **Holdings:** 1600 books; 200 clippings and special papers; 55 tapes; 80 films. **Subscriptions:** 10 journals and other serials.

★782★
U.S. Department of the Interior
Natural Resources Library
1849 18th St., NW   Ph: (202)208-5815
Washington, DC 20240   Fax: (202)219-1434
Founded: 1949. **Subjects:** Conservation, energy and power, land use, parks, American Indians, fish and wildlife, mining, law, management. **Special Collections:** Archival collection of materials published by Department of Interior (150,000 items). **Holdings:** 600,000 books; 90,000 bound periodical volumes; 7000 reels of microfilm; 40,000 unbound periodical volumes; 300,000 microfiche. **Subscriptions:** 3000 journals and other serials.

★783★
U.S. Department of Justice
Environment and Natural Resources Branch Library
950 Pennsylvania Ave., NW, Rm2333   Ph: (202)514-2768
Washington, DC 20530   Fax: (202)514-4240
Special Collections: Legislative histories. **Holdings:** 18,000 volumes. **Subscriptions:** 84 journals and other serials.

★784★
U.S. Library of Congress
American Folklife Center
Thomas Jefferson Bldg.　　　　Ph: (202)707-6590
Washington, DC 20540-8100　　Fax: (202)707-2076

Founded: 1976 **Subjects:** American folklife with emphasis on research, public programs, and technical assistance; folksong; folk music; folklife; ethnomusicology; oral history. **Special Collections:** Archive of Folk Culture. **Holdings:** 4000 books; 1000 serial titles; 45,000 hours of unpublished field recordings; manuscript collection (700,000 pages); results of current research projects including fieldnotes, sound recordings, photographs, and videotapes; 200,000 ephemera; 400,000 photographs.

★785★
U.S. Smithsonian Institution
National Anthropological Archives
National Museum of Natural History, MRC
　152
10th & Constitution Ave., NW　　Ph: (202)357-1976
Washington, DC 20560　　　　　Fax: (202)357-2208
DrJohn Homiak, Dir.

Founded: 1879 **Subjects:** Anthropology, linguistics, archeology, history of anthropology, history of American Indians, history of geography. **Special Collections:** Bureau of American Ethnology manuscript collection; photographs of American Indians; Center for the Study of Man; Department of Anthropology records; Institute for Social Anthropology records; River Basin Surveys; professional papers of anthropologists; records of anthropological organizations. **Holdings:** 4000 cubic feet of archives and private papers; 350,000 photographs; 500 recordings; 100 reels of microfilm.

★786★
University of Arizona
College of Law Library
PO Box 210176　　　　　　　　Ph: (520)621-1413
Tucson, AZ 85721-0176　　　　Fax: (520)621-3138

Founded: 1915 **Subjects:** Law. **Special Collections:** Natural resources; law relating to American Indians; Latin American law. **Holdings:** 370,000 volumes; 131,000 volumes in microform. **Subscriptions:** 4158 journals and other serials; 12 newspapers.

★787★
University of California, Berkeley
Ethnic Studies Library
510 Barrows Hall, No. 2570
University of California　　　　Ph: (510)642-1234
Berkeley, CA 94720-2570　　　Fax: (510)642-6456
Lillian Castillo-Speed, Lib.Coord.

Founded: 1969 **Subjects:** Chicano, Mexican American, Spanish speaking/surname people in U.S.; Raza; farmworkers; bilingual and biculturalgroups; Native Americans. **Special Collections:** Retrospective Newspaper Collection, 1844-1943; Chicano Art Color Transparencies (4000); Chicano Posters (800); Annual Reports of the Commissioner of Indian Affairs, 1849-1949; John Collier papers; Survey of the Conditions of the Indians of the U.S., 1929-1944; Records of the Bureau of Indian Affairs, Record Group 75; Indian Census, 1885-1941; Harvard University Peabody Museum papers and memoirs, 1896-1975; Indian Rights Association papers, 1864-1973; Bureau of American Ethnology annual reports and bulletins; Indian Claims Commission reports; water rights; California Indians. **Holdings:** 5000 volumes; 150 bound periodical volumes; 30,000 other cataloged items; 1500 microforms; 550 audiotapes; 100 videotapes; 5 films; 5000 slides; 20 maps; 1000 noncurrent journal titles; 150 linear feet of archives; 150 phonograph records. **Subscriptions:** 400 journals and other serials; 75 newspapers.

★788★
University of California, Davis
Western Research Center
Department of Special Collections
Shields Library　　　　　　　　Ph: (916)752-1621
Davis, CA 95616　　　　　　　　Fax: (916)752-3148
John Skarstad, Dir.

Founded: 1981 **Subjects:** History and development of the trans-Mississippi West, mid-19th century to present; American Indians; ethnic studies; military, local, and economic history; sociology; folklore; exploration and travel; geography; religious studies, especially the Catholic and Mormon churches; literature; art and architecture; history of printing. **Special Collections:** Books from Western fine presses; correspondence with 20th century artists, writers, and enthusiasts of the American West; original works of art. **Holdings:** 21,000 volumes. **Subscriptions:** 107 journals and other serials.

★789★
University of California, Los Angeles
American Indian Studies Center
Library
3220 Campbell Hall, Box 951548
Los Angeles, CA 90095-1548　　Ph: (310)825-7315

Founded: 1970 **Subjects:** American Indians - government relations, history, literature, art, language; Indians in California; works of Indian authorship. **Special Collections:** Indian newspapers and journals. **Holdings:** 6330 volumes; 5760 pamphlets.

★790★
University of California, Los Angeles
Department of Art History
Visual Resource Collection & Services
100 Dodd Hall
405 Hilgard Ave.　　　　　　　Ph: (310)825-0216
Los Angeles, CA 90095-1417　　Fax: (310)206-1903

Founded: 1958 **Subjects:** Painting, sculpture, applied art, and architecture - European, Islamic, Japanese, Indian, American, Chinese, African; Pre-Columbian, Oceanic, and American Indian art; contemporary art forms. **Special Collections:** The Burton Holmes Collection (hand-tinted lantern slides, 1886-1937; 19,000). **Holdings:** 300,000 slides.

★791★
University of Cincinnati
Archives and Rare Books Department
Carl Blegen Library
PO Box 210113　　　　　　　　Ph: (513)556-1959
Cincinnati, OH 45221-0113　　Fax: (513)556-2113

Founded: 1973 **Subjects:** University of Cincinnati, Southwestern Ohio, 18th century English literature, travel and exploration, North American Indians, Baseball History, History of the book; urban studies. **Holdings:** Rare Book Collection; University Archives; Urban Studies Collection; Ohio Network Collection; Baseball Research Collection; History of Design Collection; University Biographical File; university theses and dissertations; Southwest Ohio Public Records (177 reels of microfilm).

★792★
University of Florida
Samuel Proctor Oral History Program
Library
104 Anderson Hall
PO Box 115215　　　　　　　　Ph: (352)392-7168
Gainesville, FL 32611　　　　　Fax: (352)846-1983

Founded: 1967 **Subjects:** Southern history, southeastern Indians, political leaders, Florida newspapers, Florida history. **Holdings:** 3200 cassette interviews.

★793★
University of Minnesota
Law Library
120 The Law Center
229 19th Ave., S.　　　　　　　Ph: (612)625-4300
Minneapolis, MN 55455　　　　Fax: (612)625-3478
Joan S. Howland, Dir.

Founded: 1888 **Subjects:** Law - Anglo-American, foreign. **Special Collections:** Scandinavian law; American Indians; British Commonwealth legal materials, including Indian and Pakistani legal materials. **Holdings:** 571,004 volumes; 228,263 microforms. **Subscriptions:** 9550 journals and other serials.

★794★
University of Missouri—Kansas City
Snyder Collection of Americana
Miller Nichols Library
5100 Rockhill Rd.   Ph: (816)235-1532
Kansas City, MO 64110   Fax: (816)333-5584
Founded: 1937 **Subjects:** Political campaign literature; Civil War; Indians of North America; Kansas and Missouri - history, travel, biography, fiction, poetry; 19th century Americana; early Missouri and Kansas imprints; Justin McCarthy manuscripts. **Holdings:** 25,819 volumes. **Subscriptions:** 10 journals and other serials.

★795★
University of Montana
School of Law
Law Library
Missoula, MT 59812-1193   Ph: (406)243-6171
    Fax: (406)243-6358
Founded: 1911 **Subjects:** Law. **Special Collections:** Indian law. **Holdings:** 125,498 books. **Subscriptions:** 826 journals and other serials.

★796★
University of Nebraska—Lincoln
Great Plains Art Collection
205 Love Library   Ph: (402)472-6220
Lincoln, NE 68588-0475   Fax: (402)472-5131
Founded: 1980 **Subjects:** Western Americana. **Special Collections:** Christlieb Collection of Western Art; William Henry Jackson Photographs; Patricia J and Stanley H. Broder Collection of Native American Paintings; Richard Lane Collection of Western Fiction; Regina Collection of Canadian Books. **Holdings:** 2000 books; 200 paintings; 180 sculptures; 300 works on paper. **Subscriptions:** 2 journals and other serials.

★797★
University of New Mexico
Bainbridge Bunting Memorial Slide Library
College of Fine Arts   Ph: (505)277-6415
Albuquerque, NM 87131-1396   Fax: (505)277-0708
Founded: 1972 **Subjects:** History of art, architecture, photography, Native American arts, Spanish Colonial arts, Pre-Columbian arts. **Holdings:** 300,000 slides.

★798★
University of New Mexico
Center for Southwest Research
General Library   Ph: (505)277-8726
Albuquerque, NM 87131   Fax: (505)277-6019
Founded: 1950 **Subjects:** History of the American West, New Mexico history and culture, history and culture of Mexico and Latin America, Indians of the Southwest, southwestern architectural history, Hispanic and Native American studies. **Special Collections:** Doris Duke Collection (982 oral history tapes); Pioneer Foundation (527 tapes); Robb Archive of Southwestern Music; Meem Archives of Southwestern Architecture. **Holdings:** 38,500 volumes; 2100 tape recordings; 3150 linear feet of manuscript material; 80,000 photographs; 250 videocassettes. **Subscriptions:** 121 journals and other serials.

★799★
University of New Mexico
School of Law
Library
1117 Stanford, NE   Ph: (505)277-6236
Albuquerque, NM 87131-1441   Fax: (505)277-0068
Founded: 1950 **Subjects:** Law. **Special Collections:** American Indian law; Community Land Grant Law; Mexican and Latin American legal materials. **Holdings:** 197,322 volumes; 740,899 microforms (122,625 volume equivalents); 12,000 New Mexico Supreme Court records and briefs. **Subscriptions:** 3100 journals and other serials; 21 newspapers.

★800★
University of North Carolina at Chapel Hill
Kathrine R. Everett Law Library
CB 3385 Van Hecke-Wettach Bldg.   Ph: (919)962-1321
Chapel Hill, NC 27599   Fax: (919)962-1193
Founded: 1923 **Subjects:** Law. **Special Collections:** Native American law. **Holdings:** 299,290 volumes; 710,104 microforms. **Subscriptions:** 5921 journals and other serials.

★801★
University of Oklahoma
Law Library
300 Timberdell Rd.   Ph: (405)325-4311
Norman, OK 73019   Fax: (405)325-2943
Founded: 1909 **Subjects:** Law. **Special Collections:** Law - Indian, water, agriculture, natural resources; Indian land titles. **Holdings:** 186,127 volumes; 114,769 volumes in microform. **Subscriptions:** 3888 journals and other serials; 25 newspapers.

★802★
University of Oklahoma
Western History Collections
630 Parrington Oval, Rm452   Ph: (405)325-3641
Norman, OK 73019   Fax: (405)325-2943
Founded: 1927 **Subjects:** American Indian, Oklahoma, American Southwest, American Trans-Mississippi West, recent U.S. history. **Special Collections:** Cherokee Nation Papers; Patrick J. Hurley papers; E.E Dale papers; Frank E. Phillips Collection; Alan Farley Collection; Henry B. Bass Collection; Norman Brillhart Collection. **Holdings:** 65,000 books; 13,000 linear feet of manuscripts; 250,000 items in photographic archives; 20,000 microforms; 3600 maps; 1400 transcripts, tapes, and discs of oral history; 5000 pamphlets and documents; 1500 linear feet of University of Oklahoma archives; newspapers, posters, broadsides. **Subscriptions:** 52 journals and other serials; 17 newspapers.

★803★
University of the Pacific
Holt-Atherton Department of Special Collections
Stockton, CA 95211   Ph: (209)946-2404
    Fax: (209)946-2942
Founded: 1947 **Subjects:** Californiana, Western Americana, Pacific Northwest, Northern San Joaquin Valley, gold mining, Western authors, Native Americans, economic development of the West, ethnic history in California. **Special Collections:** Early California exploration; fur trade; John Muir papers (900 volumes, 16,500 items); Jack London collection; Shutes Collection on Lincoln and the Civil War; Perrin Collection on William Morris and Victoriana. **Holdings:** 30,000 books; 2928 bound periodical volumes; 75 linear feet of VF pamphlets; 51,000 photographs; 2000 maps; 3000 linear feet of manuscripts. **Subscriptions:** 153 journals and other serials.

★804★
University of Pennsylvania
The University Museum of Archaeology/Anthropology
Museum Library
33rd & Spruce Sts.   Ph: (215)898-7840
Philadelphia, PA 19104-6324   Fax: (215)573-2008
John M. Weeks, Musm.Libn.
Founded: 1887 **Subjects:** Archeology, anthropology, ethnology, museology. **Special Collections:** Brinton Collection of 19th century American Indian linguistics and ethnology (2000 titles). **Holdings:** 108,000 volumes; 5000 pamphlets; 80 reels of microfilm. **Subscriptions:** 730 journals and other serials.

★805★
University of Rochester
Government Documents and Microtext Center
Rush Rhees Library   Ph: (716)275-4484
Rochester, NY 14627-0055   Fax: (716)473-1906
Founded: 1880 **Subjects:** U.S. Congress, U.S. Bureau of the Census, New York State, women's studies, black studies, North American Indians, American and British literature. **Special Collections:** Documents - Federal Depository, New York state,

Canada, and United Nations; Microtext Goldsmiths'-Kress Library of Economic Literature; Papers of the NAACP; Early English Books; American Culture Series I and II; History of Women; Pamphlets in American History; Landmarks of Science; American Fiction. **Holdings:** 590,000 government documents in paper; 4 million microform - government documents and other; CD-ROMs. **Subscriptions:** 250 journals and other serials.

★806★
University of South Dakota
Governmental Research Library
Vermillion, SD 57069   Ph: (605)677-5702
                                 Fax: (605)677-6486

Founded: 1939 **Subjects:** State and local government, public administration, South Dakota government, political behavior, public finance, American Indians, public law, legislative apportionment. **Holdings:** 600 books; 40 bound periodical volumes. **Subscriptions:** 20 journals and other serials.

★807★
University of South Dakota
I.D. Weeks Library
Special Collections Department
Vermillion, SD 57069   Ph: (605)677-5450
                                 Fax: (605)677-5488

Founded: 1967 **Subjects:** History - Western U.S., frontier, South Dakota; American Indians. **Special Collections:** University Archives; Richardson Collections; Chilson Collection of Western Americana. **Holdings:** 10,600 books; 3575 linear feet of manuscripts.

★808★
University of South Dakota
McKusick Law Library
414 EClark   Ph: (605)677-5259
Vermillion, SD 57069   Fax: (605)677-6357

Founded: 1901 **Subjects:** Law - U.S., English, Canadian. **Special Collections:** Law - Indian, professional responsibility; arts and the law; South Dakota Supreme Court briefs (99 VF drawers); U.S. Circuit Court, 8th Circuit slip opinions. **Holdings:** 136,224 bound volumes; 8 VF drawers of pamphlets; 152,838 microfiche; 1820 reels of microfilm; 4 VF drawers of archives. **Subscriptions:** 2051 journals and other serials; 11 newspapers.

★809★
University of Tennessee at Knoxville
University Archives and Special Collections
Knoxville, TN 37996-4006   Ph: (423)974-4480
                                 Fax: (423)974-0560

Founded: 1959 **Subjects:** Tennesseana, 19th century American fiction, Southern Indians, early voyages and travels, American history from 1820 to 1870, early imprints. **Special Collections:** Estes Kefauver Collection (political papers and memorabilia; 1204 feet); Radiation Research Archives (435 feet); William Congreve Collection; Howard Baker Collection (political papers and memoribilia, 700 feet); Alex Haley Papers (literary papers and memorabilia, 120 feet); University Archives. **Holdings:** 45,000 books; 7391 feet of processed manuscripts. **Subscriptions:** 12 journals and other serials.

★810★
University of Tulsa
College of Law
Library
3120 E Fourth Place   Ph: (918)631-2459
Tulsa, OK 74104   Fax: (918)631-5022

Founded: 1923 **Subjects:** Law. **Special Collections:** American Indian law; Energy Law and Policy Collection. **Holdings:** 265,278 volumes, including microfiche; 43 CD-ROMs. **Subscriptions:** 4061 journals and other serials; 8 newspapers.

★811★
University of Tulsa
McFarlin Library
Special Collections
2933 E6th St.
Tulsa, OK 74104-3123   Ph: (918)631-2496

Founded: 1894 **Subjects:** 20th century American, British, and Irish literature; Indian history, law, and policy; World War I; Proletarian literature; American fiction regarding Vietnam; performing arts. **Special Collections:** Cyril Connolly Library and papers; Andre Deutsch Archive (London publisher, 1950-1994); Edmund Wilson Library; Richard Ellmann papers; Richard Murphy papers; V.S. Naipaul papers; Jean Rhys papers; Paul Scott papers; Muriel Spark papers; William Trevor (Cox) papers; Rebecca West papers; Stevie Smith papers; Anna Kavan papers; Alice Robertson papers; J.W. Shleppey Indian Collection; J.B. Milam Library (Cherokee materials); Indian Claims Commission Archives; University Archives. **Holdings:** 110,000 books; 1000 bound periodical volumes; 2,000,000 British and American 20th century literary manuscripts; 1,500,000 19th and 20th century historical manuscripts (primarily regional); 300 pieces of 20th century American Indian art; 150 territorial maps. **Subscriptions:** 20 journals and other serials.

★812★
University of Utah
Special Collections Department
Marriott Library   Ph: (801)581-8863
Salt Lake City, UT 84112   Fax: (801)585-3464

Founded: 1935 **Subjects:** Utah, Mountain West, Mormons, Indians. **Special Collections:** Annie Clark Tanner Memorial Trust Fund Publications; published material and university contracts; rare books (35,000 volumes); rare maps (3000 maps); Middle East rare books (300 volumes); ancient Arabic documents, 11th-15th centuries (1500 documents); Desert News, 1988 to date. **Holdings:** 97,000 books; 5525 periodical titles; 30,000 theses and dissertations; 9820 federal documents; 7,000 university printed archives, 3200 university contracts; 15,310 folders of clippings; 10,150 folders of pamphlets; 17,000 linear feet of manuscripts; 1 million photographs; 10,000 AV items; 5000 oral histories and manuscripts on microfilm; archives/records management 16,000 cubic feet (active records) 3500 linear feet (permanent historical records). **Subscriptions:** 1680 journals and other serials; 170 newspapers.

★813★
Utah History
Information Center
300 Rio Grande   Ph: (801)533-3535
Salt Lake City, UT 84101-1182   Fax: (801)533-3504

Founded: 1952 **Subjects:** History - Utah, Mormon, Western, Indian. **Special Collections:** Utah water records (200 linear feet); Works Progress Administration records (124 linear feet). **Holdings:** 25,000 books; 50,000 bound periodical volumes; 500,000 photographs; 22,000 pamphlets; 33,000 maps; 1500 oral history tapes; 3500 linear feet of manuscripts; 6000 reels of microfilm; 160 feet of clippings files; 5500 museum objects. **Subscriptions:** 220 journals and other serials.

★814★
Ute Mountain Tribal Library and Archive
Box CC   Ph: (970)565-3751
Towaoc, CO 81334   Fax: (970)565-7412

Founded: 1956 **Subjects:** Ute Indian history, Ute government, Indian tribes. **Special Collections:** Tribal government documents (25,000); tribal history pictures (200). **Holdings:** 3600 books; 30,000 archival items. **Subscriptions:** 12 journals and other serials; 6 newspapers.

★815★
Washington State Capital Museum
Library and Photo Archives
211 W21st Ave.   Ph: (253)753-2580
Olympia, WA 98501   Fax: (253)586-8322

Founded: 1941 **Subjects:** Washington history, Victoriana, museology, art. **Special Collections:** Collection of Washington photographs, including early photos of pioneers, towns, industries, Indians, and state governments; archives of Northwest Indian art. **Holdings:** 3000 historical photographs.

★816★
Washoe County Law Library
Court House
Box 11130
Reno, NV 89520

Ph: (702)328-3250
Fax: (702)328-3441

Founded: 1915 **Subjects:** Law. **Special Collections:** Nevada gambling, water rights, and Indian law. **Holdings:** 43,161 books; 4726 bound periodical volumes; 6690 volumes in microform; 21 cassettes. **Subscriptions:** 393 periodicals.

★817★
Wellesley College
Margaret Clapp Library
Special Collections
106 Central St.
Wellesley, MA 02181-8275

Ph: (617)283-2129
Fax: (617)283-3640

Founded: 1872. **Special Collections:** English Poetry Collection (including Robert and Elizabeth Barrett Browning; 12,000 volumes); Durant Collection (19th century America; 10,000 volumes); Plimpton Collection (15th and 16th century Italian literature; 1200 volumes); Book Arts Collection (4600 volumes); Alcove of North American Languages (Indian languages; 280 volumes); Elbert Collection (slavery and Reconstruction; 800 volumes); Juvenile Collection (1000 volumes); John Ruskin Collection (900 volumes); Guy Walker Collection (illustrated books; 350 volumes); Isabel and Charles Goodman Collection (book arts, fine presses, printing history; 2800 volumes). **Holdings:** 40,000 books; 60 linear feet of manuscripts and autographs.

★818★
Westchester County Department of Parks, Recreation and Conservation
Trailside Nature Museum
Ward Pound Ridge Reservation
Cross River, NY 10518

Founded: 1937 **Subjects:** Delaware culture, Native American herbalism, Algonkian tribes of the Eastern United States, Algonkian linguistics, Northeastern United States archeology, tribes of the greater New York area. **Special Collections:** Rare books on native cultures of Southern New York; taped oral history interviews with Delaware elders (50). **Holdings:** 1000 books; 500 bound periodical volumes; 10 file boxes of unbound material.

★819★
Western Carolina University
Hunter Library
Special Collections
Cullowhee, NC 28723
George Frizzell, Unit Hd.

Ph: (704)227-7474

Founded: 1953 **Subjects:** Western North Carolina, Cherokee Indians. **Special Collections:** Appalachia (1250 volumes; 250 manuscript collections); spider behavior (100 volumes); Cherokee Documents in Foreign Archives Collection, 1632-1909 (manuscript sources from foreign archives relating specifically to the Cherokee and to southern Indians in general; 821 reels of microfilm). **Holdings:** 1500 books.

★820★
Wheelwright Museum of the American Indian
Mary Cabot Wheelwright Research Library
704 Camino Lejo
Box 5153
Santa Fe, NM 87502

Ph: (505)982-4636
Fax: (505)989-7386

Founded: 1937 **Subjects:** Navajo and American Indian - religion, culture, arts; comparative religions; the Southwest. **Special Collections:** Archival material on Navajo religion, sand paintings, chants, and Southwest Indian art. **Holdings:** 2000 books; 2300 periodical volumes; 100 Navajo religion manuscripts; 300 sound recordings; 1000 slides of sandpaintings and reproductions; 100 Navajo music and prayer tapes. **Subscriptions:** 10 journals and other serials.

★821★
Whitman College
Myron Eells Library of Northwest History
Penrose Memorial Library
345 Boyer St.
Walla Walla, WA 99362

Ph: (509)527-5191
Fax: (509)527-5900

Founded: 1960 **Subjects:** Pacific Northwest - history, geography, education, politics, government, anthropology, Indians and native peoples, archeology, religion, missions, art, architecture; regional Indian art; historical fiction about the Northwest and Northwesterners; Lewis and Clark; the Oregon Trail. **Holdings:** 8000 titles in 10,000 volumes. **Subscriptions:** 150 journals and other serials.

★822★
Will Rogers Library
1515 N Florence
Claremore, OK 74017

Ph: (918)341-1564
Fax: (918)342-0361

Founded: 1936 **Subjects:** Will Rogers, American Indians, Oklahoma and regional history. **Holdings:** 60,000 books; 265 bound periodical volumes; 3 VF drawer of clippings and pamphlets. **Subscriptions:** 103 journals and other serials; 8 newspapers.

★823★
Wyandotte County Historical Society and Museum
Harry M. Trowbridge Research Library
631 N 126th St.
Bonner Springs, KS 66012
John R. Nichols, Archv.

Ph: (913)721-1078
Fax: (913)721-1394

Founded: 1956 **Subjects:** Wyandotte County and Kansas City history; Wyandot, Shawnee, and Delaware Indians. **Special Collections:** J.R. Kelley Cooperage Company business papers and ledgers, 1903-1916 (36 cubic feet); bound magazines and school texts of the late 19th century; Early, Conley, and Farrow Family Collections, 1763-1960 (30 cubic feet of papers, books, photographs); Trowbridge papers; Bureau of American Ethnology materials, papers, archaeological materials (20 cubic feet). **Holdings:** 4000 books; 1000 bound periodical volumes; clippings; 348 reels of microfilm; 6000 photographs; maps. **Subscriptions:** 10 journals and other serials.

★824★
Wyoming State Library
Supreme Court & State Library Bldg.
Cheyenne, WY 82002-0600

Ph: (307)777-7281
Fax: (307)777-6289

Subjects: Wyoming, Western Americana, North American Indians, library science. **Holdings:** 30,000 volumes; selective depository for U.S. Government publications; depository for Wyoming publications. **Subscriptions:** 50 journals and other serials.

★825★
Yakama Indian Nation
Environmental Restoration/Waste Management Library
PO Box 151
Toppenish, WA 98948

Ph: (509)452-2502
Fax: (509)452-2503

Founded: 1991 **Subjects:** Environmental science, nuclear science, Native American history. **Special Collections:** U.S. Department of Energy documents. **Holdings:** 3000 books; 50 periodical titles. **Subscriptions:** 45 journals and other serials.

★826★
Yakama Nation Library
PO Box 151
Toppenish, WA 98948

Ph: (509)865-2800
Fax: (509)865-6101

Founded: 1980 **Subjects:** American Indians of all tribes, curriculum support. **Special Collections:** Strongheart Collection (10,000 items on American Indian themes). **Holdings:** 17,703 books; 85 periodical titles. **Subscriptions:** 82 newspapers and tribal newsletters.

★827★
Yakima Valley Museum and Historical Association
Archives
2105 Tieton Dr.   Ph: (509)248-0747
Yakima, WA 98902   Fax: (509)453-4890
Martin M. Humphrey, Archv

Founded: 1956 **Subjects:** Area history and development, Yakima Indians, pioneers, irrigation history. **Special Collections:** Apple and pear box labels; William O Douglas Collection (1500 books; 11,000 slides; films; photographs); local newspaper, 1889-1952 (bound volumes); records of former Yakima Mayor Betty Edmonson; papers of state legislator and HEW chairwoman Marjorie Lynch; records of Yakima Valley Transportation Co. (railroad). **Holdings:** 6000 books; 7000 photographs; 11 file cabinets of clippings; documents; manuscripts. **Subscriptions:** 12 journals and other serials.

★828★
Yakima Valley Regional Library
Reference Department
Click Relander Collection
102 N3rd St.   Ph: (509)452-8541
Yakima, WA 98901   Fax: (509)575-2093
Cynthia Garrick, Ref.Coord

Subjects: Click Relander, Yakima newspaper publisher; Pacific Northwest history; Yakima and Wanapum Indians and their relationship with the U.S. government; Yakima Valley history and agriculture. **Holdings:** 169 boxes of letters, manuscripts, federal documents, photographs.

★829★
Yavapai-Prescott Tribal Library
530 E Merritt   Ph: (520)445-8790
Prescott, AZ 86301-2038   Fax: (520)778-9445

Founded: 1987. **Special Collections:** Indians of the Southwest collection (1300 items); archeology and anthropology of the Southwest collection (510 items). **Holdings:** 4500 books; 236 archival items. **Subscriptions:** 4 journals and other serials.

★830★
Zuni Heritage and Historic Preservation Office
Library
PO Box 339   Ph: (505)782-4113
Zuni, NM 87327   Fax: (505)782-4119

Founded: 1978 **Subjects:** Archeology, Zuni, cultural resources. **Holdings:** 3000 books; 300 bound periodical volumes; 3250 reports. **Subscriptions:** 9 journals and other serials.

Museums and Other Cultural Facilities

Alabama

★831★
Russell Cave National Monument
Rte. 1, Box 175
Bridgeport, AL 35740

Description: Site of Woodland and Mississippian period remains.

Arizona

★832★
Amerind Foundation
Museum
PO Box 400   Ph: (520)586-3666
Dragoon, AZ 85609   Fax: (520)586-4679

Description: More than 25,000 items span 10,000 years of cultural history in the Americas, focusing primarily on the native cultures of the Southwest, the Pacific Northwest, and the Arctic. An art gallery contains the works of Native Americans and includes Hopi ceremonial kachina art.

★833★
Arizona State Parks
Homolovi Ruins State Park
HCR63 Box 5   Ph: (520)289-4106
Winslow, AZ 86047-9803   Fax: (520)289-2021

★834★
Canyon de Chelly National Monument
PO Box 588
Chinle, AZ 86503   Ph: (520)674-5500
Herbert Yazhe, Superintendent

Description: Maintains collections and conducts research on the archaeology and ethnology of the Anasazi Navajo.

★835★
Casa Grande Ruins National Monument
1100 Ruins Dr.   Ph: (520)723-3172
Coolidge, AZ 85228   Fax: (520)723-7209
Bettie B. Gill, Contact

Description: Collections include items relating to Hohokam archaeology, local ethnology, and pre-Columbian artifacts.

★836★
Casa Malpais
Vistors' Center
318 W Main St.
Springerville, AZ   Ph: (520)33—5375

Description: Site of a fifty-room Pueblo ruin.

★837★
Cochise Visitor Center and Museum
c/o Willcox Chamber of Commerce
1500 N. Circle I Rd.   Ph: (520)384-2272
Willcox, AZ 85643   Fax: (520)384-0293

Description: Collections include Apache Indian artifacts.

★838★
Colorado River Indian Tribes
Museum
Rte. 1, Box 23B   Ph: (520)669-9211
Parker, AZ 85344   Fax: (520)669-5675
Weldon B. Johnson Sr., Asst.Dir.

Description: Collections include anthropological and archaeological items pertaining to the Mojave, Chemehuevi, Navajo, Hopi, Anasazi, Hohokan, and Patayan tribes.

★839★
Gila Indian Center
PO Box 457   Ph: (602)963-3981
Sacaton, AZ 85247   Fax: (602)315-3968

Description: Contains a park with reconstructed Indian villages that depict more than 2,000 years of Native American life in the Gila River Basin. The Hohokum, Papago, Maricopa, and Apache cultures are represented. A museum and craft center adjoin the park.

★840★
Heard Museum
22 E. Monte Vista Rd.   Ph: (602)252-8848
Phoenix, AZ   Fax: (602)252-9757
Description: A museum of Native American cultures and art.

★841★
Hoo-Hoogam Ki Museum
10000 E Osborn Rd
Scottsdale, AZ 85256   Ph: (602)874-8190

★842★
Hopi Cultural Center
PO Box 647
Second Mesa, AZ 86043   Ph: (602)734-2441

★843★
Hubbell Trading Post National Historic Site
PO Box 150
Ganado, AZ 86505
Description: The oldest continually operating Native American trading post.

★844★
Mohave Museum of History and Arts
400 W. Beale St.   Ph: (520)753-3195
Kingman, AZ 86401   Fax: (520)753-3195
Description: Depicts the history of northwestern Arizona with collections of turquoise, recreated Mohave and Hualapai Indian dwellings, and local artifacts and artwork.

★845★
Navajo National Monument
HC 71, Box 3   Ph: (520)672-2366
Tonalea, AZ 86044-9704   Fax: (520)672-2345
Clarence Gorman, Superintendent
Description: Collections include archeological materials of the Kayenti Anasazi and Navajo cultures.

★846★
Navajo Tribal Museum
Hwy. 264
PO Box 4950
Window Rock, AZ 86515   Ph: (520)871-6675
   Fax: (520)871-7886
Anselm Harvey, Acting Curator
Description: Collections include Navajo history, ethnology, fine arts, Southwest archaeology, geology and paleontology, and a photo archive.

★847★
Petrified Forest National Park
Petrified Forest Natl Pk, AZ 86028   Ph: (520)524-6228
Description: Location of Pueblo ruins and petroglyphs.

★848★
San Pedro Riparian National Conservation Area
1763 Paseo San Luis
Sierra Vista, AZ 85635   Ph: (520)458-3559
Description: Location of more than 250 prehistoric and historic sites, including sites attributed to the Clovis culture (9000-6000 B.C.).

★849★
Smoki Museum
PO Box 10244
Prescott, AZ 86304   Ph: (520)445-1230
Description: Patterned after early Pueblo structures both in architecture and interior design, it contains ceramics and other artifacts from the Tuzigoot, King, and Fitzmaurice ruins of Yavapai County. Paintings portray legends and ceremonials.

★850★
Tonto National Monument
Hwy. 88 30 miles n.w. of Globe
HC 02 box 4602   Ph: (520)467-2241
Roosevelt, AZ 85545   Fax: (520)467-2225
Carol Kruse, Superintendent
Description: Collections include the clothing, tools, weapons, and pottery of the Salado Indians.

★851★
Tusayan Ruin and Museum
c/o Grand Canyon National Park
PO Box 129
Grand Canyon, AZ 86023   Ph: (520)638-2305
Description: Tusayan Ruin is a small prehistoric pueblo. The museum traces the development of the Anasazi Indian culture at the canyon.

★852★
Tuzigoot National Monument
Cottonwood and Clarkdale Rd.
PO Box 68
Clarkdale, AZ 86324   Ph: (520)634-5564
Glen E. Henderson, Superintendent
Description: Collections include artifacts found during excavation of Tuzigoot and nearby ruins.

★853★
Walnut Canyon National Monument
Walnut Canyon Rd.   Ph: (602)526-3367
Flagstaff, AZ 86004   Fax: (520)527-0246
Sam R. Henderson, Superintendent
Description: A park museum located on the site of prehistoric ruins of the Sinagua Indian culture.

★854★
White Mountain Archaeological Center
HC 30
St. Johns, AZ 85936   Ph: (602)333-5857
Description: Location of the Raven archaeological site dating from 1000 to 1450 A.D. Site consists of 2 Pueblos with 800 rooms and 2 kivas.

★855★
Wupatki National Monument
HC 33, Box 444A   Ph: (520)556-7040
Flagstaff, AZ 86004   Fax: (520)679-3349
Anna Fender, Chief Ranger
Description: Exhibits include a series of displays with artifacts from the sites of the Sinagua/Anasazi cultural pattern.

★856★
Yavapai-Apache Visitor Activity Center
montezuma Castle
PO Box 219   Ph: (520)567-5276
Camp Verde, AZ 86322   Fax: (520)567-3597
Description: Exhibits depict historic and contemporary Indian lifestyles. A slide presentation on the area's prehistoric Indian cultures and a film on the Yavapai-Apache tribe are shown.

California

★857★
California State Indian Museum
2618 K St.
Sacramento, CA 95816   Ph: (916)324-0971
Jackie Jaquez, Pres.
Description: The museum houses a California Indian artifacts collection with a limited collection of North American Indian artifacts from other areas. It also maintains an Indian demonstration village.

★858★
Malki Museum
Morongo Indian Reservation
11-796 Fields Rd.
Banning, CA 92220   Ph: (909)849-7289
Katherine Siva Saubel, Pres.

Description: The museum's collection includes Cahuilla and other Southern California Indian tribe artifacts, anthropology, archaeology, history, archives, ethnology, music, and natural history.

★859★
Marin Museum of the American Indian
2200 Novato Blvd.
PO Box 864   Ph: (415)897-4064
Novato, CA 94948   Fax: (415)892-7804
Dawn Carlson, Chair.

Description: Collections include archaeological, ethnographic, and archival materials from Alaska to Peru, pertaining to Native Americans.

★860★
Santa Rosa Junior College
Jesse Peter Native American Art Museum
1501 Mendocino Ave.   Ph: (707)527-4479
Santa Rosa, CA 95401   Fax: (707)527-4816
Foley C. Benson, Dir. and Curator

Description: Collections include Native American artifacts. Conducts research pertaining to material culture of Northwest Indians with emphasis on California and the Southwest.

★861★
Southwest Museum
234 Museum Dr.
PO Box 41558
Los Angeles, CA 90041   Ph: (213)221-2164

Description: Features Native American art and artifacts.

--------- **Colorado** ---------

★862★
Adams State College Museums
Richardson Hall   Ph: (719)589-7121
Alamosa, CO 81102   Fax: (719)589-7522
Dr. Joseph Hesbrook, Curator

Description: Collections include Paleo-Indian folsom points, Pueblo Indian cultural artifacts, and Navajo weaving.

★863★
Colorado Springs Fine Arts Center
30 W. Dale St.   Ph: (719)634-5581
Colorado Springs, CO 80903   Fax: (719)634-0570
David J. Wagner, Exec.Dir.

Description: Collections include historical and contemporary Native American art.

★864★
Hovenweep National Monument
McElmo Rte.
Cortz, CO 81321   Ph: (970)749-0510

Description: Established in 1923, the monument consists of six units of Pueblo ruins located on 784 acres.

★865★
Koshare Indian Museum
115 W. 18th
PO Box 580
La Junta, CO 81050   Ph: (719)384-4411
David Bailey, CEO

Description: Collections include paintings, archaeology, anthropology, and Indian artifacts.

★866★
Lowry Ruins
Area Manager
701 Camino del Rio
Durango, CO 81301   Ph: (970)247-4082

Description: Site of a thirty-five-room Pueblo dating from 1060 to 1200 A.D.

★867★
Manitou Cliff Dwellings Museum
US Hwy. 24
PO Box 272   Ph: (719)685-5242
Manitou Springs, CO 80829   Fax: (719)685-1562

Description: Depicts the lives and architectural achievements of the Indians of the Southwest during the Great Pueblo Period (A.D. 1100-1300).

★868★
Mesa Verde National Park Museum
PO Box 8   Ph: (970)529-4465
Mesa Verde National Park, CO 81330   Fax: (970)529-4498
Donald C. Fiero, Contact

Description: Preserves Anasazi archaeological remains dating from 550-1300 A.D.

★869★
Southern Ute Indian Cultural Center
Hwy. 172
Box 737   Ph: (970)563-9583
Ignacio, CO 81137   Fax: (970)563-4641
Lillian Selbel, Chair.

Description: The center is located on the Southern Ute Indian reservation and maintains photo and artifact collections pertaining to Ute Indians and other Native American tribes. It sponsors art festivals, Native American dance recitals, hobby workshops, and lectures.

★870★
Ute Indian Museum
17253 Chipeta Dr.
PO Box 1736
Montrose, CO 81402   Ph: (970)249-3098
Glen Gross, Curator

Description: The museum is located on the site of Chief Ouray's 400-acre farm. Collections include the ethnology of the Ute Indians, Indian artifacts, history, archaeology, paintings, anthropology, costumes, and Ute Indian pottery.

★871★
Ute Mountain Tribal Park
Towaco, CO 81224   Ph: (970)565-3751
Free: 800-847-5485

Description: Site of several historic structures, petroglyphs, and Ute pictographs.

--------- **Connecticut** ---------

★872★
American Indian Archaeological Institute (AIAI)
Curtis Rd.
PO Box 1260
Washington Green, CT 06793-0260   Ph: (860)868-0518
Phillip Jones, Chair.

Description: Collections contain prehistoric and historic artifacts primarily from Connecticut and the Northwestern U.S.; ethnographic items from most North American culture areas; and contemporary native art. Facilities include the Indian Habitats Trail, a reconstructed Indian village, and an arboretum of plants the Indians used in the region over the last 10,000 years.

★873★
Tantaquidgeon Indian Museum
1819 Norwick
Rt 32
Uncasville, CT 06382   Ph: (203)848-9145
Gladys Tantaquidgeon, Owner and Curator
Description: Collections include crafts made by Mohegan craftsmen, and artifacts from Southwestern and Northern Plains Tribes.

──────── **District of Columbia** ────────

★874★
Indian Arts and Crafts Board
18th and C Sts., NW, Rm. 4004-M1B
U.S. Dept. of the Interior
Washington, DC 20240   Ph: (202)208-3773
Robert G. Hart, Gen.Manager
Description: Maintains collections of contemporary Native American arts.

★875★
National Campaign for the National Museum of the American Indian
470 L'Enfant Plz. E., S.W., Rm. 7103   Ph: (202)357-3164
Washington, DC 20560   Fax: (202)357-3369
John Colonghi, Dir.

★876★
U.S. Department of the Interior Museum
1849 C St., NW
Mail Stop 5412
Washington, DC 20240   Ph: (202)208-4743
Charles Carter, Contact   Fax: (202)208-6950
Description: Collections include Native American Indian and Eskimo handicraft and artifacts. Conducts research on North American Indian material culture.

★877★
U.S. Smithsonian Institution
National Museum of American History
Cultural History Division
American Indian Program
14th St. and Constitution Ave., NW   Ph: (202)357-2071
Washington, DC 20560   Fax: (202)633-8192
Rayna Green, Dir.

──────────── **Florida** ────────────

★878★
Ah-Tah-Thi-Ki Museum of Seminole History and Culture
Box 21-A   Ph: (941)902-1113
Clewiston, FL 33440   Fax: (941)902-1117
Description: Collection includes exhibits and artifacts of the Florida Seminole.

★879★
Indian Temple Mound Museum
139 Miraclestrip Pkwy. SE
PO Box 4009
Fort Walton Beach, FL 32549   Ph: (904)833-9595
Billy Mikel, Manager
Description: Collections include lithic and ceramic artifacts of local aboriginal origin, historic contact artifacts, ethnological and replica items, and Indian artifacts.

★880★
San Luis Archaeological and Historic Site
c/o Museum of Florida History
500 S. Bronough St.   Ph: (850)488-1484
Tallahassee, FL 32399-0250   Fax: (850)921-2503
Description: An active dig that was the site of a 17th-century Apalachee Indian village and a Spanish mission. Maintains trails with interpretive displays describing the excavations and history of the site.

★881★
Temple Mound Museum
139 Miracle Strip Pkwy.
Ft. Walton Beach, FL 32548
Description: Site of the largest Mississippian temple mound on the Gulf coast.

★882★
University of Miami
Lowe Art Museum
1301 Stanford Dr.
Coral Gables, FL 33146   Ph: (305)284-3535
Description: Maintains collection of Southwest Native American art and textiles.

──────────── **Georgia** ────────────

★883★
Chief John Ross House
826 chickamauga ave
Rossville, GA 30741   Ph: (706)866-5171
W. Larry Rose, CEO
Description: Maintains collections of arrowheads and of the Cherokee alphabet.

★884★
Chieftains Museum
501 Riverside Pkwy.
PO Box 373   Ph: (706)291-9494
Rome, GA 30162   Fax: (706)291-9494
Josephine Ransom, CEO and Dir.
Description: Collections include items from archaic Indian occupation to present time.

★885★
Etowah Indian Mounds Historical Site
813 Indian Mounds Rd. SE   Ph: (770)387-3747
Cartersville, GA 30120   Fax: (770)387-3972
Elizabeth Forehand, Superintendent
Description: Collections including archaeological excavations of a prehistoric Indian center.

★886★
Kolomoki Mounds State Park Museum
Rte. 1 PO Box 114
Blakely, GA 31723   Ph: (912)723-3398
Bill Thomas, Superintendent
Description: Collections include Indian artifacts, Mississippian mound complex, and archaeological items.

★887★
Ocmulgee National Monument
1207 Emery Hwy.   Ph: (912)752-8257
Macon, GA 31217   Fax: (912)752-8259
Mark Corey, Superintendent
Description: Collectons include Indian artifacts, and items related to Indian archaeology, anthropology, history, and ethnology.

Idaho

★888★
College of Southern Idaho
Herett Museum
315 Falls Ave.
PO Box 1238   Ph: (208)733-9554
Twin Falls, ID 83303   Fax: (208)736-4712
Jim Woods, Dir.

Description: Maintains collections on American Indians, archaeology, and ethnology.

★889★
Idaho Heritage Museum
2390 Hwy. 93, S.   Ph: (208)655-4444
Twin Falls, ID 83301   Fax: (208)655-4470

Description: Maintains collections of Indian artifacts, including arrowheads.

★890★
Nez Perce National Historic Park
Hwy. 95 S
Rt.1 Box 100   Ph: (208)843-2261
Spalding, ID 83540   Fax: (208)843-2001
Franklin C. Walker, Superintendent

Description: Collections include items relating to Nez Perce ethnology, prehistoric lithics, and 3,000 photos of the Nez Perce Indians and the local region.

Illinois

★891★
Aurora University
Schingoethe Center for Native American Cultures
Dunham Hall
347 S. Gladstone   Ph: (630)844-5402
Aurora, IL 60506   Fax: (630)892-9286
Thomas Zarle, Univ.Pres.

Description: Collections include Native American art, and cultural materials of North American peoples from pre-historic times to the present.

★892★
Cahokia Mounds State Historic Site
30 Ramey Street   Ph: (618)346-5160
Collinsville, IL 62234   Fax: (618)346-5162
Margaret Brown, Site Manager

Description: Maintains collections of prehistoric Indian artifacts.

★893★
Dickson Mounds Museum
Lewistown, IL 61542   Ph: (309)547-3721
    Fax: (309)547-3189
Dr. R.B. McMillan, Dir./Illinois State Museum

Description: Anthropology museum and site with collections including archaeological materials from West Central Illinois, Mississippi, and Middle Woodland sites. Maintains exhibits on American prehistory, osteology, and Paleo-Indian to historic cultures.

★894★
Hauberg Indian Museum
1510 46th Ave.   Ph: (309)788-9536
Rock Island, IL 61201   Fax: (309)788-9865
Neil Rangen, Superintendent

Description: A State Historic Site Museum located on the site of the main villages of the Sauk and Fox Indian Nations. Collections include dioramas containing life-size figures of Sauk and Fox Indians, depicting daily life in an Indian village.

★895★
Starved Rock State Park
Box 509   Ph: (815)667-4906
Utica, IL 61373   Fax: (815)667-5353
Jon Blume, Superintendent

Description: A historic park and museum located on the site of a former village of the Illinois Indians, which was later conquered by Ottawa and Potawatomi Indians.

Indiana

★896★
Angel Mounds State Historic Site
8215 Pollack Ave.
Evansville, IN 47715   Ph: (812)853-3956
Rebecca Means Harris, Historic Site Curator

Description: Site contains museum with collections including artifacts of Middle Mississippi Indians, photos of excavations made at Angel Mounds, and a restored Indian village.

★897★
Eiteljorg Museum of American Indian and Western Art
500 W. Washington   Ph: (317)636-9378
Indianapolis, IN 46204   Fax: (317)264-1724
Harrison Eiteljorg, Chair.

Description: Maintains collection of Native American art and artifacts, and conducts research on Native American culture.

★898★
Sonotabac Prehistoric Indian Mound
2401 Wabash Ave.
PO Box 1979
Vincennes, IN 47591

Description: Site of the largest ceremonial mound in Indiana.

Iowa

★899★
Effigy Mounds National Monument
151 Highway 76   Ph: (319)873-3491
Harpers Ferry, IA 52146   Fax: (319)873-3743
Thomas A. Munson, Superintendent

Description: Collections include Indian artifacts, ethnology, archaeological collections of mound excavations, and manuscript collections.

★900★
Sioux City American Indian Center
619 6th St.
Sioux City, IA 51105   Ph: (712)255-8957

Kansas

★901★
Coronado-Quivira Museum
105 W. Lyon
Lyons, KS 67554   Ph: (316)257-3941
Betty Romero, CEO/Dir.

Description: Collections include Coronado and Quiviran Indian artifacts.

★902★
Indian Center Museum
650 N. Seneca   Ph: (316)262-5221
Wichita, KS 67203   Fax: (316)262-4216
Richard Mitchell, Exec.Dir.
Description: Collections include Native American art and artifacts. Conducts research on Native American life, art, and religion.

★903★
Iowa, Sac and Fox Presbyterian Mission Museum
E. Mission Rd.
Rte. 1, Box 152C
Highland, KS 66035   Ph: (913)442-3304
Andrew L. Clements, Curator
Description: Collections include Indian archaeological artifacts. Conducts research on Iowa, Sac, and Fox tribes' migrations.

★904★
Mid-America All Indian Center
Library
650 N Seneca   Ph: (316)262-5221
Wichita, KS 67203   Fax: (316)262-4216

★905★
Pawnee Indian Village Museum
Rte. 1, Box 475   Ph: (913)361-2255
Republic, KS 66964   Fax: (913)361-2255
Richard Gould, Contact
Description: An archaeology museum located on the preserved Pawnee Site. Maintains original lodge floor, hearth, collections of stone, metal and bone, tools and implements, and other artifacts illustrating Pawnee Indian life and customs.

Maine

★906★
Abbe Museum
Sieur de Monts Spring
Acadia National Park
Box 286   Ph: (207)288-3519
Bar Harbor, ME 04609   Fax: (207)288-8979
Diane Kopec, Dir.
Description: An archaeology, anthropology, and ethnology museum, located on site at Sieur de Monts Spring, within Acadia National Park. Collections include archaic to modern Indian artifacts and handicrafts.

★907★
Maine Tribal Unity Museum
Quaker Hill Rd.   Ph: (207)948-3131
Unity, ME 04988   Fax: (207)948-6277
Dr. Christopher Marshall, Dir.
Description: An Indian museum with collections including Native American basketry and artifacts.

Maryland

★908★
National Colonial Farm of the Accokeek Foundation
3400 Bryan Point Rd.   Ph: (301)283-2113
Accokeek, MD 20607   Fax: (301)283-2049
Robert Ware Staus, Pres.
Description: Collections include Indian artifacts.

Massachusetts

★909★
Indian House Memorial
Main St.
PO Box 121   Ph: (413)772-0845
Deerfield, MA 01342   Fax: (413)774-5400
John Abercrombie, Pres.
Description: Collections include Native American artifacts, decorative arts, pottery, weaving, and looms.

★910★
Trustees of Reservations
572 Essex St.   Ph: (508)921-1944
Beverly, MA 01915   Fax: (508)921-1948
Herbert W. Vaughan, Chair.
Description: An open space and historic preservation project, maintaining and protecting 71 properties in Massachusetts.

Michigan

★911★
Crooked Tree Arts Council
461 E. Mitchell St.   Ph: (616)347-4337
Petoskey, MI 49770   Fax: (616)347-5414
Sean Ley, CEO and Dir.
Description: Maintains a fine arts collection with emphasis on Indians of the Great Lakes area. Areas of research include the art of Ojibway, Odawa, and Nishnawbe Indians.

★912★
Father Marquette National Memorial and Museum
Father Marquette State Park
720 Church St.   Ph: (906)643-8620
Saint Ignace, MI 49781   Fax: (906)643-9329
Description: Displays artifacts, including an Indian longhouse and canoe, and maintains exhibits which interpret early French and Indian cultures.

★913★
Marquette Mission Park and Museum of Ojibwa
Culture
500 N. State St.   Ph: (906)643-9161
Saint Ignace, MI 49781   Fax: (906)643-9380
Description: Displays include artifacts, some dating to 6,000 B.C., and reproductions relating to the Ojibwa culture.

★914★
Sabewaing Indian Museum
612 E. Bay St.   Ph: (517)883-3730
Sebewaing, MI 48759   Fax: (517)883-9171
Jim Bunke, CEO
Description: An 1849 mission home, with collections including Native American birch bark canoes, arrowheads, and headress.

Minnesota

★915★
Lac Qui Parle Indian Mission Church
RR 1, Box 125   Ph: (507)697-6321
Morton, MN 56270   Fax: (507)697-6310
Tom Ellig, Southern Dist. Man.
Description: Maintains collections and conducts research in the fields of history and archaeology.

★916★
Lower Sioux Agency History Center
RR 1, Box 125   Ph: (507)697-6321
Morton, MN 56270   Fax: (507)679-6310
Description: Exhibits and audiovisual programs portray the history of the eastern Dakota Indians since the 18th century.

★917★
Mille Lacs Indian Museum
HCR Box 195
Onamia, MN 56359   Ph: (320)532-4625
Description: Exhibits include life-size dioramas showing typical scenes of Ojibwa life for each season.

★918★
Minneapolis American Indian Center
1530 E Franklin Ave.   Ph: (612)871-4749
Minneapolis, MN 55404   Fax: (612)871-6878

★919★
Minnesota Historical Society's Grand Mound History Center
Rte. 7, Box 453
International Falls, MN 56649   Ph: (218)327-4482
Nina Archabal, CEO
Description: A prehistoric Native American burial mounds and habitation area. Research conducted on middle and late Woodland, Laurel, and Blackduck Indian cultures.

★920★
Walker Wildlife and Indian Artifacts Museum
State Hwy.200
PO Box 336
Walker, MN 56484   Ph: (218)547-1257
Renee Geving, Manager
Description: Collections include Ojibway and Chippewa Indian handicraft and artifacts from 1892-1962.

──────────── **Mississippi** ────────────

★921★
Grand Village of the Natchez Indians
400 Jefferson Davis Blvd.   Ph: (601)446-6502
Natchez, MS 39120   Fax: (601)446-6503
Elbert R. Hilliard, CEO
Description: Collection includes Indian ceramics, artifacts, and stone implements. Research fields include the culture of the Natchez Indians.

★922 ★
Winterville Indian Mounds
Rte. 3, Box 600
Greenville, MS 38703
Description: Site of Indian mounds dating to 1441 A.D.

──────────── **Missouri** ────────────

★923★
Osage Village Historic Site
PO Box 176
Jefferson City, MO 65102   Ph: (573)897-2932
Larry Grantham, Contact
Description: Houses collections of excavated materials and conducts research on Osage Indians.

──────────── **Montana** ────────────

★924★
Central Montana Museum
408 NE Main St.
PO Box 818   Ph: (406)538-5436
Lewistown, MT 59457   Fax: (406)538-5437
Frank Machler, Curator
Description: The museum includes a collection of Native American artifacts.

★925★
Chief Plenty Coups State Park
PO Box 100   Ph: (406)252-1289
Pryor, MT 59066   Fax: (406)252-6668
Annie Olson, CEO
Description: Collections include ethnographic materials of the Crow people, paintings, drawings, and pre-historic artifacts.

★926★
Flathead Indian Museum
1 Museum Ln.
PO Box 460   Ph: (406)745-2951
Saint Ignatius, MT 59865   Fax: (406)745-2951
L. Doug Allard, Contact
Description: Maintains collections of American Indian arts and crafts from major tribes throughout the United States, and traditional dress and tools of the Flathead Indians.

★927★
Museum of the Plains Indian and Crafts Center
Junction of Hwy 2 and 89 West
PO Box 410   Ph: (406)338-2230
Browning, MT 59417   Fax: (406)338-7404
Loretta Pepion, Curator
Description: Collections include: historic, contemporary, social, and ceremonial arts of the Northern Plains Indians; traditional costumes; painted tepees; and murals.

★928★
Pipestone County Historical Museum
113 S. Hiawatha
Pipestone, MT 56164   Ph: (507)825-2563
David Rambow, Dir.
Description: Collections include pipes, quilted and beaded clothing from the Dakota and Ojibwa tribes, Plains Indian saddles, feathered headdresses, and prehistoric items.

★929★
Pipestone National Monument
36 Reservation Ave.   Ph: (406)825-5464
Pipestone, MT 56164   Fax: (406)825-5466
Betty McSwain, Park Ranger
Description: Maintains a collection of Indian ceremonial pipes and pipestone objects.

──────────── **Nevada** ────────────

★930★
Lost City Museum
721 S. Hwy. 169
PO Box 807   Ph: (702)397-2193
Overton, NV 89040   Fax: (702)397-8967
Scott Miller, Dir.
Description: Collections include Puebloan artifacts excavated from Pueblo Grande de Nevada, Lost City, Paiute Indian artifacts, historic baskets, and southwestern Indian crafts.

New Mexico

★931★
Aztec Museum
125 N. Main St.   Ph: (505)334-9829
Aztec, NM 87410   Fax: (505)334-2344
Description: Collections include Indian artifacts.

★932★
Aztec Ruins National Monument
84 County Rd. 2900
PO Box 640   Ph: (505)334-6174
Aztec, NM 87410   Fax: (505)334-6372
Charles Cooper, Superintendent
Description: Collections include archaeological materials of Chaco and Mesa Verde Anasazi Indians.

★933★
Bandelier National Monument
State Rte. 4
HCR 1, Box 1, Ste. 15   Ph: (505)672-3861
Los Alamos, NM 87544-9701   Fax: (505)672-9607
Roy W. Weaver, Superintendent
Description: Collections include archaeological and ethnological items of Pueblo Indians of the Pajarito Plateau.

★934★
Chaco Culture National Historic Park
Star Rte. 4, Box 6500
Bloomfield, NM 87413   Ph: (505)786-7014
Description: Site of several historic structures.

★935★
Coronado State Monument
St. Hwy. 44
PO Box 95
Bernalillo, NM 87004   Ph: (505)867-5351
Nathan Stone, Manager
Description: Site of Tiwa Pueblo named Kuanua dating from 1300 A.D.

★936★
Eastern New Mexico University
Blackwater Draw Museum
Station 9 ENMU   Ph: (505)562-2202
Portales, NM 88130   Fax: (505)562-2910
Dr. John Montogomery, Dir.
Description: Maintains collections of Paleo-Indian archaeology and anthropology.

★937★
El Morro National Monument
Rte. 2, Box 43
Ramah, NM 87321
Description: Site of Inscription Rock and Pueblo ruins.

★938★
Gadsen Museum
Barker Rd. and Hwy. 28
Box 147
Mesilla, NM 88046   Ph: (505)526-6293
Mary Veitch Alexander, Curator and Owner
Description: Collections include Indian artifacts from the Southwest.

★939★
Indian Pueblo Cultural Center
2401 12th St., NW   Ph: (505)843-7270
Albuquerque, NM 87104   Fax: (505)842-6959
John Mihelcic, Gen.Manager
Description: Collections include contemprorary arts and crafts, architecture, daily and social dance costumes, and items relating to government, anthropology, and ethnology of the Pueblo Indians.

★940★
Institute of American Indian Arts
Museum
108 Cathedal Place   Ph: (505)988-6281
Santa Fe, NM 87501   Fax: (505)988-6273
Rick Hill, Dir.
Description: Collections include Indian artifacts, contemporary Indian arts and crafts, and an 800-tape Native American videotape archive.

★941★
Museum of Indian Arts and Culture
710 Camino Lejo
Box 2087   Ph: (505)827-6344
Santa Fe, NM 87501   Fax: (505)827-6497
Description: Displays Southwest Indian art, culture, and artifacts, including live exhibitions by Pueblo, Navajo, and Apache artists.

★942★
Museum of Indian Arts and Culture
Laboratory of Anthropology
708 Camino Lejo
PO Box 2087   Ph: (505)827-6344
Santa Fe, NM 87504-2087   Fax: (505)827-6497
Stephen A. Becker, Dir.
Description: The museum maintains exhibits relating to the material culture and ethnology of the native peoples of the Southwest, including pre-historic and historic jewelry, pottery, baskets, textiles, accessories, kachinas, sculpture, and paintings.

★943★
Petroglyph National Monument
PO Box 1293
Albuquerque, NM 87103   Ph: (505)768-3316
Description: Site of more than 15,000 petroglyphs dating from 1300 to 1680 A.D.

★944★
Pueblo of Acoma
Acoma Tourist and Visitation Center
PO Box 309   Ph: (505)552-6606
Pueblo of Acoma, NM 87034   Fax: (505)552-6600
Violet Tenorio, Dir.
Description: Collections include photograph archives and documents relating to the history of Acoma Indians, and historic to modern pottery.

★945★
Salinas National Monument
PO Box 496
Mountainair, NM 87036
Description: Site of prehistoric pithouses dating to 800 A.D.

★946★
School of American Research
Museum
660 Garcia St.
PO Box 2188   Ph: (505)982-3583
Santa Fe, NM 87504   Fax: (505)989-9809
Dr. Douglas W. Schwartz, Pres.
Description: The school maintains collections of representative historic Southwestern Pueblo Indian pottery, Navajo and Pueblo Indian textiles, Native American easel paintings, Navajo and Pueblo Indian jewelry, Southwest Indian basketry, and Kachinas and miscellaneous ethnographic objects pertaining to historic Southwest American Indian arts.

★947★
Wheelwright Museum of the American Indian
704 Camino Lejo
PO Box 5153   Ph: (505)982-4636
Santa Fe, NM 87502   Fax: (505)989-7386
Susan Brown McGreevy, Pres. Bd. of Trustees

Description: Collections include Native American artifacts and art works, musical recordings of Navajo ceremonies, Navajo sandpainting reproductions, archives, and manuscripts.

★948★
Zuni Heritage and Historic Preservation Office
PO Box 339   Ph: (505)782-5558
Zuni, NM 87327   Fax: (505)782-2393

──────── **New York** ────────

★949★
Akwesasne Museum
RR 1 box 14c   Ph: (518)358-2461
Hogansburg, NY 13655   Fax: (518)358-2649
Margaret Jacobs, CEO

Description: Collections include Mohawk traditional artifacts and basketry, contemporary Iroquoian artifacts and ethnological exhibitions.

★950★
Ganondagan State Historic Site
PO Box 239   Ph: (716)924-5848
Victor, NY 14564   Fax: (716)742-1732
Edgar Brown, Pres.

Description: The site is located at a late seventeenth-century Seneca Indian settlement. It maintains collections of Seneca artifacts and trade items of European manufacture.

★951★
Huntington Free Library
National Museum of the American Indian
9 Westchester Sq.   Ph: (718)829-7770
Bronx, NY 10461   Fax: (718)829-4875

★952★
Iroquois Indian Museum
Howes Cave, NY 12049   Ph: (518)234-8319
                          Fax: (518)296-8955
Christina B. Johannsen, Dir.

Description: Collections include contemporary art and craft work of the Iroquois Indians, pre-historic materials of the Iroquois and their immediate antecedents realting to Schoharie County, color slides, black and white prints, and a photographic collection of Iroquois arts.

★953★
Museums at Hartwick
Hartwick College   Ph: (607)431-4480
Oneonta, NY 13820   Fax: (607)431-4468

Description: Maintains extensive collections of Upper Susquehanna Native American, Southwestern, pre-Columbian, and Mesoamerican artifacts.

★954★
National Shrine of the Blessed Kateri Tekakwitha
PO Box 627   Ph: (518)853-3646
Fonda, NY 12068   Fax: (518)853-3371

Description: Collections include artifacts of North American Indians. Maintains the Caughnawaga Indian village, the only completely excavated and staked-out Iroquois village in the country.

★955★
Rochester Museum and Science Center
657 East Ave.   Ph: (716)271-1880
Rochester, NY   Fax: (716)271-5935

Description: A regional museum of natural science, history, and anthropology with permanent and changing exhibits. Features the permanent exhibit "At the Western Door," which interprets Native American-colonial European relations via more than 2,000 Seneca Indian artifacts, a 1790's furnished Seneca cabin, six life-size figure tableaus and a film.

★956★
Seneca-Iroquois National Museum
794-814 Broadstreet   Ph: (716)945-1738
Salamanca, NY 14779   Fax: (716)945-1760

Description: Located on the Alleghany Indian Reservation. Maintains collections of more than 300,000 articles which portray the life and culture of the Seneca and Iroquois Indians, including treaties, wampum belts, costumes, games, and modern art.

★957★
Six Nations Indian Museum
Roakdale Rd.
HCR 1, Box 10
Onchiota, NY 12968   Ph: (518)891-0769
John Fadden, Dir.

Description: Collections include Six Nations Indians artifacts, items relating to Iroquois culture and history, and a miniature Indian village composed of the Iroquois, Delaware, Sioux, and Abenaki tribes.

★958★
Southold Indian Museum
Bayview Rd.
PO Box 268
Southold, NY 11971   Ph: (516)765-5577
Walter L. Smith, Pres.

Description: Collections include Native American articles and artifacts, and handiworks of Eskimos.

★959★
U.S. Smithsonian Institution
Museum of the American Indian
George Gustav Heye Center
1 Bowling Green
New York, NY 10004   Ph: (212)514-3711
Carolyn Okoomian Rapkievian, Coord.

Description: Maintains collections relating to American Indian ethnology and archaeology from North America, South America, and Central America. Collections include Indian artifacts, textiles, agriculture, anthropology, paintings, sculpture, decorative arts, costumes, numismatic, music, medical, photo archives, manuscript collections, and Eskimo culture.

──────── **North Carolina** ────────

★960★
Indian Museum of the Carolinas
607 Turnpike Rd.
PO Box 666
Laurinburg, NC 28352   Ph: (910)276-5880
Dr. Margaret Houston, Dir.

Description: Collections include Indian artifacts, interpretive exhibits, and manuscript collections.

★961★
Museum of the Cherokee Indian
U.S. 441
PO Box 1599   Ph: (704)497-3481
Cherokee, NC 28719   Fax: (704)497-4985
Ken Blankenship, Dir.

Description: Collections of Cherokee Indian artifacts, relics, and archives are maintained.

★962★
Oconaluftee Indian Village
PO Box 398
Cherokee, NC 28719
Description: A replica of a 1750 Cherokee villiage.

★963★
Pembroke State University Center
Native American Resource Center
PO Box 1510
Pembroke, NC 28372   Ph: (910)521-6282
Dr. Stanley Knick, Dir.
Description: Maintains collections of Indian artifacts, art, books, cassettes, record albums, and films pertaining to Native Americans and Lumbee Indians.

★964★
Town Creek Indian Mound State Historic Site
509 Town Creek Mound Rd.   Ph: (910)439-6802
Mt. Gilead, NC 27306   Fax: (910)439-6802
Archie C. Smith Jr., Site Manager
Description: Maintains collection of Indian artifacts. Also maintains an ancient Indian mound, and reconstructed Indian structures.

--------- **North Dakota** ---------

★965★
Knife River Indian Villages National Historic Site
PO BOX 9   Ph: (701)745-3300
Stanton, ND 58571   Fax: (701)745-3708
Michael Holm, Area Manager
Description: Maintains collections of Hidatsa/Mandan cultural artifacts.

★966★
Museum of the Badlands
PO Box 198
Medora, ND 58645   Ph: (701)623-4444
Description: Collections include exhibits on the attire and crafts of North American Indian tribes.

★967★
Turtle Mountain Chippewa Heritage Center
Hwy. 5
PO Box 257
Belcourt, ND 58316   Ph: (701)477-6140
Denise Lajimodierre, CEO and Chair.
Description: Maintains collections of Chippewa Indian artifacts and contemporary art.

--------- **Ohio** ---------

★968★
Hopewell Culture National Historic Park
16062 Rte. 104
Chillicothe, OH 45601
Description: Site of 23 Hopewell culture burial mounds.

★969★
Indian Museum of Lake County, Ohio
c/o Lake Erie College
391 W. Washington
Painesville, OH 44077   Ph: (216)352-3361
Gwen G. King, Dir.
Description: Houses a pre-contact artifacts of Ohio collection, 10,000 B.C.-1650 A.D., and a crafts and art of Native North Americans collection, 1800 to present.

★970★
Mound City Group National Monument
Hopewell Culture National Historic Park
16062 State Rte. 104   Ph: (740)774-1125
Chillicothe, OH 45601   Fax: (740)774-1140
William Gibson, Superintendent
Description: Collections include archaeological artifacts from the Hopewell period.

★971★
Moundbuilders State Memorial and Museum
99 Cooper St.   Ph: (614)344-1920
Newark, OH 43055   Free: 800-600-7174
Richard Livingston, Manager
Description: Collections include art objects and other media representing achievements of the Adeba and Hopewell cultures 1000 B.C. to 700 A.D.

★972★
Piqua Historical Area
9845 N. Hardin Rd.   Ph: (937)773-2522
Piqua, OH 45356   Fax: (937)773-4311
Victoria Tabor Branson, Site Manager
Description: Collections include historic Indian tools, weapons, costumes, art, canoes, and trade items.

★973★
Serpent Mound Museum
3850 State Rte. 73
Peebles, OH 45660   Ph: (937)587-2796
William E. Gustin, Area Manager
Description: The museum's collection focuses on the Adena Indian culture.

★974★
U.S. Department of the Interior
National Park Service
Hopewell Culture National Historical Park
16062 State Rte. 104   Ph: (614)774-1125
Chillicothe, OH 45601   Fax: (614)774-1140

--------- **Oklahoma** ---------

★975★
Bacone College
Aaloa Lodge Museum
2299 Old Bacone Road
Muskogee, OK 74403-1597   Ph: (918)683-4581
Frances Donelson, Dir.
Description: The museum's collections include Native American stone artifacts, rugs, blankets, basketry, pottery, beadwork, and quillwork.

★976★
Cherokee Courthouse
Rte. 2, Box 37-1
Gore, OK 74435   Ph: (918)489-5663
John Pruitt, Curator
Description: Maintains displays and exhibits on the history of the Cherokee Indians.

★977★
Cherokee National Museum
TSA-LA-GI-Cherokee Heritage Center
Willis Rd.
PO Box 515   Ph: (918)456-6007
Tahlequah, OK 74465   Fax: (918)456-6165
Myra Moss, Exec.Dir.
Description: Collections include artifacts, paintings, a 42-structure ancient village, and a 9-structure rural village.

★978★
Chickasaw Council House Museum
Court House Sq.
PO Box 717
Tishomingo, OK 73460　　　　　Ph: (405)371-3351
Beverly J. Wyatt, Curator
Description: Collections include articles relating to the Chickasaws' life in Oklahoma Indian territory.

★979★
Creek Council House Museum
106 West 6th Street　　　　　Ph: (918)756-2324
Okmulgee, OK 74447　　　　　Fax: (918)756-3671
Janeth Slamans, Dir./Curator
Description: Collections include items relating to Indian history, archives, archaeology, and history of the Muscogee Creek Nation.

★980★
Five Civilized Tribes Museum
Honor Heights Dr.　　　　　Ph: (918)683-1701
Muskogee, OK 74401　　　　　Fax: (918)683-3070

★981★
Fort Ancient Museum
6123 State Rte. 350
Oregonia, OK 45054　　　　　Ph: (513)932-4421
Jack K. Blosser, Area Manager
Description: Maintains collection of artifacts relating to pre-historic Indian life and culture.

★982★
Indian City U.S.A.
PO Box 695
Anadarko, OK 73005　　　　　Ph: (405)247-5661
George F. Moran, Manager
Description: Collections include Indian artifacts and articles.

★983★
Memorial Indian Museum
2nd and Allen Sts.
PO Box 483
Broken Bow, OK 74728　　　　　Ph: (405)584-6531
LaMarr Smith, Dir.
Description: Collections include pre-historic Indian artifacts, modern textiles, basketry, early bead work, pre-historic Indian skeletal remains, original paintings and prints, early American glass, and fossils.

★984★
Museum of the Great Plains
601 Ferris Ave.
PO Box 68　　　　　Ph: (580)581-3460
Lawton, OK 73502　　　　　Fax: (580)581-3458
Steve Wilson, Dir.
Description: The museum maintains a photograph collection of Plains Indians.

★985★
Museum of the Red River
812 E Lincoln Road　　　　　Ph: (405)286-3616
Idabel, OK 74745　　　　　Fax: (405)286-3616
Mary Herron, Dir.
Description: The museum maintains prehistoric to contemporary American Indian collections with emphasis on local Indian history, the Caddo, and the Choctaw. It also presents interpretive exhibits of Indian cultures.

★986★
National Hall of Fame for Famous American Indians
715 East Central Blvd
PO Box 548
Anadarko, OK 73005　　　　　Ph: (405)247-5555
Allie Reynolds, Pres.
Description: Collections include sculptured bronze busts of famous American Indians in an outdoor landscaped area.

★987★
Ponca City Cultural Center and Museums
1000 E. Grand
Ponca City, OK 74601　　　　　Ph: (405)767-0427
LaWanda French, Dir.
Description: Collections include items relating to Ponca City's neighboring tribes: Ponca, Kaw, Otoe, Osage, and Tonkawa.

★988★
Seminole Nation Museum
524 S. Wewoka Ave.
Box 1532
Wewoka, OK 74884　　　　　Ph: (405)257-5580
Garvin Peck, Pres.
Description: Maintains collections of Native American art.

★989★
Sequoyah Home Site
Rte. 1, Box 141
Sallisaw, OK 74955　　　　　Ph: (918)775-2413
Dillard Jordan, Curator
Description: Collections include artifacts and exhibits relating to Native Americans (primarily Cherokee).

★990★
Southern Plains Indian Museum and Crafts Center
715 East Central Blvd
PO Box 749　　　　　Ph: (405)247-6221
Anadarko, OK 73005　　　　　Fax: (405)247-7593
Rosemary Ellison, Curator
Description: Collections include historic and contemporary Native American art.

──────────── **South Dakota** ────────────

★991★
Akta Lakota Museum
c/o St. Joseph Indian School
PO Box 89　　　　　Ph: (605)734-3455
Chamberlain, SD 57325　　　　　Fax: (605)734-3388
Description: Displays historic artifacts and artwork of Native Americans.

★992★
American Indian Culture Research Center Museum
Blue Cloud Abbey
PO Box 98　　　　　Ph: (605)432-5528
Marvin, SD 57251　　　　　Fax: (605)432-4754
Rev. Stanislaus Maudlin O.S.B., Dir.
Description: Collections include Maria pottery, Native American artifacts, and 30,000 photographs of Dakota Indians.

★993★
Bear Butte State Park
Hwy. 79
PO Box 688　　　　　Ph: (605)347-5240
Sturgis, SD 57785　　　　　Fax: (605)347-7627
William A. Gullett, Park Manager
Description: The center is located on a Native American traditional religious site and maintains a collection of Native American clothing and religious artifacts.

★994★
Buechel Memorial Lakota Museum
St. Francis Indian Mission
350 S. Oak St.
PO Box 499   Ph: (605)747-2361
Saint Francis, SD 57572   Fax: (605)747-5057
Lloyd One Star, Chair.

Description: The museum's collection is comprised of ethnographic materials of the reservation period of the Rosebud and Pine Ridge Sioux.

★995★
The Heritage Center
Red Cloud Indian School
Box 100   Ph: (605)867-5491
Pine Ridge, SD 57770   Fax: (605)867-1104
Bro. C.M. Simon S.J., Dir. and CEO

Description: Maintains the following collections: paintings by Native American artists; star quilt collection; beadwork; quill and pottery collection; Native American prints; and Northwest Coast Prints. Research fields include Native American art, Sioux artifacts, and Siouxan culture.

★996★
Indian Museum of North America
Avenue of the Chiefs, Black Hills   Ph: (605)673-4681
Crazy Horse, SD 57730   Fax: (605)673-2185
Mrs. Anne Ziolkowski, Dir.

Description: Collections include Indian art and artifacts.

★997★
Sioux Indian Museum and Crafts Center
222 New York Blvd
PO Box 1504
Rapid City, SD 57709   Ph: (605)394-2381
Paulette Montileaux, Curator

Description: The museum's collections include historic and contemporary Sioux art and architectural models of Native American arts and crafts.

★998★
Tekakwitha Fine Arts Center
PO Box 208   Ph: (605)698-7058
Sisseton, SD 57262-0208   Fax: (605)698-3801
Fr. Norman Volk, Dir.

Description: The center sponsors art festivals, concerts, hobby workshops, and the annual Coteau Heritage Festival. It maintains a collection of two-dimensional art of the Lake Traverse Dakotah Sioux Reservation.

Tennessee

★999★
Indian Heritage Council
Henry St.
Box 2302
Morristown, TN 37816   Ph: (615)581-4448

★1000★
Pinson Mounds State Archaeological Area
460 Ozier Rd.
Pinson, TN 38366

Description: Site of Woodland period mounds.

★1001★
Red Clay State Historical Park
1140 Red Clay Park Rd. SW
Cleveland, TN 37311   Ph: (423)478-0339
Lois I. Osborne, Park Manager

Description: The park's collection includes Paleo, Archaic, Mississippian, Woodland, and historic period artifacts. The park is located on the former seat of the Cherokee government and site of eleven general councils.

Texas

★1002★
Alabama-Coushatta Tribe of Texas
Indian Museum
US Hwy. 190   Ph: (409)563-4391
Rte. 3, Box 640   Free: 800-444-3507
Livingston, TX 77351   Fax: (409)563-2186
Jo Ann Battise, Tribal Admin.

Description: Located on the Alabama-Coushatta Indian reservation, the museum's collections include a dioramic display of tribes and a living Indian village. Research is conducted in the areas of tribal history and culture.

★1003★
Caddoan Mounds State Historic Site
Rte. 2, Box 85-C
Alto, TX 75925

Description: Site of a Caddoan village and ceremonial center dating to 750-1300 A.D.

Utah

★1004★
Anasazi Indian Village State Park
460 N. Hwy 12
PO Box 1429   Ph: (435)335-7308
Boulder, UT 84716   Fax: (435)335-7352
Larry Davis, Superintendent

Description: Maintains collection of artifacts representative of the Keyenta Anasazi culture during the period 1050-1200 A.D., and a diorama of Coombs Village.

★1005★
Canyonlands National Park
125 West, 200 South
Moab, UT 84532   Ph: (801)259-7164

Description: Site of several small Anasazi ruins and pictographs.

★1006★
College of Eastern Utah
Prehistoric Museum
451 East 400 North   Ph: (801)637-5060
Price, UT 84501   Fax: (801)637-2514

Description: Contains exhibits of Fremont and Anasazi Indian artifacts.

★1007★
Edge of the Cedars State Park
660 West 400 North
Box 788
Blanding, UT 84511   Ph: (435)678-2238
Stephen Olsen, Superintendent

Description: Exhibits include artifacts belonging to the prehistoric Anasazi Indian Tribe, Anasazi pottery collection, and artifacts of the Navajo, Ute, and Piute Indians.

★1008★
Natural Bridges National Monument
Box 1
Lake Powell, UT 84533   Ph: (801)259-5174

Description: Location of the Horsecollar Ruins and several small cliff dwellings and pictographs.

Washington

★1009★
Chelan County Historical Museum and Pioneer Village
600 Cotlets Way
PO Box 22
Cashmere, WA 98815   Ph: (509)782-3230

Description: Recreates the history of the Columbia River Indians before the arrival of the first pioneers and maintains an extensive collection of Indian artifacts.

★1010★
Colville Tribal Museum
PO Box 233   Ph: (509)633-0751
Coulee Dam, WA 99116   Fax: (509)633-2320

★1011★
Makah Cultural and Research Center
PO Box 160
Neah Bay, WA 98357

Description: Contains exhibits pertaining to the Makah Indian history and culture.

★1012★
Museum of Native American Cultures
2316 W. 1st Ave.   Ph: (509)456-3931
Spokane, WA 99204   Fax: (509)456-7690

Description: Displays include paintings, artifacts, ceramics, and an extensive trade bead collection from native cultures spanning the Western Hemisphere.

★1013★
Yakima Nation Cultural Center
Fort Rd.
PO Box 151   Ph: (509)865-2800
Toppenish, WA 98948   Fax: (509)865-6101

Description: Maintains dioramas and exhibits that chronicle the history of the Yakima Indians.

Wisconsin

★1014★
Lac du Flambeau Chippewa Museum and Cultural Center
PO Box 804   Ph: (715)588-3333
Lac Du Flambeau, WI 54538   Fax: (715)588-3474

Description: Houses a collection of Indian artifacts dating back to the mid-18th century, including a 24-foot dugout canoe discovered in a local lake and thought to be about 250 years old. A four seasons display demonstrates Indian activities, clothing, and living arrangements throughout the year.

Wyoming

★1015★
Cheyenne Frontier Days and Old West Museum
PO Box 2720   Ph: (307)778-7291
Cheyenne, WY 82003   Fax: (307)778-7288

Description: Displays include Oglala Sioux Indian artifacts.

★1016★
Plains Indian Museum
Buffalo Bill Historical Center
Buffalo Bill Historical Center
720 Sheridan Ave.   Ph: (307)587-4771
Cody, WY 82414   Fax: (307)587-5714

Description: Maintains an extensive collection of artifacts, ceremonial items and beadwork, dress, and weaponry of the Sioux, Blackfeet, Cheyenne, Shoshone, Crow, and Arapaho tribes.

★1017★
University of Wyoming
Anthropology Museum
University of Wyoming
Box 3431   Ph: (307)766-5136
Laramie, WY 82071   Fax: (307)766-2473

Description: Chronicals Wyoming's cultural history, Northwest Plains, and other North American Indians.

Research Centers

★1018★
American Indian Culture Research Center
Blue Cloud Abbey
PO Box 98   Ph: (605)432-5528
Marvin, SD 57251   Fax: (605)432-4754
Rev. Stanislaus Maudlin OSB, Dir.

Founded: 1967 **Research Activities and Fields:** Serves as a liaison between Indian and non-Indian cultures. Supports Indian leaders and educators in rebuilding the Indian community and educates the non-Indian public in the culture and philosophy of the Indian.

★1019★
American Indian Law Center
PO Box 4456, Sta. A   Ph: (505)277-5462
Albuquerque, NM 87196   Fax: (505)277-1035
Philip Deloria, Dir.

Founded: 1967 **Research Activities and Fields:** Legal research, policy analysis, and technical assistance to Native American tribes, organizations, and individuals, as well as governmental agencies at all levels. Development of political, administrative, and leadership capabilities of tribal governments. **Publications:** American Indian Law Newsletter, 3/year.

★1020★
American Indian Research and Development
2424 Springer Dr., Ste. 200   Ph: (405)364-0656
Norman, OK 73069   Fax: (405)364-5464
Stuart A. Tonemah, Contact

Founded: 1982 **Research Activities and Fields:** Native Americans, focusing on improving the quality of education for gifted and talented Native American Students, including developing curriculum and teaching materials and providing training and technical assistance to local and state education agencies, tribes, and other Native American organizations. Currently conducting the Native American Marrow Recruitment Project and the American Indian Teaching Training Project, also a National Evaluation study of Indian/ Native American JTPA programs.

★1021★
Arizona State University
Center for Indian Education
PO Box 871311   Ph: (602)965-6292
Tempe, AZ 85287-1311   Fax: (602)965-8115
Octaviana Trujillo, Dir.

Founded: 1959 **Research Activities and Fields:** All phases of American Indian education and related interdisciplinary issues. **Publications:** Journal of American Indian Education (JAIE), 3/year.

★1022★
Arizona State University
School of Justice Studies
PO Box 870403   Ph: (602)965-7682
Tempe, AZ 85287-0403   Fax: (602)965-9199
David Goldberg, Dir.

Founded: 1973 **Research Activities and Fields:** Social science research methods and statistics as applied to criminal, social, economic, and political justice and reforms, administering criminal justice policy, women and justice, political deviance, family violence, and grievance processes and dispute resolution. Also studies comparative justice and legality race, ethnicity, culture, and American Indian justice. Performs program evaluations and policy analysis and offers alternatives to incarceration.

★1023★
Community Research and Education Center
1609 E. Kalamazoo St., Ste.7
Lansing, MI 48912-2700   Ph: (517)485-2732
Richard Kibbey, Dir.

Founded: 1984 **Research Activities and Fields:** Neighborhood and rural economic development, housing, and issues affecting Native Americans and the disabled.

★1024★
Crow Canyon Archaeological Center
23390 County Rd. K   Ph: (970)565-8975
Cortez, CO 81321   Free: 800-422-8975
     Fax: (970)565-4859
Bruce A. Grimes, Pres.

Research Activities and Fields: Archeological investigation, including excavation and cataloging of artifacts. Specializes in Anasazi Indian culture, excavates sites in the Four Corners area of the southwest United States, and uses discoveries to describe ancient Anasazi social structure, behaviors and skill levels within the society. Center offers the public the opportunity to join research expeditions. **Publications:** Occasional Papers of the Crow Canyon Archaeological Center.

★1025★
ERIC Clearinghouse on Rural Education and Small Schools
Appalachia Educational Lab.   Ph: (304)347-0400
PO Box 1348   Free: 800-624-9120
Charleston, WV 25325   Fax: (304)347-0487

Founded: 1966 **Research Activities and Fields:** American Indian, native Alaskan, Mexican American, migrant, outdoor, and rural education and small schools. **Publications:** ERIC Digests; Handbooks; Directories.

★1026★
Humboldt State University
Center for Indian Community Development
House 93   Ph: (707)826-3711
Arcata, CA 95521   Fax: (707)826-5258
Lois J. Risling, Dir.

Founded: 1966 **Research Activities and Fields:** Community economic and organizational development, regeneration of American Indian languages and literatures and the application of computer systems to publication of Indian languages. Projects include publication of textbooks and instructional material in and about Hupa, Karuk, Tolowa, Yurok, and other Indian languages. **Publications:** The Messenger Newsletter.

★1027★
Indian Arts Research Center
Sch. of American Res.
PO Box 2188   Ph: (505)982-3584
Santa Fe, NM 87504   Fax: (505)989-9809
Michael J. Hering, Dir.

Founded: 1907 **Research Activities and Fields:** Collection of Southwest cultural materials, concentrating on Native American arts of the Southwest, such as ceramics, basketry, textiles, jewelry, paintings, and kachinas dating from the time of Spanish contact. Scholars, researchers, and Southwest American Indian artists are encouraged to utilize the facilities for research and aesthetic experience. **Publications:** Annual Report.

★1028★
Indian and Colonial Research Center
Eva Butler Library
Main St.
PO Box 525
Old Mystic, CT 06372   Ph: (203)536-9771
Joan Cohn, Pres.

Founded: 1965 **Research Activities and Fields:** Native American Indians, including the lifestyle and culture of the Pequots, Narragansetts, and Nehantics; and local history, including genealogy, oral history, old homes, and early American school books, maps, and photographs. **Publications:** Newsletter, newsletter.

★1029★
Institute of American Indian and Alaska Native Culture and Arts Development
Box 20007   Ph: (505)988-6423
Santa Fe, NM 87504-7634   Fax: (505)986-5509
Allen Schwartz, Dir.

Founded: 1962 **Research Activities and Fields:** American Indian culture, history, and fine arts.

★1030★
Institute for American Indian Studies
38 Curtis Rd.
PO Box 1260   Ph: (860)868-0518
Washington, CT 06793-0260   Fax: (860)868-1649
Alberto C. Meloni, Exec.Dir.

Founded: 1975 **Research Activities and Fields:** Discovery, preservation, and interpretation of native cultures of the Americas. **Publications:** Netop Newsletter, bimonthly.

★1031★
Institute for the Study of Traditional American Indian Arts
PO Box 66124
Portland, OR 97290   Ph: (503)233-8131
John M. Gogol, Contact

Research Activities and Fields: Native American arts and crafts.

★1032★
Makah Cultural and Research Center
PO Box 160   Ph: (360)645-2711
Neah Bay, WA 98357   Fax: (360)645-2656
Janine Bouechop, Dir.

Founded: 1979 **Research Activities and Fields:** Language, culture, and ethnohistory of the Makah people, including comparative Wakashan linguistics, anthropology, comparative Nootkan studies, and photohistory of the reservation and p eople, especially in the period of change on the reservation (1880-1920); archaeology, especially of Ozette and Hoko collections. **Publications:** Portraits in Time.

★1033★
Mississippi State University
Cobb Institute of Archaeology
Drawer AR   Ph: (601)325-3826
Mississippi State, MS 39762   Fax: (601)325-8690
Dr. Joe D. Seger, Dir.

Founded: 1971 **Research Activities and Fields:** Archeology and related fields. Emphasizes the Middle Eastern origins of Western European Civilization and the American Indians of the South, especially Mississippi. Active field research program carried out in alternate years in Mississippi and the Middle East. **Publications:** Occasional Papers; Project Reports; Brochures.

★1034★
Montana State University, Bozeman
Center for Native American Studies
Bozeman, MT 59717-2340   Ph: (406)994-3881
                                 Fax: (406)994-6879
Dr. Wayne J. Stein, Dir.

Founded: 1971 **Research Activities and Fields:** American Indian studies, including research on Montana tribal histories and culture and Indian-white relations.

★1035★
Moorhead State University
Northwest Minnesota Historical Center
Livingston Lord Library   Ph: (218)236-2343
Moorhead, MN 56563   Fax: (218)299-5924
Terry L. Shoptaugh, Dir.

Founded: 1972 **Research Activities and Fields:** Ethnicity in Northwest Minnesota, social welfare, Native Americans, politics, government, business, church history, oral history, agriculture, and women's organizations.

★1036★
Museum of the Great Plains
Elmer Thomas Park
601 Ferris Ave.
PO Box 68   Ph: (405)581-3460
Lawton, OK 73502   Fax: (405)581-3458
Steve Wilson, Dir.

Founded: 1960 **Research Activities and Fields:** Human ecology and prehistory in the Great Plains of North America and human adaptation to a plains environment, including studies in social psychology and on Pleistocene ecology of Domebo Mammoth Kill site, rise and decline of Wichita Indians, salvage excavations in Mangum Reservoir area, paleoIndian and plains archaic cultures, ethnology of Kiowa, Kiowa-Apache, and Comanche cultures, and archeological survey of Wichita Mountains. Conducts field excavations and provides information and technical consultation services for approved scholars and studies. **Publications:** Great Plains Journal, annually; Contributions of Museum of the Great Plains, occasionally; Museum Newsletter.

★1037★
Museum of New Mexico
PO Box 2087   Ph: (505)827-6450
Santa Fe, NM 87504   Fax: (505)827-6427
Thomas A. Livesay, Dir.

Founded: 1909 **Research Activities and Fields:** Archeology, ethnology, fine art, folk art, and history, including archeological and ethnological artifacts of Indians of southwestern U.S. and Mexico, Spanish colonial materials from Spain, Mexico, and New Mexico, historical and art collections from the Southwest, and folk art of the world. Conducts archeological excavations to document and catalog the prehistory and history of New Mexico. Also conducts anthropological investigations. **Publications:** El Palacio, quarterly; Preview, bimonthly.

★1038★
National Indian Policy Center
2021 K St., NW, Ste. 211   Ph: (202)973-7667
Washington, DC 20006   Fax: (202)973-7686
William Gelles, Interim Dir.

Founded: 1990 **Research Activities and Fields:** Indian issues, including public policy of concern to Native Americans and Alaska Natives; employment and training programs for urban Native Americans; and labor market experience of Indian youth.

★1039★
National Indian Training and Research Center
2121 S. Mill Ave., Ste. 216   Ph: (602)967-9484
Tempe, AZ 85282   Fax: (602)921-1015
Dr. C. Corbett, Contact

Founded: 1969 **Research Activities and Fields:** Works to promote the involvement of American Indians in leadership and professional roles in training and research projects for the social betterment of their people.

★1040★
New England Antiquities Research Association
305 Academy Rd.
Pembroke, NH 03275   Ph: (603)623-9955
Daniel J. Leary, Pres.

Founded: 1964 **Research Activities and Fields:** Anthropology, archeology, archeoastronomy, epigraphy, and geology. Native American studies concern the nature, origin, history, and purpose of stoneworks and related structures in the northeastern U.S. Current research includes archeology in Maine and New Hampshire. **Publications:** NEARA Journal, quarterly.

★1041★
Newberry Library
D'Arcy McNickle Center for American Indian History
60 W. Walton St.   Ph: (312)255-3564
Chicago, IL 60610   Fax: (312)255-3513
C. Cullen, Pres.

Founded: 1972 **Research Activities and Fields:** American Indian history, anthropology, literature, and ethnology. Programs support research in Indian-White relations, and tribal history. **Publications:** Monographs; Occasional Papers Series; Bibliographical Series.

★1042★
Northern Arizona University
American Indian Rehabilitation Research and
    Training Center
PO Box 5630   Ph: (520)523-4791
Flagstaff, AZ 86011-5630   Fax: (520)523-9127
Priscilla Lansing Sanderson, Dir.

Founded: 1983 **Research Activities and Fields:** Core areas include identifying and facilitating effective and culturally appropriate rehabilitation services for American Indians with disabilities, developing and implementing strategies to improve and maintain employment and independent living for American Indians with disabilities, increasing the awareness of high incidences and prevalence of disabilities among American Indians, and promoting the development of qualified American Indian researchers and service providers. **Publications:** American Indian Rehabilitation Newsletter; Hotline Newsletter.

★1043★
Panhandle-Plains Historical Museum
Research Center
Box 967, WTAMU Stat.   Ph: (806)656-2261
Canyon, TX 79016   Fax: (806)656-2250
Lisa S. Lambert, Archv./Libn.

Founded: 1932 **Research Activities and Fields:** Texas and Southwest history, ranching, Indians of the Great Plains, archeology of Texas Panhandle, ethnology, clothing and textiles, fine arts, antiques, and museum science.

★1044★
Pennsylvania State University
American Indian Education Policy Center
320 Rackley Bldg.   Ph: (814)865-1489
University Park, PA 16802   Fax: (814)863-7532
Dr. John Tippeconnic, Contact

Founded: 1979 **Research Activities and Fields:** Policy issues concerning American Indian education, including training needs, leadership development, and other issues related directly or indirectly to schooling for the American Indian.

★1045★
San Juan County Archaeological Research Center
    and Library
PO Box 125   Ph: (505)632-2013
Bloomfield, NM 87413   Fax: (505)632-1707
Larry L. Baker, Exec.Dir.

Founded: 1973 **Research Activities and Fields:** Southwest archaeology, history, anthropology, oral history, Native Americans, and natural science. **Publications:** SJCMA Newsletter, quarterly.

★1046★
School of American Research
PO Box 2188 Ph: (505)982-3583
Santa Fe, NM 87504 Fax: (505)989-9809
Dr. Douglas W. Schwartz, Pres.

Founded: 1907 **Research Activities and Fields:** Social sciences and humanities with emphasis on anthropology and related disciplines. **Publications:** Monographs; Advanced Seminar Series; Resident Scholar Series.

★1047★
Sinte Gleska University
Lakota Archives and Historical Research Center
PO Box 490 Ph: (605)747-2263
Rosebud, SD 57570 Fax: (605)747-2098
Marcella Cash, Archv.

Founded: 1984 **Research Activities and Fields:** Rosebud Sioux Tribe and Reservation and Sinte Gleska University.

★1048★
South Dakota Oral History Center
Dakota Hall, Rm. 12
414 E. Clark St. Ph: (605)677-5209
Vermillion, SD 57069 Fax: (605)677-6525
Leonard R. Bruguier, Dir.

Founded: 1966 **Research Activities and Fields:** Collects and preserves South Dakota and American Indian oral histories. **Publications:** The Bulletin.

★1049★
Southwest Museum
PO Box 41558 Ph: (213)221-2164
Los Angeles, CA 90041-0558 Fax: (213)224-8223
Dr. Duane King, Exec.Dir.

Founded: 1907 **Research Activities and Fields:** Archeology and ethnology of the Americas, especially history of the American Indian and Meso-America, both pre-Columbian and contemporary, illustrating development of man and his culture. **Publications:** Hodge Fund Publications; Southwest Museum Papers; Southwest Museum Leaflets.

★1050★
Taylor Museum for Southwestern Studies
30 W. Dale St. Ph: (719)634-5581
Colorado Springs, CO 80903 Fax: (719)634-0570
Cathy L. Wright, Dir.

Founded: 1936 **Research Activities and Fields:** Southwest studies, prehistoric and contemporary Hispanic and Native American material culture and ethnography, and 19th- and 20th-century American art.

★1051★
U.S. Department of Health and Human Services
Indian Health Service
Office of Planning, Evaluation, and Legislation
Division of Program Statistics
Twinbrook Metro Plaza
12300 Twinbrook Pkwy., Ste. 450 Ph: (301)443-1180
Rockville, MD 20852 Fax: (301)443-1522
Anthony J. D'Angelo, Dir.

Founded: 1983 **Research Activities and Fields:** Main function is to satisfy the American Indian and Alaska Native health statistics information needs of its clients. The Division manages a number of information systems that provide data for measuring the health status of the American Indian and Alaska Native population and appraising IHS program activities. Division's primary duty is to serve IHS management, but it also has numerous dealings with other government agencies, government contractors, academia, researchers, the media, and the general public. Division is responsible for: vital events statistics, patient care statistics, and population statistics. In addition to providing statistical data, Division also provides statistical advice on analyzing the data. **Publications:** Indian health status reports, occasionally; Trends in Indian Health, annually; Regional Differences in Indian Health, annually.

★1052★
U.S. Department of the Interior
Bureau of Indian Affairs
Office of Tribal Services
Tribal Government Services Division
Mail Stop 2611-MIB
1849 C St., N.W. Ph: (202)208-3592
Washington, DC 20240 Fax: (202)219-3008
Holly Reckord, Chf.

Founded: 1978 **Research Activities and Fields:** Primary documents research, on-site data collection, materials analysis, decision-making regarding recommendations to acknowledge or not acknowledge Indian groups; and publishing detailed reports on findings and recommendations. Principal areas of interest include: Native American history; non-federally recognized Indian tribes; post-contact Indian history and anthropology; United States-Indian relations; Indian society and governments; and dynamics of cultural/political assimilation.

★1053★
U.S. Smithsonian Institution
National Museum of the American Indian
Research Branch
Cultural Resources Department
3401 Bruckner Blvd.
Bronx, NY 10461 Ph: (212)514-3944
George Horse Capture, Dep. Asst. Dir.

★1054★
University at Albany, State University of New York
Institute for Archaeological Studies
Social Sci. 263
1400 Washington Ave. Ph: (518)442-4721
Albany, NY 12222 Fax: (518)442-5710
Prof. Richard G. Wilkinson, Contact

Founded: 1982 **Research Activities and Fields:** Archeology, including northeastern archeology, ethnology, and linguistics. Supports research conducted by faculty and graduate students on native northeastern peoples, primarily Algonquian and Iroquois tribes. Also coordinates and assists faculty with research, external funding, and teaching interests in archeology from the departments of classics, anthropology, and physics, the program in Mediterranean archeology, and the program in the Mohawk Valley of Upstate New York. **Publications:** Northeast Anthropology, journal.

★1055★
University of Arizona
Arizona State Museum
Bldg. 26 Ph: (520)621-6281
Tucson, AZ 85721-0026 Fax: (520)621-2976
Dr. George J. Gumerman, Dir.

Founded: 1893 **Research Activities and Fields:** Archeology, ethnology, ethnohistory, general ethnological studies among Indians, and special archeological research projects. Collaborates with state and local archeological and historical agencies, and with the 21 Indian tribes. **Publications:** Museum Archaeological Series; Anthropological Papers of the University of Arizona; Monograph Series.

★1056★
University of Arizona
Native American Research and Training Center
1642 E. Helen Ph: (520)621-5075
Tucson, AZ 85719 Fax: (520)621-9802
Jennie R. Joe PhD, Dir.

Founded: 1983 **Research Activities and Fields:** Health and rehabilitation of disabled and chronically ill Native Americans. Core areas include the following: needs assessment, service delivery, and evaluation as determined by or in cooperation with the disabled; empowerment that is sensitive to Indian values and needs; and vocational rehabilitation, including preventive, restorative, and occupational processes for the disabled that lead to self-sufficiency. Also studies the impact of government policy on the delivery of health care. Promotes self determination and parity among Native Americans in health and rehabilitation. Serves as a national resource for all North American tribes and Alaska natives. **Publications:** Books; Reports; Dual track videotapes.

★1057★
University of California, Davis
Michael and Margaret B. Harrison Western Research Center
Dept. of Special Collections
Shields Library
Davis, CA 95616
Ph: (916)752-1621
Fax: (916)752-3148
John Skarstad, Hd., Spec.Colls.

Founded: 1981 **Research Activities and Fields:** History and development of the trans-Mississippi West, from the mid-19th century to the present; American Indians; ethnic studies; military, local, and economic history; sociology; folklore; religious studies, especially the Catholic and Mormon churches; geography; exploration and travel; literature; art and architecture; and history of printing.

★1058★
University of California, Los Angeles
American Indian Studies Center
3220 Campbell Hall
Los Angeles, CA 90024-1548
Ph: (310)825-7315
Fax: (310)206-7060
Dr. Duane Champagne, Dir.

Founded: 1969 **Research Activities and Fields:** American Indians, including history, culture, arts, humanities, social sciences, conditions, problems, and potentialities of that ethnic group. Seeks to benefit Los Angeles Indian community and Indian community at large. Coordinates educational, research, and action-oriented programs designed to meet needs of American Indian students at the University and of American Indian communities in general. **Publications:** American Indian Culture and Research Journal; American Indian Treaties Publications; Native American Pamphlet Series.

★1059★
University of Colorado at Boulder
Center for the Study of Native Languages of the Plains and Southwest
Dept. of Linguistics
CB 295
Boulder, CO 80309-0295
Ph: (303)492-2748
Fax: (303)492-4416
Dr. Allan R. Taylor, Dir.

Research Activities and Fields: Collects data and conducts research on Native American languages of the Great Plains and Southwest, including the Siouan languages, Gros Ventre (a nearly extinct Algonquian language related to Arapaho), Kiowa, and Wichita (a nearly extinct Caddoan language).

★1060★
University of Colorado
National Center for American Indian and Alaska Native Mental Health Research
Dept. of Psychiatry
Univ. North Pavilion
4455 E. 12th Ave., A011-13
Denver, CO 80220
Ph: (303)315-9232
Fax: (303)315-9579
Dr. Spero Manson, Dir.

Founded: 1986 **Research Activities and Fields:** Center formulates, designs, conducts, and reports studies within four areas of inquiry: determining and improving the performance characteristics of self-report measures of serious psychological dysfunction and diagnostic interviews for assessing alcohol, drug, and mental (ADM) disorders; establishing the prevalence and incidence of ADM disorders and related risk factors through descriptive and experimental epidemiological investigations; developing and evaluating methods for detecting and managing ADM disorders presented in human service settings; and examining the effectiveness of interventions for preventing ADM disorders and promoting well-being. Ongoing studies include the American Indian Vietnam Veterans Project, which studies post-traumatic stress disorder and other psychological problems of Vietnam war veterans in readjusting to civilian life; Flower of Two Soils Reinterview Project, which studies emotional disorders in Native American adolescents; the Health Survey of Indian Boarding Students, which

seeks to establish the prevalence and incidence of symptoms of depression, anxiety, suicidal behavior, and substance abuse, and to clarify relative contributions of stressful life events, coping strategies, social support, mastery, and self-esteem; the Foundations of Indian Teens Project, which develops more reliable and valid measures of psychopathology among Indian adolescents, with special emphasis on trauma; and the Voices of Indian Teens Project, a survey that includes psychometrically sound constructs, including substance abuse, substance dependence, depression, anxiety, academic achievement, delinquent behavior, social support, peer values and pressure, ethnic identity, stressful life events, drinking patterns and contexts, community values, and attitudes toward alcohol. **Publications:** American Indian and Alaska Native Mental Health Research Journal, 3/year; Annual Monograph.

★1061★
University of New Mexico
New Mexico Tumor Registry
900 Camino de Salud NE
Albuquerque, NM 87131
Ph: (505)272-5541
Fax: (505)272-8572
Dr. Charles R. Key, Co-Dir.

Founded: 1966 **Research Activities and Fields:** Cancer epidemiology, with emphasis on Hispanics and American Indians. Participates in the NCI's SEER (Surveillance Epidemiology and End Results) Program. **Publications:** New Mexico Tumor Registry Newsletter, semiannually

★1062★
University of North Carolina at Pembroke
Native American Resource Center
1 Univ. Dr.
Old Main Bldg.
Pembroke, NC 28372-1510
Ph: (910)521-6282
Stanley G. Knick PhD, Dir.

Founded: 1979 **Research Activities and Fields:** The Lumbee Indians who live in the University area and American Indian tribal histories and culture, particularly the Southeastern Indian tribes. Research interests include archeology, ethnography, ethnohistory, and general American Indian studies. Research is conducted in conjuction with tribal organizations and with other University departments. **Publications:** SPIRIT!, quarterly; Robeson Trails Archaeological Survey (1988); Along the Trail: A Reader About Native Americans (1996).

★1063★
University of North Dakota
UND Center for Rural Health
501 N. Columbia Rd.
PO Box 9037
Grand Forks, ND 58202-9037
Ph: (701)777-3848
Fax: (701)777-2389
Brad Gibbens, Assoc.Dir.

Founded: 1980 **Research Activities and Fields:** Rural health care delivery, especially in the areas of health professional shortage areas, the viability of rural health facilities, aging populaiton, Native American health care, and uncompensated care. Collaborates with other research organizations throughout the nation. **Publications:** Focus on Rural Health, semiannually.

★1064★
University of South Dakota
Institute of American Indian Studies
Dakota Hall, Rm. 12
414 E. Clark St.
Vermillion, SD 57069
Ph: (605)677-5209
Fax: (605)677-6525
Leonard R. Bruguier, Dir.

Founded: 1955 **Research Activities and Fields:** Indians and their affairs, including study of Dakota/Lakota/Nakota languages. **Publications:** The Bulletin, semiannually; Reports; Papers.

★1065★
University of South Dakota
Social Science Research Institute
Vermillion, SD 57069   Ph: (605)677-5401
    Fax: (605)677-5583

Tom Allen, Dir.
Founded: 1964 **Research Activities and Fields:** Research includes studies on organizations, economic and social development, criminology, juvenile delinquency, child abuse, aged population, communications, social work and welfare, court administration, jury selection and community surveys for litigation, prison education, alcoholism, medical and educational problems on American Indian reservations, and follow-up on juvenile offenders. Conducts anthropological studies, including site preservation.

★1066★
University of South Dakota
W.H. Over State Museum
414 E. Clark   Ph: (605)677-5228
Vermillion, SD 57069   Fax: (605)624-8735
Dorothy Neuhaus, Pres., Brd.of Dirs.
Founded: 1883 **Research Activities and Fields:** Natural history, anthropology, archeology, and history of South Dakota.

★1067★
University of Utah
American West Center
1901 E. South Campus Dr., Rm. 1023   Ph: (801)581-7611
Salt Lake City, UT 84112   Fax: (801)581-7612
Dr. Patricia C. Albers, Dir.
Founded: 1964 **Research Activities and Fields:** Political, social, economic, and cultural studies of the North American West, American Indian history and traditions, other ethnic groups, oral history, and various related research projects under government and foundation grants. **Publications:** Occasional Paper Series.

Education Programs & Services

Head Start Programs

★1068★
Cocopah Tribe
Head Start Program
PO Bin G
Somerton, AZ 85350   Ph: (520)627-2811

★1069★
Colorado River Indian Tribes
Head Start Program
Rte. 1, Box 39X   Ph: (520)662-4311
Parker, AZ 85344   Fax: (520)662-4322

★1070★
Gila River Indian Community
Head Start Program
PO Box A   Ph: (520)562-3423
Sacaton, AZ 85247   Fax: (520)562-2042

★1071★
Hopi Tribe
Head Start Program
PO Box 123   Ph: (520)734-2441
Kykotsmovi, AZ 86039   Fax: (520)734-2435

★1072★
Pascua Yaqui Tribal Council
Head Start Program
7474 S. Camino De Oeste   Ph: (520)883-5189
Tucson, AZ 85746   Fax: (520)883-5014

★1073★
San Carlos Apache Tribe
Head Start Program
Box 0
San Carlos, AZ 85550   Ph: (520)475-2361

★1074★
Tohono O'Odham Nation
Head Start Program
PO Box 837
Sells, AZ 85634   Ph: (520)383-2221

★1075★
White Mountain Apache Tribe
Head Start Program
PO Box 699   Ph: (520)338-4938
Whiteriver, AZ 85941   Fax: (520)338-1598

★1076★
Hoopa Valley Business Council
Head Start Program
PO Box 1287   Ph: (530)625-4522
Hoopa, CA 95546   Fax: (530)625-4526

★1077★
Inyo Child Care Services
Head Start Program
432 N. Barlow Ln.   Ph: (760)872-3911
Bishop, CA 93514   Fax: (760)872-4857

★1078★
Ute Mountain Ute Tribe
Head Start Program
General Delivery
PO Box 308   Ph: (970)565-3751
Towaoc, CO 81334   Fax: (970)565-7412

★1079★
Miccosukee Tribe
Head Start Program
PO Box 44021, Tamiami Sta.   Ph: (305)223-8380
Miami, FL 33144   Fax: (305)223-1011

★1080★
Seminole Tribe
Head Start Program
6073 Sterling Rd.   Ph: (954)797-1441
Hollywood, FL 33024   Fax: (954)791-8565

★1081★
Nez Perce Tribal Executive Committee
Head Start Program
PO Box 365   Ph: (208)843-2253
Lapwai, ID 83540   Fax: (208)843-7327

★1082★
Shoshone-Bannock Tribes
Head Start Program
PO Box 306   Ph: (208)238-3700
Fort Hall, ID 83203   Fax: (208)237-0797

★1083★
Kickapoo Tribe of Kansas
Head Start Program
RR 1, Box 157A   Ph: (785)486-2131
Horton, KS 66439   Fax: (785)486-2801

★1084★
Grand Traverse Band of Ottawa and Chippewa Tribes
Head Start Program
2605 NW Bayshore Dr.   Ph: (616)271-3538
Suttons Bay, MI 49682   Fax: (616)271-4861

★1085★
Inter-Tribal Council of Michigan
Head Start Program
405 E. Easterday Ave.   Ph: (906)632-6896
Sault Sainte Marie, MI 49783   Fax: (906)632-1810

★1086★
Bois Forte Reservation Business Committee
Head Start Program
PO Box 16   Ph: (218)757-3261
Nett Lake, MN 55772   Fax: (218)757-3312

★1087★
Fond du Lac Reservation Business Committee
Head Start Program
1720 Biglake Rd.   Ph: (218)879-4593
Cloquet, MN 55720   Fax: (218)879-4146

★1088★
Grand Portage Reservation Business Committee
Head Start Program
PO Box 428   Ph: (218)475-2234
Grand Portage, MN 55605   Fax: (218)475-2284

★1089★
Leech Lake Reservation (Chippewa)
Head Start Program
Rte. 3, Box 100   Ph: (218)335-8257
Cass Lake, MN 56633   Fax: (218)335-8255

★1090★
Mille Lacs Reservation
Head Start Program
HCR 67, Box 194   Ph: (320)532-4181
Onamia, MN 56359   Fax: (320)532-4718

★1091★
Red Lake Reservation
Head Start Program
PO Box 53   Ph: (218)679-3396
Redlake, MN 56671   Fax: (218)679-2923

★1092★
White Earth Band of Chippewa
Head Start Program
PO Box 418   Ph: (218)983-3285
White Earth, MN 56591   Fax: (218)983-4106

★1093★
Mississippi Band of Choctaw Indians
Head Start Program
Rte. 7, Box 21   Ph: (601)656-5251
Philadelphia, MS 39350   Fax: (601)656-2763

★1094★
Blackfeet Tribal Business Council
Head Start Program
615 S. Piegan
PO Box 518   Ph: (406)338-7411
Browning, MT 59417   Fax: (406)338-7030

★1095★
Confederated Salish and Kootenai Tribes
Head Start Program
26 Round Butte Rd.   Ph: (406)676-4509
Ronan, MT 59864   Fax: (406)676-4507

★1096★
Crow Tribal Council
Head Start Program
PO Box 249   Ph: (406)638-2697
Crow Agency, MT 59022   Fax: (406)638-2364

★1097★
Fort Belknap Indian Community Council
Head Start Program
RR 1, Box 66   Ph: (406)353-2205
Harlem, MT 59526   Fax: (406)353-2797

★1098★
Fort Peck Tribes
Head Start Program
1027 Poplar   Ph: (406)768-5155
Poplar, MT 59255   Fax: (406)768-5473

★1099★
Northern Cheyenne Tribal Council
Head Start Program
PO Box 128   Ph: (406)477-6347
Lame Deer, MT 59043   Fax: (406)477-6906

★1100★
Omaha Tribal Council
Head Start Program
PO Box 357
Macy, NE 68039   Ph: (402)837-4052

★1101★
Winnebago Tribe of Nebraska
Head Start Program
PO Box 747   Ph: (402)878-2200
Winnebago, NE 68071   Fax: (402)878-2250

★1102★
Eight Northern Pueblos, Inc.
Head Start Program
PO Box 969   Ph: (505)852-4265
San Juan Pueblo, NM 87566   Fax: (505)852-4835

★1103★
Five Sandoval Indian Pueblos, Inc.
Head Start Program
1043 Highway 313   Ph: (505)867-3351
Bernalillo, NM 87004   Fax: (505)867-3514

★1104★
Jicarilla Apache Tribal Council
Head Start Program
PO Box 545   Ph: (505)759-3343
Dulce, NM 87528   Fax: (505)759-3098

★1105★
Mescalero Apache Tribal Council
Head Start Program
PO Box 176
Mescalero, NM 88340   Ph: (505)671-4494

★1106★
Pueblo of Acoma
Head Start Program
PO Box 307
Pueblo of Acoma, NM 87034   Ph: (505)552-6621

★1107★
Pueblo of Isleta
Head Start Program
PO Box 579   Ph: (505)869-3700
Isleta, NM 87022   Fax: (505)869-6034

★1108★
Pueblo of Jemez
Walatowa Head Start Program
PO Box 9   Ph: (505)834-7678
Jemez Pueblo, NM 87024   Fax: (505)834-0002

★1109★
Pueblo of Laguna
Head Start Program
PO Box 207   Ph: (505)552-6008
Laguna, NM 87026   Fax: (505)552-6398

★1110★
Pueblo of San Felipe
Head Start Program
PO Box 4346   Ph: (505)867-2816
San Felipe Pueblo, NM 87001   Fax: (505)867-8831

★1111★
Pueblo of Taos
Head Start Program
PO Box 1846   Ph: (505)758-8626
Taos, NM 87571   Fax: (505)758-5831

★1112★
Santo Domingo Tribe
Head Start Program
PO Box 40   Ph: (505)465-2214
Santo Domingo Pueblo, NM 87052   Fax: (505)465-2688

★1113★
Zuni Pueblos
Head Start Program
PO Box 339   Ph: (505)782-4481
Zuni, NM 87327   Fax: (505)782-4457

★1114★
St. Regis Band of Mohawk Indians
Head Start Program
Rte. 37   Ph: (518)358-2272
Hogansburg, NY 13655   Fax: (518)358-3585

★1115★
Qualla Indian Boundary
Head Start Program
PO Box 1178   Ph: (704)497-9416
Cherokee, NC 28719   Fax: (704)497-4212

★1116★
Little Hoop Community College
Head Start Program
PO Box 269   Ph: (701)766-4205
Fort Totten, ND 58335   Fax: (701)766-4517

★1117★
Standing Rock Sioux Tribal Council
Head Start Program
PO Box 473   Ph: (701)854-3458
Fort Yates, ND 58538   Fax: (701)854-7221

★1118★
Three Affiliated Tribes
Head Start Program
PO Box 687   Ph: (701)627-4820
New Town, ND 58763   Fax: (701)627-4401

★1119★
Turtle Mountain Band of Chippewa
Head Start Program
PO Box 900
Belcourt, ND 58316   Ph: (701)477-5688

★1120★
Central Tribes of the Shawnee Area, Inc.
Head Start Program
Rte. 5, Box 148B   Ph: (405)275-0663
Shawnee, OK 74801   Fax: (405)275-0663

★1121★
Cherokee Nation of Oklahoma
Head Start Program
PO Box 948   Ph: (918)458-5795
Tahlequah, OK 74465   Fax: (918)458-5799

★1122★
Cheyenne-Arapaho Tribe
Head Start Program
PO Box 38   Ph: (405)262-0092
Concho, OK 73022   Fax: (405)262-0745

★1123★
Chickasaw Nation of Oklahoma
Head Start Program
PO Box 1548   Ph: (405)436-2603
Ada, OK 74820   Fax: (405)436-4287

★1124★
Choctaw Nation of Oklahoma
Head Start Program
16th & Locust   Ph: (580)924-8280
PO Drawer 1210   Free: 800-522-6170
Durant, OK 74702   Fax: (580)522-6170

★1125★
Creek Nation of Oklahoma
Head Start Program
PO Box 580   Ph: (918)756-8700
Okmulgee, OK 74447   Fax: (918)758-1450

★1126★
Kickapoo Tribe of Oklahoma
Kickapoo Head Start, Inc.
PO Box 399   Ph: (405)964-3676
Mc Loud, OK 74851   Fax: (405)964-3417

★1127★
Kiowa Tribe of Oklahoma
Head Start Program
PO Box 369   Ph: (580)654-2300
Carnegie, OK 73015   Fax: (580)654-2188

★1128★
Osage Tribal Council
Head Start Program
Osage Agency Council
PO Box 1389   Ph: (918)287-1246
Pawhuska, OK 74056   Fax: (918)287-3416

★1129★
Seminole Nation of Oklahoma
Head Start Program
PO Box 1498   Ph: (405)257-6663
Wewoka, OK 74884   Fax: (405)257-3704

★1130★
TOE Missouri Tribe
Head Start Program
Rte. 1, Box 62   Ph: (580)723-4434
Red Rock, OK 74651   Fax: (580)733-4273

★1131★
Confederated Tribes of Siletz Indians
Head Start Program
PO Box 549   Ph: (541)444-2532
Siletz, OR 97380   Fax: (541)444-2307

★1132★
Confederated Tribes of the Warm Springs
  Reservation
Head Start Program
PO Box C   Ph: (541)553-1161
Warm Springs, OR 97761   Fax: (541)553-3379

★1133★
Cheyenne River Sioux Tribal Council
Head Start Program
PO Box 180   Ph: (605)964-6835
Eagle Butte, SD 57625   Fax: (605)964-8705

★1134★
Crow Creek Sioux Tribe
Head Start Program
PO Box 350   Ph: (605)245-2337
Fort Thompson, SD 57339   Fax: (605)245-2366

★1135★
Lower Brule Sioux Tribe
Head Start Program
PO Box 804   Ph: (605)473-5520
Lower Brule, SD 57548   Fax: (605)473-5879

★1136★
Oglala Sioux Tribal Council
Head Start Program
1 Preschool Rd.
PO Box 279   Ph: (605)867-5170
Porcupine, SD 57772   Fax: (605)867-5030

★1137★
Rosebud Sioux Tribal Council
Head Start Program
PO Box 430   Ph: (605)856-2391
Rosebud, SD 57570   Fax: (605)856-2039

★1138★
Rural America Initatives, Inc.
Head Start Program
919 Main St., Ste. 201   Ph: (605)341-3163
Rapid City, SD 57701   Fax: (605)341-0375

★1139★
Ute Indian Tribe
Head Start Program
PO Box 265   Ph: (801)722-4506
Fort Duchesne, UT 84026   Fax: (801)722-2083

★1140★
Chehalis Tribal Business Council
Head Start Program
420 Howanut Rd.
PO Box 536   Ph: (360)273-5911
Oakville, WA 98568   Fax: (360)273-5914

★1141★
Colville Confederated Tribes
Head Start Program
PO Box 150   Ph: (509)634-4711
Nespelem, WA 99155   Fax: (509)634-4116

★1142★
Lower Elwha-Klallam Tribe
Head Start Program
2851 Lower Elwha Rd.   Ph: (360)452-8471
Port Angeles, WA 98363   Fax: (360)452-3428

★1143★
Lummi Tribal School System
Head Start Program
2616 Kwina Rd.
Bellingham, WA 98226   Ph: (360)384-1489

★1144★
Makah Tribal Council
Head Start Program
PO Box 115   Ph: (360)645-2201
Neah Bay, WA 98357   Fax: (360)645-2359

★1145★
Muckleshoot Tribal Council
Head Start Program
39015 172nd Ave. SE   Ph: (253)939-3311
Auburn, WA 98002   Fax: (253)939-2292

★1146★
Nisqually Indian Community Council
Head Start Program
4820 She-Nah-Num Dr. SE   Ph: (360)456-5221
Olympia, WA 98503   Fax: (360)438-4838

★1147★
Nooksack Indian Tribal Council
Head Start Program
PO Box 157   Ph: (360)592-5176
Deming, WA 98244   Fax: (360)592-5721

★1148★
Port Gamble Klallam Tribe
Head Start Program
PO Box 280
Kingston, WA 98346   Ph: (360)297-2943

★1149★
Quileute Tribal Council
Head Start Program
PO Box 279   Ph: (360)374-6163
La Push, WA 98350   Fax: (360)374-6311

★1150★
Quinault Indian Nation
Head Start Program
PO Box 189   Ph: (360)962-2051
Taholah, WA 98587   Fax: (360)276-4191

★1151★
Skokomish Tribal Council
Head Start Program
N. 80 Tribal Center Rd.   Ph: (360)426-4232
Shelton, WA 98584   Fax: (360)877-5943

★1152★
Yakima Tribe
Head Start Program
PO Box 151   Ph: (509)865-5121
Toppenish, WA 98948   Fax: (509)865-6092

★1153★
Bad River Tribal Council
Head Start Program
PO Box 39   Ph: (715)682-7111
Odanah, WI 54861   Fax: (715)682-7118

★1154★
Lac Courte Oreilles Governing Board
Head Start Progr am
Rte. 2, Box 2700   Ph: (715)634-8934
Hayward, WI 54843   Fax: (715)634-4797

★1155★
Lac du Flambeau Tribal Council
Head Start Program
2899 Hwy. 47   Ph: (715)588-3303
Lac Du Flambeau, WI 54538   Fax: (715)588-3243

★1156★
Oneida Tribal Business Committee
Head Start Program
PO Box 365   Ph: (920)869-1260
Oneida, WI 54155   Fax: (920)869-4066

★1157★
Stockbridge-Munsee Tribal Council
Head Start Program
W°3429 Cherry St.   Ph: (715)793-4100
Bowler, WI 54416   Fax: (715)793-4985

★1158★
Wisconsin Winnebago Business Committee
Head Start Program
Education Department
W9814 Airport Rd.
PO Box 667   Ph: (715)284-4915
Black River Falls, WI 54615   Fax: (715)284-1760

★1159★
Shoshone and Arapahoe Tribes
Head Start Program
PO Box 308   Ph: (307)332-7163
Fort Washakie, WY 82514   Fax: (307)332-7224

Schools

★1160★
Black Mesa Community School
PO Box 97   Ph: (520)674-3632
Pinon, AZ 86510   Fax: (520)674-3632
School Type: Contract day school; grades K-8.

★1161★
Blackwater Community School
Rte. 1, Box 95   Ph: (520)215-5859
Coolidge, AZ 85228   Fax: (520)215-5862
School Type: Contract day school; grades K-2.

★1162★
Chilchinbeto Day School
PO Box 547
Kayenta, AZ 86033   Ph: (520)697-8448
School Type: BIA day school; grades K-8.

★1163★
Chinle Boarding School
PO Box 70   Ph: (520)781-6221
Many Farms, AZ 86538   Fax: (520)781-6376
School Type: BIA on-reservation boarding school; grades K-8.

★1164★
Cibecue Community School
PO Box 80068   Ph: (520)332-2444
Cibecue, AZ 85911   Fax: (520)332-2341
School Type: Grant day school; grades K-9.

★1165★
Cottonwood Day School
Navajo Rt. 4   Ph: (520)725-3256
Chinle, AZ 86503   Fax: (520)725-3243
School Type: BIA day school; grades K-8.

★1166★
Dennehotso Boarding School
PO Box 2570   Ph: (520)658-3201
Dennehotso, AZ 86535   Fax: (520)658-3221
School Type: BIA on-reservation boarding school; grades K-8.

★1167★
Dilcon Boarding School
HC 63 Box G   Ph: (520)657-3211
Winslow, AZ 86047   Fax: (520)657-3370
School Type: BIA on-reservation boarding school; grades K-8.

★1168★
Gila Crossing Day School
PO Box 10   Ph: (520)550-4834
Laveen, AZ 85339   Fax: (520)550-4252
School Type: BIA day school; grades K-6.

★1169★
Greyhills High School
PO Box 160   Ph: (520)283-6271
Tuba City, AZ 86045   Fax: (520)283-6604
School Type: Grant boarding school; grades 9-12.

★1170★
Havasupai School
PO Box 40   Ph: (520)448-2901
Supai, AZ 86435   Fax: (602)448-2551
School Type: Contract day school; grades K-8.

★1171★
Holbrook Dormitory
PO Box 758   Ph: (520)524-6222
Holbrook, AZ 86025   Fax: (520)524-2231
School Type: BIA peripheral dormitory; grades 9-12.

★1172★
Hopi Day School
PO Box 42   Ph: (520)734-2468
Kykotsmovi Village, AZ 86039   Fax: (520)734-2470
School Type: BIA day school; grades K-6.

★1173★
Hopi High School
PO Box 337   Ph: (520)738-5111
Keams Canyon, AZ 86034   Fax: (520)738-5333
School Type: BIA day school; grades 7-12.

★1174★
Hotevilla Bacavi Community School
PO Box 48   Ph: (520)734-2462
Hotevilla, AZ 86030   Fax: (520)734-2225
School Type: Contract day school; grades K-6.

★1175★
Hunters Point Boarding School
PO Box 99   Ph: (520)871-4439
Saint Michaels, AZ 86511   Fax: (520)871-4435
School Type: BIA on-reservation boarding school; grades K-5.

★1176★
John F. Kennedy Day School
PO Box 130   Ph: (520)338-4593
WhiteRiver, AZ 85941   Fax: (520)338-4592
School Type: BIA day school; grades K-8.

★1177★
Kaibeto Boarding School
PO Box 1420   Ph: (520)673-3480
Kaibito, AZ 86053   Fax: (520)673-3489
School Type: BIA on-reservation boarding school; grades K-8.

★1178★
Keams Canyon Boarding School
PO Box 397   Ph: (520)738-2385
Keams Canyon, AZ 86034   Fax: (520)738-5519
School Type: Cooperative boarding school; grades K-6.

★1179★
Leupp Schools, Inc.
PO Box HC-61, Box D   Ph: (520)686-6211
Winslow, AZ 86047   Fax: (520)686-6216
School Type: Grant boarding school; grades K-12.

★1180★
Little Singer Community School
Star Rte. Box 239   Ph: (520)526-6680
Winslow, AZ 86047   Fax: (520)526-8994
School Type: Grant day school; grades K-6.

★1181★
Low Mountain Boarding School
Chinle, AZ 86503   Ph: (520)725-3308
                                     Fax: (520)725-3306
School Type: BIA on-reservation boarding school; grades K-4.

★1182★
Lukachukai Boarding School
Navajo Rte. 13   Ph: (520)787-2301
Lukachukai, AZ 86507   Fax: (520)787-2311
School Type: BIA on-reservation boarding school; grades K-8.

★1183★
Many Farms High School
PO Box 307   Ph: (520)781-6226
Many Farms, AZ 86538   Fax: (520)781-6355
School Type: BIA on-reservation boarding school; grades 9-12.

★1184★
Moencopi Day School
PO Box 185   Ph: (520)283-5361
Tuba City, AZ 86045   Fax: (520)283-4662
School Type: BIA day school; grades K-6.

★1185★
Pine Springs Boarding School
PO Box 4198   Ph: (602)871-4198
Houck, AZ 86506-0198   Fax: (520)871-4341
School Type: BIA on-reservation boarding schools; grades K-3.

★1186★
Pinon Dormitory
PO Box 159   Ph: (520)725-3250
Pinon, AZ 86510   Fax: (520)725-3232
School Type: Contract peripheral dormitory; grades 1-5.

★1187★
Polacca Day School
PO Box 750   Ph: (520)737-2581
Polacca, AZ 86042   Fax: (520)737-2323
School Type: BIA day school; grades K-6.

★1188★
Red Lake Day School
PO Box 39   Ph: (520)283-6325
Tonalea, AZ 86044   Fax: (520)283-6326
School Type: BIA day school; grades K-8.

★1189★
Rock Point Community School
Rock Point, AZ 86545   Ph: (520)659-4224
                                     Fax: (520)659-4235
School Type: Contract day school; grades K-12.

★1190★
Rough Rock Demonstration School
RRTP#PTT
HC61 Box 1480   Ph: (520)728-3311
Chinle, AZ 86503   Fax: (520)728-3502
School Type: Grant boarding school; grades K-12.

★1191★
Salt River Day School
Rte. 1, Box 117
Scottsdale, AZ 85256   Ph: (602)946-2306
School Type: BIA day school; grades K-6.

★1192★
San Simon School
HC 02, Box 92   Ph: (520)362-2231
Sells, AZ 85634   Fax: (520)362-2405
School Type: BIA day school; grades K-8.

★1193★
Santa Rosa Boarding School
HC02 Box 400   Ph: (602)361-2331
Sells, AZ 85634   Fax: (520)361-2511
School Type: BIA on-reservation boarding school; grades K-8.

★1194★
Santa Rosa Ranch School
HCO2 Box 7570   Ph: (520)383-2359
Tucson, AZ 85634   Fax: (520)383-3960
School Type: BIA day school; grades K-8.

★1195★
Seba Dalkai Boarding School
HC-63 Box H   Ph: (520)657-3208
Winslow, AZ 86047   Fax: (520)657-3224
School Type: BIA on-reservation boarding school; grades K-6.

★1196★
Second Mesa Day School
PO Box 98   Ph: (520)737-2571
Second Mesa, AZ 86043   Fax: (520)737-2565
School Type: BIA day school; grades K-6.

★1197★
Teecnospos Boarding School
Teec Nos Pos, AZ 86514   Ph: (602)656-3451
School Type: BIA on-reservation boarding school; grades K-8.

★1198★
Theodore Roosevelt School
PO Box 567
Fort Apache, AZ 85926   Ph: (520)338-1009
School Type: BIA on-reservation boarding school; grades 4-12.

★1199★
Tohono O'Odham High School
HC 02 Box 513   Ph: (520)362-2400
Sells, AZ 85634   Fax: (520)362-2256
School Type: BIA day school; grades 9-12.

★1200★
Tuba City Boarding School
PO Box 187
Tuba City, AZ 86045   Ph: (520)283-2330
School Type: BIA on-reservation boarding school; grades K-8.

★1201★
Wide Ruins Boarding School
PO Box 309   Ph: (520)652-3251
Chambers, AZ 86502   Fax: (520)652-3252
School Type: BIA on-reservation boarding school; grades K-5.

★1202★
Miccosukee Indian School
PO Box 440021, Tamiami Station   Ph: (305)223-8380
Miami, FL 33144   Fax: (305)223-1011
School Type: Contract day school; grades K-12.

★1203★
Sho'Ban School District No. 512
PO Box 790   Ph: (208)238-4200
Fort Hall, ID 83203   Fax: (208)238-2628
School Type: Grant day school; grades 6-12.

★1204★
Sac and Fox Settlement School
1349 Meskwaki Rd.
Tama, IA 52339
Ph: (515)484-4990
Fax: (515)484-3264
School Type: Contract day school; pre-K to grades 6.

★1205★
Kickapoo Nation School
PO Box 106
Powhattan, KS 66527
Ph: (785)474-3550
School Type: Contract day school; grades K-12.

★1206★
Chitimacha Day School
3613 Chitimacha Trail
Jeanerette, LA 70544
Ph: (318)923-9960
Fax: (318)923-7346
School Type: BIA day school; grades K-8.

★1207★
Beatrice Rafferty School
RR 1 Box 338
Perry, ME 04667
Ph: (207)853-6085
Fax: (207)853-6210
School Type: Contract day school; grades K-8.

★1208★
Indian Island School
1 River Rd.
PO Box 566
Indian Island, ME 04468
Ph: (207)827-4285
Fax: (207)827-3599
School Type: Contract day school; grades K-8.

★1209★
Indian Township School
HCR 78 Box 1A
Peter Dana Point
Princeton, ME 04668
Ph: (207)796-2362
Fax: (207)796-2726
School Type: Contract day school; grades Pre-K to 8.

★1210★
Chief Bug-O-Nay-Ge-Shig School
Rte. 3, Box 100
Cass Lake, MN 56633
Ph: (218)665-2282
Fax: (218)335-3024
School Type: Grant day school; grades K-12.

★1211★
Circle of Life Survival School
PO Box 447
White Earth, MN 56591
Ph: (218)983-3285
Fax: (218)983-3641
School Type: Grant day school; grades K-12.

★1212★
Fond du Lac Ojibway School
105 University Rd.
Cloquet, MN 55720
Ph: (218)878-4642
Fax: (218)879-0102
School Type: Grant day school; grades K-12.

★1213★
Little Black Bear Elementary School
109 University Rd.
Cloquet, MN 55720
Ph: (218)878-4691
Fax: (218)878-4620

★1214★
Nay-Ah-Shing School
HCR 67 Box 194
Onamia, MN 56359
Ph: (320)532-4181
Fax: (320)532-4209
School Type: Grant day school; grades 7-12.

★1215★
Bogue Chitto Elementary School
Rte. 2, Box 274
Philadelphia, MS 39350
Ph: (601)656-8611
Fax: (601)656-8648
School Type: Grant day school; grades K-8.

★1216★
Choctaw Central High School
Rte. 7, Box 72
Philadelphia, MS 39350
Ph: (601)656-8870
Fax: (601)656-7077
School Type: Grant boarding School; grades 7-12.

★1217★
Conehatta Elementary School
Rte. 1, Box 343
Conehatta, MS 39057-9717
Ph: (601)775-8254
Fax: (601)775-9229
School Type: Grant day school; grades K-8.

★1218★
Red Water Elementary School
555 Red Water Rd.
Carthage, MS 39051
Ph: (601)267-8500
Fax: (601)267-5193
School Type: Grant day school; grades K-8.

★1219★
Standing Pine Elementary School
538 Hway 487 E.
Carthage, MS 39051
Ph: (601)267-9225
Fax: (601)267-9129
School Type: Grant day school; grades K-6.

★1220★
Tucker Elementary School
Rte. 4, Box 351
Philadelphia, MS 39350
Ph: (601)656-8775
Fax: (601)656-9341
School Type: Grant day school; grades K-8.

★1221★
Blackfeet Dormitory
PO Box 880
Browning, MT 59417
Ph: (406)338-7441
Fax: (406)388-5725
School Type: BIA peripheral dormitory; grades 1-12.

★1222★
Busby School
PO Box 150
Busby, MT 59016
Ph: (406)592-3646
Fax: (406)592-3645
School Type: Grant day school; grades K-12.

★1223★
Two Eagle River School
PO Box 160
Pablo, MT 59855
Ph: (406)675-0292
Fax: (406)675-0294
School Type: Grant day school; grades 9-12.

★1224★
Duckwater Shoshone Elementary School
PO Box 140038
Duckwater, NV 89314
Ph: (702)863-0242
Fax: (702)863-0157
School Type: Grant day school; grades K-8.

★1225★
Alamo Navajo School
PO Box 907
Magdalena, NM 87825
Ph: (505)854-2635
Fax: (505)854-2545
School Type: Grant day school; grades K-12.

★1226★
Atsa Biyaazh Community School
c/o Shiprock Alternative Schools, Inc.
PO Box 1799
Shiprock, NM 87420
Ph: (505)368-5170
Fax: (505)368-5102
Objectives: Grant day school; offers Kindergarten program.

★1227★
Aztec Dormitory
1600 Lydia Pippey Rd.
Aztec, NM 87410
Ph: (505)334-6565
Fax: (505)334-8630
School Type: BIA peripheral dormitory; grades 9-12.

★1228★
Baca Community School
PO Box 509
Prewitt, NM 87045
Ph: (505)876-2769
Fax: (505)876-2310
School Type: BIA day school; grades K-3.

★1229★
Borrego Pass School
PO Box 670
Crownpoint, NM 87313
Ph: (505)786-5237
Fax: (505)786-7078
School Type: Grant day school; grades K-8.

★1230★
Bread Springs Day School
PO Box 1117
Gallup, NM 87305
Ph: (505)778-5665
Fax: (505)778-5692
School Type: BIA Day school; grades K-3.

★1231★
Chuska Boarding School
PO Box 321
Tohatchi, NM 87325
Ph: (505)733-2280
Fax: (505)733-2222
School Type: BIA on-reservation boarding school; grades K-8.

★1232★
Crownpoint Community School
PO Box 178
Crownpoint, NM 87313
Ph: (505)786-6160
Fax: (505)786-6163
School Type: BIA on-reservation boarding school; grades K-8.

★1233★
Crystal Boarding School
Navajo, NM 87328
Ph: (505)777-2385
Fax: (505)777-2648
School Type: BIA on-reservation boarding school; grades K-6.

★1234★
Dlo'Ay Azhi Community School
PO Box 789
Thoreau, NM 87323
Ph: (505)862-7525
Fax: (505)862-7910
School Type: BIA day school; grades K-6.

★1235★
Dzilth-na-o-dith-hle Community School
35 Rd. 7585, Box 5003
Bloomfield, NM 87413
Ph: (505)632-1697
Fax: (505)632-8563
School Type: BIA day school; grades K-8, grades 9-12 (Boarding).

★1236★
Huerfano Dormitory
PO Box 639
Bloomfield, NM 87413
Ph: (505)325-3411
Fax: (505)327-3591
School Type: BIA peripheral dormitory; grades 1-12; also offers a Kindergarten day school.

★1237★
Isleta Elementary School
PO Box 550
Isleta, NM 87022
Ph: (505)869-2321
Fax: (505)869-1625
School Type: BIA day school; grades K-6.

★1238★
Jemez Day School
PO Box 139
Jemez Pueblo, NM 87024
Ph: (505)834-7304
Fax: (505)834-7081
School Type: BIA day school; grades K-6.

★1239★
Laguna Elementary School
PO Box 191
Laguna, NM 87026
Ph: (505)552-9200
Fax: (505)552-7294
School Type: BIA day school; grades K-6.

★1240★
Lake Valley Navajo School
PO Box 748
Crownpoint, NM 87313
Ph: (505)786-5392
Fax: (505)786-5956
School Type: BIA on-reservation boarding school; grades K-8.

★1241★
Mariano Lake Community School
PO Box 787
Crownpoint, NM 87313
Ph: (505)786-5265
Fax: (505)786-5203
School Type: BIA on-reservation boarding school; grades K-5.

★1242★
Na'Neelzhiin Ji'Olta
HCR 79, Box 9
Cuba, NM 87013
Ph: (505)731-2272
Fax: (505)731-2252

School Type: BIA day school; grades K-8.

★1243★
Native American Preparatory School
PO Box 160
Rowe, NM 87562-0160
Ph: (505)474-6801
Fax: (505)474-6816
School Type: Residential school for gifted and talented Native American students; grades 9-11.

★1244★
Navajo Mission Academy
1200 W. Apache
Farmington, NM 87401
Ph: (505)326-6571
Fax: (505)564-8099
School Type: Grant boarding school; grades 9-12.

★1245★
Ojo Encino Day School
HCR 79, Box 7
Cuba, NM 87013
Ph: (505)731-2333
School Type: BIA day school; grades K-8.

★1246★
Pueblo Pintado Community School
HCR 79, Box 80
Cuba, NM 87013
Ph: (505)655-3341
Fax: (505)655-3342
School Type: BIA on-reservation boarding school; grades K-8.

★1247★
Pueblo of San Felipe
San Felipe School
PO Box 4343
San Felipe Pueblo, NM 87001
Ph: (505)867-3364
Fax: (505)867-6253
School Type: BIA day school; grades K-6.

★1248★
San Ildefonso Day School
Rte. 5, Box 308
Santa Fe, NM 87501
Ph: (505)455-2366
School Type: BIA day school; grades K-6.

★1249★
San Juan Day School
PO Box 1077
San Juan Pueblo, NM 87566
Ph: (505)852-2154
School Type: BIA day school; grades K-6.

★1250★
Santa Clara Day School
PO Box 2183
Espanola, NM 87532
Ph: (505)753-4406
Fax: (505)753-8866
School Type: BIA day school; grades K-6.

★1251★
Shiprock Alternative High School
PO Box 1799   Ph: (505)368-5144
Shiprock, NM 87420   Fax: (505)368-5102
School Type: Grant day school; Kindergarten and grades 9-12.

★1252★
Shiprock Reservation Dormitory
PO Box 1180
Shiprock, NM 87420   Ph: (505)368-5114
School Type: Contract peripheral dormitory; grades 7-12.

★1253★
Sky City Community School
PO Box 428   Ph: (505)552-6959
Pueblo of Acoma, NM 87034   Fax: (505)552-9455
School Type: BIA day school; grades K-8.

★1254★
Taos Day School
Drawer X   Ph: (505)758-3652
Taos, NM 87571   Fax: (505)758-1566
School Type: BIA day school; grades K-6.

★1255★
Tesuque Day School
Rte. 11, Box 2   Ph: (505)982-1516
Santa Fe, NM 87501   Fax: (505)982-2331
School Type: BIA day school; grades K-6.

★1256★
Tohaali Community School
PO Box 9857   Ph: (505)789-3201
Newcomb, NM 87455   Fax: (505)789-3202
School Type: BIA on-reservation boarding school; grades K-8.

★1257★
To'Hajiilee-He
PO Box 438   Ph: (505)831-6426
Laguna, NM 87026   Fax: (505)836-4914
School Type: BIA day school; grades K-12.

★1258★
Tse'ii'ahi' Community School
Box 828
Crownpoint, NM 87313   Ph: (505)786-5389
School Type: BIA day school; grades K-3. **Formerly:** Standing Rock Community School.

★1259★
Wingate High School
PO Box 2
Fort Wingate, NM 87316   Ph: (505)488-5972
Objectives: BIA on-reservation boarding school; grades 9-12.

★1260★
Zia Day School
Riverside Dr.
PO Box 350   Ph: (505)867-3553
San Ysidro, NM 87053   Fax: (505)867-5079
School Type: BIA day school; grades K-6.

★1261★
Cherokee Central School
Acquini Rd.
PO Box 134   Ph: (704)497-6370
Cherokee, NC 28719   Fax: (704)497-4373
School Type: Grant day school; grades K-12.

★1262★
Dunseith Day School
PO Box 759   Ph: (701)263-4636
Dunseith, ND 58329   Fax: (701)263-4200
School Type: BIA day school; grades K-6.

★1263★
Four Winds Community School
PO Box 199   Ph: (701)766-4161
Fort Totten, ND 58335   Fax: (701)766-4766
School Type: Grant day school; grades K-8.

★1264★
Mandaree Day School
PO Box 488   Ph: (701)759-3311
Mandaree, ND 58757   Fax: (701)759-3493
School Type: Grant day school; grades K-12.

★1265★
Ojibwa Indian School
Box 600   Ph: (701)477-3108
Belcourt, ND 58316   Fax: (701)477-6039
School Type: Contract day school; grades K-8.

★1266★
Standing Rock Community School
PO Box 377   Ph: (701)854-3865
Fort Yates, ND 58538   Fax: (701)854-3878
School Type: BIA day school; grades K-12.

★1267★
Theodore Jamerson Elementary School
3315 University Dr.   Ph: (701)255-3285
Bismarck, ND 58504   Fax: (701)255-7545
School Type: Grant day school; grades K-8.

★1268★
Turtle Mountain Elementary and Middle School
PO Box 440
Belcourt, ND 58316   Ph: (701)477-6471
School Type: Cooperative day school; grades K-8.

★1269★
Turtle Mountain High School
PO Box 440
Belcourt, ND 58316   Ph: (701)477-6471
School Type: Contract day school; grades 9-12.

★1270★
Twin Buttes Day School
Rte. 1, Box 65   Ph: (701)938-4396
Halliday, ND 58636   Fax: (701)938-4398
School Type: Grant day school; grades K-8.

★1271★
Wahpeton Indian Boarding School
832 8th St. N.   Ph: (701)642-3796
Wahpeton, ND 58075   Fax: (701)642-5880
School Type: BIA off-reservation boarding school; grades 4-8.

★1272★
White Shield School
HC1, Box 45   Ph: (701)743-4350
Roseglen, ND 58775   Fax: (701)743-4501
School Type: Grant day school; grades K-12.

★1273★
Carter Seminary
2400 Chickasaw Blvd.   Ph: (580)223-8547
Ardmore, OK 73401   Fax: (580)223-6325
School Type: Grant peripheral dormitory; grades 1-12.

★1274★
Eufaula Dormitory
716 Swadley Dr.   Ph: (918)689-2522
Eufaula, OK 74432   Fax: (918)689-2438
School Type: Grant peripheral dormitory; grades 1-12.

★1275★
Jones Academy
HCR 74, Box 102-5   Ph: (918)297-2518
Hartshorne, OK 74547   Fax: (918)297-2364
School Type: Grant peripheral school; grades 1-12.

★1276★
Riverside Indian School
Rte. 1   Ph: (405)247-6673
Anadarko, OK 37005   Fax: (405)247-5529
School Type: BIA off-reservation boarding school; grades 2-12.

★1277★
Sequoyah High School
PO Box 520   Ph: (918)456-0631
Tahlequah, OK 74465   Fax: (918)456-0634
School Type: Grant off-reservation boarding school; grades 9-12.

★1278★
Chemawa Indian School
3700 Chemawa Rd. NE   Ph: (503)399-5721
Salem, OR 97305-1199   Fax: (503)399-5870
School Type: BIA off-reservation boarding school; grades 9-12.

★1279★
American Horse School
PO Box 660   Ph: (605)455-2480
Allen, SD 57714   Fax: (605)455-2249
School Type: BIA day school; grades K-8.

★1280★
Cheyenne-Eagle Butte School
PO Box 672   Ph: (605)964-8744
Eagle Butte, SD 57625   Fax: (605)964-8700
School Type: Cooperative boarding school; grades K-12.

★1281★
Crazy Horse School
PO Box 260   Ph: (605)462-6511
Wanblee, SD 57577   Fax: (605)462-6601
School Type: Grant day school; grades K-12.

★1282★
Crow Creek Reservation High School
Box 12   Ph: (605)852-2455
Stephan, SD 57346   Fax: (605)852-2401
School Type: Grant boarding school; grades 7-12.

★1283★
Enemy Swim Day School
RR 1, Box 87   Ph: (605)947-4605
Waubay, SD 57273   Fax: (605)947-4188
School Type: Contract day school; grades K-3.

★1284★
Flandreau Indian School
1000 N. Cresent St.   Ph: (605)997-2724
Flandreau, SD 57028   Fax: (605)997-2601
School Type: BIA off-reservation boarding school; grades 9-12.

★1285★
Fort Thompson Elementary School
PO Box 469   Ph: (605)245-2372
Fort Thompson, SD 57339   Fax: (605)245-2310
School Type: Cooperative day school; grades K-6.

★1286★
Little Eagle Day School
PO Box 26   Ph: (605)823-4235
Little Eagle, SD 57639   Fax: (605)823-2292
School Type: BIA day school; grades K-8.

★1287★
Little Wound Day School
PO Box 500   Ph: (605)455-2461
Kyle, SD 57752   Fax: (605)455-2340
School Type: Grant day school; grades K-12.

★1288★
Loneman Day School
PO Box 50   Ph: (605)867-5633
Oglala, SD 57764   Fax: (605)867-5109
School Type: Grant day school; grades K-8.

★1289★
Lower Brule Day School
PO Box 245   Ph: (605)473-5510
Lower Brule, SD 57548   Fax: (605)473-0217
School Type: Cooperative day school; grades K-12.

★1290★
Marty Indian School
PO Box 187   Ph: (605)384-5431
Marty, SD 57361   Fax: (605)384-5933
School Type: Grant boarding school; grades K-12.

★1291★
Pierre Indian Learning Center
3001 E. Sully   Ph: (605)224-8661
Pierre, SD 57501-4419   Fax: (605)224-8465
School Type: Contract boarding school; grades 1-8.

★1292★
Pine Ridge School
PO Box 1202   Ph: (605)867-5198
Pine Ridge, SD 57770   Fax: (605)867-5482
School Type: BIA on-reservation boarding school; grades K-12.

★1293★
Porcupine Day School
PO Box 180   Ph: (605)867-5336
Porcupine, SD 57772   Fax: (605)867-5480
School Type: Grant day school; grades K-8.

★1294★
Rock Creek Day School
PO Box 127   Ph: (605)823-4971
Bullhead, SD 57621   Fax: (605)823-4350
School Type: BIA day school; grades K-8.

★1295★
Rosebud Dormitories
PO Box 69
Mission, SD 57555   Ph: (605)856-4486
School Type: BIA peripheral dormitory; grades 1-12.

★1296★
St. Francis Indian School
PO Box 379   Ph: (605)747-2299
Saint Francis, SD 57572   Fax: (605)747-2379
School Type: Grant day school; grades K-12.

★1297★
Takini School
HC 77, Box 537   Ph: (605)538-4399
Howes, SD 57748   Fax: (605)538-4315
School Type: Grant day school; grades K-12.

★1298★
Tiospa Zina Tribal School
PO Box 719   Ph: (605)698-3953
Agency Village, SD 57262   Fax: (605)698-7873
School Type: Grant day school; grades K-12.

★1299★
White Horse Day School
Whitehorse, SD 57661   Ph: (605)733-2457
School Type: BIA day school; grades K-8.

★1300★
Wounded Knee School District
PO Box 350   Ph: (605)867-5433
Manderson, SD 57756   Fax: (605)867-1219
School Type: Grant day school; grades K-8.

★1301★
Aneth Community School
PO Drawer 600   Ph: (435)651-3271
Montezuma Creek, UT 84534   Fax: (435)651-3272
School Type: BIA on-reservation boarding school; grades K-6.

★1302★
Richfield Dormitory
PO Box 638   Ph: (435)896-5101
Richfield, UT 84701   Fax: (435)896-6157
School Type: BIA peripheral dormitory; grades 9-12.

★1303★
Lummi Tribal School System
2530 Kwina Rd.
Bellingham, WA 98225   Ph: (360)384-1489
School Type: Grant day school; K-8.

★1304★
Muckleshoot Tribal School
39015 172nd Ave., SE   Ph: (253)939-3311
Auburn, WA 98092   Fax: (253)939-5311
School Type: Grant day school; grades K-3.

★1305★
Lac Courte Oreilles Ojibwa School
Rte. 2, Box 2800   Ph: (715)634-8924
Hayward, WI 54843   Fax: (715)634-6058
School Type: Grant day school; grades K-12.

★1306★
Menominee Tribal School
Menominee Indian Tribe
PO Box 39   Ph: (715)756-2354
Neopit, WI 54150   Fax: (715)756-2364
School Type: Grant day school; grades K-8.

★1307★
Oneida Tribal School
c/o Oneida Tribe
Box 365   Ph: (920)869-2795
Oneida, WI 54155-0365   Fax: (920)869-4045
School Type: Grant day school; grades K-12.

★1308★
St. Stevens Indian School
PO Box 345   Ph: (307)856-4147
Saint Stephens, WY 82524   Fax: (307)856-3742
School Type: Grant day school; grades pre-K to 12.

Community Colleges

★1309★
Dine Community College
PO Box 126   Ph: (602)724-3311
Tsaile, AZ 86556   Fax: (602)724-3327

★1310★
Navajo Community College
PO Box 126   Ph: (602)724-3311
Tsaile, AZ 86556   Fax: (602)724-3327

★1311★
D-Q University
PO Box 409   Ph: (916)758-0470
Davis, CA 95617   Fax: (916)758-4891

★1312★
Haskell Indian Junior College
PO Box H1305   Ph: (785)749-8450
Lawrence, KS 66046   Fax: (785)749-8429

★1313★
Bay Mills Community College
12214 West Lake Shore Dr.   Ph: (906)248-3354
Brimley, MI 49715   Fax: (906)248-3351

★1314★
Fond du Lac Community College
2101 14th St.   Ph: (218)879-0800
Cloquet, MN 55720   Fax: (218)879-0814

★1315★
Blackfeet Community College
PO Box 819   Ph: (406)338-5441
Browning, MT 59417   Fax: (406)338-7808

★1316★
Dull Knife Memorial College
PO Box 98   Ph: (406)477-6215
Lame Deer, MT 59043   Fax: (406)477-6219

★1317★
Fort Belknap Community College
PO Box 159   Ph: (406)353-2607
Harlem, MT 59526   Fax: (406)353-2898

★1318★
Fort Peck Community College
PO Box 398   Ph: (406)768-5551
Poplar, MT 59255   Fax: (406)768-5552

★1319★
Little Big Horn Community College
PO Box 370   Ph: (406)638-2228
Crow Agency, MT 59022   Fax: (406)638-2229

★1320★
Salish Kootenai College
PO Box 117   Ph: (406)675-4800
Pablo, MT 59855   Fax: (406)675-4801

★1321★
Stone Child Community College
Rocky Boy RR, Box 1082   Ph: (406)395-4313
Box Elder, MT 59521   Fax: (406)395-4836

★1322★
Stone Child Community College
Rocky Boy Rte., Box 1082   Ph: (406)395-4313
Box Elder, MT 59521   Fax: (406)395-4836

★1323★
Little Priest Tribal College
PO Box 270   Ph: (402)878-2380
Winnebago, NE 68071   Fax: (402)878-2355

★1324★
Nebraska Indian Community College (Macy)
PO Box 428   Ph: (402)837-5078
Macy, NE 68039   Fax: (402)837-4183

★1325★
Nebraska Indian Community College (Niobrara)
RR 2, Box 164   Ph: (402)857-2434
Niobrara, NE 68760   Fax: (402)857-2543

★1326★
Nebraska Indian Community College (Winnebago)
PO Box 752   Ph: (402)878-2414
Winnebago, NE 68071   Fax: (402)878-2522

★1327★
Crownpoint Institute of Technology
PO Box 849   Ph: (505)786-5851
Crownpoint, NM 87313   Fax: (505)786-5644

★1328★
Southwest Indian Polytechnic Institute
Coors Rd. NW
PO Box 10140   Ph: (505)897-5347
Albuquerque, NM 87184   Fax: (505)897-5343

★1329★
Candeska Cikana Community College
PO Box 269
Fort Totten, ND 57625   Ph: (605)964-6045

★1330★
Fort Berthold Community College
PO Box 490   Ph: (701)627-3665
New Town, ND 58763   Fax: (701)627-3609

★1331★
Little Hoop Community College
Box 269   Ph: (701)766-4415
Fort Totten, ND 58335   Fax: (701)766-4077

★1332★
Sitting Bull College
HC1, Box 4   Ph: (701)854-3861
Fort Yates, ND 58538   Fax: (701)854-3403

★1333★
Turtle Mountain Community College
PO Box 340   Ph: (701)477-5605
Belcourt, ND 58316   Fax: (701)477-5028

★1334★
United Tribes Technical College
3315 University Dr.   Ph: (701)255-3285
Bismarck, ND 58501   Fax: (701)255-1844

★1335★
Cheyenne River Community College
PO Box 220   Ph: (605)964-8635
Eagle Butte, SD 57625   Fax: (605)964-1144

★1336★
Oglala Lakota College
PO Box 490   Ph: (605)455-2321
Kyle, SD 57752   Fax: (605)455-2787

★1337★
Sinte Gleska College
PO Box 490   Ph: (605)747-2263
Rosebud, SD 57570   Fax: (605)747-2098

★1338★
Sisseton Wahpeton Community College
PO Box 689   Ph: (605)698-3966
Agency Village, SD 57262   Fax: (605)698-3132

★1339★
Northwest Indian College
2522 Kwina Rd.   Ph: (360)676-2772
Bellingham, WA 98226   Fax: (360)738-0136

★1340★
Lac Courte Oreilles Ojibwa Community College
13466 W. Trepania Rd.
RR 2, Box 2357   Ph: (715)634-4790
Hayward, WI 54843-2181   Fax: (715)634-5049

Studies Programs

─────── Two-Year Programs ───────

★1341★
Bacone College
Native American Studies Program
2299 Old Bacone Rd.   Ph: (918)683-4581
Muskogee, OK 74403   Fax: (918)682-5514

★1342★
Blackfeet Community College
Native American Studies Program
Blackfeet Studies Department
Box 819   Ph: (406)338-5421
Browning, MT 59417   Fax: (406)338-3272

★1343★
College of the Redwoods
Native American Studies Program
Eureka, CA 95501   Ph: (707)445-6761

★1344★
D-Q University
Native American Studies Program
PO Box 409   Ph: (530)758-0470
Davis, CA 95617-0409   Fax: (530)758-4891

★1345★
Dull Knife Memorial College
Native American Studies Program
PO Box 98   Ph: (406)477-6215
Lame Deer, MT 59043   Fax: (406)477-6219

★1346★
Fort Peck Community College
Native American Studies Program
Box 398   Ph: (406)768-5553
Poplar, MT 59255   Fax: (406)768-5552

★1347★
Nebraska Indian Community College
Native American Studies Program
PO Box 428   Ph: (402)837-5078
Winnebago, NE 68071   Fax: (402)837-1483

★1348★
Palomar Community College
Native American Studies Program
1140 West Mission Rd.   Ph: (760)744-1150
San Marcos, CA 92069   Fax: (760)744-8123

★1349★
Rogers State College
Native American Studies Program
1701 Will Rogers Blvd.
Claremore, OK 74017   Ph: (918)341-7510

★1350★
Rose State College
Native American Studies Program
6420 S. E. 15th St.
Midwest City, OK 73110   Ph: (405)736-0203

★1351★
Salish Kootenai College
Native American Studies Program
PO Box 117   Ph: (406)675-4800
Pablo, MT 59855   Fax: (406)675-4801

★1352★
Santa Barbara City College
Native American Studies Program
721 Cliff Dr.   Ph: (805)965-0581
Santa Barbara, CA 93109   Fax: (805)963-7222

★1353★
Scottsdale Community College
Native American Studies Program
9000 E. Chaparral Rd.   Ph: (602)423-6139
Scottsdale, AZ 85250   Fax: (602)423-6200

★1354★
Standing Rock College
Sitting Bull College
HC1 Box 4   Ph: (701)854-3862
Fort Yates, ND 58538   Fax: (701)854-3403

Four-Year Programs

★1355★
Bemidji State University
Native American Studies Program
Bemidji, MN 56601   Ph: (218)755-2027
          Fax: (218)755-4048

★1356★
Black Hills State University
Native American Studies Program
USB 9502   Ph: (605)642-6343
Spearfish, SD 57799-9502   Free: 800-255-2487
          Fax: (605)642-6024

★1357★
California State University, Hayward
Hayward, CA 94542-3000   Ph: (510)885-3817

★1358★
California State University, Sacramento
Native American Studies Program
6000 J. St   Ph: (916)278-3901
Sacramento, CA 95819-6013   Fax: (916)278-5156

★1359★
Colgate University
Native American Studies Program
13 Oak Dr.   Ph: (315)824-1000
Hamilton, NY 13346   Fax: (315)228-7187

★1360★
College of St. Scholastica
Native American Studies Program
1200 Kenwood   Ph: (218)723-6046
Duluth, MN 55811   Fax: (218)723-6290

★1361★
Cornell University
410 Thurston Avenue   Ph: (607)255-5241
Ithaca, NY 14850   Fax: (607)255-0659

★1362★
Cornell University
American Indian Studies Program
600 1st St., West   Ph: (319)895-4477
Mt. Vernon, IA 52314   Free: 800-747-1112
          Fax: (319)895-4492

Remarks: Program includes Akew:kon, a residential center, library, and computer center devoted to American Indian studies.

★1363★
Dakota Wesleyan University
Native American Studies Program
1200 West University Ave.   Ph: (605)995-2650
Mitchell, SD 57301   Fax: (605)995-2699

★1364★
Dartmouth College
Native American Studies Program
Sherman House   Ph: (603)646-2875
Hanover, NH 03755   Fax: (603)646-0333

★1365★
Evergreen State College
Native American Studies Program
2700 Evergreen Parkway N.E.   Ph: (360)866-6000
Olympia, WA 98505   Fax: (360)866-6794

★1366★
Goddard College
Native American Studies Program
123 Pitkin Rd.   Ph: (802)454-8311
Plainfield, VT 05667   Fax: (802)454-8017

★1367★
Hampshire College
Native American Studies Program
893 West St.
Amherst, MA 01002-5001   Ph: (413)549-4600

★1368★
Humboldt State University
Arcata, CA 95521-8299   Ph: (707)826-4402

★1369★
Lake Superior State University
Sault Sainte Marie, MI 49783-1699   Ph: (906)635-2231
          Free: 800-682-4800
          Fax: (906)635-2111

★1370★
Montana State University-Bozeman
120 Hamilton Hall
Bozeman, MT 59717   Ph: (406)994-2452

★1371★
Montana State University-Northern
Havre, MT 59501-7751   Ph: (406)265-3704
          Free: 800-662-6132
          Fax: (406)265-3777

★1372★
Morningside College
Native American Studies Program
1501 Morningside   Ph: (712)274-5111
Sioux City, IA 51106   Free: 800-831-0806
          Fax: (712)274-5101

★1373★
Mount Senario College
Native American Studies
Ladysmith, WI 54848   Ph: (715)532-5511

★1374★
Northeastern State University
Native American Studies Program
600 North Grand Ave.   Ph: (918)456-5511
Tahlequah, OK 74464   Free: 800-722-9614
                              Fax: (918)458-2073

★1375★
Northland College
Native American Studies Program
1411 Ellis Ave.   Ph: (715)682-1224
Ashland, WI 54806   Fax: (715)682-1308

★1376★
Oglala Lakota College
Native American Studies
Kyle, SD 57752   Ph: (605)455-2321
                        Fax: (605)455-2787

★1377★
Pembroke State University
Native American Studies Program
UNCP American Indian Studies Department
PO Box 1510   Ph: (910)521-6000
Pembroke, NC 28372   Fax: (910)521-6164

★1378★
Prescott College
220 Grove Avenue   Ph: (602)776-7116
Prescott, AZ 86301-2990   Free: 800-737-0118
                                 Fax: (602)776-5137

★1379★
San Diego State University
American Indian Studies
San Diego, CA 92182-8134   Ph: (619)594-5384
                                  Fax: (619)594-2646

★1380★
Sinte Gleska College
Native American Studies
PO Box 490   Ph: (605)747-2263
Rosebud, SD 57570   Fax: (605)856-2011

★1381★
Sonoma State University
Native American Studies Program
1801 E. Cotati   Ph: (707)664-2458
Rohnert Park, CA 94928   Fax: (707)664-2505

★1382★
South Hampton College
Native American Studies Program
239 Montauk Hwy.   Ph: (516)283-4000
Southampton, NY 11968   Fax: (516)287-8464

★1383★
State University of New York at Buffalo
Native American Studies Program
Hayes Annex A; Main Street Campus
Buffalo, NY 14214   Ph: (716)878-4000

★1384★
State University of New York College at Potsdam
Potsdam, NY 13676   Ph: (315)267-2180
                           Fax: (315)267-2163

★1385★
Union Institute
Native American Studies Program
440 E. McMillan St.   Ph: (513)861-6400
Cincinnati, OH 45206-1925   Fax: (513)861-0779

★1386★
University of California, Berkeley
Native American Studies Program
30 Stephens Hall   Ph: (510)642-2261
Berkeley, CA 94720-2570   Fax: (510)643-8084

★1387★
University of California at Davis
Native American Studies Program
Tecumseh Center
2401 Hart Hall   Ph: (530)752-3237
One Shields Ave.   Free: 800-523-2847
Davis, CA 95616   Fax: (530)752-7097

★1388★
The University of Iowa
Iowa City, IA 52242   Ph: (319)335-3847
                             Free: 800-553-4692
                             Fax: (319)335-1535

★1389★
University of Minnesota, Twin Cities Campus
Native American Studies Program
107 Scott Hall   Ph: (612)624-1338
72 Pleasant St., South East   Free: 800-826-0750
Minneapolis, MN 55455   Fax: (612)624-3858

★1390★
University of Nebraska, Lincoln
Native American Studies Program
Lyman Hall, Rm. 121   Ph: (402)472-1663
Lincoln, NE 68588   Fax: (402)472-0531

★1391★
University of North Dakota
Indian Studies Department
Box 7103 U. N. D.   Ph: (701)777-3821
Grand Forks, ND 58202   Fax: (701)777-3650

★1392★
University of Oklahoma
407 West Boyd   Ph: (405)325-2151
Norman, OK 73019   Free: 800-234-6868
                          Fax: (405)325-7478

★1393★
University of Science and Arts of Oklahoma
Native American Studies Program
PO Box 82345   Ph: (405)224-3140
Chickasha, OK 73018-0001   Fax: (405)521-6244

★1394★
University of Washington
Native American Studies Program
PO Box 354305   Ph: (206)543-9082
Seattle, WA 98195   Fax: (206)616-3122

★1395★
University of Wisconsin, Milwaukee
Milwaukee, WI 53201-0413   Ph: (414)229-6164

★1396★
Washington State University
342 French Administration Building
Pullman, WA 99164-1036   Ph: (509)335-5586

★1397★
Washington State University
Native American Studies Program
Pullman, WA 99164-2314　　　　Ph: (509)335-5586
　　　　　　　　　　　　　　　　Fax: (509)335-8368

★1398★
Wichita State University
1845 North Fairmount　　　　　Ph: (316)689-3085
Wichita, KS 67260　　　　　　　Free: 800-362-2594
　　　　　　　　　　　　　　　　Fax: (316)689-3795

─────── **Graduate Programs** ───────

★1399★
Goddard College
Native American Studies Graduate Program
123 Pitkin Rd.　　　　　　　　Ph: (802)454-8311
Plainfield, VT 05667　　　　　Fax: (802)454-8017

★1400★
Oglala Lakota College
Native American Studies Graduate Program
Kyle, SD 57752　　　　　　　　Ph: (605)455-2321
　　　　　　　　　　　　　　　　Fax: (605)455-2787

★1401★
Rutgers University
Minority Advancement Program
North American Indian Studies Program
25 Bishop Pl.　　　　　　　　　Ph: (732)932-1766
New Brunswick, NJ 08903　　　Fax: (732)932-7034

★1402★
San Francisco State University
School of Ethnic Studies
American Indian Studies Program
1600 Holloway Ave.　　　　　　Ph: (415)338-1693
San Francisco, CA 94112　　　Fax: (415)338-1739

★1403★
State University of New York at Buffalo
Native American Graduate Studies Program
Hayes Annex A; Main Street Campus
Buffalo, NY 14214　　　　　　　Ph: (716)878-4000

★1404★
Union Institute
Native American Studies Doctorate Program
440 E. McMillan St.　　　　　　Ph: (513)861-6400
Cincinnati, OH 45206-1525　　Fax: (513)861-0779

★1405★
University of Arizona
College of Arts and Sciences
American Indian Studies Program
Harvill Bldg., Rm. 430
PO Box 210076　　　　　　　　　Ph: (520)621-7108
Tucson, AZ 85721　　　　　　　Fax: (520)621-7952

★1406★
University of California, Berkeley
Ethnic Studies Graduate Program
30 Stephens Hall
Berkeley, CA 94720　　　　　　Ph: (510)642-2261
Remarks: Ethnic Studies program includes Native American studies.

★1407★
University of California, Los Angeles
College of Letters and Science
American Indian Studies Program
3220 Campbell Hall
Box 951548　　　　　　　　　　Ph: (310)825-4321
Los Angeles, CA 90095　　　　Fax: (310)206-7060

★1408★
University of Hawaii at Honolulu
School of Public Health
American Indian and Alaska Native Support Program
Educational Opportunities Program
Honolulu, HI 96822

★1409★
University of North Dakota
School of Medicine
Indians into Medicine Program (INMED)
PO Box 9037　　　　　　　　　　Ph: (701)777-3037
Grand Forks, ND 58203-9037　Fax: (701)777-3277
Remarks: Offers assistance to students who are preparing to study or currently studying to become physicians, nurses and other health professionals.

Scholarships, Fellowships, & Loans

★1410★
Adolph Van Pelt Special Fund for Indian Scholarships
Association on American Indian Affairs, Inc.
PO Box 268　　　　　　　　　　Ph: (605)698-3998
Sisseton, SD 57262-0268　　　Fax: (605)698-3316
Study Level: Undergraduate. **Award Type:** Scholarship. **Purpose:** To support study by Native Americans. **Applicant Eligibility:** Applicant must be an American Indian or Alaska Native Indian affiliated with a tribe. Candidate must be enrolled in an accredited U.S. university or college, as either a graduate or undergraduate student. **Selection Criteria:** Candidates are selected based on financial aid need and merit. **Funds Available:** Up to U.S.$800/year (first year: U.S.$500). **Applicant Details:** Write for application form and guidelines. Submit form with personal essay, proof of tribal affiliation and enrollment, two letters of recommendation, budget of educational costs and resources, and most recent copy of transcripts. **Application Deadline:** June 1. Notification by July 31.

★1411★
AIGC Fellowships
American Indian Graduate Center
4520 Montgomery Blvd. NE, Ste. 1-B
Albuquerque, NM 87109-1291　Ph: (505)881-4584
Study Level: Graduate. **Award Type:** Fellowship. **Purpose:** To provide supplemental financial aid to Native American and Alaska Native graduate students pursuing master's and doctoral degrees. **Applicant Eligibility:** Applicant must be a member of a federally-recognized Native American or Alaska Native group, and enrolled full-time at an accredited graduate program in the United States. Fellowship's value is determined by applicant's level of unmet financial need. Applicants must apply for campus-based aid, including loans. **Funds Available:** Amounts ranged from U.S.$250 to U.S.$3,000. **Applicant Details:** Write or phone AIGC for application packet, available from January through May. **Application Deadline:** June 1.

★1412★
AISES A.T. Anderson Memorial Scholarship
American Indian Science and Engineering
  Society
1630 30th St., Ste. 301   Ph: (303)939-0023
Boulder, CO 80301   Fax: (303)939-8150
Study Level: Graduate. **Award Type:** Scholarship. **Applicant Eligibility:** Applicants must be American Indian or Alaskan Native college students pursuing academic programs in the sciences, engineering, health related fields, business, natural resources, and math and science secondary education. Applicants must be members of AISES with at least one-quarter American Indian or recognized as a member of a tribe, be full-time students, and maintaining a GPA of 2.0 or higher. **Funds Available:** $1,000 award for undergraduate study; $2,000 award for graduate study. **Applicant Details:** Candidates must provide proof of American Indian blood. **Application Deadline:** June 15.

★1413★
Al Qoyawayma Award
American Indian Science and Engineering
  Society
1630 30th St., Ste. 301   Ph: (303)939-0023
Boulder, CO 80301   Fax: (303)939-8150
Study Level: Undergraduate. **Award Type:** Award. **Applicant Eligibility:** Applicants must be undergraduate or graduate students who are members of the AISES. They must be double majors in science or engineering and be pursuing a degree in the arts. **Selection Criteria:** Awards are based on leadership and academic achievement. **Applicant Details:** Applications must include the applicants official academic transcript, a typed personal essay, two letters of recommendation, and a Certificate of Indian Blood (CIB)/Tribal Enrollment. Prior scholarship recipients are not required to submit their CIB and are not given special consideration during the application evaluation.

★1414★
APA Planning Fellowships
American Planning Association
1776 Massachusetts Ave., NW, Ste. 400   Ph: (202)872-0611
Washington, DC 20036-1904   Fax: (202)872-0643
Study Level: Graduate. **Award Type:** Fellowship. **Purpose:** To encourage minority students to enter the planning profession and to support graduate studies in planning. **Applicant Eligibility:** Applicants must be Black, Hispanic, or Native American citizens of the United States or Canada. They must be enrolled or accepted for enrollment in a graduate planning program accredited by the Planning Accreditation Board. They must also document the need for financial assistance. Preference will be given to full-time students. Candidates must be nominated, but self-nominations are accepted. Fellowships are tenable for the first or second year of a graduate planning program. **Selection Criteria:** Applicants are chosen based on financial need, merit, and essay. **Funds Available:** U.S.$2,000-5,000. **Applicant Details:** Write for application form and guidelines. Submit form with a letter of nomination from a professor or school official (unless self-nominated); resume; personal statement describing academic and career goals; transcripts; statement of financial independence; letter of acceptance into a graduate planning program; and verification of expenses for one academic year of graduate study. **Application Deadline:** May 15. Award decisions are made in mid-June.

★1415★
Ardell Bjugstad Memorial Scholarships
South Dakota Board of Regents
207 E. Capitol Ave.   Ph: (605)773-3455
Pierre, SD 57501-3159   Fax: (605)773-5320
Study Level: Undergraduate. **Award Type:** Scholarship. **Applicant Eligibility:** Applicants must be entering freshman students who are majoring in agricultural production, agribusiness, agricultural sciences, or natural resources. Eligible participants are South Dakota or North Dakota residents who are enrolled members of a federally recognized tribe whose reservations are located either in South or North Dakota. Students may attend any post secondary institution that offers programs in the majors specified. **Funds Available:** U.S.$500 scholarship is awarded annually.

★1416★
Association on American Indian Affairs Displaced
  Homemaker Scholarships
Association on American Indian Affairs,
  Inc.
PO Box 268   Ph: (605)698-3998
Sisseton, SD 57262-0268   Fax: (605)698-3316
Study Level: Undergraduate. **Award Type:** Scholarship. **Purpose:** To help mid-life homemakers, both men and women, who are otherwise unable to fulfill their educational goals by providing support for up to three years with scholarships that financially account for their special needs as heads of households, as single parents, or as displaced homemakers. **Applicant Eligibility:** Applicants must be mid-life Native Americans who would not otherwise be able to finish their education. They must also provide evidence of at least 25 percent American Indian heritage. **Selection Criteria:** Applicants are selected based on their special needs as head of households, as single parents, or as displaced home makers. **Funds Available:** The program augments the usual and expected financial sources of educational money. It provides funds for child care, transportation, and some basic living expenses. **Applicant Details:** Application forms must be submitted with two letters of recommendation, a one- to two-page essay outlining applicant's life experience, personal monthly budget, copy of transcripts, most recent Financial Aid letter, and copy of either a Certificate of degree of Indian blood or Tribal enrollment card. **Application Deadline:** September 1 of each academic year.

★1417★
Bureau of Indian Affairs Higher Education Grant
Hopi Tribe Grants and Scholarship
  Program
PO Box 123   Ph: (520)734-2441
Kykotsmovi, AZ 86039   Fax: (520)734-2435
Study Level: Graduate. **Award Type:** Grant. **Purpose:** To enable eligible Hopi students the opportunity to obtain their professional degrees with the hope that they will return to the reservation and provide care and expertise to the Hopi people. **Applicant Eligibility:** Applicants must be enrolled members of the Hopi Tribe and be high school graduates or have earned their GED certificate. They must be enrolled at a regionally accredited college or university and pursuing a professional degree. Students pursuing vocational certification/diplomas are not eligible. Applicants are also required to meet the minimum applicable grade point average listed as follows: entering freshman must have a minimum 2.0 cumulative high school grade point average or a composite score of 45 percent on the GED exam; undergraduates must have a minimum 2.0 cumulative grade point average for all undergraduate coursework; and graduates, post-graduates, and professional students must be in good academic standing as defined by their institution. Applicants must apply for all available funding sources before being considered for Hopi grants and they must demonstrate financial need as determined by the school financial aid office. Both full and part-time students may apply. **Selection Criteria:** Grant is based on financial need. Eligible applicants who have completed files will be renewed on a first-come first-serve basis. **Funds Available:** Up to U.S.$2,500 per semester and up to U.S.$1,250 per summer session. Part-time students are eligible for books and tuition only. Undergraduate students may be funded up to a maximum of 10 semesters/15 quarters (no more than 5 terms can funded at a community college); and graduate students may be funded for a maximum of five semesters. **Applicant Details:** Applicants will first need to apply for Federal Aid and then must complete, sign, and submit a new application form for each academic year and a separate application for the summer session(s). They must submit a Financial Aid Analysis form to the school's financial aid office and submit to the HTGSP the Certificate of Indian Blood form. They must also request their high school and college/university to submit official transcripts or GED scores to the HTGSP. Online transcripts are not considered official. **Application Deadline:** July 31 for fall semester; November 30 for spring semester; and April 30 for summer session.

★1418★
Bureau of Indian Affairs Loans and Tribal Loans
Montana Guaranteed Student Loan
  Program
PO Box 203101   Ph: (406)444-6594
Helena, MT 59620   Fax: (406)444-0684
Study Level: Undergraduate. **Award Type:** Loan. **Applicant Eligibility:** Applicants must be Native American students who are recognized as American Indian, Eskimo, or Aleut by the federal government. They must demonstrate financial need.

★1419★
CERT Scholarship
Council of Energy Resource Tribes
1999 Broadway, Ste. 2600   Ph: (303)297-2378
Denver, CO 80202-3050   Fax: (303)296-5690
Study Level: Undergraduate. **Award Type:** Scholarship. **Purpose:** To assist American Indians pursuing degrees in the fields of engineering, physical sciences, and business. **Applicant Eligibility:** Candidates must be American Indian graduate or undergraduate students in one of the above areas of study or a related field, and hold a grade point average of at least 3.0/4.0. They must have completed CERT's pre-college program for recently graduated high school seniors. Scholarships are tenable at any accredited university in the United States. **Funds Available:** U.S.$1,000. **Applicant Details:** Write to the Student Services Coordinator for application form and guidelines. **Application Deadline:** Graduates: June 1; undergraduates: June 10.

★1420★
Cherokee Nation Graduate Scholarship
Cherokee Nation
Education Dept.
PO Box 948   Ph: (918)456-0671
Tahlequah, OK 74465-0948   Fax: (918)456-6485
Study Level: Graduate. **Award Type:** Scholarship. **Purpose:** To assist members of the Cherokee Nation to attain graduate degrees. **Applicant Eligibility:** Applicant must be a certified member of the Cherokee Nation who has a bachelor's degree and is enrolled in a master's program. Candidates in fields other than those listed above may be considered, but only on a case-by-case basis. **Funds Available:** U.S.$500 full-time, $250 part-time. **Applicant Details:** Write to the Department for application form and guidelines. Submit form with a copy of Certificate of Degree of Indian Blood; transcripts, including cumulative grade point average. **Application Deadline:** Fall semester : July 1; spring semester: November 1.

★1421★
Cheyenne-Arapaho Higher Education Assistance Program Grant
Cheyenne-Arapaho Tribal Offices
PO Box 38   Ph: (405)262-0345
Concho, OK 73022   Fax: (405)262-0745
Study Level: Undergraduate. **Award Type:** Grant. **Purpose:** To increase educational level of Cheyenne and Arapaho students. **Applicant Eligibility:** Applicants must be enrolled members of the Cheyenne-Arapaho Tribes of Oklahoma, high school or GED graduates, and approved for admission by the college of their choice. The applicant must need financial aid and show reasonable assurance of completing a four-year college degree program. Graduate and/or married students are also eligible. **Funds Available:** The amount of assistance is individually determined. For renewal, a new application and Financial Needs Analysis must be submitted each year. **Applicant Details:** A completed application requires: a Financial Needs Analysis form completed by the college or university Financial Aid Office showing an estimate of college expenses; a personal letter that indicates academic goals and financial needs; a high school or college transcript or GED certificate; and indication of having filed the ACT or FAF packet, which is obtainable from high school, college, or university financial aid offices. Recipients must maintain academic standing and social conduct acceptable to the education institution attended. They may also expect personal on-campus contact by their Native American Counselor for the purpose of providing supportive services. Grade reports or transcripts must be submitted after each term. **Application Deadline:** Application and all supporting materials

must be filed by June for the first semester and November for the second semester. Renewal application must be filed by June.

★1422★
Colonial Dames Indian Nurse Scholarships
The National Society of the Colonial
  DAMES of America
Indian Nurse Scholarship Awards
2305 Gillette Dr.
Wilmington, NC 28403   Ph: (910)763-6013
Study Level: Undergraduate. **Award Type:** Scholarship. **Applicant Eligibility:** Applicants must be American Indian high school graduates enrolled full-time in an accredited nursing program, where they have achieved good scholastic standing in the pre-nursing courses. They must also be within two years of completing the degree, maintaining the GPA required by the their school, in need of financial assistance, and should have a career goal directly related to the needs of the Indian people. In addition, candidates may not have received an Indian Health Service Scholarship. **Selection Criteria:** Selection is based on need, academic standing, and career objectives. **Funds Available:** A limited number of U.S.$500, U.S.$750, and U.S.$1,000 scholarships. **Applicant Details:** Candidates must be recommended by high school counselor or school official. **Application Deadline:** All year but most scholarships are awarded in September.

★1423★
Continental Society Daughters of Indian Wars Scholarship
Daughters of Indian Wars
Scholarship Coordinator
206 Springdale Dr.
La Grange, GA 30240
Study Level: Undergraduate. **Award Type:** Scholarship. **Applicant Eligibility:** Applicants must be certified members of a federally recognized tribe of Native Americans, plan to work on a reservation, be accepted or attending an accredited college or university, and maintain at least a 3.0 grade point average while carrying at least ten quarter hours or eight semester hours. **Selection Criteria:** Awards are granted based on financial need and academic excellence. **Funds Available:** US$500. Renewable. **Applicant Details:** Applicants must submit application, letters of recommendation, statements of financial need and career objective, transcripts, and an outline of extracurricular activities. **Application Deadline:** June 15.

★1424★
Emergency Aid and Health Professions Scholarships
Association on American Indian Affairs,
  Inc.
PO Box 268   Ph: (605)698-3998
Sisseton, SD 57262-0268   Fax: (605)698-3316
Study Level: Undergraduate. **Award Type:** Scholarship. **Applicant Eligibility:** Applicants must be college-level American Indian or Alaskan Native students registered for college and in need of emergency aid. **Selection Criteria:** Candidates are selected based on financial need and limited by the availability of funds. **Funds Available:** When funds are available, individual grants average between U.S.$50 and U.S.$300. **Applicant Details:** Applicants must submit a completed application, certificate of degree of Indian blood, a one- to two-page essay describing the specific nature of the emergency need, a budget of educational costs and resources, and a most recent copy of transcripts. **Application Deadline:** Applications may be filed at any time after college classes have begun.

★1425★
Falmouth Institute Scholarship
Falmouth Institute
3918 Prosperity, Ste. 302   Ph: (703)641-9100
Fairfax, VA 22031-3333   Fax: (703)641-1558
Study Level: Undergraduate. **Award Type:** Scholarship. **Purpose:** To assist Native American high school students in furthering their education. **Applicant Eligibility:** Applicants must be American Indian high school students planning to attend a two- or four-year accredited college or university. Proof of tribal enrollment is required. **Selection Criteria:** Selection is based on scholastic

achievement and financial need. **Funds Available:** U.S.$1,000. **Applicant Details:** Application form requests must be accompanied by a self-addressed, stamped envelope. **Application Deadline:** May 1.

★1426★
Frances C. Allen Fellowships
The Newberry Library
Division of Research and Education
60 W. Walton St.
Chicago, IL 60610-3380   Ph: (312)943-9090

Study Level: Graduate. **Award Type:** Fellowship. **Purpose:** To support women of Native American heritage who are pursuing advanced education. **Applicant Eligibility:** Applicant must be a woman of American Indian heritage who is pursuing an academic program beyond the undergraduate degree. Candidate may be working in any graduate or pre-professional field, but the particular purpose of the fellowship is to encourage study in the humanities and social sciences. Fellows are expected to spend a significant amount of the fellowship term in residence at the McNickle Center, which is part of the Newberry Library. **Funds Available:** Varies. **Applicant Details:** Write or call the Center for application guidelines. **Application Deadline:** February 1.

★1427★
Hopi Supplemental Grant
Hopi Tribe Grants and Scholarship
  Program
PO Box 123   Ph: (520)734-2441
Kykotsmovi, AZ 86039   Fax: (520)734-2435

Study Level: Graduate. **Award Type:** Grant. **Purpose:** To enable eligible Hopi students the opportunity to obtain their professional degrees with the hope that they will return to the reservation and provide care and expertise to the Hopi people. **Applicant Eligibility:** Applicants must be enrolled members of the Hopi Tribe and be high school graduates or have earned their GED certificate. They must be admitted and enrolled at a regionally accredited college or university and pursuing a professional degree. Students pursuing vocational certification/diplomas are not eligible. They are also required to meet the minimum applicable grade point average listed as follows: entering freshman must have a minimum 2.0 cumulative high school grade point average or a composite score of 45 percent on the GED exam; undergraduates must have a minimum 2.0 grade point average for all undergraduate coursework; graduates, post-graduates and professional degree students must be in good academic standing as defined by their university. Applicants must apply for all available funding sources before being considered for Hopi grants and they must demonstrate financial need as determined by the school Financial Aid Office. Both full and part-time students are eligible to apply. **Selection Criteria:** Grant is based on financial need. Eligible applicants who have completed files will be renewed on a first-come first-serve basis. **Funds Available:** Up to U.S.$1,000 per semester; up to U.S.$750 per summer session. Part-time students are eligible for books and tuition only; undergraduate students may be funded for a maximum of 10 semesters/15 quarters (no more than 5 terms can be funded at a community college); graduate students may be funded for a maximum of five semesters. **Applicant Details:** Applicants must first apply for Federal Aid and then must complete, sign, and submit a new application form for each academic year and a separate application for the summer session(s). They must submit the Financial Aid Analysis form to a school financial aid office and submit to the HTGSP a Certificate of Indian Blood form. They must also request their high school and college/university to submit official transcripts or GED scores to the HTGSP. Online transcripts are not considered official. **Application Deadline:** July 31 for fall semester; November 30 for spring semester; and April 30 for summer session.

★1428★
Hopi Tribe Adult Vocational Training
Hopi Tribe Grants and Scholarship
  Program
PO Box 123   Ph: (520)734-2441
Kykotsmovi, AZ 86039   Fax: (520)734-2435

Study Level: Undergraduate. **Award Type:** Other. **Applicant Eligibility:** Applicants must be enrolled members of the Hopi Tribe. They must be looking to acquire marketable vocational skills in the

following training activities: institutional training at an accredited public or private institution (vocational training may not exceed 24 months, with the exception of registered nurse training programs, which allow for a maximum of 36 months); apprenticeship training into accredited apprenticeship programs that are recognized by industry and labor; and on-the-job training with corporations, small businesses, associations, tribes or tribal enterprises recognized by industry and labor and approved by the Hopi Tribe Adult Vocational Training Program. **Applicant Details:** Applicants will first need to apply for Federal Aid and then must complete and submit an application form. They are also required to submit to the HTGSP Certification of Indian Blood and complete a statement reflecting their educational goals and plans.

★1429★
Hopi Tribe Educational Enrichment Grant
Hopi Tribe Grants and Scholarship
  Program
PO Box 123   Ph: (520)734-2441
Kykotsmovi, AZ 86039   Fax: (520)734-2435

Study Level: All. **Award Type:** Grant. **Applicant Eligibility:** Applicants must be enrolled members of the Hopi Tribe and students who have been accepted to participate in special activities and events that offer unique opportunities to develop leadership/personal skills, or to acquire educational/preoccupational experiences. This grant is open to students from grade four through college. Additional qualifications are included in the application package.

★1430★
Hopi Tribe Private High School Scholarship
Hopi Tribe Grants and Scholarship
  Program
PO Box 123   Ph: (520)734-2441
Kykotsmovi, AZ 86039   Fax: (520)734-2435

Study Level: High School. **Award Type:** Scholarship. **Purpose:** To encourage Hopi students to achieve and maintain a high level of academic excellence. **Applicant Eligibility:** Applicants must be enrolled members of the Hopi Tribe and enrolled and accepted in an accredited private high school. Entering freshmen must have a minimum 3.50 cumulative grade point average and continuing students must have a minimum 3.25 cumulative grade point average. Additional eligibility criteria is explained on the application form. **Selection Criteria:** Scholarship is based on academic excellence. **Applicant Details:** Applicants will first need to apply for Federal Aid and then must complete and submit an application form as well as a certificate of Indian Blood form. They must also request their high school to submit official transcripts to HTGSP. Online transcripts are not considered official. A statement reflecting the applicant's educational goals and plans is also required. **Application Deadline:** July 30.

★1431★
Hopi Tribe Scholarship
Hopi Tribe Grants and Scholarship
  Program
PO Box 123   Ph: (520)734-2441
Kykotsmovi, AZ 86039   Fax: (520)734-2435

Study Level: Graduate. **Award Type:** Scholarship. **Purpose:** To enable eligible Hopi students the opportunity to obtain their professional degrees with the hope that they will return to the reservation and provide care and expertise to the Hopi people. **Applicant Eligibility:** Applicants must be enrolled members of the Hopi Tribe. Applicants must be high school graduates or have earned their GED certificate, and they must be admitted and enrolled full-time at a regionally accredited college or university and pursuing a professional degree. Students pursuing vocational certification/diplomas are not eligible. Entering freshman must be in the top ten percent of their graduating class or score a minimum of 21 on the ACT test or 930 on the SAT test; undergraduates must have a minimum of 3.0 cumulative grade point average for all undergraduate coursework; graduates, post-graduates and professional degree students must have a minimum 3.2 cumulative grade point average for all graduate coursework. **Selection Criteria:** Scholarship is based on academic excellence and applicants need not demonstrate financial need. **Funds Available:** Up to U.S.$1,000 per semester and up to U.S.$2,000 per year. The number of terms funded follows: ten terms for undergraduates, five terms for graduates, and six terms for post-graduates. **Applicant Details:** Applicants first need to apply for Federal Aid and then must complete, sign, and submit an application form as well as a Certificate of Indian Blood form. They must also request their high school and college/university to submit official transcripts or GED scores to the HTGSP. Online transcripts are not considered official. Applicants must complete a statement reflecting their educational goals and plans. Graduate and postgraduate students, if not already on file, must provide written verification of admission from the graduate college and their specific program. **Application Deadline:** July 31.

★1432★
IHS Health Professions Compensatory Preprofessional Scholarship

Indian Health Service Scholarship
  Program
Indian Health Services
Twinbrook Plaza, Ste. 100A
12300 Twinbrook Parkway   Ph: (301)443-6197
Rockville, MD 20852   Fax: (301)443-6048

Study Level: Undergraduate. **Award Type:** Scholarship. **Applicant Eligibility:** Applicants must be American Indians or Alaska Natives, high school graduates or the equivalent, in good standing at the educational institution they are attending, have the capacity to complete a health professions course of study, and must intend to serve Indian People upon completion of professional health care degree as a health care provider in the discipline for which they are taking preparatory courses. Applicants must also be enrolled, or be accepted for enrollment, in courses that will prepare them for acceptance into health professions schools. Courses may be either compensatory (required to improve science, mathematics, or other basic skills and knowledge) or preprofessional (required in order to qualify for admission into a health professions program). **Selection Criteria:** Previous recipients who meet the continued eligibility requirements will be given priority consideration. **Funds Available:** Funding is available for a maximum of two years. Recipients must apply annually to receive continued funding beyond the initial award period. The level of scholarship benefits is contingent upon the availability of funds appropriated each fiscal year by the Congress of the United States and, therefore, is subject to yearly changes. The Scholarship Program will provide a monthly stipend to cover living expenses including room and board. Recipients will receive the stipend only during the academic period covered by their awards, August 1 to May 31.

★1433★
IHS Health Professions Pre-Graduate Scholarships

Indian Health Service Scholarship
  Program
Indian Health Service
Twinbrook Plaza, Ste. 100A
12300 Twinbrook Parkway   Ph: (301)443-6197
Rockville, MD 20852   Fax: (301)443-6048

Study Level: Undergraduate. **Award Type:** Scholarship. **Applicant Eligibility:** Applicants must be American Indians or Alaska Natives. Candidates must be high school graduates or the equivalent, and must have the capacity to complete a health professions course of study. Applicants must be enrolled, or accepted for enrollment, in a baccalaureate degree program in specific preprofessional areas (pre-medicine and pre-dentistry). Applicants may be seniors, juniors, sophomores, or freshmen (priority is given to applicants in this order). Applicants must be in good standing at the educational institution they are attending. Candidates must intend to serve Indian People upon completion of professional health care education as health care providers in the disciplines for which the students are enrolled at the pregraduate level. **Funds Available:** Funding is available for a maximum of four academic years. The level of scholarship benefits is contingent upon the availability of funds appropriated each fiscal year by the Congress of the United States and, therefore, is subject to yearly changes. The Scholarship Program will provide a monthly stipend to cover living expenses, tuition and educational expenses such as cost of books, uniforms, travel, rental of a post office box to use for receiving stipend checks, and room and board. Recipients will receive the stipend only during the academic period covered by their awards, August 1 to May 31.

★1434★
Katrin H. Lamon Resident Scholarship for Native Americans

School of American Research
Resident Scholarship Program
PO Box 2188
660 Garcia St.   Ph: (505)982-3583
Santa Fe, NM 87504-2188   Fax: (505)989-9809

Study Level: Doctorate. **Award Type:** Scholarship. **Purpose:** To foster the intellectual growth of Native American scholars pursuing significant research and writing. **Applicant Eligibility:** Applicant must be a Native American and be either a postdoctoral scholar, a retired scholar, or a Ph.D. candidate who has completed all requirements for the degree except the dissertation. Candidate may be working in any world area and on any topic within anthropology or a related discipline in the humanities, social sciences, or arts. Preference is given to applicants who have completed field work or basic research and analysis, and need time to write up their results. Awards are tenable at the School of American Research. **Selection Criteria:** Applications are evaluated primarily on the basis of overall excellence and significance of the project, in addition to such factors as clarity of presentation and the applicant's record of academic accomplishments. Preference will also be given to applicants whose fieldwork or basic researc h and analysis are complete and who need time to write up their results. Fellowships are awarded competitively on the basis of evaluations by a specially covened panel of scholars who represent a broad spectrum of intellectual expertise. **Funds Available:** Housing, office, monthly stipend, and library assistance. **Applicant Details:** Write to the resident scholar coordinator for application guidelines. Submit six copies of curriculum vitae and a research proposal of up to four pages. Three letters of recommendation are also required. **Application Deadline:** December 1. Awards are announced in March.

★1435★
Louie LeFlore/Grant Foreman Scholarship

Seminole Nation Higher Education
  Program
PO Box 1498   Ph: (405)257-6629
Wewoka, OK 74884   Fax: (405)257-3704

Study Level: Undergraduate. **Award Type:** Scholarship. **Applicant Eligibility:** Candidates must be members of one of the Five Civilized Tribes (Cherokee, Creek, Choctaw, Chickasaw, or Seminole) and majoring in nursing or pre-health and health professions, with a letter of acceptance to such a program as evidence. Only Oklahoma residents living within the respective tribal service area at the time of application are eligible. Applicants must also apply for financial aid and demonstrate financial need, if required by respective tribe. **Funds Available:** $650 to one student from one of the five tribes each year. The schedule is: 93-94, Choctaw Nation; 94-95, Seminole Nation; 95-96, Chickasaw Nation; 96-97, Cherokee Nation. Scholarships are not renewable. **Application Deadline:** July 1.

★1436★
Mark Ulmer Native American Scholarships

Triangle Native American Society
PO Box 26841
Raleigh, NC 27611-6841   Ph: (919)779-5936

Study Level: Undergraduate. **Award Type:** Scholarship. **Purpose:** To help North Carolina's American Indian students obtain a college education. **Applicant Eligibility:** Applicants must be American Indians who are residents of North Carolina for at least 12 months, be attending one of the four-year institutions that comprise the University of North Carolina system, have at least a 2.0 GPA, and be enrolled for the next quarter or semester. **Selection Criteria:** Selection is based on financial need, leadership and community involvement, and academic success. **Funds Available:** Two U.S.$500 scholarships per year. **Applicant Details:** Candidates must send a completed application with official postsecondary transcripts. **Application Deadline:** June 15.

★1437★
Massachusetts Indian Association Scholarships
Massachusetts Indian Association
  Scholarship Fund
245 Rockland Rd.
Carlisle, MA 01741

Study Level: Graduate. **Award Type:** Scholarship. **Purpose:** To help Native Americans fulfill their educational goals. **Applicant Eligibility:** Applicants must be tribal members who are full-time students. **Selection Criteria:** Based on educational and professional goals, and financial need. **Funds Available:** U.S.$500 undergraduate scholarships and U.S.$1,000 graduate scholarships. **Applicant Details:** A completed application must be submitted. **Application Deadline:** September 15 and January 15.

★1438★
Michigan Indian Tuition Waiver
Michigan Commission on Indian Affairs
611 W. Ottawa St.   Ph: (517)373-0654
Lansing, MI 48933   Fax: (517)335-1642

Study Level: Undergraduate. **Award Type:** Other. **Purpose:** To provide free tuition for North American Indians to attend public state community, public junior colleges, public colleges, or public universities. **Applicant Eligibility:** Applicants must be Michigan residents for 12 consecutive months and must have not less than one-quarter blood quantum as certified by the applicant's tribal association and verified by the Michigan Commission on Indian Affairs. They must also attend a Michigan public community college or university. **Funds Available:** Cost of tuition.

★1439★
Minnesota Chippewa Tribe Grant
Minnesota Chippewa Tribe
PO Box 217   Ph: (218)335-8584
Cass Lake, MN 56633   Fax: (218)335-7712

Study Level: Undergraduate. **Award Type:** Grant. **Applicant Eligibility:** Must be a member of the Minnesota Chippewa Tribe and enrolled in an institution of postsecondary education. **Selection Criteria:** First come basis. **Funds Available:** $3,000 maximum. **Application Deadline:** June 1 for following school year.

★1440★
Montana Indian Student Fee Waiver
American Indian Minority Achievement
Office of the Commissioner of Higher
  Education
2500 Broadway   Ph: (406)444-6570
Helena, MT 59620-3101   Fax: (406)444-1469

Study Level: Doctorate. **Award Type:** Scholarship. **Purpose:** To increase accessibility to public higher education for citizens who would not be able to matriculate or to continue an educational program without financial assistance. Also to recognize meritorious achievement or service, whether academic or through exceptional accomplishment, and to assure uniform and equitable administration of fee waiver policies of students in the Montana University System. **Applicant Eligibility:** Applicants must be one-fourth or more Indian blood who are bona fide residents of the state of Montana for at least one year prior to enrollment in the Montana University System. They must also demonstrate financial need. **Funds Available:** Approximately $1,771. **Applicant Details:** Students should request an application form where applying to any Montana System campus. **Application Deadline:** Requests should be coordinated with Federal financial aid deadlines.

★1441★
Native American Journalists Association
  Scholarships
Native American Journalists Association
1433 E. Franklin Ave., No. 11   Ph: (612)874-8833
Minneapolis, MN 55404-2135   Fax: (612)874-9007

Study Level: Undergraduate. **Award Type:** Scholarship. **Purpose:** To assist Native American students pursuing a degree in journalism or a related field. **Applicant Eligibility:** Scholarship winners must be members of NAJA (student membership fee is U.S.$10). **Funds Available:** Varies each year. **Applicant Details:** Qualified applicants must send a cover letter containing name, address,

phone number, parents' names, applicant's college plans, year in school, major, and statement of post-college plans; proof of tribal enrollment; official transcript; one recommendation from a school advisor, counselor, or professional familiar with applicant's background; and sample of work, if available. **Application Deadline:** Varies.

★1442★
Native American Seminary Scholarships
Presbyterian Church (U.S.A.)
Office of Financial Aid for Studies
100 Witherspoon St.   Ph: (502)569-5000
Louisville, KY 40202-1396   Fax: (502)569-5018

Study Level: Graduate. **Award Type:** Scholarship. **Purpose:** To assist Native American graduate students preparing for professional church occupations in the Presbyterian Church. **Applicant Eligibility:** Applicant must be a U.S. citizen or permanent resident and be a Native American, Aleut, or Eskimo who is a communicant member of the Presbyterian Church (U.S.A.). Candidate must be a full-time seminary student; be enrolled in a program of Theological Education by Extension; or be employed in a professional Church occupation while pursuing a program of continuing education. Applicant should demonstrate a financial need that cannot be met through other loans, grants, scholarships, savings, and employment. Grants are tenable at schools and programs approved or administered by the Church. **Funds Available:** U.S.$1,000-3,000. **Applicant Details:** Write to the Financial Aid for Studies Office for application materials.

★1443★
New York State Indian Aid
New York State Education Department
Native American Education Unit
Education Bldg., Rm. 543   Ph: (518)474-0537
Albany, NY 12234   Fax: (518)486-2331

Study Level: Undergraduate. **Award Type:** Award. **Applicant Eligibility:** Applicants must be New York State residents who are on an official tribal roll of a New York State tribe or children of enrolled members. New York State tribes include members of the Iroquoian tribes (St. Regis Mohawk, Oneida, Onondaga, Cayuga, Seneca Nation, Tonawanda Band of Seneca, and Tuscarora), the Shinnecock tribe, and the Poospatuck tribe. In addition, students must have graduated from an accredited high school, attained a high school equivalency diploma, or are enrolled in a special 24-credit hour program at an approved, accredited postsecondary institution that will lead to degree status and a high school equivalency diploma. Recipients must also be enrolled in an approved program offered by a college, university, technical school, school of nursing, or business or trade school located in New York State. Approved programs include collegiate and non-collegiate programs registered by the New York State Education Department. Aid is not available for graduate study, for study that is not college-level, nor for study at institutions located outside New York State. There are no age restrictions on eligibility for Native American Student Aid. **Selection Criteria:** Funding is contingent upon the satisfactory progress (2.0 semester GPA) toward a degree or certificate requirements. Recipients are required to submit their grades to the Native American Education Unit at the end of each semester for which funding is received. **Funds Available:** Up to $1,550 per year for up to four years of full-time study (five years for specific programs requiring five years to complete degree requirements). Students must be enrolled in at least 12 credit hours or more to be considered full-time. Students enrolled in institutions on the trimester or quarter system must be enrolled for at least 24 credit hours per year. Funds are pro-rated for part-time status. If funding is available, students may receive aid for summer course work. Any aid received for summer school study is deducted from the student's maximum entitlement for four years of full-time college study. Payment processing takes between four and six weeks from the receipt of the voucher to the mailing of the payment; payments are sent directly to the college. Special arrangements can be made with certain schools that have nontraditional schedules, such as Empire State College. The Unit will provide information on such arrangements. Students receiving the Tuition Assistance Program Aid (TAP) may also receive this award. **Applicant Details:** Applicants must submit a completed application form, available from the State Education Department, along with proof of high school graduation, an official tribal certification form, and a letter of acceptance from the college to the State Education Department.

Students who are minors must have the signature of a parent or guardian approving their stated educational plans. After initial approval, students must notify the Unit of their interest in aid for each subsequent semester they wish to receive the award. This may be done by completing a Request for New York State Indian Aid form, which is mailed to students' homes each semester they receive aid. Proof of satisfactory academic progress (at least 2.0 GPA) must be submitted each term preceding requests for additional aid. **Application Deadline:** July 15 for the fall semester; December 31 for the spring semester; and May 20 for the summer term.

★1444★
NNAC Gifted/Talented Artist Sponsorships

National Native American Cooperative
PO Box 27626
Tucson, AZ 85726-7626   Ph: (602)622-4900

Study Level: Professional Development. **Award Type:** Other. **Purpose:** To assist in the continuation of traditional or contemporary American Indian culture. **Applicant Eligibility:** Applicants must be Native American artists. Both traditional and contemporary work is accepted. **Selection Criteria:** Selection is based upon the applicant's ability to utilize materials provided and create art that reflects a Native American cultural experience. **Funds Available:** Beads, buckskin, silver, turquoise, gold, and other raw craft materials are presented to the artist. **Applicant Details:** Applicants must forward a written request for application details to the National Native American Cooperative. **Application Deadline:** None.

★1445★
North Dakota Indian Scholarships

North Dakota University System
600 East Blvd.
State Capitol Bldg.   Ph: (701)328-2166
Bismarck, ND 58505-0300   Fax: (701)328-2961

Study Level: Undergraduate. **Award Type:** Scholarship. **Purpose:** To assist Native American students in obtaining a basic college education. **Applicant Eligibility:** Applicants must be either residents of North Dakota with one quarter degree Native American blood or enrolled members of a tribe now resident in North Dakota. They must also have been accepted for admission at an institution of higher learning or state vocational education program within North Dakota, be enrolled full-time (12 credits or more), and have a GPA of at least 2.0 on a 4.0 scale. Students participating in internships, student teaching, teaching assistance, or cooperative education programs may be eligible for a scholarship award only if participation in that program is required for the degree and only if tuition must be paid for the credits earned. **Selection Criteria:** Full-time students with a 3.5 average will be given priority in funding. **Funds Available:** Awards range from U.S.$600 to U.S.$2,000 depending upon scholastic ability, funds available, financial need, and total number of applicants in any one year. **Applicant Details:** Applications must include certification of Native American blood or tribal enrollment, a budget form completed by a financial aid officer at the institution attended by the applicant, and most recent transcript. **Application Deadline:** July 15.

★1446★
Polingaysi Qoyawayma Scholarship

American Indian Science and Engineering
   Society
1630 30th St., Ste. 301   Ph: (303)939-0023
Boulder, CO 80301   Fax: (303)939-8150

Study Level: Graduate. **Award Type:** Scholarship. **Purpose:** To promote excellence in teaching, in memory of Polingaysi Qoyawayma (Elizabeth White), who taught for 30 years on the Hopi and Navajo reservations, and who in 1954 was awarded the U.S. Department of the Interior Distinguished Service Award for teaching excellence. **Applicant Eligibility:** Applicants must be American Indian students or teachers pursuing continued teacher education in science or math. **Applicant Details:** Information is available by writing to the AISES. **Application Deadline:** June.

★1447★
Presbyterian Church Native American Education
Grants

Presbyterian Church (U.S.A.)
Office of Financial Aid for Studies
100 Witherspoon St.   Ph: (502)569-5000
Louisville, KY 40202-1396   Fax: (502)569-5018

Study Level: Graduate. **Award Type:** Grant. **Applicant Eligibility:** Candidates must be American Indians, Aleuts, or Eskimos who are United States citizens. They must have completed at least one semester at an accredited institution of higher learning. Restricted to Presbyterian students. **Funds Available:** Grants range from U.S.$200 to U.S.$1,500 annually depending on financial need and availability of funds. **Applicant Details:** Candidates must apply to their colleges for financial aid as well as filing an application with the Presbyterian Church (U.S.A.). **Application Deadline:** June 1.

★1448★
Presbyterian Church Native American Seminary
Scholarships

Presbyterian Church (U.S.A.)
Office of Financial Aid for Studies
100 Witherspoon St.   Ph: (502)569-5000
Louisville, KY 40202-1396   Fax: (502)569-5018

Study Level: Graduate. **Award Type:** Scholarship. **Applicant Eligibility:** Candidates are American Indians, Aleuts, and Eskimos who are certified by the candidate's presbytery or the Presbyterian Native American Consulting Committee. Applicants must be seminary students preparing for a church occupation and enrolled in a seminary fully accredited by the Association of Theological Schools in the United States and Canada. They may also be registered with, or under the care of, a presbytery and enrolled in a college program on Track 1 of the Native American Theological Association Program; or they may be members of the Presbyterian Church (U.S.A.) from a former UPCUSA congregation enrolled in a program of Theological Education by extension, such as the NATA Track III which is approved by a seminary fully accredited by the Association of Theological Schools in the United States and Canada. Candidates, ministers or members (former UPCUSA) in other church occupations pursuing an approved program of continuing education are also eligible. **Funds Available:** The amount of the scholarship is determined by the Office of Financial Aid for Studies based upon recommendation by the student's Financial Officer, analysis of the applicant's financial needs, and other resources and available funds. **Applicant Details:** Candidates must first contact the Financial Aid Officer of the school or seminary they attend. The officer makes a recommendation to the Office of Financial Aid for Studies.

★1449★
Santa Fe Pacific Foundation Scholarships
Scholarships

American Indian Science and Engineering
   Society
1630 30th St., Ste. 301   Ph: (303)939-0023
Boulder, CO 80301   Fax: (303)939-8150

Study Level: Undergraduate. **Award Type:** Scholarship. **Applicant Eligibility:** Applicants must be American Indians (one-quarter) who are recent high school graduates with a GPA of 2.0 or higher. They must plan to be full-time undergraduate students at a college or university majoring in the sciences, business, education, or health administration. They must also reside in states serviced by the Santa Fe Pacific Corporation and its affiliated companies, including Arizona, Colorado, Kansas, New Mexico, Oklahoma, and California. **Selection Criteria:** Selection is based on leadership and academic achievement. **Funds Available:** $2,500 for four years (8 semesters) or until baccalaureate degree is obtained, whichever occurs first. **Applicant Details:** Applicants must provide proof of American Indian blood. **Application Deadline:** March 31.

★1450★
Santa Fe Pacific Native American Scholarshipslarships
Burlington Northern Santa Fe Foundation
1700 E. Golf Rd.
Schaumburg, IL 60173-5860   Ph: (847)995-6177
Study Level: Undergraduate. **Award Type:** Scholarship. **Applicant Eligibility:** Applicants must be Native American (at least 25 percent) high school seniors residing in Arizona, Colorado, Kansas, New Mexico, Oklahoma, and San Bernardino County, California. They must also be planning to attend an accredited college or university in the United States. Affiliation with Santa Fe Pacific is not required. **Selection Criteria:** Winners are selected on the basis of academic performance, with preference g iven to students of any of the sciences, including medicine, engineering, natural and physical sciences, as well as business, education, and health administration. **Funds Available:** Awards range from $1,000 to $2,500 each.

★1451★
Sequoyah Graduate Fellowships
Association on American Indian Affairs, Inc.
PO Box 268   Ph: (605)698-3998
Sisseton, SD 57262-0268   Fax: (605)698-3316
Study Level: Graduate. **Award Type:** Fellowship. **Purpose:** To support graduate study by Native Americans. **Applicant Eligibility:** Applicant must be an American Indian or Alaska Native affiliated with a tribe. Candidate must be enrolled in a graduate program in an accredited U.S. university or college. **Selection Criteria:** Applicants are selected based on scholastic achievement. **Funds Available:** U.S.$1,500. Scholarship is paid in two installments. **Applicant Details:** Students must submit completed application, certificate of degree of Indian blood, two letters of recommendation, a one- to two-page essay describing educational goals, most recent copy of transcripts, and a budget of educational costs and resources. **Application Deadline:** July 1-September 13.

★1452★
U.S. Bureau of Indian Affairs Scholarship Grant
U.S. Bureau of Indian Affairs
Office of Indian Education Programs
1849 C St., NW   Ph: (202)208-4871
Washington, DC 20240   Fax: (202)208-3312
Study Level: Undergraduate. **Award Type:** Grant. **Applicant Eligibility:** Candidates must be Native Americans, Eskimos, or Alaska natives and be members of federally recognized tribes. They must also have been accepted at an accredited college or university. **Selection Criteria:** Based on financial need. **Funds Available:** Appropriated yearly by Congress with each tribe specifying the amount they wish to receive. **Applicant Details:** All application information is available from the Tribal Contractor or the Bureau Agency serving that tribe. There are no funds or applications available from the above address or the Central Office of the Bureau of Indian Affairs. **Application Deadline:** Set by each Tribal Contractor.

★1453★
USET Scholarships
United South & Eastern Tribes, Inc.
711 Stewarts Ferry Pike, No. 100   Ph: (615)872-7900
Nashville, TN 37214-2634   Fax: (615)872-7417
Study Level: Undergraduate. **Award Type:** Scholarship. **Purpose:** To help Native Americans obtain a college education. **Applicant Eligibility:** Candidates must be enrolled or accepted at a post-secondary educational institution. They must also be enrolled members of one of the following tribes: Chitimacha Tribe of Louisiana, Coushatta Tribe of Louisiana, Eastern Band of Cherokees, Mississippi Band of Choctaws, Miccosukee Tribe of Florida, Passamaquoddy–Indian Township, Passamaquoddy–Pleasant Point, Penobscot Nation, Seminole Tribe of Florida, Seneca Nation of Indians of New York, St. Regis Mohawks, Houlton Band of Maliseet, Poarch Band of Creeks, Narragansett Tribe, Tunica-Biloxi Tribe, Mashantucket Pequot Tribe, Gay Head Wampanoag Tribe, Oneida Nation of New York, Alabama-Coushatta, Aroostook Micmac, Catawba Nation, and Jena Band of Choctaws. **Selection Criteria:** Selection is based on financial need and scholastic standing. **Funds Available:** Four

awards of U.S.$500 are given annually. **Applicant Details:** Applicants must submit certification of tribal affiliation, college acceptance letter or proof of current enrollment, and a letter citing the proposed use of scholarship funds. **Application Deadline:** April 30.

★1454★
Washington State Student Financial Aid Programs American Indian Endowed Scholarship
Washington State Higher Education Coordinating Board
917 Lakeridge Way
PO Box 43430   Ph: (360)753-7844
Olympia, WA 98504-3430   Fax: (206)753-1784
Study Level: All. **Award Type:** Scholarship.

★1455★
Zuni Higher Education Scholarships
Zuni Higher Education and Employment Assistance
PO Box 339   Ph: (505)782-2191
Zuni, NM 87327   Fax: (505)782-2700
Study Level: Doctorate. **Award Type:** Grant. **Purpose:** To provide supplemental funds to qualified Zuni tribal members who are in need of financial assistance. **Applicant Eligibility:** Applicants must be enrolled members of the Zuni tribe who are full-time students enrolled for a minimum of 12 credit hours, be in good academic standing with a cumulative GPA of 2.0 on a 4.0 scale, and be admitted to a regionally accredited institution of higher learning in pursuit of college degrees, including the A.A., B.A., Master's, or Ph.D. Students must also apply to other financial aid sources, as the scholarship funds are intended to supplement other awards. **Selection Criteria:** Selection is based on financial need. **Funds Available:** The Higher Education Department has counselors available for any student outreach services that may be required. **Applicant Details:** Students need to complete and return a Financial Aid Form to the College Scholarship Service. The program and the institutions' offices of financial aid then consider financial aid packages relevant to each student's needs. **Application Deadline:** For the fall semester, applications must be returned by June 1 and supporting documents by June 31; for the spring semester, applications must be returned by October 1 and supporting documents by October 31; and for summer classes, applications are due April 1 and supporting documents by April 30.

Awards, Honors, & Prizes

★1456★
American Indian Lore Association Hall of Fame
American Indian Lore Association
960 Walhonding Ave.   Ph: (614)385-7136
Logan, OH 43138   Fax: (614)385-9093
Description: To recognize those individual leaders whose fields of lifetime interests are related to the various facets of Indian lifeways, including arts and crafts, music, dances, history, and folklore. The inductee need not be an American Indian by birth. A rustic wood plaque with brass engraving is awarded annually. Established in 1967 by the Sun Lodge Society of the association.

★1457★
Artist of the Year Award
Indian Arts and Crafts Association
122 La Veta Dr. NE, Ste. B   Ph: (505)265-9149
Albuquerque, NM 87108-1613   Fax: (505)265-8251
Description: To identify and encourage native American Indian artists. IACA member artists who are enrolled members of state or federally recognized Indian tribes are eligible. A monetary award of $1,500 free booths at two markets, and a lifetime membership in the Association are awarded annually. Established in 1981.

★1458★
Catlin Peace Pipe Award
Continental Confederation of Adopted
  Indians
960 Walhonding Ave.   Ph: (614)385-7136
Logan, OH 43138   Fax: (614)385-9093

Description: To recognize the outstanding achievements of those who strive to tear down negative stereotypes through Indian lore. Candidates must be nominated. Up to 10 plaques are presented annually. Established in 1970. For further information, contact Leland L. Conner.

★1459★
Cherokee National Hall of Fame
Cherokee National Historical Society
PO Box 515   Ph: (918)456-6007
Tahlequah, OK 74465   Fax: (918)456-6165

Description: To honor persons of Cherokee descent who have made outstanding contributions. A bust or other suitable monument on a native stone plaza forming the approach to the Cherokee National Museum is awarded irregularly. Established in 1970.

★1460★
D'Arcy McNickle Center for the History of the American Indian Fello wships
Newberry Library
Committee on Awards
60 W. Walton St.   Ph: (312)255-3666
Chicago, IL 60610-3380   Fax: (312)255-3513

Description: To encourage study in the humanities and social sciences. Frances C. Allen Fellowships are available to women of Indian heritage who are pursuing an academic program at any stage beyond the undergraduate degree. Candidates may be working in any graduate or pre-professional field. Length of term varies from one month to a year; stipend varies according to need. Fellows are expected to spend a significant amount of their fellowship term in residence at the McNickle Center. Applications are due February 1 of each year. Documentary Workshops and Fellowships are also available to encourage faculty who would like to include Native American materials in their teaching.

★1461★
Ely ("Eli") S. Parker Award
American Indian Science and Engineering
  Society
5661 Airport Blvd.   Ph: (303)939-0023
Boulder, CO 80301   Fax: (303)939-8150

Description: To recognize American Indians who have made significant contributions in the science, engineering, and technology fields and who have served the American Indian community in a significant manner. American Indians in the fields of science and/or engineering are eligible. A medal is awarded annually. Established in 1983 in honor of Eli S. Parker, the first American Indian engineer. Scholarships are also awarded to Indian high school graduates and college students who wish to study in the fields of science or engineering.

★1462★
Friend of the American Indian Award
American Indian Heritage Foundation
6051 Arlington Blvd.   Ph: (703)237-7500
Falls Church, VA 22044   Fax: (703)532-1921

Description: To recognize outstanding contributions on behalf of American Indians. Artists, writers, broadcasters, journalists, corporations, clubs, religious groups, civic groups, individuals, or organizations are eligible. A medal and a certificate are awarded annually. Established in 1985 by Princess Pale Moon.

★1463★
Indian Educator of the Year Award
National Coalition for Indian Education
8200 Mountain Rd. NE, Ste. 201   Ph: (505)266-6510
Albuquerque, NM 87110   Fax: (505)262-0034

Description: To recognize the most outstanding educator of Indian students in the United States each year, as demonstrated by exemplary work, leadership, and superior performance by students.

A plaque is awarded at the annual conference each April 1. Established in 1988.

★1464★
Indian Student of the Year Award
National Coalition for Indian Education
8200 Mountain Rd. NE, Ste. 201   Ph: (505)266-6510
Albuquerque, NM 87110   Fax: (505)262-0034

Description: To recognize the most outstanding Indian college or secondary school student in the United States, as demonstrated by scholarship, leadership, volunteer work, and extracurricular activities. A plaque is awarded at the annual conference each April 1. Established in 1988.

★1465★
Miss Indian World
Gathering of Nations
PO Box 75102, Sta. 14   Ph: (505)836-2810
Albuquerque, NM 87194   Fax: (505)839-0475

Description: To crown a young Indian (Native American) woman to reign as Miss Indian World. She must be an ambassador of goodwill and represent the Gathering of Nations and Native American people in the United States, Canada, and throughout the Americas (North, South, and Central). Candidates must be at least one-quarter Indian, and be 17 to 24 years of age. A traveling crown (beaded) to wear throughout the year, a banner, $1,200 cash and $1,800 travel expenses are awarded annually. Established in 1984 by Gathering of Nations Ltd.

★1466★
National Indian Health Board Award
1385 S. Colorado Blvd., Ste. A-707   Ph: (303)759-3075
Denver, CO 80222   Fax: (303)759-3674

Description: To recognize achievements in helping improve the health status of American Indian/Alaskan Native people. Each year, 6 plaques, 6 medallions, and 12 certificates are awarded at the NIHB Consumer Conference. Established in 1972. For more information, contact Yvette Joseph-Fox, Executive Director.

★1467★
Outstanding American Indian Awards
American Indian Heritage Foundation
6051 Arlington Blvd.   Ph: (703)237-7500
Falls Church, VA 22044   Fax: (703)532-1921

Description: To recognize outstanding achievements in the following categories: Youth, Man and Woman of the Year, Tribal Tribute, Corporate Cause-Related Marketing, and Celebrity Sponsorship. Monetary prizes, medals, trophies, and certificates are awarded annually during National American Indian Heritage Month. Established in 1983.

★1468★
Red Cloud Indian Art Show
Heritage Center
Red Cloud Indian School
PO Box 100   Ph: (605)867-5491
Pine Ridge, SD 57770   Fax: (605)867-1291

Description: For recognition of excellent Native American art. Any tribal member of the native peoples of North America over 18 years of age is eligible. The deadline for applications is May 22. Monetary awards of $300 are presented in the following divisions: paintings - oils, tempera, casein, encaustic polymer, and acrylic; paintings - watercolors; graphics - pencil, pen and ink, cray-pas, crayon, wash, and charcoal; mixed media; and three dimensional works - sculpture and carvings, in any media other than pottery. Native Americans who enter the Art Show are eligible. In addition to merit awards in each division, the following purchase awards are presented: Tony Begay Memorial Award of $50 in memory of Navajo artist Tony Begay by Tom Woodard of Gallup, New Mexico, to the artist whose works depict the most explicit development of an Indian theme; M. L. Woodard Award of $50 for the painting, drawing, or sketch depicting the most explicit development of an Indian theme; Bill and Sue Hensler Award of $50 for traditional representation in sculpture; Aplan Award of $100 for the outstanding young Indian artist, by Mr. and Mrs. Jim Aplan; Powers Award of $100 for the best representation of Indian women, by William K. and Marla Powers; Bonnie Erickson Award for the best representation of children; Allan and Joyce Niederman Award of $100 for the most traditional painting; Nicolaus Rostkowski Award of $100 for the best abstract painting; Gillihan Award of $100 for the most realistic rendering of an American Indian on horseback; Diederich Award of $250 to a young artist whose work shows the greatest improvement; Diederich Award of $250 for the best representation of a traditional Sioux Indian; Diederich Landscape Award of $250 for the best depiction of the Black Hills/Badlands; Diederich Landscape Award of $250 for the best depiction of Lakes, Mountains, or Prairies; Iron Cloud Family Award for best sense of humor; historic-cultural setting; Bennett County Booster Award of $100 to the most innovative artist; and Oscar Howe Memorial Award, of $100 for the best cubist painting. Awarded annually. Established in 1969.

★1469★
Samuel W. Brown, Jr. Root Cutter Award
Institute for the Study of American
 Cultures
PO Box 1658
Columbus, GA 31902

Description: To recognize achievements of individuals who have contributed to a more accurate and complete understanding of the history and culture of the peoples who inhabited the Americas before they were discovered by Christopher Columbus. Anyone is eligible for the award without restriction. A gold medallion is presented to no more than five individuals in a ceremony at the annual research conference. Established in 1989 in memory of Samuel W. Brown, Jr. (1874-1957), hereditary chief of the Yuchi Indian Tribe. Sponsored by the Yuchi Tribal Organization, Sapulpa, Oklahoma.

★1470★
Sequoyah Award
Confederation of American Indians
PO Box 5475
New York, NY 10163

Description: For recognition of significant achievement related to American Indians. Achievement primarily, but not exclusively, related to education and books is considered. A plaque or certificate is awarded at the discretion of Trustees. Established in 1980.

Publishers

★1471★
Acoma Books
PO Box 4
Ramona, CA 92065   Ph: (619)789-1288

Subjects: Native Americans, southwestern U.S.

★1472★
Akwesasne Notes
Mohawk Nation
PO Box 196   Ph: (516)558-9531
Rooseveltown, NY 13683   Fax: (516)575-2935

Description: Publishes on the history, philosophy, religion, and ecology of the native people of the Americas. Presently inactive.

★1473★
**American Committee to Advance the Study of
 Petroglyphs and Pictographs**
PO Box 158   Ph: (304)876-9431
Shepherdstown, WV 25443-0158   Fax: (304)876-9431

Description: Publishes occasional papers and a journal; offers consultant services. Distributes for Editions Sureste, S.A. (Mexico). Reaches market through direct mail. **Subjects:** Archaeology, rock art, Native American studies, anthropology.

★1474★
American Indian Basketry and Other Native Arts
PO Box 66124
Portland, OR 97266   Ph: (503)233-8131

Description: Publishes mostly monographs devoted to traditional native American arts.

★1475★
Amerind Foundation
PO Box 400   Ph: (602)586-3666
Dragoon, AZ 85609-0400   Fax: (602)586-3667

Description: Nonprofit archaeological research institution and museum specializing in the Native American cultures of the Americas. Publications result from archaeological field work. Also offers archaeological site maps, files, and photographic collections. Reaches market through direct mail. **Subjects:** American Indians, archaeology.

★1476★
Ancient City Press
PO Box 5401   Ph: (505)982-8195
Santa Fe, NM 87502   Free: 800-258-5830
                                    Fax: (505)982-8195

Description: Publishes children's books and books on Native Americans, Hispanic studies, and Western Americana. Reaches market through commission representatives, direct mail, trade sales, wholesalers, and Johnson Books. **Subjects:** Children's books, Native Americans, Hispanic studies, Western Americana.

★1477★
Angel Mounds State Historic Site
8215 Pollack Ave.   Ph: (812)853-3956
Evansville, IN 47715   Fax: (812)853-6271

Description: Publications deal with Angel Mounds, the Indians who lived there, and special exhibits. Offers a newsletter. **Subjects:** Native Americans, archaeology.

★1478★
Aquarius House
20 Battery Park, Ste. 201   Ph: (704)254-4191
Asheville, NC 28801   Fax: (704)252-9515

Description: Publishes "books reflecting a new social consciousness and practical steps toward personal transformation." Accepts unsolicited manuscripts; send self-addressed, stamped envelope with complete manuscript or outline. Distributes for Relationship Training Center chapters. Reaches market through direct mail, telephone sales, and wholesalers and distributors, including Baker & Taylor Books and New Leaf Distributing Co. **Subjects:** New age, spirituality, self-help, social change, Native American.

★1479★
Arrowstar Publishing
PO Box 427
Englewood, CO 80151   Ph: (303)231-6599

Description: American Indian-owned and operated publishing company with preference for American Indian works. Accepts unsolicited manuscripts. Reaches market through direct mail. **Subjects:** Native Americans.

★1480★
Artlist
PO Box 35552
Albuquerque, NM 87176   Ph: (505)884-8176

Description: Publishes a reference source of auction prices of American Indian art. Offers appraisals. Presently inactive. **Subjects:** American Indians, art.

★1481★
Association on American Indian Affairs
245 5th Ave., Ste. 1801   Ph: (212)689-8720
New York, NY 10016   Free: 800-895-2242
                                    Fax: (212)685-4692

Description: A private, nonprofit, national citizens organization providing technical and legal assistance to American Indian tribes and communities at their request. Also publishes the newsletter *Indian Affairs*.

★1482★
Augustana College
Center for Western Studies
PO Box 727   Ph: (605)336-4007
Sioux Falls, SD 57197   Fax: (605)337-4999
Description: Publishes historical and cultural nonfiction dealing with the West. Offers a triannual publication, *CWS Newsletter*. Accepts unsolicited manuscripts. Distributes for Nordland Heritage Foundation and University of Nebraska Press. Reaches market through direct mail and trade sales. **Subjects:** Immigration, settlement of the West, Sioux (Dakota) Indian culture, Cheyenne Indian history, Crow Indian history, Blackfoot Indian history, military history.

★1483★
Avanyu Publishing, Inc.
PO Box 27134   Ph: (505)266-6128
Albuquerque, NM 87125   Fax: (505)266-6128
Description: Publishes on the ethnography of American Indians. Accepts unsolicited manuscripts. Distributed by University of New Mexico Press. Reaches market through direct mail, commission representatives, and wholesalers. Alternate telephone number: (505) 243-8485. **Subjects:** Native Americans.

★1484★
Badlands Natural History Association
PO Box 47   Ph: (605)433-5489
Interior, SD 57750   Fax: (605)433-5404
Description: Publishes books pertaining to Badlands National Park, South Dakota history, Indians of South Dakota, geology, plants, and animals. Offers videos, postcards, and maps. Accepts unsolicited manuscripts. **Subjects:** Paleontology, geology, Native American, homesteading history, natural history. **Number of New Titles:** 1998 - 2.

★1485★
Ballena Press
PO Box 2510   Ph: (415)323-9261
Novato, CA 94948   Fax: (415)883-4280
Description: Publishes scholarly books on Native Americans in the fields of anthropology, archaeology, and history. Does not accept unsolicited manuscripts. Orders and returns should be sent to Ballena Press, Publisher's Services, PO Box 2510, Novato, CA 94948. Reaches market through direct mail. **Subjects:** Native Americans, anthropology, archaeology, history.

★1486★
Bear and Co., Inc.
PO Box 2860   Ph: (505)983-5968
Santa Fe, NM 87504-2860   Free: 800-932-3277
    Fax: (505)989-8386
Description: Publishes books "to celebrate and heal the Earth." Reaches market through direct mail, trade sales, and wholesalers. **Subjects:** Personal and social transformation, spirituality, Native American studies, indigenous studies, health and healing.

★1487★
Bear Tribe Medicine Society
PO Box 9167
Spokane, WA 99209-9167
Description: Publishes books, a magazine, *Wildfire Networking*, and video and audio cassettes. Offers lectures and educational programs. Reaches market through direct mail. **Subjects:** Native American people, earth awareness, personal and spiritual growth.

★1488★
Bear Tribe Publishing
PO Box 9167
Spokane, WA 99209
Description: Publishes books on Native American topics, including environment, philosophy, and religion. Accepts unsolicited manuscripts. **Subjects:** Native Americans, environment, religion, philosophy.

★1489★
Beechwood Books
720 Wehapa Circle
Leeds, AL 35094   Ph: (205)699-6935
Description: Publishes on Indians and history of the southeastern United States. Reaches market through direct mail and Baker & Taylor. **Subjects:** Southeastern U.S., Native Americans.

★1490★
Book World Inc./Blue Star Productions
9666 E. Riggs Rd., Ste. 194   Ph: (602)895-7995
Sun Lakes, AZ 85248   Fax: (602)895-7995
Description: Publishes on unexplained phenomena, New Age topics, Native Americans and philosophy. **Number of New Titles:** 1996 - 12.

★1491★
Bowman Books
PO Box 308   Ph: (518)584-1728
Greenfield Center, NY 12833   Fax: (518)583-9741
Description: Publishes collections of traditional storytelling with an emphasis on Native Americans and the Adirondack Mountain Region. Reaches market through Talman Company. Does not accept unsolicited manuscripts. **Subjects:** Native Americans, folklore, literature.

★1492★
Bright Horizons Specialty Distributors, Inc.
138 Springside Rd.   Ph: (704)684-8840
Asheville, NC 28803   Free: 800-437-3959
    Fax: (704)681-1790
Description: Wholesaler of titles from over 100 publishers, primarily for the tourist market. Reaches market through commission representatives, direct mail, and telephone sales. **Subjects:** Native Americans, Southwestern regional.

★1493★
Central States Archaeological Societies, Inc.
646 Knierim Pl.
Kirkwood, MO 63122   Ph: (314)821-7675
Description: Publishes books and a journal on the archaeology and history of both prehistoric and historic American Indians. Accepts unsolicited manuscripts.

★1494★
Chippewa Heritage Publications
PO Box 16736
Duluth, MN 55816-0736   Ph: (218)878-3449
Description: Publishes genealogical information relating to the Great Lakes region American Indians, with emphasis on Chippewa, Ojiwe, and Anishinabe Tribal people. Reaches market through direct mail. **Subjects:** American Indians, genealogy.

★1495★
Ciga Press
PO Box 654   Ph: (619)728-9308
Fallbrook, CA 92088   Fax: (619)728-9308
Description: Publishes some genealogical materials, but mostly publishes Osage Indian materials. Reaches market through direct mail, museums, and historical societies. Presently inactive. **Subjects:** Indian culture, history, genealogy, anthropology.

★1496★
Clear Light Publishers
823 Don Diego   Ph: (505)989-9590
Santa Fe, NM 87501   Fax: (505)989-9519
Description: Publishes art, culture, and folklore books on Native American and Southwest topics. Accepts unsolicited manuscripts. Reaches market through commission representatives, trade sales, and wholesalers. **Number of New Titles:** 1998 - 36.

★1497★
Costano Books
PO Box 355
Petaluma, CA 94953   Ph: (707)762-4848
Description: Publishes on North American Indians, lighthouses, U.S. Life-Saving Service, and maritime books. Reaches market through direct mail, commission representatives, telephone sales, direct mail, and major small press wholesalers and distributors. **Subjects:** Native Americans, maritime history, lighthouses, U.S. Life-Saving Service, travel.

★1498★
Council for Indian Education
2032 Woody Dr.   Ph: (406)248-3465
Billings, MT 59102   Fax: (406)652-0536
Description: Publishes fiction and nonfiction related to American Indian life and culture, suitable for use in the education of Native American children. Accepts unsolicited manuscripts. Reaches market through direct mail.

★1499★
Council Oak Books
1350 E. 15th St.   Ph: (918)587-6454
Tulsa, OK 74120   Free: 800-247-8850
                                          Fax: (918)583-4995
Description: A trade publishing house "dedicated to providing a national audience with excellence in fiction and nonfiction." Reaches market through commission representatives, direct mail, and trade sales. Does not accept unsolicited manuscripts. **Subjects:** Cooking, fiction, life skills, Native American history, African American history, philosophy, self-help and recovery, earth awareness, and art.

★1500★
Dancing Feather
633 N. 75 E.
Albion, IN 46701-9503   Ph: (219)636-2269
Description: Publishes American Indian philosophy and spirituality in poetic form. All profits are donated to Indian schools. Also offers lectures. Dancing Feather, a Mohawk Indian, is also known as Thomas Leonard Ebbing.

★1501★
Diablo Books
1700 Tice Valley Blvd., No. 150
Walnut Creek, CA 94595
Description: Publishes local and California Indian history. Reaches market through direct mail, wholesalers, schools, and libraries.

★1502★
Don M. Chase
916 Colorado Blvd.
Santa Rosa, CA 95405
Description: Publishes paperbound and velo-bound items of local western history and Indians. Some are first or limited editions that are numbered and signed. Reaches market through direct mail and wholesalers. Presently inactive. **Subjects:** California, Western Americana, Native Americans, church history, mountain men.

★1503★
Dream Weavers Publishing
7530 W. 10th St., No. 305   Ph: (303)237-4561
Lakewood, CO 80215   Fax: (303)232-5958
Description: Publishes fiction and non-fiction. Accepts unsolicited manuscripts; send the first chapter, double spaced. Reaches market through direct mail, telephone sales, trade sales, Ingram Book Co., and New Leaf Distributing Co. **Subjects:** New age, Native American history, humor, genealogy.

★1504★
Eaglecrafts Inc.
168 W. 12th St.   Ph: (801)393-3991
Ogden, UT 84404   Free: 800-547-3364
                                          Fax: (801)745-0903
Description: Wholesaler and craft supplier. Specializes in books on Native Americans, Indian crafts, and frontier history. Reaches market through direct mail and telephone sales. **Subjects:** Native American, early American history.

★1505★
Eagle's View Publishing
6756 North Fork Rd.   Ph: (801)393-4555
Liberty, UT 84310   Free: 800-547-3364
                                          Fax: (801)745-0903
Description: Specializes in Native American, frontier, and craft books. Also offers video cassettes and frontier/Indian clothing patterns. Reaches market through commission representatives, direct mail, telephone sales, and wholesalers. Accepts unsolicited manuscripts. **Subjects:** Beading techniques, porcupine quill decoration, crafts, jewelry, American Indians, frontier history. **Number of New Titles:** 1998 - 4.

★1506★
Earl M. Coleman Enterprises, Inc.
PO Box 720
Crugers, NY 10521-0720
Description: Publishes books on political science, social science, human rights, as well as reprints. Accepts unsolicited manuscripts. **Subjects:** Social science, political science, horticulture, Native Americans.

★1507★
Earth Art Inc.
10212 Dutch Settlement Rd.
Marcellus, MI 49067-9417   Ph: (616)646-9545
Description: Offers mailing labels of American Indian reservations, organizations, and individuals. Reaches market through direct mail and advertising. **Subjects:** American Indians, ecology, modeling, nature, education, hobbies. **Number of New Titles:** 1998 - 1.

★1508★
Eastern Washington State Historical Society
Cheney Cowles Museum
W. 2316 1st Ave.   Ph: (509)456-3931
Spokane, WA 99204   Fax: (509)456-7690
Description: Publishes to promote local history, American Indian culture, and a greater awareness of the visual arts. Offers a bimonthly newsletter, postcards, and posters. Reaches market through direct mail. **Subjects:** History, art, American Indians.

★1509★
Ervin Stuntz
6626 6A Rd.
Plymouth, IN 46563-8951
Description: Self-publisher of books on American Indians. Operates an American Indian artifacts museum. Reaches market through direct mail and telephone sales.

★1510★
Fantail Native Design
c/o Pacific Science Center
200 2nd Ave. N.   Ph: (206)443-2870
Seattle, WA 98109   Fax: (206)443-3627
Description: Publishes books related to Native American history and natural sciences. Also produces Native American prints and notecards. Reaches market through direct mail, telephone sales, and trade sales. Does not accept unsolicited manuscripts. **Subjects:** American Indians, American history.

★1511★
Five Civilized Tribes Museum
Agency Hill at Honor Heights Dr.   Ph: (918)683-1701
Muskogee, OK 74401   Fax: (918)683-3070
Description: Publishes on the history and heritage of Five Tribes and area of Muskogee, Oklahoma. **Subjects:** History, traditions, culture of the Cherokee, Chickasaw, Cxocaaw, Creek, Seminole Tribes.

★1512★
Five Flower Press
369 Montezuma, No. 254
Santa Fe, NM 87501
Description: Publishes on pre-Columbian Native American cultures. Accepts unsolicited manuscripts; query first. Reaches market through direct mail, trade sales, and SCB Distributors.

★1513★
Fogelman Publishing Co.
RD 1, Box 240   Ph: (717)437-3698
Turbotville, PA 17772-9599   Fax: (717)437-3411
Description: Publishes to educate collectors and laymen on American Indian artifacts. Offers a chronological type chart for projectiles and knives of the Northeast. Reaches market through direct mail and wholesalers. **Subjects:** American Indian artifacts. **Number of New Titles:** 1998 - 1.

★1514★
Friends of Malatesta, Inc.
PO Box 937
Ellsworth, ME 04605
Subjects: Poetry, Native Americans, anarchism.

★1515★
Fun Publishing Co.
PO Box 2049   Ph: (602)946-2093
Scottsdale, AZ 85252   Fax: (602)946-2093
Description: Publishes the Children's American Indian Book Series. **Number of New Titles:** 1997 - 5; 1998 - 5.

★1516★
Gallup Distributing Co.
205 Sunde Ave.
Gallup, NM 87301   Ph: (505)863-4304
Description: Distributor of mass market paperbacks and magazines. **Subjects:** Indian titles.

★1517★
Gallup Inter-Tribal Indian Ceremonial Association
PO Box 1   Ph: (505)863-3896
Church Rock, NM 87311   Free: 800-233-4528
                                     Fax: (505)722-5158
Description: Publishes on Indian arts and crafts. Plans to produce other pamphlets on Indian crafts, as well as an annual magazine. Offers a newsletter, cards, maps, lapel pins, T-shirts, fine art posters, Indian information service, and slides of Indian dances and Indian art. Reaches market through direct mail and magazine advertising. **Subjects:** Native American arts and crafts.

★1518★
Grandview Publishing Co.
PO Box 2863   Ph: (307)733-4593
Jackson, WY 83001   Free: 800-525-7344
                                     Fax: (307)734-0210
Description: Publishes the "Amazing Indian children" series for juveniles. Offers audio cassettes. Does not accept unsolicited manuscripts. **Subjects:** Native American children.

★1519★
Great Eagle Publishing Inc.
3020 Issaquah
Pine Lake Rd. SE, Ste. 481   Ph: (206)392-9136
Issaquah, WA 98029-7255   Fax: (206)391-7812
Description: Publishes on the frontier days in the Pacific Northwest. Reaches market through direct mail and wholesalers including Baker & Taylor Books, Pacific Pipeline Inc., Quality Books, Inc., New Leaf Distributing, Sunbelt Publications and others. Does not accept unsolicited manuscripts. **Subjects:** Native American myths, legends, medicine, Pacific Northwest. **Number of New Titles:** 1998 - 1.

★1520★
Great Elm Press
1205 Co. Rte. 60
Rexville, NY 14877   Ph: (607)225-4592
Description: Publishes works of rural orientation and general interest. Specializes in poetry and prose reflecting the affairs of Native Americans, bioregionalism, laborers, and country living. Distributes for Pagan Angel Press. Reaches market through direct mail and trade sales. **Subjects:** Poetry, prose, Native Americans, bioregionalism, laborers, country living.

★1521★
Hancock House Publishers Ltd.
Hancock Wildlife Research Center   Ph: (360)538-1114
1431 Harrison Ave.   Free: 800-938-1114
Blaine, WA 98230-5005   Fax: (360)538-2262
Description: Publishes nonfiction related to conservation, natural history, and animal husbandry. Accepts unsolicited manuscripts; send self-addressed, stamped envelope. Reaches market through commission representatives, direct mail, and wholesalers. **Subjects:** Northern biographies, Native Americans, field guides, flower guides, ornithology. **Number of New Titles:** 1998 - 30.

★1522★
Havasupai Tribal Council
PO Box 10   Ph: (602)448-2731
Supai, AZ 86435   Fax: (602)448-2551
Description: Publishes on the history of the Havasupai Indian tribe. Reaches market through direct mail.

★1523★
Heartsong Books
PO Box 370
Blue Hill, ME 04614-0370   Ph: (207)374-5170
Description: Publishes books on "Native Americans, earth awareness, spirituality and peace." Does not accept unsolicited manuscripts. Reaches market through direct mail, telephone sales, trade sales, and wholesalers and distributors, including Baker & Taylor Books and New Leaf Distributing Co. **Subjects:** Native Americans, inspiration.

★1524★
Heidelberg Graphics
2 Stansbury Ct.   Ph: (916)342-6582
Chico, CA 95928   Fax: (916)342-6582
Description: Promotes contemporary creative writing, literature for and about authors, and multicultural expression. Offers consulting to self-published authors. **Subjects:** Fiction, poetry, biography, Native Americans, graphic art.

★1525★
Heyday Books
PO Box 9145   Ph: (510)549-3564
Berkeley, CA 94709   Fax: (510)549-1889
Description: Publishes books on the natural history of California, California Indians, and California history and literature. Offers a quarterly publication, *Ne ws from Native California.* Accepts unsolicited manuscripts. **Subjects:** Bookson California Indians, history, environment.

★1526★
Hothem House
PO Box 458
Lancaster, OH 43130   Ph: (614)653-9030
Description: Publishes books on American Indian artifacts. Reaches market through direct mail and trade sales. **Subjects:** American Indians, archaeology. **Number of New Titles:** 1998 - 3; 1997 - 2.

★1527★
Impresora Sahuaro
7575 Sendero de Juana
Tucson, AZ 85718   Ph: (520)297-3089
Subjects: Minority education, books about American Indians for children.

★1528★
Indian Heritage Council Publishing
Box 2302 - Henry St.
PO Box 2302
Morristown, TN 37816   Ph: (423)581-4448
Description: Publishes on Native American religion, culture, and literature. Also offers calendars and videos. Accepts unsolicited manuscripts. Reaches market through commission representatives and direct mail. **Subjects:** Native Americans, comparative studies, history, culture, poetry. **Number of New Titles:** 1996 - 2.

★1529★
Indian Historian Press
1493 Masonic Ave.   Ph: (415)626-5235
San Francisco, CA 94117   Fax: (415)626-4923
Description: Principal interest is the American Indians of North America; also covers indigenous peoples of the western hemisphere. Does not accept unsolicited manuscripts.

★1530★
Indian Resource Development
Box 3001/MSC 3IRD
New Mexico State University   Ph: (505)646-1347
Las Cruces, NM 88003-0001   Fax: (505)646-7740
Description: Publishes materials to help American Indians develop managerial, scientific, and technical skills. Offers a semiannual newsletter aimed at recruiting high school students into college and engineering, business, and science related careers. Also offers video cassettes. Accepts unsolicited manuscripts for *Sources of Financial Aid Available to American Indian Students* and for *Indian Country Student News*. Reaches market through direct mail. **Subjects:** Native Americans, education, careers, financial aid.

★1531★
Indian Univeristy Press
Bacone College
2299 Old Bacone Road   Ph: (918)683-4581
Muskogee, OK 74403-1597   Fax: (918)687-5913
Description: Publishes materials for the teaching and preservation of Indian languages, including bilingual materials. Also publishes important writing by Indians and historical materials relating to the history of Indian territory, including family histories. Accepts one unsolicited manuscript per year. Reaches market through direct mail. **Subjects:** American Indians, Language, history.

★1532★
Institute for American Indian Studies
38 Curtis Rd.
PO Box 1260   Ph: (860)868-0518
Washington, CT 06793   Fax: (860)868-1649
Description: Publishes on New England archaeology and American Indian prehistory and history. Distributes books from other publishers. Offers a quarterly, *The Four Directions* and a quarterly newsletter, *Netop,* for members. Reaches market through direct mail. **Subjects:** American Indians, New England, archaeology, Native American cooking, ethnobotany.

★1533★
Institute for the Study of Traditional American Indian Arts
PO Box 66124
Portland, OR 97290   Ph: (503)233-8131
Subjects: Traditional American Indian arts.

★1534★
Janet Herren, Publisher
4750 Crystal Springs Dr.
Bainbridge Island, WA 98110   Ph: (206)842-3484
Description: Publishes a book on a Northwest Indian legend.

★1535★
KC Publications
PO Box 94558   Ph: (702)433-3415
Las Vegas, NV 89193-4558   Free: 800-626-9673
          Fax: (702)433-3420
Description: Publishes on national parks and Indian culture, especially Southwestern Indians. Offers calendars. Reaches market through direct mail and trade sales. Publications available in a variety of international languages. Does not accept unsolicited manuscripts. **Subjects:** Native Americans, national parks.

★1536★
Lion's Head Publishing Co.
2436 S. U.S. 33
Albion, IN 46701
Description: Presently inactive. **Subjects:** American Indians, fiction.

★1537★
MacRae Publications
1605 Cole St.
PO Box 652
Enumclaw, WA 98022   Ph: (360)825-3737
Subjects: American Indians.

★1538★
MacRae's Indian Book Distributors
1605 Cole St.
PO Box 652
Enumclaw, WA 98022   Ph: (360)825-3737
Description: Distributor. Reaches market through direct mail. **Subjects:** American Indians.

★1539★
Malki Museum Press
Morongo Indian Reservation
11-795 Fields Rd.
Banning, CA 92220   Ph: (909)849-7289
Description: Publishes books and pamphlets about the Indian peoples of California and Baja California. Also publishes the *Journal of California and Great Basin Anthropology* in cooperation with the Department of Anthropology, University of California, Riverside.

★1540★
March/Abrazo Press
PO Box 2890
Chicago, IL 60690-2890   Fax: (773)539-0013
Description: Publishes poetry of Latino experience, as well as Chicano/American Indian life. Accepts manuscripts (under forty pages) from Chicano/Native American poets only, with a self-addressed, stamped envelope and authors' biographies. Reaches market through direct mail, public readings, telephone sales, and distributors, including Literati & Co., Blackwell North America, Inc., Midwest Library Service, Emery-Pratt Co., and Baker & Taylor Books. **Subjects:** Poetry, Hispanic Americans, Native Americans. **Number of New Titles:** 1997 - 2; 1998 - 2.

★1541★
Memento Publications, Inc.
PO Box 803
Denton, TX 76202   Ph: (817)387-9286
Subjects: Indians.

★1542★
Michigan Indian Press
45 Lexington NW   Ph: (616)774-8331
Grand Rapids, MI 49504   Fax: (616)774-2810
Description: Publishes books that dispel negative stereotypes about Native Americans and instead educate the general public about Native American culture, history, heritage, and beliefs. Offers the *Turtle Talk* newsletter. Distributes for Red School House and Lotus Light. Accepts unsolicited manuscripts. Reaches market through direct mail, telephone sales, and trade sales.

★1543★
Morning Star Gallery
513 Canyon Rd.   Ph: (505)982-8187
Santa Fe, NM 87501   Fax: (505)984-2368
Description: Publishes on antique American Indian art. Does not accept unsolicited manuscripts. Reaches market through direct mail, telephone sales, and trade sales. **Subjects:** Ledger drawings, Navajo textiles, historic Pueblo pottery.

★1544★
Museum of Ojibwa Culture
500 N. State St.
St. Ignace, MI 49781   Ph: (906)643-9161
Description: Publishes books on the museum's exhibits and on 17th-century upper Michigan history. Also publishes a newsletter to friends of the museum. **Subjects:** American Indians, local history.

★1545★
National Indian Law Library
NARF
1522 Broadway   Ph: (303)447-8760
Boulder, CO 80302-6296   Fax: (303)443-7776
Description: A clearinghouse for Indian legal materials, primarily for attorneys. Reaches market through direct mail. **Subjects:** Indian law, American Indian history, tribal law.

★1546★
National Native American Cooperative
PO Box 27626
Tucson, AZ 85726   Ph: (520)622-4900
Description: Publishes a directory listing Native American tribal offices, organizations, corporations, museums, libraries, and cultural events. Publications available in microform. Offers American Indian information packets, crafts, and flags. Mailing List services also available. Reaches market through direct mail and telephone and trade sales. **Subjects:** Directory, Native Americans.

★1547★
National Woodlands Publishing Co.
8846 Green Briar Rd.   Ph: (616)275-6735
Lake Ann, MI 49650-9607   Fax: (616)275-6735
Description: Publishes original and compiled works on American Indians, including social and political issues, natural history, artifacts, historical writings, educational materials, and legends and folklore. Accepts unsolicited manuscripts; send self-addressed, stamped envelope. Reaches market through direct mail, telephone sales, trade sales, and wholesalers and distributors, including Dakota West Books, Four Winds Trading Co., and Baker & Taylor Books. **Subjects:** American Indians/Native Americans. **Number of New Titles:** 1998 - 1.

★1548★
Native American Book Publishers
5884 Winans Lake Rd.   Ph: (810)231-3728
Brighton, MI 48116   Free: 800-937-7947
                                   Fax: (810)231-3720
Description: Publishes reprints of Native American titles. Does not accept unsolicited manuscripts. Reaches market through direct mail. **Subjects:** Native Americans.

★1549★
Native American Images
PO Box 746   Ph: (512)472-3049
Austin, TX 78767   Free: 800-252-3332
                                   Fax: (512)472-7754
Description: Features exhibit posters, limited edition prints, original stone lithographs, and paintings by American Indians and Southwestern artists. Color brochures of current works available.

★1550★
Naturegraph Publishers, Inc.
3543 Indian Creek Rd.   Ph: (916)493-5353
PO Box 1075   Free: 800-390-5353
Happy Camp, CA 96039   Fax: (916)493-5240
Description: Publishes on natural history, gardening, health, and Native American studies. Offers nature card games. Accepts unsolicited manuscripts; query first. Reaches market through direct mail, trade sales, and distributors.

★1551★
Navajo Community College Press
Navajo Community College   Ph: (602)724-3311
Tsaile, AZ 86556   Fax: (602)724-3327
Description: Publishes books on the American Indian with emphasis on the Navajo in historical and contemporary contexts. Reaches market through direct mail, trade sales, and wholesalers. **Subjects:** History, life, culture, mythology, traditions, education, political aspirations, progress of the tribe, nonfiction, fiction, poetry.

★1552★
Navajo Curriculum Center
Star Rte. 1
RRDS, Box 217   Ph: (520)728-3311
Chinle, AZ 86503   Fax: (520)728-3215
Description: Publishes bilingual curriculum materials and other major publications dealing with Navajo life, history, and culture. Offers maps, cards, and calendars. Reaches market through direct mail, trade sales, and wholesalers.

★1553★
Northland Publishing
PO Box 1389
Flagstaff, AZ 86002-1389   Free: 800-346-3257
Description: Publishes books about southwestern Native American art, crafts, and culture.

★1554★
Oklahoma Historical Society
2100 N. Lincoln Blvd.   Ph: (405)522-5243
Oklahoma City, OK 73105-4997   Fax: (405)521-2492
Description: Publishes local history. Offers a quarterly journal, *The Chronicles of Oklahoma,* and a newsletter, *Mistletoe Leaves.* Accepts unsolicited manuscripts. Reaches market through direct mail and a marketing representative. List of book titles available upon request. **Subjects:** Oklahoma: railroads, governors, history, Indians, land run of 1889, biography of Sequayah, annotated guide to the chronicles of Oklahoma.

★1555★
One World Publishing
PO Box 9148   Ph: (714)842-8765
Fountain Valley, CA 92708   Fax: (714)842-0546
Description: Established primarily to publish the works of Little Crow, an American Indian teacher and interpreter of the Lakota and

Dakota oral traditions. Does not accept unsolicited manuscripts. Reaches market through direct mail.

★1556★
Origins Program
4632 Vincent Ave. S.   Ph: (612)922-8175
Minneapolis, MN 55410   Fax: (612)926-0015
Description: Publishes catalogs and books to accompany exhibitions of tribal art and books on multicultural understanding. Also offers audio and video cassettes on Indian and Eskimo topics, and on museum collections of tribal art. Reaches market through commission representatives and distributors, including Bookpeople and Quality Books, Inc. **Subjects:** Indian and Eskimo art and culture, multiculturalism.

★1557★
Pacific Pipeline
8030 S. 228th   Ph: (206)872-5523
Kent, WA 98032-2900   Free: 800-444-7323
                                   Fax: (206)395-1525
Description: Wholesaler of books to bookstores in the western U.S. Carries 60,000 titles and has about 3000 active accounts. Reaches market through direct mail and telephone sales. **Subjects:** Western U.S., Children's books, Native Americans.

★1558★
Parks-Thompson Co.
1757 W. Adams
St. Louis, MO 63122   Ph: (314)822-2409
Description: Publishes books pertaining to Indians and archaeology.

★1559★
Paupieres Publishing Co.
PO Box 707
Houma, LA 70361-0707   Ph: (504)876-9223
Description: Publishes regional fiction and nonfiction. Offers some titles in French and English. Does not accept unsolicited manuscripts. Reaches market through direct mail and trade sales. **Subjects:** Southeast Louisiana, Cajuns, Native Americans. **Number of New Titles:** 1998 - 6; 1997 - 5.

★1560★
Peter Wolf Toth
102 Arthur Ave.
Edgewater, FL 32141   Ph: (904)428-0288
Description: Publishes a book on the life and work of sculptor Peter Toth, "who is dedicating his life to honor the American Indians." Also produces postcards.

★1561★
Petereins Press
PO Box 10446
Glendale, CA 91209
Description: Established with the aim of publishing books on Chicano studies, Native American history, and on the Southwest. **Subjects:** Philosophy, religion, history.

★1562★
Prairie Provincial Press
604 W. Healey St.
Champaign, IL 61820   Ph: (217)244-0116
Description: Publishes local histories. Plans to offer software. Accepts unsolicited manuscripts with a Native American emphasis. Reaches market through direct mail and telephone sales.

★1563★
R. Schneider Publishers
312 Linwood Ave.
Stevens Point, WI 54481   Fax: (715)345-7898
Description: Publishes on the crafts and technology of the American Indian. Reaches market through direct mail, trade sales, and wholesalers. Does not accept unsolicited manuscripts. **Subjects:** Crafts and technology, primarily American Indian.

★1564★
R. V. Greeves Art Gallery
53 North Fork Rd.
PO Box 428
Fort Washakie, WY 82514   Ph: (307)332-3557
Description: Publishes a photographic essay documenting the process of sculpting and casting a bronze monument to the North American Plains Indians. Reaches market through direct mail, reviews, telephone sales, and Baker & Taylor. **Subjects:** Art, sculpture, American Indians.

★1565★
Raven Hail Books
PO Box 804
Mesa, AZ 85211-0804   Ph: (602)898-7530
Description: Self-publishes books on Cherokee Indians. Reaches market through direct mail.

★1566★
Ray Manley Publishing
238 S. Tucson Blvd.   Ph: (520)623-0307
Tucson, AZ 85716   Fax: (520)623-2524
Subjects: Indian jewelry and crafts of southwestern tribes, Indian lands.

★1567★
Ross and Haines Old Books Co.
411 2nd St.
Hudson, WI 54016   Ph: (715)381-1955
Subjects: Americana, American Indians, regional and military history.

★1568★
Shorey Publications
1109 N. 36th St.
Seattle, WA 98103   Ph: (206)633-2990
Description: Publishes facsimile reprints of older, hard-to-find books on Northwest history, Indian history, mining and gold prospecting, and how-to titles. Also produces reprints of maps. Distributed by Pacific Pipeline. Reaches market through direct mail. **Subjects:** Northwest history, Native American history, mining and gold

★1569★
Sierra Oaks Publishing Co.
1370 Sierra Oaks Ct.   Ph: (916)663-1474
Newcastle, CA 95658-9791   Fax: (916)663-1474
Description: Produces books on the history and culture of American Indians written by American Indians. Also publishes a line of children's titles on American Indian topics and legends. Reaches market through direct mail, trade sales, Pacific Pipeline, and Quality Books, Inc., Treasure Chest Publications, and S.C.B. Distributors. Does not accept unsolicited manuscripts. **Subjects:** Native Americans.

★1570★
Snowbird Publishing Co.
PO Box 729
Tellico Plains, TN 37385
Description: Publishes books on Indian issues by American Indian authors. Also publishes *The Four Directions-American Indian Literary Quarterly*. Accepts unsolicited manuscripts by Indian authors. Reaches market through direct mail. **Subjects:** American Indian fiction and non-fiction.

★1571★
Southwest Museum
PO Box 41558   Ph: (213)221-2164
Los Angeles, CA 90041-0558   Fax: (213)224-8223
Description: Publishes on native American history, anthropology, and archaeology. Offers photo cards of Indian images. Reaches market through direct mail. Does not accept unsolicited manuscripts. **Subjects:** Indian cultures, Maya monuments, archaeology sites in Los Angeles, Southwest recipes.

★1572★
Spirit Talk Press
Postal Drawer V
1992 Bear Citief Dr.
Browning, MT 59417   Ph: (406)338-2882

Description: Publishes material by and about American Indians. Accepts unsolicited manuscripts; include a self-addressed, stamped envelope. Reaches market through direct mail, trade sales, and distributors, including New Leaf Distributors, Bookpeople, Inc., and Pacific Pipeline, Inc. **Subjects:** American Indians.

★1573★
State Historical Society of North Dakota
North Dakota Heritage Center
612 E. Blvd.   Ph: (701)328-2799
Bismarck, ND 58505   Fax: (701)328-3710

Description: Publishes on the history and culture of the Northern Plains. Also publishes directories and a quarterly journal, *North Dakota History*. Offers video cassettes and posters. Accepts unsolicited manuscripts. Reaches market through direct mail and trade sales, and Saks News. **Subjects:** History, Native Americans, North Dakota.

★1574★
Sunstone Press
PO Box 2321   Ph: (505)988-4418
Santa Fe, NM 87504   Fax: (505)988-1025

Description: Publishes Southwestern history and literature for adults and children. Also preserves literature of Indian and Hispanic cultures. Offers note cards. Reaches market through commission representatives, direct mail, and wholesalers and distributors, including Baker & Taylor and Ingram Book Co. Does not accept unsolicited manuscripts; query ok, however.

★1575★
Survival News Service
PO Box 41834
Los Angeles, CA 90041   Ph: (213)255-9502

Description: Publishes on practical survival skills, American Indians, and spirituality. Also offers the monthly *Blue Rose Journal* and audio cassettes. Accepts unsolicited manuscripts. Distributes for Dover, Word Foundations, DeVrys, and others. Reaches market through direct mail. **Subjects:** American Indians, survival, spirituality.

★1576★
Sweetlight Books
16625 Heitman Rd.   Ph: (916)529-5392
Cottonwood, CA 96022-9305   Fax: (916)529-5392

Description: Publishes books "for people who love the earth." Accepts unsolicited manuscripts with a self-addressed, stamped envelope. Reaches market through direct mail and wholesalers. **Subjects:** Anthropology, Indians, natural history. **Number of New Titles:** 1998 - 1.

★1577★
Tahoma Publications/Tahoma Research Service
PO Box 44306
Tacoma, WA 98444   Ph: (206)537-7877

Description: Publishes a history of Fort Nisqually from both a British and an Indian point of view. Reaches market through direct mail. **Subjects:** Nonfiction, history, American Indians. **Number of New Titles:** 1998 - 3; 1997 - 3.

★1578★
Talking Drum Publications
295 NW Riverfront
Bend, OR 97701   Ph: (541)317-1423

Description: Publishes books and audio cassettes on shamanism aimed at metaphysical and new age audiences. Does not accept unsolicited manuscripts. Reaches market through trade sales and distributors, including New Leaf Distributing Co., Bookpeople Inc., and Pacific Pipeline Inc. **Subjects:** Shamanism, ceremonial drumming, Native American studies.

★1579★
Trees Co. Press
49 Van Buren Way
San Francisco, CA 94131   Ph: (415)334-8352

Description: Publishes on Native Americans. Reaches market through direct mail and distributors, including Bookpeople, Baker & Taylor Books, and Sunbelt Publications. **Subjects:** Native Americans, California. **Number of New Titles:** 1997 - 3; 1998 - 4.

★1580★
Trust for Native American Cultures and Crafts
POB 142
Greenville, NH 03048   Ph: (603)878-2944

Description: Disseminates information on traditional native technologies. Offers videotapes, field research, and posters. Reaches market through direct mail. **Subjects:** Native Americans.

★1581★
U.S. Smithsonian Institution
National Museum of the American Indian
3753 Broadway   Ph: (212)283-4031
New York, NY 10032-1596   Fax: (212)491-9302

Description: Publishes books in addition to offering note cards and postcards. Co-publishes with other publishers. **Subjects:** Native peoples of all the Americas, new world archaeology.

★1582★
University of Arizona Press
University of Arizona
1230 N. Park Ave., Ste. 102   Ph: (520)621-1441
Tucson, AZ 85719   Free: 800-426-3797
                                      Fax: (520)621-8899

Description: Publisher of scholarly books and books about the Southwest. **Subjects:** Arizona, American West, natural history, anthropology, archaeology, space sciences, environmental science, Native Americans, women's studies. **Number of New Titles:** 1998 - 42.

★1583★
University of California, Los Angeles
American Indian Studies Center
3220 Campbell Hall
Box 951548   Ph: (310)825-7315
Los Angeles, CA 90095-1548   Fax: (310)206-7060

Description: Publishes books, documents, and video cassettes on Native American subjects for researchers, scholars, and professionals. Offers the *American Indian Culture and Research Journal*. Accepts unsolicited manuscripts. Some publications available on microfiche. Reaches market through direct mail, trade sales, Baker & Taylor, Blackwell North America, Midwest Library Service, Inland Book Co., Pacific Pipeline, and other distributors. **Number of New Titles:** 1998 - 3.

★1584★
University of Idaho Press
16 Brink Hall   Ph: (208)885-5939
Moscow, ID 83844-1107   Free: 800-847-7377
                                      Fax: (208)885-9059

Description: Publishes scholarly books. Accepts queries with self-addressed, stamped envelopes. Request a free catalog before querying to be certain your manuscript fits the editorial program. Distributes for Idaho Geological Survey Press and Idaho State Historical Society Press. Reaches market through direct mail, trade sales, and wholesalers. Does not accept unsolicited manuscripts. **Subjects:** Regional studies, Americana, natural history, ethics, literature, western history, anthropology, American Indians, folklore. **Number of New Titles:** 1998 - 12.

★1585★
University of Montana Occasional Papers in Linguistics
University Of Montana
Linguistics Program   Ph: (406)243-5851
Missoula, MT 59812   Fax: (406)243-2016
Description: Publishes on linguistics and Native languages of the Northwest. Accepts unsolicited manuscripts; after review. **Subjects:** Native language of the Northwest. **Number of New Titles:** 1998 - 1.

★1586★
University of New Mexico
Institute for Native American Development
1812 Las Lomas NE   Ph: (505)277-3917
Albuquerque, NM 87131   Fax: (505)277-1818
Description: Provides outreach services for Native American communities in the areas of specialized seminars, research, and publications. Also offers posters. Reaches market through direct mail.

★1587★
University of Oklahoma Press
University of Oklahoma
1005 Asp Ave.   Ph: (405)325-5111
Norman, OK 73019-0445   Free: 800-627-7377
                                       Fax: (405)325-4000
Description: Publishes scholarly books on such topics as American history, American Indians, literature, and Greek and Roman history. Reaches market through commission representatives, direct mail, trade sales, and wholesalers, including Ingram Book Co., Baker & Taylor, New Leaf Distributing Co., Book Inventory Systems, Book House, Inc., and BookPeople. Does not accept unsolicited manuscripts. **Subjects:** Western U.S., American Indians, classical literature, Greek and Roman studies, literary theory, literary history, Americana, women's studies.

★1588★
University of South Dakota Press
University of South Dakota
Chi Omega 202
414 E. Clark St.   Ph: (605)677-6868
Vermillion, SD 57069-2390   Fax: (605)677-5583
Description: Nonprofit publisher of scholarly fiction and nonfiction. **Subjects:** Native American and intercultural affairs, state and regional history, archaeology, political science, education, drama, poetry.

★1589★
Werner Publications
2020 18th Ave.
Greeley, CO 80631   Ph: (970)395-1082
Description: Publishes on Western Americana and the Indian wars of the 1800's. Reaches market through direct mail and trade sales. **Subjects:** American western history.

★1590★
Westernlore Press
Box 35305   Ph: (602)297-5491
Tucson, AZ 85740   Fax: (520)624-9951
Description: Publishes historical books on the western United States and on Native Americans. Reaches market through trade sales, library jobbers, and direct mail.

★1591★
Whispering Wind Magazine
PO Box 1390
Dept. 16
Folsom, LA 70437-1390   Free: 800-301-8009
Description: Includes articles on Native American material culture. Also includes photographs, descriptions and construction techniques. **Frequency:** 6/yr. **Subscriptions:** $19.00.

Directories

★1592★
The ABC-CLIO Companion to the Native American Rights Movement
ABC-CLIO   Ph: (805)968-1911
PO Box 1911   Free: 800-422-2546
Santa Barbara, CA 93116-1911   Fax: (805)685-9685
Description: Publication includes: Organizations involved in the Native American Rights "movement." Principal content of publication is more than 500 entries that cover treaties, legislation, and landmark court cases of the movement. **Frequency:** Published 1996. **Price:** $60.

★1593★
Access
First Nations Development Institute
69 Kelley Rd.   Ph: (703)371-5615
Falmouth, VA 22405   Fax: (703)371-3505
Description: Over 300 outlets for Native American arts and crafts; national trade associations; 100 trade shows and craft fairs. Entries include: Organization name, address, phone, contact, product, cost. **Pages (approx.):** 318. **Frequency:** Published 1990; new edition possible 1994. **Price:** $21, plus $2.75 shipping.

★1594★
American Indian and Alaska Native Arts and Crafts—Source Directory
U.S. Department of the Interior
1849 C St. NW
Washington, DC 20240   Ph: (202)208-3100
Description: Native American owned and operated arts and crafts businesses throughout the U.S. Entries include: Name, address, phone, fax, contact person, products sold, and additional shop information. **Pages (approx.):** 20.

★1595★
American Indian and Alaska Native Traders Directory
Arrowstar Publishing
PO Box 427
Englewood, CO 80151   Ph: (303)231-6599
Description: 3,500 American Indian-owned and Eskimo-owned arts and crafts businesses, craft persons, and artists. Entries include: Company name, address. **Pages (approx.):** 140, Published June 1990. **Price:** $19.95, plus $1.50 shipping.

★1596★
American Indian Archival Material: A Guide to Holdings in the Southeast
Greenwood Publishing Group, Inc.   Ph: (203)226-3571
88 Post Rd. W.   Free: 800-225-5800
Westport, CT 06881   Fax: (203)222-1502
Description: manuscript repositories with significant collections on Native Americans; coverage limited to Alabama, Florida, Georgia, Kentucky, Louisiana, Mississippi, North and South Carolina, Tennessee, Virginia, and West Virginia. Entries include: Repository name, location, and description of holdings. **Pages (approx.):** 325. **Price:** $69.50.

★1597★
American Indian Index
Arrowstar Publishing
PO Box 427
Englewood, CO 80151   Ph: (303)231-6599
Description: over 6,000 Native American Indian and Native Alaskan tribes, social service organizations and agencies, newspapers, and museums. Entries include: Organization name, address, subsidiary and branch names and locations (if applicable), product or service. **Pages (approx.):** 325. **Frequency:** Irregular, latest edition 1987. **Price:** $19.95, plus $1.50 shipping.

★1598★
Arizona Commission of Indian Affairs—Tribal Directory
Arizona Commission of Indian Affairs
1400 W. Washington, Ste. 300   Ph: (602)542-3123
Phoenix, AZ 85007   Fax: (602)542-3223
Description: Indian tribes and associations, government agencies, and other organizations concerned with Indian affairs in Arizona. Entries include: For tribes–Name, office address and phone; names of officers with addresses, names and phone numbers of council and committee members, meeting and election information. For associations–Name, address, phone, names of officers, meeting details. **Pages (approx.):** 85. **Frequency:** Annual. **Price:** $6.

★1599★
California Indians: Primary Resources: A Guide to Manuscripts, Documents, Serials, Music, and Illustrations
Publishers' Services
PO Box 2510
Novato, CA 94948   Ph: (415)323-9261
Description: archives and museums with print and nonprint materials for research on California Indians; international coverage. Entries include: Archives or institution name, address, description of holdings. **Pages (approx.):** 366. **Frequency:** Irregular, previous edition 1977 (out of print); latest edition 1990. **Price:** $27, cloth; $20, paper.

★1600★
Directory of Montana's American Indians and Others
ERIC Document Reproduction Service
  (EDRS)   Ph: (703)440-1400
7420 Fullerton Road, Ste. 110   Free: 800-443-ERIC
Springfield, VA 22153-2852   Fax: (703)440-1408
Description: 250 American Indian educators and other professional involved in the education of Native Americans in Montana. Entries include: Name, address, phone of organizations and individuals, funding sources and biographical data of educators. **Pages (approx.):** 100. **Frequency:** Published 1993.

★1601★
Directory of Native Education Resources in the Appalachian Region
ERIC Document Reproduction Service
  (EDRS)   Ph: (703)440-1400
7420 Fullerton Road, Ste. 110   Free: 800-443-ERIC
Springfield, VA 22153-2852   Fax: (703)440-1408
Description: Publication includes: 60 organizations who focus on the preservation of Native American culture in the central Appalachian region. Principal content of publication is a study of Native Americans in the Appalachians. **Pages (approx.):** 18. **Frequency:** Published 1994.

★1602★
Directory of Native Education Resources in the Far West Region
ERIC Document Reproduction Service
  (EDRS)   Ph: (703)440-1400
7420 Fullerton Road, Ste. 110   Free: 800-443-ERIC
Springfield, VA 22153-2852   Fax: (703)440-1408
Description: Approximately 350 organizations found in the western U.S. who are dedicated to the welfare of Native American people. Entries include: Name, address, phone, name and title of contact, description of objectives. **Pages (approx.):** 103. **Frequency:** Published 1994.

★1603★
Directory of Native Education Resources in the Mid-Continent Region
ERIC Document Reproduction Service
  (EDRS)   Ph: (703)440-1400
7420 Fullerton Road, Ste. 110   Free: 800-443-3742
Springfield, VA 22153-2852   Fax: (703)440-1408
Description: over 300 organizations in North and South Dakota, Nebraska, Kansas, Colorado, Missouri, and Wyoming and national

organizations who provide or work to improve educational services to Native Americans. Includes private and state organizations, media and publishers, tribes, schools, and federally recognized villages. Entries include: Organization name, address, phone, contact person, and description. **Pages (approx.):** 55. **Frequency:** Periodic.

★1604★
Directory of Native Education Resources in the Northwest Region
ERIC Document Reproduction Service
  (EDRS)   Ph: (703)440-1400
7420 Fullerton Road, Ste. 110   Free: 800-443-3742
Springfield, VA 22153-2852   Fax: (703)440-1408
Description: 593 organizations in Alaska, Idaho, Montana, Oregon, and Washington and national organizations who provide or work to improve educational services to Native Americans and Alaska Natives. Includes private and state organizations, media and publishers, tribes, schools, and federally recognized villages. Entries include: Organization name, address, phone, contact person, and description. **Pages (approx.):** 74. **Frequency:** Periodic.

★1605★
Directory of Native Education Resources in the Southeast Region
ERIC Document Reproduction Service
  (EDRS)   Ph: (703)440-1400
7420 Fullerton Road, Ste. 110   Free: 800-443-3742
Springfield, VA 22153-2852   Fax: (703)440-1408
Description: Approximately 100 tribes, agencies, organizations, and institutions found in the southeastern U.S. who are dedicated to the welfare of Native American people. Entries include: Name, address, phone, name and title of contact, description of objectives. **Pages (approx.):** 37. **Frequency:** Published 1993.

★1606★
Directory of Planning and Community Development Agencies
Washington State Department of
  Community Development
906 Columbia St. SW   Ph: (206)753-2222
Olympia, WA 98504-8300   Fax: (206)753-2950
Description: nearly 400 planning and community development agencies at federal through local levels, including American Indian tribes located in the state of Washington, university and college planning departments, county extension offices, boundary review boards, hearing examiners, social service agencies, economic development organizations, community action agencies, and housing agencies. Entries include: City, county, or agency name, names of key personnel, address, and phone. **Pages (approx.):** 140. **Frequency:** Biennial, June of even years. **Price:** Free. **Formerly:** Planning Agency Directory

★1607★
Directory of Statewide Indian Programs
North Dakota Indian Affairs Commission
State Capitol
Bismarck, ND 58505   Ph: (701)224-2428
Description: about 315 tribal councils, schools and other educational programs, and other tribal, federal, state and private programs and activities on reservations; off-reservation agencies in North Dakota concerned with Indian affairs; directories issued for Standing Rock, Fort Berthold, Turtle Mountain, and Fort Totten reservations. Entries include: Name of school, agency, or program, address, phone, name of contact. **Pages (approx.):** 40. **Frequency:** Annual, January. **Price:** $2. **Formerly:** North Dakota Indian Affairs Commission–Indian Reservation Directories.

★1608★
Education Assistance for American Indians and Alaska Natives
Master of Public Health Program for
American Indians
Warren Hall, Rm. 140
Berkeley, CA 94720
Ph: (415)642-3228
Fax: (510)642-3583
Description: Publication includes: Sources of information regarding health careers, training for health careers, and financial aid available to American Indians and Alaska natives from the Bureau of Indian Affairs, institutions, tribal councils, and other sources. Entries include: Name of organization or publisher, address, name of contact, phone, service programs offered. **Frequency:** Biennial, June of even years. **Price:** Free.

★1609★
Federal Programs of Assistan ce to Native Americans
Senate Select Committee on Indian Affairs
Ph: (202)224-2251
Washington, DC 20510
Fax: (202)224-2309
Description: programs "specifically designed to benefit Indian tribes and individuals, . . .Indians or Indian tribes as eligible beneficiaries, and. . . (programs) deemed to be of special interest to Indians." Entries include: Name, description of program, eligibility requirements, application procedures, name and address of local and Washington contacts, appropriations, other information. **Pages (approx.):** 300. **Frequency:** Irregular, previous edition 1988; latest edition 1991. **Price:** Free. **Formerly:** Federal Programs of Assistance to American Indians.

★1610★
Field Directory of the California Indian Community
California Indian Assistance Program
PO Box 952054
Sacramento, CA 94252-2054
Ph: (916)327-3633
Fax: (916)323-6016
Description: Native American tribes inhabiting the more than 100 reservations and rancherias in California; government agencies dealing with Indian affairs. Entries include: For tribes–Tribe name, tribal affiliation, tribal office address and phone, names and titles of elected officials, description of tribal government; location, population, size, brief history and map of reservation. For government agencies–Name, address, phone, names and titles of key personnel. **Pages (approx.):** 143. **Frequency:** Irregular, latest edition October 1996. **Price:** Free. **Also Known As:** Reservation Field Directory.

★1611★
Financial Aid for Native Americans
Reference Service Press
5000 Windplay, Ste. 4
El Dorado Hills, CA 95762
Ph: (916)939-9620
Fax: (916)939-9626
Description: over 2,000 scholarships, fellowships, loans, grants, awards, and internships available to Native Americans from high school through the professional/postdoctoral level. Entries include: Program name, address, phone, fax, toll-free number, e-mail address, purpose, eligibility, financial data, duration, special features, limitations, number awarded, and deadline date. **Pages (approx.):** 500. **Price:** $35.

★1612★
Health of Native People of North America
Scarecrow Press, Inc.
4720 Boston Way, Ste. A
Lanham, MD 20706
Ph: (301)459-3366
Free: 800-462-6420
Fax: (301)459-2118
Description: 1,557 bibliographies, electronic resources, print abstracts, books and book chapters, conference proceedings, dissertations/theses, audiovisuals, health organizations and libraries, health facilities and agencies, and health education programs in colleges and universities that deal with some aspect of Native American health. **Pages (approx.):** 393. **Price:** $55.

★1613★
Indian America: A Traveler's Guide
John Muir Publications
PO Box 613
Santa Fe, NM 87504-0613
Ph: (505)982-4078
Free: 800-888-7504
Fax: (505)988-1680
Description: over 300 Indian tribes in the U.S. Entries include: Tribe name, council address, phone; description of activities, including public ceremonies and powwows; tribe histories. **Pages (approx.):** 448. **Frequency:** Irregular, previous edition July 1991; latest edition July 1993. **Price:** $18.95.

★1614★
Indian Country Address Book
Todd Publications
PO Box 635
Nyack, NY 10960
Ph: (914)358-6213
Free: 800-747-1056
Fax: (914)358-1059
Description: Native American contacts in the U.S. and Canada including artists, businesses, crisis intervention centers, educational institutions, employment, foods, gaming, health care, Indian centers, legal services, nations, and radio and television stations. Entries include: Contact name, address, phone and description where needed. **Pages (approx.):** 515. **Price:** $45.

★1615★
Indian Goods Retail Directory
American Business Directories, Inc.
5711 S. 86th Circle
Omaha, NE 68127
Ph: (402)593-4600
Free: 800-555-6124
Fax: (402)331-5481
Description: Number of listings: 1,820. Entries include: Name, address, phone, size of advertisement, name of owner or manager, number of employees, year first in "Yellow Pages." Compiled from telephone company "Yellow Pages," nationwide. **Frequency:** Updated continuously; printed on request. **Price:** Please inquire.

★1616★
National Directory for Eldercare Information and Referral
National Association of Area Agencies on
Aging
1112 16th St. NW, Ste. 100
Washington, DC 20036
Ph: (202)296-8130
Fax: (202)296-8134
Description: Federal, state and area offices on aging; Native American aging organizations; major national aging associations. Entries include: Name, address, phone, name of director, fax, local information and referral services, instate toll-free phone. **Pages (approx.):** 171. **Frequency:** Biennial. **Price:** $45

★1617★
Native American Directory: Alaska, Canada, United States
National Native American Cooperative
PO Box 27626
Tucson, AZ 85726
Fax: (520)292-0779
Description: More than 2,000 Native American performing arts groups, craft materials suppliers, stores and galleries, Indian-owned motels and resorts; tribal offices, museums, and cultural centers; associations and schools; newspapers, radio and television programs, and stations operated by, owned by, or specifically for Native Americans; calendar of events, including officially sanctioned powwows, conventions, arts and crafts shows, all-Indian rodeos, and Navajo rug auctions; how-to buy Indian crafts and research Indian ancestry. Entries include: Generally, organization or company name, address, descriptive comments, dates (for shows or events). **Pages (approx.):** 880. **Frequency:** Irregular, previous edition 1982; latest edition January 1996. **Price:** $65.95, postpaid; $131, library edition with wall map.

★1618★
Native American Policy Network—Directory
Native American Policy Network
Barry University
11300 NE 2nd Ave.
Miami, FL 33161
Ph: (305)899-3473
Fax: (305)899-3279
Description: about 425 professors, political leaders, and others interested in Native American politics. Entries include: Name,

address, phone. **Pages (approx.):** 15. **Frequency:** Quarterly. **Price:** $20.

★1619★
Native Education Directory: Organizations and Resources for Educators of Native Americans
ERIC Clearinghouse on Rural Education
  and Small Schools
Appalachia Educational Laboratory
1030 Quarrie St.   Ph: (304)347-0437
PO Box 1348   Free: 800-624-9120
Charleston, WV 25325-1348   Fax: (304)347-0487

Description: over 500 national and state organizations, periodicals, federal and state agencies, colleges, universities, and other groups working in the education of Native students. Entries include: Name, address, phone, name of contact, description of programs and services, e-mail, www site. **Pages (approx.):** 102. **Frequency:** Triennial, latest edition January 1997. **Price:** $12. **Formerly:** American Indian Education: A Directory of Organizations and Activities in American Indian Education.

★1620★
Native North American Almanac
Gale Research   Ph: (313)961-2242
835 Penobscot Bldg.   Free: 800-877-
Detroit, MI 48226-4094   GALE
                                    Fax: (313)961-6083

Description: Includes essays on issues of interest to Native Americans and Canadian natives, including history, economy, education, religion, culture, arts, language, law and legislation, activism, the environment, health, and media; each chapter includes, as appropriate, directories of tribal communities, organizations, government agencies, schools, and businesses relevant to the topic. Entries include: Name, address, phone, contact. **Pages (approx.):** 1,275. **Frequency:** First edition November 1993; new edition expected 1999. **Price:** $75.

★1621★
North American Indian Landmarks—A Traveler's Guide
Gale Research   Ph: (313)961-2242
835 Penobscot Bldg.   Free: 800-877-
Detroit, MI 48226-4094   GALE
                                    Fax: (313)961-6083

Description: Approximately 340 sites in the U.S. and Canada significant to Native North American history, including historical, tribal, and art museums, monuments, plaques, parks, reservations, birthplaces, grave sites, battlefields. Entries include: Site name, description, location, days and hours of operation, admission fee, phone. Paperback edition published by Visible Ink Press, an imprint of Gale Research. **Pages (approx.):** 409. **Frequency:** Published 1993. **Price:** $34.95, cloth; $17.95, paper.

★1622★
Oregon Directory of American Indian Resources
Oregon Commission on Indian Services
167 State Capitol Bldg.   Ph: (503)986-1067
Salem, OR 97310   Fax: (503)986-1071

Description: about 300 Native American Indian tribes, organizations, sponsors of educational programs, and publishers in Oregon; Oregon federal government congressional representatives; federal agencies related to Native American concerns; Oregon state government executive and legislative branch members, state agencies, and publications. Entries include: For tribes–Name, legal status, address and phone. For local agencies and organizations–Name, address, phone; statement of objectives, projects, and services offered; names and titles of key personnel. For publications–Publication title; publisher name, address, phone. For government officials–Name, address, phone; district and political affiliation. For federal agencies and commissions–Name, address, phone, name and title of contact. For regional and national organizations–Organization name, address, phone. **Pages (approx.):** 55. **Frequency:** Biennial, February of even years. **Price:** Free.

★1623★
Pow Wow on the Red Road
National Native American Co-op
PO Box 27626   Ph: (520)622-4900
Tucson, AZ 85726   Fax: (520)292-0779

Description: Over 1,200 Native American events in the U.S. and Canada for 1994-97; events listed are five years old or older. Located, cost, camping, sponsor, type of event. Given for each event (5 year directory). **Pages (approx.):** 84. **Frequency:** Irregular, latest edition 1994; new edition expected 1997. **Price:** $25.

★1624★
Powwow Calendar
Book Publishing Co. (Summertown)   Ph: (615)964-3571
PO Box 99   Free: 800-695-2241
Summertown, TN 38483   Fax: (615)964-3518

Description: Native American powwows, dances, craft fairs in the U.S. and Canada during the current calendar year. Entries include: Event name, location, phone number, date, contact person. **Pages (approx.):** 112. **Frequency:** Annual. **Price:** $8.95.

★1625★
Reference Encyclopedia of the American Indian
Todd Publications   Ph: (914)358-6213
PO Box 635   Free: 800-747-1056
Nyack, NY 10960   Fax: (914)358-1059

Description: agencies and associations of interest to Native Americans, including reservations, tribal councils, Bureaus of Indian Affairs, schools and health services, museums, cultural centers, audiovisual aids, and periodicals; approximately 2,500 Native Americans prominent in tribal affairs, business, industry, art, science, and other professions, and non-Indians active in Indian affairs and related fields. Entries include: For agencies and associations–Name, address, phone, names and titles of key personnel, description of activities. For individuals–Name, address, phone, biographical data. **Pages (approx.):** 900. **Frequency:** Biennial, Odd years. **Price:** $95, paper; $125, cloth.

★1626★
Smoke Signals: Business Directory of Indian Country U.S.A.
Arrowstar Publishing
PO Box 427
Englewood, CO 80151   Ph: (303)231-6599

Description: Approximately 3,500 American Indian and Alaska Native owned and operated businesses. Entries include: Company name, address. **Pages (approx.):** 220, Published 1990. **Price:** $24.95, plus $1.95 shipping. **Formerly:** Smoke Signals: Directory of Native Indian/Alaskan Businesses.

★1627★
Sources of Financial Aid Available to American Indian Students
Indian Resource Development
Box 3001/MSC 3IRD   Ph: (505)646-1347
Las Cruces, NM 88003-0001   Fax: (505)646-7740

Description: about 40 government agencies, private organizations, colleges and universities, and other groups offering financial aid or work experience opportunities for North American Indian college students. Entries include: Organization or institute name, address, phone, contact name, type of aid available, duration and amount, deadline, requirements, field of study, college or university selection. **Pages (approx.):** 90. **Frequency:** Annual. **Price:** $4.

★1628★
Who's Who in Indian Relics
Parks-Thompson Co.
1757 W. Adams
St. Louis, MO 63122   Ph: (314)822-2409

Description: 130 to 140 persons per volume who have outstanding collections of American Indian relics. Volume 7, published 1987, also includes roster of 1,900 other collectors. Entries include: Biography and portrait of collector, description of collection, photographs of selected items. **Pages (approx.):** 375. **Price:** $35, per volume, plus $2.50 shipping; payment with order.

Journals & Magazines

★1629★
Akwesasne Notes
Mohawk Nation
PO Box 196
Rooseveltown, NY 13683-0196   Ph: (518)358-9531
Description: Full color magazine concerning American Indian and indigenous persons worldwide. **First Published:** 1968. **Frequency:** Quarterly. **Subscriptions:** $25. **ISSN:** 0002-3949.

★1630★
American Indian Art Magazine
American Indian Art, Inc.
7314 E. Osborn Dr.   Ph: (602)994-5445
Scottsdale, AZ 85251   Fax: (602)945-9533
Description: Journal covering all areas of Native American art. **First Published:** 1975. **Frequency:** Quarterly. **Subscriptions:** $6.

★1631★
American Indian Basketry Magazine
Institute for the Study of Traditional
   American Indian Arts
PO Box 66124
Portland, OR 97290   Ph: (503)233-8131
Description: American Indian magazine featuring basketry and other native arts. **First Published:** 1979. **Frequency:** Quarterly.

★1632★
American Indian Quarterly
University of Nebraska Press
312 N. 14th St.   Ph: (402)472-3581
Lincoln, NE 68588   Fax: 800-755-1105
Description: An interdisciplinary journal featuring anthropology, history, literature, and the arts. **First Published:** 1982. **Frequency:** Quarterly. **Subscriptions:** $25. **ISSN:** 0095-182X.

★1633★
Indian Artifact Magazine
Indian Artifact Magazine, Inc.
RD 1, Box 240   Ph: (717)437-3698
Turbotville, PA 17772-9599   Fax: (717)437-3411
Description: Magazine of American Indian prehistory, including artifacts, lifestyles, customs, and archaeology. **First Published:** 1982. **Frequency:** Quarterly **ISSN:** 0736-265X.

★1634★
Indian Historian
Indian Historian Press
1493 Masonic Ave.   Ph: (415)626-5235
San Francisco, CA 94117   Fax: (415)626-4923
Description: Magazine covering American Indian culture and history. **First Published:** 1964. **Frequency:** Quarterly. **Subscriptions:** $10

★1635★
Indian Life
Intertribal Christian Communications   Ph: (204)661-9333
PO Box 3765, RPO Redwood Centre   Free: 800-665-9275
Winnipeg, MB, Canada R2W 3R6   Fax: (204)661-3482
Description: A non-denominational Christian newspaper addressing the social, cultural, and spiritual needs of North American Indians. **First Published:** 1979. **Frequency:** Bimonthly. **Subscriptions:** $7. **ISSN:** 0226-9317.

★1636★
Jicarilla Chieftain
PO Box 507   Ph: (505)759-3242
Dulce, NM 87528-0507   Fax: (505)759-3005
Description: Native American news tabloid. **First Published:** 1962. **Frequency:** Semimonthly.

★1637★
La Gente
University of California, Los Angeles
118 Kerkhoff Hall   Ph: (310)825-9836
Los Angeles, CA 90024   Fax: (310)206-3165
Description: A student publication serving the Native American, Chicano, and Latino communities. **First Published:** 1971. **Frequency:** 8/year. **Subscriptions:** $18. **Formerly:** La Gente de Aztlan.

★1638★
Native Peoples Magazine
PO Box 36820   Ph: (602)252-2236
Phoenix, AZ 85067   Free: (888)262-8483
Description: Magazine portraying the culture of native peoples of the Americas. **First Published:** 1987. **Frequency:** Quarterly. **Subscriptions:** $13.95. **ISSN:** 0895-7606.

★1639★
News from Native California
Heyday Books
PO Box 9145   Ph: (510)549-3564
Berkeley, CA 94709   Fax: (510)549-1889
Description: Magazine featuring material relating to California Indians, past and present. **First Published:** 1987. **Frequency:** Quarterly. **Subscriptions:** $19. **ISSN:** 1040-5437.

★1640★
Oklahoma Today Magazine
Oklahoma Today Magazine   Ph: (405)521-2496
PO Box 53384   Free: 800-777-1793
Oklahoma City, OK 73152   Fax: (405)521-3992
Description: Regional consumer magazine focusing on travel, nature, recreation, people and American Indian and New West issues. **First Published:** 1956. **Frequency:** Bimonthly. **ISSN:** 0030-1892.

★1641★
Whispering Wind
Written Heritage   Ph: (504)796-5433
PO Box 1390   Free: 800-301-8009
Folsom, LA 70437-1390   Fax: (504)796-9236
Description: Magazine covering historical events, crafts, and material culture of the American Indian. **First Published:** 1967. **Frequency:** Bimonthly. **Subscriptions:** $20. **ISSN:** 0300-6565.

Newsletters

★1642★
AICH Community Bulletin
American Indian Community House, Inc.
404 Lafayette St., 2nd Fl.   Ph: (212)598-0100
New York, NY 10003   Fax: (212)598-4909
Description: Reports on activities of the organization, which serves the social, educational, and cultural needs of Native Americans residing in the New York metropolitan area. Reviews news and issues of interest to American Indi ans. Recurring features include editorials, news of research, book reviews, and a calendar of events. **Pages (approx.):** 24. **Frequency:** Quarterly. **Price:** Donation requested. **Formerly:** AICH Newsletter.

★1643★
AISES Education Newsletter
AISES Publishing
5661 Airport Blvd.   Ph: (303)939-0023
Boulder, CO 80301-2339   Fax: (303)939-8150
Description: Updates Society news. Notes upcoming conferences and workshops. Recurring features include news of educational opportunities. **Pages (approx.):** 12.

★1644★
AISES Visions
American Indian Science & Engineering
  Society (AISES)
1630 30th St., Ste. 301   Ph: (303)939-0023
Boulder, CO 80301   Fax: (303)939-8150
Description: Seeks to communicate information pertinent to the Society's goal of increasing the number of American Indian scientists and engineers in the United States. Reports on recruitment efforts and activities. Recurring features include columns titled News from AISES. College Beat, Professional Chapters, Other Organizations, Programs & Events, High School News, News from the Board, Job Opportunities, and Focus on a Board Member. **Pages (approx.):** 12. **Frequency:** 2/year.

★1645★
The American Indian Community House Community Bulletin
American Indian Community House, Inc.
404 Lafayette St., 2nd Fl.   Ph: (212)598-0100
New York, NY 10003   Fax: (212)598-4909
Description: Provides community news and events concerning New York City's native community. Topics include health, performing arts, substance abuse, and education. Recurring features include notices of publications available and a calendar of events. **Pages (approx.):** 24. **Frequency:** Quarterly.

★1646★
American Indian Defense News
Big Chief International
c/o Dr. Webber
PO Box 3121
Hutchinson, KS 67504-3121   Ph: (316)665-3614
Description: Contains articles about Native Americans. **Pages (approx.):** 10. **Price:** $10, 6 issues; $14, 10 issues.

★1647★
American Indian Law Center Newsletter
American Indian Law Center, Inc.
1117 Stanford NE
Albuquerque, NM 87196   Ph: (505)277-5462
Description: Covers the latest developments in federal Indian law, legislation being considered for enactment, administration of Indian programs, and policy analysis. Reports congressional activity on issues affecting American Indians, administrative rulings, and judicial decisions. **Remarks:** Publication temporarily suspended. **Frequency:** Bimonthly. **Price:** $20.

★1648★
American Indian Libraries Newsletter
The American Indian Library Association
School of Library and Information Studies
The University of Oklahoma   Ph: (405)325-3921
Norman, OK 73019   Fax: (405)325-7648
Description: Reports news and events related to American Indian libraries/services. Reviews publications related to Native Americans. Features reservation libraries. Recurring features include reports of articles, meetings, and book reviews. **Pages (approx.):** 8. **Frequency:** Quarterly. **Price:** Included in membership; $10/year for nonmembers; $25 for institutions.

★1649★
American Indian Rehabilitation
American Indian Rehabilitation Research
  and Training Center
PO Box 5630   Ph: (520)523-4791
Flagstaff, AZ 86011   Fax: (520)523-9127
Description: Covers activities of the Center, which aims to improve the lives of American Indians with disabilities. Contains articles on rehabilitation. Recurring features include news of research, a calendar of events, reports of meetings, news of educational opportunities, book reviews, notices of publications available, and news of training activities. **Pages (approx.):** 20-24. **Frequency:** 2/year. **Formerly:** Uts'itishtaan'i.

★1650★
Bureau of Catholic Indian Missions Newsletter
Bureau of Catholic Indian Missions
2021 H St. NW
Washington, DC 20006   Ph: (202)331-8542
Description: Publishes news and concerns of the Bureau, especially those issues pertaining to the Catholic Church and the Indian community: evangelism, justice, treaties, and advocacy. Promotes healthy family living in the face of the problems affecting Indian families: divorce, drugs, suicide, and alcohol. Updates information on legislation affecting the Indian community. Recurring features include a letter from the editor, obituaries, statistics, book reviews, news of research, and a column titled Bread and Freedom. **Pages (approx.):** 4. **Frequency:** 10/year.

★1651★
Cherokee Boys Club Newsletter and CCFS Voice
Cherokee Boys Club
PO Box 507   Ph: (704)497-5001
Cherokee, NC 28719   Fax: (704)497-5818
Description: Published as a service of the Boys Club, covering activities of the Club, the Cherokee Center for Family Services, for the American Indian people indigenous to Tennessee and North Carolina. Recurring features include news of members, obituaries, awards and honors, and human service programs. **Pages (approx.):** 12. **Frequency:** Quarterly. **Formerly:** Cherokee Boys Club–Newsletter.

★1652★
Citizen Alert
PO Box 5339   Ph: (702)827-4200
Reno, NV 89513   Fax: (702)827-4299
Description: Reports on issues of environmental concern in Nevada and Great Basin, including the transportation and disposal of high-level nuclear waste, the impact of military programs on property and the environment, water importation plans, and the concerns of Native Americans. Recurring features include letters to the editor, interviews, news of research, a calendar of events, and a column titled Native Horizons. **Pages (approx.):** 16. **Frequency:** Quarterly. **Price:** Free; donation requested.

★1653★
Commission for the Catholic Missions Among the Colored People and the Indians—Quarterly
Commission for the Catholic Missions
  Among the Colored People and the
  Indians
2021 H St. NW
Washington, DC 20006   Ph: (202)331-8542
Description: Concerned with evangelism in church programs for the Black and Indian communities in the U.S. Publishes news and updates the financial status of the Commission. Reports the ordination of priests and the activities of individuals from Black and Indian communities. Recurring features include a letter from the editor and statistics. **Pages (approx.):** 4. **Frequency:** Annual.

★1654★
Cross and Feather News
Tekakwitha Conference National Center
1800 Ninth Ave. S., No. 20
Great Falls, MT 59406   Ph: (406)727-0147
Description: Carries articles addressing religious, social, and legislative issues concerning Native American Catholics. Reports on workshops, conferences, and meetings dealing with such topics as lay ministry, catechesis, youth and family concerns, chemical dependency, community life, social justice, and tribal concerns. **Pages (approx.):** 32. **Frequency:** Quarterly.

★1655★
Elder Voices
National Indian Council on Aging (NICOA)
10501 Montgomery Blvd. NE, Ste. 210   Ph: (505)292-2001
Albuquerque, NM 87111-3846   Fax: (505)292-1922
Description: Concentrates on issues affecting lives of Native American elders, such as services, entitlements, and related

legislative issues. **Pages (approx.):** 4. **Frequency:** Periodic. **Price:** Free to members; $2/year for all others. **Formerly:** NICOA News.

★1656★
Family Services Newsletter
Family Services Program
PO Box 1296
Bishop, CA 93515
Ph: (619)873-8464
Fax: (619)873-3935

Description: Focuses on concerns of Indian families, discussing issues such as drugs and alcohol, parenting, child abuse and neglect, and women's concerns. Provides information on the Program's counseling, educational, legal, and advocacy services. **Pages (approx.):** 12. **Frequency:** Quarterly.

★1657★
Field Notes
Arkansas Archeological Survey
PO Box 1249
Fayetteville, AR 72702-1249
Ph: (501)575-3556
Fax: (501)575-5453

Description: Provides news, business, and short scientific reports on Arkansas prehistory, early history, archeology, and Native Americans. Recurring features include news of research, a calendar of events, reports of meetings, book reviews, and notices of publications available. **Pages (approx.):** 15-19. **Frequency:** Bimonthly.

★1658★
Futures
Futures for Children
9600 Tennyson St. NE
Albuquerque, NM 87122-2282
Free: 800-545-6843
Fax: (505)821-4141

Description: Supports the Futures for Children program, which seeks to find sponsors for American Indian children to contribute toward the child's education and clothing. Provides sponsors, donors, and "Friends of Futures" with news concerning the Sponsorship Program, the Self-Help Program, and the International Program. Recurring features include a six-month calendar of events, lists of items for sale, and features on sponsored students. Also includes articles on organization activities, dedications, special events and columns titled Of Special Interest and From the Field. **Pages (approx.):** 4-6. **Frequency:** 2/year.

★1659★
Gower Federal Service-Miscellaneous Land Decisions
Rocky Mountain Mineral Law Foundation
7039 E. 18th Ave.
Denver, CO 80220
Ph: (303)321-8100
Fax: (303)321-7657

Description: Publishes all I.B.L.A. decisions that deal with topics such as Alaska Native allotments and claims, color or claim of title, desert land entries, grazing permits and licenses, homesteads, Indian allotments, public land surveys and classifications, and rights-of-way. **Frequency:** 5/year. **Price:** $165/year.

★1660★
Gower Federal Service-Royalty Valuation and Management
Rocky Mountain Mineral Law Foundation
7039 E. 18th Ave.
Denver, CO 80220
Ph: (303)321-8100
Fax: (303)321-7657

Description: Publishes Minerals Management Service decisions. Supplementary materials cover federal and Indian royalty valuation, management, and collection matters in 23 volumes. **Frequency:** 12/year. **Price:** $1,400, first year; $500, renewals.

★1661★
Ikhana
Office of Native American Ministry
815 2nd Ave.
New York, NY 10017
Ph: (212)922-5341
Free: 800-334-7626
Fax: (212)867-7652

Description: Focuses on American Indian affairs. Informs readers of programs and projects of groups affiliated with the Episcopal Church. Recurring features include poetry, stories, news of research, editorials, news of members, and a calendar of events. **Pages (approx.):** 4. **Frequency:** Semiannual. **Formerly:** NCIW Newsletter.

★1662★
Indian Affairs
Association on American Indian Affairs, Inc.
Box 268
Sisseton, ND 57262-0268

Description: Explores issues concerning American Indian affairs: reports on economic, political, and social conditions on reservations, inter-tribal relations, resource utilization, self-determination, legal defense, foster care programs, education, and health issues. Recurring features include book reviews and announcements of scholarship awards. **Pages (approx.):** 6. **Frequency:** 3/year. **Price:** $10/year.

★1663★
Indian Awareness Center Newsletter
Fulton County Historical Society, Inc.
37 East 375 North
Rochester, IN 46975-8384
Ph: (219)223-4436

Description: Covers projects and activities of the Center, which encourages the awareness, appreciation, and preservation of Native American culture and traditions, especially that of the Potawatomi and Miami Indians of northern Indiana. Recurring features include letters to the editor, interviews, news of research, a calendar of events, reports of meetings, news of educational opportunities, book reviews, and notices of publications available. Coordinates Trail of Death Regional Historic Trail - placing of historical markers on 1838 forced removal of Potawatomi from Indiana to Kansas. Genealogy of families descended from Trail of Death. News of Trail of Courage Living History Festival–3rd weekend of Sept. **Pages (approx.):** 20. **Frequency:** Semiannual. **Price:** $5/year for individuals; $7.50 for families and institutions.

★1664★
Indian Progress
Associated Committee of Friends on Indian Affairs (ACFIA)
PO Box 1661
Richmond, IN 47375
Ph: (317)962-9169

Description: Contains news of centers administered by the Committee. **Pages (approx.):** 4-8. **Frequency:** 3/year. **Price:** Free to individuals; $3/year for institutions.

★1665★
Indian Report
Friends Committee on National Legislation (FCNL)
245 2nd St. NE
Washington, DC 20002
Ph: (202)547-6000
Fax: (202)547-6019

Description: Serves as an educational tool of the Indian program of the Committee, reporting on legislative issues affecting Native Americans. **Pages (approx.):** 8. **Frequency:** Quarterly. **Price:** Donation requested.

★1666★
Indian Time
Mohawk Nation
PO Box 196
Rooseveltown, NY 13683-0196
Ph: (518)358-9531

Description: Provides news concerning the Akwesasne Mohawk reservation. Includes editorials, letters, and job listings. **Pages (approx.):** 8. **Frequency:** Weekly. **Price:** $40/year, U.S.; $45 elsewhere.

★1667★
The Indian Trader
The Indian Trader, Inc.
311 E. Aztec
Gallup, NM 87301
Ph: (505)722-6694
Free: 800-748-1624
Fax: (505)722-6696

Description: Spotlights American Indian culture, arts, and crafts. **Frequency:** Monthly. **Price:** $20

★1668★
Journal of Cherokee Studies
Museum of the Cherokee Indian
PO Box 1599   Ph: (704)497-3481
Cherokee, NC 28719   Fax: (704)497-4985
Description: Covers historical and cultural research of Cherokee Indians. Contains scholarly articles. **Pages (approx.):** 75-80. **Frequency:** Annual. **Price:** Museum members only.

★1669★
Ka Ri Wen Ha Wi
Akwesasne Library
R.R. 1, Box 14 C   Ph: (518)358-2240
Hogansburg, NY 13655   Fax: (518)358-2649
Description: Publishes news of the Reservation community and the Akwesasne Library/Cultural Center. Recurring features include news of members, tribal notices, a calendar of Reservation programs, and a listing of courses and job opportunities from area colleges and schools. **Pages (approx.):** 4-6. **Frequency:** Monthly.

★1670★
Las Palabras
Millicent Rogers Museum
PO Box A   Ph: (505)758-2462
Taos, NM 87571   Fax: (505)758-5751
Description: Supports the Museum's mission, which is to support "the collection and interpretation of the art, history, and culture of the Native American, Hispanic, and Anglo peoples of the Southwest, focusing on Taos and northern New Mexico." Provides in-depth information on exhibits and collections, and museum news. Includes a calendar of events. **Pages (approx.):** 12-20. **Frequency:** Annual.

★1671★
Lily of the Mohawks
Blessed Kateri Tekakwitha League
Auriesville, NY 12016   Ph: (518)853-3153
Description: Promotes the knowledge, love, and canonization of Blessed Kateri Tekakwitha (1656-1680), an American Indian who was instructed by Jesuits, lived a life of sanctity, and was made venerable in 1943 by the Roman Catholic Church and blessed by Pope John Paul II in 1980. Carries articles honoring Kateri and inspirational items. Recurring features include reports on League activities and news of members. **Pages (approx.):** 8. **Frequency:** Quarterly.

★1672★
Meeting Ground
D'Arcy McNickle Center for the History of
    the American Indian
Newberry Library
60 W Walton St.
Chicago, IL 60610   Ph: (312)943-9090
Description: Reports past, present, and future activities of the Center which is committed to "improving the quality of teaching and research in the field of Native American history." Recurring features include news of research, news of members, book reviews, reports on Chicago Indian community projects, and columns titled Director's Notes, Center Fellows, Alumni Notes, and New Books. **Pages (approx.):** 8. **Frequency:** Biennial.

★1673★
NARF Legal Review
Native American Rights Fund
1506 Broadway   Ph: (303)447-8760
Boulder, CO 80302   Fax: (303)443-7776
Description: Focuses on the concerns of the Native American Rights Fund, "a nonprofit organization specializing in the protection of Indian rights." Discusses current Indian law issues. Carries staff news, news of NARF activities, and announcements of NARF services and publications. Recurring features include a column titled Case Updates. **Pages (approx.):** 16-24. **Frequency:** Semiannual. **Formerly:** Native American Rights Fund–Announcements.

★1674★
Native Sun
Detroit American Indian Center
2272 Plymouth Rd.   Ph: (313)535-2966
Detroit, MI 48239   Fax: (313)533-1080
Description: Carries local and national news pertaining to Native Americans, including news of the Association, with emphasis on events of interest to American Indians in Wayne County. Covers pertinent legislation. Recurring features include listings of workshops, recreational activities, educational programs, recipes, poems, obituaries and birth announcements, a calendar of events, job announcements, and reports from the director of the Center. **Frequency:** Quarterly.

★1675★
The New Race
Phillip Heritage House
605 Benton
Missoula, MT 59801   Ph: (406)543-3495
Description: Contains genealogical information and family stories relating to the editor's ancestors and quest for her American Indian (Cherokee) heritage. Recurring features include letters to the editor, interviews, book reviews, and notices of publications available. **Pages (approx.):** 10-20. **Frequency:** Annual. **Price:** $10/year.

★1676★
Northwest Indian Fisheries Commission News
Northwest Indian Fisheries Commission
6730 Martin Way E.   Ph: (206)438-1180
Olympia, WA 98506   Fax: (206)753-8660
Description: Informs the public on fisheries/natural resource management activities of twenty treaty Indian tribes in Washington state. Recurring features include interviews, news of research, and a column titled Being Frank. **Pages (approx.):** 12. **Frequency:** Quarterly.

★1677★
Order of the Indian Wars—Communique
Order of the Indian Wars
PO Box 7401
Little Rock, AR 72217   Ph: (501)225-3996
Description: Centers on the study and dissemination of information on America's frontier conflicts, with as much interest in the "Indian side" as the "Army/settler side" of events in the early years of this country. Concerned about the preservation of important military sites of the Indian Wars. Recurring features include announcements of available publications and of lectures and events of interest. **Pages (approx.):** 8-12. **Frequency:** Monthly. **Price:** $20/year for members. **Also Known As:** OIW Communique.

★1678★
Pilgrim
Shrine of Our Lady of Martyrs
Noeltner Rd.
Auriesville, NY 12016   Ph: (518)853-3033
Description: Features information pertaining to saints martyred on the shrine's site including Saints Isaac Jogues, Rene Goupil, John LaLande, and Mohawk Indian Kateri Tekakwitha birthplace. **Pages (approx.):** 8. **Frequency:** 3/year.

★1679★
Pottery Southwest
Albuquerque Archaeological Society
6207 Mossman Pl. NE
Albuquerque, NM 87110   Ph: (505)828-2990
Description: Carries news and queries on prehistoric pottery of the Indians in New Mexico, Arizona, Utah, Colorado, and parts of Texas and Mexico. Recurring features include book reviews, bibliographies, and scholarly contributions from "Southwesternists" in the field of archeology. **Pages (approx.):** 7. **Frequency:** Quarterly. **Price:** $4.

★1680★
Red Cloud Country
Red Cloud Indian School
Holy Rosary Mission   Ph: (605)867-1105
Pine Ridge, SD 57770   Fax: (605)867-1104
Description: Informs donors of Red Cloud Indian School about the lives of the students on the Pine Ridge Indian Reservation. Recurring features include a Letter from the President of the Mission. **Pages (approx.):** 4.

★1681★
'Round Robbins
The Friends of the Robbins Museum
PO Box 700
Middleborough, MA 02346-0700   Ph: (508)947-9005
Description: Concerned with the preservation and study of Massachusetts' archaeological heritage; supports the Robbins Museum. Presents information on artifact collections, museum volunteers, and Native American culture. Recurring features include columns titled Friends of the Robbins Museum, Friends Special Events, and Robbin Volunteers. **Pages (approx.):** 8. **Frequency:** 2-3/year.

★1682★
The Rule
Native American Educational Services
   College
2838 W. Peterson   Ph: (312)761-5000
Chicago, IL 60659   Fax: (312)761-3808
Description: Reports news of the College. Recurring features include news of research, reports of meetings, news of educational opportunities, and a column titled President's Message. **Pages (approx.):** 16. **Frequency:** occasional.

★1683★
Seasons
Native American AIDS Prevention Center
2100 Lakeshore Ave., Ste. A   Ph: (510)444-2051
Oakland, CA 94606   Fax: (510)444-1593
Description: Features articles and artwork by Native Americans impacted by HIV/AIDS. **Frequency:** Quarterly.

★1684★
Sentinel
National Congress of American Indians
2010 Massachusetts Ave. NW, 2nd Fl.   Ph: (202)466-7767
Washington, DC 20036   Fax: (202)466-7797
Description: Focuses on national issues affecting American Indians and Alaska natives. Monitors government legislation, federal agency activities, and innovative tribal programs. Recurring features include legislation and litigation updates, profiles of important American Indians, editorials, and a calendar of events. **Pages (approx.):** 16-32. **Frequency:** Quarterly.

★1685★
Shenandoah Newsletter
Paul A. Skenandore
736 W. Oklahoma St.
Appleton, WI 54914   Ph: (414)832-9525
Description: Discusses the history and legal rights of the native peoples of Great Turtle Island. Reports news of treaty and discrimination disputes, and of the international position of American Indians in a third world setting. Recurring features include editorials. **Pages (approx.):** 21. **Frequency:** Monthly. **Price:** $14.50.

★1686★
The Source
New Mexico Office of Indian Affairs
LA, Villa Rivera Bldg.   Ph: (505)827-6440
Santa Fe, NM 87501   Fax: (505)827-6445
Description: Provides information on intergovernmental relations, commissioner activities, culture, arts, and educational issues of the American Indians. Recurring features include news of research, a calendar of events, reports of meetings, and columns titled the State

Legislature and Updates. **Pages (approx.):** 20-24. **Frequency:** 3/year.

★1687★
The Spike
The Spike
PO Box 368   Ph: (908)656-0074
Milltown, NJ 08850   Fax: (201)823-6164
Description: Discusses contemporary Native American culture from a personal perspective. Announces Native American events scheduled from Canada to Florida east of the Mississippi River. Recurring features include letters to the editor, a calendar of events, news of educational opportunities, job listings, and notices of publications available. **Pages (approx.):** 8. **Frequency:** Monthly. **Price:** $36/year, U.S.; $38, Canada.

★1688★
Spirit!
Native American Resource Center
University of North Carolina at Pembroke
Pembroke, NC 28372   Ph: (910)521-6282
Description: Gives news of projects and events. **Frequency:** Quarterly.

★1689★
University of South Dakota—Bulletin
Institute of American Indian Studies
Dakota Hall, Rm. 12
414 E. Clark St.   Ph: (605)677-5209
Vermillion, SD 57069   Fax: (605)677-6525
Description: Disseminates information on education, current affairs, and regional and national issues and activities concerning American Indians. Offers editorials and feature articles. **Pages (approx.):** 12-15. **Frequency:** Semiannual. **Price:** Donation requested.

★1690★
The WEB
American Indian Program
400 Caldwell Hall   Ph: (607)255-4308
Ithaca, NY 14853   Fax: (607)255-0185
Description: Focuses on Native American students at Cornell University. Reports on activities, awards, projects, scholarships, graduations, and alumni. Recurring features include interviews, news of research, reports of meetings, and news of educational opportunities. **Pages (approx.):** 8. **Frequency:** 2/year. **Formerly:** Update.

Newspapers

★1691★
Cherokee Advocate
Cherokee Nation
PO Box 948   Ph: (918)456-0671
Tahlequah, OK 74465   Fax: (918)456-6485
Description: Tribal newspaper. **First Published:** 1977. **Frequency:** Monthly. **Subscriptions:** $12.50.

★1692★
The Cherokee One Feather
Eastern Band of Cherokee Indians
PO Box 501   Ph: (704)497-5513
Cherokee, NC 28719   Fax: (704)497-4810
Description: Newspaper featuring news of interest to the local Cherokee tribe and to American Indians in general. **First Published:** 1967. **Frequency:** Weekly. **Subscriptions:** $40 **ISSN:** 0890-4448.

★1693★
Indian Country Today
Native American Publishing, Inc.
1920 Lombardy Dr.   Ph: (605)341-0011
Rapid City, SD 57709-2180   Fax: (605)341-6940
Description: Newspaper of national and international readership serving Native American communities. **First Published:** 7001981. **Frequency:** Weekly. **Subscriptions:** $17.50. **Formerly:** The Lakota Times.

★1694★
Lac du Flambeau News
Lac du Flambeau Band of Lake Superior
  Chippewa Indians
PO Box 67   Ph: (715)588-3303
Lac du Flambeau, WI 54538   Fax: (715)588-9408
Description: The largest Native Newspaper in Wisconsin-serving all of it's Native Communities. **First Published:** 1993. **Frequency:** Monthly. **Subscriptions:** $14.

★1695★
The Navajo Times
The Navajo Nation
PO Box 310   Ph: (520)871-6641
Window Rock, AZ 86515-0310   Fax: (520)871-6409
Description: Weekly newspaper for the Navajo people and Native Americans. **First Published:** 1959. **Frequency:** Weekly (Thurs.). **Subscriptions:** $45 **Formerly:** Navajo Times Today.

★1696★
News from Indian Country
Indian Country Communications, Inc.
Rte. 2, Box 2900 A   Ph: (715)634-5226
Hayward, WI 54843   Fax: (715)634-3243
Description: Newspaper covering national, state, and local Native American news and features. **First Published:** 1987. **Frequency:** Semimonthly. **Subscriptions:** $48, one-year subscription, first class mail; $34, one-year subscription, third class mail; $50, one-year subscription, air mail; $52, one-year subscription, surface mail. **Formerly:** LCO Journal.

★1697★
On Indian Land
Support for Native Sovereignty
PO Box 2104
Seattle, WA 98111   Ph: (206)525-5086
Description: Newspaper covering Native American issues: land, sovereignty, treaty, religious freedom, political prisoners. **First Published:** 1991. **Frequency:** Quarterly. **Subscriptions:** $12.

Radio Stations

★1698★
CKON-FM
PO Box 140
Rooseveltown, NY 13683   Ph: (518)358-3426
Frequency: 97.3. **Format:** Country, Album-Oriented Rock (AOR), Oldies, Blues, Jazz, Folk, Heavy Metal. **Owner:** Akwesasne Communication Society.

★1699★
KABR-AM
PO Box 907   Ph: (505)854-2632
Magdalena, NM 87825   Fax: (505)854-2545
Frequency: 1500 **Network Affiliation:** Independent. **Format:** News, Ethnic. **Owner:** Alamo Navajo School Board, Inc.

★1700★
KEYA-FM
PO Box 190   Ph: (701)477-5686
Belcourt, ND 58316   Fax: (701)477-3252
Frequency: 88.5 **Network Affiliation:** American Public Radio (APR), National Public Radio (NPR), Public Radio International (PRI). **Format:** Country, Oldies, Gospel, Adult Contemporary, Eclectic, Album-Oriented Rock (AOR). **Owner:** KEYA Inc.

★1701★
KIDE-FM
Box 1220   Ph: (916)625-4245
Hoopa, CA 95546   Fax: (916)625-4046
Frequency: 91.3. **Format:** Eclectic. **Owner:** Hoopa Valley Telecommunications Corp.

★1702★
KINI-FM
PO Box 419   Ph: (605)747-2291
St. Francis, SD 57572   Fax: (605)747-5791
Frequency: 96.1 **Network Affiliation:** AP. **Format:** Eclectic, News. **Owner:** Rosebud Educational Society Inc.

★1703★
KMHA-FM
HCR 3, Box 1   Ph: (701)627-3333
New Town, ND 58763   Fax: (701)627-4212
Frequency: 91.3. **Format:** Eclectic. **Owner:** Fort Berthold Communications Enterprise.

★1704★
KNNB-FM
Hwy. 73, Skill Center Rd.
PO Box 310   Ph: (520)338-5229
Whiteriver, AZ 85941   Fax: (520)338-1744
Frequency: 88.1. **Format:** Eclectic, Ethnic. **Owner:** White Mountain Apache Tribe.

★1705★
KSUT-FM
PO Box 737   Ph: (970)563-0255
Ignacio, CO 81137   Fax: (970)563-0399
Frequency: 91.3 **Network Affiliation:** National Public Radio (NPR), American Public Radio (APR). **Format:** Public Radio, Eclectic. **Owner:** KUTE, Inc.

★1706★
KTDB-FM
PO Box 40   Ph: (505)775-3215
Pinehill, NM 87357   Fax: (505)775-3551
Frequency: 89.7 **Network Affiliation:** National Public Radio (NPR). **Format:** Public Radio, Talk, Ethnic, News. **Owner:** Ramah Navajo School Board, Inc.

★1707★
KTNN-AM
PO Box 2569   Ph: (520)871-2582
Window Rock, AZ 86515   Fax: (520)871-3479
Frequency: 660. **Network Affiliation:** NBC, Interstate Radio, Alaska Public Radio. **Format:** Contemporary Country, Ethnic. **Owner:** Navajo Nation

★1708★
KWSO-FM
P.O. Box 489   Ph: (503)553-1968
Warm Springs, OR 97761   Fax: (503)553-3348
Frequency: 91.9. **Format:** Public Radio, Eclectic, Ethnic. **Owner:** Confederated Tribes of Warm Springs.

★1709★
WASG-AM
1318 S. Main St.   Ph: (205)368-2511
Atmore, AL 36502-2899   Fax: (205)368-4227
Frequency: 550. **Network Affiliation:** Talknet, ABC. **Format:** Country, Agricultural, News, Talk. **Owner:** PCI Communications, Inc.

Videos

★1710★
Abnaki: The Native People of Maine
Centre Productions, Inc.
1800 30th St., Ste. 207   Ph: (303)444-1166
Boulder, CO 80301   Free: 800-824-1166
Description: This film follows the Abnaki Indians in their efforts to accomplish their legal victory. Furthermore, we explore the historical, cultural and spiritual factors that have contributed to the survival of their Native American heritage. **Release Date:** 1984. **Length:** 29 mins. **Format:** Beta, VHS, 3/4″ U-matic Cassette.

★1711★
Aboriginal Rights: I Can Get It For You Wholesale
Native American Public Broadcasting
   Consortium
PO Box 86111
1800 N. 33rd St.
Lincoln, NE 68501   Ph: (402)472-3522
Description: This tape debates the pro side of Native American aboriginal rights, claiming precedence and respect for nature as its major arguments. **Release Date:** 1976. **Length:** 60 mins. **Format:** VHS, 3/4″ U-matic Cassette, 1″ Broadcast Type ″C″, 2″ Quadraplex Open Reel.

★1712★
Acorns: Staple Food of California Indians
University of California at Berkeley
   Extension Media Center
2176 Shattuck Ave.
Berkeley, CA 94704   Ph: (510)642-0460
Description: Pomo tribe members demonstrate traditional acorn harvesting, storing, and processing methods that have evolved over generations. **Release Date:** 1962. **Length:** 28 mins. **Format:** 3/4″ U-matic Cassette, Other than listed.

★1713★
Akwesasne: Another Point of View
Icarus Films
200 Park Ave., S., Ste. 1319
New York, NY 10003   Ph: (212)674-3375
Description: This program explores some of the social, political, and legal obstacles faced by traditional Mowhawks in recent years in their struggle to retain traditional rights. **Release Date:** 1981. **Length:** 28 mins. **Format:** 3/4″ U-matic Cassette.

★1714★
The American as Artist: A Portrait of Bob Penn
Native American Public Broadcasting
   Consortium
PO Box 86111
1800 N. 33rd St.
Lincoln, NE 68501   Ph: (402)472-3522
Description: An essay on American Indian artist Penn and his experimental work, examining both the art and his position as a Native American artist. **Release Date:** 1976. **Length:** 29 mins. **Format:** VHS, 3/4″ U-matic Cassette, 1″ Broadcast Type ″C″, 2″ Quadraplex Open Reel.

★1715★
American History for Children: Native American Life
Library Video Company   Ph: (610)667-0200
PO Box 1110   Free: 800-843-3620
Bala Cynwyd, PA 19004   Fax: (610)667-3425
Description: Covers Native American historical figures such as Pocahontas, Tecumseh, The Trail of Tears, and Mother Earth/Father Sky. **Length:** 25 **Format:** VHS

★1716★
The American Indian
Dallas County Community College District
Center for Educational
   Telecommunications
Dallas Telecourses
9596 Walnut St.   Ph: (214)952-0303
Mesquite, TX 75243   Fax: (214)952-0329
Description: This program examines the history of the American Indian from the turn of the century to the present day. **Release Date:** 1980. **Length:** 28 mins. **Format:** 3/4″ U-matic Cassette.

★1717★
American Indian: A Brief History
National Geographic Society
c/o Educational Services   Ph: (202)857-7378
PO Box 98019   Free: 800-447-0647
Washington, DC 20090   Fax: (202)857-7300
Description: Offers a history of Native American life from the time American settlers landed on the continent from Asia. **Length:** 22 **Format:** VHS

★1718★
American Indian After the White Man Came
Handel Film Corporation
8730 Sunset Blvd.
West Hollywood, CA 90069   Ph: (213)657-8990
Description: An examination of the profound impact white expansion had upon the many existing native tribes and the formation of government policies. **Release Date:** 1972. **Length:** 27 mins. **Format:** Beta, VHS, 3/4″ U-matic Cassette. **Credits:** Narrated by: Iron Eyes Cody.

★1719★
American Indian Artists: Part I
Native American Public Broadcasting
   Consortium
PO Box 86111
1800 N. 33rd St.
Lincoln, NE 68501   Ph: (402)472-3522
Description: A series looking at the work and lifestyle of six American Indian artists. **Release Date:** 1976. **Length:** 29 mins. **Format:** VHS, 3/4″ U-matic Cassette, 1″ Broadcast Type ″C″, 2″ Quadraplex Open Reel.

★1720★
American Indian Artists: Part II
Native American Public Broadcasting
   Consortium
PO Box 86111
1800 N. 33rd St.
Lincoln, NE 68501   Ph: (402)472-3522
Description: Three more American Indian artists display and discuss their work. **Release Date:** 1982. **Length:** 29 mins. **Format:** VHS, 3/4″ U-matic Cassette, 1″ Broadcast Type ″C″, 2″ Quadraplex Open Reel.

★1721★
American Indian Before the White Man
Handel Film Corporation
8730 Sunset Blvd.
West Hollywood, CA 90069   Ph: (213)657-8990
Description: A comprehensive study of the Indian, tracing the early Asiatic descendants who fanned out into Mexico and the Americas. The Apache and Navajo tribes are explored in detail. **Release Date:**

1972. **Length:** 19 mins. **Format:** Beta, VHS, 3/4″ U-matic Cassette. **Credits:** Narrated by: Iron Eyes Cody.

★1722★
American Indian Collection: Geronimo and the Apache Resistance
PBS Video
1320 Braddock Pl.
Alexandria, VA 22314-1698   Ph: (703)739-5380

Description: This presentation chronicles the years of unfair treatment handed out to the Apache tribe and the efforts of American soldiers to apprehend Geronimo and his warriors after their revolt against this tyranny. Part of the "Odyssey" series. **Release Date:** 1991. **Length:** 60 mins. **Format:** VHS.

★1723★
American Indian Collection: Myths and Moundbuilders
PBS Video
1320 Braddock Pl.
Alexandria, VA 22314-1698   Ph: (703)739-5380

Description: Recently, archaeologists discovered that huge earthen mounds scattered throughout the central U.S. were built by Indians. Part of the "Odyssey" series. **Release Date:** 1991. **Length:** 60 mins. **Format:** Beta, VHS.

★1724★
American Indian Collection: Seasons of the Navajo
PBS Video
1320 Braddock Pl.
Alexandria, VA 22314-1698   Ph: (703)739-5380

Description: An extended Navajo family deals with modern life through tribal communion in this documentary. Part of the "Odyssey" series. **Release Date:** 1991. **Length:** 60 mins. **Format:** VHS.

★1725★
American Indian Collection: Spirit of Crazy Horse
PBS Video
1320 Braddock Pl.
Alexandria, VA 22314-1698   Ph: (703)739-5380

Description: This documentary explores the culture, customs, and legacy of the great Sioux tribe and their efforts to retain their traditions and honor in a modern world. Part of the "Odyssey" series. **Release Date:** 1991. **Length:** 54 mins. **Format:** VHS.

★1726★
American Indian Collection: Winds of Change—A Matter of Promises
PBS Video
1320 Braddock Pl.
Alexandria, VA 22314-1698   Ph: (703)739-5380

Description: This documentary examines the problems facing Native Americans as they try to hold onto ancient customs and values in a modern society. The ways of the Navajo nation in Arizona and New Mexico, the Lummi tribe in Washington State, and the Onondaga in New York are detailed. Part of the "Odyssey" series. **Release Date:** 1991. **Length:** 60 mins. **Format:** VHS. **Credits:** Hosted by: N. Scott Momaday.

★1727★
American Indian Influence on the United States
Dana Productions
6249 Babcock Ave.
North Hollywood, CA 91606   Ph: (213)877-9246

Description: A look at how life in the U.S. has been influenced by the Indian—economically, sociologically, philosophically, and culturally. **Release Date:** 1972. **Length:** 20 mins. **Format:** Beta, VHS, 1/2″ Reel-EIAJ, 3/4″ U-matic Cassette, Other than listed. **Credits:** Narrated by: Barry Sullivan.

★1728★
The American Indian Series
University of California at Berkeley
  Extension Media Center
2176 Shattuck Ave.
Berkeley, CA 94704   Ph: (510)642-0460

Description: Members of several northern California Indian tribes depict unique elements of a way of life as it flourished before the imposition of European culture. **Release Date:** 196?. **Length:** 30 mins. **Format:** 3/4″ U-matic Cassette, Other than listed.

★1729★
The American Indian Speaks
Britannica Films
310 S. Michigan Ave.   Ph: (312)347-7958
Chicago, IL 60604   Fax: (312)347-7966

Description: This powerful documentary lets the Indian speak about his people and heritage, about the white man and the future. **Release Date:** 1973. **Length:** 23 mins. **Format:** Beta, VHS, 3/4″ U-matic Cassette.

★1730★
American Indian Sweat Lodge Ceremony
Artistic Video
87 Tyler Ave.
Sound Beach, NY 11789   Ph: (516)744-0449

Description: The entire ceremony, which is one of North America's oldest, is shown. **Release Date:** 1987. **Length:** 90 mins. **Format:** Beta, VHS.

★1731★
The American Indian Today
NETCHE (Nebraska ETV Council for
  Higher Education)
Box 83111
Lincoln, NE 68501   Ph: (402)472-3611

Description: This is a lesson which contains material on American Indians circa 1969. **Release Date:** 1969. **Length:** 30 mins. **Format:** 1/2″ Reel-EIAJ.

★1732★
American Indians Before European Settlement
Coronet/MTI Film & Video   Ph: (708)940-1260
108 Wilmot Rd.   Free: 800-621-2131
Deerfield, IL 60015   Fax: (708)940-3640

Description: This account of American Indian life relates their culture to their environment in five different geographic regions, prior to the coming of the European settlers. **Release Date:** 1959. **Length:** 11 mins. **Format:** Beta, VHS, 3/4″ U-matic Cassette, Other than listed.

★1733★
The American Indian's Sacred Ground
Wood Knapp & Company, Inc.
Knapp Press
5900 Wilshire Blvd.   Ph: (213)937-5486
Los Angeles, CA 90036   Free: 800-521-2666

Description: The mythical and geological aspects of the Native American sacred grounds are examined here, with discussions on architecture, communication, and the natural and spiritual world; filmed at sites throughout the United States. **Release Date:** 1991. **Length:** 60 mins. **Format:** VHS.

★1734★
American Indians: Yesterday and Today
FilmFair Communications   Ph: (818)985-0244
10621 Magnolia Blvd.   Free: 800-423-2461
North Hollywood, CA 91601   Fax: (818)980-8492

Description: In this program, Native Americans from three different tribes tell the stories of their people—how they survived the earliest days and what their lives are like today. **Release Date:** 1982. **Length:** 19 mins. **Format:** Beta, VHS, 3/4″ U-matic Cassette.

★1735★
America's Mysterious Places
Hartley Film Foundation
Cat Rock Rd.   Ph: (203)869-1818
                                 Free: 800-937-1819
Cos Cob, CT 06807   Fax: (203)869-1905
Description: A documentary investigation into America's unexplained civilizations and most mysterious ancient sites. **Length:** 60 **Format:** VHS

★1736★
Amiotte
Native American Public Broadcasting
  Consortium
PO Box 86111
1800 N. 33rd St.
Lincoln, NE 68501   Ph: (402)472-3522
Description: A film outlining the career and life of Native American artist Arthur Amiotte. **Release Date:** 1976. **Length:** 29 mins. **Format:** VHS, 3/4″ U-matic Cassette, 1″ Broadcast Type ″C″, 2″ Quadraplex Open Reel.

★1737★
Ancient America: Indians of the Southwest
Ark Media Group Ltd.   Ph: (415)863-7200
425 Alabama St.   Free: 800-727-0009
San Francisco, CA 94110   Fax: (415)864-5437
Description: Explores southwest Native American culture. Introduces Chimney Rocks, Mesa Verde, and more. Studies teh Anasazi, Mimbres, and Salado. **Length:** 60 **Format:** VHS

★1738★
Ancient America: More Than Bows and Arrows
Ark Media Group Ltd.   Ph: (415)863-7200
425 Alabama St.   Free: 800-727-0009
San Francisco, CA 94110   Fax: (415)864-5437
Description: Doctor N. Scott Momaday narrates this look at Native American traditions of the Anasazi and Iriqouis tribes. Introduces the Iriqouis League of Nations, the first democracy, ceremonial mounds and more. **Length:** 60 **Format:** VHS

★1739★
Ancient America: Nomadic Indians of the West
Ark Media Group Ltd.   Ph: (415)863-7200
425 Alabama St.   Free: 800-727-0009
San Francisco, CA 94110   Fax: (415)864-5437
Description: Explores the life and customs of the Plains Indians. Introduces the Medicine Wheel, smoke signals, sign language, and much more. **Length:** 60 **Format:** VHS

★1740★
An Ancient Gift
University of California at Berkeley
  Extension Media Center
2176 Shattuck Ave.
Berkeley, CA 94704   Ph: (510)642-0460
Description: The important role that sheep play in the lives of the Navajo is explored. **Release Date:** 1986. **Length:** 16 mins. **Format:** VHS, 3/4″ U-matic Cassette.

★1741★
Ancient Indian Cultures of Northern Arizona
Victorian Video Productions
PO Box 1540   Ph: (916)346-6184
Colfax, CA 95713-1540   Free: 800-848-0284
Description: Concentrates on the Sinagua and Anasazi people and how they survived under harsh conditions. Also looks at five national monuments: Montezuma Castle, Wupatki, Tuzigoot, Walnut Canyon, and Sunset Crater. **Release Date:** 1985. **Length:** 30 mins. **Format:** Beta, VHS.

★1742★
Ancient Spirit, Living Word: The Oral Tradition
Native American Public Broadcasting
  Consortium
PO Box 86111
1800 N. 33rd St.
Lincoln, NE 68501   Ph: (402)472-3522
Description: An exploration of the Native American oral storytelling tradition. **Release Date:** 1983. **Length:** 58 mins. **Format:** VHS, 3/4″ U-matic Cassette, 1″ Broadcast Type ″C″, 2″ Quadraplex Open Reel.

★1743★
Annie and the Old One
Phoenix/BFA Films
468 Park Ave., S.   Ph: (212)684-5910
New York, NY 10016   Free: 800-221-1274
Description: The Old One is the beloved grandmother of a little Navajo girl named Annie. Annie questions the Old One about the cycle of life. Adapted from a book by Miska Miles. **Release Date:** 1976. **Length:** 15 mins. **Format:** Beta, VHS.

★1744★
Another Wind Is Moving
University of California at Berkeley
  Extension Media Center
2176 Shattuck Ave.
Berkeley, CA 94704   Ph: (510)642-0460
Description: Since Indian schools have begun to shut down in larger and larger numbers, it is increasingly more difficult for Native Americans to learn about their culture. **Release Date:** 1986. **Length:** 59 mins. **Format:** VHS, 3/4″ U-matic Cassette.

★1745★
The Apache Indian
Coronet/MTI Film & Video   Ph: (708)940-1260
108 Wilmot Rd.   Free: 800-621-2131
Deerfield, IL 60015   Fax: (708)940-3640
Description: An examination of Apache life and culture, from ancient times to the present, from tribal ceremonies to advanced education. **Release Date:** 1975. **Length:** 10 mins. **Format:** Beta, VHS, 3/4″ U-matic Cassette, Other than listed.

★1746★
Apache Mountain Spirit
Native American Public Broadcasting
  Consortium
1800 N. 33rd St.
PO Box 86111
Lincoln, NE 68501   Ph: (402)472-3522
Description: When Robert takes up with a bad crowd, the Gaan, Apache Mountain spirits, touch and test him. He allows the spirits to direct his life and use his powers within for good purposes. **Release Date:** 1985. **Length:** 59 mins. **Format:** VHS, 1″ Broadcast Type ″C″, 3/4″ U-matic Cassette.

★1747★
The Art of Being Indian: Filmed Aspects of the Culture of the Sioux
Native American Public Broadcasting
  Consortium
PO Box 86111
1800 N. 33rd St.
Lincoln, NE 68501   Ph: (402)472-3522
Description: The refined art of being truly Sioux is thoroughly surveyed, past, present and future. Features art by Bob Penn, Seth Eastman, Stanley Morrow and George Catlin. **Release Date:** 1976. **Length:** 29 mins. **Format:** VHS, 3/4″ U-matic Cassette, 1″ Broadcast Type ″C″, 2″ Quadraplex Open Reel.

★1748★
The Art of Navajo Weaving
Arts America, Inc.
12 Havermeyer Pl.
Greenwich, CT 06830   Ph: (203)637-1454
Description: Watch as skilled veterans perform the art of Navajo weaving. This video also shows the Durango Collection, the world's largest private collection of Navajo weaving. **Release Date:** 1988. **Length:** 56 mins. **Format:** Beta, VHS.

★1749★
As Long As the Grass Is Green
Atlantis Productions
1252 La Granada Dr.
Thousand Oaks, CA 91360   Ph: (805)495-2790
Description: A summer experience with the children of the Woodland Indians of North America. Nonnarrative. **Release Date:** 1973. **Length:** 11 mins. **Format:** Beta, VHS, 3/4" U-matic Cassette.

★1750★
Basketry of the Pomo: Forms and Ornamentation
University of California at Berkeley
 Extension Media Center
2176 Shattuck Ave.
Berkeley, CA 94704   Ph: (510)642-0460
Description: This look at the basketry of the Pomo Indians of northern California illustrates the great variety of shapes and designs descriptive of animals. **Release Date:** 1962. **Length:** 21 mins. **Format:** 3/4" U-matic Cassette, Other than listed.

★1751★
Basketry of the Pomo: Introductory Film
University of California at Berkeley
 Extension Media Center
2176 Shattuck Ave.
Berkeley, CA 94704   Ph: (510)642-0460
Description: The Pomo Indians of northern California were the world's most expert basketmakers. This program shows Indians gathering raw materials for baskets, and creating baskets with graceful geometric forms. **Release Date:** 1962. **Length:** 30 mins. **Format:** 3/4" U-matic Cassette, Other than listed.

★1752★
Basketry of the Pomo: Techniques
University of California at Berkeley
 Extension Media Center
2176 Shattuck Ave.
Berkeley, CA 94704   Ph: (510)642-0460
Description: A detailed look at the basketry techniques of the Pomo Indians of northern California, showing precisely how the various weaves were executed. **Release Date:** 1962. **Length:** 33 mins. **Format:** 3/4" U-matic Cassette, Other than listed.

★1753★
Beautiful Tree: Chishkale
University of California at Berkeley
 Extension Media Center
2176 Shattuck Ave.
Berkeley, CA 94704   Ph: (510)642-0460
Description: A look at how the Pomo Indians of northern California removed poisonous tannic acid from the acorns of the tan oak chishkale (the beautiful tree) to feed the tribe. **Release Date:** 1965. **Length:** 20 mins. **Format:** 3/4" U-matic Cassette, Other than listed.

★1754★
Beyond Tradition
Home Vision Cinema   Ph: (312)878-2600
5547 N. Ravenswood Ave.   Free: 800-826-3456
Chicago, IL 60640-1199   Fax: (312)878-8648
Description: Indian art, from prehistoric to modern, is set to haunting accompaniment of guitar and flute. **Release Date:** 1982. **Length:** 45 mins. **Format:** Beta, VHS.

★1755★
Black Coal, Red Power
Indiana University Center for Media &
 Teaching Resources   Ph: (812)855-8087
Bloomington, IN 47405-5901   Fax: (812)855-8404
Description: The strip mining of coal on Navajo and Hopi reservations in Arizona is examined for its effects on the ecology and the economy of the Indian population. **Release Date:** 1972. **Length:** 41 mins. **Format:** 3/4" U-matic Cassette, Other than listed.

★1756★
The Black Hills: Who Owns the Land
NETCHE (Nebraska ETV Council for
 Higher Education)
Box 83111
Lincoln, NE 68501   Ph: (402)472-3611
Description: Examines the historical record of lands in South Dakota and the question of who owns them–the Indians? **Release Date:** 1989. **Length:** 60 mins. **Format:** Beta, VHS, 3/4" U-matic Cassette.

★1757★
Boldt Decision: Impacts and Implementation
University of Washington Instructional
 Media Services
Kane Hall, DG-10
Seattle, WA 98195   Ph: (206)543-9909
Description: A discussion of the court ruling by U.S. Judge George Boldt who ruled that treaty Indians in Washington are entitled to half the harvestable catch of salmon and steelhead. **Release Date:** 1976. **Length:** 60 mins. **Format:** 3/4" U-matic Cassette.

★1758★
Boldt Decision: Update
University of Washington Instructional
 Media Services
Kane Hall, DG-10
Seattle, WA 98195   Ph: (206)543-9909
Description: A look at the impact of the court ruling by U.S. Judge George Boldt that treaty Indians in Washington are entitled to half the harvestable catch of salmon and steelhead. **Release Date:** 1976. **Length:** 60 mins. **Format:** 3/4" U-matic Cassette.

★1759★
Box of Treasures
Documentary Educational Resources
101 Morse St.   Ph: (617)926-0491
Watertown, MA 02172   Fax: (617)926-9519
Description: This film is a focus on Kwakiutl society, a native American Indian community, and their struggle to redefine cultural identity. **Release Date:** 1986. **Length:** 28 mins. **Format:** 3/4" U-matic Cassette.

★1760★
Boy of the Navajos
Coronet/MTI Film & Video   Ph: (708)940-1260
108 Wilmot Rd.   Free: 800-621-2131
Deerfield, IL 60015   Fax: (708)940-3640
Description: The story of Tony, a present-day Navajo boy as he herds sheep in the Arizona desert, and spends evenings with his family in the hogan. **Release Date:** 1975. **Length:** 11 mins. **Format:** Beta, VHS, 3/4" U-matic Cassette, Other than listed.

★1761★
Boy of the Seminoles (Indians of the Everglades)
Coronet/MTI Film & Video   Ph: (708)940-1260
108 Wilmot Rd.   Free: 800-621-2131
Deerfield, IL 60015   Fax: (708)940-3640
Description: The story of Naha, a Seminole boy, as he travels into the swamp to return the baby alligator captured by his dog. Life among the Seminole people is illustrated. **Release Date:** 1956. **Length:** 11 mins. **Format:** Beta, VHS, 3/4" U-matic Cassette, Other than listed.

★1762★
Brave Eagle
Nostalgia Family Video
PO Box 606
Baker City, OR 97814

Ph: (503)523-9034
Free: 800-784-8362
Fax: (503)523-7115

Description: Two episodes of the television series told through the eyes of an Indian. **Length:** 60 **Format:** VHS

★1763★
The Brave Indian Chief
Facets Multimedia, Inc.
1517 W. Fullerton Ave.
Chicago, IL 60614

Ph: (312)281-9075
Free: 800-331-6197
Fax: (312)929-5437

Description: Storyteller Rafe Martin relates the tale of Indian Chief Glooscop, who travelled t he treacherous sea and battled an evil sorcerer to bring food to his starving tribe. **Length:** 30 **Format:** VHS

★1764★
Broken Journey
Native American Public Broadcasting
   Consortium
1800 N. 33rd St.
PO Box 86111
Lincoln, NE 68501

Ph: (402)472-3522

Description: Focuses on the problem of alcohol for Native Americans by listening to stories told by men and women incarcerated for alcohol related problems. Aimed at Native American youth. **Length:** 27 mins. **Format:** VHS, 1″ Broadcast Type ″C″, 3/4″ U-matic Cassette.

★1765★
Broken Rainbow
Direct Cinema Limited
PO Box 69799
Los Angeles, CA 90069-9976

Ph: (213)652-8000
Free: 800-345-6748
Fax: (213)652-2346

Description: An acclaimed documentary about the U.S. Government's relocation of 12,000 Navajo Indians. They described it as a Hopi-Navajo land settlement, but actually did it to facilitate energy development. **Release Date:** 1985. **Length:** 70 mins. **Format:** Beta, VHS, 3/4″ U-matic Cassette, Other than listed. **Credits:** Narrated by: Martin Sheen; Burgess Meredith; Buffy Sainte-Marie.

★1766★
Buckeyes: Food of California Indians
University of California at Berkeley
   Extension Media Center
2176 Shattuck Ave.
Berkeley, CA 94704

Ph: (510)642-0460

Description: This program shows how the Nisenan Indians of California harvested buckeyes and processed them by stone boiling and leaching. Buckeyes were an important staple of their diet. **Release Date:** 1961. **Length:** 13 mins. **Format:** 3/4″ U-matic Cassette, Other than listed.

★1767★
By This Song I Walk: Navajo Song
Norman Ross Publishing Inc.
330 W. 58th St.
New York, NY 10019

Ph: (212)765-8200
Free: 800-648-8850
Fax: (212)765-2393

Description: When the harmony of life is disrupted, the Navajo sings to restore balance and symmetry, as shown in this program (Navajo with English subtitles). **Release Date:** 1981. **Length:** 25 mins. **Format:** Beta, VHS, 3/4″ U-matic Cassette.

★1768★
California Riviera
New & Unique Videos
2336 Sumac Dr.
San Diego, CA 92105

Ph: (619)282-6126
Fax: (619)283-8264

Description: A look at the history, culture, archaeology, and oceanography of southern California. Included is an interview with the present members of the ancient Juaneno Indian tribe who have extensive ancestral knowledge of the area. **Release Date:** 1989. **Length:** 50 mins. **Format:** Beta, VHS.

★1769★
Calumet, Pipe of Peace
University of California at Berkeley
   Extension Media Center
2176 Shattuck Ave.
Berkeley, CA 94704

Ph: (510)642-0460

Description: This program discusses rituals surrounding the calumet, or peace pipe, which was smoked to insure safe conduct, to placate hostile nations, to control the weather, and to conclude peace treaties. **Release Date:** 1964. **Length:** 23 mins. **Format:** 3/4″ U-matic Cassette, Other than listed.

★1770★
Canyon de Chelly and Hubbell Trading Post
Victorian Video Productions
PO Box 1540
Colfax, CA 95713-1540

Ph: (916)346-6184
Free: 800-848-0284

Description: Visit these national parks of New Mexico and Arizona that contain Anasazi cliff dwellings and Navajo craftsmen. **Release Date:** 1979. **Length:** 30 mins. **Format:** Beta, VHS.

★1771★
Celebration/The Pipe is the Altar
Intermedia Arts of Minnesota, Inc.
425 Ontario St. SE
Minneapolis, MN 55414

Ph: (612)627-4444

Description: Two programs looking at various traditional Indian rituals. **Release Date:** 1980. **Length:** 26 mins. **Format:** Beta, VHS, 3/4″ U-matic Cassette.

★1772★
**A Century of Silence...Problems of the American
   Indian**
Atlantis Productions
1252 La Granada Dr.
Thousand Oaks, CA 91360

Ph: (805)495-2790

Description: This film correlates the current problems of the American Indian to the past 100 years of contact with the white culture. Also addressed, are the issues of cultural conflict, assimilation, and activism within the Indian community. **Release Date:** 197?. **Length:** 28 mins. **Format:** Beta, VHS, 3/4″ U-matic Cassette.

★1773★
Cesar's Bark Canoe
Education Development Center, Inc.
55 Chapel St., Ste. 901
Newton, MA 02160

Ph: (617)969-7100
Free: 800-225-4276

Description: Cree Indian Cesar Newashish uses a knife and axe to construct a canoe from a birch tree. With no spoken commentary, this program highlights each stage of construction with on-screen text in three languages–Cree, French, and English. **Release Date:** 1978. **Length:** 58 mins. **Format:** 3/4″ U-matic Cassette, Other than listed.

★1774★
Cherokee
Cinema Guild
1697 Broadway
New York, NY 10019

Ph: (212)246-5522
Fax: (212)246-5525

Description: This program explores the dilemma the Cherokee face in preserving their traditions and captures the beauty of the pageants and ceremonies still performed today. **Release Date:** 1976. **Length:** 26 mins. **Format:** 3/4″ U-matic Cassette, Other than listed.

★1775★
Children of the Long-Beaked Bird
Bullfrog Films, Inc.
PO Box 149
Oley, PA 19547

Ph: (215)779-8226
Free: 800-543-3764
Fax: (215)370-1978

Description: This is an intimate look at a modern Native American Family that disproves the stereotype commonly placed on American Indians. **Release Date:** 1976. **Length:** 29 mins. **Format:** Beta, VHS, 3/4″ U-matic Cassette.

★1776★
Children of the Plains Indians
CRM/McGraw-Hill Films
674 Via de la Valle
PO Box 641
Del Mar, CA 92014
Description: A view of Indian life on the Great Plains before the arrival of white settlers, featuring intimate scenes of many tribal activities. **Release Date:** 1962. **Length:** 20 mins. **Format:** Beta, VHS, 3/4″ U-matic Cassette.

★1777★
A Circle of Women
Island Visual Arts
8920 Sunset Blvd., 2nd Fl.   Ph: (213)288-5382
Los Angeles, CA 90069   Fax: (213)276-5476
Description: Modern women meet women elders of Native American Tribes in an effort to link their cultures, and create an awareness of wisdom long discarded by the modern world. **Release Date:** 1991. **Length:** 60 mins. **Format:** VHS.

★1778★
Civilized Tribes
Cinema Guild
1697 Broadway   Ph: (212)246-5522
New York, NY 10019   Fax: (212)246-5525
Description: In the Southeast part of the country, the five civilized tribes–the Seminoles, the Creek, the Choctaw, the Chickasaw, and the Cherokee–make their home. This program explores the Hollywood reservation in Florida where a village has been reconstructed to document the Seminole's earlier life. Also in Philadelphia, Miss., the Choctaw tribal people discuss their struggle to become a successful independent business community. **Release Date:** 1976. **Length:** 26 mins. **Format:** 3/4″ U-matic Cassette, Other than listed.

★1779★
Clouded Land
Intermedia Arts of Minnesota, Inc.
425 Ontario St. SE
Minneapolis, MN 55414   Ph: (612)627-4444
Description: The land claim dispute on the White Earth Reservation in Minnesota is explored by highlighting its' effect on two Indian and two non-Indian families directly involved in the conflict. **Release Date:** 1987. **Length:** 58 mins. **Format:** 3/4″ U-matic Cassette.

★1780★
Clues to Ancient Indian Life
AIMS Media
9710 De Soto Ave.
Chatsworth, CA 91311-9734   Free: 800-367-2467
          Fax: (818)341-6700
Description: The kinds of clues ancient Indians left behind, and the importance of preserving these artifacts for study are explored on this video. **Release Date:** 1962. **Length:** 10 mins. **Format:** Beta, VHS, 3/4″ U-matic Cassette.

★1781★
The Colors of Pride
National Film Board of Canada
1251 Avenue of the Americas, 16th Fl.
New York, NY 10020-1173   Ph: (212)586-5131
Description: A visit with four Indian painters whose work in recent years has stirred international interest. **Release Date:** 1973. **Length:** 28 mins. **Format:** Beta, VHS, 3/4″ U-matic Cassette.

★1782★
A Common Destiny
Mystic Fire Video
PO Box 1092
Cooper Sta.   Ph: (212)941-0999
New York, NY 10276   Fax: (212)941-1443
Description: Comprises two films: "Walking in Both Worlds" concerns Jewell Praying Wolf James, a Lummi tribesman of the Pacific Northwest who seeks Native American participation in United States land management while noting native people must walk with one foot in the Indian world and the other in the non-Indian world. "The Hopi Prophecy" tells of Thomas Banyacya, spokesman for Hopi high religious leaders, as he interprets prophetic sacred tribal symbols and calls for universal peace and spiritual connectedness with the earth. **Release Date:** 1990. **Length:** 52 mins. **Format:** VHS.

★1783★
A Common Destiny Vol. 2: The Hopi Prophecy
Wishing Well Distributing   Ph: (414)889-8501
PO Box 1008   Free: 800-888-9355
Silver Lake, WI 53170   Fax: (414)889-8591
Description: Hopi religious leader Thomas Banyacya describes the "Koyaanisqatsi," or "crazy life" state of our culture, pointing out its spiritual bankruptcy. He offers the message of a return to spiritual connectedness to Mother Earth as the only hope for mankind. **Length:** 60 **Format:** VHS

★1784★
Completing Our Circle
CRM/McGraw-Hill Films
674 Via de la Valle
PO Box 641
Del Mar, CA 92014
Description: The traditions of the Plains and West Coast Indians, the Inuit, and the first Europeans and settlers in Western Canada are shown in this program. Their art and craftsmanship are presented as a way to express both individual identity and oneness with other men. **Release Date:** 1978. **Length:** 27 mins. **Format:** Beta, VHS, 3/4″ U-matic Cassette.

★1785★
Conquista
Center for Humanities, Inc.
Communications Park
Box 1000   Ph: (914)666-4100
Mount Kisco, NY 10549   Free: 800-431-1242
Description: A look at how the history of the Old West was affected by the fateful meeting of the plains Indian and the horse. **Release Date:** 1974. **Length:** 20 mins. **Format:** Beta, VHS, 3/4″ U-matic Cassette. **Credits:** Narrated by: Richard Boone.

★1786★
Contemporary and Native American Readings
Videotakes
187 Parker Ave.
Rte. 71   Ph: (908)528-5000
Manasquan, NJ 08736   Free: 800-526-7002
Description: Chamberlain reads and interprets work from Joseph Campbell about Native Americans. He also interprets an address from Native Americans to the President regarding the obligation of Americans to protect the Earth. **Release Date:** 19??. **Length:** ? mins. **Format:** VHS. **Credits:** Narrated by: Richard Chamberlain.

★1787★
Contrary Warriors: A Film of the Crow Tribe
Direct Cinema Limited   Ph: (213)652-8000
PO Box 69799   Free: 800-345-6748
Los Angeles, CA 90069-9976   Fax: (213)652-2346
Description: The century-long struggle for survival of Native Americans is explored in this film. **Release Date:** 1986. **Length:** 60 mins. **Format:** Beta, VHS, 3/4″ U-matic Cassette.

★1788★
A Conversation with Vine Deloria, Jr.
Norman Ross Publishing Inc.   Ph: (212)765-8200
330 W. 58th St.   Free: 800-648-8850
New York, NY 10019   Fax: (212)765-2393
Description: The writer discusses the gulf between Indian and non-Indian culture and the "schizophrenia" of white expectations for the Indian. **Release Date:** 1981. **Length:** 29 mins. **Format:** Beta, VHS, 3/4″ U-matic Cassette.

★1789★
Crow Dog
Cinema Guild
1697 Broadway   Ph: (212)246-5522
New York, NY 10019   Fax: (212)246-5525
Description: A video portrait of medicine man Leonard Crow Dog, the Sioux Nation's spiritual leader and spokesperson for the traditionalist (those Sioux who wish to retain the beliefs and customs of their forefathers). **Release Date:** 1979. **Length:** 57 mins. **Format:** Beta, VHS, 3/4″ U-matic Cassette.

★1790★
Crow Dog's Paradise
Centre Productions, Inc.
1800 30th St., Ste. 207   Ph: (303)444-1166
Boulder, CO 80301   Free: 800-824-1166
Description: A look at a Sioux Indian enclave where the Crow Dog family preserves the spiritual and intellectual heritage of their traditional American Indian culture. **Release Date:** 1979. **Length:** 28 mins. **Format:** Beta, VHS, 3/4″ U-matic Cassette.

★1791★
Curse of the Lost Gold Mine
Superior Homevideo, Adivision of
PO Box 249   Ph: (847)381-0909
Barrington, IL 60010   Fax: (847)381-1178
Description: Recounts the ancient Indian legend of Slumach and the many who have searched for his gold mine and never returned. **Length:** 50 **Format:** VHS

★1792★
Dance to Give Thanks
Native American Public Broadcasting
  Consortium
1800 N. 33rd St.
PO Box 86111
Lincoln, NE 68501   Ph: (402)472-3522
Description: Looks at the 184th annual He-De-Wa-Chi (Festival of Joy) of the Omaha Indian Tribe. Learn about the history of the festival as well as see traditional and fancy dancing by tribe members. **Length:** 30 mins. **Format:** VHS, 1″ Broadcast Type "C", 3/4 U-matic Cassette.

★1793★
Dancing Awake the Drum
Wishing Well Distributing   Ph: (414)889-8501
PO Box 1008   Free: 800-888-9355
Silver Lake, WI 53170   Fax: (414)889-8591
Description: Brooke Medicine Eagle dances, drums and sings her messages of healing medicine for personal and planetary healing. **Length:** 60 **Format:** VHS

★1794★
Dancing Feathers
Beacon Films   Ph: (708)328-6700
1560 Sherman Ave., Ste. 100   Free: 800-323-9084
Evanston, IL 60201   Fax: (708)328-6706
Description: Tafia must perform a traditional Jingle Dance in a pow wow and begins to doubt her heritage. Her grandmother helps her understand. **Length:** 28 **Format:** VHS

★1795★
Daughters of the Anasazi
Facets Multimedia, Inc.
1517 W. Fullerton Ave.
Chicago, IL 60614   Ph: (312)281-9075
Description: An examination of the ancient techniques used in producing traditional pottery in the Southwest. Filmed in New Mexico. **Release Date:** 1990. **Length:** 28 mins. **Format:** VHS.

★1796★
The Day Glo Warrior
Beacon Films   Ph: (708)328-6700
1560 Sherman Ave., Ste. 100   Free: 800-323-9084
Evanston, IL 60201   Fax: (708)328-6706
Description: A Native American professional wrestler is proud of his heritage and calls himself Iron Chief Thunderhawk. His family is not impressed with his ethics. **Length:** 26 **Format:** VHS

★1797★
Desert Regions: Nomads and Traders
Phoenix/BFA Films
468 Park Ave., S.   Ph: (212)684-5910
New York, NY 10016   Free: 800-221-1274
Description: A look at the Navajo Indians of Monument Valley and the Bedouins of Jordan. **Release Date:** 1980. **Length:** 15 mins. **Format:** Beta, VHS, 3/4″ U-matic Cassette.

★1798★
Dineh: The People
Native American Public Broadcasting
  Consortium
PO Box 86111
1800 N. 33rd St.
Lincoln, NE 68501   Ph: (402)472-3522
Description: This documentary covers the impending relocation of several thousand Navajo from a joint-use land area in the Navajo Reservation. **Release Date:** 1976. **Length:** 77 mins. **Format:** VHS, 3/4″ U-matic Cassette, 1″ Broadcast Type "C", 2″ Quadraplex Open Reel.

★1799★
Dinshyin
University of California at Berkeley
  Extension Media Center
2176 Shattuck Ave.
Berkeley, CA 94704   Ph: (510)642-0460
Description: Ethnographical chronicle of the many peoples who have lived in and around the Canyon de Chelley in northeastern Arizona, focusing on the Navajo, who came to the area 700 years ago. **Release Date:** 1974. **Length:** 22 mins. **Format:** 3/4″ U-matic Cassette, Other than listed.

★1800★
Distant Voice...Thunder Words
Native American Public Broadcasting
  Consortium
1800 N. 33rd St.
PO Box 86111
Lincoln, NE 68501   Ph: (402)472-3522
Description: Discusses the role of the oral tradition in modern Native American literature. Includes interviews with storytellers and other experts. **Release Date:** 1990. **Length:** 59 mins. **Format:** VHS, 1″ Broadcast Type "C", 3/4 U-matic Cassette.

★1801★
The Divided Trail: A Native American Odyssey
Phoenix/BFA Films
468 Park Ave., S.   Ph: (212)684-5910
New York, NY 10016   Free: 800-221-1274
Description: The program follows the lives of three members of the Chicago Indian Village. One is a recovered alcoholic; another is a reformed militant; the final member has gone through a severe emotional crisis due to a conflict between her political actions and sense of personal identity. **Release Date:** 1978. **Length:** 33 mins. **Format:** Beta, VHS, 3/4″ U-matic Cassette.

★1802★
Do We Want Us To?
National AudioVisual Center
National Archives & Records
  Administration
Customer Services Section PZ
8700 Edgeworth Dr.
Capitol Heights, MD 20743-3701   Ph: (301)763-1896
Description: The story about the heritage of the Tlingket Indians helps students recognize and understand the consequences of one culture arriving in the land of another. **Release Date:** 1979. **Length:** 20 mins. **Format:** Beta, VHS, 3/4″ U-matic Cassette, Other than listed.

★1803★
Dream Catchers
Wishing Well Distributing   Ph: (414)889-8501
PO Box 1008   Free: 800-888-9355
Silver Lake, WI 53170   Fax: (414)889-8591
Description: Combines instructions on how to make traditional Native American dream catchers with authentic Native American music and music from renowned composer/pianist Gary Lamb. Hikes through 2000-year-old redwood trees and along the Monterey Bay coast are also shown. **Length:** 40 **Format:** VHS

★1804★
Dream Dances of the Kashia Pomo
University of California at Berkeley
  Extension Media Center
2176 Shattuck Ave.
Berkeley, CA 94704   Ph: (510)642-0460
Description: A look at the five dances of the Kashia Pomo Indians, the Bole Maru, nearly a century after it first evolved. The five dances reflect recent influences including Christianity and World War II. **Release Date:** 1964. **Length:** 30 mins. **Format:** 3/4″ U-matic Cassette, Other than listed.

★1805★
Dreamspeaker
Filmakers Library, Inc.
124 E. 40th
New York, NY 10016   Ph: (212)808-4980
Description: A powerful drama depicting an encounter between a disturbed youth and an Indian shaman. Presents the Indian views on death and the life cycle. **Release Date:** 1977. **Length:** 75 mins. **Format:** Beta, VHS, 3/4″ U-matic Cassette.

★1806★
The Drum
New Dimension Media, Inc.   Ph: (503)484-7125
85895 Lorane Hwy.   Free: 800-288-4456
Eugene, OR 97405   Fax: (503)484-5267
Description: A Native American ritual shows the importance of people keeping their heritage alive. **Release Date:** 1987. **Length:** 15 mins. **Format:** Beta, VHS.

★1807★
The Drum Is the Heart
Intermedia Arts of Minnesota, Inc.
425 Ontario St. SE
Minneapolis, MN 55414   Ph: (612)627-4444
Description: A program that studies the modernized rituals of the Blackfoot Indians. **Release Date:** 1982. **Length:** 29 mins. **Format:** Beta, VHS, 3/4″ U-matic Cassette.

★1808★
The Eagle and the Condor
Native American Public Broadcasting
  Consortium
PO Box 86111
1800 N. 33rd St.
Lincoln, NE 68501   Ph: (402)472-3522
Description: This tape follows the South American tour of Native American entertainers from Brigham Young University's Lamanite Generation. **Release Date:** 1976. **Length:** 29 mins. **Format:** VHS,

3/4″ U-matic Cassette, 1″ Broadcast Type ″C″, 2″ Quadraplex Open Reel.

★1809★
Early Man in North America
Films, Inc.
5547 N. Ravenswood Ave.   Ph: (312)878-2600
Chicago, IL 60640-1199   Free: 800-323-4222
Description: Early man in North America was by no means a nomadic hunter. Evidence which exists throughout the U.S. today tells of large Indian cities, advanced building structures, and other works requiring thousands of laborers. **Release Date:** 1972. **Length:** 12 mins. **Format:** Beta, VHS, 3/4″ U-matic Cassette.

★1810★
The Earth Is Our Home
Media Project, Inc.
PO Box 4093
Portland, OR 97208   Ph: (503)223-5335
Description: The film depicts the vestiges of prehistoric life ways among the Northern Paiute Indians. **Release Date:** 1979. **Length:** 30 mins. **Format:** Beta, VHS, 1/2″ Reel-EIAJ, 3/4″ U-matic Cassette.

★1811★
Earthshapers
Native American Public Broadcasting
  Consortium
1800 N. 33rd St.
PO Box 86111
Lincoln, NE 68501   Ph: (402)472-3522
Description: A look at the sacred mounds created by the Woodland Native people. **Length:** 14 mins. **Format:** VHS, 1″ Broadcast Type ″C″, 3/4″ U-matic Cassette.

★1812★
Emergence
Pictures of Record
119 Kettle Creek Rd.
Weston, CT 06883   Ph: (203)227-3387
Description: This tape is an animated reconstruction of an ancient Navajo myth about a mystic underworld. **Release Date:** 1982. **Length:** 14 mins. **Format:** VHS, 3/4″ U-matic Cassette.

★1813★
An End to Isolation
National Municipal League, Inc.
55 W. 44th St.
New York, NY 10036   Ph: (212)730-7930
Description: Explains how American Indians living in the city can assure themselves a fair share of jobs, social services, and political power. **Release Date:** 1976. **Length:** 30 mins. **Format:** 1/2″ Reel-EIAJ, 3/4″ U-matic Cassette.

★1814★
End of the Trail: The American Plains Indian
CRM/McGraw-Hill Films
674 Via de la Valle
PO Box 641
Del Mar, CA 92014
Description: This program covers the history of the American Plains Indian in the post-Civil War era. It shows the impact that the westward movement had on them and explores their folklore, pointing out the contributions they have made to generations of Americans. Available as a whole or in two parts. **Release Date:** 1967. **Length:** 16 mins. **Format:** Beta, VHS, 3/4″ U-matic Cassette.

★1815★
Excavation of Mound 7
National AudioVisual Center
National Archives & Records
  Administration
Customer Services Section PZ
8700 Edgeworth Dr.
Capitol Heights, MD 20743-3701   Ph: (301)763-1896
Description: Archaeology work in the field and in the lab to piece together the mysteries of the Pueblo Indians of New Mexico. **Release Date:** 1973. **Length:** 44 mins. **Format:** Beta, VHS, 3/4″ U-matic Cassette, Other than listed.

★1816★
The Exiles
University of California at Berkeley
  Extension Media Center
2176 Shattuck Ave.
Berkeley, CA 94704   Ph: (510)642-0460
Description: A depiction of three young American Indians who come to Los Angeles and get involved in drinking, gambling, and fighting, in anguish and frustration. **Release Date:** 1961. **Length:** 72 mins. **Format:** 3/4″ U-matic Cassette, Other than listed.

★1817★
Eyanopopi: The Heart of the Sioux
Centre Productions, Inc.
1800 30th St., Ste. 207
Boulder, CO 80301   Ph: (303)444-1166
                          Free: 800-824-1166
Description: An explanation as to why the Black Hills of South Dakota are so important to the Sioux. **Release Date:** 1990. **Length:** 30 mins. **Format:** Beta, VHS, 3/4″ U-matic Cassette.

★1818★
Faithkeeper
Mystic Fire Video
PO Box 1092
Cooper Sta.   Ph: (212)941-0999
New York, NY 10276   Fax: (212)941-1443
Description: Oren Lyons, an Onondaga chief and leader in the international environmental movement discusses with Bill Moyers the history and philosophy of Native Americans, including their respect for nature and their responsibility for future generations. **Release Date:** 1991. **Length:** 58 mins. **Format:** VHS. **Credits:** Hosted by: Bill Moyers.

★1819★
The First Americans
Troll Associates
320 Rte. 17
Mahwah, NJ 07430   Ph: (201)529-4000
Description: A tape which explains the different Indian tribes of North America, and tells about their customs. **Release Date:** 1988. **Length:** 60 mins. **Format:** VHS. **Credits:** Hosted by: Hugh Downs.

★1820★
The First Americans
New York State Education Department
Center for Learning Technologies
Media Distribution Network, Rm. C-7,
  Concourse Level
Albany, NY 12230   Ph: (518)474-1265
Description: Topics and issues related to the American Indian are discussed in a talk show format in this series of twenty programs. **Release Date:** 197?. **Length:** 30 mins. **Format:** Beta, VHS, 1/2″ Reel-EIAJ, 3/4″ U-matic Cassette, 2″ Quadraplex Open Reel.

★1821★
The First Americans
Dallas County Community College District
Center for Educational
  Telecommunications
Dallas Telecourses
9596 Walnut St.   Ph: (214)952-0303
Mesquite, TX 75243   Fax: (214)952-0329
Description: The 30,000 years of cultural development of the American Indian provide a background for the story of America. **Release Date:** 1979. **Length:** 29 mins. **Format:** 3/4″ U-matic Cassette.

★1822★
The First Americans, Part 2: Some Indians of the
  Southlands
International Film Foundation
155 W. 72nd St.
New York, NY 10023   Ph: (212)580-1111
Description: Deals with Indians who lived (and some still do) in what many refer to as the southern half of the United States. **Length:** 17 **Format:** 3/4U Special order formats

★1823★
First Frontier
Wombat Film and Video   Ph: (708)328-6700
930 Pitner   Free: 800-323-5448
Evanston, IL 60202   Fax: (708)328-6706
Description: A history of Native Americans from 1540 to 1814 including dramatizations of key events. **Release Date:** 1989. **Length:** 57 mins. **Format:** Beta, VHS, 3/4″ U-matic Cassette.

★1824★
Fleshburn
Media Home Entertainment
510 W. 6th St., Ste. 1032
Los Angeles, CA 90014   Ph: (213)236-1336
                          Fax: (213)236-1346
Description: An Indian Vietnam War veteran escapes from a mental institution to get revenge on the four psychiatrists who committed him. **Length:** 91 **Format:** Beta VHS

★1825★
Folklore of the Muscogee (Creek) People
Native American Public Broadcasting
  Consortium
PO Box 86111
1800 N. 33rd St.
Lincoln, NE 68501   Ph: (402)472-3522
Description: Dr. Ruth Arrington narrates an analysis of the significance of Creek folklore. **Release Date:** 1983. **Length:** 29 mins. **Format:** VHS, 3/4″ U-matic Cassette, 1″ Broadcast Type ″C″, 2″ Quadraplex Open Reel.

★1826★
Forest Spirits
Great Plains National (GPN)
PO Box 80669   Ph: (402)472-2007
Lincoln, NE 68501-0669   Free: 800-228-4630
Description: The plight of the Oneida and Menominee Indians comes under scrutiny in this series, in an effort to reaffirm the heritage and traditions of these North American Indians. Programs are available individually. **Release Date:** 1977. **Length:** 30 mins. **Format:** Beta, VHS, 3/4″ U-matic Cassette.

★1827★
Forever in Time: The Art of Edward S. Curtis
Cinema Guild
1697 Broadway   Ph: (212)246-5522
New York, NY 10019   Fax: (212)246-5525
Description: A biography of the man who devoted much of his life to photographing the American Indian in the early part of the twentieth century. Curtis was unable to fulfill his dream of photographing every North American tribe before his death in 1952, but he uncovered previously unknown aspects of the Battle of Little Big Horn. **Release Date:** 1990. **Length:** 50 mins. **Format:** VHS.

★1828★
The Forgotten American
Carousel Film & Video
260 5th Ave., Rm. 705
New York, NY 10001   Ph: (212)683-1660

Description: Shows how the white man exploits the American Indian. Documents hopelessness and despair, minimal food and housing, inadequate educational facilities, and limited employment opportunity. **Release Date:** 1972. **Length:** 25 mins. **Format:** Beta, VHS, 3/4″ U-matic Cassette.

★1829★
Forgotten Frontier
Native American Public Broadcasting
  Consortium
PO Box 86111
1800 N. 33rd St.
Lincoln, NE 68501   Ph: (402)472-3522

Description: A document of the Spanish missionary settlements in southern Arizona and the agricultural, political and religious influences they had on the Native Americans of the area. **Release Date:** 1976. **Length:** 29 mins. **Format:** VHS, 3/4″ U-matic Cassette, 1″ Broadcast Type ″C″, 2″ Quadraplex Open Reel.

★1830★
Forty-Seven Cents
University of California at Berkeley
  Extension Media Center
2176 Shattuck Ave.
Berkeley, CA 94704   Ph: (510)642-0460

Description: This program documents how officials of the Bureau of Indian Affairs, the Indian Claims Commission, and a lawyer representing the Pit River Indian Nation of Northern California obtained from the tribe a land settlement many of its members did not want. **Release Date:** 1973. **Length:** 45 mins. **Format:** VHS, 3/4″ U-matic Cassette.

★1831★
Four Corners of Earth
Native American Public Broadcasting
  Consortium
PO Box 86111
1800 N. 33rd St.
Lincoln, NE 68501   Ph: (402)472-3522

Description: A film documenting the cultural evolution of Seminole women. Changing traditional values in the modern world are viewed from the perspective of women living on South Florida Seminole reservations. **Release Date:** 1984. **Length:** 30 mins. **Format:** VHS, 3/4″ U-matic Cassette, 1″ Broadcast Type ″C″, 2″ Quadraplex Open Reel.

★1832★
Fulfilling the Vision
Wishing Well Distributing   Ph: (414)889-8501
PO Box 1008   Free: 800-888-9355
Silver Lake, WI 53170   Fax: (414)889-8591

Description: Examines the struggle of the Lakota Sioux generation that came of age in the 1970s and '80s to redefine the nation's identity. Adresses contemporary socioeconomic issues, spirituality, and traditional wisdom. **Length:** 30 **Format:** VHS

★1833★
Game of Staves
University of California at Berkeley
  Extension Media Center
2176 Shattuck Ave.
Berkeley, CA 94704   Ph: (510)642-0460

Description: Pomo Indians demonstrate the game of staves, a variation of dice, played by most of the Indian tribes of North America. **Release Date:** 1962. **Length:** 10 mins. **Format:** 3/4″ U-matic Cassette, Other than listed.

★1834★
Gannagaro
Native American Public Braodcasting
  Consortium
1800 N. 33rd St.
PO Box 86111
Lincoln, NE 68501   Ph: (402)472-3522

Description: Explores the Seneca, one of the five Iroquois nations of New York state, and the events that occured in 1687 when the French invaded their village and destroyed it. Combines footage from the archaelogical dig, interviews, and museum artifacts. **Release Date:** 1986. **Length:** 28 mins. **Format:** VHS, 1″ Broadcast Type ″C″, 3/4″ U-matic Cassette.

★1835★
Geronimo Jones
Learning Corporation of America
108 Wilmot Rd.   Ph: (708)940-1260
Deerfield, IL 60015-9990   Free: 800-621-2131

Description: Perceptive study of the conflict which faces an Indian boy, torn between pride in his heritage and his future in modern American society. **Release Date:** 1970. **Length:** 21 mins. **Format:** Beta, VHS, 3/4″ U-matic Cassette. **Credits:** Directed by: Bert Salzman.

★1836★
Geronimo: The Final Campaign
Centre Productions, Inc.
1800 30th St., Ste. 207   Ph: (303)444-1166
Boulder, CO 80301   Free: 800-824-1166

Description: This video takes a look at one of the most respected and well-known Indian warriors. **Release Date:** 1988. **Length:** 30 mins. **Format:** Beta, VHS, 3/4″ U-matic Cassette.

★1837★
The Gift of Santa Fe
Native American Public Broadcasting
  Consortium
1800 N. 33rd St.
PO Box 86111
Lincoln, NE 68501   Ph: (402)472-3522

Description: A visit to the internationally reknowned Santa Fe Indian Market, a weekend-long display of Native American art, including pottery, jewelry, carvings, weavings, and paintings. Features the work of Lucy M. Lewis, a 90-year-old master potter. **Length:** 22 mins. **Format:** VHS, 1″ Broadcast Type ″C″, 3/4″ U-matic Cassette.

★1838★
Girl of the Navajos
Coronet/MTI Film & Video
108 Wilmot Rd.   Ph: (708)940-1260
Deerfield, IL 60015   Free: 800-621-2131
     Fax: (708)940-3640

Description: The story of Nanabah, a Navajo girl, as she recalls her feelings of loneliness and fear the first time she had to herd her family's sheep into the canyon. **Release Date:** 1977. **Length:** 15 mins. **Format:** Beta, VHS, 3/4″ U-matic Cassette, Other than listed.

★1839★
The Girl Who Loved Wild Horses
Random House Media
Department 467
400 Hahn Rd.
Westminster, MD 21157   Free: 800-492-0782

Description: A Plains Indian girl loves the horses that live near her tribe. A Paul Globe story. **Release Date:** 1985. **Length:** 9 mins. **Format:** VHS.

★1840★
The Good Mind
Native American Public Broadcasting
  Consortium
PO Box 86111
1800 N. 33rd St.
Lincoln, NE 68501   Ph: (402)472-3522
Description: A comparative essay on Christian and American Indian beliefs, and how the two have merged. **Release Date:** 1983. **Length:** 30 mins. **Format:** VHS, 3/4″ U-matic Cassette, 1″ Broadcast Type ″C″, 2″ Quadraplex Open Reel.

★1841★
Great American Indian Heroes
Troll Associates
320 Rte. 17
Mahwah, NJ 07430   Ph: (201)529-4000
Description: A selection of brief profiles of eight different noted Indians. **Release Date:** 1988. **Length:** 82 mins. **Format:** VHS.

★1842★
The Great Movie Massacre
Video Tech
19346 3rd Ave. NW
Seattle, WA 98177   Ph: (206)546-5401
Description: The motion picture image of the Indian warrior is seen in clips from Robert Altman's "Buffalo Bill and the Indians," starring Paul Newman. From the "Images of Indians" series. **Release Date:** 1982. **Length:** 30 mins. **Format:** Beta, VHS, 3/4″ U-matic Cassette, Other than listed. **Credits:** Narrated by: Will Sampson.

★1843★
Great Spirit Within the Hole
Intermedia Arts of Minnesota, Inc.
425 Ontario St. SE
Minneapolis, MN 55414   Ph: (612)627-4444
Description: This film looks at the occasional restriction of Indian religious leaders from giving spiritual aid to Indians in prison. **Release Date:** 1983. **Length:** 60 mins. **Format:** Beta, VHS, 3/4″ U-matic Cassette.

★1844★
Hack's Choice
Beacon Films   Ph: (708)328-6700
1560 Sherman Ave., Ste. 100   Free: 800-323-9084
Evanston, IL 60201   Fax: (708)328-6706
Description: Young boy preserves the heritage of his people with the help of a family medicine bag. **Length:** 28 **Format:** VHS

★1845★
Had You Lived Then: Life in the Woodlands Before the White Man Came
AIMS Media
9710 De Soto Ave.
Chatsworth, CA 91311-9734   Free: 800-367-2467
                                     Fax: (818)341-6700
Description: Indians show how their ancestors lived before the white man came and how deer were important in the survival of the Indians. **Release Date:** 1976. **Length:** 12 mins. **Format:** Beta, VHS, 3/4″ U-matic Cassette.

★1846★
Haudensaunee: Way of the Longhouse
New York State Education Department
Center for Learning Technologies
Media Distribution Network, Rm. C-7,
  Concourse Level
Albany, NY 12230   Ph: (518)474-1265
Description: A historical overview of the lifestyles and attitudes of the Haudenosaunee Iroquois tribe. **Release Date:** 1984. **Length:** 13 mins. **Format:** Beta, VHS, 1/2″ Reel-EIAJ, 3/4″ U-matic Cassette, 2″ Quadraplex Open Reel.

★1847★
Hawk, I'm Your Brother: Stories of American Indian Culture
Hartley Film Foundation   Ph: (203)869-1818
Cat Rock Rd.   Free: 800-937-1819
Cos Cob, CT 06807   Fax: (203)869-1905
Description: Rudy is a young American Indian boy who just knows he was born to fly. His adventures with the Redtail Hawk are told in this story for the whole family. **Length:** 25 **Format:** VHS

★1848★
Health Care Crisis at Rosebud
Native American Public Broadcasting
  Consortium
PO Box 86111
1800 N. 33rd St.
Lincoln, NE 68501   Ph: (402)472-3522
Description: An exploration of the reasons behind the Rosebud Reservation's lack of physicians. **Release Date:** 1973. **Length:** 21 mins. **Format:** VHS, 3/4″ U-matic Cassette, 1″ Broadcast Type ″C″, 2″ Quadraplex Open Reel.

★1849★
Heart of the Earth Survival School/Circle of the Winds
Intermedia Arts of Minnesota, Inc.
425 Ontario St. SE
Minneapolis, MN 55414   Ph: (612)627-4444
Description: Two programs about the alternative schooling available to American Indians. **Release Date:** 1980. **Length:** 32 mins. **Format:** Beta, VHS, 3/4″ U-matic Cassette.

★1850★
Heathen Injuns and the Hollywood Gospel
Video Tech
19346 3rd Ave. NW
Seattle, WA 98177   Ph: (206)546-5401
Description: This program from the "Images of Indians" series looks at Hollywood's portrayal of Native American religion and values and the stereotyping of Indian women. **Release Date:** 1982. **Length:** 30 mins. **Format:** Beta, VHS, 3/4″ U-matic Cassette, Other than listed. **Credits:** Narrated by: Will Sampson.

★1851★
Heritage of Craftsmanship
Michigan Media
University of Michigan
400 4th St.
Ann Arbor, MI 48109   Ph: (313)764-8228
Description: A look at the role of Indian craftsmanship in Indian life, past and present. Part of the "Silent Heritage" series. **Release Date:** 1966. **Length:** 29 mins. **Format:** 3/4″ U-matic Cassette, Other than listed.

★1852★
Herman Red Elk: A Sioux Indian Artist
Native American Public Broadcasting
  Consortium
PO Box 86111
1800 N. 33rd St.
Lincoln, NE 68501   Ph: (402)472-3522
Description: A look at the work of this renowned traditional skin painter. **Release Date:** 1975. **Length:** 29 mins. **Format:** VHS, 3/4″ U-matic Cassette, 1″ Broadcast Type ″C″, 2″ Quadraplex Open Reel.

★1853★
Hisatsinom: The Ancient Ones
Native American Public Broadcasting
  Consortium
1800 N. 33rd St.
PO Box 86111
Lincoln, NE 68501   Ph: (402)472-3522

Description: Explores the culture of the Anasazi people of the Colorado and San Juan River valleys through story, song, dance, and ceremony. **Length:** 24 mins. **Format:** VHS, 1″ Broadcast Type ″C″, 3/4″ U-matic Cassette.

★1854★
The History and Problems of Winnebago Indians
NETCHE (Nebraska ETV Council for
  Higher Education)
Box 83111
Lincoln, NE 68501   Ph: (402)472-3611

Description: A native Winnebago describes the history and migration of the tribe and conditions on the Northeast Nebraska reservation in 1970. **Release Date:** 1970. **Length:** 30 mins. **Format:** 1/2″ Reel-EIAJ.

★1855★
Home of the Brave
Cinema Guild
1697 Broadway   Ph: (212)246-5522
New York, NY 10019   Fax: (212)246-5525

Description: An examination into the problems being faced by the native populations of North and South America. Of primary concern to the Indians is the increasing industrial development and pollution on their land. **Release Date:** 1984. **Length:** 53 mins. **Format:** Beta, VHS, 3/4″ U-matic Cassette.

★1856★
Honored by the Moon
Women Make Movies
225 Lafayette St., Ste. 206   Ph: (212)925-0606
New York, NY 10012   Fax: (212)925-2052

Description: An exploration of the special cultural prejudices faced by Native American lesbians and gays. **Release Date:** 1990. **Length:** 15 mins. **Format:** Beta, VHS, 3/4″ U-matic Cassette.

★1857★
The Honour of All
Native American Public Broadcasting
  Consortium
1800 N. 33rd St.
PO Box 86111
Lincoln, NE 68501   Ph: (402)472-3522

Description: Looks at the Alkali Lake Indian Band's struggle to overcome its problem with alcoholism and gives guidelines on how other communities can pull together to overcome alcoholism and drug abuse. Individual program titles: The Honour of All, Part I; The Honour of All, Part II; Sharing Innovations that Work. Tapes are available individually or as a series. **Release Date:** 1987. **Length:** 41 mins. **Format:** VHS, 1″ Broadcast Type ″C″, 3/4″ U-matic Cassette.

★1858★
Hopewell Heritage
Michigan Media
University of Michigan
400 4th St.
Ann Arbor, MI 48109   Ph: (313)764-8228

Description: This is a study of the excavation and recreation of the Hopewell Indian culture. **Release Date:** 1964. **Length:** 30 mins. **Format:** 3/4″ U-matic Cassette, Other than listed.

★1859★
The Hopi
Victorian Video Productions
PO Box 1540   Ph: (916)346-6184
Colfax, CA 95713-1540   Free: 800-848-0284

Description: A look at the everyday life of the members of this particular Indian tribe. **Release Date:** 1989. **Length:** 30 mins. **Format:** Beta, VHS.

★1860★
The Hopi Indian
Coronet/MTI Film & Video   Ph: (708)940-1260
108 Wilmot Rd.   Free: 800-621-2131
Deerfield, IL 60015   Fax: (708)940-3640

Description: The Hopi Indians hold most firmly to their traditional ways. This program shows them in daily routines and special celebrations. **Release Date:** 1975. **Length:** 11 mins. **Format:** Beta, VHS, 3/4″ U-matic Cassette, Other than listed.

★1861★
Hopi Indian Arts and Crafts
Coronet/MTI Film & Video   Ph: (708)940-1260
108 Wilmot Rd.   Free: 800-621-2131
Deerfield, IL 60015   Fax: (708)940-3640

Description: This program emphasizes Hopi skills and observes them weaving, making baskets, silversmithing, and making ceramics to sell in their cooperative store. **Release Date:** 1975. **Length:** 10 mins. **Format:** Beta, VHS, 3/4″ U-matic Cassette, Other than listed.

★1862★
Hopi Pottery
Norman Beerger Productions
3217 S. Arville St.
Las Vegas, NV 89102-7612   Ph: (702)876-2328

Description: How Hopi pottery relates to that Indian tribe's way of life is explained. **Release Date:** 1988. **Length:** 65 mins. **Format:** Beta, VHS.

★1863★
Hopi Prayer for Peace
Wishing Well Distributing   Ph: (414)864-2395
PO Box 2   Free: 800-888-9355
Wilmot, WI 53192   Fax: (414)862-2398

Description: Elders of the Hopi Nation repeat their appeal to the world for peace. **Release Date:** 1990. **Length:** 27 mins. **Format:** VHS.

★1864★
Hopi: Songs of the Fourth World
New Day Films
121 W. 27th St., Ste. 902   Ph: (212)645-8210
New York, NY 10001   Fax: (212)645-8652

Description: The life of the Hopi Indians as it remains today is implicit in their relationship with the environment. **Release Date:** 1985. **Length:** 58 mins. **Format:** Beta, VHS, 3/4″ U-matic Cassette, Other than listed.

★1865★
Hopiit
Intermedia Arts of Minnesota, Inc.
425 Ontario St. SE
Minneapolis, MN 55414   Ph: (612)627-4444

Description: A visually exciting look at the life of the Hopi Indian, which dispels many cliches about Native Americans. **Release Date:** 1982. **Length:** 15 mins. **Format:** Beta, VHS, 3/4″ U-matic Cassette.

★1866★
Hopis: Guardians of the Land
FilmFair Communications   Ph: (818)985-0244
10621 Magnolia Blvd.   Free: 800-423-2461
North Hollywood, CA 91601   Fax: (818)980-8492

Description: This program shows how the land of the Hopi Indians has been desecrated by men seeking coal and water from the soil.

Release Date: 1971. Length: 10 mins. Format: Beta, VHS, 3/4″ U-matic Cassette.

★1867★
How Hollywood Wins the West
Video Tech
19346 3rd Ave. NW
Seattle, WA 98177   Ph: (206)546-5401
Description: Scenes from "Soldier Blue" and D.W. Griffith's "America" show how the film industry has only portrayed the colonization of the West from the white man's viewpoint. From the "Images of Indians" series. Release Date: 1982. Length: 30 mins. Format: Beta, VHS, 3/4″ U-matic Cassette, Other than listed. Credits: Narrated by: Will Sampson.

★1868★
How the West Was Lost
Cinema Guild
1697 Broadway   Ph: (212)246-5522
New York, NY 10019   Fax: (212)246-5525
Description: The way of life of the Plains Indians changed dramatically with the westward movement of the white man. This program highlights the prime of Plains Indian civilization and focuses upon the contemporary Indian effort to maintain a sense of their own identity. Release Date: 1976. Length: 26 mins. Format: 3/4″ U-matic Cassette, Other than listed.

★1869★
How the West Was Won...and Honor Lost
CRM/McGraw-Hill Films
674 Via de la Valle
PO Box 641
Del Mar, CA 92014
Description: The gradual defeat of the Indians by American settlers in the 1800s is charted in this program from the "North American Indian" series. Release Date: 1971. Length: 25 mins. Format: Beta, VHS, 3/4″ U-matic Cassette.

★1870★
Hupa Indian White Deerskin Dance
Barr Films
12801 Schabarum Ave.   Ph: (818)338-7878
PO Box 7878   Free: 800-234-7878
Irwindale, CA 91706-7878   Fax: (818)814-2672
Description: Records a dance of the Hupa Indians of Northwestern California, describing the artifacts used and the traditional dance pattern and song. Release Date: 1958. Length: 11 mins. Format: Beta, VHS, 3/4″ U-matic Cassette.

★1871★
I Am Different From My Brother: Dakota Name-Giving
Native American Public Broadcasting
Consortium
PO Box 86111
1800 N. 33rd St.
Lincoln, NE 68501   Ph: (402)472-3522
Description: A documentary about the Name-Giving ceremony for three young Flandreau Dakota Sioux Indian children. Release Date: 1981. Length: 20 mins. Format: VHS, 3/4″ U-matic Cassette, 1″ Broadcast Type "C", 2″ Quadraplex Open Reel.

★1872★
I Will Fight No More Forever
New York State Education Department
Center for Learning Technologies
Media Distribution Network, Rm. C-7,
Concourse Level
Albany, NY 12230   Ph: (518)474-1265
Description: The tragic saga of the Nez Perce Indians, who were forced from their reservations in the Pacific Northwest by white settlers, which led to war and ultimate decimation. Release Date: 1982. Length: 10 mins. Format: Beta, VHS, 3/4″ U-matic Cassette.

★1873★
Iisaw: Hopi Coyote Stories
Norman Ross Publishing Inc.   Ph: (212)765-8200
330 W. 58th St.   Free: 800-648-8850
New York, NY 10019   Fax: (212)765-2393
Description: These singing tales reinforce the Hopi ethic by describing what happens to those who shirk hard work (Hopi with English subtitles). Release Date: 1981. Length: 18 mins. Format: Beta, VHS, 3/4″ U-matic Cassette.

★1874★
Images of Indians
Video Tech
19346 3rd Ave. NW
Seattle, WA 98177   Ph: (206)546-5401
Description: A five-part series that traces the stereotypical Hollywood treatment of Indians through the years. Programs are available separately. Release Date: 1982. Length: 30 mins. Format: Beta, VHS, 3/4″ U-matic Cassette, Other than listed. Credits: Narrated by: Will Sampson.

★1875★
In the Heart of Big Mountain
Upstream Productions   Ph: (206)281-9177
420 First Ave. W.   Free: (88U)PST-
Seattle, WA 98119   REAM
    Fax: (206)284-6963
Description: Examines the traumatic effects on the life of a Navajo family that was forced to relocate to one of the most remote yet traditional Indian reservations, Big Mountain, Arizona. Length: 28 Format: VHS

★1876★
In Quest of a Vision
American Educational Films
3807 Dickerson Rd.
Nashville, TN 37207   Free: 800-822-5678
Description: The culture of the Great Basin Indians is shown within the framing story of a young tribesman's journey toward spiritual fulfillment. Release Date: 1976. Length: 30 mins. Format: Beta, VHS, 3/4″ U-matic Cassette.

★1877★
In Search of the First Americans
Carolina Biological Supply Company
2700 York Rd.   Ph: (919)584-0381
Burlington, NC 27215   Free: 800-334-5551
Description: This program examines the early history of prehistoric man in North America. Release Date: 1988. Length: 28 mins. Format: Beta, VHS.

★1878★
In the White Man's Image
Native American Public Broadcasting
Consortium
1800 N. 33rd St.
PO Box 86111
Lincoln, NE 68501   Ph: (402)472-3522
Description: Explores the cultural genocide that occured in the Carlisle School for Indian Students which impacted on generations of Native Americans. At the school, students were taught to read and write English, and were placed in uniforms and drilled like soldiers in order to "civilize" them. Includes interviews with former students. Release Date: 1991. Length: 51 mins. Format: VHS, 1″ Broadcast Type "C", 3/4 U-matic Cassette.

★1879★
Indian Artists of the Southwest
Britannica Films
310 S. Michigan Ave.   Ph: (312)347-7958
Chicago, IL 60604   Fax: (312)347-7966
Description: Three Pueblo Indian tribes (Zuni, Hopi, and Navajo) introduce four of their major art forms: stone and silverwork, pottery making, weaving, and kachina carving. Release Date: 1972. Length: 15 mins. Format: Beta, VHS, 3/4″ U-matic Cassette.

★1880★
Indian Arts at the Phoenix Heard Museum
Native American Public Broadcasting
  Consortium
PO Box 86111
1800 N. 33rd St.
Lincoln, NE 68501   Ph: (402)472-3522
Description: This is a survey of the Heard Museum's collection of southwestern Indian art. **Release Date:** 1975. **Length:** 28 mins. **Format:** VHS, 3/4″ U-matic Cassette, 1″ Broadcast Type ″C″, 2″ Quadraplex Open Reel.

★1881★
Indian Boy of the Southwest
Phoenix/BFA Films
468 Park Ave., S.   Ph: (212)684-5910
New York, NY 10016   Free: 800-221-1274
Description: Toboya, a Hopi Indian boy, tells us about his life and his home. **Release Date:** 1963. **Length:** 15 mins. **Format:** Beta, VHS, 3/4″ U-matic Cassette.

★1882★
Indian Country
Cinema Guild
1697 Broadway   Ph: (212)246-5522
New York, NY 10019   Fax: (212)246-5525
Description: This program offers a thorough survey of contemporary Indian life extending to the social, religious, and political aspects. **Release Date:** 1976. **Length:** 26 mins. **Format:** 3/4″ U-matic Cassette, Other than listed.

★1883★
Indian Country
PBS Video
1320 Braddock Pl.
Alexandria, VA 22314-1698   Ph: (703)739-5380
Description: An examination of life on the Quinault Indian Reservation in Washington which assesses the effectiveness of its leader Joe De LaCruz. **Release Date:** 1988. **Length:** 60 mins. **Format:** Beta, VHS, 3/4″ U-matic Cassette.

★1884★
Indian Crafts: Hopi, Navajo, and Iroquois
Phoenix/BFA Films
468 Park Ave., S.   Ph: (212)684-5910
New York, NY 10016   Free: 800-221-1274
Description: The many diversified arts and crafts of these Indian cultures are demonstrated by their basket making, pottery making, kachina carving, weaving, jewelry making, and mask carving. **Release Date:** 1980. **Length:** 12 mins. **Format:** Beta, VHS, 3/4″ U-matic Cassette.

★1885★
Indian Family of Long Ago (Buffalo Hunters of the Plains)
Britannica Films
310 S. Michigan Ave.   Ph: (312)347-7958
Chicago, IL 60604   Fax: (312)347-7966
Description: This video presentation recreates the life of Plains Indians in the Dakotas and adjoining territories two hundred years ago. **Release Date:** 1957. **Length:** 14 mins. **Format:** Beta, VHS, 3/4″ U-matic Cassette.

★1886★
Indian Heroes of America
Atlantis Productions
1252 La Granada Dr.
Thousand Oaks, CA 91360   Ph: (805)495-2790
Description: This video presents biographical sketches of seven American Indian personalities whose lives paralleled 300 years of historic events from the coming of the white man to the final capitulation. **Release Date:** 197?. **Length:** 17 mins. **Format:** Beta, VHS, 3/4″ U-matic Cassette.

★1887★
Indian and His Homeland: American Images, 1590-1876
Finley-Holiday Film Corporation
PO Box 619
Dept. CS
Whittier, CA 90608   Free: 800-345-6707
      Fax: (213)693-4756
Description: Enhance your knowledge of the American Indian way of life, the way it was before the arrival of European civilization. Video is presented in a fascinating collage of paintings done by such artists as Catlin, Bodmer, Audubon, and Moran. **Release Date:** 1991. **Length:** 30 mins. **Format:** VHS.

★1888★
Indian Legacy
January Productions
210 6th Ave., Dept. VSF   Ph: (201)423-4666
PO Box 66   Free: 800-451-7450
Hawthorne, NJ 07507   Fax: (201)423-5569
Description: A series of five programs that will teach children about American Indians and their customs. **Release Date:** 1988. **Length:** 52 mins. **Format:** VHS.

★1889★
Indian Self-Rule
Documentary Educational Resources
101 Morse St.   Ph: (617)926-0491
Watertown, MA 02172   Fax: (617)926-9519
Description: This documentary traces the history of white-Indian relations from nineteenth century treaties through the present, as tribal leaders, historians, teachers, and other Indians gather at a 1983 conference organized to reevaluate the significance of the Indian/Reorganization Act of 1934. **Release Date:** 1986. **Length:** 58 mins. **Format:** 3/4″ U-matic Cassette.

★1890★
An Indian Summer
Atlantis Productions
1252 La Granada Dr.
Thousand Oaks, CA 91360   Ph: (805)495-2790
Description: A summer experience with Chippewa Indian children on a woodland reservation and their relationship to animals and to the environment are shown. **Release Date:** 1975. **Length:** 11 mins. **Format:** Beta, VHS, 3/4″ U-matic Cassette.

★1891★
The Indian Way
New York State Education Department
Center for Learning Technologies
Media Distribution Network, Rm. C-7,
  Concourse Level
Albany, NY 12230   Ph: (518)474-1265
Description: This program looks at how traditional Indian values clash with modern times. **Release Date:** 196?. **Length:** 30 mins. **Format:** Beta, VHS, 1/2″ Reel-EIAJ, 3/4″ U-matic Cassette, 2″ Quadraplex Open Reel.

★1892★
The Indians
Center for Humanities, Inc.
Communications Park
Box 1000   Ph: (914)666-4100
Mount Kisco, NY 10549   Free: 800-431-1242
Description: This film is a portrait of Indian life and culture in Colorado before, during, and after the white settlers came. **Release Date:** 1970. **Length:** 31 mins. **Format:** Beta, VHS, 3/4″ U-matic Cassette.

★1893★
Indians Americans
Michigan Media
University of Michigan
400 4th St.
Ann Arbor, MI 48109   Ph: (313)764-8228
Description: This video examines two extremes of American Indian life–racial and cultural extinction in the East and cultural preservation on reservations in the West. Part of the "Silent Heritage" series. **Release Date:** 1966. **Length:** 29 mins. **Format:** 3/4″ U-matic Cassette, Other than listed.

★1894★
Indians in the Americas (Revised)
Phoenix/BFA Films
468 Park Ave., S.   Ph: (212)684-5910
New York, NY 10016   Free: 800-221-1274
Description: This updated program follows America's valuable Indian heritage, from early Indian cultures to modern ones in both North and South America. **Release Date:** 1985. **Length:** 22 mins. **Format:** Beta, VHS, 3/4″ U-matic Cassette.

★1895★
Indians of California: Part 1, Village Life
Barr Films
12801 Schabarum Ave.   Ph: (818)338-7878
PO Box 7878   Free: 800-234-7878
Irwindale, CA 91706-7878   Fax: (818)814-2672
Description: This program describes life in a primitive Indian village, including trading, house building, basket making, and songs and dances. **Release Date:** 1964. **Length:** 15 mins. **Format:** Beta, VHS, 3/4″ U-matic Cassette.

★1896★
Indians of California: Part 2, Food
Barr Films
12801 Schabarum Ave.   Ph: (818)338-7878
PO Box 7878   Free: 800-234-7878
Irwindale, CA 91706-7878   Fax: (818)814-2672
Description: This program describes how primitive Indians obtained their food. Includes bow and arrow making, deer hunting, and gathering and preparing acorns. **Release Date:** 1964. **Length:** 14 mins. **Format:** Beta, VHS, 3/4″ U-matic Cassette.

★1897★
Indians of Early America
Britannica Films
310 S. Michigan Ave.   Ph: (312)347-7958
Chicago, IL 60604   Fax: (312)347-7966
Description: This film recreates activities of representative early North American Indian Tribes, including Iroquois, Sioux, and Pueblo. **Release Date:** 1957. **Length:** 22 mins. **Format:** Beta, VHS, 3/4″ U-matic Cassette.

★1898★
Iowa's Ancient Hunters
University of Iowa
Audiovisual Center
C-215 Seashore Hall
Iowa City, IA 52242   Ph: (319)335-2539
Description: This documentary shows the location and excavation of the Cherokee Dig, where remnants of three prehistoric societies have been found in northwest Iowa. **Release Date:** 1978. **Length:** 28 mins. **Format:** 3/4″ U-matic Cassette.

★1899★
The Iroquois
Michigan Media
University of Michigan
400 4th St.
Ann Arbor, MI 48109   Ph: (313)764-8228
Description: The story of the Iroquois Indian. With great pride in their unique heritage, the Iroquois Indians of New York State plan for their future despite loss of lands promised to them. Part of the

"Silent Heritage" series. **Release Date:** 1966. **Length:** 29 mins. **Format:** 3/4″ U-matic Cassette, Other than listed.

★1900★
Iroquois Social Dance I and II
Green Mountain Cine Works, Inc.
53 Hamilton Ave.
Staten Island, NY 10301   Ph: (718)981-0120
Description: Two programs, available individually, presenting social dances of the Mohawk Indians. Part I is about the dances in general; Part II illustrates the techniques. **Release Date:** 1980. **Length:** 18 mins. **Format:** Beta, 3/4″ U-matic Cassette.

★1901★
Ishi, The Ending People
Centre Productions, Inc.
1800 30th St., Ste. 207   Ph: (303)444-1166
Boulder, CO 80301   Free: 800-824-1166
Description: This film is based on the true story of the Yahi people of Northern California. It centers around a young Yahi named Ishi who came out of hiding in 1911 to tell the story of his ancient tribe. **Release Date:** 1983. **Length:** 15 mins. **Format:** Beta, VHS, 3/4″ U-matic Cassette.

★1902★
Itam Hakim Hopiit (We Someone, The Hopi)
American Federation of Arts
41 E. 65th St.   Ph: (212)988-7700
New York, NY 10021   Fax: (212)861-2487
Description: A realistic/surrealistic visualization of Hopi philosophy and prophesy. **Release Date:** 1984. **Length:** 60 mins. **Format:** Beta, VHS, 3/4″ U-matic Cassette.

★1903★
Joe KillsRight: Oglala Sioux
Downtown Community TV Center
87 Lafayette St.
New York, NY 10013   Ph: (212)966-4510
Description: A profile of Joe KillsRight, an Oglala Sioux who came to New York City to find work and found a hostile urban environment much different from the reservation. **Release Date:** 1980. **Length:** 25 mins. **Format:** 1/2″ Reel-EIAJ, 3/4″ U-matic Cassette, Other than listed.

★1904★
Journey to the Sky: A History of the Alabama Coushatta Indians
Native American Public Broadcasting
  Consortium
PO Box 86111
1800 N. 33rd St.
Lincoln, NE 68501   Ph: (402)472-3522
Description: Chief Fulton Battise tells a campfire tale of his tribe, metaphorically recounting the history of his tribe and its first meeting with white men. **Release Date:** 1980. **Length:** 53 mins. **Format:** VHS, 3/4″ U-matic Cassette, 1″ Broadcast Type "C", 2″ Quadraplex Open Reel.

★1905★
Kashia Men's Dances: Southwestern Pomo Indians
University of California at Berkeley
  Extension Media Center
2176 Shattuck Ave.
Berkeley, CA 94704   Ph: (510)642-0460
Description: This program preserves four authentic Pomo dances as performed, in elaborate costumes and headdresses, on the Kashia Reservation on the northern California coast. **Release Date:** 1963. **Length:** 40 mins. **Format:** 3/4″ U-matic Cassette, Other than listed.

★1906★
Keep Your Heart Strong
Native American Public Broadcasting
  Consortium
1800 N. 33rd St.
PO Box 86111
Lincoln, NE 68501   Ph: (402)472-3522
Description: Explores contemporary Native American culture through the Pow Wow. Explains why traditional values are important to today's culture. **Release Date:** 1986. **Length:** 58 mins. **Format:** VHS, 1″ Broadcast Type ″C″, 3/4 U-matic Cassette.

★1907★
Keeper of the Western Door
New York State Education Department
Center for Learning Technologies
Media Distribution Network, Rm. C-7,
  Concourse Level
Albany, NY 12230   Ph: (518)474-1265
Description: Various aspects of the tradition and culture of the Seneca Nations of Indians are examined in this series. **Release Date:** 198?. **Length:** 15 mins. **Format:** Beta, VHS, 1/2″ Reel-EIAJ, 3/4″ U-matic Cassette, 2″ Quadraplex Open Reel.

★1908★
Kevin Alec
The Media Guild
11722 Sorrento Valley Rd., Ste. E   Ph: (619)755-9191
San Diego, CA 92121   Fax: (619)755-4931
Description: Examines the life of an eleven-year-old boy who lives on the Fountain Indian Reserve with his grandmother. From the "Who Are You" series. **Release Date:** 1978. **Length:** 17 mins. **Format:** Beta, VHS, 3/4″ U-matic Cassette.

★1909★
Kiliwa: Hunters and Gatherers of Baja California
University of California at Berkeley
  Extension Media Center
2176 Shattuck Ave.
Berkeley, CA 94704   Ph: (510)642-0460
Description: This program documents aspects of hunting and gathering, food preparation, and shelter construction by a group of Baja California Indians. **Release Date:** 1975. **Length:** 14 mins. **Format:** 3/4″ U-matic Cassette, Other than listed.

★1910★
Lakota Quillwork: Art and Legend
One West Media
PO Box 5766
559 Onate Pl.
Santa Fe, NM 87501   Ph: (505)983-8685
Description: Lakota Indian women demonstrate their intricate craft with porcupine quills. **Release Date:** 1986. **Length:** 28 mins. **Format:** VHS, 3/4″ U-matic Cassette.

★1911★
Lament of the Reservation
CRM/McGraw-Hill Films
674 Via de la Valle
PO Box 641
Del Mar, CA 92014
Description: A record of life on an open Indian reservation, showing the sacrifices that must be made by the natives in order to remain a true Indian. Part of the "North American Indian" series. **Release Date:** 1971. **Length:** 24 mins. **Format:** Beta, VHS, 3/4″ U-matic Cassette.

★1912★
The Last of the Caddoes
Phoenix/BFA Films
468 Park Ave., S.   Ph: (212)684-5910
New York, NY 10016   Free: 800-221-1274
Description: Set in rural Texas in the 1930s, this program follows a young boy through a summer of self-discovery as he learns about

his part-Indian heritage. **Release Date:** 1982. **Length:** 29 mins. **Format:** Beta, VHS, 3/4″ U-matic Cassette.

★1913★
Last Chance for the Navajo
CRM/McGraw-Hill Films
674 Via de la Valle
PO Box 641
Del Mar, CA 92014
Description: The problems faced by Navajo Indians today are spelled out, including economic, employment and cultural difficulties. **Release Date:** 1978. **Length:** 27 mins. **Format:** Beta, VHS, 3/4″ U-matic Cassette.

★1914★
Legacy in Limbo
Native American Public Broadcasting
  Consortium
1800 N. 33rd St.
PO Box 86111
Lincoln, NE 68501   Ph: (402)472-3522
Description: Discusses the plight of the Museum of the American Indian in New York City. Because of it's small size, only a fraction of the artifacts can be displayed in the museum. The remainder sit in a Bronx warehouse. Although the museum is willing to move, politicians are blocking this step. **Release Date:** 1990. **Length:** 60 mins. **Format:** VHS, 1″ Broadcast Type ″C″, 3/4″ U-matic cassette.

★1915★
The Legend of the Boy and the Eagle
Coronet/MTI Film & Video   Ph: (708)940-1260
108 Wilmot Rd.   Free: 800-621-2131
Deerfield, IL 60015   Fax: (708)940-3640
Description: A Hopi Indian boy is caught between his love for the sacred eagle of the tribe and the conflicting values of group and individual. **Release Date:** 1990. **Length:** 21 mins. **Format:** Beta, VHS, 1/2″ Reel-EIAJ, 3/4″ U-matic Cassette, Other than listed.

★1916★
Legend Days Are Over
Pyramid Film & Video
Box 1048   Ph: (310)828-7577
2801 Colorado Ave.   Free: 800-421-2304
Santa Monica, CA 90406   Fax: (310)453-9083
Description: An elegy evoking the American Indian experience. **Release Date:** 1973. **Length:** 5 mins. **Format:** Beta, VHS, 3/4″ U-matic Cassette.

★1917★
Letter from an Apache
Pictures of Record
119 Kettle Creek Rd.
Weston, CT 06883   Ph: (203)227-3387
Description: The life of Dr. Carlos Montezuma, an Apache, and people as he remembers them, rendered in the style of 19th century Indian paintings. **Release Date:** 1983. **Length:** 12 mins. **Format:** VHS, 3/4″ U-matic Cassette. **Credits:** Narrated by: Fred Hellerman.

★1918★
Little Medicine: The Wisdom to Avoid Big Medicine
Wishing Well Distributing   Ph: (414)889-8501
PO Box 1008   Free: 800-888-9355
Silver Lake, WI 53170   Fax: (414)889-8591
Description: Drawing from Native American traditions in diet and disease prevention, helps viewers enjoy and use the world around them for simple solutions to everyday health problems. **Length:** 60 **Format:** VHS

★1919★
Live and Remember
Centre Productions, Inc.
1800 30th St., Ste. 207
Boulder, CO 80301   Ph: (303)444-1166
   Free: 800-824-1166
Description: This documentary captures the hardships and contradictions that modern Indians live with. **Release Date:** 1987. **Length:** 29 mins. **Format:** Beta, VHS, 3/4″ U-matic Cassette.

★1920★
Long Lance
National Film Board of Canada
1251 Avenue of the Americas, 16th Fl.
New York, NY 10020-1173   Ph: (212)586-5131
Description: Based on a true story, this film explores the mysterious origins of Chief Buffalo Child Long Lance. **Release Date:** 1987. **Length:** 55 mins. **Format:** Beta, VHS, 3/4″ U-matic Cassette.

★1921★
The Longest Trail
University of California at Berkeley
   Extension Media Center
2176 Shattuck Ave.
Berkeley, CA 94704   Ph: (510)642-0460
Description: View a Native American celebration in which a dance commemorates the crossing of the Bering Straits. **Release Date:** 1986. **Length:** 58 mins. **Format:** VHS, 3/4″ U-matic Cassette.

★1922★
The Longhouse People
National Film Board of Canada
1251 Avenue of the Americas, 16th Fl.
New York, NY 10020-1173   Ph: (212)586-5131
Description: Deals with the life and religion of the Iroquois Indians, showing a rain dance, a healing ceremony, and the celebration in honor of a newly chosen chief. **Release Date:** 1951. **Length:** 24 mins. **Format:** Beta, VHS, 3/4″ U-matic Cassette.

★1923★
Look What We've Done to This Land
Blue Sky Productions
PO Box 548
Santa Fe, NM 87501   Ph: (505)988-2995
Description: Questions pertinent issues of energy consumption and strip-mining in the West. Covers the effects of mining operations on Navajo and Hopi Indians. **Release Date:** 1973. **Length:** 22 mins. **Format:** 3/4″ U-matic Cassette, Other than listed.

★1924★
Lost Legacy: A Girl Called Hatter Fox
Video Gems
12228 Venice Blvd., No. 504
Los Angeles, CA 90066
Description: Tradition and technology are at odds in the life of a young Indian girl. Strong cast makes this work. Made for television and better than average. **Length:** 100 **Format:** VHS

★1925★
Loving Rebel
Centre Productions, Inc.
1800 30th St., Ste. 207
Boulder, CO 80301   Ph: (303)444-1166
   Free: 800-824-1166
Description: This documentary profiles Helen Hunt Jackson, one of the nineteenth century's foremost advocates of Native American rights. This video features readings from Jackson's poems, novels, essays and other writings as well as rare photographs and drawings of the writer's world. **Release Date:** 1987. **Length:** 25 mins. **Format:** Beta, VHS, 3/4″ U-matic Cassette.

★1926★
Lucy Covington: Native American Indian
Britannica Films
310 S. Michigan Ave.
Chicago, IL 60604   Ph: (312)347-7958
   Fax: (312)347-7966
Description: Lucy Covington, an active leader and spokesperson for the Colville Indians, retells the history of her people as it has been handed down through oral tradition. **Release Date:** 1979. **Length:** 16 mins. **Format:** Beta, VHS, 3/4″ U-matic Cassette.

★1927★
Man Belongs to the Earth
National AudioVisual Center
National Archives & Records
   Administration
Customer Services Section PZ
8700 Edgeworth Dr.
Capitol Heights, MD 20743-3701   Ph: (301)763-1896
Description: This program features Chief Dan George who offers profound insight into the native American view of nature. **Release Date:** 1974. **Length:** 22 mins. **Format:** Beta, VHS, 3/4″ U-matic Cassette, Other than listed. **Credits:** Narrated by: James Whitmore.

★1928★
Man of Lightning
Native American Public Broadcasting
   Consortium
PO Box 86111
1800 N. 33rd St.
Lincoln, NE 68501   Ph: (402)472-3522
Description: Two Cherokee folktales that delineate the nature of Indian culture before European influence are enacted. **Release Date:** 1982. **Length:** 29 mins. **Format:** VHS, 3/4″ U-matic Cassette, 1″ Broadcast Type ″C″, 2″ Quadraplex Open Reel.

★1929★
Maria! Indian Pottery of San Ildefonso
Arts America, Inc.
12 Havermeyer Pl.
Greenwich, CT 06830   Ph: (203)637-1454
Description: Noted Indian pottery maker Maria Martinez demonstrates traditional Indian ways, beginning with the spreading of sacred corn before the clay is gathered. Clay mixing, pottery construction, hand decorating, and building of the firing mound are also viewed. **Release Date:** 1972. **Length:** 27 mins. **Format:** Beta, VHS, 3/4″ U-matic Cassette, Other than listed.

★1930★
Maria of the Pueblos
Centron Films
108 Wilmot Rd.
Deerfield, IL 60015-9990   Ph: (312)940-1260
   Free: 800-621-2131
Description: This video traces the life of Maria Martinez, the world's most famous and successful Indian potter, while giving an understanding of the culture, philosophy, art, and economic conditions of the Pueblo Indians. **Release Date:** 1971. **Length:** 15 mins. **Format:** Beta, VHS, 3/4″ U-matic Cassette.

★1931★
Meet the Sioux Indian
International Film Bureau, Inc. (IFB)
332 S. Michigan Ave.
Chicago, IL 60604-4382   Ph: (312)427-4545
Description: This video shows how the Sioux Indians adapted to their environment and found food, shelter, and clothing on the Western plains. Worldwide distribution rights. **Release Date:** 1956. **Length:** 11 mins. **Format:** Beta, VHS, 3/4″ U-matic Cassette, Other than listed.

★1932★
Menominee
Native American Public Broadcasting
  Consortium
PO Box 86111
1800 N. 33rd St.
Lincoln, NE 68501   Ph: (402)472-3522

Description: The trials and current plight of the Menominee Indians of northwestern Wisconsin are related in this study. **Release Date:** 1974. **Length:** 59 mins. **Format:** VHS, 3/4" U-matic Cassette, 1" Broadcast Type "C", 2" Quadraplex Open Reel.

★1933★
A Message from Native America
Lionel Television Productions
66 1/2 Windward
Venice, CA 90291

Description: This is a recitation of Hopi and other prophecies which declare that we can have peace and joy if we return to the way of the creator, but if we continue on our present course, disaster will be the inevitable outcome. **Release Date:** 1982. **Length:** 14 mins. **Format:** Beta, VHS, 3/4" U-matic Cassette.

★1934★
The Metis
CRM/McGraw-Hill Films
674 Via de la Valle
PO Box 641
Del Mar, CA 92014

Description: This is the story of the Metis people of North America, who trace their ancestry to both Indian and European roots in the seventeenth century. **Release Date:** 1978. **Length:** 27 mins. **Format:** Beta, VHS, 3/4" U-matic Cassette.

★1935★
Minorities in Agriculture: The Winnebago
Native American Public Broadcasting
  Consortium
PO Box 86111
1800 N. 33rd St.
Lincoln, NE 68501   Ph: (402)472-3522

Description: A retrospective look at the Winnebago Indians of Nebraska, their heritage and modern troubles. **Release Date:** 1984. **Length:** 29 mins. **Format:** VHS, 3/4" U-matic Cassette, 1" Broadcast Type "C", 2" Quadraplex Open Reel.

★1936★
Minority Youth: Adam
Phoenix/BFA Films
468 Park Ave., S.   Ph: (212)684-5910
New York, NY 10016   Free: 800-221-1274

Description: Adam is an American Indian. In the show, he speaks candidly about his cultural heritage and his place in today's society. **Release Date:** 1971. **Length:** 10 mins. **Format:** Beta, VHS, 3/4" U-matic Cassette.

★1937★
Miss Indian America
Native American Public Broadcasting
  Consortium
PO Box 86111
1800 N. 33rd St.
Lincoln, NE 68501   Ph: (402)472-3522

Description: This is a filmed record of the 1973 Miss Indian America pageant held in Sheridan, Wyoming. **Release Date:** 1973. **Length:** 59 mins. **Format:** VHS, 3/4" U-matic Cassette, 1" Broadcast Type "C", 2" Quadraplex Open Reel.

★1938★
Mistress Madeleine
National Film Board of Canada
1251 Avenue of the Americas, 16th Fl.
New York, NY 10020-1173   Ph: (212)586-5131

Description: This drama focuses on a half-Native American woman during the mid-nineteenth century, whose life is nearly ruined by prejudice. **Release Date:** 1987. **Length:** 57 mins. **Format:** Beta, VHS, 3/4" U-matic Cassette.

★1939★
Monument Valley: Navajo Homeland
Finley-Holiday Film Corporation
PO Box 619
Dept. CS
Whittier, CA 90608   Free: 800-345-6707
     Fax: (213)693-4756

Description: Witness the majestic, beautiful lands of Monument Valley and learn the reasons for the Navajo bond with this, their homeland. Rare footage of Navajo customs and spiritual practices make this video a unique reference to the true identity of the Navajo Indian. **Release Date:** 1991. **Length:** 30 mins. **Format:** VHS.

★1940★
Moon Drum
Island Visual Arts
8920 Sunset Blvd., 2nd Fl.   Ph: (213)288-5382
Los Angeles, CA 90069   Fax: (213)276-5476

Description: John Whitney uses computer graphics to present Native American art and music, including the Pueblo, Hopi, Oglala Sioux, Plains, and Pacific Northwest tribes. **Release Date:** 19??. **Length:** 60 mins. **Format:** VHS.

★1941★
More Than Bows and Arrows
Video Tech
19346 3rd Ave. NW
Seattle, WA 98177   Ph: (206)546-5401

Description: A coast-to-coast look at the technology being used by Indians, Eskimos, and Aleuts. **Release Date:** 1978. **Length:** 56 mins. **Format:** Beta, VHS, 3/4" U-matic Cassette, Other than listed.

★1942★
Mother Corn
Native American Public Broadcasting
  Consortium
PO Box 86111
1800 N. 33rd St.
Lincoln, NE 68501   Ph: (402)472-3522

Description: The historical and religious role that corn plays in Hopi and Pueblo life is portrayed. **Release Date:** 1977. **Length:** 29 mins. **Format:** VHS, 3/4" U-matic Cassette, 1" Broadcast Type "C", 2" Quadraplex Open Reel.

★1943★
Mother of Many Children
National Film Board of Canada
1251 Avenue of the Americas, 16th Fl.
New York, NY 10020-1173   Ph: (212)586-5131

Description: A collection and story of womanhood as expressed through the lives of Agatha Marie Goudine, a 108-year-old woman of the Hobbema Indian tribe, and young Elizabeth and Sarah. **Release Date:** 1980. **Length:** 58 mins. **Format:** Beta, VHS, 3/4" U-matic Cassette.

★1944★
Mountain Wolf Woman
Her Own Words Productions
PO Box 5264
Madison, WI 53705   Ph: (608)271-7083

Description: Narrated by her granddaughter, Mountain Wolf Woman's story is presented in her own words. Technically excellent, with some beautiful photographs, this film presents bits and pieces of a fascinating life. **Release Date:** 1990. **Length:** 17 mins. **Format:** VHS.

★1945★
The Movie Reel Indians
Video Tech
19346 3rd Ave. NW
Seattle, WA 98177   Ph: (206)546-5401
Description: Several examples of stereotypical portrayals of American Indians in Hollywood films are shown in this final program from the "Images of Indians" series. **Release Date:** 1982. **Length:** 30 mins. **Format:** Beta, VHS, 3/4″ U-matic Cassette, Other than listed. **Credits:** Narrated by: Will Sampson.

★1946★
The Music of the Devil, the Bear and the Condor
Cinema Guild
1697 Broadway   Ph: (212)246-5522
New York, NY 10019   Fax: (212)246-5525
Description: The sacred and magical ceremonies of the Aymara Indians are the focus of this documentary. **Release Date:** 1989. **Length:** 52 mins. **Format:** Beta, VHS, 3/4″ U-matic Cassette.

★1947★
The Mystery of the Anasazi
Time-Life Video and Television
1450 E. Parham Rd.   Ph: (804)266-6330
Richmond, VA 23280   Free: 800-621-7026
Description: This film documents the attempts of archeologists in the southwestern United States to determine who the Anasazi were and where they came from. **Release Date:** 1976. **Length:** 59 mins. **Format:** Beta, VHS, 3/4″ U-matic Cassette, Other than listed.

★1948★
The Mystery of the Lost Red Paint People: The Discovery of a Prehistoric North American Sea Culture
Bullfrog Films, Inc.   Ph: (215)779-8226
PO Box 149   Free: 800-543-3764
Oley, PA 19547   Fax: (215)370-1978
Description: An expedition revealing archaeological discoveries around the periphery of the North Atlantic. **Release Date:** 1987. **Length:** 57 mins. **Format:** Beta, VHS, 3/4″ U-matic Cassette.

★1949★
Nations Within a Nation
Native American Public Broadcasting
   Consortium
1800 N. 33rd St.
PO Box 86111
Lincoln, NE 68501   Ph: (402)472-3522
Description: Examines the historical, legal, and social issues of sovereignty for tribal governments. **Length:** 59 mins. **Format:** VHS, 1″ Broadcast Type ″C″, 3/4″ U-matic Cassette.

★1950★
Native America Speaks
Lionel Television Productions
66 1/2 Windward
Venice, CA 90291
Description: Peace pipe symbolism, the religious ceremony of the sweat lodge, and the spiritual significance of group dancing are featured in segments taken from the 1979 World Symposium on Humanity, illustrating Native American culture. **Release Date:** 1980. **Length:** 25 mins. **Format:** Beta, VHS, 3/4″ U-matic Cassette.

★1951★
Native American Art—Lost and Found
American Federation of Arts
41 E. 65th St.   Ph: (212)988-7700
New York, NY 10021   Fax: (212)861-2487
Description: Fourteen American Indian artists, working in various mediums including wood carving and pottery, display their work and talk about the personal and historical meanings of such handicrafts. **Release Date:** 1986. **Length:** 22 mins. **Format:** Beta, VHS, 3/4″ U-matic Cassette.

★1952★
Native American Catholics: People of the Spirit
Franciscan Communications
1229 S. Santee St.   Ph: (213)746-2916
Los Angeles, CA 90015   Free: 800-421-8510
Description: A look at the ways that converted Indians show their faith in God. **Release Date:** 1987. **Length:** 28 mins. **Format:** Beta, VHS, 3/4″ U-matic Cassette.

★1953★
Native American Cultures in the U.S.A.: Part One
RMI Media Productions, Inc.   Ph: (913)768-1696
1365 N. Winchester   Free: 800-745-5480
Olathe, KS 66061   Fax: (913)768-0184
Description: Discusses Native American characteristics throughout history, such as rights, stereotypes, treaty disputes and land allotments. **Length:** 60 **Format:** VHS

★1954★
Native American Cultures in the U.S.A.: Part Two
RMI Media Productions, Inc.   Ph: (913)768-1696
1365 N. Winchester   Free: 800-745-5480
Olathe, KS 66061   Fax: (913)768-0184
Description: Presents a case study of the controversy regarding displaying remains of ancient Native Americans. **Length:** 60 **Format:** VHS

★1955★
Native American Images
Native American Public Broadcasting
   Consortium
PO Box 86111
1800 N. 33rd St.
Lincoln, NE 68501   Ph: (402)472-3522
Description: This is a profile of three Austin-based Native American artists: Paladine H. Roye, Donald Vann, and Steve Forbes. **Release Date:** 1984. **Length:** 29 mins. **Format:** VHS, 3/4″ U-matic Cassette, 1″ Broadcast Type ″C″, 2″ Quadraplex Open Reel.

★1956★
Native American Indian Artist Series
Arts America, Inc.
12 Havermeyer Pl.
Greenwich, CT 06830   Ph: (203)637-1454
Description: A series on Native American Artists and their art including jewelry, prints, paintings and pottery. **Release Date:** 1990. **Length:** 29 mins. **Format:** VHS.

★1957★
Native American Prophecy and Ceremony
Wishing Well Distributing   Ph: (414)864-2395
PO Box 2   Free: 800-888-9355
Wilmot, WI 53192   Fax: (414)862-2398
Description: A look at the customs of the peace pipe, ritual dancing, and the sweat lodge, combined with Native American warnings concerning the future. **Release Date:** 1990. **Length:** 25 mins. **Format:** VHS.

★1958★
Native American Series
Journal Films, Inc.   Ph: (708)328-6700
930 Pitner Ave.   Free: 800-323-5448
Evanston, IL 60202   Fax: (708)328-6706
Description: This program series is based on geological, archeological, and historical evidence and will help young people understand the origin, diversity, and life-style of the American Indian. Programs are available individually. **Release Date:** 1976. **Length:** 18 mins. **Format:** Beta, VHS, 3/4″ U-matic Cassette.

★1959★
Native American Series, Vol. 1: Nations of the Northeast
Wishing Well Distributing   Ph: (414)889-8501
PO Box 1008   Free: 800-888-9355
Silver Lake, WI 53170   Fax: (414)889-8591
Description: Descendants of the Native American nations of the Northeast come together to recount the history of their people, including segments on: the Iroquois Confederacy, the communal lifestyle and the invasion of European Christians. **Length:** 52 **Format:** VHS

★1960★
Native American Series, Vol. 2: Tribal People of the Northwest
Wishing Well Distributing   Ph: (414)889-8501
PO Box 1008   Free: 800-888-9355
Silver Lake, WI 53170   Fax: (414)889-8591
Description: Five Native American tribespeople offer insights into the origin of their people and culture, including segments on: ancient lore, the evolution of a varied culture and the devastating effect of the Gold Rush by American settlers. **Length:** 48 **Format:** VHS

★1961★
Native American Series, Vol. 3: The Tribes of the Southeast
Wishing Well Distributing   Ph: (414)889-8501
PO Box 1008   Free: 800-888-9355
Silver Lake, WI 53170   Fax: (414)889-8591
Description: Native Americans from the tribes of the Southeast tell the story of their people, including segments on stick ball, the Spanish invasion, slavery, Jacksonian democracy and the Trail of Tears. **Length:** 48 **Format:** VHS

★1962★
Native American Series, Vol. 4: The Natives of the Southwest
Wishing Well Distributing   Ph: (414)889-8501
PO Box 1008   Free: 800-888-9355
Silver Lake, WI 53170   Fax: (414)889-8591
Description: Five tribespeople relate the history of the Native American people of the Southwest, with segments on the invasion of Coronado's conquistadors, the stuggle to exist in the desert, Manifest Destiny and the resistance of Geronimo and Cochise. **Length:** 48 **Format:** VHS

★1963★
Native American Series, Vol. 5: The People of the Great Plains (Part One)
Wishing Well Distributing   Ph: (414)889-8501
PO Box 1008   Free: 800-888-9355
Silver Lake, WI 53170   Fax: (414)889-8591
Description: Native Americans of the Great Plains tell the stories of their people before the coming of the horse or the white man, including segments on the sacredness of the buffalo, harmony between man and Earth and ancient stories of their "Dog Days." **Length:** 48 **Format:** VHS

★1964★
Native American Series, Vol. 6: The People of the Great Plains (Part Two)
Wishing Well Distributing   Ph: (414)889-8501
PO Box 1008   Free: 800-888-9355
Silver Lake, WI 53170   Fax: (414)889-8591
Description: Native Americans of the Great Plains tell the story of the events that led to their downfall, including segments on the impact of the horse and rifle, the devastating effect of alcohol and the breaking of the Oregon Trail peace agreement. **Length:** 48 **Format:** VHS

★1965★
Native American Sweat Lodge Ceremony
Wishing Well Distributing   Ph: (414)864-2395
PO Box 2   Free: 800-888-9355
Wilmot, WI 53192   Fax: (414)862-2398
Description: An introduction to the physical and spiritual benefits of this centuries-old Native American custom. **Release Date:** 1990. **Length:** 90 mins. **Format:** VHS.

★1966★
The Native Americans
Cinema Guild
1697 Broadway   Ph: (212)246-5522
New York, NY 10019   Fax: (212)246-5525
Description: This series explores the reasons behind the white man's seizure of Indian land from colonial times to the present, shows why the Indian is our country's most underprivileged ethnic group, and highlights the Indians' current attempts to take their rightful place in our democracy. Programs are available individually. **Release Date:** 1981. **Length:** 26 mins. **Format:** 3/4" U-matic Cassette, Other than listed.

★1967★
Native Healer: Initiation into an Ancient Art
Wishing Well Distributing   Ph: (414)889-8501
PO Box 1008   Free: 800-888-9355
Silver Lake, WI 53170   Fax: (414)889-8591
Description: Seneca-Cherokee shaman Medicine Grizzlybear Lake speaks openly about being a medicine man. He explains how a person is called to be a healer, the trials and tests of a candidate, the use of natural tools in healing and sacred places in the earth where healing occurs. **Length:** 28 **Format:** VHS

★1968★
Native Land
Cinema Guild
1697 Broadway   Ph: (212)246-5522
New York, NY 10019   Fax: (212)246-5525
Description: The history of the native North and South Americans is traced with emphasis on the role mythology has played within their cultures. **Release Date:** 1986. **Length:** 58 mins. **Format:** Beta, VHS, 3/4" U-matic Cassette. **Credits:** Hosted by: Jamake Highwater.

★1969★
The Native Land
Atlantis Productions
1252 La Granada Dr.
Thousand Oaks, CA 91360   Ph: (805)495-2790
Description: This is an insight into Indian life and thoughts about land and heritage, told from the Indian's point of view. **Release Date:** 1976. **Length:** 17 mins. **Format:** Beta, VHS, 3/4" U-matic Cassette.

★1970★
Native Self Reliance
Bullfrog Films, Inc.   Ph: (215)779-8226
PO Box 149   Free: 800-543-3764
Oley, PA 19547   Fax: (215)370-1978
Description: A study of solar technology projects developed by six American Indians. **Release Date:** 1980. **Length:** 20 mins. **Format:** Beta, VHS, 3/4" U-matic Cassette.

★1971★
Natives of the Narrowland
Documentary Educational Resources Ph: (617)926-0491
101 Morse St.   Free: 800-569-6621
Watertown, MA 02172   Fax: (617)926-9519
Description: Explores the history of the Wampanoag tribe on New England, one of the first tribes to come into contact with Europeans, and consequently, one of the first to nearly disappear. Includes interviews with the few living members of the tribe. **Length:** 35 **Format:** VHS

★1972★
Natwaniwa: A Hopi Philosophical Statement
Norman Ross Publishing Inc.   Ph: (212)765-8200
330 W. 58th St.   Free: 800-648-8850
New York, NY 10019   Fax: (212)765-2393
Description: What the Hopi does in his field is a rehearsal for his future life, as shown in this program (Hopi with English subtitles). **Release Date:** 1981. **Length:** 27 mins. **Format:** Beta, VHS, 3/4″ U-matic Cassette.

★1973★
The Navajo
Victorian Video Productions
PO Box 1540   Ph: (916)346-6184
Colfax, CA 95713-1540   Free: 800-848-0284
Description: Spokesmen for the largest and one of the wealthiest tribes in the United States discuss the problems of preserving their culture in the advancing modern world. Part of the "Silent Heritage" series. **Release Date:** 1966. **Length:** 29 mins. **Format:** VHS, 3/4″ U-matic Cassette, Other than listed.

★1974★
The Navajo
Centre Productions, Inc.
1800 30th St., Ste. 207   Ph: (303)444-1166
Boulder, CO 80301   Free: 800-824-1166
Description: This program brings to light the fascinating blend of ancient Navajo culture with modern ideas about education and medicine that exists today within the tribe. **Release Date:** 1983. **Length:** 11 mins. **Format:** Beta, VHS, 3/4″ U-matic Cassette.

★1975★
Navajo
Native American Public Broadcasting
  Consortium
1800 N. 33rd St.
PO Box 86111
Lincoln, NE 68501   Ph: (402)472-3522
Description: Two children leave their modern lifestyle to spend time with their grandparents on a Navajo Reservation. There they learn about Navajo traditions, including the matriarchal society and the desire to live in peace with the earth. **Release Date:** 1979. **Length:** 29 mins. **Format:** VHS, 1″ Broadcast Type "C", 3/4″ U-amtic Cassette.

★1976★
Navajo: A Study in Cultural Contrast
Journal Films, Inc.   Ph: (708)328-6700
930 Pitner Ave.   Free: 800-323-5448
Evanston, IL 60202   Fax: (708)328-6706
Description: This program journeys to the southwestern desert region, the home of the Navajo. It views the environment, family structure, traditions, ceremonies, and art forms of people untouched by modern civilization. **Release Date:** 1968. **Length:** 15 mins. **Format:** Beta, VHS, 3/4″ U-matic Cassette.

★1977★
Navajo Code Talkers
One West Media
PO Box 5766
559 Onate Pl.
Santa Fe, NM 87501   Ph: (505)983-8685
Description: This video examines the contributions of Navajo cryptographers in World War II. **Release Date:** 1986. **Length:** 27 mins. **Format:** VHS, 3/4″ U-matic Cassette.

★1978★
Navajo Country
International Film Bureau, Inc. (IFB)
332 S. Michigan Ave.
Chicago, IL 60604-4382   Ph: (312)427-4545
Description: The creativity of the nomadic Navajos is presented. **Release Date:** 1983. **Length:** 10 mins. **Format:** Beta, VHS, 3/4″ U-matic Cassette, Other than listed.

★1979★
The Navajo Film Themselves
Museum of Modern Art, Circulating Film
  Library
11 W. 53rd St.
New York, NY 10019   Ph: (212)708-9530
Description: Navajo weaving and silversmithing are featured in this silent film. **Release Date:** 1966. **Length:** 18 mins. **Format:** VHS, Other than listed.

★1980★
Navajo Girl
Center for Humanities, Inc.
Communications Park
Box 1000   Ph: (914)666-4100
Mount Kisco, NY 10549   Free: 800-431-1242
Description: Daily life on an Indian reservation is depicted in this story about 10-year-old Kathy Begay and her Navajo family. **Release Date:** 1973. **Length:** 21 mins. **Format:** Beta, VHS, 3/4″ U-matic Cassette.

★1981★
Navajo Health Care Practices
University of Arizona
Biomedical Communications
Tucson, AZ 85724   Ph: (602)626-7343
Description: This program explores the traditions and healing practices of a Navajo family. **Release Date:** 1977. **Length:** 40 mins. **Format:** 3/4″ U-matic Cassette, Other than listed.

★1982★
The Navajo Indian
Coronet/MTI Film & Video   Ph: (708)940-1260
108 Wilmot Rd.   Free: 800-621-2131
Deerfield, IL 60015   Fax: (708)940-3640
Description: This is an examination of modern Navajo life, and how they adjust to contemporary changes while they continue their life as herdsman, weavers, and silversmiths. **Release Date:** 1975. **Length:** 10 mins. **Format:** Beta, VHS, 3/4″ U-matic Cassette, Other than listed.

★1983★
Navajo Land Issue
Journal Films, Inc.   Ph: (708)328-6700
930 Pitner Ave.   Free: 800-323-5448
Evanston, IL 60202   Fax: (708)328-6706
Description: This program examines a unique land issue that exists between two separate Indian tribes, the Navajo and the Hopi. **Release Date:** 197?. **Length:** 12 mins. **Format:** Beta, VHS, 3/4″ U-matic Cassette.

★1984★
Navajo: Legend of the Glittering World
Finley-Holiday Film Corporation
PO Box 619
Dept. CS
Whittier, CA 90608   Free: 800-345-6707
                                     Fax: (213)693-4756
Description: This is a look at what's left of the Navajo legacy in the Southwestern desert. **Release Date:** 1986. **Length:** 25 mins. **Format:** Beta, VHS.

★1985★
Navajo, Race for Prosperity
Cinema Guild
1697 Broadway   Ph: (212)246-5522
New York, NY 10019   Fax: (212)246-5525
Description: This program offers a contemporary view of life on the Navajo reservation and focuses upon the development of industries on the reservation. An arts and crafts cooperative provides a source of income and at the same time keeps alive the beautiful art of the Navajo. **Release Date:** 1976. **Length:** 26 mins. **Format:** 3/4″ U-matic Cassette, Other than listed.

★1986★
Navajos: The Last Red Indians
Time-Life Video and Television
1450 E. Parham Rd.   Ph: (804)266-6330
Richmond, VA 23280   Free: 800-621-7026

Description: This video documents the Navajo's fight to preserve their way of life against the inroads of the white man's culture. It contains uncensored scenes of tribal rituals and ceremonies. **Release Date:** 1972. **Length:** 35 mins. **Format:** Beta, VHS, 3/4″ U-matic Cassette, Other than listed.

★1987★
Neshnabek: The People
University of California at Berkeley
  Extension Media Center
2176 Shattuck Ave.
Berkeley, CA 94704   Ph: (510)642-0460

Description: A look at the Potowatomi Indians of Kansas is provided. **Release Date:** 1979. **Length:** 45 mins. **Format:** VHS, 3/4″ U-matic Cassette.

★1988★
The New Indians
National Geographic Society
PO Box 2118   Ph: (202)857-7378
Washington, DC 20013-2118   Free: 800-447-0647

Description: This video offers a look at contemporary tribes and the problems they face. **Release Date:** 1977. **Length:** 59 mins. **Format:** 3/4″ U-matic Cassette, Other than listed.

★1989★
The New Pequot: A Tribal Portrait
Native American Public Broadcasting
  Consortium
1800 N. 33rd St.
PO Box 86111
Lincoln, NE 68501   Ph: (402)472-3522

Description: Focuses on Connecticut's Mashantucket Pequot Indians, a tribe which was close to extinction in the 1970s, and the roadblocks they overcame to survive. **Length:** 60 mins. **Format:** VHS, 1″ Broadcast Type ″C″, 3/4″ U-matic Cassette.

★1990★
Nez Perce: Portrait of a People
Native American Public Broadcasting
  Consortium
1800 N. 33rd St.
PO Box 86111
Lincoln, NE 68501   Ph: (402)472-3522

Description: Historic photos, stories, and scenery combine to give a history of the Nez Perce tribe. **Length:** 23 mins. **Format:** VHS, 1″ Broadcast Type ″C″, 3/4″ U-matic Cassette.

★1991★
Ni'bthaska of the Umunhon
Native American Public Broadcasting
  Consortium
1800 N. 33rd St.
PO Box 86111
Lincoln, NE 68501   Ph: (402)472-3522

Description: Follows the life of a 13-year old boy from the Omaha tribe during his first summer of manhood. Condensed from the "We Are One" series. Individual program titles: Turning of the Child; Becoming a Warrior; The Buffalo Hunt. Tapes are available individually or as a series. **Release Date:** 1987. **Length:** 30 mins. **Format:** VHS, 1″ Broadcast Type ″C″, 3/4″ U-matic Cassette.

★1992★
No Address
National Film Board of Canada
1251 Avenue of the Americas, 16th Fl.
New York, NY 10020-1173   Ph: (212)586-5131

Description: This is an examination of the plight of Native Americans, lured off their reservations by the promise of jobs and a better life, only to end up homeless in large cities. **Release Date:** 1988. **Length:** 56 mins. **Format:** Beta, VHS, 3/4″ U-matic Cassette.

★1993★
No Turning Back
One West Media
PO Box 5766
559 Onate Pl.
Santa Fe, NM 87501   Ph: (505)983-8685

Description: A lengthy portrait of Boots Wagner, a Navajo Indian turned preacher, whose mission is to save the souls of the "pagan" American Indian race. **Release Date:** 1987. **Length:** 58 mins. **Format:** VHS, 3/4″ U-matic Cassette.

★1994★
North American Indian Legends
Phoenix/BFA Films
468 Park Ave., S.   Ph: (212)684-5910
New York, NY 10016   Free: 800-221-1274

Description: Legends of American Indians describe tribal traditions, explain natural events, and express values of the people. The legends in this film represent the original stories of three tribes. **Release Date:** 1973. **Length:** 21 mins. **Format:** Beta, VHS, 3/4″ U-matic Cassette.

★1995★
The North American Indian Series
CRM/McGraw-Hill Films
674 Via de la Valle
PO Box 641
Del Mar, CA 92014

Description: These three programs offer a vital new perspective on the plight of one of our most misunderstood minority groups–the American Indian. **Release Date:** 1971. **Length:** 20 mins. **Format:** Beta, VHS, 3/4″ U-matic Cassette.

★1996★
North American Indians and Edward S. Curtis
Phoenix/BFA Films
468 Park Ave., S.   Ph: (212)684-5910
New York, NY 10016   Free: 800-221-1274

Description: Vintage footage taken by Edward Curtis around the turn of the century helps viewers understand about different Indian tribes. **Release Date:** 1985. **Length:** 30 mins. **Format:** Beta, VHS, 3/4″ U-matic Cassette.

★1997★
North American Indians Today
National Geographic Society
PO Box 2118   Ph: (202)857-7378
Washington, DC 20013-2118   Free: 800-447-0647

Description: A look at Indian life today, and the problems they face. **Release Date:** 1977. **Length:** 25 mins. **Format:** 3/4″ U-matic Cassette, Other than listed.

★1998★
The Northern Plains
Michigan Media
University of Michigan
400 4th St.
Ann Arbor, MI 48109   Ph: (313)764-8228

Description: An examination of the history of the legendary Plains warriors–the Sioux and Crow tribes–who fought tenaciously against the United States for their land and means of survival. **Release Date:** 1966. **Length:** 29 mins. **Format:** 3/4″ U-matic Cassette, Other than listed.

★1999★
Now That the Buffalo's Gone
The Media Guild
11722 Sorrento Valley Rd., Ste. E   Ph: (619)755-9191
San Diego, CA 92121   Fax: (619)755-4931

Description: This program reviews the history and present-day situation of the American Indians. **Release Date:** 1969. **Length:** 75 mins. **Format:** Beta, VHS, 3/4″ U-matic Cassette.

★2000★
Obsidian Point-Making
University of California at Berkeley
  Extension Media Center
2176 Shattuck Ave.
Berkeley, CA 94704   Ph: (510)642-0460
Description: A Tolowa Indian demonstrates an ancient method of fashioning an arrow point from obsidian, using direct percussion and pressure-flaking techniques. **Release Date:** 1964. **Length:** 13 mins. **Format:** 3/4″ U-matic Cassette, Other than listed.

★2001★
Omaha Tribe: The Land, The People, The Family
NETCHE (Nebraska ETV Council for
  Higher Education)
Box 83111
Lincoln, NE 68501   Ph: (402)472-3611
Description: This series on the Omaha Tribe provides historical perspective, a view of the present population, and a close look at the life-style of a three-generation Omaha family. **Release Date:** 1979. **Length:** 30 mins. **Format:** 1/2″ Reel-EIAJ, 3/4″ U-matic Cassette.

★2002★
On the Path to Self-Reliance
Native American Public Broadcasting
  Consortium
PO Box 86111
1800 N. 33rd St.
Lincoln, NE 68501   Ph: (402)472-3522
Description: The Seminole tribe of Florida is examined amidst its current success and financial self-sufficiency. Narrated by Chairman James Billie. **Release Date:** 1982. **Length:** 45 mins. **Format:** VHS, 3/4″ U-matic Cassette, 1″ Broadcast Type ″C″, 2″ Quadraplex Open Reel.

★2003★
On the Totem Trail
Journal Films, Inc.   Ph: (708)328-6700
930 Pitner Ave.   Free: 800-323-5448
Evanston, IL 60202   Fax: (708)328-6706
Description: A school assignment about Indians helps two students discover the rich heritage of the Pacific Northwest Tribes. **Release Date:** 197?. **Length:** 30 mins. **Format:** Beta, VHS, 3/4″ U-matic Cassette.

★2004★
1,000 Years of Muscogee (Creek) Art
Native American Public Broadcasting
  Consortium
PO Box 86111
1800 N. 33rd St.
Lincoln, NE 68501   Ph: (402)472-3522
Description: Experts and anthropologists survey the history of Creek art. **Release Date:** 1982. **Length:** 28 mins. **Format:** VHS, 3/4″ U-matic Cassette, 1″ Broadcast Type ″C″, 2″ Quadraplex Open Reel.

★2005★
The Origin of the Crown Dance and Ba'ts'oosee
Norman Ross Publishing Inc.   Ph: (212)765-8200
330 W. 58th St.   Free: 800-648-8850
New York, NY 10019   Fax: (212)765-2393
Description: An Apache elder tells the story of a boy who became a gaan, a supernatural being with curative powers (Apache with English subtitles). **Release Date:** 1981. **Length:** 40 mins. **Format:** Beta, VHS, 3/4″ U-matic Cassette.

★2006★
Oscar Howe: The Sioux Painter
Centron Films
108 Wilmot Rd.   Ph: (312)940-1260
Deerfield, IL 60015-9990   Free: 800-621-2131
Description: Oscar Howe, a native Sioux Indian, has won fifteen grand or first awards in national art competitions through his

paintings. **Release Date:** 1973. **Length:** 27 mins. **Format:** Beta, VHS, 3/4″ U-matic Cassette. **Credits:** Narrated by: Vincent Price.

★2007★
Our Native American Friends
Britannica Films
310 S. Michigan Ave.   Ph: (312)347-7958
Chicago, IL 60604   Fax: (312)347-7966
Description: From the "Friends" units these three programs: Apache Indian Friends, Miccosukee Indian Friends, and Eskimo Friends, are combined to tell of different ethnic groups in the United States. **Release Date:** 1979. **Length:** 10 mins. **Format:** Beta, VHS, 3/4″ U-matic Cassette.

★2008★
Our Sacred Land
Intermedia Arts of Minnesota, Inc.
425 Ontario St. SE
Minneapolis, MN 55414   Ph: (612)627-4444
Description: A look at the tumultuous history of the restriction of Sioux's rights to visit and worship on their sacred, unreserved land. **Release Date:** 1984. **Length:** 28 mins. **Format:** Beta, VHS, 3/4″ U-matic Cassette.

★2009★
Our Totem is the Raven
Phoenix/BFA Films
468 Park Ave., S.   Ph: (212)684-5910
New York, NY 10016   Free: 800-221-1274
Description: Fifteen-year-old David, an urban Indian boy, has little interest in his cultural heritage. His grandfather takes him into the forest to give him an understanding of his forefathers. **Release Date:** 1972. **Length:** 21 mins. **Format:** Beta, VHS, 3/4″ U-matic Cassette.

★2010★
Paha Sapa
Wishing Well Distributing   Ph: (414)889-8501
PO Box 1008   Free: 800-888-9355
Silver Lake, WI 53170   Fax: (414)889-8591
Description: Chronicles the century-long struggle of the Cheyenne and Lakota peop le to regain their sacred homeland, the Black Hills of South Dakota. Told entirely by members of the Lakota and Cheyenne tribes, including descendants of legendary chiefs Red Cloud, Sitting Bull, Two Bear, Highwolf and Black Elk. **Length:** 60 **Format:** VHS

★2011★
The People Are Dancing Again
Media Project, Inc.
PO Box 4093
Portland, OR 97208   Ph: (503)223-5335
Description: This program documents the plight of Oregon's Siletz tribe and their struggle to regain federal recognition of their tribe. **Release Date:** 1976. **Length:** 28 mins. **Format:** Beta, VHS, 1/2″ Reel-EIAJ, 3/4″ U-matic Cassette.

★2012★
People of the Buffalo
Britannica Films
310 S. Michigan Ave.   Ph: (312)347-7958
Chicago, IL 60604   Fax: (312)347-7966
Description: This program demonstrates the relationship between the buffalo and the Plains Indians, showing the Indians' dependence on the creature, and explaining how the westward advance of settlers disrupted this natural relationship. **Release Date:** 1980. **Length:** 15 mins. **Format:** Beta, VHS, 3/4″ U-matic Cassette.

★2013★
People of the Dawn
CC Films
National Council of Churches
475 Riverside Dr.
Rm. 860
New York, NY 10115-0050   Ph: (212)870-2575
Description: A look at Indian tribes native to Maine, their history of broken treaties with the U.S., and their current grants of land and funds. **Release Date:** 1984. **Length:** 30 mins. **Format:** 3/4″ U-matic Cassette.

★2014★
People of the First Light
Great Plains National (GPN)
PO Box 80669   Ph: (402)472-2007
Lincoln, NE 68501-0669   Free: 800-228-4630
Description: This series tells the story of descendant tribes of the Eastern Woodland Algonquin Indians and shows how these tribes have maintained their cultural identity. Programs are available individually. **Release Date:** 1979. **Length:** 30 mins. **Format:** Beta, VHS, 3/4″ U-matic Cassette.

★2015★
People of the Macon Plateau
Native American Public Broadcasting
   Consortium
1800 N. 33rd St.
PO Box 86111
Lincoln, NE 68501   Ph: (402)472-3522
Description: Provides a picture of the tribes from the Eastern United States. **Length:** 10 mins. **Format:** VHS, 1″ Broadcast Type ″C″, 3/4″ U-matic Cassette.

★2016★
Picking Tribes
Women Make Movies
225 Lafayette St., Ste. 206   Ph: (212)925-0606
New York, NY 10012   Fax: (212)925-2052
Description: A young woman's struggle to find an identity between her Black American and Native American heritages is examined through vintage photographs and watercolor animation. **Release Date:** 1988. **Length:** 7 mins. **Format:** Beta, VHS, 3/4″ U-matic Cassette.

★2017★
Picuris Indians
Arts America, Inc.
12 Havermeyer Pl.
Greenwich, CT 06830   Ph: (203)637-1454
Description: A documentary of the lifestyle of the Picuris Indians at their ancient pueblo in the mountains of north central New Mexico. Includes ancient sacred dances performed on film for the first time. **Release Date:** 1988. **Length:** 60 mins. **Format:** VHS.

★2018★
Pine Nuts
University of California at Berkeley
   Extension Media Center
2176 Shattuck Ave.
Berkeley, CA 94704   Ph: (510)642-0460
Description: Members of the Paviotso and Paiute tribes demonstrate how the pine nuts were harvested and prepared as food, since the Indians long ago came to depend upon the pinon tree as a source of food. **Release Date:** 1961. **Length:** 13 mins. **Format:** 3/4″ U-matic Cassette, Other than listed.

★2019★
Places Not Our Own
National Film Board of Canada
1251 Avenue of the Americas, 16th Fl.
New York, NY 10020-1173   Ph: (212)586-5131
Description: A native American family is forced to live as squatters on the outskirts of town, during a drought in 1929. **Release Date:** 1987. **Length:** 56 mins. **Format:** Beta, VHS, 3/4″ U-matic Cassette.

★2020★
Politics, Peyote, and Passamaquoddy
Michigan Media
University of Michigan
400 4th St.
Ann Arbor, MI 48109   Ph: (313)764-8228
Description: A look at the Indian role in politics, their religious customs, and their languages, all of which have served to perpetuate the American Indian's independence. Part of the "Silent Heritage" series. **Release Date:** 1966. **Length:** 29 mins. **Format:** 3/4″ U-matic Cassette, Other than listed.

★2021★
Pomo Shaman
University of California at Berkeley
   Extension Media Center
2176 Shattuck Ave.
Berkeley, CA 94704   Ph: (510)642-0460
Description: The final night of an Indian healing ceremony is shown in this shortened version of "Sucking Doctor." **Release Date:** 1964. **Length:** 20 mins. **Format:** VHS, 3/4″ U-matic Cassette.

★2022★
Positively Native
Beacon Films   Ph: (708)328-6700
1560 Sherman Ave., Ste. 100   Free: 800-323-9084
Evanston, IL 60201   Fax: (708)328-6706
Description: A Boy makes a documentary illustrating native culture and receives positive feedback. **Length:** 15 **Format:** VHS

★2023★
Pow-Wow!
Centron Films
108 Wilmot Rd.   Ph: (312)940-1260
Deerfield, IL 60015-9990   Free: 800-621-2131
Description: A display of North American Indian dances at a gathering of more than twenty tribes. **Release Date:** 1980. **Length:** 16 mins. **Format:** Beta, VHS, 3/4″ U-matic Cassette.

★2024★
Powerless Politics
Anti-Defamation League of B'nai B'rith
Audio-Visual Department
823 United Nations Plaza
New York, NY 10017   Ph: (212)490-2525
Description: The impact of the Bureau of Indian Affairs on the simplest details of life on the reservation today is examined. **Release Date:** 1986. **Length:** 30 mins. **Format:** Beta, VHS, 3/4″ U-matic Cassette.

★2025★
Prehistoric Man
Center for Humanities, Inc.
Communications Park
Box 1000   Ph: (914)666-4100
Mount Kisco, NY 10549   Free: 800-431-1242
Description: A look at the developement of the Indians of the American West, from prehistoric times until the Spanish explorers. **Release Date:** 1970. **Length:** 17 mins. **Format:** Beta, VHS, 3/4″ U-matic Cassette.

★2026★
Pride, Purpose and Promise: Paiutes of the Southwest
Native American Public Broadcasting
   Consortium
PO Box 86111
1800 N. 33rd St.
Lincoln, NE 68501   Ph: (402)472-3522
Description: A profile of the Arizona and Nevada-based Paiute tribe–past, present and future. **Release Date:** 1982. **Length:** 28 mins. **Format:** VHS, 3/4″ U-matic Cassette, 1″ Broadcast Type ″C″, 2″ Quadraplex Open Reel.

★2027★
The Pride of Spirit Bay
Beacon Films   Ph: (708)328-6700
1560 Sherman Ave., Ste. 100   Free: 800-323-9084
Evanston, IL 60201   Fax: (708)328-6706
Description: Children learn that inspiration can be found in nature.
Length: 28 **Format:** VHS

★2028★
The Primal Land
Cinema Guild   Ph: (212)246-5522
1697 Broadway   Fax: (212)246-5525
New York, NY 10019
Description: A documentary contrasting Native American and Western culture. Emphasis is placed on the different perceptions of the natural environment, science, the arts, and language. **Release Date:** 1984. **Length:** 58 mins. **Format:** Beta, VHS, 3/4″ U-matic Cassette. **Credits:** Hosted by: Jamake Highwater.

★2029★
The Primal Mind
Cinema Guild   Ph: (212)246-5522
1697 Broadway   Fax: (212)246-5525
New York, NY 10019
Description: The differences between Native American and Western cultures are explored in this documentary, written and hosted by renowned author Jamake Highwater. **Release Date:** 1984. **Length:** 58 mins. **Format:** Beta, VHS, 3/4″ U-matic Cassette.

★2030★
The Probable Passing of Elk Creek
Cinema Guild   Ph: (212)246-5522
1697 Broadway   Fax: (212)246-5525
New York, NY 10019
Description: This video explores the conflict between a proposed dam, the white community it may flood, and the Indian tribal homeland it will destroy. **Release Date:** 1983. **Length:** 60 mins. **Format:** Beta, VHS, 3/4″ U-matic Cassette. **Credits:** Directed by: Robert Wilson.

★2031★
Proud Moments
Treehaus Communications
Box 249
Loveland, OH 45140   Free: 800-638-4287
Description: A look at the efforts of a nurse from Boston who works among the Navajos. **Release Date:** 1989. **Length:** 57 mins. **Format:** Beta, VHS, 3/4″ U-matic Cassette.

★2032★
Pueblo Arts
International Film Bureau, Inc. (IFB)
332 S. Michigan Ave.
Chicago, IL 60604-4382   Ph: (312)427-4545
Description: A pot is built using the coil technique of the Pueblos. **Release Date:** 198?. **Length:** 11 mins. **Format:** Beta, VHS, 3/4″ U-matic Cassette, Other than listed.

★2033★
Pueblo Peoples: First Encounters
Native American Public Broadcasting
   Consortium
1800 N. 33rd St.
PO Box 86111
Lincoln, NE 68501   Ph: (402)472-3522
Description: Using historic accounts and contemporary interpretations of events, this program discusses the Pueblos reaction to the Spanish invaders in 1539 and 1540. **Release Date:** 1991. **Length:** 30 mins. **Format:** VHS, 1″ Broadcast Type ″C″, 3/4″ U-matic Cassette.

★2034★
Pueblo Renaissance
Cinema Guild   Ph: (212)246-5522
1697 Broadway   Fax: (212)246-5525
New York, NY 10019
Description: This program provides an authentic view of the sacred traditions and the ancient religious and agricultural ceremonies of the Pueblo people. **Release Date:** 1976. **Length:** 26 mins. **Format:** 3/4″ U-matic Cassette, Other than listed.

★2035★
The Real People
Great Plains National (GPN)
PO Box 80669   Ph: (402)472-2007
Lincoln, NE 68501-0669   Free: 800-228-4630
Description: The thoughts and values of the American Indian life are examined in this series about seven tribes of the Northwest Plateau: the Spokane, Colville, Kalispel, Kooteni, Nez Perce, Coeur d'Alene and Flathead. Programs available individually. **Release Date:** 1976. **Length:** 28 mins. **Format:** Beta, VHS, 3/4″ U-matic Cassette, Other than listed.

★2036★
Red Road: Towards the Techno-Tribal
Native American Public Broadcasting
   Consortium
PO Box 86111
1800 N. 33rd St.
Lincoln, NE 68501   Ph: (402)472-3522
Description: This program views the contemporary philosophy of Native Americans in relation to the technological influences on tribal life. **Release Date:** 1984. **Length:** 27 mins. **Format:** VHS, 3/4″ U-matic Cassette, 1″ Broadcast Type ″C″, 2″ Quadraplex Open Reel.

★2037★
Red Sunday
Pyramid Film & Video
Box 1048   Ph: (310)828-7577
2801 Colorado Ave.   Free: 800-421-2304
Santa Monica, CA 90406   Fax: (310)453-9083
Description: This program examines the Battle of Little Big Horn, using a wealth of original drawings, photographs and paintings. **Release Date:** 1975. **Length:** 28 mins. **Format:** Beta, VHS, 3/4″ U-matic Cassette.

★2038★
Return of the Raven—The Edison Chiloquin Story
Televideos   Ph: 800-284-3367
PO Box 22   Free: 800-2VI-
Lorane, OR 97451   DEOS
Description: This film documents the life of Chiloquin, a Native American who struggled with the U.S. Congress in an effort to preserve traditional values, and won. **Release Date:** 1985. **Length:** 47 mins. **Format:** Beta, VHS, 3/4″ U-matic Cassette.

★2039★
Return of the Sacred Pole
Native American Public Broadcasting
   Consortium
1800 N. 33rd St.
PO Box 86000
Lincoln, NE 68501   Ph: (402)472-3522
Description: Recounts the events of returning a sacred pole, a spirit endowed artifact, to the Omaha tribe after a 100-year stay at the Peabody Museum at Harvard University. **Release Date:** 1989. **Length:** 30 mins. **Format:** VHS, 1″ Broadcast Type ″C″, 3/4″ U-matic Cassette.

★2040★
Return to Sovereignty
University of California at Berkeley
 Extension Media Center
2176 Shattuck Ave.
Berkeley, CA 94704 Ph: (510)642-0460
Description: This is a documentary about how government policy has changed concerning the American Indians. The Kickapoo tribe from Kansas are used as examples. **Release Date:** 1987. **Length:** 46 mins. **Format:** VHS, 3/4″ U-matic Cassette.

★2041★
Rolling Thunder: The Unity of Man and Nature
Facets Multimedia, Inc.
1517 W. Fullerton Ave.
Chicago, IL 60614 Ph: (312)281-9075
Description: Rolling Thunder, a medicine man of intertribal status, examines man as a dominator of nature verses man living in harmony with nature. He also talks of his visits to the spirit world and his shamanistic healing methods. **Release Date:** 19??. **Length:** 90 mins. **Format:** VHS.

★2042★
Run, Appaloosa, Run
Coronet/MTI Film & Video Ph: (708)940-1260
108 Wilmot Rd. Free: 800-621-2131
Deerfield, IL 60015 Fax: (708)940-3640
Description: An Indian girl and Holy Smoke, her stallion, share happiness and tragedy in this adventure. **Release Date:** 1966. **Length:** 48 mins. **Format:** Beta, VHS, 1/2″ Reel-EIAJ, 3/4″ U-matic Cassette, Other than listed.

★2043★
The Runaway
Native American Public Broadcasting
 Consortium
1800 N. 133rd St.
PO Box 86111
Lincoln, NE 68501 Ph: (402)472-3522
Description: Discusses the situation of 14-year old Darlene Horse, a Native American girl who ran away from a difficult home situation, including her family's problems with alcohol. **Length:** 29 mins. **Format:** VHS, 1″ Broadcast Type ″C″, 3/4 U-matic Cassette.

★2044★
Running on the Edge of the Rainbow: Laguna Stories and Poems
Norman Ross Publishing Inc. Ph: (212)765-8200
330 W. 58th St. Free: 800-648-8850
New York, NY 10019 Fax: (212)765-2393
Description: A reflection on the nature of Laguna storytelling, its functions, and the problems of being an Indian poet. **Release Date:** 1981. **Length:** 28 mins. **Format:** Beta, VHS, 3/4″ U-matic Cassette.

★2045★
Sacajawea
FilmFair Communications Ph: (818)985-0244
10621 Magnolia Blvd. Free: 800-423-2461
North Hollywood, CA 91601 Fax: (818)980-8492
Description: Still photos and animation bring to life the Indian woman who helped Lewis and Clark on their trip through the American West. **Release Date:** 1989. **Length:** 25 mins. **Format:** Beta, VHS, 3/4″ U-matic Cassette.

★2046★
Sacred Ground: The North American Indian's Relationship to the Land
Wood Knapp & Company, Inc.
Knapp Press
5900 Wilshire Blvd. Ph: (213)937-5486
Los Angeles, CA 90036 Free: 800-521-2666
Description: A look at a variety of Native American societies, focusing on mythology, anthropology, and social structure. **Release Date:** 1991. **Length:** 60 mins. **Format:** VHS. **Credits:** Hosted by: Cliff Robertson.

★2047★
Sacred Ways: Sun Dagger
Ark Media Group Ltd. Ph: (415)863-7200
425 Alabama St. Free: 800-727-0009
San Francisco, CA 94110 Fax: (415)864-5437
Description: Robert Redford hosts this look at the Anasazi Indians' celestial calendar. **Length:** 58 **Format:** VHS

★2048★
Science or Sacrilege: The Study of American Indian Remains
University of California at Santa Barbara
Instructional Development
Santa Barbara, CA 93106 Ph: (805)961-3518
Description: This program deals with the issue of whether or not American Indian Skeletal remains and artifacts should be preserved in museums for study by anthropologists and other scientists. **Release Date:** 1983. **Length:** 41 mins. **Format:** Beta, VHS, 3/4″ U-matic Cassette.

★2049★
Seasons of a Navajo
PBS Video
1320 Braddock Pl.
Alexandria, VA 22314-1698 Ph: (703)739-5380
Description: A look at the traditional Navajo way of life, including their music, folklore and ceremonies. Features scenes of Arizona's Monument Valley and the Anasazi ruins. **Release Date:** 1985. **Length:** 60 mins. **Format:** VHS, 3/4″ U-matic Cassette.

★2050★
Seminole Indians
International Film Bureau, Inc. (IFB)
332 S. Michigan Ave.
Chicago, IL 60604-4382 Ph: (312)427-4545
Description: The lives of Seminole Indians are presented in this program. **Release Date:** 1982. **Length:** 11 mins. **Format:** Beta, VHS, 3/4″ U-matic Cassette, Other than listed.

★2051★
Seyewailo: The Flower World
Norman Ross Publishing Inc. Ph: (212)765-8200
330 W. 58th St. Free: 800-648-8850
New York, NY 10019 Fax: (212)765-2393
Description: The enchanted talk of Yaqui deer songs are sung and danced to at a fiesta (Yaqui with English subtitles). **Length:** 51 **Format:** Beta VHS 3/4U

★2052★
Shadow Catcher
Phoenix/BFA Films
468 Park Ave., S. Ph: (212)684-5910
New York, NY 10016 Free: 800-221-1274
Description: This is a program about photographer-anthropologist Edward Curtis and the Indian people he worked with from 1895 to 1930. Includes all of Curtis' recoverable film footage of life among the Kwakiutl, Hopi, and Navaho Indians. **Release Date:** 1975. **Length:** 88 mins. **Format:** Beta, VHS, 3/4″ U-matic Cassette.

★2053★
The Shadow Catcher: Edward S. Curtis and the North American Indian
Mystic Fire Video Ph: (212)941-0999
524 Broadway, Ste. 604 Free: 800-292-9001
New York, NY 10012 Fax: (212)941-1443
Description: A look at the life of photographer-anthropologist Edward Curtis and the North American Indian life he recorded from 1895 to 1930. Includes all of Curtis' recoverable film footage of life among the Kwakiutl, Hopi, and Navaho Indians. **Length:** 88 **Format:** Beta VHS 3/4U

★2054★
The Shadow Walkers
Agency for Instructional Technology (AIT)
1111 W. 17th St.
Box A   Ph: (812)339-2203
Bloomington, IN 47402-0120   Free: 800-457-4509
Description: A set of programs designed to bring out the pride associated with being a Native American. **Release Date:** 1989. **Length:** 30 mins. **Format:** Beta, VHS, 3/4″ U-matic Cassette.

★2055★
Shadow of the Warrior
National AudioVisual Center
National Archives & Records
    Administration
Customer Services Section PZ
8700 Edgeworth Dr.
Capitol Heights, MD 20743-3701   Ph: (301)763-1896
Description: This video for Veterans Administration center psychology professionals deals with the lives and problems of American Indian Vietnam veterans. **Release Date:** 1985. **Length:** 42 mins. **Format:** Beta, VHS, 3/4″ U-matic Cassette.

★2056★
The Shaman's Journey
Wishing Well Distributing   Ph: (414)864-2395
PO Box 2   Free: 800-888-9355
Wilmot, WI 53192   Fax: (414)862-2398
Description: A look at Native American healing practices, coupled with a tour of Central and South American historic sites. **Release Date:** 1990. **Length:** 90 mins. **Format:** VHS.

★2057★
Shinnecock: A Story of a People
Phoenix/BFA Films
468 Park Ave., S.   Ph: (212)684-5910
New York, NY 10016   Free: 800-221-1274
Description: This video features a look at the history, heritage, and present-day status of the Shinnecock Indians. **Release Date:** 1976. **Length:** 20 mins. **Format:** Beta, VHS, 3/4″ U-matic Cassette.

★2058★
The Silent Enemy
Video Yesteryear
Box C   Ph: (203)426-2574
Sandy Hook, CT 06482   Free: 800-243-0987
Description: An interesting documentary which tells the Ojibway Indian's way of life before the arrival of the white man. The title is a reference to hunger. **Release Date:** 1930. **Length:** 110 mins. **Format:** Beta, VHS, 8mm.

★2059★
Silent Heritage: The American Indian
Michigan Media
University of Michigan
400 4th St.
Ann Arbor, MI 48109   Ph: (313)764-8228
Description: To seek the truth about the American Indian and give him an opportunity to express his views, a film crew from the University of Michigan Media Resources Center traveled to six states, interviewing representatives from major tribes. All programs available individually. **Release Date:** 1966. **Length:** 29 mins. **Format:** 3/4″ U-matic Cassette, Other than listed.

★2060★
Sinew-Backed Bow and its Arrows
University of California at Berkeley
    Extension Media Center
2176 Shattuck Ave.
Berkeley, CA 94704   Ph: (510)642-0460
Description: This program follows the construction of a sinew-backed bow–the finest of the bows used by American Indians–by a Yurok craftsman. Demonstrations of the making of arrows are also included. **Release Date:** 1961. **Length:** 24 mins. **Format:** 3/4″ U-matic Cassette, Other than listed.

★2061★
Sioux Legends
AIMS Media
9710 De Soto Ave.
Chatsworth, CA 91311-9734   Free: 800-367-2467
                                   Fax: (818)341-6700
Description: Recreates philosophies and religion of the Sioux culture and its identification with the forces of nature. **Release Date:** 1974. **Length:** 20 mins. **Format:** Beta, VHS, 3/4″ U-matic Cassette.

★2062★
The Six Nations
Cinema Guild
1697 Broadway   Ph: (212)246-5522
New York, NY 10019   Fax: (212)246-5525
Description: In upstate New York stands the Iroquois League, a federation older than the U.S. itself, consisting of the Mohawk, Oneida, Onondaga, Seneca, Cayuga, and Tuscarora tribes. This program tells how these tribes consider themselves to be a sovereign independent nation and reject the American way of life in favor of a self-sufficient existence on their own land. **Release Date:** 1976. **Length:** 26 mins. **Format:** 3/4″ U-matic Cassette, Other than listed.

★2063★
Smithsonian: Catlin and the Indians
CRM/McGraw-Hill Films
674 Via de la Valle
PO Box 641
Del Mar, CA 92014
Description: An examination of the paintings of George Catlin, who recorded the now-extinct way of life of the Plains Indians–the forms and rituals of a vanished society. From the "Smithsonian" series. **Release Date:** 1967. **Length:** 24 mins. **Format:** Beta, VHS, 3/4″ U-matic Cassette. **Credits:** Hosted by: Bill Ryan.

★2064★
Snaketown
University of California at Berkeley
    Extension Media Center
2176 Shattuck Ave.
Berkeley, CA 94704   Ph: (510)642-0460
Description: An ancient Indian site in Arizona is excavated. **Release Date:** 1969. **Length:** 45 mins. **Format:** VHS, 3/4″ U-matic Cassette.

★2065★
Something Seneca
New York State Education Department
Center for Learning Technologies
Media Distribution Network, Rm. C-7,
    Concourse Level
Albany, NY 12230   Ph: (518)474-1265
Description: A series of programs looking at modern Native American culture, for the high school student. Electronically enhanced for video. **Release Date:** 1978. **Length:** 14 mins. **Format:** Beta, VHS, 1/2″ Reel-EIAJ, 3/4″ U-matic Cassette.

★2066★
Sometimes We Feel
Barr Films
12801 Schabarum Ave.   Ph: (818)338-7878
PO Box 7878   Free: 800-234-7878
Irwindale, CA 91706-7878   Fax: (818)814-2672
Description: A young Indian tells of the proud history of his people, and explains how they are now reduced to a life of sorrow, poverty, and neglect on their desert reservation. **Release Date:** 1974. **Length:** 10 mins. **Format:** Beta, VHS, 3/4″ U-matic Cassette.

★2067★
Songs of My Hunter Heart: Laguna Songs and Poems
Norman Ross Publishing Inc.   Ph: (212)765-8200
330 W. 58th St.   Free: 800-648-8850
New York, NY 10019   Fax: (212)765-2393

Description: A look at the inroads made upon traditional Laguna Pueblo life by the discovery of uranium deposits and extensive mining. **Release Date:** 1981. **Length:** 34 mins. **Format:** Beta, VHS, 3/4″ U-matic Cassette.

★2068★
Southwest Indian Arts and Crafts
Coronet/MTI Film & Video   Ph: (708)940-1260
108 Wilmot Rd.   Free: 800-621-2131
Deerfield, IL 60015   Fax: (708)940-3640

Description: The fine workmanship of the Southwest Indians is seen in Navajo rugs, San Ildefanso and Acoma pottery, and much more. **Release Date:** 1973. **Length:** 14 mins. **Format:** Beta, VHS, 3/4″ U-matic Cassette, Other than listed.

★2069★
Southwest Indians of Early America
Coronet/MTI Film & Video   Ph: (708)940-1260
108 Wilmot Rd.   Free: 800-621-2131
Deerfield, IL 60015   Fax: (708)940-3640

Description: An examination of the prosperous ancestors of the Hopi, Pima, and Papaga Indians in the Southwestern United States. **Release Date:** 1973. **Length:** 14 mins. **Format:** Beta, VHS, 3/4″ U-matic Cassette, Other than listed.

★2070★
Spirit of the Hunt
Centre Productions, Inc.
1800 30th St., Ste. 207   Ph: (303)444-1166
Boulder, CO 80301   Free: 800-824-1166

Description: This film is a fascinating account of the spiritual elements of what the buffalo means to the Indians of the Plains of North America. **Release Date:** 1982. **Length:** 29 mins. **Format:** Beta, VHS, 3/4″ U-matic Cassette.

★2071★
Stone Age Americans
International Film Bureau, Inc. (IFB)
332 S. Michigan Ave.
Chicago, IL 60604-4382   Ph: (312)427-4545

Description: This is a study of the Indians of the Mesa Verde in Colorado, who disappeared after thirteen centuries of development. **Release Date:** 1970. **Length:** 21 mins. **Format:** Beta, VHS, 3/4″ U-matic Cassette, Other than listed.

★2072★
Stories of American Indian Culture: Hawk, I'm Your Brother
Best Film & Video Corporation   Ph: (516)487-4515
98 Cutter Mill Rd.   Free: 800-527-2189
Great Neck, NY 11021   Fax: (516)487-4834

Description: A young boy develops a special relationship with a majestic hawk and learns what it means to fly. Based on Byrd Baylor's award winning children's books, this video offers the Native American's unique perspective on life. **Release Date:** 1991. **Length:** 25 mins. **Format:** VHS. **Credits:** Narrated by: Will Rogers, Jr.

★2073★
Stories of American Indian Culture: The Other Way to Listen
Best Film & Video Corporation   Ph: (516)487-4515
98 Cutter Mill Rd.   Free: 800-527-2189
Great Neck, NY 11021   Fax: (516)487-4834

Description: Children are shown the unique Native American perspective on desert life and what one can "hear" in the desert. Based on Byrd Baylor's award winning children's books. **Release Date:** 1991. **Length:** 20 mins. **Format:** VHS. **Credits:** Narrated by: Will Rogers, Jr.

★2074★
Stories of American Indian Culture: The Way to Start a Day
Best Film & Video Corporation   Ph: (516)487-4515
98 Cutter Mill Rd.   Free: 800-527-2189
Great Neck, NY 11021   Fax: (516)487-4834

Description: Video version of Byrd Baylor's children's books which introduce young people to Native American culture, emphasizing the unique perspective on nature. This edition offers computer animated versions of illustrator Peter Parnall's work. **Release Date:** 1990. **Length:** 12 mins. **Format:** VHS. **Credits:** Narrated by: Will Rogers, Jr.

★2075★
Strength of Life—Knokavtee Scott
Native American Public Broadcasting Consortium
PO Box 86111
1800 N. 33rd St.
Lincoln, NE 68501   Ph: (402)472-3522

Description: The life and work of Cherokee/Creek jewelry craftsman Scott is explored, as is his inspirational devotion to the Spiro Mounds in Oklahoma. **Release Date:** 1984. **Length:** 27 mins. **Format:** VHS, 3/4″ U-matic Cassette, 1″ Broadcast Type "C", 2″ Quadraplex Open Reel.

★2076★
Sucking Doctor
University of California at Berkeley Extension Media Center
2176 Shattuck Ave.
Berkeley, CA 94704   Ph: (510)642-0460

Description: A group of Indians from the Southwest perform a ritual healing. **Release Date:** 1964. **Length:** 45 mins. **Format:** VHS, 3/4″ U-matic Cassette.

★2077★
Summer Legend
Churchill Films
12210 Nebraska Ave.   Ph: (213)207-6600
Los Angeles, CA 90025   Fax: (213)207-1330

Description: This is an animated version of the Micmac Indian legend that explains the changing of the seasons. **Release Date:** 1988. **Length:** 8 mins. **Format:** Beta, VHS, 3/4″ U-matic Cassette.

★2078★
Sun Bear on Earth Changes
Wishing Well Distributing   Ph: (414)864-2395
PO Box 2   Free: 800-888-9355
Wilmot, WI 53192   Fax: (414)862-2398

Description: A presentation of Native American prophecies concerning the state of the world. **Release Date:** 1990. **Length:** 60 mins. **Format:** VHS.

★2079★
Sun Bear: Vision of the Medicine Wheel
Hartley Film Foundation   Ph: (203)869-1818
Cat Rock Rd.   Free: 800-937-1819
Cos Cob, CT 06807   Fax: (203)869-1905

Description: Explains the wisdom and prophecies of the late visionary Sun Bear, and his divination of Earth changes to come. **Length:** 60 **Format:** VHS

★2080★
The Sun Dagger
Bullfrog Films, Inc.   Ph: (215)779-8226
PO Box 149   Free: 800-543-3764
Oley, PA 19547   Fax: (215)370-1978

Description: Robert Redford narrates the extraordinary culture of the Anasazi Indians who built the calendar and thrived in the harsh environment of Chaco Canyon, New Mexico, one thousand years ago. A 29 minute version is available. **Release Date:** 1983. **Length:** 58 mins. **Format:** Beta, VHS, 3/4″ U-matic Cassette.

★2081★
Surviving Columbus
PBS Video
1320 Braddock Pl.
Alexandria, VA 22314-1698   Ph: (703)739-5380

Description: A look at the first encounters between New Mexico's Pueblo Indians and the first European explorers, led by Coronado. The focus is on the explorers' search for non-existent gold, and the havoc they wrought. **Release Date:** 1990. **Length:** 30 mins. **Format:** VHS, 3/4″ U-matic Cassette.

★2082★
Tahtonka
AIMS Media
9710 De Soto Ave.
Chatsworth, CA 91311-9734   Free: 800-367-2467
                                    Fax: (818)341-6700

Description: Historic look at the Plains Indians from the pre-horse era to the Wounded Knee massacre, showing their dependence on the buffalo. **Release Date:** 1968. **Length:** 30 mins. **Format:** Beta, VHS, 3/4″ U-matic Cassette.

★2083★
Tales of the Muscogee
Centre Productions, Inc.
1800 30th St., Ste. 207   Ph: (303)444-1166
Boulder, CO 80301   Free: 800-824-1166

Description: This program is narrated, scored and illustrated by members of the Indian tribe. It examines the folklore of the tribe and demonstrates how this ancient folklore can teach today's children about morality. **Release Date:** 1983. **Length:** 15 mins. **Format:** Beta, VHS, 3/4″ U-matic Cassette.

★2084★
The Taos Pueblo
Bullfrog Films, Inc.   Ph: (215)779-8226
PO Box 149   Free: 800-543-3764
Oley, PA 19547   Fax: (215)370-1978

Description: A look at the dramatically beautiful, 1000 year-old pueblo in Taos, New Mexico to discover more about the traditions that the resident Indians are trying to preserve. **Release Date:** 1987. **Length:** 9 mins. **Format:** Beta, VHS, 3/4″ U-matic Cassette.

★2085★
That One Good Spirit—An Indian Christmas Story
Native American Public Broadcasting
  Consortium
PO Box 86111
1800 N. 33rd St.
Lincoln, NE 68501   Ph: (402)472-3522

Description: Clay animation is used to enact an Ute Christmas myth. **Release Date:** 1981. **Length:** 16 mins. **Format:** VHS, 3/4″ U-matic Cassette, 1″ Broadcast Type ″C″, 2″ Quadraplex Open Reel.

★2086★
They Promised to Take Our Land
Cinema Guild
1697 Broadway   Ph: (212)246-5522
New York, NY 10019   Fax: (212)246-5525

Description: When Europeans began to colonize the New World there were hundreds of Indian tribes spread across the continent. By 1900 the Indians had been greatly reduced in number and forced to live on tracts of land alloted by the white man. In this program, Navajo tribal chairman Peter Macdonald discusses the "rip-off" of Indian resources dating back 100 years. **Release Date:** 1976. **Length:** 26 mins. **Format:** 3/4″ U-matic Cassette, Other than listed.

★2087★
Those Who Sing Together
CRM/McGraw-Hill Films
674 Via de la Valle
PO Box 641
Del Mar, CA 92014

Description: The folklore and music of the Plains Indians and the tribes of the Pacific Northwest are chronicled in this program.

Release Date: 1978. **Length:** 28 mins. **Format:** Beta, VHS, 3/4″ U-matic Cassette.

★2088★
Thunder Warrior
Trans-World Entertainment
8899 Beverly Blvd., 8th Fl.
Los Angeles, CA 90048-2412

Description: A young Indian turns into a one-man army determined to punish the local authorities who are abusing his fellow tribe members. **Length:** 84 **Format:** Beta VHS

★2089★
A Time to Be Brave
Beacon Films
930 Pinter Ave.   Ph: (312)328-6700
Evanston, IL 60202   Free: 800-323-5448

Description: In the northern wilderness, a young Ojibway girl must overcome her fears in order to save her father's life. **Release Date:** 1982. **Length:** 28 mins. **Format:** Beta, VHS, 3/4″ U-matic Cassette.

★2090★
Tomorrow's Yesterday
Brigham Young University
101 Fletcher Building
Provo, UT 84602   Ph: (801)378-3456

Description: Shows American Indians as they were, as they are, and as they hope to be. Stresses the positive things they are doing to meet the challenge of modern civilization without losing their cultural heritage. **Release Date:** 1971. **Length:** 29 mins. **Format:** 3/4″ U-matic Cassette.

★2091★
Totem Pole
University of California at Berkeley
  Extension Media Center
2176 Shattuck Ave.
Berkeley, CA 94704   Ph: (510)642-0460

Description: The development of the seven types of totem poles is lyrically presented, and each is discussed in terms of a social system and mythology. The carving of a pole by a tribal chief is also shown. **Release Date:** 1963. **Length:** 27 mins. **Format:** 3/4″ U-matic Cassette, Other than listed.

★2092★
Track of the Moonbeast
Prism Entertainment
1888 Century Park, E., Ste. 1000   Ph: (213)277-3270
Los Angeles, CA 90067   Fax: (213)203-8036

Description: An American Indian uses mythology to capture the Moonbeast, a lizard-like creature that is roaming the deserts of New Mexico. **Release Date:** 1976. **Length:** 90 mins. **Format:** Beta, VHS. **Credits:** Cast Member: Chase Cordell; Donna Leigh Drake. Directed by: Richard Ashe.

★2093★
Trail of Broken Treaties
Cinema Guild
1697 Broadway   Ph: (212)246-5522
New York, NY 10019   Fax: (212)246-5525

Description: An examination of the past and present injustices suffe red by the Indian and a look at the attempts of Indian leaders to improve the situation. **Release Date:** 1976. **Length:** 26 mins. **Format:** 3/4″ U-matic Cassette, Other than listed.

★2094★
The Treasure: Indian Heritage
Phoenix/BFA Films
468 Park Ave., S.   Ph: (212)684-5910
New York, NY 10016   Free: 800-221-1274

Description: A contemporary study of cultural values in conflict-two teenage Indian brothers impatient with their father's traditional ways. **Release Date:** 1970. **Length:** 13 mins. **Format:** Beta, VHS, 3/4″ U-matic Cassette.

★2095★
Treaties Made, Treaties Broken
CRM/McGraw-Hill Films
674 Via de la Valle
PO Box 641
Del Mar, CA 92014
Description: The Treaty of Medicine Creek grants the Indians of Washington State fishing and hunting rights in perpetuity. Today, the treaty is in dispute. From the "North American Indian" series. **Release Date:** 1971. **Length:** 18 mins. **Format:** Beta, VHS, 3/4″ U-matic Cassette.

★2096★
The Treaty of 1868 Series
Native American Public Broadcasting
  Consortium
1800 N. 33rd St.
PO Box 86111
Lincoln, NE 68501   Ph: (402)472-3522
Description: Explores whether the Lakota Sioux Indians or the United States government own the Black Hills of South Dakota, which the Lakota regard as sacred ground. Individual program titles: The Treaty of 1868; The Black Hills Claim. Tapes are available individually or as a series. **Release Date:** 1987. **Length:** 28 mins. **Format:** VHS, 1″ Broadcast Type ″C″, 3/4″ U-matic Cassette.

★2097★
Treaty Rights or Civil Rights
Michigan Media
University of Michigan
400 4th St.
Ann Arbor, MI 48109   Ph: (313)764-8228
Description: An explanation of the importance of treaty rights and constitutional civil rights in protecting Indian reservations and preserving the Indian way of life. Part of the "Silent Heritage" series. **Release Date:** 1966. **Length:** 29 mins. **Format:** 3/4″ U-matic Cassette, Other than listed.

★2098★
The Trial of Leonard Peltier
Intermedia Arts of Minnesota, Inc.
425 Ontario St. SE
Minneapolis, MN 55414   Ph: (612)627-4444
Description: This documentary tells the unusual story of the United States Government's murder case against American Indian Movement leader Leonard Peltier. **Release Date:** 1977. **Length:** 16 mins. **Format:** 3/4″ U-matic Cassette, Other than listed.

★2099★
Turtle Shells
Native American Public Broadcasting
  Consortium
1800 N. 33rd St.
PO Box 86111
Lincoln, NE 68501   Ph: (402)472-3522
Description: Explores the crafting of Native American women's leg rattles, from choosing the turtle shell to the final fitting. Demonstrated by Christine Hannena, a Muscogee Creek Indian of Oklahoma. **Length:** 26 mins. **Format:** VHS, 1″ Broadcast Type ″C″, 3/4″ U-matic cassette.

★2100★
Two Worlds
Anti-Defamation League of B'nai B'rith
Audio-Visual Department
823 United Nations Plaza
New York, NY 10017   Ph: (212)490-2525
Description: An examination of the condition of the American Indian today and the problems rising from the effort to integrate them into the mainstream of American life. **Release Date:** 1986. **Length:** 30 mins. **Format:** Beta, VHS, 3/4″ U-matic Cassette.

★2101★
The Uncertain Future
Michigan Media
University of Michigan
400 4th St.
Ann Arbor, MI 48109   Ph: (313)764-8228
Description: A discussion of the major problems of the American Indian of today and tomorrow, such as low income, poor education, and termination of helpful government programs. Part of "Silent Heritage" series. **Release Date:** 1966. **Length:** 29 mins. **Format:** 3/4″ U-matic Cassette, Other than listed.

★2102★
Urban Indians
Downtown Community TV Center
87 Lafayette St.
New York, NY 10013   Ph: (212)966-4510
Description: This is the true story of an Oglala Sioux who came to New York City looking for a job, but wound up a drug addict. **Release Date:** 1984. **Length:** 20 mins. **Format:** 1/2″ Reel-EIAJ, 3/4″ U-matic Cassette, Other than listed.

★2103★
The Wake
National Film Board of Canada
1251 Avenue of the Americas, 16th Fl.
New York, NY 10020-1173   Ph: (212)586-5131
Description: A contemporary, single, Native American mother must face the difficulties of prejudice. **Release Date:** 1987. **Length:** 58 mins. **Format:** Beta, VHS, 3/4″ U-matic Cassette.

★2104★
Walking with Grandfather
Native American Public Broadcasting
  Consortium
1800 N. 33rd St.
PO Box 86111
Lincoln, NE 68501   Ph: (402)472-3522
Description: Stories drawn from the oral tradition of many North American Indian tribes that present basic human values. Individual program titles: The Arrival; The Woods; The Mountain; The Valley; The Stream; The Gift. Tapes are available individually or as a series. **Release Date:** 1988. **Length:** 14 mins. **Format:** VHS, 1″ Broadcast Type ″C″, 3/4″ U-matic Cassette.

★2105★
Walking in a Sacred Manner
International Film Bureau, Inc. (IFB)
332 S. Michigan Ave.
Chicago, IL 60604-4382   Ph: (312)427-4545
Description: The appreciation that Indians have for the physical, spiritual and psychological well being of man is documented. **Release Date:** 1983. **Length:** 23 mins. **Format:** Beta, VHS, 3/4″ U-matic Cassette, Other than listed.

★2106★
Warpaint and Wigs
Video Tech
19346 3rd Ave. NW
Seattle, WA 98177   Ph: (206)546-5401
Description: This program from the "Images of Indians" series shows how the movie image of the Indian has affected the self-image of Native Americans. **Release Date:** 1982. **Length:** 30 mins. **Format:** Beta, VHS, 3/4″ U-matic Cassette, Other than listed. **Credits:** Narrated by: Will Sampson.

★2107★
Warriors
Intermedia Arts of Minnesota, Inc.
425 Ontario St. SE
Minneapolis, MN 55414   Ph: (612)627-4444
Description: This film focuses on American Indians who fought in the Vietnam War. **Release Date:** 1987. **Length:** 58 mins. **Format:** 3/4″ U-matic Cassette.

★2108★
Water Is So Clear That a Blind Man Could See
Indiana University Center for Media &
   Teaching Resources   Ph: (812)855-8087
Bloomington, IN 47405-5901   Fax: (812)855-8404
Description: A look at New Mexico's Taos Indians, who believe that all life is sacred, and have lived in harmony with nature for over a century. Their land is now threatened by lumber companies. **Release Date:** 1970. **Length:** 30 mins. **Format:** 3/4″ U-matic Cassette, Other than listed.

★2109★
Way of Our Fathers
University of California at Berkeley
   Extension Media Center
2176 Shattuck Ave.
Berkeley, CA 94704   Ph: (510)642-0460
Description: Members of several northern California Indian tribes depict unique elements of a way of life as it flourished before the coming of the white man. **Release Date:** 1972. **Length:** 33 mins. **Format:** 3/4″ U-matic Cassette, Other than listed.

★2110★
We Are One: A Series
Native American Public Broadcasting
   Consortium
1800 N. 33rd St.
PO Box 86111
Lincoln, NE 68501   Ph: (402)472-3522
Description: Focuses on 13-year old Ni'bathaska and his sister Mi'onbathin and the daily activities of their lives as Omaha Indians in early 19th century Nebraska. A teacher's guide is included with each tape. Individual program titles: Morning Comes; Learning from Others; Turning of the Child; Storytelling; Becoming a Warrior; Preparing for the Summer Hunt; The Dare; The Buffalo Hunt. Tapes are available individually or as a series. **Release Date:** 1986. **Length:** 20 mins. **Format:** VHS, 1″ Broadcast Type ″C″, 3/4″ U-matic Cassette.

★2111★
We Are a River Flowing
Intermedia Arts of Minnesota, Inc.
425 Ontario St. SE
Minneapolis, MN 55414   Ph: (612)627-4444
Description: Ten-year old Fiona travels from her home in Belfast, Ireland to the Pine Ridge Indian reservation as a part of a program for children of political turmoil. This film makes a striking between the Irish and Indian societies. **Release Date:** 1985. **Length:** 40 mins. **Format:** Beta, VHS, 3/4″ U-matic Cassette.

★2112★
A Weave of Time
Direct Cinema Limited   Ph: (213)652-8000
PO Box 69799   Free: 800-345-6748
Los Angeles, CA 90069-9976   Fax: (213)652-2346
Description: A look at Navajo life in the 1930s. **Release Date:** 1987. **Length:** 60 mins. **Format:** Beta, VHS, 3/4″ U-matic Cassette.

★2113★
What Is an American, Part 2
Pyramid Film & Video
Box 1048   Ph: (310)828-7577
2801 Colorado Ave.   Free: 800-421-2304
Santa Monica, CA 90406   Fax: (310)453-9083
Description: The program explains to children how Puerto Rican and American Indian cultures have enriched our American experience. **Release Date:** 1979. **Length:** 12 mins. **Format:** Beta, VHS, 3/4″ U-matic Cassette.

★2114★
Where the Buffaloes Begin
Random House Media
Department 467
400 Hahn Rd.
Westminster, MD 21157   Free: 800-492-0782
Description: Olaf Baker's story about the lives of Native Americans is brought to life. **Release Date:** 1985. **Length:** 14 mins. **Format:** VHS. **Credits:** Narrated by: Jamake Highwater.

★2115★
White Apache
Imperial Entertainment Corporation
4640 Lankershim Blvd., 4th Fl.
North Hollywood, CA 91602
Description: Emotionally charged saga of a man barred from both Indian and White societies. The film focuses on the impact of prejudice toward a white man raised by Apaches. **Release Date:** 1988. **Length:** 90 mins. **Format:** Beta, VHS.

★2116★
White Man's Way
Native American Public Broadcasting
   Consortium
1800 N. 33rd St.
PO Box 86111
Lincoln, NE 68501   Ph: (402)472-3522
Description: Looks at the U.S. Indian School in Nebraska where, beginning in the late 1800's, Indian children from numerous tribes were sent to learn the ways of the white man and were forbidden to practice their own lifestyles. **Release Date:** 1986. **Length:** 30 mins. **Format:** VHS, 1″ Broadcast Type ″C″, 3/4″ U-matic Cassette.

★2117★
Who Discovered America
Films, Inc.
5547 N. Ravenswood Ave.   Ph: (312)878-2600
Chicago, IL 60640-1199   Free: 800-323-4222
Description: Different theories about who the Indians were and where they came from are discussed, as well as their discovery of corn, which made their world possible and still flourishes throughout today's world. **Release Date:** 1972. **Length:** 14 mins. **Format:** Beta, VHS, 3/4″ U-matic Cassette.

★2118★
Winter on an Indian Reservation
Atlantis Productions
1252 La Granada Dr.
Thousand Oaks, CA 91360   Ph: (805)495-2790
Description: A look at the lives of children on a forest reservation in the Great Lakes area. Also available in a non-narrative version. **Release Date:** 1973. **Length:** 11 mins. **Format:** Beta, VHS, 3/4″ U-matic Cassette.

★2119★
Wooden Box: Made by Steaming and Bending
University of California at Berkeley
   Extension Media Center
2176 Shattuck Ave.
Berkeley, CA 94704   Ph: (510)642-0460
Description: This program follows every stage of making the Kwakiutl box, elaborately carved and painted boxes made by steaming and bending a single wooden slab using no nails, screws, or glue. **Release Date:** 1962. **Length:** 33 mins. **Format:** 3/4″ U-matic Cassette, Other than listed.

★2120★
Woodland Indians of Early America
Coronet/MTI Film & Video   Ph: (708)940-1260
108 Wilmot Rd.   Free: 800-621-2131
Deerfield, IL 60015   Fax: (708)940-3640
Description: Authentic reconstructions and scenes in the eastern and Great Lakes regions provide settings for this study of woodland Indian life prior to European influence. **Release Date:** 1980.

Length: 10 mins. **Format:** Beta, VHS, 3/4″ U-matic Cassette, Other than listed.

★2121★
Woonspe (Education and the Sioux)
Native American Public Broadcasting
  Consortium
PO Box 86111
1800 N. 33rd St.
Lincoln, NE 68501   Ph: (402)472-3522
Description: A program that indicts the current state of Native American education. **Release Date:** 1974. **Length:** 28 mins. **Format:** VHS, 3/4″ U-matic Cassette, 1″ Broadcast Type ″C″, 2″ Quadraplex Open Reel.

★2122★
World in Our Eyes
Ark Media Group Ltd.   Ph: (415)863-7200
425 Alabama St.   Free: 800-727-0009
San Francisco, CA 94110   Fax: (415)864-5437
Description: Investigates the Native American visions of creation, from the Navajo, Zuni, Hopi and Cheyenne. **Length:** 102 **Format:** VHS

★2123★
The Wounded Knee Affair
Journal Films, Inc.   Ph: (708)328-6700
930 Pitner Ave.   Free: 800-323-5448
Evanston, IL 60202   Fax: (708)328-6706
Description: The siege of Wounded Knee, South Dakota in 1973 by a group of American Indians to draw international attention to their problems is examined. **Release Date:** 197?. **Length:** 17 mins. **Format:** Beta, VHS, 3/4″ U-matic Cassette.

★2124★
You Are on Indian Land
National Film Board of Canada
1251 Avenue of the Americas, 16th Fl.
New York, NY 10020-1173   Ph: (212)586-5131
Description: This film documents the 1969 demonstration by Mohawk Indians of the St. Regis Reserve on the international bridge between Canada and the United States near Cornwall, Ontario. **Release Date:** 1987. **Length:** 37 mins. **Format:** Beta, VHS, 3/4″ U-matic Cassette.

Internet and Online Databases

★2125★
AISESnet
University of Texas Health Science
  Center, San Antonio
Department of Biochemistry
7703 Floyd Curl Dr.
San Antonio, TX 78284-7760
Borries Demeler
URL: http://bioc02.uthscsa.edu/aisesnet.html   **Gopher:** bioc02.uthscsa.edu **Description:** The American Indian Science and Engineering Society (AISES) is a private, nonprofit organization that nurtures building of community by bridging science and technology with traditional native values. AISES provides opportunities for American Indians and Alaskan Natives to pursue studies in science, engineering, business and other academic areas. AISESnet provides AISES members with the ability to communicate through e-mail, news about AISES and American Indian activities, and employment opportunities and information sources useful in all academic fields. Main Files: What is AISES; AISES Contacts; AISES Programs; People of AISES; AISES Events, Dates, and Places; How AISES can help YOU; How YOU can help AISES; AISES Merchandise; AISES Art Auction; What is AISESnet?; AISESnet Mailing Lists; AISESnet Databases; AISESnet Career Center; and more. Related Mailing Lists: AISESnet is a moderated

distribution list distributed from the University of Montana in Missoula. **Fees:** Free.

★2126★
AISESnet: American Indian Science and Engineering Society
URL: http://bioc02.uthscsa.edu/aisesnet.html   **Description:** Site serves as an information source and membership directory for the American Indian Science and Engineering Society. Database includes names, addresses, occupations, and specialties. Also includes job information, mailing list archives, and information on educational programs.

★2127★
American Indian Resources
URL: http://www.lang.osaka-u.ac.jp/krkvls/naindex.html
Description: Provides links to Native American studies resources, including research facilities, university and college programs, and other sources of research material.

★2128★
Art of the American Indian Frontier
Detroit Institute of Arts
5200 Woodward Ave.
Detroit, MI 48202   Ph: (313)833-7900
URL: http://glrain.cic.net/diapages.htm **Description:** Art of the American Indian Frontier: A Portfolio features Native American art made between 1780 and 1920. The art, part of the Chandler-Pohrt Collection, includes clothing, bags of porcupine quill and buckskin, sashes, jewelry, pipes, and other decorative objects. Main Files: About Art of the American Indian Frontier; Ordering Information; and Plates. Beautiful, spirited works of art, all gathered in one convenient virtual location. Some of the plates are not available online. Uniquely Indian, the design and craftsmanship are witness to the creative spirit that endured even in the face of continual governmental attempts at forced assimilation. **Fees:** Free.

★2129★
Cherokee National Historical Society
Powersource

URL: http://www.powersource.com/powersource/heritage/
Description: Educational site which allows insight and easy access to Cherokee history, to read their newsletter, and to uncover related resources. Data Providers: Powersource. Main Files: Membership; Cherokee Heritage Center; First Families of the Cherokee Nation; Books and Information; Columns Newsletter; The Cherokee Nation. **Update frequency:** As needed. **Fees:** Free.

★2130★
Code Talk American Indian Website
URL: http://www.codetalk.fed.us **Description:** A database of federal government agency contacts who operate Native American programs. Also provides links to other Native American information resources.

★2131★
Costanoan-Ohlone Indian Canyon Resource
URL: http://www.ucsc.edu/costano **Gopher:** gopher.ucsc.edu Choose: The Community. **Description:** The Costanoan-Ohlone Indian Canyon Resource database provides access to information about the Costanoan-Ohlone Indians and for the California Indian Community. In addition to links to other Indian-related sites. there are full-text newsletters and articles. Main Files: Update; Visit Our Museum; 18 Treaties with America; WIYOT Tribe of California; and numerous others. Remarks: The Resource is maintained by a UCSC student. The material is all proprietary and must be attributed if small parts are used for the propagation of Californian Indian issues. **Fees:** Free.

★2132★
Dine Community College
                      Ph: (520)724-6612
URL: http://crystal.ncc.cc.nm.us/   **Description:** Boasting it's distinction as the first tribally controlled community college, this page offers readers information not only about the college itself, but

about the Navajo Nation as well. Whether or not you have an interest in the Dine College (formerly known as the Navajo Community College) or the Navajo Nation, this is a site that begs to be seen. Main Files: Attending DC; Academic Programs; Navajo & Special Programs; Auxiliaries; Navajo Nation; Directory; Help!; Web Search!; Guestbook; Calendar and News; Campuses; Continuing Education; and Visiting DC. **Update frequency:** Regularly. **Documentation:** An online help file is available. **Fees:** Free.

★2133★
The Dreamer
Four11 Corp.

URL: http://www.wp.com/gilbreath/4dreamer.htm **Description:** If you want to get just a taste of the world of Native Americans, come here to meet The Dreamer. A Potawatami who lives in a large city, he tries to preserve the knowledge and ways of his people through story, artwork, and the internet. This site is both educational and a pleasure to view. Main Files: The People; Trade Links; The Issues; Resource Links; Education; several story files. This site is truly beautiful. Welcome to the wonderful world of frames and animated GIFs! This site does not support all browsers; Netscape 2.0 or higher is necessary. Due to the amount of graphics on this site, it loads quite slowly. **Update frequency:** As needed. **Fees:** Free.

★2134★
Federally Recognized Tribes
George Washington University   Ph: (202)994-6421
   Fax: (202)994-4404
Orna Weinroth, Information Specialist
Gopher: gwis.circ.gwu.edu Choose: Centers, Institutes, and Research at GWU/Centers and Institutes/National Indian Policy Center/Useful Data. **Description:** The Federally Recognized Tribes database is a list of Indian tribal entities within the contiguous 48 states recognized as eligible to receive services from the U.S. Bureau of Indian Affairs. Data Providers: U.S. Bureau of Indian Affairs and the National Indian Policy Center. It's a comprehensive list. It would be helpful if the site contained more information about these tribes. Cherokee Nation of Oklahoma, Cheyenne-Arapaho Tribes of Oklahoma, Cheyenne River Sioux Tribe of the Cheyenne River Reservation, South Dakota, Chickasaw Nation of Oklahoma, Chicken Ranch Rancheria of Me-Wuk Indians of California, Chippewa-Cree Indians of the Rocky Boy's Reservation, Montana Chitimacha Tribe of Louisiana, Choctaw Nation of Oklahoma. **Update frequency:** Semiannual. **Fees:** Free.

★2135★
A Guide to the Great Sioux Nation
URL:
http://www.state.sd.us/state/executive/tourism/sioux/sioux.htm
Description: Presented by the State of Oklahoma, this site includes a directory of landmarks and other points of interest, pow wow schedule, information on native art galleries and shows, as well as information on tribes in Oklahoma.

★2136★
Identity
Interport Communications
1133 Broadway
New York, NY 10010   Ph: (212)989-1128
URL: http://plaza.interport.net/logomanc/heye.html **Description:** this site provides a variety of quotes and observations about Native Americans and Native American culture. There are also a wide variety of links to related sites. The site is colorful with a many small images, and it is fast loading. Main Files: National Museum of the American Indian; Torsion in the blood; Authentic Ethnic Crafts; All-American; Links to Resources and Art Sources; Native American Stereotype Awareness Project; Aboriginal Super Information Hwy.; American Indian Computer Art Project; Canadian Native Art, a collection of Canadian Native Art; Contemporary Southwest Art; Electronic gallery of the work of Cree artist Wabimeguil; The Heard Museum; Library of Congress Gopher List; MIT AISES Home Page; Native American Resources; Native Net HomePage; Pueblo Cultural Center; Shako; The Sioux Nation. This site provides much information on attitudes toward Native Americans and links to many related resources. **Update frequency:** As needed. **Fees:** Free.

★2137★
Native American Graves Protection and Repatriation Act
University of Arkansas
Center for Advanced Spatial Technologies
12 Ozark Hall   Ph: (501)575-6159
Fayetteville, AR 72701   Fax: (501)575-3846
Robert Harris, NABD Online System Coordinator
URL: http://www.cast.uark.edu/other/nps/nagpra **Telnet:** www.cast.uark.edu Login: nadb Password: nadb **Modem:** (501)575-2021 **Description:** The Native Graves Protection and Repatriation Act (NAGPRA) database contains congressional reports, proposed regulations, Review Committee activities, and Federal Register notices of Completion of Inventory and Intent to Repatriate. A directory of NAGPRA contacts for federally recognized Indian tribes, Native Alaskan villages and corporations, and Native Hawaiian organizations and a directory of NAGPRA contacts for federal agencies are available in text files. NAGPRA also includes information about permits issued for archeological and paleontological survey and excavation on federal and Indian lands under the American Antiquities Act of 1906. Data Providers: U.S. National Parks Service and the U.S. Department of the Interior. Main Files: Legal Mandates; Notices; Review Committee. Very comprehensive coverage of the Act. Not easily searchable except through WAIS or Alta Vista. On November 16, 1990 President George Bush signed into law the Native American Graves Protection and Repatriation Act, hereafter referred to as the Act. **Update frequency:** Regularly. **Fees:** Free.

★2138★
NativeWeb
David Cole, Contact
URL: http://www.nativeweb.org/ **Description:** NativeWeb contains cultural information, points of contact, a variety of indexes and hotlinks pertaining to indigenous peoples and their presence on the Net. NativeWeb's stated vision embraces ancient teachings and modern technology in order to provide a cyber-community for Earth's indigenous peoples. Main Files: Resource Center; Community Center (Listings, Message Boards, Feedback); NativeWeb News and Announcement Lists; Resource Center (Subject Index, Nations Index, Geographic Region, Index, Document Search, Submit a Web Site, New Sites this Week, Abay Yala Net, Law and Legal Issues); Community Center (Message Boards, Events, Announcements, Job Listings, E-mail Lists and Archives, News Sources); General Site Info (NativeWeb-An Internet Community, What's New, History, Awards, Volunteers, Contacting NatvieWeb, Personalize NativeWeb, Statistics); and Ongoing Projects and Sites by NativeWeb Collective Members (A Line in the Sand, Karen Strom's Native America Resources, Nevada Indian Environmental Coalition, SAIIC, Story Telling Site, Native American News, Native Events Calendar). Related Mailing Lists: NativeWeb. Subscribe by sending a message to listserv@thecity.sfsu.edu with "subscribe nativeweb your name" in the body. **Update frequency:** As needed. **Fees:** Free.

★2139★
Oklahoma NativeVoices Project
University of Kansas
Academic Computing Services
Lawrence, KS
Al Webster
URL: http://kuhttp.cc.ukans.edu/marc/language/webster/webster.html **Description:** With only one native speaker of Wyandotte and a handful of fluent speakers of Osage, Native American languages are in danger of extinction. The Oklahoma NativeVoices Project is in the process of preserving these languages by recording native speakers and making the recordings available (in Cherokee, Wyandotte, Choctaw, and Apache languages). Main Files: Osage; Cherokee; Wyandotte; Choctaw; Ft. Sill Apache; About the sound files; Overview–Oklahoma NativeVoices Project. High technology helps preserve dying languages for posterity. What a great application of the Web! You'll want more, and there isn't much there yet. I'm committed to helping Indian tribes & nations preserve their languages, mainly through my knowledge of computer & communication technology. **Fees:** Free.

★2140★
Oneida Indian Nation
Dan Umstead, Contact

URL: http://one-web.org/oneida/ **Description:** Oneida means the "People of the Standing Stone" and the Oneida Indian Nation was one of the original members of the Iroquois Confederacy. This site offers an introduction to the Nation, which includes information on the overall culture, as well as covering the topics of economic sovereignty, cultural rebirth, and mind, body, and spiritual issues. The site holds the text of press releases as well as a few audio clips. It also points to related links. Main Files: Introduction; News from the Oneida Indian Nation; Cultural and Historical Information; A Sovereign Nation Police Force; Economic Enterprises; Destination Oneida Nation; Information Links. Crisp layout; not too many gifs; audio files give samples of words in the Oneida language. Compelling historical pages document the little-known role of the Oneidas in the birth of the United States. Searching is not available, but this well-designed site is easy to navigate. **Update frequency:** As needed. **Fees:** Free.

★2141★
The People's Homepage
Concentric Network Corporation   Ph: (408)342-2800
10590 N. Tantau Ave.   Free: 800-939-4262
Cupertino, CA 95014   Fax: (408)342-2810
Nancy Thomas

URL: http://www.cris.com/nlthomas/ **Description:** These pages are dedicated to spreading this history, knowledge and culture of Native American peoples. Information ranges from legal documents to anecdotal stories. Includes Pow Wow information events and updates. Main Files: The People's Paths Message Center; Paths to Changing News; Paths to News Articles; Paths to Articles; Paths to Political and Legal Issues; Poems and Prose by Larry Kibby; Paths to Literature, Stories and Poems!; Paths to History; Pow Wow Information, Events, Updates! An interesting and entertaining site for non-natives as well as natives. It does not focus in depth on any particular people. This Internet site was created in the hope that all people, no matter what their own culture, may be able to find a bit of information that might be helpful in the understanding of American Indian Culture and other Native Cultures from all over our Mother which is called earth! **Fees:** Free.

★2142★
Raven's Tsa-La-Gi Page
California State University, San Marcos
San Marcos, CA 92096-0001   Ph: (619)750-4000
URL:
http://www.csusm.edu/public/raven/cherokee.dir/cherokee.html
Description: Have you ever wanted to learn the Cherokee language? This page offers several images of the Cherokee alphabet and tidbits of information concerning the Ani-Yunwiya (the "people"). Main Files: The People; alphabet; here for the first 19, the first column; here are the next 14, the second column; Small Cherokee Lexicon. **Update frequency:** As needed. **Fees:** Free.

★2143★
Tribal Voice

URL: http://www.tribal.com **Description:** Provides access to the Pow Wow White Pages and a variety of chat groups devoted to Native American affairs. Provides schedule of events, including concerts, theater productions, television programs and movies, educational events, seminars and conferences, festivals, and trade shows.

Alaska Natives

★2144★
Institute of American Indian and Alaska Native Culture and Arts Development
Box 20007
Santa Fe, NM 87504-7634
Ph: (505)988-6423
Fax: (505)986-5509
Allen Schwartz, Dir.
Founded: 1962 **Research Activities and Fields:** American Indian culture, history, and fine arts.

★2145★
National Indian Policy Center
2021 K St., NW, Ste. 211
Washington, DC 20006
Ph: (202)973-7667
Fax: (202)973-7686
William Gelles, Interim Dir.
Founded: 1990 **Research Activities and Fields:** Indian issues, including public policy of concern to Native Americans and Alaska Natives; employment and training programs for urban Native Americans; and labor market experience of Indian youth.

★2146★
U.S. Department of Health and Human Services
Indian Health Service
Office of Planning, Evaluation, and Legislation
Division of Program Statistics
Twinbrook Metro Plaza
12300 Twinbrook Pkwy., Ste. 450
Rockville, MD 20852
Ph: (301)443-1180
Fax: (301)443-1522
Anthony J. D'Angelo, Dir.
Founded: 1983 **Research Activities and Fields:** Main function is to satisfy the American Indian and Alaska Native health statistics information needs of its clients. The Division manages a number of information systems that provide data for measuring the health status of the American Indian and Alaska Native population and appraising IHS program activities. Division's primary duty is to serve IHS management, but it also has numerous dealings with other government agencies, government contractors, academia, researchers, the media, and the general public. Division is responsible for: vital events statistics, patient care statistics, and population statistics. In addition to providing statistical data, Division also provides statistical advice on analyzing the data. **Publications:** Indian health status reports, occasionally; Trends in Indian Health, annually; Regional Differences in Indian Health, annually.

Tribal Communities

Alaska

★2147★
Native Village of Akhiok
Box 5030
Akhiok, AK 99615
Ph: (907)836-2229
Fax: (907)836-2209
BIA Area Office: Juneau. **BIA Agency:** Anchorage.

★2148★
Akiachak Native Community
PO Box 70
Akiachak, AK 99551
Ph: (907)825-4626
Fax: (907)825-4029
BIA Area Office: Juneau. **BIA Agency:** Bethel.

★2149★
Akiak Native Community
PO Box 52165
Akiak, AK 99552
Ph: (907)765-7112
BIA Area Office: Juneau. **BIA Agency:** Bethel.

★2150★
Native Village of Akutan
PO Box 89
Akutan, AK 99553
Ph: (907)698-2228
Fax: (907)698-2301
BIA Area Office: Juneau. **BIA Agency:** Anchorage.

★2151★
Village of Alakanuk
PO Box 167
Alakanuk, AK 99554
Ph: (907)238-3313
BIA Area Office: Juneau. **BIA Agency:** Bethel.

★2152★
Alatna Village
General Delivery
Alatna, AK 99720
Ph: (907)968-2241
BIA Area Office: Juneau. **BIA Agency:** Fairbanks.

★2153★
Native Village of Aleknagik
PO Box 115
Aleknagik, AK 99555   Ph: (907)842-2229
BIA Area Office: Juneau. **BIA Agency:** Anchorage.

★2154★
Allakaket Village
PO Box 30
Allakaket, AK 99720   Ph: (907)968-2241
BIA Area Office: Juneau. **BIA Agency:** Fairbanks.

★2155★
Native Village of Ambler
PO Box 47
Ambler, AK 99786   Ph: (907)445-2181
BIA Area Office: Juneau. **BIA Agency:** Nome.

★2156★
Village of Anaktuvuk Pass
General Delivery
Anaktuvuk Pass, AK 99721   Ph: (907)661-3113
BIA Area Office: Juneau. **BIA Agency:** Fairbanks.

★2157★
Ugashik Village
909 Chugach Way
Anchorage, AK 99503
BIA Area Office: Juneau. **BIA Agency:** Anchorage.

★2158★
Village of Kanatak
c/o Becharof Corp.
1577 C St. Plz., Ste. 304   Ph: (907)263-9820
Anchorage, AK 99501   Fax: (907)274-3721
BIA Area Office: Juneau. **BIA Agency:** Anchorage.

★2159★
Angoon Community Association
PO Box 188   Ph: (907)788-3411
Angoon, AK 99820   Fax: (907)788-3821
BIA Area Office: Juneau. **BIA Agency:** Southeast.

★2160★
Native Village of Napamute
PO Box 96
Aniak, AK 99557   Ph: (907)543-2726
BIA Area Office: Juneau.

★2161★
Village of Aniak
PO Box 176
Aniak, AK 99557   Ph: (907)675-4349
BIA Area Office: Juneau. **BIA Agency:** Bethel.

★2162★
Anvik Village
General Delivery
Anvik, AK 99558   Ph: (907)663-6335
BIA Area Office: Juneau. **BIA Agency:** Fairbanks.

★2163★
Arctic Village
PO Box 22059   Ph: (907)587-5328
Arctic Village, AK 99722   Fax: (907)587-5438
BIA Area Office: Juneau. **BIA Agency:** Fairbanks.

★2164★
Native Village of Atka
PO Box 47030   Ph: (907)839-2233
Atka, AK 99574   Fax: (907)839-2234
BIA Area Office: Juneau. **BIA Agency:** Anchorage.

★2165★
Village of Atmautluak
PO Box AH   Ph: (907)553-5610
Atmautluak, AK 99559   Fax: (907)553-5610
BIA Area Office: Juneau. **BIA Agency:** Bethel.

★2166★
Atqasuk Village
General Delivery
Barrow, AK 99723
BIA Area Office: Juneau. **BIA Agency:** Fairbanks.

★2167★
Inupiat Community of Arctic Slope
PO Box 1232
Barrow, AK 99723   Ph: (907)825-6907
BIA Area Office: Juneau. **BIA Agency:** Fairbanks.

★2168★
Native Village of Barrow
Box 1139
Barrow, AK 99723   Ph: (907)852-4411
BIA Area Office: Juneau. **BIA Agency:** Fairbanks.

★2169★
Beaver Village
PO Box 24029   Ph: (907)628-6126
Beaver, AK 99724   Fax: (907)628-6815
BIA Area Office: Juneau. **BIA Agency:** Fairbanks.

★2170★
Orutsararmuit Native Council
835 Ridgecrest Dr.
PO Box 927   Ph: (907)543-2608
Bethel, AK 99559   Fax: (907)543-2639
BIA Area Office: Juneau. **BIA Agency:** Bethel.

★2171★
Native Village of Brevig Mission
PO Box 65   Ph: (907)642-4301
Brevig Mission, AK 99785   Fax: (907)642-2099
BIA Area Office: Juneau. **BIA Agency:** Nome.

★2172★
Native Village of Buckland
PO Box 67   Ph: (907)494-2171
Buckland, AK 99727   Fax: (907)494-2149
BIA Area Office: Juneau. **BIA Agency:** Nome.

★2173★
Native Village of Cantwell
PO Box 94
Cantwell, AK 99729   Ph: (907)768-2151
BIA Area Office: Juneau. **BIA Agency:** Anchorage.

★2174★
Chalkyitsik Village
PO Box 57   Ph: (907)848-8117
Chalkyitsik, AK 99788   Fax: (907)848-8986
BIA Area Office: Juneau. **BIA Agency:** Fairbanks.

★2175★
Village of Chefornak
PO Box 29
Chefornak, AK 99561   Ph: (907)867-8850
BIA Area Office: Juneau. **BIA Agency:** Bethel.

★2176★
Native Village of Chenega
PO Box 8079   Ph: (907)573-5132
Chenega Bay, AK 99574   Fax: (907)573-5120
BIA Area Office: Juneau. **BIA Agency:** Anchorage.

★2177★
Chevak Native Village
PO Box 5514
Chevak, AK 99563   Ph: (907)858-7428
BIA Area Office: Juneau. **BIA Agency:** Bethel.

★2178★
Native Village of Chickaloon
PO Box 1105
Chickaloon, AK 99674   Ph: (907)746-0505
BIA Area Office: Juneau. **BIA Agency:** Anchorage.

★2179★
Native Village of Chignik
PO Box 11   Ph: (907)749-2285
Chignik, AK 99564   Fax: (907)749-2550
BIA Area Office: Juneau. **BIA Agency:** Anchorage.

★2180★
Native Village of Chignik Lagoon
PO Box 57   Ph: (907)840-2206
Chignik Lagoon, AK 99565   Fax: (907)840-2281
BIA Area Office: Juneau. **BIA Agency:** Anchorage.

★2181★
Chignik Lake Village
PO Box 33
Chignik Lake, AK 99548   Ph: (907)845-2122
BIA Area Office: Juneau. **BIA Agency:** Anchorage.

★2182★
Chitina Traditional Village
PO Box 31
Chitina, AK 99566   Ph: (907)823-2215
BIA Area Office: Juneau. **BIA Agency:** Anchorage.

★2183★
Eklutna Native Village
26339 Eklutna Native Village Rd.   Ph: (907)688-6020
Chugiak, AK 99567   Fax: (907)688-6021
BIA Area Office: Juneau. **BIA Agency:** Anchorage.

★2184★
Chuloonawick Native Village
General Delivery
Chuloonawick, AK 99581   Ph: (907)949-1147
BIA Area Office: Juneau. **BIA Agency:** Bethel.

★2185★
Circle Native Community
General Delivery
Circle, AK 99733   Ph: (907)733-5498
BIA Area Office: Juneau. **BIA Agency:** Fairbanks.

★2186★
Village of Clark's Point
PO Box 16
Clarks Point, AK 99569   Ph: (907)236-1221
BIA Area Office: Juneau. **BIA Agency:** Anchorage.

★2187★
Native Village of Kluti-kaah
PO Box 68   Ph: (907)822-5541
Copper Center, AK 99573   Fax: (907)822-5130
BIA Area Office: Juneau. **BIA Agency:** Anchorage.

★2188★
Native Village of Eyak
PO Box 1388   Ph: (907)464-3622
Cordova, AK 99574   Fax: (907)424-5127
BIA Area Office: Juneau. **BIA Agency:** Anchorage.

★2189★
Craig Community Association
PO Box 828   Ph: (907)826-3857
Craig, AK 99821   Fax: (907)826-3980
BIA Area Office: Juneau. **BIA Agency:** Southeast.

★2190★
Native Village of Crooked Creek
PO Box 3   Ph: (907)432-2200
Crooked Creek, AK 99575   Fax: (907)432-2201
BIA Area Office: Juneau. **BIA Agency:** Bethel.

★2191★
Native Village of Deering
PO Box 89   Ph: (907)363-2138
Deering, AK 99736   Fax: (907)363-2148
BIA Area Office: Juneau. **BIA Agency:** Nome.

★2192★
Healy Lake Village
PO Box 667   Ph: (907)876-5018
Delta Junction, AK 99737   Fax: (907)876-5013
BIA Area Office: Juneau. **BIA Agency:** Fairbanks.

★2193★
Native Village of Dillingham
PO Box 216
Dillingham, AK 99576   Ph: (907)842-2384
BIA Area Office: Juneau. **BIA Agency:** Anchorage.

★2194★
Village of Eagle
PO Box 19   Ph: (907)547-2282
Eagle, AK 99738   Fax: (907)547-2338
BIA Area Office: Juneau. **BIA Agency:** Fairbanks.

★2195★
Native Village of Eek
PO Box 87   Ph: (907)536-5426
Eek, AK 99578   Fax: (907)536-5418
BIA Area Office: Juneau. **BIA Agency:** Bethel.

★2196★
Egegik Village
PO Box 189
Egegik, AK 99579   Ph: (907)233-2231
BIA Area Office: Juneau. **BIA Agency:** Anchorage.

★2197★
Native Village of Ekuk
General Delivery
Ekuk, AK 99576   Ph: (907)842-5937
BIA Area Office: Juneau. **BIA Agency:** Anchorage.

★2198★
Native Village of Elim
PO Box 39070   Ph: (907)890-3071
Elim, AK 99739   Fax: (907)890-3072
BIA Area Office: Juneau. **BIA Agency:** Nome.

★2199★
Emmonak Village
PO Box 126   Ph: (907)949-1720
Emmonak, AK 99581   Fax: (907)949-1926
BIA Area Office: Juneau. **BIA Agency:** Bethel.

★2200★
Evansville Village
PO Box 26025   Ph: (907)692-5005
Evansville, AK 99726   Fax: (907)692-5006
BIA Area Office: Juneau. **BIA Agency:** Fairbanks.

★2201★
Native Village of False Pass
PO Box 29   Ph: (907)548-2227
False Pass, AK 99583   Fax: (907)548-2256
BIA Area Office: Juneau. **BIA Agency:** Anchorage.

★2202★
Birch Creek Village
PO Box KBC   Ph: (907)221-2212
Fort Yukon, AK 99740   Fax: (907)221-2312
BIA Area Office: Juneau. **BIA Agency:** Fairbanks.

★2203★
Native Village of Ft. Yukon
Box 126
Fort Yukon, AK 99740   Ph: (907)662-2581
BIA Area Office: Juneau. **BIA Agency:** Fairbanks.

★2204★
Gulkana Village
PO Box 254   Ph: (907)822-3746
Gakona, AK 99586   Fax: (907)822-3976
BIA Area Office: Juneau. **BIA Agency:** Anchorage.

★2205★
Native Village of Chistochina
PO Box 241
Gakona, AK 99586   Ph: (907)822-3503
BIA Area Office: Juneau. **BIA Agency:** Anchorage.

★2206★
Native Village of Gakona
PO Box 124
Gakona, AK 99586   Ph: (907)822-3497
BIA Area Office: Juneau. **BIA Agency:** Anchorage.

★2207★
Galena Village
Box 244
Galena, AK 99741   Ph: (907)656-1711
BIA Area Office: Juneau. **BIA Agency:** Fairbanks.

★2208★
Native Village of Gambell
PO Box 99   Ph: (907)985-5346
Gambell, AK 99762   Fax: (907)985-5014
BIA Area Office: Juneau. **BIA Agency:** Nome.

★2209★
Native Village of Tazlina
PO Box 188   Ph: (907)822-5965
Glennallen, AK 99588   Fax: (907)822-3490
BIA Area Office: Juneau. **BIA Agency:** Anchorage.

★2210★
Chinik Eskimo Community (Golovin)
General Delivery   Ph: (907)779-3661
Golovin, AK 99762   Fax: (907)779-2214
BIA Area Office: Juneau. **BIA Agency:** Nome.

★2211★
Native Village of Goodnews Bay
PO Box 3
Goodnews Bay, AK 99589   Ph: (907)967-8929
BIA Area Office: Juneau. **BIA Agency:** Bethel.

★2212★
Organized Village of Grayling
General Delivery
Grayling, AK 99590   Ph: (907)453-5128
BIA Area Office: Juneau. **BIA Agency:** Fairbanks.

★2213★
Chilkoot Indian Association (Haines)
PO Box 490   Ph: (907)766-2810
Haines, AK 99827   Fax: (907)766-2328
BIA Area Office: Juneau. **BIA Agency:** Southeast.

★2214★
Holy Cross Village
PO Box 203
Holy Cross, AK 99602   Ph: (907)476-7134
BIA Area Office: Juneau. **BIA Agency:** Fairbanks.

★2215★
Hoonah Indian Association
PO Box 402   Ph: (907)945-3220
Hoonah, AK 99829   Fax: (907)945-3449
BIA Area Office: Juneau. **BIA Agency:** Southeast.

★2216★
Native Village of Hooper Bay
PO Box 41   Ph: (907)758-4915
Hooper Bay, AK 99604   Fax: (907)758-4066
BIA Area Office: Juneau. **BIA Agency:** Bethel.

★2217★
Native Village of Piamuit
General Delivery
Hooper Bay, AK 99604   Ph: (907)758-4420
BIA Area Office: Juneau. **BIA Agency:** Bethel.

★2218★
Hughes Village
PO Box 45029   Ph: (907)889-2239
Hughes, AK 99745   Fax: (907)889-2252
BIA Area Office: Juneau. **BIA Agency:** Fairbanks.

★2219★
Huslia Village
PO Box 32
Huslia, AK 99746   Ph: (907)829-2202
BIA Area Office: Juneau. **BIA Agency:** Fairbanks.

★2220★
Hydaburg Cooperative Association
PO Box 305   Ph: (907)285-3761
Hydaburg, AK 99922   Fax: (907)285-3667
BIA Area Office: Juneau. **BIA Agency:** Southeast.

★2221★
Igiugig Village Center
PO Box 4008
Igiugig, AK 99613   Ph: (907)533-3211
BIA Area Office: Juneau. **BIA Agency:** Anchorage.

★2222★
Native Village of Iliamna
PO Box 286
Iliamna, AK 99606   Ph: (907)571-1246
BIA Area Office: Juneau. **BIA Agency:** Anchorage.

★2223★
Ivanoff Bay Village
PO Box KIB   Ph: (907)699-2204
Ivanoff Bay, AK 99695   Fax: (907)669-2207
BIA Area Office: Juneau. **BIA Agency:** Anchorage.

★2224★
Central Council of Tlingit and Haida Tribe of Alaska
320 W. Willoughby Ave., Ste. 300   Ph: (907)586-1432
Juneau, AK 99801   Fax: (907)586-8970
BIA Area Office: Juneau. **BIA Agency:** Fairbanks.

★2225★
Douglas Indian Association
PO Box 20478
Juneau, AK 99802   Ph: (907)463-5219
BIA Area Office: Juneau. **BIA Agency:** Southeast.

★2226★
Organized Village of Kake
PO Box 316
Kake, AK 99830-0316   Ph: (907)785-6471
BIA Area Office: Juneau. **BIA Agency:** Southeast.

★2227★
Kaktovik Village
PO Box 8
Kaktovik, AK 99607   Ph: (907)640-6120
BIA Area Office: Juneau. **BIA Agency:** Fairbanks.

★2228★
Village of Kalskag
General Delivery
Kalskag, AK 99607   Ph: (907)471-2218
BIA Area Office: Juneau. **BIA Agency:** Bethel.

★2229★
Village of Kaltag
PO Box 9
Kaltag, AK 99748   Ph: (907)534-2230
BIA Area Office: Juneau. **BIA Agency:** Nome.

★2230★
Organized Village of Kasaan
One Coppercrest Dr.   Ph: (907)542-2214
Kasaan, AK 99924   Fax: (907)542-2223
BIA Area Office: Juneau. **BIA Agency:** Southeast.

★2231★
Native Village of Kasigluk
PO Box 19
Kasigluk, AK 99609   Ph: (907)477-6927
BIA Area Office: Juneau. **BIA Agency:** Bethel.

★2232★
Kenaitze Indian Tribe
PO Box 988
Kenai, AK 99611   Ph: (907)283-3633
BIA Area Office: Juneau. **BIA Agency:** Anchorage.

★2233★
Native Village of Salamatof
PO Box 2682
Kenai, AK 99611   Ph: (907)283-7864
BIA Area Office: Juneau. **BIA Agency:** Anchorage.

★2234★
Ketchikan Indian Corporation
429 Deermount Ave.
Ketchikan, AK 99901   Ph: (907)225-5158
BIA Area Office: Juneau. **BIA Agency:** Southeast.

★2235★
Organized Village of Saxman
Rte. 2, Box 2
Ketchikan, AK 99901   Ph: (907)225-4166
BIA Area Office: Juneau. **BIA Agency:** Southeast.

★2236★
Native Village of Kiana
PO Box 69
Kiana, AK 99749   Ph: (907)475-2109
BIA Area Office: Juneau. **BIA Agency:** Nome.

★2237★
Agdaagux Tribe of King Cove
PO Box 18   Ph: (907)497-2312
King Cove, AK 99612   Fax: (907)497-2444

★2238★
Native Village of Belkofski
PO Box 57   Ph: (907)497-2304
King Cove, AK 99612   Fax: (907)467-2444
BIA Area Office: Juneau. **BIA Agency:** Anchorage.

★2239★
Native Village of Kipnuk
PO Box 57   Ph: (907)896-5515
Kipnuk, AK 99614   Fax: (907)896-5240
BIA Area Office: Juneau. **BIA Agency:** Bethel.

★2240★
Native Village of Kivalina
PO Box 50051
Kivalina, AK 99750   Ph: (907)645-2153
BIA Area Office: Juneau. **BIA Agency:** Nome.

★2241★
Klawock Cooperative Association
PO Box 112
Klawock, AK 99925   Ph: (907)755-2265
BIA Area Office: Juneau. **BIA Agency:** Southeast.

★2242★
Chilkat Indian Village (Klukwan)
PO Box 210   Ph: (907)767-5505
Klukwan, AK 99827-0210   Fax: (907)767-5515
BIA Area Office: Juneau. **BIA Agency:** Southeast.

★2243★
Native Village of Kobuk
General Delivery
Kobuk, AK 99751   Ph: (907)948-2214
BIA Area Office: Juneau. **BIA Agency:** Nome.

★2244★
Shoonaq' Tribe of Kodiak
PO Box 1974
Kodiak, AK 99615   Ph: (907)486-4449
BIA Area Office: Juneau.

★2245★
Kokhanok Village
PO Box 1007   Ph: (907)282-2202
Kokhanok, AK 99606   Fax: (907)282-2202
BIA Area Office: Juneau. **BIA Agency:** Anchorage.

★2246★
Koliganek Village
PO Box 5057   Ph: (907)596-3434
Koliganek, AK 99576   Fax: (907)596-3462
BIA Area Office: Juneau. **BIA Agency:** Anchorage.

★2247★
Native Villiage of Kongiganak
PO Box 5069   Ph: (907)557-5226
Kongiganak, AK 99559   Fax: (907)557-5226
BIA Area Office: Juneau. **BIA Agency:** Bethel.

★2248★
Native Village of Bill Moore's Slough
PO Box 20037
Kotlik, AK 99620   Ph: (907)899-4712
BIA Area Office: Juneau. **BIA Agency:** Bethel.

★2249★
Native Village of Hamilton
PO Box 20130   Ph: (907)899-4313
Kotlik, AK 99620   Fax: (907)899-4826
BIA Area Office: Juneau. **BIA Agency:** Bethel.

★2250★
Village of Kotlik
PO Box 20096
Kotlik, AK 99620   Ph: (907)899-4326
BIA Area Office: Juneau. **BIA Agency:** Bethel.

★2251★
Native Village of Kotzebue
PO Box 296
Kotzebue, AK 99752   Ph: (907)442-3467
BIA Area Office: Juneau. **BIA Agency:** Nome.

★2252★
Native Village of Koyuk
PO Box 30   Ph: (907)963-3651
Koyuk, AK 99753   Fax: (907)963-2353
BIA Area Office: Juneau. **BIA Agency:** Nome.

★2253★
Organized Village of Kwethluk
PO Box 84   Ph: (907)757-6814
Kwethluk, AK 99621   Fax: (907)757-6328
BIA Area Office: Juneau. **BIA Agency:** Bethel.

★2254★
Native Village of Kwigillingok
PO Box 49
Kwigillingok, AK 99622   Ph: (907)588-8114
BIA Area Office: Juneau. **BIA Agency:** Bethel.

★2255★
Native Village of Larsen Bay
PO Box 35
Larsen Bay, AK 99624   Ph: (907)847-2207
BIA Area Office: Juneau. **BIA Agency:** Anchorage.

★2256★
Levelock Village
Box 70   Ph: (907)287-3030
Levelock, AK 99625   Fax: (907)287-3032
BIA Area Office: Juneau. **BIA Agency:** Anchorage.

★2257★
Lime Village
PO Box LVD   Ph: (907)526-5112
Lime Village, AK 99627   Fax: (907)526-5225
BIA Area Office: Juneau. **BIA Agency:** Bethel.

★2258★
Village of Lower Kalskag
PO Box 27
Lower Kalskag, AK 99626   Ph: (907)471-2307
BIA Area Office: Juneau. **BIA Agency:** Bethel.

★2259★
Manley Hot Springs Village
General Delivery   Ph: (907)672-3177
Manley Hot Springs, AK 99756   Fax: (907)672-3200
BIA Area Office: Juneau. **BIA Agency:** Fairbanks.

★2260★
Manokotak Village
PO Box 169
Manokotak, AK 99628   Ph: (907)289-1027
BIA Area Office: Juneau. **BIA Agency:** Anchorage.

★2261★
Native Village of Marshall
PO Box 10   Ph: (907)679-6302
Marshall, AK 99585   Fax: (907)679-6187
BIA Area Office: Juneau. **BIA Agency:** Bethel.

★2262★
McGrath Native Village
PO Box 134
McGrath, AK 99627   Ph: (907)524-3024
BIA Area Office: Juneau. **BIA Agency:** Bethel.

★2263★
Metlakatla Indian Community
PO Box 8   Ph: (907)886-4441
Metlakatla, AK 99926   Fax: (907)886-7997
BIA Area Office: Portland. **BIA Agency:** Metlakatla.

★2264★
Minto Village
PO Box 26   Ph: (907)798-7181
Minto, AK 99758   Fax: (907)798-7556
BIA Area Office: Juneau. **BIA Agency:** Fairbanks.

★2265★
Naknek Native Village
PO Box 106   Ph: (907)246-4277
Naknek, AK 99633   Fax: (907)246-4419
BIA Area Office: Juneau. **BIA Agency:** Anchorage.

★2266★
Native Village of Napakiak
General Delivery
Napakiak, AK 99634   Ph: (907)589-2227
BIA Area Office: Juneau. **BIA Agency:** Bethel.

★2267★
Native Village of Nanwalek
PO Box 8028   Ph: (907)281-9219
Napakiak via Homer, AK 99603   Fax: (907)281-2252
BIA Area Office: Juneau. **BIA Agency:** Anchorage.

★2268★
Napaskiak Native Village
PO Box 6009   Ph: (907)737-7364
Napaskiak, AK 99559   Fax: (907)737-7039
BIA Area Office: Juneau. **BIA Agency:** Bethel.

★2269★
Native Village of Nelson Lagoon
PO Box 12-NLG   Ph: (907)989-2234
Nelson Lagoon, AK 99571   Fax: (907)989-2233
BIA Area Office: Juneau. **BIA Agency:** Anchorage.

★2270★
Nenana Native Association
PO Box 356
Nenana, AK 99760   Ph: (907)832-5662
BIA Area Office: Juneau. **BIA Agency:** Fairbanks.

★2271★
New Stuyahok Village
General Delivery   Ph: (907)693-3173
New Stuyahok, AK 99636   Fax: (907)693-3148
BIA Area Office: Juneau. **BIA Agency:** Anchorage.

★2272★
Newhalen Village
PO Box 165   Ph: (907)571-1410
Newhalen via Iliamna, AK 99606   Fax: (907)571-1537
BIA Area Office: Juneau. **BIA Agency:** Anchorage.

★2273★
Newtok Village
PO Box WWT
Newtok, AK 99559　　　　　　　Ph: (907)237-2314
BIA Area Office: Juneau. **BIA Agency:** Bethel.

★2274★
Native Village of Nightmute
General Delivery
Nightmute, AK 99690　　　　　　Ph: (907)647-6213
BIA Area Office: Juneau. **BIA Agency:** Bethel.

★2275★
Umkumiut Native Village
General Delivery
Nightmute, AK 99690　　　　　　Ph: (907)647-6213
BIA Area Office: Juneau. **BIA Agency:** Bethel.

★2276★
Nickolai Village
Nickolai Rural Branch
Nikolai, AK 99691　　　　　　　Ph: (907)524-2226
BIA Area Office: Juneau. **BIA Agency:** Bethel.

★2277★
Native Village of Nikolski
PO Box 109　　　　　　　　　　Ph: (907)576-2225
Nikolski, AK 99638　　　　　　　Fax: (907)576-2205
BIA Area Office: Juneau. **BIA Agency:** Anchorage.

★2278★
Native Village of Noatak
PO Box 89
Noatak, AK 99761　　　　　　　Ph: (907)485-2173
BIA Area Office: Juneau. **BIA Agency:** Nome.

★2279★
King Island Native Community
PO Box 992
Nome, AK 99762　　　　　　　　Ph: (907)443-5494
BIA Area Office: Juneau. **BIA Agency:** Nome.

★2280★
Nome Eskimo Community
PO Box 1090　　　　　　　　　Ph: (907)443-2246
Nome, AK 99762　　　　　　　　Fax: (907)443-3539
BIA Area Office: Juneau. **BIA Agency:** Nome.

★2281★
Nondalton Village
PO Box 49　　　　　　　　　　Ph: (907)294-2254
Nondalton, AK 99640　　　　　　Fax: (907)294-2254
BIA Area Office: Juneau. **BIA Agency:** Anchorage.

★2282★
Noorvik Native Communities
PO Box 71　　　　　　　　　　Ph: (907)636-2144
Noorvik, AK 99763　　　　　　　Fax: (907)636-2202
BIA Area Office: Juneau. **BIA Agency:** Nome.

★2283★
Northway Village
PO Box 516
Northway, AK 99764　　　　　　Ph: (907)778-2271
BIA Area Office: Juneau. **BIA Agency:** Fairbanks.

★2284★
Native Village of Nuiqsut
General Delivery
Nuiqsut, AK 99723　　　　　　　Ph: (907)480-6714
BIA Area Office: Juneau. **BIA Agency:** Fairbanks.

★2285★
Native Village of Nunapitchuk
PO Box 130
Nunapitchuk, AK 99641　　　　　Ph: (907)543-5705
BIA Area Office: Juneau. **BIA Agency:** Bethel.

★2286★
Village of Old Harbor
PO Box 62
Old Harbor, AK 99643　　　　　Ph: (907)286-2215
BIA Area Office: Juneau. **BIA Agency:** Anchorage.

★2287★
Oscarville Traditional Council
PO Box 6119　　　　　　　　　Ph: (907)737-7591
Oscarville, AK 99559　　　　　　Fax: (907)737-7211
BIA Area Office: Juneau. **BIA Agency:** Bethel.

★2288★
Native Village of Ouzinkie
PO Box 130　　　　　　　　　　Ph: (907)680-2259
Ouzinkie, AK 99644　　　　　　　Fax: (907)680-2214
BIA Area Office: Juneau. **BIA Agency:** Anchorage.

★2289★
Pedro Bay Village
PO Box 4720　　　　　　　　　Ph: (907)850-2225
Pedro Bay, AK 99647　　　　　　Fax: (907)850-2227
BIA Area Office: Juneau. **BIA Agency:** Anchorage.

★2290★
Native Village of Perryville
PO Box 101　　　　　　　　　　Ph: (907)853-2203
Perryville, AK 99648　　　　　　Fax: (907)853-2230
BIA Area Office: Juneau. **BIA Agency:** Anchorage.

★2291★
Petersburg Indian Association
PO Box 1418　　　　　　　　　Ph: (907)772-3636
Petersburg, AK 99833　　　　　　Fax: (907)772-3637
BIA Area Office: Juneau. **BIA Agency:** Southeast.

★2292★
Native Village of Pilot Point
PO Box 449　　　　　　　　　　Ph: (907)797-2208
Pilot Point, AK 99649　　　　　　Fax: (907)797-2258
BIA Area Office: Juneau. **BIA Agency:** Anchorage.

★2293★
Pilot Station Traditional Council
PO Box 5040
Pilot Station, AK 99650　　　　　Ph: (907)549-3512
BIA Area Office: Juneau. **BIA Agency:** Bethel.

★2294★
Platinum Traditional Village
General Delivery
Platinum, AK 99651　　　　　　Ph: (907)979-8126
BIA Area Office: Juneau. **BIA Agency:** Bethel.

★2295★
Native Village of Point Hope
PO Box 91
Point Hope, AK 99766　　　　　Ph: (907)368-2453
BIA Area Office: Juneau. **BIA Agency:** Nome.

★2296★
Native Village of Point Lay
PO Box 101
Point Lay, AK 99759　　　　　　Ph: (907)833-2428
BIA Area Office: Juneau. **BIA Agency:** Fairbanks.

★2297★
Port Graham Village
PO Box PGV   Ph: (907)284-2227
Port Graham, AK 99603   Fax: (907)284-2222
BIA Area Office: Juneau. **BIA Agency:** Anchorage.

★2298★
Native Village of Port Heiden
PO Box 49007
Port Heiden, AK 99549   Ph: (907)837-2218
BIA Area Office: Juneau. **BIA Agency:** Anchorage.

★2299★
Native Village of Port Lions
PO Box 69   Ph: (907)454-2234
Port Lions, AK 99550   Fax: (907)454-2434
BIA Area Office: Juneau. **BIA Agency:** Anchorage.

★2300★
Portage Creek Village
c/o Choggiung
Portage Creek, AK 99576   Ph: (907)842-5218
BIA Area Office: Juneau. **BIA Agency:** Anchorage.

★2301★
Native Village of Kwinhagak
General Delivery   Ph: (907)556-8166
Quinhagak, AK 99655   Fax: (907)556-8166
BIA Area Office: Juneau. **BIA Agency:** Bethel.

★2302★
Rampart Village
PO Box 67029   Ph: (907)358-3312
Rampart, AK 99767   Fax: (907)348-3115
BIA Area Office: Juneau. **BIA Agency:** Fairbanks.

★2303★
Village of Red Devil
PO Box 5
Red Devil, AK 99656   Ph: (907)447-3225
BIA Area Office: Juneau. **BIA Agency:** Bethel.

★2304★
Native Village of Ruby
Box 28
Ruby, AK 99768   Ph: (907)468-4406
BIA Area Office: Juneau. **BIA Agency:** Fairbanks.

★2305★
Iqurmuit Tribe Russian Mission
PO Box 9   Ph: (907)584-5511
Russian Mission, AK 99657   Fax: (907)584-5511

★2306★
St. George Island Village
PO Box 940
Saint George Island, AK 99591 Ph: (907)859-2205
BIA Area Office: Juneau. **BIA Agency:** Anchorage.

★2307★
Qagun Tayagungin Tribe of Sand Point
Box 447   Ph: (907)383-3525
Sand Point, AK 99661   Fax: (907)383-5356

★2308★
Native Village of Savoonga
PO Box 129
Savoonga, AK 99769   Ph: (907)984-6414
BIA Area Office: Juneau. **BIA Agency:** Nome.

★2309★
Native Village of Scammon Bay
PO Box 126   Ph: (907)558-5113
Scammon Bay, AK 99662   Fax: (907)558-5626
BIA Area Office: Juneau. **BIA Agency:** Bethel.

★2310★
Native Village of Selawik
PO Box 59
Selawik, AK 99770   Ph: (907)484-2225
BIA Area Office: Juneau. **BIA Agency:** Nome.

★2311★
Seldovia Village Tribe
PO Drawer L   Ph: (907)234-7898
Seldovia, AK 99663   Fax: (907)234-7637
BIA Area Office: Juneau. **BIA Agency:** Bethel.

★2312★
Shageluk Native Village
General Delivery   Ph: (907)473-8239
Shageluk, AK 99665   Fax: (907)473-8239
BIA Area Office: Juneau. **BIA Agency:** Bethel.

★2313★
Native Village of Shaktoolik
PO Box 100   Ph: (907)955-3701
Shaktoolik, AK 99771   Fax: (907)955-2352
BIA Area Office: Juneau. **BIA Agency:** Nome.

★2314★
Native Village of Sheldon's Point
General Delivery
Sheldon Point, AK 99666   Ph: (907)498-4226
BIA Area Office: Juneau. **BIA Agency:** Bethel.

★2315★
Native Village of Shishmaref
PO Box 72110   Ph: (907)649-3821
Shishmaref, AK 99772   Fax: (907)647-3583
BIA Area Office: Juneau. **BIA Agency:** Nome.

★2316★
Native Village of Shungnak
PO Box 63
Shungnak, AK 99773   Ph: (907)437-2170
BIA Area Office: Juneau. **BIA Agency:** Nome.

★2317★
Sitka Tribe of Alaska
456 Katlia St.   Ph: (907)747-3207
Sitka, AK 99835   Fax: (907)747-4915
BIA Area Office: Juneau. **BIA Agency:** Southeast.

★2318★
Village of Sleetmute
PO Box 30
Sleetmute, AK 99668   Ph: (907)449-4223
BIA Area Office: Juneau. **BIA Agency:** Bethel.

★2319★
Native Village of Solomon
PO Box 243   Ph: (907)443-2844
Solomon, AK 99762   Fax: (907)443-5098
BIA Area Office: Juneau.

★2320★
South Naknek Village
PO Box 70106   Ph: (907)246-6566
South Naknek, AK 99670   Fax: (907)246-6565
BIA Area Office: Juneau. **BIA Agency:** Anchorage.

★2321★
Native Village of Algaaciq
PO Box 48   Ph: (907)438-2932
St. Mary's, AK 99658   Fax: (907)428-2932
BIA Area Office: Juneau. **BIA Agency:** Bethel.

★2322★
Native Village of Pitka's Point
PO Box 127   Ph: (907)438-2833
St. Mary's, AK 99658   Fax: (907)438-2569
BIA Area Office: Juneau. **BIA Agency:** Bethel.

★2323★
Native Village of St. Michael
PO Box 3   Ph: (907)923-3222
St. Michael, AK 99659   Fax: (907)923-3142
BIA Area Office: Juneau. **BIA Agency:** Nome.

★2324★
Aleut Community of St. Paul Island and St. George
PO Box 86   Ph: (907)546-2211
St. Paul Island, AK 99660   Fax: (907)546-2407
BIA Area Office: Juneau. **BIA Agency:** Anchorage.

★2325★
Stebbins Community Association
PO Box 71002   Ph: (907)934-3561
Stebbins, AK 99671   Fax: (907)934-3560
BIA Area Office: Juneau. **BIA Agency:** Nome.

★2326★
Village of Stoney River
PO Box SRV   Ph: (907)537-3209
Stoney River, AK 99557   Fax: (907)537-3236
BIA Area Office: Juneau.

★2327★
Takotna Village
PO Box TYC
Takotna, AK 99675   Ph: (907)298-2212
BIA Area Office: Juneau. **BIA Agency:** Bethel.

★2328★
Native Village of Tanacross Village
PO Box 76009   Ph: (907)883-5024
Tanacross, AK 99776   Fax: (907)883-4497
BIA Area Office: Juneau. **BIA Agency:** Bethel.

★2329★
Native Village of Tanana
PO Box 77093   Ph: (907)366-7160
Tanana, AK 99777   Fax: (907)366-7195
BIA Area Office: Juneau. **BIA Agency:** Fairbanks.

★2330★
Native Village of Tatitlek
PO Box 171
Tatitlek, AK 99677   Ph: (907)325-2311
BIA Area Office: Juneau. **BIA Agency:** Anchorage.

★2331★
Telida Village
General Delivery
Telida, AK 99629   Ph: (907)843-8115
BIA Area Office: Juneau. **BIA Agency:** Bethel.

★2332★
Native Village of Mary's Igloo
PO Box 572
Teller, AK 99778   Ph: (907)642-3731
BIA Area Office: Juneau.

★2333★
Native Village of Teller
PO Box 590   Ph: (907)642-3381
Teller, AK 99778   Fax: (907)642-4014
BIA Area Office: Juneau. **BIA Agency:** Nome.

★2334★
Native Village of Tetlin
PO Box TTL   Ph: (907)324-2130
Tetlin, AK 99780   Fax: (907)324-2131
BIA Area Office: Juneau. **BIA Agency:** Fairbanks.

★2335★
Traditional Village of Togiak
PO Box 209   Ph: (907)493-5920
Togiak, AK 99678   Fax: (907)493-5932
BIA Area Office: Juneau. **BIA Agency:** Anchorage.

★2336★
Tuluksak Native Community
PO Box 156
Tuluksak, AK 99679   Ph: (907)695-6828
BIA Area Office: Juneau. **BIA Agency:** Bethel.

★2337★
Native Village of Tuntutuliak
PO Box WTL   Ph: (907)256-2128
Tuntutuliak, AK 99680   Fax: (907)256-2441
BIA Area Office: Juneau. **BIA Agency:** Bethel.

★2338★
Native Village of Tununak
PO Box 77
Tununak, AK 99681   Ph: (907)652-6527
BIA Area Office: Juneau. **BIA Agency:** Bethel.

★2339★
Twin Hills Village
PO Box TWA   Ph: (907)525-4821
Twin Hills, AK 99576   Fax: (907)525-4820
BIA Area Office: Juneau. **BIA Agency:** Anchorage.

★2340★
Native Village of Tyonek
PO Box 82009   Ph: (907)583-2201
Tyonek, AK 99682-0009   Fax: (907)583-2442
BIA Area Office: Juneau. **BIA Agency:** Anchorage.

★2341★
Qawalangin Tribe of Unalaska
PO Box 334   Ph: (907)581-2920
Unalaska, AK 99685   Fax: (907)581-3644
BIA Area Office: Juneau. **BIA Agency:** Anchorage.

★2342★
Native Village of Venetie
PO Box 99   Ph: (907)849-8165
Venetie, AK 99781   Fax: (907)849-8513
BIA Area Office: Juneau. **BIA Agency:** Fairbanks.

★2343★
Village of Wainwright
PO Box 184
Wainwright, AK 99782   Ph: (907)763-2726
BIA Area Office: Juneau. **BIA Agency:** Fairbanks.

★2344★
Native Village of Wales
PO Box 549   Ph: (907)664-3511
Wales, AK 99783   Fax: (907)664-3641
BIA Area Office: Juneau. **BIA Agency:** Nome.

★2345★
Knik Village
PO Box 871565   Ph: (907)373-2161
Wasilla, AK 99687   Fax: (907)373-2161
BIA Area Office: Juneau. **BIA Agency:** Anchorage.

★2346★
Native Village of White Mountain
PO Box 82
White Mountain, AK 99784   Ph: (907)638-3651
BIA Area Office: Juneau. **BIA Agency:** Nome.

★2347★
Wrangell Cooperative Association
PO Box 868   Ph: (907)874-3747
Wrangell, AK 99929   Fax: (907)874-3482
BIA Area Office: Juneau. **BIA Agency:** Southeast.

★2348★
Native Village of Yakutat
PO Box 418   Ph: (907)784-3932
Yakutat, AK 99689   Fax: (907)784-3595
BIA Area Office: Juneau. **BIA Agency:** Southeast.

National Organizations

★2349★
National Native American AIDS Prevention
134 Linden St.
Oakland, CA 94607   Ph: (510)444-2051
Description: Network of concerned Native people. Works to stop the spread of HIV and related diseases, including sexually transmitted disease and tuberculosis, among American Indians, Alaska Natives, and Native Hawaiians by improving their health status through empowerment and self determination. Serves as a resource to Native communities and to support community efforts by providing education and information services, thereby ehancing the physical, spiritual, and economic health of Native people. Sponsors educational programs. Maintains speakers' bureau. Compiles statistics. **Founded:** 1987. **Publications:** Season; Newsletter, quarterly

Regional, State/Provincial, & Local Organizations

★2350★
Alaska Federation of Natives
1577 C St., Ste. 100   Ph: (907)274-3611
Anchorage, AK 99501   Fax: (907)276-7989
Julie Kitka, Pres.
Description: Alaska Natives (Aleut, Eskimo, an d Indian) and regional and profit corporations. To act as lobbyist and advocate on behalf of villages, regional profit, and nonprofit native corporations on social, economic, political, and cultural issues; to provide technical assistance to these groups. Operates Alaska Native Sobriety Movement.

★2351★
Alaska Native Tourism Council
1577 C St. No. 304   Ph: (907)274-5400
Anchorage, AK 99501   Fax: (907)263-9971

★2352★
Bristol Bay Native Corp. Education Foundation
800 Cordova St.
Anchorage, AK 99501-3717

★2353★
Institute of Alaska Native Arts
PO Box 80583
Fairbanks, AK 99708   Ph: (907)456-7419
Caroline Atuk-Derrick, Exec.Dir.
Description: Seeks to provide opportunities for the development of Eskimo, Aleut, and Indian art and artists.

★2354★
World Eskimo-Indian Olympics
PO Box 72433
Fairbanks, AK 99701   Ph: (907)452-6646
Chris Anderson, Gen.Mgr.
Description: Seeks to perpetuate and preserve the Native Games of the Circumpolar North. Educates the public of its importance.

★2355★
Ahtna
PO Box 649   Ph: (907)822-3476
Glennallen, AK 99588   Fax: (907)822-3495
Roy S. Ewan, Pres.
Description: Athabascan Indians living in a Ahtna village in south central Alaska. Promotes the economic and social welfare of Ahtna regions. Works to protect traditional customs and regulate use of Ahtna lands.

★2356★
Alaska Native Sisterhood
PO Box 749
Haines, AK 99827-0749

★2357★
Maniilaq Association
PO Box 256
Kotzebue, AK 99752   Ph: (907)442-3311
Description: Tribal organization serving 11 Alaskan Eskimo villages ranging from 60 to 3000 in population. Works to: promote health and social welfare in the Northwest Arctic Borough region of Alaska; preserve and promote the Eskimo customs, arts, and language; advance education in all forms; stimulate economic activity and social understanding between natives and nonnatives. Maintains group home, senior citizen center, nursing wing, social rehabilitation center, and youth camp; manages Maniiaq Medical Center. Provides women's crisis program, prematernal home, and placement and children's services. Programs include: Adult Education; Agriculture; Counseling Services; Dental and Eye Care; Emergency Medical Services; Environmental Health Services; Health Aide Training; Health Education; Housing Improvement; Maternal-Child Health; Public Assistance; Public Health Nursing; Realty; Safety Education; Substance Abuse Treatment; Tribal Doctors; WIC. **Founded:** 1966. **Members:** 6, 500. **Regional Groups:** 4. **Local Groups:** 13. **Publications:** Maniilaq Directory, annual; Northwest Arctic NUNA Newsletter, 10/year; Annual Report

★2358★
Association of Interior Eskimos
PO Box 56062
North Pole, AK 99705   Ph: (907)488-6340
John L. Heffle Sr., Pres.
Description: Seeks to preserve and perpetuate the Eskimo culture and heritage.

★2359★
South East Alaska Indian Cultural Center
106 Metlakatla St.   Ph: (907)747-8061
Sitka, AK 99835   Fax: (907)747-5938
Kathie Wasserman, Exec.Dir.

Arizona

★2360★
Arizona American Eskimo Association
35406 N. 9th St.
Phoenix, AZ 85027-7418

Oklahoma

★2361★
American Eskimo Association, Oklahoma Chapter
3416 SE 104th
Moore, OK 73165   Ph: (405)794-6421
Dick Kortemeier, Exec. Officer.

Federal Government Agencies

★2362★
U.S. Department of Justice
Office of Justice Programs
American Indian and Alaska Native Program
Indiana Bldg.
633 Indiana Ave., NW
Washington, DC 20530   Ph: (202)616-9053
Norena Henry, Dir.

Federal Domestic Assistance Programs

★2363★
U.S. Department of Agriculture
Cooperative State Research, Education and
  Extension Service
Tribal Colleges Education Equity Grants
Higher Education Programs
Rm. 3433-S
Washington, DC 20250   Ph: (202)720-1973
Catalog Number: 10.221 **Objectives:** To enhance educational opportunities at the 29 Tribal Colleges designated as the 1994 Land-Grant Institutions by strengthening their teaching programs in the food and agricultural sciences in targeted need areas. **Applicant Eligibility:** Bay Mills Community College, Blackfeet Community College, Cheyenne River Community College, D-Q University, Dullknife Memorial College, Fond Du Lac Community College, Fort Belknap Community College, Fort Berthold Community College, Fort Peck Community College, LacCourte Orielles Ojibwa Community College, Little Big Horn Community College, Little Hoop Community College, Nebraska Indian Community College, Northwest Indian College, Oglala Lakota College, Salish Kootenai College, Sinte Gleska University, Sisseton Wahpeton Community College, Standing Rock College, Stonechild Community College, Turtle Mountain Community College, Navajo Community College, United Tribes Technical College, Southwest Indian Polytechnic Institute, Institute of American Indian and Alaska Native Culture and Arts Development, Crownpoint Institute of Technology, Haskell Indian Junior College, Leech Lake Tribal College, and College of the Monoamine Nation. **Types of Assistance:** Formula Grants. **Beneficiary Eligibility:** The 1994 Institutions-Bay Mills Community College, Blackfeet Community College, Cheyenne River Community College, D-Q University, dullknife Memorial College, Fond Du Lac Community College, Fort Belknap Community College, Fort Berthold Community College, Fort Peck Community College, LacCourte Orielles Ojibwa Community College, Little Big Horn Community College, Little Hoop Community College, Nebraska Indian Community College, Northwest Indian College, Oglala Lakota College, Salish Kootenai

College, Sinte Gleska University, Sisseton Wahpeton Community College, Standing Rock College, Stonechild Community College, Turtle Mountain Community College, Navajo Community College, United Tribes Technical College, Southwest Indian Polytechnic Institute, Institute of America Indian and Alaska Native Culture and Arts Development, Crownpoint Institute of Technology, Haskell Indian Junior College, Leech Lake Tribal College, and College of the Monoamine Nation.

★2364★
U.S. Department of Agriculture
Farm Service Agency
Indian Tribes and Tribal Corporation Loans
Loan Marketing Division
AG Box 0522
Washington, DC 20250   Ph: (202)720-1632
Catalog Number: 10.421. **Objectives:** To enable federally recognized Indian tribes and tribal corporations to acquire land within tribal reservations and Alaskan communities. **Applicant Eligibility:** Limited to any Indian tribe recognized by the Secretary of the Interior or tribal corporation established pursuant to the Indian Reorganization Act which does not have adequate uncommitted funds to acquire lands within the tribe's reservation or in a community in Alaska incorporated by the Secretary of the Interior pursuant to the Indian Reorganization Act. Must be unable to obtain sufficient credit elsewhere at reasonable rates and terms and must be able to show reasonable prospects of success as determined by an acceptable repayment plan and a satisfactory management plan for the land being acquired. **Types of Assistance:** Direct Loans; Guaranteed/Insured Loans. **Beneficiary Eligibility:** American Indian Tribe or tribal corporation recognized by the Secretary of the Interior.

★2365★
U.S. Department of Education
Office of Elementary and Secondary Education,
Alaska Native Educational Planning, Curriculum
  Development, Teacher Training, and Recruitment
  Program
School Improvement Programs
600 Independence Ave., SW
Washington, DC 20202   Ph: (202)260-1431
Catalog Number: 84.320 **Objectives:** To provide funds to Alaska Native organizations or educational entities to operate Alaska Native language, for the following purposes (1) The consolidation of existing educational plans, recommendations, and research into implementation methods and strategies to improve schooling for Alaska Natives; (2) the adoption and implementation of specific educational plans; (3) the development of curricula to address the needs of elementary and secondary Alaska Natives students, including innovative programs, pilots, and demonstration programs that reflect cultural diversity or contributions of Alaska Native people; (4) the development and implementation of preteacher training programs to ensure student teachers are prepared to address the cultural diversity and unique needs of Alaska Native students; (5) the development and implementations of teacher recruitment programs; and (6) the development and implementation of inservice teacher training programs to ensure teachers are better prepared to address the uniqueness of Alaska Native students. **Applicant Eligibility:** Alaska Native organizations or educational entities with experience in developing or operating Alaska Native programs or programs of instruction conducted in Alaska Native languages, or to partnerships involving Alaska Native organizations. **Types of Assistance:** Direct Payments for Specified Use. **Beneficiary Eligibility:** Elementary and secondary Alaska Native students will be the beneficiaries.

★2366★
U.S. Department of Education
Office of Elementary and Secondary Education
Alaska Native Home Based Education for Preschool
  Children (Alaska Native Education)
School Improvement Programs
600 Independence Ave., SW
Washington, DC 20202   Ph: (202)260-1431
Catalog Number: 84.321 **Objectives:** To provide funds to Alaska Native organizations or educational entities to implement home

instruction programs for Alaska Native preschool youngsters. The objective of such programs shall be to develop parents as educators for their children and assure active involvement of parents in the education of their children from the earliest ages. Home based education programs for Alaska Native children shall include the following: (1) Parent-infant programs for parents and their children 0-3 years old; (2) preschool programs for four and five years old; (3) training, education, and support programs to teach parents skills in observation, reading readiness, story telling and critical thinking; (4) continued research and development; and (5) a long-term follow-up and assessment program. **Applicant Eligibility:** Alaska Native organizations or educational entities with experience in developing or operating Alaska Native programs or programs of instruction conducted in Alaska Native languages, or to partnerships involving Alaska Native organizations. **Types of Assistance:** Direct Payments for Specified Use. **Beneficiary Eligibility:** Elementary and secondary Alaska Native students will be the beneficiaries.

★2367★
U.S. Department of Education
Office of Elementary and Secondary Education
Alaska Native Student Enrichment Program (Alaska Native Education)
School Improvement Programs
600 Independence Ave., SW
Washington, DC 20202   Ph: (202)260-1431

Catalog Number: 84.322 **Objectives:** To provide funds to Alaska Native organizations or educational entities with experience in developing or operating Alaska Native programs, for enrichment programs for Alaska Native students in the areas of science and mathematics education. The program will be designed to : (1) Prepare qualified students from rural areas who are preparing to enter village high schools to excel in sciences and mathematics; and (2) provide support services to the families of such students to benefit from the program. **Applicant Eligibility:** Alaska Native organizations or educational entities with experience in developing or operating Alaska Native languages, or to partnerships involving Alaska Native organizations. **Types of Assistance:** Direct Payments for Specified Use. **Beneficiary Eligibility:** Alaska Native students from rural areas preparing to enter a village high school.

★2368★
U.S. Department of Education
Office of Elementary and Secondary Education
Indian Education —Grants to Local Educational Agencies
Office of Indian Education
600 Independence Ave., SW
Washington, DC 20202   Ph: (202)260-1441

Catalog Number: 84.060. **Objectives:** Support local educational agencies in their efforts to reform elementary and secondary school programs that serve Indian students in order to ensure that programs are based on challenging state content standards and student performance standards that are used for all students, and are designed to assist Indian students meet those standards in reaching the National Education goals. **Applicant Eligibility:** Local educational agencies (LEAs) that enroll at least 10 Indian children or in which Indians constitute at least 50 percent of the total enrollment. These requirements do not apply to LEAs serving Indian children in Alaska, California, and Oklahoma or located on, or in proximity to, an Indian reservation. **Types of Assistance:** Formula Grants; Project Grants. **Beneficiary Eligibility:** Eligible Indian children enrolled in eligible local educational agencies, tribal schools, and BIA schools.

★2369★
U.S. Department of Health and Human Services
Administration on Aging
American Indian, Alaskan Native, & Native Hawaiian Programs
Special Programs for the Aging, Title VI—Part B Grants to Native Hawaiians
330 Independence Ave. SW
Washington, DC 20201   Ph: (202)619-2957

Catalog Number: 93.655. **Objectives:** To promote the delivery of supportive services, including nutrition services to older Indians, Alaskan Natives, and Native Hawaiians. Services are comparable to services provided under Title III of the Older Americans Act of 1965, as amended. **Applicant Eligibility:** Includes public or nonprofit organizations which serve Native Hawaiian Elders, which represent at least 50 Indians or Hawaiians 60 years of age or older. Applicants must document that they have or will have the ability to deliver social and nutrition services. **Types of Assistance:** Project grants. **Beneficiary Eligibility:** Indians or Native Hawaiians who are 60 years of age and older, and in the case of nutrition, their spouses.

★2370★
U.S. Department of Health and Human Services
Administration for Children and Families
Tribal Work Grants (Grants for Indian Tribes that Received JOBS Funds)
Office of the Director
Office of Family Assistance
Aerospace Bldg., 5th Fl.
370 L'Enfant Promenade, SW
Washington, DC 20447   Ph: (202)401-9275

Catalog Number: 93.594 **Objectives:** To allow Tribes to operate a program to make work activities available to members of the Indian tribe. **Applicant Eligibility:** An Indian tribe or Alaska Native organization that conducted a Job Opportunities and Basic Skills Training program in fiscal year 1995. **Types of Assistance:** Formula Grants. **Beneficiary Eligibility:** Members of the Indian tribe or Alaska Native organization.

★2371★
U.S. Department of Health and Human Services
Indian Health Service
Health Management Development Program
Division of Acquisitions and Grants
  Operations
2300 Twinbrook Pkwy., Ste. 100
Rockville, MD 20857   Ph: (301)443-5204

Catalog Number: 93.228. **Objectives:** To improve the quality of the health of American Indians and Native Alaskans by providing a full range of curative, preventive and rehabilitative health services; and to increase the capability of American Indians and Native Alaskans to assume operation of all or part of an existing Indian Health Service direct-operated health care program. **Applicant Eligibility:** Federally-recognized tribes and tribal organizations. **Types of Assistance:** Project Grants. **Beneficiary Eligibility:** Individuals who are members of an eligible applicant tribe, band, group, or village and who may be regarded as within the scope of the Indian health and medical service program and who are regarded as an Indian by the community in which he lives as evidenced by such factors as tribal membership, enrollment, residence on tax exempt land, ownership of restricted property, active participation in tribal affairs or other relevant factors in keeping with general Bureau of Indian Affairs practices in the jurisdiction.

★2372★
U.S. Department of Health and Human Services
Indian Health Service
Health Professions Preparatory Scholarship Program for Indians
12300 Twinbrook Pkwy., Ste. 100
Rockville, MD 20852   Ph: (301)443-0243
Wes Picciotti, Contact

Catalog Number: 93.971. **Objectives:** To make scholarships to American Indians and Alaska Natives for the purpose of completing compensatory pre-professional education to enable the recipient to qualify for enrollment or re-enrollment in a health professions school. **Applicant Eligibility:** Scholarship awards are made to individuals of American Indian or Native Alaskan descent, who have successfully completed high school education or high school equivalency and who have been accepted for enrollment in a compensatory, pre-professional general education course or curriculum. **Types of Assistance:** Project Grants. **Beneficiary Eligibility:** Individuals of American Indian or Native Alaskan descent.

★2373★
U.S. Department of Health and Human Services
Indian Health Service
Health Professions Scholarship Program
12300 Twinbrook Pkwy., Ste. 100
Rockville, MD 20852   Ph: (301)443-0243
Catalog Number: 93.972. **Objectives:** To promote service delivery improvement through research studies, and application of knowledge. **Applicant Eligibility:** Individuals of American Indian or Native Alaskan descent are given priority. Applicants for new awards: (1) must be accepted by an accredited U.S. educational institution for a full-time course of study leading to a degree in medicine, osteopathy, dentistry, or othe r participating health profession which is deemed necessary by the Indian Health Service; (2) be eligible for or hold an appointment as a Commissioned Officer in the Regular or Reserve Corps of the Public Health Service; or (3) be eligible for civilian service in the Indian Health Service. **Types of Assistance:** Project Grants.

★2374★
U.S. Department of Health and Human Services
Indian Health Service
Indian Health Service Research
12300 Twinbrook Pkwy., Ste. 100
Rockville, MD 20852   Ph: (301)443-5204
Catalog Number: 93.905. **Objectives:** To conduct research and developmental activities in areas of Indian health care which further the performance of health responsibilities of the Indian Health Service. **Applicant Eligibility:** There are two groups of eligible applicants: (1) Federally recognized Indian tribes and tribal organizations which are contracting with the Indian Health Service under the authority of the Indian Self-Determination and Education Assistance Act; and (2) Indian Health Service components, including Service units and area offices. /TYP Direct payment for specified use. **Beneficiary Eligibility:** American Indian Tribes and Alaska Natives.

★2375★
U.S. Department of Health and Human Services
Indian Health Services
Health Professions Recruitment Program for Indians
12300 Twinbrook Pkwy., Ste. 100
Rockville, MD 20852   Ph: (301)443-5204
Catalog Number: 93.970. **Objectives:** (1) To identify American Indians and Alaska Natives with a potential for education or training in the health professions, and to encourage and assist them to enroll in health or allied health professional schools (2) to increasae the number of nurses, nurse midwives, nurse practitioners and nurse anesthetists who deliver health care services to American Indians and Alaska Natives; and (3) to place health professional residents for short-term assignments at Indian Health Service facilities as a recruitment aid. **Applicant Eligibility:** Public or private nonprofit health or educational entities or Indian tribes or tribal organizations as specifically provided in legislative authority. **Types of Assistance:** Project Grants. **Beneficiary Eligibility:** Preference is given to applicants in the following order of priority: (1) Indian tribes; (2) tribal organizations; (3) urban Indian organizations and other Indian health organizations; or (4) other public or nonprofit health or educational entities.

★2376★
U.S. Department of Health and Human Services
Indian Health Services
Research and Demonstration Projects for Indian
  Health
Division of Acquisition and Grants
  Operations
12300 Twinbrook Pkwy., Ste. 100
Rockville, MD 20852   Ph: (301)443-5204
Catalog Number: 93.933. **Objectives:** To promote improved health care among American Indians and Alaska Natives through research studies, and demonstration projects. **Applicant Eligibility:** Federally recognized Indian tribes; tribal organizations; nonprofit intertribal organizations; nonprofit urban Indian organizations contracting with the Indian Health Service under Title V of the Indian Health Care Improvement Act; public or private nonprofit health and education entities; and State and local government health agencies. **Types of Assistance:** Project Grants. **Beneficiary Eligibility:** American Indians/Alaska Natives will be the ultimate beneficiaries of the funded projects either directly or indirectly depending upon the nature of the project. For example, those individuals who participate in research studies and receive services will be direct beneficiaries while those impacted by policy changes resulting from analyses of Indian health care issues will be indirect beneficiaries.

★2377★
U.S. Department of Housing and Urban Development
Public and Indian Housing
Washington, DC 20410   Ph: (202)708-0950
Catalog Number: 14.850. **Objectives:** To provide and operate cost-effective, decent, safe and sanitary dwellings for lower income families through an authorized local Public Housing Agency (PHA) or Indian Housing Authority (IHA). **Applicant Eligibility:** Public Housing Agencies and Indian Housing Authorities established in accordance with State or Tribal law are eligible. Other lower income individuals may be served under certain limited cirumstances. **Types of Assistance:** Direct payments for specified use. **Beneficiary Eligibility:** Lower income families composed of citizens or eligible immigrants. "Families" include individuals who are 62 years old or older, disabled , or handicapped, or the remaining member of a tenant family.

★2378★
U.S. Department of the Interior
Bureau of Indian Affairs
Alaskan Indian Allotments and Subsistence
    Preference - Alaska National Interest Lands
    Conservation Act
Office of Trust Responsibilities
1849 C St., NW
MB-4510 MIB
Washington, DC 20240   Ph: (202)208-5831
Catalog Number: 15.055 **Applicant Eligibility:** Federally Recognized Indian Tribal Governments in Alaska, Native American Organizations authorized by the Tribes and individual Alaska Natives **Types of Assistance:** Direct Payments for Specified Use. **Beneficiary Eligibility:** Federally Recognized Alaskan Indian Tribal Governments and their members.

★2379★
U.S. Department of the Interior
Bureau of Indian Affairs
Higher Education Grant Program
Office of Indian Educational Programs
1849 C St., NW
MS3512 - MIB
Washington, DC 20245   Ph: (202)219-1127
Catalog Number: 15.114. **Objectives:** To provide finanical aid to eligible Indian students to enable them to attended accredited institutions of higher education. **Applicant Eligibility:** Must be a member of an Indian tribe or Alaska Native Village being served by the Bureau, be enrolled or accepted for enrollment in an accredited college, and have financial need as determined by the institution's financial aid office. **Types of Assistance:** Project Grants. **Beneficiary Eligibility:** Same as applicant eligibility.

★2380★
U.S. Department of the Interior
Bureau of Indian Affairs
Indian Loans—Economic Development
Office of Economic Development
1849 C St. NW, MS 2061
Washington, DC 20240   Ph: (202)208-5324
Catalog Number: 15.124. **Objectives:** To provide assistance to federally recognized Indian tribal governments, and individual America Indians in obtaining financing from private sources to promote business development initiatives on or near federally recognized Indian reservations. **Applicant Eligibility:** Federally recognized Indian tribal governments, Native American organizations authorized by Indian tribal governments, and individual American Indians. **Types of Assistance:** Direct Loans;

Guaranteed/Insured Loans; Provisions of Specialized Services. **Beneficiary Eligibility:** Same as applicant eligibility.

★2381★
U.S. Department of the Interior
Bureau of Indian Affairs
Indian Social Services—Child Welfare Assistance
Office of Tribal Services
1849 C St., NW
Washington, DC 20240   Ph: (202)208-2721

Catalog Number: 15.103. **Objectives:** To provide foster home care and appropriate institutional (non-medical) care for dependent, neglected, and handicapped Indian children in need of protection residing on or near reservations, including those children living in Bureau of Indian Affairs service area jurisdictions in Alaska and Oklahoma, when these services are not available from State or local public agencies. **Applicant Eligibility:** Dependent, neglected, and handicapped Indian children in need of protection whose families live on or near Indian reservations or in jurisdictions under the Bureau of Indian Affairs in Alaska and Oklahoma, and who are not elgible for similar Federal, State, or county funded programs. Applications may be made by a parent, guardian or person having custody of the child, or by court referral. **Types of Assistance:** Direct Payments for Specified Use. **Beneficiary Eligibility:** Members of federally recognized Indian tribes.

★2382★
U.S. Department of the Interior
Bureau of Indian Affairs
Real Estate Programs - Indian Lands
Office of Trust Responsibilities
Division of Real Estate Services
1849 C St., NW
MS-4510 MIB
Washington, DC 20240   Ph: (202)208-7737

Catalog Number: 15.040 **Objectives:** To provide real property management, counseling, and land use planning services to individual Indian allottees and Indian tribal and Alaska Native entities who own an interest in almost 56 million acres of trust land; to provide real estate appraisal services required in processing land transactions, and to protect and enhance the Indian leasehold estate by providing individual Indian landowners and Indian tribes with lease compliance activities . **Applicant Eligibility:** Federally Recognized Indian Tribal Governments, Native American Organizations authorized by tribes, and individual American Indians. **Types of Assistance:** Direct Payments for Specified Use. **Beneficiary Eligibility:** Federally Recognized Indian Tribal Governments and their members.

★2383★
U.S. Department of the Interior
Indian Arts and Crafts Development
Indian Arts and Crafts Board
Main Interior Bldg., Rm. 4004
Washington, DC 20240   Ph: (202)208-3773

Catalog Number: 15.850. **Objectives:** To encourage and promote the development of American Indian arts and crafts. **Applicant Eligibility:** American Indian and Alaska Native individuals and organizations, federally recognized Indian tribal governments, State and local governments, and nonprofit organizations. **Types of Assistance:** Use of Property, Facilities, and Equipment; Advisory Services and Counseling; Investigation of Complaints. **Beneficiary Eligibility:** Same as applicant eligibility.

★2384★
U.S. Department of Labor
Employment and Training Administration
Native American Employment and Training Programs
Division of Indian and Native American
   Programs
200 Constitution Ave., NW, Rm. N4641
Washington, DC 20210   Ph: (202)219-8502

Catalog Number: 17.251. **Objectives:** To afford job training to Native Americans facing serious barriers to employment, who are in special need of such training to obtain productive employment. To reduce the economic disadvantages among Indians and others of Native American descent and to advance the economic and social development of such people. **Applicant Eligibility:** Indian tribes, bands or groups, Alaska Native villages or groups, and Hawaiian Native communities meeting the eligibility criteria, public bodies or private nonprofit agencies selected by the Secretary. Tribes, bands and groups may also form consortia in order to qualify for designation as a grantee. An independently eligible grantee shall be an Indian or Native American entity which has: (1) An identifiable Native American resident population of at least 1,000 individuals (for new grantees) within its designated service area, and (2) the capability to administer Indian and Native American employment and training programs. **Types of Assistance:** Formula Grants. **Beneficiary Eligibility:** Members of State or federally recognized Indian tribes, bands and other individuals of Native American descent, such as, but not limited to, the Kalamaths in Oregon, Micmac and Miliseet in Maine, the Lumbees in North Carolina and South Carolina, Indians variously descibed as terminated or landless, Eskimos and Aleuts in Alaska, and Hawaiian Natives. ("Hawaiian Native" means an individual any of whose ancestors were natives prior to 1778 of the area which now comprises the State of Hawaii.) Applicants must also be economically disadvantaged, unemployed, or underemployed. A Native American grantee may apply in some cases enroll participants who are not economically disadvantaged, unemployed, or underemployed in upgrading and retraining programs.

State/Provincial & Local Government Agencies

Alaska

★2385★
Anchorage Equal Opportunity Office
PO Box 196650
Anchorage, AK 99519-6650   Ph: (907)343-4897
Lillian Lack, Equal Opportunity Dir.

Library Collections

★2386★
Alaska Yukon Library
327 E13th Ave., No1   Ph: (907)272-6647
Anchorage, AK 99501   Fax: (907)272-6647

Founded: 1988 **Subjects:** Alaska Natives, Circumpolar indigenous peoples, Native Americans, Pacific Island indigenous peoples. **Holdings:** Books; reports; archives; microfiche; vertical files of clippings; monographs; original documents.

★2387★
Nome Library/Kegoayah Kozga Public Library
200 Front St.
Box 1168   Ph: (907)443-5133
Nome, AK 99762   Fax: (907)443-3762

Founded: 1905 **Subjects:** Alaska, Eskimo and Gold Rush artifacts. **Special Collections:** Alaskana (75 rare volumes). **Holdings:** 14,000 books; 3000 cassette tapes; 1200 AV programs; old photographs; bilingual and oral history materials. **Subscriptions:** 70 journals and other serials.

★2388★
North Slope Borough School District
Media Center
Library
PO Box 960   Ph: (907)852-8950
Barrow, AK 99723   Fax: (907)852-8969
Special Collections: Inupiaq language and culture collection (300 items). **Holdings:** 8000 books; 3500 AV items. **Subscriptions:** 75 journals and other serials; 2 newspapers.

★2389★
St. Herman's Theological Seminary
Library
414 Mission Rd.   Ph: (907)486-3524
Kodiak, AK 99615   Fax: (907)486-5935
Subjects: Orthodox theology and history, Alaskan history, Native American culture, Alaskan Church History, Russian and Siberian studies. **Special Collections:** Archives of the Russian Orthodox Diocese of Alaska, 1823-1940 (10 cubic meters); Ilvani File (tapes of interviews with Kodiak senior citizens). **Holdings:** 100 cassette tapes; 10,000 ethnographic photographs.

★2390★
Sheldon Museum and Cultural Center
Box 269   Ph: (907)766-2366
Haines, AK 99827   Fax: (907)766-2368
Cynthia L. Jones
Founded: 1925 **Subjects:** Tlingit art and culture; Alaskan history. **Special Collections:** Porcupine Mining Company account books, 1897-1916; logbooks from two harbor boats, 1910-1930. **Holdings:** 1150 books; 5600 feet of home movies; Haines and Skagway newspapers on microfilm; AV programs on historical and resource subjects; photographs, 1897 to present; autographed correspondence; journals, manuscripts, deeds from circa 1900; maps; charts. **Subscriptions:** 12 journals and other serials.

★2391★
Tongass Historical Museum
Library
629 Dock St.   Ph: (907)225-5600
Ketchikan, AK 99901   Fax: (907)225-5602
Founded: 1967 **Subjects:** Alaska - forestry, mining, fishing, Indians. **Special Collections:** Ketchikan Spruce Mills manuscript collection (500 cubic feet); regional photographs of Alaskan industries and Indians (10,000). **Holdings:** 500 books; 700 cubic feet of regional archives. **Subscriptions:** 5 journals and other serials; 2 newspapers.

★2392★
University of Alaska, Fairbanks
Alaska Native Language Center
Research Library
PO Box 757680   Ph: (907)474-7874
Fairbanks, AK 99775-7680   Fax: (907)474-6365
Founded: 1972 **Subjects:** Alaskan native, Athabaskan, Eyak, Tlingit, Haida, Tsimshian, and Eskimo-Aleut languages; Amerindian linguistics. **Holdings:** 10,000 books, journals, unpublished papers, field notes, and archival materials.

★2393★
University of Alaska, Fairbanks
Alaska and Polar Regions Department
Elmer E. Rasmuson Library
PO Box 756808   Ph: (907)474-7261
Fairbanks, AK 99775-6808   Fax: (907)474-6365
Founded: 1965 **Subjects:** Alaska - history, anthropology, ecology, geology, mining, forestry, fisheries; Arctic; Antarctic. **Special Collections:** Alaska Book Collection (books on Alaska, published before 1868); Alaska cartography; University Archives; papers of Alaska builders; Alaska Native and pioneer oral histories. **Holdings:** 110,000 monograph and serial volumes (8000 with microfiche copies); 5000 rare books (4000 with microfiche copies); 15,000 manuscripts maps; 900 rare printed maps; 11,000 feet archives and manuscripts; 600,000 photographs; 3200 reels of archival film and

videotape; 3500 reels of newspapers (microfilm); 8000 oral history audiocassettes. **Subscriptions:** 110 journals and other serials.

Museums and Other Cultural Facilities

★2394★
Alaska Indian Arts
23 Ft. Seward Dr.
PO Box 271
Haines, AK 99827   Ph: (907)766-2160
Carl W. Heinmiller, CEO
Description: Collections include Tlingit Indian costumes, Indian art, and ethnology. It maintains a totem village with tribal house and totem poles.

★2395★
Alaska State Museum
395 Whittier St.
Juneau, AK 99801   Ph: (907)465-2976
Description: Preserves and exhibits the culture and art of Alaska's native peoples.

★2396★
Anchorage Museum of History and Art
121 W. 7th Ave.   Ph: (907)343-4326
Anchorage, AK 99501   Fax: (907)343-6149
Patricia B. Wolf, Dir.
Description: The museum contains collections of Alaskan art and artifacts of all periods.

★2397★
Baranov Museum
Erskine House
101 Marine Way   Ph: (907)486-5920
Kodiak, AK 99615   Fax: (907)486-3166
Peggy Dyson, Pres.
Description: Collections include items from the Kodiak and Aleutian Islands and Eskimo artifacts.

★2398★
Clausen Memorial Museum
203 Fram St.
PO Box 708
Petersburg, AK 99833   Ph: (907)772-3598
Michale Edgington, Exec.Dir.
Description: The museum's collections reflect the diversity of the peoples who have lived in the area, including Tlingit, European, and Asian. Collections include a Tlingit canoe and tools.

★2399★
Cook Inlet Historical Society
121 W. 7th Ave.   Ph: (907)343-4326
Anchorage, AK 99501   Fax: (907)343-6149
William E. Davis, Pres.
Description: The society maintains a collection of native artifacts.

★2400★
Etolin Canoe
Tongass National Forest
Wrangell, AK 99929

★2401★
Fort William H. Seward
PO Box 530   Ph: (907)766-2234
Haines, AK 99827   Free: 800-458-3579
                                    Fax: (907)766-3155
Description: Accommodates carvers who use traditional Indian methods for creating totems, dance masks, and other items. Maintains a replica of a tribal house, and several totem poles.

★2402★
Kotzebue Museum
PO Box 46   Ph: (907)442-3401
Kotzebue, AK 99752   Fax: (907)442-3742
Caleb Pungowiyi, City Manager and CEO

Description: Collections contain Eskimo artifacts, arts and crafts, costumes, and Indian artifacts.

★2403★
Sealaska Heritage Foundation
1 Sealaska Plz., Ste. 201   Ph: (907)463-4844
Juneau, AK 99801   Fax: (907)586-1807

★2404★
Sheldon Jackson Museum
104 College Dr.   Ph: (907)747-8981
Sitka, AK 99835   Fax: (907)747-3004
Irene Schuler, Pres.

Description: Collections include: Haida argillite carvings; Eskimo implements, ivory carvings, masks, skin clothing, baskets, kayaks, umiak; Athapaskan birchbark canoes, skin clothing, implements; Tlingit totem poles, Shaman charms, baskets, ceremonial equipment and garments.

★2405★
Sheldon Museum and Cultural Center
11 Main St.
PO Box 269   Ph: (907)766-2366
Haines, AK 99827   Fax: (907)766-2368
Cynthia L. Jones, Curator

Description: The center maintains a collection of Tlingit and other Northwest Coast Indian artifacts, including some Eskimo/Athapascan.

★2406★
Simon Paneak Memorial Museum
PO Box 21085   Ph: (907)661-3413
Anaktuvuk Pass, AK 99721   Fax: (907)661-3414
Jeslie Kaleak, CEO

Description: The museum maintains a collection on Nunamuit Eskimo history and traditions.

★2407★
Tongass Historical Museum
629 Dock St.   Ph: (907)225-5600
Ketchikan, AK 99901   Fax: (907)225-5901
Roxana Adams, Dir.

Description: Collections contain Indian artifacts, as well as objects and photos relating to the Tlingit, Haida, and Tsimshian cultures.

★2408★
Totem Heritage Center
629 Dock St.   Ph: (907)225-5900
Ketchikan, AK 99901   Fax: (907)225-5901
Roxana Adams, Dir.

Description: The center maintains an Alaska Totem collection and a collection of Northwest Coast Indian art. It sponsors a Native Arts Studies program and awards a certificate of merit in carving/design or textile arts.

★2409★
Wrangell Museum
PO Box 1050
Wrangell, AK 98929   Ph: (907)874-3770

Description: Contains collection of Tlingit Indian hand tools, spruce root and cedar baskets, ceremonial headdresses and blankets.

───────── **California** ─────────

★2410★
Marin Museum of the American Indian
2200 Novato Blvd.
PO Box 864   Ph: (415)897-4064
Novato, CA 94948   Fax: (415)892-7804
Dawn Carlson, Chair.

Description: Collections include archaeological, ethnographic, and archival materials from Alaska to Peru, pertaining to Native Americans.

───────── **District of Columbia** ─────────

★2411★
U.S. Department of the Interior Museum
1849 C St., NW
Mail Stop 5412   Ph: (202)208-4743
Washington, DC 20240   Fax: (202)208-6950
Charles Carter, Contact

Description: Collections include Native American Indian and Eskimo handicraft and artifacts. Conducts research on North American Indian material culture.

───────── **New York** ─────────

★2412★
Southold Indian Museum
Bayview Rd.
PO Box 268
Southold, NY 11971   Ph: (516)765-5577
Walter L. Smith, Pres.

Description: Collections include Native American articles and artifacts, and handiworks of Eskimos.

★2413★
U.S. Smithsonian Institution Museum of the American Indian
George Gustav Heye Center
1 Bowling Green
New York, NY 10004   Ph: (212)514-3711
Carolyn Okoomian Rapkievian, Coord.

Description: Maintains collections relating to American Indian ethnology and archaeology from North America, South America, and Central America. Collections include Indian artifacts, textiles, agriculture, anthropology, paintings, sculpture, decorative arts, costumes, numismatic, music, medical, photo archives, manuscript collections, and Eskimo culture.

Research Centers

★2414★
Dartmouth College Institute of Arctic Studies
6214 Steele Hall   Ph: (603)646-1278
Hanover, NH 03755-3577   Fax: (603)646-1279
Oran Young, Dir.

Founded: 1989 **Research Activities and Fields:** Arctic and northern studies, including ice engineering, visions of the Arctic in art and literature, and problems of health care delivery in northern communities. Focus is on human/environment relationships in the circumpolar north, including small scale common property arrangements, the role of social institutions or resource regimes, and the impact of ideas, values, and belief systems on the formation and operation of these regimes. **Publications:** Northern Notes Annual Journal, journal, annually.

★2415★
McGill University
McGill Subarctic Research Station
PO Box 790   Ph: (418)585-2489
Schefferville, PQ, Canada G0G 2T0 Fax: (418)585-2489
Dr. Wayne Pollard, Sci.Dir.

Founded: 1954 **Research Activities and Fields:** Subarctic environment, including studies on snow, ice, permafrost, hydrology, caribou ecology, entomology, geology, Naskapi land use and hunting, peatlands, phytosociology, phenology, subarctic vegetation, snowcover, snowmelt, geomorphology, periglacial processes, meteorology, climatology, biological productivity, limnology, soils, stringbog and muskeg, plant ecology, acid rain, demography, social sciences, and Canadian Indians. **Publications:** McGill Subarctic Research Papers, semiannually.

★2416★
St. Herman's Theological Seminary
414 Mission Rd.   Ph: (907)486-3524
Kodiak, AK 99615   Fax: (907)486-5935
Very Rev. Michael Oleksa, Contact

Research Activities and Fields: Alaska history, Native American culture, Alaskan Church history, Russian and Siberian studies, and the Russian Orthodox Diocese of Alaska.

★2417★
U.S. Smithsonian Institution
National Museum of the American Indian
Research Branch
Cultural Resources Department
3401 Bruckner Blvd.
Bronx, NY 10461   Ph: (212)514-3944
George Horse Capture, Dep. Asst. Dir.

★2418★
University of Alaska, Anchorage
Institute for Circumpolar Health Studies
3211 Providence Dr.   Ph: (907)786-4020
Anchorage, AK 99508   Fax: (907)786-4019
Dr. John M. Booker, Dir.

Founded: 1988 **Research Activities and Fields:** Health care issues in Alaska and the Circumpolar North, provides research instruction and information between the university, state agencies and the international community.

★2419★
University of Alaska, Fairbanks
Alaska Native Language Center
PO Box 757680   Ph: (907)474-7874
Fairbanks, AK 99775-7680   Fax: (907)474-6586
Dr. Michael E. Krauss, Dir.

Founded: 1972 **Research Activities and Fields:** Linguistic research and documentation of the twenty native Indian, Aleut, and Eskimo languages of Alaska, including preparation of comprehensive native language dictionaries, which currently cover 12 Alaskan languages.

★2420★
University of Colorado
National Center for American Indian and Alaska
  Native Mental Health Research
Dept. of Psychiatry
Univ. North Pavilion
4455 E. 12th Ave., A011-13   Ph: (303)315-9232
Denver, CO 80220   Fax: (303)315-9579
Dr. Spero Manson, Dir.

Founded: 1986 **Research Activities and Fields:** Center formulates, designs, conducts, and reports studies within four areas of inquiry: determining and improving the performance characteristics of self-report measures of serious psychological dysfunction and diagnostic interviews for assessing alcohol, drug, and mental (ADM) disorders; establishing the prevalence and incidence of ADM disorders and related risk factors through descriptive and experimental epidemiological investigations; developing and evaluating methods for detecting and managing ADM disorders presented in human service settings; and examining the effectiveness of interventions for preventing ADM disorders and promoting well-being. Ongoing studies include the American Indian Vietnam Veterans Project, which studies post-traumatic stress disorder and other psychological problems of Vietnam war veterans in readjusting to civilian life; Flower of Two Soils Reinterview Project, which studies emotional disorders in Native American adolescents; the Health Survey of Indian Boarding Students, which seeks to establish the prevalence and incidence of symptoms of depression, anxiety, suicidal behavior, and substance abuse, and to clarify relative contributions of stressful life events, coping strategies, social support, mastery, and self-esteem; the Foundations of Indian Teens Project, which develops more reliable and valid measures of psychopathology among Indian adolescents, with special emphasis on trauma; and the Voices of Indian Teens Project, a survey that includes psychometrically sound constructs, including substance abuse, substance dependence, depression, anxiety, academic achievement, delinquent behavior, social support, peer values and pressure, ethnic identity, stressful life events, drinking patterns and contexts, community values, and attitudes toward alcohol. **Publications:** American Indian and Alaska Native Mental Health Research Journal, 3/year; Annual Monograph.

Education Programs & Services

Head Start Programs

★2421★
Association of Village Council Presidents
Head Start Program
PO Box 219   Ph: (907)543-3521
Bethel, AK 99559   Fax: (907)543-5590

★2422★
Bristol Bay Native Association
Head Start Program
PO Box 310   Ph: (907)842-4059
Dillingham, AK 99576   Fax: (907)842-2338

★2423★
Cook Inlet Tribal Council
Head Start Program
1818 West Northern Lights   Ph: (907)276-4323
Anchorage, AK 99517   Fax: (907)278-0627

★2424★
Fairbanks Native Association
Head Start Program
201 1st Ave., Ste. 200   Ph: (907)452-1648
Fairbanks, AK 99701   Fax: (907)456-5311

★2425★
Kawerak, Inc.
Head Start Program
Pouch 948   Ph: (907)443-5231
Nome, AK 99762   Free: 800-443-5294
                            Fax: (907)443-5570

★2426★
Metlakatla Indian Community Council
Head Start Program
PO Box 8   Ph: (907)886-5151
Metlakatla, AK 99926   Fax: (907)886-5314

★2427★
Tanana Chiefs Conference
Head Start Program
122 1st Ave., Ste. 600   Ph: (907)452-8251
Fairbanks, AK 99701   Fax: (907)459-3592

★2428★
Tlingit and Haida Central Council
Head Start Program
320 W. Willoughby, Ste. 300   Ph: (907)586-1432
Juneau, AK 99801   Fax: (907)463-7324

Studies Programs

Four-Year Programs

★2429★
University of Alaska, Fairbanks
Alaska Native Studies, Inupiaq Eskimo Studies, and
   Yupik Eskimo Studies Programs
PO Box 756300
Fairbanks, AK 99775-0885   Ph: (907)474-6243

★2430★
University of Alaska, Fairbanks
Alaskan Native Studies Program
PO Box 756300
Fairbanks, AK 99775   Ph: (907)474-6243

Graduate Programs

★2431★
University of Hawaii at Honolulu
School of Public Health
American Indian and Alaska Native Support Program
Educational Opportunities Program
Honolulu, HI 96822

Scholarships, Fellowships, & Loans

★2432★
AIGC Fellowships
American Indian Graduate Center
4520 Montgomery Blvd. NE, Ste. 1-B
Albuquerque, NM 87109-1291   Ph: (505)881-4584
Study Level: Graduate. **Award Type:** Fellowship. **Purpose:** To provide supplemental financial aid to Native American and Alaska Native graduate students pursuing master's and doctoral degrees. **Applicant Eligibility:** Applicant must be a member of a federally-recognized Native American or Alaska Native group, and enrolled full-time at an accredited graduate program in the United States. Fellowship's value is determined by applicant's level of unmet financial need. Applicants must apply for campus-based aid, including loans. **Funds Available:** Amounts ranged from U.S.$250 to U.S.$3,000. **Applicant Details:** Write or phone AIGC for application packet, available from January through May. **Application Deadline:** June 1.

★2433★
AISES A.T. Anderson Memorial Scholarship
American Indian Science and Engineering
   Society
1630 30th St., Ste. 301   Ph: (303)939-0023
Boulder, CO 80301   Fax: (303)939-8150
Study Level: Graduate. **Award Type:** Scholarship. **Applicant Eligibility:** Applicants must be American Indian or Alaskan Native college students pursuing academic programs in the sciences, engineering, health related fields, business, natural resources, and math and science secondary education. Applicants must be members of AISES with at least one-quarter American Indian or

recognized as a member of a tribe, be full-time students, and maintaining a GPA of 2.0 or higher. **Funds Available:** $1,000 award for undergraduate study; $2,000 award for graduate study. **Applicant Details:** Candidates must provide proof of American Indian blood. **Application Deadline:** June 15.

★2434★
Bureau of Indian Affairs Loans and Tribal Loans
Montana Guaranteed Student Loan
   Program
PO Box 203101   Ph: (406)444-6594
Helena, MT 59620   Fax: (406)444-0684
Study Level: Undergraduate. **Award Type:** Loan. **Applicant Eligibility:** Applicants must be Native American students who are recognized as American Indian, Eskimo, or Aleut by the federal government. They must demonstrate financial need.

★2435★
Emergency Aid and Health Professions Scholarships
Association on American Indian Affairs,
   Inc.
PO Box 268   Ph: (605)698-3998
Sisseton, SD 57262-0268   Fax: (605)698-3316
Study Level: Undergraduate. **Award Type:** Scholarship. **Applicant Eligibility:** Applicants must be college-level American Indian or Alaskan Native students registered for college and in need of emergency aid. **Selection Criteria:** Candidates are selected based on financial need and limited by the availability of funds. **Funds Available:** When funds are available, individual grants average between U.S.$50 and U.S.$300. **Applicant Details:** Applicants must submit a completed application, certificate of degree of Indian blood, a one- to two-page essay describing the specific nature of the emergency need, a budget of educational costs and resources, and a most recent copy of transcripts. **Application Deadline:** Applications may be filed at any time after college classes have begun.

★2436★
IHS Health Professions Compensatory
   Preprofessional Scholarship
Indian Health Service Scholarship
   Program
Indian Health Services
Twinbrook Plaza, Ste. 100A
12300 Twinbrook Parkway   Ph: (301)443-6197
Rockville, MD 20852   Fax: (301)443-6048
Study Level: Undergraduate. **Award Type:** Scholarship. **Applicant Eligibility:** Applicants must be American Indians or Alaska Natives, high school graduates or the equivalent, in good standing at the educational institution they are attending, have the capacity to complete a health professions course of study, and must intend to serve Indian People upon completion of professional health care degree as a health care provider in the discipline for which they are taking preparatory courses. Applicants must also be enrolled, or be accepted for enrollment, in courses that will prepare them for acceptance into health professions schools. Courses may be either compensatory (required to improve science, mathematics, or other basic skills and knowledge) or preprofessional (required in order to qualify for admission into a health professions program). **Selection Criteria:** Previous recipients who meet the continued eligibility requirements will be given priority consideration. **Funds Available:** Funding is available for a maximum of two years. Recipients must apply annually to receive continued funding beyond the initial award period. The level of scholarship benefits is contingent upon the availability of funds appropriated each fiscal year by the Congress of the United States and, therefore, is subject to yearly changes. The Scholarship Program will provide a monthly stipend to cover living expenses including room and board. Recipients will receive the stipend only during the academic period covered by their awards, August 1 to May 31.

★2437★
IHS Health Professions Pre-Graduate Scholarships
Indian Health Service Scholarship
  Program
Indian Health Service
Twinbrook Plaza, Ste. 100A
12300 Twinbrook Parkway   Ph: (301)443-6197
Rockville, MD 20852   Fax: (301)443-6048
Study Level: Undergraduate. **Award Type:** Scholarship. **Applicant Eligibility:** Applicants must be American Indians or Alaska Natives. Candidates must be high school graduates or the equivalent, and must have the capacity to complete a health professions course of study. Applicants must be enrolled, or accepted for enrollment, in a baccalaureate degree program in specific preprofessional areas (pre-medicine and pre-dentistry). Applicants may be seniors, juniors, sophomores, or freshmen (priority is given to applicants in this order). Applicants must be in good standing at the educational institution they are attending. Candidates must intend to serve Indian People upon completion of professional health care education as health care providers in the disciplines for which the students are enrolled at the pregraduate level. **Funds Available:** Funding is available for a maximum of four academic years. The level of scholarship benefits is contingent upon the availability of funds appropriated each fiscal year by the Congress of the United States and, therefore, is subject to yearly changes. The Scholarship Program will provide a monthly stipend to cover living expenses, tuition and educational expenses such as cost of books, uniforms, travel, rental of a post office box to use for receiving stipend checks, and room and board. Recipients will receive the stipend only during the academic period covered by their awards, August 1 to May 31.

★2438★
**Presbyterian Church Native American Education
  Grants**
Presbyterian Church (U.S.A.)
Office of Financial Aid for Studies
100 Witherspoon St.   Ph: (502)569-5000
Louisville, KY 40202-1396   Fax: (502)569-5018
Study Level: Graduate. **Award Type:** Grant. **Applicant Eligibility:** Candidates must be American Indians, Aleuts, or Eskimos who are United States citizens. They must have completed at least one semester at an accredited institution of higher learning. Restrict ed to Presbyterian students. **Funds Available:** Grants range from U.S.$200 to U.S.$1,500 annually depending on financial need and availability of funds. **Applicant Details:** Candidates must apply to their colleges for financial aid as well as filing an application with the Presbyterian Church (U.S.A.). **Application Deadline:** June 1.

★2439★
**Presbyterian Church Native American Seminary
  Scholarships**
Presbyterian Church (U.S.A.)
Office of Financial Aid for Studies
100 Witherspoon St.   Ph: (502)569-5000
Louisville, KY 40202-1396   Fax: (502)569-5018
Study Level: Graduate. **Award Type:** Scholarship. **Applicant Eligibility:** Candidates are American Indians, Aleuts, and Eskimos who are certified by the candidate's presbytery or the Presbyterian Native American Consulting Committee. Applicants must be seminary students preparing for a church occupation and enrolled in a seminary fully accredited by the Association of Theological Schools in the United States and Canada. They may also be registered with, or under the care of, a presbytery and enrolled in a college program on Track 1 of the Native American Theological Association Program; or they may be members of the Presbyterian Church (U.S.A.) from a former UPCUSA congregation enrolled in a program of Theological Education by extension, such as the NATA Track III which is approved by a seminary fully accredited by the Association of Theological Schools in the United States and Canada. Candidates, ministers or members (former UPCUSA) in other church occupations pursuing an approved program of continuing education are also eligible. **Funds Available:** The amount of the scholarship is determined by the Office of Financial Aid for Studies based upon recommendation by the student's Financial Officer, analysis of the applicant's financial needs, and other resources and available funds. **Applicant Details:** Candidates must first contact the Financial Aid Officer of the school or seminary

they attend. The officer makes a recommendation to the Office of Financial Aid for Studies.

★2440★
Sequoyah Graduate Fellowships
Association on American Indian Affairs,
  Inc.
PO Box 268   Ph: (605)698-3998
Sisseton, SD 57262-0268   Fax: (605)698-3316
Study Level: Graduate. **Award Type:** Fellowship. **Purpose:** To support graduate study by Native Americans. **Applicant Eligibility:** Applicant must be an American Indian or Alaska Native affiliated with a tribe. Candidate must be enrolled in a graduate program in an accredited U.S. university or college. **Selection Criteria:** Applicants are selected based on scholastic achievement. **Funds Available:** U.S.$1,500. Scholarship is paid in two installments. **Applicant Details:** Students must submit completed application, certificate of degree of Indian blood, two letters of recommendation, a one- to two-page essay describing educational goals, most recent copy of transcripts, and a budget of educational costs and resources. **Application Deadline:** July 1-September 13.

★2441★
U.S. Bureau of Indian Affairs Scholarship Grant
U.S. Bureau of Indian Affairs
Office of Indian Education Programs
1849 C St., NW   Ph: (202)208-4871
Washington, DC 20240   Fax: (202)208-3312
Study Level: Undergraduate. **Award Type:** Grant. **Applicant Eligibility:** Candidates must be Native Americans, Eskimos, or Alaska natives and be members of federally recognized tribes. They must also have been accepted at an accredited college or university. **Selection Criteria:** Based on financial need. **Funds Available:** Appropriated yearly by Congress with each tribe specifying the amount they wish to receive. **Applicant Details:** All application information is available from the Tribal Contractor or the Bureau Agency serving that tribe. There are no funds or applications available from the above address or the Central Office of the Bureau of Indian Affairs. **Application Deadline:** Set by each Tribal Contractor.

Awards, Honors, & Prizes

★2442★
Indian Achievement Award
National Urban Indian Council
100068 University Park St.
Denver, CO 80250-0168   Ph: (303)750-2695
Description: For recognition of service to off-reservation American Indian and Alaska native people and programs. A plaque is presented annually. Established in 1983.

★2443★
Indian Achievement Award
National Urban Indian Council
100068 University Park St.
Denver, CO 80250-0168   Ph: (303)750-2695
Description: For recognition of service to off-reservation American Indian and Alaska native people and programs. A plaque is presented annually. Established in 1983.

★2444★
Miss Indian World
Gathering of Nations
PO Box 75102, Sta. 14   Ph: (505)836-2810
Albuquerque, NM 87194   Fax: (505)839-0475
Description: To crown a young Indian (Native American) woman to reign as Miss Indian World. She must be an ambassador of goodwill and represent the Gathering of Nations and Native American people in the United States, Canada, and throughout the Americas (North, South, and Central). Candidates must be at least one-quarter Indian, and be 17 to 24 years of age. A traveling crown (beaded) to

wear throughout the year, a banner, $1,200 cash and $1,800 travel expenses are awarded annually. Established in 1984 by Gathering of Nations Ltd.

Publishers

★2445★
Alaska Northwest Books
PO Box 10306   Ph: (503)226-2402
Portland, OR 97210   Free: 800-452-3032

Description: Publishes large format photo essay books on international, national and regional areas. Also publishes calendars. Distributes for Whitecap Books and Epicenter Press. Reaches market through commission representatives, direct mail, trade sales, and wholesalers and distributors. Does not accept unsolicited manuscripts. **Subjects:** Travel reference, cookbooks, Alaska, children's, Native Americans, gardening, nature.

★2446★
Indian Historian Press
1493 Masonic Ave.   Ph: (415)626-5235
San Francisco, CA 94117   Fax: (415)626-4923

Description: Principal interest is the American Indians of North America; also covers indigenous peoples of the western hemisphere. Does not accept unsolicited manuscripts.

★2447★
Origins Program
4632 Vincent Ave. S.   Ph: (612)922-8175
Minneapolis, MN 55410   Fax: (612)926-0015

Description: Publishes catalogs and books to accompany exhibitions of tribal art and books on multicultural understanding. Also offers audio and video cassettes on Indian and Eskimo topics, and on museum collections of tribal art. Reaches market through commission representatives and distributors, including Bookpeople and Quality Books, Inc. **Subjects:** Indian and Eskimo art and culture, multiculturalism.

★2448★
Tanadgusix Corp.
St. Paul Island, AK 99660   Ph: (907)546-2312
      Fax: (907)546-2366

Subjects: Aleut history, St. Paul guide.

★2449★
U.S. Smithsonian Institution
National Museum of the American Indian
3753 Broadway   Ph: (212)283-4031
New York, NY 10032-1596   Fax: (212)491-9302

Description: Publishes books in addition to offering note cards and postcards. Co-publishes with other publishers. **Subjects:** Native peoples of all the Americas, new world archaeology.

Directories

★2450★
American Indian and Alaska Native Arts and Crafts—Source Directory
U.S. Department of the Interior
1849 C St. NW
Washington, DC 20240   Ph: (202)208-3100

Description: Native American owned and operated arts and crafts businesses throughout the U.S. Entries include: Name, address, phone, fax, contact person, products sold, and additional shop information. **Pages (approx.):** 20.

★2451★
American Indian and Alaska Native Traders Directory
Arrowstar Publishing
PO Box 427
Englewood, CO 80151   Ph: (303)231-6599

Description: 3,500 American Indian-owned and Eskimo-owned arts and crafts businesses, craft persons, and artists. Entries include: Company name, address. **Pages (approx.):** 140, Published June 1990. **Price:** $19.95, plus $1.50 shipping.

★2452★
American Indian Index
Arrowstar Publishing
PO Box 427
Englewood, CO 80151   Ph: (303)231-6599

Description: over 6,000 Native American Indian and Native Alaskan tribes, social service organizations and agencies, newspapers, and museums. Entries include: Organization name, address, subsidiary and branch names and locations (if applicable), product or service. **Pages (approx.):** 325. **Frequency:** Irregular, latest edition 1987. **Price:** $19.95, plus $1.50 shipping.

★2453★
Directory of Native Education Resources in the Northwest Region
ERIC Document Reproduction Service
  (EDRS)   Ph: (703)440-1400
7420 Fullerton Road, Ste. 110   Free: 800-443-3742
Springfield, VA 22153-2852   Fax: (703)440-1408

Description: 593 organizations in Alaska, Idaho, Montana, Oregon, and Washington and national organizations who provide or work to improve educational services to Native Americans and Alaska Natives. Includes private and state organizations, media and publishers, tribes, schools, and federally recognized villages. Entries include: Organization name, address, phone, contact person, and description. **Pages (approx.):** 74. **Frequency:** Periodic.

★2454★
Education Assistance for American Indians and Alaska Natives
Master of Public Health Program for
  American Indians
Warren Hall, Rm. 140   Ph: (415)642-3228
Berkeley, CA 94720   Fax: (510)642-3583

Description: Publication includes: Sources of information regarding health careers, training for health careers, and financial aid available to American Indians and Alaska natives from the Bureau of Indian Affairs, institutions, tribal councils, and other sources. Entries include: Name of organization or publisher, address, name of contact, phone, service programs offered. **Frequency:** Biennial, June of even years. **Price:** Free.

★2455★
National Directory of Minority-Owned Business Firms
Todd Publications   Ph: (914)358-6213
PO Box 635   Free: 800-747-1056
Nyack, NY 10960   Fax: (914)358-1059

Description: Over 40,000 minority-owned businesses in the U.S. Entries include: Contact name, phone, number of employees, certification status, start-up date, and key word business descriptions. **Pages (approx.):** 1,500. **Frequency:** Biennial. **Price:** $195.

★2456★
Native American Directory: Alaska, Canada, United States
National Native American Cooperative
PO Box 27626
Tucson, AZ 85726   Fax: (520)292-0779

Description: More than 2,000 Native American performing arts groups, craft materials suppliers, stores and galleries, Indian-owned motels and resorts; tribal offices, museums, and cultural centers; associations and schools; newspapers, radio and television programs, and stations operated by, owned by, or specifically for

Native Americans; calendar of events, including officially sanctioned powwows, conventions, arts and crafts shows, all-Indian rodeos, and Navajo rug auctions; how-to buy Indian crafts and research Indian ancestry. Entries include: Generally, organization or company name, address, descriptive comments, dates (for shows or events). **Pages (approx.):** 880. **Frequency:** Irregular, previous edition 1982; latest edition January 1996. **Price:** $65.95, postpaid; $131, library edition with wall map.

★2457★
Native North American Almanac
Gale Research   Ph: (313)961-2242
835 Penobscot Bldg.   Free: 800-877-
Detroit, MI 48226-4094   GALE
     Fax: (313)961-6083

Description: Includes essays on issues of interest to Native Americans and Canadian natives, including history, economy, education, religion, culture, arts, language, law and legislation, activism, the environment, health, and media; each chapter includes, as appropriate, directories of tribal communities, organizations, government agencies, schools, and businesses relevant to the topic. Entries include: Name, address, phone, contact. **Pages (approx.):** 1,275. **Frequency:** First edition November 1993; new edition expected 1999. **Price:** $75.

★2458★
Native North American Almanac
Gale Research   Ph: (313)961-2242
835 Penobscot Bldg.   Free: 800-877-
Detroit, MI 48226-4094   GALE
     Fax: (313)961-6083

Description: Includes essays on issues of interest to Native Americans and Canadian natives, including history, economy, education, religion, culture, arts, language, law and legislation, activism, the environment, health, and media; each chapter includes, as appropriate, directories of tribal communities, organizations, government agencies, schools, and businesses relevant to the topic. Entries include: Name, address, phone, contact. **Pages (approx.):** 1,275. **Frequency:** First edition November 1993; new edition expected 1999. **Price:** $75.

★2459★
Smoke Signals: Business Directory of Indian Country U.S.A.
Arrowstar Publishing
PO Box 427
Englewood, CO 80151   Ph: (303)231-6599

Description: Approximately 3,500 American Indian and Alaska Native owned and operated businesses. Entries include: Company name, address. **Pages (approx.):** 220, Published 1990. **Price:** $24.95, plus $1.95 shipping. **Formerly:** Smoke Signals: Directory of Native Indian/Alaskan Businesses.

Journals & Magazines

★2460★
Alaska People Magazine
PO Box 190648   Ph: (907)277-3675
Anchorage, AK 99519   Fax: (907)277-3857

Description: Lifestyle magazine featuring information of interest to the Alaskan community. **First Published:** 1994. **Frequency:** Quarterly. **Subscriptions:** $19.95, five issues; $29.95, ten issues.

★2461★
The Alaskan Viewpoint
HCR 64, Box 453
Seward, AK 99664   Ph: (907)288-3168

Description: True stories on lives of Alaskan women. **First Published:** 1986. **Frequency:** Semiannual. **Subscriptions:** $7.

Newsletters

★2462★
Sentinel
National Congress of American Indians
2010 Massachusetts Ave. NW, 2nd Fl.   Ph: (202)466-7767
Washington, DC 20036   Fax: (202)466-7797

Description: Focuses on national issues affecting American Indians and Alaska natives. Monitors government legislation, federal agency activities, and innovative tribal programs. Recurring features include legislation and litigation updates, profiles of important American Indians, editorials, and a calendar of events. **Pages (approx.):** 16-32. **Frequency:** Quarterly.

Newspapers

★2463★
Tundra Times
Eskimo, Indian, Aleut Publishing Co.   Ph: (907)349-2512
PO Box 92247   Free: 800-764-2512
Anchorage, AK 99509-2247   Fax: (907)349-0335

Description: Statewide Native American newspaper. **First Published:** 1962. **Frequency:** Biweekly (Wed.). **Subscriptions:** $30.

Radio Stations

★2464★
KBRW-AM
1695 Okpik St.
PO Box 109   Ph: (907)852-6811
Barrow, AK 99723   Fax: (907)852-2274

Frequency: 680 **Network Affiliation:** Public Radio International (PRI), National Public Radio (NPR), Alaska Public Radio. **Format:** Public Radio, Eclectic, Educational. **Owner:** Silakkuagvik Communications, Inc.

★2465★
KDLG-AM
Box 670   Ph: (907)842-5281
Dillingham, AK 99576   Fax: (907)842-5645

Frequency: 670. **Network Affiliation:** Alaska Radio Network, Public Radio International (PRI), AP. **Format:** Public Radio, Full Service. **Owner:** Dillingham City Schools.

★2466★
KFSK-FM
PO Box 149   Ph: (907)772-3808
Petersburg, AK 99833   Fax: (907)772-9296

Frequency: 100.9. **Format:** News, Soft Rock. **Owner:** Narrows Broadcasting Corp.

★2467★
KNBA-FM
810 E 9th Ave.
Anchorage, AL 99501

Frequency: 90.3. **Format:** National Native News.

★2468★
KOTZ-AM
Box 78　　　　　　　　　　　Ph: (907)442-3435
Kotzebue, AK 99752-0078　　　Fax: (907)442-2292
Frequency: 720 **Network Affiliation:** American Public Radio (APR), Alaska Radio Network. **Format:** Public Radio, News, Eclectic. **Owner:** Kotzubue Broadcasting Inc.

★2469★
KSKO-AM
PO Box 70　　　　　　　　　　Ph: (907)524-3001
McGrath, AK 99627　　　　　　Fax: (907)524-3436
Frequency: 870 **Network Affiliation:** Public Radio International (PRI). **Format:** News, Public Radio, Contemporary Hit Radio (CHR), Album-Oriented Rock (AOR). **Owner:** Kuskokwim Public Broadcasting Corp.

★2470★
KUHB-FM
Pribilof School District
St. Paul Island, AK 99660　　　Ph: (907)546-2254
Frequency: 91.9. **Format:** Country, Album-Oriented Rock (AOR). **Owner:** Pribilof School District.

★2471★
KYUK-AM
640 Radio St.　　　　　　　　Ph: (907)543-3131
Pouch 468　　　　　　　　　　Free: 800-478-3640
Bethel, AK 99559　　　　　　　Fax: (907)543-3130
Frequency: 640 **Network Affiliation:** National Public Radio (NPR), Alaska Public Radio, Public Radio International (PRI). **Format:** Eclectic, Adult Contemporary, Country, Oldies. **Owner:** Bethel Broadcasting Inc.

Videos

★2472★
Angoon One Hundred Years Later
Native American Public Broadcasting
　Consortium
PO Box 86111
1800 N. 33rd St.
Lincoln, NE 68501　　　　　　Ph: (402)472-3522
Description: A commemoration of the destruction of the Tlingit Indian village of Angoon, Alaska in 1882 by the U.S. Naval Force. **Release Date:** 1982. **Length:** 30 mins. **Format:** VHS, 3/4″ U-matic Cassette, 1″ Broadcast Type ″C″, 2″ Quadraplex Open Reel.

★2473★
Angotee
International Film Bureau, Inc. (IFB)
332 S. Michigan Ave.
Chicago, IL 60604-4382　　　　Ph: (312)427-4545
Description: A documentary account of an Eskimo boy's life from infancy to maturity. **Release Date:** 1953. **Length:** 31 mins. **Format:** Beta, VHS, 3/4″ U-matic Cassette, Other than listed.

★2474★
At the Autumn River Camp: Parts 1 and 2
Education Development Center, Inc.
55 Chapel St., Ste. 901　　　　Ph: (617)969-7100
Newton, MA 02160　　　　　　Free: 800-225-4276
Description: The autumn existence of the Netsilik Eskimos is related in these programs. Hunting, fishing, sewing tent roofs, and igloo building are a few of the jobs that are handled by the Native Alaskans. **Release Date:** 1967. **Length:** 30 mins. **Format:** 3/4″ U-matic Cassette, Other than listed.

★2475★
At the Caribou Crossing Place: Parts 1 and 2
Education Development Center, Inc.
55 Chapel St., Ste. 901　　　　Ph: (617)969-7100
Newton, MA 02160　　　　　　Free: 800-225-4276
Description: A documentary of the day-to-day existence of a family of Netsilik Eskimos. **Release Date:** 1967. **Length:** 30 mins. **Format:** 3/4″ U-matic Cassette, Other than listed.

★2476★
At the Spring Sea Ice Camp: Parts 1-3
Education Development Center, Inc.
55 Chapel St., Ste. 901　　　　Ph: (617)969-7100
Newton, MA 02160　　　　　　Free: 800-225-4276
Description: A record of the everyday life of a family of Netsilik Eskimos, as they hunt seals through the sea-ice in the springtime. **Release Date:** 1967. **Length:** 27 mins. **Format:** 3/4″ U-matic Cassette, Other than listed.

★2477★
At the Winter Sea Ice Camp: Parts 1-4
Education Development Center, Inc.
55 Chapel St., Ste. 901　　　　Ph: (617)969-7100
Newton, MA 02160　　　　　　Free: 800-225-4276
Description: A way of life that is no more is seen in the lifestyle of the Netsilik Eskimos. We see them at work during the frigid Canadian winter, when special care must be taken to survive. **Release Date:** 1967. **Length:** 35 mins. **Format:** 3/4″ U-matic Cassette, Other than listed.

★2478★
Building a Kayak: Parts 1 and 2
Education Development Center, Inc.
55 Chapel St., Ste. 901　　　　Ph: (617)969-7100
Newton, MA 02160　　　　　　Free: 800-225-4276
Description: Two Netsilik Eskimos show the work involved in building a kayak from seal skins, sinews, bone and scraps of wood. **Release Date:** 1967. **Length:** 32 mins. **Format:** 3/4″ U-matic Cassette, Other than listed.

★2479★
Easter in Igloolik: Peter's Story
Bullfrog Films, Inc.　　　　　Ph: (215)779-8226
PO Box 149　　　　　　　　　Free: 800-543-3764
Oley, PA 19547　　　　　　　　Fax: (215)370-1978
Description: Viewers are provided with a look at life in a modern Arctic Eskimo community. **Release Date:** 1987. **Length:** 24 mins. **Format:** Beta, VHS, 3/4″ U-matic Cassette. **Credits:** Cast Member: Peter Arnatsiaq.

★2480★
Eskimo Artist: Kenojuak
National Film Board of Canada
1251 Avenue of the Americas, 16th Fl.
New York, NY 10020-1173　　　Ph: (212)586-5131
Description: Kenojuak, an eskimo artist, depicts her works and sources of inspiration. She transfers her designs into stone, which express her beliefs and understandings of the ecological unity. **Release Date:** 1964. **Length:** 20 mins. **Format:** Beta, VHS, 3/4″ U-matic Cassette.

★2481★
Eskimo Family
Britannica Films　　　　　　　Ph: (312)347-7958
310 S. Michigan Ave.　　　　　Fax: (312)347-7966
Chicago, IL 60604
Description: Follows Anakudluk and his family on their annual trek from winter camp to spring hunting grounds. **Release Date:** 1959. **Length:** 17 mins. **Format:** Beta, VHS, 3/4″ U-matic Cassette.

★2482★
The Eskimo: Fight for Life
Education Development Center, Inc.
55 Chapel St., Ste. 901   Ph: (617)969-7100
Newton, MA 02160   Free: 800-225-4276
Description: Six families of Netsilik heritage are seen hunting the frozen ice masses for food and animal skins, building an igloo, conversing with each other, and enacting their food sharing ritual. Aside from showing the Netsilik's daily activities, the program focuses particularly on the eskimo's patience, industry, strength, and family security. Part of the "Eskimo Survival" series. **Release Date:** 1971. **Length:** 51 mins. **Format:** 3/4″ U-matic Cassette, Other than listed.

★2483★
Eskimo (Inuit) Legends Series
Beacon Films   Ph: (708)328-6700
1560 Sherman Ave., Ste. 100   Free: 800-323-9084
Evanston, IL 60201   Fax: (708)328-6706
Description: Series of nine stories about eskimo legends. **Length:** 6 **Format:** VHS

★2484★
The Eskimo in Life and Legend (The Living Stone)
Britannica Films
310 S. Michigan Ave.   Ph: (312)347-7958
Chicago, IL 60604   Fax: (312)347-7966
Description: Relates the dramatic story of a great seal hunter who carved the image of his wish from a piece of stone-a wish that later came true. Shows the Eskimo way of life, his legends, and his art. **Release Date:** 1960. **Length:** 22 mins. **Format:** Beta, VHS, 3/4″ U-matic Cassette.

★2485★
Eskimo Summer
Education Development Center, Inc.
55 Chapel St., Ste. 901   Ph: (617)969-7100
Newton, MA 02160   Free: 800-225-4276
Description: This program includes all of the Netsilik activities on the land. In spring, they begin to fish, gather moss and heather, and search for bird eggs. Summer activities include building a kayak for caribou hunting. As summer progresses they move farther inland to trap salmon returning up river, hunt caribou, and prepare to return to the sea and ice. Part of the "People of the Seal" series. **Release Date:** 19??. **Length:** 52 mins. **Format:** 3/4″ U-matic Cassette, Other than listed.

★2486★
Eskimo Survival Series
Education Development Center, Inc.
55 Chapel St., Ste. 901   Ph: (617)969-7100
Newton, MA 02160   Free: 800-225-4276
Description: A series of programs on the North American Eskimo: a look at their lives, their homes, their rituals and their struggles. Highlighted are the Netsilik Eskimos. Programs are available individually. **Release Date:** 1971. **Length:** 54 mins. **Format:** 3/4″ U-matic Cassette, Other than listed.

★2487★
Eskimo Winter
Education Development Center, Inc.
55 Chapel St., Ste. 901   Ph: (617)969-7100
Newton, MA 02160   Free: 800-225-4276
Description: As the sea freezes, the Netsilik move far out into the Bay, search for seal holes, and build their igloos near good seal-hunting spots. The program concentrates on seal hunting, on which the Eskimos' lives depend. We are shown how the families divide up the food and put every part of the animal to good use, after which they begin their annual inland trek. Part of the "People of the Seal" series. **Release Date:** 19??. **Length:** 52 mins. **Format:** 3/4″ U-matic Cassette, Other than listed.

★2488★
Eskimos: A Changing Culture
Phoenix/BFA Films
468 Park Ave., S.   Ph: (212)684-5910
New York, NY 10016   Free: 800-221-1274
Description: Using the Eskimos of Nunivak Island in the Bering Sea, this show examines the changes as they have occurred in the lifetime of the present generation. **Release Date:** 1971. **Length:** 17 mins. **Format:** Beta, VHS, 3/4″ U-matic Cassette.

★2489★
Expressions of Eskimo Culture
Michigan Media
University of Michigan
400 4th St.
Ann Arbor, MI 48109   Ph: (313)764-8228
Description: Inuit (Eskimo) culture is shown, as expressed in rich and beautiful prints and carvings. **Release Date:** 1979. **Length:** 29 mins. **Format:** 3/4″ U-matic Cassette, Other than listed.

★2490★
Eyes of the Spirit
KET, The Kentucky Network Enterprise
 Division   Ph: (606)233-3000
2230 Richmond Rd., Ste. 213   Free: 800-354-9067
Lexington, KY 40502   Fax: (606)266-3562
Description: A look at Yup'ik Eskimo mask carvers in action. **Release Date:** 1983. **Length:** 30 mins. **Format:** Beta, VHS, 3/4″ U-matic Cassette.

★2491★
Fishing at the Stone Weir, Parts I and II
Education Development Center, Inc.
55 Chapel St., Ste. 901   Ph: (617)969-7100
Newton, MA 02160   Free: 800-225-4276
Description: In the summertime, a group of Netsilik Eskimos fish by the side of the river using three-pronged leisters, spearing the fish and stringing them on a thong. **Release Date:** 1967. **Length:** 30 mins. **Format:** 3/4″ U-matic Cassette, Other than listed.

★2492★
From the First People
Documentary Educational Resources
101 Morse St.   Ph: (617)926-0491
Watertown, MA 02172   Fax: (617)926-9519
Description: This program is about change and contemporary life in Shungnak, a village on the Kobuk River in northwestern Alaska. **Release Date:** 1977. **Length:** 45 mins. **Format:** 3/4″ U-matic Cassette.

★2493★
Group Hunting on the Spring Ice, Parts I-III
Education Development Center, Inc.
55 Chapel St., Ste. 901   Ph: (617)969-7100
Newton, MA 02160   Free: 800-225-4276
Description: Late in June, the hunters of a Netsilik Eskimo tribe go out in search of seal pups for food. **Release Date:** 1967. **Length:** 30 mins. **Format:** 3/4″ U-matic Cassette, Other than listed.

★2494★
Haa Shagoon
University of California at Berkeley
 Extension Media Center
2176 Shattuck Ave.
Berkeley, CA 94704   Ph: (510)642-0460
Description: One day in the life of the Tlingit Indian tribe from Alaska is documented. **Release Date:** 1983. **Length:** 29 mins. **Format:** VHS, 3/4″ U-matic Cassette.

★2495★
High Arctic: Life with the Northernmost Eskimos
Cornell University
Audio Visual Resource Center
8 Business & Technology Park   Ph: (607)255-2091
Ithaca, NY 14850   Fax: (607)255-9946
Description: This tape looks at the culture and society of a tribe of Eskimos who make their home a few hundred miles from the North Pole. **Release Date:** 1963. **Length:** 65 mins. **Format:** Beta, VHS, 1/2″ Reel-EIAJ, 3/4″ U-matic Cassette, 2″ Quadraplex Open Reel.

★2496★
Hitting Sticks—Healing Hearts
River Tracks Productions
PO Box 9
Manley Hot Springs, AK 99756
Description: This documentary, produced at the request of village elders, provides an in-depth view of an Athabaskan memorial potlatch in the village of Minto, Alaska. This video centers on death, grieving, love, community, music, and tradition. **Release Date:** 1991. **Length:** 58 mins. **Format:** VHS.

★2497★
Hunters of the Seal
Time-Life Video and Television
1450 E. Parham Rd.   Ph: (804)266-6330
Richmond, VA 23280   Free: 800-621-7026
Description: Documents the dramatic contrast between the old and the new for the Netsilik Eskimo, and their struggle to find meaning in their new lives. **Release Date:** 1976. **Length:** 30 mins. **Format:** Beta, VHS, 3/4″ U-matic Cassette, Other than listed.

★2498★
Huteetl: A Koyukon Memorial Potlatch
River Tracks Productions
PO Box 9
Manley Hot Springs, AK 99756
Description: Documents the final death rites for a young couple who died in a plane crash in 1981. A memorial potlatch was given over a year later and more than 200 people joined the residents of Hughes, Alaska, for the week-long celebration releasing the deceased spirit. **Release Date:** 1983. **Length:** 55 mins. **Format:** VHS.

★2499★
Inuit Kids
Bullfrog Films, Inc.   Ph: (215)779-8226
PO Box 149   Free: 800-543-3764
Oley, PA 19547   Fax: (215)370-1978
Description: A film which helps children get the feel of Arctic life by sharing moments in the lives of two thirteen year old boys. **Release Date:** 1987. **Length:** 15 mins. **Format:** Beta, VHS.

★2500★
Inuit Legends Series
Beacon Films
930 Pinter Ave.   Ph: (312)328-6700
Evanston, IL 60202   Free: 800-323-5448
Description: These programs are three Eskimo legends of courage and sacrifice in puppet animation for young viewers. **Release Date:** 1982. **Length:** 6 mins. **Format:** Beta, VHS, 3/4″ U-matic Cassette.

★2501★
Jigging for Lake Trout
Education Development Center, Inc.
55 Chapel St., Ste. 901   Ph: (617)969-7100
Newton, MA 02160   Free: 800-225-4276
Description: In springtime, the Netsilik Eskimos go fishing through lake ice for freshwater trout. **Release Date:** 1967. **Length:** 32 mins. **Format:** 3/4″ U-matic Cassette, Other than listed.

★2502★
Lumaaq—An Eskimo Legend
National Film Board of Canada
1251 Avenue of the Americas, 16th Fl.
New York, NY 10020-1173   Ph: (212)586-5131
Description: Without commentary, this program depicts the story of a legend widely believed by the Povungnituk Eskimos. **Release Date:** 1975. **Length:** 8 mins. **Format:** Beta, VHS, 3/4″ U-matic Cassette.

★2503★
Matthew Aliuk: Eskimo in Two Worlds
Learning Corporation of America
108 Wilmot Rd.   Ph: (708)940-1260
Deerfield, IL 60015-9990   Free: 800-621-2131
Description: This is the story of a proud people's struggle for cultural survival in a changing world. **Release Date:** 1973. **Length:** 18 mins. **Format:** Beta, VHS, 3/4″ U-matic Cassette.

★2504★
More Than Bows and Arrows
Video Tech
19346 3rd Ave. NW
Seattle, WA 98177   Ph: (206)546-5401
Description: A coast-to-coast look at the technology being used by Indians, Eskimos, and Aleuts. **Release Date:** 1978. **Length:** 56 mins. **Format:** Beta, VHS, 3/4″ U-matic Cassette, Other than listed.

★2505★
Old Dances, New Dancers
KET, The Kentucky Network Enterprise
   Division   Ph: (606)233-3000
2230 Richmond Rd., Ste. 213   Free: 800-354-9067
Lexington, KY 40502   Fax: (606)266-3562
Description: A filmed record of the first annual Young People's Eskimo Dance Awareness Festival in Chevak, Alaska. **Release Date:** 1983. **Length:** 30 mins. **Format:** Beta, VHS, 3/4″ U-matic Cassette.

★2506★
On the Spring Ice
Documentary Educational Resources
101 Morse St.   Ph: (617)926-0491
Watertown, MA 02172   Fax: (617)926-9519
Description: The danger of moving ice and walrus hunting are the topics of this program. **Release Date:** 1975. **Length:** 45 mins. **Format:** 3/4″ U-matic Cassette.

★2507★
Our Native American Friends
Britannica Films
310 S. Michigan Ave.   Ph: (312)347-7958
Chicago, IL 60604   Fax: (312)347-7966
Description: From the "Friends" units these three programs: Apache Indian Friends, Miccosukee Indian Friends, and Eskimo Friends, are combined to tell of different ethnic groups in the United States. **Release Date:** 1979. **Length:** 10 mins. **Format:** Beta, VHS, 3/4″ U-matic Cassette.

★2508★
People of the Seal Series
Education Development Center, Inc.
55 Chapel St., Ste. 901   Ph: (617)969-7100
Newton, MA 02160   Free: 800-225-4276
Description: A summary of the entire migratory cycle of the Netsilik Eskimo, from summer to winter, including their seasonal activities and rituals. Programs are available individually. **Release Date:** 19??. **Length:** 52 mins. **Format:** 3/4″ U-matic Cassette, Other than listed.

★2509★
Sananguagat: Inuit Masterworks
National Film Board of Canada
1251 Avenue of the Americas, 16th Fl.
New York, NY 10020-1173 Ph: (212)586-5131
Description: This program alternates between an exhibition of Eskimo carvings and views of the daily life in the Iglootik settlement of the Northwest Territories. **Release Date:** 1974. **Length:** 25 mins. **Format:** Beta, VHS, 3/4″ U-matic Cassette.

★2510★
Songs In Minto Life
One West Media
PO Box 5766
559 Onate Pl.
Santa Fe, NM 87501 Ph: (505)983-8685
Description: The interrelationship between songs and life of the Minto Indians of Alaska is documented here. **Release Date:** 1986. **Length:** 30 mins. **Format:** VHS, 3/4″ U-matic Cassette.

★2511★
Stalking Seal on the Spring Ice, Parts I and II
Education Development Center, Inc.
55 Chapel St., Ste. 901 Ph: (617)969-7100
Newton, MA 02160 Free: 800-225-4276
Description: On the shore of Pelly Bay, a family of Netsilik Eskimos stalk a seal, kill it and then use the animal for food, sinew and clothing. **Release Date:** 1967. **Length:** 30 mins. **Format:** 3/4″ U-matic Cassette, Other than listed.

★2512★
Tanana River Rat
River Tracks Productions
PO Box 9
Manley Hot Springs, AK 99756
Description: Focusing on contemporary life in Interior Alaska, this film portrays the story of two brothers who are forced to come together after being separated by the 1991 Alaska Native land claims. **Release Date:** 1989. **Length:** 57 mins. **Format:** VHS.

★2513★
They Never Asked Our Fathers
Native American Public Broadcasting
  Consortium
1800 N. 33rd St.
PO Box 86111
Lincoln, NE 68501 Ph: (402)472-3522
Description: Focuses on the Yup'ik Eskimos of Nunivaq, who have lost their land to the U.S. government. Includes historic photographs, documents, interviews, and scenes of life in the Bering Sea area. **Release Date:** 1982. **Length:** 58 mins. **Format:** VHS, 1″ Broadcast Type ″C″, 3/4″ U-matic Cassette.

★2514★
Tukiki and His Search for a Merry Christmas
Coronet/MTI Film & Video Ph: (708)940-1260
108 Wilmot Rd. Free: 800-621-2131
Deerfield, IL 60015 Fax: (708)940-3640
Description: The Christmastime adventures of a small Eskimo boy named Tukiki are related. **Release Date:** 1980. **Length:** 25 mins. **Format:** Beta, VHS, 3/4″ U-matic Cassette, Other than listed.

★2515★
Tununeremiut: The People of Tununak
Documentary Educational Resources
101 Morse St.
Watertown, MA 02172 Ph: (617)926-0491
Fax Fax: (617)926-9519
Description: This program portrays aspects of the lives of the Eskimos of Tununak in Alaska. **Release Date:** 1972. **Length:** 35 mins. **Format:** 3/4″ U-matic Cassette.

★2516★
The Wedding of Palo
Video Yesteryear
Box C Ph: (203)426-2574
Sandy Hook, CT 06482 Free: 800-243-0987
Description: The classic documentary co-filmed by Danish explorer Rasmussen about Eskimo life in a northern district of Greenland. **Release Date:** 1935. **Length:** 72 mins. **Format:** Beta, VHS. **Credits:** Directed by: Knud Rasmussen; Knud Rasmussen; Friedrich Dalsheim.

★2517★
World Eskimo Art
New York State Education Department
Center for Learning Technologies
Media Distribution Network, Rm. C-7,
  Concourse Level
Albany, NY 12230 Ph: (518)474-1265
Description: How Eskimo art relates to the Eskimo lifestyle is examined. **Release Date:** 1971. **Length:** 30 mins. **Format:** Beta, VHS, 1/2″ Reel-EIAJ, 3/4″ U-matic Cassette, 2″ Quadraplex Open Reel.

★2518★
Yesterday, Today: The Netsilik Eskimo
Education Development Center, Inc.
55 Chapel St., Ste. 901 Ph: (617)969-7100
Newton, MA 02160 Free: 800-225-4276
Description: A look at one day in the life of a Netsilik Eskimo family for whom life is no longer a constant struggle. They have left their igloos for rented government housing, receive their government provided family allowance checks to use at the co-op store, and hunt from snowmobiles. We are shown how their traditional self-sufficient way of life has been replaced by the interdependency and specialization of modern life. Part of the "Eskimo Survival" series. **Release Date:** 1971. **Length:** 57 mins. **Format:** 3/4″ U-matic Cassette, Other than listed.

★2519★
You Can't Grow Potatoes Up There!
Kinetic Film Enterprises, Ltd.
255 Delaware Ave., Ste. 340
Buffalo, NY 14202 Ph: (716)856-7631
Description: This program illustrates the importance of seal hunting in the traditional life of the Arctic Inuit Eskimos. **Release Date:** 1981. **Length:** 27 mins. **Format:** 3/4″ U-matic Cassette.

Internet and Online Databases

★2520★
**Circumpolar and Aboriginal North America
  Resources**
Nunavut Implementation Commission

URL: http://www.nunanet.com/nic/WWWVL-ANA.html **Description:** Provides links to information resources on the peoples and environment of the Arctic Circle, as well as other aboriginal groups throughout the world.

★2521★
Eskimo Words for Snow
Utopia Inc.
200 Fifth Ave. Ph: (617)768-5500
Waltham, MA 02154 Fax: (617)768-5555
URL: http://www.utopia.com/mailings/rre/Eskimo.words.for.snow.html **Description:** Eskimo Words for Snow is a list of lexemes referring to snow and related notions in one Eskimo language, Central Alaskan Yupik (or just Yup'ik Eskimo). The list is organized according to lexeme meanings. Data Providers: Alaska Native Language Center, University of Alaska, Fairbanks. Everything you need to be the life of the party in

Nome. Site is plain ASCII text, although it is searchable. This is a list of lexemes rather than of words. Roughly, a lexeme can be thought of as an independent vocabulary item or dictionary entry. It's different from a word since a lexeme can give rise to more than one distinctly inflected word. **Update frequency:** Not updated. **Fees:** Free.

★2522★
Native American Graves Protection and Repatriation Act
University of Arkansas
Center for Advanced Spatial Technologies
12 Ozark Hall　　　　　　　　Ph: (501)575-6159
Fayetteville, AR 72701　　　　Fax: (501)575-3846
Robert Harris, NABD Online System Coordinator
URL:　　　http://www.cast.uark.edu/other/nps/nagpra　　**Telnet:** www.cast.uark.edu Login: nadb Password: nadb **Modem:** (501)575-2021 **Description:** The Native Graves Protection and Repatriation Act (NAGPRA) database contains congressional reports, proposed regulations, Review Committee activities, and Federal Register notices of Completion of Inventory and Intent to Repatriate. A directory of NAGPRA contacts for federally recognized Indian tribes, Native Alaskan villages and corporations, and Native Hawaiian organizations and a directory of NAGPRA contacts for federal agencies are available in text files. NAGPRA also includes information about permits issued for archeological and paleontological survey and excavation on federal and Indian lands under the American Antiquities Act of 1906. Data Providers: U.S. National Parks Service and the U.S. Department of the Interior. Main Files: Legal Mandates; Notices; Review Committee. Very comprehensive coverage of the Act. Not easily searchable except through WAIS or Alta Vista. On November 16, 1990 President George Bush signed into law the Native American Graves Protection and Repatriation Act, hereafter referred to as the Act. **Update frequency:** Regularly. **Fees:** Free.

Native Hawaiians

National Organizations

★2523★
Aloha International
PO Box 665
Kilauea, HI 96754   Ph: (808)828-0302

Description: Nondenominational religious order of individuals dedicated to creating peace and environmental harmony through the use of Huna (Hawaiian word meaning "hidden" or "secret"). Huna is a system of psychology used to remedy emotional and physical problems based on the knowledge of how the physical, mental, and spiritual levels of consciousness function effectively when used properly. Conducts classes, courses, lectures, tour groups, seasonal celebrations, and workshops; administers training in Huna techniques to individuals, group leaders, and counselors; offers Hawaiian shaman training. Participates in spiritual healing; sponsors voluntary research projects; organizes spiritual cooperatives (kokuas). Maintains reference library. **Founded:** 1973. **Members:** 10,000 **Publications:** Aloha News, Newsletter, semiannual; The Aloha Spirit, Booklet; Basic Huna, Brochure. **Formerly:** Huna International.

★2524★
Foundation for Pacific Dance
PO Box 621435
Littleton, CO 80162   Ph: (303)933-2157

Description: Seeks to preserve and promote traditional authentic Hawaiian and Pacific dance and culture. Maintains speakers' bureau and performing group. Also hosts workshops and seminars. **Founded:** 1987. **Formerly:** (1991) Pacific Dance Association.

★2525★
Institute for the Advancement of Hawaiian Affairs
86-649 Puuhulu Rd.
Waianae, HI 96792   Ph: (808)696-5157

Description: Works to raise awareness of all aspects of Hawaiian culture. Promotes discussion on such issues as traditional healing practices, self-determination of indigenous peoples, national independence, and the impact of tourism on Hawaiian people. **Founded:** 1985.

★2526★
National Native American AIDS Prevention
134 Linden St.
Oakland, CA 94607   Ph: (510)444-2051

Description: Network of concerned Native people. Works to stop the spread of HIV and related diseases, including sexually transmitted disease and tuberculosis, among American Indians, Alaska Natives, and Native Hawaiians by improving their health status through empowerment and self determination. Serves as a resource to Native communities and to support community efforts by providing education and information services, thereby ehancing the physical, spiritual, and economic health of Native people. Sponsors educational programs. Maintains speakers' bureau. Compiles statistics. **Founded:** 1987. **Publications:** Season; Newsletter, quarterly

★2527★
Pele Defense Fund
PO Box 404
Volcano, HI 96785   Ph: (808)935-1663

Description: Individuals following traditional Hawaiian religious practices, particularly worship of Pele, the volcano goddess. Seeks to: perpetuate Hawaiian religion and culture through revitalization of beliefs, traditions, and practices regarding nature and the earth; gather and disseminate funds for research grants and an ethnographic research project; disseminate research findings through publications and other media to educate Hawaiian communities and the general public. Lobbies local and federal governments; opposes geothermal development in Hawaii as desecration of the goddess Pele. Conducts public forums. Sponsors religious ceremonies and activities. **Founded:** 1985.

★2528★
Polynesian Cultural Center
55-370 Kamehameha Hwy.
Laie, HI 96762   Ph: (808)293-3333

Description: Presents, preserves, and perpetuates the arts, crafts, culture, and lore of Fijian, Hawaiian, Maori, Marquesan, Tahitian, Tongan, Samoan, and other Polynesian peoples. Seeks to preserve and dramatize ancient cultures in a manner that is entertaining, informative, and educational. Polynesian islanders demonstrate traditional ways of life in villages of authentic huts at the center, which is located on a 42-acre site on the north shore of the island of Oahu, 38 miles from Waikiki. Offers visitors guided tours, extemporaneous dancing by Tahitian and other Polynesian peoples, crafts demonstrations, and an evening show featuring up to 150 performers. Shares cultural information and experience with approximately one million visitors per year. Maintains collection of Polynesian artifacts. Funds the Institute for Polynesian Studies, located at Brigham Young University - Hawaii campus. Revenue from the center has been used to provide educational and employment opportunities for more than 26,000 Polynesian young people since 1963. **Founded:** 1963.

Regional, State/Provincial, & Local Organizations

Hawaii

★2529★
Institute for Native Pacific Culture and Education
PO Box 11365
Honolulu, HI 96828   Ph: (808)262-7650
Sherlyn Franklin Goog, Pres.
Description: Provides educational services.

★2530★
Native Hawaiian Chamber of Commerce
c/o Leighton Laakea K.L. Suganuma,
   Pres.
PO Box 597   Ph: (808)531-3744
Honolulu, HI 96809   Fax: (808)536-8699

Federal Domestic Assistance Programs

★2531★
U.S. Department of Education
Office of the Assistant Secretary for Elementary and Secondary Education
School Improvement Programs
Native Hawaiian Family-Based Education Centers
School Improvement Program
600 Independence Ave., SW
Washington, DC 20202   Ph: (202)260-2502
Catalog Number: 84.209. **Objectives:** To expand the operation of Family-Based Education Centers, which include prenatal and preschool programs, follow-up and assessment, and research and develoopment, through the Hawaiian Islands. **Applicant Eligibility:** Native Hawaiian organizations including Native Hawaiian educational organizations may apply. **Types of Assistance:** Direct Payments for Specified Use. **Beneficiary Eligibility:** Infants up to three years old and their parents, also preschoolers four and five years old and their parents will benefit.

★2532★
U.S. Department of Education
Office of Elementary and Secondary Education
Native Hawaiian Community-Based Education Learning Center
600 Maryland Ave., SW
Washington, DC 20202   Ph: (202)260-2502
Catalog Number: 84.296 **Objectives:** To support collaborative efforts between community-based Native Hawaiian organizations and community colleges, to develop, establish, and operate a minimum of three community-based education learning centers. **Applicant Eligibility:** Community-based Native Hawaiian organizations and community colleges in Hawaii. **Types of Assistance:** Project Grants. **Beneficiary Eligibility:** Preschool, elementary and secondary students, and adult students will benefit.

★2533★
U.S. Department of Education
Office of Elementary and Secondary Education
Native Hawaiian Curriculum Development, Teacher Training and Recruitment
600 Maryland Ave., SW
Washington, DC 20202   Ph: (202)260-2502
Catalog Number: 84.297 **Objectives:** To fund native Hawaiian programs designed to conduct instruction in the Native Hawaiian language for curriculum development or teacher training. **Applicant Eligibility:** Native Hawaiian education organization or education entities with experience in developing or operating native Hawaiian programs or programs of instruction conducted in the native Hawaiian language. **Types of Assistance:** Project Grants. **Beneficiary Eligibility:** Elementary and secondary students will benefit.

★2534★
U.S. Department of Education
Office of Elementary and Secondary Education
Native Hawaiian Gifted and Talented
School Improvement Program
600 Independence Ave., SW
Washington, DC 20202   Ph: (202)260-2502
Catalog Number: 84.210. **Objectives:** To provide financial assistance to the University of Hawaii at Hilo to :(1) Establish a Native Hawaiian Gifted and Talented Center at the University of Hawaii at Hilo; and (2) to demonstrate programs designed to address the special needs of Native Hawaiian elementary and secondary school students who are gifted and talented. Support services are also provided to their families as needed. **Applicant Eligibility:** Native Hawaiian educational organizations or educational entities may apply. **Types of Assistance:** Project grants. **Beneficiary Eligibility:** Gifted and talented native Hawaiian elementary and secondary educational students will benefit.

★2535★
U.S. Department of Education
Office of Special Education and Rehabilitative Services
Native Hawaiian Special Education
600 Independence Ave., SW
Washington, DC 20202   Ph: (202)265-9099
Catalog Number: 84.221. **Objectives:** To operate projects addressing the special education needs of Native Hawaiian students. **Applicant Eligibility:** State of Hawaii or Native Hawaiian organizations may apply. **Types of Assistance:** Project Grants. **Beneficiary Eligibility:** Native Hawaiian students with handicaps served by grantees will benefit.

★2536★
U.S. Department of Education
Office of Vocational and Adult Education
Native Hawaiian Vocational Education
Division of National Programs
600 Independence Ave., SW
Washington, DC 20202   Ph: (202)205-5563
Catalog Number: 84.259 **Objectives:** To make grants to organizations primarily serving and representing Native Hawaiians for programs or portions of programs authorized by, and consistent with, the Carl D. Perkins Vocational and Applied Technology Education Act. **Applicant Eligibility:** Any organization primarily serving and representing Native Hawaiians and recognized by the Governor of Hawaii may apply. **Types of Assistance:** Project Grants (Cooperative Agreements). **Beneficiary Eligibility:** Native Hawaiians will benefit.

★2537★
U.S. Department of Education
Office of Vocational and Adult Education
Vocational Education—Indian Setaside
Division of National Programs
600 Independence Ave., SW
Washington, DC 20202-7242   Ph: (202)205-5680

Catalog Number: 84.101. **Objectives:** To make grants to or enter contracts with Indian tribes or tribal organizations and to organizations primarily serving and representing Hawaiian Natives to plan, conduct, and administer programs or portions of programs authorized by and consistent with the Carl D. Perkins Vocational Education Act. **Applicant Eligibility:** A tribal organization or an Indian tribe eligible to contract with the Secretary of the Interior for the administration of programs under the Indian Self-Determination and Education Assistance Act of 1975 or under the Act of April 16, 1934. **Types of Assistance:** Project Grants (Cooperative Agreements); Project Grants (Contracts). **Beneficiary Eligibility:** Federally recognized Indian tribes and Hawaiian Natives will benefit.

★2538★
U.S. Department of Health and Human Services
Administration on Aging
American Indian, Alaskan Native, & Native Hawaiian Programs
Special Programs for the Aging, Title VI—Part B Grants to Native Hawaiians
330 Independence Ave. SW
Washington, DC 20201   Ph: (202)619-2957

Catalog Number: 93.655. **Objectives:** To promote the delivery of supportive services, including nutrition services to older Indians, Alaskan Natives, and Native Hawaiians. Services are comparable to services provided under Title III of the Older Americans Act of 1965, as amended. **Applicant Eligibility:** Includes public or nonprofit organizations which serve Native Hawaiian Elders, which represent at least 50 Indians or Hawaiians 60 years of age or older. Applicants must document that they have or will have the ability to deliver social and nutrition services. **Types of Assistance:** Project grants. **Beneficiary Eligibility:** Indians or Native Hawaiians who are 60 years of age and older, and in the case of nutrition, their spouses.

★2539★
U.S. Department of Health and Human Services
Health Resources and Services Administration
Native Hawaiian Health Systems
4350 East-West Hwy., 11th Fl.
Bethesda, MD 20814   Ph: (301)594-4260

Catalog Number: 93.932. **Objectives:** To raise the health status of Native Hawaiians living in Hawaii to the highest possible level through the provision of comprehensive health promotion and disease prevention services, as well as primary health services, and to provide existing Native Hawaiian health care programs with all resources necessary to effectuate this policy. **Applicant Eligibility:** An entity qualifies to apply if it is a "Native Hawaiian health system." the term Native Hawaiian health care system is defined as an entity (1) which is organized under the laws of the State of Hawaii; (2) which provides or arranges for health care services through practitioners licensed by the State of Hawaii, where licensure requirements are applicable; (3) which is a public or nonprofit private entity; (4) in which Native Hawaiian health practitioners significantly participate in the planning, management, monitoring, and evaluation of health care services; (5) which may be composed of as many Native Hawaiian health centers as necessary to meet the health care needs of each island's Native Hawaiians; and (6) which is recognized by Papa Ola Lokahi (a consortium of Hawaiian and Native Hawaiian organizations) for the purpose of planning, conducting, or administering programs or portions of programs, authorized by this act for the benefit of Native Hawaiians, and is certified by Papa Ola Lokahi as having the qualifications and the capacity to provide the services and meet the requirements of this Act. **Types of Assistance:** Project Grants. **Beneficiary Eligibility:** Native Hawaiians.

★2540★
U.S. Department of Labor
Employment and Training Administration
Native American Employment and Training Programs
Division of Indian and Native American
     Programs
200 Constitution Ave., NW, Rm. N4641
Washington, DC 20210   Ph: (202)219-8502

Catalog Number: 17.251. **Objectives:** To afford job training to Native Americans facing serious barriers to employment, who are in special need of such training to obtain productive employment. To reduce the economic disadvantages among Indians and others of Native American descent and to advance the economic and social development of such people. **Applicant Eligibility:** Indian tribes, bands or groups, Alaska Native villages or groups, and Hawaiian Native communities meeting the eligibility criteria, public bodies or private nonprofit agencies selected by the Secretary. Tribes, bands and groups may also form consortia in order to qualify for designation as a grantee. An independently eligible grantee shall be an Indian or Native American entity which has: (1) An identifiable Native American resident population of at least 1,000 individuals (for new grantees) within its designated service area, and (2) the capability to administer Indian and Native American employment and training programs. **Types of Assistance:** Formula Grants. **Beneficiary Eligibility:** Members of State or federally recognized Indian tribes, bands and other individuals of Native American descent, such as, but not limited to, the Kalamaths in Oregon, Micmac and Miliseet in Maine, the Lumbees in North Carolina and South Carolina, Indians variously descibed as terminated or landless, Eskimos and Aleuts in Alaska, and Hawaiian Natives. ("Hawaiian Native" means an individual any of whose ancestors were natives prior to 1778 of the area which now comprises the State of Hawaii.) Applicants must also be economically disadvantaged, unemployed, or underemployed. A Native American grantee may apply in some cases enroll participants who are not economically disadvantaged, unemployed, or underemployed in upgrading and retraining programs.

State/Provincial & Local Government Agencies

★2541★
Hawaii Health Department
Affirmative Action Office
1250 Punchbowl St.   Ph: (808)586-4612
Honolulu, HI 96813   Fax: (808)586-4444

Library Collections

★2542★
Bernice P. Bishop Museum
Library
1525 Bernice St.   Ph: (808)848-4148
Honolulu, HI 96817-0916   Fax: (808)845-4133
Duane E. Wenzel, Lib.Chm.

Founded: 1889 **Subjects:** Anthropology, archaeology, entomology, botany, malacology, marine biology, vertebrate and invertebrate zoology, Hawaiiana, exploration, history, linguistics, geology. **Special Collections:** Fuller Collection of Pacific Books (anthropology; 2500 volumes); 19th century Hawaiian language newspapers; Carter Collection of Hawaiiana (1500 volumes); early Pacific voyages; Pacific island language texts. **Holdings:** 100,000 volumes; 1500 microfiche; 1000 reels of microfilm; 17,000 pamphlets. **Subscriptions:** 1100 journals and other serials.

★2543★
**Hawaii (State) Department of Accounting and
General Services**
State Archives
Iolani Palace Grounds   Ph: (808)586-0329
Honolulu, HI 96813   Fax: (808)586-0330
Founded: 1906 **Subjects:** Hawaiian history and government.
Special Collections: Captain Cook Collection (Cook and discovery
of the Hawaiian Islands); historic photograph collection (Hawaiian
monarchs, major towns, Waikiki, sugar and pineapple industries,
and historic events, 1800s-1980s; 107,000 photographs and
negatives). **Holdings:** 4038 books; 160 bound periodical volumes;
620 cubic feet of private manuscript collections; 9293 cubic feet of
official archives; 3294 reels of microfilm; 11,000 aerial photographs;
1855 maps.

★2544★
Hawaii State Public Library System
Hawaii State Library
Edna Allyn Room
478 S. King St.   Ph: (808)586-3510
Honolulu, HI 96813   Fax: (808)586-3584
Subjects: Children's books, Hawaiiana, foreign books for children.
Special Collections: Historical collection of out-of-print and rare
children's books; alphabet books; counting books; autographed
Nene Award books. **Holdings:** 81,824 books; 387 book/cassette
kits. **Subscriptions:** 44 journals and other serials.

★2545★
Hawaii State Public Library System
Hawaii State Library
Hawaii and Pacific Section I
478 S. King St.   Ph: (808)586-3535
Honolulu, HI 96813   Fax: (808)586-3586
Joyce Miyamoto, Hd.
Founded: 1913 **Subjects:** Hawaiiana, Pacifica. **Special
Collections:** Hawaii and the Pacific Collection (85,269 volumes);
State Documents Collection (59,122); Admiral Thomas Papers
(130); Phillips Collection (1705 items). **Holdings:** 85,269 books;
1284 bound periodical volumes; 86,500 pamphlets and newspaper
clippings; 65,012 state documents on microfiche. **Subscriptions:**
1557 journals and other serials.

★2546★
Hawaiian Historical Society
Library
560 Kawaiahao St.
Honolulu, HI 96813   Ph: (808)537-6271
Barbara E. Dunn, Adm.Dir.
Founded: 1892 **Subjects:** Pacific and round the world voyages,
history of Hawaiian Islands and Polynesia, local biography. **Special
Collections:** Newspapers printed in Hawaiian Islands, 1836-1900;
Hawaiian language imprints, 1822-1900 (600 volumes). **Holdings:**
12,000 volumes; 2808 pamphlets; 5 VF drawers of manuscripts; 10
VF drawers of clippings; 5 VF drawers of photographs; early
newspapers on microfilm; 3 VF drawers of maps; 1 VF drawer of
broadsides; 50 photograph albums and scrapbooks.
Subscriptions: 28 journals and other serials.

★2547★
Hawaiian Mission Children's Society Library
Mission Houses Museum
553 S. King St.   Ph: (808)531-0481
Honolulu, HI 96813   Fax: (808)545-2280
Marilyn L. Reppun, Hd.Libn.
Founded: 1908 **Subjects:** 19th century Hawaiian history, history of
Protestant missionaries in Hawaii, voyages to Hawaii. **Special
Collections:** Manuscripts of American Protestant missionaries,
1820-1900 (includes unpublished letters, journals, reports);
Hawaiian language materials; early Hawaiian newspapers; archives
of the Congregational Church in Hawaii, Micronesia, and the
Marquesas. **Holdings:** 12,000 books; 400 bound periodical
volumes; 6 drawers of microfilm; 245 linear feet of manuscript
material; engravings; drawings; daguerreotypes; photographs.
Subscriptions: 15 journals and other serials.

★2548★
Lyman House Memorial Museum
Kathryn E. Lyle Memorial Library
276 Haili St.   Ph: (808)935-5021
Hilo, HI 96720   Fax: (808)969-7685
Charlene Dahlquist
Founded: 1932 **Subjects:** Hawaii - history and pre-Cook history,
volcanology, geology, shells, religions; local family genealogies;
Pacific islands; missionaries in Hawaii; Hilo and environment.
Special Collections: Lyman Family; Hilo Boarding School; Kohala
Sugar Co; Hamakua Sugar Co. **Holdings:** 4000 books; 14,000
photographs; 200 blueprints; 6 charts; 84 daguerreotypes; 40,000
pieces of ephemera; 735 glassplates; 5 journals; 2000 letters; 190
maps; 13 newsletters; 200 prints; 6000 clippings; 660 New England
newspapers, 1806-1900; historical materials on early Hawaii.

★2549★
Maui Historical Society
Library
2375-A Main St.
Wailuku, HI 96793   Ph: (808)244-3326
Founded: 1975 **Subjects:** Hawaii, Maui. **Special Collections:**
Historic photographs and maps. **Holdings:** 600 books; 6 VF
drawers of mounted clippings; 10 VF drawers of photographs; 1
drawer of slides; 8 VF drawers of historical files by subject; 5 VF
drawers of archeological files; 22.5 linear feet of archives and
manuscripts. **Subscriptions:** 4 journals and other serials.

★2550★
U.S. Department of the Interior
National Park Service
Haleakala National Park
Library
Box 369   Ph: (808)572-9306
Makawao, HI 96768   Fax: (808)572-1304
Founded: 1916 **Subjects:** Botany, zoology, Hawaiiana, geology,
ecology, parks, archeology. **Special Collections:** IBP-Island
Ecosystems (of Hawaii; 75). **Holdings:** 1100 books pamphlets.
Collection of pertinent subject material. **Subscriptions:** 2 journals
and other serials.

★2551★
U.S. Department of the Interior
National Park Service
Hawaii Volcanoes National Park
Library
PO Box 52   Ph: (808)985-6000
Hawaii National Park, HI 96718   Fax: (808)985-8640
Founded: 1916 **Subjects:** Volcanology, zoology, botany, ancient
culture of Hawaiians. **Holdings:** 3130 books; 470 bound periodical
volumes; 1825 pamphlets; 2000 black/white photographs; 3000
slides. **Subscriptions:** 17 journals and other serials.

★2552★
U.S. Department of the Interior
National Park Service
Pu'uhonua o Honaunau National Historical Park
Library
Box 129   Ph: (808)328-2288
Honaunau, HI 96726   Fax: (808)328-9485
Founded: 1961 **Subjects:** Hawaiian culture and history; National
Park Service. **Holdings:** 800 books; 180 manuscripts.

★2553★
University of Hawaii
Special Collections
Archives and Manuscripts
Sinclair Library
2425 Campus Rd.   Ph: (808)956-7923
Honolulu, HI 96822   Fax: (808)956-5968
DrNancy Morris, Lib.Spec.
Founded: 1968 **Subjects:** University of Hawaii. **Holdings:**
Noncurrent official records of the university, faculty, and staff;

miscellaneous historical material about the university; manuscript material related to Hawaii and the Pacific.

★2554★
University of Hawaii
Special Collections
Hawaiian Collection
Hamilton Library
2550 The Mall
Honolulu, HI 96822   Ph: (808)956-8264
DrChieko Tachihata, Cur.   Fax: (808)956-5968

Founded: 1927 **Subjects:** Hawaiian Islands, languages, Captain Cook, state and county government documents, children's literature, Hawaiian language materials, ethnic materials. **Special Collections:** Rare Hawaiiana; 19th century Hawaiian business and literary manuscripts (20 linear feet); oral history collections (30.5 linear feet of reel-to-reel tapes, audio cassettes, bound transcripts). **Holdings:** 125,511 volumes; 10,434 REE; audiovisual materials; 54 linear feet of pamphlets; audiotapes of oral history; oral history transcripts; University of Hawaii theses and dissertations. **Subscriptions:** 2077 journals and other serials.

Museums and Other Cultural Facilities

★2555★
Bailey House Museum
2375A Main St.   Ph: (808)244-3326
Wailuku, HI 96793   Fax: (808)244-3920
John Cooper, Exec.Dir.

Description: Collections include Native Hawaiian artifacts. Conducts research on local history and archaeology of Maui County.

★2556★
Bernice Pauahi Bishop Museum
1525 Bernice St.
PO Box 19000-A   Ph: (808)847-3511
Honolulu, HI 96817-0916   Fax: (808)841-8968
Siegfried S. Kagawa, Pres.

Description: The state museum of cultural and natural history with exhibits relating to Hawaii and the Pacific, including a collection of Hawaiian royal artifacts.

★2557★
Hawaii Children's Museum
Kauai Children's Discovery Museum
6458 B Kahuna Rd.   Ph: (808)823-8222
Kapaa, HI 96746   Fax: (808)821-2558

Description: Has hands-on exhibits relating to Hawaiian and other cultures.

★2558★
Hulihee Palace
75-5718 Alii Dr.   Ph: (808)329-1877
Kailua Kona, HI 96740   Fax: (808)329-1321
Julia L. Soehren, 4th Vice-Regent and CEO

Description: Collections include ancient Hawaiian artifacts.

★2559★
Iolani Palace
King and Richards Sts.
PO Box 2259   Ph: (808)522-0822
Honolulu, HI 96804   Fax: (808)532-1051
Alice F. Guild, Managing Dir.

Description: Collections include artifacts of the Hawaiian monarchy (1882-1893), and original artifacts of Iolani Palace.

★2560★
Kamuela Museum
PO Box 507
Kamuela, HI 96743   Ph: (808)885-4724

Description: Includes a large Hawaiian cultural collection, including royal artifacts and pieces that were originally in the Iolani palace.

★2561★
Kauai Museum
4428 Rice St.
PO Box 248   Ph: (808)245-6931
Lihue, HI 96766   Fax: (808)245-6864
Dan Dahl, Dir.

Description: Maintains Hawaiiana collection with particular emphasis on items of the island of Kauai, a Kauai photo collection, and ethnic and heritage displays.

★2562★
Lahaina Restoration Foundation
120 Dickenson   Ph: (808)661-3262
Maui, HI 96761   Fax: (808)661-9309
James C. Luckey, Exec.Dir.

Description: Collections include Hawaiian stone artifacts and tools.

★2563★
Lyman Mission House Memorial Museum
276 Haili St.   Ph: (808)935-5021
Hilo, HI 96720   Fax: (808)969-7685
Richard Henderson, Pres.

Description: Collections include 19th and early 20th century Hawaiian Artists' Gallery, Hawaiian cultural relics, and ethnic displays of seven national groups living in Hawaii.

★2564★
Mission Houses Museum
553 S. King St.   Ph: (808)531-0481
Honolulu, HI 96813   Fax: (808)545-2280
Deborah Pope, CEO

Description: Maintains collection of Polynesian artifacts, including domestic artifacts, household furnishings, and Hawaiian language materials.

★2565★
Moanalua Gardens Foundation
1352 Pineapple Pl.   Ph: (808)839-5334
Honolulu, HI 96819   Fax: (808)839-3658
Paulie K. Jennings, Exec.Dir.

Description: Collections include items relating to Hawaiian cultural history.

★2566★
Pu'uhonua O Honaunau National Historical Park
PO Box 129   Ph: (808)328-2326
Honaunau, HI 96726   Fax: (808)328-9485
Jerry Y. Shimoda, Superintendent

Description: Maintains collections of Hawaiian artifacts and burial remains.

★2567★
Queen Emma Summer Palace
2913 Pali Hwy.   Ph: (808)595-3167
Honolulu, HI 96817   Fax: (808)595-4395
Mildred Nolan, CEO and Regent

Description: Former home of Queen Emma and King Kamehameha IV. Collections include household furnishings and personal effects of Queen Emma and her family, period pieces, portraits, photographs, Hawaiian artifacts, tapa, feather work, and Hawaiian quilts.

Education Programs & Services

Schools

★2568★
Hale Kako'o Punana Leo/Hilo
1744 Kino'ole St.   Ph: (808)959-4979
Hilo, HI 96720   Fax: (808)959-4725
School Type: Hawaiian Immersion schools support center.

★2569★
Hale Kako'o Punana Leo/Honolulu
2002-L Hunnewell St.   Ph: (808)941-0584
Honolulu, HI 96822   Fax: (808)941-0584
School Type: Hawaiian Immersion schools support and materials development center.

★2570★
Kamehameha Schools/Bernice Pauahi Bishop Estate (KS/BE)
Education Group
Program Services Division
1887 Makuakane St.   Ph: (808)842-8211
Honolulu, HI 96817-1887   Fax: (808)842-8875
Description: Exists to carry out the legacy of Bernice Pauahi Bishop (Ke Ali'i Pauahi, the last direct descendent of the royal line of Kamehameha). KS/BE offers a variety of educational services, both independently and in conjunction with the Hawaii State Department of Education, and gives preference to children of Hawaiian ancestry. Programs include: Parent-Infant Program; Traveling Pre-schools; 23 Center-based Pre-Schools; KEEP—Kamehameha's Elementary Education Program (elementary language arts); Pre-service Education for Teachers of Minorities (PETOM); Kamehameha Elementary School (grades K-6); Kamehameha Secondary School (grades 7-12; college prep); Alternative and Continuing Education programs; Hawaiian Studies Institute; Summer programs; Kamehameha Schools Intermediate Reading Program (KSIRP); Post-High Scholarship and Counseling Program; Kamehameha Talent Search; Native Hawaiian Higher Education Program; Native Hawaiian Health Professions Scholarship Program; and the Native Hawaiian Drug-Free Schools and Communities Program. Operates the KS Press, which publishes a small group of educational materials with a focus on Hawaiian studies.

★2571★
Kapa'a Elementary School
4886 Kawaihau Rd.   Ph: (808)821-4424
Kapaa, HI 96746   Fax: (808)821-4431
School Type: Hawaiian Immersion school; grades 1-8.

★2572★
Kualapu'u Elementary School
PO Box 102   Ph: (808)567-6126
Kualapuu, HI 96757   Fax: (808)567-6514
School Type: Hawaiian Immersion school; grades 1-8.

★2573★
Pa'ia Elementary School
955 Baldwin Ave.   Ph: (808)579-8261
Paia, HI 96779   Fax: (808)579-8769
School Type: Hawaiian Immersion school; grades 1-8.

★2574★
Punana Leo O Hilo
1744 Kino'ole St.   Ph: (808)959-4700
Hilo, HI 96720   Fax: (808)959-4725
School Type: Hawaiian Immersion preschool.

★2575★
Punana Leo O Honolulu
1313 Kamehameha IV Rd.   Ph: (808)841-6655
Honolulu, HI 96819   Fax: (808)841-6655
School Type: Hawaiian Immersion preschool.

★2576★
Punana Leo O Kaua'i
PO Box 2093   Ph: (808)245-1755
Puhi, HI 96766   Fax: (808)245-8672
School Type: Hawaiian Immersion Preschool.

★2577★
Punana Leo O Maui
PO Box 337   Ph: (808)244-5676
Wailuku, HI 96793   Fax: (808)244-0534

★2578★
Punana Leo O Moloka'I
PO Box 102   Ph: (808)567-9211
Kualapuu, HI 96757   Fax: (808)567-6514
School Type: Hawaiian Immersion preschool.

★2579★
Pu'ohala Elementary School
45-233 Kulauli St.   Ph: (808)233-5660
Kaneohe, HI 96744   Fax: (808)233-5663
School Type: Hawaiian Immersion school; grades 1-8.

★2580★
Waiau Elementary School
98-450 Ho'okanike St.   Ph: (808)453-6530
Pearl City, HI 96782   Fax: (808)453-6541
School Type: Hawaiian Immersion School; grades 1-8.

Studies Programs

Four-Year Programs

★2581★
University of Hawaii at Hilo
Hawaiian Studies Program
523 W. Lanikaula St.
Hilo, HI 96720-4091

★2582★
University of Hawaii at Manoa
Hawaiian Studies Program
Honolulu, HI 96822   Ph: (808)948-8975

Publishers

★2583★
Aka Press
PO Box 1372
Wailuku, HI 96793
Description: Publishes travel books and books on Hawaii and Hawaiiana. Reaches market through direct mail, reviews, trade sales, Pacific Trade Group, and BookPeople.

★2584★
Aloha Publishing
PO Box 240165
Honolulu, HI 96824-0165   Fax: (808)926-0865
Description: Specializes in Hawaiian history for visitors. Accepts unsolicited manuscripts. Reaches market through commission representatives, trade sales, and Booklines Hawaii, Ltd.

★2585★
Bamboo Ridge Press
PO Box 61781
Honolulu, HI 96839-1781   Ph: (808)626-1481
Description: Publishes books by or about Hawaii's people. Publications include collections of short stories, anthologies of contemporary Hawaiian literature, collections of legends, and collections of poetry. Reaches market through direct mail, telephone sales, and wholesalers.

★2586★
Barnhart Press
PO Box 27940   Ph: (213)462-0767
Los Angeles, CA 90027   Fax: (213)462-0767
Description: Publishes on ancient Kahuna secrets from old Hawaii, interfaced with contemporary self-help. Does not accept unsolicited manuscripts. **Subjects:** Magic, Hawaii.

★2587★
Bess Press
3565 Harding Ave.   Ph: (808)734-7159
Honolulu, HI 96816   Free: 800-910-2377
                                 Fax: (808)732-3627
Description: A regional publisher of Asian, Pacific, and Hawaiian history, language, and cultural materials. Also publishes adult and children's trade books. Offers a map of Hawaii and an eight-part filmstrip package on the Hawaiians of old. Reaches market through wholesalers. Accepts unsolicited manuscripts. **Number of New Titles:** 1998 - 12.

★2588★
Bishop Museum Press
1525 Bernice Street   Ph: (808)847-3511
Honolulu, HI 96817-0916   Fax: (808)841-8968
Description: Publishes popular and scientific titles on natural and cultural history of Hawaii and the Pacific. Reaches market through trade sales, wholesalers, and direct contact. **Subjects:** Natural history, cultural history, Hawaiiana, Pacifiana.

★2589★
Editions Ltd.
PO Box 10558   Ph: (808)735-7644
Honolulu, HI 96816   Fax: (808)732-2164
Description: Publishes limited editions and collectors' books on Hawaiian history, sociology, religion, and art. Also produces calendars and maps. Reaches market through direct mail and wholesalers. Does not accept unsolicited manuscripts. **Subjects:** Hawaii, history, art, maps.

★2590★
Hammeter Publishing Corp.
250 S. Hotel St., No. 201
Honolulu, HI 96813-2831   Fax: (808)529-9023
Subjects: Hawaiiana, art, architecture, travel.

★2591★
Hawaiian Island Concepts
PO Box 1069   Ph: (808)572-2606
Wailuku, HI 96793   Fax: (808)573-1362
Description: Publishes educational children's books with Hawaiian themes. Accepts unsolicited manuscripts; query first for guidelines. Reaches market through commission representatives, direct mail, telephone sales, trade sales, and wholesalers and distributors, including Native Books, Booklines Hawaii, Inc., Quality Books, Inc., and Baker & Taylor Books. Pacific pipeline distributors. **Number of New Titles:** 1998 - 3.

★2592★
Heritage Press of Pacific
1279-203 Ala Kapuna St.   Ph: (808)839-1238
Honolulu, HI 96819   Fax: (808)839-1238
Description: Publishes non-fiction and fiction. Reaches market through direct mail. Does not accept unsolicited manuscripts. **Subjects:** Hawaiian history, Hawaiian tales, Pearl Harbor.

★2593★
Hui Hanai
1300 Halona St.
Honolulu, HI 96817   Ph: (808)955-5256
Description: The Hui Hanai is an auxiliary of the Queen Lilioukalani Children's Center. Publishes on Hawaiian ethnohistory and sociology. All books are distributed exclusively by Booklines.

★2594★
Kamehameha Schools Press
1887 Makuakane St.   Ph: (808)842-8876
Honolulu, HI 96817   Fax: (808)842-8875
Description: Publishes on Hawaiian studies. Offers posters. **Subjects:** Hawaiian history, culture and language. **Number of New Titles:** 1998 - 5; 1996 - 5.

★2595★
Lani Goose Publications, Inc.
583 Kamoku St., Ste. 3803
Honolulu, HI 96826   Ph: (808)947-7330
Description: Publishes legends of Hawaii with read-along cassettes for elementary-age children. Reaches market through Booklines Hawaii, Ltd. **Subjects:** Hawaii.

★2596★
Lyman House Memorial Museum
276 Haili St.   Ph: (808)935-5021
Hilo, HI 96720   Fax: (808)969-7685
Description: Publishes on Hawaiian history. Also offers newsletters. Reaches market through direct mail and museum gift shop. Does not accept unsolicited manuscripts. **Subjects:** Hawaii history. **Number of New Titles:** 1998 - 1.

★2597★
Makapu'u Press
PO Box 264   Ph: (503)388-2892
Bend, OR 97709   Fax: (503)388-2892
Description: Publishes illustrated books on Hawaiian and Japanese culture. Reaches market through telephone sales and personal contact. **Subjects:** Hawaiiana, natural history, folklore.

★2598★
Na Kane O Ka Malo Press
PO Box 970
Waipahu, HI 96797-0970   Ph: (808)677-9513
Description: Publishes on the history, current events, and future of Hawaii. Offers audio tapes and decals. Accepts unsolicited manuscripts; Hawaiian works only. Reaches market through direct mail, trade sales, New Leaf Distributing Co., De Vorss & Co., Booklines Hawaii. Accepts unsolicited manuscripts. **Subjects:** Hawaiian religion, philosophy, history, politics, environmental thought sovereignty movement, alternative futures.

★2599★
Petroglyph Press, Ltd.
160 Kamehameha Ave.   Ph: (808)935-6006
Hilo, HI 96720-2834   Fax: (808)935-1553
Subjects: Hawaiiana.

★2600★
University of Hawaii Press
University of Hawaii
2840 Kolowalu St.
Honolulu, HI 96822

Ph: (808)956-8257
Free: 800-956-2840
Fax: (808)988-6052

Description: Publishes scholarly and regional books on Asia and the Pacific. Offers maps, audio cassettes, and calendars. Accepts unsolicited manuscripts. Distributes for Seoul National University Press, University of the Philippines Press, and Polynesian Press. Reaches market through direct mail and trade sales. **Subjects:** Asia, the Pacific, Hawaii. **Number of New Titles:** 1998 - 70.

★2601★
Wizard Publications
PO Box 991
Lihue, HI 96766-0991

Ph: (808)822-3991
Fax: (808)822-3991

Description: Publishes travel and adventure books about the Hawaiian Islands. Does not accept unsolicited manuscripts. Reaches market through direct mail and wholesalers and distributors, including Pacific Pipeline Inc., Bookpeople Inc., and Quality Books, Inc. **Subjects:** Hawaii, travel.

★2602★
Wonder View Press
823 Olive Ave.
Wahiawa, HI 96786

Ph: (808)621-2288
Fax: (808)621-4971

Description: Specializes in local-interest publications with emphasis on histories of Hawaiian locales, people, and traditions. Reaches market through direct mail, trade sales, and Pacific Trade Group.

Newsletters

★2603★
Aloha News
Huna International
PO Box 665
Kilauea, HI 96754-0665

Ph: (808)828-0302
Fax: (808)828-2839

Description: Explores the process of personal growth and fulfillment through Huna, a Hawaiian word referring to the invisible knowledge and power of the mind and an ancient philosophy focusing on the fulfillment of an individual's potential. Offers information on basic Huna techniques and spiritual healing. Recurring features include news of the organization and its members. **Pages (approx.):** varies. **Frequency:** Semiannual. **Price:** Donation requested.

Radio Stations

★2604★
KAHU-AM
PO Box 4727
Hilo, HI 96720

Ph: (808)959-2056
Fax: (808)959-4507

Frequency: 1060. **Format:** Ethnic, Hawaiian. **Owner:** KANI Communications Inc.

★2605★
KCCN-AM
900 Fort St., Ste. 400
Honolulu, HI 96813

Ph: (808)536-2728

Frequency: 1420. **Format:** Ethnic. **Owner:** Diamond Head Radio Inc.

★2606★
KMVI-AM
311 Ano St.
Kahului, HI 96732-1304

Ph: (808)877-5566
Fax: (808)877-2137

Frequency: 550 **Network Affiliation:** CNN Radio. **Format:** Adult Contemporary, Ethnic, Religious. **Owner:** Media.

★2607★
KUAI-AM
4469 Waialo Rd.
PO Box 720
Eleele, HI 96705-0720

Ph: (808)335-3171
Fax: (808)335-3834

Frequency: 720 **Network Affiliation:** Mutual Broadcasting System. **Format:** Full Service, Ethnic. **Owner:** American Islands Broadcasting Corp.

Internet and Online Databases

★2608★
Hawaii - Independent and Sovereign Nation-State
Hawaii OnLine
737 Bishop St., Mauka Tower
Ste. 2350
Honolulu, HI 96813

Ph: (808)791-1000
Free: 800-207-1880
Fax: (808)534-0089

URL: http://www.aloha.net/nation/hawaii-nation.html **Description:** The Nation of Hawaii database provides information regarding the legal foundation for the restoration of Hawaiian independence. The information includes the historical background, documents, current news, and images. Main Files: What's New at this site; Background Information; Legal Foundation; Policy Statements; Historical Information; News Articles; Music; Images; Support Hawaiian Self-Determination; Contact Information; Hawaiian Sovereignty and Culture LINKS; and more. Related Mailing Lists: To subscribe to the Hawaiian Sovereignty Listserver send e-mail to listproc@hawaii.edu and put KANAKAMAOLIALLIES-L first-name last-name in the body of the message. **Update frequency:** Regularly. **Fees:** Free.

★2609★
Huna from Hawaii
Aloha International
PO Box 665
Kilauea, HI 96754

Ph: (808)828-0302
Fax: (808)828-0302

URL: http://planet-hawaii.com/huna **Description:** Huna is a spiritual part of Hawaiian culture. To help keep it alive, Aloha International sponsors workshops, teacher fellowships, cultural exhibits, and this web site. Ample information is provided here regarding Huna; topics include teaching resources, a calendar of events, books and other media related to Huna, and a place to share thoughts. Main Files: Village Center; Teaching Hut; Sharing Hut; Activity Hut; Resource Hut. **Update frequency:** As needed. **Fees:** Free.

★2610★
Native American Graves Protection and Repatriation Act
University of Arkansas
Center for Advanced Spatial Technologies
12 Ozark Hall
Fayetteville, AR 72701
Robert Harris, NABD Online System Coordinator

Ph: (501)575-6159
Fax: (501)575-3846

URL: http://www.cast.uark.edu/other/nps/nagpra **Telnet:** www.cast.uark.edu Login: nadb Password: nadb **Modem:** (501)575-2021 **Description:** The Native Graves Protection and Repatriation Act (NAGPRA) database contains congressional reports, proposed regulations, Review Committee activities, and Federal Register notices of Completion of Inventory and Intent to Repatriate. A directory of NAGPRA contacts for federally recognized Indian tribes, Native Alaskan villages and corporations, and Native Hawaiian organizations and a directory of NAGPRA contacts for federal agencies are available in text files. NAGPRA also includes information about permits issued for archeological and paleontological survey and excavation on federal and Indian lands under the American Antiquities Act of 1906. Data Providers: U.S.

National Parks Service and the U.S. Department of the Interior. Main Files: Legal Mandates; Notices; Review Committee. Very comprehensive coverage of the Act. Not easily searchable except through WAIS or Alta Vista. On November 16, 1990 President George Bush signed into law the Native American Graves Protection and Repatriation Act, hereafter referred to as the Act. **Update frequency:** Regularly. **Fees:** Free.

Aboriginal Canadians

★2611★
Dartmouth College
Institute of Arctic Studies
6214 Steele Hall   Ph: (603)646-1278
Hanover, NH 03755-3577   Fax: (603)646-1279
Oran Young, Dir.

Founded: 1989 **Research Activities and Fields:** Arctic and
northern studies, including ice engineering, visions of the Arctic in
art and literature, and problems of health care delivery in northern
communities. Focus is on human/environment relationships in the
circumpolar north, including small scale common property
arrangements, the role of social institutions or resource regimes,
and the impact of ideas, values, and belief systems on the formation
and operation of these regimes. **Publications:** Northern Notes
Annual Journal, journal, annually.

★2612★
University of Alaska, Anchorage
Institute for Circumpolar Health Studies
3211 Providence Dr.   Ph: (907)786-4020
Anchorage, AK 99508   Fax: (907)786-4019
Dr. John M. Booker, Dir.

Founded: 1988 **Research Activities and Fields:** Health care
issues in Alaska and the Circumpolar North, provides research
instruction and information between the university, state agencies
and the international community.

★2613★
Native Peoples Magazine
PO Box 36820   Ph: (602)252-2236
Phoenix, AZ 85067   Free: (888)262-
                                              8483

Description: Magazine portraying the culture of native peoples of
the Americas. **First Published:** 1987. **Frequency:** Quarterly.
Subscriptions: $13.95. **ISSN:** 0895-7606.

Tribal Communities

Alberta

★2614★
Whitefish Lake First Nation (Atikameg)
General Delivery   Ph: (403)767-3914
Atikameg, AB, Canada T0G 0C0   Fax: (403)767-3814

★2615★
Kehewin Cree Nation
PO Box 6218   Ph: (403)826-3333
Bonnyville, AB, Canada T9N 2G8   Fax: (403)826-2355

★2616★
Peigan First Nation
PO Box 70   Ph: (403)965-3940
Brocket, AB, Canada T0K 0H0   Fax: (403)965-2030

★2617★
Duncan's First Nation
PO Box 148
Brownvale, AB, Canada T0H 0L0   Ph: (403)597-3777

★2618★
Woodland Cree First Nation
General Delivery
Cadotte Lake, AB, Canada T0H 0N0   Ph: (403)629-3803

★2619★
Dene Tha' First Nation
PO Box 120   Ph: (403)321-3775
Chateh, AB, Canada T0H 0S0   Fax: (403)321-3886

★2620★
Bigstone Cree First Nation
General Delivery
Desmarais, AB, Canada T0G 0T0   Ph: (403)891-3836

★2621★
Driftpile First Nation
General Delivery
Driftpile, AB, Canada T0G 0V0   Ph: (403)355-3868

★2622★
Paul First Nation
PO Box 89
Duffield, AB, Canada T0E 0N0   Ph: (403)892-2691

★2623★
Sucker Creek First Nation
PO Box 65
Enilda, AB, Canada T0G 0W0   Ph: (403)523-4426

★2624★
Enoch Cree Nation No. 440
PO Box 29   Ph: (403)470-4505
Enoch, AB, Canada T7X 3Y3   Fax: (403)470-3380

★2625★
Athabasca Chipewyan First Nation
PO Box 366
Fort Chipewyan, AB, Canada T0P 1B0   Ph: (403)697-3730

★2626★
Mikisew Cree First Nation
PO Box 90
Fort Chipewyan, AB, Canada T0P 1B0   Ph: (403)697-3740

★2627★
Fort McKay First Nation
PO Box 5360
Fort McMurray, AB, Canada T9H 3G4   Ph: (403)828-4220

★2628★
Fort McMurray No. 468 First Nation
Box 6130   Ph: (403)334-2293
Fort McMurray, AB, Canada T9H 4W1   Fax: (403)334-2457

★2629★
Tallcree First Nation
PO Box 100   Ph: (403)927-3727
Fort Vermilion, AB, Canada T0H 1N0   Fax: (403)927-4375

★2630★
Frog Lake First Nation
General Delivery   Ph: (403)943-3737
Frog Lake, AB, Canada T0A 1M0   Fax: (403)943-3966

★2631★
Frog Lake Indian Band
Frog Lake, AB, Canada T0A 1M0   Ph: (403)943-3980
   Fax: (403)943-3966

★2632★
Alexis First Nation
PO Box 7
Glenevis, AB, Canada T0E 0X0   Ph: (403)967-2225

★2633★
Whitefish Lake First Nation (Goodfish)
Box 271   Ph: (403)636-7000
Goodfish Lake, AB, Canada T0A 1R0   Fax: (403)636-7006

★2634★
Cold Lake First Nation
PO Box 1769
Grand Centre, AB, Canada T0A 1T0   Ph: (403)594-7183

★2635★
Kapawe'no First Nation
Box 10   Ph: (403)751-3800
Grouard, AB, Canada T0G 1C0   Fax: (403)649-3873

★2636★
Beaver First Nation
PO Box 270   Ph: (403)927-3544
High Level, AB, Canada T0H 1Z0   Fax: (403)927-3496

★2637★
Little Red River Cree Nation
PO Box 1165
High Level, AB, Canada T0H 1Z0   Ph: (403)759-3912

★2638★
Ermineskin First Nation
PO Box 219
Hobbema, AB, Canada T0C 1N0   Ph: (403)420-0008

★2639★
Louis Bull Tribe First Nation
PO Box 130
Hobbema, AB, Canada T0C 1N0   Ph: (403)423-2064

★2640★
Montana First Nation
PO Box 70
Hobbema, AB, Canada T0C 1N0   Ph: (403)585-3744

★2641★
Samson First Nation
PO Box 159
Hobbema, AB, Canada T0C 1N0   Ph: (403)421-4926

★2642★
Horse Lake First Nation
PO Box 303
Hythe, AB, Canada T0H 2C0   Ph: (403)356-2248

★2643★
Swan River First Nation
PO Box 270
Kinuso, AB, Canada T0G 1K0   Ph: (403)775-3536

★2644★
Beaver Lake First Nation
PO Box 960
Lac La Biche, AB, Canada T0A 2C0   Ph: (403)623-4549

★2645★
Heart Lake First Nation
PO Box 447
Lac La Biche, AB, Canada T0A 2C0   Ph: (403)623-2130

★2646★
Alexander First Nation
PO Box 3419   Ph: (403)939-5887
Morinville, AB, Canada T8R 1S3   Fax: (403)939-6166

★2647★
Stoney Tribal Administration First Nation (Bearspaw)
PO Box 40
Morley, AB, Canada T0L 1N0   Ph: (403)881-3770

★2648★
Stoney Tribal Administration First Nation (Chiniki)
PO Box 40
Morley, AB, Canada T0L 1N0   Ph: (403)881-3770

★2649★
Stoney Tribal Administration First Nation (Wesley)
PO Box 40
Morley, AB, Canada T0L 1N0   Ph: (403)881-3770

★2650★
Lubicon Lake First Nation
PO Box 6731   Ph: (403)629-3945
Peace River, AB, Canada T8S 1S5   Fax: (403)629-3939

★2651★
Loon River Cree First Nation
Box 189   Ph: (403)649-3883
Red Earth Creek, AB, Canada T0G 1X0   Fax: (403)649-3873

★2652★
O'Chiese First Nation
PO Box 1570
Rocky Mountain House, AB, Canada T0M
1T0   Ph: (403)989-3943

★2653★
Sunchild First Nation
PO Box 747
Rocky Mountain House, AB, Canada T0M
1T0   Ph: (403)989-3740

★2654★
Saddle Lake First Nation
PO Box 100 Ph: (403)726-3829
Saddle Lake, AB, Canada T0A 3T0 Fax: (403)726-3788

★2655★
Siksika First Nation
PO Box 1100 Ph: (403)264-7250
Siksika, AB, Canada T0H 3W0 Fax: (403)734-5110

★2656★
Sawridge First Nation
PO Box 326
Slave Lake, AB, Canada T0G 2A0 Ph: (403)849-4311

★2657★
Blood Tribe First Nation
PO Box 60
Standoff, AB, Canada T0L 1Y0 Ph: (403)737-3753

★2658★
Tsuu T'Ina Nation
9911 Chula Blvd. Ph: (403)281-4455
Tsuu T'ina, AB, Canada T2W 6H6 Fax: (403)251-6061

★2659★
Sturgeon Lake First Nation
PO Box 757
Valleyview, AB, Canada T0H 3N0 Ph: (403)524-3307

─────── **British Columbia** ───────

★2660★
Westbank Indian Band
515 Hwy. 97 S. Ph: (250)769-5666
301 Kelowna, BC, Canada V1Z 3J2 Fax: (250)769-4377

★2661★
Canim Lake Indian Band
PO Box 1030 Ph: (250)397-2227
100 Mile House, BC, Canada V0K 2E0 Fax: (250)397-2769

★2662★
Sumas First Nation
3092 Sumas Mountain Rd.
RR 4 Ph: (250)852-4040
Abbotsford, BC, Canada V2S 4N4 Fax: (250)852-3834

★2663★
Chehalis Indian Band
Chehalis Rd.
RR 1, Compt. 66
Agassiz, BC, Canada V0M 1A0 Ph: (250)796-2116

★2664★
Seabird Island Band
PO Box 650 Ph: (250)796-2177
Agassiz, BC, Canada V0M 1A0 Fax: (250)796-3729

★2665★
Skawahlook Band
PO Box 388 Ph: (250)796-9877
Agassiz, BC, Canada V0M 1A0 Fax: (250)796-9877

★2666★
Ahousaht First Nation
General Delivery Ph: (250)670-9563
Ahousaht, BC, Canada V0R 1A0 Fax: (250)670-9696

★2667★
Tlowitsis-Mumtagila Band
PO Box 150 Ph: (250)974-5501
Albert Bay, BC, Canada V3J 1A0 Fax: (250)974-8904

★2668★
Namgis First Nation
PO Box 210 Ph: (250)974-5556
Alert Bay, BC, Canada V0N 1A0 Fax: (250)974-5900

★2669★
Tanakteuk First Nation
PO Box 330
Alert Bay, BC, Canada V0N 1A0 Ph: (250)974-2179

★2670★
Tlatlasikwala Band
c/o Whe-La-La-U Area Council
PO Box 270 Ph: (250)974-2000
Alert Bay, BC, Canada V0N 1A0 Fax: (250)974-2010

★2671★
Anaham Indian Band
General Delivery
Alexis Creek, BC, Canada V0L 1A0 Ph: (250)394-4212

★2672★
Ulkatcho Indian Band
General Delivery Ph: (250)742-3260
Anahim Lake, BC, Canada V0L 1C0 Fax: (250)742-3411

★2673★
Ashcroft Indian Band
PO Box 440 Ph: (250)453-9154
Ashcroft, BC, Canada V0K 1A0 Fax: (250)453-9156

★2674★
Oregon Jack Creek Indian Band
PO Box 940 Ph: (250)453-9098
Ashcroft, BC, Canada V0K 1A0 Fax: (250)453-9097

★2675★
Dax Ka Nation
c/o Taku River Tlinglit
PO Box 132 Ph: (250)651-7615
Atlin, BC, Canada V0W 1A0 Fax: (250)651-7714

★2676★
Taku River Tlingit First Nation
Box 132 Ph: (250)651-7615
Atlin, BC, Canada V0W 1A0 Fax: (250)651-7714

★2677★
North Thompson Band
PO Box 220
Barriere, BC, Canada V0E 1E0 Ph: (250)672-9995

★2678★
Bella Coola Indian Band
PO Box 65
Bella Coola, BC, Canada V0T 1C0 Ph: (250)799-5613

★2679★
Nuxalk Indian Band
PO Box 65 Ph: (250)799-5613
Bella Coola, BC, Canada V0T 1C0 Fax: (250)799-5426

★2680★
Boothroyd Indian Band
PO Box 295 Ph: (250)867-9211
Boston Bar, BC, Canada V0K 1C0 Fax: (250)867-9747

★2681★
Boston Bar Indian Band
SS 1
Boston Bar, BC, Canada V0K 1C0 Ph: (250)867-9349

★2682★
Pauquachin Indian Band
PO Box 517   Ph: (250)656-0191
Brentwood Bay, BC, Canada V0S 1K0   Fax: (250)656-6134

★2683★
Blueberry River Indian Band
PO Box 3009   Ph: (250)630-2584
Buick Creek, BC, Canada V0C 2R0   Fax: (250)630-2588

★2684★
Broman Lake Indian Band
PO Box 760
Burns Lake, BC, Canada V0J 1E0   Ph: (250)698-7309

★2685★
Cheslatta Carrier Nation
PO Box 909   Ph: (250)694-3334
Burns Lake, BC, Canada V0J 1E0   Fax: (250)694-3632

★2686★
Lake Babine Nation (Nat'oot'en Nation)
PO Box 879
Burns Lake, BC, Canada V0J 1E0   Ph: (250)692-6957

★2687★
Nee-Tahi-Buhn Band
RR 2, Box 28   Ph: (250)694-3492
Burns Lake, BC, Canada V0J 1E0   Fax: (250)694-3530

★2688★
Bonaparte Indian Band
PO Box 669   Ph: (250)457-9624
Cache Creek, BC, Canada V0K 1H0   Fax: (250)457-9550

★2689★
Pavilion Indian Band
PO Box 609   Ph: (250)256-4204
Cache Creek, BC, Canada V0K 1H0   Fax: (250)256-4058

★2690★
Campbell River Indian Band
1400 Weiwaikum Rd.   Ph: (250)286-6949
Campbell River, BC, Canada V9W 5W8   Fax: (250)286-8838

★2691★
Ehattesaht Tribe
201-938 Island Hwy, Box 716   Ph: (250)287-4353
Campbell River, BC, Canada V9W 6J3   Fax: (250)287-2330

★2692★
Homalco Indian Band
1400 Weiwaikum
PO Box 789   Ph: (250)923-4979
Campbell River, BC, Canada V9W 6Y4   Fax: (250)923-4987

★2693★
Kwiakah Indian Band
1440 Island Hwy.
Campbell River, BC, Canada V9W 2E3   Ph: (250)286-1295

★2694★
Mamaleleqala Qwe'Qwa'Sot'Enox Band
1400 Weiwaikum Rd.   Ph: (250)287-2955
Campbell River, BC, Canada V9W 5W8   Fax: (250)287-4655

★2695★
Adams Lake Indian Band
PO Box 588   Ph: (250)679-8841
Chase, BC, Canada V0E 1M0   Fax: (250)679-8813

★2696★
Little Shuswap Band
PO Box 1100   Ph: (250)679-3203
Chase, BC, Canada V0E 1M0   Fax: (250)679-3220

★2697★
Neskonlith Indian Band
PO Box 608   Ph: (250)679-3295
Chase, BC, Canada V0E 1M0   Fax: (250)679-5306

★2698★
Halalt Indian Band
8017 Chemainus Rd., RR 1
Chemainus, BC, Canada V0R 1K0   Ph: (250)246-4736

★2699★
Penelakut Indian Band
PO Box 360   Ph: (250)246-2321
Chemainus, BC, Canada V0R 1K0   Fax: (250)246-2725

★2700★
Saulteaux Indian Band
PO Box 414   Ph: (250)788-3955
Chetwynd, BC, Canada V0C 1J0   Fax: (250)788-9158

★2701★
Alexis Creek Indian Band
PO Box 69   Ph: (250)481-3335
Chilanko Forks, BC, Canada V0L 1H0   Fax: (250)481-1197

★2702★
Kwaw-Kwaw-Apilt Indian Band
PO Box 412   Ph: (250)792-3058
Chilliwack, BC, Canada V2P 6H7   Fax: (250)858-8488

★2703★
Popkum First Nation
62-45185 Wolfe Rd.   Ph: (250)858-3366
Chilliwack, BC, Canada V2P 1V5   Fax: (250)858-4790

★2704★
Skwah Indian Band
PO Box 178
Chilliwack, BC, Canada V2P 6H7   Ph: (250)792-9204

★2705★
Squiala Indian Band
44974 Ashwell Rd.
PO Box 392   Ph: (250)792-8300
Chilliwack, BC, Canada V2P 6J7   Fax: (250)792-4522

★2706★
High Bar Indian Band
PO Box 45   Ph: (250)455-2279
Clinton, BC, Canada V0K 1K0   Fax: (250)459-2355

★2707★
Quatsino Indian Band
PO Box 100   Ph: (250)949-6245
Coal Harbour, BC, Canada V0N 1K0   Fax: (250)949-6249

★2708★
Kwayhquitlim First Nation
65 Colony Farm Rd.   Ph: (250)540-0680
Coquitlam, BC, Canada V3C 3V4   Fax: (250)540-0772

★2709★
Comox Indian Band
3320 Comox Rd.
Courtenay, BC, Canada V9N 3P8   Ph: (250)339-4545

★2710★
St. Mary's Indian Band
RR3, Site 15, Comp. 55   Ph: (250)426-5717
Cranbrook, BC, Canada V1C 6H3   Fax: (250)426-8935

★2711★
Lower Kootenay First Nation
PO Box 1107   Ph: (250)428-4428
Creston, BC, Canada V0B 1G0   Fax: (250)428-7686

★2712★
Soowahlie Indian Band
4070 Soowahlie Rd.　　　Ph: (250)858-4603
Cultus Lake, BC, Canada V0X 1H0　　Fax: (250)858-2350

★2713★
Anderson Lake First Nation
PO Box 88　　　Ph: (250)452-3221
D'Arcy, BC, Canada V0N 1L0　　Fax: (250)452-3295

★2714★
Tsawwassen First Nation
N. Tsawwassen Dr., Bldg. 132　Ph: (250)943-2112
Delta, BC, Canada V4K 3N2　　Fax: (250)943-9226

★2715★
Lakahahmen Indian Band
41290 Lougheed Hwy.
RR1　　　Ph: (250)826-7976
Deroche, BC, Canada V0M 1G0　Fax: (250)826-0362

★2716★
Canoe Creek Indian Band
General Delivery　　Ph: (250)440-5645
Dog Creek, BC, Canada V0L 1J0　Fax: (250)440-5679

★2717★
Cowichan First Nation
5760 Allenby Rd.
PO Box 880　　Ph: (250)748-3196
Duncan, BC, Canada V9L 3Y2　Fax: (250)748-1233

★2718★
Spallumcheen First Nation
PO Box 430　　Ph: (250)838-6496
Enderby, BC, Canada V0E 1V0　Fax: (250)838-2131

★2719★
Nadleh Whut'en
PO Box 36　　Ph: (250)690-7211
Fort Fraser, BC, Canada V0J 1N0　Fax: (250)690-7316

★2720★
Kwantlen First Nation
PO Box 117
92 Gabriel Rd.　　Ph: (250)888-2488
Fort Langley, BC, Canada V0X 1J0　Fax: (250)888-2442

★2721★
Fort Nelson Indian Band
293 Alaska Hwy.
RR 1　　　Ph: (250)774-7257
Fort Nelson, BC, Canada V0C 1R0　Fax: (250)774-7260

★2722★
Prophet River First Nation
PO Box 3250　　Ph: (250)774-6555
Fort Nelson, BC, Canada V0C 1R0　Fax: (250)774-2270

★2723★
Nak'Azdli First Nation
PO Box 1329　　Ph: (250)996-7171
Fort Saint James, BC, Canada V0J 1P0　Fax: (250)996-8010

★2724★
Tl'azt'en Nation
PO Box 670　　Ph: (250)648-3212
Fort Saint James, BC, Canada V0J 1P0　Fax: (250)648-3266

★2725★
Gitwinksihlkw Indian Band
PO Box 1　　Ph: (250)633-2294
Gitwinksihlkw, BC, Canada V0J 3T0　Fax: (250)633-2539

★2726★
Mowachaht/Muchalaht Band
PO Box 459　　Ph: (250)283-2015
Gold River, BC, Canada V0P 1G0　Fax: (250)283-2335

★2727★
Dease River Band (British Columbia/Yukon)
General Delivery　　Ph: (250)239-3000
Good Hope Lake, BC, Canada V0C 2Z0　Fax: (250)239-3003

★2728★
Tobacco Plains First Nation
PO Box 761　　Ph: (250)887-3461
Grasmere, BC, Canada V0B 1R0　Fax: (250)887-3424

★2729★
Stone Indian Band
General Delivery　　Ph: (250)394-4295
Hanceville, BC, Canada V0L 1K0　Fax: (250)394-4407

★2730★
Douglas Indian Band
PO Box 339
Harrison Hot Springs, BC, Canada V0M　Ph: (250)820-3082
1K0　　Fax: (250)820-2661

★2731★
Hartley Bay Indian Band
General Delivery　　Ph: (250)841-2500
Hartley Bay, BC, Canada V0V 1A0　Fax: (250)841-2581

★2732★
Gitanmaax First Nation
PO Box 440
Hazelton, BC, Canada V0J 1Y0　Ph: (250)842-6364

★2733★
Glen Vowell Indian Band
PO Bo x 157　　Ph: (250)842-5241
Hazelton, BC, Canada V0J 1Y0　Fax: (250)842-5601

★2734★
Chawathil Indian Band
PO Box 1659　　Ph: (250)869-9994
Hope, BC, Canada V0X 1L0　Fax: (250)869-7614

★2735★
Ohamil Indian Band
RR 2, Site 22, C4　　Ph: (250)869-2627
Hope, BC, Canada V0X 1L0　Fax: (250)869-9903

★2736★
Peters Indian Band
16650 Peters Rd.
RR 2　　　Ph: (250)794-7059
Hope, BC, Canada V0X 1L0　Fax: (250)794-7885

★2737★
Union Bar Indian Band
PO Box 788　　Ph: (250)869-9466
Hope, BC, Canada V0X 1L0　Fax: (250)869-9466

★2738★
Yale First Nation
PO Box 1869　　Ph: (250)863-2443
Hope, BC, Canada V0X 1L0　Fax: (250)863-2467

★2739★
Shuswap Indian Band
PO Box 790　　Ph: (250)342-6361
Invermere, BC, Canada V0A 1K0　Fax: (250)342-2948

★2740★
Iskut Band
PO Box 30   Ph: (250)234-3331
Iskut, BC, Canada V0J 1K0   Fax: (250)234-3200

★2741★
Kamloops Indian Band
315 Yellowhead Hwy.   Ph: (250)828-9700
Kamloops, BC, Canada V2H 1H1   Fax: (250)828-8833

★2742★
Shuswap Nation
355 Yellowhead Highway   Ph: (250)828-9789
Kamloops, BC, Canada V2H 1H1   Fax: (250)374-6331

★2743★
Whispering Pines Indian Band
RR 1, Site 8, Comp. 4   Ph: (250)579-5772
Kamloops, BC, Canada V2C 1Z3   Fax: (250)579-8367

★2744★
Lower Similkameen Band
PO Box 100   Ph: (250)499-5528
Keremeos, BC, Canada V0X 1N0   Fax: (250)499-5335

★2745★
Upper Similkameen Indian Band
PO Box 310   Ph: (250)499-2221
Keremeos, BC, Canada V0X 1N0   Fax: (250)499-5117

★2746★
Kincolith Indian Band
General Delivery   Ph: (250)326-4212
Kincolith, BC, Canada V0V 1B0   Fax: (250)326-4208

★2747★
Tsawataineuk Indian Band
Kingcome Village
Kingcome Inlet, BC, Canada V0N 2B0

★2748★
Kispiox Indian Band
RR 1, Box 25   Ph: (250)842-5248
Kispiox, BC, Canada V0J 1Y0   Fax: (250)842-5604

★2749★
Kitamaat Indian Band (Haisla Nation)
Haisla
PO Box 1101   Ph: (250)639-9361
Kitamaat Village, BC, Canada V0T 2B0   Fax: (250)639-2840

★2750★
Kitkatla Indian Band
General Delivery   Ph: (250)848-2214
Kitkatla, BC, Canada V0V 1C0   Fax: (250)848-2238

★2751★
Gitanyow Band
PO Box 340   Ph: (250)849-5222
Kitwanga, BC, Canada V0J 2A0   Fax: (250)849-5787

★2752★
Gitwangak First Nation
PO Box 400   Ph: (250)849-5591
Kitwanga, BC, Canada V0J 2A0   Fax: (250)849-5353

★2753★
Kitasoo First Nation
General Delivery   Ph: (250)839-1255
Klemtu, BC, Canada V0T 1L0   Fax: (250)839-1256

★2754★
Chemainus Indian Band
RR 1
Silverstrand Rd.   Ph: (250)245-7155
Ladysmith, BC, Canada V0R 2E0   Fax: (250)245-3012

★2755★
Scowlitz Indian Band
PO Box 76   Ph: (250)826-5813
Lake Errock, BC, Canada V0M 1N0 Fax: (250)826-6222

★2756★
Nanoose First Nation
209 Mallard Way   Ph: (250)390-3661
Lantzville, BC, Canada V0R 2H0   Fax: (250)390-3365

★2757★
Bridge River Indian Band
PO Box 190   Ph: (250)256-7423
Lillooet, BC, Canada V0K 1V0   Fax: (250)256-7999

★2758★
Cayoose Creek Indian Band
PO Box 484   Ph: (250)256-4136
Lillooet, BC, Canada V0K 1V0   Fax: (250)256-4138

★2759★
Fountain Indian Band
PO Box 1330   Ph: (250)256-4227
Lillooet, BC, Canada V0K 1V0   Fax: (250)256-7570

★2760★
Lillooet Indian Band
PO Box 615   Ph: (250)256-4118
Lillooet, BC, Canada V0K 1V0   Fax: (250)256-4544

★2761★
Kanaka Bar Indian Band
PO Box 400   Ph: (250)455-2279
Lytton, BC, Canada V0K 1Z0   Fax: (250)455-2772

★2762★
Lytton Indian Band
PO Box 20   Ph: (250)455-2304
Lytton, BC, Canada V0K 1Z0   Fax: (250)455-2291

★2763★
Nlaka'Pamux Nation
PO Box 430   Ph: (250)455-2711
Lytton, BC, Canada V0K 1Z0   Fax: (250)455-2565

★2764★
Siska Indian Band
PO Box 358   Ph: (250)455-2219
Lytton, BC, Canada V0K 1Z0   Fax: (250)455-2539

★2765★
Skuppah Indian Band
PO Box 116   Ph: (250)455-2279
Lytton, BC, Canada V0K 1Z0   Fax: (250)455-2772

★2766★
Matsqui Indian Band
31989 Harris Rd.
RR #1, PO Box 229   Ph: (250)826-6145
Matsqui, BC, Canada V0X 1S0   Fax: (250)826-7009

★2767★
McLeod Lake Indian Band
General Delivery   Ph: (250)750-4415
McLeod Lake, BC, Canada V0J 2G0 Fax: (250)750-4420

★2768★
Coldwater Indian Band
PO Bag 4600   Ph: (250)378-6174
Merritt, BC, Canada V0K 2B0 Fax: (250)378-5351

★2769★
Lower Nicola Indian Band
RR 1, Site 17, Comp. 18   Ph: (250)378-5157
Merritt, BC, Canada V0K 2B0   Fax: (250)378-6188

★2770★
Nooaitch Indian Band
PO Bag 6000   Ph: (250)378-6141
Merritt, BC, Canada V0K 2B0 Fax: (250)378-9119

★2771★
Shackan Indian Band
Bag 6000   Ph: (250)378-6141
Merritt, BC, Canada V0K 2B0 Fax: (250)378-6141

★2772★
Upper Nicola Indian Band
PO Bag 3700   Ph: (250)350-3342
Merritt, BC, Canada V0K 2B0 Fax: (250)350-3311

★2773★
Malahat Indian Band
PO Box 111   Ph: (250)743-3231
Mill Bay, BC, Canada V0R 2P0 Fax: (250)743-3251

★2774★
Samahquam Indian Band
PO Box 3068   Ph: (250)820-2265
Mission, BC, Canada V2V 4J3 Fax: (250)820-0935

★2775★
West Moberly Indian Band
General Delivery   Ph: (250)788-3663
Moberly Lake, BC, Canada V0X 1X0 Fax: (250)788-9792

★2776★
Moricetown Indian Band
RR 1, Site 15, Box 1   Ph: (250)847-2133
Moricetown, BC, Canada V0J 2N0 Fax: (250)847-9291

★2777★
Mount Currie Indian Band
PO Box 165   Ph: (250)894-6115
Mount Currie, BC, Canada V0N 2K0 Fax: (250)894-6841

★2778★
Nanaimo Indian Bands
1145 Totem Rd.   Ph: (250)753-3481
Nanaimo, BC, Canada V9R 1H1   Fax: (250)753-3492

★2779★
Nemaiah Valley First Nation
Nemaiah Valley Post Office
Nemaiah Valley, BC, Canada V0L 1X0

★2780★
Gitlakdamix Band
PO Box 233   Ph: (250)633-2215
New Aiyansh, BC, Canada V0J 1A0 Fax: (250)633-2514

★2781★
Hagwilget Indian Band
PO Box 460   Ph: (250)842-6258
New Hazelton, BC, Canada V0J 2J0 Fax: (250)842-6924

★2782★
Squamish Nation
320 Seymour Blvd.   Ph: (250)980-4553
North Vancouver, BC, Canada V7L 2J3 Fax: (250)980-4523

★2783★
Osoyoos Band
RR 3, Site 25, Comp. 1   Ph: (250)498-4906
Oliver, BC, Canada V0H 1T0   Fax: (250)498-6577

★2784★
Skookumchuck Indian Band
PO Box 190   Ph: (250)894-5262
Pemberton, BC, Canada V0N 2L0 Fax: (250)894-6188

★2785★
Penticton Indian Band
Site 80, Comp. 19, RR 2   Ph: (250)493-0048
Penticton, BC, Canada V2A 6J7 Fax: (250)493-2882

★2786★
Katzie Indian Band
10946 Katzie Rd.   Ph: (250)465-8961
Pitt Meadows, BC, Canada V3Y 2G8 Fax: (250)465-5949

★2787★
Ditidaht Indian Band
PO Box 340   Ph: (250)745-3333
Port Alberni, BC, Canada V9Y 7M8 Fax: (250)745-3332

★2788★
Nuu-chan-nulth Tribal Council
PO Box 1383   Ph: (250)724-5757
Port Alberni, BC, Canada V9Y 7M2 Fax: (250)723-0463

★2789★
Opetchesaht First Nation
PO Box 211   Ph: (250)724-4041
Port Alberni, BC, Canada V9Y 7M7 Fax: (250)724-1232

★2790★
Uchucklesant Band
Box 157   Ph: (250)724-1832
Port Alberni, BC, Canada V9Y 7M7 Fax: (250)724-1806

★2791★
Gwa'Sala-Nakwaxda'xw Indian Band
PO Box 998   Ph: (250)949-8343
Port Hardy, BC, Canada V0N 2P0 Fax: (250)949-7402

★2792★
Kwakiutl Indian Band
PO Box 1440   Ph: (250)949-6012
Port Hardy, BC, Canada V0N 2P0 Fax: (250)949-6066

★2793★
Oweekeno Nation
PO Box 3500   Ph: (250)949-2107
Port Hardy, BC, Canada V0N 2P0 Fax: (250)949-2107

★2794★
Kwa-Wa-Aineuk Indian Band
PO Box 344   Ph: (250)949-8732
Port McNeill, BC, Canada V0N 2R0 Fax: (250)949-8732

★2795★
Pacheenaht Band
General Delivery   Ph: (250)647-5521
Port Renfrew, BC, Canada V0S 1K0 Fax: (250)647-5561

★2796★
Lax-Kw'-alaams Indian Band
206 Shashaak St.   Ph: (250)625-3293
Port Simpson, BC, Canada V0V 1H0 Fax: (250)625-3246

★2797★
Sliammon Band
Sliammon Rd.
RR 2
Powell River, BC, Canada V8A 4Z3 Ph: (250)483-9646

★2798★
Fort Ware Band
3-1257 4th Ave.   Ph: (250)563-4161
Prince George, BC, Canada V2L 3J5   Fax: (250)563-2668

★2799★
Metlakatla Indian Band
PO Box 459   Ph: (250)628-3234
Prince Rupert, BC, Canada V8J 3R2   Fax: (250)628-9205

★2800★
Qualicum Indian Band
5850 River Rd.   Ph: (250)757-9337
Qualicum Beach, BC, Canada V9K 1Z5   Fax: (250)757-9898

★2801★
Cape Mudge Indian Band
PO Box 220   Ph: (250)285-3316
Quathiaski Cove, BC, Canada V0P 1N0   Fax: (250)285-2400

★2802★
Alexandria Band
RR 2, PO Box 4
Rancherie Group   Ph: (250)993-4324
Quesnel, BC, Canada V2J 3H6   Fax: (250)993-5798

★2803★
Kluskus Indian Band
4-651 Wade Ave.   Ph: (250)992-8186
Quesnel, BC, Canada V5T 1E2   Fax: (250)992-3929

★2804★
Nazko Indian Band
1954 Hilborn Rd.   Ph: (250)992-9810
Quesnel, BC, Canada V2L 3P7   Fax: (250)992-7854

★2805★
Red Bluff Indian Band
PO Box 4693   Ph: (250)747-2900
Quesnel, BC, Canada V2J 5H8   Fax: (250)747-1341

★2806★
Toosey Indian Band
PO Box 80   Ph: (250)659-5655
Riske Creek, BC, Canada V0L 1T0   Fax: (250)659-5601

★2807★
Doig River Indian Band
PO Box 55   Ph: (250)827-3776
Rose Prairie, BC, Canada V0C 2H0   Fax: (250)827-3778

★2808★
Cheam Indian Band
10704 Hwy. 9   Ph: (250)794-7924
Rosedale, BC, Canada V0X 1X0   Fax: (250)794-7456

★2809★
Tsawout Indian Band
Box 121   Ph: (250)652-9101
Saanichton, BC, Canada V0S 1M0   Fax: (250)652-9114

★2810★
Aitchelitz Indian Band
8150 Aitkens Rd., RR 1
Sardis, BC, Canada V2R 1A9   Ph: (250)792-2404

★2811★
Skowkale Indian Band
PO Box 159   Ph: (250)792-0730
Sardis, BC, Canada V2R 1A7   Fax: (250)792-1153

★2812★
Tzeachten Indian Band
Box 278
Bldg. E Tzeachten Community Centre
45585 Promontory Rd.   Ph: (250)858-3888
Sardis, BC, Canada V2R 1A6   Fax: (250)858-3382

★2813★
Yakweakwioose Indian Band
7176 Chilliwack River Rd.
RR 2
Sardis, BC, Canada V2R 1B1   Ph: (250)858-1775

★2814★
Skeetchestn Indian Band
PO Box 178   Ph: (250)373-2493
Savona, BC, Canada V0K 2J0   Fax: (250)373-2494

★2815★
Sechelt Indian Band
PO Box 740   Ph: (250)687-8641
Sechelt, BC, Canada V0N 3A0   Fax: (250)687-3490

★2816★
Seton Lake Indian Band
Site 3, Box 76   Ph: (250)259-8227
Shalalth, BC, Canada V0N 3C0   Fax: (250)259-8384

★2817★
Tseycum Indian Band
PO Box 1210 Totem Lane   Ph: (250)656-0858
Sidney, BC, Canada V8L 5S4   Fax: (250)656-0868

★2818★
Kwicksutaineuk-Ah-Kwaw-Ah-Mish Band
General Delivery   Ph: (250)949-3500
Simoon Sound, BC, Canada V0P 1S0   Fax: (250)949-3500

★2819★
Skidegate Indian Band
PO Box 1301
Skidegate Haida Gwaii, BC, Canada V0T   Ph: (250)559-4496
   1S1   Fax: (250)559-8247

★2820★
Beecher Bay Band
3843 E. Sooke Rd.
RR 1, PO Box 4
Sooke, BC, Canada V0S 1N0   Ph: (250)478-3535

★2821★
Gitsegukla Indian Band
36 Cascade Ave.
RR 1   Ph: (250)849-5043
South Hazelton, BC, Canada V0J 2R0   Fax: (250)849-5276

★2822★
Cook's Ferry Band
PO Box 130   Ph: (250)458-2224
Spences Bridge, BC, Canada V0K 2L0   Fax: (250)458-2312

★2823★
Klahoose Indian Band
PO Box 9
Squirrel Cove Cortes Island, BC, Canada   Ph: (250)935-6536
   V0P 1K0   Fax: (250)935-6997

★2824★
Takla Lake Indian Band
General Delivery
Takla Landing Via Fort James, BC,   Ph: (250)564-3704
   Canada V0J 2T0   Fax: (250)564-3704

★2825★
Tahltan Indian Band
Telegraph Creek, BC, Canada V0J 2W0　Ph: (250)235-3241
　　　　　　　　　　　　　　　　　Fax: (250)235-3244

★2826★
Kitselas Indian Band
4562 Queensway　　　　　　　Ph: (250)635-5084
Terrace, BC, Canada V8G 3X6　Fax: (250)635-5335

★2827★
Kitsumkalum Band/House of Sim-Oi-Ghes
PO Box 544　　　　　　　　　Ph: (250)635-6177
Terrace, BC, Canada V8G 4B5　Fax: (250)635-4622

★2828★
Hesquiaht Band
PO Box 2000　　　　　　　　Ph: (250)724-8570
Tofino, BC, Canada V0R 2Z0　Fax: (250)724-8570

★2829★
Tla-o-qui-aht First Nation
PO Box 18　　　　　　　　　Ph: (250)725-3223
Tofino, BC, Canada V0R 2Z0　Fax: (250)725-4233

★2830★
Toquaht Band
Box 759　　　　　　　　　　Ph: (250)726-4230
Ucluelet, BC, Canada V0R 3A0　Fax: (250)726-4403

★2831★
Ucluelet Band
Box 699　　　　　　　　　　Ph: (250)726-7342
Ucluelet, BC, Canada V0R 3A0　Fax: (250)726-7552

★2832★
Musqueam Indian Band
6370 Salish Dr.　　　　　　Ph: (250)263-3261
Vancouver, BC, Canada V6N 2C6　Fax: (250)263-4212

★2833★
Stony Creek Indian Band
RR 1, Site 12, Comp. 26　　Ph: (250)567-9293
Vanderhoof, BC, Canada V0J 3A0　Fax: (250)567-2998

★2834★
Okanagan Indian Band
Westside Rd.　　　　　　　Ph: (250)542-4328
Vernon, BC, Canada V1T 7Z3　Fax: (250)542-4990

★2835★
Esquimalt Indian Band
1000 Thomas Rd.　　　　　Ph: (250)381-7861
Victoria, BC, Canada V9A 7K7　Fax: (250)381-9309

★2836★
Songhees Indian Band
1500 A-Admirals Rd.　　　　Ph: (250)386-1043
Victoria, BC, Canada V9A 2R1　Fax: (250)386-4161

★2837★
Heiltsuk Band
PO Box 880　　　　　　　　Ph: (250)957-2381
Waglisla, BC, Canada V0T 1Z0　Fax: (250)957-2544

★2838★
Semiahmoo Band
16010 Beach Rd.
RR 7　　　　　　　　　　　Ph: (250)536-3101
White Rock, BC, Canada V4B 5A8　Fax: (250)536-6116

★2839★
Alkali Lake First Nation (Esketemc First Nation)
PO Box 4479　　　　　　　Ph: (250)440-5611
Williams Lake, BC, Canada V2G 2V5　Fax: (250)440-5721

★2840★
Soda Creek Indian Band
RR 4, Site 15, Comp. 2　　Ph: (250)297-6323
Williams Lake, BC, Canada V2G 4M8　Fax: (250)297-6300

★2841★
Williams Lake Indian Band
Sugarcane
RR 3, Box 4　　　　　　　Ph: (250)296-3507
Williams Lake, BC, Canada V2G 1M3　Fax: (250)296-4750

★2842★
Columbia Lake Band
PO Box 130　　　　　　　Ph: (250)342-6301
Windermere, BC, Canada V0B 2L0　Fax: (250)342-9693

★2843★
Halfway River Band
PO Box 59
Wonowon, BC, Canada V0C 2N0　Ph: (250)787-4451

★2844★
Spuzzum Indian Band
RR 1　　　　　　　　　　Ph: (250)863-2395
Yale, BC, Canada V0K 2S0　Fax: (250)863-2213

★2845★
Nuchatlaht Tribe
PO Box 40
Zeballos, BC, Canada V0P 2A0　Ph: (250)724-8609

———————— **Manitoba** ————————

★2846★
Berens River First Nation
Berens River Post Office
Berens River, MB, Canada R0B 0A0　Ph: (204)382-2161

★2847★
Birdtail Sioux First Nation
PO Box 22
Beulah, MB, Canada R0M 0B0　Ph: (204)568-4540

★2848★
Gamblers First Nation
PO Box 293
Binscarth, MB, Canada R0J 0G0　Ph: (204)532-2464

★2849★
Wuskwi Sipihk First Nation
PO Box 220　　　　　　　Ph: (204)236-4201
Birch River, MB, Canada R0L 0E0　Fax: (204)236-4786

★2850★
Bloodvein First Nation
General Delivery
Bloodvein, MB, Canada R0C 0J0　Ph: (204)395-2148

★2851★
Dakota Ojibway Tribal Council
702 Douglas St.　　　　　Ph: (204)729-3682
Brandon, MB, Canada R7A 5V2　Fax: (204)726-5966

★2852★
Barren Lands First Nation
General Delivery
Brochet, MB, Canada R0B 0B0　Ph: (204)323-2300

★2853★
Pine Creek First Nation
PO Box 70　　　　　　　Ph: (204)524-2478
Camperville, MB, Canada R0L 0J0　Fax: (204)524-2832

★2854★
O-Chi-Chak-Ko-Sipi First Nation
General Delivery   Ph: (204)732-2490
Crane River, MB, Canada R0L 0M0   Fax: (204)732-2596

★2855★
Cross Lake First Nation
PO Box 10   Ph: (204)676-2218
Cross Lake, MB, Canada R0B 0J0   Fax: (204)676-2117

★2856★
Jackhead First Nation
General Delivery   Ph: (204)394-2366
Dallas, MB, Canada R0C 0S0   Fax: (204)394-2271

★2857★
Chemawawin First Nation
PO Box 9   Ph: (204)329-2161
Easterville, MB, Canada R0C 0V0   Fax: (204)329-2017

★2858★
Ebb and Flow First Nation
Ebb and Flow, MB, Canada R0L 0R0   Ph: (204)448-2134

★2859★
Keeseekoowenin First Nation
PO Box 100
Elphinstone, MB, Canada R0J 0N0   Ph: (204)625-2004

★2860★
Rolling River
PO Box 145   Ph: (204)636-2211
Erickson, MB, Canada R0J 0P0   Fax: (204)636-7823

★2861★
Fairford First Nation
Fairford, MB, Canada R0C 0X0   Ph: (204)659-5705

★2862★
Fort Alexander First Nation
PO Box 3   Ph: (204)367-2287
Fort Alexander, MB, Canada R0E 0P0   Fax: (204)367-4315

★2863★
Sagkeeng First Nation, Band No. 262
Fort Alexander Indian Reserve, MB,   Ph: (204)367-2287
  Canada R0E 0P0   Fax: (204)367-4315

★2864★
Fox Lake First Nation
PO Box 369   Ph: (204)652-2954
Gilliam, MB, Canada R0B 0L0   Fax: (204)652-6519

★2865★
Roseau River First Nation
PO Box 30
Ginew, MB, Canada R0A 2R0   Ph: (204)427-2312

★2866★
God's River First Nation
General Delivery   Ph: (204)366-2011
God's River, MB, Canada R0B 0N0   Fax: (204)366-2282

★2867★
Grand Rapids First Nation
PO Box 500   Ph: (204)639-2219
Grand Rapids, MB, Canada R0C 1E0   Fax: (204)639-2503

★2868★
Sioux Valley First Nation
PO Box 38
Griswold, MB, Canada R0M 0S0   Ph: (204)855-2671

★2869★
Dauphin River First Nation
PO Box 58   Ph: (204)659-5370
Gypsumville, MB, Canada R0C 1J0   Fax: (204)659-4458

★2870★
Lake St. Martin First Nation
PO Box 69
Gypsumville, MB, Canada R0C 1J0   Ph: (204)659-4539

★2871★
Little Saskatchewan First Nation
General Delivery   Ph: (204)659-4584
Gypsumville, MB, Canada R0C 1J0   Fax: (204)659-2071

★2872★
War Lake First Nation
General Delivery
Ilford, MB, Canada R0B 0S0   Ph: (204)288-4315

★2873★
Garden Hill First Nation
General Delivery   Ph: (204)456-2085
Island Lake, MB, Canada R0B 0T0   Fax: (204)456-2338

★2874★
God's Lake First Nation
Island Lake, MB, Canada R0B 0M0   Ph: (204)456-2085
     Fax: (204)456-2338

★2875★
Fisher River First Nation
PO Box 367   Ph: (204)645-2171
Koostatak, MB, Canada R0C 1S0   Fax: (204)645-2745

★2876★
Northlands First Nation
Lac Brochet, MB, Canada R0B 2E0   Ph: (204)337-2001

★2877★
Little Grand Rapids First Nation
General Delivery
Little Grand Rapids, MB, Canada R0B   Ph: (204)397-2264
  0V0   Fax: (204)397-2340

★2878★
Sandy Bay First Nation
PO Box 109   Ph: (204)843-2462
Marius, MB, Canada R0H 0T0   Fax: (204)843-2706

★2879★
Buffalo Point First Nation
PO Box 37
Middlebro, MB, Canada R0A 1B0   Ph: (204)437-2133

★2880★
Mosakahiken Cree Nation
General Delivery   Ph: (204)678-2113
Moose Lake, MB, Canada R0B 0Y0   Fax: (204)678-2292

★2881★
Nelson House First Nation
General Delivery
Nelson House, MB, Canada R0B 1A0   Ph: (204)484-2332

★2882★
Norway House Cree Nation
PO Box 250   Ph: (204)359-6786
Norway House, MB, Canada R0B 1B0   Fax: (204)359-4186

★2883★
Little Black River First Nation
O'Hanley, MB, Canada R0E 1K0   Ph: (204)367-4411

★2884★
Oxford House First Nation
Oxford House, MB, Canada R0B 1C0   Ph: (204)538-2156

★2885★
Peguis First Nation
PO Box 10   Ph: (204)645-2359
Peguis Reserve, MB, Canada R0C 3J0   Fax: (204)645-2360

★2886★
Oak Lake First Nation
PO Box 146   Ph: (204)854-2959
Pipestone, MB, Canada R0M 1T0   Fax: (204)854-2525

★2887★
Dakota Plains First Nation
PO Box 110
Portage La Prairie, MB, Canada R1N 3B2   Ph: (204)252-2288

★2888★
Dakota Tipi First Nation
PO Box 1569
Portage La Prairie, MB, Canada R1N 3P1   Ph: (204)857-4381

★2889★
Long Plain First Nation
PO Box 430   Ph: (204)252-2731
Portage La Prairie, MB, Canada R1N 3B7   Fax: (204)252-2012

★2890★
Mathias Colomb First Nation
General Delivery
Pukatawagan, MB, Canada R0B 1G0   Fax: (204)553-2419

★2891★
Red Sucker Lake First Nation
General Delivery   Ph: (204)469-5041
Red Sucker Lake, MB, Canada R0B 1H0   Fax: (204)469-5325

★2892★
St. Theresa Point First Nation
Saint Theresa Point, MB, Canada R0B
1J0   Ph: (204)462-2106

★2893★
Brokenhead Ojibway Nation
General Delivery   Ph: (204)766-2494
Scanterbury, MB, Canada R0E 1W0   Fax: (204)766-2306

★2894★
Shamattawa First Nation
PO Box 102   Ph: (204)565-2340
Shamattawa, MB, Canada R0B 1K0   Fax: (204)565-2321

★2895★
Tootinaowaziibeeng
General Delivery   Ph: (204)546-3334
Shortdale, MB, Canada R0L 1W0   Fax: (204)546-3090

★2896★
Waterhen First Nation
Skownan, MB, Canada R0L 1Y0   Ph: (204)628-3373

★2897★
Split Lake Cree First Nation
General Delivery   Ph: (204)342-2045
Split Lake, MB, Canada R0B 1P0   Fax: (204)342-2270

★2898★
Swan Lake First Nation
PO Box 368
Swan Lake, MB, Canada R0G 2S0   Ph: (204)836-2101

★2899★
Sayisi Dene First Nation
General Delivery   Ph: (204)684-2022
Tadoule Lake, MB, Canada R0B 2C0   Fax: (204)684-2069

★2900★
Opaskwayak Cree Nation
PO Box 297   Ph: (204)623-5483
The Pas, MB, Canada R9A 1K4   Fax: (204)623-5263

★2901★
Poplar River First Nation
General Delivery   Ph: (204)244-2267
Via Negginan, MB, Canada R0B 0Z0   Fax: (204)244-2690

★2902★
Sapotaweyak Cree Nation
General Delivery   Ph: (204)587-2012
Via Pelican Rapids, MB, Canada R0L 1L0   Fax: (204)587-2072

★2903★
Lake Manitoba First Nation
Vogar, MB, Canada R0C 3C0   Ph: (204)768-3492

★2904★
Hollow Water First Nation
Wanipigow, MB, Canada R0E 2E0   Ph: (204)363-7278

★2905★
Wasagamack First Nation
Wasagamack, MB, Canada R0B 1Z0   Ph: (204)457-2337

★2906★
Waywayseecappo First Nation Treaty Four
PO Box 9
Waywayseecappo, MB, Canada R0J 1S0   Fax: (204)859-2403

★2907★
York Factory First Nation
General Delivery   Ph: (204)341-2180
York Landing, MB, Canada R0B 2B0   Fax: (204)341-2322

——————— **New Brunswick** ———————

★2908★
Pabineau Indian Band
RR 5, Box 1, Site 26   Ph: (506)548-9211
Bathurst, NB, Canada E2A 3Y8   Fax: (506)548-9849

★2909★
Buctouche Micmac Band
RR #2, Box 9, Site 1   Ph: (506)743-6493
Buctouche, NB, Canada E0E 1G0   Fax: (506)743-8995

★2910★
Eel River Bar Band
PO Box 1660   Ph: (506)684-3360
Dalhousie, NB, Canada E0K 1B0   Fax: (506)684-5840

★2911★
Fort Folly Indian Band
PO Box 21   Ph: (506)379-6224
Dorchester, NB, Canada E0A 1M0   Fax: (506)379-6641

★2912★
Kingsclear Indian Band
RR 6, Comp. 19, Site 6   Ph: (506)363-3028
Fredericton, NB, Canada E3B 4X7   Fax: (506)363-4324

★2913★
Burnt Church First Nation
RR #2   Ph: (506)776-1200
Legaceville, NB, Canada E0C 1K0   Fax: (506)776-1215

★2914★
Eel Ground Indian Band
RR I, Box 9, Site 23
Newcastle, NB, Canada E1V 3L8
Ph: (506)627-4600
Fax: (506)627-4602

★2915★
Red Bank Indian Band
PO Box 120
Red Bank, NB, Canada E0C 1W0
Ph: (506)836-2366

─────── **Newfoundland** ───────

★2916★
Innu Nation
PO Box 119
Sheshatshiu, Labrador, Canada A0P 1M0
Ph: (709)497-8398
Fax: (709)497-8396

─────── **Northwest Territories** ───────

★2917★
Aklavik First Nation
PO Box 118
Aklavik, NT, Canada X0E 0A0
Ph: (403)978-2029

★2918★
Acho Dene Koe First Nation
General Delivery
Fort Liard, NT, Canada X0G 0A0
Ph: (403)770-4141

★2919★
Nahanni Butte Indian Band
General Delivery
Nahanni Butte, NT, Canada X0E 0N0
Ph: (403)695-7223

★2920★
Dene Nation
PO Box 2338
Yellowknife, NT, Canada X1A 2P7
Ph: (403)873-4081

─────── **Ontario** ───────

★2921★
Wapekeka First Nation
Angling Lake, ON, Canada P0V 1B0
Ph: (807)537-2315

★2922★
Whitesand First Nation
PO Box 68
Armstrong, ON, Canada P0T 1A0
Ph: (807)583-2177

★2923★
Attawapiskat First Nation
PO Box 248
Attawapiskat, ON, Canada P0L 1A0
Ph: (705)997-2166

★2924★
Wahta Mohawks
PO Box 327
Bala, ON, Canada P0C 1A0
Ph: (705)756-2354
Fax: (705)756-2376

★2925★
Temagami First Nation
Bear Island Post Office
Bear Island, ON, Canada P0H 1C0
Ph: (705)237-8943
Fax: (705)237-8959

★2926★
Lake Nipigon Ojibway First Nation
Rocky Bay Reserve
PO Box 241
Beardmore, ON, Canada P0T 1G0
Ph: (807)875-2785

★2927★
Bearskin Lake First Nation
Post Office
Bearskin Lake, ON, Canada P0V 1E0
Ph: (807)363-2518

★2928★
Big Trout Lake First Nation
Big Trout Lake, ON, Canada P0V 1G0
Ph: (807)537-2263

★2929★
Whitefish River First Nation
Birch Island, ON, Canada P0P 1A0
Ph: (705)285-4335

★2930★
Mississauga No. 8 First Nation
PO Box 1299
Blind River, ON, Canada P0R 1B0
Ph: (705)356-1621
Fax: (705)356-1740

★2931★
Caldwell First Nation
215 Main St.
Bothwell, ON, Canada N0P 1C0
Ph: (519)695-3920
Fax: (519)695-2538

★2932★
Magnetawan First Nation
RR #1
PO Box 15
Britt, ON, Canada P0G 1B0
Ph: (705)383-2477
Fax: (705)383-2566

★2933★
Constance Lake First Nation
General Delivery
Calstock, ON, Canada P0L 1B0
Ph: (807)463-4511
Fax: (807)463-2222

★2934★
Wahnapitae First Nation
PO Box 1119
Capreol, ON, Canada P0M 1H0
Ph: (705)858-4133

★2935★
Cat Lake First Nation
Cat Lake, ON, Canada P0V 1J0
Ph: (807)347-2100
Fax: (807)347-2116

★2936★
Brunswick House First Nation
PO Box 1178
Chapleau, ON, Canada P0M 1K0
Ph: (705)864-0174
Fax: (705)864-1960

★2937★
Chapleau Cree First Nation
4 Beech St.
PO Box 400
Chapleau, ON, Canada P0M 1K0
Ph: (705)864-0784
Fax: (705)864-1760

★2938★
Chapleau Ojibway First Nation
PO Box 279
Chapleau, ON, Canada P0M 1K0
Ph: (705)864-2910
Fax: (705)864-2391

★2939★
North Spirit Lake First Nation
PO Box 70
Cochenour, ON, Canada P0V 1G0

★2940★
New Post First Nation
RR #2, Box 2, Comp. 0
Cochrane, ON, Canada P0L 1C0
Ph: (705)272-5685

★2941★
Mohawks of Akwesasne
PO Box 579
Cornwall, ON, Canada K6H 5T3   Ph: (613)575-2250
   Fax: (613)575-2181

★2942★
Curve Lake First Nation
Curve Lake Post Office
Curve Lake, ON, Canada K0L 1R0   Ph: (705)657-8045

★2943★
Serpent River First Nation
48 Indian Rd.
Cutler, ON, Canada P0P 1B0   Ph: (705)844-2418
   Fax: (705)844-2757

★2944★
Deer Lake First Nation
PO Box 335
Deer Lake, ON, Canada P0V 1N0   Ph: (807)775-2141
   Fax: (807)775-2220

★2945★
Mohawks of the Bay of Quinte
RR No. 1
Deseronto, ON, Canada K0K 1X0   Ph: (613)396-3424

★2946★
Naicatchewenin First Nation
RR 1
Devlin, ON, Canada P0W 1C0   Ph: (807)486-3407

★2947★
Wabigoon Lake First Nation
Site 112, Box 24
Dinorwic, ON, Canada P0V 1P0   Ph: (807)938-6684
   Fax: (807)938-1166

★2948★
Eagle Lake First Nation
PO Box 10
Eagle River, ON, Canada P0V 1S0   Ph: (807)755-5526
   Fax: (807)755-5696

★2949★
Wabauskang First Nation
PO Box 418
Ear Falls, ON, Canada P0V 1T0   Ph: (807)529-3174
   Fax: (807)529-3007

★2950★
Rainy River First Nation
PO Box 450
Emo, ON, Canada P0W 1E0   Ph: (807)482-2479

★2951★
Chippewas of Kettle and Stony Point First Nation
53 Indian Ln.
RR No. 1
Forest, ON, Canada N0N 1J0   Ph: (519)786-2125

★2952★
Fort Albany First Nation
General Delivery
Fort Albany, ON, Canada P0L H1W   Ph: (705)278-1044
   Fax: (705)278-1193

★2953★
Couchiching First Nation
c/o PO Box 723
Fort Frances, ON, Canada P9A 3N1   Ph: (807)274-3228
   Fax: (807)274-6458

★2954★
Lac La Croix First Nation
PO Box 640
Fort Frances, ON, Canada P9A 3M9   Ph: (807)485-2431
   Fax: (807)485-2583

★2955★
Nicikousemenecaning First Nation
PO Box 68
Fort Frances, ON, Canada P9A 3M5   Ph: (807)481-2536
   Fax: (807)481-2511

★2956★
Stanjikoming First Nation
PO Box 609
Fort Frances, ON, Canada P9A 3M6   Ph: (807)274-2188
   Fax: (807)274-4774

★2957★
Fort Severn First Nation
Fort Severn, ON, Canada P0V 1W0   Ph: (807)478-2572

★2958★
Missanabie Cree First Nation
RR4, Hwy 17E, Bell's Point
Garden River, ON, Canada P6A 5K9   Ph: (705)254-2705
   Fax: (705)254-3292

★2959★
Ojibways of Garden River First Nation
RR No. 4, Site 5, Box 7
Garden River, ON, Canada P6A 5K9   Ph: (705)946-6300
   Fax: (705)946-1415

★2960★
Mattagami First Nation
PO Box 99
Gogama, ON, Canada P0M 1W0   Ph: (705)894-2072
   Fax: (705)894-2887

★2961★
Algonquins of Golden Lake
Golden Lake, ON, Canada K0J 1X0   Ph: (613)625-2800

★2962★
Grassy Narrows First Nation
General Delivery
Grassy Narrows, ON, Canada P0X 1B0   Ph: (807)925-2201

★2963★
Gull Bay First Nation
General Delivery
Gull Bay, ON, Canada P0T 1P0   Ph: (807)982-2101
   Fax: (807)982-2290

★2964★
Mississaugas of New Credit
RR No. 6
Hagersville, ON, Canada N0A 1H0   Ph: (416)768-1133
   Fax: (416)768-1225

★2965★
Ojibways of the Pic River (Heron Bay)
General Delivery
Heron Bay, ON, Canada P0T 1R0   Ph: (807)229-1749
   Fax: (807)229-1944

★2966★
Lac Seul First Nation
PO Box 100
Hudons, ON, Canada P0V 2A0   Ph: (807)582-3211
   Fax: (807)582-3493

★2967★
Kasabonika Lake First Nation
General Delivery
Kasabonika Lake, ON, Canada P0V 1Y0   Ph: (807)535-2547
   Fax: (807)535-1152

★2968★
Kashechewan First Nation
General Delivery
Village of Kaschechew an
General Delivery
Kashechewan, ON, Canada P0L 1S0   Ph: (705)275-4440

★2969★
Ojibways of Hiawatha First Nation
RR No. 2
Keene, ON, Canada K0L 2G0   Ph: (705)295-4421
   Fax: (705)295-4424

★2970★
Washagamis Bay First Nation
PO Box 625
Keewatin, ON, Canada P0X 1C0   Ph: (807)543-2532

★2971★
Wauzhushk Onigum First Nation (Rat Portage)
PO Box 1850   Ph: (807)548-5663
Kenora, ON, Canada P9M 3X8   Fax: (807)548-4877

★2972★
Kingfisher Lake First Nation
General Delivery   Ph: (807)532-2067
Kingfisher Lake, ON, Canada P0V 1Z0 Fax: (807)532-2063

★2973★
Lansdowne House First Nation
General Delivery   Ph: (807)479-2570
Lansdowne House, ON, Canada P0T 2L0 Fax: (807)479-1138

★2974★
Ojibways of Sucker Creek
RR 1, Box 21   Ph: (705)368-2228
Little Current, ON, Canada P0P 1K0   Fax: (705)368-3563

★2975★
Ginoogaming First Nation
PO Box 89
Long Lac, ON, Canada P0T 2A0   Fax: (807)876-2495

★2976★
Long Lake No. 58 First Nation
PO Box 609   Ph: (807)876-2292
Long Lac, ON, Canada P0T 2A0   Fax: (807)876-2757

★2977★
Rocky Bay First Nation
General Delivery   Ph: (807)885-3401
Macdiarmid, ON, Canada P0T 2B0   Fax: (807)885-3231

★2978★
Moose Deer Point First Nation
PO Box 119
Mactier, ON, Canada P0C 1H0   Ph: (705)375-5209

★2979★
Sagamok Anishriawbek First Nation
PO Box 610   Ph: (705)865-2421
Massey, ON, Canada P0P 1P0   Fax: (705)865-3307

★2980★
Matachewan First Nation
PO Box 208   Ph: (705)565-2230
Matachewan, ON, Canada P0K 1M0   Fax: (705)565-2585

★2981★
Wahgoshig First Nation
PO Box 629   Ph: (705)567-4891
Matheson, ON, Canada P0K 1N0   Fax: (705)567-4891

★2982★
Seine River First Nation
PO Box 124   Ph: (807)599-2224
Mine Centre, ON, Canada P0W 1H0   Fax: (807)599-2865

★2983★
Pic Mobert First Nation
General Delivery
Mobert, ON, Canada P0M 2J0   Fax: (807)822-2850

★2984★
Moose Cree First Nation
PO Box 190   Ph: (705)658-4619
Moose Factory, ON, Canada P0L 1W0   Fax: (705)658-4734

★2985★
Big Grassy First Nation
General Delivery   Ph: (807)488-5614
Morson, ON, Canada P0W 1J0   Fax: (807)488-5533

★2986★
Big Island First Nation
General Delivery
Morson, ON, Canada P0W 1J0   Ph: (807)488-5602

★2987★
Chippewas of the Thames First Nation
R.R. No. 1   Ph: (519)289-5555
Muncey, ON, Canada N0L 1Y0   Fax: (519)289-2230

★2988★
Munsee-Delaware First Nation
RR 1
Muncey, ON, Canada N0L 1Y0   Ph: (519)289-5396

★2989★
Muskrat Dam First Nation
General Delivery   Ph: (807)471-2573
Muskrat Dam, ON, Canada P0V 2B0   Fax: (807)471-2540

★2990★
Aroland First Nation
PO Box 390
Nakina, ON, Canada P0T 2H0   Ph: (807)329-5970

★2991★
Marten Falls First Nation
General Delivery
Ogoki Post   Ph: (807)349-2509
Nakina, ON, Canada P0T 2L0   Fax: (807)349-2511

★2992★
Whitefish Lake First Nation
PO Box 39   Ph: (705)692-3423
Naughton, ON, Canada P0M 2M0   Fax: (705)692-5010

★2993★
Ojibways of Onegaming Band(Sabaskong)
PO Box 160   Ph: (807)484-2162
Nestor Falls, ON, Canada P0X 1K0   Fax: (807)484-2737

★2994★
Mishkegogamang First Nation
General Delivery   Ph: (807)928-2414
New Osnaburg, ON, Canada P0V 2H0   Fax: (807)928-2077

★2995★
New Slate Falls First Nation
General Delivery
New Slate Falls, ON, Canada P0V 2P0

★2996★
Flying Post First Nation
PO Box 1027   Ph: (807)887-3071
Nipigon, ON, Canada P0T 2J0   Fax: (807)887-1138

★2997★
Lake Helen First Nation (Red Rock)
PO Box 1030   Ph: (807)887-2510
Nipigon, ON, Canada P0T 2J0   Fax: (807)887-3446

★2998★
Shawanaga First Nation
RR 1
Nobel, ON, Canada P0G 1G0   Ph: (705)366-2526

★2999★
Six Nations of the Grand River Territory
PO Box 5000   Ph: (519)445-2201
Ohsweken, ON, Canada N0A 1M0   Fax: (519)445-4208

★3000★
Wasauksing First Nation
PO Box 253   Ph: (705)746-2531
Parry Sound, ON, Canada P2A 2X4   Fax: (705)746-5984

★3001★
Whitefish Bay First Nation
Pawitik Post Office Ph: (807)226-5411
Pawitik, ON, Canada P0X 1L0 Fax: (807)226-5389

★3002★
Beausoleil First Nation
Cedar Point Post Office Ph: (705)247-2051
Penetanguishene, ON, Canada L0K 1C0 Fax: (705)247-2239

★3003★
Henvey Inlet First Nation
Pickerel, ON, Canada P0G 1J0 Ph: (705)857-2331

★3004★
Eabametoong First Nation
Eabamet Lake Post Office
PO Box 70 Ph: (807)242-7361
Pickle Lake, ON, Canada P0T 2H0 Fax: (807)242-1440

★3005★
Pikangikum First Nation
General Delivery Ph: (807)773-5578
Pikangikum, ON, Canada P0V 1L0 Fax: (807)773-5536

★3006★
Mississaugas of Scugog First Nation
RR 5, 22521 Island Rd. Ph: (905)985-3337
Port Perry, ON, Canada L9L 1B6 Fax: (905)985-8828

★3007★
Mnjikaning First Nation
Post Office 35 Ph: (705)325-3611
Rama, ON, Canada L0K 1T0 Fax: (705)325-2230

★3008★
M'Njikaning First Nation
PO Box 35 Ph: (705)325-3611
Rama, ON, Canada L0K 1T0 Fax: (705)325-0879

★3009★
McDowell Lake First Nation
PO Box 740 Ph: (807)727-1168
Red Lake, ON, Canada P0V 2M0 Fax: (807)727-1168

★3010★
Poplar Hill First Nation
PO Box 5004 Ph: (807)772-8838
Red Lake, ON, Canada P0V 2M0 Fax: (807)772-8876

★3011★
Mississaugas of Alderville First Nation
PO Box 4 Ph: (905)352-2011
Roseneath, ON, Canada K0K 2X0 Fax: (905)352-3242

★3012★
Sachigo Lake First Nation
Sachigo Lake, ON, Canada P0V 2P0 Ph: (807)595-2577

★3013★
Kee-Way-Win First Nation
General Delivery Ph: (807)774-1210
Sandy Lake, ON, Canada P0V 1V0 Fax: (807)774-1210

★3014★
Sandy Lake First Nation
Sandy Lake, ON, Canada P0V 1V0 Ph: (807)774-3421

★3015★
Chippewas of Sarnia First Nation
978 Tashmoo Ave.
Sarnia, ON, Canada N7T 7H5 Ph: (519)336-8410

★3016★
Batchewana First Nation
Rankin Reserve
236 Frontenac St., RR4
Sault Ste. Marie, ON, Canada P6A 5K9 Ph: (705)759-0914

★3017★
Saugeen First Nation
General Delivery Ph: (807)584-2989
Savant Lake, ON, Canada P0V 2S0 Fax: (807)584-2243

★3018★
Pays Plat First Nation
PO Box 819
Scheiber, ON, Canada P0T 2S0 Ph: (807)824-2541

★3019★
Sheguiandah First Nation
PO Box 101 Ph: (705)368-2781
Sheguiandah, ON, Canada P0P 1W0 Fax: (705)368-3697

★3020★
Sheshegwaning First Nation
Sheshegwanin, ON, Canada P0P 1X0 Ph: (705)283-3292

★3021★
Iskutewizaagegan First Nation (Shoal Lake No. 39)
Kejick Post Office Ph: (807)733-2560
Shoal Lake, ON, Canada P0X 1E0 Fax: (807)733-3106

★3022★
Shoal Lake No. 40 First Nation
Kejick Post Office Ph: (807)733-2315
Shoal Lake, ON, Canada P0X 1E0 Fax: (807)733-3115

★3023★
Cockburn Island First Nation
General Delivery
Silverwater, Manitoulin Island, ON, Ph: (705)283-3963
  Canada P0P 1Y0 Fax: (705)283-3964

★3024★
Northwest Angle No. 37 First Nation
PO Box 267 Ph: (807)226-5353
Sioux Narrows, ON, Canada P0X 1N0 Fax: (807)226-1164

★3025★
Chippewas of Saugeen First Nation
RR 1 Ph: (519)797-2781
Southampton, ON, Canada N0H 2L0 Fax: (519)797-2978

★3026★
Oneidas of the Thames First Nation
RR 2 Ph: (519)652-3244
Southwold, ON, Canada N0L 2G0 Fax: (519)652-9287

★3027★
Nipissing First Nation
RR 1
Sturgeon Falls, ON, Canada P0H 2G0 Ph: (705)753-2050

★3028★
Nibinamik First Nation
General Delivery
Summer Beaver, ON, Canada P0T 3B0 Ph: (807)593-2131

★3029★
Chippewas of Georgina Island
RR No. 2, Box 12 Ph: (705)437-1337
Sutton West, ON, Canada L0E 1R0 Fax: (705)437-4597

★3030★
Georgina Island First Nation
RR 2 Ph: (705)437-3748
Sutton West, ON, Canada L0E 1R0 Fax: (705)437-4597

★3031★
Delaware of the Thames First Nation (Moravian Town)
RR 3   Ph: (519)692-3936
Thamesville, ON, Canada N0P 2K0   Fax: (519)692-5522

★3032★
Thessalon First Nation
RR 2, Box 9   Ph: (705)842-2323
Thessalon, ON, Canada P0R 1L0   Fax: (705)842-2332

★3033★
Fort William First Nation
PO Box 786   Ph: (807)623-9543
Thunder Bay, ON, Canada P7C 4W6   Fax: (807)623-5190

★3034★
Lac des Milles Lacs First Nation
PO Box 36 Stn. F   Ph: (807)344-1328
Thunder Bay, ON, Canada P7C 4V5   Fax: (807)623-2008

★3035★
Sand Point First Nation
600 Victoria Ave. PO/CP 27089   Ph: (807)622-1144
Thunder Bay, ON, Canada P7C 5Y7   Fax: (807)622-6431

★3036★
Dokis First Nation
Dokis Bay   Ph: (807)763-2200
Via Monetville, ON, Canada P0M 2K0   Fax: (807)763-2087

★3037★
Chippewas of Beausoleil First Nation
Cedar Point Post Office
Via Penetanguishene, ON, Canada L0K   Ph: (705)247-2051
1P0   Fax: (705)247-2239

★3038★
Ojibways of Walpole Island
RR 3   Ph: (519)627-1481
Wallaceburg, ON, Canada N8A 4K9   Fax: (519)627-0440

★3039★
Michipicoten First Nation
RR No. 1, Ste. 7, Box 1   Ph: (705)856-4455
Wawa, ON, Canada P0S 1K0   Fax: (705)856-1642

★3040★
North Caribou Lake First Nation
Weagamow Lake, ON, Canada P0V 2Y0   Ph: (807)469-5191

★3041★
Webequi First Nation
PO Box 176   Ph: (807)353-6531
Webequie, ON, Canada P0T 3A0   Fax: (807)353-1218

★3042★
West Bay First Nation
PO Box 2   Ph: (705)377-5362
West Bay, ON, Canada P0P 1G0   Fax: (705)377-4980

★3043★
Wabasseemoong Independent Nation (Islington)
Whitedog Post Office   Ph: (807)927-2068
Whitedog, ON, Canada P0X 1P0   Fax: (807)927-2071

★3044★
Chippewas of Nawash
RR No. 5
Wiarton, ON, Canada N0H 2T0   Ph: (519)534-1689

★3045★
Wikweminkong Unceded First Nation
PO Box 112   Ph: (705)859-3122
Wikweminkong, ON, Canada P0P 2J0   Fax: (705)859-3851

★3046★
Wunnumin Lake First Nation
PO Box 105   Ph: (807)442-2559
Wunnumin Lake, ON, Canada P0V 2Z0   Fax: (807)442-2627

Prince Edward Island

★3047★
Abegweit First Nation
Po Box 220   Ph: (902)675-3842
Cornwall, PE, Canada C0A 1H0   Fax: (902)675-2286

Quebec

★3048★
Wolinak First Nation
4670, rue Kolipaio   Ph: (819)294-6696
Becancour, PQ, Canada G0X 1B0   Fax: (819)294-6697

★3049★
Betsiamites First Nation
2, rue Ashini, C.P. 40   Ph: (418)567-2265
Betsiamites, PQ, Canada G0H 1B0   Fax: (418)567-8560

★3050★
Mistissini First Nation
Mistassini Lake, Baie-du-Poste
Chibougamau, PQ, Canada G0W 1C0   Fax: (418)923-3115

★3051★
Chisasibi First Nation
PO Box 150   Ph: (819)855-2878
Chisasibi, PQ, Canada J0M 1E0   Fax: (819)855-2875

★3052★
Cree Nation of Chisasibi
Chisasibi, PQ, Canada J0M 1E0   Ph: (819)855-2878
      Fax: (819)855-2875

★3053★
Cree Nation of Eastmain
Eastmain, PQ, Canada J0M 1W0   Ph: (819)977-0211
      Fax: (819)977-0281

★3054★
Eastmain First Nation
Eastmain, PQ, Canada J0M 1W0   Ph: (819)977-0211

★3055★
Bande indienne de Gaspe
C.P. 69, Fontenelle
Gaspe, PQ, Canada G0E 1H0   Ph: (418)368-6005

★3056★
Mohawks of Kahnawake
PO Box 720
Kahnawake, PQ, Canada J0L 1B0   Ph: (514)632-7500

★3057★
Kanesatake First Nation
681 Ste. Philomene   Ph: (514)479-8373
Kanesatake, PQ, Canada J0N 1E0   Fax: (514)479-8249

★3058★
Naskapis of Quebec First Nation
PO Box 5111   Ph: (418)585-2686
Kawawchikamach, PQ, Canada G0G 2Z0   Fax: (418)585-3130

★3059★
Kipawa First Nation
Kebaoweck Indian Reserve
PO Box 756   Ph: (819)627-3455
Kipawa, PQ, Canada J0Z 3R0   Fax: (819)627-9428

★3060★
La Romaine First Nation
Conceil des Montagnais de la Romaine   Ph: (418)229-2917
La Romaine, PQ, Canada G0G 1M0   Fax: (418)229-2921

★3061★
Conseil de la Nation Atikamekw
317, rue St. Joseph
CP 848   Ph: (819)523-6153
La Tuque, PQ, Canada G9X 3P6   Fax: (819)523-5101

★3062★
Lac Simon First Nation
Conceil de Bande du Lac Simon
Lac Simon   Ph: (819)449-5170
Lac Simon, PQ, Canada J9E 3C9 Fax: (819)449-5673

★3063★
Essipit First Nation
27 rue de la Reserve, C.P. 820   Ph: (418)233-2509
Les Escoumins, PQ, Canada G0T 1K0   Fax: (418)233-2888

★3064★
Listuguj First Nation
17 Riverside West
PO Box 298   Ph: (418)788-2904
Listuguj, PQ, Canada G0C 2R0   Fax: (418)788-2058

★3065★
Listuguj Mi'gmaq First Nation
PO Box 298
17 Riverside W   Ph: (418)788-2248
Listuguj, PQ, Canada G0C 2R0   Fax: (418)788-2058

★3066★
Conseil Attikamek-Montagnais
80 Boulevard Bastien
Village des Hurons
Lorette, PQ, Canada G0A 4V0   Ph: (418)842-0277

★3067★
Manawan First Nation
135 rue Kicik   Ph: (819)971-8813
Manawan, PQ, Canada J0K 1M0   Fax: (819)971-8848

★3068★
Conseil de la Nation Algonquine Anishnabeg
314 Hill St.
PO Box 313   Ph: (819)449-1225
Maniwaki, PQ, Canada J9E 3C9   Fax: (819)449-8064

★3069★
Kitigan Zibi Anishinabeg First Nation
PO Box 309
Maniwaki, PQ, Canada J9E 3C9   Ph: (819)449-5170

★3070★
Gesgapegiag First Nation
Maria Indian Reserve
PO Box 1280   Ph: (418)759-3441
Maria, PQ, Canada G0C 1Y0   Fax: (418)759-5856

★3071★
Lac St. Jean First Nation
151, rue Ouiatchouan   Ph: (418)275-2473
Mashteuiatsh, PQ, Canada G0W 2H0   Fax: (418)275-6212

★3072★
Mingan First Nation
C.P. 319   Ph: (418)949-2234
Mingan, PQ, Canada G0G 1V0   Fax: (418)949-2085

★3073★
Cree Nation of Mistissini
Mistissini, PQ, Canada G0W 1C0   Ph: (418)923-3253
                                 Fax: (418)923-3115

★3074★
Malecites of Viger
5805, rue Chauveau   Ph: (514)251-1454
Montreal, PQ, Canada H1N 1H5   Fax: (514)251-8114

★3075★
Natashquan First Nation
Conceil des Montagnais de Natshquan   Ph: (418)726-3529
Natashquan, PQ, Canada G0G 2E0   Fax: (418)726-3606

★3076★
Cree Nation of Nemaska
Nemaska, PQ, Canada J0Y 3B0   Ph: (819)673-2512
                               Fax: (819)673-2542

★3077★
Nemaska First Nation
Lac Champion
Nemiscau, PQ, Canada J0Y 3B0   Ph: (819)673-2512

★3078★
Temiskaming First Nation
PO Box 336
Notre Dame du Nord, PQ, Canada J0Z   Ph: (819)723-2335
   3B0   Fax: (819)723-2353

★3079★
Odanak First Nation
58 rue Sibosis   Ph: (514)568-2819
Odanak, PQ, Canada J0G 1H0   Fax: (514)568-3553

★3080★
Cree Nation of Ouji-Bougoumou
Ouji-Bougoumou, PQ, Canada G0W 3C0   Ph: (418)748-2617
                                     Fax: (418)745-3911

★3081★
Abitibiwinni First Nation
180, rue Abitibiwinni   Ph: (819)732-6591
Pikogan, PQ, Canada J9T 3A3   Fax: (819)732-1569

★3082★
Barriere Lake First Nation
La Verendrye Park
Rapid Lake, PQ, Canada J0W 2G0   Ph: (819)824-1734

★3083★
Obedjiwan First Nation
Reserve d'Obedjiwan   Ph: (819)974-8837
Roberval, PQ, Canada G0W 3B0   Fax: (819)974-8828

★3084★
Pakua Shipi First Nation
Conceil des Montagnais de Pakua Shipi   Ph: (418)947-2622
Saint Augustin, PQ, Canada G0G 2R0   Fax: (418)947-2622

★3085★
Schefferville First Nation
C.P. 1390   Ph: (418)585-2601
Scheferville, PQ, Canada G0G 2T0   Fax: (418)585-3856

★3086★
Mamit Innuat
700 boulevard Laure, bureau 208   Ph: (418)968-4890
Sept-Iles, PQ, Canada G4R 1Y1   Fax: (418)968-2370

★3087★
Uashat Mak Mani-Utenam First Nation
1089, rue Dequen, C.P. 8000   Ph: (418)962-0327
Sept-iles, PQ, Canada G4R 4L9   Fax: (418)968-0937

★3088★
Huronne-Wendat First Nation
145, rue Chef-Michel-Laveau
Village-des-Hurons Wendake, PQ, Canada   Ph: (418)843-3767
   G0A 4V0   Fax: (418)842-1108

★3089★
Cree Nation of Waskaganish
Waskaganish, PQ, Canada J0M 1R0   Ph: (819)895-8843
    Fax: (819)895-8901

★3090★
Waskaganish Band
PO Box 60
Waskaganish, PQ, Canada J0M 1R0   Ph: (819)895-8843

★3091★
Cree Nation of Waswanipi
Waswanipi, PQ, Canada J0Y 3C0   Ph: (819)753-2587
    Fax: (819)753-2555

★3092★
Waswanipi First Nation
Waswanipi River, PQ, Canada J0Y 3C0   Ph: (819)753-2587
    Fax: (819)753-2555

★3093★
Cree Nation of Wemindji
16 Beaver Rd.   Ph: (819)978-0264
Wemindji, PQ, Canada J0M 1L0   Fax: (819)978-0258

★3094★
Wemindji First Nation
Cree Nation of Wemindji   Ph: (819)978-0264
Weminedji, PQ, Canada J0M 1L0   Fax: (819)978-0258

★3095★
Weymontachie First Nation
C.P. 37   Ph: (819)666-2237
Weymontachie, PQ, Canada G0X 3R0   Fax: (819)666-2209

★3096★
Cree Nation of Whapmagoostui
Whapmagoostui, PQ, Canada J0M 1G0   Ph: (819)929-3384
    Fax: (819)929-3203

★3097★
Whapmagoostui First Nation
PO Box 390   Ph: (819)929-3384
Whapmagoostui, PQ, Canada J0M 1G0   Fax: (819)929-3203

★3098★
Long Point First Nation
PO Box 1
Winneway River, PQ, Canada J0Z 2J0   Ph: (819)722-2441

——————— **Saskatchewan** ———————

★3099★
Okanese First Nation
PO Box 759   Ph: (306)334-2532
Balcarres, SK, Canada S0G 0C0   Fax: (306)334-2545

★3100★
Peepeekisis First Nation
PO Box 518   Ph: (306)334-2573
Balcarres, SK, Canada S0G 0C0   Fax: (306)334-2280

★3101★
Star Blanket First Nation
PO Box 456   Ph: (306)334-2206
Balcarres, SK, Canada S0G 0C0   Fax: (306)334-2606

★3102★
One Arrow First Nation
PO Box 147   Ph: (306)423-5900
Bellevue, SK, Canada S0K 3Y0   Fax: (306)467-2337

★3103★
Black Lake First Nation
PO Box 27   Ph: (306)284-2044
Black Lake, SK, Canada S0J 0H0   Fax: (306)284-2101

★3104★
Cowessess First Nation
PO Box 607
Broadview, SK, Canada S0G 0K0   Ph: (306)696-2520

★3105★
Kahkewistahaw First Nation
PO Box 609
Broadview, SK, Canada S0G 0K0   Ph: (306)696-3291

★3106★
Mosquito Grizzly Bear's Head First Nation
PO Box 177   Ph: (306)937-7707
Cando, SK, Canada S0K 0V0   Fax: (306)937-7747

★3107★
Red Pheasant First Nation
PO Box 70   Ph: (306)937-7717
Cando, SK, Canada S0K 0V0   Fax: (306)937-7727

★3108★
Canoe Lake First Nation
Canoe Narrows, SK, Canada S0M 0K0   Ph: (306)829-2150

★3109★
White Bear First Nation
PO Drawer 700
Carlyle, SK, Canada S0C 0R0   Ph: (306)577-2461

★3110★
Moosomin First Nation
PO Box 98   Ph: (306)386-2206
Cochin, SK, Canada S0M 0L0   Fax: (306)386-2098

★3111★
Saulteaux First Nation
PO Box 159   Ph: (306)386-2424
Cochin, SK, Canada S0M 0L0   Fax: (306)386-2444

★3112★
Cumberland House Cree Nation
PO Box 220   Ph: (306)888-2226
Cumberland House, SK, Canada S0E 0S0   Fax: (306)888-2084

★3113★
Piapot First Nation
General Delivery   Ph: (306)781-4848
Cupar, SK, Canada S0G 5K0   Fax: (306)781-4853

★3114★
Big River First Nation
PO Box 340   Ph: (306)724-4700
Debden, SK, Canada S0J 0S0   Fax: (306)724-2161

★3115★
Buffalo River Dene Nation
Dillon, SK, Canada S0M 0S0   Ph: (306)282-2033

★3116★
Beardy's and Okemasis First Nation
PO Box 340
Duck Lake, SK, Canada S0K 1J0   Ph: (306)467-4523

★3117★
Fond Du Lac Denesuline Nation
General Delivery   Ph: (306)686-2102
Fond Du Lac, SK, Canada S0J 0W0   Fax: (306)686-2040

★3118★
Fond du Lac First Nation
PO Box 211   Ph: (306)686-2102
Fond du Lac, SK, Canada S0G 0W0   Fax: (306)686-2040

★3119★
Muscowpetung First Nation
PO Box 1310   Ph: (306)723-4747
Fort Qu'Appelle, SK, Canada S0G 1S0   Fax: (306)723-4710

★3120★
Pasqua First Nation No. 79
PO Box 968
Fort Qu'Appelle, SK, Canada S0G 1S0   Ph: (306)332-5697

★3121★
Standing Buffalo First Nation
PO Box 128   Ph: (306)332-4685
Fort Qu'Appelle, SK, Canada S0G 1S0   Fax: (306)332-5953

★3122★
Sweet Grass First Nation
PO Box 147
Gallivan, SK, Canada S0M 0X0   Ph: (306)937-2990

★3123★
Little Black Bear First Nation
PO Box 40   Ph: (306)334-2269
Goodeve, SK, Canada S0A 1C0   Fax: (306)334-2721

★3124★
Sakimay First Nation
PO Box 339
Grenfell, SK, Canada S0G 2B0   Ph: (306)697-2831

★3125★
Cote First Nation 366
PO Box 1659
Kamsack, SK, Canada S0A 1S0   Ph: (306)542-2694

★3126★
Keeseekoose First Nation
PO Box 1120   Ph: (306)542-2516
Kamsack, SK, Canada S0A 2V0   Fax: (306)542-2586

★3127★
Pheasant Rump Nakota
PO Box 238   Ph: (306)462-2002
Kisby, SK, Canada S0C 1L0   Fax: (306)462-2003

★3128★
Lac La Ronge First Nation
PO Box 480
La Ronge, SK, Canada S0J 1L0   Ph: (306)425-2183

★3129★
Mistawasis First Nation
PO Box 250
Leask, SK, Canada S0J 1M0   Ph: (306)466-4800

★3130★
Muskeg Lake First Nation
PO Box 248   Ph: (306)466-4959
Leask, SK, Canada S0J 1R0   Fax: (306)466-4951

★3131★
Pelican Lake First Nation
PO Box 9
Leoville, SK, Canada S0J 1N0   Ph: (306)984-2313

★3132★
Muskowekwan First Nation
PO Box 298
Lestock, SK, Canada S0A 2G0   Ph: (306)274-2061

★3133★
Island Lake First Nation
PO Box 460   Ph: (306)837-2188
Loon Lake, SK, Canada S0M 1L0   Fax: (306)837-2266

★3134★
Makwa Sahgaiehcan First Nation
PO Box 340
Loon Lake, SK, Canada S0M 1L0   Ph: (306)837-2150

★3135★
Nekaneet First Nation
PO Box 548   Ph: (306)662-3660
Maple Creek, SK, Canada S0N 1N0   Fax: (306)662-4160

★3136★
Flying Dust First Nation
8001 Flying Dust Reserve   Ph: (306)236-4437
Meadow Lake, SK, Canada S9X 1T8   Fax: (306)236-3373

★3137★
James Smith First Nation
PO Box 1059
Melfort, SK, Canada S0E 1A0   Ph: (306)864-3636

★3138★
Montreal Lake First Nation
PO Box 340   Ph: (306)663-5349
Montreal Lake, SK, Canada S0J 1Y0   Fax: (306)663-5320

★3139★
Key First Nation
PO Box 70
Norquay, SK, Canada S0A 2V0   Ph: (306)594-2020

★3140★
Onion Lake First Nation
PO Box 100
Onion Lake, SK, Canada S0M 2E0   Ph: (403)847-2200

★3141★
Shoal Lake of the Cree Nation
Pakwaw Lake, SK, Canada S0E 1G0   Ph: (306)768-3551

★3142★
English River Band
General Delivery   Ph: (306)396-2066
Patuanak, SK, Canada S0M 2H0   Fax: (306)396-2155

★3143★
Little Pine First Nation
PO Box 70
Paynton, SK, Canada S0M 2J0   Ph: (306)398-4942

★3144★
Poundmaker First Nation
PO Box 220
Paynton, SK, Canada S0M 2J0   Ph: (306)398-4971

★3145★
Peter Ballantyne Cree Nation
Pelican Narrows, SK, Canada S0P 0E0   Ph: (306)632-2125

★3146★
Joseph Bighead First Nation
PO Box 309
Pierceland, SK, Canada S0M 2K0   Ph: (306)839-2277

★3147★
Wahpeton Dakota Nation
PO Box 128   Ph: (306)764-6649
Prince Albert, SK, Canada S0G 0C0   Fax: (306)764-6637

★3148★
Day Star First Nation
PO Box 277
Punnichy, SK, Canada S0A 3C0   Ph: (306)835-2834

★3149★
Gordon First Nation
PO Box 248   Ph: (306)835-2232
Punnichy, SK, Canada S0A 3C0   Fax: (306)835-2036

★3150★
Kawacatoose First Nation
PO Box 640   Ph: (306)835-2125
Raymore, SK, Canada S0A 3J0   Fax: (306)835-2178

★3151★
Red Earth First Nation
PO Box 109   Ph: (306)768-3640
Red Earth, SK, Canada S0E 1K0   Fax: (306)768-3440

★3152★
Lucky Man First Nation
1038 Packham Pl., Ste. 225   Ph: (306)374-2828
Saskatoon, SK, Canada S7N 4K4   Fax: (306)934-2853

★3153★
Whitecap Dakota/Sioux First Nation (Moose Woods)
RR 5, Box 28, Site 507   Ph: (306)477-0908
Saskatoon, SK, Canada S7K 3J8   Fax: (306)374-5899

★3154★
Ahtahkakoop First Nation
PO Box 220   Ph: (306)468-2326
Shell Lake, SK, Canada S0J 1J0   Fax: (306)468-2344

★3155★
Sturgeon Lake First Nation
Site 12, RR 1
PO Box 5
Shellbrook, SK, Canada S0J 2E0   Ph: (306)764-1872

★3156★
Carry the Kettle First Nation
PO Box 57
Sintaluta, SK, Canada S0G 4N0   Ph: (306)727-2135

★3157★
Witchekan Lake First Nation
PO Box 879
Spiritwood, SK, Canada S0J 2M0   Ph: (306)883-2787

★3158★
Ocean Man
PO Box 157
Stoughton, SK, Canada S0G 4T0   Ph: (306)457-2697

★3159★
Kinistin First Nation
PO Box 2590   Ph: (306)594-2020
Tisdale, SK, Canada S0A 2V0   Fax: (306)594-2545

★3160★
Thunderchild First Nation
PO Box 600   Ph: (306)845-3424
Turtleford, SK, Canada S0M 2Y0   Fax: (306)845-3230

★3161★
Fishing Lake First Nation
PO Box 508
Wadena, SK, Canada S0A 4J0   Ph: (306)338-3838

★3162★
Waterhen Lake First Nation
PO Box 9   Ph: (306)236-6717
Waterhen Lake, SK, Canada S0M 3B0   Fax: (306)236-4866

★3163★
Ochapowace First Nation
PO Box 550   Ph: (306)696-2425
Whitewood, SK, Canada S0G 4T0   Fax: (306)696-3146

★3164★
Hatchet Lake First Nation
General Delivery   Ph: (306)633-2003
Wollaston Lake, SK, Canada S0J 3C0   Fax: (306)633-2040

★3165★
Wood Mountain First Nation
PO Box 104   Ph: (306)266-4420
Wood Mountain, SK, Canada S0H 4L0   Fax: (306)266-2023

★3166★
Yellowquill First Nation
PO Box 40   Ph: (306)322-2281
Yellowquill, SK, Canada S0A 3A0   Fax: (306)322-2304

─────── **Yukon** ───────

★3167★
White River First Nation First Nation
General Delivery
Beaver Creek, YT, Canada Y0B 1A0   Ph: (403)862-7802

★3168★
Champagne and Aishihik First Nations
Box 5309
Haines Junction, YT, Canada Y0B 1L0   Ph: (403)634-2288

★3169★
Na-Cho Ny'A'K-Dun First Nation
Box 220
Mayo, YT, Canada Y0B 1M0   Ph: (403)996-2265

★3170★
Vuntut Gwitch'in First Nation
Box 94
Old Crow, YT, Canada Y0B 1N0   Ph: (403)966-3261

National Organizations

★3171★
Association for Native Development in the Performing and Visual Arts
204 9 St. Joseph St.
Toronto, ON, Canada M4Y 1J6   Ph: (416)972-0871

★3172★
Canadian Alliance in Solidarity with the Native People
16 Spadina Rd., Ste. 302
Toronto, ON, Canada M5R 2S7   Ph: (905)964-0169
Description: Native and non-native individuals. Seeks to educate the public about issues of concern to native people, such as spirituality, self-determination, child welfare, and the environment. Assists Native peoples in obtaining services and benefits to which

they are entitled. Works to provide support for the indigenous peoples of the world. Conducts workshops and panel discussions. **Founded:** 1960. **Members:** 1200. **Regional Groups:** 5. **Local Groups:** 7. **Publications:** Indian Giver: A Legacy of North American Native Peoples; Native Rights in Canada; The Phoenix, quarterly; Resource/Reading List. **Formerly:** (1972) Indian-Eskimo Association of Canada; (1984) Canadian Association in Support of the Native Peoples.

★3173★
Canadian Native Arts Foundation
77 Mowat Ave., Ste. 508   Ph: (416)588-3328
Toronto, ON, Canada M6K 3E3   Fax: (416)588-9198

★3174★
Multicultural Heritage Centre
PO Box 2188   Ph: (403)963-2777
Stony Plain, AB, Canada T7Z 1X7 Fax: (403)963-0935
Judy Unterschultz, Exec. Dir.

★3175★
Secwepemc Cultural Education Society and Native Heritage Park
355 Yellowhead Hwy.   Ph: (250)828-9801
Kamloops, BC, Canada V2H 1H1   Fax: (250)372-1127
Stephen Conway, Exec. Dir.

Federal Government Agencies

★3176★
Canada National Aboriginal Management Board
Portage IV, #4F00
140, Promenade du Portage
Hull, PQ, Canada K1A 0J9   Ph: (819)994-2274

★3177★
Fisheries and Oceans Canada
Aboriginal Affairs Office
200 Kent St.   Ph: (613)991-0181
Ottawa, ON, Canada K1A 0E6   Fax: (613)993-7651

★3178★
Health Canada
First Nations and Inuit Health Program
Ottawa, ON, Canada K1A 0L3   Ph: (613)052-7177
                                 Fax: (613)941-5366

★3179★
Indian and Northern Affairs Canada
Affaires indiennes et du Nord Canada
Tour Nord
Les Terrasses de la Chaudiere
10 Wellington St.   Ph: (819)997-0380
Hull, PQ, Canada K1A 0H4   Fax: (819)953-3017

★3180★
Indian and Northern Affairs Canada
Alberta Policy and Strategic Direction Sector
Canada Pl., #630
9700 Jasper Ave.   Ph: (403)495-2773
Edmonton, AB, Canada T5J 4G2   Fax: (403)495-4088
Ken Kirby, Regional Dir. Gen.

★3181★
Indian and Northern Affairs Canada
Atlantic Policy and Strategic Direction Sector
40 Havelock St.
PO Box 160   Ph: (902)661-6200
Amherst, NS, Canada B4H 3Z3   Fax: (902)661-6237
George Fotheringham, Regional Dir. Gen.

★3182★
Indian and Northern Affairs Canada
British Columbia Policy and Strategic Direction Sector
1550 Alberni St., #340   Ph: (604)666-7891
Vancouver, BC, Canada V6G 3C5   Fax: (604)666-2546
John Watson, Regional Dir. Gen.

★3183★
Indian and Northern Affairs Canada
Indian Taxation Advisory Board
90 Elgin St., 2nd Fl.   Ph: (613)954-9769
Ottawa, ON, Canada K1A 0H4   Fax: (613)954-2073

★3184★
Indian and Northern Affairs Canada
Manitoba Policy and Strategic Direction Sector
275 Portage Ave., #1100   Ph: (204)983-4928
Winnipeg, MB, Canada R3B 3A3   Fax: (204)983-7820
Brenda Kustra, Regional Dir. Gen.

★3185★
Indian and Northern Affairs Canada
Northwest Territories Policy and Strategic Direction Sector
PO Box 1500
Yellowknife, NT, Canada X1A 2R3 Ph: (403)669-2500
Warren Johnson, Regional Dir. Gen.

★3186★
Indian and Northern Affairs Canada
Ontario Policy and Strategic Direction Sector
25 St. Clair Ave., East, 5th Fl. Ph: (416)973-6234
Toronto, ON, Canada M4T 1M2   Fax: (416)954-6329
John Donnelly, Acting Regional Dir. Gen.

★3187★
Indian and Northern Affairs Canada
Quebec Policy and Strategic Direction Sector
320, rue St. Joseph est
CP 51127
Succ Comptoir postal
Quebec, PQ, Canada G1K 8Z7   Free: 800-263-5592
                                 Fax: (418)648-4040

Jerome Lapierre, Acting Regional Dir. Gen.

★3188★
Indian and Northern Affairs Canada
Saskatchewan Policy and Strategic Direction Sector
2221 Cornwall St.   Ph: (306)780-5945
Regina, SK, Canada S4P 4M2   Fax: (306)780-5733
Myler Savill, Regional Dir. Gen.

★3189★
Indian and Northern Affairs Canada
Yukon Policy and Strategic Direction Sector
300 Main St., #345
Whitehorse, YT, Canada Y1A 2B5   Ph: (403)667-3100
Mike Ivanski, Regional Dir. Gen.

★3190★
Industry Canada
Aboriginal Business Canada
235 Queen St.   Ph: (613)954-2788
Ottawa, ON, Canada K1A 0H5   Fax: (613)954-2303

★3191★
Yukon Territory Office of Aboriginal Language Services
PO Box 2703
Whitehorse, YT, Canada Y1A 2C6   Ph: (403)667-5812
Mike Smith, Dir.

State/Provincial & Local Government Agenies

Alberta

★3192★
Alberta Family and Social Services Office
Aboriginal Affairs Office
7th St. Plz.
10030 - 107 St.   Ph: (403)422-5925
Edmonton, AB, Canada T5J 3E4   Fax: (403)427-4019
Cliff Supernault, Chief Exec. Off.

British Columbia

★3193★
British Columbia Attorney General and Minister Responsible for Multiculturalism, Human Rights and Immigration
Parliament Bldgs. #156
Victoria, BC, Canada V8V 1X4   Ph: (250)356-3027
Hon. Ujjal Dosanjh, Attorney Gen. & Minister

★3194★
British Columbia Ministry of Aboriginal Affairs
908 Pandora Ave.   Ph: (250)356-8281
Victoria, BC, Canada V8V 1X4   Fax: (250)387-1785

★3195★
British Columbia Ministry of Social Services
Aboriginal Services
Parliament Bldgs.
614 Humboldt St., 7th Fl.   Ph: (250)387-6485
Victoria, BC, Canada V8V 1X4   Fax: (250)356-7801
Mavis Henry, Deputy Dir.

Manitoba

★3196★
Manitoba Northern Affairs Office
Native Affairs Secretariat
59 Elizabeth Dr.   Ph: (204)677-6607
Thompson, MB, Canada R8N 1X4   Fax: (204)677-6753
Harvey Bostrom, Dir.

New Brunswick

★3197★
New Brunswick Department of Intergovernmental and Aboriginal Affairs
Affaires intergouvernementales et
autochtones
PO Box 6000   Ph: (506)453-2384
Fredericton, NB, Canada E3B 5H1   Fax: (506)453-2995

Newfoundland

★3198★
Labrador and Aboriginal Affairs Secretariat
Confederation Bldg.
PO Box 8700
St. John's, NF, Canada A1B 4J6   Ph: (709)729-5645
Harold Marshall, Sec.

Northwest Territories

★3199★
Northwest Territories Ministry of Intergovernmental and Aboriginal Affairs
Precambrian Bldg., 7th Fl.
PO Box 1320
Yellowknife, NT, Canada X1A 2L9   Ph: (403)873-7143
Hon. James Antoine, Minister

Ontario

★3200★
Ontario Attorney General and Minister Responsible for Native Affairs
720 Bay St., 11th Fl.   Ph: (416)326-4000
Toronto, ON, Canada M5G 2K1   Fax: (416)326-4016
Hon. Charles Harnick, Attorney Gen. & Minister

★3201★
Ontario Ministry of Citizenship, Culture and Recreation
Culture Division
Native American Branch
77 Bloor St. West, 6th Fl.   Ph: (416)314-7414
Toronto, ON, Canada M7A 2R9   Fax: (416)314-7428
Allan Chrisjohn, Dir.

★3202★
Ontario Ministry of Community and Social Services
Office of Aboriginal Healing and Wellness
Hepburn Block
80 Grosvenor St., 6th Fl.   Ph: (416)325-5666
Toronto, ON, Canada M7A 1E9   Fax: (416)325-5172
Carrie Hayward, Mgr.

★3203★
Ontario Native Affairs Secretariat
595 Bay St., #1009   Ph: (416)326-4740
Toronto, ON, Canada M5G 2C2   Fax: (416)326-4017

Quebec

★3204★
Quebec Secretariat for Native Affairs
Secretariat aux affaires autochtones
Edifice H #875
Grande-Allee est, 2e etage   Ph: (819)644-5848
Quebec, PQ, Canada G1R 4Y8   Fax: (819)644-9659

Saskatchewan

★3205★
Saskatchewan Indian and Metis Affairs Secretariat
1870 Albert St., 3rd Fl.   Ph: (306)787-6250
Regina, SK, Canada S4P 3V7   Fax: (306)787-6336

★3206★
Saskatchewan Minister for Indian and Metis Affairs, Status of Women, and Gaming Authority
Legislative Bldg. Ph: (306)787-0354
Regina, SK, Canada S4S 0B3 Fax: (306)787-2202
Hon. Joanne Crofford, Minister

Library Collections

★3207★
Northwest Territory Canadian and French Heritage Center
Minnesota Genealogical Society Library
PO Box 29397
Brooklyn Center, MN 55429
Jean Jensen, Libn.

Subjects: Quebec, Canada, Canadians in the U.S., Metis Indians, Franco-Americans. **Holdings:** 2000 books; 100 bound periodical volumes; 1600 microforms; 100 manuscripts; 30 AV programs. **Subscriptions:** 1000 journals and other serials.

Museums and Other Cultural Facilities

─────────── **Alberta** ───────────

★3208★
Luxton Museum of the Plains Indian
c/o Buffalo Nations Cultural Society
PO Box 850 Ph: (403)762-2388
Banff, AB, Canada T0L 0C0 Fax: (403)762-2388
Pete Brewster, Exec. Dir.

★3209★
Medicine Hat Museum and Art Gallery
1302 Bomfort Ph: (403)527-6266
Medicine Hat, AB, Canada T1A 5E6 Fax: (403)528-2464
Description: Collections include Indian artifacts.

★3210★
Sarcee People's Museum
3700 Anderson Rd., SW
Calgary, AB, Canada T2W 3C4 Ph: (403)238-2677

─────────── **British Columbia** ───────────

★3211★
Campbell River Museum and Archives
407 Island Ph: (250)287-3103
Vanconer Island, BC, Canada V9W 4Z7 Fax: (250)286-0109
Description: Displays artifacts crafted by Indians of Northern Vancouver Island, principally Kwakiutl, Nuu-cha-nulth, and Salishan.

★3212★
'Ksan Indian Village
Box 326 Ph: (250)842-5544
Hazelton, BC, Canada B0J 1Y0 Fax: (250)842-6533
Description: A Gitksan Indian village consisting of seven tribal houses.

★3213★
Kwagiulth Museum and Cultural Centre
Box 8 Ph: (250)285-3733
Quathiaski Cove, BC, Canada V0P 1N0 Fax: (250)285-3753
Description: Displays items used in potlatch, a ceremonial feast of the Indians of the Northwest. The collection includes masks, rattles, whistles, head and neck rings, and various other headgear, and photographs of traditional Kwakiutl villages at the turn of the century.

★3214★
Museum of Northern British Columbia
PO Box 669 Ph: (250)624-3207
Prince Rupert, BC, Canada B8J 3S1 Fax: (250)627-8009
Description: Contains objects from the Northwest coast Indian culture. Reconstructed models, maps, graphic displays, and an ethnological collection explain pioneer history and the lifestyles of the coastal Indian groups from prehistoric times through their first contact with explorers. A modern Indian carving shed is on the museum grounds.

★3215★
Saanichton Historical Artifacts Society
7321 Lochside Dr.
RR #3
Saanichton, BC, Canada V0S 1M0 Ph: (250)652-5522
Robert Norwood, Curator

★3216★
U'Mista Cultural Centre
Box 253 Ph: (250)974-5403
Alert Bay, BC, Canada V0N 1A0 Fax: (250)974-5499
Description: Displays a collection of masks, cedar baskets, copper items, and other artifacts from Indian Potlatches.

─────────── **Manitoba** ───────────

★3217★
Eskimo Museum
La Verendrye St.
Box 10
Churchill, MB, Canada R0B 0E0 Ph: (204)675-2030
Description: Displays artifacts and exhibits featuring contemporary and historic eskimo culture. Kayaks from the pre-Dorset period dating back to 2000 B.C., a collection of Cree and Chipewyah Indian art, and Eskimo carvings are also displayed.

─────────── **Newfoundland** ───────────

★3218★
Piulimatsivik - Nain Museum
PO Box 247
Nain, NF, Canada A0P 1L0 Ph: (709)922-2821
Rev. Renatus Hunter, Supervisor

─────────── **Northwest Territories** ───────────

★3219★
Northern Life Museum
110 King St.
Box 420 Ph: (403)872-2859
Fort Smith, NT, Canada X0E 0P0 Fax: (867)867-5808
Description: Collections include Indian artifacts, and Inuit tools and artifacts.

★3220★
Nuantta Sunaqutangit Museum
PO Box 605
Iqaluit, NT, Canada X0A 0H0   Ph: (819)979-5537
Denise Kekkema, Curator

──────────── **Ontario** ────────────

★3221★
Canadian Museum of Civilization
100 Laurier St.   Ph: (613)776-7000
Hull, ON, Canada J8X 4H2   Fax: (613)776-8300
Description: Exhibits illustrate Canada's history, prehistory, periods of migration, and native settlement.

★3222★
Huron Indian Village
Box 638   Ph: (705)526-2844
Midland, ON, Canada L4R 4P4   Fax: (705)527-6622
Description: A reconstructed village that interprets 16th-century life of the Huron Indians of the region.

★3223★
**Museum of Indian Archaeology and Lawson
  Prehistoric Village**
Lawson-Jury Bldg.
1600 Attawandaron Rd.   Ph: (519)473-1360
London, ON, Canada N6G 3M6   Fax: (519)473-1363
Description: Depicts 11,000 years of Indian habitation in southwestern Ontario. Includes an excavation site and exhibits arranged according to five periods of development.

★3224★
**North American Indian Travel College
The Living Museum**
RR 3
Cornwall Island, ON, Canada K6H 5R7   Ph: (613)932-9452
Description: A re-created village consisting of traditional buildings of the Cree, Ojibway, and Iroquois tribes. Depicts Indian lifestyles typical of the early 18th-century; museum contains cultural artifacts.

★3225★
Sainte-Marie Among the Hurons
Sainte-Marie-au-Pays-des-Hurons
c/o Economic Development, Trade and
  Tourism,
Huronia Historical Parks
PO Box 160   Ph: (705)526-7838
Midland, ON, Canada L4R 4K8   Fax: (705)526-9193
John Barrett-Hamilton, Gen. Mgr.

★3226★
Ska-Nah-Doht Indian Village
Longwoods Rd. Conservation Area
8449 Irish Dr. RR1   Ph: (519)264-2420
Mt. Brydges, ON, Canada N0L 1W0   Fax: (519)264-1562
Description: A re-created village depicting the Iroquois culture in southwestern Ontario about the year 1000. Offers a slide show and displays devoted to conservation and Indian artifacts.

★3227★
Thunder Bay Art Gallery
1080 Keewatin St.
PO Box 1193   Ph: (807)577-6427
Thunder Bay, ON, Canada P7C 4X9   Fax: (807)577-3781
Description: Collections include Indian artifacts, and contemporary Indian art.

★3228★
Woodland Indian Cultural Education Centre
184 Mohawk St.
PO Box 1506   Ph: (519)759-2650
Brantford, ON, Canada N3T 5V6   Fax: (519)759-8912
Description: Exhibits include artifacts, art, clothing, and the Indian Hall of Fame, which commemorates the contributions of 21 individuals.

──────────── **Quebec** ────────────

★3229★
Abenakis Museum
108 Waban-AKI   Ph: (514)568-2600
Odanak, PQ, Canada J0G 1H0   Fax: (514)568-5959
Description: Displays relate the history of the Abenaki tribe of Odanak.

★3230★
Chapelle des Indiens
CP 69
Tadoussac, PQ, Canada G0T 2A0   Ph: (418)235-4324
Yvon Cholette, Cure

★3231★
**Musee des Abenakis d'Odanak
Societe historique d'Odanak**
108 Waban-Aki   Ph: (514)568-2600
Odanak, PQ, Canada J0G 1H0   Fax: (514)568-5959
Nicole O'Bomsawin, Directrice

★3232★
Musee Kateri Tekakwitha
PO Box 70
Kahnawake, PQ, Canada J0L 1B0   Ph: (514)632-6030
Leon Lajoie, Directeur/Conservateur

──────────── **Saskatchewan** ────────────

★3233★
Regina Plains Museum
1801 Scarth St.
Regina, SK, Canada S4P 2G9
Description: Collections include exhibits on the Plains Indian culture, the Metis pilgrimage, and the Riel rebellion.

Research Centers

★3234★
**Carleton University
Centre for Aboriginal Education, Research, and
  Culture**
2206 Dunton Tower
1125 Colonel By Dr.
Ottawa, ON, Canada K1S 5B6   Ph: (613)520-4494
Madeleine Dion Stout, Dir.
Research Activities and Fields: Aboriginal peoples, focusing on historical and contemporary issues.

★3235★
Carleton University
Northern and Native Studies Program
School of Canadian Studies
1125 Colonel By Dr.   Ph: (613)520-2366
Ottawa, ON, Canada K1S 5B6   Fax: (613)788-3903
Madeleine Dion Stout, Coord.

Founded: 1981 **Research Activities and Fields:** Teaching and research on the Canadian north and native people of Canada, as well as Aboriginal governance and economic development.

★3236★
Centre for Nutrition and the Environment of
Indigenous People
McDonald Campus
21,111 Lakeshore Rd.
Ste. Anne de Bellevue, PQ, Canada H9X   Ph: (514)398-7544
    3V9   Fax: (514)398-1020
Dr. Harriet Kuhnlein, Dir.

Research Activities and Fields: Food and nutrition concerns for Indigenous Peoples, and the environmental concerns inherent in Indigenous societies.

★3237★
Human Rights Institute of Canada
303-246 Queen St.   Ph: (613)232-2920
Ottawa, ON, Canada K1P 5E4   Fax: (613)232-3735

Founded: 1974 **Research Activities and Fields:** Laws and policies of Canada and human rights problems in Canada and other parts of the world, particularly in regard to the Canadian Constitution, Middle East, government, native peoples, marriage and divorce, status of women, rights of children, discrimination against women in Senate appointments, and United Nations. Performs contract research for government bodies and private organizations. Specializes in U.N. conventions and agreements accepted by Canada.

★3238★
Lakehead University
Centre for Northern Studies
955 Oliver Rd.   Ph: (807)343-8787
Thunder Bay, ON, Canada P7B 5E1   Fax: (807)345-2394
Margaret E. Johnston, Dir.

Research Activities and Fields: Indigenous people in Canada.

★3239★
London Museum of Archaeology
Lawson-Jury Bldg.
1600 Attawandaron Rd.   Ph: (519)473-1360
London, ON, Canada N6G 3M6   Fax: (519)473-1363
William D. Finlayson, Dir.

Founded: 1933 **Research Activities and Fields:** Prehistoric and historic archeology of Southwestern Ontario, including excavation, restoration, and interpretation of a prehistoric Neutral village. Develops a system of computer programs to process archeological materials. **Publications:** Museum Notes; Bulletins, occasionally; Research Reports **Formerly:** Museum of Indian Archaeology.

★3240★
McGill University
McGill Subarctic Research Station
PO Box 790   Ph: (418)585-2489
Schefferville, PQ, Canada G0G 2T0   Fax: (418)585-2489
Dr. Wayne Pollard, Sci.Dir.

Founded: 1954 **Research Activities and Fields:** Subarctic environment, including studies on snow, ice, permafrost, hydrology, caribou ecology, entomology, geology, Naskapi land use and hunting, peatlands, phytosociology, phenology, subarctic vegetation, snowcover, snowmelt, geomorphology, periglacial processes, meteorology, climatology, biological productivity, limnology, soils, stringbog and muskeg, plant ecology, acid rain, demography, social sciences, and Canadian Indians. **Publications:** McGill Subarctic Research Papers, semiannually.

★3241★
Memorial University of Newfoundland
Archaeology Unit
Queen's College
Prince Phillip Dr.   Ph: (709)737-8869
St. John's, NF, Canada A1C 5S7   Fax: (709)737-2374
J.A. Tuck, Dir.

Founded: 1980 **Research Activities and Fields:** Archeology, with emphasis on the sixteenth century whaling communities in Labrador, sixteenth and seventeenth century English colonies in Newfoundland, prehistoric Eskimo and Indian occupations of Newfoundland and Labrador, and ethnoarcheological studies in Mexico. Also studies the prehistory of the Maritime Provinces and occasionally undertakes international expeditions, including sites in Sri Lanka. **Publications:** Reports in Archeology.

★3242★
Queen's University at Kingston
Agnes Etherington Art Centre
University Ave. & Queen's Crescent   Ph: (613)545-2190
Kingston, ON, Canada K7L 3N6   Fax: (613)545-6765
Dr. David McTavish, Dir.

Founded: 1957 **Research Activities and Fields:** Studies and exhibits historical and contemporary art from permanent collections, including work from Canada, Great Britain, Europe (with emphasis on seventeenth-century Dutch and Flemish painting), and Africa. Also focuses on Inuit art of Canada, including prints by Kenojuak, Pitseolak, and Lucy. Mounts 30 exhibitions annually, including travelling exhibitions from other institutions. **Publications:** Catalog of the Permanent Collection of Paintings, Drawings, and Sculpture.

★3243★
University College of Cape Breton
Beaton Institute
Box 5300   Ph: (902)563-1329
Sydney, NS, Canada B1P 6L2   Fax: (902)562-8899
Dr. R.J. Morgan, Dir.

Founded: 1957 **Research Activities and Fields:** Cape Breton Island, including its history, labor history, Gaelic literature, folklore, political and industrial history, traditional Scottish music, genealogy, and Mikmaq history.

★3244★
University of Saskatchewan
Native Law Centre
101 Diefenbaker Place   Ph: (306)966-6189
Saskatoon, SK, Canada S7N 5B8   Fax: (306)966-6207
Ruth Thompson, Dir. of Prog.

Founded: 1975 **Research Activities and Fields:** Native law, including Canadian law relating to aboriginal people (Indian, Metis, and Inuit) and aboriginal rights in international law. Also develops legal education opportunities for native students and promotes the development of law and the legal system in ways which accommodate the advancement of native communities in Canadian society. **Publications:** Monographs; Canadian Native Law Reporter, quarterly; Justice as Healing, newsletter.

★3245★
University of Western Ontario
Centre for Research and Teaching of Canadian
Native Languages
Anthropology Dept.   Ph: (519)661-3430
Social Sci. Bldg.   Fax: (519)661 -
London, ON, Canada N6A 5C2   2157
Dr. Regina Darnell, Actg.Dir.

Founded: 1978 **Research Activities and Fields:** Canadian native languages, languages of Ontario, and government policy on native languages. **Publications:** Monograph Series.

Education Programs & Services

——— Community Colleges ———

★3246★
Red Crow Community College
PO Box 1258   Ph: (403)737-2400
Cardston, AB, Canada T0K 0K0   Fax: (403)737-2101

★3247★
Saskatchewan Indian Federated College
University of Regina
118 College W.   Ph: (306)584-8333
Regina, SK, Canada S4S 0A2   Fax: (306)584-0955

Studies Programs

——— Four-Year Programs ———

★3248★
Brandon University
Native Studies Program
270 18th St.   Ph: (204)727-9740
Brandon, MB, Canada R7A 6A9   Free: 800-852-2704
                                     Fax: (204)726-0473

★3249★
Laurentian University
Native Studies Program
Ramsey Lake Rd.   Ph: (705)673-5661
Sudbury, ON, Canada P3E 2C6   Free: 800-461-4030
                                     Fax: (705)673-4912

★3250★
St. Thomas University
Native Studies Program
Fredericton, NB, Canada E3B 5G3   Ph: (506)452-7700
                                     Fax: (506)452-0547

★3251★
University College of Cape Breton
Sydney, NS, Canada B1P 6L2   Ph: (902)539-5300
                                     Fax: (902)562-0119

★3252★
University of Lethbridge
Native Studies Program
4401 University Dr.   Ph: (403)329-2758
Lethbridge, AB, Canada T1K 3M4   Fax: (403)380-1855

★3253★
University of Regina
Native Studies Program
Saskatchewan Indian Federated College   Ph: (306)585-4591
Regina, SK, Canada S4S 0A2   Fax: (306)779-6290

★3254★
University of Saskatchewan
Native Studies Department
McLean Hall, Rm. 102
106 Wiggins Rd.   Ph: (306)966-6718
Saskatoon, SK, Canada S7N 5E6   Fax: (306)966-4242

★3255★
University of Toronto
Native Studies Program
Toronto, ON, Canada M5S 1A1   Ph: (416)978-6125

——— Graduate Programs ———

★3256★
Trent University
Native Studies Program
2151 E. Beg Dr.   Ph: (705)748-1215
Peterborough, ON, Canada K9J 7B8   Fax: (705)748-1416

★3257★
University of Regina
Interdisciplinary Studies Program
Regina, SK, Canada S4S 0A2   Ph: (306)585-4161
                                     Fax: (306)585-4893

Remarks: Program includes Indian Studies.

Scholarships, Fellowships, & Loans

★3258★
CN Native Education Awards
CN Native Educational Awards Program
Employment Equity
PO Box 8100
Montreal, PQ, Canada H3C 3N4

Study Level: Undergraduate. **Award Type:** Award. **Applicant Eligibility:** Applicants must be Canadian native students attending post-secondary institutions. They must be in need of financial assistance, seriously interested in preparing for a career in the transportation industry, provide proof of acceptance into post-secondary institution, maintain full-time student status, and have a good academic record. **Selection Criteria:** Financial need is considered. **Funds Available:** Five awards of C$1,500 each. **Applicant Details:** Completed application forms must be submitted. For applications, write to: 935 De La Gaucuetiere, Montreal, Quebec H3B 2M9. **Application Deadline:** June 30.

★3259★
Cultural Grants
Canada - Department of Indian and
    Northern Affairs
10 Wellington St.   Ph: (819)997-0380
Hull, PQ, Canada K1A 0H4   Fax: (819)953-4941

Study Level: Professional Development. **Award Type:** Grant. **Purpose:** To encourage projects by and about Canadian Inuit. **Applicant Eligibility:** Applicant must be a Canadian Inuit who wishes to undertake a project related to the promotion or preservation of his/her native culture. **Funds Available:** C$5,000 maximum. **Applicant Details:** Submit a letter of application to the Department, including an explanation of the project and a budget outline. **Application Deadline:** None.

★3260★
Petro-Canada Education Awards for Native Students
Petro-Canada Inc.
PO Box 2844
Calgary, AB, Canada T2P 3E3

Study Level: Undergraduate. **Award Type:** Award. **Applicant Eligibility:** Candidates must be of Canadian or Inuit ancestry and pursuing full-time studies in disciplines applicable to the oil and gas industry. **Selection Criteria:** Financial need, grades, applicability of course of studies. **Funds Available:** A number of awards valued up to $5,000 are available. **Applicant Details:** Letter, resume, transcript of grades, and proof of enrollment. **Application Deadline:** June 15 each year.

Awards, Honors, & Prizes

★3261★
Miss Indian World
Gathering of Nations
PO Box 75102, Sta. 14   Ph: (505)836-2810
Albuquerque, NM 87194   Fax: (505)839-0475
Description: To crown a young Indian (Native American) woman to reign as Miss Indian World. She must be an ambassador of goodwill and represent the Gathering of Nations and Native American people in the United States, Canada, and throughout the Americas (North, South, and Central). Candidates must be at least one-quarter Indian, and be 17 to 24 years of age. A traveling crown (beaded) to wear throughout the year, a banner, $1,200 cash and $1,800 travel expenses are awarded annually. Established in 1984 by Gathering of Nations Ltd.

Publishers

★3262★
Akwesasne Notes
Mohawk Nation
PO Box 196   Ph: (516)558-9531
Rooseveltown, NY 13683   Fax: (516)575-2935
Description: Publishes on the history, philosophy, religion, and ecology of the native people of the Americas. Presently inactive.

★3263★
Bill Hanson Consulting
310 Garrison Crescent   Ph: (306)374-0288
Saskatoon, SK, Canada S7H 2Z8 Fax: (306)955-3500
Description: Publishes a handbook on programming for aboriginal people. Reaches market through direct mail and telephone sales. **Subjects:** American Indians.

★3264★
Butterfly Books Ltd.
PO Box 294
Maple Creek, SK, Canada S0N 1N0
Description: Originated as publishing division of Walter P. Stewart Consultant Ltd. Publishes on photo-journalism, Canada, and North American Indians; offers the magazine *Photo-Essai*.

★3265★
Cherev Canada Inc.
RR 3, PO Box 698   Ph: (519)986-4353
Markdale, ON, Canada N0C 1H0   Free: 800-263-2408
                               Fax: (519)986-3103
Description: Publishes on New Age topics. Offers audio and video cassettes and music. Does not accept unsolicited manuscripts. Distributes for over 500 publishers, including the entire APC Trade West list of publishers. Reaches market through direct mail, telephone sales, and trade sales. **Subjects:** Metaphysical, self-help, New Age, Native Americans.

★3266★
Cherev Canada Inc.
PO Box 698   Ph: (519)986-4353
R.R. 3   Free: 800-263-2408
Markdale, ON, Canada N0C 1H0   Fax: (519)968-3103
Description: Distributes for 107 publishers in U.S., Canada and Europe. Sells to 550 independent stores and chains. Reincorporated in 1990 as Cherev Canada Inc. Operates for profit. Reaches market through direct mail and telephone sales. **Subjects:** New Age, metaphysical, self-help, Native Americans.

★3267★
Council for Yukon Indians
11 Nisutlin Dr.
Whitehorse, YT, Canada Y1A 3S4
Description: Negotiates with the Government of Canada and plans for the implementation, in the Yukon Territory, of a Land Claims Settlement that reflects the needs and aspirations of those Indian people with aboriginal rights in the Yukon Territory. Reaches market through public meetings. **Subjects:** The Yukon Indian people.

★3268★
Gabriel Dumont Institute of Native Studies and Applied Research
2nd Fl., 505 23rd St. East   Ph: (306)934-5073
Saskatoon, SK, Canada S7K 4K7 Fax: (306)244-0252
Description: Publishes on the native history and culture of Saskatchewan. Offers video and audio cassettes and the periodical, *Journal of Indigenous Studies*. Reaches market through direct mail.

★3269★
Good Medicine Books
PO Box 844
Skookumchuck, BC, Canada V0B 2E0
Description: Publishes on Native American culture, history, and natural lifestyles; also publishes on railroad and western history. Offers videotapes, audio cassettes, and cards and calendars on the Canadian railways. Does not accept unsolicited manuscripts. Reaches market through direct mail. **Subjects:** Native Indians.

★3270★
Indian Historian Press
1493 Masonic Ave.   Ph: (415)626-5235
San Francisco, CA 94117   Fax: (415)626-4923
Description: Principal interest is the American Indians of North America; also covers indigenous peoples of the western hemisphere. Does not accept unsolicited manuscripts.

★3271★
IROQRAFTS
RR 2, Ohsweken
Six Nations Reserve, ON, Canada N0A   Ph: (519)445-0414
   1M0   Fax: (519)445-0580
Description: Publishes titles of importance in the history and culture of the Iroquois peoples and of other North American Indians. Reaches market through direct mail. Does not accept unsolicited manuscripts. **Subjects:** Iroquois Indians.

★3272★
Metis Association of the Northwest Territories
PO Box 1375
Yellowknife, NT, Canada X1A 2P1   Ph: (403)873-3505
Description: Publishes on the history and culture of the northern Metis. Offers a newsletter.

★3273★
Millenia Press
1335-B Richardson St.   Ph: (604)385-9270
Victoria, BC, Canada V8S 1P6   Fax: (604)360-2463
Description: Publishes academic and trade books. Does not accept unsolicited manuscripts; send query and sample chapters. Reaches market through commission representatives, direct mail, trade sales, and wholesalers and distributors, including BookWorld Companies, Bookpeople Inc., New Leaf Distributing Co., and Marginal Distribution. **Subjects:** Anthropology, religion, Native American studies.

★3274★
Namaka Community Historical Committee
RR 1
Strathmore, AB, Canada T1P 1J6   Ph: (403)934-4515
Description: Publishes Indian community history to help outsiders understand the native people and their customs. Presently inactive. **Subjects:** Family history,

★3275★
Ojibway-Cree Cultural Centre
210 Spruce St.S., Ste. 304   Ph: (705)267-7911
Timmins, ON, Canada P4N 2M7   Fax: (705)267-4988
Description: Involved in developing native-oriented materials including videotapes for elementary classroom use. Concerned both with the historical as well as the contemporary aspect of Canada's native peoples. Offers cassette tapes, posters, a coloring book, and teacher's manuals. Reaches market through direct mail. **Subjects:** Nisnawbe-Aski nation history, seasons, hymns, teacher's manual, teacher's guide.

★3276★
Pemmican Publications Inc.
1635 Burrows Ave., No. 2   Ph: (204)589-6346
Winnipeg, MB, Canada R2X 0T1   Fax: (204)589-2063
Description: Specializes in work about, by, and for Metis and Aboriginal people, including history, social studies, fiction, short stories, etc. Accepts unsolicited manuscripts. Reaches market through commission representatives, direct mail, and trade sales. **Subjects:** Metis people, Aboriginies, history.

★3277★
Press Gang Publishers
101-225 E. 17th Ave.
Vancouver, BC, Canada V5V 1A6   Fax: (604)876-7892
Description: Publishes books by Canadian women which explore themes of personal and political struggles for equality. Also offers posters. Reaches market through commission representatives, direct mail, trade sales, and wholesalers. Accepts unsolicited manuscripts. **Subjects:** Feminism, women's studies, health, labor, criminology, lesbian studies, Native studies. **Number of New Titles:** 1998 - 5.

★3278★
Secwepemc Cultural Education Society
345 Yellowhead Hwy.
Kamloops, BC, Canada V2H 1H1   Ph: (604)374-0616
Description: Publishes books either written by or about Shuswap people. Offers social studies curriculum, oral histories, supplementary teaching resources, children stories, Shuswap language materials, and periodicals. Also offers slides, a newspaper, maps, games, teaching kits, calendars, posters, art prints, cassette tapes, and cards. Reaches market through direct mail, telephone sales, and trade sales. **Subjects:** Native Indians.

★3279★
Skelep Publishing
345 Yellowhead Hwy.
Kamloops, BC, Canada V2H 1H1   Ph: (604)374-0616
Description: Publishes materials to preserve and record Shuswap language, history, and culture. Offers cassette tapes, slides, and video cassettes. Accepts unsolicited manuscripts on the Shuswap culture. Reaches market through direct mail and trade sales.

★3280★
Theytus Books Ltd.
PO Box 20040   Ph: (604)493-7181
Penticton, BC, Canada V2A 8K3   Fax: (604)493-5302
Description: Publishes native Indian and curriculum development materials, especially locally developed material. Accepts unsolicited manuscripts; include a self-addressed, stamped envelope. Reaches market through commission representatives, direct mail, trade sales, Raincoast Book Distribution Ltd., and John Coutts Library Services.

★3281★
Thunder Bay Art Gallery
PO Box 1193   Ph: (807)577-6427
Thunder Bay, ON, Canada P7C 4X9   Fax: (807)577-3781
Description: A public art gallery specializing in contemporary Native art. Publications consist of catalogs produced for exhibitions. Offers *Imprint,* a quarterly newsletter. Reaches market through direct mail and trade sales. Operates a gift shop, art sales, and rental service. Does not accept unsolicited manuscripts. **Subjects:**

Canadian art history, First Nations Contemporary Visual. **Number of New Titles:** 1998 - 2.

★3282★
Thunderbird Publications
PO Box 193
Peterborough, ON, Canada K9J 6Z8
Description: Publishes a book on the spiritual and physical lives of Canadian Indian shamans. Does not accept unsolicited manuscripts. Reaches market through direct mail and telephone sales. **Subjects:** Canadian Indians, religion.

★3283★
University of New Brunswick
Micmac-Maliseet Institute
Fredericton, NB, Canada E3B 6E3   Ph: (506)453-4840
    Fax: (506)453-4784
Description: Publishes Indian studies and local history. Reaches market through direct mail. **Number of New Titles:** 1998 - 1.

★3284★
Watson and Dwyer Publishing Ltd.
P.O Box 86
905 Corydon   Ph: (204)284-0985
Winnipeg, MB, Canada R3M 3S3   Fax: (204)453-8320
Description: Publishes social history of the fur trade, social history of Northwest and Arctic regions, and history of northern aviation and tractor trains. Also covers aviation history, native art and social history of the Inuit and Indian. Accepts unsolicited manuscripts. Reaches market through commission representatives and direct mail.

★3285★
Winnipeg Art Gallery
300 Memorial Blvd.
Winnipeg, MB, Canada R3C 1V1   Fax: (204)788-4998
Description: Publishes informative books relating to its exhibitions. Also offers a magazine of Gallery-related information and events. **Subjects:** Contemporary art, art history, Inuit art, decorative art.

Directories

★3286★
Arrowfax National Aboriginal Directory
Arrowfax Inc.
102-90 Garry St.
Winnipeg, MB, Canada R3C 4H1   Free: 800-665-0037
    Fax: (204)943-6332
Description: 12,000 Canadian Aboriginal communities, professional services, and social and professional organizations. Entries include: Name, address, phone, fax. **Pages (approx.):** 400. **Frequency:** Irregular, previous edition November 1991; latest edition April 1996. **Price:** $44.

★3287★
Directory of Substance Abuse Organizations in Canada
Canadian Centre on Substance Abuse
75 Albert St., Ste. 300   Ph: (613)235-4048
Ottawa, ON, Canada K1P 5E7   Fax: (613)235-8101
Description: Over 2,000 organizations involved with treating substance abuse, including national non-governmental organizations, provincial/territorial agencies and regional offices, aboriginal organizations. Entries include: Name, address, phone, fax. **Price:** Please inquire.

★3288★
First Nations Tribal Directory
Arrowfax Inc. Ph: (204)943-6234
102-90 Garry St. Free: 800-665-0037
Winnipeg, MB, Canada R3C 4H1 Fax: (204)943-6332
Description: Approximately 15,000 Native American and Aboriginal Canadian listings, including tribes, Internet resources, gaming operations, and businesses. Entries include: Organization or company name, address, phone, description. **Frequency:** Latest edition 1996. **Price:** $44.

★3289★
First Nations Tribal Directory
Arrowfax Inc. Ph: (204)943-6234
102-90 Garry St. Free: 800-665-0037
Winnipeg, MB, Canada R3C 4H1 Fax: (204)943-6332
Description: Approximately 15,000 Native American and Aboriginal Canadian listings, including tribes, Internet resources, gaming operations, and businesses. Entries include: Organization or company name, address, phone, description. **Frequency:** Latest edition 1996. **Price:** $44.

★3290★
Indian America: A Traveler's Guide
John Muir Publications Ph: (505)982-4078
PO Box 613 Free: 800-888-7504
Santa Fe, NM 87504-0613 Fax: (505)988-1680
Description: over 300 Indian tribes in the U.S. Entries include: Tribe name, council address, phone; description of activities, including public ceremonies and powwows; tribe histories. **Pages (approx.):** 448. **Frequency:** Irregular, previous edition July 1991; latest edition July 1993. **Price:** $18.95.

★3291★
Indian Country Address Book
Todd Publications Ph: (914)358-6213
PO Box 635 Free: 800-747-1056
Nyack, NY 10960 Fax: (914)358-1059
Description: Native American contacts in the U.S. and Canada including artists, business es, crisis intervention centers, educational institutions, employment, foods, gaming, health care, Indian centers, legal services, nations, and radio and television stations. Entries include: Contact name, address, phone and description where needed. **Pages (approx.):** 515. **Price:** $45.

★3292★
National Directory of Minority-Owned Business Firms
Todd Publications Ph: (914)358-6213
PO Box 635 Free: 800-747-1056
Nyack, NY 10960 Fax: (914)358-1059
Description: Over 40,000 minority-owned businesses in the U.S. Entries include: Contact name, phone, number of employees, certification status, start-up date, and key word business descriptions. **Pages (approx.):** 1,500. **Frequency:** Biennial. **Price:** $195.

★3293★
Native American Directory: Alaska, Canada, United States
National Native American Cooperative
PO Box 27626
Tucson, AZ 85726 Fax: (520)292-0779
Description: More than 2,000 Native American performing arts groups, craft materials suppliers, stores and galleries, Indian-owned motels and resorts; tribal offices, museums, and cultural centers; associations and schools; newspapers, radio and television programs, and stations operated by, owned by, or specifically for Native Americans; calendar of events, including officially sanctioned powwows, conventions, arts and crafts shows, all-Indian rodeos, and Navajo rug auctions; how-to buy Indian crafts and research Indian ancestry. Entries include: Generally, organization or company name, address, descriptive comments, dates (for shows or events). **Pages (approx.):** 880. **Frequency:** Irregular, previous edition 1982; latest edition January 1996. **Price:** $65.95, postpaid; $131, library edition with wall map.

★3294★
Native North American Almanac
Gale Research Ph: (313)961-2242
835 Penobscot Bldg. Free: 800-877-
Detroit, MI 48226-4094 GALE
  Fax: (313)961-6083
Description: Includes essays on issues of interest to Native Americans and Canadian natives, including history, economy, education, religion, culture, arts, language, law and legislation, activism, the environment, health, and media; each chapter includes, as appropriate, directories of tribal communities, organizations, government agencies, schools, and businesses relevant to the topic. Entries include: Name, address, phone, contact. **Pages (approx.):** 1,275. **Frequency:** First edition November 1993; new edition expected 1999. **Price:** $75.

★3295★
Native North American Almanac
Gale Research Ph: (313)961-2242
835 Penobscot Bldg. Free: 800-877-
Detroit, MI 48226-4094 GALE
  Fax: (313)961-6083
Description: Includes essays on issues of interest to Native Americans and Canadian natives, including history, economy, education, religion, culture, arts, language, law and legislation, activism, the environment, health, and media; each chapter includes, as appropriate, directories of tribal communities, organizations, government agencies, schools, and businesses relevant to the topic. Entries include: Name, address, phone, contact. **Pages (approx.):** 1,275. **Frequency:** First edition November 1993; new edition expected 1999. **Price:** $75.

★3296★
North American Indian Landmarks—A Traveler's Guide
Gale Research Ph: (313)961-2242
835 Penobscot Bldg. Free: 800-877-
Detroit, MI 48226-4094 GALE
  Fax: (313)961-6083
Description: Approximately 340 sites in the U.S. and Canada significant to Native North American history, including historical, tribal, and art museums, monuments, plaques, parks, reservations, birthplaces, grave sites, battlefields. Entries include: Site name, description, location, days and hours of operation, admission fee, phone. Paperback edition published by Visible Ink Press, an imprint of Gale Research. **Pages (approx.):** 409. **Frequency:** Published 1993. **Price:** $34.95, cloth; $17.95, paper.

★3297★
Pow Wow on the Red Road
National Native American Co-op
PO Box 27626 Ph: (520)622-4900
Tucson, AZ 85726 Fax: (520)292-0779
Description: Over 1,200 Native American events in the U.S. and Canada for 1994-97; events listed are five years old or older. Located, cost, camping, sponsor, type of event. Given for each event (5 year directory). **Pages (approx.):** 84. **Frequency:** Irregular, latest edition 1994; new edition expected 1997. **Price:** $25.

★3298★
Powwow Calendar
Book Publishing Co. (Summertown) Ph: (615)964-3571
PO Box 99 Free: 800-695-2241
Summertown, TN 38483 Fax: (615)964-3518
Description: Native American powwows, dances, craft fairs in the U.S. and Canada during the current calendar year. Entries include: Event name, location, phone number, date, contact person. **Pages (approx.):** 112. **Frequency:** Annual. **Price:** $8.95.

Journals & Magazines

★3299★
Akwesasne Notes
Mohawk Nation
PO Box 196
Rooseveltown, NY 13683-0196   Ph: (518)358-9531
Description: Full color magazine concerning American Indian and indigenous persons worldwide. **First Published:** 1968. **Frequency:** Quarterly. **Subscriptions:** $25. **ISSN:** 0002-3949.

★3300★
Indian Life
Intertribal Christian Communications   Ph: (204)661-9333
PO Box 3765, RPO Redwood Centre   Free: 800-665-9275
Winnipeg, MB, Canada R2W 3R6   Fax: (204)661-3482
Description: A non-denominational Christian newspaper addressing the social, cultural, and spiritual needs of North American Indians. **First Published:** 1979. **Frequency:** Bimonthly. **Subscriptions:** $7. **ISSN:** 0226-9317.

Newsletters

★3301★
Mal-I-Mic-News
New Brunswick Aboriginal Peoples Council
PO Box 3370
Fredericton, NB, Canada E3B 5A2   Ph: (506)452-6671
Description: Provides off reserve aboriginal people with information on functions, workshops, and job opportunities at the Council. Also provides articles on land claims, education as well as human interest stories. Recurring features include reports of meetings, housing, local news, and current events. **Pages (approx.):** 16. **Frequency:** Bimonthly. **Price:** $12/year for nonmembers.

★3302★
The Phoenix
Canadian Alliance in Solidarity with the
  Native Peoples
PO Box 574, Sta. P   Ph: (416)972-1573
Toronto, ON, Canada M5S 2T1   Fax: (416)972-6232
Description: Covers native issues, history, and culture. Promotes cultural education. **Pages (approx.):** 25. **Frequency:** Quarterly.

★3303★
Sagitawa Friendship Centre Newsletter
Sagitawa Friendship Centre
10108-100 Ave.   Ph: (403)624-2443
Peace River, AB, Canada T8S 1R7   Fax: (403)624-2728
Description: Presents news of the Centre, which is a focal point of activities and information pertaining to Native Canadians. Recurring features include a calendar of events, reports of meetings, news of educational opportunities, job listings, poems, and stories. **Frequency:** Quarterly

★3304★
Shastri Newsletter
Shastri Indo-Canadian Institute
University of Calgary
2500 University Dr. NW   Ph: (403)220-7467
Calgary, AB, Canada T2N 1N4   Fax: (403)289-0100
Description: Discusses Canadian and Indian relations. Features such topics as developmental projects and educational programs. Recurring features include reports of meetings, news of educational opportunities, notices of publications available, and news of members. **Pages (approx.):** 8.

★3305★
The Spike
The Spike
PO Box 368   Ph: (908)656-0074
Milltown, NJ 08850   Fax: (201)823-6164
Description: Discusses contemporary Native American culture from a personal perspective. Announces Native American events scheduled from Canada to Florida east of the Mississippi River. Recurring features include letters to the editor, a calendar of events, news of educational opportunities, job listings, and notices of publications available. **Pages (approx.):** 8. **Frequency:** Monthly. **Price:** $36/year, U.S.; $38, Canada.

Newspapers

★3306★
Kainai News
Blood Tribe Comm. News
PO Box 410   Ph: (403)737-2121
Standoff, AB, Canada T0L 1Y0   Fax: (403)737-2336
Description: Newspaper for Indian communities. **First Published:** 1968. **Frequency:** Weekly.

★3307★
Nunatsiaq News
Nunatext Publishing Corp.
Box 8
Iqaluit, NT, Canada X0A 0H0   Free: 800-263-1452
Description: Community newspaper (English and Inuktitut). **First Published:** 1972. **Frequency:** Weekly (Fri.). **Subscriptions:** $50, Canada; $80 U.S. **ISSN:** 0702-7915.

★3308★
Wawatay News
Wawatay Native Communications Society   Ph: (807)737-2951
16 5th Ave.   Free: 800-243-9059
Sioux Lookout, ON, Canada P8T 1B7   Fax: (807)737-3224
Description: Newspaper (tabloid) for 92 Indian reserves in northern Ontario (English and Oji-Cree). **First Published:** 1974. **Frequency:** Biweekly.

Radio Stations

★3309★
CFWE-FM
PO Box 2250   Ph: (403)623-3333
Lac la Biche, AB, Canada T0A 2C0   Fax: (403)623-3302
Frequency: 89.9. **Format:** Country, Ethnic. **Owner:** Aboriginal Multi-Media Society of Alberta, Native Perspective Div.

★3310★
CHON-FM
4228 A 4th Ave.
Whitehorse, YT, Canada Y1A 1K1   Ph: (403)668-6629
Frequency: 98.1 **Network Affiliation:** Independent. **Format:** Country, Album-Oriented Rock (AOR), Adult Contemporary. **Owner:** Northern Native Broadcasting, Yukon.

★3311★
CKQN-FM
General Delivery
Baker Lake, NT, Canada X0C 0A0   Ph: (819)793-2962
Frequency: 99.3 **Network Affiliation:** Canadian Broadcasting Corporation (CBC)/Societe Radio-Canada (SRC). **Format:** Ethnic. **Owner:** Qamani'tuap Naalautaa Society.

★3312★
WRN-FM
16-5th Ave.
PO Box 1180
Sioux Lookout, ON, Canada P0V 2T0   Ph: (807)737-2951
                                        Fax: (807)737-3224
Frequency: 89.1 **Network Affiliation:** Broadcast News. **Format:** News. **Owner:** Wawatay Native Communications Society.

Videos

★3313★
....And The Word Was God
Video Out
1102 Homer St.
Vancouver, BC, Canada V6B 2X6   Ph: (604)688-4336
Description: A poetic narrative video focusing on the Cree-speaking natives of northern Saskatchewan. **Release Date:** 1987. **Length:** 28 mins. **Format:** Beta, VHS, 3/4″ U-matic Cassette.

★3314★
Augusta
Phoenix/BFA Films
468 Park Ave., S.
New York, NY 10016   Ph: (212)684-5910
                        Free: 800-221-1274
Description: A portrait of an 88-year-old woman, born a daughter of a Shuswap chief in Canada. She lives today in Cariboo country of British Columbia without running water or electricity. Augusta lost her status as an Indian in 1903, when she married a white man. **Release Date:** 1978. **Length:** 17 mins. **Format:** Beta, VHS, 3/4″ U-matic Cassette.

★3315★
The Ballad of Crowfoot
CRM/McGraw-Hill Films
674 Via de la Valle
PO Box 641
Del Mar, CA 92014
Description: This program is a graphic history of the Canadian West, filmed by Indians who wanted to reflect the traditions, attitudes, and problems of their own people. **Release Date:** 1972. **Length:** 10 mins. **Format:** Beta, VHS, 3/4″ U-matic Cassette.

★3316★
Beavertail Snowshoes
Trust for Native American Cultures &
  Crafts
PO Box 142
Greenville, NH 03348   Ph: (603)878-2944
Description: A look at the construction of beavertail snowshoes by the Eastern Cree Indians of Mistassini Lake, Quebec. **Release Date:** 1990. **Length:** 40 mins. **Format:** Beta, VHS, 3/4″ U-matic Cassette.

★3317★
Building an Algonquin Birchbark Canoe
Trust for Native American Cultures &
  Crafts
PO Box 142
Greenville, NH 03348   Ph: (603)878-2944
Description: The endangered art of canoe building is demonstrated by a pair of elderly Algonquin Indians in Maniwaki, Quebec. **Release Date:** 1990. **Length:** 54 mins. **Format:** Beta, VHS, 3/4″ U-matic Cassette.

★3318★
Canada's Original Peoples: Then and Now
Native American Public Broadcasting
  Consortium
PO Box 86111
1800 N. 33rd St.
Lincoln, NE 68501   Ph: (402)472-3522
Description: A tour of the Indian artifacts in the Royal Ontario Museum and the history they indicate. **Release Date:** 1977. **Length:** 20 mins. **Format:** VHS, 3/4″ U-matic Cassette, 1″ Broadcast Type ″C″, 2″ Quadraplex Open Reel.

★3319★
Circle of the Sun
National Film Board of Canada
1251 Avenue of the Americas, 16th Fl.
New York, NY 10020-1173   Ph: (212)586-5131
Description: The Spectacle of the Sun Dance is demonstrated by the Blood Indians of Alberta, as the young generation breaks ties with their people to fit into the changing society. **Release Date:** 1960. **Length:** 29 mins. **Format:** Beta, VHS, 3/4″ U-matic Cassette.

★3320★
Completing Our Circle
CRM/McGraw-Hill Films
674 Via de la Valle
PO Box 641
Del Mar, CA 92014
Description: The traditions of the Plains and West Coast Indians, the Inuit, and the first Europeans and settlers in Western Canada are shown in this program. Their art and craftsmanship are presented as a way to express both individual identity and oneness with other men. **Release Date:** 1978. **Length:** 27 mins. **Format:** Beta, VHS, 3/4″ U-matic Cassette.

★3321★
Concerned Aboriginal Women
Video Out
1102 Homer St.
Vancouver, BC, Canada V6B 2X6   Ph: (604)688-4336
Description: A moving documentary about the occupation by native women of the federal Indian and Northern Affairs office in Vancouver, British Columbia. **Release Date:** 1981. **Length:** 60 mins. **Format:** Beta, VHS, 3/4″ U-matic Cassette.

★3322★
Cree Hunters of Mistassini
National Film Board of Canada
1251 Avenue of the Americas, 16th Fl.
New York, NY 10020-1173   Ph: (212)586-5131
Description: The Cree Indians of northern Quebec live with the land in a way that reflects not only a set of ecological principles and religious beliefs, but an entire way of life that they are afraid of losing. **Release Date:** 1974. **Length:** 58 mins. **Format:** Beta, VHS, 3/4″ U-matic Cassette.

★3323★
Daughters of the Country
National Film Board of Canada
1251 Avenue of the Americas, 16th Fl.
New York, NY 10020-1173   Ph: (212)586-5131
Description: This series examines the prejudices Canadians have had against native North Americans in four different periods in time, focusing on four women. **Release Date:** 1986. **Length:** 57 mins. **Format:** Beta, VHS, 3/4″ U-matic Cassette.

★3324★
Doctor, Lawyer, Indian Chief
National Film Board of Canada
1251 Avenue of the Americas, 16th Fl.
New York, NY 10020-1173   Ph: (212)586-5131
Description: This film documents the achievements of five Native American Canadian women who have overcome problems and prejudices to attain a variety of positions, including one who is an

Indian Chief. **Release Date:** 1986. **Length:** 29 mins. **Format:** Beta, VHS, 3/4″ U-matic Cassette.

★3325★
How to Build An Igloo
National Film Board of Canada
1251 Avenue of the Americas, 16th Fl.
New York, NY 10020-1173   Ph: (212)586-5131
Description: A demonstration of igloo building in Canada's far north. **Release Date:** 1987. **Length:** 18 mins. **Format:** Beta, VHS, 3/4″ U-matic Cassette.

★3326★
Indian Hide Tanning
Trust for Native American Cultures &
   Crafts
PO Box 142
Greenville, NH 03348   Ph: (603)878-2944
Description: Eastern Cree Indians of Mistassini, Quebec demonstrate the methods used in the tanning of moose and caribou hides. The hides are then used to make moccasins, mittens, and snowshoes. **Release Date:** 1990. **Length:** 38 mins. **Format:** Beta, VHS, 3/4″ U-matic Cassette.

★3327★
John Cat
National Film Board of Canada
1251 Avenue of the Americas, 16th Fl.
New York, NY 10020-1173   Ph: (212)586-5131
Description: Based on a story by W.P. Kinsella, this drama concerns the violence and prejudice that two young Canadian Indians encounter. **Release Date:** 1987. **Length:** 24 mins. **Format:** Beta, VHS, 3/4″ U-matic Cassette.

★3328★
Joshua's Soapstone Carving
Coronet/MTI Film & Video   Ph: (708)940-1260
108 Wilmot Rd.   Free: 800-621-2131
Deerfield, IL 60015   Fax: (708)940-3640
Description: Inuit culture is explored as this film shows the carving craft of young Joshua Qumaluk. **Release Date:** 1982. **Length:** 25 mins. **Format:** Beta, VHS, 3/4″ U-matic Cassette, Other than listed.

★3329★
Kamik
National Film Board of Canada   Ph: (212)596-1770
1251 Avenue of the Americas, 16th Fl.   Free: 800-542-2164
New York, NY 10020-1173   Fax: (212)596-1779
Description: Studies the dying art of Kamik, the making of seal skin boots. Documents the art and struggles of an Inuit woman as her community undergoes a cultural transformation. **Length:** 15 **Format:** VHS

★3330★
Keep the Circle Strong
Cinema Guild
1697 Broadway   Ph: (212)246-5522
New York, NY 10019   Fax: (212)246-5525
Description: Mike Auger is a Canadian Cree Indian who traveled to Bolivia to work with the Amayra Indians. In the process, he rediscovered his own cultural roots, and came to terms with some of the anger and confusion he experienced as a young man. **Release Date:** 1990. **Length:** 28 mins. **Format:** VHS.

★3331★
The Last Days of Okak
National Film Board of Canada
1251 Avenue of the Americas, 16th Fl.
New York, NY 10020-1173   Ph: (212)586-51 31
Description: A documentary about the plague of Spanish influenza that wiped out an Inuit settlement on the Northern Labrador coast. **Release Date:** 1987. **Length:** 24 mins. **Format:** Beta, VHS, 3/4″ U-matic Cassette.

★3332★
Legends and Life of the Inuit
National Film Board of Canada
1251 Avenue of the Americas, 16th Fl.
New York, NY 10020-1173   Ph: (212)586-5131
Description: Five folktales from this Native American community are presented. **Release Date:** 1987. **Length:** 58 mins. **Format:** Beta, VHS, 3/4″ U-matic Cassette.

★3333★
Magic in the Sky
National Film Board of Canada
1251 Avenue of the Americas, 16th Fl.
New York, NY 10020-1173   Ph: (212)586-5131
Description: This program looks at the impact of television on Arctic Eskimos. **Release Date:** 1983. **Length:** 57 mins. **Format:** Beta, VHS, 3/4″ U-matic Cassette.

★3334★
Mariculture: The Promise of the Sea
Video Out
1102 Homer St.
Vancouver, BC, Canada V6B 2X6   Ph: (604)688-4336
Description: This program looks at an Indian community involved in a mariculture project. **Release Date:** 1981. **Length:** 21 mins. **Format:** Beta, VHS, 3/4″ U-matic Cassette.

★3335★
National Native Artists' Symposium
Video Out
1102 Homer St.
Vancouver, BC, Canada V6B 2X6   Ph: (604)688-4336
Description: The gathering of Indian artists from across Canada at this symposium is documented. **Release Date:** 1983. **Length:** 59 mins. **Format:** Beta, VHS, 3/4″ U-matic Cassette.

★3336★
North of 60 Degrees: Destiny Uncertain
Native American Public Broadcasting
   Consortium
PO Box 86111
1800 N. 33rd St.
Lincoln, NE 68501   Ph: (402)472-3522
Description: A series that examines the Canadian wilderness both as it is now and as it was known to Indians in the past. **Release Date:** 1983. **Length:** 29 mins. **Format:** VHS, 3/4″ U-matic Cassette, 1″ Broadcast Type ″C″, 2″ Quadraplex Open Reel.

★3337★
Potlatch People
Cinema Guild
1697 Broadway   Ph: (212)246-5522
New York, NY 10019   Fax: (212)246-5525
Description: The attempts to preserve the culture of the Pacific Northwest Indian are vividly presented in scenes of excavations underway in British Columbia and at museums where many of the prized artifacts are now on display. **Release Date:** 1976. **Length:** 26 mins. **Format:** 3/4″ U-matic Cassette, Other than listed.

★3338★
Rendezvous Canada, 1606
National Film Board of Canada
1251 Avenue of the Americas, 16th Fl.
New York, NY 10020-1173   Ph: (212)586-5131
Description: This film examines the clash of cultures between the natives and the European settlers in Canada around 1606, and the influences that each culture had on the other. **Release Date:** 1988. **Length:** 29 mins. **Format:** Beta, VHS, 3/4″ U-matic Cassette.

★3339★
Richard Cardinal: Cry From a Diary of a Metis Child
National Film Board of Canada Ph: (212)596-1770
1251 Avenue of the Americas, 16th Fl. Free: 800-542-2164
New York, NY 10020-1173 Fax: (212)596-1779
Description: Documentary look at a young Native American boy who was victimized and committed suicide. **Length:** 29 **Format:** VHS

★3340★
Richard's Totem Pole (Canada)
Coronet/MTI Film & Video Ph: (708)940-1260
108 Wilmot Rd. Free: 800-621-2131
Deerfield, IL 60015 Fax: (708)940-3640
Description: A 16-year-old Gitskan Indian living in British Columbia helps his father carve a 30-foot totem pole. He learns about his heritage and culture while working on it. Part of the "World Cultures and Youth" series. **Release Date:** 1981. **Length:** 25 mins. **Format:** Beta, VHS, 3/4″ U-matic Cassette, Other than listed.

★3341★
School in the Bush
National Film Board of Canada Ph: (212)596-1770
1251 Avenue of the Americas, 16th Fl. Free: 800-542-2164
New York, NY 10020-1173 Fax: (212)596-1779
Description: Documentary study of Cree Indians and how they educate their children in the traditional ways of their culture. **Length:** 15 **Format:** VHS

★3342★
The Spirit Within
National Film Board of Canada Ph: (212)596-1770
1251 Avenue of the Americas, 16th Fl. Free: 800-542-2164
New York, NY 10020-1173 Fax: (212)596-1779
Description: Visits prisons where Native American inmates practice spiritual ceremonies and customs. **Length:** 51 **Format:** VHS

★3343★
Standing Alone
National Film Board of Canada
1251 Avenue of the Americas, 16th Fl.
New York, NY 10020-1173 Ph: (212)586-5131
Description: The story of Pete Standing Alone, a Blood Indian who, as a young man was more at home in the white man's culture than in his own. After becoming a father, he re-enters Indian society. **Release Date:** 1987. **Length:** 58 mins. **Format:** Beta, VHS, 3/4″ U-matic Cassette.

★3344★
Tales of Wesakachak
Native American Public Broadcasting
Consortium
PO Box 86111
1800 N. 33rd St.
Lincoln, NE 68501 Ph: (402)472-3522
Description: This series for children relates orally conveyed Canadian Creek folktales. **Release Date:** 1984. **Length:** 15 mins. **Format:** VHS, 3/4″ U-matic Cassette, 1″ Broadcast Type "C", 2″ Quadraplex Open Reel.

★3345★
Telling Our Story
University of Calgary Dept. of
Communications Media
2500 University Dr. NW Ph: (403)220-3709
Calgary, AB, Canada T2N 1N4 Fax: (403)282-4497
Description: Northern Alberta Indians discover and share their cultural heritage through innovative drama presentations. **Release Date:** 1983. **Length:** 20 mins. **Format:** Beta, VHS, 3/4″ U-matic Cassette, 1″ Broadcast Type "C".

★3346★
White Justice
Cinema Guild
1697 Broadway Ph: (212)246-5522
New York, NY 10019 Fax: (212)246-5525
Description: The Canadian Criminal Justice system and its effect on the Inuits of northern Quebec is examined, particularly the clash of white and native cultures. **Release Date:** 1987. **Length:** 57 mins. **Format:** Beta, VHS, 3/4″ U-matic Cassette.

★3347★
Women Within Two Cultures
Women in Focus
849 Beatty St.
Vancouver, BC, Canada V6B 2M6 Ph: (604)872-2250
Description: The influences of white settlers on the British Columbia West Coast Indian women is depicted in this program. **Release Date:** 1976. **Length:** 30 mins. **Format:** 3/4″ U-matic Cassette, Other than listed.

★3348★
You Are on Indian Land
National Film Board of Canada
1251 Avenue of the Americas, 16th Fl.
New York, NY 10020-1173 Ph: (212)586-5131
Description: This film documents the 1969 demonstration by Mohawk Indians of the St. Regis Reserve on the international bridge between Canada and the United States near Cornwall, Ontario. **Release Date:** 1987. **Length:** 37 mins. **Format:** Beta, VHS, 3/4″ U-matic Cassette.

Internet and Online Databases

★3349★
Circumpolar and Aboriginal North America Resources
Nunavut Implementation Commission

URL: http://www.nunanet.com/nic/WWWVL-ANA.html **Description:** Provides links to information resources on the peoples and environment of the Arctic Circle, as well as other aboriginal groups throughout the world.

★3350★
The First Perspective Online
MBnet Networking Inc.
University of Manitoba
603 Engineering Bldg.
Winnipeg, MB, Canada R3T 2N2 Ph: (204)474-7325
URL: http://www.mbnet.mb.ca/firstper/ **Description:** The First Perspective is Canada's source on indigenous peoples. The paper is divided into news, native law, opinions, and events, and is sorted by topics like aboriginal political news, international news, sports, pow wow schedules, women, health & healing, education and training, etc. It also includes cartoons. Main Files: News; Events; Opinion; Ottawa Watch; Law Cases; Directory; Cartoon; Feedback; Subscriptions; About FP Online. **Update frequency:** Monthly. **Fees:** Free.

★3351★
Identity
Interport Communications
1133 Broadway
New York, NY 10010 Ph: (212)989-1128
URL: http://plaza.interport.net/logomanc/heye.html **Description:** this site provides a variety of quotes and observations about Native Americans and Native American culture. There are also a wide variety of links to related sites. The site is colorful with a many small images, and it is fast loading. Main Files: National Museum of the American Indian; Torsion in the blood; Authentic Ethnic Crafts; All-American; Links to Resources and Art Sources; Native American Stereotype Awareness Project; Aboriginal Super Information Hwy.;

American Indian Computer Art Project; Canadian Native Art, a collection of Canadian Native Art; Contemporary Southwest Art; Electronic gallery of the work of Cree artist Wabimeguil; The Heard Museum; Library of Congress Gopher List; MIT AISES Home Page; Native American Resources; Native Net HomePage; Pueblo Cultural Center; Shako; The Sioux Nation. This site provides much information on attitudes toward Native Americans and links to many related resources. **Update frequency:** As needed. **Fees:** Free.

General Resources

★3352★

Ad Hoc Committee on the Human Rights and Genocide Treaties
c/o Jewish Labor Comm.
25 E. 21st St.
New York, NY 10010   Ph: (212)477-0707

Description: Affiliated national organizations, including labor, religious, civic, nationality, and fraternal groups. Promotes understanding of and public support for U.S. ratification of United Nations treaties on racial discrimination, forced labor, and genocide. Prepares and distributes educational materials on the UN human rights conventions. **Founded:** 1964.

★3353★

Affirmative Action Coordinating Center
126 W. 119th St.
New York, NY 10026   Ph: (212)864-4000

Description: Network of organizations that believe affirmative action programs are legal and essential if the effects of hundreds of years of repression to minorities and women are to be overcome. Collects, indexes, and analyzes information on the status of pending litigation, and legislative and administrative rulings affecting affirmative action programs. Acts as clearinghouse and resource center in developing legal intervention strategies and sharing skills and reference materials among attorneys working to defend and expand affirmative action programs. **Founded:** 1978. **Members:** 150. **Publications:** News, quarterly.

★3354★

Alliance of Minority Women for Business and Political Development
PO Box 13858
Silver Spring, MD 20911-0858   Ph: (301)585-8051

Description: Organizations in support of minority women in business and politics. Seeks to increase number of minority women business owners as elected officials, especially on the state level. Political action committee supports candidates through fundraising, endorsements, and training. **Founded:** 1988. **Members:** 210. **Publications:** Power in Color and Gender, quarterly.

★3355★

American Civil Liberties Union
132 W. 43rd St.
New York, NY 10036   Ph: (212)944-9800

Description: Champions the rights set forth in the Bill of Rights of the U.S. Constitution: freedom of speech, press, assembly, and religion; due process of law and fair trial; equality before the law regardless of race, color, sexual orientation, national origin, political opinion, or religious belief. Activities include litigation, advocacy, and public education. Sponsors litigation projects on topics such as women's rights, gay and lesbian rights, and children's rights. **Founded:** 1920. **Members:** 275,000. **State Groups:** 50. **Local Groups:** 200.

★3356★

American Civil Liberties Union Foundation
125 Broad St., 18th Fl.
New York, NY 10004   Ph: (212)549-2500

Description: Established as the tax-exempt arm of the American Civil Liberties Union. Purposes are legal defense, research, and public education on behalf of civil liberties including freedom of speech, press, and other First Amendment rights. Sponsors projects on topics such as children's rights, capital punishment, censorship, women's rights, immigration, prisoners' rights, national security, voting rights, and equal employment opportunity. Conducts research and public education projects to enable citizens to know and assert their rights. Seeks funds to protect liberty guaranteed by the Bill of Rights and the Constitution. **Founded:** 1966. **Regional Groups:** 2. **Publications:** Civil Liberties; Newsletter, quarterly; First Principles, monthly; Annual Report. **Formerly:** (1969) Roger Baldwin Foundation of ACLU.

★3357★

American Council for the Advancement of Human Rights
1875 Connecticut Ave. NW, Ste. 1140
Washington, DC 20009

Description: To advance human rights on an international basis. Works for the codification of human rights norms on an international basis. Monitors compliance with the Helsinki Accords especially in Poland and Czechoslovakia. (The Helsinki Accords is a treaty pledging support of human rights and was signed by 35 countries, including the U.S. and USSR, in 1975.) Worked on the passage of the Genocide Convention, a treaty forbidding the mass extermination of human beings. (Though signed by the U.S. and introduced in the Senate immediately following World War II, the Genocide Convention was not ratified by the Senate until 1986.) Plans to focus concern on other international human rights treaties, including the American Convention on Human Rights, the International Covenant on Economic, Social an d Cultural Rights, the Treaty on the Abolition of All Forms of Sex Discrimination, the Treaty on the Elimination of All Forms of Racial Discrimination, and the International Covenant on Political and Civil Rights. **Founded:** 1978.

★3358★
American Indian Law Center
PO Box 4456, Sta. A
Albuquerque, NM 87196   Ph: (505)277-5462

Description: Located at the University of New Mexico School of Law, funded primarily by government and foundation contracts and grants, and from contracts with Indian tribes and Indian organizations. Purpose is to render services, primarily research and training, of a broad legal and governmental nature. The demands of society on Indian tribal governments as well as their own entry into many areas of property rights and civil rights open many new frontiers in Indian law. The center and its staff of Indian law school graduates and attorneys constitute a major resource in assisting the tribes, as well as private and public agencies, in research of basic Indian law. Assists tribes in making legal decisions when assistance is necessary. Serves on a cooperative basis with other related programs in Indian affairs. Helped found and currently provides staff support to the Commission on State-Tribal Relations, a group of elected tribal, state, and municipal officials interested in cooperative intergovernmental relations on Indian reservations. Provides individualized training programs for tribal judges and tribal prosecutors in addition to others tailored to the needs of tribal communities. Offers Pre-Law Summer Institute for American Indians who have been accepted into or who indicate an interest in attending a law school. Provides assistance to Alaskan natives. Sponsors seminars; maintains library and audiovisual materials. **Founded:** 1967. **Publications:** American Indian Law Newsletter; Newsletter.

★3359★
American Indian Library Association
University of Pittsburgh
207 Hillman Library
Pittsburgh, PA 15260   Ph: (512)471-3959

Description: Individuals and institutions interested in promoting the development, maintenance, and improvement of libraries, library systems, and cultural and information services on reservations and in communities of Native Americans and Native Alaskans. Develops and encourages adoption of standards for Indian libraries; provides technical assistance to Indian tribes on establishing and maintaining archives systems. Works to enhance the capability of libraries to assist Indians who are writing tribal histories and to perpetuate knowledge of Indian language, history, legal rights, and culture. Seeks support for the establishment of networks for exchange of information among Indian tribes. Communicates the needs of Indian libraries to legislators and the library community. Coordinates development of courses, workshops, institutes, and internships on Indian library services. **Founded:** 1979. **Publications:** American Indian Libraries Newsletter; Newsletter, quarterly.

★3360★
American Native Press Research Association
University of Arkansas at Little Rock
Department of English
2801 S. University Ave.
Little Rock, AR 72204   Ph: (501)569-3160

Description: Membership includes contributors to the American Indian and Alaska Native Periodicals Project, nonprofit educational and cultural insti tutions, and individuals interested in the study of the American native press. Purpo ses are to: promote and foster academic research concerning the American native pres s, those involved in it, and American native periodical literature as a whole; disseminate research results; refine methodologies for discussing the American native press. **Founded:** 1984. **Members:** 70

★3361★
Americans for Indian Opportunity
681 Juniper Hill Rd.
Bernalillo, NM 87004   Ph: (505)867-0278

Description: Promotes cultural, political, and economic self-sufficiency for American Indian tribes and individuals, and political self-government for members of American Indian tribes. Seeks to: help American Indians, Eskimos, and Aleuts establish self-help programs at the local level; improve communications among Native Americans and with non-Indians; educate the public on the achievements and current needs of Native Americans. Supports projects in education, health, housing, the environment, and

leadership. Assists in establishing local centers with similar goals. Monitors federal agencies to ensure the fair and proper administration of Indian pro grams and to obtain federal programs and grants of benefit to Indians on a local or national scale. Conducts research; compiles statistics. **Founded:** 1970. **Publications:** Core Cultural Values; Messing with Mother Nature Can Be Hazardous to Your Health; You Don't Have to Be Poor to Be Indian.

★3362★
Amnesty International USA
322 8th Ave.   Ph: (212)807-8400
New York, NY 10001   Free: 800-AMN-ESTY

Description: Works impartially for the release of men, women, and children detained anywhere for their conscientiously held beliefs, color, ethnic origin, sex, religion, or language, provided they have neither used nor advocated violence. Opposes torture, "disappearances," and executions without reservation and advocates fair and prompt trials for all political prisoners. Has consultative status with the United Nations and the Council of Europe, has cooperative relations with the Inter-American Commission on Human Rights, and has observer status with the Organization of African Unity. Was the recipient of the 1977 Nobel Prize for Peace. Volunteers participate in networks: Educators; Freedom Writers; Health Professionals; Legal Professionals; Religion; Urgent Action; Women. **Founded:** 1961. **Members:** 290,000. **Regional Groups:** 1800. **Local Groups:** 400. **Publications:** Amnesty Action; Newsletter, 3/year; Amnesty International Report, annual.

★3363★
Anti-Repression Resource Team
PO Box 8040
State College, PA 16803-8040   Ph: (814)237-3095

Description: Combats all forms of political repression including: police violence and misconduct; Ku Klux Klan and Nazi terrorism; spying and covert action by secret police and intelligence agencies. Focuses on research, writing, lecturing, organizing, and publishing. Conducts training workshops for church, labor, and community organizations. Maintains library of materials on spying, repression, covert action, terrorism, and civil liberties. Maintains speakers' bureau. **Founded:** 1979.

★3364★
Archaeological Conservancy
5301 Central Ave. NE, Ste. 1218
Albuquerque, NM 87108   Ph: (505)266-1540

Description: People interested in preserving prehistoric and historic sites for interpretive or research purposes (most members are not professional archaeologists). Seeks to acquire for permanent preservation, through donation or purchase, the ruins of past American cultures, primarily those of American Indians. Works throughout the U.S. to preserve cultural resources presently on private lands and protect them from the destruction of looters, modern agricultural practices, and urban sprawl. Operates with government agencies, universities, and museums to permanently preserve acquired sites. **Founded:** 1979. **Members:** 13,000. **Publications:** American Archaeology Magazine, quarterly.

★3365★
Association of American Indian Physicians
1235 Sovereign Row, Ste. C-7
Oklahoma City, OK 73108   Ph: (405)946-7072

Description: Physicians (M.D. or D.O.) of American Indian descent. Encourages American Indians to enter the health professions. Provides a forum for the interchange of ideas and information of mutual interest to physicians of Indian descent. Establishes contracts with government agencies to provide consultation and other expert opinion regarding health care of American Indians and Alaskan Natives; receives contracts and grant monies and other forms of assistance from these sources. Supports and encourages all other agencies and organizations, Indian and non-Indian, working to improve health conditions of American Indians and Alaskan Natives. Locates scholarship funds for Indian professional students; provides counseling assistance; preserves American Indian culture. Conducts seminars for students interested in health careers and for counselors in government and other schools where

American Indian children are taught. **Founded:** 1971. **Members:** 220. **Publications:** Newsletter, quarterly.

★3366★
Association of Community Tribal Schools
616 4th Ave. W.
Sisseton, SD 57262-1349   Ph: (605)698-3112
Description: American Indian-controlled schools organized under the Indian Self-Determination and Educational Assistance Act and Tribally Controlled Schools Act; American Indian schools seeking status under these acts; interested individuals and organizations. Advocates Indian self-determination and Indian-controlled school. Provides technical assistance in making self-determination contracts; offers school board training assistance. **Founded:** 1982. **Members:** 30. **Regional Groups:** 2. **Formerly:** (1987) Association of Contract Tribal Schools.

★3367★
A Better Chance
419 Boylston St.
Boston, MA 02116   Ph: (617)421-0950
Description: Identifies, recruits, and places academically talented and motivated minority students into leading independent secondary schools and selected public schools. Students receive need-based financial assistance from member schools. Prepares students to attend selective colleges and universities and encourages their aspirations to assume positions of responsibility and leadership in American society. Conducts research and provides technical assistance on expanded educational opportunities for minority group students in secondary and higher education. **Founded:** 1963. **Publications:** Letters to Member Schools, annual; Annual Report; Brochure.

★3368★
Bureau of Catholic Indian Missions
2021 H St. NW
Washington, DC 20006   Ph: (202)331-8542
Description: Purpose is to conduct religious, charitable, and educational activities at American Indian and Eskimo missions. Maintains speakers' bureau; conducts research programs. **Founded:** 1874. **Publications:** Bureau of Catholic Indian Missions–Newsletter; Newsletter, 10/year.

★3369★
Campaign for Amnesty and Human Rights for Political Prisoners
2048 W. Division St.
Chicago, IL 60622   Ph: (312)278-6706
Description: Community, religious, and political activists. Works to improve the conditions of political prisoners in U.S. prisons; abolish U.S. prison control units. (Control units are sections of a prison where prisoners deemed to present security risks are segregated from the general prison population.) Conducts letter-writing campaigns, sponsors delegations to meet prison officials, holds press conferences, and prepares and disseminates documentation of human rights violations to other human rights organizations. Operates speakers' bureau. **Founded:** 1989. **Members:** 30. **Regional Groups:** 3. **Publications:** Can't Jail the Spirit; Newsletter, periodic. **Formerly:** (1992) Campaign for Amnesty and Human Rights for Political Prisoners.

★3370★
Campaign for Political Rights
201 Massachusetts Ave. NE, Rm. 316
Washington, DC 20002   Ph: (202)547-4705
Description: Serves as national network of committed people and religious, civil liberties, environmental, academic, foreign policy, disarmament, press, women's, Native American, black, and Latino organizations. Objectives are to end intelligence agency abuse at home and abroad; and to promote government accountability and access to information about government policies and actions. Provides educational materials and films, organizing assistance, press and publicity advice, and referral services for organizations. **Founded:** 1977. **Publications:** ALERT, monthly; Organizing Notes. **Formerly:** Campaign to Stop Government Spying.

★3371★
Catholic Interracial Council of New York
899 10th Ave.
New York, NY 10019   Ph: (212)237-8255
Description: Promotes interracial justice. Works in cooperation with local parishes and governmental and voluntary groups to combat bigotry and discrimination and to promote social justice for all racial, religious, and ethnic groups. Sponsors research, educational forums, and community action programs. Maintains speakers' bureau. **Founded:** 1934. **Members:** 1600. **Publications:** Interracial Review, quarterly; News, quarterly.

★3372★
Center for the Advancement of the Covenant
Philosophy Department
1600 Holloway Ave.
San Francisco, CA 94132   Ph: (415)338-1596
Description: Publicizes the United States ratification of the 1992 International Covenant on Civil and Political Rights and the rights it contains. Organizes an effective network of nongovernmental organizations to work toward federal, state, and local government compliance with the Covenant. Works with the San Francisco University's Global Peace Studies program. Helps to develop internships; sponsors programs and educational projects. **Founded:** 1992.

★3373★
Center for Alternative Mining Development Policy
210 Avon St., Ste. 4
La Crosse, WI 54603   Ph: (608)784-4399
Description: Native Americans, farmers, and those living in urban areas concerned about threats to the environment of the Lake Superior region. Seeks to provide information and technical assistance to Indian tribes and rural communities affected by plans for mining development. Focuses on issues such as mining taxation, groundwater qualtiy, hazards of uranium exploration, and the environmental impact of metallic sulfide mi ning. Operates speakers' bureau. Consults with similar international and national groups. **Founded:** 1977. **Members:** 600. **Publications:** Anishinaabe Niijii (Friends of the Chippewa) Video; Keepers of the Water; Video; LAND GRAB: The Corporate Theft of Wisconsin's Mineral Resources; The Mineral Province of Wisconsin; Minerals and the Future of the Lake Superior Region; The New Resource Wars: Native and Environmental Struggles Against Multinational Corporations.

★3374★
Center of Concern
3700 13th St. NE
Washington, DC 20017   Ph: (202)635-2757
Description: People working with grass roots and international networks to show the connections between global and local justice. Promotes social analysis, theological reflection, policy advocacy, research, and public education on global and local issues such as poverty, underemployment, unemployment, hunger, women's rights, economic justice, and social development. **Founded:** 1971. **Publications:** Catholic Social Teaching: Our Best Kept Secret Book; Center Focus Newsletter, bimonthly; Hope and Crisis in Africa Book; Opting for the Poor: The Task for North Americans; Book; Social Analysis: Linking Faith and Justice Book; Trouble and Beauty: Women Encounter Catholic Social Teaching Book.

★3375★
Center for National Policy Review
1025 Vermont Ave. NW, Ste. 360
Washington, DC 20005   Ph: (202)783-5640
Description: Conducts nonpartisan research and review of national policies with urban and racial implications. Objectives are: to aid civil rights and public interest groups in representing and presenting the concerns of their memberships before federal administrative agencies and judicial bodies; to provide a useful learning experience for students of law, public administration and the social sciences. Conducts program for law interns. Maintains library. **Founded:** 1970. **Publications:** Annual Report; Jobs Watch, bimonthly.

★3376★
Center for the Study of Human Rights
Columbia University
1108 International Affairs Bldg.
New York, NY 10027   Ph: (212)854-2479
Description: Academic advisers (23) and directors (10). Promotes teaching and research in the field of human rights. Sponsors interdisciplinary human rights research. Offers advice, fellowships, training and other assistance in conducting and financing such research; provides assistance in teaching and curriculum development. Offers consultation service, which provides information on human rights research, resources, and education and training programs at other institutions. **Founded:** 1977. **Members:** 34. **Publications:** Center for the Study of Human Rights–Newsletter, quarterly; Conference Proceedings, annual; Human Rights: A Topical Bibliography; Human Rights Syllabi, Annual Report; Papers.

★3377★
Center for World Indigenous Studies
1001 Cooper Point Rd. SW, Ste. 140-214
Olympia, WA 98502
Description: Research and education organization dedicated to wider understanding and appreciation of the ideas and knowledge of indigenous peoples. Fosters a better understanding between peoples through the publication of literature written and voiced by leading contributors from Fourth World nations. Seeks to establish cooperation between nations and to democratize relations between nations and states. Sponsors educational and research programs. **Founded:** 1984. **Publications:** Fourth World Journal; Indian Self-Governance; Indian War and Peace in Nicaragua.

★3378★
Children's Watch International
22 Towbridge St.
Cambridge, MA 02139   Ph: (617)492-4890
Description: Seeks to improve the quality of children's status and to shelter and care for children's human rights. "Represents and publicizes the needs and human rights of children who are victims of violence, in both domestic situations, such as child prostitution or child labor in hazardous industry, and in armed conflicts in national, international, civil, and ethnic conflicts. Develops and evaluates information on the human rights violations of children throughout the world." Organizes celebrations for children. Monitors nation's compliance with the UN convention on the Rights of the Child. **Founded:** 1994. **Publications:** Children's Watch Annual Report

★3379★
Citizens in Defense of Civil Liberties
14 Beacon St., No. 407
Boston, MA 02108
Description: Lawyers, legal workers, civil liberties activists, and researchers. Works to defend civil liberties through educational programs and publications. Conducts seminars; sponsors professional training of lawyers and legal workers. Resources include: biographical archives, 100 volume library, a collection of 50,000 items from FBI COINTELPRO (Counter Intelligence Program) files, and other research materials. Compiles statistics. **Founded:** 1979. **Members:** 2, 000. **Publications:** The Bulwark, quarterly; Civil Rights and Public Misconduct, quarterly; The Public Eye, quarterly.

★3380★
Coalition of Minority Policy Professionals
PO Box 45260
Washington, DC 20026   Ph: (301)608-0038
Description: Multicultural members of the public policy community. Works to ensure that minorities play an active role in developing and implementing public policy. Enhances the development of professional people of color in the public policy community. Stimulates the interest of minority students in public policy careers. Participates in the policy process by providing analyses and perspectives on issues and their effects on minority groups. Serves as a clearinghouse for volunteer and career opportunities; maintains an employment bank for members; provides career placement and counseling to assist students in the policy arena. **Founded:** 1988.

Members: 100. **State Groups:** 2. **Publications:** The Exchange Newsletter, quarterly.

★3381★
Committee for Action for Rural Indians
401 Liberty St.
Petoskey, MI 49770   Ph: (616)347-0059
Description: Native Americans who do not live on a reservation. Provides information and referral services to non-reservation Native Americans. Conducts alcohol and substance abuse recovery programs. **Publications:** none. **Founded:** 1972. **Formerly:** Native American Recovery Center.

★3382★
Committee on Professional Ethics, Rights and Freedom
c/o American Political Science Association
1527 New Hampshire Ave. NW
Washington, DC 20036   Ph: (202)483-2512
Description: Committee of the American Political Science Association. Concerned with the support of professional ethics, human rights, and academic freedom of political scientists. Reviews individual cases of violations and sometimes recommends action to APSA on cases and policies. **Founded:** 1969. **Formerly:** (1980) Committee on Professional Ethics and Academic Freedom.

★3383★
Common Destiny Alliance
College of Education
University of Maryland
4114 Benjamin Bldg.
College Park, MD 20742-1121   Ph: (301)405-2334
Description: Organizations and scholars interested in working to end prejudice. Fosters the viewpoint that cultural diversity is "a resource that can help the nation attain goals such as improving economic productivity and the academic achievement of all children." Seeks to end racial isolation in schools, neighborhoods, and the work force. Promotes social policies, especially those related to education, that encourage racial and ethnic understanding and cooperation. Conducts research to identify the causes of racism and means to overcome racism. **Founded:** 1991.

★3384★
Concerned American Indian Parents
CUHCC Clinic
2001 Bloomington Ave.
Minneapolis, MN 55404   Ph: (612)627-6888
Description: Serves as a network for American Indian parents and others interested in abolishing symbols that are degrading to American Indians, such as the Redskins and Indians logos adopted by sports teams in the U.S. Seeks to make the future easier for American Indian children by educating the public about the racial messages inherent in such symbols. **Founded:** 1987.

★3385★
Congressional Friends of Human Rights Monitors
House of Representatives
1432 Longworth Bldgs.
Washington, DC 20515   Ph: (202)225-6465
Description: Not an official congressional caucus; a coalition of members of the U.S. House and Senate. Promotes human rights on an international level. Writes letters on behalf of individuals who monitor human rights violations and victims worldwide. Group was initiated by Americas Watch, U.S. Helsinki Watch Committee, and Lawyers Committee for Human Rights. **Founded:** 1983.

★3386★
Consortium for Graduate Study in Management
200 S. Hanley Rd., Ste. 1102
St. Louis, MO 63105-3415   Ph: (314)935-6324
Description: Graduate fellowship program operated by Indiana University, New York University, University of Michigan, University of North Carolina, University of Virginia, Washington University, University of Rochester, University of Southern California, University of Texas-Austin, University of California-Berkely, and the University of Wisconsin to hasten the entry of minorities into managerial

positions in business. Program includes three-day orientation program, summer business internships and career placement, and involves minority groups such as American Indians, Afro-Americans, Mexican-Americans, Puerto Ricans, and Dominicans who hold U.S. citizenship. Recruits nationally on campuses and in minority communities. Fellowships provide tuition for up to two years; loans are available to meet additional need. **Founded:** 1967. **Members:** 11. **Publications:** Consortium Review Newsletter, 3/year. **Formerly:** (1971) Consortium for Graduate Study in Business for Negros.

★3387★
Continental Confederation of Adopted Indians
960 Walhonding Ave.
Logan, OH 43138   Ph: (614)385-7136

Description: Non-Indians who have been presented with honorary tribal chieftainship, an official Indian name, or recipients of any other Indian-oriented awards. Persons so honored include Wayne Newton, Reginald Laubin, and Ann Miller. Membership also open to blooded Indians. Maintains Indian Lore Hall of Fame. Maintains speakers' bureau. **Founded:** 1950. **Members:** 150.

★3388★
Council for Alternatives to Stereotyping in Entertainment
139 Corson Ave.
Staten Island, NY 10301   Ph: (718)720-5378

Description: Individuals in the arts and entertainment industry. Seeks to educate the public on the widespread, undesirable effects inflicted upon the entertainment industry by stereotyping. Disseminates information on self-image, reality perception, and receptivity to accurate performance feedback. Maintains speakers' bureau and 1000 volume library. **Founded:** 1982. **Members:** 25. **Publications:** Case Cares, quarterly.

★3389★
Council on Career Development for Minorities
1341 W. Mockingbird Ln., Ste. 722-E
Dallas, TX 75247   Ph: (214)631-3677

Description: Works to heighten the awareness and employability of African American, Hispanic American, and Native American college students and to improve career counseling and referral services offered to them. Provides programs to help minority students improve test-taking and learning skills. Promotes the inclusion of career education into college curricula and the establishment of career counseling and placement services. Conducts consultative visits by teams of specialists who evaluate the needs of a given institution and make recommendations for the creation or improvement of counseling and placement services. Serves as a consultant to colleges involving government grants. Sponsors training activities such as annual institutes for new and experienced counseling personnel. Also provides professional development programs that offer training in techniques and theory of career development and current labor market and employment trends. Conducts Corporate Orientation Program which provides sophomore-level minority students with the opportunity to study actual college-to-work transitional business activities and learn factors that affect their employability and chances for promotion in the world to work. Offers workshops for college presidents from historically black colleges to improve awareness of the role and importance of career counseling and placement on the college campus. Also offers consultations to advise employers on policies, practices, and strategies for the recruitment and retention of college-trained minorities; provides training for recruiting personnel on minority interviewing techniques. Sends association representatives to meetings of similar organizations. Maintains Julius A. Thomas Fellowship Program to grant minority students the opportunity for graduate studies in counseling; awards one or two fellowship grants annually. **Founded:** 1964. **Publications:** CCDM Annual Report, annual; CCDM Minority Student Recruitment Guide, biennial; CCDM Newsletter; CCDM World Newsletter, quarterly; Corporate Orientation Program, annual; Council on Career Development for Minorities, annual. **Formerly:** (1984) College Placement Services.

★3390★
Council of Energy Resource Tribes
1999 Broadway, Ste. 2600
Denver, CO 80202   Ph: (303)297-2378

Description: American Indian tribes owning energy resources. Promotes the general welfare of members through the protection, conservation, control, and prudent management of their oil, coal, natural gas, uranium, geothermal, oil shale, and other resources. Provides on-site technical assistance to tribes in all aspects of energy resource management, economic development, human resource development, and environmental protection. Conducts youth education and professional/technical training programs aimed at enhancing tribal planning and management capacities. **Founded:** 1975. **Members:** 57. **Publications:** CERT Report Newsletter, quarterly; D.C. Update Newsletter, periodic; Discover Indian Reservations U.S.A. Book.

★3391★
Council for Native American Indians
280 Broadway, Ste. 316
New York, NY 10007   Ph: (212)732-0485

Description: Individuals interested in the holistic philosophies and teachings of the earlier indigenous groups of North and Central America. Conducts research on the social, economic, and political relationships between the indigenous groups and the 16th century settlers in New York City and Long Island, NY areas. Conducts educational series for children that teaches concepts of discipline through the methods and techniques of the ancient peoples. Sponsors charitable programs; compiles statistics. **Founded:** 1974. **Members:** 843. **Publications:** Earth Walk and Four Directions for Peace; Medicine Lodge Newsletter, periodic.

★3392★
Council for Opportunity in Graduate Management Education
Central Plz.
675 Massachusetts Ave.
Cambridge, MA 02139   Ph: (617)491-8370

Description: Universities working to promote the flow of minorities into positions of managerial responsibility. Seeks to increase the number of Afro-Americans, American Indians, Asian Americans, and Hispanic-Americans graduating from master's degree programs at member schools. Presents fellowships to selected students planning to attend a regular, full-time graduate management program at one of the member schools. Students need not have completed any work or study in business or related fields prior to application, but U.S. citizenship and residency are required. **Founded:** 1970. **Members:** 10. **Publications:** Council for Opportunities in Graduate Management Education, annual.

★3393★
Department of Civil Rights, AFL-CIO
815 16th St. NW
Washington, DC 20006   Ph: (202)637-5270

Description: Staff arm AFL-CIO Civil Rights Committee. Serves as official liaison with women's and civil rights organizations and government agencies working in the field of equal opportunity; helps to implement state and federal laws and AFL-CIO civil rights policies; aids affiliates in the development of affirmative programs to expand opportunities for minorities and women; prepares and disseminates special materials on civil rights; speaks at union and civil rights institutes, conferences, and conventions; helps affiliates resolve complaints involving unions under Title VII of the 1964 Civil Rights Act and Executive Order 11246. **Founded:** 1955. **Publications:** AFL-CIO and Civil Rights, biennial.

★3394★
Emissary Foundation
5569 N. County Rd. 29
Loveland, CO 80538-9515   Ph: (303)679-4222

Description: Supports and participates in activities "that magnify the finest qualities of character in every field of human endeavor." Considers "all things as manifestations of one universal spirit." Maintains that alignment with, and expression of, this spirit can lead to clarity of thought and "perception essential to effectiveness in living" and encourages individuals to extend this spirit's influence into the world. Emphasizes accepting individual responsibility for creative change as the foundation for leadership and "collective transformation." Works with environmental organizations and programs, community building, Native American programs, and United Nations programs. **Founded:** 1981. **Regional Groups:** 13. **Local Groups:** 50. **Publications:** Facing the Intensity of the 90s Magazine, quarterly; Audiotapes; Booklets; Books; Brochures; Videos. **Formerly:** (1984) Foundation of Universal Unity; (1993) Emissary Foundation International.

★3395★
Equal Rights Congress
4167 S. Normandy Ave.
Los Angeles, CA 90037   Ph: (213)291-1092

Description: National minority organizations united to struggle for equality of all people who have been discriminated against because of nationality, color, religion, sex, or economic status. Conducts educational program and seminars; provides training and technical assistance for organizing; maintains speakers' bureau and biographical archives; compiles statistics; sponsors competitions. **Founded:** 1976. **Regional Groups:** 2. **Local Groups:** 35. **Publications:** Equal Rights Advocate, bimonthly; Southern Advocate, bimonthly.

★3396★
Film/Video Arts
817 Broadway, 2nd Fl.
New York, NY 10003   Ph: (212)673-9361

Description: Seeks to encourage media production as an artistic, educational, and vocational experience for people who might not otherwise find such opportunities. Services include film and video workshops for individuals and organizations. Provides subsidized access to film, videotape, and sound equipment for nonprofit organizations and individual artists, and provides the use of postproduction facilities for film and video editing, sound transfers, and film to tape transfers. Offers scholarship assistance to African-Americans, Asians, Latinos, and Native Americans pursuing careers in media arts. Provides matching grants for film speakers to appear at New York community organizations. **Founded:** 1968. **Members:** 1200. **Publications:** Intermediary; Newsletter quarterly.

★3397★
First Nations Development Institute
The Stores Bldg
11917 Main St.
Fredericksburg, VA 22408   Ph: (540)371-5615

Description: Aims to help Native American tribes achieve self-sufficiency using culturally appropriate development methods; promotes economic development and commercial enterprises of reservation-based Indian tribes and non-profit organizations through technical assistance, grants and loans. **Founded:** 1980. **Publications:** Business Alert Newsletter, bimonthly; Indian Giver Newsletter, quarterly.

★3398★
For Mother Earth
Old First Presbyterian Church
1101 Bryden Rd.
Columbus, OH 43205   Ph: (614)252-9255

Description: Sponsors Walk Across America and Europe to increase public awareness of injustice to indigenous people, especially Native Americans. Works to: repeal Public Law 93-531 which advocates forced relocation of the Dine (Navajo) from their homelands; end nuclear testing, which occurs on the land of indigenous persons; support the inclusion of indigenous nations into the United Nations (see separate entry); train community organizers; conduct educational series on interrelated issues. Offers children's services. Conducts educational, charitable, and research programs. Compiles statistics. Maintains speakers' bureau and museum; operates placement service. Affiliated with the Ohio Peace March for Global Nuclear Disarmament. **Founded:** 1989. **Regional Groups:** 87. **State Groups:** 24. **Publications:** For Mother Earth Newsletter, periodic; Ohio Peace March for Global Nuclear Disarmament.

★3399★
Four Arrows
PO Box 1332
Ottawa, ON, Canada K1P 5R4   Ph: (613)234-5887

Description: Individuals seeking to protect the human and political rights of indigenous peoples of the Americas. Promotes intercultural exchange, spiritual strength, and communication among Indian people; encourages self-sufficiency projects; supports revitalization of Indian communities through culture, tradition, and spiritual strength. Sponsors programs in education and agricultural development for Mexican Indian youth. Has sponsored development projects in Guatemala. **Founded:** 1968. **Members:** 100. **Regional Groups:** 4. **Publications:** Guatemala: The Horror and the Hope. **Also Known As:** Las Cuatro Flechas. **Formerly:** (1977) White Roots of Peace.

★3400★
Fourth World Documentation Project
PO Box 2574
Olympia, WA 98507-2574

Description: A project of the Center for World Indigenous Studies. Gathers documents pertaining to the global economy and international development including essays, position papers, government reports, treaties, and United Nations documents, and processes them into electronic text for global distribution on computer networks. **Founded:** 1992.

★3401★
Freedom Fund
4534 1/2 University Way NE
Seattle, WA 98105   Ph: (206)547-7644

Description: Individuals who seek to raise public awareness of human rights violations throughout the world and encourage grassroots solutions to these problems. Gathers material aid for victims of human rights abuses; makes available funding to organizations that provide direct relief. Has provided aid to South African political prisoners, Soviet refuseniks, Native Americans, and refugees from Afghanistan and Central America. Has sponsored caravans to provide relief supplies to human rights victims in Guatemala and to Native Americans at Big Mountain reservation in Arizona. **Founded:** 1984. **Publications:** World Insight Newsletter, bimonthly.

★3402★
Futures for Children
9600 Tennyson St. NE   Ph: (505)821-2828
Albuquerque, NM 87122-2282   Free: 800-545-6843

Description: Community development organization working to encourage and motivate people in underdeveloped areas to improve their communities through self-help programs. Is currently working in Colombia, Costa Rica, Honduras, and among American Indian tribes in the southwestern United States. Maintains speakers' bureau and children's services. Provides technical assistance. **Founded:** 1961. **Publications:** Guidebook for Community Counselors; Storyteller Newsletter, quarterly; Annual Report.

★3403★
Futures for Children
9600 Tennyson St., NE
Albuquerque, NM 87122

Description: Provides opportunities for cross-cultural friendships; provides support and incentives for Native American children to stay in school; works to strengthen traditional values among Native peoples and build self-reliance in Native American communities.

★3404★
Gathering of Nations
3200 Coors Blvd. NW, No. K-235
Albuquerque, NM 87120-1269   Ph: (505)836-2810

Description: Native Americans. Promotes the expression of Native American culture and religion, including Native American song and dance. Sponsors pow wows and periodic song, dance, and Miss Indian World competitions. **Founded:** 1984. **Publications:** Program Book; Magazine, annual.

★3405★
Great Lakes Indian Fish and Wildlife Commission
PO Box 9
Odanah, WI 54861   Ph: (715)682-6619

Description: Chippewa tribes concerned with wildlife conservation in the Great Lakes region. Assists member tribes in the conservation and management of fish, wildlife, and natural resources. Promotes tribal self-government; encourages ecosystem protection. Sponsors educational and research programs; maintains a speakers' bureau. **Founded:** 1983. **Members:** 11. **Regional Groups:** 11. **Publications:** Chippewa Treaty Rights; MASINAIGAN; Annual Report; Manuals; Reports.

★3406★
Human Rights Advocates
PO Box 5675
Berkeley, CA 94705   Ph: (510)540-8017

Description: International human rights lawyers and professionals. Objectives are to provide education about the application of human rights law and to promote this body of law domestically and internationally. Organizes public conferences, lectures, and seminars; submits amicus curiae briefs. Maintains library of current United Nations documents and materials on human rights organizations. Has consultative status with ECOSOC. **Founded:** 1978. **Members:** 100. **Publications:** Human Rights Advocates–Newsletter; International Human Rights Law: What It Is and How It Can Be Used in State and Federal Courts.

★3407★
Human Rights Advocates International
341 Madison Ave., 20th Fl.
New York, NY 10017   Ph: (212)986-5555

Description: Law firms, attorneys, academicians, and individuals worldwide interested in constitutional law and human rights. Protects and promotes human rights by coordinating and providing legal services, constitutional law resources, counseling, and investigations of alleged human rights violations. Represents exiles, individual citizens, and member states of the United Nations. Acts as sole representative for Amerasian children in Vietnam. Offers seminars on human rights law and international organization affairs; operates speakers' bureau. Conducts research on constitutionalism. **Founded:** 1979. **Members:** 300. **Publications:** Constitutions of Dependencies and Special Sovereignties; Constitutions of the Countries of the World.

★3408★
Human Rights Watch
350 5th Ave. No. 34 Fl
New York, NY 10118   Ph: (212)972-8400

Description: Organization which promotes and monitors human rights worldwide. Evaluates the human rights practices of governments in accordance with standards recognized by international laws and agreements including the United Nations Declaration of Human Rights and the Helsinki Accords. Identifies government abuses of human rights such as kidnapping, torture, and imprisonment for nonviolent association, exile, psychiatric abuse, and censorship; publicizes and protests against these violations. Also observes the human rights practices of nongovernmental groups, such as guerrilla groups, that are in sustained armed conflict with governments and measures these practices against internal war standards set forth in the Geneva Conventions and Protocols. Reports on discrepancies between the claims made by governments with respect to human rights and their actual practices; urges governments to bring actual practices in line with stated claims; works in conjunction with international bodies such as the Organization of American States (see separate entry), the UN, and the Helsinki Review Conferences. Sponsors missions to countries accused of human rights abuses; meets with government officials, local human rights and relief groups, church officials, labor leaders, journalists, and others with information on human rights practices; conducts interviews with victims of human rights abuses, their families, and witnesses. Attends court proceedings and examines court records. Observes elections and reports on conditions as a means to promote fair and free elections. Evaluates the U.S. government's performance in promoting human rights worldwide; observes U.S. domestic practices of human rights, particularly the treatment of visitors to the U.S. or refugees who are denied asylum or discriminated against on ideological, political, or racial grounds; also generates pressure to enforce U.S. laws that require governments receiving U.S. economic, military, or diplomatic assistance to adhere to appropriate human rights practices. Testifies before congressional hearings. Serves as an umbrella organization for HRW/Africa, HRW/Americas, HRW/Asra, HRW/Helsinki, HRW/Middle East, HRW/Children's Rights Project, HRW/Women's Rights Project, HRW/Prison Project, HRW/Arms Project, HRW/Fund for Free Expression. Has organized Congressional Friends of Human Rights Monitors. **Founded:** 1987. **Members:** 8000. **Regional Groups:** 5. **Publications:** Human Rights Watch Publications Catalog, semiannual; Human Rights Watch Quarterly Newsletter; Human Rights Watch: Questions and Answers; Brochure; Human Rights Watch World Report, annual.

★3409★
Indian Arts and Crafts Association
122 La Veta Dr. NE, Ste. B
Albuquerque, NM 87108   Ph: (505)265-9149

Description: Indian craftspeople and artists, museums, dealers, collectors, and others. Works to promote, preserve, protect, and enhance the understanding of authentic American Indian arts and crafts. Sets code of ethics for members and standards for the industry. Conducts consumer education seminars, meetings, and display programs; works with related government groups. Operates speakers' bureau. **Founded:** 1974. **Members:** 700. **Publications:** Buyer's Guide/Membership Directory; Brochures; Indian Arts and Crafts Association–Directory, annual; Indian Arts and Crafts Association–Newsletter, monthly; Membership Directory/Buyer's Guide annual.

★3410★
Indian Educators Federation
PO Box 2020
Farmington, NM 87499   Ph: (505)327-7733

Description: Professional educators employed in federal schools operated by the Bureau of Indian Affairs. To protect the rights and interests of teachers in Indian education; to promote quality educational opportunities for Indian students. Maintains speakers' bureau. **Founded:** 1967. **Members:** 400. **Formerly:** (1994) National Council of BIA Educators.

★3411★
Indian Heritage Council
Henry St.
Box 2302
Morristown, TN 37816   Ph: (423)581-4448

Description: American Indians and interested others. Promotes and supports American Indian endeavors. Seeks a deeper understanding between American Indians and others of the cultural, educational, spiritual, and historical aspects of Native Americans. Conducts research and educational programs. Sponsors charitable events; operates speakers' bureau. Publishes books, poems, manuscripts written by members or Native Americans. **Founded:** 1988. **Members:** 1, 000. **State Groups:** 3. **Local Groups:** 6. **Publications:** Great American Indian Bible; Indian Drug Usage; Native American Play; Native American Poetry; Native American Predictions; Vision Quest.

★3412★
Indian Law Resource Center
602 N. Ewing St.
Helena, MT 59601   Ph: (406)449-2006

Description: A legal, environmental, and human rights organization for Indian tribes and other indigenous peoples in the Western Hemisphere. Works to enable Indian people to survive as distinct peoples with unique cultures. Combats discrimination and injustice in the law and in public policy. Engages in human rights advocacy and environmental protection on behalf of Indians in the UN and U.S. courts; holds consultative status as a nongovernmental organization with the UN Economic and Social Council; offers free legal help. Conducts research and educational programs. **Founded:** 1978. **Publications:** Indian Rights-Human Rights; Handbook; Indian Rights, Human Rights;

★3413★
Indigenous Communications Association
948 Sage St.
Grants, NM 87020   Ph: (505)775-3215
Description: Radio stations in the continental U.S. and Canada, mainly located on Indian reservations. Provides development, advocacy, and technical support to member stations, including: financial resource development and management; advocacy and communications that promote station stability and growth; station staff development and training; international, national, and regional program production and dissemination; cross-cultural programming. Conducts fundraising. **Founded:** 1991. **Members:** 25 Brochure. **Formerly:** Coalition of Native American Public Radio Stations.

★3414★
Indigenous Women's Network
101 Pereida
San Antonio, TX 78210   Ph: (210)924-0991
Description: Individuals seeking to increase visibility of the indigenous women of the Western Hemisphere. Encourages the resolution of contemporary problems through traditional values. Operates speakers' bureau; sponsors educational programs; conducts research. **Founded:** 1989. **Members:** 300. **Publications:** Indigenous Environmental Perspectives - A North American Primer Booklet; Indigenous Woman Magazine, semiannual.

★3415★
Inroads
10 S. Broadway
St. Louis, MO 63102   Ph: (314)241-7488
Description: Participants are U.S. corporations that sponsor internships for minority students and pledge to develop career opportunities for the interns. Prepares black, Hispanic, and Native American high school and college students for leadership positions within major American business corporations in their own communities. Screens and places over 4000 individuals for internships with more than 1000 American business corporations per year. Offers professional training seminars on time management, business presentation skills, team building, and decision making. Provides personal and professional guidance to pre-college and college interns. **Founded:** 1970. **Regional Groups:** 4. **Local Groups:** 50. **Publications:** INROADS Newsletter, quarterly; Annual Report.

★3416★
Institute for Encyclopedia of Human Ideas on Ultimate Reality and Meaning
15 St. Mary St.
Toronto, ON, Canada M4Y 2R5   Ph: (416)922-2476
Description: Professors teaching at universities and experts involved in scientific research with an interest in interdisciplinary work and in promoting the project of the encyclopedia. Purposes are to study, in its historical development, all that humankind has ever thought about ultimate reality and the meaning of human existence from its early history until the present, and to publish the result first in the quarterly journal and later in an encyclopedia bearing the same name. Conducts a reflective, structural, and systematic investigation and study of the materials contained in the encyclopedia. Maintains library and 22 committees including: Anthropology; Arabic and Islamic Studies; Biblical Studies; Chemistry; Japanese Studies; North American Indian Studies; Philosophy and Comparative Literature; Physics; Prehistoric State; Protestant Studies; Theater Arts. **Founded:** 1970. **Members:** 400. **Publications:** American Philosophers Ideas on Ultimate Reality; Encyclopedia of Human Reality and Meaning; International Society for the Study of Human Ideas on Ultimate Reality and Meaning; Ultimate Reality and Meaning: Interdisciplinary Studies in the Philosophy of Understanding; Journal, quarterly; URAM Cumulative Index.

★3417★
Institute of the Northamerican West
110 Cherry St., Ste. 202
Seattle, WA 98104   Ph: (206)623-9597
Description: Works to improve the mutual understanding of issues of transboundary significance to western Canada, Mexico, and the U.S., and enhance quality of life in the region through the implementation of educational programs and other projects. Areas of concern include: the history, management, conservation, preservation, and development of land and water resources; land use policy and controls; pollution controls; energy policy; management of economic growth; preservation and enhancement of scenic beauty, trade, tourism, and recreation; immigration; tax policies regarding natural resources; native peoples' relationships and claims to resources; cultural values of populations in the western North American continent. Conducts research. **Founded:** 1984.

★3418★
Institute for Research and Education on Human Rights
PO Box 6106
Kansas City, MO 64110
Description: Engages in charitable, educational, and social welfare activities designed to protect and advance human rights and to increase public understanding of the consequences of the denial of those rights. Offers research and documentation service for schools and universities regarding human rights. Educational programs include lectures, media and speaking tours, and participation in conferences and seminars on human rights. Bestows annual award for outstanding work in the promotion and defense of human rights. **Founded:** 1983. **Publications:** Hammer, quarterly.

★3419★
Institute for the Study of American Cultures
1004 Broadway
PO Box 1658
Columbus, GA 31902   Ph: (706)571-2800
Description: Supports and promotes unbiased research into the origin and history of the American Indians and their pre-Columbian ancestors. Promotes a revisionist examination of the discovering of America by Columbus. Uses research technology in the fields of archaeology, anthropology, linguistics, epigraphy, music, and history to determine the "truth and relevancy of new discoveries without allegiance to any historical or ethnological paradigm." Sponsors research projects. Maintains the Pre-Columbian Research Center and Museum. **Founded:** 1983. **Members:** 300. **Publications:** Admiral Piri, Amerigo Vespucci, and Utopia; Columbus, the Man; Dene and NaDene Ingian Migration 1233 A.D., Escape from Genghis Khan to America; Lost America: The Story of Pre-Columbian Iron Age in America; The Nexus: Spoken Language Connection between the Mayar Asemetic During Pre-Columbian Times; The Norse Discovery of America.

★3420★
Institute for the Study of Genocide
899 10th Ave., Rm. 325
New York, NY 10019   Ph: (212)582-2537
Description: Professors, scholars, and other individuals. United to further research and scholarship on the causes, prevention, and consequences of genocide. Goals are to: sponsor historical, contemporary, and predictive research on the causes of genocide, mass political killing, and other violations of human rights of people; research and evaluate responses to genocide; monitor contemporary reports of human rights violations; considers deterrents to genocide and strategies to impede genocide and to assist the potential victims. Establishes liaison with related groups internationally and with archives and libraries specializing in the history of indigenous peoples. Reports on collections of scholarly material and related lectures and seminars. **Founded:** 1982. **Members:** 50. **Publications:** ISG Newsletter, semiannual.

★3421★
Inter-American Commission on Human Rights
1889 F St. NW, 8th Fl.
Washington, DC 20006   Ph: (202)458-6002
Description: Citizens of member nations of the Organization of American States. Promotes and protects human rights in the Caribbean, and North, Central, and South America. Maintains 5000 volume library specializing in human rights law. **Founded:** 1960. **Members:** 7. **Publications:** Special County Reports; Annual Report; Reports.

★3422★
Interfaith Council for Human Rights
8403 Arlington Blvd., Ste. 100
Fairfax, VA 22031 Ph: (703)876-6800

Description: A division of the National Ecumenical Coalition. Mainline religious denominations, including Catholic, Methodist, and Moslem. Promotes and defends civil rights through national educational activities. Organizes opposition to the New Right which the council says is an "extremist" group; coordinates programs which "attempt to keep the New Right in check." Supports the Equal Rights Amendment; conducts research, lobbying activities, AIDS education, and charitable programs; maintains speakers' bureau; compiles statistics. **Founded:** 1978. **Members:** 3, 200. **Regional Groups:** 6. **State Groups:** 50. **Local Groups:** 435. **Publications:** Legislative Update, weekly; Newsletter, monthly.

★3423★
International Association of Official Human Rights Agencies
444 N. Capitol St., Ste. 408
Washington, DC 20001 Ph: (202)624-5410

Description: Governmental human rights agencies with legal enforcement powers. Objectives are to foster better human relations and to enhance human rights procedures under the law. Conducts training services that include: administration and management training; technical assistance in civil rights compliance and curriculum development for colleges and universities, business, industry, and other organizations; training for administrators and commissioners to promote awareness and capability in current literature, theory, and philosophy relative to equal opportunity. Maintains ongoing liaison with federal agencies involved with civil rights enforcement in order to coordinate development of state legislation. Has developed and conducted training and technical assistance workshops for regional planning units and state planning agencies. Plans to establish a human rights training institute. Sponsors workshops; compiles statistics. **Founded:** 1949. **Members:** 187. **Regional Groups:** 5. **Publications:** IAOHRA Newsletter; Newsletter, quarterly; Membership Directory, annual.

★3424★
International Federation for the Protection of the Rights of Ethnic, Religious, Linguistic and Other Minorities
11-25 30th Ave.
Long Island City, NY 11102 Ph: (718)728-3330

Description: Individuals united in protecting the human rights of ethnic, religious, and linguistic minorities. Reports human rights violations. **Founded:** 1984: Newsletter, quarterly; Reports.

★3425★
International Human Rights Law Group
1601 Connecticut Ave. NW, Ste. 700
Washington, DC 20009 Ph: (202)232-8500

Description: Attorneys, government officials, law students, scholars, and interested individuals seeking to protect human rights. Legal strategies include filing complaints with regional and international human rights commissions, litigation before federal courts and government agencies, and preparing congressional testimony and legal analyses on violations of international human rights norms. Sponsors election-observing missions; provides information on international election observing. **Founded:** 1978. **Members:** 200. **Publications:** Guidelines for International Election Observing; U.S. Legislation Relating Human Rights to U.S. Foreign Policy; U.S. Ratification of Human Rights Treaties: With or Without Reservation.

★3426★
International Indian Treaty Council
54 Mint St., Ste. 400
San Francisco, CA 94103 Ph: (415)512-1501

Description: Organization of traditional Indian nations formed to draw attention to Indian problems and Indian rights. Maintains NGO status with the United Nations; makes regular presentations to the UN Commission on Human Rights; cosponsored a conference in Geneva, Switzerland in 1981 on Indigenous People and the Land. Cooperates with other human rights organizations. **Founded:** 1974. **Publications:** Treaty Council News, quarterly.

★3427★
International League for Human Rights
432 Park Ave. S., Rm. 1103
New York, NY 10016 Ph: (212)684-1221

Description: Individuals and national affiliates promoting human rights, including political and civil rights, racial and religious freedom, and the implementation of the Universal Declaration of Human Rights. Serves as nongovernmental agency accredited by the United Nations, International Labor Organization, United Nations Educational, Scientific and Cultural Organization, and Council of Europe (see separate entries). Participates in studies and programs on human rights. Advocates effective procedures to protect human rights, including protection of minorities; deals with issues of torture, political imprisonment, due process of law, racial discrimination, genocide, apartheid, treatment of prisoners, status of women, and religious freedom; promotes ability of local human rights groups to exist and work unimpeded by government. Intervenes directly with governments concerning violations of human rights. Sends special investigators to areas where human rights violations exist and sends observers to political trials. **Founded:** 1942. **Members:** 2, 700. **Regional Groups:** 35. **Publications:** In Brief; Petitions Before the UN Trusteeship Council; Report of a Medical Fact-Finding Mission to El Salvador; Report; Booklets; Books; Pamphlets. **Formerly:** (1976) International League for the Rights of Man.

★3428★
International Society for Human Rights/U.S.A. Section
PO Box 90
Toms River, NJ 08754 Ph: (908)341-1441

Description: U.S. section of the International Society for Human Rights, comprising individuals interested in preserving human rights, freedom, and democracy. Supports human rights activities in the C.I.S., Poland, Czechoslovakia, Romania, Germany, Cuba, Nicaragua, South Africa, Chile, and elsewhere. Works to establish nonviolent means of human rights defense in totalitarian countries. Organizes working groups within the U.S. and maintains contact with U.S. organizations seeking similar goals. Provides material and moral support for persons or groups who are persecuted for promoting human rights; initiates letter writing campaigns. Believes that the United Nations Declaration of Human Rights is not observed by all member countries and that the advancement of international tolerance and realization of human rights worldwide are vital steps toward securing world peace. Past activities have included: Save Professor Sakharov Campaign; monitoring of El Salvadoran elections; petitions to win release of Cuban political prisoners and campaigns to free political prisoners in Yugoslavia, Poland, and Romania; efforts to further religious freedom in the former Soviet Union. Current projects include: economic human rights in Eastern Europe; return of churches and places of worship in the C.I.S. to believers; rights of minorities in C.I.S. republics. Maintains speakers' bureau; operates charitable program. **Founded:** 1982. **Members:** 265. **Regional Groups:** 3. **Local Groups:** 1. **Publications:** Apartheid–How Much Longer?; Human Rights Around the World; Human Rights Review; Newsletter, quarterly; Human Rights Violation in SWAPO Camps in Angola and Zambia; In the Grip of the Sandinistas; The Middle Road for South Africa: The Way Between a Continuation of the Status Quo and Bloody Revolution.

★3429★
Internet: International Human Rights Documentation Network
8 York St., Ste. 202
Ottawa, ON, Canada K1N 5S6 Ph: (613)789-7407

Description: Scholars, activists, and policymakers concerned with the promotion and protection of internationally recognized standards of human rights. Goals are to foster communication among scholars, activists, and policymakers in the field and to function as an information clearinghouse, responding to questions about current research, publications, teaching resources, and activities of human rights organizations. **Founded:** 1976. **Members:** 1600. **Publications:** Funding Human Rights: An International Directory of Funding Organizations; Directory; Human Rights Reporter, semiannual; Human Rights Thesaurus; The Human Rights Tribune; Magazine, quarterly; Teaching About Genocide; Directories. **Formerly:** (1991) Human Rights INTERNET.

★3430★
Interracial Council for Business Opportunity
51 Madison Ave., Ste. 2212
New York, NY 10010   Ph: (212)779-4360

Description: Assists minorities and women in developing, owning, and managing business ventures with substantial employment and economic impact. Services include business feasibility studies, financing, market development, and other technical assistance to start or expand women-and minority-owned companies. Offers free management training courses. **Founded:** 1963. **Publications:** Annual Report; Newsletter, monthly.

★3431★
James Willard Schultz Society
135 Wildwood Dr.
New Bern, NC 28562   Ph: (919)637-5985

Description: Individuals and libraries interested in the life and writings of James Willard Schultz (1859-1947), enthusiast of the American Indian and author of children's books, stories, and autobiographical works on Indian culture and adventures. Objectives are to: preserve the memory and promote the works of Schultz; restore Indian names to natural features in Glacier National Park, MT; promote Montana history; help preserve the heritage of the Blackfoot Indian. Is conducting search for previously unpublished works by Schultz and related material. **Founded:** 1976. **Members:** 300. **Publications:** Piegan Storyteller Newsletter, quarterly.

★3432★
Lawyers Committee for Human Rights
330 7th Ave., 10th Fl.
New York, NY 10001   Ph: (212)629-6170

Description: Public interest law center that works to promote international human rights and refugee law and legal procedures. Focuses on cases where volunteer lawyers may help promote international human rights standards. Is involved in the pro bono representation of indigent political asylum applicants in the U.S. Investigates human rights issues in the justice system for follow-ups with local lawyers, U.S. foreign policy issues in markers, and intergovernmental organizations. Conducts training sessions and educational workshops for attorneys on international human rights and refugee law. Bestows Roger Baldwin Medal of Liberty every two years to individuals and organizations making a significant contribution to human rights in any part of the world. **Founded:** 1978. **Members:** 800. **Publications:** Lawyers Committee for Human Rights–Newsbriefs, quarterly. **Formerly:** Lawyers Committee for International Human Rights.

★3433★
Leadership Conference on Civil Rights
1629 K St. NW, Ste. 1010
Washington, DC 20006   Ph: (202)466-3311

Description: Coalition of national organizations working to promote passage of civil rights, social and economic legislation, and enforcement of laws already on the books. Has released studies examining former President Ronald Reagan's tax and budget programs in areas including housing, elementary and secondary education, social welfare, and Indian affairs, and tax cuts. Has evaluated the enforcement of activities in civil rights by the U.S. Department of Justice; has also reviewed civil rights activities of the U.S. Department of Education. **Founded:** 1950. **Members:** 185. **Publications:** LCCR Memo. **Formerly:** Civil Rights Mobilization.

★3434★
Leonard Peltier Defense Committee
PO Box 583
Lawrence, KS 66044   Ph: (913)842-5774

Description: Seeks to gain justice for Leonard Peltier through promotion, education, and public speaking. Works to improve the lives of American Indians and prisoners. Provides information on social, judicial and cultural issues. **Founded:** 1976. **Regional Groups:** 188. **Publications:** Spirit of Crazy Horse Newsletter, bimonthly.

★3435★
Maine Folklife Center
5773 S. Stevens Hall
Orono, ME 04469   Ph: (207)581-1891

Description: Works to research and record the folk history of Maine and the Maritimes, Native American legends, women in the Depression Era and World War II, labor history, textile folk arts and artists. Maintains the Northeast Archives of Folklore and Oral History. **Founded:** 1957. **Members:** 325. **Publications:** A Catalog of the First 1800 Accessions; Northeast Folklore J ournal.

★3436★
Marquette League for Catholic Indian Missions
1011 1st Ave.
New York, NY 10022

Description: Provides financial support for the material welfare of Catholic Indian missions in the United States. **Founded:** 1904.

★3437★
MCAP Group
89-50 164th St., Ste. 2B
Jamaica, NY 11432   Ph: (718)657-6444

Description: Provides bonding, financial, technical, and management assistance to minority and small construction contractors in cities for the purpose of assisting the contractors to compete for a more equitable share of the construction industry. Services include: surety bonding program; financial and construction management; financial analysis; construction project management, including estimating, engineering, joint venture, and consortia arrangements; procurement referrals for several federally funded building programs. Sponsors conferences and workshops on matters of particular interest to minority contractors, such as bonding and nonprofit housing. Operates MCAP Bonding and Insurance Agency, a for-profit subsidiary. **Founded:** 1970. **Formerly:** (1989) Minority Contractors Assistance Project.

★3438★
Meiklejohn Civil Liberties Institute
PO Box 673
Berkeley, CA 94701   Ph: (510)848-0599

Description: Established to collect attorney workpapers and unreported rulings filed in courts in cases involving civil rights, due process, and civil liberties, in order to assist attorneys and legal workers confronted with similar issues. Concentrates effort on a peace law and education project, with a brief bank of legal case files and in-depth findings and reports relating to current issues about U.S. military policies and conventional and nuclear war. Operates speakers' bureau. **Founded:** 1965. **Publications:** Alexander Meiklejohn: Teacher of Freedom Book; The Cold War Against Labor; Booklets; Event Journal, annual; The Ford Hunger March; Human Rights and Peace Law Docket: 1945-1993, 1995 edition, biennial; Human Rights Docket.

★3439★
MESHWORK
1333 H St. NW
Washington, DC 20005

Description: Minority professional associations. Provides contact information and idea exchange among members. **Members:** 55. **Publications:** MESHWORK Directory. **Also Known As:** Mathematics, Engineering, Science and Health: A Network of Minority Professional Associations.

★3440★
Mesoamerican Archeology Study Unit
PO Box 1442
Riverside, CA 92502

Description: A study unit of the American Topical Association. Philatelists with an interest in the pre-Columbian cultures of the Americas. Promotes the collection, research, study, display, and exhibition of philatelic material related to the native peoples of this period, their artifacts, and archaeological sites. Offers language translation services; facilitates the exchange of information among members. **Founded:** 1974. **Members:** 81. **Publications:** Codex Filatelica Newsletter, bimonthly; New World Archeology on Stamps Manual.

★3441★
Minorities International Network for Trade
60 Madison Ave.
New York, NY 10010-1600   Ph: (212)725-3312
Description: Minority professionals interested in furthering the understanding of international culture and trade issues among minority communities of the U.S. Serves as an educative and social network for pooling resources and disseminating such information, contacts, and assistance. Fosters and promotes cultural, social, and economic ties between members and businesses in the U.S. and in developing nations in Africa, the Caribbean, Asia, and Latin America. Maintains commercial, social, cultural, and governmental dialogues with foreign governments and their business communities. Provides seminars; bestows awards; conducts educational programs. **Founded:** 1987. **Members:** 80. **Publications:** MINT Newsletter, quarterly.

★3442★
Minority Business Enterprise Legal Defense and Education Fund
900 Second St., Ste. 8
Washington, DC 20002
Description: Minority businesspersons united to defend, enhance, and expand minority business. Acts as advocate and legal representative for the minority business community, offering legal representation in matters of national or regional importance. **Founded:** 1980. **Members:** 2,000. **Publications:** MBE Vanguard Newsletter, quarterly.

★3443★
Minority Business Information Institute
130 5th Ave., 10th Fl.
New York, NY 10011   Ph: (212)242-8000
Description: Not an association. Maintains 2200 volume library of books, periodicals, and reports focusing on minority businesses. **Founded:** 1970. **Publications:** Index to Black Enterprise, periodic.

★3444★
Minority Rights Group U.S.A.
c/o Sue Roff
35 Claremont Ave., Box 4S
New York, NY 10027   Ph: (212)864-7986
Description: A branch of Minority Rights Group. Aims are to: secure justice for minority or majority groups suffering discrimination by investigating their situation and publicizing the facts internationally; help prevent violations of human rights by using publicity and to prevent such problems from developing into dangerous and destructive conflicts; foster, by its research findings, international understanding of the factors that create prejudiced treatment and group tensions; promote the growth of a world conscience regarding human rights. Sponsors seminars on minority issues; commissions multidisciplinary research into the causes of minority problems and their solutions. Granted consultative status by the United Nations. Maintains library. **Founded:** 1968. **Publications:** Newsletter, bimonthly.

★3445★
Music for the Rights of Man
178 E. 70th St.
New York, NY 10021   Ph: (212)734-3230
Description: To promote and draw attention to human rights issues through musical performances. Conducts concerts, seminars, and workshops by musicians to focus attention on violations of human rights. Sponsors fundraising activities to support nonviolent human rights organizations that serve cultural, educational, or medical needs. **Founded:** 1984. **Also Known As:** Musique-Esperance.

★3446★
The Mustard Seed
PO Box 400   Ph: (818)791-5123
Pasadena, CA 91114-7000   Free: 800-943-2484
Description: An international, interdenominational Christian ministry which provides services to aboriginal/tribal peoples of Pacific rim countries. We currently work in Indonesia, Taiwan, and Papua New Guinea. Service projects include medical clinics, residential homes for children, the handicapped, and the elderly,

economic development projects, relief services, and care for unwedmothers. Educational project includes day care, K-12 schools, vocational training, teacher training education, and pastoral training. Evangleism projects include prision ministries, new church development, and support for evangelists and pastors. Discipleship projects include, Bible conferences, Sunday school training events, and Church development seminars. **Founded:** 1954. **Publications:** Seeds of Hope Newsletter, quarterly.

★3447★
NAIM Ministries
PO Box 151
Point Roberts, WA 98281   Ph: (604)946-1227
Description: Professionals, such as teachers and engineers, who also have some theological training. Objective is to establish indigenous Native American churches in urban centers and on reservations. Conducts economic, educational, social, and rehabilitation programs. Offers alcohol treatment and cross-cultural communication seminars. **Founded:** 1949. **Members:** 144. **Publications:** Dear Team, monthly; Infocus Newsletter, quarterly; Intercesor Newsletter, bimonthly. **Formerly:** North America Indian Mission; (1986) Marine Medical Mission.

★3448★
National Action Council for Minorities in Engineering
Empire State Bldg., Ste. 2212
350 Fifth Ave.
New York, NY 10118-2299   Ph: (212)279-2626
Description: Seeks to increase the number of African American, Latino, and Native American students enrolled in and graduating from engineering schools. Through the Corporate Scholars Program, offers comprehensive scholarships to engineering students that include leadership development, corporate mentors and summer internships. Through the Engineering Vanguard Program works with local and regional organizations to motivate and encourage precollege students to engage in engineering careers. Conducts educational and research programs; operates diversity seminars for engineering schools. Compiles statistics. **Founded:** 1980. **Publications:** Academic Gamesmanship: Becoming a "Master" Engineering Student Book; NACME News; Newsletter, semiannual; The Sky's Not the Limit Brochure; Annual Report, annual.

★3449★
National Alliance Against Racist and Political Repression
407 S. Dearborn, Ste. 540
Chicago, IL 60605   Ph: (312)939-2750
Description: Religious, community, and human relations organizations united to safeguard the Bill of Rights and constitutional freedoms and to ensure the just application of state and local laws. Has initiated and developed three organizations: Citizens Alert (deals with police and community problems); Illinois Gay and Lesbian Task Force; and Illinois Prisons and Jails Project (monitoring county and state prisons). Other areas of activity include media accountability, cable television license ordinances, rights of minors, juvenile justice, national and state legislation, and rights of immigrants. Maintains library and archives. **Founded:** 1970. **Members:** 53. **Formerly:** (1995) Alliance to End Repression.

★3450★
National American Indian Court Judges Association
Attn. Judicial Branch
PO Box 652
Okumulgee, OK 74447   Ph: (918)758-1400
Description: American Indian court judges. Seeks to improve the American Indian court system throughout the United States by furthering knowledge and understanding of it, and maintaining its integrity in providing equal protection to all persons. Offers periodic training sessions on criminal law and family law/child welfare. Conducts research and continuing education programs. **Founded:** 1968. **Members:** 256. **Publications:** Indian Courts Newsletter, periodic.

★3451★
National Association of Human Rights Workers
c/o Ronald McElreath
Florida Commission on Human Relations
Bldg. F., Ste. 240
325 John Knox Rd.
Tallahassee, FL 32303   Ph: (904)488-7082
Description: Professional association of governmental or private organization employees working in the areas of civil rights, civil liberties, interracial and interethnic relations, and religious understanding. Maintains speakers' bureau; conducts research programs; compiles statistics. **Founded:** 1947. **Members:** 350. **Regional Groups:** 4. **Local Groups:** 16. **Publications:** Journal of Intergroup Relations Journal, quarterly; NAHRW Newsletter, bimonthly. **Formerly:** National Association of Intergroup Relations Officials.

★3452★
National Association of Medical Minority Educators
Marquette University
Office of Multicultural Concerns
Milwaukee, WI 53233   Ph: (414)288-5861
Description: Educators, administrators, and practitioners of medicine, osteopathic medicine, dentistry, veterinary medicine, optometry, podiatry, public health, and allied health. Promotes the increase of medical minority personnel; admissions of minority students to health professionals schools; retention and graduation of minority students in health profession schools; recruitment and development of minority faculty administrators and managerial personnel in the health professions; delivery of quality health care for minority populations; and recruitment, retention, and development of minority students in pre-health profession programs. Sponsors workshops for high school counselors and junior high and high school science teachers; provides training for minority affairs workers and officers. Offers annual student development sessions and recruitment fairs. Conducts research programs and systematic studies. **Founded:** 1975. **Members:** 200. **Regional Groups:** 4. **Publications:** Financing Your Medical Education Book, annual; James Stills Quarterly - NAMME Edition Newsletter, quarterly.

★3453★
National Association of Minority Automobile Dealers
1111 14th St. NW Ste., 720
Washington, DC 20005   Ph: (202)789-3140
Description: Automobile dealers. Acts as liaison between membership, the federal government, the community, and industry representatives; seeks to better the business conditions of its members on an ongoing basis. Acts as confidential spokesperson for dealers. Offers business analysis, financial counseling, and short- and long-term management planning. Conducts research programs; compiles statistics. **Founded:** 1980. **Members:** 500. **Publications:** Newsletter, bimonthly.

★3454★
National Association of Minority Media Executives
PO Box 310
5746 Union Mill Rd.   Free: (888)968-
Clifton, VA 20124   7658
Description: Senior minority managers and executives. Strives to increase the number of minorities in senior management positions and to promote cultural diversity in the communications industry. Conducts research and educational programs. **Founded:** 1990. **Members:** 115. **Publications:** NAMME Guide to Minority Media Associations Booklet, annual.

★3455★
National Association of Minority Women in Business
906 Grand Ave., Ste. 200
Kansas City, MO 64106   Ph: (816)421-3335
Description: Minority women in business ownership and management positions; college students. Serves as a network for the exchange of ideas and information on business opportunities for minority women in the public and private sectors. Conducts research; sponsors workshops, conferences, seminars, and luncheons. Maintains speakers' bureau, hall of fame, and placement service; compiles statistics; bestows awards to women who have made significant contributions to the field. **Founded:** 1972.

Members: 5000. **Publications:** Today Newsletter, bimonthly; Brochures.

★3456★
National Business League
1511 K St. NW, Ste. 432
Washington, DC 20005   Ph: (202)737-4430
Description: Organizational vehicle for minority businesspeople. Promotes the economic development of minorities. Encourages minority ownership and management of small businesses and supports full minority participation within the free enterprise system. Maintains file of minority vendors and corporate procurement and purchasing agents. Conducts special projects. **Founded:** 1900. **Members:** 10,000. **Local Groups:** 127. **Publications:** Corporate Guide for Minority Vendors, annual; National Memo Membership Directory, monthly; President's Briefs Bulletin, monthly. **Formerly:** National Negro Business League.

★3457★
National Catholic Conference for Interracial Justice
3033 4th St. NE
Washington, DC 20017-1102   Ph: (202)529-6480
Description: Catholic organization working for interracial justice and social concerns in America. Initiates programs within and outside the Catholic church to end discrimination in community development, education, and employment. **Founded:** 1959. **Members:** 6,000. **Publications:** Commitment Newsletter, quarterly; LASER: Creating Unity in Diversity; Martin Luther King Jr. Holiday Celebration Packet; Pentecost: A Feast for all Peoples; Workshops on Racism; Pamphlets.

★3458★
National Center for Minority Business Research and Development
PO Box 36068   Ph: (410)323-0162
Towson, MD 21286-6068   Free: 800-466-2627
Description: Works to provide minority and women entrepreneurs with resources to succeed in the marketplace. Creates and supports partnerships and joint ventures; guarentees procured loans for women and minority businesses; offers financial tools and resources; provides professional services and technical assistance; researches and analyzes market trends; advises minority business on market conditions and developing markets; maintains Hall of Fame. **Founded:** 1993. **Members:** 15,000. **Publications:** The Voice of Women and Minority Businesses Newsletter, monthly.

★3459★
National Committee on Pay Equity
1126 16th St. NW, Rm. 411
Washington, DC 20036   Ph: (202)331-7343
Description: Individuals (250) and organizations (178) such as women's groups, labor unions, professional associations, minority and civil rights groups, and governmental and educational groups. Educates the public about the historical, legal, and economic basis for pay inequities between men and women and white people and people of color. Sponsors speakers' bureau; acts as an information clearinghouse on pay equity activities. Promotes grassroots activism. **Founded:** 1979. **Members:** 428. **Publications:** Bargaining for Pay Equity: A Strategy Briefing Paper: The Wage Gap; Paper; Erase the Bias: A Pay Equity Guide to Eliminating Race and Sex Bias from Wage Setting Systems.; The Intersection Between Pay Equity and Workplace Representation; Newsnotes; Pay Equity Activity in the Public Sector, 1979-1989.

★3460★
National Consortium on Alternatives for Youth at Risk
5250 17th St., Ste. 107   Ph: (941)378-4793
Sarasota, FL 34235   Free: 800-245-7133
Description: Works to research and disseminate information on the needs of youth and on programs that meet these needs. Researches alternatives for youth-at-risk; surveys programs to validate success; acquaints practitioners with alternative programs; educates the public on the needs of youth-at-risk. **Founded:** 1989. **Publications:** Green Sheet/Mailing; Newsletter, monthly.

★3461★
National Consortium for Educational Access
161 Spring St., Ste. 800   Ph: (404)332-7270
Atlanta, GA 30303   Free: 800-869-1013

Description: Historically Black colleges and universities, Hispanic and Hispanic serving institutions, and other Ph.D.-granting institutions. Seeks to increase the number of African Americans, Hispanic Americans, and Native Americans who hold a Ph.D. and are interested in furthering their academic careers as faculty at the collegiate level. Emphasis is primarily on scientific, technological, and other disciplines where they are underrepresented. **Founded:** 1984. **Members:** 115. **Publications:** Annual Report.

★3462★
National Council for Culture and Art
1600 Broadway, Ste. 611C
New York, NY 10019

Description: Artists, civic and business leaders, professional performers, and visual arts organizations. Purpose is to provide exposure and employment opportunities for rural Americans, disabled Americans, and other minorities including blacks, Hispanics, American Indians, and European-Americans. Sponsors arts programs and spring and fall concert series. Operates Opening Night, a cable television show. Bestows annual Monarch Award and President's Award, and sponsors annual Monarch Scholarship Program. Offers children's and placement services; conducts charitable program; maintains hall of fame. Plans to conduct Minority Playwrights Forum, Dance Festival U.S.A., Vocal and Instrumental Competition, Film and Video Festival, and Concerts U.S.A. **Founded:** 1980. **Members:** 1,500. **Publications:** Monarch Herald Newsletter, quarterly.

★3463★
National Indian Health Board
1385 S. Colorado Blvd., Ste. A-708
Denver, CO 80222   Ph: (303)759-3075

Description: Indians of all tribes and natives of Alaskan villages. Advocates the improvement of health conditions which directly or indirectly affect American Indians and Alaskan Natives. Seeks to inform the public of the health condition of Native Americans; represents Indians and their interests. Conducts seminars and workshops on health subjects. Provides technical assistance to members and Indian organizations. **Founded:** 1969. **Members:** 12. **Regional Groups:** 12. **Publications:** Conference Report, annual

★3464★
National Institute for Resources in Science and Engineering
4302 Star Ln.
Rockville, MD 20852   Ph: (301)770-1437

Description: Offers technical assistance to community-based organizations, Hispanic professional engineering societies, and college and university student groups that wish to increase the number of minority engineers. Provides assistance and information on governmental and private sector opportunities in science and engineering to Hispanics and American Indians. Consults with university officials concerning minority engineers and disseminates that information to congressional offices studying minority participation in engineering education. Assists in accessing government resources. Conducts workshops. **Founded:** 1980.

★3465★
National Institute for Women of Color
1301 20th St. NW, Ste. 702
Washington, DC 20036

Description: Aims to: enhance the strengths of diversity; promote educational and economic equity for black, Hispanic, Asian-American, Pacific-Islander, American Indian, and Alaskan Native women. Focuses on mutual concerns and needs, bringing together women who have traditionally been isolated. (NIWC uses the phrase "women of color" to convey unity, self-esteem, and political status and to avoid using the term "minority," which the institute feels has a negative psychological and social impact.) Serves as a networking vehicle to: link women of color on various issues or programs; promote women of color for positions on boards and commissions; ensure that women of color are visible as speakers or presenters at major women's conferences, as well as planners or

program developers; support and initiate programs; educate women and the public about the status and culture of the various racial/ethnic groups they represent; promote cooperative efforts between general women's organizations and women of color, while raising awareness about issues and principles of feminism. Sponsors seminars and workshops. Provides technical assistance; conducts internship and leadership development programs; compiles statistics. **Founded:** 1981. **Publications:** Brown Papers.

★3466★
National Minority Business Council
235 E. 42nd St.
New York, NY 10017   Ph: (212)573-2385

Description: Minority businesses in all areas of industry and commerce. Seeks to increase profitability by developing marketing, sales, and management skills in minority businesses. Acts as an informational source for the national minority business community. Programs include: a legal services plan that provides free legal services to members in such areas as sales contracts, copyrights, estate planning, and investment agreement; a business referral service that develops potential customer leads; an international trade assistance program that provides technical assistance in developing foreign markets; an executive banking program that teaches members how to package a business loan for bank approval; a procurement outreach program for minority and women business owners. Conducts continuing management education and provides assistance in teaching youth the free enterprise system. **Founded:** 1972. **Members:** 400. **Publications:** Corporate Minority Vendor Directory, annual; Corporate Purchasing Directory, annual; NMBC Business Report, biennial.

★3467★
National Minority Supplier Development Council
15 W. 39th St., 9th Fl.
New York, NY 10018   Ph: (212)944-2430

Description: Minority businesspersons, corporations, government agencies, and other organizations who are members of regional purchasing councils or who have agreed to participate in the program. Regional councils certify and match minority-owned businesses with member corporations which want to purchase goods and services. Conducts sales training programs for minority entrepreneurs, and buyer training program for corporate minority purchasing programs. Compiles statistics. **Founded:** 1972. **Members:** 175. **Regional Groups:** 44. **Publications:** Minority Supplier News; Minority Vendor Directory, periodic; National Minority Supplier Development Council–Annual Report. **Formerly:** (1980) National Minority Purchasing Council.

★3468★
National Native American Chamber of Commerce
225 Valencia St.
San Francisco, CA 94103

Description: Supports the development of regional and local chambers of commerce for Native Americans. Advocates business related education for Native American youth and businesspeople. **Founded:** 1985. **Regional Groups:** 12. **Local Groups:** 50.

★3469★
National Native American Cooperative
PO Box 27626
Tucson, AZ 85726   Ph: (520)622-4900

Description: Native American artists and craftsmen, cultural presenters, dance groups, and individuals interested in preserving American Indian crafts, culture, and traditional education. Provides incentives to Native Americans to encourage the preservation of their culture; offers assistance marketing American Indian crafts and locating material that is difficult to find. Supplies referral information on public health, education, career counseling, scholarships and funding sources, marketing, models, and dance. Sponsors crafts and cultural demonstrations. Is currently developing a North American Indian Trade and Information Center. Compiles statistics; operates speakers' bureau. Maintains museum. **Founded:** 1969. **Members:** 2,700. **Publications:** Indian Information Packets; Native American Directory: Alaska, Canada, U.S.; Directory, quinquennial; Pow Wow on the Red Road.

★3470★
National Tribal Chairman's Association
818 18th St. NW, Ste. 840
Washington, DC 20006   Ph: (202)293-0031
Description: Federally recognized tribes and their leaders. Provides a united front for elected Indian leaders to consult with government officials; assists Indian groups in obtaining full rights from federal agencies; monitors federal programs that affect Indians. **Founded:** 1971. **Members:** 182. **Publications:** List of Tribes and Tribal Leaders, quarterly; Newsbrief, periodic.

★3471★
National Tribal Environmental Council
2221 Rio Grande NW
Albuquerque, NM 87104   Ph: (505)242-2175
Description: Native American tribes. Focuses on the environmental concerns of Native Americans. Seeks to strengthen environmental management of lands by Native American tribes. Acts as a clearinghouse for environmental information. Monitors legislation related to the environment. Maintains speakers' bureau. **Founded:** 1991. **Members:** 88. **Publications:** Tribal Vision Newsletter, quarterly.

★3472★
National Urban Indian Council
100068 University Pk. St.
Denver, CO 80250-0168
Description: According to the 1990 U.S. census, more than 50% of the American Indians and Alaska Natives in the U.S. now reside off their reservations. Because of this transition and the resulting problems that have arisen, the council was formed to serve as a coalition through which urban-based American Indian and Alaskan Native groups could communicate among themselves and with the public for mutual support and sharing of information. Compiles statistics; operates speakers' bureau and private personnel placement service. Conducts research. **Founded:** 1977. **Members:** 500. **Regional Groups:** 10. **Local Groups:** 150. **Publications:** American Indian Review, quarterly; American Indians Source Document; Urban Indians Bulletin.

★3473★
Nations Ministries
Box 70
Honobia, OK 74549   Ph: (918)755-4570
Description: Individuals and churches conducting evangelical Christian ministry on American Indian reservations in the U.S. Maintains speakers' bureau. **Founded:** 1983. **Publications:** Indian Nations News, bimonthly.

★3474★
Native American Community Board
PO Box 572
Lake Andes, SD 57356-0572   Ph: (605)487-7072
Description: Works toward the educational, social, and economic advancement of American Indians. Maintains Native American Women Health Education Resource Center, which provides selfhelp programs and workshops on issues such as fetal alcohol syndrome, AIDS awareness, family planning, domestic abuse and crisis, reproductive rights, and child development. Conducts adult education classes; offers support services to Native Americans seeking employment and educational opportunities. Conducts charitable programs; offers children's services; maintains speakers' bureau and placement service. Compiles statistics. Is concerned with treaty and environmental issues involving Native Americans. **Founded:** 1984. **Publications:** Wicozanni-Wowapi; Newsletter, quarterly; Brochures; Pamphlets.

★3475★
Native American Educational Services College
2838 W. Peterson
Chicago, IL 60659   Ph: (773)761-5000
Description: An educational program accredited by the Commission on Institutions of Higher Education of the North Central Association of Colleges and Schools Indian communities (2 urban, 2 reservations). Maintains 5000 volume library on historical and contemporary American Indian topics. **Founded:** 1974. **Members:**

15. **Publications:** College Catalog Directory, biennial; NAES-Rule, quarterly; Native Child Advocate, quarterly. **Formerly:** Native American Educational Service.

★3476★
Native American (Indian) Chamber of Commerce
PO Box 27626
Tucson, AZ 85726-7626   Ph: (520)622-4900
Description: Promotes research and education on Native American issues including: health, education, tribal and cultural information, and current events. Maintains speakers' bureau; compiles statistics. **Founded:** 1990. **Members:** 200. **Regional Groups:** 2. **Publications:** Native American Directory, Alaska, Canada and U.S.; Directory, periodic; Pow-Wow on the Red Road.

★3477★
Native American Law Students Association
Indian Law Clinic
University of Montana Law School
Missoula, MT 59812   Ph: (406)243-6480
Description: American Indian or Native Alaskan law students. Promotes unity, communication, and cooperation among Indian law students; seeks to provide financial aid and summer employment opportunities for members; encourages development of educational opportunities such as tutorial programs, research projects, and curriculum development in Indian law; offers a forum for discussion of legal problems relating to law affecting American Indians. Maintains speakers' bureau of students in the field of Indian law. Operates no library; however, members have access to the extensive Indian law collection at the University of New Mexico. **Founded:** 1970. **Members:** 160. **Regional Groups:** 6. **Local Groups:** 14. **Formerly:** (1990) American Indian Law Students Association.

★3478★
Native American Policy Network
Barry University
11300 2nd Ave. NE
Miami, FL 33161   Ph: (305)899-3473
Description: Academicians; Indian and political leaders; policymakers. Objective is to foster research in all areas of Native American policy. Organizes panels and seminars at the annual conventions of the American Political Science Association and Western Social Science Association (see separate entries). **Founded:** 1979. **Members:** 425. **Publications:** NAPN Directory; Directory, periodic; NAPN Newsletter; Newsletter.

★3479★
Native American Public Telecommunications
PO Box 83111   Ph: (402)472-3522
Lincoln, NE 68501   Free: 800-793-4250
Description: Seeks to inform, educate, and encourage the awareness of tribal histories, cultures, languages, opportunities, and aspirations through the fullest participation of American Indians and Alaska Natives in creating and employing all forms of educational and public telecommunications programs and services, thereby supporting tribal sovereignty. NAPT's mission is accomplished through: producing and developing educational telecommunication programs for all media including television and public radio; distributing and encouraging the broadest use of such educational telecommunications programs; providing training opportunities to encourage increasing numbers of American Indians and Alaska Natives to produce quality programs; promoting increased control and use of information technologies by American Indians and Alaska Natives; providing leadership in creating awareness of and developing telecommunications policies favorable to American Indians and Alaska Natives; and building partnerships to develop and implement telecommunications projects with tribal nations, Indian organizations, and native communities. **Founded:** 1977. **Publications:** Vision Maker Brochure; Catalog; Newsletter, quarterly. **Formerly:** Native American Public Broadcasting Consortium.

★3480★
Native American Rights Fund
1506 Broadway
Boulder, CO 80302   Ph: (303)447-8760
Description: Represents Indian individuals, organizations and tribes in legal matters of national significance. Provides legal counsel in these areas of concern: tribal existence; protection of tribal resources; human rights, including educational matters and religious freedom; accountability of federal, state, and tribal governments; Indian law development. **Founded:** 1970. **Publications:** NARF Legal Review; Newsletter, biennial; National Indian Law Library Catalogue quarterly.

★3481★
Native American Scholarship Fund
8200 Mountain Rd. NE, No. 203
Albuquerque, NM 87110-7835   Ph: (505)262-2351
Description: Raises funds to provide Native American students with merit scholarships for university study, primarily in math, engineering, science, business, education, and computers, at undergraduate and graduate levels. Conducts research and educational programs. Maintains speakers' bureau and placement service. Compiles statistics. **Founded:** 1986. **Publications:** Exemplory Programs in Indian Education Book.

★3482★
Native American Science Education Association
c/o Stafford Kay
Phelps-Stokes Fund
11 Dupont Cir. NW
Washington, DC 20036
Description: Individuals interested in improving math and science education for Native Americans. Operates 30 programs including: Indian Science Teachers Education Program, which recruits and trains Native Americans to become high school math and science teachers; Introduce Science to Students Using the Environment series, which is a program guide for primary and secondary school teachers interested in teaching math and science. Bestows scholarships. **Founded:** 1982. **Members:** 2500. **Regional Groups:** 3. **Publications:** Kuitatk Newsletter.

★3483★
Native Americans for a Clean Environment
PO Box 1671
Tahlequah, OK 74465
Description: Individuals devoted to halting contamination of the environment by nuclear waste and to promoting forms of energy production that are safer than nuclear power. Seeks to educate the public on safe disposal methods and the advantages of using renewable energy sources. Provides speakers for lectures on the nuclear industry, food irradiation, and uranium mining. Maintains library. **Founded:** 1985. **Members:** 500. **Publications:** NACE News Newsletter, monthly; Raffinate Brochure.

★3484★
Native Hawaiian Culture and Arts Program
Bishop Museum
1525 Bernice St.
Honolulu, HI 96817-0916   Ph: (808)847-8237
Description: Individuals, organizations, and agencies interested in the preservation and perpetuation of traditional Native Hawaiian culture, arts, and values. Works to research, recover, and develop native practices and ceremonies; fosters personal pride among Native Hawaiians and enhances awareness and appreciation of Native Hawaiian history among all peoples. Sponsors cultural research with emphasis on values, language, lore, ceremony, and protocol. Facilitates access to natural and cultural resources; disseminates information on current research and findings. Encourages improved psychological, social, cultural, and economic well-being of Native Hawaiians. Promotes and assists in the development of Native Hawaiian professionals; operates speakers' bureau. Maintains museum. **Founded:** 1986. **Members:** 13. **Local Groups:** 1.

★3485★
Natives of the Four Directions Cultural Center
131 Berkeley Sq., No. 308
Berkeley, CA 94704
Description: Encourages people to return to their indigenous roots; to study, know and participate in their ancestral cultures. Offers lectures, seminars, educational and cultural events; conducts classes in Native languages, history and traditional art forms; sponsors theater, poetry and music concerts; conducts research. **Founded:** 1994. **Members:** 50. **Publications:** Teacalli News Newsletter, quarterly; Brochures.

★3486★
NGO Committee on Human Rights
866 United Nations Plz., Ste. 120
New York, NY 10017-1822   Ph: (212)756-3500
Description: Representatives of non-governmental organizations (NGOs) at the United Nations. Works to make human rights a priority for the United Nations. Serves as a forum for discussion and education on human rights issues, especially those relating to the work of the United Nations. **Members:** 120.

★3487★
North American Indian Association
22720 Plymouth Rd.
Detroit, MI 48239   Ph: (313)535-2966
Description: Individuals of at least one-quarter North American Indian blood and their families. Membership centered in the Detroit, MI, area; open to natives and non-natives. Objectives are to: establish a meeting center for North American Indians; preserve and promote Indian culture; assist Indians in obtaining higher education; help each other in time of need; work for the betterment of all Indians. Provides employment and training programs, adult counseling services, and children's services. Operates Native American Gallery. Offers speakers' bureau. **Founded:** 1940. **Members:** 300. **Publications:** Native Sun Newsletter, quarterly. **Also Known As:** Detroit American Indian Center. **Formerly:** (1965) North American Indian Club.

★3488★
North American Indian Chamber of Commerce
PO Box 27626
Tucson, AZ 85726-7626   Ph: (520)622-4900
Description: Acts as a clearinghouse of information on American Indians. Collects and disseminates information at major American Indian events, conferences, and gatherings. Sponsors educational programs. **Founded:** 1983. **Members:** 2,700. **Publications:** Indian America, quarterly; Native American Directory; Pow Wows on the Red Road.

★3489★
North American Indian Women's Association
32 Lambert Branch Rd.
Cherokee, NC 28719-9703
Description: Women, 18 years and older, who are members of federally recognized tribes. Seeks to foster the general well-being of Indian people through unity of purpose. Promotes inter-tribal communication, awareness of the Native American culture, betterment of family life, health, and education, and strengthening of communication among Native Americans. **Founded:** 1970. **Regional Groups:** 6. **Local Groups:** 19.

★3490★
North American Native American Indian Information and Trade Center
PO Box 27626
Tucson, AZ 85762   Ph: (520)622-4900
Description: A project of the National Native American Cooperative Provides educational programs to individuals interested in Native American culture. Serves as a clearinghouse of information on American Indians including special events and sales of arts and crafts. Maintains trading post of Indian crafts. Also maintains speakers' bureau and museum. Compiles statistics. **Founded:** 1991. **Publications:** American Indian Information Packet; Indian America, annual; Native American Directory: Alaska, Canada, U.S.; Pow Wow on the Red Road.

★3491★
North American Native Fishes Association
c/o Bruce Gebhardt
123 W. Mt. Airy Ave.
Philadelphia, PA 19119   Ph: (215)247-0384

Description: Ichthyologists and other scientists, students, sportsmen, naturalists, and aquarists. Increases appreciation of native species through observation, study, research, and restoration and improvement of the natural habitat; gathers and disseminates information about native fishes; and promotes practical laws for the preservation of native fishes in the wild and in the home aquarium. Operates a "trading post" program through which members exchange fish and eggs from all parts of North America. Provides speakers; conducts specialized study groups. **Founded:** 1972. **Members:** 350. **Publications:** American Currents Journal, quarterly; Covers native fish research sources.; Bibliographies; Darter; Newsletter.

★3492★
Organization of North American Indian Students
Northern Michigan University
Box 26, University Center
Marquette, MI 49855   Ph: (906)227-2138

Description: University students of American Indian ancestry and other interested students. Encourages pride and identity in Indian culture and tradition; establishes communications among the native communities; promotes scholarship among Indian students attending institutions of higher learning. Sponsors basket weaving seminars, powwows, social and cultural gatherings, and annual Indian Awareness Week. **Founded:** 1971. **Members:** 40.

★3493★
Pan-American Indian Association
8335 Sevigny
Fort Meyers, FL 33917   Ph: (941)731-7029

Description: Americans of Native American descent; students and other interested individuals. Assists persons with Native American heritage in researching their tribal roots. Provides genealogical and historical aids. Provides speakers' bureau and educational programs. **Founded:** 1984. **Members:** 3,700. **Regional Groups:** 20. **State Groups:** 5. **Local Groups:** 15. **Publications:** Whirling Rainbow-Voice of the People Journal, quarterly.

★3494★
Panel of American Women
c/o Nancy Boylan
205 19th St. NE, Apt. 108
Canton, OH 44714   Ph: (216)453-6160

Description: Groups of women volunteers in cities all over the United States promoting understanding among people of all races and religions. Members present panel-type programs for church, school, and civic groups, discussing their personal experiences in confronting prejudice and discrimination. Each panel usually includes a moderator and four or five panelists representing Protestant, Catholic, Jewish, Black, Hispanic, Native American, and/or other ethnic groups, depending on the ethnic makeup of the community. The panels discuss issues affecting women and the prejudices they and their families have met in schools, housing, employment, and other situations; panels then answer questions from the audience. Also sponsors youth panels. Acts as a community resource, putting organizations in touch with agencies or providing them with resource materials. **Founded:** 1957. **Members:** 150. **Regional Groups:** 2. **Local Groups:** 14. **Publications:** National Panel of American Women.

★3495★
Physicians for Human Rights
100 Boylston St., Ste. 702
Boston, MA 02116   Ph: (617)695-0041

Description: Health professionals, concerned citizens, and scientists. Aims to bring the skills of the medical profession to the protection of human rights. Works to: prevent the participation of doctors in torture; defend imprisoned health professionals; prevent physical and psychological abuse of citizens by governments. Has conducted over 50 missions to more than 35 countries including Cambodia, Iraq, Kenya, Somalia, former Yugoslavia, and Haiti. Maintains speakers' bureau; conducts educational programs.

Founded: 1986. **Members:** 5,000. **Publications:** Medical Action Alert, monthly; Medical Testimony on Victims of Torture: A Physician's Guide to Political Asylum Cases Book; Record, 3/year. **Formerly:** (1987) American Committee for Human Rights.

★3496★
Plan of Action for Challenging Times
PACT-Educ. Opportunities Clearinghouse
635 Divisadero St.
San Francisco, CA 94117   Ph: (415)922-2550

Description: Program to benefit minority and/or low-income students who have not, in most cases, utilized their educational potential by reason of circumstances inherent in their background, mainly lack of encouragement, motivation, and finances. Students must be citizens or permanent residents of the U.S. Serves the city and county of San Francisco, CA; African-Americans represent the greatest percentage of students served. Assists Mexican-Americans, Asians, Native Americans, and low-income Caucasians. Students are identified through agency, school, and community referrals offering counseling services, college and financial aid information, and college admissions procedures. Provides college admissions, financial aid, and career counseling services; offers assistance with application forms; organizes campus visits, meetings between college recruiters and students, and visits to corporations and public institutions to observe various professions; conducts financial aid workshops; sponsors presentations to organizations, churches, and clubs. PACT has developed a screening process and a system of commitments from colleges. Supported by U.S. Department of Education under Educational Talent Search Program. **Founded:** 1966.

★3497★
Political Rights Defense Fund
New York, NY 10003

Description: To provide legal defense for persons who have been denied their constitutionally guaranteed civil liberties. Opposes governmental and corporate victimization of persons based on their political beliefs and backgrounds. Opposes government spying, harassment, and disruption of labor unions, civil rights groups, and socialist activists. Opposes: the use of wiretaps, bugs, burglaries, and informants; deportation of foreign-born students and workers whose ideas differ from those of the U.S. government; the firing of persons for their political views or activities. Has directed efforts toward the Socialist Workers Party v. the Attorney General of the United States lawsuit which challenges the U.S. government's alleged use of illegal methods to gather information to be used against socialists and political activists; the court found in favor of the SWP, though the ruling is now under appeal. **Founded:** 1973. **Local Groups:** 45.

★3498★
The Prejudice Institute/Center for the Applied Study of Ethnoviolence
2743 Maryland Ave.
Baltimore, MD 21218   Ph: (410)830-2435

Description: Purpose is to study and respond to the problems of prejudice, discrimination, conflict, and violence. Collects, analyzes, produces, and disseminates information and materials on programs of prevention and response. Conducts research on the causes and prevalence of prejudice and violence and their effects on victims and society; provides technical assistance to public agencies, voluntary organizations, schools, and communities in conflict; analyzes and drafts model legislation; conducts educational and training programs. **Founded:** 1984. **Publications:** Bigotry and Cable TV Report; Campus Ethnoviolence and the Policy Options Report; Community Response to Bias Crimes and Incidents; The Ecology of Anti-Gay Violence,Artical hnoviolence at Work Report; Ethnoviolence in the Workplace: Summary of Major Findings. **Formerly:** Center for the Applied Study of Prejudice and Ethnoviolence; (1986) Institute for Prevention and Control of Violence and Extremism.

★3499★
Rural Coalition
PO Box 5199
Arlington, VA 22205   Ph: (703)534-1845

Description: Organizations and individuals concerned with issues directly affecting low income and disadvantaged rural Americans. Objective is to work for effective public policies and to develop a strong rural constituency for progressive change to benefit rural people. Subscribes to the following principles: justice and equal opportunity regardless of sex, race, or place of residence; availability of goods and services essential to a decent quality of life; control and use of resources by rural people; development of rural, community-based organizations. Works through grass roots task forces on agriculture, employment, community development, military intrusion, national policy, American Indian, and natural resources issues. Provides technical assistance and information to local and regional groups. **Founded:** 1978. **Members:** 145. **Regional Groups:** 30. **Local Groups:** 90. **Publications:** Minority Land Loss Study; National Rural Agenda; Northern Cheyenne Groundwater Study; Rural Poverty in Perspective; Saturn - a Case Study of Industrial Recruitment in Rural America; Update Newsletter, quarterly.

★3500★
Section of Individual Rights and Responsibilities
750 N. Lake Shore Dr.
Chicago, IL 60611   Ph: (312)988-5000

Description: A section of the American Bar Association. Lawyers, law students, and other individuals. Concentrates on law and public policy as they relate to civil and constitutional rights, civil liberties, and human rights in the United States and internationally. Projects include representation of the homeless, people with AIDS, and those facing capital sentences. Administers ABA International Human Rights Trial Observer Project. **Founded:** 1967. **Members:** 4,000. **Publications:** Human Rights Magazine, quarterly; Newsletter, semiannual.

★3501★
Society for the Study of Indigenous Languages of the Americas
Humboldt State University
Native American Studies
Arcata, CA 95521   Ph: (707)826-4324

Description: All persons interested in the scientific study of the languages of the native peoples of North, Central, and South America. Promotes the study of indigenous linguistics in the Americas. **Founded:** 1981. **Members:** 850. **Publications:** Indigenous Languages of the Americas Monograph; Learning Aids; SSILA Newsletter, quarterly; Directory, annual.

★3502★
South and Meso-American Indian Information Center
PO Box 28703
Oakland, CA 94604   Ph: (510)834-4263

Description: Provides information about the problems currently facing Indians in South and Central America and Mexico. (These problems include the increasing control of agriculture in the region by large corporations and the damage done to the Amazonian rainforest environment by developers and others.) Encourages interchange between Indian organizations in North, Central and South America; coordinates visits of leaders of Indian nations of Mexico, South and Central America. Broadcasts South and Central American Indian Update (radio program). **Founded:** 1983. **Members:** 1,500. **Publications:** ABYA YALA News Journal, quarterly; Daughters of Abya Yala: Testimonies of Indian Women Organizing Throughout the Continent; 1992 International Directory and Resource Guide for 500 Years of Resistance, Directory; Film; Reports. **Formerly:** (1985) South American Indian Information Center; (1988) South and Central American Indian Information Center.

★3503★
Southwest Voter Registration Education Project
403 E. Commerce, Ste. 220   Ph: (210)222-0224
San Antonio, TX 78205   Free: 800-404-VOTE

Description: Church, civic, labor, and fraternal groups that organize coalitions to register minority voters in the southwest and 13 western states. Conducts nonpartisan voter education projects and research on Hispanic and Native American political organization participation in the southwest. Seeks reapportionment of gerrymandered counties and cities. Trains regional coordinators for voter registration campaigns. Compiles statistics. **Founded:** 1975. **Publications:** National Hispanic Voter Registration Campaign; Newsletters, bimonthly; Reports, bimonthly.

★3504★
Survival International, U.S.A.
2121 Decatur Pl. NW
Washington, DC 20008   Ph: (202)265-1077

Description: Individuals concerned with the rights of tribal peoples. Supports tribal groups in their efforts towards self-determination; helps them protect their lands, environment, and way of life. **Founded:** 1979. **Members:** 1,100. **Publications:** Survival International News, semiannual.

★3505★
Tekakwitha Conference National Center
PO Box 67 68
Great Falls, MT 59406-6768   Ph: (406)727-0147

Description: Catholic missionaries among American Indians; Eskimo and American Indian deacons and laypersons involved in ministry. Develops Catholic evangelization in the areas of Native American ministry, catechesis, liturgy, family life, evangelical liberation, ecumenical cooperation, and urban ministry, spirituality, and theology. Provides a forum for the exchange of ideas among Catholic Native Americans, Eskimos, and missionaries. Encourages development of Native American ministry by Indian people and attempts to assure Native American representation in the decision-making bodies of the church. **Founded:** 1939. **Members:** 12,000. **Regional Groups:** 3. **Publications:** Cross and Feather News, quarterly.

★3506★
Thunderbird American Indian Dancers
c/o Louis Mofsie
McBurney YMCA
215 W. 23rd St.
New York, NY 10011   Ph: (201)587-9633

Description: Indians and non-Indians who raise money for the Thunderbird Indian Scholarship Fund for Indian Students. Offers cultural classes in crafts, singing, dancing, and language. Sponsors Indian studies program for Indian youngsters. **Founded:** 1956. **Members:** 30.

★3507★
Traditions for Tomorrow
PO Box 5835, J.F.K. Sta.
Boston, MA 02114

Description: Serves to protect and promote the cultural environments of indigenous populations, supporting their efforts to strengthen their cultural identities. Acts as a partner with indigenous communities, proposing cultural projects through fund raising initiatives and assisting communities in social organization, so that they may be fully responsible for their own development. Contributes to international development awareness building among international, national, non-governmental organizations and the press; participates in discussion and debate on the objectives and means for international development as it relates to indigenous populations. Maintains that development should be founded on two preliminary principles: that it contributes to the development of cultural identity among indigenous communities and does not infringe on their traditional modes of expression; that it allows communities full responsibility for their own future development, thus asserting the right to dignity of indigenous populations.

★3508★
United Indians of All Tribes Foundation
Daybreak Star Arts Center
Discovery Park
PO Box 99100
Seattle, WA 98199   Ph: (206)285-4425
Description: Provides social, cultural, and educational services to the urban Native American Community owns and operates the Daybreak Star Indian Cultural Center which houses the permanent art collection of the foundation. Hosts yearly cultural activities for the native and non-native American community. **Founded:** 1970. **Members:** 13. **Publications:** Daybreak Star Press Magazine, monthly.

★3509★
United National Indian Tribal Youth
4010 Lincoln Blvd., Ste. 202
PO Box 25042
Oklahoma City, OK 73125   Ph: (405)424-3010
Description: Youth councils and individuals. Strives to foster the spiritual, mental, physical, and social development of American Indian and Alaska Native youth and to help build a strong, unified, and self-reliant Native America through involvement of its youth. Works to combat negative peer pressure and develop and use talents of Native youth. Conducts youth leadership seminars; assists in the development of tribal, village, and community youth councils; helps youth to formally voice their concerns and opinions at Congressional and Senate hearings. Sponsors Unity Network and National UNITY Council. **Founded:** 1976. **Members:** 168. **Publications:** Unity News Newspaper, quarterly.

★3510★
United Native Americans
2434 Faria Ave.
Pinole, CA 94564
Description: Indians and interested non-Indians. Purposes are to: promote the general welfare of Americans; find employment; provide legal aid, housing, food, lodging, and counseling for Indians. Aided in establishing Native American studies program at University of California at Berkeley. Maintains speakers' bureau. Sells historical posters of Indians. **Founded:** 1968. **Members:** 12,000. **Local Groups:** 18. **Publications:** Warpath, monthly.

★3511★
Women of All Red Nations
4511 N. Hermitage
Chicago, IL 60640
Description: Seeks to empower Native American women through education and advocacy programs. Provides a forum for members to express concerns and exchange information. **Founded:** 1990. **Members:** 25. **Publications:** WARN Newsletter; Newsletter, monthly.

★3512★
World Emergency Relief
2075 Corte Del Norgal Ste. S
Carlsbad, CA 92009   Ph: (760)930-8001
Description: Promotes micro-economic development and institutional advancement for Native Americans and underdeveloped countries. Provides domestic and international emergency relief and orphan support services. **Publications:** World Report; Newsletter, quarterly.

Regional, State/Provincial, & Local Organizations

─────── **Alabama** ───────

★3513★
Birmingham Urban League
PO Box 11269
Birmingham, AL 35202   Ph: (205)326-0162
Ms. Laquita S. Bell, Exec.Dir.
Description: Seeks to assist, encourage, and engage in activities designed to improve the economic and social conditions of minorities in Jefferson county, AL. Provides housing, education, job training, and employment opportunities. **Affiliated With:** National Urban League.

★3514★
American Civil Liberties Union, Alabama Affiliate
207 Montgomery St Ste 825   Ph: (205)262-0304
Montgomery, AL 36104   Fax: (205)269-5666
Olivia Turner, Contact.

★3515★
Alabama Coalition for Equity
14131 Market St.
Moulton, AL 35650-1415
DeWayne W. Key, Exec. Officer.

─────── **Alaska** ───────

★3516★
American Civil Liberties Union, Alaska Affiliate
PO Box 201844   Ph: (907)258-0044
Anchorage, AK 99520   Fax: (907)258-0288
Description: Individuals united to protect civil rights as guaranteed by the Bill of Rights of the U.S. Constitution and the Declaration of Rights of the Alaska State Constitution.

★3517★
United Minority Coalition
Box 020014
Juneau, AK 99802   Ph: (907)780-6739
Ben E. Holganza, Pres.
Description: Asians, blacks, hispanics, and other minorities in Alaska united to promote community development. Organizes Martin Luther King, Jr. Day activities.

─────── **Arizona** ───────

★3518★
American Civil Liberties Union of Arizona
PO Box 17148
Phoenix, AZ 85011   Ph: (602)650-1967
Louis L. Rhodes, Exec. Officer.

★3519★
Arizona Human Rights Funds
40 N Central, Ste. 2700
Phoenix, AZ 85004-0000

★3520★
Arizonans for Fairness Coalition
PO Box 34766
Phoenix, AZ 85067-4766   Ph: (602)258-7985
Michele Hallet, Contact

★3521★
American Civil Liberties Union, Tempe-Mesa Chapter
1008 East Concorda Dr.
Tempe, AZ 85282   Ph: (602)966-7039
William Wootten, Chairperson
Description: Champions the rights of people set forth in the Declaration of Independence and the Constitution of the United States. **Affiliated With:** American Civil Liberties Union.

★3522★
Amnesty International Group 88
PO Box 44120
Tucson, AZ 85733-4120   Ph: (602)323-0164
Richard Smyer, Coord.
Description: Individuals in southern Arizona interested in the protection of human rights. Promotes research, publicity, and lobbying on human rights. Sponsors annual Peace Fair and semiannual street fairs. **Affiliated With:** Amnesty International of the U.S.A..

★3523★
Tucson Urban League
2305 South Park Ave.   Ph: (602)791-9522
Tucson, AZ 85713   Fax: (602)623-9364
Ray Clarke, Pres./CEO
Description: Individuals working to promote and protect civil rights and liberties, especially in the areas of housing and employment. **Affiliated With:** National Urban League.

─────────── **Arkansas** ───────────

★3524★
American Civil Liberties Union of Arkansas
103 W. Capitol, Ste. 1120
Little Rock, AR 72201-5727   Ph: (501)374-2660
Rita Spillenger, Exec.Dir.
Description: Champions the rights of people set forth in the Declaration of Independence and the Constitution of the U.S. **Affiliated With:** American Civil Liberties Union.

★3525★
Urban League of Arkansas
2200 Main St.
PO Box 164039
Little Rock, AR 72216-4039   Ph: (501)372-3037
Mrs. J. Sandra Key, Pres.-CEO
Description: Promotes the protection of equal rights and opportunities for minorities. Sponsors annual Equal Opportunity Week Observance events. Conducts charitable activities. **Affiliated With:** National Urban League.

─────────── **California** ───────────

★3526★
California Native Circle
P.O. Box 513
Covelo, CA 95428

★3527★
Amnesty International, U.S.A., Southern California
900 W Washington Blvd.
Culver City, CA 90232   Ph: (310)815-0450

★3528★
Fontana Native American Center
PO Box 1258
Fontana, CA 92334-1258

★3529★
Fresno Minority Business Development Center
4944 E Clinton Way Ste 103
Fresno, CA 93727-1527   Ph: (209)252-7551

★3530★
Orange County Urban League
12391 Lewis St., No. 102
Garden Grove, CA 92640-3241   Ph: (714)748-9976

★3531★
Hollywood-Mid Los Angeles Fair Housing Council
7080 Hollywood Blvd., No. 816   Ph: (213)464-1141
Hollywood, CA 90028   Fax: (213)464-7756
Debra Rodriguez, Exec.Dir.
Description: Civil rights organizations investigating housing discrimination. Conducts charitable activities. Provides counseling on landlord-tenant rights and responsibilities.

★3532★
American Civil Liberties Union of Southern California
1616 Beverly Blvd.   Ph: (213)977-9500
Los Angeles, CA 90026-5752   Fax: (213)250-3919
Description: Individuals promoting the protection of civil rights and liberties. Advocates on behalf of public interest law. **Affiliated With:** American Civil Liberties Union.

★3533★
Californians Against Discrimination and Preferences
777 S Figueroa St., Ste. 3400
Los Angeles, CA 90017-5834

★3534★
Center for Human Rights and Constitutional Law
256 South Occidental Blvd.
Los Angeles, CA 90057   Ph: (213)388-8693
Peter Schey, Exec.Dir.

★3535★
Ethnic Coalition of Southern California, USC Civic and Community Relations
835 W 34th St. No. 102
Los Angeles, CA 90089-0751   Ph: (213)740-5480

★3536★
Golden State Minority Federation
1999 W Adams Blvd.
Los Angeles, CA 90018   Ph: (213)731-7771

★3537★
Indian Diamond and Colorstone Association
550 S Hill St., Ste. 1395
Los Angeles, CA 90013-2414

★3538★
Multi-Racial Americans of Southern California
12228 Venice Blvd., Ste. 452
Los Angeles, CA 90066-3814   Ph: (310)836-1535
Roberta Brown, Pres.
Description: Parents of multiracial children, multiracial adults, interracial, intercultural, and interfaith couples, and families that have adopted transracially. Seeks to broaden self and public understanding of society by facilitating interethnic dialogue and providing cultural, educational, and recreational activities.

★3539★
Westside Fair Housing Council
1849 Surtelle Blvd., No. 670   Ph: (310)477-9260
Los Angeles, CA 90025   Fax: (310)475-9326
Kathryn Divine, Exec.Dir.
Description: Individuals in Culver City, Gardena, Redondo Beach, West Hollywood, Inglewood and West Los Angeles, CA dedicated to equal housing opportunities and an end to discrimination in the marketing, rental, and sale of housing.

★3540★
American Civil Liberties Union, Santa Clara Valley
  Chapter
PO Box 215
Los Gatos, CA 95031   Ph: (408)293-2584
Christine Beraldo, Chairperson
Description: Champions the rights of people set forth in the
Declaration of Independence and the Constitution of the U.S.
Affiliated With: American Civil Liberties Union.

★3541★
Human Rights Association
32 Eucalyptus Knoll
Mill Valley, CA 94941-2258

★3542★
All Tribes Cultural Arts Program
PO Box 8813
Moreno Valley, CA 92552-8813
Russell R. Drew, Contact.

★3543★
American Civil Liberties Union, Marin Chapter
PO Box 434
Novato, CA 94948   Ph: (415)453-0222
Description: Seeks to protect the rights of people set forth in the
Declaration of Independence and the Constitution. **Affiliated With:**
American Civil Liberties Union.

★3544★
Bay Area Urban League
2201 Broadway Ave.   Ph: (510)271-1846
Oakland, CA 94612-3593   Fax: (510)839-8109
Walter Brame, Pres.
Description: Individuals, organizations, and corporations in the
Oakland, CA area promoting equal opportunity in education,
employment, housing, and health and welfare services. **Affiliated
With:** National Urban League.

★3545★
Minorities Alcoholic Treatment Alternative
1315 Fruitvale Ave.
Oakland, CA 94601   Ph: (510)261-7120
Regina Chavarin, Exec.Dir.

★3546★
Minority Contractors Association of Northern
  California
825 Eighth Ave.
Oakland, CA 94606   Ph: (415)763-2330

★3547★
National Committee for Responsive Philanthropy,
  California Chapter
Bay Area Black United Fund   Ph: (510)763-7270
1300 Clay St., Ste. 330   Free: 800-533-
Oakland, CA 94612   WECA
                              Fax: (510)763-1155
Cheryl Garner-Shaw, Exec.Dir.
Description: Works to improve the quality of life in minority
communities by providing financial, volunteer, and technical
assistance to community-based agencies. **Publications:** none.

★3548★
American Civil Liberties Union, Monterey County
  Chapter
PO Box 1112
Pacific Grove, CA 93950   Ph: (408)622-9894
Richard Criley, Exec.Dir.
Description: Champions the rights of people set forth in the
Declaration of Independence and the Constitution of the U.S.
Publications: none. **Affiliated With:** American Civil Liberties
Union.

★3549★
Greater Riverside Area Urban League
2060 University Ave., No. 203   Ph: (909)682-2766
Riverside, CA 92507   Fax: (909)682-2318
Yolanda Nava, Interim Exec.Dir.
Description: Works to secure equality of economic opportunity for
minorities and disadvantaged people. Operates Project Star for at-
risk youth between the ages of 14 and 21. Maintains Leadership
Development Institute for minority males.

★3550★
Children's Alternative Learning Program
PO Box 506
Rodeo, CA 94572-0506

★3551★
Sacramento Urban League
4900 Broadway No.1600   Ph: (916)368-3280
Sacramento, CA 95820-1531   Fax: (916)368-3293
James C. Shelby, Pres./CEO.

★3552★
American Civil Liberties Union of San Diego and
  Imperial Counties
PO Box 87131   Ph: (619)232-2121
San Diego, CA 92138-7131   Fax: (619)232-0036
Linda Hills, Exec.Dir.
Description: Champions the rights of people set forth in the Bill of
Rights and the Constitution of the U.S. **Affiliated With:** American
Civil Liberties Union.

★3553★
San Diego Urban League
4261 Market St.   Ph: (619)263-3115
San Diego, CA 92102   Fax: (619)263-3660
John W. Johnson, Pres. & CEO
Description: Assists African-Americans and other people of color in
achieving economic and social equality. Provides employment,
training, health care, and housing assistance.

★3554★
American Civil Liberties Union of Northern California
1663 Mission St., Ste. 460   Ph: (415)621-2488
San Francisco, CA 94103   Fax: (415)255-1478
Dorothy M. Ehrlich, Exec.Dir.
Description: Champions the rights of people set forth in the
Declaration of Independence and the Constitution of the U.S.
Sponsors forums, debates, and radio shows. **Affiliated With:**
American Civil Liberties Union.

★3555★
Amnesty International, U.S.A., Northern California
500 Sansome St., No. 615
San Francisco, CA 94111   Ph: (415)291-9233

★3556★
Coalition for Civil Rights
1663 Mission St., Ste. 550
San Francisco, CA 94103   Ph: (415)621-0672

★3557★
Colombia Human Rights Information Committee
PO Box 40155
San Francisco, CA 94140   Fax: (415)206-1326
Description: North Americans and Colombians united to inform the
public about human rights violations in Colombia. Maintains
speakers' bureau. Conducts cultural events and educational
programs.

★3558★
Santa Clara Valley Urban League
75 S. 20th St.
San Jose, CA 95116-2216   Ph: (408)971-0117
Susan Logan, Interim Exec.Dir.

★3559★
California Council for the Defense of Freedom
2679 E California Blvd.
San Marino, CA 91108-1404

★3560★
Human Rights Resource Center
615 B St.
San Rafael, CA 94901   Ph: (415)453-0404
Luther Wallace, Exec.Dir.

Description: Community-based agency serving law enforcement agencies, educational agencies, nonprofit organizations, and businesses in Marin County and the greater Bay area of California. Works to end discrimination based on race, gender, age, sexual preference, or national origin. Encourages respect for cultural diversity and indivi dual differences; promotes the right of everyone to social and economic justice. Maintains speakers' bureau.

★3561★
American Civil Liberties Union, Singles Chapter
8435 Burnet Ave., No. 104
Sepulveda, CA 91343   Ph: (818)893-2276
Myron Faverman, Exec. Officer

Description: Single civil libertarians in the Los Angeles, CA area. Provides civil rights education and social activities. **Affiliated With:** American Civil Liberties Union.

★3562★
American Civil Liberties Union, Mid-Peninsula Chapter
PO Box 3676
Stanford, CA 94305   Ph: (415)328-0732
Iris Barrie, Chm.

Description: Champions the rights of people set forth in the U.S. Bill of Rights. Provides legal services in defense of civil liberties. **Affiliated With:** American Civil Liberties Union.

————— **Colorado** —————

★3563★
Pikes Peak Minority Business Foundation
2140 D Academy Circle
Colorado Springs, CO 80909-0000

★3564★
Urban League of the Pikes Peak Region
125 N. Parkside Dr.
PO Box 1979
Colorado Springs, CO 80901-1979   Ph: (719)634-1525
                                         Fax: (719)634-3357
Description: Works to promote and protect civil rights and liberties, especially in the areas of housing and employment. **Affiliated With:** National Urban League.

★3565★
American Civil Liberties Union, Colorado Affiliate
400 Corona St.   Ph: (303)777-5482
Denver, CO 80218   Fax: (303)777-1773
James Joy, Exec.Dir.

★3566★
American Civil Liberties Union Foundation
511 16th St., Ste. 300
Denver, CO 80202   Ph: (303)893-4163
Stephen Pevar, Staff Council.

★3567★
American Civil Liberties Union, Mountain States
6825 E Tennessee Ave., Ste. 530   Ph: (303)321-4828
Denver, CO 80224   Fax: (303)321-4851

★3568★
American Civil Liberties Union, Mountain States Chapter
511 16th St. Ste, 300   Ph: (303)321-4828
Denver, CO 80202-4228   Fax: (303)321-4851
Dorothy Davidson, Exec.Dir.

★3569★
Colorado Alliance to Restore Equality
1625 Broadway, Ste. 2450
Denver, CO 80202-4722

★3570★
Urban League of Metropolitan Denver
1525 Josephine St.
Denver, CO 80206   Ph: (303)388-5861
Thomas B. Jenkins, Pres. & CEO

Description: Individuals and corporations organized to provide social services to those in need.

★3571★
Jeffco Citizens for Human Rights
PO Box 261112
Lakewood, CO 80226-9112

————— **Connecticut** —————

★3572★
Minority Entrepreneurs Network Association
955 Connecticut Ave.
Bridgeport, CT 06607-1200

★3573★
Minority Business Association of Greater Danbury
51-1/2 Maple Ave.
Danbury, CT 06810-5806

★3574★
American Civil Liberties Union, Connecticut
32 Grand St.   Ph: (203)247-9823
Hartford, CT 06106   Fax: (203)728-0287

★3575★
Connecticut Civil Liberties Union
32 Grand St.   Ph: (203)247-9823
Hartford, CT 06106   Fax: (203)728-0287
Joseph S. Grabarz Jr., Exec.Dir.

Description: Seeks to protect rights of citizens as described in the U.S. Constitution and Bill of Rights. Maintains Connecticut Civil Liberties Union Foundation. **Affiliated With:** American Civil Liberties Union.

★3576★
Urban League of Greater New Haven
1 State St.
New Haven, CT 06511-5707   Ph: (203)624-4168
Martha Wright, Interim Dir.

★3577★
Urban League of Southwestern Connecticut
46 Atlantic St.
Stamford, CT 06901   Ph: (203)356-7784
Dr. Curtiss E. Porter, Pres./CEO

Description: Works to eliminate racial segregation and discrimination in southwestern CT.

★3578★
Nipmuc Indian Association of Connecticut
PO Box 411
Thompson, CT 06277-0411

Delaware

★3579★
American Civil Liberties Union of Delaware
First Federal Plaza
702 King St., Ste. 600A
Wilmington, DE 19801
Max Bell, Pres.

Ph: (302)654-3966
Fax: (302)654-3689

Description: Provides public education on civil liberties guaranteed by the U.S. Constitution and other statutory rights. Recruits attorneys for litigation for civil liberties cases for people unable to afford counsel. Provides informal legal counseling. **Affiliated With:** American Civil Liberties Union.

★3580★
Minority Business Association of Delaware
PO Box 9751
Wilmington, DE 19809-0751

Description: Represents members' interests; conducts lobbying activities. Holds seminars and workshops.

District of Columbia

★3581★
American Civil Liberties Union of the National Capital Area
1400 20th St. NW, Ste. 119
Washington, DC 20036

Ph: (202)457-0800

Description: Champions the rights of people as set forth in the Bill of Rights and the Constitution. Cases that occur in the District of Columbia and Prince George's or Montgomery County, Maryland. **Affiliated With:** American Civil Liberties Union.

★3582★
Amnesty International U.S.A., Mid-Atlantic Region
1118 22nd St. NW
Washington, DC 20037
Jodi Lango, Regional Dir.

Ph: (202)775-5161
Fax: (202)775-5992

Description: Human rights organization serving Washington DC, Maryland, Virginia, Pennsylvania, Delaware, and West Virginia. Works for the immediate and unconditional release of prisoners of conscience; for fair and prompt trials for political prisoners; and for an end to torture, executions, political killings, and disappearances. **Affiliated With:** Amnesty International of the U.S.A..

★3583★
District of Columbia Department of Human Rights and Minority Business Development
441 4th St. NW, Ste. 970N
Washington, DC 20009

Ph: (202)724-1385
Fax: (202)724-3786

★3584★
District of Columbia Student Coalition Against Apartheid and Racism
PO Box 18291
Washington, DC 20036
Raynard T. Davis, Exec.Dir.

Ph: (202)483-4593
Fax: (202)328-3369

Description: Students and youths in the Washington, DC area united to oppose racism in the United States and Apartheid in South Africa. Sponsors educational, children's, and research programs; conducts workshops and anti-racism seminars. Develops community grassroots groups; networks with national and international organizations; writes and distributes literature. Maintains speakers' bureau.

★3585★
Washington Urban League
3501 14th St., NW
Washington, DC 20010

Ph: (202)265-8200

Florida

★3586★
American Civil Liberties Union, Palm Beach Chapter
28 Burning Tree Ln.
Boca Raton, FL 33431-3918
Sam Clark, Chm.

Ph: (407)833-8936

Description: Individuals in Martin and Palm Beach counties, FL seeking to protect rights granted to U.S. citizens under the Bill of Rights of the U.S. Constitution. **Affiliated With:** American Civil Liberties Union.

★3587★
Citizens Commission on Human Rights
512 Cleveland St., No. 103
Clearwater, FL 34615-4008

★3588★
Minority Builders Coalition of Broward County
771 NW 22nd Rd.
Ft. Lauderdale, FL 33311
Lloyd Brown, Pres.

Ph: (305)792-1121

★3589★
Sonny Billie Foundation for Native Culture Studies
6430 NE 21st Rd.
Ft. Lauderdale, FL 33308-1060

★3590★
Urban League of Broward County
Romart Bldg.
11 NW 36th Ave.
Ft. Lauderdale, FL 33311

Ph: (305)584-0777

★3591★
First Coast United Against Discrimination
PO Box 3795
Jacksonville, FL 32206-0795

★3592★
American Civil Liberties Union, Florida Affiliate
225 NE 34th St., No. 102
Miami, FL 33137
Robyn Blumner, Exec.Dir.

Ph: (305)576-2336
Fax: (305)576-1106

Description: Protects and defends constitutional rights through litigation, public education, and lobbying. **Affiliated With:** American Civil Liberties Union.

★3593★
Miami Equity Associates
8603 S Dixie Hwy., Ste. 304
Miami, FL 33143-7807

★3594★
Urban League of Greater Miami
8500 NW 25th Ave.
Miami, FL 33147

Ph: (305)696-4450

★3595★
Keewaydin Institute
260 Bay Rd.
Naples, FL 33940-7950

★3596★
Metropolitan Orlando Urban League
2512 W. Colonial Dr.
Orlando, FL 32804
Shirley J. Boykin, Pres.

Ph: (407)841-7654
Fax: (407)841-0360

Description: Seeks to enable minority and disadvantaged people in central Florida to fully participate in the social and economic life of the community.

★3597★
Pinellas County Urban League
333 31st St. S.
St. Petersburg, FL 33713   Ph: (813)327-2081
Description: Civic, professional, business, labor, and religious leaders working to eliminate racial segregation and discrimination and to achieve parity for blacks and other minorities in all areas of life. **Affiliated With:** National Urban League.

★3598★
Tallahassee Urban League
923 Bainbridge Rd.
Tallahassee, FL 32303   Ph: (904)222-6111

★3599★
American Civil Liberties Union, Greater Tampa Chapter
PO Box 1481
Tampa, FL 33601-1481   Ph: (813)237-8182
Roger A. Sanderson, Chair
Description: Attorneys and other individuals interested in promoting and defending civil liberties in Hernando, Hillsborough, Sumter, Pasco, and Polk counties, Florida. **Affiliated With:** American Civil Liberties Union.

★3600★
Hillsborough Organization for Progress and Equality
1702 Ave. Republica de Cuba
Tampa, FL 33605

★3601★
Tampa-Hillsborough Urban League
1405 Tampa Park Plaza   Ph: (813)229-8117
Tampa, FL 33605   Fax: (813)221-4937
Description: Civic and fraternal organizations, corporations, religious institutions, and students interested in promoting civil rights and equal opportunities. Offers youth/parent training and housing, employment. **Affiliated With:** National Urban League.

★3602★
Palm Beach County Human Rights Council
333 Colonial Rd.
West Palm Beach, FL 33405-4335

★3603★
Palm Beach County Urban League
1700 N. Australian Ave.
West Palm Beach, FL 33407   Ph: (407)833-1461

★3604★
Urban League of Palm Beach County
1700 Australian Ave.
West Palm Beach, FL 33407   Ph: (407)833-1461
Percy H. Lee, Pres.
Description: Attorneys, corporations, and county employees. Promotes equal opportunity for all residents. **Affiliated With:** National Urban League.

★3605★
American Civil Liberties Union, Central Florida Chapter
PO Box 3084
Winter Park, FL 32790   Ph: (407)539-0615
Warren Keiner, Chm.
Description: Works to protect and defend the civil rights and liberties of individuals in Lake, Orange, Osceola, and Seminole counties, FL.

─────────── **Georgia** ───────────

★3606★
Minority Enterprise in Clarke County Athens
1127 W. Hancock Ave.
Athens, GA 30606-3029   Ph: (706)543-5513
Sharon B. Pickett Atty., Chief Admin. Officer
Description: Promotes success of minority-owned businesses in the Athens, GA area. Offers a technical assistance program and an economic development loan program in conjunction with Athens First Bank and Trust Company.

★3607★
American Civil Liberties Union, Georgia Affiliate
142 Mitchell St. SW, No. 301   Ph: (404)523-5398
Atlanta, GA 30303   Fax: (404)577-0181
Teresa Nelson, Exec.Dir.
Description: Works to defend the civil liberties of the people in Georgia. **Affiliated With:** American Civil Liberties Union.

★3608★
American Civil Liberties Union, Southern Regional Office
44 Forsyth St. NW, Ste. 202   Ph: (404)523-2721
Atlanta, GA 30303   Fax: (404)653-0331
Laughlin McDonald, Dir.

★3609★
Atlanta Urban League
100 Edgewood Ave. NE, Ste. 600
Atlanta, GA 30303   Ph: (404)659-1150
Description: Business, political, and religious leaders. Works to eliminate racism and discrimination and to achieve parity for blacks and other minorities in all areas of life.

★3610★
Augusta Minority Business Development Center
1394 Lancy-Walker Blvd.   Ph: (706)722-0994
Augusta, GA 30901   Fax: (706)722-1730
Kelley McKie, Dir.
Description: Minority business owners. Provides management and technical assistance to minority businesses. Sponsors Minority Entrepreneur Development Week. Conducts charitable activities. **Publications:** none.

★3611★
Central Savannah River Area Business League
1394 Larry-Walker Blvd.   Ph: (706)722-0994
Augusta, GA 30901   Fax: (706)722-1730
Mr. Clarence Baylor, Pres.
Description: Local business people, officials, corporations, and interested individuals. Advocates and promotes economic development for the minority business community. Operates the Augusta Minority Business Development Center (AMBDC) and a local revolving loan fund for minority businesses. Conducts charitable activities. Sponsors Minority Entrepreneur Development Week, Black Expo activities, and an annual awards banquet. **Publications:** none. **Affiliated With:** National Business League.

★3612★
Columbus Urban League
806 1st Ave.
Columbus, GA 31901   Ph: (404)323-3687

★3613★
Metro Columbus Urban League
802 1st Ave.   Ph: (706)323-3687
Columbus, GA 31901   Fax: (706)596-2144
Description: Membership organization committed to eliminating the effects of racism in the Greater Columbus area. **Affiliated With:** National Urban League.

★3614★
Citizens Commission of Human Rights
PO Box 1812
Tucker, GA 30085   Ph: (404)972-9077
Dwight Mathey, Exec. Officer.

─────────── **Hawaii** ───────────

★3615★
American Civil Liberties Union of Hawaii
PO Box 3410   Ph: (808)545-1722
Honolulu, HI 96801   Fax: (808)545-2993
Vanessa Y Chong, Dir.

─────────── **Idaho** ───────────

★3616★
American Civil Liberties Union of Idaho
PO Box 1897   Ph: (208)344-5243
Boise, ID 83701-1897   Fax: (208)344-7201
Jack Van Valkenburgh, Exec.Dir.

Description: Champions the rights of people set forth in the Constitution of the United States. **Affiliated With:** American Civil Liberties Union.

★3617★
Amnesty International, Boise Chapter
PO Box 7846
Boise, ID 83707   Ph: (208)345-3223
Kathryn C. Anderson, Membership Coord.

Description: Works for the release of prisoners of conscience. Supports fair and prompt trials for all political prisoners. Advocates an end to torture and execution of prisoners. Offers human rights education; operates speakers' bureau.

★3618★
Bonner County Human Rights Task Force
212 N 4th, Ste. 189
Sandpoint, ID 83864-1424

─────────── **Illinois** ───────────

★3619★
Madison County Urban League
210 William St.
PO Box 8093   Ph: (618)463-1906
Alton, IL 62002   Fax: (618)463-9021
Edward Hightower, Bd.Chm.

Description: To promote, encourage, assist, and engage in activities to improve the economic and social conditions of blacks and other minorities. **Publications:** none. **Affiliated With:** National Urban League.

★3620★
Quad County Urban League
808 E. Galena, Ste. B   Ph: (708)851-2203
Aurora, IL 60505   Fax: (708)851-2703
Theodia Gillespie, Pres.

Description: Multi-racial community-based organization seeking to secure equal opportunities for all disadvantaged persons and minorities. **Publications:** none. **Convention/Meeting:** none. **Affiliated With:** National Urban League.

★3621★
Urban League of Champaign County
17 Taylor St.
Champaign, IL 61820   Ph: (217)356-1364
Mr. Tracy Parsons, Pres. and CEO

Description: Works to eliminate racial prejudice and discrimination in Champaign County, IL.

★3622★
American Civil Liberties Union of Illinois
203 N. LaSalle, No. 1405   Ph: (312)201-9740
Chicago, IL 60601   Free: 800-572-1092
                              Fax: (312)201-9760
Jay A. Miller, Exec.Dir.

Description: Seeks to defend civil liberties and the Bill of Rights through litigation, lobbying and education. **Affiliated With:** American Civil Liberties Union.

★3623★
Amnesty International U.S.A., Midwest Regional Office
53 W. Jackson, Rm. 1162   Ph: (312)427-2060
Chicago, IL 60604-3507   Fax: (312)427-2589

Description: Individuals in the midwestern U.S. interested in promoting human rights throughout the world. Participates in letter writing campaigns. **Affiliated With:** Amnesty International of the U.S.A..

★3624★
Artists for Racial Unity
5701 S Woodlawn Ave.
Chicago, IL 60637-1602

★3625★
Chicago Urban League
4510 S. Michigan Ave.
Chicago, IL 60653   Ph: (312)285-5800
James W. Compton, Pres./CEO

Description: Strives to eliminate racial discrimination and segregration in Chicago, IL and works for the achievement of equal opportunity and parity for African-Americans, other minorities, and the poor. Focuses efforts on education, economic development, and community empowerment.

★3626★
Des Plaines Citizens Rights Committee
PO Box 2884
Des Plaines, IL 60017-2884

★3627★
Oak Park Housing Center
1041 South Blvd.   Ph: (708)848-7150
Oak Park, IL 60302   Fax: (708)848-7165
Roberta L. Raymond, Co.Exec.Dir.

Description: Individuals and corporations. Promotes fair housing and a racially diverse community. Provides counseling, liaison with real estate companies, and affirmative marketing programs; makes available housing referral services.

★3628★
Tri-County Urban League
317 S. MacArthur Hwy.
Peoria, IL 61605-3892   Ph: (309)673-7474
Frank Campbell, Exec.Dir.

★3629★
Hope Fair Housing Center
2100 Manchester Rd., Ste. 1070., Bldg B
Wheaton, IL 60187   Ph: (708)690-6500
Bernard J. Kleina, Exec.Dir.

Description: Acts as an advocate for minorities, families with children, the handicapped, and others experiencing housing discrimination. Seeks to increase the availability of affordable housing.

Indiana

★3630★
Ft. Wayne Urban League
227 E. Washington
Ft. Wayne, IN 46802　　　　Ph: (219)424-6326
Rick C. Frazier, Pres. & CEO

Description: To promote, encourage, assist, and engage in activities to improve the economic and social conditions of blacks and other minorities. Provides services in the areas of advocacy, education, employment, and economic development. Operates job assistance and placement program, senior community service program, and teen group. Sponsors annual Black college tour and College and Career Day. **Affiliated With:** National Urban League.

★3631★
Gary Minority Business Development Center
567 Broadway　　　　Ph: (219)883-5802
Gary, IN 46402　　　　Fax: (219)882-9042
Jeffrey Q. Williams, Contact

Description: Promotes establishment and prosperity of minority-owned businesses.

★3632★
American Civil Liberties Union of Indiana
445 N. Pennsylvania St., Ste. 911
Indianapolis, IN 46204　　　　Ph: (317)635-4056
Sheila Kennedy, Exec. Officer.

★3633★
American Civil Liberties Union, Indiana
445 N Pennsylvania St., Ste. 911　　Ph: (317)635-4056
Indianapolis, IN 46204　　　　Fax: (317)635-4105

★3634★
Indianapolis Urban League
850 N. Meridian St.　　　　Ph: (317)639-9404
Indianapolis, IN 46204　　　　Fax: (317)684-2183
Sam H. Jones, Pres.

★3635★
Marion Area Urban League
1221 W. 12th St.
Marion, IN 46953　　　　Ph: (317)664-3933
Cleo Richardson, Pres. & CEO

Description: Engages in activities to improve the economic and social conditions of blacks and other minorities in Grant County, IN. Sponsors ethnic festival and summer day camp. **Affiliated With:** National Urban League.

★3636★
Urban League of South Bend and St. Joseph County
914 Lincolnway W.
PO Box 4043　　　　Ph: (219)287-2800
South Bend, IN 46634-4043　　　Fax: (219)287-6073
Verge Gillam, Managing Dir.

Description: To promote, encourage, assist, and engage in activities to improve the economic and social conditions of blacks and other minorities. Emphasizes education, employment, health, housing, and family life. **Affiliated With:** National Urban League.

Iowa

★3637★
Peace Network, Cedar Rapids
4949 Council St., NE
Cedar Rapids, IA 52402　　　　Ph: (319)363-3927
John M. Ely Jr., Moderator

Description: To promote peace and the preservation of human rights. Sponsors public affairs forums and town meetings.

★3638★
American Civil Liberties Union, Iowa Chapter
Exchange Bldg.
446 Insurance　　　　Ph: (515)243-3576
Des Moines, IA 50309　　　Fax: (515)243-3988
Cryss D. Farley, Exec.Dir.

★3639★
Friends of the Des Moines Human Rights Commission
PO Box 93861
Des Moines, IA 50393-3861

★3640★
Free World Research
Box 458
Farnhamville, IA 50538-0458

★3641★
American Civil Liberties Union, Hawkeye Chapter
History Department
Cornell College
Mt. Vernon, IA 52314　　　　Ph: (319)895-4314
Robert D. Givens, Pres.

Description: Champions the rights of people set forth in the Declaration of Independence and the Constitution of the U.S. **Affiliated With:** American Civil Liberties Union.

Kansas

★3642★
Kansas Human Rights Commission
Landon State Off. Bldg. No. 851-S
Topeka, KS 66612　　　　Ph: (913)296-3206

★3643★
Wichita Urban League
1405 N. Minneapolis
Wichita, KS 67214　　　　Ph: (316)262-2463
Otis G. Milton, Pres.

Kentucky

★3644★
Minority Contractors Bond Assurance Fund of Kentucky
PO Box 490
Crestwood, KY 40014-0490

★3645★
ACT - Lexington
PO Box 11442
Lexington, KY 40575　　　　Ph: (606)281-5151
David C. Radez, Treas.

Description: Provides AIDS education, support, training, and referral. Coordinates and funds AIDS education for other community organizations. **Convention/Meeting:** none. **Publications:** none.

★3646★
Urban League of Lexington-Fayette County
167 W. Main St., Rm. 406　　　Ph: (606)233-1561
Lexington, KY 40507　　　　Fax: (606)233-7260
Porter G. Peeples, Pres./CEO.

★3647★
American Civil Liberties Union of Kentucky
425 W. Muhammad Ali Blvd., Ste. 230　Ph: (502)581-1181
Louisville, KY 40202　　　　Fax: (502)589-9687
Everett Hoffman, Exec.Dir.

Affiliated With: American Civil Liberties Union.

★3648★
Louisville Urban League
1535 W. Broadway
Louisville, KY 40203   Ph: (502)585-4622

Louisiana

★3649★
Baton Rouge Business Development Center
2036 Woodale Blvd., Ste. D   Ph: (504)924-0186
Baton Rouge, LA 70806   Fax: (504)924-0036
Warren O. Birkett Jr., Contact
Description: Provides management and technical services to minority-owned businesses.

★3650★
People's Organization for Social Equality
715 S Sibley   Ph: (504)464-1632
Metairie, LA 70003-6743   Fax: (504)464-1632
Richard Glass Jr.

★3651★
American Civil Liberties Union Louisiana Affiliate
PO Box 70496   Ph: (504)522-0617
New Orleans, LA 70172   Fax: (504)522-0618
Joe Cook, Exec.Dir.
Description: To protect individual freedom of speech, association, religion, protest, press, due proces of law and equal protection of the law among other embodied in the U.S. and state constitution without regard to ones social or economic status.

★3652★
Urban League of Greater New Orleans
1929 Blenville St.
New Orleans, LA 70112   Ph: (504)524-4667
Clarence L. Barney, Pres. & CEO
Description: Individuals interested in promoting and protecting civil rights and liberties for minorities, especially in the areas of employment and housing. **Affiliated With:** National Urban League.

★3653★
American Civil Liberties Union, Northwest Louisiana Chapter
PO Box 17   Ph: (318)954-1113
Shreveport, LA 71101   Fax: (318)954-0989
Description: Champions the rights of people set forth in the Declaration of Independence and Constitution of the United States.

Maine

★3654★
American Civil Liberties Union, Maine Affiliate
97A Exchange St.
Portland, ME 04101   Ph: (207)774-8087
Sally Sutton, Dir.

★3655★
Maine Civil Liberties Union
97A Exchange St.
Portland, ME 04101   Ph: (207)774-5444
Sally Sutton, Exec.Dir.
Description: Interested persons organized to promote civil liberties. Engages in lobbying, litigation, and education. **Affiliated With:** American Civil Liberties Union.

Maryland

★3656★
American Civil Liberties Union of Maryland
2219 St. Paul St.   Ph: (410)889-8555
Baltimore, MD 21218   Fax: (410)366-7838
Description: Organization dedicated to the protection of civil rights and civil liberties through litigation, lobbying, and public education. **Affiliated With:** American Civil Liberties Union.

★3657★
Baltimore Urban League
1150 Mondawmin Concourse
Baltimore, MD 21215   Ph: (301)523-8150
Description: Civic, professional, business, labor, and religious leaders working to eliminate racial segregation and discrimination and to achieve parity for blacks and other minorities in all areas of life. **Affiliated With:** National Urban League.

★3658★
Coalition for Open Doors
2219 St. Paul St.   Ph: (301)889-8555
Baltimore, MD 21218   Fax: (301)576-0937
Susan Goering, Dir.
Description: Individuals and groups in Maryland working to open private club membership to women and minorities.

★3659★
Airport Minority Advisory Council
4733 Bethesda Ave., Ste. 200A
Bethesda, MD 20814-5228

Massachusetts

★3660★
Belmont Against Racism
290 Payson Rd.
Belmont, MA 02178-3427   Ph: (617)489-2353
Douglas Reynolds, Pres.
Description: Works to end racism in the city of Belmont. **Publications:** none.

★3661★
American Civil Liberties Union, Massachussetts
99 Chauncey St., Ste. 310   Ph: (617)482-3170
Boston, MA 02111   Fax: (617)451-0009

★3662★
Massachusetts Minority Business Round Table
69 Neponset Ave.
Boston, MA 02122-3321
Albert Shaw, Exec. Officer.

★3663★
New England Alliance of Multiracial Families
14 Monument St.
Medford, MA 02155-6716

★3664★
Urban League of Eastern Massachusetts
88 Warren St.
Roxbury, MA 02119   Ph: (617)442-4519
Description: Individuals, corporations, and foundations. Offers employment placement and recruitment services and advocacy for youth and senior citizens. Issues publications. **Affiliated With:** National Urban League.

★3665★
Amnesty International, U.S.A., Northeast
58 Day St.
Somerville, MA 02144   Ph: (617)623-0202

★3666★
Worcester Minority Business Council
717 Main St.
Worcester, MA 01610-3164

Michigan

★3667★
American Civil Liberties Union, Michigan Chapter
1249 Washington Blvd., Ste. 2910   Ph: (313)961-4662
Detroit, MI 48226-1822   Fax: (313)961-9005
Howard Simon, Exec.Dir.

★3668★
Amnesty International U.S.A., Group 78
15769 Auburn
Detroit, MI 48223   Ph: (313)531-7647
Ken and Geraldine Grunow, Coordinators
Description: People who write letters of appeal to free prisoners of conscience. Advocates for fair and prompt trials for political prisoners and an end to torture and the death penalty in all cases. **Affiliated With:** Amnesty International of the U.S.A..

★3669★
Council of Urban League Executives
208 Mack Ave.   Ph: (313)832-4600
Detroit, MI 48201   Fax: (313)832-3222
N. Charles Anderson, Pres.
Description: Chief executive officers of Michigan affiliates of the National Urban League.

★3670★
Detroit Urban League
208 Mack Ave.   Ph: (313)832-4600
Detroit, MI 48201   Fax: (313)832-3222
N. Charles Anderson, Pres./CEO
Description: Works to enable African-Americans, and other minorities, to reach their full potential. Programs and services focus on the areas of employment, health and substance abuse, male and female responsibility, nutritional education, senior citizen development, and education. **Affiliated With:** National Urban League.

★3671★
Fair Housing Center of Metropolitan Detroit
1249 Washington Blvd., Ste. 1340
Detroit, MI 48226   Ph: (313)963-1274
Clifford C. Schrupp, Exec.Dir.
Description: Individuals and organizations supporting fair and equal housing in the Detroit, MI area.

★3672★
Michigan Coalition for Human Rights
4800 Woodward Ave.   Ph: (313)833-4407
Detroit, MI 48201-1399   Fax: (313)831-0259
Kathryn Savoie, Exec.Dir.
Description: Multiracial interfaith organization dedicated to providing resources for human rights issues, including South Africa, the death penalty, and racism. **Publications:** none. **Affiliated With:** Clergy and Laity Concerned.

★3673★
Michigan Minority Business Development Council
230 Fisher Bldg.
3011 W. Grand Blvd.   Ph: (313)873-3200
Detroit, MI 48202   Fax: (313)873-4783
Ronald E. Hall, Pres.
Description: Seeks to promote the minority business community by providing corporate members with qualified minority suppliers. Sponsors annual dinner and golf outing.

★3674★
Urban League of Flint Housing Center
202 East Boulevard Dr.
Flint, MI 48503   Ph: (313)239-2195
Melvin Brannon, Dir.

★3675★
Grand Rapids Urban League
745 Eastern St. SE   Ph: (616)245-2207
Grand Rapids, MI 49503   Fax: (616)245-6510
Walter M. Brame, Pres.
Description: No further information was available for this edition
Affiliated With: National Urban League.

★3676★
Greater Lansing Urban League
300 N. Washington Sq., Ste. 100   Ph: (517)487-3608
Lansing, MI 48933   Fax: (517)487-3625
Mr. Cleophus Boyd Jr., Exec.Dir.
Description: Works to eliminate racial segregation and discrimination in Lansing, MI. Conducts charitable activities. Employment development through skills training and referrals. **Affiliated With:** National Urban League.

★3677★
Urban League of Greater Muskegon
1095 3rd St., Ste. 201   Ph: (616)726-6019
Muskegon, MI 49441   Fax: (616)722-2728
Gloria Gardner, Exec. Officer
Description: Community service organization. Attempts to bring together people of many different ethnic groups and backgrounds with vested interests to openly exchange views for the purpose of bridging understanding and increasing acceptance of each others' differences. Works to improve the conditions of African Americans and other minority groups in Muskegon County. **Affiliated With:** National Urban League.

★3678★
Pontiac Area Urban League
295 W. Huron St.
Pontiac, MI 48341   Ph: (810)335-8730
Jacquelin E. Washington, Pres.
Description: Works to eliminate racial segregation and discrimination.

★3679★
Saginaw County Minority Business Development Center
901 S Washington
Saginaw, MI 48601-2554

★3680★
Minority Advisory Panel
23500 Northwestern Hwy., Ste. E-258
Southfield, MI 48075-3369

Minnesota

★3681★
American Civil Liberties Union, Minnesota Chapter
1021 Broadway W.
Minneapolis, MN 55411-2503   Ph: (612)522-2423
William Roath, Exec.Dir.
Description: Seeks to ensure civil rights for residents of Minnesota.

★3682★
Minnesota Advocates for Human Rights
310 4th Ave S #1000   Ph: (612)341-3302
Minneapolis, MN 55415-1012   Fax: (612)341-2971
Barbara A. Frey, Exec. Officer
Description: Works to prevent human rights violations including torture, executions, genocide, and wrongful detention. Protects the

human rights of refugees, torture victims, political dissidents, women, children, oppressed ethnic groups, indigenous people and other vulnerable individuals. Investigates and exposes violations; educates the public; represents human rights victims; promotes the universal acceptance of international standards; and trains and assists groups that protect human rights.

★3683★
Amnesty International, Rochester Chapter
500 1st Ave. SW
Rochester, MN 55902   Ph: (507)288-5982
Gerald Weinrich, Exec. Officer

Description: Human rights organization working to secure the immediate and unconditional release of all prisoners of conscience.

★3684★
Common Action for Racial Equality
PO Box 6281
Rochester, MN 55903   Ph: (507)282-6917
Larry Stafford, Exec. Officer.

★3685★
Human Rights Commission of Rochester
201 4th St. SE, Rm. 135   Ph: (507)285-8086
Rochester, MN 55904   Fax: (507)285-8256

Description: Individuals appointed by the mayor to resolve complaints of age, sex, race, and religious discrimination.

★3686★
Central Minnesota Freedom Task Force
810 W St. Germaine, Ste. 5
St. Cloud, MN 56301-3508
Tracy L. Jensen, Exec. Officer.

★3687★
St. Paul Tenants Union
500 Laurel Ave.
St. Paul, MN 55102   Ph: (612)221-0501
Joan Pearson, Exec.Dir.

Description: Tenants living in low to moderate income housing. Provides legal information concerning the rights and responsibilities of tenants. Also provides community organizing assistance to tenants seeking to enforce their rights. Seeks to end housing inequalities.

—————————— **Mississippi** ——————————

★3688★
American Civil Liberties Union, Mississippi Affiliate
PO Box 2242   Ph: (601)355-6464
Jackson, MS 39225   Fax: (601)355-6465
David Ingebretsen, Exec.Dir.

Description: Constitutional defense organization.

★3689★
Urban League of Greater Jackson
3405 Medgar Evers Blvd.
Jackson, MS 39213   Ph: (601)981-4211
Clayton Hodge, Dir.

—————————— **Missouri** ——————————

★3690★
American Civil Liberties Union, Mid-Missouri Chapter
1612 Wilson Ave.
Columbia, MO 65201   Ph: (314)442-0285
John Coffman, Contact

Description: Individuals united to protect the rights of the individual as set forth in the U.S. Constitution. **Affiliated With:** American Civil Liberties Union.

★3691★
American Civil Liberties Union, Kansas and Western Missouri Chapter
706 W. 42nd St., Ste. 108   Ph: (816)756-3113
Kansas City, MO 64111   Fax: (816)756-0945
Dick Kurtenbach, Exec.Dir.

★3692★
Kansas City Minority Business Development Center
1101 Walnut, Ste. 1900   Ph: (816)471-1520
Kansas City, MO 64106   Fax: (816)471-7923
Stanley L. Peeples, Exec. Officer

Description: Provides management and technical assistance to minority entrepreneurs.

★3693★
Urban League of Kansas City
1710 Paseo
Kansas City, MO 64108   Ph: (816)471-0550

Description: Individuals interested in promoting and protecting civil rights and liberties for minorities, especially in the areas of employment and housing. **Affiliated With:** National Urban League.

★3694★
Citizens Commission on Human Rights
3212 Tally Ho
St. Charles, MO 63301-0027

★3695★
American Civil Liberties Union, East Missouri
4557 Laclede Ave.   Ph: (314)361-2111
St. Louis, MO 63108   Fax: (314)361-3135

★3696★
Urban League of Metropolitan St. Louis
3701 Grandel Sq.
St. Louis, MO 63108   Ph: (314)371-0040
James H. Buford, Contact

Description: Individuals interested in promoting and protecting civil rights and liberties for minorities, especially in the areas of employment and housing. **Affiliated With:** National Urban League.

—————————— **Montana** ——————————

★3697★
American Civil Liberties Union, Montana Chapter
Box 3012   Ph: (406)248-1086
Billings, MT 59103   Fax: (406)248-7763
Scott Crichton, Exec.Dir.

Description: Works to defend rights provided by the U.S. Constitution and Bill of Rights. Provides educational programs and litigation and lobbying services. **Affiliated With:** American Civil Liberties Union.

★3698★
Medicine Wheel Alliance
PO Box 37   Ph: (406)477-6215
Huntley, MT 59037   Fax: (406)245-2353
Nicol Price, Coord.

Description: Native American Indians and non-Natives interested in working towards the preservation of Sacred land areas and teaching federal compliance to grassroots groups under Historic Preservation Act.

Nebraska

★3699★
American Civil Liberties Union, Nebraska Chapter
PO Box 81455   Ph: (402)476-8091
Lincoln, NE 68501   Fax: (402)476-8135
Marlayn Cragun, Exec.Dir.

★3700★
Urban League of Nebraska
3024 N. 24th
Omaha, NE 68110   Ph: (402)453-9730
Description: Community service agency. Seeks to eliminate discrimination and segregation, increase the economic and political empowerment of minorities, and help all Americans share equally in the rewards and responsibilities of full citizenship. **Affiliated With:** National Urban League.

Nevada

★3701★
American Civil Liberties Union of Nevada
325 S 3rd St.
Las Vegas, NV 89101-6003   Ph: (702)786-8260
Shelley Chase, Exec.Dir.
Description: Champions the rights of people set forth in the Declaration of Independence and the U.S. Constitution. **Affiliated With:** American Civil Liberties Union.

New Hampshire

★3702★
American Civil Liberties Union, New Hampshire
18 Low Ave.   Ph: (603)225-3080
Concord, NH 03301   Fax: (603)226-0203

★3703★
Civil Liberties Union, New Hampshire Chapter
18 Low Ave.
Concord, NH 03301   Ph: (603)225-3080
Claire T. Ebel, Exec.Dir.
Description: Individuals interested in preserving freedoms guaranteed in the Bill of Rights of the American Constitution. **Affiliated With:** American Civil Liberties Union.

New Jersey

★3704★
Minority Contractors and Coalition of Trade Workers of New Jersey
338 Stegmen Pkwy.
Jersey City, NJ 07305-1409
Don Wilson, Contact.

★3705★
American Civil Liberties Union, New Jersey
2 Washington Pl.   Ph: (201)642-2084
Newark, NJ 07102   Fax: (201)642-6523

★3706★
American Civil Liberties Union of New Jersey
2 Washington Pl.
Newark, NJ 07102   Ph: (201)642-2084
Edward Martone, Exec.Dir.
Description: Advocates and litigates for prison reform, separation of church and state, reproductive freedom, and the Bill of Rights. Offers counseling and referral services. Maintains speakers' bureau. **Affiliated With:** American Civil Liberties Union.

★3707★
Essex County Urban League
3 William St., Ste. 300
Newark, NJ 07102   Ph: (201)624-6660
Description: Works to eliminate racial segregation and discrimination in the Essex County, NJ area. Provides word processing, job training, and employment center. Supports Youth AIDS Prevention Project (YAPP), Adolescent Mothers Program, and the William and Mary Ashby Day Care Center. Sponsors independent living skills for foster teens, youth male responsibility project, emergency assistance for families, housing counseling, and male responsibility. **Affiliated With:** National Urban League.

★3708★
Newark Minority Business Development Center
60 Park Pl., Ste. 1404
Newark, NJ 07102   Ph: (201)623-7712

New Mexico

★3709★
American Civil Liberties Union of New Mexico
PO Box 80915   Ph: (505)266-5915
Albuquerque, NM 87198   Fax: (505)266-5916
Jennie Lusk, Exec.Dir.
Description: Champions the rights of people set forth in the Bill of Rights to the U.S. Constitution and the New Mexico State Constitution. **Affiliated With:** American Civil Liberties Union.

New York

★3710★
Urban League of the Albany Area
95 Livingston Ave.
Albany, NY 12207   Ph: (518)463-3121
Joseph Grigg, Pres. & CEO
Description: Individuals promoting equal opportunities for blacks and other minorities in Albany, Schenectady, and Troy, NY.

★3711★
NIA: A Minority Womens Professional Network'
PO Box 813
Wakefield Sta.
Bronx, NY 10466   Ph: (718)518-3248
DeRhone Sutton, Pres.
Description: Seeks to provide minority women with an outlet for professional growth, personal enhancement and community service. **Publications:** none. **Affiliated With:** National Association for Female Executives.

★3712★
Brooklyn Minority Business Development Center
30 Flatbush Ave., Ste. 423
Brooklyn, NY 11217   Ph: (718)522-5880
Gabe Mustesa, Exec.Dir.

★3713★
Williamsburg/Brooklyn Minority Business Development Center
12 Heywood St.
Brooklyn, NY 11211   Ph: (718)522-5620

★3714★
Buffalo Urban League
15 E. Genessee St.   Ph: (716)854-7625
Buffalo, NY 14203   Fax: (716)854-8960
Leroy R. Coles, Pres./CEO
Description: Works to eliminate racial segregation and discrimination in Buffalo, NY. Sponsors fundraisers, and Equal Opportunity Day. **Affiliated With:** National Urban League.

★3715★
Upstate New York Regional Minority
4455 Genesee St.
Buffalo, NY 14225-1928

★3716★
Women for Human Rights and Dignity Development Corp.
2528 Main St.
Buffalo, NY 14214-2010

★3717★
Urban League of Long Island
219 Carleton Ave.   Ph: (516)232-2482
Central Islip, NY 11722-4501   Fax: (516)232-3849
Description: Works to protect and enhance the civil and human rights of blacks and other minorities. Conducts youth enrichment & senior citizens programs. **Affiliated With:** National Urban League.

★3718★
Queens Minority Business Development Center
110-29 Horace Harding Expy.
Corona, NY 11368   Ph: (718)699-2400

★3719★
Open Island
320 Old Country Rd.   Ph: (516)535-3662
Garden City, NY 11530   Fax: (516)877-0218
Linda Leaf, Dir.
Description: Promotes fair housing.

★3720★
Association of Minority Business Enterprises of New York
250 Fulton Ave. No. 505
Hempstead, NY 11550-3901   Ph: (516)489-0120

★3721★
Cultural and Historical Events for Native American Children
Webster Bldg.
2000 Lehigh Station Rd.
Henrietta, NY 14467   Ph: (716)359-5047
Jeanette Miller, Coord.

★3722★
Northeastern Native American Association
106 52 150 St.
Jamaica, NY 11435-5100

★3723★
Nassau/Suffolk Minority Business Development Center
150 Broad Hollow Rd., Ste. 304   Ph: (516)549-5454
Melville, NY 11747   Fax: (516)549-5703
Erik J. Burgos CPA, Exec.Dir.
Description: Provides management, financial, marketing, and procurement assistance to minority businesses and entrepreneurs.

★3724★
American Civil Liberties Union, New York
132 W 43rd, 2nd Fl.   Ph: (212)382-0557
New York, NY 10036   Fax: (212)354-2583

★3725★
Catholic Interracial Council of New York
899 10th Ave.   Ph: (212)237-8255
New York, NY 10019   Fax: (212)237-8607
Gerald W. Lynch, Pres.
Description: Aim is to promote interracial justice. Works in cooperation with local parishes and governmental and voluntary groups to combat bigotry and discrimination. Promotes social justice for all racial, religious, and ethnic groups. Sponsors research,

educational forums, workshops, and community action programs. **Convention/Meeting:** none.

★3726★
Institute for Social and Economic Rights
228 W 71st St., Apt. 14H
New York, NY 10023-3736

★3727★
Local Education Alternatives Resource Network
100 E 42nd St.
New York, NY 10017-5613

★3728★
Musicians Against Racism-Sexism
433 Park Ave. S, 3rd Fl.
New York, NY 10016-8002

★3729★
National Minority Business Council
235 E. 42nd St.   Ph: (212)573-2385
New York, NY 10017   Fax: (212)573-4462

★3730★
New York Civil Rights Coalition
3 West 35th St. (PH)
New York, NY 10001   Ph: (212)563-5636
Michael Meyers, Exec.Dir.
Description: To kindle in Americans a spirit of unity and commitment to achieving a truly open and just society, where the individual enjoys the blessings of liberty free of racial prejudice, stigma, caste or discrimination. Works purposefully toward an integrated society; inclusive neighborhoods; strong, diverse and interracial educational systems, both public and private. Advocates equal opportunity in employment and voting rights, and unfettered participation in the civic affairs of our democracy.

★3731★
Veterans for Human Rights of Greater New York
346 Broadway, Ste. 811
New York, NY 10013-3990
German F. Lopez, Contact.

★3732★
National Association for the Advancement of Colored People, Rochester Chapter 2172
550 Meigs St.
Rochester, NY 14607   Ph: (716)461-1395
Rev. Norvel Goff, Pres.

★3733★
New York Civil Liberties Union, Genesee Valley Chapter
121 N Fitzhugh St.
Rochester, NY 14614   Ph: (716)454-4334

★3734★
Rochester Minority Business Development Center
350 North St.
Rochester, NY 14605   Ph: (716)232-6120

★3735★
Urban League of Rochester
265 Clinton Ave. N   Ph: (716)325-6530
Rochester, NY 14605   Fax: (716)325-4864
William G. Clark, Pres./CEO
Description: The Urban League of Rochester, New York, seeks to enable African Americans, Hispanics, the poor, and other disadvantaged minorities to realize their full human rights and potential, and advocates for the well-being of the entire Rochester community. Through a comprehensive offering of programs and services designed to meet the special needs of minorities, the Urban League provides opportunities for families, youths, people with disabilities, tenants, homeowners, and business owners to help them develop their maximum potential.

★3736★
Friends of Lt. George Lener
102 Benedict Ave.
Staten Island, NY 10314-2411
Robert Farrell, Contact.

★3737★
Urban League of Onondaga County
505 E. Fayette St.   Ph: (315)472-6955
Syracuse, NY 13202   Fax: (315)472-6445
Leon E. Modeste, Pres.

★3738★
Long Island Community Housing Resource Board
300 Sunrise Hwy.
West Babylon, NY 11704   Ph: (516)661-4800
Barbara O'Brian, Chairperson

Description: Representatives of community groups, the housing industry, and the Long Island Board of Realtors. Works to encourage voluntary compliance with fair housing laws, to develop training for the real estate industry, and to promote education for schools, organizations, and the media.

★3739★
Yonkers Minority Business Association
PO Box 917
Yonkers, NY 10703-0917

─────── **North Carolina** ───────

★3740★
Center for Women's Economic Alternatives
PO Box 1033
Ahoskie, NC 27910   Ph: (919)332-4179
Bernice Sesoms, Exec.Dir.

Description: Provides workplace and benefits education. Maintains referral service.

★3741★
Carolinas Minority Supplier Development Councils
Hatteras Bldg., Ste. 106
5624 Executive Center Dr.
Charlotte, NC 28212   Ph: (704)536-2884
                             Fax: (704)536-8856
Malcom Graham, Exec.Dir.

Description: Strives to enhance business opportunities for minority-owned companies. Works to develop mutually beneficial networking opportunities between corporate employees. **Affiliated With:** National Minority Supplier Development Council.

★3742★
Charlotte-Mecklenburg Urban League
500 N. Tryon St.
Charlotte, NC 28202-2232   Ph: (704)376-9834
Madine Hester Fails, Pres. & CEO

Description: Companies, organizations, and individuals in Cabarrus, Mecklenburg, and Union counties, NC organized to enable blacks and other minorities to reach their full potential and achieve parity with other Americans. Holds annual Equal Opportunity Day Dinner. **Affiliated With:** National Urban League.

★3743★
Charlotte Minority Business Development Center
700 E. Stonewall St., Ste. 360
Charlotte, NC 28202   Ph: (704)334-7522
Robert M. Sampson, Project Dir.

Description: Aims to develop positive minority business and community development. Funded by the United States Department of Commerce; operated by the Charlotte Area Business League.

★3744★
Metro-Charlotte Minority Chamber
PO Box 36862
Charlotte, NC 28236-6862

★3745★
American Civil Liberties Union of North Carolina
PO Box 28004   Ph: (919)834-3390
Raleigh, NC 27611   Fax: (919)828-3265
Deborah Ross, Exec. Legal Dir.

Description: Works to defend civil liberties as set forth in the Bill of Rights through litigation, lobbying, and public education. Holds bimonthly board meeting.

★3746★
North Carolina Human Relations Commission
217 W. Jones St.
Raleigh, NC 27603   Ph: (919)733-7996
Eddie Lawrence, Dir.

Description: Advocates, enforces, and promotes equality of opportunity in the area of housing, fair employment practices, public accommodations, education, justice, and governmental services for all people in North Carolina.

★3747★
Children's Advocacy Group
206 N. Spruce St.
Winston-Salem, NC 27101   Ph: (919)723-9678
Martha Young, Exec. Officer

Description: Works to protect the civil rights of children. Helps children receive available services. **Publications:** none. **Convention/Meeting:** none.

★3748★
Winston-Salem Urban League
201 W. 5th St.   Ph: (910)725-5614
Winston-Salem, NC 27101   Fax: (910)725-5713
Delores J. Smith, CEO & Pres.

─────── **North Dakota** ───────

★3749★
Amnesty International, North Dakota Chapter
2033 St. Bennedict Dr.
Bismarck, ND 58501   Ph: (701)255-4528
Erling N. Sannes, Contact

Description: Human rights organization working to free prisoners of conscience. Promotes fair and prompt trials for all political prisoners. Seeks to abolish torture and executions. **Convention/Meeting:** none. **Publications:** none.

─────── **Ohio** ───────

★3750★
Canal Winchester Tribe
10737 Miller Ave.
Canal Winchester, OH 43110-9592
Thomas L. Sharrow, Contact.

★3751★
American Civil Liberties Union of Ohio, Cincinnati Chapter
103 William Howard Taft   Ph: (513)961-5566
Cincinnati, OH 45219   Fax: (513)961-2180
Christine Link, Exec.Dir.

Description: Individuals in southwestern Ohio seekin g to "champion the rights of people set forth in the Declaration of Independence and the Constitution." Maintains speakers' bureau; engages in litigation. **Affiliated With:** American Civil Liberties Union.

★3752★
Urban League of Greater Cincinnati
2400 Reading Rd.
Cincinnati, OH 45202   Ph: (513)721-2237
Sheila J. Adams, Exec.Dir.
Affiliated With: National Urban League.

★3753★
Urban League of Greater Cleveland
1255 Euclid Ave., No.205
Cleveland, OH 44115-1807   Ph: (216)421-0999

★3754★
American Civil Liberties Union of Ohio
85 E. Gay St., No. 806
Columbus, OH 43215-3118   Ph: (614)228-8951
Elinor Alger, Exec.Dir.

★3755★
Columbus Urban League
788 Mt. Vernon Ave.   Ph: (614)257-6300
Columbus, OH 43203   Fax: (614)257-6327
Samuel Gresham Jr., Pres.
Affiliated With: National Urban League.

★3756★
Dayton Urban League
United Way Bldg., Rm. 200
184 Salem Ave.
Dayton, OH 45406   Ph: (513)220-6666
Willie F. Walker, Pres.
Description: Works to eliminate racial segregation and discrimination in Dayton, OH.

★3757★
Lorain County Urban League
401 Broad St.
Elyria, OH 44035   Ph: (216)323-3364
Delbert Lancaster, Dir.

★3758★
Euclid Community Concerns
291 E. 222nd St., No. 233   Ph: (216)731-7302
Euclid, OH 44123   Fax: (216)731-7302
Kirsten Gail, Exec.Dir.
Description: Individuals promoting racial, religious, ethnic, and cultural diversity and cooperation in Euclid, OH. Works to ensure neighborhood safety, stability, and attractiveness.

★3759★
Rural Residential Alternatives
301 S. Front St.
Hamilton, OH 45011-2901

★3760★
Hillcrest Housing Service
5010 Mayfield Rd., Ste. 207   Ph: (216)691-9696
Lyndhurst, OH 44124   Fax: (216)691-9699
Maria Thompson, Exec.Dir.
Description: Cities and school districts supporting integration in eastern suburban Cleveland, OH communities and schools. Operates housing service for Blacks. Provides affirmative action training for real estate agents. Supports legislation concerning fair housing and integration.

★3761★
OGCA Civil Rights Defense Fund
PO Box 9007
Maumee, OH 43537-9007
John Snyder, Contact.

★3762★
Worthington Human Relations Council
6795 Bowerman St. W.
Worthington, OH 43085   Ph: (614)885-2379
Marguerite Turnbull, Pres.

★3763★
Youngstown Area Urban League
1350 5th Ave., Ste. 300   Ph: (330)744-4111
Youngstown, OH 44504   Fax: (330)744-1140
William Ronald Miller, CEO

Oklahoma

★3764★
Choctaw Nation Indian Home Corp.
PO Drawer 1210
Durant, OK 74702-1210

★3765★
American Civil Liberties Union of Oklahoma
1411 Classen, Ste. 318   Ph: (405)524-8511
Oklahoma City, OK 73106   Fax: (405)524-2296
Joann Bell, Dir.
Description: Professional men and women in Oklahoma seeking to preserve the civil rights of all individuals. Sponsors Bill of Rights Day every December. **Affiliated With:** American Civil Liberties Union.

★3766★
Oklahoma Minority Supplier Development Council
525 Central Park Dr., Ste. 106
Oklahoma City, OK 73105-1703

★3767★
Urban League of Greater Oklahoma City
Urban League Community Center
3017 Martin Luther King   Ph: (405)424-5243
Oklahoma City, OK 73111   Fax: (405)424-3382
Leonard D. Benton, Contact
Description: Individuals interested in promoting and protecting civil rights and liberties for minorities, especially in the areas of employment and housing. Conducts charitable activities. **Affiliated With:** National Urban League.

Oregon

★3768★
American Civil Liberties Union of Oregon, Southern District
PO Box 50426
Eugene, OR 97405   Ph: (503)345-6162
David Fidanque, Exec.Dir.
Description: Works for preservation of civil liberties as guaranteed in the U.S. Constitution and Bill of Rights.

★3769★
American Civil Liberties Union of Oregon
705 Board of Trade Bldg.
310 SW 4th. Ave.
Portland, OR 97240-0585   Ph: (503)227-3186
David J. Fidanque, Exec.Dir.
Description: Champions the rights of people set forth in the Constitution of the U.S and the Bill of Rights.

★3770★
Citizens Commission on Human Rights of Oregon
PO Box 8842   Ph: (503)228-3279
Portland, OR 97207-8842   Free: 800-869-2247
Jan Meekcoms, Pres.
Description: Investigates and exposes psychiatric violations of human rights. **Convention/Meeting:** none.

★3771★
Coalition for Human Dignity
PO Box 40344
Portland, OR 97420
Scot Nakagawa, Program Coordinator.

Pennsylvania

★3772★
Urban League of Lancaster County
502 S. Duke St.   Ph: (717)394-1966
Lancaster, PA 17602   Fax: (717)295-5044
Paul Culbreth, Pres.
Description: Assists minorities to "cultivate and exercise their full human potential." Seeks to ensure full inclusion of participants in the economic and social life of the community.

★3773★
Citizens to Abolish Domestic Apartheid
PO Box 21
North Versailles, PA 15137-0021

★3774★
Breaking Chains
PO Box 27356
Philadelphia, PA 19118-0356

★3775★
Delaware Valley Minority Business Resource Council
1835 Market St., 8th Fl.
Philadelphia, PA 19103-2968
Keith Lake, Exec.Dir.

★3776★
American Civil Liberties Union, Pennsylvania Affiliate
237 Oakland Ave.
Pittsburgh, PA 15213   Ph: (412)681-7736
Witold Walczak, Dir.

Rhode Island

★3777★
American Civil Liberties Union, Rhode Island Affiliate
212 Union St., Rm. 211   Ph: (401)831-7171
Providence, RI 02903   Fax: (401)831-7175
Steve Brown, Pres.

★3778★
Rhode Island Justice Alliance
177 Union St.
Providence, RI 02903-3407

★3779★
Urban League of Rhode Island
246 Prairie Ave.
Providence, RI 02905   Ph: (401)351-5000

South Carolina

★3780★
American Civil Liberties Union, South Carolina
Middleburg Plz, Ste. 104
2712 Middleburg Dr.
Columbia, SC 29204   Ph: (803)799-5151

★3781★
Columbia Urban League
1400 Barnwell St.
Columbia, SC 29201   Ph: (803)799-8150

★3782★
Urban League of the Upstate, Inc.
15 Regency Hill Dr.   Ph: (864)244-3862
Greenville, SC 29607   Fax: (864)244-6134
William B. Whitney, Pres./CEO

South Dakota

★3783★
Red Feather
131 Greygoose Rd.
Pierre, SD 57501-6108

★3784★
Soaring Eagle Foundation
1001 Fir Dr.
Rapid City, SD 57701-2034

Tennessee

★3785★
Urban League of Greater Chattanooga
730 Martin Luther King Blvd.
PO Box 11106
Chattanooga, TN 37401   Ph: (423)756-1765
Jerome W. Page, Pres.

★3786★
Knoxville Area Urban League
2416 Magnolia Ave.
PO Box 1911   Ph: (615)524-5511
Knoxville, TN 37901   Fax: (615)525-5154
Rosemary Durant-Giles, Pres./CEO.

★3787★
American Civil Liberties Union, Tennessee
PO Box 120160   Ph: (615)320-7142
Nashville, TN 37212   Fax: (615)320-7260

★3788★
Belmont-Hillsboro Neighbors
PO Box 120712   Ph: (615)297-2629
Nashville, TN 37212   Fax: (615)343-9957
Gene TeSelle, Corr.Sec.
Description: Seeks to maintain good relations in interracial neighborhood. Conducts planning, zoning, and codes enforcement activities; also, the door to door distribution every 2-months of a newsletter.

★3789★
Nashville Urban League
1219 9th Ave. N.   Ph: (615)254-0525
Nashville, TN 37208   Fax: (615)254-0636
Rhonda Cantrell Dunn, Pres.
Description: Promotes equal opportunity and the creation of an open, integrated, pluralistic society. Provides employment services, a youth learning center, drug and alcohol abuse prevention

programs, housing services, and a homicide reduction program. **Affiliated With:** National Urban League.

───────────── **Texas** ─────────────

★3790★
American Civil Liberties Union, Texas Affiliate
1004 West Ave.   Ph: (512)441-0077
Austin, TX 78764   Fax: (512)441-3195
Jay Jacobson, Exec. Officer.
Affiliated With: American Civil Liberties Union.

★3791★
Amnesty International, Austin Chapter
PO Box 4951
Austin, TX 78765   Ph: (512)469-0966
Peggy O'Shaugnessy, Pres.
Description: Human rights organization. **Affiliated With:** Amnesty International of the U.S.A..

★3792★
Austin Area Urban League
1825 E. 38 1/2th St.   Ph: (512)478-7176
Austin, TX 78722   Fax: (512)478-1239
Herman Lessard Jr., Pres./CEO
Affiliated With: National Urban League.

★3793★
Austin Minority/Women Alliance
1301 E. 7th St.
Austin, TX 78702   Ph: (512)474-6526
George Villalva, Pres.

★3794★
Clearinghouse for Native American Concerns of Austin
PO Box 19572
Austin, TX 78728   Ph: (512)346-1437
Rosemary Smith, Exec.Dir.

★3795★
Human Rights Review Council of Austin
4312 Speedway, No. 110
Austin, TX 78751   Ph: (512)452-4755
W. T. Handy, Pres.
Description: Oversees and investigates human rights agencies and organizations.

★3796★
Texas Association of Minority Business Enterprises
PO Box 6206
Austin, TX 78762-6206

★3797★
Texas Civil Liberties Union
1004 West Ave.
Austin, TX 78701   Ph: (512)477-5849

★3798★
Golden Triangle Minority Business Council
PO Box 1623
Beaumont, TX 77704-1623
Description: Represents members' interests; conducts lobbying activities. Holds seminars and workshops.

★3799★
Corpus Christi Minority Business Development Center
3649 Leopard, Ste. 514   Ph: (512)887-7961
Corpus Christi, TX 78408   Fax: (512)884-5128

★3800★
Dallas Urban League
3625 N. Hall St., Ste. 700   Ph: (214)528-8038
Dallas, TX 75219-5118   Fax: (214)528-9166

★3801★
Four Winds Intertribal Society
401 Hogan Circle
Harker Heights, TX 76543-2040

★3802★
Association of Minority Contractors of Houston
15131 Bathurst
Houston, TX 77053   Ph: (713)433-3303

★3803★
Houston Area Urban League
3215 Fannin
Houston, TX 77004   Ph: (713)526-5127

★3804★
Lubbock Civil Liberties Union
Box 4033
Lubbock, TX 79409   Ph: (806)793-3754
B. H. Newcomb, Pres.
Description: Seeks to protect the rights of individuals as set forth in the Declaration of Independence and the U.S. Constitution. Promotes legislation that protects human rights in the U.S.; seeks to educate the public about civil liberties. Conducts special and educational events. **Publications:** none. **Affiliated With:** American Civil Liberties Union.

───────────── **Utah** ─────────────

★3805★
American Civil Liberties Union, Utah Affiliate
Boston Bldg.
9 Exchange Pl., Ste. 715   Ph: (801)521-9289
Salt Lake City, UT 84111   Fax: (801)532-2850
Carol Gnade, Exec.Dir.

───────────── **Vermont** ─────────────

★3806★
Minority Business Association
64 North St.
Burlington, VT 05401-5109

★3807★
American Civil Liberties Union, Vermont Affiliate
110 E. State St.   Ph: (802)223-6304
Montpelier, VT 05602-3114   Fax: (802)223-6304
Leslie Williams, Exec.Dir.
Description: Protects constitutional rights of all Vermonters. **Affiliated With:** American Civil Liberties Union.

───────────── **Virginia** ─────────────

★3808★
Airport Minority Advisory Council
1800 Diagnoal Rd., Ste. 210
Alexandria, VA 22314-2840

★3809★
Tidewater Regional Minority Purchasing Council
1216 Granby St., Ste. 9   Ph: (804)627-8471
Norfolk, VA 23510-2622   Fax: (804)627-3272
Description: Corporations, minority business owners, and local governments. Promotes economic opportunities for minority business enterprises. **Affiliated With:** National Minority Supplier Development Council.

★3810★
Urban League of Hampton Roads
840 Church St., Apt. HIJ
Norfolk, VA 23510-3031   Ph: (804)627-0864

★3811★
American Civil Liberties Union, Virginia
6 N 6th St., Ste. 400   Ph: (804)644-8022
Richmond, VA 23219-2419   Fax: (804)649-2733

★3812★
Housing Opportunities Made Equal
1218 W. Cary St.   Ph: (804)354-0641
Richmond, VA 23220   Fax: (804)354-0690
Description: Promotes equal opportunity housing. Offers housing counseling and information, and community education and outreach. Provides emergency financial assistance to people in danger of eviction or foreclosure; makes available downpayment assistance to first-time home buyers. Provides emergency financial assistance to people with AIDS.

★3813★
Urban League of Greater Richmond
101 E. Clay St.
Richmond, VA 23219   Ph: (804)649-8407
Randolph C. Kendall Jr., Pres. & CEO
Description: Promotes minority involvement in the community through social work in Chesterfield, Hanover, and Henrico counties, VA. **Affiliated With:** National Urban League.

★3814★
Virginia Regional Minority Supplier Development Council
111 E. Main St., 3rd Fl.   Ph: (804)780-2322
Richmond, VA 23219   Fax: (804)780-3171
Adele Johnson-Crawley, Pres.

——————— **Washington** ———————

★3815★
Northwest Minority Supplier Development Council
3605 NW. 132nd Ave., Ste. 414   Ph: (206)453-6686
Bellevue, WA 98006   Fax: (206)453-7066
Beverly Klein, Exec.Dir.

★3816★
American Civil Liberties Union, Washington
705 2nd Ave., Ste. 300
Seattle, WA 98104   Ph: (206)624-2180
Description: To defend and extend civil liberties.

★3817★
Seattle Minority Business Development Center-IMPACT Business Consultants
10740 Meridian N, Ste. 102   Ph: (206)363-6167
Seattle, WA 98133   Fax: (206)363-6164
Grace Gallegos, Exec. Officer
Description: Provides management and technical assistance to minority-owned businesses. **Publications:** none.

★3818★
Seattle Urban League
105 14th Ave.
Seattle, WA 98122   Ph: (206)461-3792

★3819★
Urban League of Metropolitan Seattle
105 14th Ave.   Ph: (206)461-3792
Seattle, WA 98122   Fax: (206)461-8425
Dr. R. Y. Woodhouse, Pres. & CEO
Description: Seeks to eliminate racism and the conditions that promote poverty by creating equal opportunities for all minorities. **Affiliated With:** National Urban League.

★3820★
Tacoma Urban League
2550 South Yakima Ave.   Ph: (206)383-2007
Tacoma, WA 98405   Fax: (206)383-4818
Thomas Dixon, Pres.
Description: Seeks to eliminate racial segregation and to achieve parity for blacks and other minorities in every phase of American life. Sponsors charitable events. **Publications:** none. **Affiliated With:** National Urban League.

——————— **West Virginia** ———————

★3821★
American Civil Liberties Union, West Virginia Affiliate
PO Box 3952   Ph: (304)345-9246
Charleston, WV 25339-3952   Fax: (304)345-9262
Hilary L. Chiz, Dir.
Description: Supports and promotes civil liberties. Conducts education, legislative advocacy, and litigation activities. **Affiliated With:** American Civil Liberties Union.

★3822★
West Virginia Human Rights Commission
1321 Plaza E., Rm. 106
Charleston, WV 25301   Ph: (304)348-2616
Phyllis H. Carter, Exec.Dir.
Description: To encourage and bring about mutual understanding and respect among all groups within the state and to eliminate all discrimination in employment, places of public accommodation, housing, and other areas.

——————— **Wisconsin** ———————

★3823★
Urban League of Greater Madison
151 E. Gorham   Ph: (608)251-8550
Madison, WI 53703   Fax: (608)251-0944
J.M. Mickler Sr., Pres./CEO.

★3824★
American Civil Liberties Union of Wisconsin
207 E. Buffalo St., No. 325   Ph: (414)272-4032
Milwaukee, WI 53202-5712   Fax: (414)272-0182
Christopher Ahmuty, Exec. Dir.
Description: Individuals interested in promoting constitutional rights through lobbying, public education, and litigation. **Affiliated With:** American Civil Liberties Union.

★3825★
Milwaukee Minority Business Development Center
144 2 N Farwell, Ste. 500   Ph: (414)289-3422
Milwaukee, WI 53202   Fax: (414)289-3424
Gregory L. McKinney, Exec.Officer

Description: Develops, supports, and promotes minority businesses. Provides management and technical assistance. Offers marketing, accounting, bonding, and financial planning services.

★3826★
Milwaukee Urban League
2800 W. Wright St.
Milwaukee, WI 53210   Ph: (414)374-5850
Jacqueline Shropshire, Interim Pres.

★3827★
Great Lakes Indian, Fish and Wildlife Committee
PO Box 9
Odanah, WI 54861   Ph: (715)682-8825
J. Thannum, Contact

Description: Indian tribes. Assists tribes in preservation and conservation of wildlife within ceded territories.

★3828★
Racine Treaty Support Group
1243 Kentucky
Racine, WI 53405   Ph: (414)634-2606
Julie McGuire, Exec. Officer

Description: Information clearinghouse for Native Americans and those interested in Native American issues in Racine, WI.

★3829★
Urban League of Racine and Kenosha
718-22 N. Memorial Dr.
Racine, WI 53404   Ph: (414)637-8532
Thelma Orr, Interim Pres.

Description: Works to eliminate racial segregation and discrimination in Racine and Kenosha, WI through advocacy, education, employment assistance, and special programs for teens and seniors. **Publications:** none. **Affiliated With:** National Urban League.

——————————— **Wyoming** ———————————

★3830★
American Civil Liberties Union, Wyoming
PO Box A
Laramie, WY 82070   Ph: (307)745-4515

Federal Government Agencies

★3831★
Canadian Human Rights Commission
Commission canadienne des droits de la
   personne
Place de Ville, Tower A, #1300
320 Queen St.   Ph: (613)995-1151
Ottawa, ON, Canada K1A 1E1   Fax: (613)996-9661

★3832★
U.S. Commission on Civil Rights
624 Ninth St., NW
Washington, DC 20425   Ph: (202)376-7417
Mary F. Berry, Chairperson

★3833★
U.S. Commission on Civil Rights
Office of Civil Rights Evaluation
624 Ninth St., NW
Washington, DC 20425   Ph: (202)376-8582
Frederick Isler, Asst. Staff Dir.

★3834★
U.S. Congress
Congressional Empowerment Caucus
Rayburn House Office Bldg.
Washington, DC 20515   Ph: (202)225-2011
Brian Taylor, Legislative Asst.

★3835★
U.S. Congress
U.S. House of Representatives
Congressional Human Rights Caucus
2373 Rayburn House Office Bldg.
Washington, DC 20515   Ph: (202)225-4835
Kelley Eckels Currie, Legislative Asst.

★3836★
U.S. Department of Agriculture
Food, Nutrition and Consumer Services
Office of Civil Rights
Park Office Center
3101 Park Center Dr.   Ph: (703)305-2195
Alexandria, VA 22302   Fax: (703)305-2387
Gloria McColl, Dir.

★3837★
U.S. Department of Agriculture
Food Safety
Civil Rights Staff
Independence Ave. 12th and 14th Sts.,
   SW   Ph: (202)205-0285
Washington, DC 20250   Fax: (202)205-0588
Cynthia P. Mercado, Dir.

★3838★
U.S. Department of Agriculture
Natural Resources and Environment
Civil Rights Staff
Rosslyn Plaza Bldg. E
1621 N. Kent St.
Arlington, VA 22209   Ph: (703)235-2931
Luther Burse, Dir.

★3839★
U.S. Department of Agriculture
Office of Civil Rights Enforcement
Jamie L. Whitten Federal Bldg., Rm. 326-
   W
Washington, DC 20250   Ph: (202)720-5212
George Robertson, Dir.

★3840★
U.S. Department of Commerce
Bureau of the Census
Equal Employment Opportunity Office
Herbert Clark Hoover Bldg.
14th St. and Constitution Ave., NW
Washington, DC 20230   Ph: (301)457-2853
Carol Shaw, EEO Off.

★3841★
U.S. Department of Commerce
Minority Business Development Agency
Herbert Clark Hoover Bldg.
14th St. and Constitution Ave., NW
Washington, DC 20230   Ph: (202)482-5061
Joan Parrott-Fonseca, Dir.

★3842★
U.S. Department of Commerce
National Institute of Standards and Technology
Civil Rights Office
Quince Orchard and Clopper Rds.   Ph: (301)975-2037
Gaithersburg, MD 20899   Fax: (301)948-3716
Alvin C. Lewis, Dir.

★3843★
U.S. Department of Commerce
Office of Civil Rights
Herbert Clark Bldg.
14th St, and Constitution Ave., NW   Ph: (202)482-0625
Washington, DC 20230   Fax: (202)482-5375
Courtland V. Cox, Dir.

★3844★
U.S. Department of Commerce
Patent and Trademark Office
Office of Civil Rights
Crystal Park Bldg. 1
2011 Crystal Dr.
Arlington, VA 22202   Ph: (703)305-8292
Wayne R. Yoshino, Dir.

★3845★
U.S. Department of Defense
Acquisition and Technology
Office of Small and Disadvantaged Business
  Utilization
3061 Defense Pentagon
Washington, DC 20301-3061   Ph: (703)697-9383
Robert L. Neal Jr., Dir.

★3846★
U.S. Department of Defense
Department of the Air Force
Manpower, Reserve Affairs, Installations, and
  Environment
Equal Opportunity Office
1660 Air Force, Pentagon
Washington, DC 20330-1660   Ph: (703)697-6586
Dennis M. Collins, Deputy Dir.

★3847★
U.S. Department of Defense
Department of the Air Force
Small and Disadvantaged Business Utilization
1060 Air Force
Pentagon
Washington, DC 20330-1060   Ph: (703)697-1950
Anthony J. DeLuca, Dir.

★3848★
U.S. Department of Defense
Department of the Army
Chief of Staff of the Army
Office of Equal Employment Opportunity
The Pentagon   Ph: (202)761-0098
Washington, DC 20301   Fax: (202)761-0872
John R. Sellmansberger, Equal Employment Mgr.

★3849★
U.S. Department of Defense
Department of the Army
Chief of Staff of the Army
Office of Small and Disadvantaged Business
  Utilization
The Pentagon   Ph: (202)761-4609
Washington, DC 20301   Fax: (202)761-0725
Diane S. Sisson, Dir.

★3850★
U.S. Department of Defense
Department of the Army
Equal Employment Opportunity Compliance and
  Complaints Review Agency
Crystal Mall Bldg. #4
1941 Jefferson Davis Hwy.
Arlington, VA 22202   Ph: (703)607-1447
Delores C. Symons, Dir.

★3851★
U.S. Department of Defense
Department of the Army
Equal Opportunity Agency
Crystal Mall Bldg. #4
1941 Jefferson Davis Hwy.
Arlington, VA 22202   Ph: (703)607-1976
Luther Santiful, Dir.

★3852★
U.S. Department of Defense
Department of the Navy
Civil Personnel Policy/Equal Employment Opportunity
  Office
The Pentagon
Washington, DC 20301   Ph: (703)695-2248
Betty Welch, Deputy Asst. Sec.

★3853★
U.S. Department of Defense
Department of the Navy
Small and Disadvantaged Business Utilization Office
The Pentagon
Washington, DC 20301   Ph: (703)602-2690
Don L. Hathaway, Dir.

★3854★
U.S. Department of Defense
Personnel and Readiness
Equal Opportunity Office
The Pentagon
Washington, DC 20301   Ph: (703)695-0105
Clairborne D. Haughton, Principal Dir.

★3855★
U.S. Department of Education
Office of the Assistant Secretary for Civil Rights
Federal Office Bldg. 10
600 Independence Ave. SW   Ph: (202)205-5557
Washington, DC 20202   Fax: (202)205-9862
Norman V. Cantu, Asst. Sec.

★3856★
U.S. Department of Education
Office of Hearings and Appeals
Civil Rights Reviewing Authority
Federal Office Bldg. 10B
Independence Ave. SW
Washington, DC 20202   Ph: (202)619-9700
Richard Slippen, Staff Dir.

★3857★
U.S. Department of Energy
Office of Economic Impact and Diversity
Office of Civil Rights
Forrestal Bldg.
1000 Independence Ave. SW   Ph: (202)586-2218
Washington, DC 20585-0904   Fax: (202)586-0888
Willie Garrett, Deputy Dir.

★3858★
U.S. Department of Energy
Office of Economic Impact and Diversity
Office of Small and Disadvantaged Business
  Utilization
Forrestal Bldg.
1000 Independence Ave. SW   Ph: (202)586-7377
Washington, DC 20585-0903   Fax: (202)586-5488
Percy McCraney, Deputy Dir.

★3859★
U.S. Department of Health and Human Services
Administration for Children and Families
EEO/Civil Rights and Special Initiatives Staff
370 L'Enfant Promenade SW
Washington, DC 20447   Ph: (202)401-9376
Virginia Apodoca, Dir.

★3860★
U.S. Department of Health and Human Services
Equal Employment Opportunity Programs Group
Hubert H. Humphrey Bldg.
200 Independence Ave. SW
Washington, DC 20201   Ph: (202)690-6555
Bonita White, Dir.

★3861★
U.S. Department of Health and Human Services
Health Care Financing Administration
Equal Employment Opportunity Staff
7500 Security Blvd.   Ph: (410)786-5110
Baltimore, MD 21244   Fax: (410)786-9549
Joanne Hitchcock, Dir.

★3862★
U.S. Department of Health and Human Services
Office for Civil Rights
Wilbur J. Cohen Bldg.
300 Independence Ave. SW   Ph: (202)619-0403
Washington, DC 20201   Fax: (202)619-3818
Dennis Hayashi, Dir.

★3863★
U.S. Department of Health and Human Services
Office of the General Counsel
Civil Rights Division
Wilbur J. Cohen Bldg.
330 Independence Ave. SW
Washington, DC 20447   Ph: (202)619-0900
George Lyon, Assoc. Gen. Counsel

★3864★
U.S. Department of Health and Human Services
Office of Public Health and Science
Bureau of Primary Health Care
Office of Minority and Women's Health
4350 East-West Hwy.
Bethesda, MD 20814   Ph: (301)594-4490
Sharon Barrett, Dir.

★3865★
U.S. Department of Health and Human Services
Office of Public Health and Science
Food and Drug Administration
Industry and Small Business Liaison Staff
Parklawn Bldg.
5600 Fishers Lane   Ph: (301)827-3430
Rockville, MD 20857   Fax: (301)443-5153
Beverly Corey, Team Leader

★3866★
U.S. Department of Health and Human Services
Office of Public Health and Science
Food and Drug Administration
Office of Equal Employment Opportunity and Civil
  Rights
Parklawn Bldg.
5600 Fishers Lane   Ph: (301)443-5541
Rockville, MD 20857   Fax: (301)480-6167
Rosamelia T. Lecea, Dir.

★3867★
U.S. Department of Health and Human Services
Office of Public Health and Science
Health Resources and Services Administration
Office of Equal Opportunity and Civil Rights
Parklawn Bldg.
5600 Fishers Lane
Rockville, MD 20857   Ph: (301)443-5636
J. Calvin Adams, Dir.

★3868★
U.S. Department of Health and Human Services
Office of Public Health and Science
National Cancer Institute
Equal Employment Opportunity Office
9000 Rockville Pike, Bldg. 31
Rockville, MD 20892   Ph: (301)496-6266

★3869★
U.S. Department of Health and Human Services
Office of Public Health and Science
National Institutes of Health
Minority Programs Office
National Institutes of Health, Bldg. 1
9000 Rockville Pike
Bethesda, MD 20892   Ph: (301)402-1366
John Ruffin, Assoc. Dir.

★3870★
U.S. Department of Health and Human Services
Office of Public Health and Science
National Institutes of Health
Office of Equal Opportunity
9000 Rockville Pike, Bldg. 31
Bethesda, MD 20892   Ph: (301)496-6301
Naomi Churchill, Dir.

★3871★
U.S. Department of Health and Human Services
Office of Public Health and Science
Office of Deputy Assistant Secretary for Minority
  Health
Rockwall Bldg. 2
5515 Security Lane
Rockville, MD 20852   Ph: (301)443-5084
Clay E. Simpson, Dep. Asst. Sec. Minority Health

★3872★
U.S. Department of Health and Human Services
Office of Public Health and Science
Office of Minority Health
Parklawn Bldg.
5600 Fishers Lane
Rockville, MD 20857   Ph: (301)443-2964
Ilena Herrell, Dir.

★3873★
U.S. Department of Health and Human Services
Office of Public Health and Science
Research Grants Division
Employment Opportunity Specialist
Rockledge Bldg. 1
6701Rockledge Dr.   Ph: (301)435-1279
Bethesda, MD 20892-7965   Fax: (301)480-3965
Margarite Curtis-Farrell, Employment Opportunity Specialist

★3874★
U.S. Department of Health and Human Services
Office of Small and Disadvantaged Business
  Utilization
Hubert H. Humphrey Bldg.
200 Independence Ave. SW
Washington, DC 20201   Ph: (202)690-7300
Verl Zanders, Dir.

★3875★
U.S. Department of Housing and Urban Development
Assistant Secretary for Fair Housing and Equal
  Opportunity
451 Seventh St., SW
Washington, DC 20410   Ph: (202)708-4252

★3876★
U.S. Department of Housing and Urban Development
Civil Rights and Litigation
Office of Assisted Housing and Community
  Development
451 Seventh St., SW
Washington, DC 20410   Ph: (202)708-0212
Robert S. Kenison, Assoc. Gen. Counsel

★3877★
U.S. Department of Housing and Urban Development
Civil Rights and Litigation
Office of Litigation and Fair Housing Enforcement
451 Seventh St., SW   Ph: (202)708-0300
Washington, DC 20410   Fax: (202)708-3351
Carole W. Wilson, Assoc. Gen. Counsel

★3878★
U.S. Department of Housing and Urban Development
Civil Rights and Litigation
Office of Program Enforcement
451 Seventh St., SW   Ph: (202)708-2568
Washington, DC 20410   Fax: (202)619-8351
John W. Herold, Assoc. Gen. Counsel

★3879★
U.S. Department of Housing and Urban Development
Office of Departmental Equal Employment
  Opportunity
451 Seventh St., SW
Washington, DC 20410   Ph: (202)708-3633
Mari Barr, Dir.

★3880★
U.S. Department of Housing and Urban Development
Office of Small and Disadvantaged Business
  Utilization
451 Seventh St., SW   Ph: (202)708-3350
Washington, DC 20410   Fax: (202)708-7642
Joseph M. Pilijay, Small Business Specialist

★3881★
U.S. Department of the Interior
Bureau of Indian Affairs
Equal Employment Opportunity Staff
1849 C St., NW
Washington, DC 20240   Ph: (202)208-3600
John C. Nicholas, Dir.

★3882★
U.S. Department of the Interior
Office for Equal Opportunity
1849 C St., NW
Washington, DC 20240   Ph: (202)208-5693
E. Melodee Smith, Dir.

★3883★
U.S. Department of the Interior
Office of Small and Disadvantaged Business
  Utilization
1849 C St., NW
Washington, DC 20240   Ph: (202)208-7438
Ralph W. Rausch, Deputy Dir.

★3884★
U.S. Department of Justice
Civil Rights Division
Educational Opportunities Section
Home Owners Loan Corp. Bldg.
320 First St., NW   Ph: (202)514-4092
Washington, DC 20534   Fax: (202)307-1379
Kenneth A. Mines, Sect. Chief

★3885★
U.S. Department of Justice
Civil Rights Division
Employment Litigation Section
Home Owners Loan Corp. Bldg.
320 First St., NW   Ph: (202)514-3831
Washington, DC 20534   Fax: (202)307-1379
Katherine A. Baldwin, Sect. Chief

★3886★
U.S. Department of Justice
Civil Rights Division
Housing and Civil Enforcement Section
Home Owners Loan Corp. Bldg.
320 First St., NW   Ph: (202)514-4713
Washington, DC 20534   Fax: (202)307-1379
Paul F. Hancock, Sect. Chief

★3887★
U.S. Department of Justice
Civil Rights Division
Office of Complaint Adjudication
Home Owners Loan Corp. Bldg.
320 First St., NW   Ph: (202)514-2172
Washington, DC 20534   Fax: (202)307-1379
Mark L. Gross, Complaint Adjudication Off.

★3888★
U.S. Department of Justice
Civil Rights Division
Special Litigation Section
Home Owners Loan Corp. Bldg.
320 First St., NW   Ph: (202)514-6255
Washington, DC 20534   Fax: (202)307-1379
Steven H. Rosenbaum, Sect. Chief

★3889★
U.S. Department of Justice
Civil Rights Division
Voting Section
Home Owners Loan Corp. Bldg.
320 First St., NW   Ph: (202)514-6018
Washington, DC 20534   Fax: (202)307-1379
Elizabeth Johnson, Sect. Chief

★3890★
U.S. Department of Justice
Drug Enforcement Agency
Equal Employment Opportunity Staff
Washington, DC 20537   Ph: (202)307-8888
Marian E. Moss, Off.

★3891★
U.S. Department of Justice
Immigration and Naturalization Service
Office of Equal Employment Opportunity
Discrimination Complaints Branch
Washington, DC 20536   Ph: (202)514-2732
JoAn Taylor, Chief

★3892★
U.S. Department of Justice
Office of Justice Programs
Office for Civil Rights
Indiana Bldg.
633 Indiana Ave., NW
Washington, DC 20530   Ph: (202)307-0690
Inez Alfonzo-Lasso, Dir.

★3893★
U.S. Department of Labor
Civil Rights Center
Frances Perkins Bldg.
200 Constitution Ave., NW   Ph: (202)219-8927
Washington, DC 20210   Fax: (202)219-5658
Annabelle T. Lockhart, Dir.

★3894★
U.S. Department of Labor
Office of Small Business and Minority Affairs
Frances Perkins Bldg.
200 Constitution Ave., NW   Ph: (202)219-9148
Washington, DC 20210   Fax: (202)219-9167
June M. Robinson, Dir.

★3895★
U.S. Department of Labor
Office of the Solicitor
Civil Rights Division
Frances Perkins Bldg.
200 Constitution Ave., NW   Ph: (202)219-8286
Washington, DC 20210   Fax: (202)219-5037
James D. Henry, Assoc. Solicitor

★3896★
U.S. Department of State
Equal Employment Opportunity and Civil Rights
  Office
2201 C St., NW
Washington, DC 20520   Ph: (202)647-9294
Deidre Davis, Dep. Asst. Sec.

★3897★
U.S. Department of Transportation
Federal Aviation Administration
Office of the Assistant Administrator for Civil Rights
Nassif Bldg.
400 Seventh St., SW   Ph: (202)267-3254
Washington, DC 20590   Fax: (202)267-5565
Fanny Rivera, Asst. Admin.

★3898★
U.S. Department of Transportation
Federal Highway Administration
Office of Civil Rights
400 Seventh St., SW
Washington, DC 20590   Ph: (202)366-0693
Edward W. Morris Jr., Dir.

★3899★
U.S. Department of Transportation
Federal Transit Administration
Office of Civil Rights
400 Seventh St., SW
Washington, DC 20590   Ph: (202)366-4018
Arthur A. Lopez, Dir.

★3900★
U.S. Department of Transportation
National Highway Traffic Safety Administration
Office of Civil Rights
400 Seventh St., SW
Washington, DC 20590   Ph: (202)366-0972
George Quick, Dir.

★3901★
U.S. Department of Transportation
Office of Civil Rights
Nassif Bldg.
400 Seventh St., SW   Ph: (202)366-4648
Washington, DC 20590   Fax: (202)366-9371
Jacklyn Miles, Administrative Off.

★3902★
U.S. Department of Transportation
Office of Small and Disadvantaged Business
  Utilization
Nassif Bldg.   Ph: (202)366-1930
400 Seventh St., SW   Free: 800-532-1169
Washington, DC 20590   Fax: (202)366-1930
Luz A. Hopewell, Dir.

★3903★
U.S. Department of Transportation
Research and Special Programs Administration
Office of Civil Rights
400 Seventh St., SW
Washington, DC 20590   Ph: (202)366-9638

★3904★
U.S. Department of Transportation
U.S. Coast Guard
Office of Civil Rights
Nassif Bldg.
400 Seventh St., SW   Ph: (202)267-1562
Washington, DC 20590   Fax: (202)267-4282
Walter R. Somerville, Chief

★3905★
U.S. Department of the Treasury
Internal Revenue Service
Equal Employment Opportunity and Diversity
  Division
Treasury Bldg. Annex
Pennsylvania Ave. and Madison Pl., NW
Washington, DC 20220   Ph: (202)622-5400
Edward Chavez, Natl. Dir.

★3906★
U.S. Department of the Treasury
Internal Revenue Service
Equal Opportunity and Organizational Management
  Division
111 Constitution Ave., NW
Washington, DC 20224   Ph: (202)622-9090
Paulette Sewell, Dir.

★3907★
U.S. Department of the Treasury
Office of Small Business Programs
Treasury Bldg. Annex
Pennsylvania Ave. and Madison Pl., NW
Washington, DC 20220   Ph: (202)622-0530
T. J. Garcia, 202622-0530

★3908★
U.S. Department of the Treasury
U.S. Customs Service
Equal Opportunity Office
1301 Constitution Ave., NW   Ph: (202)927-0210
Washington, DC 20229   Fax: (202)927-1380
Martha Green-McDonald, Satff Chief

★3909★
U.S. Department of Veterans Affairs
Center for Minority Veterans
810 Vermont Ave., NW
Washington, DC 20420   Ph: (202)273-6708
Lt. Col. Willie L. Hensley, Exec. Dir.

★3910★
U.S. Department of Veterans Affairs
Equal Employment Opportunity Office
Westory Bldg.
607 14th St., NW   Ph: (202)482-6701
Washington, DC 20001   Fax: (202)482-6760
Gerald K. Hinch, Deputy Asst. Sec.

★3911★
U.S. Department of Veterans Affairs
Office of Small and Disadvantaged Business
  Utilization
810 Vermont Ave., NW   Ph: (202)565-8124
Washington, DC 20420   Fax: (202)565-8156
Scott F. Dennison, Dir.

★3912★
U.S. Environmental Protection Agency
Office of Civil Rights
401 M St., SW   Ph: (202)260-4575
Washington, DC 20460   Fax: (202)260-4580
Dan J. Rondeau, Dir.

★3913★
U.S. Environmental Protection Agency
Office of Small and Disadvantaged Business
  Utilization
401 M St., SW   Ph: (703)305-7777
Washington, DC 20460   Free: 800-368-5888
                               Fax: (703)305-6606
Leon H. Hampton, Dir.

★3914★
U.S. Equal Employment Opportunity Commission
1801 L St., NW   Ph: (202)663-4900
Washington, DC 20507   Free: 800-669-4000
Gilbert F. Casellas, Chm.

★3915★
U.S. Federal Communications Commission
Office of Workplace Diversity
1919 M St., NW   Ph: (202)418-1799
Washington, DC 20554   Fax: (202)418-0379
Jack W. Gravely, Dir.

★3916★
U.S. Federal Deposit Insurance Corporation
Office of Equal Opportunity
550 17th St., NW
Washington, DC 20429   Ph: (202)942-3103
Jo-Ann Henry, Dir.

★3917★
U.S. Federal Maritime Commission
Office of Equal Employment Opportunity
800 North Capitol St., NW
Washington, DC 20573   Ph: (202)523-5806

★3918★
U.S. General Accounting Office
Office of Affirmative Action/Civil Rights Office
441 9th St. NW
Washington, DC 20548   Ph: (202)512-6388
Nilda Aponte, Dir.

★3919★
U.S. General Services Administration
Office of Equal Employment Opportunity
18th and F St., NW
Washington, DC 20405   Ph: (202)501-0767
Yvonne T. Jones, Assoc. Admin.

★3920★
U.S. General Services Administration
Office of Small and Disadvantaged Business
  Utilization
18th and F St., NW   Ph: (202)501-1021
Washington, DC 20405   Fax: (202)208-3938
Dietra Ford, Assoc. Admin.

★3921★
U.S. Information Agency
Office of Civil Rights
301 Fourth St., SW   Ph: (202)619-5151
Washington, DC 20547   Fax: (202)260-0406
Hattie P. Baldwin, Dir.

★3922★
U.S. International Development Cooperation Agency
Agency for International Development
Office of Equal Employment Opportunity
State Dept. Bldg.
320 21st St., NW   Ph: (703)875-7292
Washington, DC 20523   Fax: (703)875-5408
Jessalyn L Pendarvis, Dir.

★3923★
U.S. International Development Cooperation Agency
Agency for International Development
Office of Small and Disadvantaged Business
  Utilization
Minority Resource Center
Gannet Bldg.
1100 Wilson Blvd.   Ph: (703)875-1551
Arlington, VA 22209   Fax: (703)875-1862
Ivan R. Ashley, Dir.

★3924★
U.S. Legal Services Corporation
Office of Administration, Human Resources and
  Equal Opportunity
750 First St., NE   Ph: (202)336-8877
Washington, DC 20002-4250   Fax: (202)336-8959
Joan Kennedy, Dir.

★3925★
U.S. Merit Systems Protection Board
Office of Equal Employment Opportunity
1120 Vermont Ave., NW   Ph: (202)653-6180
Washington, DC 20419   Fax: (202)653-7130
Janice E. Fritts, Dir.

★3926★
U.S. National Aeronautics and Space Administration
Office of Equal Opportunity Programs
Affirmative Employment and Diversity Policy Division
2 Independence Sq.
300 E St., SW
Washington, DC 20546   Ph: (202)358-0958
James A. Westbrooks, Dir.

★3927★
U.S. National Aeronautics and Space Administration
Office of Equal Opportunity Programs
Discrimination Complaints Division
2 Independence Sq.
300 E St., SW   Ph: (202)358-2180
Washington, DC 20546   Fax: (202)358-2829
Brenda Manuel-Alexander, Dir.

★3928★
U.S. National Aeronautics and Space Administration
Office of Equal Opportunity Programs
Minority University Research and Education Division
2 Independence Sq.
300 E St., SW   Ph: (202)358-0970
Washington, DC 20546   Fax: (202)358-3745
Bettie L. White, Dir.

★3929★
U.S. National Science Foundation
Design, Manufacture and Industrial Innovation Division
Office of Small Business Research and Development
Office of Small and Disadvantaged Business Utilization
4201 Wilson Blvd.
Arlington, VA 22230   Ph: (703)306-1330
Donald Senich, Head

★3930★
U.S. National Science Foundation
Design, Manufacture and Industrial Innovation Division
Small Business Innovation Research Programs
4201 Wilson Blvd.
Arlington, VA 22230   Ph: (703)306-1391
Anthony Centodocati, Program Mgr.

★3931★
U.S. National Science Foundation
Design, Manufacture and Industrial Innovation Division
Small Business Technology Transfer Program
4201 Wilson Blvd.
Arlington, VA 22230   Ph: (703)306-1391
Darryl G. Gorman, Program Mgr.

★3932★
U.S. National Science Foundation
Directorate for Education and Human Resources
Graduate Education Division
Graduate and Minority Graduate Fellowships Programs
4201 Wilson Blvd.   Ph: (703)306-1694
Arlington, VA 22230   Fax: (703)306-0399
Susan W. Duby, Program Dir.

★3933★
U.S. National Science Foundation
Human Resource Development Division
Alliance for Minority Participation Program
4201 Wilson Blvd.
Arlington, VA 22230   Ph: (703)306-1632
William E. McHenry, Dir.

★3934★
U.S. National Science Foundation
Office of Equal Opportunity
4201 Wilson Blvd.
Arlington, VA 22230   Ph: (703)306-1020
Jean W. Riggs, Equal Opportunity Programs Coordinator

★3935★
U.S. Nuclear Regulatory Commission
Office of Small Business/Civil Rights
Nuclear Regulatory Commission
Washington, DC 20555   Ph: (301)415-7380
Irene P. Little, Dir.

★3936★
U.S. Office of Personnel Management
Office of Human Resources and Equal Employment Opportunity
Equal Employment Opportunity Division
Nuclear Regulatory Commission
Washington, DC 20555   Ph: (202)606-2460
Alicia McPhie, Chief

★3937★
U.S. Peace Corps
American Diversity Program
Esplanade Bldg.
1990 K St., NW
Washington, DC 20526   Ph: (202)606-3324
Mabel Dobarro, Diversity & EEO Mgr.

★3938★
U.S. Peace Corps
Volunteer Recruitment and Selection
Minority Recruitment
Esplanade Bldg.
1990 K St., NW
Washington, DC 20526   Ph: (202)606-3454
Raymond Gonzales, Dir.

★3939★
U.S. Postal Service
Diversity Development Office
475 L'Enfant Plaza West, SW
Washington, DC 20260   Ph: (202)268-6566
Robert F. Harris, Vice Pres.

★3940★
U.S. Small Business Administration
Office of Equal Employment Opportunity and Civil Rights Compliance
409 Third St., SW
Washington, DC 20416   Ph: (202)205-6750
Erline M, Patrick, Asst. Admin.

★3941★
U.S. Small Business Administration
Office of Minority Enterprise Development
409 Third St., SW
Washington, DC 20416   Ph: (202)205-6412
Calvin Jenkins, Assoc. Admin.

★3942★
U.S. Small Business Administration
Office of Small Business Development Centers
409 Third St., SW
Washington, DC 20416   Ph: (202)205-6766
Johnnie L. Albertson, Assoc. Admin.

★3943★
U.S. Smithsonian Institution
Office of Equal Employment and Minority Affairs
955 L'Enfant Plaza North, SW   Ph: (202)287-3487
Washington, DC 20560   Fax: (202)287-3492
Era L. Marshall, Dir.

★3944★
U.S. Social Security Administration
Office of Civil Rights and Equal Opportunity
West High Rise Bldg.
6401 Security Blvd.   Ph: (410)965-1977
Baltimore, MD 21235   Fax: (410)966-0941
Miguel A. Torrado, Dir.

★3945★
Yukon Human Rights Commission
205 Rogers St.
Whitehorse, YT, Canada Y1A 1X1   Ph: (403)667-6226

★3946★
Yukon Human Rights Panel of Adjudicators
208 Main St. #202
Whitehorse, YT, Canada Y1A 2B2   Ph: (403)667-7667

Federal Domestic Assistance Programs

★3947★
U.S. Department of Agriculture
Cooperative State Research, Education, and Extension Service
Higher Education and Multicultural Scholars Program (Minority Scholars Program)
Education Programs
South Building, Rm. 3912
Washington, DC 20250-2251   Ph: (202)720-7854

Catalog Number: 10.220 **Objectives:** To increase the ethnic and cultural diversity of the food and agricultural scientific and professional work force, and to advance the educational achievement of minority Americans, by providing grants to colleges and universities that have a demonstrable capacity to attract, educate, and graduate minority students for careers as agriscience and agribusiness professionals, and have unique capabilities for achieving the objective of full representation of minority groups in the fields of agriculture, natural resources, forestry, veterinary medicine, home economics, and disciplines closely allied to the food and agricultural system. **Applicant Eligibility:** Proposals may be submitted by all U.S. colleges and universities with baccalaureate or higher degree programs in agriculture, natural resources, forestry, veterinary medicine, home economics, and disciplines closely allied to the food and agricultural system, including land-grant colleges and universities, colleges and universities having significant minority enrollments and a demonstrable capacity to carry out the teaching of food and agricultural sciences, and other colleges and universities have a demonstrable capacity to carry out the teaching of food and agricultural sciences. **Types of Assistance:** Project Grants. **Beneficiary Eligibility:** Funds awarded under this program are used to support full-time undergraduate students pursuing a baccalaureate degree in an area of the food and agricultural sciences or a closely allied field. Persons eligible to receive scholarships under this program are students, who either. are enrolled or have been accepted for full-time baccalaureate degree candidates, and who are members of minority groups traditionally under-represented in food and agricultural scientific and professional fields including AfricanAmericans, Hispanics, Asians, Native-Americans, Alaskan Natives and Pacific Islanders.

★3948★
U.S. Department of Agriculture
Cooperative State Research, Education and Extension Service,
Tribal Colleges Education Equity Grants
USDA, Rm. 3433-S
Washington, DC 20250   Ph: (202)720-1973

Catalog Number: 10.221 **Objectives:** To enhance educational opportunities at the 29 Tribal Colleges designated as the 1994 Land-Grant Institutions by strengthening their teaching programs in the food and agricultural sciences in targeted need areas. **Applicant Eligibility:** Bay Mills Community College, Blackfeet Community College, Cheyenne River Community College, D-Q University, Dullknife Memorial College, Fond Du Lac Community College, Fort Belknap Community College, Fort Berthold Community College, Fort Peck Community College, LacCourte Orielles Ojibwa Community College, Little Big Horn Community College, Little Hoop Community College, Nebraska Indian Community College, Northwest Indian College, Oglala Lakota College, Salish Kootenai College, Sinte Gleska University, Sisseton Wahpeton Community College, Standing Rock College, Stonechild Community College, Turtle Mountain Community College, Navajo Community College, United Tribes Technical College, Southwest Indian Pllytechnic Institute, Institute of American Indian and Alaska Native Culture and Arts Development, Crownpoint Institute of Technology, Haskell Indian Junior College, Leech Lake Tribal College, and College of the Monoamine Nation. **Types of Assistance:** Formula Grants. **Beneficiary Eligibility:** The 1984 Institutions-Bay Mills Community College, Blackfeet Community College, Cheyenne River Community College, D-Q University, Dullknife Memorial College, Fond Du Lac Community College, Fort Peck Community College, LacCourte Orielles Ojibwa Community College, Little Big Horn Community College, Little Hoop Community College, Nebraska Indian Community College, Northwest Indian College, Oglala Lakota College, Salish Kootenai College, Sinte Gleska University, Sisseton Wahpeton Community College, Turtle Mountain Community College, Navajo Community College, United Tribes Technical College, Southwest Indian Polytechnic Institute, Institute of American Indian and Alaska Native Culture and Arts Development, Crownpoint Institute of Technology, Haskell Indian Junior College, Leech Lake Tribal College, and College of the Monoamine Nation.

★3949★
U.S. Department of Agriculture
Cooperative State Research, Education and Extension Service
Tribal Colleges Endowment Program
USDA, Rm. 3433-S
Washington, DC 20250   Ph: (202)720-1973

Catalog Number: 10.222 **Objectives:** To enhance educational opportunities at the 29 Tribal colleges designated as the 1994 Land-Grant institutions by strengthening their teaching programs in the food and agricultural sciences in targeted need areas. **Applicant Eligibility:** Bay Mills Community College, Blackfeet Community College, Cheyenne River Community College, D-Q University, Dullknife Memorial College, Fond Du Lac Community College, Fort Belknap Community College, Fort Berthold Community College, Fort Peck Community College, LacCourte Orielles Ojibwa Community College, Little Big Horn Community College, Little Hoop Community College, Oglala Lakota College, Salish Kootenai College, Sinte Gleska University, Sisseton Wahpeton Community College, Standing Rock College, Stonechild Community College, Turtle Mountain Community College, Navajo Community College, United Tribes Technical College, Southwest Indian Polytechnic Institute, Institute of American Indian and Alaska Native Culture and Arts Development, Crownpoint Insititute of Technology, Haskell Indian Junior College, Leech Lake Tribal College, and College of the Menominee Nation. **Types of Assistance:** Formula Grants. **Beneficiary Eligibility:** The 1994 Institutions -Bay Mills Community College, Cheyenne River Community College, D-Q University, Dullknife Memorial College, Fond Du Lac Community, Fort Belknap Community College, Little Hoop Community College, Nebraska Indian Community College, Northwest Indian College, Oglala Lakota College, Salish Kootenai College, Sinte Gleska University, Sisseton Wahpeton Community College, Standing Rock College, Stonechild Community College, Turtle Mountain Community College, Navajo Community College, United Tribes Technical College, Southwest

Indian Polytechnic Institute, Institute of American Indian and Alaska Native Culture and Arts Development, Crownpoint Institute of Technology, Haskell Indian Junior College, Leech Lake Tribal College, and College of the Menominee Nation

★3950★
U.S. Department of Agriculture
Cooperative State Research, Education and
   Extension Service
Tribal Colleges Endowment Program
Higher Education Programs
Rm. 3433-S
Washington, DC 20250   Ph: (202)720-1973

Catalog Number: 10.222 **Objectives:** To enhance educational opportunities at the 29 Tribal colleges designated as the 1994 Land-Grant Institutions by strenthening their teaching programs in the food and agricultural sciences in targeted need areas. **Applicant Eligibility:** Bay Mills Community College, Blackfeet Community College, Cheyenne River Community College, D-Q University, Dullknife Memorial College, Fond Du Lac Community College, Fort Belknap Community College, Fort Berthold Community College, Fort Peck Community College, LacCourte Orielles Ojibwa Community College, Little Big Horn Community College, Little Hoop Community College, Nebraska Indian Community College, Northwest Indian College, Oglala Lakota College, Salish Kootenai College, Sinte Gleska University, Sisseton Wahpeton Community College, Standing Rock College, Stonechild Community College, Turtle Mountain Community College, Navajo Community College, United Tribes Technical College, Southwest Indian Polytechnic Institiue, Institute of American Indian and Alaska Native Culture and Arts Development, Crownpoint Institute of Technology, Haskell Indian Junior College, Leech Lake Tribal College, and College of the Menominee Nation. **Types of Assistance:** Formula Grants. **Beneficiary Eligibility:** The 1994 Institutions-Bay Mills Community College, Cheyenne River Community College, D-Q University, Dullknife Memorial College, Fond Du Lac Community, Fort Belknap Community College, Little Hoop Community College, Nebraska Indian Community College, Northwest Indian College, Oglala Lakota College, Salish Kootenai College, Sinte Gleska University, Sisseton Wahpeton Community College, Standing Rock College, Stonechild Community College, Turtle Mountain Community College, Navajo Community College, United Tribes Technical College, Southwest Indian Polytechnic Institute, Institute of American Indian and Alaska Native Culture and Arts Development, Crownpoint Institute of Technology, Haskell Indian Junior College, Leech Lake Tribal College, and College of the Menominee Nation.

★3951★
U.S. Department of Commerce
Minority Business Development Agency
Minority Business Development Centers
Office of Strategic Planning & Operations
14th & Constitution Ave. NW, Rm. 5087
Washington, DC 20230   Ph: (202)482-3237

Catalog Number: 11.800. **Objectives:** To provide business development services for a minimal fee to minority firms and individuals interested in entering, expanding or improving their efforts in the marketplace. Minority business development center operators provide a wide range of services to clients, from initial consultations to the identification and resolution of specific business problems. **Applicant Eligibility:** No restrictions. **Types of Assistance:** Project grants (cooperative agreements). **Beneficiary Eligibility:** Recipient is to provide assistance to minority-owned businesses or minorities interested in starting a business.

★3952★
U.S. Department of Commerce
Minority Business Development Agency
Minority Business Resource Development
Office of Strategic Planning & Operations
14th & Constitution Ave. NW, Rm. 5087
Washington, DC 20230   Ph: (202)482-3237

Catalog Number: 11.802. **Objectives:** The resource development activity provides for the indirect business assistance program conducted by MBDA. These programs encourage minority business development by identifying and developing private markets and capital sources; decreasing minority dependence on government

programs; expanding business information and business services through trade associations; promoting and supporting the mobilization of resources of Federal agencies and State and local governments at the local level; and assisting minorities in entering new and growing markets. **Applicant Eligibility:** Restricted to established business, industry, professional, and trade associations, and chambers of commerce. **Types of Assistance:** Project grants (cooperative agreements). **Beneficiary Eligibility:** Restricted to established business, industry, professional, and trade associations, and chambers of commerce.

★3953★
U.S. Department of Commerce
Minority Business Development Agency
Minority Business Resource Development (Public
   and Private)
Office of Strategic Planning & Operations
14th and Constitution Ave., NW, Rm.
  5087
Washington, DC 20230   Ph: (202)482-3237

Catalog Number: 11.802 **Objectives:** The resource development activity provides for the indirect business assistance programs conducted by MBDA. These programs encourage minority business development by identifying and developing private markets and capital sources; expanding business information and business services through trade associations; promoting and supporting the mobilization of resources of Federal agencies and State and local governments at the local level, and assisting minorities in entering new and growing markets. **Applicant Eligibility:** Applicants for this program are established businesses, professional organizations, individuals, trade associations and chambers of commerce. **Types of Assistance:** Project Grants. **Beneficiary Eligibility:** Beneficiaries of this program are minority business persons/firms.

★3954★
U.S. Department of Education
Office of Assistant Secretary for Educational
   Research and Improvement
Eisenhower Regional Mathematics and Science
   Education Consortia
Office of Reform Assistance and
  Dissemination
Washington, DC 20208-5572   Ph: (202)219-2087

Catalog Number: 84.319 **Objectives:** To enable educational entities to establish and operate regional mathematics and science education consortia, to disseminate exemplary mathematics and science curricular materials, and to provide technical assistance for the implementation of teaching methods and assessment tools for use by K-12 students, teachers, and administrators. **Applicant Eligibility:** State and local educational agencies, elementary or secondary schools, institutions of higher education, nonporfit organizations, regional educational laboratories, or any combination of these entities. Applicants must have demonstrated expertise in mathematics and science education. **Types of Assistance:** Project Grants. **Beneficiary Eligibility:** State and local educational agencies, institutions of higher education, and nonprofit organizations will benefit.

★3955★
U.S. Department of Education
Office of Assistant Secretary for Postsecondary
   Education
Minority Science Improvement
Division of Higher Education Incentive
  Programs
Office of Postsecondary Education
Washington, DC 20202   Ph: (202)260-3261

Catalog Number: 84.120. **Objectives:** (1) To assist institutions improve the quality of preparation of their students for graduate work or careers in physical and social science; (2) to improve access of undergraduate minority students to careers in the physical and social sciences, mathematics and engineering; (3) to improve access for precollege minority students to careers in physical and social science and engineering through precollege enrichment programs conducted through eligible colleges and universities; and (4) to improve the capability of predominantly minority institutions for self-assessment, management and evaluation of their physical and social science programs and dissemination of their results. **Applicant Eligibility:** Private and public accredited two- and four-year institutions of higher education whose enrollments are predominantly (50% or more) American Indian, Alaskan Native, Black, Hispanic, Pacific Islander, or any combination of these or other disadvantaged ethnic minorities who are underrepresented in science and engineering. Proposals may also be submitted by professional scientific societies, and all nonprofit accredited colleges and universities. **Types of Assistance:** Project grants. **Beneficiary Eligibility:** Same as above; also nonprofit science-oriented societies, and all nonprofit accredited colleges and universities.

★3956★
U.S. Department of Education
Office of Assistant Secretary for Postsecondary Education
TRIO—Upward Bound
Division of Student Services
Education Outreach Branch
Federal Office Bldg. 6
600 Independence Ave., SW, Rm. 5065
Washington, DC 20202-5249   Ph: (202)708-4804

Catalog Number: 84.047. **Objectives:** To generate skills and motivation necessary for success in education beyond high school among low-income and potential first-generation college students and veterans. **Applicant Eligibility:** Institutions of higher education, public and private agencies and organizations, and in exceptional cases, secondary schools. **Types of Assistance:** Project grants. **Beneficiary Eligibility:** Low-income individuals and potential first-generation college students who have a need for academic support in order to successfully pursue a program of postsecondary education. Two-thirds of the participants must be low-income individuals who are potential first generation college students. The remaining participants must be either low-income individuals or potential first generation college students. Except for veterans, who can be served regardless of age, project participants must be between 13 and 19 years old, have completed the eighth grade, but who have not entered the twelfth grade (exceptions allowed).

★3957★
U.S. Department of Education
Office of Elementary and Secondary Education
Desegregation Assistance, Civil Rights Training, and Advisory Service
Equity and Educational Excellence Div.
Office of Elementary and Secondary
  Education
600 Independence Ave., SW
Washington, DC 20202   Ph: (202)260-2495

Catalog Number: 84.004. **Objectives:** To provide technical assistance and training services to school districts to cope with educational problems occasioned by race, sex, and national origin desegregation. **Applicant Eligibility:** State educational agencies, desegregation assistance centers, any private nonprofit organizations or any public agency (other than SEA or school board). **Types of Assistance:** Project grants. **Beneficiary Eligibility:** Educational personnel and elementary and secondary students in local school districts will benefit.

★3958★
U.S. Department of Education
Office of Elementary and Secondary Education
Magnet Schools Assistance in Desegregating Districts
Equity and Educational Excellence Div.
Portals Bldg., Rm. 4500m. 2040
500 Independence Ave., SW
Washington, DC 20202-6140   Ph: (202)260-2476

Catalog Number: 84.165. **Objectives:** To provide grants to eligible local educational agencies for use in magnet schools that are part of approved desegregation plans and that are designed to bring together students from different social, economic, racial, and ethnic backgrounds. **Applicant Eligibility:** Educational agencies. **Types of Assistance:** Project grants. **Beneficiary Eligibility:** Educational agencies.

★3959★
U.S. Department of Education
Office of Postsecondary Education
Minority Teacher Recruitment
600 Independence Ave., SW
Washington, DC 20202-5153   Ph: (202)260-3207

Catalog Number: 84.262 **Objectives:** (1) To improve recruiting and training opportunities in education for minority teachers in elementary and secondary schools; (2) to increase the number of minority teachers, including language minority teachers, in elementary and secondary schools; and (3) to identify and encourage minority students in the seventh through twelfth grades to aspire to and prepare for careers as elementary and secondary school teachers. **Applicant Eligibility:** Teacher Partnership Program: Institutions of higher education as defined in Section 1201 of the Higher Education Act of 1965, in partnership with: (1) One or more institutions of higher education; and (2) one or more local education agency; or community based organizations may apply. Teacher Placement Program: Institutions of higher education that have schools or departments of education may apply. **Types of Assistance:** Project Grants. **Beneficiary Eligibility:** Minority individuals seeking opportunities in education; minority teachers, including language minority teachers, in elementary and secondary schools; minority students in the seventh through twelfth grades seeking careers in elementary and secondary schools teaching will benefit.

★3960★
U.S. Department of Energy
Office of Minority Economic Impact
Management and Technical Assistance for Minority Business Enterprise
Office of Economic Impact and Diversity
1000 Independence Ave. SW
Washington, DC 20585   Ph: (202)586-8698

Catalog Number: 81.082. **Objectives:** To support increased participation of minority business enterprises (MBE's) in the Department of Energy's high technology research and development contracting activities. **Applicant Eligibility:** Minority businesses. **Types of Assistance:** Advisory services and counseling. **Beneficiary Eligibility:** Minority businesses wanting to do business with the Department of Energy.

★3961★
U.S. Department of Health and Human Services
Health Resources and Services Administration
Scholarships for Health Professions Students from Disadvantaged Backgrounds
Division of Student Assistance
5600 Fishers Ln., Rm. 8-34
Rockville, MD 20857   Ph: (301)443-4776

Catalog Number: 93.95. **Objectives:** To make funds available for grants to schools of medicine, nursing, osteopathic medicine, dentistry, pharmacy, podiatric medicine, optometry, veterinary medicine, allied health, or public health, or schools that offer graduate programs in clinical psychology for the purpose of assisting such schools in providing scholarships to individuals from disadvantaged backgrounds who are enrolled (or accepted for enrollment) as full-time students in the schools. **Applicant Eligibility:** Accredited public or private nonprofit schools of medicine. **Types of Assistance:** Project grants. **Beneficiary Eligibility:** Students who are (1) citizens, U.S. nationals, aliens lawfully admitted for permanent residency in the U.S., or citizens of the Commonwealth of the Northern Mariana Islands, the Trust Territory of the Pacific Islands, or citizens of the Republic of Marshall Islands, and the Federated States of Micronesia.

★3962★
U.S. Department of Health and Human Services
National Institutes of Health
Minority Access to Research Careers (MARC)
National Institute of General Medical
   Sciences
45 Center Drive MSC 6200
Bethesda, MD 20892-6200   Ph: (301)594-3900

Catalog Number: 93.880 **Objectives:** To assist minority institutions to develop and strengthen their biomedical research training capabilities. As a result, these schools are able to motivate and interest students in, as well as prepare them for, pursuing doctoral study and biomedical research careers. **Applicant Eligibility:** Any nonfederal public or private nonprofit 4-year university or college with substantial enrollment of underrepresented minority students may apply for an institutional National Research Service Award. Individual National Research Service awardees must be nominated and sponsored by a public or nonprofit private institution having staff and facilities appropriate to the proposed research training program. All awardees must be citizens or noncitizens national of the United States, or must have been lawfully admitted to the United States for permanent residence. Predoctoral awardees must have completed the baccalaureate degree and must have been accepted into a Ph.D. or combined professional degree-Ph.D. training program in the biomedical or behavioral sciences. Predoctoral faculty fellows must have been full-time faculty in the biomedical sciences for at least 3 years before the date of application. Senior faculty fellows must have received the Ph.D. or equivalent degree at least 7 years before the date of application. **Types of Assistance:** Project Grants. **Beneficiary Eligibility:** Any nonfederal public or private nonprofit 4-year university or college with a substantial enrollment of ethnic minority students.

★3963★
U.S. Department of Health and Human Services
National Institutes of Health
Minority Biomedical Research Support
National Institute of General Medical
   Science
45 Center Dr., MSC 6200
Bethesda, MD 20892   Ph: (301)494-5135

Catalog Number: 93.375. **Objectives:** To address the lack of representation of minorities in biomedical research by increasing the pool of minorities pursuing research careers. **Applicant Eligibility:** Four-year colleges, universities, and health profession schools with over 50% minority enrollment; four-year institutions with significant, but not necessarily over 50% enrollment, provided they have a history of encouragement and assistance to minorities; two-year colleges with 50% minority enrollment. **Types of Assistance:** Project grants. **Beneficiary Eligibility:** Minority students and faculty, and investigators at eligible institutions.

★3964★
U.S. Department of Health and Human Services
Office of Public Health and Science
Office of Minority Health
Family and Community Violence Prevention Program
   (Family Life Centers)
Division of Program Operations
Rockwall II Building
5515 Security Ln., Ste. 1000
Rockville, MD 20852   Ph: (301)594-0769

Catalog Number: 93.910 **Objectives:** To establish a consortium of nineteen Family Life Centers on the campuses of minority institutions of higher education to : (1)Assess local community resources for violence prevention projects; (2) Coordinate activities with existing violence prevention projects; (3) Design and implement educational interventions addressing interpersonal family violence; and (4)Design and implement a project to identify students from dysfunctional families and support them with coping strategies. **Applicant Eligibility:** Eligible Applicants: A consortium of historically and predominantly black colleges and universities. **Types of Assistance:** Project Grants (Cooperative Agreements). **Beneficiary Eligibility:** Blacks, Hispanics, Latinos, American Indians are the beneficiar ies groups.

★3965★
U.S. Department of Health and Human Services
Office of Public Health and Science
Office of Minority Health
Minority Community Health Coalition Demonstration
Division of Program Operations
Rockwall II Bldg., Ste. 1000
5515 Security Ln.
Rockville, MD 20852   Ph: (301)594-0758

Catalog Number: 93.137. **Objectives:** To demonstrate that coalitions of local community organizations can be formed to effectively promote health and effect disease risk factors within minority populations, through unique and innovative methods of modifying the behavioral and environmental factors involved. **Applicant Eligibility:** Public organizations, private nonprofit organizations, and for-profit organizations. **Types of Assistance:** Project grants. **Beneficiary Eligibility:** Members of the four major minority groups: Asian/Pacific Islanders, Blacks, Hispanics, American Indians, or a subgroup of any of these groups.

★3966★
U.S. Department of Health and Human Services
Office of the Secretary
Civil Rights Compliance Activities
Policy and Special Projects Staff
Hubert H. Humphrey Bldg., Rm. 502-E
200 Independence Ave. SW
Washington, DC 20201   Ph: (202)619-0403

Catalog Number: 93.001. **Objectives:** To eliminate unlawful discrimination and ensure equal opportunities for beneficiaries and potential beneficiaries of Federal financial assistance provided by the Department of Health and Human Services (HHS), as well as to eliminate unlawful discrimination against those involved in programs and activities conducted by HHS on the basis of any individual's handicap(s). The Office for Civil Rights (OCR) enforces various civil rights laws and regulations that prohibit discrimination on a variety of bases including race, color, national origin, handicaps, and age. OCR also enforces the community services assurance under which health care facilities assisted by the Hill-Burton Act must provide health care services to all persons residing in the service area without discrimination. Finally, OCR enforces the nondiscrimination provisions enacted under the health care and other block grants administered by the Department, and nondiscrimination provisions of the Family Violence Prevention and Services Act, which prohibit discrimination on all of the bases listed above, as well as sex and religion. **Applicant Eligibility:** Anyone who believes he or she has been discriminated against and recipients of Federal financial assistance who desire technical assistance and information for the purpose of assuring their complicance with nondiscrimination laws. **Types of Assistance:** Investigation of complaints; dissemination of technical information. **Beneficiary Eligibility:** Individuals subject to discrimination and recipients who require technical assistance and information.

★3967★
U.S. Department of Housing and Urban Development
Assistant Secretary for Fair Housing and Equal
   Opportunity
Equal Opportunity in Housing
451 7th St. SW, Rm. 5402   Ph: (202)708-0836
Washington, DC 20410   Free: 800-927-9275

Catalog Number: 14.400. **Objectives:** To provide fair housing throughout the United States; to create an administrative enforcement system which is subject to judicial review. **Applicant Eligibility:** Any individual aggrieved by a discriminatory housing practice because of race, color, religion, sex, or national origin may file a complaint with the Department of Housing and Urban Development. Litigation may be initiated by the individual aggrieved and under certain conditions by the Attorney General. **Types of Assistance:** Investigation of complaints. **Beneficiary Eligibility:** Individuals.

★3968★
U.S. Department of Housing and Urban Development
Assistant Secretary for Fair Housing and Equal
  Opportunity
Fair Housing Assistance Program—State and Local
451 7th St. SW, Rm. 5216
Washington, DC 20410   Ph: (202)708-0455
Catalog Number: 14.401. **Objectives:** To provide to those state and local agencies to whom HUD must refer Title VIII complaints both the incentive and the resources required to develop an effective work force to handle complaints, provide technical assistance, training, and other fair housing projects to assure that HUD referred complaints are properly and efficiently handled. **Applicant Eligibility:** State and local governments administering state and local fair housing laws and ordinances which have been recognized by HUD as providing sustantially equivalent rights and remedies as those provided by Title VIII of the Civil Rights Act of 1968, and which have executed formal Memoranda of Understanding with HUD to process Title VIII complaints. **Types of Assistance:** Project grants (cooperative agreements). **Beneficiary Eligibility:** Any person or group of persons aggrieved by a discriminatory housing practice because of race, color, religion, sex, or national origin.

★3969★
U.S. Department of Housing and Urban Development
Assistant Secretary for Fair Housing and Equal
  Opportunity
Non-Discrimination in the Community Development
  Block Grant Program
451 7th St. SW, Rm. 5236
Washington, DC 20410   Ph: (202)708-0404
Catalog Number: 14.406. **Objectives:** Section 109 of Title I of the Housing and Community Development Act of 1974, as amended prohibits discrimination in Community Development Block Grant Programs on the basis of race, color, national origin, sex, handicap, and age. **Applicant Eligibility:** Any individual feeling aggrieved because of an alleged discriminatory action in a Title I program on the basis of race, color, national origin, handicap, or age may file a complaint with the Department of Housing and Urban Development. **Types of Assistance:** Investigation of complaints. **Beneficiary Eligibility:** Aggrieved individuals.

★3970★
U.S. Department of Housing and Urban Development
Assistant Secretary for Fair Housing and Equal
  Opportunity
Non-Discrimination in Federally Assisted Programs
451 7th St. SW, Rm. 5236
Washington, DC 20410   Ph: (202)708-0404
Catalog Number: 14.405. **Objectives:** Title VI of The Civil Rights Act of 1964 prohibits discrimination on the basis of race, color, or national origin in federally assisted programs. **Applicant Eligibility:** Any individual feeling aggrieved because of an alleged discriminatory action on the basis of race, color, or national origin may file a complaint with the Department of Housing and Urban Development. **Types of Assistance:** Investigation of complaints. **Beneficiary Eligibility:** Aggrieved individuals.

★3971★
U.S. Department of Housing and Urban Development
Office of Native American Programs
Public and Indian Housing
Public and Indian Housing - Indian Loan Guarantee
  Program (Loan Guarantees for Indian Housing)
Deputy Assistant Secretary for Native
  American Programs
1999 Broadway, Ste. 3390
Box 90
Denver, CO 80202   Ph: (303)675-1600
Catalog Number: 14.865 **Objectives:** To provide homeownership opportunities to Native Americans, Tribes and Indian Housing Authorities on Indian land, through a guaranteed mortgage loan program available through private financial institutions. **Applicant Eligibility:** The loan applicant must be a Native American, which includes Alaska Natives, or an Indian Housing Authority or a Tribe

which meets certain requirements. **Types of Assistance:** Guaranteed/Insured Loans. **Beneficiary Eligibility:** The homeowner is the ultimate beneficiary of the program. When the Indian Housing Authority or Tribe is the homebuyer, they may then rent the property. In these cases, the person renting the home would be an indirect beneficiary.

★3972★
U.S. Department of the Interior
Bureau of Indian Affairs
Administrative Cost Grants for Indian Schools
Office of Indian Education Programs
1849 C St., NW
MS 3512 MIB
Washington, DC 20240   Ph: (202)219-1129
Catalog Number: 15.046 **Objectives:** To provide grants to tribes and tribal organizations operating schools for the purpose of paying administrative and indirect costs. **Applicant Eligibility:** Federally Recognized Indian Tribal Governments or Tribal Organizations operating a Bureau of Indian Affairs funded schools. **Types of Assistance:** Project Grants. **Beneficiary Eligibility:** Indian Tribal Governments or tribal organizations operating an elementary or secondary school under a grant or Self-determination contract with the Bureau of Indian Affairs.

★3973★
U.S. Department of the Interior
Bureau of Indian Affairs
Agriculture on Indian Lands
Office of Trust Responsibilities
Division of Water and Land Resources
1849 C St., NW
Washington, DC 20240   Ph: (202)208-3598
Catalog Number: 15.034 **Objectives:** To protect and restore the agronomic and rangeland resources on trust lands and facilitate the development of renewable agricultural resources in accordance with principles of sustained yield management to maintain productivity under multiple use concepts. **Applicant Eligibility:** Federally Recognized Indian Tribal Governments and Native American Organizations authorized by Indian tribal governments. **Types of Assistance:** Direct Payments for Specified Use; Advisory Services and Counseling; Provision of Special Services **Beneficiary Eligibility:** Federally Recognized Indian Tribal Governments and their members; Native American Organizations; and individual American Indian land owners.

★3974★
U.S. Department of the Interior
Bureau of Indian Affairs
Aid to Tribal Governments
Chief, Division of Tribal Government
  Services
1849 C St., NW
MS-4641 MIB
Washington, DC 20240   Ph: (202)208-4097
Catalog Number: 15.020 **Objectives:** To provide funds to Indian tribal governments to support general tribal government operations, to maintain up-to-date tribal enrollment, to conduct tribal elections, and to develop appropriate tribal policies, legislation, and regulations. **Applicant Eligibility:** Federally Recognized Indian Tribal Governments. **Types of Assistance:** Direct Payments for Specified Use. **Beneficiary Eligibility:** Federally Recognized Indian Tribal Governments and members of American Indian Tribes.

★3975★
U.S. Department of the Interior
Bureau of Indian Affairs
Assistance for Indian Children with Severe
  Disabilities
Office of Indian Education Programs
1849 C St., NW
MS 3512 MIB
Washington, DC 20240   Ph: (202)208-6675
Catalog Number: 15.045 **Objectives:** To provide for the special education and related services of Indian children with severe disabilities. **Applicant Eligibility:** Members or direct descendants of

members of Federally recognized tribes and enrolled in a BIA-funded school. **Types of Assistance:** Direct Payments for Specified Use. **Beneficiary Eligibility:** Indian children enrolled in a Bureau-funded school who are between the ages of five and twenty-one who have been determined by a multi-disciplinary team comprised of parents, teachers, school administrators and other concerned parties to be in need of specialized services available only in residential settings. Children whose fifth birthday occurs on or before December 31 or whose twenty-second birthday occurs during the course of the regular school year shall be regarded as eligible children for the entire school year.

★3976★
U.S. Department of the Interior
Bureau of Indian Affairs
Assistance to Tribally Controlled Community
  Colleges and Universities
Office of Indian Educational Programs
1849 C St., NW
MS-3512-MIB
Washington, DC 20240   Ph: (202)219-1127

Catalog Number: 15.027 **Objectives:** To provide grants for the operation and improvement of tribally controlled community colleges to insure continued and expanded educational opportunities for Indian students, and to allow for the improvement and expansion of the physical resources of such institutions. **Applicant Eligibility:** Colleges sponsored by Federally Recognized Indian Tribes or tribal organizations which are governed by a board of directors, are in operation more than one year, admit students with a certificate of graduation from a secondary institution or equivalent, provide certificates, associate, baccalaureate and graduate degrees, are nonprofit and nonsectarian. **Types of Assistance:** Project Grants. **Beneficiary Eligibility:** Indian students who are a member of or are at least a one-fourth degree Indian blood descendant of a member of an Indian tribe which is eligible for the special programs and services provided by the United States through the Bureau of Indian Affairs to Indians because of their status as Indians.

★3977★
U.S. Department of the Interior
Bureau of Indian Affairs
Attorney Fees - Indian Rights
Office of Trust Responsibilities
1849 C St., NW
MS-4510 MIB
Washington, DC 20240   Ph: (202)208-7216

Catalog Number: 15.053 **Objectives:** To assist Federally Recognized Tribes in protecting their treaty rights and other rights established through Executive Order or court action. **Applicant Eligibility:** Federally Recognized Indian Tribal Governments. **Types of Assistance:** Direct Payments for Specified Use. **Beneficiary Eligibility:** Federally Recognized Indian Tribes and their members.

★3978★
U.S. Department of the Interior
Bureau of Indian Affairs
Bureau of Indian Affairs Facilities - Operations and
  Maintenance
Facilities Management and Construction
  Center
201 3rd St., NW, Ste. 500
PO Box 1248
Albuquerque, NM 87103   Ph: (505)766-2825

Catalog Number: 15.048 **Objectives:** To provide funds for basic operating services to Bureau-owned or Bureau-operated non-education facilities and to maintain these facilities in a safe operating condition for the conduct of Bureau programs. **Applicant Eligibility:** Federally Recognized Indian Tribal Governments who have Bureau-owned or Bureau-operated facilities on their reservation. **Types of Assistance:** Direct Payments for Specified Use. **Beneficiary Eligibility:** Federally Recognized Indian Tribal Governments and occupants and visitors of Bureau-owned or Bureau-operated facilities.

★3979★
U.S. Department of the Interior
Bureau of Indian Affairs
Consolidated Tribal Government Program
Division of Self-Determination Services
1849 C St., NW
MS-4603 MIB
Washington, DC 20240   Ph: (202)208-5727

Catalog Number: 15.021 **Objectives:** To provide funds for certain programs of an ongoing nature to Indian Tribal Governments in a manner which minimizes program administrative requirements and maximizes flexibility. **Applicant Eligibility:** Federally Recognized Indian Tribal Governments. **Types of Assistance:** Direct Payments for Specified Use. **Beneficiary Eligibility:** Federally Recognized Indian Tribal Governments and members of American Indian Tribes.

★3980★
U.S. Department of the Interior
Bureau of Indian Affairs
Construction and Repair of Indian Detention
  Facilities
Office of Law Enforcement Services
417 Gold SW, Ste. 120
PO Box 66
Albuquerque, NM 87103   Ph: (505)248-7937

Catalog Number: 15.063 **Objectives:** To provide safe, functional, code and standards compliant, economical, and energy-efficient adult and/or juvenile detention facilities. **Applicant Eligibility:** Federally Recognized Indian Tribal Governments who have a prioritized Law Enforcement project for construction of a detention facility or a prioritized Facilities Improvement and Repair project for a Bureau detention facility for which funds have been appropriated. **Types of Assistance:** Direct Payments for Specified Use. **Beneficiary Eligibility:** Federally Recognized Indian Tribal Governments.

★3981★
U.S. Department of the Interior
Bureau of Indian Affairs
Endangered Species on Indian Lands
Office of Trust Responsibilities
Division of Water and Land Resources
1849 C St., NW
MS-4513 MIB
Washington, DC 20240   Ph: (202)208-4837

Catalog Number: 15.051 **Objectives:** To comply with the Endangered Species Act, the Northern Spotted Owl Recovery plan, and to implement the Cheyenne River Prairie Management Plan on Indian lands. **Applicant Eligibility:** Federally Recognized Indian Tribal Governments and Native American Organizations authorized by Indian tribal governments whose reservations are in areas inhabited by these specific endangered species. **Types of Assistance:** Direct Payments for Specified Use; Dissemination of Technical Information; Advisory Services and Counseling. **Beneficiary Eligibility:** Federally Recognized Indian Tribal Governments and Native American Organizations authorized by Indian tribal governments.

★3982★
U.S. Department of the Interior
Bureau of Indian Affairs
Environmental Quality Services - Indian Programs
Office of Trust Responsibilities
Branch of Environmental Services
1849 C St., NW
MS-4510 MIB
Washington, DC 20240

Catalog Number: 15.041 **Objectives:** To determine environmental impacts of Federal projects on Indian lands and to identify hazardous waste sites. **Applicant Eligibility:** Federally Recognized Indian Tribal Governments and Native American Organizations authorized by the Tribes. **Types of Assistance:** Direct Payments for Specified Use. **Beneficiary Eligibility:** Federally Recognized Indian tribes.

★3983★
U.S. Department of the Interior
Bureau of Indian Affairs
Fish, Wildlife, and Parks Programs on Indian Lands
Office of Trust Responsibilities
Division of Water and Land Resources
849 C St., NW
MS-4513 MIB
Washington, DC 20240   Ph: (202)208-4088

Catalog Number: 15.039 **Objectives:** To promote the conservation, development, and utilization of fish, wildlife, and recreational resources for sustenance, cultural enrichment, economic support, and maximum benefit of Indians. **Applicant Eligibility:** Federally Recognized Indian Tribal Governments and Native American Organizations authorized by Indian tribal governments. **Types of Assistance:** Direct Payments for Specified Use. **Beneficiary Eligibility:** Federally Recognized Indian Tribal Governments and their members and Native American Organizations.

★3984★
U.S. Department of the Interior
Bureau of Indian Affairs
Forestry on Indian Lands
Office of Trust Responsibilities
Division of Forestry
1849 C St., NW
MS-4513 MIB
Washington, DC 20240   Ph: (202)208-4439

Catalog Number: 15.035 **Objectives:** To maintain, protect, enhance, and develop Indian forest resources through the execution of forest management activities. **Applicant Eligibility:** Federally Recognized Indian Tribal Governments and Native American Organizations (currently limited to the Intertribal Timber Council) authorized by Indian tribal governments. **Types of Assis tance:** Direct Payments for Specified Use; Provision of Specialized Services; Advisory Services and Counseling. **Beneficiary Eligibility:** Federally Recognized Indian Tribal Governments and their members and Native American Organizations.

★3985★
U.S. Department of the Interior
Bureau of Indian Affairs
Indian Adult Education
Office of Indian Education Programs
1849 C St., NW
MS-3512-MB
Washington, DC 20240   Ph: (202)219-1129

Catalog Number: 15.026 **Objectives:** To improve the educational opportunities for Indian adults who lack the level of literacy skills necessary for effective citizenship and productive employment and to encourage the establishment of adult education programs. **Applicant Eligibility:** Federally Recognized Indian Tribal Governments. **Types of Assistance:** Direct Payments for Specified Use. **Beneficiary Eligibility:** Federally Recognized Indian Tribal Governments and members of American Indian Tribes.

★3986★
U.S. Department of the Interior
Bureau of Indian Affairs
Indian Child and Family Education (FACE)
Office of Indian Education Programs
1849 C St., NW
MS-3512 MIB
Washington, DC 20240   Ph: (202)219-1127

Catalog Number: 15.043 **Objectives:** To begin educating children at an early age through parental involvement, to increase high school graduation rates among Indian parents, and to encourage life-long learning. **Applicant Eligibility:** Federally Recognized Indian Tribal Governments and tribal organizations authorized by Indian tribal governments on reservations with Bureau-funded schools may apply to administer the program. **Types of Assistance:** Project Grants; Training. **Beneficiary Eligibility:** Parents and their Indian children under 5 years of age who live on a reservation with a Bureau-funded school.

★3987★
U.S. Department of the Interior
Bureau of Indian Affairs
Indian Community Fire Protection
Director, Office of Tribal Service
1849 C St., NW
MA-4603-MIB
Washington, DC 20240   Ph: (202)208-3463

Catalog Number: 15.031 **Objectives:** To provide funds to perform fire protection services to Indian Tribal Governments that do not receive fire protection support from State or local government. **Applicant Eligibility:** Federally Recognized Indian Tribal Governments performing fire protection services on their reservation. **Types of Assistance:** Direct Payments for Specified Use. **Beneficiary Eligibility:** Federally Recognized Indian Tribal Governments.

★3988★
U.S. Department of the Interior
Bureau of Indian Affairs
Indian Economic Development
Office of Economic Development
1849 C St., NW
MS-2061
Washington, DC 20240

Catalog Number: 15.032 **Objectives:** To assist Federally Recognized Indian Tribal Governments to develop resources to improve their economics through administration of credit programs and other economic development assistance activities. **Applicant Eligibility:** Federally Recognized Indian Tribal Governments. **Types of Assistance:** Direct Payments for Specified Use. **Beneficiary Eligibility:** Federally Recognized Indian Tribal Governments and their members. Complete information on beneficiary eligibility is found in 25 CFR, Parts 26 and 27.

★3989★
U.S. Department of the Interior
Bureau of Indian Affairs
Indian Education Facilities, Operations, and Maintenance
Office of Indian Education Programs
1849 C St., NW
MS-3512- MIB
Washington, DC 20240   Ph: (202)219-1129

Catalog Number: 15.047 **Objectives:** To provide funds to Indian - controlled schools for facilities operations and maintenance. **Applicant Eligibility:** Federally Recognized Indian Tribal Governments or tribal organizations currently served by a BIA-funded elementary or secondary school or peripheral dormitory. **Types of Assistance:** Direct Payments for Specified Use. **Beneficiary Eligibility:** Federally Recognized Indian Tribal Governments.

★3990★
U.S. Department of the Interior
Bureau of Indian Affairs
Indian Graduate Student Scholarships (Special Higher Education Scholarships)
American Indian Graduate Ctr.
4520 Montgomery Blvd., Ste. 1-B
Albuquerque, NM 87109   Ph: (505)881-4584

Catalog Number: 15.059 **Objectives:** To provide financial aid to eligible Indian students to enable them to obtain advanced degrees. **Applicant Eligibility:** Individual applicants must be Indian students who are members of Federally Recognized Indian Tribes, who have been admitted to a graduate program and have unmet financial need. **Types of Assistance:** Project Grants. **Beneficiary Eligibility:** Members of Federally Recognized Indian Tribes who are a member of or are at least one-fourth degree Indian blood descendant of a member of an Indian tribe which is eligible for the special programs and services provided by the United States through the Bureau of Indian Affairs to Indians because of their status as Indians.

★3991★
U.S. Department of the Interior
Bureau of Indian Affairs
Indian Job Placement - United Sioux Tribes
  Development Corporation
Office of Economic Development
Division of Job Placement and Training
1849 C St., NW
MS-2061 MIB
Washington, DC 20240   Ph: (202)208-2671
Catalog Number: 15.061 **Objectives:** To provide job development, counseling, social adjustment guidance, and referrals to job training programs and other assistance programs through the United Sioux Tribes Development Corporation, located in Pierre, South Dakota. **Applicant Eligibility:** Application to administer the program is limited to the United Sioux Tribes Development Corporation. Individual American Indian applicants must be a member of a Federally Recognized Indian Tribe, be in need of financial assistance, and reside on or near an Indian reservation under the jurisdiction of the Bureau of Indian Affairs. **Types of Assistance:** Advisory Services and Counseling; Direct Payments with Unrestricted Use. **Beneficiary Eligibility:** Must be an American Indian member of a Federally Recognized Indian Tribe and reside on or near an Indian reservation under the jurisdiction of the Bureau of Indian Affairs. Complete information on beneficiary eligibility is found in 25 CFR, Parts 26 and 27.

★3992★
U.S. Department of the Interior
Bureau of Indian Affairs
Indian Law Enforcement
Office of Law Enforcement Services
417 Gold SW, Ste. 120
PO Box 66
Albuquerque, NM 87103   Ph: (505)248-7937
Catalog Number: 15.030 **Objectives:** To provide funds to Indian tribal Government to operate police departments and detention facilities. **Applicant Eligibility:** federally Recognized Indian Tribal Governments exercising Federal criminal law enforcement authority over crimes under the Major Crimes Act (18 U.S.C. 1153) on their reservation. **Types of Assistance:** Direct Payments for Specified Use. **Beneficiary Eligibility:** Federally Recognized Indian Tribal Governments.

★3993★
U.S. Department of the Interior
Bureau of Indian Affairs
Indian Post Secondary Schools (Haskell and SIPI)
Southwestern Indian Polytechnic Institute
9169 Coors Rd., NW   Ph: (505)897-5362
Albuquerque, NM 81774   Free: 800-586-SIPI
Catalog Number: 15.058 **Objectives:** To provide postsecondary educational opportunities for American Indian Students. **Applicant Eligibility:** A member of a Federally Recognized Indian tribe. **Types of Assistance:** Training. **Beneficiary Eligibility:** American Indians.

★3994★
U.S. Department of the Interior
Bureau of Indian Affairs
Indian Rights Protection
Office of Trust Responsibilities
Division of Real Estate Services
1849 C St., NW
MS-4510 MIB
Washington, DC 20240   Ph: (202)208-7737
Catalog Number: 15.036 **Objectives:** To protect Indian rights guaranteed through treaty or statute by obtaining the services or information needed to litigate challenges to these rights. **Applicant Eligibility:** Federally Recognized Indian Tribal Governments and Native American Organizations authorized by Indian tribal governments. **Types of Assistance:** Direct Payments for Specified Use. **Beneficiary Eligibility:** Federally Recognized Indian Tribal Governments and their members.

★3995★
U.S. Department of the Interior
Bureau of Indian Affairs
Indian School Equalization Program (ISEP)
Office of Indian Education Program
1849 C St., NW
MS 3512 MIB
Washington, DC 20240   Ph: (202)219-1129
Catalog Number: 15.042 **Objectives:** To provide funding for primary and secondary education. **Applicant Eligibility:** Federally Recognized Indian Tribes or tribal organizations currently served by a Bureau of Indian Affairs funded school. **Types of Assistance:** Direct Payments for Specified Use. **Beneficiary Eligibility:** Children between the ages of 5 and 21 who are a member of or are at least a one-fourth degree Indian blood descendant of a member of an Indian tribe which is eligible for the special programs and services provided by the United States through the Bureau of Indian Affairs to Indians because of their status as Indians.

★3996★
U.S. Department of the Interior
Bureau of Indian Affairs
Indian Schools - Student Transportation
Office of Indian Education Programs
1849 C St., NW
MS 3512 MIB
Washington, DC 20240   Ph: (202)219-1129
Catalog Number: 15.044 **Objectives:** To provide funds to each school for the round trip transportation of students between home and the school site. **Applicant Eligibility:** Federally Recognized Indian Tribes or tribal organizations currently served by a Bureau of Indian Affairs funded school. **Types of Assistance:** Direct Payments for Specified Use. **Beneficiary Eligibility:** Children between the ages of 5 and 21 who are members of or are at least a one-fourth degree Indian blood descendant of a member of an Indian tribe which is eligible for the special programs and services provided by the United States through the Bureau of Indian Affairs to Indians because of their status as Indians.

★3997★
U.S. Department of the Interior
Bureau of Indian Affairs
Indian Self-Determination Contract Support
Division of Self-Determination Services
1849 C St., NW
MS-4603 MIB
Washington, DC 20240   Ph: (202)208-5727
Catalog Number: 15.024 **Objectives:** To provide funds to Federally Recognized Indian Tribal Governments and to tribal organizations to fund some or all of the indirect costs incurred in administering Federal programs for which direct appropriations are made to the Bureau of Indian Affairs. **Applicant Eligibility:** Federally Recognized Indian Tribal Governments and tribal organizations authorized by Indian Tribal Governments. **Types of Assistance:** Direct Payments for Specified Use. **Beneficiary Eligibility:** Federally Recognized Indian Tribal Governments.

★3998★
U.S. Department of the Interior
Bureau of Indian Affairs
Indian Social Services - Child Welfare Assistance
Rehabilitation Services Administration
Office of Special Education and
  Rehabilitation Services
Washington, DC 20202   Ph: (202)205-8292
Catalog Number: 15.103 **Objectives:** To provide foster home care and appropriate institutional (non-medical) care for dependent, neglected, and handicapped Indian children in need of protection residing on or near reservations, including those children living in Bureau of Indian Affairs service area jurisdictions in Alaska and Oklahoma, when these services are not available from State or local public agencies. **Applicant Eligibility:** Dependent, neglected, and handicapped Indian children in need of protection whose families live on or near Indian reservations or in Bureau of Indian Affairs service area jurisdictions in Alaska and Oklahoma, and who are not eligible for similar Federal, State or county funded programs. **Types

of Assistance: Direct Payments for Specified Use. **Beneficiary Eligibility:** Member of a federally recognized Indian Tribe.

★3999★
U.S. Department of the Interior
Bureau of Indian Affairs
Indian Vocational Training - United Tribes Technical
College
Office of Economic Development
Division of Job Placement and Training
1849 C St., NW
MS-2061 MIB
Washington, DC 20240

Catalog Number: 15.060 **Objectives:** To provide vocational training to individual American Indians through the United Tribes Technical College, located in Bismarck, North Dakota. **Applicant Eligibility:** Application to administer the program is limited to the United Tribes Technical College. Individual American Indian applicants must be a member of a Federally Recognized Indian Tribe, be in need of financial assistance, and reside on or near an Indian reservation under the jurisdiction of the Bureau of Indian Affairs. **Types of Assistance:** Training; Direct Payments with Unrestricted Use. **Beneficiary Eligibility:** Individual American Indians who are members of a Federally Recognized Indian Tribe and reside on or near an Indian reservation under the jurisdiction of the Bureau of Indian Affairs. Complete information on beneficiary eligibility is found in 25 CFR, Parts 26 and 27.

★4000★
U.S. Department of the Interior
Bureau of Indian Affairs
Irrigation Operations and Maintenance on Indian
Lands
Office of Trust Responsibilities
1849 C St., NW
MS-4513 MIB
Washington, DC 20240   Ph: (202)208-5480

Catalog Number: 15.049 **Objectives:** To conserve water and operate and maintain the irrigation water delivery systems on Indian irrigation projects and maintain the dams in a safe, economical, beneficial ,and equitable manner. **Applicant Eligibility:** Federally Recognized Indian Tribal Governments and Native American Organizations authorized by Indian tribal governments. **Types of Assistance:** Direct Payments for Specified Use; Use of Property, Facilities, and Equipment; Provision of Specialized Services. **Beneficiary Eligibility:** Federally Recognized Indian Tribal Governments and their members and Native American Organization.

★4001★
U.S. Department of the Interior
Bureau of Indian Affairs
Litigation Support for Indian Rights
Office of Trust Responsibilities
1849 C St., NW
MS-4510 MIB
Washington, DC 20240   Ph: (202)208-7216

Catalog Number: 15.052 **Applicant Eligibility:** Federally Recognized Indian Tribal Governments and Native American Organizations authorized by these Tribes. **Beneficiary Eligibility:** Federally Recognized Indian Tribes and their members.

★4002★
U.S. Department of the Interior
Bureau of Indian Affairs
Minerals and Mining on Indian Lands
Office of Trust Responsibilities
Division of Energy and Minerals
12136 W. Bayaud Ave., Ste. 300
Lakewood, CO 80228   Ph: (303)969-5270

Catalog Number: 15.038 **Objectives:** To assist and support the inventory and prudent development of energy and mineral resources on Indian lands. **Applicant Eligibility:** Federally Recognized Indian Tribal Governments and Native American Organizations authorized by Indian tribal governments. **Types of Assistance:** Direct Payments for Specified Use; Provision of

Specialized Services; Dissemination of Technical Information. **Beneficiary Eligibility:** Federally Recognized Indian Tribal Governments and their members, Native American Organizations, and/or individual American Indian mineral property owners.

★4003★
U.S. Department of the Interior
Bureau of Indian Affairs
Real Estate Programs - Indian Lands
Office of Trust Responsibilities
Division of Real Estate Services
1849 C St., NW
MS-4510 MIB
Washington, DC 20240   Ph: (202)208-7737

Catalog Number: 15.040 **Objectives:** To provide real property management, counseling, and land use planning services to individual Indian allottees and Indian tribal and Alaska Native entities who own an interest in almost 56 million acres of trust land; to provide real estate appraisal services required in processing land transactions, and to protect and enhance the Indian leasehold estate by providing individual Indian landowners and Indian tribes with lease compliance activities . **Applicant Eligibility:** Federally Recognized Indian Tribal Governments, Native American Organizations authorized by tribes, and individual American Indians. **Types of Assistance:** Direct Payments for Specified Use. **Beneficiary Eligibility:** Federally Recognized Indian Tribal Governments and their members.

★4004★
U.S. Department of the Interior
Bureau of Indian Affairs
Replacement and Repair of Indian Schools
Facilities Management and Construction
  Ctr.
201 3rd St., NW, Ste. 500
PO Box 1248
Albuquerque, NM 87103   Ph: (505)766-2825

Catalog Number: 15.062 **Applicant Eligibility:** Federally Recognized Indian Tribal Governments and Tribal Organizations, including School Boards, who have a prioritized Replacement School Construction or Facilities Improvement and Repair project for which funds have been appropriated. **Types of Assistance:** Direct Payments for Specified Use. **Beneficiary Eligibility:** Indian children attending Bureau owned or funded primary and secondary schools and/or Indian children residing in Bureau owned or funded dormitories.

★4005★
U.S. Department of the Interior
Bureau of Indian Affairs
Road Maintenance - Indian Roads
Office of Trust Responsibilities
Division of Transportation
1849 C St., NW
MS-4510-MIB
Washington, DC 20240   Ph: (202)208-4359

Catalog Number: 15.033 **Objectives:** To provide limited routine maintenance on paved, gravel, earth, and unimproved roads; bridges; and airstrips. **Applicant Eligibility:** Federally Recognized Indian tribal Governments and Native American Organizations authorized by Tribal governments which have jurisdiction over roads or other facilities that qualify for this program. **Types of Assistance:** Direct Payments for Specified Use. **Beneficiary Eligibility:** Federally Recognized Indian Tribal Governments and individual American Indians.

★4006★
U.S. Department of the Interior
Bureau of Indian Affairs
Safety of Dams on Indian Lands
Office of Trust Responsibilities
Division of Water and Land Resources
1849 C St., NW
MS-4513 MIB
Washington, DC 20240   Ph: (202)208-5480

Catalog Number: 15.065 **Objectives:** To improve the structural integrity of dams on Indian lands. **Applicant Eligibility:** Federally Recognized Indian Tribal Governments and Native American Organizations authorized by Indian tribal governments to be benefited by the award. **Types of Assistance:** Direct Payments for Specified Use. **Beneficiary Eligibility:** Federally Recognized Indian Tribal Governme nts and their members and Native American Organizations.

★4007★
U.S. Department of the Interior
Bureau of Indian Affairs
Services to Indian Children, Elderly and Families
Division of Social Services
1849 C St., NW
MS-4627-MIB
Washington, DC 20240   Ph: (202)208-2479

Catalog Number: 15.025 **Objectives:** To provide funds to Federally Recognized Indian Tribal Governments to administer welfare assistance programs for both adults and children; to support caseworkers and counselors; and to support tribal programs to reduce the incidence of substance abuse and alcohol abuse in Indian country. **Applicant Eligibility:** Federally Recognized Indian Tribal Governments. **Types of Assistance:** Direct Payments for Specified Use. **Beneficiary Eligibility:** Federally Recognized Indian Tribal Governments, adult Indians in need of financial assistance or social services counseling, Indian children who require foster care services, and Indian youth requiring temporary, emergency shelter.

★4008★
U.S. Department of the Interior
Bureau of Indian Affairs
Structural Fire Protection - Bureau of Indian Affairs
  Facilities (Fire Protection)
Structural Fire Protection Program
Facilities Management and Construction
  Ctr.
201 3rd St., NW, Ste. 500
PO Box 1248
Albuquerque, NM 87103   Ph: (505)766-2825

Catalog Number: 15.064 **Objectives:** To provide for the installation of fire protection and prevention equipment in schools, dormitories, detention centers and other BIA facilities. **Applicant Eligibility:** Federally Recognized Indian Tribal Governments and Tribal Organizations, including School Boards, who have a prioritized Fire Protection project for which funds have been appropriated. **Types of Assistance:** Direct Payments for Specified Use. **Beneficiary Eligibility:** Indian children attending Bureau owned or funded primary and secondary schools and/or residing in Bureau owned or funded dormitories and occupants and visitors of detention centers and other BIA facilities.

★4009★
U.S. Department of the Interior
Bureau of Indian Affairs
Tribal Courts
Division of Tribal Government Services
1849 C St., NW
MS-4641-MIB
Washington, DC 20240   Ph: (202)208-4400

Catalog Number: 15.029 **Objectives:** To provide funds to federally Recognized Indian Tribal Governments to operate a judicial branch of government. **Applicant Eligibility:** Federally Recognized Indian Tribal Governments exercising law enforcement jurisdiction on their reservations. **Types of Assistance:** Direct Payments for Specified Use. **Beneficiary Eligibility:** Federally Recognized Indian Tribal Governments.

★4010★
U.S. Department of the Interior
Bureau of Indian Affairs
Tribal Self-Governance
1849 C St., NW
MS-2548-MIB
Washington, DC 20240   Ph: (202)219-0240

Catalog Number: 15.022 **Objectives:** To further the goals of Indian Self-Determination by providing funds to Indian tribes to administer a wide range of programs with maximum administrative and programmatic flexibility. **Applicant Eligibility:** Federally Recognized Indian Tribal Governments and tribal consortia authorized by the Federally Recognized Indian Tribal Governments to be serves. **Types of Assistance:** Direct Payments for Specified Use. **Beneficiary Eligibility:** Federally Recognized Indian Tribal Governments and their members.

★4011★
U.S. Department of the Interior
Bureau of Indian Affairs
Tribal Self-Governance Grants
Office of Self-Governance
1849 C St., NW
MS-2548-MIB
Washington, DC 20240   Ph: (202)219-0240

Catalog Number: 15.023 **Objectives:** To support tribal self-governance planning, negotiation, and related activities; to meet initial management expenses associated with self-governance program. Funds are also used to support grants to provide education, training, and dissemination of information relative to tribal self-governance. **Applicant Eligibility:** Federally Recognized Indian Tribal Governments and tribal consortia authorized by Indian Tribal governments. **Types of Assistance:** Project Grants. **Beneficiary Eligibility:** Federally Recognized Indian Tribal Governments and their members.

★4012★
U.S. Department of the Interior
Bureau of Indian Affairs
Tribally Controlled Community College Endowments
Office of Indian Education Programs
1849 C St., NW
MS-3512-MIB
Washington, DC 20240   Ph: (202)291-2127

Catalog Number: 15.028 **Objectives:** to provide grants to establish endowments for the Tribally Controlled Community Colleges. **Applicant Eligibility:** Colleges chartered by Federally Recognized Indian Tribes which are governed by an Indian board of directors, are in operation more than one year, admit students with a certificate of graduation from a secondary institutions or equivalent, provide certificates, associate, baccalaureate and graduate degrees. **Types of Assistance:** Project Grants. **Beneficiary Eligibility:** Indian students who are a member of or are at least a one-fourth degree Indian blood descendant of a member of an Indian tribe which is eligible for the special programs and services provided by the United States through the Bureau of Indian Affairs to Indians because of their status as Indians.

★4013★
U.S. Department of the Interior
Bureau of Indian Affairs
Unresolved Indian Hunting and Fishing Rights
Office of Trust Responsibilities
Division of Water and Land Resources
1849 C St., NW
MS-4513 MIB
Washington, DC 20240

Catalog Number: 15.050 **Objectives:** To assist tribes in clarifying and defining their off-reservation hunting and fishing rights. **Applicant Eligibility:** Federally Recognized Indian Tribal Governments and Native American Organizations authorized by Indian tribal governments. **Types of Assistance:** Direct Payments for Specified Use. **Beneficiary Eligibility:** Federally Recognized Indian Tribal Governments and their members and Native American Organizations.

★4014★
U.S. Department of the Interior
Bureau of Indian Affairs
Unresolved Indian Rights Issues
Office of Trust Responsibilities
Division of Real Estate Services
1849 C St., NW
MS-4510 MIB
Washington, DC 20240   Ph: (202)208-7737

Catalog Number: 15.054 **Objectives:** To protect Indian rights associated with natural resources in the context of the Secretary's trust responsibility to protect, maintain, and manage Indian natural resources and environment on trust lands. **Applicant Eligibility:** Federally Recognized Indian Tribal Governments, Native American Organizations authorized by a Tribe. **Types of Assistance:** Direct Payments for Specified Use. **Beneficiary Eligibility:** Federally Recognized Indian Tribal Governments.

★4015★
U.S. Department of the Interior
Bureau of Indian Affairs
Waste Management - Indian Lands
Office of Trust Responsibilities
Branch of Environmental Services
1849 C St., NW
MS-4510 MIB
Washington, DC 20240   Ph: (202)208-3606

Catalog Number: 15.056 **Objectives:** To conduct surveys of Bureau of Indian Affairs controlled Federal lands and facilities, and of Indian lands, in order to identify hazardous waste sites, evaluate the potential threat to health and the environment, and develop the necessary remedial actions; to train area, agency and tribal staff in waste management principles; and to respond to emergencies and alleviate adverse health or environmental impacts. **Applicant Eligibility:** Federally Recognized Indian Tribal Governments and Native American Organizations authorized by the Tribes. **Types of Assistance:** Direct Payments for Specified Use. **Beneficiary Eligibility:** Federally Recognized Indian Tribal Governments and their members.

★4016★
U.S. Department of Justice
Civil Rights Division
Criminal Section
Civil Rights Prosecution
PO Box 66018
Washington, DC 20035-6018   Ph: (202)514-3204

Catalog Number: 16.109 **Objectives:** To reduce significantly police and other official criminal misconduct, and to eliminate or substantially reduce violent activity by private citizens (including organized hate groups) against others because of their race, religion, national origin, or sex, which interferes with the Federal and constitutional rights of individuals. **Applicant Eligibility:** All persons. **Types of Assistance:** Investigation of Complaints. **Beneficiary Eligibility:** All persons.

★4017★
U.S. Department of Justice
Civil Rights Division
Desegregation of Public Education
Educational Opportunities Litigation
  Section
PO Box 65958
Washington, DC 20530   Ph: (202)514-4092

Catalog Number: 16.100. **Objectives:** To secure equal educational opportunity for persons regardless of race, color, religion, sex, or national origin. **Applicant Eligibility:** Parent or group of parents in the case of public schools. An individual or his parents in the case of a public college. **Types of Assistance:** Provision of specialized services. **Beneficiary Eligibility:** Same as applicant eligibility.

★4018★
U.S. Department of Justice
Civil Rights Division
Equal Employment Opportunity
Employment Litigation Section
PO Box 65968
Washington, DC 20530   Ph: (202)514-2007

Catalog Number: 16.101. **Objectives:** To enforce Federal laws providing equal employment opportunities for all without regard to race, religion, national origin or sex, and where authorized, handicap condition. **Applicant Eligibility:** All persons. **Types of Assistance:** Provision of specialized services. **Beneficiary Eligibility:** All persons.

★4019★
U.S. Department of Justice
Civil Rights Division
Fair Housing and Equal Credit Opportunity
Housing & Civil Enforcement Section
PO Box 65998
Washington, DC 20530   Ph: (202)514-2007

Catalog Number: 16.103. **Objectives:** To provide freedom from discrimination on the basis of race, color, religion, sex or national origin in connection with the sale, rental, and financing of housing and other related activities. (Fair Housing Act). The Equal Credit Opportunity Act (ECOA) prohibits discrimination in credit transactions on the basis of race, color, religion, national origin, sex, marital status, or age (provided the applicant has the capacity to contract,) because all or a part of the applicant's income is derived from a public assistance program, or because the applicant has in good faith exercised any right under the Consumer Credit Protection Act. **Applicant Eligibility:** All persons. **Types of Assistance:** Provision of specialized services. **Beneficiary Eligibility:** All persons.

★4020★
U.S. Department of Justice
Civil Rights DivisionProtection of Voting Rights
Voting Section
PO Box 66128
Washington, DC 20530   Ph: (202)514-2007
Amy Casner, Contact

Catalog Number: 16.104. **Objectives:** To provide protection of an individual's right to register and vote in all local, state, and federal elections without discrimination on account of race, color, membership in a language minority group, or age; to assure the rights of persons who are disabled or are unable to read or write to receive assistance in voting for a person of their choice, to assure the right to vote in federal elections to U.S. citizens residing overseas, and to assure access to registration and voting to the elderly and handicapped. **Applicant Eligibility:** All U.S. citizens of voting age. **Types of Assistance:** Provision of specialized services. **Beneficiary Eligibility:** Same as applicant eligibility.

★4021★
U.S. Department of Justice
Community Relations Service
PO Box 66128
Washington, DC 20530   Ph: (301)514-2007

Catalog Number: 16.200. **Objectives:** To assist communities in resolving disputes, disagreeements, and difficulties arising from discrimination based on race, color, or national origin. **Applicant Eligibility:** Any person, group, community, or state or local governmental unit that seeks to alleviate tensions related to race, color, or national origin may be considered for CRS assistance. **Types of Assistance:** Provision of specialized services. **Beneficiary Eligibility:** Same as applicant eligibility.

★4022★
U.S. Department of Justice
Federal Bureau of Investigation
Indian Country Investigations.
935 Pennsylvania Ave., NW
Washington, DC 20535   Ph: (202)324-3000

Catalog Number: 16.308 **Objectives:** To provide training to the Bureau of Indian Affairs (BIA) and Tribal Law Enforcement Officers in conjunction with the Bureau of Indian Affairs and the Federal Law Enforcement Training Center (FLETC) to better enforce investigations on Indian territories. Coordination of the development of training curriculum with the BIA and the FLETC; and FBI training Instructors. To coordinate investigative activities within Indian Country. **Applicant Eligibility:** BIA Investigators, Tribal Law Enforcement Officers and other law enforcement officers assigned to work in Indian Country. **Types of Assistance:** Training. **Beneficiary Eligibility:** BIA Investigators, Tribal Law Enforcement Officers and other law enforcement officers assigned to work in Indian Country.

★4023★
U.S. Department of Justice
Office of Justice Programs
Violence Against Women Discretionary Grants for Indian Tribal Governments
633 Indiana Ave., NW
Washington, DC 20532   Ph: (202)307-6026

Catalog Number: 16.587 **Objectives:** To assist Indian tribal governments to develop and strengthen effective law enforcement and prosecution strategies to combat violent crimes against women, and to develop and strengthen victim services in cases involving crimes against women. **Applicant Eligibility:** Indian tribal governments may make individual applications or apply as a consortium. **Types of Assistance:** Project Grants (Discretionary) **Beneficiary Eligibility:** Indian tribal governments and nonprofit nongovernmental victim services programs.

★4024★
U.S. Department of Labor
Employment Standards Administration
Non-Discrimination and Affirmative Action by Federal Contractors and Federally Assisted Construction Contractors
Office of Federal Contract Compliance
  Programs
Washington, DC 20210   Ph: (202)523-9475

Catalog Number: 17.301. **Objectives:** To assure non-discrimination and affirmative action in employment by covered federal contractors, including Federal construction contractors, and federally assisted construction contractors. **Applicant Eligibility:** Complaints against Federal contractors and federally assisted construction contractors which allege class-type discrimination on the basis of race, sex, religion, or national origin may be filed. **Types of Assistance:** Dissemination of technical information and investigation of complaints. **Beneficiary Eligibility:** Employees, former employees, or applicants with a government contractor or federally involved contractor, including construction contractors.

★4025★
U.S. Equal Employment Opportunity Commission
Employment Discrimination - Equal Pay Act
Office of Communications and Legislative
  Affairs
1801 L St., NW
Washington, DC 20507   Ph: (202)663-4900

Catalog Number: 30.010 **Objectives:** To prohibit sex discrimination in the payment of wages to men and women performing equal work in the same establishment. **Applicant Eligibility:** An Employee on behalf of himself and other employees similarly situated who believes he has been paid in violation of the Equal Pay Act in any State of the United States, the District of Columbia or any territory or possession of the United States. **Types of Assistance:** Advisory Services and Counseling; Investigation of Complaints. **Beneficiary Eligibility:** Individuals covered by the Fair Labor Standards Act of 1938, as amended.

★4026★
U.S. Equal Employment Opportunity Commission
Employment Discrimination—Private Bar Program
Office of General Counsel
Washington, DC 20507   Ph: (202)663-7028

Catalog Number: 30.005. **Objectives:** (a) To assist aggrieved individuals who have obtained notices of rights to sue in contacting members of the private bar, (b) to provide technical assistance to

aggrieved parties and their attorneys in Title VII, Equal Pay and Age Discriminiation in Employment Act cases, (c) to establish the attorney referral mechanism; and (d) to coordinate the strategies of the private bar with those of the Commission. **Applicant Eligibility:** Any individual who has received a notice of right to sue from the Commission. **Types of Assistance:** Provision of specialized services. **Beneficiary Eligibility:** Same as applicant eligibility.

★4027★
U.S. Equal Employment Opportunity Commission
Employment Discrimination Project Contracts - Indian Tribes
Charge Resolution Review Program
1801 L St., NW, Rm. 8030
Washington, DC 20507   Ph: (202)663-4944

Catalog Number: 30.009 **Objectives:** To insure the protection of employment rights of Indians working on or near reservations. **Applicant Eligibility:** Must be a land based American Indian Tribe that has a tribal employment rights office established under an ordinance passed by the tribal council. **Types of Assistance:** Project Grants (Contracts). **Beneficiary Eligibility:** American Indians employed or seeking employment on or near reservations with Tribal Employment Rights office having contracts.

★4028★
U.S. Equal Employment Opportunity Commission
Employment Discrimination—State and Local Fair Practices Agency Contracts
Program Development & Coordination
  Division
Systematic Investigation & Individual
  Compliance Programs
1801 L St. NW, Rm. 8030
Washington, DC 20507   Ph: (202)663-4944

Catalog Number: 30.002. **Objectives:** To assist EEOC in the enforcement of Title VII of the Civil Rights Act of 1964, as amended, and of the Age Discrimination in Employment Act of 1967 by investigating and resolving charges of employment discrimination based on race, color, religion, sex, national origin, or age. **Applicant Eligibility:** Offical state and local government agencies charged with the administration and enforcement of fair employment practices laws. **Types of Assistance:** Direct payments for specified use. **Beneficiary Eligibility:** Employees, potential employees, and former employees covered by Title VII of the Civil Rights Act o 1964 as amended, or the Age Discrimination in Employment Act of 1967.

★4029★
U.S. Equal Employment Opportunity Commission
Employment Discrimination—Title VII of the Civil Rights Act of 1964
Office of Communications & Legislative
  Affai rs
Public Information Unit
1801 L St. NW   Free: (202)663-
Washington, DC 20507   4900

Catalog Number: 30.001. **Objectives:** To provide for enforcement of the Federal prohibition against employment discrimination in the private and public sector based on race, color, religion, sex, or national origin. **Applicant Eligibility:** Any aggrieved individual or individuals, labor union, association, legal representative, or unincorporated organization, filing on behalf of an aggrieved individual who have reason to believe that an unlawful employment practice within the meaning of Title VII, as amended, has beem committed by an employer with more than 15 employees, employment agency, labor organization, or joint labor-management committee. **Types of Assistance:** Investigation of complaints. **Beneficiary Eligibility:** Potential employees, employees and former employees of the named respondents in a charge who have been subject to unlawful employment practices.

★4030★
U.S. Small Business Administration
Business Loans for 8(A) Program Participants
Loan Policy and Procedures Branch
409 Third St., SW
Washington, DC 20416   Ph: (202)205-6570
Catalog Number: 59.042 **Objectives:** To provide guaranteed loans to small business contractors receiving assistance under the subsection 7(j) 10 and section 8(a) of the Small Business Act (15 U.S.C. 636 (a)), who are unable to obtain financing on reasonable terms in the private credit marketplace, but can demonstrate an ability to repay loans granted. Terms not to exceed 25 years. These loans are provided for under the 7(a) guarantee program. **Applicant Eligibility:** A small business concern owned by socially and economically disadvantaged person(s) eligible for assistance under the SBA Programs 59.006 and 59.009. **Types of Assistance:** Guaranteed/Insured Loans. **Beneficiary Eligibility:** Small businesses socially and economically disadvantaged.

★4031★
U.S. Small Business Administration
Management and Technical Assistance for Socially and Economically Disadvantaged Businesses (7(J) Development Assistant Program)
Associate Administrator for Minority
  Enterprise Development
409 3rd St., SW
Washington, DC 20416   Ph: (202)205-6410
Catalog Number: 59.007 **Objectives:** To provide management and technical assistance through qualified individuals, public or private organizations to 8(a) certified firms and other existing or potential businesses which are economically and socially disadvantaged; businesses operating in areas of high unemployment or low income; firms owned by low-income persons; or participants in activities authorized by Sections 7(j) and 8(a) of the Small Business Act. **Applicant Eligibility:** State and local governments, educational institutions, public or private organizations and businesses, Indian tribes and individuals that have the capability to provide the necessary assistance, as described in each program solicitation announcement. **Types of Assistance:** Project Grants (Cooperative Agreements). **Beneficiary Eligibility:** Socially and economically disadvantaged persons and businesses owned and operated by participants in the 8(a) program, (59.006) businesses operating in areas of low-income or high-unemployment, and firms owned by low-income individuals.

★4032★
U.S. Small Business Administration
Microloan Demonstration Program
Office of Financial Assistance
Microenterprise Development Branch
409 3rd St., SW, 8th Fl.
Mail Code 7881
Washington, DC 20416   Ph: (202)205-6490
Catalog Number: 59.046 **Objectives:** To assist women, low-income, and minority entrepreneurs, business owners, and other individuals possessing the capability to operate successful business concerns and to assist small business concerns in those areas suffering from a lack of credit due to economic downturns. Under the Program, the Small Business Administration (SBA) will make loans or provide guaranties to private, non-profit, and quasi-governmental organizations (intermediary lenders) who will use the loan funds to make short-term, fixed interest rate microloans in amounts up to $25,000 to start-up, newly established, and growing small business concerns. These microloans are to be used exclusively for working capital, inventory, supplies, furniture, fixtures, machinery, and/or equipment. In addition, the SBA will make grants to participating intermediary lenders to provide marketing, management, and technical assistance to borrowers receiving microloans. In addition, the SBA will make grants to non-profit organizations, which are not intermediary lenders, to provide marketing, management, and technical assistance to low-income individuals seeking private sector financing for their businesses. Under the Program, SBA will also provide training for intermediary lenders and non-lenders participating in the Program. **Applicant Eligibility:** An applicant is considered eligible to apply if it meets the definition of an intermediary lender as published in program materials, 13CFR, and PL 102-140, and meets published minimum experience and capability requirements. **Types of Assistance:** Formula Grants; Project Grants; Direct Loans. **Beneficiary Eligibility:** Small businesses, minority entrepreneurs, nonprofit entities, business owners, women and low-income, and other individuals possessing the capability to operate successful business concerns.

★4033★
U.S. Small Business Administration
Minority Business Development (Section 8(a) Program)
Office of AA/MSBDCOD
409 3rd St. SW
Washington, DC 20416   Ph: (202)205-6410
Catalog Number: 59.006. **Objectives:** To foster business ownership by individuals who are both socially and economically disadvantaged; and to promote the competitive viability of such firms by providing such available contract, financial, technical, and managerial assistance as may be necessary to become independent and self-sustaining in a normal competitive environment. **Applicant Eligibility:** Qualification as a socially and economically disadvantaged person on the basis of clear and convincing evidence. **Types of Assistance:** Provision of specialized services. **Beneficiary Eligibility:** Socially and economically disadvantaged individuals.

★4034★
U.S. Small Business Administration
Office of Minority Small Business and Capital Ownership Development
Management and Technical Assistance for Socially and Economically Disadvantaged Business
409 3rd St. SW
Washington, DC 20416   Ph: (202)205-6410
Catalog Number: 59.007. **Objectives:** To provide management and technical assistance through qualified individuals, public or private organizations to existing or potential businesses which are economically and socially disadvantaged or which are located in areas of high concentration of unemployment; or are participants in activities authorized by Sections 7(i), 7(j) and 8(a) of the Small Business Act. **Applicant Eligibility:** State and local governments, educational institutions, public or private organizations that have the capability to provide the necessary assistance. **Types of Assistance:** Project grants (cooperative agreements). **Beneficiary Eligibility:** Businesses or potential businesses which are economically and socially disadvantaged, or participants in the 8(a) program.

State/Provincial & Local Government Agencies

Alabama

★4035★
Birmingham Minority Business Development Center
2026 2nd Ave. N, Ste. 1901
Birmingham, AL 35203   Ph: (205)324-3525

★4036★
Mobile Minority Business Development Center
801 Executive Park Dr., Ste. 102   Ph: (334)471-5165
Mobile, AL 36609   Fax: (334)471-4022

★4037★
Montgomery Minority Business Development Center
770 S. McDonough St., Ste. 207
Montgomery, AL 36104   Ph: (205)834-7598

──────────── **Alaska** ────────────

★4038★
Alaska Equal Employment Opportunity Division
3601 C St., Ste. 250   Ph: (907)269-7495
Anchorage, AK 99503   Fax: (907)269-7497
Thelma Buchholdt, Exec. Dir.

★4039★
Alaska Human Rights Commission
800 A St., Ste. 204   Ph: (907)276-7474
Anchorage, AK 99501-3669   Fax: (907)278-8588
Paula Haley, Exec. Dir.

★4040★
Alaska Minority Business Development Center
1577 C St. Plaza, Ste. 304
Anchorage, AK 99501-5133   Ph: (907)274-5400

──────────── **Arizona** ────────────

★4041★
Phoenix Minority Business Development Center
1661 East Camelback, Ste. 210
Phoenix, AZ 85016   Ph: (602)277-7707

──────────── **Arkansas** ────────────

★4042★
Arkansas Industrial Development Commission
Minority Business Division
1 Capitol Mall   Ph: (501)682-5060
Little Rock, AR 72201   Fax: (501)682-7394

★4043★
Little Rock Minority Business Development Center
100 S. Main, Ste. 438
Little Rock, AR 72201   Ph: (501)682-9100

──────────── **California** ────────────

★4044★
Anaheim Minority Business Development Center
6 Hutton Center Dr., Ste. 1050
Santa Ana, CA 92707   Ph: (714)434-0444

★4045★
Bakersfield Minority Business Development Center
2300 Tulare St., Ste. 210
Fresno, CA 93721-2226   Ph: (805)837-0291

★4046★
Fresno Minority Business Development Center
4944 E Clinton Way Ste 103
Fresno, CA 93727-1527   Ph: (209)252-7551

★4047★
Oxnard Minority Business Development Center
451 West 5th St.
Oxnard, CA 93030   Ph: (805)483-1123

★4048★
San Diego Minority Business Development Center
6363 Alvarado Ct., Ste. 225
San Diego, CA 92120   Ph: (619)594-3684

★4049★
San Francisco Human Rights Commission
25 Van Ness Ave., Ste. 800   Ph: (415)252-2500
San Francisco, CA 94102   Fax: (415)431-5764
Marivic Bamba, Dir.

★4050★
San Francisco/Oakland Minority Business
  Development Center No. 1
150 Almaden Blvd., 6th Fl.
San Jose, CA 95113-2009   Ph: (415)989-2920

★4051★
San Francisco Small Business Advisory Commission
401 Van Ness Ave., Rm. 339
San Francisco, CA 94102   Ph: (415)554-6249
Barbara Kolesar, Dir.

★4052★
San Jose Minority Business Development Center
150 Almaden Blvd., Ste. 600
San Jose, CA 95150   Ph: (408)275-9000

★4053★
Stockton Minority Business Development Center
305 N. El Dorado St., Ste. 305
Stockton, CA 95202-2306   Ph: (209)477-2098

──────────── **Colorado** ────────────

★4054★
Colorado Equal Employment Opportunity Department
PO Box 1575   Ph: (719)385-5900
Colorado Springs, CO 80901   Fax: (719)578-6601
Steve Masias, Dir.

★4055★
Denver Minority Business Development Center
930 W. 7th Ave.   Ph: (303)623-5660
Denver, CO 80204   Fax: (303)623-9015

──────────── **Connecticut** ────────────

★4056★
Bridgeport Affirmative Action Department
45 Lyon Terrace
Bridgeport, CT 06604   Ph: (203)576-8227
Alvin Penn, Affirmative Action Dir.

★4057★
Connecticut Children and Families Department
Affirmation Action Division
505 Hudson St.   Ph: (860)550-6303
Hartford, CT 06106   Fax: (860)566-7947

★4058★
Connecticut Environmental Protection Department
Affirmative Action Division
79 Elm St.   Ph: (860)424-3035
Hartford, CT 06106-5127   Fax: (860)424-4051

★4059★
Connecticut Human Rights and Opportunities
  Commission
21 Grand St.   Ph: (860)541-3449
Hartford, CT 06106   Fax: (860)246-3419
Louis Martin, Dir.

★4060★
Connecticut Social Services Department
Affirmative Action Division
25 Sigourney St.   Ph: (860)424-5036
Hartford, CT 06016   Fax: (860)424-5129

★4061★
Connecticut State Board of Education
Affirmation Action Office
165 Capitol Ave.   Ph: (860)566-7619
Hartford, CT 06145   Fax: (860)566-1080

─────────── **District of Columbia** ───────────

★4062★
District of Columbia Diversity and Special Services
Office
441 4th St. NW, Ste. 1160N   Ph: (202)727-1620
Washington, DC 20001   Fax: (202)727-0875
Ayo Bryant, Dir.

★4063★
District of Columbia Human Rights Commission
441 4th St. NW   Ph: (202)727-0656
Washington, DC 20001   Fax: (202)727-3781
James M. Loots, Chairperson

★4064★
District of Columbia Human Rights and Minority
Business Development Office
441 4th St. NW, Ste. 970   Ph: (202)724-1385
Washington, DC 20031   Fax: (202)724-3786
Gerald Draper, Dir.

★4065★
Minority Business Development Agency—Directory of
Regional and District Offices and Funded
Organizations
U.S. Minority Business Development
 Agency
Washington, DC 20230   Ph: (202)501-4698

★4066★
Washington Minority Business Development Center
1133-15th St., NW, Ste. 1120   Ph: (202)785-2886
Washington, DC 20005   Fax: (202)785-2890

─────────── **Florida** ───────────

★4067★
Florida Human Relations Commission
325 John Knox Rd.
Bldg. F, Ste 240   Ph: (904)488-7082
Tallahassee, FL 32303-4149   Fax: (904)488-5291
Ronald McElrath, Exec. Dir.

★4068★
Florida Labor and Employment Security Department
Civil Rights Office
2012 Capitol Circle SE, Hartman Bldg.   Ph: (904)488-5905
Tallahassee, FL 32399-2152   Fax: (904)488-8930

★4069★
Jacksonville Minority Business Development Center
218 W. Adams St., Ste. 300
Jacksonville, FL 32202-3502   Ph: (904)353-3826

★4070★
Miami/Ft. Lauderdale Minority Business Development
Center
1200 NW 78th Ave., Ste. 301   Ph: (305)591-7355
Miami, FL 33126   Fax: (305)477-7241

★4071★
Orlando Human Relations Office
400 S. Orange Ave.
Orlando, FL 32801   Ph: (407)246-2122
Albert Nelson

★4072★
Orlando Minority Business Development Center
7200 Lake Ellenor Dr., Ste.242
Orlando, FL 32809   Ph: (407)422-6234

★4073★
Tampa/St. Petersburg Minority Business
Development Center
4601 W. Kennedy Blvd., Ste. 200   Ph: (813)289-8824
Tampa, FL 33609   Fax: (813)289-8954

★4074★
West Palm Beach Minority Business Development
Center
2001 Broadway, Ste. 301
Riviera Beach, FL 33404   Ph: (407)393-2530

─────────── **Georgia** ───────────

★4075★
Atlanta Minority Business Development Center
75 Piedmont Ave., NE Ste. 256
Atlanta, GA 30303   Ph: (404)586-0973

★4076★
Augusta Equal Employment Office
Municipal Bldg.
530 Green St.
Augusta, GA 30911   Ph: (706)821-1786
Brenda Byrd-Pelaez, Equal Employment Off.

★4077★
Augusta Minority Business Development Center
1394 Lancy-Walker Blvd.   Ph: (706)722-0994
Augusta, GA 30901   Fax: (706)722-1730

★4078★
Columbus Minority Business Development Center
1214 1st Ave., Ste. 430
Columbus, GA 31902-1696   Ph: (404)324-4253

★4079★
Georgia Attorney General (Law Department)
Civil Rights Litigation Section
40 Capitol Square SW   Ph: (404)656-6197
Atlanta, GA 30334-1300   Fax: (404)651-9148

★4080★
Georgia Equal Opportunity Commission
229 Peachtree St. NE
710 Cain Towers   Ph: (404)656-1736
Atlanta, GA 30303   Fax: (404)656-4399
Mustafa Aziz, Admin.

★4081★
Georgia Human Relations Commission
225 Peachtree St. NE
1207 S Tower   Ph: (404)651-9115
Atlanta, GA 30303   Fax: (404)656-6046
Joy Berry, Exec. Dir.

★4082★
Savannah Minority Business Development Center
31 W. Congress St., Ste. 201
Savannah, GA 31401   Ph: (912)236-6708

──────── **Hawaii** ────────

★4083★
Hawaii Home Lands Department
PO Box 1879   Ph: (808)586-3800
Honolulu, HI 96805   Fax: (808)586-3899
Kali Watson, Chm.

★4084★
Honolulu Minority Business Development Center
1001 Bishop St., Ste. 2900
Honolulu, HI 96813   Ph: (808)536-0066

──────── **Idaho** ────────

★4085★
Idaho Human Rights Commission
PO Box 83720   Ph: (208)334-2873
Boise, ID 83720-0040   Fax: (208)334-2664
Marilyn T. Shuler, Dir.

──────── **Illinois** ────────

★4086★
Chicago Commission on Human Relations
510 N. Peshtigo Ct., Ste. 6A   Ph: (312)744-4100
Chicago, IL 60611   Fax: (312)744-1081
Clarence N. Wood, Commissioner

★4087★
Chicago Minority Business Development Center No.
2
700 1 Prudential Plaza
Chicago, IL 60601   Ph: (312)565-4710

★4088★
Chicago Minority Business Development Mega
Center
105 W. Adam 7th Fl.
Chicago, IL 60603   Ph: (312)977-9190

★4089★
Illinois Human Rights Commission
100 W Randolph St., Ste. 5-100   Ph: (312)814-6269
Chicago, IL 60601   Fax: (312)814-6271
Gail Bradshaw, Exec. Dir.

──────── **Indiana** ────────

★4090★
Coalition for Minority Business Development
Resource Directory
Indianapolis Chamber of Commerce
320 N. Meridian St., Ste. 200   Ph: (317)464-2242
Indianapolis, IN 46204   Fax: (317)464-2217

★4091★
Gary Minority Business Development Center
567 Broadway   Ph: (219)883-5802
Gary, IN 46402   Fax: (219)882-9042

★4092★
Indiana Administration Department
Minority Business Development Division
402 W Washington St., Rm. W474   Ph: (317)232-3073
Indianapolis, IN 46204   Fax: (317)233-5022
Elena Looper, Dir.

★4093★
Indiana Civil Rights Commission
100 N Senate Ave., Rm. N103   Ph: (317)232-2600
Indianapolis, IN 46204   Fax: (317)232-6580
Sandra D Leek, Dir.

★4094★
Indiana Health Department
Public Hea lth Services
Minority Health Office
2 Meridian St.   Ph: (317)233-7596
Indianapolis, IN 46204-1325   Fax: (317)233-7847

★4095★
Indiana Personnel Department
Affirmative Action Division
IGCS
402 W Washington St.   Ph: (317)232-3164
Indianapolis, IN 46204   Fax: (317)232-3089

──────── **Iowa** ────────

★4096★
Davenport Civil Rights Department
226 W. 4th St.   Ph: (319)326-0717
Davenport, IA 52801   Fax: (319)328-6726
Brenda Drew-Peeples, Dir.

★4097★
Dubuque Human Rights Office
City Hall
50 W 13th St.   Ph: (319)589-4190
Dubuque, IA 52001-4864   Fax: (319)589-4149
Elizabeth Creger, Dir.

★4098★
Iowa Civil Rights Commission
211 E Maple St., 2nd Fl.   Ph: (515)281-8084
Des Moines, IA 50309   Fax: (515)242-5840
Don Grove, Exec. Dir.

──────── **Kansas** ────────

★4099★
Kansas Human Rights Commission
900 SW Jackson St., Ste. 851 S   Ph: (913)296-3206
Topeka, KS 66612-1258   Fax: (913)296-0589

★4100★
Topeka Human Relations Office
215 SE 7th St.
Topeka, KS 66603   Ph: (785)368-3867
Dr. Don Miller, Human Relations Dir.

──────── **Kentucky** ────────

★4101★
Kentucky Finance and Administration Cabinet
Equal Employment Opportunity and Contract
Compliance Division
383 Capitol Annex   Ph: (502)564-2874
Frankfort, KY 40601   Fax: (502)564-6785

★4102★
Kentucky Human Rights Commission
332 W Broadway, 7th Fl.   Ph: (502)595-4024
Louisville, KY 40202   Fax: (502)595-4801
Beverly L. Watts, Exec. Dir.

★4103★
Kentucky Transportation Cabinet
Minority Affairs and Equal Employment Opportunity
Office
1002 State Office Bldg.
501 High St.   Ph: (502)564-3601
Frankfort, KY 40622   Fax: (502)564-4809

──────── **Louisiana** ────────

★4104★
Baton Rouge Business Development Center
2036 Woodale Blvd., Ste. D   Ph: (504)924-0186
Baton Rouge, LA 70806   Fax: (504)924-0036

★4105★
Louisiana Economic Development Department
Minority and Women's Business Division
PO Box 94185   Ph: (504)342-5388
Baton Rouge, LA 70804-9185   Fax: (504)342-9095

★4106★
Louisiana Office of the Governor
Human Rights Office
State Capitol, 5th Fl   Ph: (504)342-6969
Baton Rouge, LA 70804   Fax: (504)342-2063
Leah Raby, Exec. Dir.

★4107★
Louisiana Social Services Department
Civil Rights Division
PO Box 3776   Ph: (504)342-2700
Baton Rouge, LA 70821   Fax: (504)342-8636

★4108★
New Orleans Economic Development and Policy
Planning Division
Small and Disadvantaged Business Office
1515 Poydras St., 12th Fl.
New Orleans, LA 70112   Ph: (504)565-6971
Arnold Baker

★4109★
New Orleans Intergovernmental Relations Division
Human Relations Commission
1300 Perdido St., Ste. 2E10
New Orleans, LA 70112   Ph: (504)565-7916
Earl Jackson

★4110★
New Orleans Minority Business Development Center
1683 N. Claiborne
New Orleans, LA 70116   Ph: (504)947-1491

──────── **Maine** ────────

★4111★
Maine Human Rights Commission
51 State House Station   Ph: (207)624-6050
Augusta, ME 04333   Fax: (207)624-6063
Patricia Ryan, Exec. Dir.

──────── **Maryland** ────────

★4112★
Baltimore Minority Business Development Center
2901 Druid Park Dr., Ste. 201
Baltimore, MD 21215   Ph: (301)383-2214

★4113★
Maryland Human Relations Commission
6 St. Paul St., 9th Fl., Ste. 900   Ph: (410)767-8600
Baltimore, MD 21202   Fax: (410)333-1841
Henry B. Ford, Exec. Dir.

★4114★
Maryland Human Resources Department
Equal Opportunity Division
311 Saratoga St.   Ph: (410)767-7861
Baltimore, MD 21201   Fax: (410)333-0099

──────── **Massachusetts** ────────

★4115★
Boston Economic Development Department
Minority and Women Business Enterprises Office
1 City Hall Plaza
Boston, MA 02201   Ph: (617)635-4084
Brooke Woodson, Dir.

★4116★
Boston Minority Business Development Center
985 Commonwealth Ave.
Boston, MA 02215   Ph: (617)353-7060

★4117★
Massachusetts Affirmative Action Office
1 Ashburton Pl., Rm. 213   Ph: (617)727-7441
Boston, MA 02106   Fax: (617)727-0568
Mark D. Bolling, Dir.

★4118★
Massachusetts Commission Against Discrimination
1 Ashburton Pl., Rm. 601   Ph: (617)727-3990
Boston, MA 02108   Fax: (617)720-6053
Charles E. Walker Jr., Chm.

★4119★
Massachusetts Economic Development Department
Minority and Women's Business Division
100 Cambridge St.   Ph: (617)727-8692
Boston, MA 02202   Fax: (617)727-5915
France Lopez, Dir.

★4120★
Massachusetts Public Protection Bureau
Civil Rights and Civil Liberties Division
1 Ashburton Pl.   Ph: (617)727-2200
Boston, MA 02106   Fax: (617)727-5762

──────── **Michigan** ────────

★4121★
Detroit Human Rights Office
City-County Bldg.
2 Woodward Ave.   Ph: (313)224-4955
Detroit, MI 48226   Fax: (313)224-4433
John Roy Castillo, Dir.

★4122★
Flint Equal Opportunity Office
1101 S. Saginaw St.   Ph: (810)766-7295
Flint, MI 48502   Fax: (810)766-7218
Charles Winfrey, Equal Opportunity Off.

★4123★
Lansing Human Relations and Community Services
 Office
City Hall
124 W. Michigan
Lansing, MI 48933   Ph: (517)483-4477
Arthur Walker, Dir.

★4124★
Michigan Attorney General
Civil Rights Division
PO Box30212   Ph: (517)256-2557
Lansing, MI 48909   Fax: (517)335-4213

★4125★
Michigan Civil Rights Department
201 N Washington Sq., 7th Fl.   Ph: (517)335-3165
Lansing, MI 48913   Fax: (517)335-6513
Dr. Nanette Lee Reynolds, Dir.

★4126★
Michigan Civil Rights Department
Detroit Office
Plaza Bldg.
1200 6th St.   Ph: (313)256-2578
Detroit, MI 48226   Fax: (313)256-1035
Dr. Nanette Lee Reynolds, Dir.

★4127★
Michigan Civil Service Department
Equal Employment Opportunity and Affirmative
 Action Office
PO Box 30002   Ph: (517)373-2961
Lansing, MI 48909   Fax: (517)373-3103

★4128★
Michigan Family Independence Agency
Affirmative Action Office
235 S Grand Ave.
PO Box 30037   Ph: (517)373-8520
Lansing, MI 48909   Fax: (517)373-8471

★4129★
Michigan Minority Business Development Council
230 Fisher Bldg.
3011 W. Grand Blvd.   Ph: (313)873-3200
Detroit, MI 48202   Fax: (313)873-4783

★4130★
Michigan Transportation Department
Equal Employment Opportunity Office
Box 30050   Ph: (517)373-6732
Lansing, MI 48909   Fax: (517)373-6457

★4131★
Saginaw County Minority Business Development
 Center
901 S Washington
Saginaw, MI 48601-2554

——————— **Minnesota** ———————

★4132★
Minneapolis Civil Rights Office
309 2nd Ave. S, Rm. 239
Minneapolis, MN 55415   Ph: (612)673-2144
Kenneth White, Dir.

★4133★
Minneapolis Minority Business Development Center
2021 E. Hennepin Ave., Ste. LL 35   Ph: (612)331-5576
Minneapolis, MN 55413   Fax: (612)331-1045

★4134★
Minnesota Attorney General
Human Rights Division
1200 NCL Tower
St. Paul, MN 55101-2130   Ph: (612)296-9417

★4135★
Minnesota Employee Relations Department
Equal Opportunity Division
200 Centennial Office Bldg.
658 Cedar St.   Ph: (612)296-8272
St. Paul, MN 55155   Fax: (612)296-1990

★4136★
Minnesota Human Rights Department
190 E 5th St., Ste. 700   Ph: (612)296-5665
St. Paul, MN 55101   Fax: (612)296-1736
Dolores Fridge, Commissioner

★4137★
Minnesota Human Services Department
Equal Opportunity, Affirmative Action and Civil
 Rights Division
444 Lafayette Rd.   Ph: (612)296-3510
St. Paul, MN 55155   Fax: (612)296-5868

——————— **Mississippi** ———————

★4138★
Jackson Minority Business Development Center
5220 Keele St.
Jackson, MS 39206-4332   Ph: (601)362-2260

★4139★
Mississippi Economic and Community Development
 Department
Minority Business Office
PO Box 849   Ph: (601)359-3797
Jackson, MS 39205   Fax: (601)359-2832

★4140★
Mississippi Health Department
Minority Affairs Office
PO Box 1700   Ph: (601)960-7950
Jackson, MS 39215-1700   Fax: (601)960-7931

——————— **Missouri** ———————

★4141★
Kansas City Human Relations Office
414 E. 12th St.
Kansas City, MO 64106   Ph: (816)274-1194
Michael Bates, Dir.

★4142★
Kansas City Minority Business Development Center
1101 Walnut, Ste. 1900   Ph: (816)471-1520
Kansas City, MO 64106   Fax: (816)471-7923

★4143★
Missouri Health Department
Minority Health Office
PO Box 570   Ph: (573)526-1683
Jefferson City, MO 65102   Fax: (573)751-6010

★4144★
Missouri Human Rights Commission
3315 W Truman Blvd.   Ph: (573)751-3325
Jefferson City, MO 65102-1129 Fax: (573)751-2905
Steven Skolnick, Dir.

★4145★
St. Louis Civil Rights Enforcement Agency
906 Olive St., Ste. 1100   Ph: (314)622-3301
St. Louis, MO 63101   Fax: (314)622-4190
Jaqueline Lester, Exec. Dir.

★4146★
St. Louis Minority Business Development Center
500 Washington Ave., Ste. 1200
St. Louis, MO 63101   Ph: (314)621-6232

——————— **Montana** ———————

★4147★
Montana Labor and Industry Department
Human Rights Commission
PO Box 1728   Ph: (406)444-2884
Helena, MT 59624   Fax: (406)444-1394

★4148★
Montana Office of the Governor
Indian Affairs Coordinator
Capitol Building   Ph: (406)444-3702
Helena, MT 59620-0801   Fax: (406)444-5529
Wyman McDonald, Coordinator

——————— **Nebraska** ———————

★4149★
Lincoln Human Rights/Equal Opportunity Office
129 N. 10th St.
Lincoln, NE 68508   Ph: (402)441-7624
Enrique Brossky

★4150★
Nebraska Equal Opportunity Commission
PO Box 94934   Ph: (402)471-2024
Lincoln, NE 68509-4934 Fax: (402)471-4059
Alfonzo Whitaker, Exec. Dir.

★4151★
Nebraska Labor Department
Civil Rights Division
PO Box 94600
Lincoln, NE 68509-4600 Fax: (402)471-2318

——————— **Nevada** ———————

★4152★
Las Vegas Minority Business Development Center
716 South 6th St.
Las Vegas, NV 89101   Ph: (702)384-3293

★4153★
Nevada Employment Training and Rehabilitation
  Department
Equal Employment Opportunity Office
500 East 3rd St., Rm. 200 Ph: (702)687-4651
Carson City, NV 89713   Fax: (702)687-8351
Maureen Cole, EEO Off.

★4154★
Nevada Equal Rights Commission
1515 E. Tropicana Ave., Ste. 590 Ph: (702)486-7161
Las Vegas, NV 89119   Fax: (702)486-7054
William Stewart, Admin.

★4155★
Nevada Personnel Department
Affirmative Action Office
209 E. Musser St.   Ph: (702)687-3509
Carson City, NV 89710   Fax: (702)687-5017

——————— **New Hampshire** ———————

★4156★
New Hampshire Human Rights Commission
163 Loudon Rd.   Ph: (603)271-2767
Concord, NH 03301-5151 Fax: (603)271-6339
Raymond S. Perry Jr., Exec. Dir.

——————— **New Jersey** ———————

★4157★
Harlem Minority Business Development Center
270 Sylvan Ave.
Englewood Cliffs, NJ 07632 Ph: (201)661-8044

★4158★
New Jersey Attorney General
Law and Public Safety Department
Civil Rights Division
383 W. State St.
Trenton, NJ 08625-0089 Ph: (609)984-3101

★4159★
New Jersey Commerce and Economic Development
  Department
Development for Small Business, Women and
  Minorities Division
CN 820
20 W State St.   Ph: (609)292-3860
Trenton, NJ 08625-0820 Fax: (609)777-4097

★4160★
New Jersey Community Affairs Department
Affirmative Action Office
CN 800
101 S. Broad St.   Ph: (609)292-6830
Trenton, NJ 08625-0800 Fax: (609)984-6696
Lorraine Aldridge, Affirmative Action Off.

★4161★
New Jersey Personnel Department
Equal Employment Opportunity/Affirmative Action
  Division
CN 317
44 S. Clinton Ave.   Ph: (609)777-0919
Trenton, NJ 08625-0317 Fax: (609)984-3631

★4162★
New Jersey Transportation Department
Civil Rights Office
CN 601
1035 Pkwy. Ave.   Ph: (609)530-3009
Trenton, NJ 08625-0601 Fax: (609)530-3894

★4163★
Newark Minority Business Development Center
60 Park Pl., Ste. 1404
Newark, NJ 07102   Ph: (201)623-7712

New Mexico

★4164★
Albuquerque Minority Business Development Center
718 Central SW   Ph: (505)843-7114
Albuquerque, NM 87102   Fax: (505)242-2030

★4165★
New Mexico Labor Department
Human Rights Division
1596 Pacheco St.   Ph: (505)827-6838
Santa Fe, NM 87505   Fax: (505)827-6878
Richard Galaz, Dir.

New York

★4166★
Brooklyn Minority Business Development Center
30 Flatbush Ave., Ste. 423
Brooklyn, NY 11217   Ph: (718)522-5880

★4167★
Buffalo Minority Business Development Center
523 Delaware Ave.
Buffalo, NY 14202   Ph: (716)885-0336

★4168★
Manhattan Minority Business Development Center
51 Madison Ave., Ste. 2212
New York, NY 10010   Ph: (212)779-4360

★4169★
Nassau/Suffolk Minority Business Development Center
150 Broad Hollow Rd., Ste. 304   Ph: (516)549-5454
Melville, NY 11747   Fax: (516)549-5703

★4170★
New York City Community Assistance Unit
51 Chambers St., Rm. 630   Ph: (212)788-7418
New York, NY 10007   Fax: (212)788-7754
Rosemarie C. O'Keefe, Commissioner

★4171★
New York Empire State Development Corporation
Minority and Women's Business Development Office
1 Commerce Plz.   Ph: (518)474-6346
Albany, NY 12245   Fax: (518)473-9374

★4172★
New York Mental Retardation and Developmental
Disabilities Agency
Equal Opportunity Office
44 Holland Ave.   Ph: (518)473-8084
Albany, NY 12229   Fax: (518)473-1271

★4173★
New York Secretary of State
State Department
Affirmative Action Office
41 State St.   Ph: (518)474-2750
Albany, NY 12231   Fax: (518)474-4765

★4174★
New York State Agricultural and Markets Department
Affirmative Action Program
1 Winners Circle   Ph: (518)457-4418
Albany, NY 12235   Fax: (518)457-3087

★4175★
New York State Civil Service Department
Affirmative Action Office
State Office Campus, Bldg. 1   Ph: (518)457-6935
Albany, NY 12239-0001   Fax: (518)457-7547
Barbara Wooten, Affirmative Action Off.

★4176★
New York State Education Department
Affirmative Action Office
Education Bldg.
Washington Ave.   Ph: (518)474-1265
Albany, NY 12234   Fax: (518)473-4909

★4177★
New York State Equal Employment Opportunity
Division
100 Church St.   Ph: (212)788-1010
New York, NY 10007   Fax: (212)788-1621
Linda G. Howard, EEO Off.

★4178★
New York State General Services Office
Affirmative Action Office
Coming Tower
Empire State Plz., 41st Fl.
Albany, NY 12242
Martha Sherwood, Affirmative Action Off.

★4179★
New York State Housing and Community Renewal
Division
Affirmative Action Unit
1 Fordham Plz.   Ph: (718)563-5848
Bronx, NY 10454   Fax: (718)563-5840

★4180★
New York State Human Rights Commission
40 Rector St.   Ph: (212)306-7550
New York, NY 10006   Fax: (212)306-7658
Marta B. Varela, Chairman/Commissioner

★4181★
New York State Human Rights Division
55 W 125th St.   Ph: (212)961-8790
New York, NY 10027   Fax: (212)961-8552
Edward Marcado, Commissioner

★4182★
New York State Labor Department
Equal Opportunity Development Division
State Campus, Bldg. 12   Ph: (518)457-8119
Albany, NY 12240   Fax: (518)457-6908

★4183★
Queens Minority Business Development Center
110-29 Horace Harding Expy.
Corona, NY 11368   Ph: (718)699-2400

★4184★
Rochester Minority Business Development Center
350 North St.
Rochester, NY 14605   Ph: (716)232-6120

★4185★
Williamsburg/Brooklyn Minority Business
Development Center
12 Heywood St.
Brooklyn, NY 11211   Ph: (718)522-5620

North Carolina

★4186★
Charlotte Minority Business Development Center
700 E. Stonewall St., Ste. 360
Charlotte, NC 28202   Ph: (704)334-7522

★4187★
Durham Equal Opportunity/Equity Assurance Office
101 City Hall Plaza   Ph: (919)560-4180
Durham, NC 27701   Fax: (919)687-0896
Cora Cole-McFadden

★4188★
**Environment, Health and Natural Resources
  Department**
Health Director's Office
Minority Health Office
PO Box 27687   Ph: (919)715-4125
Raleigh, NC 27611   Fax: (919)715-3060

★4189★
Fayetteville Minority Business Development Center
114 1/2 Anderson St.
Fayetteville, NC 28302   Ph: (919)483-7513

★4190★
**North Carolina Environmental, Health and Natural
  Resources Department**
Equal Employment Opportunity Office
PO Box 27687   Ph: (919)733-4984
Raleigh, NC 27611-7687   Fax: (919)715-3060

★4191★
**Raleigh/Durham Minority Business Development
  Center**
205 Fayetteville Street Mail, Ste. 200   Ph: (919)833-6122
Raleigh, NC 27601-1362   Fax: (919)821-3572

North Dakota

★4192★
North Dakota Labor Department
Equal Employment Opportunity Division
600 E. Boulevard Ave., 15th Fl.   Ph: (701)328-2660
Bismarck, ND 58505-0340   Fax: (701)328-2031

★4193★
North Dakota Transportation Department
Civil Rights Office
608 E. Boulevard Ave.   Ph: (701)328-2576
Bismarck, ND 58505-0700   Fax: (701)328-4545

Ohio

★4194★
Cincinnati Economic Development Department
Small Business Division
City Hall
801 Plum St., Rm. 15
Cincinnati, OH 45202   Ph: (513)352-3952
Patricia King

★4195★
Cincinnati Equal Employment Opportunity Office
City Hall
801 Plum St., Rm. 15
Cincinnati, OH 45202   Ph: (513)352-2444
Wendell Young

★4196★
Cincinnati Human Relations Department
City Hall
801 Plum St., Rm. 15
Cincinnati, OH 45202   Ph: (513)352-3237
Arzell Nelson, Exec. Dir.

★4197★
**Cleveland Minority Business Development Center No.
  1**
601 Lakeside, Ste. 335   Ph: (216)664-4150
Cleveland, OH 44114   Fax: (216)664-3870

★4198★
**Cleveland Minority Business Development Center No.
  2**
6200 Frank Rd. NW
Canton, OH 44720-7299   Ph: (330)494-6170

★4199★
Columbus Minority Business Development Center
37 N. High St.
Columbus, OH 43215   Ph: (614)225-6910

★4200★
Ohio Agricultural Department
Equal Employment Opportunity and Training Section
8995 E. Main St.
Reynoldsburg, OH 43068

★4201★
Ohio Attorney General
Civil Rights Section
30 E. Broad St.
Columbus, OH 43215-3428   Ph: (614)466-7900

★4202★
Ohio Civil Rights Commission
220 Parsons St., Ste. 4020   Ph: (614)466-2785
Columbus, OH 43215-5385   Fax: (614)644-8776
Francis Smith, Exec. Dir.

★4203★
Ohio Development Department
Minority Business Development Office
PO Box 1001   Ph: (614)466-5700
Columbus, OH 43216-1001   Fax: (614)644-0745

★4204★
Ohio Health Department
Equal Employment Opportunity Office
246 N High St.   Ph: (614)752-4935
Columbus, OH 43266-0588   Fax: (614)644-0085

★4205★
Ohio Health Department
Minority Affairs Office
PO Box 118   Ph: (614)644-1101
Columbus, OH 43266-0588   Fax: (614)644-0085

★4206★
Ohio Office of the Governor
Multicultural Affairs Office
77 S. High St., 30th Fl.   Ph: (614)644-0813
Columbus, OH 43266-0601   Fax: (614)466-9354

Oklahoma

★4207★
Oklahoma City Minority Business Development
Center
1500 NE 4th St., Ste. 101
Oklahoma City, OK 73117   Ph: (405)235-0430

★4208★
Oklahoma Employment Security Commission
Equal Employment Opportunity Office
PO Box 52003   Ph: (405)557-0200
Oklahoma City, OK 73152-2003   Fax: (405)557-7258

★4209★
Oklahoma Health Department
Affirmative Action Division
1000 NE 10th St.   Ph: (405)271-4171
Oklahoma City, OK 73117-1299   Fax: (405)271-3431

★4210★
Oklahoma Human Rights Commission
2102 N. Lincoln Blvd., Rm 480   Ph: (405)521-3441
Oklahoma City, OK 73105   Fax: (405)522-3534
Grace Monson, Dir.

★4211★
Oklahoma Human Services Department
Affirmative Action Office
PO Box 25352   Ph: (405)521-2234
Oklahoma City, OK 73125   Fax: (405)521-6458

★4212★
Tulsa Human Rights Office
707 S. Houston , Ste. 303
Tulsa, OK 74127   Ph: (918)596-7820
Dyanne Mason, Dir.

★4213★
Tulsa Minority Business Development Center
240 E. Apache St.
Tulsa, OK 74106   Ph: (918)592-1995

Oregon

★4214★
Oregon Office of the Governor
Affirmative Action Office
State Capitol Bldg., Rm. 254   Ph: (503)378-1111
Salem, OR 97310   Fax: (503)378-6827
Raleigh Lewis, Dir.

★4215★
Oregon Transportation Department
Human Resources and Organization Development
  Branch
Civil Rights Section
Transportation Bldg,, Rm. 102   Ph: (503)986-3700
Salem, OR 97310   Fax: (503)986-3446

★4216★
Portland Minority Business Development Center
8959 SW Barbur Blvd., Ste. 102
Portland, OR 97219   Ph: (503)245-9253

Pennsylvania

★4217★
Pennsylvania Aging Department
Affirmative Action Office
Rachel Carson State Office Bldg.
400 Market St., 6th Fl.
Harrisburg, PA 17101-2301   Ph: (717)783-1550

★4218★
Pennsylvania Education Department
Postsecondary and Higher Education Office
Equal Employment Opportunity Office
333 Market St.   Ph: (717)783-9531
Harrisburg, PA 17126-0333   Fax: (717)783-0583

★4219★
Pennsylvania General Services Department
Minority Development Office
North Office Bldg., Rm. 515   Ph: (717)787-7629
Harrisburg, PA 17125   Fax: (717)772-2026

★4220★
Pennsylvania Human Relations Commission
PO Box 3145   Ph: (717)787-4410
Harrisburg, PA 17105-3145   Fax: (717)787-0420
Homer C. Floyd, Exec. Dir.

★4221★
Pennsylvania Public Welfare Department
Affirmative Action Office
Box 2675   Ph: (717)787-9695
Harrisburg, PA 17105   Fax: (717)787-2062

★4222★
Pennsylvania Transportation Department
Equal Opportunity Bureau
555 Walnut St., 9th Fl.
Forum Place   Ph: (717)787-5891
Harrisburg, PA 17101-1900   Fax: (717)787-5491

★4223★
Philadelphia Mayor's Action Center
City Hall, Rm. 143
Philadelphia, PA 19107   Ph: (215)686-6216
Renee R. Grundy, Dir.

★4224★
Pittsburgh Minority Business Development Center
168 S 19th St.
Pittsburgh, PA 15203-1856   Ph: (412)921-1155

Puerto Rico

★4225★
Mayaguez Minority Business Development Center
70 W. Mendez Bigo
Mayaguez, PR 00680   Ph: (809)833-7783

★4226★
Ponce Minority Business Development Center
19 Salud St.
Ponce, PR 00731   Ph: (809)840-8100

Rhode Island

★4227★
Providence Human Relations Office
151 Weybosset St.
Providence, RI 02903   Ph: (401)421-3708
Christine Roundtree, Exec. Dir.

★4228★
Rhode Island Administration Department
Human Resources Office
Minority Business Enterprise
1 Capital Hill   Ph: (401)277-6246
Providence, RI 02908-5868   Fax: (401)277-6378

★4229★
Rhode Island Education Department
Elementary and Secondary Office
Equity and Access Office
Shepard Bldg.
255 Westminster St.   Ph: (401)277-4979
Providence, RI 02903   Fax: (401)277-6178

★4230★
Rhode Island Human Rights Commission
10 Abbott Park Pl.   Ph: (401)277-2661
Providence, RI 02903-3768   Fax: (401)277-2616

★4231★
Rhode Island Transportation Department
Equal Employment Opportunity Office
2 Capitol Hill, Rm 210   Ph: (401)277-3260
Providence, RI 02903   Fax: (401)277-6038

South Carolina

★4232★
Charleston Minority Business Development Center
701 E. Bay St., Ste. 1539
Charleston, SC 29403   Ph: (803)724-3477

★4233★
South Carolina Human Affairs Commission
Fair Housing Division
PO Box 4490   Ph: (803)737-7800
Columbia, SC 29240   Fax: (803)253-4191

South Dakota

★4234★
South Dakota Education and Cultural Affairs
  Department
Education Division
Equal Employment Opportunity
700 Governors Dr.   Ph: (605)773-4257
Pierre, SD 57501-2291   Fax: (605)773-6139

Tennessee

★4235★
Memphis Minority Business Development Center
5 3rd St., Ste. N 2020
Memphis, TN 38103   Ph: (901)527-2298

★4236★
Nashville Minority Business Development Center
PO Box 22561   Ph: (615)255-0432
Nashville, TN 37202-2561   Fax: (615)255-2377

★4237★
Tennessee Attorney General's Office
Civil Rights and Claims Division
450 James Robertson Pkwy.   Ph: (615)741-2091
Nashville, TN 37243-2009   Fax: (615)741-2009

★4238★
Tennessee Economic and Community Development
  Department
Minority Business Enterprise Division
320 6th Ave. N. 8th Fl.   Ph: (615)741-2545
Nashville, TN 37243-0405   Fax: (615)741-7306

★4239★
Tennessee Health Department
Minority Health Office
426 5th Ave. N, 3rd Fl.   Ph: (615)741-9443
Nashville, TN 37247-0101   Fax: (615)741-0544

★4240★
Tennessee Human Rights Commission
530 Church St., Ste. 400   Ph: (615)741-5825
Nashville, TN 37243   Free: 800-325-9664
          Fax: (615)532-2197

Warren N. Moore, Exec. Dir.

★4241★
Tennessee Personnel Department
Employee Development and Equal Employment
  Opportunity Division
James K. Polk Bldg., 2nd Fl.   Ph: (615)741-4845
Nashville, TN 37243-0635   Fax: (615)532-0728
Rosie Wilson

Texas

★4242★
Austin Minority Business Development Center
301 Congress Ave., Ste. 1020
Austin, TX 78701   Ph: (512)476-9700

★4243★
Beaumont Minority Business Development Center
550 Fannin, Ste. 106A
Beaumont, TX 77701   Ph: (409)835-1377

★4244★
Brownsville Minority Business Development Center
2100 Boca Chica, Ste. 301   Ph: (210)546-3400
Brownsville, TX 78521-2265   Fax: (210)546-3527

★4245★
Corpus Christi Minority Business Development
  Center
3649 Leopard, Ste. 514   Ph: (512)887-7961
Corpus Christi, TX 78408   Fax: (512)884-5128

★4246★
Dallas/Ft. Worth Minority Business Development
  Center
1445 Ross Ave., Ste. 800
Dallas, TX 75202   Ph: (214)855-7373

★4247★
El Paso Minority Business Development Center
1312-A E. Rio Grande St.
El Paso, TX 79902   Ph: (915)544-2700

★4248★
Fort Worth Human Relations Department
1000 Throckmorton St.   Ph: (817)871-7567
Fort Worth, TX 76102   Fax: (817)871-6196
Michael Ivey, Human Relations Commissioner

★4249★
Houston Citizen Assistance Office
PO Box 1562
Houston, TX 77251-1562   Ph: (713)247-1888
Jesse Cantu, Dir.

★4250★
Houston Minority Business Development Center
1200 Smith St., Ste. 2870
Houston, TX 77002   Ph: (713)650-3831

★4251★
Laredo Minority Business Development Center
1602 Victoria St.   Ph: (210)726-8815
Laredo, TX 78040-4954   Fax: (210)726-1051

★4252★
Lubbock Human Relations Department
PO Box 2000
Lubbock, TX 79457   Ph: (806)767-3000
Anthony Jones, Dir.

★4253★
Lubbock/Midland-Odessa Minority Business
  Development Center
1220 Broadway, Ste. 509
Lubbock, TX 79401   Ph: (806)762-6232

★4254★
McAllen Minority Business Development Center
1701 W. Bus. Hwy. 83, Ste. 1108
McAllen, TX 78501   Ph: (512)687-5224

★4255★
San Antonio Minority Business Development Center
1222 N. Main, Ste. 750
San Antonio, TX 78212   Ph: (210)558-2480

★4256★
Texas Higher Education Coordinating Board
Access and Equity Division
PO Box 12788   Ph: (512)483-6101
Austin, TX 78711   Fax: (512)483-6169

★4257★
Texas Transportation Department
Civil Rights Division
125 E. 11th St.   Ph: (512)305-9501
Austin, TX 78701-2483   Fax: (512)463-9389

───────────── **Utah** ─────────────

★4258★
Salt Lake City Minority Business Development
  Center
350 East 500 S., Ste. 101
Salt Lake City, UT 84111   Ph: (801)328-8181

★4259★
Utah Industrial Commission
Anti-Discrimination Division
PO Box 146600   Ph: (801)530-6921
Salt Lake City, UT 84114-6600   Fax: (801)530-6804

───────────── **Vermont** ─────────────

★4260★
Vermont Human Services Agency
Economic Opportunity Office
103 S Main St, State Complex   Ph: (802)241-2453
Waterbury, VT 05671-0201   Fax: (802)241-2979

───────────── **Virgin Islands** ─────────────

★4261★
Virgin Islands Minority Business Development Center
81-AB Princess Gade
St. Thomas, VI 00804   Ph: (809)774-7215

───────────── **Virginia** ─────────────

★4262★
Alexandria Human Rights Office
301 King St.
Alexandria, VA 22314   Ph: (703)838-6390
Robert Steindler, Human Rights Administrator

★4263★
Newport News Minority Business Development
  Center
6060 Jefferson Ave., Ste. 6016   Ph: (804)245-8743
Newport News, VA 23605   Fax: (804)245-0115

★4264★
Norfolk Minority Business Development Center
355 Crawford Pkwy., Ste. 608
Portsmouth, VA 23701   Ph: (804)399-0888

★4265★
Virginia Commerce and Trade Office
Employment Commission
Equal Employment Office
703 E Main St.   Ph: (804)786-3025
Richmond, VA 23219   Fax: (804)225-3923
Alexis Thornton-Crump, EEO Off.

★4266★
Virginia Health and Human Resources Office
Public Health Programs
Minority Health Office
PO Box 2448   Ph: (804)786-4891
Richmond, VA 23218   Fax: (804)784-0814

★4267★
Virginia Human Rights Council
Washington Bldg., 12th Fl.
1100 Bank St.   Ph: (804)255-2292
Richmond, VA 23219   Fax: (804)255-3294
Roxie Raines-Kornegay, Dir.

★4268★
Virginia Minority Business Enterprises Department
200-202 N 9th St. Office Bldg., 11th Fl   Ph: (804)786-5560
Richmond, VA 23219   Fax: (804)371-7359
Ken A P Smith, Dir.

★4269★
Virginia Transportation Office
Administration Department
Equal Employment Opportunity Division
1401 East Broad St.   Ph: (804)786-2085
Richmond, VA 23219   Fax: (804)786-2940

───────────── **Washington** ─────────────

★4270★
Seattle Civil Rights Office
700 3rd Ave., Ste. 250
Seattle, WA 98104   Ph: (206)684-4500
Germaine Covington, Dir.

★4271★
**Seattle Minority Business Development Center,
IMPACT Business Consultants**
10740 Meridian N, Ste. 102   Ph: (206)363-6167
Seattle, WA 98133   Fax: (206)363-6164

★4272★
Washington Human Rights Commission
PO Box 422490   Ph: (360)753-6770
Olympia, WA 98504-2490   Fax: (360)586-2282
Idolina Reta, Exec. Dir.

──────────── **West Virginia** ────────────

★4273★
West Virginia Human Rights Commission
1321 Plaza E, Rm 108A   Ph: (304)558-2616
Charleston, WV 25301-1400   Fax: (304)558-0085
Herman H. Jones, Exec. Dir.

★4274★
**West Virginia Minority and Small Business
Development Agency**
950 Kanawha Blvd. E, Ste. 200   Ph: (304)558-2960
Charleston, WV 25301-0311   Fax: (304)588-0127
Hazel Kroesser-Palmer, Dir.

──────────── **Wisconsin** ────────────

★4275★
Milwaukee Minority Business Development Center
1442 N Farwell, Ste. 500   Ph: (414)289-3422
Milwaukee, WI 53202   Fax: (414)289-3424

★4276★
**Wisconsin Health and Social Services Department
Affirmative Action and Civil Rights Office**
PO Box 1768   Ph: (608)266-3465
Madison, WI 53707-7850   Fax: (608)266-7882

──────────── **Alberta** ────────────

★4277★
Alberta Human Rights and Citizenship Commission
Standard Life Centre, #1600
10405 Jasper Ave.   Ph: (403)427-3116
Edmonton, AB, Canada T5J 4R7   Fax: (403)422-3563

★4278★
Alberta Human Rights Secretariat
Standard Life Centre
10405 Jasper Ave., 7th Fl.   Ph: (403)427-3116
Edmonton, AB, Canada T5J 4R7   Fax: (403)422-3563

★4279★
Alberta Multiculturalism Commission
Standard Life Centre
10405 Jasper Ave., 9th Fl.   Ph: (403)427-2927
Edmonton, AB, Canada T5J 4R7   Fax: (403)422-6348

──────────── **British Columbia** ────────────

★4280★
British Columbia Council of Human Rights
844 Courtney St., 2nd Fl.   Ph: (250)387-3710
Victoria, BC, Can ada V8V 1X4   Fax: (250)387-3643

──────────── **Manitoba** ────────────

★4281★
Manitoba Human Rights Commission
259 Portage Ave., #301   Ph: (204)945-3007
Winnipeg, MB, Canada R3B 2A9   Fax: (204)945-1292

★4282★
**Manitoba Minister for Culture, Heritage and
Citizenship, and Multiculturalism**
Legislative Bldg.   Ph: (204)945-3729
Winnipeg, MB, Canada R3C 0V8   Fax: (204)945-5223
Hon. Harold Gilshammer, Minister

──────────── **New Brunswick** ────────────

★4283★
New Brunswick Human Rights Commission
751 Brunswick St.
PO Box 6000   Ph: (506)453-2301
Fredericton, NB, Canada E3B 5H1   Fax: (506)453-2653

──────────── **Newfoundland** ────────────

★4284★
**Newfoundland and Labrador Human Rights
Commission**
PO Box 8700   Ph: (709)729-2709
St. John's, NF, Canada A1B 4J6   Fax: (709)729-0790

──────────── **Nova Scotia** ────────────

★4285★
Nova Scotia Human Rights Commission
Lord Nelson Arcade
5675 Spring Garden Rd., 7th Fl.
PO Box 2221   Ph: (902)424-4111
Halifax, NS, Canada B3J 3C4   Fax: (902)424-0596

──────────── **Ontario** ────────────

★4286★
Ontario Human Rights Commission
400 University Ave., 12th Fl.   Ph: (416)314-4500
Toronto, ON, Canada M7A 2R9   Fax: (416)314-4533

──────────── **Prince Edward Island** ────────────

★4287★
Prince Edward Island Human Rights Commission
3 Queen St.
PO Box 2000   Ph: (902)368-4180
Charlottetown, PE, Canada C1A 7N8   Fax: (902)368-4236

──────────── **Saskatchewan** ────────────

★4288★
Saskatchewan Human Rights Commission
122-3 Ave. N, 8th Fl.   Ph: (306)933-5952
Saskatoon, SK, Canada S7K 2H6   Fax: (306)933-7863

Library Collections

★4289★
Cultural Survival, Inc.
96 Mt. Auburn St.   Ph: (617)441-5400
Cambridge, MA 02138-5017   Fax: (617)441-5417
Heather Armitage, Dir.

Founded: 1972 **Subjects:** Indigenous populations, ethnic minorities, human rights, development, social impact, culture change. **Holdings:** 10,000 clippings; 1000 reports and documents. **Subscriptions:** 150 journals and other serials; 20 newspapers.

★4290★
U.S. National Archives and Records Administration
National Archives - Pacific Region
1000 Commodore Dr.   Ph: (415)876-9009
San Bruno, CA 94066-2350   Fax: (415)876-9233
Waverly B. Lowell, Dir.

Founded: 1969 **Subjects:** Archival records of the Federal Government in Nevada (except Clark County), Northern California, Hawaii, American Samoa, Guam, the Trust Territory of the Pacific Islands. **Special Collections:** Records of the Government of American Samoa; records of the Bureau of Indian Affairs in California and Nevada; Chinese immigration records; records of naval shipyards at Pearl Harbor, HI, and Mare Island, CA; records relating to World War II industry, labor, housing, and racial discrimination in employment; records of federal district courts in Northern California, Hawaii, and Nevada; records of The Immigration and Naturalization Service; and of the U.S. Court of Appeals for the Ninth Circuit; records relating to scientific and technical research in agriculture, aviation, civil and military engineering, fisheries, forestry, high-energy physics, river basins, and waterways; records relating to maritime history; national parks and national forests; migratory labor; land use; mining; records of U.S. Penitentiary at Alcatraz; records of the San Francisco mint. **Holdings:** 44,000 cubic feet of original records; 55,000 reels of microfilm. **Subscriptions:** 6 journals and other serials.

★4291★
U.S. National Archives and Records Administration
National Archives - Southwest Region
501 Felix at Hemphill, Bldg. 1
Box 6216   Ph: (817)334-5515
Fort Worth, TX 76115   Fax: (817)334-5621
Kent Carter, Dir., Regional Adm.

Founded: 1969 **Subjects:** Inactive records of U.S. government agencies in Texas, Oklahoma, Arkansas, New Mexico, Louisiana. **Special Collections:** U.S. census reports, 1790-1920; index to some Civil War service records; passenger records from various ports; Bureau of Indian Affairs records from the state of Oklahoma. **Holdings:** 68,000 cubic feet of records; 70,000 reels of microfilm.

★4292★
U.S. National Archives and Records Administration
Still Picture Branch
8601 Adelphi Rd.
Room 5360   Ph: (301)713-6625
College Park, MD 20740-6001   Fax: (301)713-7436
James Hastings, Actg.Chf.

Founded: 1935 **Subjects:** AV materials; still photography; posters; United States - history, politics, government. **Special Collections:** Included in the wide-ranging files are historical photographs from such agencies as: American Commission for the Protection and Salvage of Artistic and Historic Monuments in War Areas, 1943-1946 (German destruction of monuments; vandalism of historic buildings; architectural damage caused by war activities in Europe and Japan; works of art); Department of Defense, 1775-1982 (Army, Navy, Air Force, Marine Corps personnel, activities, installations, ordnance, transport; includes Revolutionary War, Mathew Brady Civil War photographs, western exploration, surveys, settlement, minor military expeditions, Spanish-American War, World War I, history of flight, scenic photographs, recruiting and war loan posters, effects of atomic bombing of Japan, occupation of Germany and Japan, U.S. Navy, Army, Air Force, Marine Corps photographs of

World War II, the Korean War, and Vietnam War); Harmon Foundation Donated Materials; Collection of Photographs, 1922-1966 (art works by black American and African artists; prominent black Americans; foreign art objects; activities of blacks on campuses of southern colleges; exhibits of black artists' works and art workshops); Department of the Interior, 1850-1973 (geological surveys-Hayden, Powell, King & Wheeler surveys; western land development; coastal fishing; wildlife; power, irrigation, soil conservation projects; national parks and recreation; U.S. territories; Indian affairs; Antarctic exploration; Bureau of Mines activities and Russell Lee photographs of coal mining activities in 1946); War Relocation Authority photos of relocation of Japanese Americans; NASA 1920-1965 (history of aviation and rocketry research and development; lunar surface photographs); Tennessee Valley Authority, 1933-1941 (dams, scenery, recreational areas; Lewis Hine photographs of families forced to leave their land); Department of the Treasury, 1917-1977 (posters for war bonds and E bonds campaigns; stills from World War I promotional movies; Bureau of Engraving and printing activities); Office of War Information, 1940-1950 (World War II military operations and U.S. home front; U.S. and foreign posters; international conferences and personalities; views of American life and culture for foreign distribution); United States Information Agency (USIA) (photographs documenting American social, political, and cultural history, 1948-1984). **Holdings:** 8.5 million archival photographs and graphics from U.S. Federal Government agencies that document American and world cultural, social, environmental, economic, technological, political history of a non governmental nature as well as activities of military and civilian governmental agencies; historical photographs of precursors of contemporary governmental activity; 12,000 posters (ca 1800 to present). **Subscriptions:** 2 journals and other serials.

Research Centers

★4293★
Brown University
Center for the Study of Race and Ethnicity in
   America
Box 1886   Ph: (401)863-3080
Providence, RI 02912   Fax: (401)863-7589
Fayneese Miller, Dir.

Research Activities and Fields: Racial and ethnic minorities in America, focusing on African Americans, Asian Americans, Latinos, and Native Americans. Emphasis is on interdisciplinary, comparative, and analytical studies of race, gender, and class. **Publications:** Newsletter, quarterly.

★4294★
Center for Third World Organizing
1218 E. 21st St.   Ph: (510)533-7583
Oakland, CA 94606   Fax: (510)533-0923
Mr. Francis Calpotura, Co-Dir.

Founded: 1980 **Research Activities and Fields:** Policies and programs critical to people of color in the U.S. Research includes studies on welfare, free enterprise zones, subminimum wage, toxics, and immigration. Creates a network of African-American, Latino, Asian, and Native American communities and develops links to community activists and progressives in the U.S. and abroad. **Publications:** Occasional Papers Series; Minority Trendsletter, quarterly; Issue Pac Series, quarterly.

★4295★
Colorado State University
Center for Applied Studies in American Ethnicity
Fort Collins, CO 80523-1790   Ph: (970)491-2418
    Fax: (970)491-2717
Dr. Paul Wong, Dir.

Founded: 1993 **Research Activities and Fields:** Native American language preservation, issues of Native American identity, Asian American independent film making, formation of multi-ethnic communities in south central Colorado, changes and continuities within 19th and 20th century black communities, race, ethnicity, and nationality in the United States; race and fairness in sentencing;

ethnicity/race in comparative perspective; minority educational issues and social policy. **Publications:** CASAE News.

★4296★
Cultural Survival Center
96 Mt. Auburn   Ph: (617)441-5400
Cambridge, MA 02138   Fax: (617)441-5417
Marie Tocco, Dir.

Founded: 1972 **Research Activities and Fields:** Indigenous populations, ethnic minorities, human rights, social impact, cultural development and change, and conflict management. **Publications:** Cultural Survival Quarterly; Occasional Reports.

★4297★
Kansas State University
Multicultural Research and Resource Center
KSU Libraries   Ph: (785)532-7470
Manhattan, KS 66506   Fax: (785)532-6144
Molly Royse, Coord.

Founded: 1971 **Research Activities and Fields:** African Americans, Hispanic Americans, Native Americans, and Asian Americans.

★4298★
Princeton University
Woodrow Wilson School of Public and International Affairs
Bendheim-Thomas Center for Child Wellbeing
21 Prospect Ave.   Ph: (609)258-4875
Princeton, NJ 08544   Fax: (609)258-1039
Prof. Sara McLanahan, Dir.

Research Activities and Fields: Child Health and development, evaluations of specific policies and Programs.

★4299★
University of Colorado at Boulder
Center for Studies of Ethnicity and Race in America
Ketchum 30
CB 339   Ph: (303)492-8852
Boulder, CO 80309-0339   Fax: (303)492-7799
Dr. Evelyn Hu-DeHart, Dir.

Founded: 1988 **Research Activities and Fields:** Comparative race and ethnicity and specific ethnic groups, including Afro-American, American Indian, Asian-American, and Chicano studies; African and Asian diasporal studies.

★4300★
University of Guelph
Institute for Environmental Policy
Blackwood Hall, Rm. 101   Ph: (519)824-4120
Guelph, ON, Canada N1G 2W1   Fax: (519)763-4686
Isobel Heathcote PhD, Dir.

Research Activities and Fields: National and international forest stewardship, including agroforestry, soil retention and stability, water quality and quantity, fish and wildlife habitat, ecological requirements, resource use, mineral extraction, atmospheric and climatic stability, and indigenous peoples and cultures.

★4301★
University of Maryland at College Park
Casey Journalism Center for Children and Families
8701-B Adelphi Rd.   Ph: (301)445-4971
Adelphi, MD 20783-1716   Fax: (301)445-9659
Reese Cleghorn, Dean

Founded: 1993 **Research Activities and Fields:** Issues and institutions affecting disadvantaged children and their families, including public policy, welfare reform, poverty, and violence. **Publications:** Newsletter, quarterly.

Scholarships, Fellowships, & Loans

★4302★
ABF Summer Research Fellowships in Law and Social Science for Minority Undergraduate Students
American Bar Foundation
750 N. Lake Shore Dr.   Ph: (312)988-6500
Chicago, IL 60611-4403   Fax: (312)988-6281

Study Level: Undergraduate. **Award Type:** Fellowship. **Purpose:** To acquaint undergraduate minority students with research in the field of law and social science. **Applicant Eligibility:** Applicants must be citizens or permanent residents of the United States. They must be of American Indian, African, Mexican, or Puerto Rican descent. Candidates should have completed at least the sophomore year of college and must not have received a bachelor's degree by the time the fellowship begins. Applicants must have a grade point average of at least 3.0 on a 4.0 scale and be moving toward an academic major in one of the social science disciplines. They must be able to work at the American Bar Foundation's offices in Chicago for 35 hours per week during the period of the fellowship. **Funds Available:** U.S.$3,500. **Applicant Details:** A formal application must be submitted, along with a personal statement, official transcripts, and one letter of reference from a faculty member familiar with the student's work. **Application Deadline:** March 1. Recipients are announced by April 15.

★4303★
ADHA Minority Scholarships Program
American Dental Hygienists' Association
Institute for Oral Health
444 N. Michigan Ave., Ste. 3400 Ph: (312)440-8944
Chicago, IL 60611   Fax: (312)440-8929

Study Level: Undergraduate. **Award Type:** Scholarship. **Purpose:** To provide financial assistance for minority groups currently underrepresented in the dental hygiene program. **Applicant Eligibility:** Applicants must be members of minority groups, including Native Americans, African-Americans, Hispanics, Asians, and males. Male applicants are not required to be members of minority groups. Applicants must have completed a minimum of one year in a dental hygiene curriculum. They must have a minimum grade point average of 3.0 on a 4.0 scale for the time they have been enrolled in a dental hygiene curriculum. Applicants must be full-time students during the academic year for which they are applying. Candidates must be able to document financial need of at least U.S.$1,500. **Funds Available:** Funds for financial assistance are limited because they consist of donations and grants from various sources. **Applicant Details:** A formal application must be filed. Upon request, a scholarship application packet is sent to interested candidates. **Application Deadline:** Completed packets and all other application materials must be filed by June 1. All applicants are notified in September whether or not they have been selected as recipients.

★4304★
Advanced Industrial Concepts (AIC) Materials Science Program
U.S. Department of Energy
Oak Ridge Institute for Science Education
PO Box 117   Ph: (423)576-3000
Oak Ridge, TN 37831-0117   Fax: (423)576-3643

Study Level: Graduate. **Award Type:** Fellowship. **Purpose:** To establish and maintain cooperative linkages between Oak Ridge National Laboratory (ORNL) and universities with program that lead to degrees or degree options in materials science and related disciplines. **Applicant Eligibility:** Applicants must be African American or Native American graduating seniors and graduate students who have not completed their first year. **Funds Available:** Tuition and fees up to US$6,000 per year; US$1,200 per month in stipends plus US$300 dislocation allowance during research appointment. Renewable for up to 24 months. **Applicant Details:** Write or telephone for further details. **Application Deadline:** Late February.

★4305★
Affirmative Action Scholarship Program
Special Libraries Association
Scholarship Committee
Membership Dept.
1700 18th St. NW   Ph: (202)234-4700
Washington, DC 20009   Fax: (202)265-9317
Study Level: Graduate. **Award Type:** Scholarship. **Purpose:** To support individuals pursuing Master's degrees in library and information sciences. **Applicant Eligibility:** Candidate must be enrolled, or about to enroll, as a graduate student in an accredited library or information science program in the United States or Canada. Preference is given to individuals interested in careers in special librarianship and to students in financial need. In addition to the requirements listed above, applicant for an Affirmative Action Scholarship must be a member of a minority group (African-American, Hispanic, Asian or Pacific Islander, American Indian or Alaskan Native). **Funds Available:** U.S.$6,000. **Applicant Details:** Write to the manager for application guidelines. **Application Deadline:** October 31.

★4306★
American Economic Association/Federal Reserve System Minority Graduate Fellowships in Economics
American Economic Association
c/o Joint Center for Political and
  Economic Studies
1090 Vermont Ave., Ste. 1100
Washington, DC 20005
Study Level: Graduate. **Award Type:** Fellowship. **Applicant Eligibility:** Applicants must be U.S. citizens who are African American, Hispanic or Native American and are enrolled in an accredited graduate program in economics in the United States. Preference will be given to applicants whose areas of concentration are of special interest to the Federal Reserve System. The applicant must also be in residence at the institution and cannot be employed without prior permission from the fellowship committee. **Selection Criteria:** Based on academic performance. **Funds Available:** The fellowships provide a monthly stipend of $900. **Applicant Details:** Applicants must send the following information: a completed application form; GRE scores; copies of undergraduate and graduate transcripts; current resume, which should include a complete employment history; a detailed description of the proposed dissertation (3-5 pages); a personal statement from the nominee which discusses the nominee's career plans or aspirations; copies of letters of recommendation for graduate school; a letter of recommendation from the nominee's primary dissertation advisor; a statement from the director of graduate studies or chairman of the Economics Department listing the requirements for the PhD in Economics and specifying the candidate's progress toward fulfilling each of those requirements. The application must be signed by the director of graduate studies or the chairman of the Department of Economics. Either signature indicates compliance with the following three conditions: the nominee is enrolled in full-time study toward a PhD in Economics in an accredited U.S. institution; the nominee is a U.S. citizen and; the nominating institution agrees to provide a tuition waiver without requiring research or teaching assistantship. **Application Deadline:** March 1.

★4307★
ASM Predoctoral Minority Fellowships
American Society for Microbiology
1325 Massachusetts Ave., NW   Ph: (202)942-9295
Washington, DC 20005-4171   Fax: (202)942-9329
Study Level: Doctorate. **Award Type:** Fellowship. **Purpose:** To support doctoral studies by minorities. **Applicant Eligibility:** Applicant must be a U.S. citizen or permanent resident and a member of an ethnic minority, including: Blacks, Hispanics, Native American Indians, Alaskan Natives, and Pacific Islanders. Candidate must be enrolled full-time in a doctoral program at a U.S. institution. Studies must be related to the clinical, medical, veterinary, or industrial aspects of microbiology. **Selection Criteria:** Selection is based on academic achievement, evidence of a successful research plan, and relevant career goals in the microbiological sciences. **Funds Available:** U.S.$12,000. **Applicant Details:** Write or call the assistant for application form and guidelines. **Application Deadline:** May 1

★4308★
AT & T Bell Laboratories Cooperative Research Fellowships for Minorities
AT & T Bell Laboratories
Special Programs
600 Mountain Ave., Rm. 3D316   Ph: (908)582-4822
Murray Hill, NJ 07974   Fax: (908)582-7383
Study Level: Graduate. **Award Type:** Fellowship. **Purpose:** To identify and develop scientific and engineering research ability among members of underrepresented minority groups, and to increase their representation in the sciences and engineering. **Applicant Eligibility:** Applicants must be members of underrepresented minority groups (Blacks, Native American Indians, and Hispanics) who are graduate students in programs leading to doctoral degrees in the following disciplines: chemistry, chemical engineering, communications science, computer science and engineering, electrical engineering, information science, materials science, mathematics, mechanical engineering, operations research, physics, and statistics. Awards are made only to U.S. citizens or permanent residents, and who are admitted to full-time study in a graduate program approved by AT&T Bell Laboratories. **Selection Criteria:** Candidates are selected on the basis of scholastic attainment in their field of specialization, and other evidence of their ability and potential as research scientists. A personal interview with AT&T Bell Laboratories scientists and engineers is arranged to select an appropriate summer mentor. **Funds Available:** Nine to 12 fellowships are awarded annually. The fellowship provides full tuition, an annual stipend of U.S.$13,200 (paid bi-monthly September through May), books, fees, and related travel expenses. Fellowship recipients may not accept any other fellowship support. Fellowships may be renewed on a yearly basis for four years, contingent upon satisfactory progress toward the doctoral degree. If needed, the fellowship will be renewed after four years subject to an annual review by the CRFP committee. Fellowship holders are invited to resume employment at AT&T Bell Laboratories during subsequent summers, but may elect to continue supervised university study or research; fellowship support would be continued (with the exception of the living stipend). During periods of summer employment, fellowship holders receive salaries commensurate with those earned by employees at approximately the same level of training. **Applicant Details:** Applications should include: a completed application form; official transcripts of grades from all undergraduate schools attended; a statement of interest; letters of recommendation from college professors who can evaluate the applicant's scientific aptitude and potential for research (additional letters of recommendation are also invited); Graduate Record Examination scores on the Aptitude Test and the appropriate Advanced Test (scores are required and should be submitted by listing on the GRE registration form Institution Code R2041, AT&T Bell Laboratories). **Application Deadline:** Applications and all supporting documentation, preferably in one package, must be received by January 15.

★4309★
AT & T Bell Laboratories Summer Research Program for Minorities and Women
AT & T Bell Laboratories
Special Programs
600 Mountain Ave., Rm. 3D316   Ph: (908)582-4822
Murray Hill, NJ 07974   Fax: (908)582-7383
Study Level: Undergraduate. **Award Type:** Fellowship. **Purpose:** To attract students into scientific careers, including patent law, by placing participants in working contact with experienced research scientists, engineers, and patent lawyers. **Applicant Eligibility:** Applicants must be women and/or members of underrepresented minority groups (Blacks, Native American Indians, and Hispanics). The program is primarily directed toward undergraduate students who have completed their third year of college. Emphasis is placed on the following disciplines: ceramic engineering, chemistry, chemical engineering, communications science, computer science and engineering, electrical engineering, information science, materials science, mathematics, mechanical engineering, operations research, physics, and statistics. Applicants should be U.S. citizens or permanent residents of the United States. **Selection Criteria:** Candidates are selected based on academic achievement, personal motivation, and compatibility of student interests with current AT&T Bell Laboratories activities. **Funds Available:** Salaries are commensurate with those of regular AT&T Bell Laboratories employees of comparable education. During the

summer, living accommodations at a nearby college are arranged for students who desire them. Bus transportation between campus housing facilities and AT&T Bell Laboratories is provided. Participants are free to make their own arrangements for board and transportation. Upon reporting to work, each summer employee will be reimbursed for air or surface travel expenses to New Jersey, in an amount not to exceed the cost of round trip economy class airfare. **Application Deadline:** Applications and all supporting documentation, preferably in one package, must be received by December 1.

★4310★
Aura E. Severinghaus Award
National Medical Fellowships, Inc.
110 W. 32nd St., 8th Fl.   Ph: (212)714-0933
New York, NY 10001-3205   Fax: (212)239-9718
Study Level: Doctorate. **Award Type:** Scholarship. **Applicant Eligibility:** Candidates must be African Americans, mainland Puerto Ricans, Mexican-Americans, and American Indians in their senior year who are enrolled at Columbia University College of Physicians and Surgeons. **Selection Criteria:** Selections are based on academic excellence, and community service and leadership. **Funds Available:** One nonrenewable award of $2,000 is presented annually. **Applicant Details:** Application is by nomination by the committee of faculty at Columbia University College of Physicians and Surgeons only. **Application Deadline:** Nominations are requested in September.

★4311★
CIC Predoctoral Fellowships
Committee on Institutional Cooperation
CIC Predoctoral Fellowships Program
Indiana University   Ph: (812)855-0822
Bloomington, IN 47405   Fax: (812)855-8741
Study Level: Graduate. **Award Type:** Fellowship. **Purpose:** To increase the representation of Native Americans, African Americans, Mexican-Americans, and Puerto Ricans among Ph.D. recipients in humanities, social sciences, natural sciences, mathematics, and engineering at select universities. **Applicant Eligibility:** Applicant must be a U.S. citizen. Candidate must be African American, American Indian, Mexican American, or Puerto Rican and must hold or receive a bachelor's degree from a regionally accredited college or university by August of the year of matriculation into a graduate program. Students who have received master's degrees or who are currently enrolled in graduate study may also apply. Fellowships are for doctoral study, and continued support is contingent upon satisfactory performance and progress toward the degree. Fellowships are tenable at any of the 11 CIC universities: University of Chicago, University of Illinois at Chicago, Indiana University, University of Iowa, University of Michigan, Michigan State University, University of Minnesota, Northwestern University, Ohio State University, Pennsylvania State University, Purdue University, University of Wisconsin, Madison, and University of Wisconsin, Milwaukee. Currently enrolled graduate students at CIC university campuses are not eligible to apply. **Funds Available:** Humanities U.S.$10,500 plus tuition; Social Sciences U.S.$10,000/year plus full tuition. **Applicant Details:** Write or call the CIC office for brochures or application. **Application Deadline:** January 5.

★4312★
CLA Scholarship for Minority Students in Memory of Edna Yelland
California Library Association
717 K St., Ste. 300   Ph: (916)447-8541
Sacramento, CA 95814-3477   Fax: (916)447-8394
Study Level: Undergraduate. **Award Type:** Scholarship. **Purpose:** To encourage and support ethnic minority students in the attainment of a graduate degree in library or information science. **Applicant Eligibility:** Applicants must be enrolled or accepted for enrollment in a master's program in an ALA accredited California library school; be American Indian, African American, Mexican American, Latino/Hispanic, Asian American, Pacific Islander, or Filipino; be a California resident at the time of the application and a U.S. citizen or permanent U.S. resident; and provide evidence of financial need. **Selection Criteria:** Individuals will be considered for oral interviews based upon the merits of the written application. Scholarship selections are based on applicant's adherence to instructions and

the professional presentation of the application package. **Funds Available:** The amount of each scholarship as well as the actual number granted depends upon the available funds and the financial need of the applicants. **Applicant Details:** Application forms can be requested from the California Library Association. **Application Deadline:** Applications must be received by May 31, and awards will be announced in July. Two interview sessions will be conducted in June, one in Southern California, the other in Northern California.

★4313★
Consortium Graduate Study Management Fellowships for Minorities
Consortium for Graduate Study in Management
200 S. Hanley, Ste. 1102   Ph: (314)935-5614
St. Louis, MO 63105-3415   Fax: (314)935-5014
Study Level: Graduate. **Award Type:** Fellowship. **Purpose:** To hasten the entry of minorities into managerial positions in business. **Applicant Eligibility:** Applicants must be U.S. citizens and members of one of the following minority groups: African-American, Hispanic, or Native American. They must already have an undergraduate degree and be qualified for admission to an M.B.A. program at one of the Consortium universities. Fellowships are tenable at the business schools of the University of California at Berkeley, Indiana University, the University of Michigan, New York University, the University of North Carolina at Chapel Hill, University of Rochester, University of Southern California, the University of Texas at Austin, Washington University in St. Louis, University of Virginia, and University of Wisconsin. Fellows are selected on merit and are awarded full tuition and fees. **Funds Available:** Tuition and fees. **Application Deadline:** February 1.

★4314★
Corporate Sponsored Scholarships for Minority Undergraduate Physics Majors
American Physical Society
One Physics Ellipse   Ph: (301)209-3200
College Park, MD 20740-3842   Fax: (301)209-0865
Study Level: Undergraduate. **Award Type:** Scholarship. **Purpose:** To significantly increase the level of underrepresented minority participation in physics in this country. **Applicant Eligibility:** Any Black, Hispanic, or American Indian U.S. citizen who is majoring or plans to major in physics and who is a high school senior, or college freshman or sophomore is eligible. **Selection Criteria:** A Selection Committee of the APS Committee on Minorities in Physics and appointed by the APS President will select the scholarship recipients and match the recipient with an available scholarship from a host corporate sponsor. The Selection committee will provide an accomplished physicist as a mentor for each scholarship recipient. It is the intention of the Selection Committee to give approximately half the awards to students in institutions with historically or predominately Black, Hispanic, or American Indian enrollment. **Funds Available:** U.S.$2,000 for tuition, room, or board, and U.S.$500 awarded to each college or university physics department that hosts one or more APS minority undergraduate scholars. The scholarship may be renewed one time. **Applicant Details:** Applicants must submit a completed application form with a personal statement. Three completed reference forms and a copy of applicant's high school and/or college transcripts should be mailed directly to the APS office. ACT, SAT, and any other scholastic aptitude test scores must be sent directly to the APS office by the testing service. **Application Deadline:** February 26.

★4315★
Council on Social Work Education Minority Fellowships
Minority Fellowship Programs
Council on Social Work Education
1600 Duke St., Ste. 300   Ph: (703)683-8080
Alexandria, VA 22314-3421   Fax: (703)683-8099
Study Level: Doctorate. **Award Type:** Fellowship. **Purpose:** To increase the number of ethnic minority mental health researchers, and to equip minority individuals for the provision of leadership, teaching, consultation, training, policy development and administration in mental health and substance abuse programs. **Applicant Eligibility:** Open to U.S. citizens or those who have permanent residence status, who are members of a minority group, including (but not limited to) persons who are American

Indian/Alaskan Native, Asian/Pacific Islander, Black, or Hispanic. Applicant must have a master's degree in social work and plan to begin full-time study leading to a doctoral degree in social work, or be currently enrolled full-time in a social work doctoral program. **Funds Available:** Monthly stipend for living expenses; tuition support may be available. **Applicant Details:** Write for application form and guidelines. Submit completed application to the national selection committee. **Application Deadline:** February 28. Notification by June 1.

★4316★
Crusade Scholarships
United Methodist General Board of Global
  Ministries
Mission Personnel Resources Program
  Department
475 Riverside Drive, Suite 1470   Ph: (212)870-3662
New York, NY 10115   Fax: (212)870-3774
Study Level: Graduate. **Award Type:** Scholarship. **Purpose:** To support individuals who show promise of providing leadership for the church and society. **Applicant Eligibility:** Applicants must be U.S. citizens who are members of an ethnic/racial minority (African American, Asian American, Hispanic American, Native American). Scholarships are also available to international persons who are members of the United Methodist Church or other churches in which the United Methodist Church has a relationship. International persons must have the recommendation of the home scholarship committee and remain in the home country until the application process has been completed. Preference is given to members of the United Methodist Church or those entering Christian vocations. **Funds Available:** Varies. **Applicant Details:** Write to the scholarship officer for application form and guidelines. **Application Deadline:** February 1.

★4317★
Fellowship Program in Academic Medicine
National Medical Fellowships, Inc.
110 W. 32nd St., 8th Fl.   Ph: (212)714-0933
New York, NY 10001-3205   Fax: (212)239-9718
Study Level: Doctorate. **Award Type:** Fellowship. **Purpose:** To foster mentor relationships between outstanding minority medical students and prominent biomedical scientists through a program of laboratory training. **Applicant Eligibility:** Candidate must be a U.S. citizen and a member of one of the following groups that are traditionally under-represented in the medical profession: African Americans, Mainland Puerto Ricans, Mexican Americans, Native Americans, Native Hawaiians, and Alaskan Aleuts. Candidate must be a student enrolled in a medical school at a U.S. institution who is nominated by the medical school dean. Nominee must have an interest in and talent for academic or research medicine. Preference is given to third-year students, although second-and fourth-year students may also be considered. Fellows study in research laboratories with established senior investigators in the biomedical sciences. The candidate is responsible for seeking a qualified mentor who is willing to support the fellowship application and oversee the proposed research project. **Funds Available:** U.S.$6,000. **Applicant Details:** Write to NMF for guidelines. Medical school dean must submit letter of nomination with transcripts. Candidate must complete fellowship application, including personal statement. Mentor must submit letter of commitment in support of application with a detailed research proposal. Additional letters of recommendation from faculty are also required. **Application Deadline:** Nominations must be submitted by November 15.

★4318★
Ford Foundation Postdoctoral Fellowships for Minorities
National Research Council
Fellowship Office
2101 Constitution Ave., NW
Washington, DC 20418   Ph: (202)334-2872
Study Level: Postdoctorate. **Award Type:** Fellowship. **Purpose:** To support postdoctoral research by U.S. minority scholars. **Applicant Eligibility:** Applicant must be a U.S. citizen or national and a member of one of the following minority groups: Alaskan Native, Native American Indian, Black/African American, Mexican American/Chicano, Native Pacific Islander, or Puerto Rican.

Applicant must have held a Ph.D. or Sc.D. degree for not more than seven years by the application deadline. Candidate must be engaged in, or planning to begin, a teaching or research career, and the proposed fellowship must further his/her career in education. Fellowships are intended for full-time research at an institution of higher learning, normally in the United States. Candidates must have the endorsement, as well as the support of a faculty member who is willing to act as fellowship sponsor. Awards will not be made to individuals in professions such as medicine, law, social work, or library science; or in such areas as business administration and management, fine arts, health sciences, home economics, speech pathology and audiology, personnel and guidance, or education. **Funds Available:** U.S.$25,000, plus U.S.$3,000 for travel and relocation. **Applicant Details:** Write for application form and guidelines, available in September. Submit form with proposed plan of study or research, curriculum vitae, a list of publications and courses taught, transcri pts, and an abstract of dissertation. Four letters of reference, one of which should be from the department chair at home institution, and a letter of endorsement from proposed host institution should be sent directly to the Fellowship Office. **Application Deadline:** January 6. Notification by early April.

★4319★
Ford Foundation Predoctoral and Dissertation Fellowships for Minorities
National Research Council
Fellowship Office
2101 Constitution Ave., NW
Washington, DC 20418   Ph: (202)334-2872
Study Level: Doctorate. **Award Type:** Fellowship. **Purpose:** To support graduate research by U.S. minority scholars. **Applicant Eligibility:** Applicant must be a U.S. citizen or national and a member of one of the following minority groups: Alaskan Native, Native American Indian, African Americans, Mexican American/Chicano, Native Pacific Islander, or Puerto Rican. Applicant for the Predoctoral Fellowship must be beginning, or planning to begin, a Ph.D. or Sc.D. degree program in one of the fields listed above. Applicant for the Dissertation Fellowship must have finished all required coursework for the Ph.D. or Sc.D. degree except the dissertation defense, and expect to complete dissertation during the fellowship year. Awards will not be made to individuals studying in fields such as medicine, law, social work, library science, business administration and management, fine arts, health sciences, home economics, speech pathology and audiology, personnel and guidance, fine arts, performing arts, or education. Fellowships are tenable at any accredited U.S. institution of higher learning. **Selection Criteria:** Merit. **Funds Available:** Dissertation: U.S.$18,000; Predoctoral: U.S.$12,000/year. **Applicant Details:** Write for application materials and guidelines, available in September. First, submit a preliminary application Office Card, which will be included with application materials. The Fellowship Office will send a complete application packet to qualified candidates. Then, submit forms with proposed plan of study/research, a description of previous research experience, and official transcripts. Predoctoral candidates must also submit Graduate Record Examination scores. Dissertation candidates must include verification of doctoral degree status, a curriculum vitae, an abstract of dissertation and reference reports from four referees. **Application Deadline:** Part 1: November 3; Part 2: December 1. Notification in early April.

★4320★
GEM Master's Engineering Fellowships for Minorities
Natl. Consort. Grad. Degrees for
  Minorities in Eng. & Sci.
GEM Central Office
PO Box 537   Ph: (219)631-1091
Notre Dame, IN 46556   Fax: (219)287-1486
Study Level: Graduate. **Award Type:** Fellowship. **Purpose:** To provide opportunities for minority students to obtain a master's degree in engineering through a program of paid summer engineering internship and financial aid. **Applicant Eligibility:** Applicant must be a U.S. citizen and a member of one of the ethnic groups under-represented in engineering: American Indian, Black American, Mexican American, Puerto Rican, and other Hispanics. Fellowships are for master's study; applicant must have a minimum academic status of junior-year enrollment in an accredited engineering discipline. Master's studies must take place at a GEM member institution. Acceptance in the fellowship program does not

guarantee acceptance to a graduate program. Fellows are required to spend a paid summer research internship at a GEM member employer location. **Funds Available:** U.S.$20,000-40,000: includes full tuition and fees, annual stipend, and paid summer research internship **Applicant Details:** Write to the Central Office for application guidelines and a list of participating academic institutions and employers. **Application Deadline:** December 1. Awards are announced February 1.

★4321★
GEM Ph.D. Engineering Fellowships for Minorities
Natl. Consort. Grad. Degrees for
Minorities in Eng. & Sci.
GEM Central Office
PO Box 537   Ph: (219)631-1091
Notre Dame, IN 46556   Fax: (219)287-1486

Study Level: Doctorate. **Award Type:** Fellowship. **Purpose:** To increase/produce members in engineering faculties and industries. **Applicant Eligibility:** Applicant must be a U.S. citizen and a member of one of the ethnic groups under-represented in engineering: American Indian, Black American, Mexican American, Puerto Rican, and other Hispanics. Fellowships are for doctoral study at GEM member institutions; applicant must hold an M.S. degree in engineering and be accepted to an approved doctoral program, or have three years of graduate studying remaining to complete the Ph.D. Candidate must demonstrate financial need and a strong interest in teaching and/or industrial research. Fellowships include summer research at a research-based company. Fellows must also be willing to accept a teaching/research assistantship after the first year. **Funds Available:** U.S.$60,000-100,000: includes full tuition and fees, annual stipend, and paid summer research. **Applicant Details:** Write to the Central Office for application guidelines and a list of participating academic institutions and employers. **Application Deadline:** December 1. Awards are made February 1.

★4322★
GEM Ph.D. Science Fellowship Program
Natl. Consort. Grad. Degrees for
Minorities in Eng. & Sci.
GEM Central Office
PO Box 537   Ph: (219)631-1091
Notre Dame, IN 46556   Fax: (219)287-1486

Study Level: Doctorate. **Award Type:** Fellowship. **Purpose:** To provide opportunities for minority students to obtain a Ph.D. degree in the natural sciences through a program of paid summer internship and financial aid. **Applicant Eligibility:** Applicant must be a U.S. citizen and a member of one of the ethnic groups under-represented in the sciences: American Indian, Black American, Mexican American, Puerto Rican, and other Hispanics. Applicant must be a junior, senior, or baccalaureate degree recipient in an accredited science discipline with an academic record that reflects the ability to succeed in a Ph.D. program. Fellowships are tenable at a GEM Ph.D. Science Program member university. Fellow must intern with a member employer during one summer of the program. **Funds Available:** Tuition, fees, and a stipend of U.S.$,12,000, plus funds earned during summer internship. **Applicant Details:** Write to the Central Office for application guidelines. **Application Deadline:** December 1. Awards are announced February 1.

★4323★
Gerber Prize for Excellence in Pediatrics
National Medical Fellowships, Inc.
110 W. 32nd St., 8th Fl.   Ph: (212)714-0933
New York, NY 10001-3205   Fax: (212)239-9718

Study Level: Doctorate. **Award Type:** Award. **Applicant Eligibility:** Candidates must be African Americans, American Indians, Mexican Americans, and mainland Puerto Ricans who are seniors at the University of Michigan Medical School, Michigan State University School of Human Medicine, or Wayne State University School of Medicine. Candidates must plan to pursue careers in pediatric medicine and must match to pediatric residency programs. Students must demonstrate academic excellence, especially in pediatrics, as well as leadership and financial need. **Selection Criteria:** Nominations are reviewed by a special committee, the members of which individually review and rank each candidate. The student with the best average score is designated the Gerber Scholar. **Funds Available:** One $2,000 non-renewable

award is presented annually. **Applicant Details:** Candidates must be nominated by their medical school deans and the chairmen of the departments of pediatrics at their medical schools. The school's dean must submit letters of nomination that fully discuss the candidate's overall academic accomplishments and extracurricular involvement, and the pediatrics chairman must submit a recommendation that discusses the performance in pediatrics rotations and includes faculty evaluations. An official academic transcripts is also required. **Application Deadline:** Nominations are requested in January.

★4324★
GOALS Fellowships
Industrial Relations Council on GOALS
PO Box 4363   Ph: (517)351-6122
East Lansing, MI 48826-4363   Fax: (517)351-1960

Study Level: Graduate. **Award Type:** Fellowship. **Purpose:** To recruit minority students. **Applicant Eligibility:** Applicants must be African American, Hispanic, Native Alaskan, Native American, or Native Hawaiian U.S. citizens. They must use the fellowship for full-time graduate study in human resource management or relations at any of the 13 participating consortium universities. Participating universities are Loyola University, Cornell University, University of Illinois (Champaign-Whara), Georgia State, University of Massachusetts–Amherst, Michigan State University, University of Minnesota, Ohio State University, University of Oregon, Rutgers University, University of South Carolina, West Virginia University, and University of Wisconsin. Candidates must also have an undergradate degree in one of the social sciences, such as economics, psychology, sociology, or political science, or have concentrations in business administration, communications, or social work. **Selection Criteria:** Candidates are ranked according to overall academic ability by a selection committee. **Funds Available:** Fellowships include either whole or partial waiver of tuition and fees and stipends of up to U.S.$7,800 per academic year. The number of fellowships awarded each year varies depending on funds donated by corporate sponsors. **Applicant Details:** Students must be accepted at one of the 13 consortium graduate schools to be eligible. Candidates must then apply directly to the school for the GOALS fellowship and be nominated by the school's director. **Application Deadline:** Depends on the university. Many graduate programs require that necessary documents be received by the middle of January for the following fall term.

★4325★
Golden State Minority Foundation Scholarships
Golden State Minority Foundation
1055 Wilshire Blvd., Ste. 1115   Ph: (213)482-6300
Los Angeles, CA 90017   Fax: (213)482-6305

Study Level: Undergraduate. **Award Type:** Scholarship. **Applicant Eligibility:** Applicants must attend school in or be a resident of southern California, study business administration, economics, or a related field; be a qualified minority (African-American, Hispanic, Native American, or other underrepresented minority); have a minimum GPA of 3.0 on a 4.0 scale; be a U.S. citizen or legal resident; be of at least junior standing (60 units of college credit); work no more than 28 hours per week; and have full-time status at an accredited four-year college or university. **Applicant Details:** Applications are on file at most schools' financial aid offices or can be obtained by sending a self-addressed stamped envelope. Applications are only sent out on application periods. **Application Deadline:** Southern California - February 1 to April 1.

★4326★
James H. Robinson M.D. Memorial Prizes in Surgery
National Medical Fellowships, Inc.
110 W. 32nd St., 8th Fl.   Ph: (212)714-0933
New York, NY 10001-3205   Fax: (212)239-9718

Study Level: Doctorate. **Award Type:** Prize. **Purpose:** To recognize outstanding performance in surgery by a student. **Applicant Eligibility:** Candidate must be a U.S. citizen and a member of one of the following groups that are traditionally under-represented in the medical profession: African Americans, Mainland Puerto Ricans, Mexican Americans, Native Americans, Native Hawaiians, and Alaskan Aleuts. Candidate must be a senior student enrolled in a medical school at a U.S. institution who is nominated by both the medical school dean and the chair of the department of surgery. **Funds Available:** U.S.$500. **Applicant Details:** The letter of nomination from the dean should fully discuss academic and extracurricular accomplishments. The letter from the department chair should delineate performance in the surgical disciplines and include faculty evaluations. Transcripts are also required. **Application Deadline:** November.

★4327★
Jimmy A. Young Memorial Scholarships
American Respiratory Care Foundation
11030 Ables Ln.   Ph: (214)243-2272
Dallas, TX 75229-4593   Fax: (214)484-2720

Study Level: Undergraduate. **Award Type:** Scholarship. **Purpose:** To assist minority students in respiratory therapy programs based on academic achievement. **Applicant Eligibility:** Applicants must be United States citizens or submit a copy of their immigrant visa. They must be members of minority groups, which include American Indians, Asian or Pacific Islanders, Black-Americans, Spanish-Americans, and Mexican-Americans. They must provide evidence of enrollment in an AMA-approved respiratory care program and have a minimum grade point average of 3.0 on a 4.0 scale. **Funds Available:** U.S.$1,000. **Applicant Details:** Candidates must submit official transcripts of grades, and two letters of recommendation from the program director and medical director that verifies the applicant is deserving and a member of a designated minority group. An original essay on some facet of respiratory care is also required. **Application Deadline:** Applications are accepted between April 1 and June 30. Scholarships are awarded by September 1.

★4328★
KNTV Minority Scholarships
KNTV Television
645 Park Ave.   Ph: (408)286-1111
San Jose, CA 95110   Fax: (408)295-5461

Study Level: Undergraduate. **Award Type:** Scholarship. **Purpose:** To assist local students who plan to attend or are attending a four-year college in the field of broadcast television to pay for college expenses. **Applicant Eligibility:** Students must be either Black, Hispanic, Asian/Pacific Islander, or American Indian and residents of Santa Clara, Santa Cruz, Monterey, or San Benito Counties. The award is contingent on the acceptability of student for admission to an accredited California four-year college or university. The major should be broadcast television. Students must have at least one full year of undergraduate work remaining and must carry a minimum of 12 semester units during each semester of the school year. **Selection Criteria:** Scholarships are given to students with financial need who demonstrate interest and potential in the field of broadcast televison. **Funds Available:** Two U.S.$1,000 scholarships. **Applicant Details:** Contact KNTV for applications. **Application Deadline:** April.

★4329★
LITA/OCLC Minority Scholarship and LITA/LSSI Minority Scholarships
American Library Association
Library and Information Technology
   Association
50 E. Huron St.   Ph: (312)280-4270
Chicago, IL 60611-2729   Fax: (312)280-3257

Study Level: Graduate. **Award Type:** Scholarship. **Purpose:** To encourage minority students committed to a career in library automation and information technology. **Applicant Eligibility:** Applicant must be a U.S. or Canadian citizen, a member of a principle minority group, and a student entering a ALA-accredited master's program of library education, with an emphasis on library automation. **Funds Available:** U.S.$2,500. **Applicant Details:** Write to the ALA at the above address for application form and guidelines. **Application Deadline:** April 1.

★4330★
Metropolitan Life Foundation Awards for Academic Excellence in Medicine
National Medical Fellowships, Inc.
110 W. 32nd St., 8th Fl.   Ph: (212)714-0933
New York, NY 10001-3205   Fax: (212)239-9718

Study Level: Doctorate. **Award Type:** Award. **Applicant Eligibility:** Applicants must be African American, Mexican American, Native American, or mainland Puerto Rican second- and third-year medical students who attend medical schools or have legal residence in the following cities only: San Francisco, California; Tampa, Florida; Atlanta, Georgia; Aurora, Illinois (Chicago); Wichita, Kansas; New York, New York; Tulsa, Oklahoma; Pittsburgh, Pennsylvania; Scranton, Pennsylvania; Warwick, Rhode Island (Providence); Greenville, South Carolina; and San Antonio, Texas. Candidates must demonstrate outstanding academic achievement, leadership, and potential for distinguished contributions to medicine, as well as financial need. **Selection Criteria:** NFL staff review the candidates' dossiers and select the students they judge most deserving of these scholarships. **Funds Available:** Up to ten $2,500 nonrenewable scholarships are presented annually. **Applicant Details:** Candidates must be nominated by medical school deans. Schools are required to submit letters of recommendation and official academic transcripts for each nominee. Students are required to submit scholarship applications, including personal statements, and verification of financial need. **Application Deadline:** Nominations are requested in August.

★4331★
Minority Dental Student Scholarship Program
ADA Endowment Fund and Assistance
   Fund Inc.
211 E. Chicago Ave., 17th Fl.   Ph: (312)440-2567
Chicago, IL 60611   Fax: (312)440-2822

Study Level: Doctorate. **Award Type:** Scholarship. **Purpose:** To assist students from minority groups that are traditionally under-represented in the fields of medicine and dentistry. **Applicant Eligibility:** Applicants must be U.S. citizens entering the second year of a U.S. dental school. They must also be African-Americans, Native Americans, or Hispanics. **Selection Criteria:** 2.5 GPA; demonstrate financial need; 2 letters of reference; and a typed summary of personal/professional goals. **Funds Available:** U.S.$2,000. **Applicant Details:** Write to the Fund for guidelines. Applications are sent to schools. **Application Deadline:** July 1. Notification in mid-August.

★4332★
Minority Faculty Fellowships at Indiana University
Indiana University
Minority Faculty Fellowship Program
Memorial Hall West 111
Indiana University, Bloomington   Ph: (812)855-0543
Bloomington, IN 47405   Fax: (812)855-4869

Study Level: Professional Development. **Award Type:** Fellowship. **Purpose:** To acquaint minority faculty with opportunities at the University, and to identify potential candidates for longer-term positions. **Applicant Eligibility:** Applicant must be a U.S. citizen or permanent resident, and must be Hispanic, Black, or Native American. Candidate must either have completed the Ph.D. within the last four years, or be nearing completion of the doctorate. There are no restrictions on the discipline, provided that a program in that discipline exists at the University. Applications are accepted for both summer term and academic year appointments. Summer fellows teach one course during their session in residence. Academic year fellows teach in both the fall and spring terms. **Funds Available:** Fellows will receive a salary equivalent to that of a University faculty member of the same rank, plus a research and living stipen d of U.S.$3,000. **Applicant Details:** Write to the director for application form and guidelines. An interview may be required. **Application Deadline:** Preferential consideration dates are October 1 for Summer; November 15 for academic year. The department chairperson or dean of the school will notify all candidates of the outcome.

★4333★
Minority Geoscience Scholarships
American Geological Institute
4220 King St.   Ph: (703)379-2480
Alexandria, VA 22302-1502   Fax: (703)379-7563

Study Level: Undergraduate. **Award Type:** Scholarship. **Purpose:** To aid outstanding minority students in the geosciences. **Applicant Eligibility:** Applicant must be a U.S. citizen, and be a geoscience or geoscience-education major. Candidate must be a member of one of the following groups in the geosciences: Black, Hispanic, Native American (American Indian, Eskimo, Hawaiian, and Samoan). Applicant must have a good academic record, meet financial need criteria, and be currently enrolled in an accredited institution in the United States. **Funds Available:** U.S.$10,000 maximum. **Applicant Details:** Write for application form. Submit form with official transcripts from all colleges attended (SAT, ACT, and/or GRE scores are requested), and three letters of recommendation from persons qualified to judge applicants academic performance and character. **Application Deadline:** February 1.

★4334★
MLA Scholarship for Minority Students
Medical Library Association
6 N. Michigan Ave., Ste. 300   Ph: (312)419-9094
Chicago, IL 60602-4805   Fax: (312)419-8950
Study Level: Graduate. **Award Type:** Scholarship. **Purpose:** To recognize and encourage students showing excellence in scholarship and potential for accomplishment in health sciences librarianship. **Applicant Eligibility:** Candidate must be a citizen or permanent resident of the United States or Canada and a member of one of the following minority groups: African-American, Asian, Hispanic, Native or Pacific Islander. Applicant must be entering a graduate library school accredited by the American Library Association, and have at least one-half of his/her academic requirements to complete during the year following the granting of the scholarship. Past recipients of MLA scholarships are ineligible. **Funds Available:** U.S.$2,000. **Applicant Details:** Write to the Professional Development Department assistant for application form and guidelines. Submit form with three letters of reference, official transcripts, and a statement of career objectives. **Application Deadline:** December 1. Scholarship recipients are notified in April.

★4335★
NACA Multi-Cultural Scholarship
National Association for Campus Activities
Educational Foundation
13 Harbison Way   Ph: (803)732-6222
Columbia, SC 29212-3401   Fax: (803)749-1047
Study Level: Professional Development. **Award Type:** Scholarship. **Purpose:** To increase the participation of ethnic minorities in the field of campus activities by providing economic assistance to qualified minority group members to allow attendance at NACA-sponsored training workshops, regional conferences or national conventions. **Applicant Eligibility:** Applicants must be identified as members of African American, Hispanic American, Native American, Pacific Islander, or Asian-American ethnic minority groups who are interested in training in campus activities. **Selection Criteria:** Financial need is considered as a criterion only to choose among applicants who have successfully met the first three criteria. **Funds Available:** Up to three scholarships are available for registration to NACA-sponsored training workshops, regional conferences and national conventions. Travel is not included. **Applicant Details:** In addition to a completed application form, candidates must submit at least one letter of recommendation, which is to be forwarded separately to the National Office. This letter should be from someone well acquainted with the applicant and they should address their involvement in the student's activities and potential in the field. It should also affirm the applicant's ethnic minority status, financial need, and commitment to stay in the field at least one year following the program for which a scholarship is being sought. Applicants must demonstrate their minority status, their past, present, and potential involvement in activities, their professional development objectives, and their financial need. When documenting their financial need, applicants should describe their institution's procedures and policy for funding expenses, and explain why such funding is unavailable for the program being sought. **Application Deadline:** Applications must be filed by May 1.

★4336★
NACME Corporate Scholars Program
National Action Council for Minorities in
   Engineering, Inc.
3 W. 35th St.
New York, NY 10001-2281   Ph: (212)279-2626
Study Level: Undergraduate. **Award Type:** Scholarship. **Applicant Eligibility:** Applicants must be African American, Hispanic, or American Indian students who are studying engineering. **Selection Criteria:** Students must demonstrate engineering leadership potential in areas where imminent need is anticipated. **Funds**

Available: Scholars receive between U.S.$12,000 and $20,000 each during their college careers. They also receive summer internship opportunities with their corporate sponsors, research and development work experience, academic and career mentoring, and professional development opportunities. **Applicant Details:** Scholarships are administered by participating colleges and universities. Students must be nominated through participating universities. They should apply to the dean of admissions or contact NACME.

★4337★
NACME Incentive Grants Program
National Action Council for Minorities in
   Engineering, Inc.
3 W. 35th St.
New York, NY 10001-2281   Ph: (212)279-2626
Study Level: Undergraduate. **Award Type:** Scholarship. **Applicant Eligibility:** Applicants must be African American, Hispanic, or American Indian students who are studying engineering. **Selection Criteria:** Selection is based on the student's potential for success in engineering. **Funds Available:** Between U.S.$3,000 and $18,000 is available to each student over the course of their education. **Applicant Details:** Scholarships are administered by participating colleges and universities. Students must be nominated through participating universities. They should contact the dean of admissions for application information or contact NACME.

★4338★
NACME TechForce Scholarships
National Action Council for Minorities in
   Engineering, Inc.
3 W. 35th St.
New York, NY 10001-2281   Ph: (212)279-2626
Study Level: Undergraduate. **Award Type:** Scholarship. **Applicant Eligibility:** Candidates must be exceptional African American, Hispanic, or American Indian high school seniors who plan to pursue careers in engineering. **Selection Criteria:** Students must demonstrate academic excellence, leadership skills, and commitment to engineering as a career. **Funds Available:** Ten primary finalists receive awards of U.S.$1,000 each per year, renewable for four years. Two top scholars receive an additional $2,500 per year for four years. Additionally, ten semifinalists each receive $500. **Applicant Details:** Students must be nominated through participating pre-college engineering programs.

★4339★
National FFA Foundation Minority Scholarships
National FFA Foundation
5632 Mt. Vernon Memorial Hwy.
PO Box 15160
Alexandria, VA 22309-0160   Ph: (703)360-3600
Study Level: Undergraduate. **Award Type:** Scholarship. **Applicant Eligibility:** Applicants must be FFA members pursuing college degrees in any area of agriculture and must represent a minority ethnic group (American Indian or Alaskan Native, Asian or Pacific Islander, African American, or Hispanic). FFA members from any state, Puerto Rico, the Virgin Islands, or the District of Columbia are eligible. **Funds Available:** One $10,000 scholarship and three $5,000 scholarships. Winners of the $10,000 scholarship will have to provide documentation of college expenses (tuition, books, room and board) to the National FFA in order to receive allotment of funds. They must also maintain full-time student status and a GPA of 2.0 on a 4.0 scale. A copy of quarter, trimester, or semester grades will be sent to FFA after each grading period. **Applicant Details:** Application material is available from the FFA. **Application Deadline:** March 1.

★4340★
National Miss Indian U.S.A. Scholarship
American Indian Heritage Foundation
6051 Arlington Blvd.   Ph: (703)237-7500
Falls Church, VA 22044   Fax: (703)532-1921
Study Level: Graduate. **Award Type:** Scholarship. **Purpose:** To promote young Indian women who continue with their Indian culture and heritage along with making a place for themselves in the white man's world. **Applicant Eligibility:** Women must be 18-26 years old, never married, pregnant, or cohabitated, and must be high

school graduates. Applicant must have an Indian sponsor such as: tribe, business, or organization with a valid governing board. The women must also have a belief of and practice tribal culture and heritage. They must exhibit such positive characteristics as: listening to their elders, joining in pow-wows, and promoting Indian language if possible. **Funds Available:** First place winner receives a $12,000 cash award, $7,000 to the school of choice, and $5,000 for wardrobe. **Applicant Details:** Applications must be requested. There is a $500 application fee. **Application Deadline:** September 15.

★4341★
Nelson A. Rockefeller Minority Internships
WRKL
PO Box 910
Pomona, NY 10970   Ph: (914)354-2000

Study Level: Undergraduate. **Award Type:** Internship. **Purpose:** To give applicants an opportunity to work in the broadcasting industry and identify potential areas of specialization. **Applicant Eligibility:** Candidates must be Black, Hispanic, American Indian, Aleut, or Asiatic. They must be high school or undergraduate students between the ages of 17 and 21. Candidates must also be residents of New York, or students attending school in New York, who are first-time entrants in the internship program and the broadcasting industry. **Selection Criteria:** Applicants are judged on written and verbal communication skills. **Funds Available:** Interns are paid by the hour based on the current minimum wage. **Applicant Details:** Applicants must submit a personalized letter of application expressing their area of interest. Finalists are then chosen for an interview. **Application Deadline:** April 30.

★4342★
NMA Scholarships
National Medical Fellowships, Inc.
110 W. 32nd St., 8th Fl.   Ph: (212)714-0933
New York, NY 10001-3205   Fax: (212)239-9718

Study Level: Graduate. **Award Type:** Scholarship. **Applicant Eligibility:** Applicants must be U.S. citizens who are African American, Puerto Rican, Mexican American, or Native American. **Selection Criteria:** Scholarship selections are based on needs. **Applicant Details:** Applications are available in April. **Application Deadline:** August 31.

★4343★
NMF Scholarships for Minority Students
National Medical Fellowships, Inc.
110 W. 32nd St., 8th Fl.   Ph: (212)714-0933
New York, NY 10001-3205   Fax: (212)239-9718

Study Level: Doctorate. **Award Type:** Scholarship. **Purpose:** To assist U.S. students from minority groups to obtain an education in medicine. **Applicant Eligibility:** Applicant must be a U.S. citizen and a member of one of the following groups that are traditionally under-represented in the medical profession: African Americans, Mainland Puerto Ricans, Mexican Americans, Native Americans, Native Hawaiians, and Alaskan Aleuts. Candidate must be accepted to or enrolled in the first or second year of medical school at a U.S. institution. **Funds Available:** Varies, depending on need, cost of education, and other sources of aid. **Applicant Details:** Write to NMF for application materials, available April through July. **Application Deadline:** August 31/May 31 for renewal students.

★4344★
Planning and The Black Community Division of APA Undergraduate Minority Scholarship
American Planning Association
1776 Massachusetts Ave., NW, Ste. 400   Ph: (202)872-0611
Washington, DC 20036-1904   Fax: (202)872-0643

Study Level: Undergraduate. **Award Type:** Scholarship. **Purpose:** To recognize outstanding minority students in undergraduate planning programs in the United States. **Applicant Eligibility:** Applicants must be African American, Hispanic American, or Native American students with a demonstrated interest in working in the planning profession or as an advocate for improving, enhancing, or maintaining the quality of life in black communities. They must apply in their second or third year of undergraduate study, be working towards a baccalaureate degree in planning or related field (architecture, community development, environmental science,

public administration, or urban studies), have a minimum of 30 semester hours or 45 quarter hours at the time of application, have demonstrated financial need, and have a minimum GPA of 2.85 on a 4.0 scale. **Selection Criteria:** Preference is given to applicants who demonstrate a record of service to the black community, are enrolled in planning programs and those recognized by the Planning Accreditation Board, and are members of the American Planning Association and/or the Planning and the Black Community Division. **Funds Available:** U.S.$2,500. **Applicant Details:** Applicants must send a completed application accompanied by a two- to five-page, double-spaced essay that identifies critical problems facing minority communities in the 21st century and indicates alternative planning strategies to resolve these problems; at least two letters of recommendation (for nominated candidates, one of the two letters must be from a professor or school official); and an official copy of college or university transcripts. **Application Deadline:** May 15. Award decisions are made in July.

★4345★
Presbyterian Church Student Opportunity Scholarships
Presbyterian Church (U.S.A.)
Office of Financial Aid for Studies
100 Witherspoon St.   Ph: (502)569-5000
Louisville, KY 40202-1396   Fax: (502)569-5018

Study Level: Undergraduate. **Award Type:** Scholarship. **Purpose:** Student Opportunity Scholarships have been established for young persons of limited opportunities from ethnic minority groups. **Applicant Eligibility:** Applicants must be Asian, Black, Hispanic, Native American and members of the Presbyterian Church (U.S.A.). Candidates must be entering college as incoming full-time freshmen and must have applied to the college for financial aid. They must also be United States citizens or permanent residents. **Funds Available:** Scholarships range from U.S.$100 to U.S.$1,400 and are individually determined based on financial need and funds available. **Application Deadline:** April 1 of the candidate's senior year in high school.

★4346★
Racial/Ethnic Leadership Supplemental Grants
Presbyterian Church (U.S.A.)
Office of Financial Aid for Studies
100 Witherspoon St.   Ph: (502)569-5000
Louisville, KY 40202-1396   Fax: (502)569-5018

Study Level: Graduate. **Award Type:** Grant. **Purpose:** To assist minority graduate students preparing for professional church occupations in the Presbyterian Church. **Applicant Eligibility:** Applicant must be a U.S. citizen or permanent resident and be an Asian, Black, Hispanic, or Native American who is a communicant member of the Presbyterian Church (U.S.A.). Candidate must be enrolled at least half-time in a graduate program which prepares him/her for a professional career with the Church. Applicant should demonstrate a financial need that cannot be met through other loans, grants, scholarships, savings, and employment. Grants are tenable at U.S. and Canadian seminaries and theological institutions administered or approved by the Church. Funds are awarded for the first professional degree only, and are not available for doctoral study, summer terms, or internships. **Funds Available:** U.S.$1,000. **Applicant Details:** Write to the Financial Aid for Studies Office for application materials, or contact school financial aid office. Application forms must be submitted to the Church by the school financial aid officer on behalf of the candidate.

★4347★
Society of Actuaries/Casualty Actuarial Society Scholarships for Minority Students
Society of Actuaries
475 N. Martingale Rd., Ste. 800   Ph: (847)706-3500
Schaumburg, IL 60173-2226   Fax: (847)706-3599

Study Level: Undergraduate. **Award Type:** Scholarship. **Purpose:** The scholarship program is designed to aid minority students interested in pursuing actuarial careers. **Applicant Eligibility:** Candidates must be members of a minority group (i.e., African Americans, Hispanics, or Native Americans). They must be either U.S. citizens or have permanent-resident visas. Candidates must also be undergraduate students admitted to an accredited college or university offering either a program in actuarial science or courses that will serve to prepare the student for an actuarial career.

Applicants must have demonstrated mathematical ability and evidence some understanding of the field, and must have taken the Scholastic Aptitude Test (SAT), the ACT, or exam 100 of the Actuarial Examinations. **Selection Criteria:** Scholarships are awarded on the basis of individual merit and financial need. **Funds Available:** The number and amount of the scholarships are determined by a committee of members of the Society of Actuaries and the Casualty Actuarial Society. The number and amount of the awards vary from year to year. **Applicant Details:** Applicants must submit the Financial Aid Form (FAF) to the College Scholarship Service (CSS) of the College Board not later than March 31 and give CSS permission to forward information to the Society. Applicants must also submit two nomination forms, completed by their instructors or academic advisors, a financial statement, and a transcript of grades. **Application Deadline:** May 1.

★4348★
Times Mirror Minority Editorial Training Program
Los Angeles Times
Times Mirror Sq.   Ph: (213)237-4435
Los Angeles, CA 90053   Fax: (213)237-4712

Study Level: Professional Development. **Award Type:** Other. **Purpose:** To provide 18 journalists an opportunity to train for two years at Times Mirror newspapers. **Applicant Eligibility:** Applicants must be minorities (African Americans, Asian Americans, and Native Americans) who are legal residents of the United States with any amount of experience or no experience at all. Applicants must provide proof of eli gibility to work two years at newsroom locations. They must hold a driver's and have a car in good condition. Reporters must know how to type and photographers must have basic equipment in good condition, although they will have access to METPRO camera/ equipment pool. **Selection Criteria:** Selections are based on written essays, a review of written work or photographs, college transcripts, recommendations, writing tests and personal interviews. **Funds Available:** The program provides paid training for reporters, photographers, and copy editors at daily newspapers. Reporting and photography trainees spend the first year at the Los Angeles Times; editing trainees spend the first year at Newsday in Long Island, New York. Second year trainees are assigned to newsrooms of the Times Mirror newspapers and will receive the compensation and benefits applicable at the newspaper which they work and are subject to the employment terms and conditions of those newspapers. Reporting and photography trainees spend the first year at the Los Angeles Times; editing trainees spend the first year at Newsday in Long Island, New York. Second year trainees are assigned to newsrooms of Times Mirror newspapers. **Application Deadline:** Application deadline is January 1. All trainees must be ready to enter the program in June.

★4349★
Underrepresented Minority Investigators Award in Asthma and Allergy
American Academy of Allergy, Asthma &
  Immunology
611 E. Wells St., 4th Fl.   Ph: (414)272-6071
Milwaukee, WI 53202-3889   Fax: (414)276-3349

Study Level: Postdoctorate. **Award Type:** Award. **Purpose:** To assist underrepresented minority postdoctoral scientists to concentrate research efforts in the fields of asthma and allergy. **Applicant Eligibility:** Applicants must be U.S. citizens or permanent residents and members of a minority group traditionally underrepresented in biomedical or behavioral research such as African Americans, Hispanics, Native Americans or Pacific Islanders. Applicants should also be postdoctoral scientists in NIH and non-NIH funded programs with an M.D. **Funds Available:** U.S.$30,000/year. **Applicant Details:** Write for further information and application form. Original application plus five copies should be submitted to: Sri Ram, Ph.D., Director of Lung Diseases, NHLBI, 5333 W. Bard Ave., Rm. 6A09, Bethesda, MD 20892 U.S.A. **Application Deadline:** March 31.

★4350★
W. K. Kellogg Foundation Fellowships in Community Medicine
National Medical Fellowships, Inc.
110 W. 32nd St., 8th Fl.   Ph: (212)714-0933
New York, NY 10001-3205   Fax: (212)239-9718

Study Level: Doctorate. **Award Type:** Fellowship. **Applicant Eligibility:** Applicants must be African American, Mexican American, Native American, or mainland Puerto Rican second- and third-year medical students. They must be in good academic standing, attend accredited United States medical schools, and demonstrate outstanding leadership, community involvement, and potential for responsible roles in health care delivery. They must also have a desire to work in community-based health centers that provide high quality, managed care for those people who lack access to health services because of geographic isolation, lack of providers, or financial barriers. **Selection Criteria:** Fellows are selected by a committee of persons prominent in community medicine and primary care. **Funds Available:** Fifteen $5,000 non-renewable awards are presented annually. Students work with senior staff members and advisory boards at community and migrant health centers through the country for eight to twelve week periods. **Applicant Details:** Candidates must be nominated by medical school deans. Schools must submit letters of nomination and official academic transcripts for each nominee. Medical school faculty members willing to serve as academic advisors must submit letters of commitment in support of each student's application. Students are required to complete fellowship applications and include personal statements. **Application Deadline:** Nominations are requested in October.

★4351★
William and Charlotte Cadbury Award and Franklin C. McClean Award
National Medical Fellowships, Inc.
110 W. 32nd St., 8th Fl.   Ph: (212)714-0933
New .York, NY 10001-3205   Fax: (212)239-9718

Study Level: Doctorate. **Award Type:** Award. **Purpose:** To recognize outstanding academic achievement, leadership and community service by medical students. **Applicant Eligibility:** Candidate must be a U.S. citizen and a member of one of the following groups that are traditionally under-represented in the medical profession: African Americans, Blacks, Mainland Puerto Ricans, Mexican Americans, Native Americans, Native Hawaiians, and Alaskan Aleuts. Candidate must be a senior student enrolled in a medical school at a U.S. institution who is nominated for the award by the medical school dean. **Funds Available:** McClean Award: U.S.$3,000; Cadbury Award: U.S.$2,000. **Applicant Details:** Nominating letter from dean must be submitted to NMF with letters of recommendation and transcripts. **Application Deadline:** June 15.

Awards, Honors, & Prizes

★4352★
Aggrey Medal
Phelps-Stokes Fund
10 E. 87th St.
New York, NY 10028   Ph: (212)427-8100

Description: To recognize individuals who have made significant contributions in one of the charter areas of interest of the Phelps-Stokes Fund, i.e., education for Africans, African Americans, and American Indians. A silver medal is awarded from time to time by the Board of Trustees of the Phelps-Stokes Fund. Established in 1986 to honor Dr. J.E.K. Aggrey, the renowned African educator who was a member of the first Phelps-Stokes African Education Commission (1920-21), and one of the period's foremost proponents of racial equality.

★4353★
National Indian Health Board Award
1385 S. Colorado Blvd., Ste. A-707   Ph: (303)759-3075
Denver, CO 80222   Fax: (303)759-3674
Description: To recognize achievements in helping improve the health status of American Indian/Alaskan Native people. Each year, 6 plaques, 6 medallions, and 12 certificates are awarded at the NIHB Consumer Conference. Established in 1972. For more information, contact Yvette Joseph-Fox, Executive Director.

Publishers

★4354★
Alpha Publications Inc.
1079 De Kalb Pike
Blue Bell, PA 19422
    Ph: (610)277-6342
Subjects: Ethnic Books.

★4355★
American Civil Liberties Union
132 W. 43rd St.   Ph: (212)944-9800
New York, NY 10036   Fax: (212)869-9065
Description: An organization which defends individual rights guaranteed by the Constitution through litigation, legislative lobbying, and public education. Publishes *ACLU Rights Handbook Series* consisting of twenty titles, an annual members' newsletter titled *Civil Liberties,* and periodic pamphlets, videos, reports and brochures. Does not accept unsolicited manuscripts.

★4356★
American National Heritage Association
PO Box 4827
Alexandria, VA 22303-0827   Ph: (703)960-6322
Description: Seeks to preserve the multicultural ethnic history of the United States and its peoples by researching, compiling, writing, and publishing books on the subject in several languages. Also offers a magazine, *Quinto Lingo* and a cassette *Sound of Quinto Lingo.* Accepts unsolicited manuscripts. Reaches market through direct mail. **Subjects:** History, languages.

★4357★
Amnesty International USA
322 8th Ave.   Ph: (212)807-8400
New York, NY 10001   Free: 800-266-3789
    Fax: (212)627-1451
Description: A world-wide movement of people working for the release of prisoners of conscience, for fair trials for political prisoners, and for an end of torture and executions. A human rights organization that works on behalf of anyone imprisoned because of their political, religious, or ethnic beliefs, and who has neither committed nor advocated violence. Publishes reports and briefing papers on human rights abuses throughout the world. Also offers a quarterly newsletter, *Amnesty Action.* Publications are available in Spanish, French, and Arabic. Reaches market through direct mail and trade sales. Does not accept unsolicited manuscripts. **Subjects:** Human rights, civil rights, treatment of prisoners, peace.

★4358★
Anthropology Film Center Foundation
1626 Canyon Rd.   Ph: (505)983-4127
Santa Fe, NM 87501-6138   Fax: (505)983-4127
Description: Provides consultation and research services, seminars, publications, teaching, research films, and reports on visual anthropology/documentary filmmaking. Distributed by Zia Cine, Inc.

★4359★
Archives of Social History
PO Box 763
Stony Brook, NY 11790
Subjects: Civil rights, social history.

★4360★
Blue Bird Publishing
2266 S. Dobson, Ste. 275   Ph: (602)831-6063
Mesa, AZ 85202   Fax: (602)831-1829
Description: Publishes educational material for libraries. Accepts unsolicited manuscripts. Reaches market through commission representatives, direct mail, Baker & Taylor Books, Quality Books, Inc., Pacific Pipeline Inc., and Spring Arbor Distributors. **Subjects:** Home schooling, social issues, parenting, multicultural.

★4361★
Books Beyond Borders
PO Box 18929   Ph: (303)449-6440
Boulder, CO 80308-1929   Free: 800-347-6440
    Fax: (303)449-7918
Description: Publishes nonfiction books on multicultural, women's studies, health & healing, metaphysical. Accepts unsolicited manuscripts. **Subjects:** Multicultural, metaphysical, woman's studies, health/healing.

★4362★
Bowling Green State University
Popular Press
Bowling Green, OH 43403   Ph: (419)372-7866
    Fax: (419)372-8095
Description: Publishes materials for use as classroom texts. Reaches market through direct mail. Accepts unsolicited manuscripts. **Subjects:** Folklore, popular culture, women's studies, Afro-American studies, Caribbean culture, cultural diversity, multiculturalism.

★4363★
California State University, Fullerton
Oral History Program
P.O.B 34080   Ph: (714)773-3580
Fullerton, CA 92634   Fax: (714)773-3580
Description: Seeks to record oral recollections, edit, index, and process select ones into bound volumes and make them available to libraries and interested persons. Reaches market through direct mail and telephone sales. **Subjects:** Local history, political history, ethnic studies, family history.

★4364★
Clover Park Press
PO Box 5067
Santa Monica, CA 90409   Ph: (310)452-7657
Description: Publishes fiction and nonfiction books on multiculturalism, biography, travel, California history, and translations of women's writings from the Third World. Accepts unsolicited manuscripts–query first. **Subjects:** Biography, multiculturalism, history, travel.

★4365★
Clyde Press
373 Lincoln Pkwy.
Buffalo, NY 14216   Ph: (716)875-4713
Description: Publishes firsthand accounts of the native and ethnic folklore of America, researched from the author's collections. Reaches market through direct mail and wholesalers, including Baker & Taylor, Ballen Books, and Legacy Books. **Subjects:** Folklore, anthropology, children, ethnic themes, games.

★4366★
Cobblehill Books
375 Hudson St.   Ph: (212)366-2628
New York, NY 10014   Fax: (212)366-2011
Description: Publishes children's books from pre-school through high school. Accepts unsolicited manuscripts only for picture book length; query letters for longer. Reaches market through trade sales and wholesalers. Cobblehill Books is an affiliate of Dutton Children's Books which is a division of Penguin USA. **Subjects:** Nature, animals, multicultural, novels by previous authors. **Number of New Titles:** 1998 - 20.

★4367★
Columbia University
Center for the Study of Human Rights
420 W. 118th St., No. 1108 IAB   Ph: (212)854-2479
New York, NY 10027-3365   Fax: (212)316-4578
Description: Promotes teaching and research in international human rights. Publishes occasional papers, reports, proceedings, and course syllabi. Reports and documents copyrighted.

★4368★
Commune-A-Key Publishing, Inc.
730 Butte Ave.   Ph: (916)926-6305
Mount Shasta, CA 96067   Free: 800-983-0600
                                        Fax: (916)926-6305
Description: Publishes books geared to health care professionals and lay caregivers on psychology, selfhelp, and recovery. Accepts unsolicited manuscripts. Reaches market through commission representatives, direct mail, telephone and trade sales, and Atrium Publishers' Group. **Subjects:** Native American spirituality and healing, psychology, self-help, recovery, inspirational.

★4369★
Content Communications
PO Box 4763   Ph: (913)233-9066
Topeka, KS 66604   Fax: (913)232-0835
Description: Publishes books on diversity topics, such as ethnicity, racial relations, and class issues. Accepts unsolicited manuscripts. **Subjects:** Multiculturalism. **Number of New Titles:** 1998 - 2.

★4370★
Council on Interracial Books for Children, Inc.
1841 Broadway
New York, NY 10023
Description: Publishes "to identify–and more recently to counteract–racism, sexism, and other anti-human values in children's learning materials and in society." Offers books, maps, filmstrips, catalogs, and booklists. Reaches market through direct mail.

★4371★
Cultural Survival, Inc.
46 Brattle St.   Ph: (617)441-5400
Cambridge, MA 02138-3705   Fax: (617)441-5417
Description: A nonprofit organization founded by a group of social scientists concerned with the fate of tribal peoples and ethnic minorities around the world. Publications serve to inform the general public, educators, and policy makers in the US and abroad to stimulate action on behalf of these societies. Reaches market through direct mail and distributors. **Subjects:** Human rights, anthropology, social sciences.

★4372★
Dayton Human Relations Council
40 S. Main St., Ste. 721
Dayton, OH 45402
Description: Makes large segment of the community aware of the services and programs of the Human Relations Council. Reaches market through direct mail and distribution points. **Subjects:** Unlawful discriminatory practices in employment, public accommodations, housing, credit transactions.

★4373★
Eclectic Travel Editions
1515 Capalina Rd., No. 25
Box 221040
San Diego, CA 92192   Fax: (619)471-1998
Description: Publishes novels with an emphasis on international travel and other cultures. **Subjects:** Muticulturalism, travel.

★4374★
Five Star Publications
4696 W. Tyson St.   Ph: (602)940-8182
Chandler, AZ 85226-2903   Free: 800-545-7827
                                        Fax: (602)940-8787
Description: Publishes children's books, books on child and senior care, cookbooks, and directories. Also offers book production and marketing through Publishers Support Services. Distributes for Navajo Community College Press. Reaches market through commission representatives, direct mail, and wholesalers. **Subjects:** Publishing, Native Americans, education, cooking, childcare, cooking.

★4375★
Human Rights Internet
c/o Human Rights Centre
University of Ottawa
57 Louis Pasteur   Ph: (613)564-3492
Ottawa, ON, Canada K1N 6N5   Fax: (613)564-4054
Description: A non-partisan, not-for-profit corporation aimed at developing communication and cooperation among academics, activists, and policy-makers for the promotion and protection of international human rights. Publishes books, several periodicals, including *HRI Reporter,* and microfiche. **Subjects:** International human rights, political prisoners, censorship, minorities, labor, women.

★4376★
Human Rights Watch
485 5th Ave.   Ph: (212)290-4700
New York, NY 10017   Fax: (212)972-0905
Description: Nonprofit human rights organization publishing books and newsletters on human rights practices in more than sixty countries worldwide. Practices covered include arbitrary imprisonment, censorship, disappearances, due process of law, murder, poor prison conditions, torture, and violations of laws of war. Joint publishes with Yale University Press. Reaches market through direct mail, trade sales, and membership. Does not accept unsolicited manuscripts. **Subjects:** Human rights, social issues.

★4377★
Institute on Pluralism and Group Identity
165 E. 56th St.
New York, NY 10022   Ph: (212)251-8800
Description: Publishes material designed to promote a better understanding of American pluralism.

★4378★
Inter-American Commission on Human Rights
1889 F St. NW   Ph: (202)458-6002
Washington, DC 20006   Fax: (202)458-3992
Description: Monitors human rights compliance in OAS member states in conformance with the American Convention on Human Rights and the American Declaration of the Rights and Duties of Man. Publishes annual reports and reports on individual countries.

★4379★
Keyla Inc.
PO Box 1647   Ph: (404)508-9457
Pine Lake, GA 30072-1647   Fax: (404)508-9457
Description: Publishes and distributes books and games on multiculturalism. **Subjects:** Ethnic groups, history.

★4380★
Language Learning Systems, Inc.
PO Box 4827   Ph: (703)960-6322
Alexandria, VA 22303-0827   Fax: (703)329-0930
Description: Publishes all books for the American National Heritage Association. **Subjects:** Education, history, ethnic traditions.

★4381★
Media Forum International, Ltd.
RR 1, Box 107   Ph: (802)592-3444
West Danville, VT 05873   Fax: (802)592-3000
Description: Publishes books and offers services, including newsletter and brochure development, editing, video and film projects, consulting, and media training programs abroad. Alternate address is PO Box 265, Peacham, VT 05862. Reaches market through direct mail and trade sales. **Subjects:** Ethnic interests, biographies, food, cooking.

★4382★
Meiklejohn Civil Liberties Institute
PO Box 673   Ph: (510)848-0599
Berkeley, CA 94701   Fax: (510)848-6008
Description: Publishes books dealing with law, human rights, and civil rights. Reaches market through direct mail.

★4383★
Mitchell Lane Publishers, Inc.
17 Matthew Bathon Ct.   Ph: (410)392-5036
Elkton, MD 21921   Free: 800-814-5484
                           Fax: (410)392-4781
Description: Publishes biographies for juveniles. Reaches market through Chelsea House Publishers and People's Publishing Group. **Subjects:** Multicultural, biography. **Number of New Titles:** 1998 - 10; 1996 - 7.

★4384★
Morten Publishing Co., Inc.
136 Wedgewood
Barrington, IL 60010   Ph: (708)381-1440
Description: Publishes a genealogical reference of lineages of Americans of all ethnic backgrounds. Reaches market through direct mail, advertising, and wholesalers. **Subjects:** Genealogy.

★4385★
Multicultural History Society of Ontario
43 Queen's Park Crescent E.   Ph: (416)979-2973
Toronto, ON, Canada M5S 2C3   Fax: (416)979-7947
Description: Publishes on history, immigration and multiculturalism. Also publishes a newsletter. Offers microform publications. Does not accept unsolicited manuscripts. Reaches market through University of Toronto Press. **Number of New Titles:** 1996 - 3; 1997 - 2.

★4386★
National Center for Urban Ethnic Affairs
PO Box 20
Washington, DC 20064   Ph: (202)232-3600
Description: Established to develop neighborhood programs and policies which are grounded in the appreciation of ethnic cultural diversity. **Subjects:** Ethnicity, Americans, urban affairs.

★4387★
North American Printing
680 E. C. Row   Ph: (519)966-1970
PO Box 1150   Free: 800-759-1300
Windsor, ON, Canada N9A 6P8   Fax: (519)966-6701
Description: Publishes on ethnic art and history. Offers printing and binding services. Reaches market through commission representatives and direct mail.

★4388★
Persimmon Press
118 Tillinghast Pl.   Ph: (716)838-3633
Buffalo, NY 14216   Fax: (716)852-0093
Description: Publishes monographs on prehistoric archaeology and "how the New World became peopled." Accepts unsolicited manuscripts. Distributes for Buffalo Museum of Science, Atlantic Archaeology, Ltd., and St. Johns, Newfoundland. Reaches market through direct mail and Center for the Study of the First Americans. **Subjects:** Archeology, physical anthorpology, palaeontology.

★4389★
Place in the Woods
3900 Glenwood Ave.   Ph: (612)374-2120
Golden Valley, MN 55422-5302   Fax: (612)593-5593
Description: Publishes biographical research and analysis of minority achievements, especially of leaders not covered in textbooks. Accepts unsolicited manuscripts; query first. Reaches market through direct mail, distribution in the Reading Is Fundamental, Head Start, and Migrant Education programs nationwide, and through wholesalers and jobbers. **Subjects:** Humanities, minorities, affirmative action, equal employment opportunity, reading, education. **Number of New Titles:** 1998 - 6.

★4390★
Probe Communications International Inc.
347 Fifth Ave.   Ph: (212)679-2670
New York, NY 10016   Fax: (212)679-1380
Description: Publishes diaries and history books, as well as culinary titles. Accepts unsolicited manuscripts. **Subjects:** Children's books, history, world cultures, religions.

★4391★
Project Equality, Inc.
6301 Rockhill Rd., Ste. 315   Ph: (816)361-9222
Kansas City, MO 64131   Fax: (816)361-8997
Description: A national interfaith program promoting equal employment opportunity among member religious and nonprofit organizations and suppliers of goods and services to such organizations. Publishes *Update, Action,* and *EEO News,* a quarterly newsletter. Also publishes annual *Buyers Guide* listing all participating employers. Reaches market through direct mail and member organizations. **Subjects:** Civil and human rights.

★4392★
Proof Press
PO Box 1256
Berkeley, CA 94701   Ph: (510)521-8741
Subjects: Social studies.

★4393★
Rainbow Educational Media Inc.
4540 Preslyn Dr.   Ph: (919)954-7550
Raleigh, NC 27616   Free: 800-331-4047
                           Fax: (919)954-7554
Description: Producer of educational videocassettes and interactive videodiscs for elementary children. Reaches market through commission representatives and direct mail. **Subjects:** American history, art, science, multiculturism, guidance, literature, holidays, health, geography, language arts, community studies. **Number of New Titles:** 1998 - 25.

★4394★
Social Justice
PO Box 40601   Ph: (415)647-4472
San Francisco, CA 94140   Fax: (510)528-4731
Description: Educational research and journal publishing center with a progressive global perspective on crime, international law, institutions, human rights, and social justice. Reaches market through direct mail and trade sales. Accepts unsolicited manuscripts. **Subjects:** Law, crime, prisons, sociology, civil and political rights, race and gender issues.

★4395★
Treccani
12 E. 46th St.   Ph: (212)986-3180
New York, NY 10017   Fax: (212)986-3264
Description: Publishes on cultural interests. Offers video cassettes. Reaches market through direct mail and telephone sales.

★4396★
University of Massachusetts
Horace Mann Bond Center for Equal Education
University Library 2220
School of Education
Amherst, MA 01003   Ph: (413)545-0327
Description: Publishes magazines, pamphlets, and books dealing with the education of minorities.

★4397★
Ward Hill Press
PO Box 04-0424   Ph: (718)816-9449
Staten Island, NY 10304   Free: 800-535-4340
                                      Fax: (718)816-4056
Description: Publishes adult how-to books and young adult books that focus on American history and multiculturalism. Prefers query letters prior to submissions. Reaches market through direct mail, trade sales, and wholesalers and distributors. Submission guidelines available; send SASE. Does not accept unsolicited manuscripts. **Subjects:** Young adult books that focus on American history and multiculturalism, how-to automotive books for adults.

★4398★
Washington State University Press
Washington State University
PO Box 645910   Ph: (509)335-3518
Pullman, WA 99164-5910   Free: 800-354-7360
                                      Fax: (509)335-8568
Description: Publishes books on history, culture, and politics of the West, particularly the Pacific Northwest Accepts. Accepts unsolicited manuscripts; queries preferred. Reaches market through direct mail, commission representatives, trade sales, Ingram Book, Pacific Pipeline Inc., Baker & Taylor Books, and Northwest News. **Subjects:** Pacific Northwest regional topics, history, ethnic studies. **Number of New Titles:** 1998 - 10.

★4399★
World Citizens
96 Laverne Ave.   Ph: (415)383-8766
Mill Valley, CA 94941   Free: 800-247-6553
Description: Publishes multicultural novels and books. Reaches market through Inland Book Co. **Subjects:** Multiculturalism, novels.

★4400★
WREE (Women for Racial and Economic Equality)
198 Broadway, Rm. 606
New York, NY 10038   Ph: (212)385-1103
Subjects: Women's issues, racism.

Directories

★4401★
Directory of Indian Owned Businesses
All Indian Pueblo Council, Inc.
3939 San Pedro NE, Ste. D
Albuquerque, NM 87190   Ph: (505)889-9092
Description: about 200 firms offering professional, commercial, and industrial products and services in New Mexico. Entries include: Firm name, address, phone, name and title of owner or chief executive, product or service. **Pages (approx.):** 30. **Frequency:** Annual. **Price:** $5.

★4402★
Directory of Minority Arts Organizations
Civil Rights Division
1100 Pennsylvania Ave. NW, Rm. 812   Ph: (202)682-5454
Washington, DC 20506   Fax: (202)682-5674
Description: almost 1,000 performing groups, presenters, galleries, art and media centers, literary organizations, and community centers with significant arts programming that have leadership and constituency that is predominantly Asian-American, Black, Hispanic,

Native American, or multi-racial. Entries include: Organization name, address, phone, name and title of contact, description of activities. **Pages (approx.):** 120. **Frequency:** Irregular, previous edition 1982; latest edition February 1987. **Price:** Free.

★4403★
Directory of Minority Media
San Francisco Redevelopment Agency
770 Golden Gate Ave.   Ph: (415)749-2400
San Francisco, CA 94102-3120   Fax: (415)749-2526
Description: more than 60 radio stations, television stations, and publications oriented toward Asian Americans, African Americans, Native Americans, and Hispanic Americans in northern California. Entries include: Name of medium, name of contact, address, phone. **Pages (approx.):** 4. **Frequency:** Annual. **Price:** Free.

★4404★
Directory of People of Color in the Visual Arts
College Art Association
275 7th Ave.   Ph: (212)691-1051
New York, NY 10001   Fax: (212)627-2381
Description: Approximately 700 African-American, Latino, Native American, Asian, Pacific Islander, and other "people of color" who are artists, art historians, museum professionals, arts educators, gallery professionals, or otherwise involved in the visual arts. Entries include: Name, address, phone, telex, professional information. **Pages (approx.):** 72. **Price:** $9.

★4405★
Ethnic Genealogy: A Research Guide
Greenwood Publishing Group, Inc.
88 Post Rd. W.   Ph: (203)226-3571
Westport, CT 06881   Free: 800-225-5800
                                      Fax: (203)222-1502
Description: genealogical organizations and societies, and libraries and historical societies with significant collections for research in genealogy of Native Americans, Asian Americans, African Americans, Hispanic Americans, and other ethnic groups. **Pages (approx.):** 440. **Price:** $69.50, payment must accompany order.

★4406★
Grants for Minorities
Foundation Center
79 5th Ave.   Ph: (212)620-4230
New York, NY 10003-3076   Free: 800-424-9836
                                      Fax: (212)807-3677
Description: foundations and organizations which have awarded grants in the preceding year for ethnic groups and minority populations, including African Americans, Hispanics, Asian Americans, Native Americans, gays and lesbians, and immigrants and refugees. Entries include: Foundation name, address, limitations on grants; recipient name and location, grant amount, date authorized, duration and purpose of grant, data source. Part of "Grant Guides" series. **Pages (approx.):** 384. **Frequency:** Annual, October. **Price:** $75, plus $4.50 shipping; payment must accompany order.

★4407★
Guide to Multicultural Resources
Highsmith Press
W5527 Hwy. 106   Ph: (920)563-9571
Fort Atkinson, WI 53538-0800   Free: 800-558-2110
                                      Fax: (920)563-4801
Description: over 3,600 minority and multicultural organizations and associations involved with the African, Asian, Hispanic, and Native American communities. Entries include: Organization name, address, phone, e-mail, contact names, description of organization, information or publications available, websites, listservs, budget, membership. **Pages (approx.):** 580. **Frequency:** Biennial, January of odd years. **Price:** $49.

★4408★
How and Where to Research Your Ethnic-American Cultural Heritage
R & E Publishers
2132 Otoole Ave.   Ph: (408)432-3443
San Jose, CA 95131   Fax: (408)432-9221
Description: historical societies, cultural institutes, libraries, archives, publishers, and other sources for genealogical research

into German, Russian, Native American, Polish, African, Japanese, Jewish, Irish, Mexican, Italian, Chinese, Hungarian, Austrian, Croatian, Vietnamese, Dutch, English, French, Spanish, Filipino, Puerto Rican, Portuguese, Cuban, and Scandinavian backgrounds; 24 separate volumes cover each ethnic group. Entries include: Institution name, address, phone. **Pages (approx.):** 30. **Price:** $4.50

★4409★
Minority CPAs
San Francisco Redevelopment Agency
770 Golden Gate Ave.   Ph: (415)749-2400
San Francisco, CA 94102-3120   Fax: (415)749-2526

Description: over 80 Spanish-speaking, Asian, Black or Native American certified public accounting (CPA) firms in Northern California; minority CPA associations. Entries include: For firms-Name, address, phone. For associations–Name, address, phone, name of president. **Pages (approx.):** 5. **Frequency:** Annual, latest edition December 1996. **Price:** Free.

★4410★
Minority Health Resources Directory
ANROW Publishing
1700 Research Blvd., Ste. 400   Ph: (301)294-5400
Rockville, MD 20852-3142   Fax: (301)294-5401

Description: 360 federal government programs and agencies, organizations, and foundations offering health services and products to minority group members. Entries include: Name, address, phone, description, activities for minorities, publications and other communications, meetings and conferences. **Pages (approx.):** 355 **Frequency:** Published 1991. **Price:** $50, plus $6.95 shipping.

★4411★
Minority Law Firms
San Francisco Redevelopment Agency
770 Golden Gate Ave.   Ph: (415)749-2400
San Francisco, CA 94102-3120   Fax: (415)749-2526

Description: over 200 Spanish-speaking, Asian, Black, or Native American law firms and lawyers in northern California; minority bar associations. Entries include: For firms–Name, address, phone. For associations–Name, address, phone, name of president. **Pages (approx.):** 13. **Frequency:** Annual. **Price:** Free.

★4412★
Minority Organizations: A National Directory
Garrett Park Press
PO Box 190   Ph: (301)946-2553
Garrett Park, MD 20896   Fax: (301)949-3958

Description: over 9,700 groups composed of or intended to serve members of minority groups, including Alaska Natives, American Indians, Blacks, Hispanics, and Asian Americans. Entries include: Organization name, address, description of activities, purpose, publications, etc. **Pages (approx.):** 514. **Frequency:** Irregular, previous edition 1987; latest edition 1992. **Price:** $50.

★4413★
Minority Student Enrollments in Higher Education: A Guide to Institutions with. . .Asian, Black, Hispanic, and Native American Students
Garrett Park Press
PO Box 190   Ph: (301)946-2553
Garrett Park, MD 20896   Fax: (301)949-3958

Description: about 500 colleges and universities at which one or more minority (Asian, Black, Hispanic, or Native American) constitutes at least 20% of the student body. Entries include: Institution name, address, phone, total enrollment, highest level of degree offered, partial list of major programs offered, minority groups representing at least one-fifth of the total enrollment. **Pages (approx.):** 80. **Frequency:** Irregular, previous edition 1988; latest edition 1993. **Price:** $14, payment with order; $15, billed.

★4414★
Montana Vacation Guide
Travel Montana
Department of Commerce   Ph: (406)444-2654
1424 9th Ave.   Free: 800-847-4868
Helena, MT 59620   Fax: (406)444-1800

Description: over 300 attractions, historic sites, national and state parks, cultural centers, Indian reservations and museums in Montana. Entries include: Name of site, address or location, description, key to location on state map. **Pages (approx.):** 48. **Frequency:** Annual, January. **Price:** Free.

★4415★
Multicultural Student's Guide to College
Noonday Press   Ph: (212)741-6900
19 Union Sq. W.   Free: 800-788-6262
New York, NY 10003   Fax: (212)633-9385

Description: over 200 colleges and universities selected on the basis of reputation and degree of ethnic diversity; emphasis placed on programs and services for Black, Hispanic, Asian, and Native American students. Entries include: School name, address, phone, names of admissions director and multicultural student recruiter, tuition and fees, application deadlines; statistics on non-white students including freshman admissions and percentage of total student body, popular majors, scholarships available only to non-white students, organizations, notable non-white alumni, faculty breakdown by ethnic group, detailed description of activities, programs, and campus life. **Pages (approx.):** 650. **Price:** $25.

★4416★
National Database of Arts Organizations of Color
National Assembly of State Arts Agencies
1010 Vermont Ave. NW, Ste. 920
Washington, DC 20005   Ph: (202)347-6352

Description: over 1,100 orchestras, dance companies, theaters, museums, media organizations, presenters, and service organizations representing African American, Native American, Latino, and Asian cultures. Entries include: Organization name, address, phone, discipline, ethnicity. **Frequency:** Updated continuously; printed on request. **Formerly:** National Directory of Multi-Cultural Arts Organizations.

★4417★
National Directory of Minority-Owned Business Firms
Todd Publications   Ph: (914)358-6213
PO Box 635   Free: 800-747-1056
Nyack, NY 10960   Fax: (914)358-1059

Description: Over 40,000 minority-owned businesses in the U.S. Entries include: Contact name, phone, number of employees, certification status, start-up date, and key word business descriptions. **Pages (approx.):** 1,500. **Frequency:** Biennial. **Price:** $195.

★4418★
New Mexico Vacation Guide
New Mexico Department of Tourism   Ph: (505)827-7400
PO Box 20003   Free: 800-545-2040
Santa Fe, NM 87503   Fax: (505)827-7402

Description: About 800 annual events, 60 state and national parks and monuments, eight recreation areas, numerous ruins and ghost towns, 22 Native American reservations and pueblos, historic sites, five horse racetracks, numerous ski areas and resorts, plus lodging and restaurant listings. Entries include: For events–Name, date location, description, time, fees, contact address, phone. For others–Name, location, descri ption. **Pages (approx.):** 184. **Frequency:** Annual, winter. **Price:** Free. **Formerly:** New Mexico Vacation Planner.

★4419★
North Dakota Department of Transportation Disadvantaged Business Enterprise Directory
North Dakota Department of
Transportation
608 E. Boulevard Ave.   Ph: (701)328-2576
Bismarck, ND 58505-0700   Fax: (701)328-1415
Description: 81 North Dakota Department of Transportation-certified disadvantaged business enterprises (DBEs), which provide product/service related to the development, construction, maintenance, and operation of transportation systems. Entries include: Company name, address, phone, fax, name and title of owner or contact; business listings also show line of business, equipment available, number of employees, territory served, year established. **Pages (approx.):** 49. **Frequency:** Annual, January. **Price:** Free. **Formerly:** Minority Business Directory.

★4420★
The Source: A Guidebook of American Genealogy
Ancestry, Inc.   Ph: (801)426-3500
PO Box 476   Free: 800-531-1790
Salt Lake City, UT 84110   Fax: (801)426-3501
Description: Publication includes: Lists of federal archives, record centers, state archives, and historical societies, research libraries, heraldry and lineage societies, genealogy publications and publishers, sources of business records, and fraternal organizations. Entries include: Name of the genealogical source, location, contents of the record, means of access, use in research or family history. Main content of the publication is discussion of records useful for research in American genealogy, including Native Americans, Jewish Americans, and African Americans. **Pages (approx.):** 783. **Frequency:** Irregular, latest edition 1997. **Price:** $49.95, plus $4.50 shipping.

★4421★
Talent Roster of Outstanding Minority Transfer Students from Two-Year Colleges
The College
45 Columbus Ave.
New York, NY 10023-6992   Ph: (212)713-8000
Description: 5,000 minority graduates of two-year colleges selected by their colleges on the basis of grade point average. Entries include: Name, address, grade point average, intended major. **Pages (approx.):** 200. **Frequency:** Annual, fall. **Price:** Free. **Formerly:** Talent Roster of Outstanding Minority Community College Graduates.

Journals & Magazines

★4422★
Abstracts in Anthropology
Baywood Publishing Co., Inc.   Ph: (516)691-1270
26 Austin Ave.   Free: 800-638-7819
Amityville, NY 11701   Fax: (516)691-1770
Description: Abstracting service covering archaeology, cultural and physical anthropology, and linguistics. **First Published:** 1970 8/year. **Subscriptions:** $304, U.S. & Canada; $314.50, other countries. **ISSN:** 0001-3455.

★4423★
Affirmative Action Register
Affirmative Action, Inc.   Ph: (314)991-1335
8356 Olive Blvd.   Free: 800-537-0655
St. Louis, MO 63132   Fax: (314)997-1788
Description: Journal for business, academe, and the government to use in recruiting females, Native Americans, minorities, veterans, and the handicapped. **First Published:** 1974. **Frequency:** Monthly. **ISSN:** 0146-2113.

★4424★
American Antiquity
Society for American Archaeology
900 2nd St. NE, No. 12   Ph: (202)789-8200
Washington, DC 20002   Fax: (202)789-0284
Description: Journal on the archaeology of the New World. **First Published:** 1935. **Frequency:** Quarterly. **Subscriptions:** $175. **ISSN:** 0002-7316.

★4425★
The Atlanta Tribune
L & L Communications, Inc.
875 Old Roswell Rd., Ste. C-100   Ph: (770)587-0501
Roswell, GA 30076   Fax: (770)642-6501
Description: Minority business newsmagazine. **Frequency:** Biweekly. **Subscriptions:** $24.

★4426★
Beads
Society of Bead Researchers
1600 Liverpool Court   Ph: (613)990-4814
Ottawa, ON, Canada K1A 0M5   Fax: (613)952-1756
Description: Research journal featuring information on beads of all materials and periods. **First Published:** 1989. **Frequency:** 1/year. **Subscriptions:** $20, U.S. and Canada; $30, overseas. **ISSN:** 0843-5499.

★4427★
Interculture
Intercultural Institute of Montreal   Ph: (514)288-7229
Montreal, PQ, Canada H2T 2W1   Fax: (514)844-6800
Description: Journal covering cross-cultural themes. **First Published:** 1968. **Frequency:** Semiannual. **Subscriptions:** $23. **ISSN:** 0828-797X.

★4428★
Journal of American Ethnic History
Transaction Periodicals Consortium
Dept. 3093   Ph: (908)445-2280
New Brunswick, NJ 08903   Fax: (908)932-3138
Description: Journal addressing various aspects of American immigration and ethnic history including background of emigration, ethnic and racial groups, native Americans, and immigration policies. **First Published:** 1981. **Frequency:** Quarterly. **Subscriptions:** $30. **ISSN:** 0278-5927.

★4429★
Journal of Intergroup Relations
National Association of Human Rights
Workers
115 S. Andrews Ave., No. A-640   Ph: (954)357-6046
Fort Lauderdale, FL 33301   Fax: (954)357-5746
Description: Magazine focusing on civil rights and race relations issues. **Frequency:** Quarterly.

★4430★
Mammoth Trumpet
Center for the First American
Oregon State University   Ph: (541)737-4595
Corvallis, OR 97331   Fax: (541)737-3651
Description: Scholarly journal covering U.S. anthropology and archaeology. **Frequency:** Quarterly **ISSN:** 8755-6898.

★4431★
Minority Business Entrepreneur
3528 Torrance Blvd., Ste. 101   Ph: (310)540-9398
Torrance, CA 90503-4826   Fax: (310)792-8263
Description: Business magazine for ethnic minority and women business owners. **Frequency:** Bimonthly. **Subscriptions:** $15.

★4432★
Rural History
Cambridge University Press   Ph: (212)924-3900
40 W. 20th St.   Free: 800-221-4512
New York, NY 10011-4211   Fax: (212)691-3239
Description: Interdisciplinary journal. Focuses on, but is not limited to, Western studies. **First Published:** 1990. **Frequency:** Semiannual **ISSN:** 0956-7933.

Newsletters

★4433★
Chronicle of Minority Business
Association of African American Women
  Business Owners
PO Box 13858
Silver Spring, MD 20911-0933   Ph: (301)585-8051
Description: Provides information for minority business owners. **Frequency:** Quarterly.

★4434★
Civil Rights
Wakeman/Walworth, Inc.   Ph: (703)549-8606
300 N. Washington St.   Free: 800-876-2545
Alexandria, VA 22314   Fax: (703)549-1372
Description: Covers state civil rights and affirmative action legislation, including ethnic, race, and sex discrimination; judicial decisions regarding desegregation; discrimination compensation; gay rights; and civil rights of the disabled. **Frequency:** Weekly.

★4435★
EduQuest Connections
Mejia & Associates, Inc.
1047 E. 29th St.   Ph: (718)253-5113
Brooklyn, NY 11210   Fax: (718)253-1434
Description: Provides information written and compiled by business owners, business educators, consultants, and journalists for small and home-based business owners. Addresses links between education and business, training, investments, health issues, telecommunications, and technological trends. Recurring features include interviews, an international news column, news of research, a calendar of events, reports of meetings, news of educational opportunities, job listings, book reviews, notices of publications available, and columns titled Connect Your Business, Trends, Demographics, Commentary, Health & Fitness, The Book Review, and Bulletin Board. **Pages (approx.):** 12. **Frequency:** Monthly. **Price:** $24.95.

★4436★
Federal Computer Market Report
Computer Age
714 Church St.   Ph: (703)739-8500
Alexandria, VA 22314-4202   Fax: (703)739-8505
Description: Keeps commercial vendors and government buyers up-to-date with trends in government computer contracting. Covers procurement regulations, technical evaluation criteria, minority subcontracting, and other topics of interest. Recurring features include listings of contract opportunities and major government acquisitions. **Frequency:** Semimonthly.

★4437★
Human Rights Watch UPDATE
Human Rights Watch
485 5th Ave.   Ph: (212)290-4700
New York, NY 10017   Fax: (212)972-0905
Description: Reports on work on behalf of human rights in Angola, Britain, Bosnia, Burundi, Honduras, Israel, Mexico, and the U.S. Recurring features include news of research and notices of publications available. **Frequency:** 10x/yr.

★4438★
Indiana Minority Business Report
8458 Lynhaven Pl.
Indianapolis, IN 46256-3701   Ph: (317)845-0665
Description: Profiles successful minority-owned businesses and reports on new Indiana legislation affecting minority-run businesses. Recurring features include interviews. **Frequency:** Bimonthly.

★4439★
Iowa Civil Rights Communicator
Iowa Civil Rights Commission   Ph: (515)281-4121
211 E. Maple St., 2nd Fl.   Free: 800-457-4416
Des Moines, IA 50309   Fax: (515)242-5840
Description: Serves as the official newsletter of the Commission, which seeks to "eliminate discrimination" and to establish equality and justice for all persons within the state through civil rights enforcement and advocacy. Features news of civil rights legislation and court decisions. Identifies civil rights issues of particular interest to Iowa residents, as well as discussing issues of general interest. Includes articles written by civil rights professionals. **Frequency:** Semiannual.

★4440★
LAMA's Watch on Washington
Latin American Management Association
419 New Jersey Ave. SE
Washington, DC 20003-4007   Ph: (202)546-3803
Description: Contains national news on minority and small business issues, including legislation and regulations. **Frequency:** Bimonthly.

★4441★
Maryknoll Justice and Peace Office—NewsNotes
Maryknoll Justice and Peace Office
PO Box 29132   Ph: (202)832-1780
Washington, DC 20017   Fax: (202)832-5195
Description: Covers international justice and peace issues Africa, the Middle East, Latin America, and Asia and the Pacific. Recurring features include List of resources. **Frequency:** Bimonthly.

★4442★
Michigan Civil Rights Commission Newsletter
Michigan Civil Rights Commission
Information Division
Dept. of Civil Rights
201 N. Washington Sq., Ste. 700   Ph: (517)373-0089
Lansing, MI 48913   Fax: (517)335-6513
Description: Informs the public of specific issues affecting the Civil Rights Commission's jurisdiction, including legislative developments. Covers news of the Commission regarding elections and appointments. Recurring features include notices of publications. **Frequency:** Quarterly.

★4443★
National Association of Investment Companies Newsletter
National Association of Investment
  Counselors
1111 14th St., Ste. 700
Washington, DC 20005   Ph: (202)289-4336
Description: Presents "issues, events and trends of vital concern to the MESBIC industry and to minority small business." Focuses on legislative trends and actions. **Frequency:** Monthly

★4444★
National Business League—National Memo
National Business League
1511 K St. NW, Ste. 432   Ph: (202)737-4430
Washington, DC 20005   Fax: (202)466-4432
Description: Discusses minority business development, especially the role of the League in furthering continued advances. Features news about economic trends, government policies and issues, private sector trends, minority business trade association activity, and chapter activities. Recurring features include reports of meetings, news of educational opportunities, book reviews, notices

of publications available, a calendar of events, and a column titled From the President's Desk. **Remarks:** Publication temporarily suspended. **Frequency:** Quarterly.

★4445★
News from MCLI
Meiklejohn Civil Liberties Institute
PO Box 673   Ph: (510)848-0599
Berkeley, CA 94701   Fax: (510)848-6008
Description: Monitors and reports the organization's ongoing work with human rights. Lists recent human rights and peace law publications and projects. Recurring features include news of research, job listings, and notices of publications available. **Frequency:** Irregular.

★4446★
Notes for a New World
Fine Arts Center Development Office
University of Massachusetts
Box 31810
Amherst, MA 01003-1810
Description: Spotlights New World Theater, "a multiracial theater founded in 1979 which produces plays about the Black, Latino, Asian, and Native American experiences." Features artists, directors, playwrights, and actors affiliated with the theater. Recurring features include columns titled Between The Lines and Auditions. **Pages (approx.):** 12. **Frequency:** Quarterly.

★4447★
The Organizer
National Alliance Against Racist and
  Political Repression
953 E. Sahara Ave., Ste. 215   Ph: (702)406-3330
Las Vegas, NV 89104-3016   Fax: (702)406-3542
Description: Reports on the activities of task forces within the Alliance concerned with issues such as repressive legislation, political prisoners, police crimes, labor rights, prisoners' rights, racism, and political repression. Recurring features include information on the Alliance's national priority cases and activities planned around each case. **Frequency:** Quarterly.

★4448★
Quaker Service Bulletin
American Friends Service Committee   Ph: (215)241-7048
1501 Cherry St.   Free: (888)588-
Philadelphia, PA 19102   AFSC
                                              Fax: (215)241-7275
Description: Concerned with the issues of peace, reconciliation, nonmilitary solutions to conflicts, social change, and other issues of international concern. Also covers domestic issues, such as education, youth and militarism, social justice, minority rights, criminal justice, rights of immigrants, the homeless, Indian rights, and hunger, "focusing particularly on empowerment." Recurring features include news of the current work of the Committee, editorials, and news of AFSC staff members. Also available on microfilm. **Frequency:** 2/year.

★4449★
Set-Aside Alert
Small Business Press, Inc.
1925 N. Lynn St., Ste. 1000   Ph: (703)243-9868
Arlington, VA 22209-1707   Fax: (703)243-2317
Description: Addresses issues of interest to 8(a) SDB minority- and women-owned businesses that have federal government clientele. Covers networking and contact opportunities. Recurring features include interviews, a calendar of events, reports of meetings, and columns titled legal, accounting, marketing, and finance columns. **Frequency:** 24/year.

★4450★
Today
National Association of Minority Women in
  Business
906 Grand Ave., Ste. 200   Ph: (816)421-3335
Kansas City, MO 64106   Fax: (816)421-3336
Description: Serves as a network for the exchange of ideas and information on business opportunities for minority women in the public and private sectors. Discusses topics of concern to minority women in business ownership and management positions. Recurring features include highlights of pertinent legislative developments, news of members, news of research, notices of educational opportunities, and a calendar of events. Also includes items on women who have made significant contributions to the field. **Frequency:** Bimonthly.

★4451★
UUACTION Alert Legislative Network
Unitarian Universalist Assn. of Churches
  in North America
100 Maryland Ave. NE   Ph: (202)547-0254
Washington, DC 20002   Fax: (202)594-2854
Description: Monitors public policy and legislative developments concerning the military budget, arms control and disarmament, human and civil rights, religious liberties, and economic justice. **Frequency:** Periodic.

Videos

★4452★
The ABA Commission on Minorities and Judicial Administration Division
American Bar Association
Commission on Public Understanding
  About the Law
750 N. Lakeshore Dr.
Chicago, IL 60611   Ph: (312)988-5000
Description: Issues of prejudice in the courtroom are discussed. **Release Date:** 1988. **Length:** 15 mins. **Format:** Beta, VHS, 3/4" U-matic Cassette.

★4453★
AIDS and the Native American Family
Upstream Productions   Ph: (206)281-9177
420 First Ave. W.   Free: (888)778-
Seattle, WA 98119   7326
                                             Fax: (206)284-6963
Description: Addresses the need for family and cultural support of Native Americans with the AIDS virus. **Length:** 11 **Format:** VHS

★4454★
Alice Elliott
University of California at Berkeley
  Extension Media Center
2176 Shattuck Ave.
Berkeley, CA 94704   Ph: (510)642-0460
Description: The artist who makes Indian-style baskets is profiled. **Release Date:** 1977. **Length:** 45 mins. **Format:** VHS, 3/4" U-matic Cassette.

★4455★
And Justice for Some
Downtown Community TV Center
87 Lafayette St.
New York, NY 10013   Ph: (212)966-4510
Description: This documentary examines the unfairness of the justice system towards minorities. **Release Date:** 1983. **Length:** 7 mins. **Format:** 1/2" Reel-EIAJ, 3/4" U-matic Cassette, Other than listed.

★4456★
Are People All the Same?
Pyramid Film & Video
Box 1048   Ph: (310)828-7577
2801 Colorado Ave.   Free: 800-421-2304
Santa Monica, CA 90406   Fax: (310)453-9083
Description: This part of the "Who We Are" series features live action and animation showing children the meaning of race and the uniqueness of each and every person. **Release Date:** 1977. **Length:** 9 mins. **Format:** Beta, VHS, 3/4" U-matic Cassette.

★4457★
Combating Racism
Chinese for Affirmative Action
17 Walter Lum Pl.
San Francisco, CA 94108   Ph: (415)982-0801
Description: In this program various community representatives from San Francisco are interviewed as to what can be done to combat racism. Among those interviewed were Leaonard Carter, George Tamsak, Mack Hall, Shone Martinez, John Chinn, and Margaret Cruz. **Release Date:** 1973. **Length:** 30 mins. **Format:** 1/2" Reel-EIAJ.

★4458★
Equal Opportunity
Barr Films
12801 Schabarum Ave.   Ph: (818)338-7878
PO Box 7878   Free: 800-234-7878
Irwindale, CA 91706-7878   Fax: (818)814-2672
Description: This program explores the meaning of equal opportunity within the context of affirmative action, racial discrimination, past discrimination, union contracts, seniority, fairness and the Bill of Rights. **Release Date:** 1983. **Length:** 22 mins. **Format:** Beta, VHS, 3/4" U-matic Cassette.

★4459★
Mental Health Needs of Minority Children
Social Psychiatry Research Institute
150 E. 69th St.
New York, NY 10021   Ph: (212)628-4800
Description: This program describes the special problems of minority groups, blacks, Hispanics and native Americans, with an emphasis on preventive work with children in school settings so as to avoid the continued high incidence of neurosis and psychoses in this population. **Release Date:** 1981. **Length:** 50 mins. **Format:** 1/2" Reel-EIAJ, 3/4" U-matic Cassette.

★4460★
Minorities in Journalism: Making a Difference
PBS Video
1320 Braddock Pl.
Alexandria, VA 22314-1698   Ph: (703)739-5380
Description: A look at how minority students can enter and get ahead in the various branches of journalism - print, radio, and TV. **Release Date:** 1989. **Length:** 25 mins. **Format:** VHS, 3/4" U-matic Cassette.

★4461★
Native American Herbology for Beginners
Wishing Well Distributing   Ph: (414)889-8501
PO Box 1008   Free: 800-888-9355
Silver Lake, WI 53170   Fax: (414)889-8591
Description: Focuses on the spiritual Native American approach to herbology, and the nine herbs most useful in avoiding harsh over-the-counter medications. Also outlines the identification of medicinal herbs and their preparation for use. **Length:** 55 **Format:** VHS

★4462★
Opportunities in Criminal Justice
William Greaves Productions
80 8th Ave., Ste. 1701
New York, NY 10011   Ph: (212)206-1213
Description: The wide variety of career opportunities available to women and minorities in the criminal justice system. **Release Date:**

1978. **Length:** 25 mins. **Format:** Beta, VHS. **Credits:** Narrated by: Bill Cosby.

★4463★
Prejudice: A Lesson to Forget
American Educational Films
3807 Dickerson Rd.
Nashville, TN 37207   Free: 800-822-5678
Description: An interview with people who exhibit unconscious prejudices against minorities. **Release Date:** 1973. **Length:** 17 mins. **Format:** Beta, VHS, 3/4" U-matic Cassette. **Credits:** Narrated by: Joseph Campanella.

★4464★
Prejudice: Causes, Consequences, Cures
CRM/McGraw-Hill Films
674 Via de la Valle
PO Box 641
Del Mar, CA 92014
Description: This program focuses on research findings and their implications for dealing with prejudice against women and racial, national, and ethnic groups. **Release Date:** 1974. **Length:** 24 mins. **Format:** Beta, VHS, 3/4" U-matic Cassette.

★4465★
The Prejudice Film
Motivational Media
12001 Ventura Pl., No. 202   Ph: (818)508-6553
Studio City, CA 91604   Free: 800-331-8454
Description: The historical background of contemporary forms of prejudice are examined in this program. **Release Date:** 1984. **Length:** 28 mins. **Format:** Beta, VHS, 3/4" U-matic Cassette. **Credits:** Narrated by: David Hartman.

★4466★
Racism and Minority Groups: Part 1
University of Washington Instructional
  Media Services
Kane Hall, DG-10
Seattle, WA 98195   Ph: (206)543-9909
Description: Each of the major racial minorities is presented in historic and current respective and members of each group respond to the series' presentations. Programs available individually. **Release Date:** 1973. **Length:** 30 mins. **Format:** 3/4" U-matic Cassette.

★4467★
Racism and Minority Groups: Part 2
University of Washington Instructional
  Media Services
Kane Hall, DG-10
Seattle, WA 98195   Ph: (206)543-9909
Description: These programs are a continuation of "Racism and Minority Groups 1." Programs are available individually. **Release Date:** 1973. **Length:** 30 mins. **Format:** 3/4" U-matic Cassette.

★4468★
The Red Road to Sobriety
Wishing Well Distributing   Ph: (414)889-8501
PO Box 1008   Free: 800-888-9355
Silver Lake, WI 53170   Fax: (414)889-8591
Description: Chronicles how the governments of North America used alcohol against Native Americans as a tool for land acquisition, and how the media and school systems manufactured the stereotype of "the drunken Indian" to justify the government's dishonest actions. Also examines the cultural revitalization movement now flourishing throughout the U.S. and Canada. **Length:** 60 **Format:** VHS

★4469★
Storm of Strangers
Films, Inc.
5547 N. Ravenswood Ave.   Ph: (312)878-2600
Chicago, IL 60640-1199   Free: 800-323-4222

Description: This series introduces America's ethnic and racial minorities to each other. **Release Date:** 1983. **Length:** 29 mins. **Format:** Beta, VHS, 3/4″ U-matic Cassette.

★4470★
Sweating Indian Style: Conflicts over Native American Ritual
Documentary Educational Resources   Ph: (617)926-0491
101 Morse St.   Free: 800-569-6621
Watertown, MA 02172   Fax: (617)926-9519

Description: Focuses on a group of New Age women who construct a sweat lodge and prepare for their own ceremony. Also looks at some Native American groups who condemn this practice and believe that it should not be shared with outside cultures. **Length:** 57 **Format:** VHS

★4471★
What Color Is Skin
Pyramid Film & Video
Box 1048   Ph: (310)828-7577
2801 Colorado Ave.   Free: 800-421-2304
Santa Monica, CA 90406   Fax: (310)453-9083

Description: This part of the "Who We Are" series combines live action and animation to show that individual skin coloring is determined by the amount of melanin in the skin. **Release Date:** 1977. **Length:** 9 mins. **Format:** Beta, VHS, 3/4″ U-matic Cassette.

Internet and Online Databases

★4472★
ACLU Freedom Network
American Civil Liberties Union
132 W. 43rd St.
New York, NY 10036   Fax: (212)944-9065

URL: http://www.aclu.org **Description:** The ACLU's web site is filled with news, articles and information pertaining to nearly every issue related to individual rights in the United States. A search engine in the Library area allows for searches on specific topics, but so many topic areas are laid out on the home page that it is not always necessary to use the search engine to find current information. Main Files: In Congress; In the Courts; Students; News and Events; About the ACLU; Join the ACLU; The Store; Library; Act Now; In the States; Church and State; Criminal Justice; Cyber-Liberties; Death Penalty; Free Speech; HIV/AIDS; Immigrants' Rights; Lesbian and Gay Rights; National Security; Racial Equality; Reproductive Rights; Students' Rights; Voting Rights; Women's Rights; Workplace Rights; Index; Join; Home; Search; Feedback.

★4473★
An Adoptee's Right to Know
Plumsite

Shea Grimm

URL: http://www.plumsite.com/shea/ **Description:** This site contains directions on how to search, links to state and federal laws, including pending legislation as well as to other adoption-related sites. Shea's site provides more information on transracial adoption and the issues involving adoption of Native American children. The content of this site is quite informative and should be of interest to anyone planning to adopt–it should also be noted that this site is quite attractive. The sparse use of graphics and the unique color scheme make it quite pleasing to the eye. Main Files: Searching; Legal and Activist Resources; General Information. **Update frequency:** As needed. **Fees:** Free.

★4474★
Affrimative Action Manual
The Bureau of National Affairs, Inc.   Ph: (202)452-4132
123 25th St., NW   Free: 800-960-1220
Washington, DC 20037   Fax: (202)452-4062

Description: Online database. Contains the complete text of a special report on affirmative action. Includes historical background, a review of currently applicable federal regulations, and a summary of decisions from the Supreme Court. Also provides case studies of employer-initiated affirmative action programs, essays, and a selected bibliography. Corresponds to *Affirmative Action Today: A Legal and Regulatory Analysis.* **Available through:** HRIN Corporation, 7200 Wisconsin Ave., Ste. 601, Bethesda, MD 20814, (301)961-6760, toll-free 800-638-8094.

★4475★
American Civil Liberties Union Freedom Network
American Civil Liberties Union
132 W. 43rd St.   Ph: (212)944-9800
New York, NY 10036   Fax: (212)944-9065

URL: http://www.aclu.org/ **Description:** In the wake of the 1996 Telecommunications Act, the ACLU Freedom Network will doubtless assume a more prominent role in the Internet. Even as the bill was signed by President Clinton, the ACLU was already submitting legislation that challenges the act. The ACLU's home page is a comprehensive and well-organized repository of civil rights history and information. The site contains hypertext links to several civil liberty issues, including Church and State; Criminal Justice; Cyber-Liberties; Death Penalty; Free Speech; HIV / AIDS; Immigrants' Rights; Lesbian and Gay Rights; National Security; Racial Equality; Reproductive Rights; Students' Rights; Voting Rights; Women's Rights; and Workplace Rights. Main Files: In Congress; In the Courts; Students; News and Events; About the ACLU; Join the ACLU; The Store; Library; Act Now!; and In the States. If you feeling as if your civil rights are being trampled upon, then this site will probably have whatever information you seek. The web site's "text only" option is somewhat misleading in that only the home page switches from graphics to text; all other hypertext links are still presented graphically. The American Civil Liberties Union is the nation's foremost advocate of individual rights–litigating, legislating, and educating the public on a broad array of issues affecting individual freedom in the United States. **Update frequency:** Regularly. **Fees:** Free.

★4476★
Amnesty International On-line
Internex Online
20 Bay St., Ste. 1625   Ph: (416)363-8518
Toronto, ON, Canada M5J 2N8   Fax: (416)363-8713
Ray Mitchell

URL: http://www.amnesty.org/ **Gopher:** gopher.igc.apc.org Choose: Organizations. **Description:** Amnesty International Online contains information about and from Amnesty International (AI), an organization concerned with the protection of human rights. It includes facts and figures about AI, reports of human rights violations, and the Universal Declaration of Human Rights, among other features. Main Files: Stop Press; About AI; Campaigns; Act Now; AI Library; News Release; AI Interactive; AI Sections; and Other Sites. This site is filled with important information not only about the organization but also the issues. Maybe it's a temporary problem, but at time of review, this was one of the slowest-loading sites in history–painfully slow. Human rights violations around the world are reported virtually every day of the week and sorting out fact from fiction is an essential task for Amnesty International. **Update frequency:** Daily. **Fees:** Free.

★4477★
AskERIC Home Page
Syracuse University   Ph: (315)443-3640
Center for Science & Technology   Free: 800-464-9107
Syracuse, NY 13244-4100   Fax: (315)443-5448

URL: http://ericir.syr.edu/ **Description:** AskERIC is an education information service of the ERIC System. The service is comprised of three major components: AskERIC Q & A Service where teachers, library media specialists, administrators, and others involved in the field of education can send a message requesting education information to AskERIC. Drawing on their extensive resources,

AskERIC information specialists, will respond within 48 hours with ERIC database searches, ERIC Digests, and Internet resources. To request education information, address an email message (via the Internet) to: askeric@ericir.syr.edu. AskERIC Virtual Library contains selected resources for education and general interest. The files include News and Information about ERIC and AskERIC; Map of the Library; Search AskERIC Menu Items; AskERIC Toolbox; Frequently Asked Questions (FAQ's) about ERIC & AskERIC; AskERIC InfoGuides; Lesson Plans (over 700); Education Listservs Archives; ERIC Clearinghouses/Components; ERIC Digests File; ERIC Bibliographic Database (RIE and CIJE); Bibliographies; News & Announcements of Interest to Educators; Other Education Resources; Education Conferences; Electronic Journals, Books, and Reference Tools; Internet Guides and Directories; and Gophers and Library Catalogs. AskERIC R&D was formed so that ERIC could continue to use state of the art technology to provide outstanding service to the education community. According to the site, current R&D projects include providing access to fulltext ERIC documents on the Internet, improved interface to the ERIC database on the Internet, automating the distributed question answering service, and multimedia development of the Virtual Library. Main Files: About Ask Eric; Q & A Service; Virtual Library; New and Noteworthy; R & D; Search ERIC Database; Ask ERIC Sponsors; Feedback; Search. Remarks: ERIC is the Educational Resources Information Center (ERIC), a federally funded national information system that provides access to education related resources. The ERIC Clearinghouse on Information and Technology (ERIC/IT), sponsor of the AskERIC Project, is one of 16 ERIC Clearinghouses nationwide. AskERIC is funded by the U.S. Department of Education - Office of Educational Research and Improvement (OERI). Outstanding site with very strong search capabilities. The design gets a little weak when linking into gopher areas. Because AskERIC is also a Sun SITE repository, AskERIC is able to expand the quality and quantity of its resources and services to the education community.

★4478★
Center for World Indigenous Studies
1001 Cooper Point Rd. SW, Ste. 140-214
c/o John Burrows   Free: (888)286-
Olympia, WA 98502   2947
                          Fax: (360)956-1087

URL: http://www.halcyon.com/FWDP/cwisinfo.html   **Description:** Improving the conditions of indigenous peoples around the world is the main focus of this site. Offers programs of study and internships to individuals interested in Fourth World Studies. Catalog of publications and databases available on disks. Provides information about the ongoing Fourth World Documentation Project and related internal links include Africa; Asia; Europe; North America; Mexico and Caribbean; Central and South America; Melanesia, Polynesia and Micronesia; and General/International. Main Files: Who We Are; What We Do; Contact Us; What's New; News; Search. **Update frequency:** Regularly. **Fees:** Database of Indigenous Organizations around the world and a database of all U.S. federally recognized tribes available on 5 1/2" and 3 1/4" disks for $10.00.

★4479★
DISCovering Multicultural America
Gale Research   Ph: (313)961-2242
835 Penobscot Bldg.   Free: 800-347-4253
Detroit, MI 48226-4094   Fax: (313)961-6815

Description: Online database. Provides text, video and sound clips, statistics, and photographs linked to the culture, history, and current status of America's largest and most-studied groups: African Americans, Asian Americans, Hispanic Americans, and Native North Americans. For each ethnic group, provides seven categories of information, including biographies, historical and topical essays, ethnic landmarks, significant documents, timeline, organizations, and full-text periodical articles. Contains morte than 2000 biographical sketchs for contempory and historial figures; more than 350 significant documents; 3100 timeline events; 5000 contact organizations; 500 full-text periodical articles from 25 ethnic publications; and 1500 photos, 70 audio clips, and 25 video clips. Enables the user to search by individual, organization, document, place, event, time period, subject, gender, or occupation. **Available through:** GaleNet (Available by subscription; contact Gale Research for details).

★4480★
EcoJustice Network
Institute for Global Communications
18 DeBoom St.   Ph: (415)442-0220
San Francisco, CA 94107   Fax: (415)546-1976
Antonio Diaz, EcoNet Program Coordinator
URL: http://www.igc.apc.org/envjustice/   **Gopher:** gopher.igc.apc.org Choose: Publications and News Services on the IGC Networks Gopher. **Description:** The EcoJustice Directory is the revised and expanded edition of the earlier directory, with information on people of color groups that are concerned with environmental issues. Coverage includes the United States, Canada, and Mexico, and entries include contact and general information for the groups. The purpose is to provide a networking tool for people of color to press their environmental concerns. Data Providers: Dr. Robert Bullard at the Environmental Justice Resource Center, Clark Atlanta University. Main Files: New and Featured; Organizations @igc; Reports & Articles @igc; EcoJustice Actions; The People of Color Environmental Groups Directory; Maps; About the Project; Government Resources; Other Links; African American Networking; Asian Community Online (ACON); Toxics, Hazards & Waste. **Update frequency:** Annual. **Fees:** Free.

★4481★
EEOC Policies and Programs
The Bureau of National Affairs, Inc.   Ph: (202)452-4132
1231 25th St. NW   Free: 800-960-1220
Washington, DC 20037   Fax: (202)452-4062

Description: Online database. Contains the complete text of *EEO Policies and Programs,* a special report on procedures undertaken by U.S businesses to meet equal employment opportunity (EEO) and affirmative action goals. Includes sample policies, procedures, and forms for use in program monitoring and compliance. Source of information is the Personnel Policy Forum Survey conducted by BNA. **Available through:** HRIN Corporation, 7200 Wisconsin Ave., Ste. 601, Bethesda, MD 20814, (301)961-6760, toll-free 800-638-8094.

★4482★
Ethnic NewsWatch
SoftLine Information, Inc.   Ph: (203)975-8292
20 Summer St.   Free: 800-524-7922
Stamford, CT 06901   Fax: (203)975-8347

Description: Online database. Contains the complete text of more than 250,000 articles, editorials, and reviews published in approximately 1800 ethnic and minority newspapers, magazines, and journals published in the United States. Provides multicultural coverage of subjects of interest to African Americans, Hispanics, Latinos, Chicanos, Native Americans, Asians, Jewish, Arab, and European Americans. Includes a directory providing bibliographic information for each publication covered. **Available through:** NEXIS, 9443 Springboro Pike, PO Box 933, Dayton, OH 45401-0933, (513)865-6800, toll-free 800-543-6862 (ENW: Transaction pricing, per-search pricing, and connect hour charging options available; contact vendor for details).

★4483★
Fair Employment Practices Newsletter
The Bureau of National Affairs, Inc.   Ph: (202)452-4132
1231 25th St., NW   Free: 800-960-1220
Washington, DC 20037   Fax: (202)452-4062

Description: Online database. Contains the complete text of *Fair Employment Practices Newsletter,* covering federal and state activities relating to equal employment opportunity. Covers the Equal Employment Opportunity Commission (EEOC), the Office of Federal Contract Compliance Programs (OFCCP), court action in discrimination suits, new laws and regulations, and affirmative action programs. **Available through:** HRIN Corporation, 7200 Wisconsin Ave., Ste. 601, Bethesda, MD, 20814, (301)961-6760, toll-free 800-638-8094.

★4484★
Federal Information Exchange, Inc.
555 Quince Orchard Rd., Ste. 36   Ph: (301)975-0103
Gaithersburg, MD 20878   Fax: (301)975-0109
URL: http://www.fie.com/   **Gopher:** gopher.fie.com   **Telnet:** fedix.fie.com **Modem:** (301)258-0953 **Description:** If you need to

locate funding for research and education or contact the right people within the federal system, you can do that and more with this site. The site provides contact information, educational programs, and services, equipment grants, and procurement notices, as well as supplying information on students and faculty, educational programs, and research centers for minority colleges and universities. Main Files: FEDIX Opportunity Alert; Federal Opportunities; Minority Colleges; Federal Equipment; Electronic Research Administration; Research and Educational Resources; Scholarship Resource Network; About FIE; What's New; Comments. The FIE offers telecommunications and computer support services. Warning! This site contains lots of information to wade through. Today, FIE's full range of electronic interfacing and technical support services can give you the competitive edge you need to succeed. **Fees:** Free.

★4485★
Fourth World Documentation Project
Center for World Indigenous Studies
PO Box 2574   Ph: (360)786-9679
Olympia, WA 98507-2574   Fax: (360)956-1087
URL: http://www.halcyon.com/FWDP/fwdp.html **Description:** Organized by the Center for World Indigenous Studies in 1992, the mission of The Fourth World Documentation Project is to document and make available to tribal governments, researchers and organizations, important documents relating to the social, political, strategic, economic and human rights situations being faced by Fourth World nations and create an historical archive of the political struggles waged by Indigenous Nations to assert their rights as sovereign nations. Whew! The FWDP gathers documents from nations and organizations around the world and processes them into electronic text for distribution on the Internet, Peace Net and other computer networks. The Fourth World Documentation Project Archive contains more than 400 full text documents from Indigenous Nations in the Americas, Africa, Europe, Asia, Melanesia and the Pacific, forming a vital resource for tribal officials and researchers, activists or anyone interested in the state of the world's Indigenous Nations. Documents include: Speeches, articles and essays by leading Fourth World writers, political analysts and leaders. Compacts, treaties and agreements between Indigenous Nations and States. Compacts, treaties and agreements between Indigenous Nations and States. More than 70 United Nations documents covering the last 11 years of work by the Working Group on Indigenous Populations–including various drafts of the UN Draft Declaration on the Rights of Indigenous Peoples. Position Papers and resolutions by tribal governments and inter-tribal organizations, including: The World Council of Indigenous Peoples, The National Congress of American Indians, The Affiliated Tribes of Northwest Indians, The Conference of Tribal Governments and the Navajo Nation's Navajo-Hopi Land Commission; and Background on the Center for World Indigenous Studies including programs, publications, contributors and philosophy. Main Files: What is the FWDP; Helping the FWDP; Background on CWIS; Internship Opportunities; CWIS Notes; CWIS Publication Catalogue; Other Indigenous Resources; What's New in the FWDP; and Document Submissions. Very comprehensive coverage of these little-known areas. Countries that formerly did not get a whole lot of attention are documented at this site. Documents are sometimes technical/official-like and you'll really have to concentrate if you want to understand them. This site is dedicated to the nations of the Fourth World and our elders. Our goal is to present the online community with the greatest possible access to Fourth World documents and resources.

★4486★
Georgetown University - Catalogue of Projects in Electronic Text
Georgetown University
Reiss Science Bldg., Rm. 238
37th and O Sts., NW   Ph: (202)687-6096
Washington, DC 20057   Fax: (202)687-6003
Paul Mangiafico, Humanities Computing Consultant
Gopher: Georgetown University - Academic Computer Center Gopher gopher.georgetown.edu **Telnet:** guvax3.georgetown.edu Login: CPET **Description:** The Georgetown University Catalogue of Projects in Electronic Text is an online database of projects worldwide in various disciplines and languages. The database includes such topics as: art; music; linguistic studies in some 36 languages; literature studies in 29 different languages; other

disciplines such as archaeology, information services, rhetoric, and science; religious studies including Biblical Studies, Buddhist Studies, Christian Theology, Hindu Studies, and Islamic Studies, and Cultural Studies, including African, American, Classical, Indian, Medieval, Mesopotamian, and Native American Studies. Main Files: Information on the CFET Database; How to Access; Information on the Digests; Digests by Discipline; Digests by Language. Remarks: The actual database is in telnet. The documentation is in gopher. Extensive listings. Searching this database requires much patience. The electronic text projects documented in the database are machine-readable files of primary materials from humanities disciplines. **Documentation:** A free user's guide is available. **Fees:** Free.

★4487★
Human Rights Country Reports
U.S. Department of Agriculture

URL: http://www.hri.org/docs/USSD-Rights **Description:** The Country Reports on Human Rights database covers internationally recognized individual, political, civil, and worker rights, as set forth in the Universal Declaration of Human Rights, and provides information on the status of internationally recognized human rights in some 193 countries. Each report includes information on the political climate, historical background, respect for human rights, use of excessive force, respect for political rights, government attitude, discrimination, workers' rights, women's rights, and the freedoms of speech, press, religion, peaceful assembly, and movement. Remarks: The initial information is gathered by the embassies through government officials, military sources, journalists, labor unions, jurists, academics, and human rights monitors. Very comprehensive information. Some type of search interface would make this site even better. The willingness of nations to begin to hold each other accountable for human rights abuses is a reflection of the work of individuals to hold their own governments accountable. **Update frequency:** Annual. **Fees:** Free.

★4488★
Human Rights Library
University of Minnesota
Minneapolis, MN 55455   Ph: (612)625-5000
URL: http://www.umn.edu/humanrts/ **Description:** A repository of full-text official documents, arranged according to issuing organization; plus educational materials, profiles of information sources; and bibliographies. Treaties and such are presented with their dates of passage and other pertinent details. Main Files: What's New; Search Our Documents; Treaties and Other Instruments; U.N. Documents; Regional Materials; U.S. Human Rights Documents; Bibliographies; Human Rights Education; Asylum and Refugee Materials; Links to Other Sites; Search Elsewhere on the Web; Tips on Using Our Documents; European Mirror; Africa Mirror; Send Us Your Comments; University of Minnesota Human Rights Center; Africa Human Rights Resource Center; University of Minnesota Law School; West Group; Ford Foundation, U.S. Institute of Peace; DIANA; Diana Vincent Daviss; Staff; Honors; Use; and University of Minnesota. **Update frequency:** As needed. **Fees:** Free.

★4489★
Human Rights Quarterly
Project Muse
The John Hopkins University Press
2715 North Charles St.   Ph: (410)516-6900
Baltimore, MD 21218-4319   Fax: (410)516-6998
URL: http://muse.jhu.edu/journals/humanrightsquarterly/ **Description:** This publication draws on experts from around the world to report on information and developments within the United Nations and regional human rights organizations (governmental and non-governmental). It includes current work in human rights research and policy analysis, a review of books, philosophical essays, and other explorations of the Universal Declaration of Human Rights. Through these efforts, the journal seeks to define national and international human rights policies. The site also contains links to other Johns Hopkins University publications. Main Files: Project Muse; Subscribing; Volumes; Copyright Info; Editorial Info; Current Pricing; Indexing/Abstracting; Advertising Info; Booksellers Terms; Submission Guideline; Urban Morgan Institute for Human Rights; Journals.

★4490★
The Human Rights Web Home Page
Human Rights Web

Ph: (408)736-2237

URL: http://www.hrweb.org/ **Description:** The Human Rights Web Page provides information about human rights both as a concept and as a political reality. These pages provide both information on human rights and various links to resources on the Internet regarding human rights. Main Files: Human Rights Emergencies; What are Human Rights?: An Introduction to Human Rights, A Short History of the Human Rights Movement, Biographies of Prisoners of Conscience; Human Rights Legal and Political Documents; What can I do to Promote Human Rights?; Human Rights Resources; and Human Rights Web Administrative Page. **Update frequency:** As needed. **Fees:** Free.

★4491★
Illinois Human Rights Commission Decisions
Chicago-Kent College of Law
565 W. Adams
Chicago, IL 60661

URL: http://www.kentlaw.edu/hrc/ **Description:** The Illinois Human Rights Commission Decisions contains precedential orders and decisions of the Illinois Human Rights Commission. Currently, the library is limited to every precedential decision issued from April 1991 to date, except for six that are not available in electronic form. The administrative law judge's recommended order & decision are not included from 1991 to 1993. Main Files: Welcome to the Illinois HRC Decisions Repository; Searching; HRC decisions–In browsable ASCII Text; HRC decisions–In binary WordPerfect v5.1; Emergency amendments (eff 1-1-96) to procedural rules–in ASCII text; and Emergency amendments (eff 1-1-96) to procedural rules–in WordPerfect 5.1 format. A great resource that will expand the availability of these materials. They need to (and promise to) expand. Our goal is to provide the legal community with ready access to these decisions and offer a convenient and reliable method to research them. **Update frequency:** Monthly. **Fees:** Free.

★4492★
Index of Native American Resources on the Internet
URL: http://hanksville.phast.umass.edu/misc/NAresources.html **E-mail:** kstrom@hanksville.phast.umass.edu **Description:** Site designed to provide information resources to Native Americans. Contains links to sites dealing with such topics as Native American culture, history, education, lanuages, health, genealogy, and art.

★4493★
International Human Rights Database
University of Cincinnati College of Law
Center for Electronic Text in the Law
Cincinnati, OH

URL: http://www.law.uc.edu/Diana/ **Description:** DIANA: International Human Rights Database promotes the creation, preservation, organization, and dissemination of primary and secondary electronic materials critical to human rights research and advocacy. DIANA creates an electronic library of human rights material, from treaties, secondary sources, court decisions, legal briefs, and current information from international non-governmental human rights organizations. Main Files: About DIANA; Browse DIANA; Search DIANA; Bibliography; Other DIANA sites; Help. **Fees:** Free.

★4494★
Learning Aids for North American Indian Languages
University of California, Davis
Davis, CA 95616
Victor Golla

Ph: (916)752-3237
Fax: (916)752-7097

URL: http://cougar.ucdavis.edu/nas/SSILA/names.html **Description:** These pages serve as a directory for locating material valuable in the study of native north American languages. Most languages are covered, including hybrid languages like the Chinook Jargon. Although most of the materials listed are not available on the web, complete contact information is given. Data Providers: Native American Studies Dept. of the University of California at Davis. Main Files: Learning Materials; Bookstore. A useful bibliographic source. Most materials not available online.

Dictionaries, Descriptive Grammars, Pedagogic Materials, Collections of Bilingual Narratives, Tapes, etc. **Fees:** Free.

★4495★
The Legal Information Institute
Cornell University - Law School
The Legal Information Institute
Myron Taylor Hall
Ithaca, NY 14853

URL: http://www.law.cornell.edu **Description:** The Legal Information Institute database offers hypertext searching to recent Supreme Court decisions (which are distributed on the day of decision under project Hermes) and the LII's e-mail address directory of faculty and staff at U.S. law schools. It is also host to the Nasdaq Financial Executive Journal. In addition, many hypertext documents in the fields of law and legal education are available, including a Gallery of the Justices and their work, the Civil Rights Code of the United States and the Uniform Commercial Code. A tour of the site for new users is available, as well as a shortcut list of heavily used sources for experienced users. Main Files: LII's hypertext front-end to recent Supreme Court decisions; historic decisions; recent opinions of the New York Court of Appeals; liibulletin-ny; the full U.S. Code; E-mail address directory of faculty and staff at U.S. law schools; Cornell Law Review; information about Cello; hypertext law materials on disk; Cornell Law School; Cornell Law Library; and Items of Special Current Interest. The site provides a tour for new visitors and a shortcut to heavily used resources for experienced users. The paragraph listing of resources is more trouble to navigate than a bulleted list would be. The Fair Housing Act (FHA or Act) prohibits discrimination in housing against, inter alios, persons with handicaps. Section 3607(b)(1) of the Act entirely exempts from the FHA's compass-any reasonable local, State, or Federal restrictions regarding the maximum number of occupants permitted to occupy a dwelling.42 U. S. C. 3607(b)(1). **Update frequency:** Regularly. **Fees:** Free.

★4496★
Minority Business Entrepreneur
MBE magazine
3528 Torrance Blvd., Ste. 101
Torrance, CA 90503

Fax: (310)792-8263

URL: http://www.mbemag.com/ **Description:** This is the flagship site of a small but well-positioned Southwest publisher with a focus on start-up businesses and new opportunities for those outside the pinstriped mainstream. Main Files: Women's Business Exclusive; Table of Contents; Publisher's Page; Current Events; Mission Statement; Back Issues; Advertising Benefits; Media kit order form; Business Opportunities; How to Subscribe; MBE Business Resources Directory; Calendar of Events; Send Letters to the Editor; Send Comments on this Website; Create Your Own Web Site; Search Our Web Site; Web Weaving By Infostreet, Inc. There's a good range of resources available here. Magazine covers are reproduced but the subjects remain unidentified. MBE is a bimonthly publication for and about minority and women business owners.

★4497★
Minority Business and Professional Directory
CommerceNet, Inc.
4005 Miranda Avenue, Ste. 175
Palo Alto, CA 94304

Ph: (415)858-1930
Fax: (415)858-1936

URL: http://www.minbizdir.com/ **Description:** The Minority Business and Professional Directory (MBPD) is a directory/yellow pages of the minority/woman-owned business community. The directory may be browsed by business name, or searched by keyword. Listings provide the name, address (including city, state and zip), phone and fax numbers, and the type and nature of the business. Access to information on minority businesses often difficult to locate. This site provides that needed information. The site is strictly a directory, no images or informative documents, other than addresses. The Minority Business and Professional Directory (MBPD) is a magazine style directory/yellow pages of the minority/woman-owned business community. **Update frequency:** As needed. **Fees:** Free.

★4498★
The Minority Health Network
University of Pittsburgh
Pittsburgh, PA
Emma Barinas-Mitchell

URL: http://www.pitt.edu/ejb4/min/ **Description:** The Minority Health Network provides information about health issues of minorities. It also provides links to other health related databases. Information is cited by disease and/or by minority group. There is a calendar of important events. From the "Publications" menu option, there is access to Electronic Journals, articles and documents. Main Files: What Is?: The Minority Health Network (MHNet); What Is?: The Global Health Network (GHNet); Minority Health Resources: By Minority Group; Disease Specific; By Subject; Upcoming Events; Publications; Other links of interest; Feedback: Your additions/comm ents to the MHNet. MHNet provides access to hard to locate information on American Indians/Native Alaskans, African Americans, Asian/Pacific Islander Americans, Hispanics, and people with disabilities. There's not a large quantity of information at this time, more is needed to make this a number one resource for health care professionals. The Minority Health Network (MHNet) is a world wide web based information source for individuals interested in the health of minority groups. The authors of this homepage understand that the term 'minority' typically is one used in the United States and lacking in many respects, but because of its widespread use and in order to facilitate identification of this web site, it will be preserved. Within the context of our homepage, 'minority' will be used to refer to all people of color and people who are underrepresented economically and socially. **Update frequency:** As needed. **Fees:** Free.

★4499★
Multilaterals Project
Cornell University - Law School
The Legal Information Institute
Ithaca, NY

URL: http://www.tufts.edu /fletcher/multilaterals.html **Gopher:** fatty.law.cornell.edu Choose: Foreign and International Law: Primary Documents and Commentary. **Description:** The Multilaterals Project database provides information on treaties agreed to by more than two nations or parties. The database is subdivided into sections, including treaties for air, sea, land, and various other matters. Main Files: Multilateral Conventions organized by subject; Search the text files of the Multilaterals Project; and About the Multilaterals Project. A massive and well-organized resource with the full text of dozens of important treaties. For this kind of site, audio and video should also be included. The provisions of this Convention shall in no way affect the right of Parties to adopt, in accordance with international law, domestic measures additional to those referred to in paragraphs 1 and 2 above, nor shall they affect additional domestic measures already taken by a Party, provided that these measures are not incompatible with their obligations under this Convention. **Update frequency:** As needed. **Fees:** Free.

★4500★
Native Americans Studies Collections
Stanford University Libraries

URL: http://www-library.stanford.edu/depts/ssrg/native/indian.html **Description:** Catalog to Native American resources, including archeology, art and music, biography and oral history, film and media, government documents, language and literature, and religion. All resources listed are available in the Stanford University Library General Reference Collection.

★4501★
1994-95 People of Color Environmental Groups Directory
Institute for Global Communications
18 DeBoom St.
San Francisco, CA 94107   Fax: (415)546-1976
Antonio Diaz, EcoNet Program Coordinator

URL: http://www.igc.apc.org/envjustice/ **Gopher:** gopher.igc.apc.org Choose: Publications and News Services on the IGC Networks Gopher. **Description:** The 1994-95 People of Color Environmental Groups Directory is the revised and expanded edition of the earlier directory, with information on people of color groups that are concerned with environmental issues. Coverage includes the United States, Canada, and Mexico, and entries include contact and general information for the groups. The purpose is to provide a networking tool for people of color to press their environmental concerns. Data Providers: Dr. Robert Bullard at the Environmental Justice Resource Center, Clark Atlanta University. Main Files: About the 1994-95 People of Color Environmental Groups Directory; People of Color Groups in the United States; People of Color Groups in Mexico; People of Color Groups in Canada; Legal Resource Groups; and Search the 94-95 Directory. A good tool for networking, organized and searchable. The web address just provides a link to the gopher. Also, could use links directly to the groups. This revised and expanded edition of the *People of Color Environmental Groups Directory* by Dr. Robert Bullard includes a resource guide, and group listings from Canada and Mexico. **Update frequency:** Annual. **Fees:** Free.

★4502★
On-Line for Peace and Justice
PeaceNet
942 Market St., Rm. 708
San Francisco, CA 94102   Ph: (415)495-0526

URL: http://www.igc.apc.org/peacenet/ **Description:** This site contains a sample of the information related to peace and justice that is available to PeaceNet subscribers. It provides action alerts; headlines concerning current issues; special interest features, and other information. Users may select from a topical list of issues to gain information about the topic. Main Files: Action Alerts (includes an Alerts Archive); Highlights; Headlines (includes a Headlines Archive); Features; and Select an Issue. **Fees:** Free.

★4503★
PeaceNet
Institute for Global Communications
Presidio Bldg. 1012, 1st Fl.
Torney Ave.
PO Box 29904   Ph: (415)561-6100
San Francisco, CA 94129-0904   Fax: (415)561-6101

URL: http://www.peacenet.apc.org/peacenet/ **Gopher:** gopher.igc.apc.org **Description:** PeaceNet is a computer network serving advocates for peace, social justice and human rights around the world. It promotes the prevention of warfare, elimination of militarism and poverty, protection of the environment, economic justice, participatory democracy, nonviolent conflict resolution, and sustainable development. It includes newsletters, events calenders, press releases, legislative alerts, and news services. There is also a database of directories and articles. Main Files: About PeaceNet; PeaceNet Info-Compass Headline News; New and Featured Items; Issue Pages; Directory of PeaceNet Member Organizations; and Search PeaceNet's Website. Lots of pertinent info and links to connect you to more. Seems as if it could include more, and there's a subscription required for that. PeaceNet is a repository for current information about issues ranging from disarmament, economic justice, immigrant rights, the prison system, indigenous peoples, poverty, children's rights and many others. **Update frequency:** As needed. **Fees:** Free. There are fees for subscribing to PeaceNet, details included on site.

★4504★
Pow Wow Pages and Native Events
GLRAIN Project
2901 Hubbard Dr.   Ph: (313)998-6103
Ann Arbor, MI 48105-2467   Fax: (313)998-6105
Mike Dashner

URL: http://glrain.cic.net/events.htm **Description:** The Pow Wow Pages and Native Events site is a section of the award-winning Great Lakes Regional American Indian Network. The site provides information about upcoming Native American events and pow wows throughout the United States and Canada. Some files in the Native Events section are regional. Within them, you can click by month to upcoming events, including pow wows, in your area. Listings in the Pow Wow Pages section are links to the web pages of major pow wows. Most of these web pages include colorful graphics and photographs, a schedule of events, admission fees and times, staff, performers, vendors, lodging information, and the address, phone number (and usually, e-mail address) of the host. And, at the end, each pow wow web page has a For More Information file. In that file are links to pages that tell the rules and etiquette for attending and participating in pow wows. Main Files: Great Lakes Tribal Economic Development Conference; Moccasin Telegraph; Tribal Voice Pow Wow List; Southwest Celebrations; Lenni Lenape Pow wow List; Native Events Calendar; Los Angeles area pow wows. **Update frequency:** Continuous **Fees:** Free.

Index

The alphabetical Master Name and Keyword Index provides access to all entries included in NAID, as well as former or alternate names which appear within its text. The index also provides access to entries via inversions on significant keywords appearing in an entry name. Index references are to book entry numbers rather than page numbers. Entry numbers appear in **boldface** type if the reference is to the unit for which information is provided in NAID and in lightface if the reference is to a program, former, or alternate name included within the text of the cited entry.

(7(J) Development Assistant Program); Management and Technical Assistance for Socially and Economically Disadvantaged Businesses • Business Administration; U.S. Small **4031**

8(A) Program Participants; Business Loans for • Business Administration; U.S. Small **4030**

Aaloa Lodge Museum • Bacone College **975**

The ABA Commission on Minorities and Judicial Administration Division **4452**

Abbe Museum **906**

The ABC-CLIO Companion to the Native American Rights Movement **1592**

Abegweit First Nation **3047**

Abenaki Indian Center **488**

Abenaki Tribe of New Hampshire **222**

Abenaki Tribe of Vermont **325**

Abenakis d'Odanak; Musee des • Societe historique d'Odanak **3231**

Abenakis Museum **3229**

ABF Summer Research Fellowships in Law and Social Science for Minority Undergraduate Students **4302**

Abitibiwinni First Nation **3081**

Abnaki: The Native People of Maine **1710**

Aboriginal Affairs; British Columbia Ministry of **3194**

Aboriginal Affairs; New Brunswick Department of Intergovernmental and **3197**

Aboriginal Affairs; Northwest Territories Ministry of Intergovernmental and **3199**

Aboriginal Affairs Office • Fisheries and Oceans Canada **3177**

Aboriginal Affairs Secretariat; Labrador and **3198**

Aboriginal Business Canada • Industry Canada **3190**

Aboriginal Directory; Arrowfax National **3286**

Aboriginal Healing and Wellness; Office of • Ontario Ministry of Community and Social Services **3202**

Aboriginal Language Services; Yukon Territory Office of **3191**

Aboriginal Management Board; Canada National **3176**

Aboriginal Multi-Media Society of Alberta **3309**

Aboriginal North America Resources; Circumpolar and **2520, 3349**

Aboriginal Research Club **366**

Aboriginal Rights: I Can Get It For You Wholesale **1711**

Aboriginal Women; *Concerned* **3321**

Abrazo Press; March/ **1540**

Absentee-Shawnee Tribe **287**

Abstracts in Anthropology **4422**

Academic Freedom; Committee on Professional Ethics and **3382**

Access **1593**

Access and Equity Division • Texas Higher Education Coordinating Board **4256**

Accokeek Foundation; National Colonial Farm of the **908**

Acho Dene Koe First Nation **2918**

ACLU Freedom Network **4472**

ACLU; Roger Baldwin Foundation of **3356**

Acoma Books **1471**

Acoma Pueblo **234, 944**
    Head Start Program **1106**

Acorns: Staple Food of California Indians **1712**

ACT - Lexington **3645**

Action for Rural Indians; Committee for **3381**

Actuarial Society Scholarships for Minority Students; Society of Actuaries/ Casualty **4347**

Ad Hoc Committee on the Human Rights and Genocide Treaties **3352**

Adams Lake Indian Band **2695**

Adams State College Museums **862**

ADHA Minority Scholarships Program **4303**

Administration for Children and Families • Tribal Work Grants (Grants for Indian Tribes that Received JOBS Funds) • U.S. Department of Health and Human Services **556, 2370**

Administration for Native Americans • U.S. Department of Health and Human Services • Administration for Children and Families **531**

Administrative Cost Grants for Indian Schools • U.S. Department of the Interior • Bureau of Indian Affairs **3972**

Adolescent Mothers Program **3707**

Adolph Van Pelt Special Fund for Indian Scholarships **1410**

Adopted Indians; Continental Confederation of **3387**

An Adoptee's Right to Know **4473**

Adult Education Association; National Indian **506**

Adult Education; Indian • U.S. Department of the Interior • Bureau of Indian Affairs **3985**

Adult Vocational Training; Hopi Tribe **1428**

Advanced Industrial Concepts (AIC) Materials Science Program **4304**

Affirmation Action Division • Connecticut Children and Families Department **4057**

Affirmation Action Office • Connecticut State Board of Education **4061**

Affirmative Action and Civil Rights Division; Equal Opportunity, • Human Services Department; Minnesota **4137**

Affirmative Action and Civil Rights Office • Wisconsin Health and Social Services Department **4276**

Affirmative Action Coordinating Center **3353**

Affirmative Action Department; Bridgeport **4056**

Affirmative Action Division
    Connecticut Environmental Protection Department **4058**
    Connecticut Social Services Department **4060**
    Indiana Personnel Department **4095**
    Oklahoma Health Department **4209**

Affirmative Action Division; Equal Employment Opportunity/ • New Jersey Personnel Department **4161**

Affirmative Action Office
    Civil Service Department; New York State **4175**
    Nevada Personnel Department **4155**
    New Jersey Community Affairs Department **4160**
    New York Secretary of State • State Department **4173**
    New York State Education Department **4176**
    New York State General Services Office **4178**
    Oklahoma Human Services Department **4211**
    Oregon Office of the Governor **4214**
    Pennsylvania Aging Department **4217**
    Pennsylvania Public Welfare Department **4221**

Affirmative Action Office; Equal Employment Opportunity and • Civil Service Department; Michigan **4127**

Affirmative Action Office; Massachusetts **4117**

Affirmative Action Program • New York State Agricultural and Markets Department **4174**

Affirmative Action Register **4423**

Affirmative Action Scholarship Program **4305**

Affirmative Action Unit • New York State Housing and Community Renewal Division **4179**

Affirmative Employment and Diversity Policy Division • U.S. National Aeronautics and Space Administration • Office of Equal Opportunity Programs **3926**

Affirmative Action Manual **4474**

AFL-CIO; Department of Civil Rights, **3393**

African-American and Native-American Family History; Kansas Institute for **462**

Agdaagux Tribe of King Cove **2237**

Aggrey Medal **4352**

Aging; National Indian Council on **413**

Agnes Etherington Art Centre • Queen's University at Kingston **3242**

Agriculture on Indian Lands • U.S. Department of the Interior • Bureau of Indian Affairs **3973**

Agriculture: The Winnebago; Minorities in **1935**

Agua Caliente Tribe **98**

Ah-Tah-Thi-Ki Museum of Seminole History and Culture **878**

Ahousaht First Nation **2666**

Ahtahkakoop First Nation **3154**

Ahtna **2355**

AICH Community Bulletin **1642**

Aid Available to American Indian Students; Sources of Financial **1627**

Aid to Tribal Governments • U.S. Department of the Interior • Bureau of Indian Affairs **3974**

AIDS and the Native American Family **4453**

AIDS Prevention Center; National Native American **443**

AIDS Prevention; National Native American **419, 2349, 2526**

AIDS Prevention Project (YAPP); Youth **3707**

AIGC Fellowships **1411, 2432**

Airport Minority Advisory Council **3659, 3808**

(AISES); American Indian Science and Engineering Society **385**

AISES A.T. Anderson Memorial Scholarship **1412, 2433**

AISES Education Newsletter **1643**

AISES Visions **1644**

AISESnet **2125**

AISESnet: American Indian Science and Engineering Society **2126**

Aishihik First Nations; Champagne and **3168**

Aitchelitz Indian Band **2810**

Ak Chin Indian Community **8**

Aka Press **2583**

Akew:kon **1362**

Akhiok; Native Village of **2147**

Akiachak Native Community **2148**

Akiak Native Community **2149**

Aklavik First Nation **2917**

Akta Lakota Museum **991**

Akutan; Native Village of **2150**

Akwesasne: Another Point of View **1713**

Akwesasne Library Cultural Center **599**

Akwesasne; Mohawks of **2941**

Akwesasne Museum **949**

Akwesasne Notes **1472, 1629, 3262, 3299**

Al Qoyawayma Award **1413**

Alabama Attorney General • Civil Rights Division **578**

Alabama Coalition for Equity **3515**

Alabama Coushatta Indians; Journey to the Sky: A History of the **1904**

Alabama-Coushatta Tribe of Texas **320**
     Indian Museum **1002**

Alabama-Quassarte Tribal Town **271**

Alakanuk; Village of **2151**

Alamo Navajo School **1225**

Alaska, Canada, United States; Native American Directory: **1617, 2456, 3293**

Alaska; Central Council of Tlingit and Haida Tribe of **2224**

Alaska Equal Employment Opportunity Division **4038**

Alaska Federation of Natives **2350**

Alaska Human Rights Commission **4039**

Alaska Indian Arts **2394**

Alaska Minority Business Development Center **4040**

Alaska National Interest Lands Conservation Act; Alaskan Indian Allotments and Subsistence Preference - • U.S. Department of the Interior • Bureau of Indian Affairs **2378**

Alaska Native Arts and Crafts—Source Directory; American Indian and **1594, 2450**

Alaska Native Culture and Arts Development; Institute of American Indian and **1029, 2144**

(Alaska Native Education); Alaska Native Home Based Education for Preschool Children • U.S. Department of Education • Office of Elementary and Secondary Education **2366**

(Alaska Native Education); Alaska Native Student Enrichment Program • U.S. Department of Education • Office of Elementary and Secondary Education **2367**

Alaska Native Educational Planning, Curriculum Development, Teacher Training, and Recruitment Program • U.S. Department of Education • Office of Elementary and Secondary Education, **2365**

Alaska Native Home Based Education for Preschool Children (Alaska Native Education) • U.S. Department of Education • Office of Elementary and Secondary Education **2366**

Alaska Native Language Center
     Research Library • University of Alaska, Fairbanks **2392**
     University of Alaska, Fairbanks **2419**

Alaska Native Mental Health Research; National Center for American Indian and **408**
     University of Colorado **1060, 2420**

Alaska Native Periodicals Project; American Indian and **3360**

Alaska Native Sisterhood **2356**

Alaska Native Sobriety Movement **2350**

Alaska Native Student Enrichment Program (Alaska Native Education) • U.S. Department of Education • Office of Elementary and Secondary Education **2367**

Alaska Native Tourism Council **2351**

Alaska Native Traders Directory; American Indian and **1595, 2451**

Alaska Natives; Education Assistance for American Indians and **1608, 2454**

Alaska Northwest Books **2445**

Alaska People Magazine **2460**

Alaska and Polar Regions Department • University of Alaska, Fairbanks **2393**

Alaska State Museum **2395**

Alaska Yukon Library **2386**

Alaskan Businesses; Smoke Signals: Directory of Native Indian/ **1626, 2459**

Alaskan Indian Allotments and Subsistence Preference - Alaska National Interest Lands Conservation Act • U.S. Department of the Interior • Bureau of Indian Affairs **2378**

The Alaskan Viewpoint **2461**

Alatna Village **2152**

Albany Equal Employment Opportunity and Fair Housing Office **592**

Alberta Family and Social Services Office • Aboriginal Affairs Office **3192**

Alberta Human Rights and Citizenship Commission **4277**

Alberta Human Rights Secretariat **4278**

Alberta Multiculturalism Commission **4279**

Albuquerque Family and Community Services Office • Human Rights Section **590**

Albuquerque Minority Business Development Center **4164**

Alcoholic Treatment Alternative; Minorities **3545**

Alcoholics; National Association for Native American Children of **407**

Alec; Kevin **1908**

Aleknagik; Native Village of **2153**

Aleut Community of St. Paul Island and St. George **2324**

Alexander First Nation **2646**

Alexandria Band **2802**

Alexandria Human Rights Office **4262**

Alexis Creek Indian Band **2701**

Alexis First Nation **2632**

Algaaciq; Native Village of **2321**

Algonquian Confederacy Quinnipiac Tribal Council **449**

Algonquin Birchbark Canoe; Building an **3317**

Algonquine Anishnabeg; Conseil de la Nation **3068**

Algonquins of Golden Lake **2961**

Alice Elliott **4454**

Aliuk: Eskimo in Two Worlds; Matthew **2503**

Alkali Lake First Nation (Esketemc First Nation) **2839**

All Indian Pueblo Council **367**

All Tribes Cultural Arts Program **3542**

Allakaket Village **2154**

Allan and Joyce Niederman Award **1468**

Allen County Historical Society • Elizabeth M. MacDonell Memorial Library **600**

Allen Fellowships; Frances C. **1426**, 1460
Allergy; Underrepresented Minority Investigators Award in Asthma and **4349**
Alliance to End Repression 3449
Alliance of Minority Women for Business and Political Development **3354**
Aloha International **2523**
Aloha News **2603**
Aloha Publishing **2584**
Alpha Publications Inc. **4354**
Alternative Education; National Center for American Indian 384
Alturas Rancheria **26**
Amah Mutsum Band of Mission Indians **137**
Amarillo Public Library • Local History Collection **601**
Ambler; Native Village of **2155**
American Antiquity **4424**
The American as Artist: A Portrait of Bob Penn **1714**
American Association of Minority Enterprise Small Business Investment Companies 406
American Civil Liberties Union **3355, 4355**
American Civil Liberties Union, Alabama Affiliate **3514**
American Civil Liberties Union, Alaska Affiliate **3516**
American Civil Liberties Union of Arizona **3518**
American Civil Liberties Union of Arkansas **3524**
American Civil Liberties Union, Central Florida Chapter **3605**
American Civil Liberties Union, Colorado Affiliate **3565**
American Civil Liberties Union, Connecticut **3574**
American Civil Liberties Union of Delaware **3579**
American Civil Liberties Union, East Missouri **3695**
American Civil Liberties Union, Florida Affiliate **3592**
American Civil Liberties Union Foundation **3356, 3566**
American Civil Liberties Union Freedom Network **4475**
American Civil Liberties Union, Georgia Affiliate **3607**
American Civil Liberties Union, Greater Tampa Chapter **3599**
American Civil Liberties Union of Hawaii **3615**
American Civil Liberties Union, Hawkeye Chapter **3641**
American Civil Liberties Union of Idaho **3616**
American Civil Liberties Union of Illinois **3622**
American Civil Liberties Union of Indiana **3632, 3633**
American Civil Liberties Union, Iowa Chapter **3638**
American Civil Liberties Union, Kansas and Western Missouri Chapter **3691**
American Civil Liberties Union of Kentucky **3647**
American Civil Liberties Union Louisiana Affiliate **3651**
American Civil Liberties Union, Maine Affiliate **3654**
American Civil Liberties Union, Marin Chapter **3543**
American Civil Liberties Union of Maryland **3656**
American Civil Liberties Union, Massachussetts **3661**
American Civil Liberties Union, Michigan Chapter **3667**
American Civil Liberties Union, Mid-Peninsula Chapter **3562**
American Civil Liberties Union, Mid-Missouri Chapter **3690**
American Civil Liberties Union, Minnesota Chapter **3681**
American Civil Liberties Union, Mississippi Affiliate **3688**
American Civil Liberties Union, Montana Chapter **3697**
American Civil Liberties Union, Monterey County Chapter **3548**
American Civil Liberties Union, Mountain States **3567**
American Civil Liberties Union, Mountain States Chapter **3568**
American Civil Liberties Union of the National Capital Area **3581**
American Civil Liberties Union, Nebraska Chapter **3699**
American Civil Liberties Union of Nevada **3701**
American Civil Liberties Union, New Hampshire **3702**
American Civil Liberties Union, New Jersey **3705, 3706**
American Civil Liberties Union of New Mexico **3709**
American Civil Liberties Union, New York **3724**
American Civil Liberties Union of North Carolina **3745**
American Civil Liberties Union of Northern California **3554**
American Civil Liberties Union, Northwest Louisiana Chapter **3653**
American Civil Liberties Union of Ohio **3754**
American Civil Liberties Union of Ohio, Cincinnati Chapter **3751**
American Civil Liberties Union of Oklahoma **3765**
American Civil Liberties Union of Oregon **3769**
American Civil Liberties Union of Oregon, Southern District **3768**
American Civil Liberties Union, Palm Beach Chapter **3586**
American Civil Liberties Union, Pennsylvania Affiliate **3776**
American Civil Liberties Union, Rhode Island Affiliate **3777**
American Civil Liberties Union of San Diego and Imperial Counties **3552**

American Civil Liberties Union, Santa Clara Valley Chapter **3540**
American Civil Liberties Union, Singles Chapter **3561**
American Civil Liberties Union, South Carolina **3780**
American Civil Liberties Union of Southern California **3532**
American Civil Liberties Union, Southern Regional Office **3608**
American Civil Liberties Union, Tempe-Mesa Chapter **3521**
American Civil Liberties Union, Tennessee **3787**
American Civil Liberties Union, Texas Affiliate **3790**
American Civil Liberties Union, Utah Affiliate **3805**
American Civil Liberties Union, Vermont Affiliate **3807**
American Civil Liberties Union, Virginia **3811**
American Civil Liberties Union, Washington **3816**
American Civil Liberties Union, West Virginia Affiliate **3821**
American Civil Liberties Union of Wisconsin **3824**
American Civil Liberties Union, Wyoming **3830**
American Committee to Advance the Study of Petroglyphs and Pictographs **1473**
American Committee for Human Rights 3495
American Council for the Advancement of Human Rights **3357**
American Economic Association/Federal Reserve System Minority Graduate Fellowships in Economics **4306**
American Eskimo Association, Oklahoma Chapter **2361**
American Folklife Center • U.S. Library of Congress **784**
American History for Children: Native American Life **1715**
American Horse School **1279**
The American Indian **1716**
American Indian: A Brief History **1717**
American Indian After the White Man Came **1718**
American Indian and Alaska Native Arts and Crafts—Source Directory **1594, 2450**
American Indian and Alaska Native Periodicals Project **3360**
American Indian and Alaska Native Traders Directory **1595, 2451**
American Indian Archaeological Institute 401, **872**
American Indian Archival Material: A Guide to Holdings in the Southeast **1596**
American Indian Art Magazine **1630**
American Indian Artists: Part I **1719**
American Indian Artists: Part II **1720**
American Indian Arts Council **368**
American Indian Basketry Magazine **1631**
American Indian Basketry and Other Native Arts **1474**
American Indian Before the White Man **1721**
American Indian Bible College • Dorothy Cummings Memorial Library **602**
American Indian Center of Central Florida **452**
American Indian Center of Santa Clara Valley, Inc. • Indian Center Library **603**
American Indian Collection: Geronimo and the Apache Resistance **1722**
American Indian Collection: Myths and Moundbuilders **1723**
American Indian Collection: Seasons of the Navajo **1724**
American Indian Collection: Spirit of Crazy Horse **1725**
American Indian Collection: Winds of Change—A Matter of Promises **1726**
American Indian College Fund **369**
American Indian Community House **492**
The American Indian Community House Community Bulletin **1645**
American Indian Community Leadership Council **475**
American Indian Council of Central California **441**
American Indian Council of Mariposa County **442**
American Indian Cultural Society of North Florida **495**
American Indian Culture Research Center **370, 1018**
  Museum **992**
American Indian Defense News **1646**
American Indian Development Association **371**
American Indian Education Center **498**
American Indian Education Policy Center • Pennsylvania State University **1044**
American Indian Fund 388
American Indian Graduate Center **372**
American Indian Health Care Association **373**
American Indian Heritage Foundation **374**
American Indian Higher Education Consortium **375**
American Indian Historical Society **376**
American Indian Index **1597, 2452**
American Indian Influence on the United States **1727**
American Indian Institute **377**

American Indian Language Center **503**
American Indian Law Center **1019, 3358**
American Indian Law Center Newsletter **1647**
American Indian Law Students Association 3477
American Indian Liberation Crusade **378**
American Indian Libraries Newsletter **1648**
American Indian Library Association **3359**
American Indian Library Collection • Oakland Public
  Library **718**
American Indian Lore Association **379**
American Indian Lore Association Hall of Fame **1456**
American Indian Movement **380**
American Indian Museum Studies Program • Smithsonian
  Institution; U.S. • Center for Museum Studies **549**
American Indian Quarterly **1632**
American Indian Refugees **381**
American Indian Registry for the Performing Arts **382**
American Indian Rehabilitation **1649**
American Indian Rehabilitation Research and Training Center •
  Northern Arizona University **1042**
American Indian Research and Development **1020**
American Indian Research Project • South Dakota Oral History
  Center • Library **604**
American Indian Resource Center • County of Los Angeles
  Public Library **632**
American Indian Resource and Education Coalition, Austin
  Chapter **520**
American Indian Resources **2127**
American Indian Ritual Object Repatriation Foundation **383**
American Indian Scholarships 372
American Indian Science and Education Center **384**
American Indian Science and Engineering Society 2125
American Indian Science and Engineering Society
  (AISES) **385**
The American Indian Series **1728**
The American Indian Speaks **1729**
American Indian Studies Center
    Library • University of California, Los Angeles **789**
    University of California, Los Angeles **1058, 1583**
American Indian Summer Seminar **386**
American Indian Sweat Lodge Ceremony **1730**
The American Indian Today **1731**
American Indian Trade and Information Center; North 3469
American Indians of All Nations **493**
American Indians Before European Settlement **1732**
The American Indian's Sacred Ground **1733**
American Indians in Texas **525**
American Indians: Yesterday and Today **1734**
American National Heritage Association **4356**
American Native Press Research Association **3360**
American Philosophical Society • Library **605**
American West Center • University of Utah **1067**
Americans for Indian Opportunity **3361**
Americans for Restitution and Righting of Old Wrongs 387
America's Mysterious Places **1735**
Amerind Foundation **1475**
    Museum **832**
Amiotte **1736**
Amnesty and Human Rights for Political Prisoners; Campaign
  for 3369, **3369**
Amnesty International, Austin Chapter **3791**
Amnesty International, Boise Chapter **3617**
Amnesty International Group 88 **3522**
Amnesty International, North Dakota Chapter **3749**
Amnesty International On-line **4476**
Amnesty International, Rochester Chapter **3683**
Amnesty International USA **3362, 4357**
Amnesty International U.S.A., Group 78 **3668**
Amnesty International U.S.A., Mid-Atlantic Region **3582**
Amnesty International U.S.A., Midwest Regional Office **3623**
Amnesty International, U.S.A., Northeast **3665**
Amnesty International, U.S.A., Northern California **3555**
Amnesty International, U.S.A., Southern California **3527**
Anaham Indian Band **2671**
Anaheim Minority Business Development Center **4044**
Anaktuvuk Pass; Village of **2156**
Anasazi; Daughters of the **1795**
Anasazi Indian Village State Park **1004**
Anasazi; The Mystery of the **1947**
Anchorage Equal Opportunity Office **2385**
Anchorage Museum of History and Art **2396**

Ancient America: Indians of the Southwest **1737**
Ancient America: More Than Bows and Arrows **1738**
Ancient America: Nomadic Indians of the West **1739**
Ancient City Press **1476**
An Ancient Gift **1740**
Ancient Indian Cultures of Northern Arizona **1741**
Ancient Ones; Hisatsinom: The **1853**
Ancient Spirit, Living Word: The Oral Tradition **1742**
And Justice for Some **4455**
....And The Word Was God **3313**
Anderson Lake First Nation **2713**
Anderson Memorial Scholarship; AISES A.T. **1412, 2433**
Aneth Community School **1301**
Angel Mounds State Historic Site **896, 1477**
    Library **606**
Angoon Community Association **2159**
Angoon One Hundred Years Later **2472**
Angotee **2473**
Ani-Stohini/Unami Nation **326**
Aniak; Village of **2161**
Anishnabeg; Conseil de la Nation Algonquine **3068**
Annie and the Old One **1743**
Another Wind Is Moving **1744**
Antelope Valley Paiute Tribe **48**
Anthropological Archives; National • Smithsonian Institution;
  U.S. **785**
Anthropology; Abstracts in **4422**
Anthropology Film Center Foundation **4358**
Anti-Discrimination Division • Utah Industrial Commission **4259**
Antiquities Research Association; New England **1040**
Antiquity; American **4424**
Anti-Repression Resource Team **3363**
Anvik Village **2162**
APA Planning Fellowships **1414**
Apache Business Committee **262**
Apache; Camp Verde Yavapai- **2**
Apache Community Council (Fort McDowell); Mohave- **5**
Apache Community Council; Yavapai- **3**
Apache Community of Ebarb; Choctaw- **466**
The Apache Indian **1745**
Apache; Letter from an **1917**
Apache Mountain Spirit **1746**
*Apache Resistance; American Indian Collection: Geronimo and
  the* **1722**
Apache Survival Coalition **437**
Apache Tribal Council; Jicarilla • Head Start Program **1104**
Apache Tribal Council; Mescalero • Head Start Program **1105**
Apache Tribe; Fort Sill **265**
Apache Tribe; Jicarilla **227**
Apache Tribe; Mescalero **232**
Apache Tribe; San Carlos **13**
    Head Start Program **1073**
Apache Tribe; White Mountain **20**
    Head Start Program **1075**
Apache Visitor Activity Center; Yavapai- **856**
Apartheid; Citizens to Abolish Domestic **3773**
Apartheid and Racism; District of Columbia Student Coalition
  Against **3584**
Aplan Award **1468**
Appalachia Educational Laboratory • Schools; ERIC
  Clearinghouse on Rural Education and Small **641**
Appalachian Region; Directory of Native Education Resources
  in the **1601**
Aquarius House **1478**
Arapaho Higher Education Assistance Program Grant;
  Cheyenne- **1421**
Arapaho Tribe; Cheyenne- **269**
    Head Start Program **1122**
Arapahoe Business Council **364**
Arapahoe Tribes; Shoshone and • Head Start Program **1159**
Archaeological Area; Pinson Mounds State **1000**
Archaeological Center; Crow Canyon **1024**
Archaeological Center; White Mountain **854**
Archaeological Conservancy **3364**
Archaeological and Historic Site; San Luis **880**
Archaeological Institute; American Indian 401, **872**
Archaeological Research Center and Library; San Juan
  County **1045**
Archaeological Societies, Inc.; Central States **1493**
Archaeological Society; Shepaug Valley 401

Archaeological Studies; Institute for • University at Albany, State University of New York 1054
Archaeology; Cobb Institute of • Mississippi State University 1033
Archaeology and Lawson Prehistoric Village; Museum of Indian 3223
Archaeology; London Museum of 3239
Archaeology; Museum of Indian 3239
Archaeology Unit • Memorial University of Newfoundland 3241
Archeology Study Unit; Mesoamerican 3440
Archival Material: A Guide to Holdings in the Southeast; American Indian 1596
Archives; Campbell River Museum and 3211
Archives of Social History 4359
Arctic Slope; Inupiat Community of 2167
Arctic Studies; Institute of • Dartmouth College 2414, 2611
Arctic Village 2163
Ardell Bjugstad Memorial Scholarships 1415
Are People All the Same? 4456
Arizona American Eskimo Association 2360
Arizona; Ancient Indian Cultures of Northern 1741
Arizona Attorney General • Civil Rights Section 579
Arizona Commission of Indian Affairs—Tribal Directory 1598
Arizona Historical Society • Library/Archives 607
Arizona Human Rights Funds 3519
Arizona State Museum • University of Arizona 1055
Arizona State Parks
        Homolovi Ruins State Park 833
        Homolovi Ruins State Park Library 608
Arizona State University
        Center for Indian Education 1021
        School of Justice Studies 1022
Arizonans for Fairness Coalition 3520
Arkansas Industrial Development Commission • Minority Business Division 4042
Arkansas State University Museum • Library/Archives 609
Aroland First Nation 2990
Aroostook Band of Micmacs 163
Arragon Library; Rex • Art Museum; Portland 732
ARROW 387
Arrowfax National Aboriginal Directory 3286
Arrowstar Publishing 1479
Art of the American Indian Frontier 2128
Art; Anchorage Museum of History and 2396
The Art of Being Indian: Filmed Aspects of the Culture of the Sioux 1747
Art Centre; Agnes Etherington • Queen's University at Kingston 3242
Art Collection; Great Plains • University of Nebraska—Lincoln 796
Art; Eiteljorg Museum of American Indian and Western 897
Art Gallery; Medicine Hat Museum and 3209
Art Gallery; R. V. Greeves 1564
Art Gallery; Thunder Bay 3227, 3281
Art Gallery; Winnipeg 3285
Art and Legend; Lakota Quillwork: 1910
Art—Lost and Found; Native American 1951
Art Magazine; American Indian 1630
Art Museum; J.B. Speed • Library 664
Art Museum; Jesse Peter Native American • Santa Rosa Junior College 860
Art Museum; Joslyn • Art Reference Library 667
Art Museum; Portland • Rex Arragon Library 732
Art; National Council for Culture and 3462
The Art of Navajo Weaving 1748
Art Reference Library • Brooklyn Museum 619
Art Show; Red Cloud Indian 1468
Art; Thomas Gilcrease Institute of American History and • Library 757
Artifact Magazine; Indian 1633
Artifacts Museum; Walker Wildlife and Indian 920
Artifacts Society; Saanichton Historical 3215
Artist: A Portrait of Bob Penn; The American as 1714
Artist; Herman Red Elk: A Sioux Indian 1852
Artist Series; Native American Indian 1956
Artist Sponsorships; NNAC Gifted/Talented 1444
Artist of the Year Award 1457
Artists: Part I; American Indian 1719
Artists: Part II; American Indian 1720
Artists for Racial Unity 3624

Artists Resource Collection; Native American 653
Artists of the Southwest; Indian 1879
Artists' Symposium; National Native 3335
Artlist 1480
Arts; Alaska Indian 2394
Arts; American Indian Basketry and Other Native 1474
Arts; Association for Native Development in the Performing and Visual 3171
Arts Center; Colorado Springs Fine 863
        Reference Library and Taylor Museum Library 630
Arts Center; Tekakwitha Fine 998
Arts Council; American Indian 368
Arts Council; Crooked Tree 911
Arts Council; Zuni Cultural 491
Arts and Crafts Association; Indian 3409
Arts and Crafts Board; Indian 874
        U.S. Department of the Interior 762
Arts and Crafts Board; U.S. Indian 546
Arts and Crafts; Hopi Indian 1861
Arts and Crafts—Source Directory; American Indian and Alaska Native 1594, 2450
Arts and Crafts; Southwest Indian 2068
Arts and Culture; Museum of Indian 941
        Laboratory of Anthropology 942
Arts Development; Institute of American Indian and Alaska Native Culture and 1029, 2144
Arts; Directory of People of Color in the Visual 4404
Arts; Film/ Video 3396
Arts; Flint Institute of • Library 645
Arts; Institute of Alaska Native 2353
Arts; Institute of American Indian 400
        Library 661
        Museum 940
Arts; Institute for the Study of Traditional American Indian 403, 1031, 1533
Arts Organizations of Color; National Database of 4416
Arts Organizations; Directory of Minority 4402
Arts Organizations; National Directory of Multi-Cultural 4416
Arts at the Phoenix Heard Museum; Indian 1880
Arts Program; All Tribes Cultural 3542
Arts Program; Native Hawaiian Culture and 3484
Arts; Pueblo 2032
Arts Research Center; Indian 1027
As Long As the Grass Is Green 1749
Ashcroft Indian Band 2673
Asian, Black, Hispanic, and Native American Students; Minority Student Enrollments in Higher Education: A Guide to Institutions with. . . 4413
AskERIC Home Page 4477
ASM Predoctoral Minority Fellowships 4307
Assistance for Indian Children with Severe Disabilities • U.S. Department of the Interior • Bureau of Indian Affairs 3975
Assistance to Native Americans; Federal Programs of 1609
Assistance Project; Minority Contractors 3437
Assistance to Tribally Controlled Community Colleges and Universities • U.S. Department of the Interior • Bureau of Indian Affairs 3976
Association on American Indian Affairs 388, 1481
Association on American Indian Affairs Displaced Homemaker Scholarships 1416
Association of American Indian Physicians 3365
Association of Community Tribal Schools 3366
Association of Contract Tribal Schools 3366
Association of Interior Eskimos 2358
Association of Minority Business Enterprises of New York 3720
Association of Minority Contractors of Houston 3802
Association for Native Development in the Performing and Visual Arts 3171
Association of Village Council Presidents • Head Start Program 2421
Asthma and Allergy; Underrepresented Minority Investigators Award in 4349
A.T. Anderson Memorial Scholarship; AISES 1412, 2433
At the Autumn River Camp: Parts 1 and 2 2474
At the Caribou Crossing Place: Parts 1 and 2 2475
At the Spring Sea Ice Camp: Parts 1-3 2476
AT & T Bell Laboratories Cooperative Research Fellowships for Minorities 4308
AT & T Bell Laboratories Summer Research Program for Minorities and Women 4309

At the Winter Sea Ice Camp: Parts 1-4 **2477**
Athabasca Chipewyan First Nation **2625**
Atherton Department of Special Collections; Holt- • University of the Pacific **803**
Athletic Association; National Indian **412, 510**
(Atikameg); Whitefish Lake First Nation **2614**
Atikamekw; Conseil de la Nation **3061**
Atka; Native Village of **2164**
Atkins Museum of Art; Nelson- • Slide Library **711**
Atlanta Minority Business Development Center **4075**
The Atlanta Tribune **4425**
Atlanta Urban League **3609**
Atmautluak; Village of **2165**
Atqasuk Village **2166**
Atsa Biyaazh Community School **1226**
Attawapiskat First Nation **2923**
Attikamek-Montagnais; Conseil **3066**
Attorney Fees - Indian Rights • U.S. Department of the Interior • Bureau of Indian Affairs **3977**
Attorney General; Alabama • Civil Rights Division **578**
Attorney General; Arizona • Civil Rights Section **579**
Attorney General (Law Department); Georgia • Civil Rights Litigation Section **4079**
Attorney General; Michigan • Civil Rights Division **4124**
Attorney General and Minister Responsible for Multiculturalism, Human Rights and Immigration; British Columbia **3193**
Attorney General and Minister Responsible for Native Affairs; Ontario **3200**
Attorney General; Minnesota • Human Rights Division **4134**
Attorney General; New Jersey • Law and Public Safety Department • Civil Rights Division **4158**
Attorney General; Ohio • Civil Rights Section **4201**
Attorney General's Office; Tennessee • Civil Rights and Claims Division **4237**
Augusta **3314**
Augusta Equal Employment Office **4076**
Augusta Minority Business Development Center **3610, 4077**
Augustana College • Center for Western Studies **610, 1482**
Augustine Band of Mission Indians **30**
Aura E. Severinghaus Award **4310**
Aurora University • Schingoethe Center for Native American Cultures **891**
Austin Area Urban League **3792**
Austin Minority Business Development Center **4242**
Austin Minority/Women Alliance **3793**
Automobile Dealers; National Association of Minority **3453**
Autumn River Camp: Parts 1 and 2; At the **2474**
Avanyu Publishing, Inc. **1483**
Aztec Dormitory **1227**
Aztec Museum **931**
Aztec Ruins National Monument **932**
Azurite Cherokee Cultural Center **501**
B. Robinson Department of Special Collections **611**
Baca Community School **1228**
Bacavi Community School; Hotevilla **1174**
Bacone College
    Aaloa Lodge Museum **975**
    Library • Special Collections **612**
    Native American Studies Program **1341**
Bad River Tribal Council • Head Start Program **1153**
Bad River Tribe **361**
Badlands; Museum of the **966**
Badlands Natural History Association **1484**
Bailey House Museum **2555**
Bainbridge Bunting Memorial Slide Library • University of New Mexico **797**
Baja California; Kiliwa: Hunters and Gatherers of **1909**
Bakersfield Minority Business Development Center **4045**
Bakken Memorial Library; Lavola • Douglas County Museum **637**
Baldwin Foundation of ACLU; Roger **3356**
The Ballad of Crowfoot **3315**
Ballantyne Cree Nation; Peter **3145**
Ballena Press **1485**
Baltimore Minority Business Development Center **4112**
Baltimore Urban League **3657**
Bamboo Ridge Press **2585**
Bande indienne de Gaspe **3055**
Bandelier National Monument **933**
Bannock Tribes; Shoshone- • Head Start Program **1082**
Bar Association; Texas Indian **522**

Baraga Association; Bishop • Archives **613**
Baranov Museum **2397**
Barnhart Press **2586**
Barona Rancheria **81**
Barren Lands First Nation **2852**
Barriere Lake First Nation **3082**
Barrow; Native Village of **2168**
Basketry Magazine; American Indian **1631**
Basketry and Other Native Arts; American Indian **1474**
Basketry of the Pomo: Forms and Ornamentation **1750**
Basketry of the Pomo: Introductory Film **1751**
Basketry of the Pomo: Techniques **1752**
Batchewana First Nation **3016**
Baton Rouge Business Development Center **3649, 4104**
Ba'ts'oosee; The Origin of the Crown Dance and **2005**
Battle Mountain Band **202**
Bay Area Urban League **3544**
Bay Mills Community College **1313**
Beads **4426**
Bear Butte State Park **993**
Bear and Co., Inc. **1486**
Bear River Band of Rohnerville Rancheria **56**
Bear Tribe Medicine Society **1487**
Bear Tribe Publishing **1488**
Beardy's and Okemasis First Nation **3116**
Bearskin Lake First Nation **2927**
(Bearspaw); Stoney Tribal Administration First Nation **2647**
Beaton Institute • University College of Cape Breton **3243**
Beatrice Rafferty School **1207**
Beaumont Minority Business Development Center **4243**
Beausoleil First Nation **3002**
Beausoleil First Nation; Chippewas of **3037**
Beautiful Tree: Chishkale **1753**
Beaver First Nation **2636**
Beaver Lake First Nation **2644**
Beaver Village **2169**
Beavertail Snowshoes **3316**
Beecher Bay Band **2820**
Beechwood Books **1489**
Begay Memorial Award; Tony **1468**
Belkofski; Native Village of **2238**
Bella Coola Indian Band **2678**
Belmont Against Racism **3660**
Belmont-Hillsboro Neighbors **3788**
Bemidji State University • Native American Studies Program **1355**
Bendheim-Thomas Center for Child Wellbeing • Princeton University • Woodrow Wilson School of Public and International Affairs **4298**
Bennett County Booster Award **1468**
Benton Paiute Reservation **32**
Berens River First Nation **2846**
Bernice Ford Price Reference Library • Historical Society; Oklahoma • Museum of the Western Prairie **722**
Bernice P. Bishop Museum • Library **2542**
Bernice Pauahi Bishop Estate; Kamehameha Schools/ **2570**
Bernice Pauahi Bishop Museum **2556**
Berry Creek Rancheria **95**
Berry Library-Learning Center; E.Y. • Special Collections • Black Hills State University **615**
Bess Press **2587**
Betsiamites First Nation **3049**
A Better Chance **3367**
Beyond Tradition **1754**
BIA Educators; National Council of **3410**
Bible College; American Indian • Dorothy Cummings Memorial Library **602**
Bible Institute of Seattle; Lutheran • Library **680**
Big Bend Rancheria **33**
Big Grassy First Nation **2985**
Big Island First Nation **2986**
Big Lagoon Rancheria **126**
Big Pine Reservation **34**
Big River First Nation **3114**
Big Sandy Rancheria **29**
Big Trout Lake First Nation **2928**
Big Valley Rancheria **80**
Bighead First Nation; Joseph **3146**
Bigstone Cree First Nation **2620**
Bill Hanson Consulting **3263**
Bill Moore's Slough; Native Village of **2248**

Bill and Sue Hensler Award 1468
Billings Library; Parmly • Montana Room 726
Biloxi Tribe of Louisiana; Tunica- 159
Birch Creek Village 2202
Birdtail Sioux First Nation 2847
Birmingham Minority Business Development Center 4035
Birmingham Urban League 3513
Bishop Baraga Association • Archives 613
Bishop Estate; Kamehameha Schools/ Bernice Pauahi 2570
Bishop Museum; Bernice P. • Library 2542
Bishop Museum; Bernice Pauahi 2556
Bishop Museum Press 2588
Bishop Reservation Tribe 35
Bitter Root Valley Historical Society • Ravalli County Museum •
    Miles Romney Memorial Library 614
Bjugstad Memorial Scholarships; Ardell 1415
Black Coal, Red Power 1755
Black Hills State University
        E.Y. Berry Library-Learning Center • Special
        Collections 615
        Native American Studies Program 1356
The Black Hills: Who Owns the Land 1756
Black, Hispanic, and Native American Students; Minority
    Student Enrollments in Higher Education: A Guide to
    Institutions with. . . Asian, 4413
Black Lake First Nation 3103
Black Mesa Community School 1160
Blackbear Bosin Collection 688
Blackfeet Community College 1315
        Native American Studies Program • Blackfeet Studies
        Department 1342
Blackfeet Dormitory 1221
Blackfeet Tribal Business Council 191
        Head Start Program 1094
Blackwater Community School 1161
Blackwater Draw Museum • Eastern New Mexico
    University 936
Blessed Kateri Tekakwitha League 389
Blood Tribe First Nation 2657
Bloodvein First Nation 2850
Blue Bird Publishing 4360
Blue Cloud Abbey • Library 616
Blue Lake Rancheria 36
Blue Rose Journal 1575
Blue Star Productions; Book World Inc./ 1490
Blueberry River Indian Band 2683
Board of Indian Appeals • U.S. Department of the Interior 538
Board; Long Island Community Housing Resource 3738
Board of Minneapolis; Indian Health 478
Bob Penn; The American as Artist: A Portrait of 1714
Bogue Chitto Elementary School 1215
Bois Forte Reservation Business Committee • Head Start
    Program 1086
Boldt Decision: Impacts and Implementation 1757
Boldt Decision: Update 1758
Bonaparte Indian Band 2688
Bond Assurance Fund of Kentucky; Minority Contractors 3644
Bond Center for Equal Education; Horace Mann • University of
    Massachusetts 4396
Bonding and Insurance Agency; MCAP 3437
Bonner County Human Rights Task Force 3618
Bonnie Erickson Award 1468
Book Publishers; Native American 1548
Book World Inc./Blue Star Productions 1490
Books Beyond Borders 4361
Boothroyd Indian Band 2680
Borrego Pass School 1229
Boston Bar Indian Band 2681
Boston Economic Development Department • Minority and
    Women Business Enterprises Office 4115
Boston Indian Council 470
Boston Minority Business Development Center 4116
Bougoumou; Cree Nation of Ouji- 3080
Bow and its Arrows; Sinew-Backed 2060
Bowers Museum of Cultural Art • Research Library 617
Bowling Green State University • Popular Press 4362
Bowman Books 1491
Box of Treasures 1759
Boy and the Eagle; The Legend of the 1915
Boy of the Navajos 1760
Boy of the Seminoles (Indians of the Everglades) 1761

Boys Club Newsletter and CCFS Voice; Cherokee 1651
Boys Club—Newsletter; Cherokee 1651
Brandon University • Native Studies Program 3248
Braun Research Library • Southwest Museum 753
Brave Eagle 1762
The Brave Indian Chief 1763
Bread Springs Day School 1230
Breaking Chains 3774
Brevig Mission; Native Village of 2171
Bridge River Indian Band 2757
Bridgeport Affirmative Action Department 4056
Bridgeport Indian Colony 38
Bridgeton Public Library • Special Collections 618
Bright Horizons Specialty Distributors, Inc. 1492
Bristol Bay Native Association • Head Start Program 2422
Bristol Bay Native Corp. Education Foundation 2352
British Columbia Attorney General and Minister Responsible for
    Multiculturalism, Human Rights and Immigration 3193
British Columbia Council of Human Rights 4280
British Columbia Ministry of Aboriginal Affairs 3194
British Columbia Ministry of Social Services • Aboriginal
    Services 3195
British Columbia; Museum of Northern 3214
(British Columbia/Yukon); Dease River Band 2727
Broadcasting Consortium; Native American Public 420, 3479
Broken Journey 1764
Broken Rainbow 1765
Brokenhead Ojibway Nation 2893
Broman Lake Indian Band 2684
Brooklyn Minority Business Development Center 3712, 4166
Brooklyn Museum • Art Reference Library 619
Brown and Bain, P.A. • Library 620
Brown, Jr. Root Cutter Award; Samuel W. 1469
Brown Library; John Carter 666
Brown University • Center for the Study of Race and Ethnicity
    in America 4293
Brownsville Minority Business Development Center 4244
Brunswick House First Nation 2936
Buckeyes: Food of California Indians 1766
Buckland; Native Village of 2172
Buctouche Micmac Band 2909
Buechel Memorial Lakota Museum 994
Buena Vista Rancheria 73
Buffalo Bill Historical Center
        McCracken Research Library 621
        Plains Indian Museum 1016
*(Buffalo Hunters of the Plains); Indian Family of Long
    Ago* 1885
Buffalo Minority Business Development Center 4167
Buffalo Point First Nation 2879
Buffalo River Dene Nation 3115
Buffalo Urban League 3714
Building an Algonquin Birchbark Canoe 3317
Building a Kayak: Parts 1 and 2 2478
Bunting Memorial Slide Library; Bainbridge • University of New
    Mexico 797
Bureau of Catholic Indian Missions 3368
Bureau of Catholic Indian Missions Newsletter 1650
Bureau of Indian Affairs
        Administrative Cost Grants for Indian Schools • U.S.
        Department of the Interior 3972
        Agriculture on Indian Lands • U.S. Department of the
        Interior 3973
        Aid to Tribal Governments • U.S. Department of the
        Interior 3974
        Alaskan Indian Allotments and Subsistence Preference -
        Alaska National Interest Lands Conservation Act • U.S.
        Department of the Interior 2378
        Assistance for Indian Children with Severe Disabilities •
        U.S. Department of the Interior 3975
        Assistance to Tribally Controlled Community Colleges and
        Universities • U.S. Department of the Interior 3976
        Attorney Fees - Indian Rights • U.S. Department of the
        Interior 3977
        Bureau of Indian Affairs Facilities - Operations and
        Maintenance • U.S. Department of the Interior 3978
        Consolidated Tribal Government Program • U.S.
        Department of the Interior 3979
        Construction and Repair of Indian Detention Facilities •
        U.S. Department of the Interior 3980

Bureau of Indian Affairs (continued)
  Endangered Species on Indian Lands • U.S. Department of the Interior **3981**
  Environmental Quality Services - Indian Programs • U.S. Department of the Interior **3982**
  Equal Employment Opportunity Staff • U.S. Department of the Interior **3881**
  Fish, Wildlife, and Parks Programs on Indian Lands • U.S. Department of the Interior **3983**
  Forestry on Indian Lands • U.S. Department of the Interior **3984**
  Indian Adult Education • U.S. Department of the Interior **3985**
  Indian Child and Family Education (FACE) • U.S. Department of the Interior **3986**
  Indian Community Fire Protection • U.S. Department of the Interior **3987**
  Indian Economic Development • U.S. Department of the Interior **3988**
  Indian Education Facilities, Operations, and Maintenance • Office of Indian Education Programs • U.S. Department of the Interior **3989**
  Indian Gaming Management Staff • U.S. Department of the Interior **539**
  Indian Graduate Student Scholarships (Special Higher Education Scholarships) • U.S. Department of the Interior **3990**
  Indian Job Placement - United Sioux Tribes Development Corporation • U.S. Department of the Interior **3991**
  Indian Law Enforcement • U.S. Department of the Interior **3992**
  Indian Post Secondary Schools (Haskell and SIPI) • U.S. Department of the Interior **3993**
  Indian Rights Protection • U.S. Department of the Interior **3994**
  Indian School Equalization Program (ISEP) • U.S. Department of the Interior **3995**
  Indian Schools - Student Transportation • U.S. Department of the Interior **3996**
  Indian Self-Determination Contract Support • U.S. Department of the Interior **3997**
  Indian Social Services - Child Welfare Assistance • U.S. Department of the Interior **3998**
  Indian Vocational Training - United Tribes Technical College • U.S. Department of the Interior **3999**
  Irrigation Operations and Maintenance on Indian Lands • Office of Trust Responsibilities • U.S. Department of the Interior **4000**
  Litigation Support for Indian Rights • U.S. Department of the Interior **4001**
  Minerals and Mining on Indian Lands • U.S. Department of the Interior **4002**
  Navajo-Hopi Indian Settlement Program • U.S. Department of the Interior **574**
  Office of American Indian Trust • U.S. Department of the Interior **540**
  Office of Indian Education Programs • U.S. Department of the Interior **541**
  Office of Tribal Services
    Tribal Government Services Division • U.S. Department of the Interior **1052**
    U.S. Department of the Interior **542**
  Office of Trust Responsibilities • U.S. Department of the Interior **543**
  Real Estate Programs - Indian Lands • U.S. Department of the Interior **2382, 4003**
  Replacement and Repair of Indian Schools • U.S. Department of the Interior **4004**
  Road Maintenance - Indian Roads • U.S. Department of the Interior **4005**
  Services to Indian Children, Elderly and Families • U.S. Department of the Interior **4007**
  Southwestern Indian Polytechnic Institute • Library • U.S. Department of the Interior **761**
  Structural Fire Protection - Bureau of Indian Affairs Facilities (Fire Protection) • U.S. Department of the Interior **4008**
  Tribal Courts • U.S. Department of the Interior **4009**
  Tribal Self-Governance • U.S. Department of the Interior **4010**
  Tribal Self-Governance Grants • U.S. Department of the Interior **4011**
  Tribally Controlled Community College Endowments • U.S. Department of the Interior **4012**
  Unresolved Indian Hunting and Fishing Rights • U.S. Department of the Interior **4013**
  Unresolved Indian Rights Issues • U.S. Department of the Interior **4014**
  Waste Management - Indian Lands • U.S. Department of the Interior **4015**
Bureau of Indian Affairs Facilities (Fire Protection); Structural Fire Protection - • U.S. Department of the Interior • Bureau of Indian Affairs **4008**
Bureau of Indian Affairs Facilities - Operations and Maintenance • U.S. Department of the Interior • Bureau of Indian Affairs **3978**
Bureau of Indian Affairs Higher Education Grant **1417**
Bureau of Indian Affairs Loans and Tribal Loans **1418, 2434**
Bureau of Indian Affairs Scholarship Grant; U.S. **1452, 2441**
Burlingame Special Collections/Archives; Merrill G. • Montana State University - Libraries **697**
Burns-Paiute Tribe **295**
Burnt Church First Nation **2913**
Busby School **1222**
Business Administration; U.S. Small
  Business Loans for 8(A) Program Participants **4030**
  Management and Technical Assistance for Socially and Economically Disadvantaged Businesses (7(J) Development Assistant Program) **4031**
  Microloan Demonstration Program **4032**
  Minority Business Development (Section 8(a) Program) **4033**
  Office of Equal Employment Opportunity and Civil Rights Compliance **3940**
  Office of Minority Enterprise Development **3941**
  Office of Minority Small Business and Capital Ownership Development • Management and Technical Assistance for Socially and Economically Disadvantaged Business **4034**
  Office of Native American Affairs **548**
  Office of Small Business Development Centers **3942**
Business Advisory Commission; San Francisco Small **4051**
Business Association of Delaware; Minority **3580**
Business Association of Greater Danbury; Minority **3573**
Business Association; Minority **3806**
Business Association; Yonkers Minority **3739**
Business; Chronicle of Minority **4433**
Business Committee; Apache **262**
Business Committee; Bois Forte Reservation • Head Start Program **1086**
Business Committee; Chippewa- Cree **190**
Business Committee (Chippewa); Grand Portage Reservation **179**
Business Committee (Chippewa); Mille Lacs Reservation **183**
Business Committee; Fond du Lac Reservation • Head Start Program **1087**
Business Committee; Grand Portage Reservation • Head Start Program **1088**
Business Committee; Kalispel **351**
Business Committee; Oneida Tribal • Head Start Program **1156**
Business Committee; Wisconsin Winnebago • Head Start Program **1158**
Business Consultants; Seattle Minority Business Development Center- IMPACT **3817, 4271**
Business Council; Arapahoe **364**
Business Council; Blackfeet Tribal **191**
  Head Start Program **1094**
Business Council; Chehalis **339**
Business Council; Chehalis Tribal • Head Start Program **1140**
Business Council; Colville **338**
Business Council; Golden Triangle Minority **3798**
Business Council; Goshute **324**
Business Council; Hoopa Valley • Head Start Program **1076**
Business Council; Lummi **329**
Business Council of Michigan; Native American **477**
Business Council; National Minority **3466, 3729**
Business Council; Shoshone **365**
Business Council; Shoshone Paiute **216**
Business Council; Three Affiliated Tribes **260**
Business Council; Worcester Minority **3666**

Business Development Agency—Directory of Regional and District Offices and Funded Organizations; Minority **4065**
Business Development Agency; Minority • U.S. Department of Commerce **3841**
Business Development Agency; West Virginia Minority and Small **4274**
Business Development Center; Alaska Minority **4040**
Business Development Center; Albuquerque Minority **4164**
Business Development Center; Anaheim Minority **4044**
Business Development Center; Atlanta Minority **4075**
Business Development Center; Augusta Minority **3610, 4077**
Business Development Center; Austin Minority **4242**
Business Development Center; Bakersfield Minority **4045**
Business Development Center; Baltimore Minority **4112**
Business Development Center; Baton Rouge **3649, 4104**
Business Development Center; Beaumont Minority **4243**
Business Development Center; Birmingham Minority **4035**
Business Development Center; Boston Minority **4116**
Business Development Center; Brooklyn Minority **3712, 4166**
Business Development Center; Brownsville Minority **4244**
Business Development Center; Buffalo Minority **4167**
Business Development Center; Charleston Minority **4232**
Business Development Center; Charlotte Minority **3743, 4186**
Business Development Center; Columbus Minority **4078, 4199**
Business Development Center; Corpus Christi Minority **3799, 4245**
Business Development Center; Dallas/Ft. Worth Minority **4246**
Business Development Center; Denver Minority **4055**
Business Development Center; El Paso Minority **4247**
Business Development Center; Fayetteville Minority **4189**
Business Development Center; Fresno Minority **3529, 4046**
Business Development Center; Gary Minority **3631, 4091**
Business Development Center; Harlem Minority **4157**
Business Development Center; Honolulu Minority **4084**
Business Development Center; Houston Minority **4250**
Business Development Center- IMPACT Business Consultants; Seattle Minority **3817, 4271**
Business Development Center; Jackson Minority **4138**
Business Development Center; Jacksonville Minority **4069**
Business Development Center; Kansas City Minority **3692, 4142**
Business Development Center; Laredo Minority **4251**
Business Development Center; Las Vegas Minority **4152**
Business Development Center; Little Rock Minority **4043**
Business Development Center; Lubbock/ Midland- Odessa Minority **4253**
Business Development Center; Manhattan Minority **4168**
Business Development Center; Mayaguez Minority **4225**
Business Development Center; McAllen Minority **4254**
Business Development Center; Memphis Minority **4235**
Business Development Center; Miami/Ft. Lauderdale Minority **4070**
Business Development Center; Milwaukee Minority **3825, 4275**
Business Development Center; Minneapolis Minority **4133**
Business Development Center; Mobile Minority **4036**
Business Development Center; Montgomery Minority **4037**
Business Development Center; Nashville Minority **4236**
Business Development Center; Nassau/Suffolk Minority **3723, 4169**
Business Development Center; New Orleans Minority **4110**
Business Development Center; Newark Minority **3708, 4163**
Business Development Center; Newport News Minority **4263**
Business Development Center; Norfolk Minority **4264**
Business Development Center No. 1; Cleveland Minority **4197**
Business Development Center No. 1; San Francisco/ Oakland Minority **4050**
Business Development Center No. 2; Chicago Minority **4087**
Business Development Center No. 2; Cleveland Minority **4198**
Business Development Center; Oklahoma City Minority **4207**
Business Development Center; Orlando Minority **4072**
Business Development Center; Oxnard Minority **4047**
Business Development Center; Phoenix Minority **4041**
Business Development Center; Pittsburgh Minority **4224**
Business Development Center; Ponce Minority **4226**
Business Development Center; Portland Minority **4216**
Business Development Center; Queens Minority **3718, 4183**
Business Development Center; Raleigh/Durham Minority **4191**
Business Development Center; Rochester Minority **3734, 4184**
Business Development Center; Saginaw County Minority **3679, 4131**
Business Development Center; St. Louis Minority **4146**

Business Development Center; Salt Lake City Minority **4258**
Business Development Center; San Antonio Minority **4255**
Business Development Center; San Diego Minority **4048**
Business Development Center; San Jose Minority **4052**
Business Development Center; Savannah Minority **4082**
Business Development Center; Stockton Minority **4053**
Business Development Center; Tampa/St. Petersburg Minority **4073**
Business Development Center; Tulsa Minority **4213**
Business Development Center; Virgin Islands Minority **4261**
Business Development Center; Washington Minority **4066**
Business Development Center; West Palm Beach Minority **4074**
Business Development Center; Williamsburg/Brooklyn Minority **3713, 4185**
Business Development Council; Michigan Minority **3673, 4129**
Business Development; District of Columbia Department of Human Rights and Minority **3583**
Business Development Mega Center; Chicago Minority **4088**
Business Development Office; District of Columbia Human Rights and Minority **4064**
Business Development Resource Directory; Coalition for Minority **4090**
Business Directory of Indian Country U.S.A.; Smoke Signals: **1626, 2459**
Business Directory; Minority **4419**
Business Division; Minority • Arkansas Industrial Development Commission **4042**
Business Enterprise Directory; North Dakota Department of Transportation Disadvantaged **4419**
Business Enterprise Legal Defense and Education Fund; Minority **3442**
Business Enterprises Department; Virginia Minority **4268**
Business Enterprises of New York; Association of Minority **3720**
Business Enterprises Office; Minority and Women • Economic Development Department; Boston **4115**
Business Enterprises; Texas Association of Minority **3796**
Business Entrepreneur, Minority **4431, 4496**
Business Firms; National Directory of Minority-Owned **2455, 3292, 4417**
Business Foundation; Pikes Peak Minority **3563**
Business Information Institute; Minority **3443**
Business Innovation Research Programs; Small • U.S. National Science Foundation • Design, Manufacture and Industrial Innovation Division **3930**
Business Investment Companies; American Association of Minority Enterprise Small **406**
Business League; Central Savannah River Area **3611**
Business League; National **3456**
Business League—National Memo; National **4444**
Business Loans for 8(A) Program Participants • Business Administration; U.S. Small **4030**
Business; National Association of Minority Women in **3455**
Business Office; Small and Disadvantaged • Policy Planning Division; New Orleans Economic Development and **4108**
Business Opportunity; Inter racial Council for **3430**
Business Paiute-Shoshone Tribe; Fallon **208**
Business and Political Development; Alliance of Minority Women for **3354**
Business and Professional Directory; Minority **4497**
Business Report; Indiana Minority **4438**
Business Research and Development; National Center for Minority **3458**
Business Resource Council; Delaware Valley Minority **3775**
Business Resource Development (Public and Private); Minority • U.S. Department of Commerce • Minority Business Development Agency **3953**
Business Round Table; Massachusetts Minority **3662**
Business Technology Transfer Program; Small • U.S. National Science Foundation • Design, Manufacture and Industrial Innovation Division **3931**
Business Utilization; Small and Disadvantaged • U.S. Department of Defense • Department of the Air Force **3847**
Businesses (7(J) Development Assistant Program); Management and Technical Assistance for Socially and Economically Disadvantaged • Business Administration; U.S. Small **4031**
Businesses; Directory of Indian Owned **4401**
Butler Library; Eva • Colonial Research Center, Inc.; Indian and **658**
Butterfly Books Ltd. **3264**

By This Song I Walk: Navajo Song 1767
Cabazon Indians of California 72
Cadbury Award and Franklin C. McClean Award; William and Charlotte 4351
Caddo Tribe 267
Caddoan Mounds State Historic Site 1003
Caddoes; The Last of the 1912
Cahokia Mounds State Historic Site 892
Cahuilla Band of Mission Indians 27
Cahuilla Indians; Ramona Band of 28
Caldwell First Nation 2931
California; Cabazon Indians of 72
California Council for the Defense of Freedom 3559
California Health Services Department • Civil Rights Office 580
California Indian Community; Field Directory of the 1610
California Indians; Acorns: Staple Food of 1712
California Indians: Primary Resources: A Guide to Manuscripts, Documents, Serials, Music, and Illustrations 1599
California; Kiliwa: Hunters and Gatherers of Baja 1909
California Native American Heritage Commission 581
California Native Circle 3526
California; News from Native 1639
California: Part 1, Village Life; Indians of 1895
California: Part 2, Food; Indians of 1896
California Riviera 1768
California State Indian Museum 857
California State University, Fullerton • Oral History Program 4363
California State University, Hayward 1357
California State University, Sacramento • Native American Studies Program 1358
Californians Against Discrimination and Preferences 3533
Calumet, Pipe of Peace 1769
Camp Verde Yavapai-Apache 2
Campaign for Amnesty and Human Rights for Political Prisoners 3369, 3369
Campaign for Political Rights 3370
Campaign to Stop Government Spying 3370
Campbell River Indian Band 2690
Campbell River Museum and Archives 3211
Campo Band of Mission Indians 41
Canada, 1606; Rendezvous 3338
Canada; Directory of Substance Abuse Organizations in 3287
Canada; Indian- Eskimo Association of 3172
Canada; Indian and Northern Affairs • Ontario Policy and Strategic Direction Sector 3186
Canada National Aboriginal Management Board 3176
(Canada); Richard's Totem Pole 3340
Canada, United States; Native American Directory: Alaska, 1617, 2456, 3293
Canada's Original Peoples: Then and Now 3318
Canadian Alliance in Solidarity with the Native People 3172
Canadian Association in Support of the Native Peoples 3172
Canadian Human Rights Commission 3831
Canadian Museum of Civilization 3221
Canadian Native Arts Foundation 3173
Canadian Native Languages; Centre for Research and Teaching of • University of Western Ontario 3245
Canal Winchester Tribe 3750
Candeska Cikana Community College 1329
Canim Lake Indian Band 2661
Canoe; Building an Algonquin Birchbark 3317
Canoe; Cesar's Bark 1773
Canoe Creek Indian Band 2716
Canoe Lake First Nation 3108
Cantwell; Native Village of 2173
Canyon de Chelly and Hubbell Trading Post 1770
Canyon de Chelly National Monument 834
Canyon De Chelly National Monument • Library • U.S. Department of the Interior • National Park Service 764
Canyonlands National Park 1005
Cape Mudge Indian Band 2801
Career Development for Minorities; Council on 3389
Careers (MARC); Minority Access to Research • U.S. Department of Health and Human Services • National Institutes of Health 3962
Carleton University
 Centre for Aboriginal Education, Research, and Culture 3234
 Northern and Native Studies Program 3235

Carmel Mission Indians; Coastanoan Band of 92
Carolinas; Indian Museum of the 960
Carolinas Minority Supplier Development Councils 3741
Carry the Kettle First Nation 3156
Carson Colony 203
Carter Collection of Hawaiiana (1500 volumes) 2542
Carter Seminary 1273
Carving; Joshua's Soapstone 3328
Casa Grande Ruins National Monument 835
Casa Malpais 836
Casey Journalism Center for Children and Families • University of Maryland at College Park 4301
Casualty Actuarial Society 4347
Casualty Actuarial Society Scholarships for Minority Students; Society of Actuaries/ 4347
Cat; John 3327
Cat Lake First Nation 2935
Catalogue of Projects in Electronic Text; Georgetown University - 4486
Catawba Indian Nation 307
Catholic Conference for Interracial Justice; National 3457
Catholic Indian Missions; Bureau of 3368
Catholic Indian Missions; Marquette League for 3436
Catholic Indian Missions Newsletter; Bureau of 1650
Catholic Interracial Council of New York 3371, 3725
Catholic Missions Among the Colored People and the Indians— Quarterly; Commission for the 1653
Catholics: People of the Spirit; Native American 1952
Catlin and the Indians; Smithsonian: 2063
Catlin Peace Pipe Award 1458
Cayoose Creek Indian Band 2758
Cayuga Indian Nation 252
The Cayuga Museum • Library 622
Cayuga Tribe; Seneca- 278
Cedarville Rancheria 42
Celebration/The Pipe is the Altar 1771
Center for the Advancement of the Covenant 3372
Center for Alternative Mining Development Policy 3373
Center for Applied Studies in American Ethnicity • Colorado State University 4295
Center for the Applied Study of Ethnoviolence; The Prejudice Institute/ 3498
Center for the Applied Study of Prejudice and Ethnoviolence 3498
Center of Concern 3374
Center for Human Rights and Constitutional Law 3534
Center for Indian Community Development • Humboldt State University 1026
Center for Indian Education • Arizona State University 1021
Center for National Policy Review 3375
Center for Native American Studies • Montana State University, Bozeman 1034
Center for Religion, Ethics and Social Policy • Durland Alternatives Library 623
Center; Roswell Museum and Art • Research Library 735
Center for Southwest Research • University of New Mexico 798
Center of Southwest Studies • Fort Lewis College 646
Center for Studies of Ethnicity and Race in America • University of Colorado at Boulder 4299
Center for the Study of Human Rights 3376 Columbia University 4367
Center for Study of Indian Territory; Five Civilized Tribes Museum and • Library 644
Center for the Study of Native Languages of the Plains and Southwest • University of Colorado at Boulder 1059
Center for the Study of Race and Ethnicity in America • Brown University 4293
Center for Third World Organizing 4294
Center for Western Studies • Augustana College 610, 1482
Center for Women's Economic Alternatives 3740
Center for World Indigenous Studies 3377, 4478
Central Council of Tlingit and Haida Tribe of Alaska 2224
Central Michigan University • Clarke Historical Library 624
Central Minnesota Freedom Task Force 3686
Central Montana Museum 924
Central Savannah River Area Business League 3611
Central States Archaeological Societies, Inc. 1493
Central Tribes of the Shawnee Area, Inc. • Head Start Program 1120

Centre for Aboriginal Education, Research, and Culture •
Carleton University **3234**
Centre for Northern Studies • Lakehead University **3238**
Centre for Nutrition and the Environment of Indigenous
People **3236**
Centre for Research and Teaching of Canadian Native
Languages • University of Western Ontario **3245**
A Century of Silence...Problems of the American Indian **1772**
Ceremonial Association; Gallup Inter-Tribal Indian **1517**
Ceremonial Association; Inter- Tribal Indian **404**
CERT Scholarship **1419**
Cesar's Bark Canoe **1773**
CFWE-FM **3309**
Chaco Culture National Historic Park **934**
Chairman's Association; National Tribal **3470**
Chalkyitsik Village **2174**
Chamber of Commerce; National Native American **3468**
Chamber of Commerce; Native American (Indian) **3476**
Chamber of Commerce; North American Indian **3488**
Champagne and Aishihik First Nations **3168**
Chapelle des Indiens **3230**
Chapleau Cree First Nation **2937**
Chapleau Ojibway First Nation **2938**
Chapman Library • Philbrook Museum of Art **728**
Charleston Minority Business Development Center **4232**
Charlotte-Mecklenburg Urban League **3742**
Charlotte Minority Business Development Center **3743, 4186**
Chase; Don M. **1502**
Chattanooga Equal Employment Opportunity and Better
Housing Office **597**
Chattanooga Inter-Tribal Association at UTC **517**
Chawathil Indian Band **2734**
Cheam Indian Band **2808**
Chefornak; Village of **2175**
Chehalis Business Council **339**
Chehalis Indian Band **2663**
Chehalis Tribal Business Council • Head Start Program **1140**
Chelan County Historical Museum and Pioneer Village **1009**
Chemainus Indian Band **2754**
Chemawa Indian School **1278**
Chemawawin First Nation **2857**
Chemehuevi Tribe **65**
Chemical Dependency Association; Northern Plains Native
American **515**
Chenega; Native Village of **2176**
Cherev Canada Inc. **3265, 3266**
Cherokee **1774**
Cherokee Advocate **1691**
Cherokee Boys Club—Newsletter **1651**
Cherokee Boys Club Newsletter and CCFS Voice **1651**
Cherokee Central School **1261**
Cherokee Courthouse **976**
Cherokee Cultural Center; Azurite **501**
Cherokee; Eastern Band of **253**
Cherokee Indian; Museum of the **961**
        Archives **699**
Cherokee Mark Norman Ugaku Gigege; Kwatani Mission of
Chickamuga **316**
Cherokee Nation Graduate Scholarship **1420**
Cherokee Nation of Oklahoma **290**
        Head Start Program **1121**
Cherokee National Archives • Historical Society, Inc.; Cherokee
National **625**
Cherokee National Hall of Fame **1459**
Cherokee National Historical Society **390, 2129**
Cherokee National Historical Society, Inc. • Cherokee National
Archives **625**
Cherokee National Museum **977**
The Cherokee One Feather **1692**
Cherokee Studies; Journal of **1668**
Cherokee Tennessee River Band Chickamauga; Free **317**
Cherokees of the Southeastern U.S.; Chickamogee **430**
Cheslatta Carrier Nation **2685**
Chevak Native Village **2177**
Cheyenne-Arapaho Higher Education Assistance Program
Grant **1421**
Cheyenne-Arapaho Tribe **269**
        Head Start Program **1122**
Cheyenne-Eagle Butte School **1280**
Cheyenne Frontier Days and Old West Museum **1015**
Cheyenne River Community College **1335**

Cheyenne River Sioux Tribal Council • Head Start
Program **1133**
Cheyenne River Sioux Tribe **308**
Cheyenne Tribal Council; Northern • Head Start
Program **1099**
Cheyenne Tribe; Northern **194**
Chicago Commission on Human Relations **4086**
Chicago Minority Business Development Center No. 2 **4087**
Chicago Minority Business Development Mega Center **4088**
Chicago Urban League **3625**
Chickaloon; Native Village of **2178**
Chickamauga; Free Cherokee Tennessee River Band **317**
Chickamogee Cherokees of the Southeastern U.S. **430**
Chickamuga Cherokee Mark Norman Ugaku Gigege; Kwatani
Mission of **316**
Chickasaw Council House Library **626**
Chickasaw Council House Museum **978**
Chickasaw Nation of Oklahoma **261**
        Head Start Program **1123**
Chicken Ranch Rancheria **75**
Chico Rancheria; Mechoopda Maidu Indian Tribe of **43**
(Chicora Shakori) Indian People; Chicora Siouan **306**
Chicora Siouan (Chicora Shakori) Indian People **306**
Chief Bug-O-Nay-Ge-Shig School **1210**
Chief John Ross House **883**
Chief Plenty Coups State Park **925**
Chieftain; Jicarilla **1636**
Chieftains Museum **884**
Chignik Lagoon; Native Village of **2180**
Chignik Lake Village **2181**
Chignik; Native Village of **2179**
Chilchinbeto Day School **1162**
Child Care Services; Inyo • Head Start Program **1077**
Child and Family Education (FACE); Indian • U.S. Department
of the Interior • Bureau of Indian Affairs **3986**
Child Welfare Assistance; Indian Social Services - • U.S.
Department of the Interior • Bureau of Indian Affairs **3998**
Child Wellbeing; Bendheim-Thomas Center for • Princeton
University • Woodrow Wilson School of Public and
International Affairs **4298**
Children (Alaska Native Education); Alaska Native Home Based
Education for Preschool • U.S. Department of Education •
Office of Elementary and Secondary Education **2366**
Children of Alcoholics; National Association for Native
American **407**
Children of the Bear Indian Council **459**
Children, Elderly and Families; Services to Indian • U.S.
Department of the Interior • Bureau of Indian Affairs **4007**
Children and Families; Casey Journalism Center for •
University of Maryland at College Park **4301**
Children; Futures for **3402, 3403**
Children, Inc.; Council on Interracial Books for **4370**
Children of the Long-Beaked Bird **1775**
Children; Mental Health Needs of Minority **4459**
Children of the Plains Indians **1776**
Children with Severe Disabilities; Assistance for Indian • U.S.
Department of the Interior • Bureau of Indian Affairs **3975**
Children's Advocacy Group **3747**
Children's Alternative Learning Program **3550**
Children's Center; Queen Lilioukalani **2593**
Children's Museum • Resource Center **628**
Children's Museum; Hawaii **2557**
Children's Museum of Indianapolis • Rauh Memorial
Library **627**
Children's Watch International **3378**
Chilkat Indian Village (Klukwan) **2242**
Chilkoot Indian Association (Haines) **2213**
Chiloquin Story; Return of the Raven—The Edison **2038**
Chilula Tribe **57**
Chinik Eskimo Community (Golovin) **2210**
(Chiniki); Stoney Tribal Administration First Nation **2648**
Chinle Boarding School **1163**
Chipewyan First Nation; Athabasca **2625**
Chippewa-Cree Business Committee **190**
(Chippewa); Fond du Lac **178**
(Chippewa); Grand Portage Reservation Business
Committee **179**
Chippewa Heritage Center; Turtle Mountain **967**
Chippewa Heritage Publications **1494**
Chippewa Indians of Michigan; Lac Vieux Desert Band of Lake
Superior **174**

(Chippewa); Leech Lake Reservation 176
    Head Start Program 1089
(Chippewa); Mille Lacs Reservation Business Committee 183
Chippewa Museum and Cultural Center; Lac du
    Flambeau 1014
Chippewa Tribal Executive Committee; Minnesota 177
Chippewa Tribe Grant; Minnesota 1439
Chippewa Tribe; Saginaw 171
Chippewa Tribe; Sault Ste. Marie 172
Chippewa Tribe; Sokaogon 356
Chippewa Tribes; Grand Traverse Band of Ottawa and • Head
    Start Program 1084
Chippewa; Turtle Mountain Band of • Head Start
    Program 1119
(Chippewa); White Earth 187
Chippewa; White Earth Band of • Head Start Program 1092
Chippewas of Beausoleil First Nation 3037
Chippewas of Georgina Island 3029
Chippewas of Kettle and Stony Point First Nation 2951
Chippewas of Nawash 3044
Chippewas of Sarnia First Nation 3015
Chippewas of Saugeen First Nation 3025
Chippewas of the Thames First Nation 2987
Chisasibi; Cree Nation of 3052
Chisasibi First Nation 3051
Chishkale; Beautiful Tree: 1753
Chistochina; Native Village of 2205
Chitimacha Day School 1206
Chitimacha Tribe of Louisiana 156
Chitina Traditional Village 2182
Choctaw-Apache Community of Ebarb 466
Choctaw Central High School 1216
Choctaw Indians; Jena Band of 158
Choctaw Indians; Mississippi Band of 188
    Head Start Program 1093
Choctaw Nation Indian Home Corp. 3764
Choctaw Nation of Oklahoma 270
    Head Start Program 1124
CHON-FM 3310
Christmas Story; That One Good Spirit—An Indian 2085
Chronicle of Minority Business 4433
Chukchansi Yokotch of Mariposa 89
Chuloonawick Native Village 2184
Chumash; Coastal Band of 87
Chuska Boarding School 1231
Cibecue Community School 1164
CIC Predoctoral Fellowships 4311
Ciga Press 1495
Cincinnati Economic Development Department • Small Business
    Division 4194
Cincinnati Equal Employment Opportunity Office 4195
Cincinnati Human Relations Department 4196
Cincinnati; Urban League of Greater 3752
Circle of Life Survival School 1211
Circle Native Community 2185
Circle of the Sun 3319
Circle of the Winds; Heart of the Earth Survival School/ 1849
A Circle of Women 1777
Circumpolar and Aboriginal North America Resources 2520,
    3349
Circumpolar Health Studies; Institute for • University of Alaska,
    Anchorage 2418, 2612
Citizen Alert 1652
Citizen Assistance Office; Houston 4249
Citizen Band of Potawatami 288
Citizens to Abolish Domestic Apartheid 3773
Citizens Alert 3449
Citizens Commission on Human Rights 3587, 3614, 3694
Citizens Commission on Human Rights of Oregon 3770
Citizens in Defense of Civil Liberties 3379
Citizens for Human Rights; Jeffco 3571
Citizens Rights Committee; Des Plaines 3626
Civil Liberties; Citizens in Defense of 3379
Civil Liberties Division; Civil Rights and • Massachusetts Public
    Protection Bureau 4120
Civil Liberties Institute; Meiklejohn 3438, 4382
Civil Liberties Union, Alabama Affiliate; American 3514
Civil Liberties Union, Alaska Affiliate; American 3516
Civil Liberties Union; American 3355, 4355
Civil Liberties Union of Arizona; American 3518
Civil Liberties Union of Arkansas; American 3524

Civil Liberties Union, Central Florida Chapter; American 3605
Civil Liberties Union, Colorado Affiliate; American 3565
Civil Liberties Union; Connecticut 3575
Civil Liberties Union, Connecticut; American 3574
Civil Liberties Union of Delaware; American 3579
Civil Liberties Union, East Missouri; American 3695
Civil Liberties Union, Florida Affiliate; American 3592
Civil Liberties Union Foundation; American 3356, 3566
Civil Liberties Union Foundation; Connecticut 3575
Civil Liberties Union Freedom Network; American 4475
Civil Liberties Union, Genesee Valley Chapter; New York 3733
Civil Liberties Union, Georgia Affiliate; American 3607
Civil Liberties Union, Greater Tampa Chapter; American 3599
Civil Liberties Union of Hawaii; American 3615
Civil Liberties Union, Hawkeye Chapter; American 3641
Civil Liberties Union of Idaho; American 3616
Civil Liberties Union of Illinois; American 3622
Civil Liberties Union of Indiana; American 3632, 3633
Civil Liberties Union, Iowa Chapter; American 3638
Civil Liberties Union, Kansas and Western Missouri Chapter;
    American 3691
Civil Liberties Union of Kentucky; American 3647
Civil Liberties Union Louisiana Affiliate; American 3651
Civil Liberties Union; Lubbock 3804
Civil Liberties Union; Maine 3655
Civil Liberties Union, Maine Affiliate; American 3654
Civil Liberties Union, Marin Chapter; American 3543
Civil Liberties Union of Maryland; American 3656
Civil Liberties Union, Massachussetts; American 3661
Civil Liberties Union, Michigan Chapter; American 3667
Civil Liberties Union, Mid-Peninsula Chapter; American 3562
Civil Liberties Union, Mid-Missouri Chapter; American 3690
Civil Liberties Union, Minnesota Chapter; American 3681
Civil Liberties Union, Mississippi Affiliate; American 3688
Civil Liberties Union, Montana Chapter; American 3697
Civil Liberties Union, Monterey County Chapter;
    American 3548
Civil Liberties Union, Mountain States; American 3567
Civil Liberties Union, Mountain States Chapter; American 3568
Civil Liberties Union of the National Capital Area;
    American 3581
Civil Liberties Union, Nebraska Chapter; American 3699
Civil Liberties Union of Nevada; American 3701
Civil Liberties Union, New Hampshire; American 3702
Civil Liberties Union, New Hampshire Chapter 3703
Civil Liberties Union, New Jersey; American 3705, 3706
Civil Liberties Union of New Mexico; American 3709
Civil Liberties Union, New York; American 3724
Civil Liberties Union of North Carolina; American 3745
Civil Liberties Union of Northern California; American 3554
Civil Liberties Union, Northwest Louisiana Chapter;
    American 3653
Civil Liberties Union of Ohio; American 3754
Civil Liberties Union of Ohio, Cincinnati Chapter;
    American 3751
Civil Liberties Union of Oklahoma; American 3765
Civil Liberties Union of Oregon; American 3769
Civil Liberties Union of Oregon, Southern District;
    American 3768
Civil Liberties Union, Palm Beach Chapter; American 3586
Civil Liberties Union, Pennsylvania Affiliate; American 3776
Civil Liberties Union, Rhode Island Affiliate; American 3777
Civil Liberties Union of San Diego and Imperial Counties;
    American 3552
Civil Liberties Union, Santa Clara Valley Chapter;
    American 3540
Civil Liberties Union, Singles Chapter; American 3561
Civil Liberties Union, South Carolina; American 3780
Civil Liberties Union of Southern California; American 3532
Civil Liberties Union, Southern Regional Office; American 3608
Civil Liberties Union, Tempe-Mesa Chapter; American 3521
Civil Liberties Union, Tennessee; American 3787
Civil Liberties Union; Texas 3797
Civil Liberties Union, Texas Affiliate; American 3790
Civil Liberties Union, Utah Affiliate; American 3805
Civil Liberties Union, Vermont Affiliate; American 3807
Civil Liberties Union, Virginia; American 3811
Civil Liberties Union, Washington; American 3816
Civil Liberties Union, West Virginia Affiliate; American 3821
Civil Liberties Union of Wisconsin; American 3824
Civil Liberties Union, Wyoming; American 3830

Civil Personnel Policy/Equal Employment Opportunity Office •
  U.S. Department of Defense • Department of the Navy **3852**
Civil Rights **4434**
Civil Rights, AFL-CIO; Department of **3393**
Civil Rights Center • U.S. Department of Labor **3893**
Civil Rights and Civil Liberties Division • Massachusetts Public
  Protection Bureau **4120**
Civil Rights and Claims Division • Attorney General's Office;
  Tennessee **4237**
Civil Rights; Coalition for **3556**
Civil Rights Coalition; New York **3730**
Civil Rights Commission; Indiana **4093**
Civil Rights Commission; Iowa **4098**
Civil Rights Commission Newsletter; Michigan **4442**
Civil Rights Commission; Ohio **4202**
Civil Rights Communicator; Iowa **4439**
Civil Rights Defense Fund; OGCA **3761**
Civil Rights Department; Davenport **4096**
Civil Rights Department; Michigan **4125**
    Detroit Office **4126**
Civil Rights Division
    Attorney General; Alabama **578**
    Attorney General; Michigan **4124**
    Attorney General; New Jersey • Law and Public Safety
      Department **4158**
    Colorado Regulatory Agencies Department **583**
    Educational Opportunities Section • U.S. Department of
      Justice **3884**
    Employment Litigation Section • U.S. Department of
      Justice **3885**
    Housing and Civil Enforcement Section • U.S. Department
      of Justice **3886**
    Louisiana Social Services Department **4107**
    Nebraska Labor Department **4151**
    Office of Complaint Adjudication • U.S. Department of
      Justice **3887**
    Special Litigation Section • U.S. Department of
      Justice **3888**
    U.S. Department of Health and Human Services • Office
      of the General Counsel **3863**
    U.S. Department of Labor • Office of the Solicitor **3895**
    Voting Section • U.S. Department of Justice **3889**
Civil Rights Division; Equal Opportunity, Affirmative Action and
  • Human Services Department; Minnesota **4137**
Civil Rights Enforcement Agency; St. Louis **4145**
Civil Rights; Leadership Conference on **3433**
Civil Rights and Litigation
    Office of Assisted Housing and Community Development •
      U.S. Department of Housing and Urban
      Development **3876**
    Office of Litigation and Fair Housing Enforcement • U.S.
      Department of Housing and Urban Development **3877**
    Office of Program Enforcement • U.S. Department of
      Housing and Urban Development **3878**
Civil Rights Litigation Section • Attorney General (Law
  Department); Georgia **4079**
Civil Rights Office
    California Health Services Department **580**
    Florida Labor and Employment Security Department **4068**
    New Jersey Transportation Department **4162**
    North Dakota Transportation Department **4193**
    U.S. Department of Commerce • National Institute of
      Standards and Technology **3842**
Civil Rights Office; Affirmative Action and • Wisconsin Health
  and Social Services Department **4276**
Civil Rights Office; Equal Employment Opportunity and
    Delaware Transportation Department **585**
    U.S. Department of State **3896**
Civil Rights Office; Minneapolis **4132**
Civil Rights Office; Seattle **4270**
Civil Rights Prosecution • U.S. Department of Justice • Civil
  Rights Division • Criminal Section **4016**
Civil Rights Reviewing Authority • U.S. Department of
  Education • Office of Hearings and Appeals **3856**
Civil Rights Section
    Attorney General; Ohio **4201**
    Oregon Transportation Department • Human Resources
      and Organization Development Branch **4215**
Civil Rights Staff
    U.S. Department of Agriculture
      Food Safety **3837**

    Natural Resources and Environment **3838**
Civil Rights; *Treaty Rights or* **2097**
Civil Rights; U.S. Commission on **3832**
    Office of Civil Rights Evaluation **3833**
Civil Service Department; Michigan • Equal Employment
  Opportunity and Affirmative Action Office **4127**
Civil Service Department; New York State • Affirmative Action
  Office **4175**
Civilization; Canadian Museum of **3221**
Civilized Tribes **1778**
Civilized Tribes Foundation; Five **396**
Civilized Tribes Museum and Center for Study of Indian
  Territory; Five • Library **644**
Civilized Tribes Museum; Five **980, 1511**
CKON-FM **1698**
CKQN-FM **3311**
CLA Scholarship for Minority Students in Memory of Edna
  Yelland **4312**
Claims Commission Archives; Indian 811
Claims Division; Civil Rights and • Attorney General's Office;
  Tennessee **4237**
Clapp Library; Margaret • Special Collections • Wellesley
  College **817**
Clark Collection; General John S. 622
Clarke Historical Library • Central Michigan University **624**
Clark's Point; Village of **2186**
Clausen Memorial Museum **2398**
Clear Light Publishers **1496**
Clearinghouse for Native American Concerns of Austin **3794**
Cleveland Minority Business Development Center No. 1 **4197**
Cleveland Minority Business Development Center No. 2 **4198**
Click Relander Collection • Yakima Valley Regional Library •
  Reference Department **828**
Cliff Dwellings Museum; Manitou **867**
Cline Library • Special Collections and Archives Department •
  Northern Arizona University **715**
Clouded Land **1779**
Clover Park Press **4364**
Cloverdale Rancheria **118**
Club of Indian Women **458**
Clues to Ancient Indian Life **1780**
Clyde Press **4365**
CN Native Education Awards **3258**
Coalition for Civil Rights **3556**
Coalition for Human Dignity **3771**
Coalition for Indian Education 410
Coalition for Indian Education; National **410**
Coalition for Minority Business Development Resource
  Directory **4090**
Coalition of Minority Policy Professionals **3380**
Coalition of Native American Public Radio Stations 3413
Coalition for Open Doors **3658**
Coalition of Trade Workers of New Jersey; Minority Contractors
  and **3704**
Coast Indian Community of the Resighini Rancheria **79**
Coastal Band of Chumash **87**
Coastanoan Band of Carmel Mission Indians **92**
Cobb Institute of Archaeology • Mississippi State
  University **1033**
Cobblehill Books **4366**
Cochise Visitor Center and Museum **837**
Cochiti Pueblo **226**
Cockburn Island First Nation **3023**
Cocopah Tribe **16**
    Head Start Program **1068**
Code Talk American Indian Website **2130**
Coeur D'Alene Tribe 150
Cold Lake First Nation **2634**
Cold Springs Rancheria **125**
Coldwater Indian Band **2768**
Coleman Enterprises, Inc.; Earl M. **1506**
Colgate University • Native American Studies Program **1359**
College of Eastern Utah • Prehistoric Museum **1006**
College Endowments; Tribally Controlled Community • U.S.
  Department of the Interior • Bureau of Indian Affairs **4012**
College Fund; American Indian **369**
College; Indian Vocational Training - United Tribes Technical •
  U.S. Department of the Interior • Bureau of Indian
  Affairs **3999**
College; Multicultural Student's Guide to **4415**
College Placement Services **3389**

College of the Redwoods • Native American Studies Program **1343**
College of St. Scholastica • Native American Studies Program **1360**
College of Southern Idaho • Herett Museum **888**
Colleges Education Equity Grants; Tribal • U.S. Department of Agriculture • Cooperative State Research, Education and Extension Service, **3948**
Colleges Endowment Program; Tribal
    Higher Education Programs • U.S. Department of Agriculture • Cooperative State Research, Education and Extension Service **3950**
    U.S. Department of Agriculture • Cooperative State Research, Education and Extension Service **3949**
Colleges; Talent Roster of Outstanding Minority Transfer Students from Two-Year **4421**
Colleges and Universities; Assistance to Tribally Controlled Community • U.S. Department of the Interior • Bureau of Indian Affairs **3976**
Colomb First Nation; Mathias **2890**
Colombia Human Rights Information Committee **3557**
Colonial Dames Indian Nurse Scholarships **1422**
Colonial Farm of the Accokeek Foundation; National **908**
Colonial Research Center, Inc.; Indian and • Eva Butler Library **658**
Colonial Research Center; Indian and **1028**
Color; National Institute for Women of **3465**
Colorado Alliance to Restore Equality **3569**
Colorado Equal Employment Opportunity Department **4054**
Colorado Local Affairs Department • Minority Business Office **582**
Colorado Regulatory Agencies Department • Civil Rights Division **583**
Colorado River Indian Tribes
    Head Start Program **1069**
    Museum **838**
    Public Library and Archives **629**
Colorado River Tribal Council **9**
Colorado Springs Fine Arts Center **863**
    Reference Library and Taylor Museum Library **630**
Colorado State University • Center for Applied Studies in American Ethnicity **4295**
Colored People and the Indians—Quarterly; Commission for the Catholic Missions Among the **1653**
The Colors of Pride **1781**
Colorstone Association; Indian Diamond and **3537**
Colton Memorial Library; Harold S. • Museum of Northern Arizona **702**
Columbia Lake Band **2842**
Columbia University • Center for the Study of Human Rights **4367**
Columbia Urban League **3781**
Columbus Minority Business Development Center **4078, 4199**
Columbus Urban League **3612, 3755**
Columbus Urban League; Metro **3613**
Colusa Rancheria **49**
Colville Business Council **338**
Colville Confederated Tribes • Head Start Program **1141**
Colville Tribal Museum **1010**
Comanche Tribe **273**
Combating Racism **4457**
Commission Against Discrimination; Massachusetts **4118**
Commission for the Catholic Missions Among the Colored People and the Indians—Quarterly **1653**
Commission on State-Tribal Relations **3358**
Committee for Action for Rural Indians **3381**
Committee for Human Rights; American **3495**
Committee on Professional Ethics and Academic Freedom **3382**
Committee on Professional Ethics, Rights and Freedom **3382**
Common Action for Racial Equality **3684**
A Common Destiny **1782**
Common Destiny Alliance **3383**
A Common Destiny Vol. 2: The Hopi Prophecy **1783**
Commune-A-Key Publishing, Inc. **4368**
Communications Association; Indigenous **3413**
Community Action; Native Americans for **433**
Community Assistance Unit; New York City **4170**
Community Board; Native American **3474**
Community Concerns; Euclid **3758**

Community Development Agencies; Directory of Planning and **1606**
Community Development; Center for Indian • Humboldt State University **1026**
Community Development Department; Mississippi Economic and • Minority Business Office **4139**
Community Development Department; Tennessee Economic and • Minority Business Enterprise Division **4238**
Community Housing Resource Board; Long Island **3738**
Community Medicine; W. K. Kellogg Foundation Fellowships in **4350**
Community Research and Education Center **1023**
Community Services Office; Lansing Human Relations and **4123**
Community Tribal Schools; Association of **3366**
Comox Indian Band **2709**
Complaints Review Agency; Equal Employment Opportunity Compliance and • U.S. Department of Defense • Department of the Army **3850**
Completing Our Circle **1784, 3320**
Concerned Aboriginal Women **3321**
Concerned American Indian Parents **3384**
Conehatta Elementary School **1217**
Confederated Salish and Kootenai Tribal Council • Tribal Council **195**
Confederated Salish and Kootenai Tribes • Head Start Program **1095**
Confederated Tribes of Coos, Lower Umpqua, and Suislaw Indians **297**
Confederated Tribes of the Grande Ronde Tribe **299**
Confederated Tribes of Siletz Indians • Head Start Program **1131**
Confederated Tribes of the Umatilla Indian Reservation **300**
Confederated Tribes of the Warm Springs Reservation **303**
    Head Start Program **1132**
Congressional Empowerment Caucus • U.S. Congress **3834**
Congressional Friends of Human Rights Monitors **3385**
Congressional Human Rights Caucus • U.S. Congress • U.S. House of Representatives **3835**
Congressional Native American Caucus • U.S. Congress • U.S. House of Representatives **529**
Connecticut Children and Families Department • Affirmation Action Division **4057**
Connecticut Civil Liberties Union **3575**
Connecticut Civil Liberties Union Foundation **3575**
Connecticut Environmental Protection Department • Affirmative Action Division **4058**
Connecticut Human Rights and Opportunities Commission **4059**
Connecticut Social Services Department • Affirmative Action Division **4060**
Connecticut State Board of Education • Affirmation Action Office **4061**
Connecticut; Urban League of Southwestern **3577**
Conquista **1785**
Conseil Attikamek-Montagnais **3066**
Conseil de la Nation Algonquine Anishnabeg **3068**
Conseil de la Nation Atikamekw **3061**
Conservancy; Archaeological **3364**
Consolidated Tribal Government Program • U.S. Department of the Interior • Bureau of Indian Affairs **3979**
Consortium for Graduate Study in Management **3386**
Consortium Graduate Study Management Fellowships for Minorities **4313**
Constance Lake First Nation **2933**
Constitutional Law; Center for Human Rights and **3534**
Construction and Repair of Indian Detention Facilities • U.S. Department of the Interior • Bureau of Indian Affairs **3980**
Contemporary and Native American Readings **1786**
Content Communications **4369**
Continental Confederation of Adopted Indians **3387**
Continental Society Daughters of Indian Wars Scholarship **1423**
Contract Compliance Division; Equal Employment Opportunity and • Kentucky Finance and Administration Cabinet **4101**
Contractors Assistance Project; Minority **3437**
Contractors Bond Assurance Fund of Kentucky; Minority **3644**
Contractors and Coalition of Trade Workers of New Jersey; Minority **3704**
Contrary Warriors: A Film of the Crow Tribe **1787**

Control of Violence and Extremism; Institute for Prevention
   and 3498
A Conversation with Vine Deloria, Jr. 1788
Cook College and Theological School • Mary Mildred McCarthy
   Library 631
Cook Inlet Historical Society 2399
Cook Inlet Native Association 391
Cook Inlet Tribal Council • Head Start Program 2423
Cook's Ferry Band 2822
Cooperative; National Native American 1546, 3469
Coos, Lower Umpqua, and Suislaw Indians; Confederated
   Tribes of 297
Coquille Indian Tribe 298
Cornell University 1361
      American Indian Studies Program 1362
Coronado-Quivira Museum 901
Coronado State Monument 935
Corporate Orientation Program 3389
Corporate Scholars Program; NACME 4336
Corporate Sponsored Scholarships for Minority Undergraduate
   Physics Majors 4314
Corpus Christi Minority Business Development Center 3799,
   4245
Correll Collection; J.L. 708
Cortina Rancheria 44
Cosmit Band of Mission Indians; Inaja and 113
Costano Books 1497
Costanoan-Ohlone Indian Canyon Resource 2131
Costanoan People; Indian Canyon Nation of 68
Cote First Nation 366 3125
Cottonwood Day School 1165
Couchiching First Nation 2953
Council for Alternatives to Stereotyping in Entertainment 3388
Council on Career Development for Minorities 3389
Council of Energy Resource Tribes 3390
Council for Indian Education 392, 1498
Council on Interracial Books for Children, Inc. 4370
Council for Native American Indians 3391
Council Oak Books 1499
Council for Opportunity in Graduate Management
   Education 3392
Council on Social Work Education Minority Fellowships 4315
Council of Three Rivers American Indian Center 512
Council of Urban League Executives 3669
Council for Yukon Indians 3267
Counselor Certification; Southwest Indian Substance
   Abuse 436
Counselors Association; National Indian 414
County of Los Angeles Public Library • American Indian
   Resource Center 632
Court Judges Association; National American Indian 3450
Courts; Tribal • U.S. Department of the Interior • Bureau of
   Indian Affairs 4009
*Coushatta Indians; Journey to the Sky: A History of the
   Alabama* 1904
Coushatta Tribe of Louisiana 157
Coushatta Tribe of Texas; Alabama- 320
      Indian Museum 1002
Covenant; Center for the Advancement of the 3372
Covington: Native American Indian; Lucy 1926
Cow Creek Band of Umpqua Indians 301
Cowessess First Nation 3104
Cowichan First Nation 2717
Coyote Valley Reservation 104
CPAs; Minority 4409
Crafts Association; Indian Arts and 3409
Crafts Board; Indian Arts and 874
      U.S. Department of the Interior 762
Crafts Board; U.S. Indian Arts and 546
Crafts Center; Museum of the Plains Indian and 927
Crafts Center; Sioux Indian Museum and 997
Crafts Center; Southern Plains Indian Museum and 990
Crafts; Hopi Indian Arts and 1861
Crafts—Source Directory; American Indian and Alaska Native
   Arts and 1594, 2450
Crafts; Southwest Indian Arts and 2068
Crafts; Trust for Native American Cultures and 1580
Craftsmanship; Heritage of 1851
Craig Community Association 2189
Cranford Historical Society • Museum Library 633
Crazy Horse; American Indian Collection: Spirit of 1725

Crazy Horse Memorial • Library 634
Crazy Horse Memorial Foundation 393
Crazy Horse School 1281
Cree Business Committee; Chippewa- 190
Cree Cultural Centre; Ojibway- 3275
Cree First Nation; Chapleau 2937
Cree First Nation; Loon River 2651
Cree First Nation; Mikisew 2626
Cree First Nation; Missanabie 2958
Cree First Nation; Split Lake 2897
Cree First Nation; Woodland 2618
Cree Hunters of Mistassini 3322
Cree Nation of Chisasibi 3052
Cree Nation; Cumberland House 3112
Cree Nation of Eastmain 3053
Cree Nation; Kehewin 2615
Cree Nation; Little Red River 2637
Cree Nation of Mistissini 3073
Cree Nation of Nemaska 3076
Cree Nation No. 440; Enoch 2624
Cree Nation of Ouji-Bougoumou 3080
Cree Nation; Peter Ballantyne 3145
Cree Nation; Shoal Lake of the 3141
Cree Nation of Waskaganish 3089
Cree Nation of Waswanipi 3091
Cree Nation of Wemindji 3093
Cree Nation of Whapmagoostui 3096
(Creek) Art; 1,000 Years of Muscogee 2004
Creek Council House Museum 979
      Library • Creek Indian Memorial Association 635
Creek Indian Memorial Association 394
      Creek Council House Museum • Library 635
Creek Indians; Poarch Band of 1
Creek Nation; Muscogee 280
Creek Nation of Oklahoma • Head Start Program 1125
(Creek) People; Folklore of the Muscogee 1825
Criminal Justice; Opportunities in 4462
Crooked Creek; Native Village of 2190
Crooked Tree Arts Council 911
Cross and Feather News 1654
Cross Lake First Nation 2855
Crow Canyon Archaeological Center 1024
Crow Creek Reservation High School 1282
Crow Creek Sioux Tribe 310
      Head Start Program 1134
Crow Dog 1789
Crow Dog's Paradise 1790
Crow Tribal Council • Head Start Program 1096
Crow Tribe 192
Crow Tribe; Contrary Warriors: A Film of the 1787
Crowfoot; The Ballad of 3315
Crown Dance and Ba'ts'oosee; The Origin of the 2005
Crownpoint Community School 1232
Crownpoint Institute of Technology 1327
Crusade Scholarships 4316
Crystal Boarding School 1233
Cultural Affairs Department; South Dakota Education and •
   Education Division • Equal Employment Opportunity 4234
Cultural Art; Bowers Museum of • Research Library 617
Cultural Arts Council; Zuni 491
Cultural Arts Program; All Tribes 3542
Cultural Center; Akwesasne Library 599
Cultural Center; Azurite Cherokee 501
Cultural Center; Hopi 842
Cultural Center; Indian Pueblo 367, 939
Cultural Center; Lac du Flambeau Chippewa Museum
   and 1014
Cultural Center and Museums; Ponca City 987
      Library 731
Cultural Center; Natives of the Four Directions 3485
Cultural Center; Polynesian 2528
Cultural Center; Sheldon Museum and 2390, 2405
Cultural Center; South East Alaska Indian 2359
Cultural Center; Southern Ute Indian 448, 869
Cultural Center; Yakima Nation 1013
Cultural Centre; Kwagiulth Museum and 3213
Cultural Centre; Ojibway- Cree 3275
Cultural Centre; U'Mista 3216
Cultural Contrast; Navajo: A Study in 1976
Cultural Education Centre; Woodland Indian 3228

Cultural Education Society and Native Heritage Park; Secwepemc **3175**
Cultural Education Society; Secwepemc **3278**
Cultural Exchange Committee; Native American **499**
Cultural Grants **3259**
Cultural Heritage; How and Where to Research Your Ethnic-American **4408**
Cultural and Historical Events for Native American Children **3721**
Cultural Non Profit Society; Mid-Winter Pow-Wow and **485**
Cultural Program; Native American Resource Center Elementary-Secondary Native American Student **494**
Cultural and Research Center; Makah **1011, 1032**
Cultural Society of North Florida; American Indian **495**
Cultural Survival Center **4296**
Cultural Survival, Inc. **4289, 4371**
Culture; Ah-Tah-Thi-Ki Museum of Seminole History and **878**
Culture and Art; National Council for **3462**
Culture and Arts Development; Institute of American Indian and Alaska Native **1029, 2144**
Culture and Arts Program; Native Hawaiian **3484**
Culture; Centre for Aboriginal Education, Research, and • Carleton University **3234**
Culture Division • Native American Branch • Culture and Recreation; Ontario Ministry of Citizenship, **3201**
Culture and Education; Institute for Native Pacific **2529**
Culture; Eskimos: A Changing **2488**
Culture; Expressions of Eskimo **2489**
Culture; Hawk, I'm Your Brother: Stories of American Indian **1847, 2072**
Culture, Heritage and Citizenship, and Multiculturalism; Manitoba Minister for **4282**
Culture; Marquette Mission Park and Museum of Ojibwa **913**
Culture; Museum of Indian Arts and **941**
    Laboratory of Anthropology **942**
Culture; Museum of Ojibwa **1544**
Culture; The Mystery of the Lost Red Paint People: The Discovery of a Prehistoric North American Sea **1948**
Culture National Historic Park; Chaco **934**
Culture National Historic Park; Hopewell **968**
Culture and Recreation; Ontario Ministry of Citizenship, • Culture Division • Native American Branch **3201**
Culture Research Center; American Indian **370, 1018**
    Museum **992**
Culture of the Sioux; The Art of Being Indian: Filmed Aspects of the **1747**
Culture Studies; Sonny Billie Foundation for Native **3589**
Culture: The Other Way to Listen; Stories of American Indian **2073**
Culture: The Way to Start a Day; Stories of American Indian **2074**
Cultures and Crafts; Trust for Native American **1580**
Cultures; Institute for the Study of American **3419**
Cultures; Museum of Native American **1012**
Cultures of Northern Arizona; Ancient Indian **1741**
Cultures in the U.S.A.: Part One; Native American **1953**
Cultures in the U.S.A.: Part Two; Native American **1954**
Cultures; Women Within Two **3347**
Cumberland House Cree Nation **3112**
Cummings Memorial Library; Dorothy • Bible College; American Indian **602**
Curriculum Development, Teacher Training and Recruitment; Native Hawaiian • U.S. Department of Education • Office of Elementary and Secondary Education **2533**
Curse of the Lost Gold Mine **1791**
Curtis and the North American Indian; The Shadow Catcher: Edward S. **2053**
Curtis; North American Indians and Edward S. **1996**
Curve Lake First Nation **2942**
Custer Collection; General George Armstrong • Monroe County Library System **695**
Cuyapaipe Band of Mission Indians **23**
D-Q University **1311**
    Native American Studies Program **1344**
Dakota Name-Giving; I Am Different From My Brother: **1871**
Dakota Nation; Wahpeton **3147**
Dakota Ojibway Tribal Council **2851**
Dakota Plains First Nation **2887**
Dakota/Sioux First Nation (Moose Woods); Whitecap **3153**
Dakota Tipi First Nation **2888**

Dakota Wesleyan University • Native American Studies Program **1363**
Dakota Women of All Red Nations **395**
Dallas/Ft. Worth Intertribal Association **524**
Dallas/Ft. Worth Minority Business Development Center **4246**
Dallas Urban League **3800**
Dams on Indian Lands; Safety of • U.S. Department of the Interior • Bureau of Indian Affairs **4006**
Dance Association; Pacific **2524**
Dance; Foundation for Pacific **2524**
Dance to Give Thanks **1792**
Dance I and II; Iroquois Social **1900**
Dancers Family Club; Talako Indian **453**
Dancers; Thunderbird American Indian **3506**
Dances, New Dancers; Old **2505**
Dances: Southwestern Pomo Indians; Kashia Men's **1905**
Dancing Awake the Drum **1793**
Dancing Feather **1500**
Dancing Feathers **1794**
D'Arcy McNickle Center for American Indian History • Newberry Library **1041**
D'Arcy McNickle Center for the History of the American Indian Fello wships **1460**
Dartmouth College
    Institute of Arctic Studies **2414, 2611**
    Native American Studies Program **1364**
Daughters of the Anasazi **1795**
Daughters of the Country **3323**
Daughters of Indian Wars Scholarship; Continental Society **1423**
Dauphin River First Nation **2869**
Davenport Civil Rights Department **4096**
Davis Library; Harwell Goodwin • Special Collections • Samford University **739**
Dax Ka Nation **2675**
The Day Glo Warrior **1796**
Day Star First Nation **3148**
Dayton Human Relations Council **4372**
Dayton Urban League **3756**
De Soto National Memorial • Library • U.S. Department of the Interior • National Park Service **765**
Dease River Band (British Columbia/Yukon) **2727**
Deer Lake First Nation **2944**
Deering; Native Village of **2191**
Defense of Freedom; California Council for the **3559**
Defense Fund; OGCA Civil Rights **3761**
Delaware First Nation; Munsee- **2988**
Delaware State Department • Human Relations Division **584**
Delaware of the Thames First Nation (Moravian Town) **3031**
Delaware Transportation Department • Equal Employment Opportunity and Civil Rights Office **585**
Delaware Tribe of Eastern Oklahoma **266**
Delaware Tribe of Western Oklahoma **263**
Delaware Valley Minority Business Resource Council **3775**
Deloria, Jr.; A Conversation with Vine **1788**
Dene Nation **2920**
Dene Nation; Buffalo River **3115**
Dene Tha' First Nation **2619**
Denesuline Nation; Fond Du Lac **3117**
Dennehotso Boarding School **1166**
Dental Student Scholarship Program; Minority **4331**
Denver Minority Business Development Center **4055**
Department of Civil Rights, AFL-CIO **3393**
Des Plaines Citizens Rights Committee **3626**
Desert Regions: Nomads and Traders **1797**
Detention Facilities; Construction and Repair of Indian • U.S. Department of the Interior • Bureau of Indian Affairs **3980**
Detroit American Indian Center **3487**
Detroit Human Rights Office **4121**
Detroit Public Library • History and Travel Department **636**
Detroit Urban League **3670**
Development Agencies; Directory of Planning and Community **1606**
Development; American Indian Research and **1020**
Development Center; Baton Rouge Business **3649**
Development Center; Brooklyn Minority Business **3712**
Development Center; Fresno Minority Business **3529**
Development Center; Gary Minority Business **3631**
Development Center; Newark Minority Business **3708**
Development Corporation; New York Empire State • Minority and Women's Business Development Office **4171**

Development Corporation; United Sioux Tribes of South Dakota **516**
Development Council; Northwest Minority Supplier **3815**
Development Institute; First Nations **3397**
Development; National Center for American Indian Enterprise **409**
Development; Seventh Generation Fund for Indian **425**
Devils Lake Sioux Tribe **258**
Diablo Books **1501**
Diamond and Colorstone Association; Indian **3537**
Dickson Mounds Museum **893**
Diederich Award **1468**
Diederich Landscape Award **1468**
Dignity Development Corp.; Women for Human Rights and **3716**
Dilcon Boarding School **1167**
Dillingham; Native Village of **2193**
Dine Community College **1309, 2132**
Dineh: The People **1798**
Dinshyin **1799**
Directory of Indian Owned Businesses **4401**
Directory of Minority Arts Organizations **4402**
Directory of Minority Media **4403**
Directory of Montana's American Indians and Others **1600**
Directory of Native Education Resources in the Appalachian Region **1601**
Directory of Native Education Resources in the Far West Region **1602**
Directory of Native Education Resources in the Mid-Continent Region **1603**
Directory of Native Education Resources in the Northwest Region **1604, 2453**
Directory of Native Education Resources in the Southeast Region **1605**
Directory of People of Color in the Visual Arts **4404**
Directory of Planning and Community Development Agencies **1606**
Directory of Statewide Indian Programs **1607**
Directory of Substance Abuse Organizations in Canada **3287**
Disadvantaged Business Enterprise Directory; North Dakota Department of Transportation **4419**
DISCovering Multicultural America **4479**
Discrimination Complaints Branch • U.S. Department of Justice • Immigration and Naturalization Service • Office of Equal Employment Opportunity **3891**
Discrimination Complaints Division • U.S. National Aeronautics and Space Administration • Office of Equal Opportunity Programs **3927**
Discrimination Division; Anti- • Utah Industrial Commission **4259**
Discrimination; First Coast United Against **3591**
Discrimination; Massachusetts Commission Against **4118**
Discrimination and Preferences; Californians Against **3533**
Displaced Homemaker Scholarships; Association on American Indian Affairs **1416**
Dissertation Fellowships for Minorities; Ford Foundation Predoctoral and **4319**
Distant Voice...Thunder Words **1800**
District of Columbia Department of Human Rights and Minority Business Development **3583**
District of Columbia Diversity and Special Services Office **4062**
District of Columbia Human Rights Commission **4063**
District of Columbia Human Rights and Minority Business Development Office **4064**
District of Columbia Student Coalition Against Apartheid and Racism **3584**
Ditidaht Indian Band **2787**
Diversity Development Office • U.S. Postal Service **3939**
Diversity Division; Equal Employment Opportunity and • U.S. Department of the Treasury • Internal Revenue Service **3905**
Diversity Policy Division; Affirmative Employment and • U.S. National Aeronautics and Space Administration • Office of Equal Opportunity Programs **3926**
Diversity and Special Services Office; District of Columbia **4062**
The Divided Trail: A Native American Odyssey **1801**
Dlo'Ay Azhi Community School **1234**
Do We Want Us To? **1802**
Dr. John Woodenlegs Memorial Library • Dull Knife Memorial College **638**

Doctor, Lawyer, Indian Chief **3324**
Document Collection; Sac and Fox **737**
Documentation Project; Fourth World **3400, 4485**
Documents, Serials, Music, and Illustrations; California Indians: Primary Resources: A Guide to Manuscripts, **1599**
d'Odanak; Musee des Abenakis • Societe historique d'Odanak **3231**
d'Odanak; Societe historique • d'Odanak; Musee des Abenakis **3231**
Doig River Indian Band **2807**
Dokis First Nation **3036**
Domestic Apartheid; Citizens to Abolish **3773**
Don M. Chase **1502**
Dorothy Cummings Memorial Library • Bible College; American Indian **602**
Douglas County Museum • Lavola Bakken Memorial Library **637**
Douglas Indian Association **2225**
Douglas Indian Band **2730**
Dream Catchers **1803**
Dream Dances of the Kashia Pomo **1804**
Dream Weavers Publishing **1503**
The Dreamer **2133**
Dreamspeaker **1805**
Dresslerville Colony of the Washoe Tribe of Nevada and California **209**
Driftpile First Nation **2621**
The Drum **1806**
The Drum Is the Heart **1807**
Dry Creek Rancheria **62**
Dubuque Human Rights Office **4097**
Duckwater Shoshone Elementary School **1224**
Duckwater Shoshone Tribe of the Duckwater Reservation **204**
Dull Knife Memorial College **1316**
   Dr. John Woodenlegs Memorial Library **638**
   Native American Studies Program **1345**
Dumont Institute of Native Studies and Applied Research; Gabriel **3268**
Duncan's First Nation **2617**
Dunlap Band of Mono Indians **53**
Dunseith Day School **1262**
Durham Equal Opportunity/Equity Assurance Office **4187**
Durland Alternatives Library • Policy; Center for Religion, Ethics and Social **623**
Dzilth-na-o-dith-hle Community School **1235**
Eabametoong First Nation **3004**
Eagle Butte School; Cheyenne- **1280**
The Eagle and the Condor **1808**
Eagle Lake First Nation **2948**
Eagle; Village of **2194**
Eaglecrafts Inc. **1504**
Eagle's View Publishing **1505**
Earl M. Coleman Enterprises, Inc. **1506**
Earlham College • Friends Collection **639**
Early Man in North America **1809**
Earth Art Inc. **1507**
Earth; For Mother **3398**
The Earth Is Our Home **1810**
Earthshapers **1811**
East Tennessee Discovery Center • Library **640**
East Tennessee Indian League **518**
Easter in Igloolik: Peter's Story **2479**
Eastern Band of Cherokee **253**
Eastern New Mexico University • Blackwater Draw Museum **936**
Eastern Shawnee Tribe of Oklahoma **189**
Eastern Tribes; United South and **429**
Eastern Washington State Historical Society **1508**
Eastmain; Cree Nation of **3053**
Eastmain First Nation **3054**
Ebb and Flow First Nation **2858**
Ebbing; Thomas Leonard **1500**
Eclectic Travel Editions **4373**
EcoJustice Network **4480**
Economic Alternatives; Center for Women's **3740**
Economic Development Department; Boston • Minority and Women Business Enterprises Office **4115**
Economic Development Department; Cincinnati • Small Business Division **4194**
Economic Development Department; Louisiana • Minority and Women's Business Division **4105**

Economic Development Department; Massachusetts • Minority and Women's Business Division **4119**

Economic Development Department; New Jersey Commerce and • Development for Small Business, Women and Minorities Division **4159**

Economic Development Department; Utah Community and • Indian Affairs Division **598**

Economic Development; Indian • U.S. Department of the Interior • Bureau of Indian Affairs **3988**

Economic Development and Policy Planning Division; New Orleans • Small and Disadvantaged Business Office **4108**

Economic Opportunity Office • Vermont Human Services Agency **4260**

Economic Rights; Institute for Social and **3726**

Economically Disadvantaged Businesses (7(J) Development Assistant Program); Management and Technical Assistance for Socially and • Business Administration; U.S. Small **4031**

Economics; American Economic Association/ Federal Reserve System Minority Graduate Fellowships in **4306**

ECOSOC **3406**

Edge of the Cedars State Park **1007**

Edison Chiloquin Story; Return of the Raven—The **2038**

Editions Ltd. **2589**

Editorial Training Program; Times Mirror Minority **4348**

Edna Yelland; CLA Scholarship for Minority Students in Memory of **4312**

Education Assistance for American Indians and Alaska Natives **1608, 2454**

Education Assistance Program Grant; Cheyenne- Arapaho Higher **1421**

Education Association; National Indian **415**

Education Association; Native American Science **3482**

Education Awards; CN Native **3258**

Education Awards for Native Students; Petro-Canada **3260**

Education Center; American Indian **498**

Education Center; American Indian Science and **384**

Education Center; Community Research and **1023**

Education; Center for Indian • Arizona State University **1021**

Education Centre; Woodland Indian Cultural **3228**

Education; Coalition for Indian **410**

Education Consortia; Eisenhower Regional Mathematics and Science • U.S. Department of Education • Office of Assistant Secretary for Educational Research and Improvement **3954**

Education Consortium; American Indian Higher **375**

Education; Council for Indian **392, 1498**

Education; Council for Opportunity in Graduate Management **3392**

Education Directory: Organizations and Resources for Educators of Native Americans; Native **1619**

Education Division; Indian • North Dakota Public Instruction Department **593**

Education Equity Grants; Tribal Colleges • U.S. Department of Agriculture • Cooperative State Research, Education and Extension Service, **3948**

Education (FACE); Indian Child and Family • U.S. Department of the Interior • Bureau of Indian Affairs **3986**

Education Facilities, Operations, and Maintenance; Indian • Office of Indian Education Programs • U.S. Department of the Interior • Bureau of Indian Affairs **3989**

Education Foundation; Bristol Bay Native Corp. **2352**

Education Fund; Minority Business Enterprise Legal Defense and **3442**

Education Grant; Bureau of Indian Affairs Higher **1417**

Education Grants; Presbyterian Church Native American **1447, 2438**

Education; Horace Mann Bond Center for Equal • University of Massachusetts **4396**

Education on Human Rights; Institute for Research and **3418**

Education; Indian Adult • U.S. Department of the Interior • Bureau of Indian Affairs **3985**

Education Learning Center; Native Hawaiian Community-Based • U.S. Department of Education • Office of Elementary and Secondary Education **2532**

Education Minority Fellowships; Council on Social Work **4315**

Education; Montana Council for Indian **392**

Education and Multicultural Scholars Program (Minority Scholars Program); Higher • U.S. Department of Agriculture • Cooperative State Research, Education, and Extension Service **3947**

Education; National Center for American Indian Alternative **384**

Education; National Coalition for Indian **410**

Education; Native Hawaiian Vocational • U.S. Department of Education • Office of Vocational and Adult Education **2536**

Education Policy Center; American Indian • Pennsylvania State University **1044**

Education for Preschool Children (Alaska Native Education); Alaska Native Home Based • U.S. Department of Education • Office of Elementary and Secondary Education **2366**

Education Program; Indian Science Teachers **3482**

Education Program; Native Hawaiian Higher **2570**

Education Project; Southwest Voter Registration **3503**

Education, Research, and Culture; Centre for Aboriginal • Carleton University **3234**

Education Resource Center; Native American Women Health **3474**

Education Resources in the Appalachian Region; Directory of Native **1601**

Education Resources in the Far West Region; Directory of Native **1602**

Education; Resources for Indian Student **440**

Education Resources in the Mid-Continent Region; Directory of Native **1603**

Education Resources in the Northwest Region; Directory of Native **1604, 2453**

Education Resources in the Southeast Region; Directory of Native **1605**

(Education and the Sioux); Woonspe **2121**

Education and Small Schools; ERIC Clearinghouse on Rural **1025**

    Appalachia Educational Laboratory **641**

Education Society and Native Heritage Park; Secwepemc Cultural **3175**

Education Society; Secwepemc Cultural **3278**

Educational Access; National Consortium for **3461**

Educational Enrichment Grant; Hopi Tribe **1429**

Educational Opportunities Section • U.S. Department of Justice • Civil Rights Division **3884**

Educational Planning, Curriculum Development, Teacher Training, and Recruitment Program; Alaska Native • U.S. Department of Education • Office of Elementary and Secondary Education, **2365**

Educational Resources Information Center (ERIC) **4477**

Educational Service Inc.; Native American • Central Library and Resource Center **704**

Educational Service; Native American **3475**

Educational Services College; Native American **3475**

Educational Society; Native American Traditions Ideas and Values **451**

Educator of the Year Award; Indian **1463**

Educators Federation; Indian **3410**

Educators; National Association of Medical Minority **3452**

Educators; National Council of BIA **3410**

EduQuest Connections **4435**

Edward S. Curtis and the North American Indian; The Shadow Catcher: **2053**

Edward S. Curtis; North American Indians and **1996**

Eek; Native Village of **2195**

Eel Ground Indian Band **2914**

Eel River Bar Band **2910**

EEOC Policies and Programs **4481**

Effigy Mounds National Monument **899**

Egegik Village **2196**

Ehattesaht Tribe **2691**

Eight Northern Pueblos, Inc. • Head Start Program **1102**

Eisenhower Regional Mathematics and Science Education Consortia • U.S. Department of Education • Office of Assistant Secretary for Educational Research and Improvement **3954**

Eiteljorg Museum of American Indian and Western Art **897**

Eklutna Native Village **2183**

Ekuk; Native Village of **2197**

El Morro National Monument **937**

El Paso Minority Business Development Center **4247**

Elder Voices **1655**

Eldercare Information and Referral; National Directory for **1616**

Elderly and Families; Services to Indian Children, • U.S. Department of the Interior • Bureau of Indian Affairs **4007**

Elem Indian Colony of Pomo Indians **45**

Elim; Native Village of **2198**

Elizabeth M. MacDonell Memorial Library • Historical Society; Allen County **600**

Elk Valley Rancheria **51**

Elko Band of The Te-Moak Tribe of Western Shoshone Indians **205**

Ely Colony Council **207**

Ely ("Eli") S. Parker Award **1461**

Emergence **1812**

Emergency Aid and Health Professions Scholarships **1424, 2435**

Emergency Relief; World **3512**

Emissary Foundation **3394**

Emissary Foundation International **3394**

Emmonak Village **2199**

Employee Development and Equal Employment Opportunity Division • Tennessee Personnel Department **4241**

Employment Discrimination - Equal Pay Act • Equal Employment Opportunity Commission; U.S. **4025**

Employment Discrimination Project Contracts - Indian Tribes • Equal Employment Opportunity Commission; U.S. **4027**

Employment Discrimination—State and Local Fair Practices Agency Contracts • U.S. Equal Employment Opportunity Commission **4028**

Employment Discrimination—Title VII of the Civil Rights Act of 1964 • U.S. Equal Employment Opportunity Commission **4029**

Employment Litigation Section • U.S. Department of Justice • Civil Rights Division **3885**

Employment Opportunity Specialist • U.S. Department of Health and Human Services • Office of Public Health and Science • Research Grants Division **3873**

Empowerment Caucus; Congressional • U.S. Congress **3834**

Encyclopedia of Human Ideas on Ultimate Reality and Meaning; Institute for **3416**

An End to Isolation **1813**

End of the Trail: The American Plains Indian **1814**

Endangered Species on Indian Lands • U.S. Department of the Interior • Bureau of Indian Affairs **3981**

Enemy Swim Day School **1283**

Energy Resource Tribes; Council of **3390**

Engineering Fellowships for Minorities; GEM Master's **4320**

Engineering Fellowships for Minorities; GEM Ph.D. **4321**

Engineering; National Action Council for Minorities in **3448**

Engineering; National Institute for Resources in Science and **3464**

Engineering, Science and Health: A Network of Minority Professional Associations; Mathematics, **3439**

Engineering Society (AISES); American Indian Science and **385**

Engineering Society; AISESnet: American Indian Science and **2126**

Engineering Society; American Indian Science and **2125**

English River Band **3142**

Enoch Cree Nation No. 440 **2624**

Enterprise Development; National Center for American Indian **409**

Enterprises; Texas Association of Minority Business **3796**

Entertainment; Council for Alternatives to Stereotyping in **3388**

Entrepreneurs Network Association; Minority **3572**

Environment, Health and Natural Resources Department • Health Director's Office • Minority Health Office **4188**

Environment of Indigenous People; Centre for Nutrition and the **3236**

Environment; Introduce Science to Students Using the **3482**

Environment; Native Americans for a Clean **3483**

Environment and Natural Resources Branch Library • U.S. Department of Justice **783**

Environmental Council; National Tribal **3471**

Environmental Groups Directory; 1994-95 People of Color **4501**

Environmental Policy; Institute for • University of Guelph **4300**

Environmental Quality Services - Indian Programs • U.S. Department of the Interior • Bureau of Indian Affairs **3982**

Environmental Restoration/Waste Management Library • Yakama Indian Nation **825**

Equal Employment Office • Virginia Commerce and Trade Office • Employment Commission **4265**

Equal Employment Office; Augusta **4076**

Equal Employment Opportunity • Cultural Affairs Department; South Dakota Education and • Education Division **4234**

Equal Employment Opportunity/Affirmative Action Division • New Jersey Personnel Department **4161**

Equal Employment Opportunity and Affirmative Action Office • Civil Service Department; Michigan **4127**

Equal Employment Opportunity and Better Housing Office; Chattanooga **597**

Equal Employment Opportunity and Civil Rights Office
Delaware Transportation Department **585**
U.S. Department of State **3896**

Equal Employment Opportunity Commission; U.S. **3914**
Employment Discrimination - Equal Pay Act **4025**
Employment Discrimination Project Contracts - Indian Tribes **4027**

Equal Employment Opportunity Compliance and Complaints Review Agency • U.S. Department of Defense • Department of the Army **3850**

Equal Employment Opportunity and Contract Compliance Division • Kentucky Finance and Administration Cabinet **4101**

Equal Employment Opportunity Department; Colorado **4054**

Equal Employment Opportunity and Diversity Division • U.S. Department of the Treasury • Internal Revenue Service **3905**

Equal Employment Opportunity Division
North Dakota Labor Department **4192**
Virginia Transportation Office • Administration Department **4269**

Equal Employment Opportunity Division; Alaska **4038**

Equal Employment Opportunity Division; Employee Development and • Tennessee Personnel Department **4241**

Equal Employment Opportunity Division; New York State **4177**

Equal Employment Opportunity and Fair Housing Office; Albany **592**

Equal Employment Opportunity Office
Kansas Human Resources Department **587**
Michigan Transportation Department **4130**
Nevada Employment Training and Rehabilitation Department **4153**
North Carolina Environmental, Health and Natural Resources Department **4190**
Ohio Health Department **4204**
Oklahoma Employment Security Commission **4208**
Pennsylvania Education Department • Postsecondary and Higher Education Office **4218**
Rhode Island Transportation Department **4231**
U.S. Department of Commerce • Bureau of the Census **3840**
U.S. Department of Veterans Affairs **3910**

Equal Employment Opportunity Office; Cincinnati **4195**

Equal Employment Opportunity Office; Civil Personnel Policy/ • U.S. Department of Defense • Department of the Navy **3852**

Equal Employment Opportunity Programs Group • U.S. Department of Health and Human Services **3860**

Equal Employment Opportunity Staff
U.S. Department of Health and Human Services • Health Care Financing Administration **3861**
U.S. Department of the Interior • Bureau of Indian Affairs **3881**
U.S. Department of Justice • Drug Enforcement Agency **3890**

Equal Employment Opportunity and Training Section • Ohio Agricultural Department **4200**

Equal Opportunity **4458**

Equal Opportunity, Affirmative Action and Civil Rights Division • Human Services Department; Minnesota **4137**

Equal Opportunity Agency • U.S. Department of Defense • Department of the Army **3851**

Equal Opportunity Bureau • Pennsylvania Transportation Department **4222**

Equal Opportunity Commission; Georgia **4080**

Equal Opportunity Commission; Nebraska **4150**

Equal Opportunity Development Division • New York State Labor Department **4182**

Equal Opportunity Division
Human Resources Department; Maryland **4114**
Minnesota Employee Relations Department **4135**

Equal Opportunity/Equity Assurance Office; Durham **4187**

Equal Opportunity Office
New York Mental Retardation and Developmental Disabilities Agency **4172**
U.S. Department of Defense
Department of the Air Force • Manpower, Reserve Affairs, Installations, and Environment **3846**
Personnel and Readiness **3854**
U.S. Department of the Treasury • U.S. Customs Service **3908**

Equal Opportunity Office; Anchorage **2385**
Equal Opportunity Office; Flint **4122**
Equal Opportunity Office; Lincoln Human Rights/ **4149**
Equal Opportunity and Organizational Management Division •
    U.S. Department of the Treasury • Internal Revenue
    Service **3906**
Equal Pay Act; Employment Discrimination - • Equal
    Employment Opportunity Commission; U.S. **4025**
Equal Rights Commission; Nevada **4154**
Equal Rights Congress **3395**
Equality; Hillsborough Organization for Progress and **3600**
Equality; People's Organization for Social **3650**
Equity and Access Office • Rhode Island Education
    Department • Elementary and Secondary Office **4229**
Equity; Alabama Coalition for **3515**
Equity Associates; Miami **3593**
Equity Assurance Office; Durham Equal Opportunity/ **4187**
ERIC Clearinghouse on Information and Technology
    (ERIC/IT) **4477**
ERIC Clearinghouse on Rural Education and Small
    Schools **1025**
        Appalachia Educational Laboratory **641**
Erickson Award; Bonnie **1468**
Ermineskin First Nation **2638**
Ervin Stuntz **1509**
(Esketemc First Nation); Alkali Lake First Nation **2839**
Eskimo Art; World **2517**
Eskimo Artist: Kenojuak **2480**
Eskimo Association; Arizona American **2360**
Eskimo Association of Canada; Indian- **3172**
Eskimo Association, Oklahoma Chapter; American **2361**
Eskimo Community (Golovin); Chinik **2210**
Eskimo Community; Nome **2280**
Eskimo Family **2481**
The Eskimo: Fight for Life **2482**
Eskimo-Indian Olympics; World **2354**
Eskimo (Inuit) Legends Series **2483**
Eskimo Legend; Lumaaq—An **2502**
The Eskimo in Life and Legend (The Living Stone) **2484**
Eskimo Museum **3217**
Eskimo Summer **2485**
Eskimo Survival Series **2486**
Eskimo in Two Worlds; Matthew Aliuk: **2503**
Eskimo Winter **2487**
Eskimo Words for Snow **2521**
Eskimo; Yesterday, Today: The Netsilik **2518**
Eskimos: A Changing Culture **2488**
Eskimos; Association of Interior **2358**
Eskimos; High Arctic: Life with the Northernmost **2495**
Esquimalt Indian Band **2835**
Esselen Nation **119**
Essex County Urban League **3707**
Essipit First Nation **3063**
Etherington Art Centre; Agnes • Queen's University at
    Kingston **3242**
Ethics and Academic Freedom; Committee on
    Professional **3382**
Ethics, Rights and Freedom; Committee on Professional **3382**
Ethics and Social Policy; Center for Religion, • Durland
    Alternatives Library **623**
Ethnic Affairs; National Center for Urban **4386**
Ethnic-American Cultural Heritage; How and Where to
    Research Your **4408**
Ethnic Coalition of Southern California, USC Civic and
    Community Relations **3535**
Ethnic Genealogy: A Research Guide **4405**
Ethnic History; Journal of American **4428**
Ethnic NewsWatch **4482**
Ethnic, Religious, Linguistic and Other Minorities; International
    Federation for the Protection of the Rights of **3424**
Ethnic Studies Library • University of California, Berkeley **787**
Ethnicity in America; Center for the Study of Race and •
    Brown University **4293**
Ethnicity; Center for Applied Studies in American • Colorado
    State University **4295**
Ethnicity and Race in America; Center for Studies of •
    University of Colorado at Boulder **4299**
Ethnoviolence; Center for the Applied Study of Prejudice
    and **3498**
Ethnoviolence; The Prejudice Institute/ Center for the Applied
    Study of **3498**

Etolin Canoe **2400**
Etowah Indian Mounds Historical Site **885**
Euclid Community Concerns **3758**
Eufaula Dormitory **1274**
Eva Butler Library • Colonial Research Center, Inc.; Indian
    and **658**
Evansville Village **2200**
Events; Pow Wow Pages and Native **4504**
Everett Law Library; Kathrine R. • University of North Carolina
    at Chapel Hill **800**
Evergreen State College • Native American Studies
    Program **1365**
Excavation of Mound 7 **1815**
Executives; National Association of Minority Media **3454**
The Exiles **1816**
Expressions of Eskimo Culture **2489**
Extremism; Institute for Prevention and Control of Violence
    and **3498**
E.Y. Berry Library-Learning Center • Special Collections •
    Black Hills State University **615**
Eyak; Native Village of **2188**
Eyanopopi: The Heart of the Sioux **1817**
Eyes of the Spirit **2490**
Faculty Fellowships at Indiana University; Minority **4332**
Fair Employment Practices Newsletter **4483**
Fair Housing Center of Metropolitan Detroit **3671**
Fair Housing Council; Hollywood-Mid Los Angeles **3531**
Fair Housing Council; Westside **3539**
Fairbanks Native Association • Head Start Program **2424**
Fairford First Nation **2861**
Fairness Coalition; Arizonans for **3520**
Faithkeeper **1818**
Fallon Business Paiute-Shoshone Tribe **208**
Falmouth Institute Scholarship **1425**
False Pass; Native Village of **2201**
Families; Casey Journalism Center for Children and •
    University of Maryland at College Park **4301**
Families; Services to Indian Children, Elderly and • U.S.
    Department of the Interior • Bureau of Indian Affairs **4007**
Family; AIDS and the Native American **4453**
Family Club; Talako Indian Dancers **453**
Family and Community Services Office; Albuquerque • Human
    Rights Section **590**
Family and Community Violence Prevention Program (Family
    Life Centers) • U.S. Department of Health and Human
    Services • Office of Public Health and Science • Office of
    Minority Health **3964**
Family Education (FACE); Indian Child and • U.S. Department
    of the Interior • Bureau of Indian Affairs **3986**
Family Independence Agency; Michigan • Affirmative Action
    Office **4128**
(Family Life Centers); Family and Community Violence
    Prevention Program • U.S. Department of Health and Human
    Services • Office of Public Health and Science • Office of
    Minority Health **3964**
Family Services Newsletter **1656**
Famous American Indians; National Hall of Fame for **986**
Fantail Native Design **1510**
Farrell Library • Minority Resource Research Center • Kansas
    State University **671**
Father Marquette National Memorial and Museum **912**
Fayette County; Urban League of Lexington- **3646**
Fayetteville Minority Business Development Center **4189**
Federal Computer Market Report **4436**
Federal Information Exchange, Inc. **4484**
Federal Programs of Assistance to Native Americans **1609**
Federal Reserve System Minority Graduate Fellowships in
    Economics; American Economic Association/ **4306**
Federally Recognized Tribes **2134**
Fellowship Program in Academic Medicine **4317**
Fellowship Program; Julius A. Thomas **3389**
Festival Association; National Indian **416**
FFA Foundation Minority Scholarships; National **4339**
Field Directory of the California Indian Community **1610**
Field Museum • Webber Resource Center: Native Cultures of
    the Americas **642**
Field Notes **1657**
Fillmore County Historical Society • Historical Center **643**
Film Center Foundation; Anthropology **4358**
Film Commissions; Tribal **382**
Film/Video Arts **3396**

Financial Aid Available to American Indian Students; *Sources of 1530,* **1627**
Financial Aid for Native Americans **1611**
Financial Aid Programs American Indian Endowed Scholarship; Washington State Student **1454**
Fire Protection - Bureau of Indian Affairs Facilities (Fire Protection); Structural • U.S. Department of the Interior • Bureau of Indian Affairs **4008**
Fire Protection; Indian Community • U.S. Department of the Interior • Bureau of Indian Affairs **3987**
The First Americans **1819-1821**
First Americans; In Search of the **1877**
The First Americans, Part 2: Some Indians of the Southlands **1822**
First Coast United Against Discrimination **3591**
First Frontier **1823**
First Nations Development Institute **3397**
First Nations and Inuit Health Program • Health Canada **3178**
First Nations Tribal Directory **3289**
The First Perspective Online **3350**
Fish and Wildlife Commission; Great Lakes Indian **3405**
Fish and Wildlife Committee; Great Lakes Indian, **3827**
Fish, Wildlife, and Parks Programs on Indian Lands • U.S. Department of the Interior • Bureau of Indian Affairs **3983**
Fisher River First Nation **2875**
Fisheries Commission News; Northwest Indian **1676**
Fisheries and Oceans Canada • Aboriginal Affairs Office **3177**
Fishes Association; North American Native **3491**
Fishing Lake First Nation **3161**
Fishing Rights; Unresolved Indian Hunting and • U.S. Department of the Interior • Bureau of Indian Affairs **4013**
Fishing at the Stone Weir, Parts I and II **2491**
Five Civilized Tribes Foundation **396**
Five Civilized Tribes Museum **980, 1511**
Five Civilized Tribes Museum and Center for Study of Indian Territory • Library **644**
Five Flower Press **1512**
Five Sandoval Indian Pueblos, Inc. • Head Start Program **1103**
Five Star Publications **4374**
Flambeau News; Lac du **1694**
Flandreau Indian School **1284**
Flandreau Santee Sioux **309**
Flathead Indian Museum **926**
Fleshburn **1824**
Flint Equal Opportunity Office **4122**
Flint Institute of Arts • Library **645**
Florida Human Relations Commission **4067**
Florida Labor and Employment Security Department • Civil Rights Office **4068**
Flying Dust First Nation **3136**
Flying Post First Nation **2996**
Fogelman Publishing Co. **1513**
Folklife Center; American • U.S. Library of Congress **784**
Folklife Center; Maine **3435**
Folklore of the Muscogee (Creek) People **1825**
Fond Du Lac Denesuline Nation **3117**
Fond du Lac (Chippewa) **178**
Fond du Lac Community College **1314**
Fond du Lac First Nation **3118**
Fond du Lac Ojibway School **1212**
Fond du Lac Reservation Business Committee • Head Start Program **1087**
Fontana Native American Center **3528**
For Mother Earth **3398**
Ford Foundation Postdoctoral Fellowships for Minorities **4318**
Ford Foundation Predoctoral and Dissertation Fellowships for Minorities **4319**
Foreman Scholarship; Louie LeFlore/Grant **1435**
Forest County Potawatomi Executive Council **355**
Forest Spirits **1826**
Forestry on Indian Lands • U.S. Department of the Interior • Bureau of Indian Affairs **3984**
Forever in Time: The Art of Edward S. Curtis **1827**
The Forgotten American **1828**
Forgotten Frontier **1829**
Fort Albany First Nation **2952**
Fort Alexander First Nation **2862**
Fort Ancient Museum **981**
Fort Belknap Community College **1317**
Fort Belknap Indian Community **193**

Fort Belknap Indian Community Council • Head Start Program **1097**
Fort Berthold Community College **1330**
Fort Bidwell Reservation **60**
Fort Folly Indian Band **2911**
Fort Hall Community **148**
Fort Independence Reservation **71**
Fort Laramie National Historic Site • Library • U.S. Department of the Interior • National Park Service **766**
Fort Larned National Historic Site • Library • U.S. Department of the Interior • National Park Service **767**
Fort Lewis College • Center of Southwest Studies **646**
Fort McDermitt Paiute and Shoshone Tribe **213**
Fort McDowell Mohave-Apache **4**
(Fort McDowell); Mohave- Apache Community Council **5**
Fort McKay First Nation **2627**
Fort McMurray No. 468 First Nation **2628**
Fort Mohave Tribe **93**
Fort Nelson Indian Band **2721**
Fort Peck Community College **1318**
   Native American Studies Program **1346**
Fort Peck Tribal Council **196**
Fort Peck Tribes • Head Start Program **1098**
Fort Severn First Nation **2957**
Fort Sill Apache Tribe **265**
Fort Snelling Branch Library • Historical Society; Minnesota **690**
Fort Thompson Elementary School **1285**
Fort Verde State Park • Library **647**
Fort Ware Band **2798**
Ft. Wayne Urban League **3630**
Fort William First Nation **3033**
Fort William H. Seward **2401**
Fort Worth Human Relations Department **4248**
Ft. Yukon; Native Village of **2203**
(Fort Yuma); Quechan Tribe **22**
Forty-Seven Cents **1830**
Foundation for Pacific Dance **2524**
Foundation of Universal Unity **3394**
Fountain Indian Band **2759**
Four Arrows **3399**
Four Corners of Earth **1831**
Four Directions Cultural Center; Natives of the **3485**
Four Winds Community School **1263**
Four Winds Intertribal Society **3801**
Fourth World Documentation Project **3400, 4485**
Fox Document Collection; Sac and **737**
Fox Lake First Nation **2864**
Fox National Public Library; Sac and **737**
Fox Oral History Collection; Sac and **737**
Fox Photography Collection; Sac and **737**
Fox Presbyterian Mission Museum; Iowa, Sac and **903**
Fox; Sac and **289**
Fox Settlement School; Sac and **1204**
Fox Tribe; Sac and **154**
Frances C. Allen Fellowships **1426,** 1460
The Frank Phillips Foundation, Inc. • Woolaroc Museum • Library **648**
Franklin C. McClean Award; William and Charlotte Cadbury Award and **4351**
Free Cherokee Tennessee River Band Chickamauga **317**
Free World Research **3640**
Freedom; California Council for the Defense of **3559**
Freedom; Committee on Professional Ethics and Academic **3382**
Freedom; Committee on Professional Ethics, Rights and **3382**
Freedom Fund **3401**
Freedom Network; ACLU **4472**
Freedom Task Force; Central Minnesota **3686**
Freedom Writers **3362**
Fresno County Free Library • Special Collections **649**
Fresno Minority Business Development Center **3529, 4046**
Friend of the American Indian Award **1462**
Friends of Caddo Adais Indian **464**
Friends Collection • Earlham College **639**
Friends of the Des Moines Human Rights Commission **3639**
Friends of Lt. George Lener **3736**
Friends of Malatesta, Inc. **1514**
Friends of the Oglala Lakota **487**
Frog Lake First Nation **2630**
Frog Lake Indian Band **2631**

From the First People 2492
Frontier; Art of the American Indian 2128
Frontier Gateway Museum • Library 650
Fruitlands Museums • Library 651
Fulfilling the Vision 1832
Fun Publishing Co. 1515
Futures 1658
Futures for Children 3402, 3403
Gabriel Dumont Institute of Native Studies and Applied Research 3268
Gadsen Museum 938
Gakona; Native Village of 2206
Galena Village 2207
Gallup Distributing Co. 1516
Gallup Inter-Tribal Indian Ceremonial Association 1517
Gambell; Native Village of 2208
Gamblers First Nation 2848
Game of Staves 1833
Gaming Association; United South and Eastern Tribes 450
Gaming Authority; Saskatchewan Minister for Indian and Metis Affairs, Status of Women, and 3206
Gaming Commission; U.S. National Indian 547
Gaming Management Staff; Indian • U.S. Department of the Interior • Bureau of Indian Affairs 539
Gannagaro 1834
Ganondagan State Historic Site 950
Garden Hill First Nation 2873
Garden River First Nation; Ojibways of 2959
Gary Minority Business Development Center 3631, 4091
Gaspe; Bande indienne de 3055
Gathering of Nations 3404
Gay Head; Wampanoag Tribe of 165
GEM Master's Engineering Fellowships for Minorities 4320
GEM Ph.D. Engineering Fellowships for Minorities 4321
GEM Ph.D. Science Fellowship Program 4322
Genealogical Society Library; Minnesota • Heritage Center; Northwest Territory Canadian and French 3207
Genealogy: A Research Guide; Ethnic 4405
Genealogy; The Source: A Guidebook of American 4420
General George Armstrong Custer Collection • Monroe County Library System 695
General John S. Clark Collection 622
Genocide; Institute for the Study of 3420
Genocide Treaties; Ad Hoc Committee on the Human Rights and 3352
Gente; La 1637
George Armstrong Custer Collection; General • Monroe County Library System 695
George C. Ruhle Library • U.S. Department of the Interior • National Park Service • Glacier National Park 768
Georgetown University - Catalogue of Projects in Electronic Text 4486
Georgia Attorney General (Law Department) • Civil Rights Litigation Section 4079
Georgia Equal Opportunity Commission 4080
Georgia Human Relations Commission 4081
Georgina Island; Chippewas of 3029
Georgina Island First Nation 3030
Geoscience Scholarships; Minority 4333
Gerald R. Sherratt Library • Special Collections Department • Southern Utah University 752
Gerber Prize for Excellence in Pediatrics 4323
Geronimo and the Apache Resistance; American Indian Collection: 1722
Geronimo Jones 1835
Geronimo: The Final Campaign 1836
Gesgapegiag First Nation 3070
The Gift of Santa Fe 1837
Gifted/Talented Artist Sponsorships; NNAC 1444
Gila Crossing Day School 1168
Gila Indian Center 839
Gila River Indian Community 12
    Head Start Program 1070
Gilcrease Institute of American History and Art; Thomas • Library 757
Gillihan Award 1468
Ginoogaming First Nation 2975
Girl of the Navajos 1838
The Girl Who Loved Wild Horses 1839
Gitanmaax First Nation 2732
Gitanyow Band 2751

Gitlakdamix Band 2780
Gitsegukla Indian Band 2821
Gitwangak First Nation 2752
Gitwinksihlkw Indian Band 2725
Glacier National Park • George C. Ruhle Library • U.S. Department of the Interior • National Park Service 768
Glen Vowell Indian Band 2733
Global Peace Studies 3372
GOALS Fellowships 4324
Goddard College
    Native American Studies Graduate Program 1399
    Native American Studies Program 1366
God's Lake First Nation 2874
God's River First Nation 2866
Golden Lake; Algonquins of 2961
Golden State Minority Federation 3536
Golden State Minority Foundation Scholarships 4325
Golden Triangle Minority Business Council 3798
Goldwater Library; Robert • Metropolitan Museum of Art 687
(Golovin); Chinik Eskimo Community 2210
Good Medicine Books 3269
The Good Mind 1840
(Goodfish); Whitefish Lake First Nation 2633
Goodnews Bay; Native Village of 2211
Gordon B. Olson Library • Minot State University 692
Gordon First Nation 3149
Goshute Business Council 324
Government Documents and Microtext Center • University of Rochester 805
Government Spying; Campaign to Stop 3370
Governmental Research Library • University of South Dakota 806
Gower Federal Service-Miscellaneous Land Decisions 1659
Gower Federal Service-Royalty Valuation and Management 1660
Graduate Center; American Indian 372
Graduate Fellowships; Sequoyah 1451, 2440
Graduate Management Education; Council for Opportunity in 3392
Graduate Scholarship; Cherokee Nation 1420
Graduate Student Scholarships (Special Higher Education Scholarships); Indian • U.S. Department of the Interior • Bureau of Indian Affairs 3990
Graduate Study in Management; Consortium for 3386
Graduate Study Management Fellowships for Minorities; Consortium 4313
Grand Mound History Center; Minnesota Historical Society's 919
Grand Portage National Monument • Library • U.S. Department of the Interior • National Park Service 769
Grand Portage Reservation Business Committee • Head Start Program 1088
Grand Portage Reservation Business Committee (Chippewa) 179
Grand Rapids First Nation 2867
Grand Rapids Urban League 3675
Grand River Territory; Six Nations of the 2999
Grand Traverse Band of Ottawa and Chippewa Tribes • Head Start Program 1084
Grand Traverse Tribal Council 173
Grand Village of the Natchez Indians 921
Grande Ronde Tribe; Confederated Tribes of the 299
Grandview Publishing Co. 1518
Grant Guides 4406
Grant School Association; Navajo Area 434
Grants for Indian Schools; Administrative Cost • U.S. Department of the Interior • Bureau of Indian Affairs 3972
Grants for Indian Tribal Governments; Violence Against Women Discretionary • U.S. Department of Justice • Office of Justice Programs 4023
Grants for Minorities 4406
Grants; Tribal Colleges Education Equity • U.S. Department of Agriculture • Cooperative State Research, Education and Extension Service, 3948
Grants; Tribal Self-Governance • U.S. Department of the Interior • Bureau of Indian Affairs 4011
Grassy Narrows First Nation 2962
Graves Protection and Repatriation Act; Native American 2137, 2522, 2610
Grayling; Organized Village of 2212
Great American Indian Heroes 1841

Great Eagle Publishing Inc. **1519**
Great Elm Press **1520**
Great Lakes Indian Fish and Wildlife Commission **3405**
Great Lakes Indian, Fish and Wildlife Committee **3827**
The Great Movie Massacre **1842**
Great Plains Art Collection • University of Nebraska—
Lincoln **796**
Great Plains; Museum of the **984, 1036**
Great Spirit Within the Hole **1843**
Greater Lansing Urban League **3676**
Greater Riverside Area Urban League **3549**
Greenville Rancheria **63**
Greeves Art Gallery; R. V. **1564**
Greyhills High School **1169**
Grindstone Rancheria **54**
Group Hunting on the Spring Ice, Parts I-III **2493**
A Guide to the Great Sioux Nation **2135**
Guide to Multicultural Resources **4407**
Gulkana Village **2204**
Gull Bay First Nation **2963**
Gwa'Sala-Nakwaxda'xw Indian Band **2791**
Haa Shagoon **2494**
Hack's Choice **1844**
*Had You Lived Then: Life in the Woodlands Before the White
Man Came* **1845**
Hagwilget Indian Band **2781**
Haida Central Council; Tlingit and • Head Start Program **2428**
Haida Tribe of Alaska; Central Council of Tlingit and **2224**
Hail Books; Raven **1565**
(Haines); Chilkoot Indian Association **2213**
(Haisla Nation); Kitamaat Indian Band **2749**
Halalt Indian Band **2698**
Hale Kako'o Punana Leo/Hilo **2568**
Hale Kako'o Punana Leo/Honolulu **2569**
Haleakala National Park • Library • U.S. Department of the
Interior • National Park Service **2550**
Halfway River Band **2843**
Haliwa-Saponi Tribe **254**
Hall of Fame; American Indian Lore Association **1456**
Hall of Fame; Cherokee National **1459**
Hall of Fame for Famous American Indians; National **986**
Hamilton; Native Village of **2249**
Hammeter Publishing Corp. **2590**
Hampshire College • Native American Studies Program **1367**
Hancock House Publishers Ltd. **1521**
Hannahville Indian Community **175**
Hanson Consulting; Bill **3263**
Harlem Minority Business Development Center **4157**
Harold S. Colton Memorial Library • Museum of Northern
Arizona **702**
Harrison Western Research Center; Michael and Margaret B. •
University of California, Davis **1057**
Harry M. Trowbridge Research Library • Historical Society and
Museum; Wyandotte County **823**
Hartley Bay Indian Band **2731**
Hartwick College • Stevens-German Library • Special
Collections **652**
Harwell Goodwin Davis Library • Special Collections • Samford
University **739**
Haskell Indian Junior College **1312**
Hatchet Lake First Nation **3164**
Hatter Fox; Lost Legacy: A Girl Called **1924**
Hauberg Indian Museum **894**
Haudensaunee: Way of the Longhouse **1846**
Havasupai School **1170**
Havasupai Tribal Council **1522**
Havasupai Tribe **17**
Hawaii; American Civil Liberties Union of **3615**
Hawaii Children's Museum **2557**
Hawaii Health Department • Affirmative Action Office **2541**
Hawaii at Hilo; University of • Hawaiian Studies
Program **2581**
Hawaii Home Lands Department **4083**
Hawaii at Honolulu; University of • School of Public Health •
American Indian and Alaska Native Support Program **1408,
2431**
Hawaii; Huna from **2609**
Hawaii - Independent and Sovereign Nation-State **2608**
Hawaii at Manoa; University of • Hawaiian Studies
Program **2582**
Hawaii Press; University of • University of Hawaii **2600**

Hawaii (State) Department of Accounting and General Services
• State Archives **2543**
Hawaii State Public Library System
Hawaii State Library
Edna Allyn Room **2544**
Hawaii and Pacific Section I **2545**
Hawaii; University of
Special Collections
Archives and Manuscripts **2553**
Hawaiian Collection **2554**
Hawaii Volcanoes National Park • Library • U.S. Department of
the Interior • National Park Service **2551**
Hawaiian Affairs; Institute for the Advancement of **2525**
Hawaiian Chamber of Commerce; Native **2530**
Hawaiian Collection • Hawaii; University of • Special
Collections **2554**
Hawaiian Community-Based Education Learning Center; Native
• U.S. Department of Education • Office of Elementary and
Secondary Education **2532**
Hawaiian Culture and Arts Program; Native **3484**
Hawaiian Curriculum Development, Teacher Training and
Recruitment; Native • U.S. Department of Education • Office
of Elementary and Secondary Education **2533**
Hawaiian Drug-Free Schools and Communities Program;
Native **2570**
Hawaiian Health Professions Scholarship Program;
Native **2570**
Hawaiian Higher Education Program; Native **2570**
Hawaiian Historical Society • Library **2546**
Hawaiian Island Concepts **2591**
Hawaiian Mission Children's Society Library • Mission Houses
Museum **2547**
Hawaiian Studies Institute **2570**
Hawaiian Vocational Education; Native • U.S. Department of
Education • Office of Vocational and Adult Education **2536**
Hawk, I'm Your Brother: Stories of American Indian
Culture **1847**
Healer: Initiation into an Ancient Art; Native **1967**
Healing and Wellness; Office of Aboriginal • Ontario Ministry of
Community and Social Services **3202**
Health: A Network of Minority Professional Associations;
Mathematics, Engineering, Science and **3439**
Health Board Award; National Indian **1466, 4353**
Health Board of Minneapolis; Indian **478**
Health Board; National Indian **3463**
Health Canada • First Nations and Inuit Health Program **3178**
Health Care Association; American Indian **373**
Health Care Crisis at Rosebud **1848**
Health Care Practices; Navajo **1981**
Health Coalition; Nebraska Urban Indian **486**
Health Department; Mississippi • Minority Affairs Office **4140**
Health Department; Missouri • Minority Health Office **4143**
Health Department; Ohio • Minority Affairs Office **4205**
Health Education Resource Center; Native American
Women **3474**
Health of Native People of North America **1612**
Health Network; The Minority **4498**
Health Professions Compensatory Preprofessional Scholarship;
IHS **1432, 2436**
Health Professions Pre-Graduate Scholarships; IHS **1433,
2437**
Health Professions Scholarship Program; Native
Hawaiian **2570**
Health Professions Scholarships; Emergency Aid and **1424,
2435**
Health Project; Sacramento Urban Indian **445**
Health Research; National Center for American Indian and
Alaska Native Mental **408**
University of Colorado **1060, 2420**
Health Resources Directory; Minority **4410**
Health; San Diego American Indian **446**
Health Service; Indian • U.S. Department of Health and Human
Services • Office of Public Health and Science **533**
Health Studies; Institute for Circumpolar • University of Alaska,
Anchorage **2418, 2612**
Healy Lake Village **2192**
Heard Museum **840**
Library and Archives **653**
Heart of the Earth Survival School **380**
Heart of the Earth Survival School/Circle of the Winds **1849**
Heart Lake First Nation **2645**

Heartsong Books **1523**
Heathen Injuns and the Hollywood Gospel **1850**
Heidelberg Graphics **1524**
Heiltsuk Band **2837**
Helena Indian Alliance **483**
Helping Our People Endure **465**
Hensler Award; Bill and Sue **1468**
Henvey Inlet First Nation **3003**
Herbology for Beginners; Native American **4461**
Heritage Association; American National **4356**
The Heritage Center **995**
    Library **654**
Heritage Center; Kansas • Library **669**
Heritage Center; Northwest Territory Canadian and French •
    Minnesota Genealogical Society Library **3207**
Heritage Center; Totem **759, 2408**
Heritage Center; Turtle Mountain Chippewa **967**
Heritage Centre; Multicultural **3174**
Heritage and Citizenship, and Multiculturalism; Manitoba
    Minister for Culture, **4282**
Heritage Commission; California Native American **581**
Heritage Council; Indian **999, 3411**
Heritage Council Publishing; Indian **1528**
Heritage of Craftsmanship **1851**
Heritage Foundation; American Indian **374**
Heritage Foundation; Sealaska **2403**
Heritage and Historic Preservation Office; Zuni **948**
    Library **830**
Heritage; Hopewell **1858**
Heritage; How and Where to Research Your Ethnic-American
    Cultural **4408**
Heritage Museum; Idaho **889**
Heritage Museums; Siouxland • Library **749**
Heritage Park; Secwepemc Cultural Education Society and
    Native **3175**
Heritage Press of Pacific **2592**
Heritage Publications; Chippewa **1494**
Heritage: The American Indian; Silent **2059**
Heritage; The Treasure: Indian **2094**
Herman Red Elk: A Sioux Indian Artist **1852**
Heroes of America; Indian **1886**
(Heron Bay); Ojibways of the Pic River **2965**
Herren, Publisher; Janet **1534**
Hesquiaht Band **2828**
Heyday Books **1525**
Hiawatha First Nation; Ojibways of **2969**
Hide Tanning; Indian **3326**
High Arctic: Life with the Northernmost Eskimos **2495**
High Bar Indian Band **2706**
Higher Education: A Guide to Institutions with. . .Asian, Black,
    Hispanic, and Native American Students; Minority Student
    Enrollments in **4413**
Higher Education Consortium; American Indian **375**
Higher Education and Multicultural Scholars Program (Minority
    Scholars Program) • U.S. Department of Agriculture •
    Cooperative State Research, Education, and Extension
    Service **3947**
Hightower - Regional Library; Sara • Special Collections **742**
Hillcrest Housing Service **3760**
Hillsborough Organization for Progress and Equality **3600**
Hilo; Hale Kako'o Punana Leo/ **2568**
Hilo; Punana Leo O **2574**
Hisatsinom: The Ancient Ones **1853**
Hispanic, and Native American Students; Minority Student
    Enrollments in Higher Education: A Guide to Institutions with.
    . . Asian, Black, **4413**
Historian; Indian **1634**
Historian Press; Indian **1529, 2446, 3270**
Historic Park; Chaco Culture National **934**
Historic Park; Hopewell Culture National **968**
Historic Park; Nez Perce National **890**
Historic Preservation Office; Zuni Heritage and **948**
    Library **830**
Historic Site; Angel Mounds State **896, 1477**
    Library **606**
Historic Site; Caddoan Mounds State **1003**
Historic Site; Cahokia Mounds State **892**
Historic Site; Ganondagan State **950**
Historic Site; Hubbell Trading Post National **843**
Historic Site; Knife River Indian Villages National **965**
Historic Site; Osage Village **923**

Historic Site; Pawnee Indian Village State • Library **727**
Historic Site; San Luis Archaeological and **880**
Historic Site; Town Creek Indian Mound State **964**
Historical Area; Piqua **972**
Historical Artifacts Society; Saanichton **3215**
Historical Association; Yakima Valley Museum and •
    Archives **827**
Historical Center; Buffalo Bill • McCracken Research
    Library **621**
Historical Committee; Namaka Community **3274**
Historical Events for Native American Children; Cultural
    and **3721**
Historical Library; Illinois State **657**
Historical Museum; Hoard • Library **655**
Historical Museum; Marathon County • Library **682**
Historical Museum; Panhandle- Plains • Research Center **725,**
    1043
Historical Museum and Pioneer Village; Chelan County **1009**
Historical Museum; Pipestone County **928**
Historical Museum; Skagit County • Historical Reference
    Library **750**
Historical Museum; Tongass **2407**
    Library **2391**
Historical Park; Pu'uhonua O Honaunau National **2566**
Historical Park; Red Clay State **1001**
    Library **733**
Historical Research Center; Lakota Archives and • Sinte
    Gleska University **1047**
Historical Site; Etowah Indian Mounds **885**
Historical Societies; Sharlot Hall/ Prescott •
    Library/Archives **748**
Historical Society; Allen County • Elizabeth M. MacDonell
    Memorial Library **600**
Historical Society; American Indian **376**
Historical Society; Arizona • Library/Archives **607**
Historical Society; Bitter Root Valley • Ravalli County Museum
    • Miles Romney Memorial Library **614**
Historical Society; Cherokee National **390, 2129**
Historical Society; Cook Inlet **2399**
Historical Society; Cranford • Museum Library **633**
Historical Society; Eastern Washington State **1508**
Historical Society; Fillmore County • Historical Center **643**
Historical Society; Hawaiian • Library **2546**
Historical Society, Inc.; Cherokee National • Cherokee National
    Archives **625**
Historical Society, Inc.; Martin County • Pioneer Museum •
    Library **685**
Historical Society; Indian **394**
Historical Society of Iowa; State • Library/Archives **754**
Historical Society; Kankakee County • Musuem **668**
Historical Society; Kansas State • Library & Archives
    Division **670**
Historical Society; Lehigh County • Scott Andrew Trexler II
    Memorial Library **678**
Historical Society; Maui • Library **2549**
Historical Society; Minnesota
    Fort Snelling Branch Library **690**
    Library & Archives **691**
Historical Society; Missouri
    Archives **693**
    Library **694**
Historical Society; Montana • Library/Archives **696**
Historical Society and Museum; Wyandotte County • Harry M.
    Trowbridge Research Library **823**
Historical Society; Nebraska State
    John G. Neihardt State Historic Site • Research
       Library **709**
    Library **710**
Historical Society; Nevada • Library **712**
Historical Society of North Dakota; State **1573**
Historical Society; Northern Indiana • Library **716**
Historical Society; Oklahoma **1554**
    Archives and Manuscript Division **720**
    Division of Library Resources **721**
    Museum of the Western Prairie • Bernice Ford Price
       Reference Library **722**
Historical Society of Wisconsin; State • Library **755**
Historical Society's Grand Mound History Center;
    Minnesota **919**
*History of the Alabama Coushatta Indians; Journey to the Sky:
    A* **1904**

History; American Indian: A Brief **1717**
History of the American Indian Fello wships; D'Arcy McNickle Center for the **1460**
History; Archives of Social **4359**
History and Art; Anchorage Museum of **2396**
History and Art; Thomas Gilcrease Institute of American • Library **757**
History and Arts; Mohave Museum of **844**
History Association; Badlands Natural **1484**
History Center; Lower Sioux Agency **916**
History Center; Minnesota Historical Society's Grand Mound **919**
History Center; South Dakota Oral **1048**
History for Children: Native American Life; American **1715**
History Collection; Sac and Fox Oral **737**
History and Culture; Ah-Tah-Thi-Ki Museum of Seminole **878**
History; D'Arcy McNickle Center for American Indian • Newberry Library **1041**
History; Journal of American Ethnic **4428**
History; Kansas Institute for African-American and Native-American Family **462**
History and Problems of Winnebago Indians; The **1854**
History; Rural **4432**
History Society of Ontario; Multicultural **4385**
History; Utah • Information Center **813**
Hitting Sticks—Healing Hearts **2496**
Ho-Chunk Nation **363**
Hoard Historical Museum • Library **655**
Hoh Tribe **332**
Holbrook Dormitory **1171**
Holdings in the Southeast; American Indian Archival Material: A Guide to **1596**
Hollow Water First Nation **2904**
Hollywood Gospel; Heathen Injuns and the **1850**
Hollywood-Mid Los Angeles Fair Housing Council **3531**
Hollywood Wins the West; How **1867**
Holt-Atherton Department of Special Collections • University of the Pacific **803**
Holy Cross Village **2214**
Homalco Indian Band **2692**
Home Based Education for Preschool Children (Alaska Native Education); Alaska Native • U.S. Department of Education • Office of Elementary and Secondary Education **2366**
Home of the Brave **1855**
Home Corp.; Choctaw Nation Indian **3764**
Home Lands Department; Hawaii **4083**
Homemaker Scholarships; Association on American Indian Affairs Displaced **1416**
Homolovi Ruins State Park • Arizona State Parks **833**
Homolovi Ruins State Park Library • Arizona State Parks **608**
Honolulu; Hale Kako'o Punana Leo/ **2569**
Honolulu Minority Business Development Center **4084**
Honolulu; Punana Leo O **2575**
Honored by the Moon **1856**
The Honour of All **1857**
Hoo-Hoogam Ki Museum **841**
Hoonah Indian Association **2215**
Hoopa Valley Business Council • Head Start Program **1076**
Hoopa Valley Indian Reservation **69**
Hooper Bay; Native Village of **2216**
Hope Fair Housing Center **3629**
Hopewell Culture National Historic Park **968**
Hopewell Culture National Historical Park
    Library • U.S. Department of the Interior • National Park Service **770**
    U.S. Department of the Interior • National Park Service **974**
Hopewell Heritage **1858**
The Hopi **1859**
Hopi Coyote Stories; Iisaw: **1873**
Hopi Cultural Center **842**
Hopi Day School **1172**
Hopi High School **1173**
The Hopi Indian **1860**
Hopi Indian Arts and Crafts **1861**
Hopi Indian Settlement Program; Navajo- • U.S. Department of the Interior • Bureau of Indian Affairs **574**
Hopi, Navajo, and Iroquois; Indian Crafts: **1884**
Hopi Philosophical Statement; Natwaniwa: A **1972**
Hopi Pottery **1862**
Hopi Prayer for Peace **1863**

Hopi Prophecy; A Common Destiny Vol. 2: The **1783**
Hopi: Songs of the Fourth World **1864**
Hopi Supplemental Grant **1427**
Hopi Tribal Council **7**
Hopi Tribe • Head Start Program **1071**
Hopi Tribe Adult Vocational Training **1428**
Hopi Tribe Educational Enrichment Grant **1429**
Hopi Tribe Private High School Scholarship **1430**
Hopi Tribe Scholarship **1431**
Hopiit **1865**
Hopis: Guardians of the Land **1866**
Hopland Reservation **70**
Horace Mann Bond Center for Equal Education • University of Massachusetts **4396**
Horse Lake First Nation **2642**
Horsecollar Ruins **1008**
Hotevilla Bacavi Community School **1174**
Hothem House **1526**
Houlton Band of Maliseet Indians **160**
House of Sim-Oi-Ghes; Kitsumkalum Band/ **2827**
Housing Center; Hope Fair **3629**
Housing Center of Metropolitan Detroit; Fair **3671**
Housing Center; Oak Park **3627**
Housing Center; Urban League of Flint **3674**
Housing and Civil Enforcement Section • U.S. Department of Justice • Civil Rights Division **3886**
Housing Council; Hollywood-Mid Los Angeles Fair **3531**
Housing Council; Westside Fair **3539**
Housing - Indian Loan Guarantee Program (Loan Guarantees for Indian Housing); Public and Indian • U.S. Department of Housing and Urban Development • Office of Native American Programs • Public and Indian Housing **3971**
Housing Office; Albany Equal Employment Opportunity and Fair **592**
Housing Opportunities Made Equal **3812**
Housing Resource Board; Long Island Community **3738**
Housing Service; Hillcrest **3760**
Houston Area Urban League **3803**
Houston Citizen Assistance Office **4249**
Houston Minority Business Development Center **4250**
Hovenweep National Monument **864**
How to Build An Igloo **3325**
How Hollywood Wins the West **1867**
How the West Was Lost **1868**
How the West Was Won...and Honor Lost **1869**
How and Where to Research Your Ethnic-American Cultural Heritage **4408**
Howe: The Sioux Painter; Oscar **2006**
Hualapai Tribal Council **10**
Hubbell Trading Post; Canyon de Chelly and **1770**
Hubbell Trading Post National Historic Site **843**
Huerfano Dormitory **1236**
Hughes Village **2218**
Hui Hanai **2593**
Hulihee Palace **2558**
Human Affairs Commission; South Carolina • Fair Housing Division **4233**
Human Dignity; Coalition for **3771**
Human Relations; Chicago Commission on **4086**
Human Relations Commission • New Orleans Intergovernmental Relations Division **4109**
Human Relations Commission; Florida **4067**
Human Relations Commission; Georgia **4081**
Human Relations Commission; Maryland **4113**
Human Relations Commission; North Carolina **3746**
Human Relations Commission; Pennsylvania **4220**
Human Relations and Community Services Office; Lansing **4123**
Human Relations Council; Dayton **4372**
Human Relations Council; Worthington **3762**
Human Relations Department; Cincinnati **4196**
Human Relations Department; Fort Worth **4248**
Human Relations Department; Lubbock **4252**
Human Relations Division • Delaware State Department **584**
Human Relations Office; Kansas City **4141**
Human Relations Office; Orlando **4071**
Human Relations Office; Providence **4227**
Human Relations Office; Topeka **4100**
Human Resources Department; Maryland • Equal Opportunity Division **4114**
Human Rights Advocates **3406**

Human Rights Advocates International **3407**
Human Rights Agencies; International Association of
   Official **3423**
Human Rights; American Committee for **3495**
Human Rights; American Council for the Advancement
   of **3357**
Human Rights Association **3541**
Human Rights; British Columbia Council of **4280**
Human Rights Caucus; Congressional • U.S. Congress • U.S.
   House of Representatives **3835**
Human Rights; Center for the Study of **3376**
     Columbia University **4367**
Human Rights; Citizens Commission of **3614**
Human Rights and Citizenship Commission; Alberta **4277**
Human Rights Commission • Montana Labor and Industry
   Department **4147**
Human Rights Commission; Alaska **4039**
Human Rights Commission; Canadian **3831**
Human Rights Commission Decisions; Illinois **4491**
Human Rights Commission; District of Columbia **4063**
Human Rights Commission; Friends of the Des Moines **3639**
Human Rights Commission; Idaho **4085**
Human Rights Commission; Illinois **4089**
Human Rights Commission; Kansas **4099**
Human Rights Commission; Kentucky **4102**
Human Rights Commission; Maine **4111**
Human Rights Commission; Manitoba **4281**
Human Rights Commission; Missouri **4144**
Human Rights Commission; New Brunswick **4283**
Human Rights Commission; New Hampshire **4156**
Human Rights Commission; New York State **4180**
Human Rights Commission; Newfoundland and Labrador **4284**
Human Rights Commission; Nova Scotia **4285**
Human Rights Commission; Oklahoma **4210**
Human Rights Commission; Ontario **4286**
Human Rights Commission; Prince Edward Island **4287**
Human Rights Commission; Rhode Island **4230**
Human Rights Commission of Rochester **3685**
Human Rights Commission; San Francisco **4049**
Human Rights Commission; Saskatchewan **4288**
Human Rights Commission; Tennessee **4240**
Human Rights Commission; Washington **4272**
Human Rights Commission; West Virginia **3822, 4273**
Human Rights Commission; Yukon **3945**
Human Rights and Constitutional Law; Center for **3534**
Human Rights Council; Palm Beach County **3602**
Human Rights Council; Virginia **4267**
Human Rights Country Reports **4487**
Human Rights Database; International **4493**
Human Rights Department; Minnesota **4136**
Human Rights and Dignity Development Corp.; Women
   for **3716**
Human Rights Division
     Attorney General; Minnesota **4134**
     New Mexico Labor Department **4165**
Human Rights Division; New York State **4181**
Human Rights Documentation Network; Internet:
   International **3429**
Human Rights/Equal Opportunity Office; Lincoln **4149**
Human Rights and Genocide Treaties; Ad Hoc Committee on
   the **3352**
Human Rights of Greater New York; Veterans for **3731**
Human Rights and Immigration; British Columbia Attorney
   General and Minister Responsible for Multiculturalism, **3193**
Human Rights Information Committee; Colombia **3557**
Human Rights Institute of Canada **3237**
Human Rights; Institute for Research and Education on **3418**
Human Rights; Inter-American Commission on **3421, 4378**
Human Rights; Interfaith Council for **3422**
Human Rights; International League for **3427**
Human Rights INTERNET **3429, 4375**
Human Rights Law Group; International **3425**
Human Rights; Lawyers Committee for **3432**
Human Rights; Lawyers Committee for International **3432**
Human Rights Library **4488**
Human Rights; Michigan Coalition for **3672**
Human Rights; Minnesota Advocates for **3682**
Human Rights and Minority Business Development Office;
   District of Columbia **4064**
Human Rights Monitors; Congressional Friends of **3385**
Human Rights; NGO Committee on **3486**

Human Rights Office • Louisiana Office of the Governor **4106**
Human Rights Office; Alexandria **4262**
Human Rights Office; Detroit **4121**
Human Rights Office; Dubuque **4097**
Human Rights Office; Tulsa **4212**
Human Rights and Opportunities Commission;
   Connecticut **4059**
Human Rights of Oregon; Citizens Commission on **3770**
Human Rights Panel of Adjudicators; Yukon **3946**
Human Rights; Physicians for **3495**
Human Rights for Political Prisoners; Campaign for Amnesty
   and **3369, 3369**
Human Rights Quarterly **4489**
Human Rights Resource Center **3560**
Human Rights Review Council of Austin **3795**
Human Rights Secretariat; Alberta **4278**
Human Rights Section • Family and Community Services
   Office; Albuquerque **590**
Human Rights Trial Observer Project; International **3500**
Human Rights/U.S.A. Section; International Society for **3428**
Human Rights Watch **3408, 4376**
Human Rights Watch UPDATE **4437**
The Human Rights Web Home Page **4490**
Human Rights Workers; National Association of **3451**
Human Services Department; Minnesota • Equal Opportunity,
   Affirmative Action and Civil Rights Division **4137**
Humboldt State University **1368**
     Center for Indian Community Development **1026**
Huna from Hawaii **2609**
Huna International **2523**
Hunter Library • Special Collections • Western Carolina
   University **819**
Hunters; Iowa's Ancient **1898**
Hunters Point Boarding School **1175**
Hunters of the Seal **2497**
Hunting and Fishing Rights; Unresolved Indian • U.S.
   Department of the Interior • Bureau of Indian Affairs **4013**
Huntington Free Library
     National Museum of the American Indian **951**
        Library **656**
Hupa Indian White Deerskin Dance **1870**
Huron Indian Village **3222**
Huronne-Wendat First Nation **3088**
Hurons; Sainte-Marie Among the **3225**
Huslia Village **2219**
Huteetl: A Koyukon Memorial Potlatch **2498**
Hydaburg Cooperative Association **2220**
I Am Different From My Brother: Dakota Name-Giving **1871**
I Will Fight No More Forever **1872**
I.D. Weeks Library • Special Collections Department •
   University of South Dakota **807**
Idaho Heritage Museum **889**
Idaho Human Rights Commission **4085**
Identity **2136, 3351**
Igiugig Village Center **2221**
Igloo; How to Build An **3325**
Igloolik: Peter's Story; Easter in **2479**
IHS Health Professions Compensatory Preprofessional
   Scholarship **1432, 2436**
IHS Health Professions Pre-Graduate Scholarships **1433, 2437**
Iisaw: Hopi Coyote Stories **1873**
Ikhana **1661**
Iliamna; Native Village of **2222**
Illinois Human Rights Commission **4089**
Illinois Human Rights Commission Decisions **4491**
Illinois State Historical Library **657**
Illustrations; California Indians: Primary Resources: A Guide to
   Manuscripts, Documents, Serials, Music, and **1599**
Images of Indians **1874**
IMPACT Business Consultants; Seattle Minority Business
   Development Center- **3817, 4271**
Impresora Sahuaro **1527**
In the Heart of Big Mountain **1875**
In Quest of a Vision **1876**
In Search of the First Americans **1877**
In the White Man's Image **1878**
Inaja and Cosmit Band of Mission Indians **113**
Independent and Sovereign Nation-State; Hawaii - **2608**
Index of Native American Resources on the Internet **4492**
Indian Achievement Award **2443**

Indian Adult Education • U.S. Department of the Interior •
  Bureau of Indian Affairs **3985**
Indian Affairs **1662**
Indian Affairs; Bureau of
        Office of Tribal Services • U.S. Department of the
        Interior **542**
        Office of Trust Responsibilities • U.S. Department of the
        Interior **543**
Indian Affairs Division • U.S. Department of the Interior •
  Office of the Solicitor **544**
Indian and Alaska Native Periodicals Project; American 3360
Indian America: A Traveler's Guide **1613, 3290**
Indian Archaeological Institute; American 401
Indian Artifact Magazine **1633**
Indian Artists of the Southwest **1879**
Indian Arts and Crafts Association **3409**
Indian Arts and Crafts Board **874**
        U.S. Department of the Interior **762**
Indian Arts and Crafts Board; U.S. **546**
Indian Arts at the Phoenix Heard Museum **1880**
Indian Arts Research Center **1027**
Indian Awareness Center Newsletter **1663**
Indian Boy of the Southwest **1881**
Indian Canyon Nation of Costanoan People **68**
Indian Center; Detroit American 3487
Indian Center Library • American Indian Center of Santa Clara
  Valley, Inc. **603**
Indian Center Museum **902**
Indian Child and Family Education (FACE) • U.S. Department
  of the Interior • Bureau of Indian Affairs **3986**
Indian City U.S.A. **982**
Indian Claims Commission Archives 811
Indian and Colonial Research Center **1028**
Indian and Colonial Research Center, Inc. • Eva Butler
  Library **658**
Indian Community Fire Protection • U.S. Department of the
  Interior • Bureau of Indian Affairs **3987**
Indian Country **1882, 1883**
Indian Country Address Book **1614, 3291**
Indian Country Investigations. • U.S. Department of Justice •
  Federal Bureau of Investigation **4022**
Indian Country Student News 1530
Indian Country Today **1693**
Indian Crafts: Hopi, Navajo, and Iroquois **1884**
Indian Detention Facilities; Construction and Repair of • U.S.
  Department of the Interior • Bureau of Indian Affairs **3980**
Indian Diamond and Colorstone Association **3537**
Indian Economic Development • U.S. Department of the Interior
  • Bureau of Indian Affairs **3988**
Indian Education; Center for • Arizona State University **1021**
Indian Education Division • North Dakota Public Instruction
  Department **593**
Indian Education Facilities, Operations, and Maintenance •
  Office of Indian Education Programs • U.S. Department of
  the Interior • Bureau of Indian Affairs **3989**
Indian Education; Montana Council for 392
Indian Education Office • Oklahoma School Improvement and
  Standards **595**
Indian Educator of the Year Award **1463**
Indian Educators Federation **3410**
Indian-Eskimo Association of Canada 3172
*Indian Family of Long Ago (Buffalo Hunters of the
  Plains)* **1885**
Indian Fund; American 388
Indian Gaming Management Staff • U.S. Department of the
  Interior • Bureau of Indian Affairs **539**
Indian Goods Retail Directory **1615**
Indian Graduate Student Scholarships (Special Higher
  Education Scholarships) • U.S. Department of the Interior •
  Bureau of Indian Affairs **3990**
Indian Health Board of Minneapolis **478**
Indian Health Service
        Office of Planning, Evaluation, and Legislation • Division
        of Program Statistics • U.S. Department of Health and
        Human Services **1051, 2146**
        Office of Tribal Self-Governance • U.S. Department of
        Health and Human Services • Office of Public Health
        and Science **534**
        U.S. Department of Health and Human Services • Office
        of Public Health and Science **533**

Indian Health Services • Office of Tribal Activities • U.S.
  Department of Health and Human Services • Office of Public
  Health and Science **535**
Indian Heritage Council **999, 3411**
Indian Heritage Council Publishing **1528**
Indian Heroes of America **1886**
Indian Hide Tanning **3326**
Indian and His Homeland: American Images, 1590-1876 **1887**
Indian Historian **1634**
Indian Historian Press **1529, 2446, 3270**
Indian Historical Society 394
Indian House Memorial **909**
Indian Island School **1208**
Indian Job Placement - United Sioux Tribes Development
  Corporation • U.S. Department of the Interior • Bureau of
  Indian Affairs **3991**
Indian Lands; Agriculture on • U.S. Department of the Interior
  • Bureau of Indian Affairs **3973**
Indian Lands; Endangered Species on • U.S. Department of
  the Interior • Bureau of Indian Affairs **3981**
Indian Lands; Fish, Wildlife, and Parks Programs on • U.S.
  Department of the Interior • Bureau of Indian Affairs **3983**
Indian Lands; Forestry on • U.S. Department of the Interior •
  Bureau of Indian Affairs **3984**
Indian Lands; Irrigation Operations and Maintenance on •
  Office of Trust Responsibilities • U.S. Department of the
  Interior • Bureau of Indian Affairs **4000**
Indian Lands; Minerals and Mining on • U.S. Department of
  the Interior • Bureau of Indian Affairs **4002**
Indian Lands; Real Estate Programs - • U.S. Department of
  the Interior • Bureau of Indian Affairs **2382, 4003**
Indian Lands; Safety of Dams on • U.S. Department of the
  Interior • Bureau of Indian Affairs **4006**
Indian Lands; Waste Management - • U.S. Department of the
  Interior • Bureau of Indian Affairs **4015**
Indian Law Enforcement • U.S. Department of the Interior •
  Bureau of Indian Affairs **3992**
Indian Law Resource Center **3412**
Indian Legacy **1888**
Indian Life **1635, 3300**
Indian Loan Guarantee Program (Loan Guarantees for Indian
  Housing); Public and Indian Housing - • U.S. Department of
  Housing and Urban Development • Office of Native American
  Programs • Public and Indian Housing **3971**
Indian Managers; Management Institute: Training for 409
Indian; Museum of the American • Smithsonian Institution;
  U.S. **959, 2413**
Indian Museum of the Carolinas **960**
        Library **659**
Indian Museum of Lake County, Ohio **969**
Indian Museum of North America **996**
Indian Museum Studies Program; American • Smithsonian
  Institution; U.S. • Center for Museum Studies **549**
Indian and Northern Affairs Canada **3179**
        Alberta Policy and Strategic Direction Sector **3180**
        Atlantic Policy and Strategic Direction Sector **3181**
        British Columbia Policy and Strategic Direction
        Sector **3182**
        Indian Taxation Advisory Board **3183**
        Manitoba Policy and Strategic Direction Sector **3184**
        Northwest Territories Policy and Strategic Direction
        Sector **3185**
        Ontario Policy and Strategic Direction Sector **3186**
        Quebec Policy and Strategic Direction Sector **3187**
        Saskatchewan Policy and Strategic Direction Sector **3188**
        Yukon Policy and Strategic Direction Sector **3189**
Indian Post Secondary Schools (Haskell and SIPI) • U.S.
  Department of the Interior • Bureau of Indian Affairs **3993**
Indian Progress **1664**
Indian Pueblo Cultural Center 367, **939**
Indian Rehabilitation Research and Training Center; American •
  Northern Arizona University **1042**
Indian Report **1665**
Indian Resource Development **1530**
Indian Rights Association **397**
Indian Rights; Attorney Fees - • U.S. Department of the
  Interior • Bureau of Indian Affairs **3977**
Indian Rights Issues; Unresolved • U.S. Department of the
  Interior • Bureau of Indian Affairs **4014**
Indian Rights; Litigation Support for • U.S. Department of the
  Interior • Bureau of Indian Affairs **4001**

Indian Rights Protection • U.S. Department of the Interior • Bureau of Indian Affairs **3994**
Indian School Equalization Program (ISEP) • U.S. Department of the Interior • Bureau of Indian Affairs **3995**
Indian Schools; Replacement and Repair of • U.S. Department of the Interior • Bureau of Indian Affairs **4004**
Indian Schools - Student Transportation • U.S. Department of the Interior • Bureau of Indian Affairs **3996**
Indian Science Teachers Education Program **3482**
Indian Self-Determination Contract Support • U.S. Department of the Interior • Bureau of Indian Affairs **3997**
Indian Self-Rule **1889**
Indian Social Services - Child Welfare Assistance • U.S. Department of the Interior • Bureau of Indian Affairs **3998**
Indian Student of the Year Award **1464**
Indian Studies Center; American • University of California, Los Angeles **1058**
An Indian Summer **1890**
Indian Temple Mound Museum **879**
    Library **660**
Indian Time **1666**
Indian Township School **1209**
Indian Trade and Information Center; North American **3469**
The Indian Trader **1667**
Indian Univeristy Press **1531**
Indian Vocational Training - United Tribes Technical College • U.S. Department of the Interior • Bureau of Indian Affairs **3999**
The Indian Way **1891**
Indian Youth of America **398**
Indiana Administration Department • Minority Business Development Division **4092**
Indiana Civil Rights Commission **4093**
Indiana Health Department • Public Health Services • Minority Health Office **4094**
Indiana Minority Business Report **4438**
Indiana Personnel Department • Affirmative Action Division **4095**
Indianapolis Urban League **3634**
The Indians **1892**
indians Americans **1893**
Indians in the Americas (Revised) **1894**
Indians of California: Part 1, Village Life **1895**
Indians of California: Part 2, Food **1896**
Indians of Early America **1897**
Indians Into Medicine **399**
Indigenous Communications Association **489, 3413**
Indigenous Languages of the Americas; Society for the Study of **3501**
Indigenous Studies; Center for World **3377, 4478**
Indigenous Women's Network **3414**
Individual Rights and Responsibilities; Section of **3500**
Industry Canada • Aboriginal Business Canada **3190**
Industry and Small Business Liaison Staff • U.S. Department of Health and Human Services • Office of Public Health and Science • Food and Drug Administration **3865**
Information Center; North American Indian Trade and **3469**
Information Center; South and Meso-American Indian **3502**
Innu Nation **2916**
Inroads **3415**
Institute for the Advancement of Hawaiian Affairs **2525**
Institute of Alaska Native Arts **2353**
Institute of American Indian and Alaska Native Culture and Arts Development **1029, 2144**
Institute of American Indian Arts **400**
    Library **661**
    Museum **940**
Institute for American Indian Studies **401, 1030, 1532**
    Library **662**
    University of South Dakota **1064**
Institute for Archaeological Studies • University at Albany, State University of New York **1054**
Institute of Arctic Studies • Dartmouth College **2414, 2611**
Institute for Circumpolar Health Studies • University of Alaska, Anchorage **2418, 2612**
Institute for the Development of Indian Law **402**
Institute for Encyclopedia of Human Ideas on Ultimate Reality and Meaning **3416**
Institute for Environmental Policy • University of Guelph **4300**
Institute for Native American Development • University of New Mexico **1586**

Institute for Native Pacific Culture and Education **2529**
Institute of the Northamerican West **3417**
Institute on Pluralism and Group Identity **4377**
Institute for Polynesian Studies **2528**
Institute for Prevention and Control of Violence and Extremism **3498**
Institute for Research and Education on Human Rights **3418**
Institute for Social and Economic Rights **3726**
Institute for the Study of American Cultures **3419**
Institute for the Study of Genocide **3420**
Institute for the Study of Traditional American Indian Arts **403, 1031, 1533**
Insurance Agency; MCAP Bonding and **3437**
Inter-American Commission on Human Rights **3421, 4378**
Inter-Tribal Council of California **444**
Inter-Tribal Council of Michigan **476**
    Head Start Program **1085**
Inter-Tribal Council of Tolba Menahan **473**
Inter-Tribal Indian Ceremonial Association **404**
Inter-Tribal Indian Ceremonial Association; Gallup **1517**
Interculture **4427**
Interfaith Council for Human Rights **3422**
Intergroup Relations; Journal of **4429**
Intergroup Relations Officials; National Association of **3451**
Intermountain Cultural Resource Center • Library • U.S. Department of the Interior • National Park Service **771**
International Association of Official Human Rights Agencies **3423**
International Federation for the Protection of the Rights of Ethnic, Religious, Linguistic and Other Minorities **3424**
International Human Rights Database **4493**
International Human Rights Law Group **3425**
International Human Rights; Lawyers Committee for **3432**
International Human Rights Trial Observer Project **3500**
International Indian Treaty Council **3426**
International League for Human Rights **3427**
International League for the Rights of Man **3427**
International Society for Human Rights/U.S.A. Section **3428**
Internet; Index of Native American Resources on the **4492**
Internet: International Human Rights Documentation Network **3429**
Internships; Nelson A. Rockefeller Minority **4341**
Interracial Books for Children, Inc.; Council on **4370**
Interracial Council for Business Opportunity **3430**
Interracial Council of New York; Catholic **3371, 3725**
Interracial Justice; National Catholic Conference for **3457**
Intertribal Association; Dallas/Ft. Worth **524**
Intertribal Society; Four Winds **3801**
Introduce Science to Students Using the Environment **3482**
Inuit Health Program; First Nations and • Health Canada **3178**
Inuit Kids **2499**
Inuit; Legends and Life of the **3332**
Inuit Legends Series **2500**
(Inuit) Legends Series; Eskimo **2483**
Inuit Masterworks; Sananguagat: **2509**
Inupiat Community of Arctic Slope **2167**
Investment Companies; American Association of Minority Enterprise Small Business **406**
Investment Companies; National Association of **406**
Investment Companies Newsletter; National Association of **4443**
Inyo Child Care Services • Head Start Program **1077**
Iolani Palace **2559**
Iowa Civil Rights Commission **4098**
Iowa Civil Rights Communicator **4439**
Iowa, Sac and Fox Presbyterian Mission Museum **903**
Iowa Tribe of Kansas and Nebraska **155**
Iowa Tribe of Oklahoma **283**
Iowa's Ancient Hunters **1898**
Iqurmuit Tribe Russian Mission **2305**
Iron Cloud Family Award **1468**
IROQRAFTS **3271**
The Iroquois **1899**
Iroquois; Indian Crafts: Hopi, Navajo, and **1884**
Iroquois Indian Museum **952**
    Library **663**
Iroquois National Museum; Seneca- **956**
Iroquois Social Dance I and II **1900**
Irrigation Operations and Maintenance on Indian Lands • Office of Trust Responsibilities • U.S. Department of the Interior • Bureau of Indian Affairs **4000**

Ishi, The Ending People **1901**
Iskut Band **2740**
Iskutewizaagegan First Nation (Shoal Lake No. 39) **3021**
Island Lake First Nation **3133**
Isleta Elementary School **1237**
Isleta Pueblo **229**
    Head Start Program **1107**
(Islington); Wabasseemoong Independent Nation **3043**
Itam Hakim Hopiit (We Someone, The Hopi) **1902**
Ivanoff Bay Village **2223**
Jackhead First Nation **2856**
Jackson Minority Business Development Center **4138**
Jackson Museum; Sheldon **2404**
Jackson Rancheria **74**
Jacksonville Minority Business Development Center **4069**
Jamerson Elementary School; Theodore **1267**
James H. Robinson M.D. Memorial Prizes in Surgery **4326**
James Smith First Nation **3137**
James Willard Schultz Society **3431**
Jamestown Band of S'Klallam Indians **343**
Jamul Band of Mission Indians **76**
Janet Herren, Publisher **1534**
J.B. Speed Art Museum • Library **664**
Jeffco Citizens for Human Rights **3571**
Jefferson National Expansion Memorial • Library and Archives
  • U.S. Department of the Interior • National Park
  Service **772**
Jemez Day School **1238**
Jemez Pueblo **230**
    Walatowa Head Start Program **1108**
Jena Band of Choctaw Indians **158**
Jesse Peter Native American Art Museum • Santa Rosa Junior
  College **860**
Jesuit Oregon Province • Archives **665**
Jicarilla Apache Tribal Council • Head Start Program **1104**
Jicarilla Apache Tribe **227**
Jicarilla Chieftain **1636**
Jigging for Lake Trout **2501**
Jimmy A. Young Memorial Scholarships **4327**
J.L. Correll Collection **708**
Job Placement - United Sioux Tribes Development Corporation;
  Indian • U.S. Department of the Interior • Bureau of Indian
  Affairs **3991**
Joe KillsRight: Oglala Sioux **1903**
John Carter Brown Library **666**
John Cat **3327**
John F. Kennedy Day School **1176**
John G. Neihardt State Historic Site • Research Library •
  Historical Society; Nebraska State **709**
John Ross House; Chief **883**
John S. Clark Collection; General **622**
John Vaughan Library/LRC • Special Collections and Archives
  • Northeastern Oklahoma State University **714**
John Woodenlegs Memorial Library; Dr. • Dull Knife Memorial
  College **638**
Jones Academy **1275**
Jones; Geronimo **1835**
Joseph Bighead First Nation **3146**
Joshua's Soapstone Carving **3328**
Joslyn Art Museum • Art Reference Library **667**
Journal of American Ethnic History **4428**
Journal of Cherokee Studies **1668**
Journal of Intergroup Relations **4429**
Journalism Center for Children and Families; Casey •
  University of Maryland at College Park **4301**
Journalism: Making a Difference; Minorities in **4460**
Journalists Association Scholarships; Native American **1441**
*Journey to the Sky: A History of the Alabama Coushatta
  Indians* **1904**
Juaneno Band of Mission Indians 84-A **110**
Juaneno Band of Mission Indians 84-B **111**
Judges Association; National American Indian Court **3450**
Julius A. Thomas Fellowship Program **3389**
Justice Alliance; Rhode Island **3778**
Justice; National Catholic Conference for Inter racial **3457**
Justice; On-Line for Peace and **4502**
Ka Ri Wen Ha Wi **1669**
KABR-AM **1699**
Kahkewistahaw First Nation **3105**
Kahnawake; Mohawks of **3056**
KAHU-AM **2604**

Kaibab Paiute Tribe **6**
Kaibeto Boarding School **1177**
Kainai News **3306**
Kake; Organized Village of **2226**
Kaktovik Village **2227**
Kalispel Business Committee **351**
Kalskag; Village of **2228**
Kaltag; Village of **2229**
Kamehameha Elementary School **2570**
Kamehameha Schools/Bernice Pauahi Bishop Estate **2570**
Kamehameha Schools Press **2594**
Kamehameha Secondary School **2570**
Kamik **3329**
Kamloops Indian Band **2741**
Kamuela Museum **2560**
Kanaka Bar Indian Band **2761**
Kanatak; Village of **2158**
Kanesatake First Nation **3057**
Kankakee County Historical Society • Musuem **668**
Kansas City Human Relations Office **4141**
Kansas City Minority Business Development Center **3692,
  4142**
Kansas Commerce and Housing Department • Minority
  Business Office **586**
Kansas Heritage Center • Library **669**
Kansas Human Resources Department • Equal Employment
  Opportunity Office **587**
Kansas Human Rights Commission **3642, 4099**
Kansas Institute for African-American and Native-American
  Family History **462**
Kansas; Kickapoo Tribe of **152**
    Head Start Program **1083**
Kansas State Historical Society • Library & Archives
  Division **670**
Kansas State University
    Farrell Library • Minority Resource Research Center **671**
    Multicultural Research and Resource Center **4297**
Kapa'a Elementary School **2571**
Kapawe'no First Nation **2635**
Karuk Tribe of California **64**
Kasaan; Organized Village of **2230**
Kasabonika Lake First Nation **2967**
Kashechewan First Nation **2968**
Kashia Men's Dances: Southwestern Pomo Indians **1905**
Kashia Pomo; Dream Dances of the **1804**
Kasigluk; Native Village of **2231**
Kateri Tekakwitha League; Blessed **389**
Kateri Tekakwitha; Musee **3232**
Kateri Tekakwitha; National Shrine of the Blessed **954**
Kathrine R. Everett Law Library • University of North Carolina
  at Chapel Hill **800**
Kathryn E. Lyle Memorial Library • Lyman House Memorial
  Museum **2548**
Katrin H. Lamon Resident Scholarship for Native
  Americans **1434**
Katzie Indian Band **2786**
Kauai Museum **2561**
Kaua'i; Punana Leo O **2576**
Kaw Tribe of Oklahoma **272**
Kawacatoose First Nation **3150**
Kawerak, Inc. • Head Start Program **2425**
Kayak: Parts 1 and 2; Building a **2478**
KBRW-AM **2464**
KC Publications **1535**
KCCN-AM **2605**
KDLG-AM **2465**
Keams Canyon Boarding School **1178**
Kee-Way-Win First Nation **3013**
Keep the Circle Strong **3330**
Keep Your Heart Strong **1906**
Keeper of the Western Door **1907**
Keeseekoose First Nation **3126**
Keeseekoowenin First Nation **2859**
Keewaydin Institute **3595**
Kegoayah Kozga Public Library; Nome Library/ **2387**
Kehewin Cree Nation **2615**
Kellogg Foundation Fellowships in Community Medicine; W.
  K. **4350**
Kenaitze Indian Tribe **2232**
Kendall College
    Library • Special Collections **672**

Kendall College (continued)
    Mitchell Indian Museum • Library **673**
Kennedy Day School; John F. **1176**
Kenneth J. Shouldice Library • Michigan & Marine Collections •
  Lake Superior State University **676**
Kenosha; Urban League of Racine and **3829**
Kentucky Finance and Administration Cabinet • Equal
  Employment Opportunity and Contract Compliance
  Division **4101**
Kentucky Human Rights Commission **4102**
Kentucky Transportation Cabinet • Minority Affairs and Equal
  Employment Opportunity Office **4103**
Kern Valley Indian Community **77**
Ketchikan Indian Corporation **432, 2234**
Kettle and Stony Point First Nation; Chippewas of **2951**
Kevin Alec **1908**
Keweenaw Bay Tribe **168**
Key First Nation **3139**
KEYA-FM **1700**
Keyla Inc. **4379**
KFSK-FM **2466**
Ki He Kah Steh of Skiatook Oklahoma **505**
Kialegee Tribal Town **292**
Kiana; Native Village of **2236**
Kickapoo Nation School **1205**
Kickapoo Tribe of Kansas **152**
    Head Start Program **1083**
Kickapoo Tribe of Oklahoma **274**
    Kickapoo Head Start, Inc. **1126**
Kickapoo Tribe of Texas **318**
KIDE-FM **1701**
Kiliwa: Hunters and Gatherers of Baja California **1909**
KillsRight: Oglala Sioux; Joe **1903**
Kincolith Indian Band **2746**
King Cove; Agdaagux Tribe of **2237**
King Island Native Community **2279**
Kingfisher Lake First Nation **2972**
Kingsclear Indian Band **2912**
KINI-FM **1702**
Kinistin First Nation **3159**
Kiowa Tribe **268**
Kiowa Tribe of Oklahoma • Head Start Program **1127**
Kipawa First Nation **3059**
Kipnuk; Native Village of **2239**
Kispiox Indian Band **2748**
Kitamaat Indian Band (Haisla Nation) **2749**
Kitasoo First Nation **2753**
Kitigan Zibi Anishinabeg First Nation **3069**
Kitkatla Indian Band **2750**
Kitselas Indian Band **2826**
Kitsumkalum Band/House of Sim-Oi-Ghes **2827**
Kivalina; Native Village of **2240**
Klahoose Indian Band **2823**
Klallam Tribe; Lower Elwha- • Head Start Program **1142**
Klallam Tribe; Port Gamble • Head Start Program **1148**
Klamath County Museum • Research Library **674**
Klamath General Council **296**
Klawock Cooperative Association **2241**
(Klukwan); Chilkat Indian Village **2242**
Kluskus Indian Band **2803**
Kluti-kaah; Native Village of **2187**
KMHA-FM **1703**
KMVI-AM **2606**
KNBA-FM **2467**
Knife River Indian Villages National Historic Site **965**
Knik Village **2345**
KNNB-FM **1704**
Knokavtee Scott; Strength of Life— **2075**
Knoxville Area Urban League **3786**
KNTV Minority Scholarships **4328**
Kobuk; Native Village of **2243**
Kodiak; Shoonaq' Tribe of **2244**
Kokhanok Village **2245**
Koliganek Village **2246**
Kolomoki Mounds State Park Museum **886**
Kongiganak; Native Villiage of **2247**
Kootenai Tribal Council; Confederated Salish and • Tribal
  Council **195**
Kootenai Tribe **147**
Kootenai Tribes; Confederated Salish and • Head Start
  Program **1095**

Koshare Indian Library • Koshare Indian Museum **675**
Koshare Indian Museum **865**
    Koshare Indian Library **675**
Kotlik; Village of **2250**
KOTZ-AM **2468**
Kotzebue Museum **2402**
Kotzebue; Native Village of **2251**
Koyuk; Native Village of **2252**
Koyukon Memorial Potlatch; Huteetl: A **2498**
KS Press **2570**
'Ksan Indian Village **3212**
KSKO-AM **2469**
KSUT-FM **1705**
KTDB-FM **1706**
KTNN-AM **1707**
KUAI-AM **2607**
Kualapu'u Elementary School **2572**
KUHB-FM **2470**
Kwa-Wa-Aineuk Indian Band **2794**
Kwagiulth Museum and Cultural Centre **3213**
Kwakiutl Indian Band **2792**
Kwantlen First Nation **2720**
Kwatani Mission of Chickamuga Cherokee Mark Norman Ugaku
  Gigege **316**
Kwaw-Kwaw-Apilt Indian Band **2702**
Kwayhquitlim First Nation **2708**
Kwethluk; Organized Village of **2253**
Kwiakah Indian Band **2693**
Kwicksutaineuk-Ah-Kwaw-Ah-Mish Band **2818**
Kwigillingok; Native Village of **2254**
Kwinhagak; Native Village of **2301**
KWSO-FM **1708**
KYUK-AM **2471**
La Gente **1637**
La Jolla Band **132**
La Posta Band **82**
La Romaine First Nation **3060**
Labrador and Aboriginal Affairs Secretariat **3198**
Labrador Human Rights Commission; Newfoundland and **4284**
Lac Courte Oreilles Governing Board • Head Start
  Program **1154**
Lac Courte Oreilles Ojibwa Community College **1340**
Lac Courte Oreilles Ojibwa School **1305**
Lac Courte Oreilles Tribe **357**
Lac du Flambeau Chippewa Museum and Cultural
  Center **1014**
Lac du Flambeau News **1694**
Lac du Flambeau Tribal Council • Head Start Program **1155**
Lac du Flambeau Tribe **360**
Lac La Croix First Nation **2954**
Lac La Ronge First Nation **3128**
Lac des Milles Lacs First Nation **3034**
Lac Qui Parle Indian Mission Church **915**
Lac St. Jean First Nation **3071**
Lac Seul First Nation **2966**
Lac Simon First Nation **3062**
Lac Vieux Desert Band of Lake Superior Chippewa Indians of
  Michigan **174**
Laguna Elementary School **1239**
Laguna Pueblo **231**
    Head Start Program **1109**
Laguna Songs and Poems; Songs of My Hunter Heart: **2067**
*Laguna Stories and Poems; Running on the Edge of the
  Rainbow:* **2044**
Lahaina Restoration Foundation **2562**
Lakahahmen Indian Band **2715**
Lake Babine Nation (Nat'oot'en Nation) **2686**
Lake County, Ohio; Indian Museum of **969**
Lake Erie Native American Council **496**
Lake Helen First Nation (Red Rock) **2997**
Lake Manitoba First Nation **2903**
Lake Nipigon Ojibway First Nation **2926**
Lake St. Martin First Nation **2870**
Lake Superior Chippewa Indians of Michigan; Lac Vieux Desert
  Band of **174**
Lake Superior State University **1369**
    Kenneth J. Shouldice Library • Michigan & Marine
      Collections **676**
Lake Valley Navajo School **1240**
Lakehead University • Centre for Northern Studies **3238**

Lakota Archives and Historical Research Center • Sinte Gleska University **1047**
Lakota College; Oglala **1336**
    Library **719**
Lakota Foundation **500**
Lakota; Friends of the Oglala **487**
Lakota Museum; Akta **991**
Lakota Museum; Buechel Memorial **994**
Lakota Oyate Akicita Okolaciye **513**
Lakota Quillwork: Art and Legend **1910**
The Lakota Times **1693**
LAMA's Watch on Washington **4440**
Lament of the Reservation **1911**
Lamon Resident Scholarship for Native Americans; Katrin H. **1434**
Lancaster County; Urban League of **3772**
Land Decisions; Gower Federal Service- Miscellaneous **1659**
Landmarks—A Traveler's Guide; North American Indian **1621, 3296**
Lands; Agriculture on Indian • U.S. Department of the Interior • Bureau of Indian Affairs **3973**
Lands Conservation Act; Alaskan Indian Allotments and Subsistence Preference - Alaska National Interest • U.S. Department of the Interior • Bureau of Indian Affairs **2378**
Lands; Endangered Species on Indian • U.S. Department of the Interior • Bureau of Indian Affairs **3981**
Lands; Fish, Wildlife, and Parks Programs on Indian • U.S. Department of the Interior • Bureau of Indian Affairs **3983**
Lands; Forestry on Indian • U.S. Department of the Interior • Bureau of Indian Affairs **3984**
Lands; Irrigation Operations and Maintenance on Indian • Office of Trust Responsibilities • U.S. Department of the Interior • Bureau of Indian Affairs **4000**
Lands; Minerals and Mining on Indian • U.S. Department of the Interior • Bureau of Indian Affairs **4002**
Lands; Real Estate Programs - Indian • U.S. Department of the Interior • Bureau of Indian Affairs **2382, 4003**
Lands; Waste Management - Indian • U.S. Department of the Interior • Bureau of Indian Affairs **4015**
Language Center; Alaska Native • University of Alaska, Fairbanks **2419**
Language Learning Systems, Inc. **4380**
Language Services; Yukon Territory Office of Aboriginal **3191**
Languages of the Americas; Society for the Study of Indigenous **3501**
Languages; Centre for Research and Teaching of Canadian Native • University of Western Ontario **3245**
Languages; Learning Aids for North American Indian **4494**
Languages of the Plains and Southwest; Center for the Study of Native • University of Colorado at Boulder **1059**
Lani Goose Publications, Inc. **2595**
Lansdowne House First Nation **2973**
Lansing Human Relations and Community Services Office **4123**
Lansing Urban League; Greater **3676**
Laredo Minority Business Development Center **4251**
Larsen Bay; Native Village of **2255**
Las Cuatro Flechas **3399**
Las Palabras **1670**
Las Vegas Minority Business Development Center **4152**
Las Vegas Paiute Tribe **210**
The Last of the Caddoes **1912**
Last Chance for the Navajo **1913**
The Last Days of Okak **3331**
Latah-Nez Perce Voices for Human Rights **457**
Laurentian University • Native Studies Program **3249**
Lavola Bakken Memorial Library • Douglas County Museum **637**
Law Branch Library • U.S. Department of the Interior **763**
Law Center; American Indian **1019, 3358**
Law Center Newsletter; American Indian **1647**
Law Centre; Native • University of Saskatchewan **3244**
Law Enforcement; Indian • U.S. Department of the Interior • Bureau of Indian Affairs **3992**
Law Firms; Minority **4411**
Law Group; International Human Rights **3425**
Law; Institute for the Development of Indian **402**
Law Library
    University of Minnesota **793**
    University of Montana • School of Law **795**
    University of Oklahoma **801**

Law Library; Kathrine R. Everett • University of North Carolina at Chapel Hill **800**
Law Library; McKusick • University of South Dakota **808**
Law Library; National Indian **1545**
    Rights Fund; Native American **707**
Law Library; Washoe County **816**
Law Resource Center; Indian **3412**
Law and Social Science for Minority Undergraduate Students; ABF Summer Research Fellowships in **4302**
Law Students Association; American Indian **3477**
Law Students Association; Native American **3477**
Lawson Indian Library; Roberta Campbell **728**
Lawson Prehistoric Village; Museum of Indian Archaeology and **3223**
Lawyers Committee for Human Rights **3432**
Lawyers Committee for International Human Rights **3432**
Lax-Kw'-alaams Indian Band **2796**
Laytonville Rancheria **83**
Le Brun Library • Montclair Art Museum **698**
Leadership Conference on Civil Rights **3433**
Leadership Council; American Indian Community **475**
Leadership Supplemental Grants; Racial/Ethnic **4346**
League for the Rights of Man; International **3427**
Learning Aids for North American Indian Languages **4494**
Leech Lake Reservation (Chippewa) **176**
    Head Start Program **1089**
Leeward Community College Library • Special Collections **677**
LeFlore/Grant Foreman Scholarship; Louie **1435**
Legacy in Limbo **1914**
Legal Defense Association; Native American **460**
Legal Defense and Education Fund; Minority Business Enterprise **3442**
The Legal Information Institute **4495**
Legal Review; NARF **1673**
The Legend of the Boy and the Eagle **1915**
Legend Days Are Over **1916**
Legends and Life of the Inuit **3332**
Legends Series; Eskimo (Inuit) **2483**
Legislative Network; UUACTION Alert **4451**
Lehigh County Historical Society • Scott Andrew Trexler II Memorial Library **678**
Lener; Friends of Lt. George **3736**
Leonard Peltier Defense Committee **3434**
Leonard Peltier; The Trial of **2098**
Letter from an Apache **1917**
Leupp Schools, Inc. **1179**
Levelock Village **2256**
Lexington-Fayette County; Urban League of **3646**
Liberties Union, Alabama Affiliate; American Civil **3514**
Liberties Union of New Mexico; American Civil **3709**
Liberties Union, Northwest Louisiana Chapter; American Civil **3653**
Libraries Newsletter; American Indian **1648**
Library Association; American Indian **3359**
Library of Northwest History; Myron Eells • Whitman College **821**
Lilioukalani Children's Center; Queen **2593**
Lillooet Indian Band **2760**
Lily of the Mohawks **1671**
Lime Village **2257**
Lincoln Human Rights/Equal Opportunity Office **4149**
Linguistic and Other Minorities; International Federation for the Protection of the Rights of Ethnic, Religious, **3424**
Linguistics; University of Montana Occasional Papers in **1585**
Lion's Head Publishing Co. **1536**
Listuguj First Nation **3064**
Listuguj Mi'gmaq First Nation **3065**
LITA/LSSI Minority Scholarships; LITA/OCLC Minority Scholarship and **4329**
LITA/OCLC Minority Scholarship and LITA/LSSI Minority Scholarships **4329**
Litigation Support for Indian Rights • U.S. Department of the Interior • Bureau of Indian Affairs **4001**
Little Big Horn Community College **1319**
Little Bighorn Battlefield National Monument • White Swan Library • U.S. Department of the Interior • National Park Service **773**
Little Black Bear Elementary School **1213**
Little Black Bear First Nation **3123**
Little Black River First Nation **2883**
Little Eagle Day School **1286**

Little Grand Rapids First Nation **2877**
Little Hoop Community College **1331**
    Head Start Program **1116**
Little Medicine: The Wisdom to Avoid Big Medicine **1918**
Little Pine First Nation **3143**
Little Priest Tribal College **1323**
Little Red River Cree Nation **2637**
Little River Band of Ottawa Indians **170**
Little Rock Minority Business Development Center **4043**
Little Saskatchewan First Nation **2871**
Little Shuswap Band **2696**
Little Singer Community School **1180**
Little Wound Day School **1287**
Live and Remember **1919**
(Loan Guarantees for Indian Housing); Public and Indian
    Housing - Indian Loan Guarantee Program • U.S. Department
    of Housing and Urban Development • Office of Native
    American Programs • Public and Indian Housing **3971**
Loans for 8(A) Program Participants; Business • Business
    Administration; U.S. Small **4030**
Loans; Bureau of Indian Affairs Loans and Tribal **1418**, **2434**
Local Education Alternatives Resource Network **3727**
London Museum of Archaeology **3239**
Lone Pine Reservation **88**
Loneman Day School **1288**
Long Island Community Housing Resource Board **3738**
Long Lake No. 58 First Nation **2976**
Long Lance **1920**
Long Plain First Nation **2889**
Long Point First Nation **3098**
The Longest Trail **1921**
Longhouse; Haudensaunee: Way of the **1846**
The Longhouse People **1922**
Look What We've Done to This Land **1923**
Loon River Cree First Nation **2651**
Lorain County Urban League **3757**
Lore Association; American Indian **379**
Lore Association Hall of Fame; American Indian **1456**
Los Angeles Public Library • History and Genealogy
    Department **679**
Los Coyotes Band of Mission Indians **135**
Lost City Museum **930**
Lost Legacy: A Girl Called Hatter Fox **1924**
Louie LeFlore/Grant Foreman Scholarship **1435**
Louis Bull Tribe First Nation **2639**
Louisiana Economic Development Department • Minority and
    Women's Business Division **4105**
Louisiana Office of the Governor • Human Rights Office **4106**
Louisiana Social Services Department • Civil Rights
    Division **4107**
Louisville Urban League **3648**
Lovelock Paiute Tribe **212**
Loving Rebel **1925**
Low Mountain Boarding School **1181**
Lowe Art Museum • University of Miami **882**
Lower Brule Day School **1289**
Lower Brule Sioux Tribe **311**
    Head Start Program **1135**
Lower Eastern Ohio Mekoce Shawnee **502**
Lower Elwha Community Council **341**
Lower Elwha-Klallam Tribe • Head Start Program **1142**
Lower Kalskag; Village of **2258**
Lower Kootenay First Nation **2711**
Lower Nicola Indian Band **2769**
Lower Similkameen Band **2744**
Lower Sioux Agency History Center **916**
Lower Sioux Mdewakanton Community **182**
Lower Umpqua, and Suislaw Indians; Confederated Tribes of
    Coos, **297**
Lowry Ruins **866**
Lubbock Civil Liberties Union **3804**
Lubbock Human Relations Department **4252**
Lubbock/Midland-Odessa Minority Business Development
    Center **4253**
Lubicon Lake First Nation **2650**
Lucky Man First Nation **3152**
Lucy Covington: Native American Indian **1926**
Lukachukai Boarding School **1182**
Lumaaq—An Eskimo Legend **2502**
Lummi Business Council **329**

Lummi Tribal School System **1303**
    Head Start Program **1143**
Lutheran Bible Institute of Seattle • Library **680**
Luxton Museum of the Plains Indian **3208**
Lyle Memorial Library; Kathryn E. • Lyman House Memorial
    Museum **2548**
Lyman House Memorial Museum **2596**
    Kathryn E. Lyle Memorial Library **2548**
Lyman Mission House Memorial Museum **2563**
Lytton Indian Band **2762**
M. L. Woodard Award **1468**
MacDonell Memorial Library; Elizabeth M. • Historical Society;
    Allen County **600**
Macon Plateau; People of the **2015**
MacRae Publications **1537**
MacRae's Indian Book Distributors **1538**
(Macy); Nebraska Indian Community College **1324**
Madison County Urban League **3619**
Magic in the Sky **3333**
Magnetawan First Nation **2932**
Maine; Abnaki: The Native People of **1710**
Maine Civil Liberties Union **3655**
Maine Folklife Center **3435**
Maine Human Rights Commission **4111**
Maine; Passamaquoddy Tribe of[Princeton, ME] **164**
Maine Tribal Unity Museum **907**
Makah Cultural and Research Center **1011**, **1032**
Makah Tribal Council • Head Start Program **1144**
Makah Tribe **337**
Makapu'u Press **2597**
Makwa Sahgaiehcan First Nation **3134**
Mal-I-Mic-News **3301**
Malahat Indian Band **2773**
Malatesta, Inc.; Friends of **1514**
Malecites of Viger **3074**
Maliseet Indians; Houlton Band of **160**
Maliseet Institute; Micmac- • University of New
    Brunswick **3283**
Malki Museum **858**
Malki Museum, Inc. • Archives **681**
Malki Museum Press **1539**
Mamaleleqala Qwe'Qwa'Sot'Enox Band **2694**
Mamit Innuat **3086**
Mammoth Trumpet **4430**
Man Belongs to the Earth **1927**
Man of Lightning **1928**
Management; Consortium for Graduate Study in **3386**
Management Education; Council for Opportunity in
    Graduate **3392**
Management; Gower Federal Service- Royalty Valuation
    and **1660**
Management Institute: Training for Indian Managers **409**
Management and Technical Assistance for Socially and
    Economically Disadvantaged Businesses (7(J) Development
    Assistant Program) • Business Administration; U.S.
    Small **4031**
Managers; Management Institute: Training for Indian **409**
Manawan First Nation **3067**
Manchester/Point Arena Rancheria **101**
Mandaree Day School **1264**
Manhattan Minority Business Development Center **4168**
Maniilaq Association **2357**
Manitoba Human Rights Commission **4281**
Manitoba Minister for Culture, Heritage and Citizenship, and
    Multiculturalism **4282**
Manitoba Northern Affairs Office • Native Affairs
    Secretariat **3196**
Manitou Cliff Dwellings Museum **867**
Manley Hot Springs Village **2259**
Manley Publishing; Ray **1566**
Manokotak Village **2260**
Manuscripts, Documents, Serials, Music, and Illustrations;
    California Indians: Primary Resources: A Guide to **1599**
Many Farms High School **1183**
Manzanita General Council **37**
Marathon County Historical Museum • Library **682**
March/Abrazo Press **1540**
Margaret B. Harrison Western Research Center; Michael and •
    University of California, Davis **1057**
Margaret Clapp Library • Special Collections • Wellesley
    College **817**

Maria! Indian Pottery of San Ildefonso **1929**
Maria of the Pueblos **1930**
Mariano Lake Community School **1241**
Maricopa Indian Community; Salt River Pima- **14**
Mariculture: The Promise of the Sea **3334**
Marin Museum of the American Indian **859, 2410**
    Library **683**
Marine Medical Mission **3447**
Marion Area Urban League **3635**
Mark Ulmer Native American Scholarships **1436**
Marquette League for Catholic Indian Missions **3436**
Marquette Mission Park and Museum of Ojibwa Culture **913**
Marquette National Memorial and Museum; Father **912**
Marquette University Libraries • Department of Special
    Collections and University Archives **684**
Marshall; Native Village of **2261**
Marten Falls First Nation **2991**
Martin County Historical Society, Inc. • Pioneer Museum •
    Library **685**
Martinez Tribe; Torres- **124**
Marty Indian School **1290**
Mary Cabot Wheelwright Research Library • Wheelwright
    Museum of the American Indian **820**
Mary Mildred McCarthy Library • Cook College and Theological
    School **631**
Maryknoll Justice and Peace Office—NewsNotes **4441**
Maryland Human Relations Commission **4113**
Maryland Human Resources Department • Equal Opportunity
    Division **4114**
Mary's Igloo; Native Village of **2332**
Mashantucket Pequot Nation **140**
Mashantucket Pequot Tribe **141**
Mashpee Wampanoag Indian Tribal Council **472**
Mashpee Wampanoag Tribe **166**
Massachusetts Affirmative Action Office **4117**
Massachusetts Commission Against Discrimination **4118**
Massachusetts Economic Development Department • Minority
    and Women's Business Division **4119**
Massachusetts Indian Association Scholarships **1437**
Massachusetts Minority Business Round Table **3662**
Massachusetts Public Protection Bureau • Civil Rights and Civil
    Liberties Division **4120**
Matachewan First Nation **2980**
Materials Science Program; Advanced Industrial Concepts
    (AIC) **4304**
Mathematics, Engineering, Science and Health: A Network of
    Minority Professional Associations **3439**
Mathematics and Science Education Consortia; Eisenhower
    Regional • U.S. Department of Education • Office of
    Assistant Secretary for Educational Research and
    Improvement **3954**
Mathias Colomb First Nation **2890**
Matsqui Indian Band **2766**
Mattagami First Nation **2960**
Matthew Aliuk: Eskimo in Two Worlds **2503**
Maui Historical Society • Library **2549**
Maui; Punana Leo O **2577**
Mayaguez Minority Business Development Center **4225**
Mayor's Action Center; Philadelphia **4223**
McAllen Minority Business Development Center **4254**
MCAP Bonding and Insurance Agency **3437**
MCAP Group **3437**
McCarthy Library; Mary Mildred • Cook College and
    Theological School **631**
McClean Award; William and Charlotte Cadbury Award and
    Franklin C. **4351**
McCracken Research Library • Historical Center; Buffalo
    Bill **621**
McDowell Lake First Nation **3009**
McFarlin Library • Special Collections • University of
    Tulsa **811**
McGill Subarctic Research Station • McGill University **2415,
3240**
McGill University • McGill Subarctic Research Station **2415,
3240**
McGrath Native Village **2262**
McKusick Law Library • University of South Dakota **808**
McLeod Lake Indian Band **2767**
McNickle Center for American Indian History; D'Arcy •
    Newberry Library **1041**

McNickle Center for the History of the American Indian Fello
    wships; D'Arcy **1460**
Mdewakanton Community; Lower Sioux **182**
Meaning; Institute for Encyclopedia of Human Ideas on
    Ultimate Reality and **3416**
Mechoopda Maidu Indian Tribe of Chico Rancheria **43**
Media; Directory of Minority **4403**
Media Executives; National Association of Minority **3454**
Media Forum International, Ltd. **4381**
Medical Center; Phoenix Indian • Library **729**
Medical Minority Educators; National Association of **3452**
Medical Mission; Marine **3447**
Medicine; Fellowship Program in Academic **4317**
Medicine Hat Museum and Art Gallery **3209**
Medicine; Indians Into **399**
Medicine; Metropolitan Life Foundation Awards for Academic
    Excellence in **4330**
Medicine Society; Bear Tribe **1487**
Medicine; W. K. Kellogg Foundation Fellowships in
    Community **4350**
Medicine Wheel Alliance **3698**
Medicine Wheel; Sun Bear: Vision of the **2079**
Meet the Sioux Indian **1931**
Meeting Ground **1672**
Meherrin Indian Tribe **256**
Meiklejohn Civil Liberties Institute **3438, 4382**
Mekoce Shawnee; Lower Eastern Ohio **502**
Mellor Collection; William J. **717**
Memento Publications, Inc. **1541**
Memorial Association; Creek Indian **394**
Memorial Foundation; Crazy Horse **393**
Memorial Indian Museum **983**
Memorial and Museum; Moundbuilders State **971**
Memorial University of Newfoundland • Archaeology Unit **3241**
Memphis Minority Business Development Center **4235**
Menominee **1932**
Menominee Indian Tribe of Wisconsin **359**
Menominee Tribal School **1306**
Mental Health Needs of Minority Children **4459**
Mental Health Research; National Center for American Indian
    and Alaska Native **408**
        University of Colorado **1060, 2420**
Merrill G. Burlingame Special Collections/Archives • Montana
    State University - Libraries **697**
Mesa Grande Band of Mission Indians **114**
Mesa Verde National Park Museum **868**
Mescalero Apache Tribal Council • Head Start Program **1105**
Mescalero Apache Tribe **232**
MESHWORK **3439**
Mesoamerican Archeology Study Unit **3440**
Meso-American Indian Information Center; South and **3502**
A Message from Native America **1933**
The Metis **1934**
Metis Affairs Secretariat; Saskatchewan Indian and **3205**
Metis Affairs, Status of Women, and Gaming Authority;
    Saskatchewan Minister for Indian and **3206**
Metis Association of the Northwest Territories **3272**
Metis Child; Richard Cardinal: Cry From a Diary of a **3339**
Metlakatla Indian Band **2799**
Metlakatla Indian Community **2263**
Metlakatla Indian Community Council • Head Start
    Program **2426**
Metro-Charlotte Minority Chamber **3744**
Metro Columbus Urban League **3613**
Metropolitan Life Foundation Awards for Academic Excellence
    in Medicine **4330**
Metropolitan Museum of Art
        Department of the Arts of Africa, Oceania, and the
            Americas • Photograph Study Collection **686**
        Robert Goldwater Library **687**
Metropolitan Orlando Urban League **3596**
Miami Equity Associates **3593**
Miami/Ft. Lauderdale Minority Business Development
    Center **4070**
Miami Nation of Indians **151**
Miami Tribe of Oklahoma **275**
Miccosukee Indian School **1202**
Miccosukee Tribe • Head Start Program **1079**
Miccosukee Tribe of Florida **145**
Michael and Margaret B. Harrison Western Research Center •
    University of California, Davis **1057**

Michigan Attorney General • Civil Rights Division **4124**
Michigan Civil Rights Commission Newsletter **4442**
Michigan Civil Rights Department **4125**
    Detroit Office **4126**
Michigan Civil Service Department • Equal Employment
  Opportunity and Affirmative Action Office **4127**
Michigan Coalition for Human Rights **3672**
Michigan Family Independence Agency • Affirmative Action
  Office **4128**
Michigan Indian Affairs Commission **588**
Michigan Indian Press **1542**
Michigan Indian Tuition Waiver **1438**
Michigan Minority Business Development Council **3673, 4129**
Michigan Transportation Department • Equal Employment
  Opportunity Office **4130**
Michipicoten First Nation **3039**
Micmac Band; Buctouche **2909**
Micmac-Maliseet Institute • University of New Brunswick **3283**
Micmacs; Aroostook Band of **163**
Microloan Demonstration Program • Business Administration;
  U.S. Small **4032**
Mid-America All Indian Center • Library **688, 904**
Mid-Continent Region; Directory of Native Education Resources
  in the **1603**
Mid-Winter Pow-Wow and Cultural Non Profit Society **485**
Middletown Rancheria **91**
Midland-Odessa Minority Business Development Center;
  Lubbock/ **4253**
Mi'gmaq First Nation; Listuguj **3065**
Mikisew Cree First Nation **2626**
Miles Romney Memorial Library • Historical Society; Bitter Root
  Valley • Ravalli County Museum **614**
Mille Lacs Indian Museum **917**
Mille Lacs Reservation • Head Start Program **1090**
Mille Lacs Reservation Business Committee (Chippewa) **183**
Millenia Press **3273**
Milwaukee Minority Business Development Center **3825, 4275**
Milwaukee Urban League **3826**
Minerals and Mining on Indian Lands • U.S. Department of the
  Interior • Bureau of Indian Affairs **4002**
Mingan First Nation **3072**
Mining Development Policy; Center for Alternative **3373**
Mining on Indian Lands; Minerals and • U.S. Department of
  the Interior • Bureau of Indian Affairs **4002**
Ministries; NAIM **3447**
Ministries; Nations **3473**
Minneapolis American Indian Center **918**
Minneapolis Civil Rights Office **4132**
Minneapolis Minority Business Development Center **4133**
Minneapolis Public Library • Special Collections
  Department **689**
Minnesota Advocates for Human Rights **3682**
Minnesota Attorney General • Human Rights Division **4134**
Minnesota Chippewa Tribal Executive Committee **177**
Minnesota Chippewa Tribe Grant **1439**
Minnesota Employee Relations Department • Equal Opportunity
  Division **4135**
Minnesota Genealogical Society Library • Heritage Center;
  Northwest Territory Canadian and French **3207**
Minnesota Historical Society
    Fort Snelling Branch Library **690**
    Library & Archives **691**
Minnesota Historical Society's Grand Mound History
  Center **919**
Minnesota Human Rights Department **4136**
Minnesota Human Services Department • Equal Opportunity,
  Affirmative Action and Civil Rights Division **4137**
Minnesota Indian Affairs Council **589**
(Minnesota Mdewakanton Sioux); Prairie Island
  Community **186**
Minorities in Agriculture: The Winnebago **1935**
Minorities Alcoholic Treatment Alternative **3545**
Minorities; Council on Career Development for **3389**
Minorities in Engineering; National Action Council for **3448**
Minorities; International Federation for the Protection of the
  Rights of Ethnic, Religious, Linguistic and Other **3424**
Minorities International Network for Trade **3441**
Minorities in Journalism: Making a Difference **4460**
*Minorities and Judicial Administration Division; The ABA
  Commission on* **4452**

Minority Access to Research Careers (MARC) • U.S.
  Department of Health and Human Services • National
  Institutes of Health **3962**
Minority Advisory Panel **3680**
Minority Affairs Office • Health Department; Mississippi **4140**
Minority Builders Coalition of Broward County **3588**
Minority Business Association **3806**
Minority Business Association of Delaware **3580**
Minority Business Association of Greater Danbury **3573**
Minority Business Development Agency
    American Indian Program • U.S. Department of
      Commerce **552**
    U.S. Department of Commerce **3841**
Minority Business Development Agency—Directory of Regional
  and District Offices and Funded Organizations **4065**
Minority Business Directory **4419**
Minority Business Division • Arkansas Industrial Development
  Commission **4042**
Minority Business Enterprise Legal Defense and Education
  Fund **3442**
Minority Business Entrepreneur **4431, 4496**
Minority Business Information Institute **3443**
Minority Business and Professional Directory **4497**
Minority Business Resource Development (Public and Private) •
  U.S. Department of Commerce • Minority Business
  Development Agency **3953**
Minority Contractors Assistance Project **3437**
Minority Contractors Association of Northern California **3546**
Minority Contractors Bond Assurance Fund of Kentucky **3644**
Minority Contractors and Coalition of Trade Workers of New
  Jersey **3704**
Minority CPAs **4409**
Minority Dental Student Scholarship Program **4331**
Minority Enterprise in Clarke County Athens **3606**
Minority Entrepreneurs Network Association **3572**
Minority Faculty Fellowships at Indiana University **4332**
Minority Geoscience Scholarships **4333**
The Minority Health Network **4498**
Minority Health Office • Health Department; Missouri **4143**
Minority Health Resources Directory **4410**
Minority Law Firms **4411**
Minority Organizations: A National Directory **4412**
Minority Professional Associations; Mathematics, Engineering,
  Science and Health: A Network of **3439**
Minority Resource Research Center • Kansas State University
  • Farrell Library **671**
Minority Rights Group U.S.A. **3444**
Minority Student Enrollments in Higher Education: A Guide to
  Institutions with. . .Asian, Black, Hispanic, and Native
  American Students **4413**
Minority Teacher Recruitment • U.S. Department of Education •
  Office of Postsecondary Education **3959**
Minority and Women Business Enterprises Office • Economic
  Development Department; Boston **4115**
Minority Youth: Adam **1936**
Minot State University • Gordon B. Olson Library **692**
Minto Life; Songs In **2510**
Minto Village **2264**
Miscellaneous Land Decisions; Gower Federal Service- **1659**
Mishkegogamang First Nation **2994**
Miss Indian America **1937**
Miss Indian U.S.A. Scholarship; National **4340**
Miss Indian World **1465, 2444, 3261**
Missanabie Cree First Nation **2958**
Mission Academy; Navajo **1244**
Mission of Chickamuga Cherokee Mark Norman Ugaku Gigege;
  Kwatani **316**
Mission Children's Society Library; Hawaiian • Mission Houses
  Museum **2547**
Mission Church; Lac Qui Parle Indian **915**
Mission House Memorial Museum; Lyman **2563**
Mission Houses Museum **2564**
    Mission Children's Society Library; Hawaiian **2547**
Mission Indians 84-A; Juaneno Band of **110**
Mission Indians 84-B; Juaneno Band of **111**
Mission Indians; Amah Mutsum Band of **137**
Mission Indians; Augustine Band of **30**
Mission Indians; Cahuilla Band of **27**
Mission Indians; Campo Band of **41**
Mission Indians; Coastanoan Band of Carmel **92**
Mission Indians; Cuyapaipe Band of **23**

Mission Indians; Inaja and Cosmit Band of **113**
Mission Indians; Jamul Band of **76**
Mission Indians; Los Coyotes Band of **135**
Mission Indians; Mesa Grande Band of **114**
Mission Indians; Morongo Band of **31**
Mission Indians; Pala Band of **97**
Mission Indians; Pauma Band of **100**
Mission Indians; Pechanga Band of **123**
Mission Indians; Rincon Band of **133**
Mission Museum; Iowa, Sac and Fox Presbyterian **903**
Mission Park and Museum of Ojibwa Culture; Marquette **913**
Missions Among the Colored People and the Indians—
    Quarterly; Commission for the Catholic **1653**
Missions; Bureau of Catholic Indian **3368**
Missions; Marquette League for Catholic Indian **3436**
Missions Newsletter; Bureau of Catholic Indian **1650**
Mississauga No. 8 First Nation **2930**
Mississaugas of Alderville First Nation **3011**
Mississaugas of New Credit **2964**
Mississaugas of Scugog First Nation **3006**
Mississippi Band of Choctaw Indians **188**
    Head Start Program **1093**
Mississippi Economic and Community Development Department
    • Minority Business Office **4139**
Mississippi Health Department • Minority Affairs Office **4140**
Mississippi State University • Cobb Institute of
    Archaeology **1033**
Missoula Indian Center **484**
Missouri Health Department • Minority Health Office **4143**
Missouri Historical Society
    Archives **693**
    Library **694**
Missouri Human Rights Commission **4144**
Missouri Tribe; TOE • Head Start Program **1130**
Missouria Tribe; Otoe- **286**
Mistassini; Cree Hunters of **3322**
Mistawasis First Nation **3129**
Mistissini; Cree Nation of **3073**
Mistissini First Nation **3050**
Mistress Madeleine **1938**
Mitchell Indian Museum • Library • Kendall College **673**
Mitchell Lane Publishers, Inc. **4383**
MLA Scholarship for Minority Students **4334**
Mnjikaning First Nation **3007, 3008**
Moanalua Gardens Foundation **2565**
Moapa Indian Reservation; Moapa Paiute Band of the **214**
Moapa Paiute Band of the Moapa Indian Reservation **214**
Moberly Indian Band; West **2775**
Mobert First Nation; Pic **2983**
Mobile Minority Business Development Center **4036**
Moencopi Day School **1184**
Mohave-Apache Community Council (Fort McDowell) **5**
Mohave-Apache; Fort McDowell **4**
Mohave Museum of History and Arts **844**
Mohave Tribe; Fort **93**
Mohawk Indians; St. Regis Band of • Head Start
    Program **1114**
Mohawks of Akwesasne **2941**
Mohawks of the Bay of Quinte **2945**
Mohawks of Kahnawake **3056**
Mohawks; Lily of the **1671**
Moloka'l; Punana Leo O **2578**
Mono Indians; Dunlap Band of **53**
Mono Indians; North Fork Band of **46**
Mono Lake Indian Community **84**
Monroe County Library System • General George Armstrong
    Custer Collection **695**
Montagnais; Conseil Attikamek- **3066**
Montana Council for Indian Education **392**
Montana First Nation **2640**
Montana Historical Society • Library/Archives **696**
Montana Indian Student Fee Waiver **1440**
Montana Labor and Industry Department • Human Rights
    Commission **4147**
Montana Museum; Central **924**
Montana Office of the Governor • Indian Affairs
    Coordinator **4148**
Montana State University-Bozeman **1370**
    Center for Native American Studies **1034**
Montana State University - Libraries • Merrill G. Burlingame
    Special Collections/Archives **697**

Montana State University-Northern **1371**
Montana Vacation Guide **4414**
Montana's American Indians and Others; Directory of **1600**
Montclair Art Museum • Le Brun Library **698**
Montgomery Minority Business Development Center **4037**
Montreal Lake First Nation **3138**
Monument; Coronado State **935**
Monument; Effigy Mounds National **899**
Monument; Mound City Group National **970**
Monument Valley: Navajo Homeland **1939**
Moon Drum **1940**
Moore's Slough; Native Village of Bill **2248**
Mooretown Rancheria **96**
Moorhead State University • Northwest Minnesota Historical
    Center **1035**
Moose Cree First Nation **2984**
Moose Deer Point First Nation **2978**
(Moose Woods); Whitecap Dakota/ Sioux First Nation **3153**
Moosomin First Nation **3110**
(Moravian Town); Delaware of the Thames First Nation **3031**
More Than Bows and Arrows **1941, 2504**
Moricetown Indian Band **2776**
Morning Star Gallery **1543**
Morning Star Institute **405**
Morningside College • Native American Studies Program **1372**
Morongo Band of Mission Indians **31**
Morten Publishing Co., Inc. **4384**
Mosakahiken Cree Nation **2880**
Mosquito Grizzly Bear's Head First Nation **3106**
Mother Corn **1942**
Mother of Many Children **1943**
Mound City Group National Monument **970**
Mound History Center; Minnesota Historical Society's
    Grand **919**
Mound Museum; Serpent **973**
Moundbuilders; American Indian Collection: Myths and **1723**
Moundbuilders State Memorial and Museum **971**
Mounds Historical Site; Etowah Indian **885**
Mounds Museum; Dickson **893**
Mounds National Monument; Effigy **899**
Mounds State Park Museum; Kolomoki **886**
Mount Currie Indian Band **2777**
Mount Senario College • Native American Studies **1373**
Mountain Wolf Woman **1944**
The Movie Reel Indians **1945**
Mowachaht/Muchalaht Band **2726**
Muckleshoot Tribal Council • Head Start Program **1145**
Muckleshoot Tribal School **1304**
Muckleshoot Tribe **328**
Multi-Cultural Scholarship; NACA **4335**
Multi-Media Society of Alberta; Aboriginal **3309**
Multicultural Affairs Office • Ohio Office of the Governor **4206**
Multicultural America; DISCovering **4479**
Multicultural Heritage Centre **3174**
Multicultural History Society of Ontario **4385**
Multicultural Research and Resource Center • Kansas State
    University **4297**
Multicultural Resources; Guide to **4407**
Multicultural Scholars Program (Minority Scholars Program);
    Higher Education and • U.S. Department of Agriculture •
    Cooperative State Research, Education, and Extension
    Service **3947**
Multicultural Student's Guide to College **4415**
Multiculturalism Commission; Alberta **4279**
Multiculturalism, Human Rights and Immigration; British
    Columbia Attorney General and Minister Responsible
    for **3193**
Multiculturalism; Manitoba Minister for Culture, Heritage and
    Citizenship, and **4282**
Multilaterals Project **4499**
Multi-Racial Americans of Southern California **3538**
Multiracial Families; New England Alliance of **3663**
Mumtagila Band; Tlowitsis- **2667**
Munsee-Delaware First Nation **2988**
Munsee Tribal Council; Stockbridge- • Head Start
    Program **1157**
Munsee Tribe; Stockbridge- **354**
Muscogee (Creek) Art; 1,000 Years of **2004**
Muscogee Creek Nation **280**
Muscogee; Tales of the **2083**
Muscowpetung First Nation **3119**

Musee des Abenakis d'Odanak • Societe historique
  d'Odanak **3231**
Musee Kateri Tekakwitha **3232**
Museum of the American Indian • Smithsonian Institution;
  U.S. **959, 2413**
Museum of the Badlands **966**
Museum of the Cherokee Indian **961**
    Archives **699**
Museum Foundation; Plains Indians and Pioneers **508**
Museum of the Great Plains **984, 1036**
Museum of Indian Archaeology **3239**
Museum of Indian Archaeology and Lawson Prehistoric
  Village **3223**
Museum of Indian Arts and Culture **941**
    Laboratory of Anthropology **942**
The Museum of Mobile • Museum Reference Library **700**
Museum of Native American Cultures **1012**
Museum of New Mexico **1037**
    Photo Archives **701**
Museum of Northern Arizona • Harold S. Colton Memorial
  Library **702**
Museum of Northern British Columbia **3214**
Museum of Ojibwa Culture **1544**
Museum of the Plains Indian and Crafts Center **927**
Museum of the Red River **985**
Museum Studies Program; American Indian • Smithsonian
  Institution; U.S. • Center for Museum Studies **549**
Museum of the Western Prairie • Bernice Ford Price Reference
  Library • Historical Society; Oklahoma **722**
Museums at Hartwick **953**
The Music of the Devil, the Bear and the Condor **1946**
Music, and Illustrations; California Indians: Primary Resources:
  A Guide to Manuscripts, Documents, Serials, **1599**
Music for the Rights of Man **3445**
Musicians Against Racism-Sexism **3728**
Musique-Esperance **3445**
Muskeg Lake First Nation **3130**
Muskegon County Museum • Archives **703**
Muskegon; Urban League of Greater **3677**
Muskowekwan First Nation **3132**
Muskrat Dam First Nation **2989**
Musqueam Indian Band **2832**
The Mustard Seed **3446**
Muwekma Ohlone Tribe **109**
Myron Eells Library of Northwest History • Whitman
  College **821**
The Mystery of the Anasazi **1947**
The Mystery of the Lost Red Paint People: The Discovery of a
  Prehistoric North American Sea Culture **1948**
Na-Cho Ny'A'K-Dun First Nation **3169**
Na Kane O Ka Malo Press **2598**
NACA Multi-Cultural Scholarship **4335**
NACME Corporate Scholars Program **4336**
NACME Incentive Grants Program **4337**
NACME TechForce Scholarships **4338**
Nadleh Whut'en **2719**
Nahanni Butte Indian Band **2919**
Naicatchewenin First Nation **2946**
NAIM Ministries **3447**
Nain Museum; Piulimatsivik - **3218**
Nak'Azdli First Nation **2723**
Naknek Native Village **2265**
Nakwaxda'xw Indian Band; Gwa'Sala- **2791**
Namaka Community Historical Committee **3274**
Nambe Pueblo **239**
Namgis First Nation **2668**
Nanaimo Indian Bands **2778**
Na'Neelzhiin Ji'Olta **1242**
Nanoose First Nation **2756**
Nanwalek; Native Village of **2267**
Napakiak; Native Village of **2266**
Napamute; Native Village of **2160**
Napaskiak Native Village **2268**
NARF Legal Review **1673**
Narragansett Indian Tribe **305**
Nashville Minority Business Development Center **4236**
Nashville Urban League **3789**
Naskapis of Quebec First Nation **3058**
Nassau/Suffolk Minority Business Development Center **3723,
  4169**
Natashquan First Nation **3075**

Natchez Indians; Grand Village of the **921**
Natchez Trace Parkway • Library & Visitor Center • U.S.
  Department of the Interior • National Park Service **774**
Nation-State; Hawaii - Independent and Sovereign **2608**
National Aboriginal Management Board; Canada **3176**
National Action Council for Minorities in Engineering **3448**
National Alliance Against Racist and Political Repression **3449**
National American Indian Court Judges Association **3450**
National Anthropological Archives • Smithsonian Institution;
  U.S. **785**
National Association for the Advancement of Colored People,
  Rochester Chapter 2172 **3732**
National Association of Human Rights Workers **3451**
National Association of Intergroup Relations Officials **3451**
National Association of Investment Companies **406**
National Association of Investment Companies
  Newsletter **4443**
National Association of Medical Minority Educators **3452**
National Association of Minority Automobile Dealers **3453**
National Association of Minority Media Executives **3454**
National Association of Minority Women in Business **3455**
National Association for Native American Children of
  Alcoholics **407**
National Business League **3456**
National Business League—National Memo **4444**
National Campaign for the National Museum of the American
  Indian **875**
National Catholic Conference for Interracial Justice **3457**
National Center for American Indian and Alaska Native Mental
  Health Research **408**
    University of Colorado **1060, 2420**
National Center for American Indian Alternative Education **384**
National Center for American Indian Enterprise
  Development **409**
National Center for Minority Business Research and
  Development **3458**
National Center for Urban Ethnic Affairs **4386**
National Coalition for Indian Education **410**
National Colonial Farm of the Accokeek Foundation **908**
National Committee on Pay Equity **3459**
National Committee for Responsive Philanthropy, California
  Chapter **3547**
National Congress of American Indian Fund **387**
National Congress of American Indians **411**
National Consortium on Alternatives for Youth at Risk **3460**
National Consortium for Educational Access **3461**
National Council of BIA Educators **3410**
National Council for Culture and Art **3462**
National Database of Arts Organizations of Color **4416**
National Directory for Eldercare Information and Referral **1616**
National Directory of Minority-Owned Business Firms **2455,
  3292, 4417**
National Directory of Multi-Cultural Arts Organizations **4416**
National FFA Foundation Minority Scholarships **4339**
National Hall of Fame for Famous American Indians **986**
National Indian Activities Association **412**
National Indian Adult Education Association **506**
National Indian Athletic Association **412, 510**
National Indian Council on Aging **413**
National Indian Counselors Association **414**
National Indian Education Association **415**
National Indian Festival Association **416**
National Indian Gaming Commission; U.S. **547**
National Indian Health Board **3463**
National Indian Health Board Award **1466, 4353**
National Indian Law Library **1545**
    Rights Fund; Native American **707**
National Indian Policy Center **1038, 2145**
National Indian Training and Research Center **417, 1039**
National Indian Youth Council **418**
National Institute for Resources in Science and
  Engineering **3464**
National Institute for Women of Color **3465**
National Minority Business Council **3466, 3729**
National Minority Purchasing Council **3467**
National Minority Supplier Development Council **3467**
National Miss Indian U.S.A. Scholarship **4340**
National Monument; Canyon de Chelly **834**
National Monument; Navajo **845**
National Monument; Tonto **850**
National Monument; Tuzigoot **852**

National Monument; Walnut Canyon **853**
National Monument; Wupatki **855**
National Museum of American History • Cultural History
   Division • American Indian Program • U.S. Smithsonian
   Institution **877**
National Museum of the American Indian
      Huntington Free Library **951**
      Library • Huntington Free Library **656**
National Museum of the American Indian; National Campaign
   for the **875**
National Native American AIDS Prevention **419, 2349, 2526**
National Native American AIDS Prevention Center **443**
National Native American Chamber of Commerce **3468**
National Native American Cooperative **1546, 3469**
National Native Artists' Symposium **3335**
National Park Museum; Mesa Verde **868**
National Park Service
   Canyon De Chelly National Monument • Library • U.S.
     Department of the Interior **764**
   De Soto National Memorial • Library • U.S. Department of
     the Interior **765**
   Fort Laramie National Historic Site • Library • U.S.
     Department of the Interior **766**
   Fort Larned National Historic Site • Library • U.S.
     Department of the Interior **767**
   Glacier National Park • George C. Ruhle Library • U.S.
     Department of the Interior **768**
   Grand Portage National Monument • Library • U.S.
     Department of the Interior **769**
   Haleakala National Park • Library • U.S. Department of
     the Interior **2550**
   Hawaii Volcanoes National Park • Library • U.S.
     Department of the Interior **2551**
   Hopewell Culture National Historical Park
      Library • U.S. Department of the Interior **770**
      U.S. Department of the Interior **974**
   Intermountain Cultural Resource Center • Library • U.S.
     Department of the Interior **771**
   Jefferson National Expansion Memorial • Library and
     Archives • U.S. Department of the Interior **772**
   Little Bighorn Battlefield National Monument • White Swan
     Library • U.S. Department of the Interior **773**
   Natchez Trace Parkway • Library & Visitor Center • U.S.
     Department of the Interior **774**
   Navajo National Monument • Library • U.S. Department of
     the Interior **775**
   Ocmulgee National Monument Library • U.S. Department
     of the Interior **776**
   Olympic National Park • Visitor Center - Library • U.S.
     Department of the Interior **777**
   Pipestone National Monument • Library & Archives • U.S.
     Department of the Interior **778**
   Point Reyes National Seashore • Library • U.S.
     Department of the Interior **779**
   Pu'uhonua o Honaunau National Historical Park • Library
     • U.S. Department of the Interior **2552**
   Scotts Bluff National Monument • Library • U.S.
     Department of the Interior **780**
   Sitka National Historical Park • Library • U.S. Department
     of the Interior **781**
National Policy Review; Center for **3375**
National Shrine of the Blessed Kateri Tekakwitha **954**
National Tribal Chairman's Association **3470**
National Tribal Environmental Council **3471**
National UNITY Council **3509**
National Urban Indian Council **3472**
National Woodlands Publishing Co. **1547**
Nations; Gathering of **3404**
Nations Ministries **3473**
Nations Within a Nation **1949**
Native America Speaks **1950**
Native American Appreciation Day **467**
Native American Art—Lost and Found **1951**
Native American Artists Resource Collection **653**
Native American Book Publishers **1548**
Native American Branch • Culture and Recreation; Ontario
   Ministry of Citizenship, • Culture Division **3201**
Native American Business Council of Michigan **477**
Native American Catholics: People of the Spirit **1952**
Native American Caucus; Congressional • U.S. Congress •
   U.S. House of Representatives **529**

Native American Center **482**
Native American Center of Southeastern Minnesota **479**
Native American Coalition of Boise **456**
Native American Community Board **3474**
Native American Cultural Exchange Committee **499**
Native American Cultures; Schingoethe Center for • Aurora
   University **891**
Native American Cultures in the U.S.A.: Part One **1953**
Native American Cultures in the U.S.A.: Part Two **1954**
Native American Directory: Alaska, Canada, United
   States **1617, 2456, 3293**
Native American Educational Service **3475**
Native American Educational Service Inc. • Central Library and
   Resource Center **704**
Native American Educational Services College **3475**
Native American Expressions **514**
Native American Graves Protection and Repatriation Act **2137,**
   2522, 2610
Native American Herbology for Beginners **4461**
Native American Heritage Foundation **374**
Native American Images **1549, 1955**
Native American Indian Artist Series **1956**
Native American Indian Center of Central Ohio • Library **705**
Native American (Indian) Chamber of Commerce **3476**
Native American Indian Inter-Tribal Association of Venutra
   County **447**
Native American Inter-Tribal Association of Texas **523**
Native American Inter-Tribal Foundation **468**
Native American Journalists Association Scholarships **1441**
Native American Law Students Association **3477**
Native American Legal Defense Association **460**
Native American Policy Network **3478**
Native American Policy Network—Directory **1618**
Native American Preparatory School **1243**
Native American Preservation Association of Georgia **455**
Native American Preservation Society **461**
Native American Prophecy and Ceremony **1957**
Native American Public Broadcasting Consortium **420**, 3479
Native American Public Telecommunications **3479**
   Library **706**
Native American Recovery Center **3381**
Native American Research and Training Center • University of
   Arizona **1056**
Native American Resource Center
   Pembroke State University Center **963**
   University of North Carolina at Pembroke **1062**
Native American Resource Center Elementary-Secondary Native
   American Student Cultural Program **494**
Native American Rights Fund **3480**
   National Indian Law Library **707**
Native American Scholarship Fund **3481**
Native American Science Education Association **3482**
Native American Seminary Scholarships **1442**
Native American Series **1958**
Native American Series, Vol. 1: Nations of the Northeast **1959**
Native American Series, Vol. 2: Tribal People of the
   Northwest **1960**
Native American Series, Vol. 3: The Tribes of the
   Southeast **1961**
Native American Series, Vol. 4: The Natives of the
   Southwest **1962**
Native American Series, Vol. 5: The People of the Great
   Plains (Part One) **1963**
Native American Series, Vol. 6: The People of the Great
   Plains (Part Two) **1964**
Native American Sports Council **421**
Native American Student Organization, Austin Chapter **521**
Native American Sweat Lodge Ceremony **1965**
Native American Traditions Ideas and Values Educational
   Society **451**
Native American War Dead Memorial **528**
Native American Women Health Education Resource
   Center **3474**
The Native Americans **1966**
Native Americans for a Clean Environment **3483**
Native Americans for Community Action **433**
Native Americans Studies Collections **4500**
Native Education Directory: Organizations and Resources for
   Educators of Native Americans **1619**
Native Hawaiian Chamber of Commerce **2530**

Native Hawaiian Community-Based Education Learning Center •
U.S. Department of Education • Office of Elementary and
Secondary Education **2532**
Native Hawaiian Culture and Arts Program **3484**
Native Hawaiian Curriculum Development, Teacher Training and
Recruitment • U.S. Department of Education • Office of
Elementary and Secondary Education **2533**
Native Hawaiian Drug-Free Schools and Communities
Program **2570**
Native Hawaiian Health Professions Scholarship Program **2570**
Native Hawaiian Higher Education Program **2570**
Native Hawaiian Vocational Education • U.S. Department of
Education • Office of Vocational and Adult Education **2536**
Native Healer: Initiation into an Ancient Art **1967**
Native Land **1968, 1969**
Native Languages; Centre for Research and Teaching of
Canadian • University of Western Ontario **3245**
Native Law Centre • University of Saskatchewan **3244**
Native North American Almanac **1620, 2458, 3295**
Native Peoples Magazine **1638, 2613**
Native Self Reliance **1970**
Native Sobriety Movement; Alaska **2350**
Native Studies Program; Northern and • Carleton
University **3235**
Native Sun **1674**
Native Village of Akhiok **2147**
Native Village of Akutan **2150**
Native Village of Aleknagik **2153**
Native Village of Algaaciq **2321**
Native Village of Ambler **2155**
Native Village of Atka **2164**
Native Village of Barrow **2168**
Native Village of Belkofski **2238**
Native Village of Bill Moore's Slough **2248**
Native Village of Brevig Mission **2171**
Native Village of Buckland **2172**
Native Village of Cantwell **2173**
Native Village of Chenega **2176**
Native Village of Chickaloon **2178**
Native Village of Chignik **2179**
Native Village of Chignik Lagoon **2180**
Native Village of Chistochina **2205**
Native Village of Crooked Creek **2190**
Native Village of Deering **2191**
Native Village of Dillingham **2193**
Native Village of Eek **2195**
Native Village of Ekuk **2197**
Native Village of Elim **2198**
Native Village of Eyak **2188**
Native Village of False Pass **2201**
Native Village of Ft. Yukon **2203**
Native Village of Gakona **2206**
Native Village of Gambell **2208**
Native Village of Goodnews Bay **2211**
Native Village of Hamilton **2249**
Native Village of Hooper Bay **2216**
Native Village of Iliamna **2222**
Native Village of Kasigluk **2231**
Native Village of Kiana **2236**
Native Village of Kipnuk **2239**
Native Village of Kivalina **2240**
Native Village of Kluti-kaah **2187**
Native Village of Kobuk **2243**
Native Village of Kotzebue **2251**
Native Village of Koyuk **2252**
Native Village of Kwigillingok **2254**
Native Village of Kwinhagak **2301**
Native Village of Larsen Bay **2255**
Native Village of Marshall **2261**
Native Village of Mary's Igloo **2332**
Native Village of Nanwalek **2267**
Native Village of Napakiak **2266**
Native Village of Napamute **2160**
Native Village of Nelson Lagoon **2269**
Native Village of Nightmute **2274**
Native Village of Nikolski **2277**
Native Village of Noatak **2278**
Native Village of Nuiqsut **2284**
Native Village of Nunapitchuk **2285**
Native Village of Ouzinkie **2288**
Native Village of Perryville **2290**

Native Village of Piamuit **2217**
Native Village of Pilot Point **2292**
Native Village of Pitka's Point **2322**
Native Village of Point Hope **2295**
Native Village of Point Lay **2296**
Native Village of Port Heiden **2298**
Native Village of Port Lions **2299**
Native Village of Ruby **2304**
Native Village of St. Michael **2323**
Native Village of Salamatof **2233**
Native Village of Savoonga **2308**
Native Village of Scammon Bay **2309**
Native Village of Selawik **2310**
Native Village of Shaktoolik **2313**
Native Village of Sheldon's Point **2314**
Native Village of Shishmaref **2315**
Native Village of Shungnak **2316**
Native Village of Solomon **2319**
Native Village of Tanacross Village **2328**
Native Village of Tanana **2329**
Native Village of Tatitlek **2330**
Native Village of Tazlina **2209**
Native Village of Teller **2333**
Native Village of Tetlin **2334**
Native Village of Tuntutuliak **2337**
Native Village of Tununak **2338**
Native Village of Tyonek **2340**
Native Village of Venetie **2342**
Native Village of Wales **2344**
Native Village of White Mountain **2346**
Native Village of Yakutat **2348**
Native Villiage of Kongiganak **2247**
Native Voices Public Television **422**
Natives of the Four Directions Cultural Center **3485**
Natives of the Narrowland **1971**
NativeWeb **2138**
(Nat'oot'en Nation); Lake Babine Nation **2686**
Natural Bridges National Monument **1008**
Natural History Association; Badlands **1484**
Natural Resources Branch Library; Environment and • U.S.
Department of Justice **783**
Natural Resources Library • U.S. Department of the
Interior **782**
Naturegraph Publishers, Inc. **1550**
Natwaniwa: A Hopi Philosophical Statement **1972**
The Navajo **1973-1975**
Navajo: A Study in Cultural Contrast **1976**
Navajo; American Indian Collection: Seasons of the **1724**
Navajo Area Grant School Association **434**
Navajo Area School Board Association **423**
Navajo Chapter; Ramah **235**
Navajo Code Talkers **1977**
Navajo Community College **1310**
Navajo Community College Press **1551**
Navajo Country **1978**
Navajo Curriculum Center **1552**
The Navajo Film Themselves **1979**
Navajo Girl **1980**
Navajo Health Care Practices **1981**
Navajo Homeland; Monument Valley: **1939**
Navajo-Hopi Indian Settlement Program • U.S. Department of
the Interior • Bureau of Indian Affairs **574**
The Navajo Indian **1982**
Navajo, and Iroquois; Indian Crafts: Hopi, **1884**
Navajo Land Issue **1983**
Navajo; Last Chance for the **1913**
Navajo: Legend of the Glittering World **1984**
Navajo Mission Academy **1244**
Navajo Nation **21**
Navajo Nation Library System **708**
Navajo National Council **423**
Navajo National Monument **845**
    Library • U.S. Department of the Interior • National Park
    Service **775**
Navajo, Race for Prosperity **1985**
Navajo School; Alamo **1225**
Navajo School; Lake Valley **1240**
Navajo; Seasons of a **2049**
Navajo Song; By This Song I Walk: **1767**
The Navajo Times **1695**
Navajo Tribal Museum **846**

Navajo Weaving; The Art of **1748**
Navajos; Boy of the **1760**
Navajos; Girl of the **1838**
Navajos: The Last Red Indians **1986**
Nawash; Chippewas of **3044**
Nay-Ah-Shing School **1214**
Nazko Indian Band **2804**
NCAI Fund **411**
Nebraska Equal Opportunity Commission **4150**
Nebraska Indian Community College • Native American Studies
　Program **1347**
Nebraska Indian Community College (Macy) **1324**
Nebraska Indian Community College (Niobrara) **1325**
Nebraska Indian Community College (Winnebago) **1326**
Nebraska Labor Department • Civil Rights Division **4151**
Nebraska State Historical Society
　　John G. Neihardt State Historic Site • Research
　　　Library **709**
　　Library **710**
Nebraska Urban Indian Health Coalition **486**
Nebraska; Winnebago Tribe of • Head Start Program **1101**
Nee-Tahi-Buhn Band **2687**
Neighbors; Belmont-Hillsboro **3788**
Neihardt State Historic Site; John G. • Research Library •
　Historical Society; Nebraska State **709**
Nekaneet First Nation **3135**
Nelson A. Rockefeller Minority Internships **4341**
Nelson-Atkins Museum of Art • Slide Library **711**
Nelson House First Nation **2881**
Nelson Lagoon; Native Village of **2269**
Nemaiah Valley First Nation **2779**
Nemaska; Cree Nation of **3076**
Nemaska First Nation **3077**
Nenana Native Association **2270**
Neshnabek: The People **1987**
Neskonlith Indian Band **2697**
Netop, **1532**
Netsilik Eskimo; Yesterday, Today: The **2518**
Nevada Employment Training and Rehabilitation Department •
　Equal Employment Opportunity Office **4153**
Nevada Equal Rights Commission **4154**
Nevada Historical Society • Library **712**
Nevada Personnel Department • Affirmative Action Office **4155**
New Brunswick Department of Intergovernmental and Aboriginal
　Affairs **3197**
New Brunswick Human Rights Commission **4283**
New England Alliance of Multiracial Families **3663**
New England Antiquities Research Association **1040**
New Hampshire Human Rights Commission **4156**
New Haven; Urban League of Greater **3576**
The New Indians **1988**
New Jersey Attorney General • Law and Public Safety
　Department • Civil Rights Division **4158**
New Jersey Commerce and Economic Development
　Department • Development for Small Business, Women and
　Minorities Division **4159**
New Jersey Community Affairs Department • Affirmative Action
　Office **4160**
New Jersey Personnel Department • Equal Employment
　Opportunity/Affirmative Action Division **4161**
New Jersey Transportation Department • Civil Rights
　Office **4162**
New Mexico Indian Affairs Office **591**
New Mexico Labor Department • Human Rights Division **4165**
New Mexico; Museum of **1037**
New Mexico Tumor Registry • University of New Mexico **1061**
New Mexico Vacation Guide **4418**
New Orleans Economic Development and Policy Planning
　Division • Small and Disadvantaged Business Office **4108**
New Orleans Intergovernmental Relations Division • Human
　Relations Commission **4109**
New Orleans Minority Business Development Center **4110**
The New Pequot: A Tribal Portrait **1989**
New Post First Nation **2940**
The New Race **1675**
New Slate Falls First Nation **2995**
New Stuyahok Village **2271**
New World; Notes for a **4446**
New York City Community Assistance Unit **4170**
New York Civil Liberties Union, Genesee Valley Chapter **3733**
New York Civil Rights Coalition **3730**

New York Empire State Development Corporation • Minority
　and Women's Business Development Office **4171**
New York Mental Retardation and Developmental Disabilities
　Agency • Equal Opportunity Office **4172**
New York; Oneida Indian Nation of **247**
New York Secretary of State • State Department • Affirmative
　Action Office **4173**
New York State Agricultural and Markets Department •
　Affirmative Action Program **4174**
New York State Civil Service Department • Affirmative Action
　Office **4175**
New York State Education Department • Affirmative Action
　Office **4176**
New York State Equal Employment Opportunity Division **4177**
New York State General Services Office • Affirmative Action
　Office **4178**
New York State Housing and Community Renewal Division •
　Affirmative Action Unit **4179**
New York State Human Rights Commission **4180**
New York State Human Rights Division **4181**
New York State Indian Aid **1443**
New York State Labor Department • Equal Opportunity
　Development Division **4182**
Newark Minority Business Development Center **3708, 4163**
Newberry Library **713**
　　D'Arcy McNickle Center for American Indian History **1041**
Newfoundland and Labrador Human Rights Commission **4284**
Newhalen Village **2272**
Newport News Minority Business Development Center **4263**
News from Indian Country **1696**
News from MCLI **4445**
News from Native California 1525, **1639**
Newtok Village **2273**
Nez Perce National Historic Park **890**
Nez Perce: Portrait of a People **1990**
Nez Perce Tribal Executive Committee **149**
　　Head Start Program **1081**
NGO Committee on Human Rights **3486**
NIA: A Minority Womens Professional Network' **3711**
Nibinamik First Nation **3028**
Ni'bthaska of the Umunhon **1991**
Nicikousemenecaning First Nation **2955**
Nickolai Village **2276**
Nicolaus Rostkowski Award **1468**
Niederman Award; Allan and Joyce **1468**
Nightmute; Native Village of **2274**
Nikolski; Native Village of **2277**
1994-95 People of Color Environmental Groups Directory **4501**
(Niobrara); Nebraska Indian Community College **1325**
Nipissing First Nation **3027**
Nipmuc Indian Association of Connecticut **3578**
Nipmucs; Quinsigamond Band of the **167**
Nisqually Indian Community Council • Head Start
　Program **1146**
Nisqually Tribe **340**
Nlaka'Pamux Nation **2763**
NMA Scholarships **4342**
NMF Scholarships for Minority Students **4343**
NNAC Gifted/Talented Artist Sponsorships **1444**
No Address **1992**
No Turning Back **1993**
Noatak; Native Village of **2278**
Nome Eskimo Community **2280**
Nome Library/Kegoayah Kozga Public Library **2387**
Nomlaki Indians; Paskenta Band of **136**
Non Profit Society; Mid-Winter Pow-Wow and Cultural **485**
Nondalton Village **2281**
Nooaitch Indian Band **2770**
Nooksack Indian Tribal Council • Head Start Program **1147**
Nooksack Tribe **331**
Noorvik Native Communities **2282**
Norfolk Minority Business Development Center **4264**
North America; Health of Native People of **1612**
North America Indian Mission **3447**
North American Indian Alliance **481**
North American Indian Association **474, 3487**
North American Indian Center of Boston **471**
North American Indian Chamber of Commerce **3488**
North American Indian Club **3487**
North American Indian Landmarks—A Traveler's Guide **1621,**
　3296

North American Indian Legends 1994
The North American Indian Series 1995
North American Indian Students; Organization of 3492
North American Indian Trade and Information Center 3469
North American Indian Travel College • The Living
  Museum 3224
North American Indian Women's Association 3489
North American Indians and Edward S. Curtis 1996
North American Indians Today 1997
North American Native American Indian Information and Trade
  Center 3490
North American Native Fishes Association 3491
North American Printing 4387
North Caribou Lake First Nation 3040
North Carolina Environmental, Health and Natural Resources
  Department • Equal Employment Opportunity Office 4190
North Carolina Human Relations Commission 3746
North Dakota Department of Transportation Disadvantaged
  Business Enterprise Directory 4419
North Dakota Indian Affairs Commission—Indian Reservation
  Directories 1607
North Dakota Indian Scholarships 1445
North Dakota Labor Department • Equal Employment
  Opportunity Division 4192
North Dakota Public Instruction Department • Indian Education
  Division 593
North Dakota Transportation Department • Civil Rights
  Office 4193
North Fork Band of Mono Indians 46
North Fork Rancheria 107
North of 60 Degrees: Destiny Uncertain 3336
North Slope Borough School District • Media Center •
  Library 2388
North Spirit Lake First Nation 2939
North Thompson Band 2677
Northeast; Native American Series, Vol. 1: Nations of
  the 1959
Northeastern Native American Association 3722
Northeastern Oklahoma State University • John Vaughan
  Library/LRC • Special Collections and Archives 714
Northeastern State University • Native American Studies
  Program 1374
Northern Affairs Office; Manitoba • Native Affairs
  Secretariat 3196
Northern Arizona University
      American Indian Rehabilitation Research and Training
        Center 1042
      Cline Library • Special Collections and Archives
        Department 715
Northern Cheyenne Tribal Council • Head Start Program 1099
Northern Cheyenne Tribe 194
Northern Indiana Historical Society • Library 716
Northern Life Museum 3219
Northern and Native Studies Program • Carleton
  University 3235
The Northern Plains 1998
Northern Plains Native American Chemical Dependency
  Association 515
Northern Studies; Centre for • Lakehead University 3238
Northland College • Native American Studies Program 1375
Northland Publishing 1553
Northlands First Nation 2876
Northway Village 2283
Northwest Angle No. 37 First Nation 3024
Northwest History; Myron Eells Library of • Whitman
  College 821
Northwest Indian College 1339
Northwest Indian Fisheries Commission News 1676
Northwest Minority Supplier Development Council 3815
Northwest; Native American Series, Vol. 2: Tribal People of
  the 1960
Northwest Region; Directory of Native Education Resources in
  the 1604, 2453
Northwest Territories Ministry of Intergovernmental and
  Aboriginal Affairs 3199
Northwest Territory Canadian and French Heritage Center •
  Minnesota Genealogical Society Library 3207
Northwestern Band of Shoshone Nation 146
Northwestern Florida Creek Indian Council 454
Northwestern Oklahoma State University • Library 717
Norway House Cree Nation 2882

Notes for a New World 4446
Nova Scotia Human Rights Commission 4285
Now That the Buffalo's Gone 1999
Nuantta Sunaqutangit Museum 3220
Nuchatlaht Tribe 2845
Nuiqsut; Native Village of 2284
Nunapitchuk; Native Village of 2285
Nunatsiaq News 3307
Nurse Scholarships; Colonial Dames Indian 1422
Nutrition and the Environment of Indigenous People; Centre
  for 3236
Nuu-chan-nulth Tribal Council 2788
Nuxalk Indian Band 2679
O-Chi-Chak-Ko-Sipi First Nation 2854
Oak Lake First Nation 2886
Oak Park Housing Center 3627
Oakland Minority Business Development Center No. 1; San
  Francisco/ 4050
Oakland Public Library • American Indian Library
  Collection 718
Obedjiwan First Nation 3083
Obsidian Point-Making 2000
Occaneechi Band of the Saponi Nation 255
Ocean Man 3158
Ochapowace First Nation 3163
O'Chiese First Nation 2652
Ocmulgee National Monument 887
Ocmulgee National Monument Library • U.S. Department of the
  Interior • National Park Service 776
Oconaluftee Indian Village 962
Odanak First Nation 3079
Odessa Minority Business Development Center; Lubbock/
  Midland- 4253
Office of Aboriginal Healing and Wellness • Ontario Ministry of
  Community and Social Services 3202
Office; Chattanooga Equal Employment Opportunity and Better
  Housing 597
Office of Tribal Services • Tribal Government Services Division
  • U.S. Department of the Interior • Bureau of Indian
  Affairs 1052
Official Human Rights Agencies; International Association
  of 3423
OGCA Civil Rights Defense Fund 3761
Oglala Lakota College 1336
      Library 719
      Native American Studies 1376
      Native American Studies Graduate Program 1400
Oglala Lakota; Friends of the 487
Oglala Sioux; Joe KillsRight: 1903
Oglala Sioux Tribal Council • Head Start Program 1136
Oglala Sioux Tribe 313
Ohamil Indian Band 2735
Ohio Agricultural Department • Equal Employment Opportunity
  and Training Section 4200
Ohio Attorney General • Civil Rights Section 4201
Ohio Center for Native American Affairs 497
Ohio Civil Rights Commission 4202
Ohio Development Department • Minority Business
  Development Office 4203
Ohio Health Department
      Equal Employment Opportunity Office 4204
      Minority Affairs Office 4205
Ohio Office of the Governor • Multicultural Affairs Office 4206
Ojibwa Community College; Lac Courte Oreilles 1340
Ojibwa Culture; Marquette Mission Park and Museum of 913
Ojibwa Culture; Museum of 1544
Ojibwa Indian School 1265
Ojibwa School; Lac Courte Oreilles 1305
Ojibway-Cree Cultural Centre 3275
Ojibway First Nation; Chapleau 2938
Ojibway First Nation; Lake Nipigon 2926
Ojibway School; Fond du Lac 1212
Ojibway Tribal Council; Dakota 2851
Ojibways of Garden River First Nation 2959
Ojibways of Hiawatha First Nation 2969
Ojibways of Onegaming Band(Sabaskong) 2993
Ojibways of the Pic River (Heron Bay) 2965
Ojibways of Sucker Creek 2974
Ojibways of Walpole Island 3038
Ojibwe; Sandy Lake Band of 181
Ojo Encino Day School 1245

Okak; The Last Days of 3331
Okanagan Indian Band 2834
Okanese First Nation 3099
Okemasis First Nation; Beardy's and 3116
Oklahoma; Cherokee Nation of 290
    Head Start Program 1121
Oklahoma; Chickasaw Nation of 261
    Head Start Program 1123
Oklahoma; Choctaw Nation of 270
    Head Start Program 1124
Oklahoma City Minority Business Development Center 4207
Oklahoma; Creek Nation of • Head Start Program 1125
Oklahoma; Eastern Shawnee Tribe of 189
Oklahoma Employment Security Commission • Equal
    Employment Opportunity Office 4208
Oklahoma Health Department • Affirmative Action
    Division 4209
Oklahoma Historical Society 1554
    Archives and Manuscript Division 720
    Division of Library Resources 721
    Museum of the Western Prairie • Bernice Ford Price
        Reference Library 722
Oklahoma Human Rights Commission 4210
Oklahoma Human Services Department • Affirmative Action
    Office 4211
Oklahoma Indian Affairs Commission 594
Oklahoma; Kickapoo Tribe of 274
    Kickapoo Head Start, Inc. 1126
Oklahoma; Kiowa Tribe of • Head Start Program 1127
Oklahoma; Miami Tribe of 275
Oklahoma Minority Supplier Development Council 3766
Oklahoma NativeVoices Project 2139
Oklahoma; Ottawa Tribe of 276
Oklahoma; Peoria Indian Tribe of 277
Oklahoma School for the Blind • Parkview Library 723
Oklahoma School Improvement and Standards • Indian
    Education Office 595
Oklahoma; Seminole Nation of • Head Start Program 1129
Oklahoma Today Magazine 1640
Old Dances, New Dancers 2505
Old Harbor; Village of 2286
Old West Museum; Sunset Trading Post- • Library 756
Olson Library; Gordon B. • Minot State University 692
Olympic National Park • Visitor Center - Library • U.S.
    Department of the Interior • National Park Service 777
Olympics; World Eskimo-Indian 2354
Omaha Tribal Council • Head Start Program 1100
Omaha Tribe 197
Omaha Tribe: The Land, The People, The Family 2001
On Indian Land 1697
On-Line for Peace and Justice 4502
On the Path to Self-Reliance 2002
On the Spring Ice 2506
On the Totem Trail 2003
One Arrow First Nation 3102
1,000 Years of Muscogee (Creek) Art 2004
One World Publishing 1555
Onegaming Band(Sabaskong); Ojibways of 2993
Oneida Indian Nation 2140
Oneida Indian Nation of New York 247
Oneida Tribal Business Committee • Head Start
    Program 1156
Oneida Tribal School 1307
Oneida Tribe 362
Oneidas of the Thames First Nation 3026
Onion Lake First Nation 3140
Onondaga County; Urban League of 3737
Onondaga Nation 250
Ontario Attorney General and Minister Responsible for Native
    Affairs 3200
Ontario Human Rights Commission 4286
Ontario Ministry of Citizenship, Culture and Recreation •
    Culture Division • Native American Branch 3201
Ontario Ministry of Community and Social Services • Office of
    Aboriginal Healing and Wellness 3202
Ontario Native Affairs Secretariat 3203
Opaskwayak Cree Nation 2900
Open Doors; Coalition for 3658
Open Island 3719
Opetchesaht First Nation 2789
Opportunities in Criminal Justice 4462

Oral History Center; South Dakota 1048
    Library • American Indian Research Project 604
Oral History Collection; Sac and Fox 737
Oral History Program • California State University,
    Fullerton 4363
Oral History Program; Samuel Proctor • Library • University of
    Florida 792
Oral Tradition; Ancient Spirit, Living Word: The 1742
Orange County Urban League 3530
Order of the Indian Wars—Communique 1677
Oregon Directory of American Indian Resources 1622
Oregon Jack Creek Indian Band 2674
Oregon Office of the Governor • Affirmative Action
    Office 4214
Oregon Transportation Department • Human Resources and
    Organization Development Branch • Civil Rights
    Section 4215
Organization of North American Indian Students 3492
Organizations: A National Directory; Minority 4412
Organizations; Directory of Minority Arts 4402
Organized Village of Grayling 2212
Organized Village of Kake 2226
Organized Village of Kasaan 2230
Organized Village of Kwethluk 2253
Organized Village of Saxman 2235
The Organizer 4447
Orientation Program; Corporate 3389
The Origin of the Crown Dance and Ba'ts'oosee 2005
Original Peoples: Then and Now; Canada's 3318
Origins Program 1556, 2447
Orlando Human Relations Office 4071
Orlando Minority Business Development Center 4072
Orlando Urban League; Metropolitan 3596
Orutsararmuit Native Council 2170
Osage Nation of Oklahoma 281
Osage Tribal Council • Head Start Program 1128
Osage Village Historic Site 923
Oscar Howe Memorial Award 1468
Oscar Howe: The Sioux Painter 2006
Oscarville Traditional Council 2287
Osoyoos Band 2783
Otoe-Missouria Tribe 286
Ottawa and Chippewa Tribes; Grand Traverse Band of • Head
    Start Program 1084
Ottawa Indians; Little River Band of 170
Ottawa Tribe of Oklahoma 276
Ouji-Bougoumou; Cree Nation of 3080
Our Native American Friends 2007, 2507
Our Sacred Land 2008
Our Totem is the Raven 2009
Ouray Tribe; Unitah and 323
Outstanding American Indian Awards 1467
Ouzinkie; Native Village of 2288
Over State Museum; W.H. • University of South Dakota 1066
Oweekeno Nation 2793
Oxford House First Nation 2884
Oxnard Minority Business Development Center 4047
Pabineau Indian Band 2908
Pacheenaht Band 2795
Pacific Culture and Education; Institute for Native 2529
Pacific Dance Association 2524
Pacific Dance; Foundation for 2524
Pacific Pipeline 1557
PACT 3496
Paha Sapa 2010
Pa'ia Elementary School 2573
Painter, Oscar Howe: The Sioux 2006
Paintings; Patricia J and Stanley H. Broder Collection of Native
    American 796
Paiute Band of the Moapa Indian Reservation; Moapa 214
Paiute Business Council; Shoshone 216
Paiute Indian Tribe of Utah 321
Paiute Reservation; Benton 32
Paiute and Shoshone Tribe; Fort McDermitt 213
Paiute Tribe; Antelope Valley 48
Paiute Tribe; Burns- 295
Paiute Tribe; Kaibab 6
Paiute Tribe; Las Vegas 210
Paiute Tribe; Pyramid Lake 215
Paiute Tribe; San Juan Southern 18
Paiute Tribe; Summit Lake 220

Paiute Tribe; Walker River 218
Paiute Tribe; Yerington 221
Paiutes of the Southwest; Pride, Purpose and Promise: 2026
Pakua Shipi First Nation 3084
Pala Band of Mission Indians 97
Palm Beach County Human Rights Council 3602
Palm Beach County Urban League 3603
Palomar Community College
    Library • Special Collections 724
    Native American Studies Program 1348
Pan-American Indian Association 3493
Paneak Memorial Museum; Simon 2406
Panel of American Women 3494
Panhandle-Plains Historical Museum • Research Center 725,
   1043
Parents; Concerned American Indian 3384
Parker Award; Ely ("Eli") S. 1461
Parks Programs on Indian Lands; Fish, Wildlife, and • U.S.
   Department of the Interior • Bureau of Indian Affairs 3983
Parks-Thompson Co. 1558
Parmly Billings Library • Montana Room 726
Pascua Yaqui Tribal Council • Head Start Program 1072
Pascua Yaqui Tribe 19
Paskenta Band of Nomlaki Indians 136
Pasqua First Nation No. 79 3120
Passamaquoddy; Politics, Peyote, and 2020
Passamaquoddy Tribe 162
Passamaquoddy Tribe of Maine [Princeton, ME] 164
Patricia J and Stanley H. Broder Collection of Native American
   Paintings 796
Paucatuck Eastern Pequot Tribe 142
Paul First Nation 2622
Pauma Band of Mission Indians 100
Paupieres Publishing Co. 1559
Pauquachin Indian Band 2682
Pavilion Indian Band 2689
Pawnee Indian Village Museum 905
Pawnee Indian Village State Historic Site • Library 727
Pawnee Tribe 282
Pay Equity; National Committee on 3459
Pays Plat First Nation 3018
Peace and Justice; On-Line for 4502
Peace Network, Cedar Rapids 3637
Peace Pipe Award; Catlin 1458
Peace; White Roots of 3399
PeaceNet 4503
Pechanga Band of Mission Indians 123
Pediatrics; Gerber Prize for Excellence in 4323
Pedro Bay Village 2289
Peepeekisis First Nation 3100
Peguis First Nation 2885
Peigan First Nation 2616
Pele Defense Fund 2527
Pelican Lake First Nation 3131
Peltier Defense Committee; Leonard 3434
Peltier; The Trial of Leonard 2098
Pembroke State University • Native American Studies Program
   • UNCP American Indian Studies Department 1377
Pembroke State University Center • Native American Resource
   Center 963
Pemmican Publications Inc. 3276
Penelakut Indian Band 2699
Penn; The American as Artist: A Portrait of Bob 1714
Pennsylvania Aging Department • Affirmative Action
   Office 4217
Pennsylvania Association of Native Americans 511
Pennsylvania Education Department • Postsecondary and
   Higher Education Office • Equal Employment Opportunity
   Office 4218
Pennsylvania General Services Department • Minority
   Development Office 4219
Pennsylvania Human Relations Commission 4220
Pennsylvania Public Welfare Department • Affirmative Action
   Office 4221
Pennsylvania State University • American Indian Education
   Policy Center 1044
Pennsylvania Transportation Department • Equal Opportunity
   Bureau 4222
Penobscot Indian Nation 161
Penticton Indian Band 2785
The People Are Dancing Again 2011

People of the Buffalo 2012
People of Color Environmental Groups Directory; 1994-
   95 4501
People of the Dawn 2013
People of the First Light 2014
People of the Macon Plateau 2015
People of the Seal Series 2508
The People's Homepage 2141
People's Organization for Social Equality 3650
Peoria Indian Tribe of Oklahoma 277
Pequot: A Tribal Portrait; The New 1989
Pequot Nation; Mashantucket 140
Pequot Tribe; Mashantucket 141
Pequot Tribe; Paucatuck Eastern 142
Performing Arts; American Indian Registry for the 382
Performing and Visual Arts; Association for Native Development
   in the 3171
Periodicals Project; American Indian and Alaska Native 3360
Perryville; Native Village of 2290
Persimmon Press 4388
Peter Ballantyne Cree Nation 3145
Peter Native American Art Museum; Jesse • Santa Rosa
   Junior College 860
Peter Wolf Toth 1560
Petereins Press 1561
Peters Indian Band 2736
Petersburg Indian Association 2291
Petrified Forest National Park 847
Petro-Canada Education Awards for Native Students 3260
Petroglyph National Monument 943
Petroglyph Press, Ltd. 2599
Petroglyphs and Pictographs; American Committee to Advance
   the Study of 1473
Peyote, and Passamaquoddy; Politics, 2020
Pheasant Rump Nakota 3127
Philadelphia Mayor's Action Center 4223
Philanthropy, California Chapter; National Committee for
   Responsive 3547
Philbrook Museum of Art • Chapman Library 728
Phillips Foundation, Inc.; The Frank • Woolaroc Museum •
   Library 648
Philosophical Society; American • Library 605
The Phoenix 3302
Phoenix Heard Museum; Indian Arts at the 1880
Phoenix Indian Center 435
Phoenix Indian Medical Center • Library 729
Phoenix Minority Business Development Center 4041
Phoenix Public Library • Arizona Room 730
Photography Collection; Sac and Fox 737
Physicians; Association of American Indian 3365
Physicians for Human Rights 3495
Physics Majors; Corporate Sponsored Scholarships for Minority
   Undergraduate 4314
Piamuit; Native Village of 2217
Piapot First Nation 3113
Pic Mobert First Nation 2983
Pic River (Heron Bay); Ojibways of the 2965
Picayune Rancheria 47
Picking Tribes 2016
Pictographs; American Committee to Advance the Study of
   Petroglyphs and 1473
Picuris Indians 2017
Picuris Pueblo 233
Pierre Indian Learning Center 1291
Pikangikum First Nation 3005
Pikes Peak Minority Business Foundation 3563
Pilgrim 1678
Pilot Point; Native Village of 2292
Pilot Station Traditional Council 2293
Pima-Maricopa Indian Community; Salt River 14
Pine Creek First Nation 2853
Pine Nuts 2018
Pine Ridge School 1292
Pine Springs Boarding School 1185
Pinellas County Urban League 3597
Pineoleville Rancheria 129
Pinon Dormitory 1186
Pinson Mounds State Archaeological Area 1000
Pioneer Museum • Library • Historical Society, Inc.; Martin
   County 685
Pioneers Museum Foundation; Plains Indians and 508

The Pipe is the Altar, Celebration/ **1771**
Pipestone County Historical Museum **928**
Pipestone National Monument **929**
    Library & Archives • U.S. Department of the Interior •
    National Park Service **778**
Piqua Historical Area **972**
Pit River Tribe **40**
Pitka's Point; Native Village of **2322**
Pittsburgh Minority Business Development Center **4224**
Piulimatsivik - Nain Museum **3218**
Place in the Woods **4389**
Placement Services; College **3389**
Places Not Our Own **2019**
Plains First Nation; Dakota **2887**
Plains Historical Museum; Panhandle- • Research Center **725**
Plains Indian and Crafts Center; Museum of the **927**
Plains Indian; End of the Trail: The American **1814**
Plains Indian; Luxton Museum of the **3208**
Plains Indian Museum • Buffalo Bill Historical Center **1016**
Plains Indians; Children of the **1776**
Plains Indians and Pioneers Museum Foundation **508**
Plains; Museum of the Great **984, 1036**
Plains; The Northern **1998**
Plains (Part One); Native American Series, Vol. 5: The People
    of the Great **1963**
Plains (Part Two); Native American Series, Vol. 6: The People
    of the Great **1964**
Plains and Southwest; Center for the Study of Native
    Languages of the • University of Colorado at Boulder **1059**
Plan of Action for Challenging Times **3496**
Planning and Community Development Agencies; Directory
    of **1606**
Planning and The Black Community Division of APA
    Undergraduate Minority Scholarship **4344**
Plat First Nation; Pays **3018**
Platinum Traditional Village **2294**
Plenty Coups State Park; Chief **925**
Pluralism and Group Identity; Institute on **4377**
Poarch Band of Creek Indians **1**
Point Arena Rancheria; Manchester/ **101**
Point Hope; Native Village of **2295**
Point Lay; Native Village of **2296**
Point Reyes National Seashore • Library • U.S. Department of
    the Interior • National Park Service **779**
Pojoaque Pueblo **240**
Pokagon Band of Potawatomi Indians **169**
Pokanoket Tribe **304**
Polacca Day School **1187**
Policy; Center for Alternative Mining Development **3373**
Policy Center; National Indian **1038, 2145**
Policy; Center for Religion, Ethics and Social • Durland
    Alternatives Library **623**
Policy Network—Directory; Native American **1618**
Policy Network; Native American **3478**
Policy Planning Division; New Orleans Economic Development
    and • Small and Disadvantaged Business Office **4108**
Policy Professionals; Coalition of Minority **3380**
Policy Review; Center for National **3375**
Polingaysi Qoyawayma Scholarship **1446**
Political Development; Alliance of Minority Women for Business
    and **3354**
Political Prisoners; Campaign for Amnesty and Human Rights
    for **3369, 3369**
Political Repression; National Alliance Against Racist and **3449**
Political Rights; Campaign for **3370**
Political Rights Defense Fund **3497**
Politics, Peyote, and Passamaquoddy **2020**
Polynesian Cultural Center **2528**
Polynesian Studies; Institute for **2528**
Pomo; Dream Dances of the Kashia **1804**
Pomo: Forms and Ornamentation; Basketry of the **1750**
Pomo Indians; Elem Indian Colony of **45**
Pomo Indians; Kashia Men's Dances: Southwestern **1905**
Pomo: Introductory Film; Basketry of the **1751**
Pomo Shaman **2021**
Pomo: Techniques; Basketry of the **1752**
Ponca City Cultural Center and Museums **987**
    Library **731**
Ponca Creek Tribe of Nebraska **198**
Ponca He-Thush-Ka Society **504**
Ponca Tribe **284**

Ponce Minority Business Development Center **4226**
Pontiac Area Urban League **3678**
Popkum First Nation **2703**
Poplar Hill First Nation **3010**
Poplar River First Nation **2901**
Popular Press • Bowling Green State University **4362**
Porcupine Day School **1293**
Port Gamble Klallam Tribe • Head Start Program **1148**
Port Gamble S'Klallam Tribe **333**
Port Graham Village **2297**
Port Heiden; Native Village of **2298**
Port Lions; Native Village of **2299**
(Port Madison); Suquamish Tribe **346**
Portage Creek Village **2300**
Portland Art Museum • Rex Arragon Library **732**
Portland Minority Business Development Center **4216**
Positively Native **2022**
Post Secondary Schools (Haskell and SIPI); Indian • U.S.
    Department of the Interior • Bureau of Indian Affairs **3993**
Potawatomi Executive Council; Forest County **355**
Potawatomi Indians; Pokagon Band of **169**
Potawatomi Tribe; Prairie Band **153**
Potlatch; Huteetl: A Koyukon Memorial **2498**
Potlatch People **3337**
Potter Valley Rancheria **130**
Pottery; Hopi **1862**
Pottery Southwest **1679**
Poundmaker First Nation **3144**
Pow-Wow! **2023**
Pow-Wow and Cultural Non Profit Society; Mid-Winter **485**
Pow Wow Pages and Native Events **4504**
Pow Wow on the Red Road **1623, 3297**
Pow Wow White Pages **2143**
Powerless Politics **2024**
Powers Award **1468**
Powhatan Renape Nation **223**
Powwow Calendar **1624, 3298**
Prairie Band Potawatomi Tribe **153**
Prairie Island Community (Minnesota Mdewakanton Sioux) **186**
Prairie Provincial Press **1562**
Pre-Columbian Research Center and Museum **3419**
Preferences; Californians Against Discrimination and **3533**
Prehistoric Man **2025**
Prehistoric Museum • College of Eastern Utah **1006**
Prejudice: A Lesson to Forget **4463**
Prejudice: Causes, Consequences, Cures **4464**
Prejudice and Ethnoviolence; Center for the Applied Study
    of **3498**
The Prejudice Film **4465**
The Prejudice Institute/Center for the Applied Study of
    Ethnoviolence **3498**
Presbyterian Church Native American Education Grants **1447,
    2438**
Presbyterian Church Native American Seminary
    Scholarships **1448, 2439**
Presbyterian Church Student Opportunity Scholarships **4345**
Presbyterian Mission Museum; Iowa, Sac and Fox **903**
Preschool Children (Alaska Native Education); Alaska Native
    Home Based Education for • U.S. Department of Education •
    Office of Elementary and Secondary Education **2366**
Prescott College **1378**
Prescott Historical Societies; Sharlot Hall/ •
    Library/Archives **748**
Prescott Tribal Library; Yavapai- **829**
Prescott Tribe; Yavapai- **11**
Preservation Society; Native American **461**
Press Gang Publishers **3277**
Press Research Association; American Native **3360**
Prevention and Control of Violence and Extremism; Institute
    for **3498**
Price Reference Library; Bernice Ford • Historical Society;
    Oklahoma • Museum of the Western Prairie **722**
Pride, Purpose and Promise: Paiutes of the Southwest **2026**
The Pride of Spirit Bay **2027**
The Primal Land **2028**
The Primal Mind **2029**
Prince Edward Island Human Rights Commission **4287**
Princeton University • Woodrow Wilson School of Public and
    International Affairs • Bendheim-Thomas Center for Child
    Wellbeing **4298**

Prisoners; Campaign for Amnesty and Human Rights for Political 3369, **3369**
The Probable Passing of Elk Creek **2030**
Probe Communications International Inc. **4390**
Proctor Oral History Program; Samuel • Library • University of Florida **792**
Professional Ethics and Academic Freedom; Committee on 3382
Professional Ethics, Rights and Freedom; Committee on **3382**
Progress and Equality; Hillsborough Organization for **3600**
Project Equality, Inc. **4391**
Project Star 3549
Proof Press **4392**
Prophet River First Nation **2722**
Proud Moments **2031**
Providence Human Relations Office **4227**
Public Broadcasting Consortium; Native American **420**, 3479
Public and Indian Housing - Indian Loan Guarantee Program (Loan Guarantees for Indian Housing) • U.S. Department of Housing and Urban Development • Office of Native American Programs • Public and Indian Housing **3971**
Public Radio Stations; Coalition of Native American 3413
Public Telecommunications; Native American **3479**
Public Television; Native Voices **422**
Publishers; Native American Book **1548**
Pueblo of Acoma **234, 944**
        Head Start Program **1106**
Pueblo Arts **2032**
Pueblo; Cochiti **226**
Pueblo Council; All Indian **367**
Pueblo Cultural Center; Indian 367, **939**
Pueblo; Isleta **229**
        Head Start Program **1107**
Pueblo; Jemez **230**
        Walatowa Head Start Program **1108**
Pueblo; Laguna **231**
        Head Start Program **1109**
Pueblo; Nambe **239**
Pueblo Peoples: First Encounters **2033**
Pueblo; Picuris **233**
Pueblo Pintado Community School **1246**
Pueblo; Pojoaque **240**
Pueblo Renaissance **2034**
Pueblo; San Felipe **236**
        Head Start Program **1110**
        San Felipe School **1247**
Pueblo; San Ildefonso **241**
Pueblo; San Juan **237**
Pueblo; Sandia **224**
Pueblo; Santa Ana **225**
Pueblo; Santa Clara **228**
Pueblo; Santo Domingo **243**
Pueblo; Taos **244, 2084**
        Head Start Program **1111**
Pueblo; Tesuque **242**
Pueblo; Ysleta del Sur **319**
Pueblo; Zia **238**
Pueblo; Zuni **245**
Pueblos, Inc.; Eight Northern • Head Start Program **1102**
Pueblos, Inc.; Five Sandoval Indian • Head Start Program **1103**
Pueblos; Maria of the **1930**
Pueblos; Zuni • Head Start Program **1113**
Punana Leo O Hilo **2574**
Punana Leo O Honolulu **2575**
Punana Leo O Kaua'i **2576**
Punana Leo O Maui **2577**
Punana Leo O Moloka'l **2578**
Pu'ohala Elementary School **2579**
Purchasing Council; National Minority 3467
Purchasing Council; Tidewater Regional Minority **3809**
Pu'uhonua o Honaunau National Historical Park • Library • U.S. Department of the Interior • National Park Service **2552**
Pu'uhonua O Honaunau National Historical Park **2566**
Puyallup Tribe **347**
Pyramid Lake Paiute Tribe **215**
Qagun Tayagungin Tribe of Sand Point **2307**
Qamani'tuap Naalautaa Society 3311
Qawalangin Tribe of Unalaska **2341**
Qoyawayma Award; Al **1413**
Qoyawayma Scholarship; Polingaysi **1446**

Quad County Urban League **3620**
Quaker Service Bulletin **4448**
Qualicum Indian Band **2800**
Qualla Indian Boundary • Head Start Program **1115**
Quapaw Tribe **285**
Quartz Valley Reservation **55**
Quassarte Tribal Town; Alabama- **271**
Quatsino Indian Band **2707**
Quebec First Nation; Naskapis of **3058**
Quebec Secretariat for Native Affairs **3204**
Quechan Tribe (Fort Yuma) **22**
Queen Emma Summer Palace **2567**
Queen Lilioukalani Children's Center 2593
Queens Minority Business Development Center **3718, 4183**
Queen's University at Kingston • Agnes Etherington Art Centre **3242**
Quileute Tribal Council • Head Start Program **1149**
Quileute Tribe **335**
Quinault Indian Nation **348**
        Head Start Program **1150**
Quinnipiac Tribal Council; Algonquian Confederacy **449**
Quinsigamond Band of the Nipmucs **167**
Quinte; Mohawks of the Bay of **2945**
Quivira Museum; Coronado- **901**
R. Schneider Publishers **1563**
R. V. Greeves Art Gallery **1564**
Race in America; Center for Studies of Ethnicity and • University of Colorado at Boulder **4299**
Race and Ethnicity in America; Center for the Study of • Brown University **4293**
racial Council for Business Opportunity; Inter **3430**
racial Council of New York; Catholic Inter **3725**
Racial/Ethnic Leadership Supplemental Grants **4346**
racial Justice; National Catholic Conference for Inter **3457**
Racial Unity; Artists for **3624**
Racine and Kenosha; Urban League of **3829**
Racine Treaty Support Group **3828**
Racism; Belmont Against **3660**
Racism; District of Columbia Student Coalition Against Apartheid and **3584**
Racism and Minority Groups: Part 1 **4466**
Racism and Minority Groups: Part 2 **4467**
Racism-Sexism; Musicians Against **3728**
Racist and Political Repression; National Alliance Against **3449**
Radio Stations; Coalition of Native American Public 3413
Rafferty School; Beatrice **1207**
Rainbow Educational Media Inc. **4393**
Rainy River First Nation **2950**
Raleigh/Durham Minority Business Development Center **4191**
Ramah Navajo Chapter **235**
Ramona Band of Cahuilla Indians **28**
Rampart Village **2302**
Rancheria; Alturas **26**
(Rat Portage); Wauzhushk Onigum First Nation **2971**
Rauh Memorial Library • Children's Museum of Indianapolis **627**
Ravalli County Museum • Miles Romney Memorial Library • Historical Society; Bitter Root Valley **614**
Raven Hail Books **1565**
Raven's Tsa-La-Gi Page **2142**
Ray Manley Publishing **1566**
Real Estate Programs - Indian Lands • U.S. Department of the Interior • Bureau of Indian Affairs **2382, 4003**
The Real People **2035**
Reality and Meaning; Institute for Encyclopedia of Human Ideas on Ultimate **3416**
Recovery Center; Native American 3381
Red Bank Indian Band **2915**
Red Bluff Indian Band **2805**
Red Clay State Historical Park **1001**
        Library **733**
Red Cliff Tribe **353**
Red Cloud Country **1680**
Red Cloud Indian Art Show **1468**
Red Crow Community College **3246**
Red Devil; Village of **2303**
Red Earth First Nation **3151**
Red Elk: A Sioux Indian Artist; Herman **1852**
Red Feather **3783**
Red Lake Band of Chippewa Indians of Minnesota **185**
Red Lake Day School **1188**

Red Lake Reservation • Head Start Program **1091**
Red Nations; Dakota Women of All **395**
Red Nations; Women of All **395, 3511**
Red Paint People: The Discovery of a Prehistoric North American Sea Culture; The Mystery of the Lost **1948**
Red Pheasant First Nation **3107**
Red River; Museum of the **985**
The Red Road to Sobriety **4468**
Red Road: Towards the Techno-Tribal **2036**
(Red Rock); Lake Helen First Nation **2997**
Red Sucker Lake First Nation **2891**
Red Sunday **2037**
Red Water Elementary School **1218**
Redding Rancheria **103**
Redwood Valley Rancheria **105**
Redwoods; College of the • Native American Studies Program **1343**
Reference Encyclopedia of the American Indian **1625**
Refugees; American Indian **381**
Regina Plains Museum **3233**
Rehabilitation; American Indian **1649**
Relander Collection; Click • Yakima Valley Regional Library • Reference Department **828**
Relics; Who's Who in Indian **1628**
Relief; World Emergency **3512**
Religion, Ethics and Social Policy; Center for • Durland Alternatives Library **623**
Religious, Linguistic and Other Minorities; International Federation for the Protection of the Rights of Ethnic, **3424**
Renape Nation; Powhatan **223**
Rendezvous Canada, 1606 **3338**
Reno-Sparks Indian Colony **217**
Repatriation Act; Native American Graves Protection and **2137, 2522, 2610**
Repatriation Foundation; American Indian Ritual Object **383**
Replacement and Repair of Indian Schools • U.S. Department of the Interior • Bureau of Indian Affairs **4004**
Repression; Alliance to End **3449**
Repression=ANTIREPRESSION Resource Team; Anti- **3363**
Research Association; American Native Press **3360**
Research Careers (MARC); Minority Access to • U.S. Department of Health and Human Services • National Institutes of Health **3962**
Research Club; Aboriginal **366**
Research and Education on Human Rights; Institute for **3418**
Research; Gabriel Dumont Institute of Native Studies and Applied **3268**
Reservation Directories; North Dakota Indian Affairs Commission—Indian **1607**
Reservation; Lament of the **1911**
Reservations; Trustees of **910**
Residential Alternatives; Rural **3759**
Resighini Rancheria; Coast Indian Community of the **79**
Resource Board; Long Island Community Housing **3738**
Resource Center; Native American • Pembroke State University Center **963**
Resources for Indian Student Education **440**
Responsibilities; Section of Individual Rights and **3500**
Responsive Philanthropy, California Chapter; National Committee for **3547**
Return of the Raven—The Edison Chiloquin Story **2038**
Return of the Sacred Pole **2039**
Return to Sovereignty **2040**
Rex Arragon Library • Art Museum; Portland **732**
Rhode Island Administration Department • Human Resources Office • Minority Business Enterprise **4228**
Rhode Island Education Department • Elementary and Secondary Office • Equity and Access Office **4229**
Rhode Island Human Rights Commission **4230**
Rhode Island Justice Alliance **3778**
Rhode Island Transportation Department • Equal Employment Opportunity Office **4231**
Richard Cardinal: Cry From a Diary of a Metis Child **3339**
Richard's Totem Pole (Canada) **3340**
Richfield Dormitory **1302**
Right to Know; An Adoptee's **4473**
Rights Advocates; Human **3406**
Rights Advocates International; Human **3407**
Rights, AFL-CIO; Department of Civil **3393**
Rights Agencies; International Association of Official Human **3423**

Rights; American Committee for Human **3495**
Rights; American Council for the Advancement of Human **3357**
Rights Association; Human **3541**
Rights Association; Indian **397**
Rights; Attorney Fees - Indian • U.S. Department of the Interior • Bureau of Indian Affairs **3977**
Rights; British Columbia Council of Human **4280**
Rights; Campaign for Political **3370**
Rights; Center for the Study of Human **3376**
Rights; Citizens Commission on Human **3587, 3614, 3694**
Rights and Citizenship Commission; Alberta Human **4277**
Rights; Civil **4434**
Rights or Civil Rights; Treaty **2097**
Rights; Coalition for Civil **3556**
Rights Coalition; New York Civil **3730**
Rights Commission; Alaska Human **4039**
Rights Commission; Canadian Human **3831**
Rights Commission Decisions; Illinois Human **4491**
Rights Commission; District of Columbia Human **4063**
Rights Commission; Friends of the Des Moines Human **3639**
Rights Commission; Idaho Human **4085**
Rights Commission; Illinois Human **4089**
Rights Commission; Indiana Civil **4093**
Rights Commission; Iowa Civil **4098**
Rights Commission; Kansas Human **3642, 4099**
Rights Commission; Kentucky Human **4102**
Rights Commission; Maine Human **4111**
Rights Commission; Manitoba Human **4281**
Rights Commission; Missouri Human **4144**
Rights Commission; Nevada Equal **4154**
Rights Commission; New Brunswick Human **4283**
Rights Commission; New Hampshire Human **4156**
Rights Commission; New York State Human **4180**
Rights Commission; Newfoundland and Labrador Human **4284**
Rights Commission Newsletter; Michigan Civil **4442**
Rights Commission; Nova Scotia Human **4285**
Rights Commission; Ohio Civil **4202**
Rights Commission; Oklahoma Human **4210**
Rights Commission; Ontario Human **4286**
Rights Commission; Prince Edward Island Human **4287**
Rights Commission; Rhode Island Human **4230**
Rights Commission of Rochester; Human **3685**
Rights Commission; San Francisco Human **4049**
Rights Commission; Saskatchewan Human **4288**
Rights Commission; Tennessee Human **4240**
Rights Commission; Washington Human **4272**
Rights Commission; West Virginia Human **3822, 4273**
Rights Commission; Yukon Human **3945**
Rights Committee; Des Plaines Citizens **3626**
Rights Communicator; Iowa Civil **4439**
Rights Congress; Equal **3395**
Rights and Constitutional Law; Center for Human **3534**
Rights Council; Palm Beach County Human **3602**
Rights Council; Virginia Human **4267**
Rights Country Reports; Human **4487**
Rights Database; International Human **4493**
Rights Defense Fund; OGCA Civil **3761**
Rights Defense Fund; Political **3497**
Rights Department; Davenport Civil **4096**
Rights Department; Michigan Civil **4125**
    Detroit Office **4126**
Rights Department; Minnesota Human **4136**
Rights and Dignity Development Corp.; Women for Human **3716**
Rights Division; New York State Human **4181**
Rights Documentation Network; Internet: International Human **3429**
Rights Enforcement Agency; St. Louis Civil **4145**
Rights/Equal Opportunity Office; Lincoln Human **4149**
Rights of Ethnic, Religious, Linguistic and Other Minorities; International Federation for the Protection of the **3424**
Rights and Freedom; Committee on Professional Ethics, **3382**
Rights Fund; Native American **3480**
    National Indian Law Library **707**
Rights Funds; Arizona Human **3519**
Rights and Genocide Treaties; Ad Hoc Committee on the Human **3352**
Rights of Greater New York; Veterans for Human **3731**
Rights Group U.S.A.; Minority **3444**
Rights: I Can Get It For You Wholesale; Aboriginal **1711**

Rights and Immigration; British Columbia Attorney General and Minister Responsible for Multiculturalism, Human **3193**
Rights Information Committee; Colombia Human **3557**
Rights Institute of Canada; Human **3237**
Rights; Institute for Research and Education on Human **3418**
Rights; Institute for Social and Economic **3726**
Rights; Inter-American Commission on Human **3421, 4378**
Rights; Interfaith Council for Human **3422**
Rights; International League for Human **3427**
Rights Internet; Human **4375**
Rights Issues; Unresolved Indian • U.S. Department of the Interior • Bureau of Indian Affairs **4014**
Rights; Jeffco Citizens for Human **3571**
Rights; Latah-Nez Perce Voices for Human **457**
Rights Law Group; International Human **3425**
Rights; Lawyers Committee for Human **3432**
Rights; Leadership Conference on Civil **3433**
Rights Library; Human **4488**
Rights; Litigation Support for Indian • U.S. Department of the Interior • Bureau of Indian Affairs **4001**
Rights of Man; International League for the **3427**
Rights of Man; Music for the **3445**
Rights; Michigan Coalition for Human **3672**
Rights; Minnesota Advocates for Human **3682**
Rights and Minority Business Development; District of Columbia Department of Human **3583**
Rights and Minority Business Development Office; District of Columbia Human **4064**
Rights Monitors; Congressional Friends of Human **3385**
Rights Movement; The ABC-CLIO Companion to the Native American **1592**
Rights; NGO Committee on Human **3486**
Rights Office; Alexandria Human **4262**
Rights Office; Detroit Human **4121**
Rights Office; Dubuque Human **4097**
Rights Office; Minneapolis Civil **4132**
Rights Office; Seattle Civil **4270**
Rights Office; Tulsa Human **4212**
Rights and Opportunities Commission; Connecticut Human **4059**
Rights of Oregon; Citizens Commission on Human **3770**
Rights Panel of Adjudicators; Yukon Human **3946**
Rights; Physicians for Human **3495**
Rights for Political Prisoners; Campaign for Amnesty and Human **3369, 3369**
Rights Protection; Indian • U.S. Department of the Interior • Bureau of Indian Affairs **3994**
Rights Quarterly; Human **4489**
Rights Resource Center; Human **3560**
Rights and Responsibilities; Section of Individual **3500**
Rights Review Council of Austin; Human **3795**
Rights Secretariat; Alberta Human **4278**
Rights Task Force; Bonner County Human **3618**
Rights; Treaty Rights or Civil **2097**
Rights; U.S. Commission on Civil **3832**
    Office of Civil Rights Evaluation **3833**
Rights; Unresolved Indian Hunting and Fishing • U.S. Department of the Interior • Bureau of Indian Affairs **4013**
Rights/U.S.A. Section; International Society for Human **3428**
Rights Watch; Human **3408, 4376**
Rights Watch UPDATE; Human **4437**
Rights Web Home Page; The Human **4490**
Rights Workers; National Association of Human **3451**
Rincon Band of Mission Indians **133**
Ritual Object Repatriation Foundation; American Indian **383**
Riverside Indian School **1276**
Road Maintenance - Indian Roads • U.S. Department of the Interior • Bureau of Indian Affairs **4005**
Robert Goldwater Library • Metropolitan Museum of Art **687**
Roberta Campbell Lawson Indian Library **728**
Robinson Department of Special Collections; B. **611**
Robinson M.D. Memorial Prizes in Surgery; James H. **4326**
Robinson Rancheria **94**
Rochester Minority Business Development Center **3734, 4184**
Rochester Museum and Science Center **955**
    Library **734**
Rock Creek Day School **1294**
Rock Point Community School **1189**
Rockefeller Minority Internships; Nelson A. **4341**
Rocky Bay First Nation **2977**
Roger Baldwin Foundation of ACLU **3356**

Rogers Library; Will **822**
Rogers State College • Native American Studies Program **1349**
Rohnerville Rancheria **58**
Rohnerville Rancheria; Bear River Band of **56**
Rolling River **2860**
Rolling Thunder: The Unity of Man and Nature **2041**
Romaine First Nation; La **3060**
Roosevelt School; Theodore **1198**
Rose State College • Native American Studies Program **1350**
Roseau River First Nation **2865**
Rosebud Dormitories **1295**
Rosebud; Health Care Crisis at **1848**
Rosebud Sioux Tribal Council • Head Start Program **1137**
Rosebud Sioux Tribe **314**
Ross and Haines Old Books Co. **1567**
Ross House; Chief John **883**
Rostkowski Award; Nicolaus **1468**
Roswell Museum and Art Center • Research Library **735**
Rough Rock Demonstration School **1190**
'Round Robbins **1681**
Round Valley Reservation **50**
Rowan University Library • Stewart Room • Rowan University of New Jersey **736**
Rowan University of New Jersey • Rowan University Library • Stewart Room **736**
Royalty Valuation and Management; Gower Federal Service- **1660**
Ruby; Native Village of **2304**
Ruhle Library; George C. • U.S. Department of the Interior • National Park Service • Glacier National Park **768**
Ruins National Monument; Aztec **932**
The Rule **1682**
Rumsey Rancheria **39**
Run, Appaloosa, Run **2042**
The Runaway **2043**
Running on the Edge of the Rainbow: Laguna Stories and Poems **2044**
Running Strong for American Indian Youth **424**
Rural America Initatives, Inc. • Head Start Program **1138**
Rural Coalition **3499**
Rural History **4432**
Rural Indians; Committee for Action for **3381**
Rural Residential Alternatives **3759**
Russell Cave National Monument **831**
Russian Mission; Iqurmuit Tribe **2305**
Rutgers University • Minority Advancement Program • North American Indian Studies Program **1401**
Saanichton Historical Artifacts Society **3215**
Sabewaing Indian Museum **914**
Sac and Fox **289**
Sac and Fox Document Collection **737**
Sac and Fox National Public Library **737**
Sac and Fox Oral History Collection **737**
Sac and Fox Photography Collection **737**
Sac and Fox Presbyterian Mission Museum; Iowa, **903**
Sac and Fox Settlement School **1204**
Sac and Fox Tribe **154**
Sacajawea **2045**
Sachigo Lake First Nation **3012**
Sacramento Urban Indian Health Project **445**
Sacramento Urban League **3551**
Sacred Ground; The American Indian's **1733**
Sacred Ground: The North American Indian's Relationship to the Land **2046**
Sacred Ways: Sun Dagger **2047**
Saddle Lake First Nation **2654**
Safety of Dams on Indian Lands • U.S. Department of the Interior • Bureau of Indian Affairs **4006**
Sagamok Anishriawbek First Nation **2979**
Saginaw Chippewa Tribe **171**
Saginaw County Minority Business Development Center **3679, 4131**
Sagitawa Friendship Centre Newsletter **3303**
Sagkeeng First Nation, Band No. 262 **2863**
St. Croix Tribe **358**
St. Francis Indian School **1296**
Saint Francis; School Sisters of • Archives **744**
St. George; Aleut Community of St. Paul Island and **2324**
St. George Island Village **2306**

St. Herman's Theological Seminary **2416**
  Library **2389**
St. Joseph Museum • Library **738**
St. Louis Civil Rights Enforcement Agency **4145**
St. Louis Minority Business Development Center **4146**
St. Mary's Indian Band **2710**
St. Michael; Native Village of **2323**
St. Paul Island and St. George; Aleut Community of **2324**
St. Paul Tenants Union **3687**
St. Regis Band of Mohawk Indians **248**
  Head Start Program **1114**
St. Scholastica; College of • Native American Studies
  Program **1360**
St. Stevens Indian School **1308**
St. Theresa Point First Nation **2892**
St. Thomas University • Native Studies Program **3250**
Sainte-Marie Among the Hurons **3225**
Sakimay First Nation **3124**
Salamatof; Native Village of **2233**
Salinan Nation **78**
Salinas National Monument **945**
Salish Kootenai College **1320**
  Native American Studies Program **1351**
Salish and Kootenai Tribal Council; Confederated • Tribal
  Council **195**
Salish and Kootenai Tribes; Confederated • Head Start
  Program **1095**
Salt Lake City Minority Business Development Center **4258**
Salt River Day School **1191**
Salt River Pima-Maricopa Indian Community **14**
Samahquam Indian Band **2774**
Samford University • Harwell Goodwin Davis Library • Special
  Collections **739**
Samson First Nation **2641**
Samuel Proctor Oral History Program • Library • University of
  Florida **792**
Samuel W. Brown, Jr. Root Cutter Award **1469**
San Antonio Minority Business Development Center **4255**
San Carlos Apache Tribe **13**
  Head Start Program **1073**
San Diego American Indian Health **446**
San Diego Minority Business Development Center **4048**
San Diego Museum of Man • Scientific Library **740**
San Diego Public Library • Special Collections • Wangenheim
  Room **741**
San Diego State University • American Indian Studies **1379**
San Diego Urban League **3553**
San Felipe Pueblo **236**
  Head Start Program **1110**
  San Felipe School **1247**
San Francisco Human Rights Commission **4049**
San Francisco/Oakland Minority Business Development Center
  No. 1 **4050**
San Francisco Small Business Advisory Commission **4051**
San Francisco State University • School of Ethnic Studies •
  American Indian Studies Program **1402**
San Ildefonso Day School **1248**
San Ildefonso; Maria! Indian Pottery of **1929**
San Ildefonso Pueblo **241**
San Jose Minority Business Development Center **4052**
San Juan County Archaeological Research Center and
  Library **1045**
San Juan Day School **1249**
San Juan Pueblo **237**
San Juan Southern Paiute Tribe **18**
San Luis Archaeological and Historic Site **880**
San Manuel Tribe **67**
San Pasqual Tribe **134**
San Pedro Riparian National Conservation Area **848**
San Simon School **1192**
Sananguaqat: Inuit Masterworks **2509**
Sand Point First Nation **3035**
Sandia Pueblo **224**
Sandoval Indian Pueblos, Inc.; Five • Head Start
  Program **1103**
Sandy Bay First Nation **2878**
Sandy Lake Band of Ojibwe **181**
Sandy Lake First Nation **3014**
Santa Ana Pueblo **225**
Santa Barbara City College • Native American Studies
  Program **1352**

Santa Clara Day School **1250**
Santa Clara Pueblo **228**
Santa Clara Valley Urban League **3558**
Santa Fe Pacific Foundation Scholarships Scholarships **1449**
Santa Fe Pacific Native American Scholarshipslarships **1450**
Santa Rosa Boarding School **1193**
Santa Rosa Junior College • Jesse Peter Native American Art
  Museum **860**
Santa Rosa Ranch School **1194**
Santa Rosa Rancheria **85**
Santa Rosa Reservation **66**
Santa Ynez Tribe **112**
Santa Ysabel Tribe **115**
Sante Fe Indian School **400**
Santee Sioux; Flandreau **309**
Santee Sioux Tribe **199**
Santo Domingo Pueblo **243**
Santo Domingo Tribe • Head Start Program **1112**
Saponi Nation; Occaneechi Band of the **255**
Saponi Tribe; Haliwa- **254**
Sapotaweyak Cree Nation **2902**
Sara Hightower - Regional Library • Special Collections **742**
Sarcee People's Museum **3210**
Sarnia First Nation; Chippewas of **3015**
Saskatchewan Human Rights Commission **4288**
Saskatchewan Indian Federated College **3247**
Saskatchewan Indian and Metis Affairs Secretariat **3205**
Saskatchewan Minister for Indian and Metis Affairs, Status of
  Women, and Gaming Authority **3206**
Saugeen First Nation **3017**
Saugeen First Nation; Chippewas of **3025**
Sauk-Suiattle Tribe **330**
Sault Ste. Marie Chippewa Tribe **172**
Saulteaux First Nation [Cochin, SK, Canada] **3111**
Saulteaux Indian Band **2700**
Savannah Minority Business Development Center **4082**
Savannah River Area Business League; Central **3611**
Savoonga; Native Village of **2308**
Sawridge First Nation **2656**
Saxman; Organized Village of **2235**
Sayisi Dene First Nation **2899**
Scammon Bay; Native Village of **2309**
Schaghticoke Indian Tribe **143**
Schefferville First Nation **3085**
Schingoethe Center for Native American Cultures • Aurora
  University **891**
Schneider Publishers; R. **1563**
Scholars Program (Minority Scholars Program); Higher
  Education and Multicultural • U.S. Department of Agriculture •
  Cooperative State Research, Education, and Extension
  Service **3947**
Scholars Program; NACME Corporate **4336**
Scholarship Fund; Native American **3481**
Scholarship Service for American Indian Students; United **384**
Scholarships; American Indian **372**
Scholarships (Special Higher Education Scholarships); Indian
  Graduate Student • U.S. Department of the Interior • Bureau
  of Indian Affairs **3990**
School of American Research **1046**
  Library **743**
  Museum **946**
School Association; Navajo Area Grant **434**
School Board Association; Navajo Area **423**
School in the Bush **3341**
School Equalization Program (ISEP); Indian • U.S. Department
  of the Interior • Bureau of Indian Affairs **3995**
School; Heart of the Earth Survival **380**
School Sisters of Saint Francis • Archives **744**
Schools; Administrative Cost Grants for Indian • U.S.
  Department of the Interior • Bureau of Indian Affairs **3972**
Schools; Association of Community Tribal **3366**
Schools; Association of Contract Tribal **3366**
Schools; ERIC Clearinghouse on Rural Education and
  Small **1025**
  Appalachia Educational Laboratory **641**
Schools (Haskell and SIPI); Indian Post Secondary • U.S.
  Department of the Interior • Bureau of Indian Affairs **3993**
Schools; Replacement and Repair of Indian • U.S. Department
  of the Interior • Bureau of Indian Affairs **4004**
Schools - Student Transportation; Indian • U.S. Department of
  the Interior • Bureau of Indian Affairs **3996**

Schultz Society; James Willard **3431**
Science Education Association; Native American **3482**
Science and Education Center; American Indian **384**
Science Education Consortia; Eisenhower Regional Mathematics and • U.S. Department of Education • Office of Assistant Secretary for Educational Research and Improvement **3954**
Science and Engineering; National Institute for Resources in **3464**
Science and Engineering Society (AISES); American Indian **385**
Science and Engineering Society; AISESnet: American Indian **2126**
Science and Engineering Society; American Indian **2125**
Science Fellowship Program; GEM Ph.D. **4322**
Science and Health: A Network of Minority Professional Associations; Mathematics, Engineering, **3439**
Science Program; Advanced Industrial Concepts (AIC) Materials **4304**
Science or Sacrilege: The Study of American Indian Remains **2048**
Science; Society for Advancement of Chicanos and Native Americans in **426**
Science to Students Using the Environment; Introduce **3482**
Science Teachers Education Program; Indian **3482**
Scott Andrew Trexler II Memorial Library • Historical Society; Lehigh County **678**
Scott; Strength of Life— Knokavtee **2075**
Scotts Bluff National Monument • Library • U.S. Department of the Interior • National Park Service **780**
Scottsdale Community College • Native American Studies Program **1353**
Scowlitz Indian Band **2755**
Seabird Island Band **2664**
Sealaska Heritage Foundation **2403**
Seasons **1683**
Seasons of a Navajo **2049**
Seattle Civil Rights Office **4270**
Seattle Minority Business Development Center- IMPACT Business Consultants **3817, 4271**
Seattle Urban League **3818**
Seba Dalkai Boarding School **1195**
Sechelt Indian Band **2815**
Second Mesa Day School **1196**
Section of Individual Rights and Responsibilities **3500**
Secwepemc Cultural Education Society **3278**
Secwepemc Cultural Education Society and Native Heritage Park **3175**
Seine River First Nation **2982**
Selawik; Native Village of **2310**
Seldovia Village Tribe **2311**
Self-Determination Contract Support; Indian • U.S. Department of the Interior • Bureau of Indian Affairs **3997**
Self-Governance Grants; Tribal • U.S. Department of the Interior • Bureau of Indian Affairs **4011**
Self-Governance; Tribal • U.S. Department of the Interior • Bureau of Indian Affairs **4010**
Semiahmoo Band **2838**
Seminary Scholarships; Native American **1442**
Seminary Scholarships; Presbyterian Church Native American **1448, 2439**
Seminole History and Culture; Ah-Tah-Thi-Ki Museum of **878**
Seminole Indians **2050**
Seminole Nation **293**
Seminole Nation Museum **988**
Seminole Nation of Oklahoma • Head Start Program **1129**
Seminole Tribal Library System • Seminole Tribe of Florida **745**
Seminole Tribe • Head Start Program **1080**
Seminole Tribe of Florida **144**
    Seminole Tribal Library System **745**
Seminoles (Indians of the Everglades); Boy of the **1761**
Seneca-Cayuga Tribe **278**
Seneca-Iroquois National Museum **956**
Seneca Nation of Indians **251**
Seneca Nation Library **746**
Sentinel **1684, 2462**
Sequoyah Award **1470**
Sequoyah Graduate Fellowships **1451, 2440**
Sequoyah High School **1277**
Sequoyah Home Site **989**

Serials, Music, and Illustrations; California Indians: Primary Resources: A Guide to Manuscripts, Documents, **1599**
Serpent Mound Museum **973**
Serpent River First Nation **2943**
Services to Indian Children, Elderly and Families • U.S. Department of the Interior • Bureau of Indian Affairs **4007**
Set-Aside Alert **4449**
Seton Lake Indian Band **2816**
Seton Memorial Library **747**
Settlement Program; Navajo- Hopi Indian • U.S. Department of the Interior • Bureau of Indian Affairs **574**
Seventh Generation Fund for Indian Development **425**
Severinghaus Award; Aura E. **4310**
Seward; Fort William H. **2401**
Sexism; Musicians Against Racism- **3728**
Seyewailo: The Flower World **2051**
Shackan Indian Band **2771**
Shadow Catcher **2052**
The Shadow Catcher: Edward S. Curtis and the North American Indian **2053**
The Shadow Walkers **2054**
Shadow of the Warrior **2055**
Shageluk Native Village **2312**
Shakopee Mdewakanton Sioux **184**
Shaktoolik; Native Village of **2313**
The Shaman's Journey **2056**
Shamattawa First Nation **2894**
Sharlot Hall/Prescott Historical Societies • Library/Archives **748**
Shastri Newsletter **3304**
Shawanaga First Nation **2998**
Shawnee Area, Inc.; Central Tribes of the • Head Start Program **1120**
Shawnee County Allied Tribes **463**
Shawnee; Lower Eastern Ohio Mekoce **502**
Shawnee Tribe; Absentee- **287**
Shawnee Tribe of Oklahoma; Eastern **189**
Sheguiandah First Nation **3019**
Sheldon Jackson Museum **2404**
Sheldon Museum and Cultural Center **2390, 2405**
Sheldon's Point; Native Village of **2314**
Shenandoah Newsletter **1685**
Shepaug Valley Archaeological Society **401**
Sherratt Library; Gerald R. • Special Collections Department • Southern Utah University **752**
Sherwood Valley Rancheria **131**
Sheshegwaning First Nation **3020**
Shingle Springs Rancheria **116**
Shinnecock: A Story of a People **2057**
Shiprock Alternative High School **1251**
Shiprock Reservation Dormitory **1252**
Shishmaref; Native Village of **2315**
Shoal Lake of the Cree Nation **3141**
(Shoal Lake No. 39); Iskutewizaagegan First Nation **3021**
Shoal Lake No. 40 First Nation **3022**
Shoalwater Tribe **349**
Sho'Ban School District No. 512 **1203**
Shoonaq' Tribe of Kodiak **2244**
Shorey Publications **1568**
Shoshone and Arapahoe Tribes • Head Start Program **1159**
Shoshone-Bannock Tribes • Head Start Program **1082**
Shoshone Business Council **365**
Shoshone Elementary School; Duckwater **1224**
Shoshone Indians; Te-Moak Tribe of Western **206**
Shoshone Nation; Northwestern Band of **146**
Shoshone Paiute Business Council **216**
Shoshone Tribe of the Duckwater Reservation; Duckwater **204**
Shoshone Tribe; Fort McDermitt Paiute and **213**
Shouldice Library; Kenneth J. • Michigan & Marine Collections • Lake Superior State University **676**
Shrine of the Blessed Kateri Tekakwitha; National **954**
Shungnak; Native Village of **2316**
Shuswap Indian Band **2739**
Shuswap Nation **2742**
Sierra Oaks Publishing Co. **1569**
Siksika First Nation **2655**
The Silent Enemy **2058**
Silent Heritage: The American Indian **2059**
Siletz Indians; Confederated Tribes of • Head Start Program **1131**
Siletz Tribe **302**
Sill Apache Tribe; Fort **265**

Sim-Oi-Ghes; Kitsumkalum Band/ House of **2827**
Simon Paneak Memorial Museum **2406**
Sinew-Backed Bow and its Arrows **2060**
Sinte Gleska College **1337**
    Native American Studies **1380**
Sinte Gleska University • Lakota Archives and Historical
    Research Center **1047**
Siouan (Chicora Shakori) Indian People; Chicora **306**
*Sioux; The Art of Being Indian: Filmed Aspects of the Culture
    of the* **1747**
Sioux City American Indian Center **900**
Sioux Community; Upper **180**
Sioux; Eyanopopi: The Heart of the **1817**
Sioux First Nation; Birdtail **2847**
Sioux First Nation (Moose Woods); Whitecap Dakota/ **3153**
Sioux; Flandreau Santee **309**
Sioux Indian Artist; Herman Red Elk: A **1852**
Sioux Indian; Meet the **1931**
Sioux Indian Museum and Crafts Center **997**
Sioux; Joe KillsRight: Oglala **1903**
Sioux Legends **2061**
Sioux Nation; A Guide to the Great **2135**
Sioux Painter, Oscar Howe: The **2006**
Sioux Tribal Council; Cheyenne River • Head Start
    Program **1133**
Sioux Tribal Council; Oglala • Head Start Program **1136**
Sioux Tribal Council; Rosebud • Head Start Program **1137**
Sioux Tribal Council; Standing Rock • Head Start
    Program **1117**
Sioux Tribe; Cheyenne River **308**
Sioux Tribe; Crow Creek **310**
    Head Start Program **1134**
Sioux Tribe; Devils Lake **258**
Sioux Tribe; Lower Brule **311**
    Head Start Program **1135**
Sioux Tribe; Oglala **313**
Sioux Tribe; Rosebud **314**
Sioux Tribe; Santee **199**
Sioux Tribe; Sisseton- Wahpeton **315**
Sioux Tribe; Standing Rock **259**
Sioux Tribe; Yankton **312**
Sioux Tribes Development Corporation; Indian Job Placement -
    United • U.S. Department of the Interior • Bureau of Indian
    Affairs **3991**
Sioux Tribes of South Dakota Development Corporation;
    United **516**
Sioux Valley First Nation **2868**
Siouxland Heritage Museums • Library **749**
Siska Indian Band **2764**
Sisseton Wahpeton Community College **1338**
Sisseton-Wahpeton Sioux Tribe **315**
Sisterhood; Alaska Native **2356**
Sitka National Historical Park • Library • U.S. Department of
    the Interior • National Park Service **781**
Sitka Tribe of Alaska **2317**
Sitting Bull College **1332**
The Six Nations **2062**
Six Nations of the Grand River Territory **2999**
Six Nations Indian Museum **957**
Ska-Nah-Doht Indian Village **3226**
Skagit County Historical Museum • Historical Reference
    Library **750**
Skagit Tribe; Upper **342**
Skawahlook Band **2665**
Skeetchestn Indian Band **2814**
Skelep Publishing **3279**
Skidegate Indian Band **2819**
S'Klallam Indians; Jamestown Band of **343**
S'Klallam Tribe; Port Gamble **333**
Skokomish Tribal Council • Head Start Program **1151**
Skokomish Tribe **344**
Skookumchuck Indian Band **2784**
Skowkale Indian Band **2811**
Skull Valley Tribe **322**
Skuppah Indian Band **2765**
Skwah Indian Band **2704**
Sky City Community School **1253**
Sleetmute; Village of **2318**
Sliammon Band **2797**
Slough; Native Village of Bill Moore's **2248**

Small Business Administration; U.S.
    Business Loans for 8(A) Program Participants **4030**
    Management and Technical Assistance for Socially and
      Economically Disadvantaged Businesses (7(J)
      Development Assistant Program) **4031**
    Microloan Demonstration Program **4032**
    Office of Equal Employment Opportunity and Civil Rights
      Compliance **3940**
    Office of Minority Enterprise Development **3941**
    Office of Native American Affairs **548**
    Office of Small Business Development Centers **3942**
Small Business Advisory Commission; San Francisco **4051**
Small Business Development Agency; West Virginia Minority
    and **4274**
Small Business Innovation Research Programs • U.S. National
    Science Foundation • Design, Manufacture and Industrial
    Innovation Division **3930**
Small Business Investment Companies; American Association of
    Minority Enterprise 406
Small Business Liaison Staff; Industry and • U.S. Department
    of Health and Human Services • Office of Public Health and
    Science • Food and Drug Administration **3865**
Small Business Technology Transfer Program • U.S. National
    Science Foundation • Design, Manufacture and Industrial
    Innovation Division **3931**
Small and Disadvantaged Business Office • Policy Planning
    Division; New Orleans Economic Development and **4108**
Small and Disadvantaged Business Utilization • U.S.
    Department of Defense • Department of the Air Force **3847**
Small and Disadvantaged Business Utilization Office • U.S.
    Department of Defense • Department of the Navy **3853**
Smith First Nation; James **3137**
Smith River Rancheria **117**
Smithsonian: Catlin and the Indians **2063**
Smithsonian Institution; U.S.
    Center for Museum Studies • American Indian Museum
      Studies Program **549**
    Museum of the American Indian **959, 2413**
    National Anthropological Archives **785**
    National Museum of the American Indian **1581, 2449**
      Research Branch • Cultural Resources
        Department **1053, 2417**
    Office of Equal Employment and Minority Affairs **3943**
Smoke Signals: Business Directory of Indian Country
    U.S.A. **1626, 2459**
Smoke Signals: Directory of Native Indian/Alaskan
    Businesses 1626, 2459
Smoki Museum **849**
The Smoki Museum, Inc. • Library **751**
Snaketown **2064**
Snowbird Publishing Co. **1570**
Snyder Collection of Americana • University of Missouri—
    Kansas City **794**
Soapstone Carving; Joshua's **3328**
Soaring Eagle Foundation **3784**
Soboba **108**
Sobriety Movement; Alaska Native 2350
Sobriety; The Red Road to **4468**
Social and Economic Rights; Institute for **3726**
Social Equality; People's Organization for **3650**
Social History; Archives of **4359**
Social Justice **4394**
Social Policy; Center for Religion, Ethics and • Durland
    Alternatives Library **623**
Social Science for Minority Undergraduate Students; ABF
    Summer Research Fellowships in Law and **4302**
Social Science Research Institute • University of South
    Dakota **1065**
Social Services - Child Welfare Assistance; Indian • U.S.
    Department of the Interior • Bureau of Indian Affairs **3998**
Social Work Education Minority Fellowships; Council on **4315**
Societe historique d'Odanak • d'Odanak; Musee des
    Abenakis **3231**
Society of Actuaries/Casualty Actuarial Society Scholarships for
    Minority Students **4347**
Society for Advancement of Chicanos and Native Americans in
    Science **426**
Society for the Study of Indigenous Languages of the
    Americas **3501**
Soda Creek Indian Band **2840**
Sokaogon Chippewa Tribe **356**

Solidarity with the Native People; Canadian Alliance in 3172
Solomon; Native Village of **2319**
Something Seneca **2065**
Sometimes We Feel **2066**
Songhees Indian Band **2836**
Songs of the Fourth World; Hopi: **1864**
Songs In Minto Life **2510**
Songs of My Hunter Heart: Laguna Songs and Poems **2067**
Sonny Billie Foundation for Native Culture Studies **3589**
Sonoma State University • Native American Studies
    Program **1381**
Sonotabac Prehistoric Indian Mound **898**
Soowahlie Indian Band **2712**
The Source **1686**
The Source: A Guidebook of American Genealogy **4420**
*Sources of Financial Aid Available to American Indian
    Students* 1530, **1627**
South American Indian Information Center 3502
South Carolina Human Affairs Commission • Fair Housing
    Division **4233**
South and Central American Indian Information Center 3502
South Dakota—Bulletin; University of **1689**
South Dakota Education and Cultural Affairs Department •
    Education Division • Equal Employment Opportunity **4234**
South Dakota Office of the Governor • Indian Affairs
    Office **596**
South Dakota Oral History Center **1048**
    Library • American Indian Research Project **604**
South East Alaska Indian Cultural Center **2359**
South and Eastern Tribes; United **429**
South Fork Band of the Te-Moak Tribe of Western Shoshone
    Indians **211**
South Hampton College • Native American Studies
    Program **1382**
South and Meso-American Indian Information Center **3502**
South Naknek Village **2320**
Southeast; American Indian Archival Material: A Guide to
    Holdings in the **1596**
Southeast; Native American Series, Vol. 3: The Tribes of
    the **1961**
Southeastern Tribes; United 429
Southern Plains Indian Museum and Crafts Center **990**
Southern Utah University • Gerald R. Sherratt Library • Special
    Collections Department **752**
Southern Ute Indian Cultural Center **448, 869**
Southern Ute Tribe **138**
Southold Indian Museum **958, 2412**
Southwest; Center for the Study of Native Languages of the
    Plains and • University of Colorado at Boulder **1059**
Southwest; Indian Artists of the **1879**
Southwest Indian Arts and Crafts **2068**
Southwest; Indian Boy of the **1881**
Southwest Indian Polytechnic Institute **1328**
Southwest Indian Substance Abuse Counselor Certification **436**
Southwest Indians of Early America **2069**
Southwest Museum **861, 1049, 1571**
    Braun Research Library **753**
Southwest; Native American Series, Vol. 4: The Natives of
    the **1962**
Southwest; Pride, Purpose and Promise: Paiutes of the **2026**
Southwest Research; Center for • University of New
    Mexico **798**
Southwest Studies; Center of • Fort Lewis College **646**
Southwest Voter Registration Education Project **3503**
Southwestern Association on Indian Affairs **490**
Southwestern Indian Polytechnic Institute • Library • U.S.
    Department of the Interior • Bureau of Indian Affairs **761**
Southwestern Studies; Taylor Museum for **1050**
Sovereign Nation-State; Hawaii - Independent and **2608**
Sovereignty Program; Tribal 425
Spallumcheen First Nation **2718**
Sparks Indian Colony; Reno- **217**
(Special Higher Education Scholarships); Indian Graduate
    Student Scholarships • U.S. Department of the Interior •
    Bureau of Indian Affairs **3990**
Speed Art Museum; J.B. • Library **664**
The Spike **1687, 3305**
Spirit! **1688**
Spirit of the Hunt **2070**
Spirit Talk Press **1572**
The Spirit Within **3342**

Split Lake Cree First Nation **2897**
Spokane Tribe **352**
Sponsorships; NNAC Gifted/Talented Artist **1444**
Sports Council; Native American **421**
Spuzzum Indian Band **2844**
Spying; Campaign to Stop Government 3370
Squamish Nation **2782**
Squaxin Island Tribe **345**
Squiala Indian Band **2705**
Stalking Seal on the Spring Ice, Parts I and II **2511**
Standing Alone **3343**
Standing Buffalo First Nation **3121**
Standing Pine Elementary School **1219**
Standing Rock College • Sitting Bull College **1354**
Standing Rock Community School 1258, **1266**
Standing Rock Sioux Tribal Council • Head Start
    Program **1117**
Standing Rock Sioux Tribe **259**
Stanjikoming First Nation **2956**
Stanley H. Broder Collection of Native American Paintings;
    Patricia J and 796
Star Blanket First Nation **3101**
Starved Rock State Park **895**
State Historical Society of Iowa • Library/Archives **754**
State Historical Society of North Dakota **1573**
State Historical Society of Wisconsin • Library **755**
State-Tribal Relations; Commission on 3358
State University of New York at Buffalo
    Native American Graduate Studies Program **1403**
    Native American Studies Program **1383**
State University of New York College at Potsdam **1384**
Staves; Game of **1833**
Stebbins Community Association **2325**
Stereotyping in Entertainment; Council for Alternatives to **3388**
Stewart Consultant Ltd.; Walter P. 3264
Stewarts Point Rancheria **120**
Stillaguamish Tribe **327**
Stockbridge-Munsee Tribal Council • Head Start
    Program **1157**
Stockbridge-Munsee Tribe **354**
Stockton Minority Business Development Center **4053**
Stone Age Americans **2071**
Stone Child Community College **1321, 1322**
Stone Indian Band **2729**
Stoney River; Village of **2326**
Stoney Tribal Administration First Nation (Bearspaw) **2647**
Stoney Tribal Administration First Nation (Chiniki) **2648**
Stoney Tribal Administration First Nation (Wesley) **2649**
Stony Creek Indian Band **2833**
Stony Point First Nation; Chippewas of Kettle and **2951**
*Stories of American Indian Culture: Hawk, I'm Your
    Brother* **2072**
*Stories of American Indian Culture: The Other Way to
    Listen* **2073**
*Stories of American Indian Culture: The Way to Start a
    Day* **2074**
Storm of Strangers **4469**
Strength of Life—Knokavtee Scott **2075**
Structural Fire Protection - Bureau of Indian Affairs Facilities
    (Fire Protection) • U.S. Department of the Interior • Bureau
    of Indian Affairs **4008**
Student Coalition Against Apartheid and Racism; District of
    Columbia **3584**
Student Education; Resources for Indian **440**
Student Enrollments in Higher Education: A Guide to
    Institutions with. . .Asian, Black, Hispanic, and Native
    American Students; Minority **4413**
Student Fee Waiver; Montana Indian **1440**
Student News; *Indian Country* **1530**
Student Opportunity Scholarships; Presbyterian Church **4345**
Student Organization, Austin Chapter; Native American **521**
Student Organization; Tiyospaya American Indian **428**
Student Scholarship Program; Minority Dental **4331**
Student Scholarships (Special Higher Education Scholarships);
    Indian Graduate • U.S. Department of the Interior • Bureau
    of Indian Affairs **3990**
Student Transportation; Indian Schools - • U.S. Department of
    the Interior • Bureau of Indian Affairs **3996**
Student of the Year Award; Indian **1464**
Students Association; American Indian Law 3477
Students Association; Native American Law 3477

Students; Organization of North American Indian **3492**
Students; Sources of Financial Aid Available to American
   Indian **1627**
Students from Two-Year Colleges; Talent Roster of Outstanding
   Minority Transfer **4421**
Students; United Scholarship Service for American Indian **384**
Students Using the Environment; Introduce Science to **3482**
Studies Institute; Hawaiian **2570**
Study of Ethnoviolence; The Prejudice Institute/ Center for the
   Applied **3498**
Study of Prejudice and Ethnoviolence; Center for the
   Applied **3498**
Stuntz; Ervin **1509**
Sturgeon Lake First Nation **2659**
Sturgeon Lake First Nation [Shellbrook, SK, Canada] **3155**
Subarctic Research Station; McGill • McGill University **2415**,
3240
Subsistence Preference - Alaska National Interest Lands
   Conservation Act; Alaskan Indian Allotments and • U.S.
   Department of the Interior • Bureau of Indian Affairs **2378**
Substance Abuse Counselor Certification; Southwest
   Indian **436**
Substance Abuse Organizations in Canada; Directory of **3287**
Sucker Creek First Nation **2623**
Sucker Creek; Ojibways of **2974**
Sucking Doctor **2076**
Suffolk Minority Business Development Center; Nassau/ **4169**
Suiattle Tribe; Sauk- **330**
Suislaw Indians; Confederated Tribes of Coos, Lower Umpqua,
   and **297**
Sumas First Nation **2662**
Summer Legend **2077**
Summer Palace; Queen Emma **2567**
Summer Research Fellowships in Law and Social Science for
   Minority Undergraduate Students; ABF **4302**
Summer Research Program for Minorities and Women; AT & T
   Bell Laboratories **4309**
Summer Seminar; American Indian **386**
Summit Lake Paiute Tribe **220**
Sun Bear on Earth Changes **2078**
Sun Bear: Vision of the Medicine Wheel **2079**
The Sun Dagger **2080**
Sunaqutangit Museum; Nuantta **3220**
Sunchild First Nation **2653**
Sunset Trading Post-Old West Museum • Library **756**
Sunstone Press **1574**
Supplier Development Council; National Minority **3467**
Supplier Development Council; Oklahoma Minority **3766**
Support Group; Racine Treaty **3828**
Suquamish Tribe (Port Madison) **346**
Sur Pueblo; Ysleta del **319**
Surgery; James H. Robinson M.D. Memorial Prizes in **4326**
Survival of American Indians Association **427**
Survival International, U.S.A. **3504**
Survival News Service **1575**
Survival School; Heart of the Earth **380**
Surviving Columbus **2081**
Susanville Rancheria **121**
Swan Lake First Nation **2898**
Swan River First Nation **2643**
Sweat Lodge Ceremony; American Indian **1730**
Sweat Lodge Ceremony; Native American **1965**
Sweating Indian Style: Conflicts over Native American
   Ritual **4470**
Sweet Grass First Nation **3122**
Sweetlight Books **1576**
Swinomish Tribe **334**
Sycuan Tribe **24**
Ta-Kwa-Teu-Nee-Ya-Y Collection **649**
Table Bluff Rancheria **86**
Table Mountain Rancheria **61**
Tacoma Urban League **3820**
Tahltan Indian Band **2825**
Tahoma Publications/Tahoma Research Service **1577**
Tahoma Research Service; Tahoma Publications/ **1577**
Tahtonka **2082**
Takini School **1297**
Takla Lake Indian Band **2824**
Takotna Village **2327**
Taku River Tlingit First Nation **2676**
Talako Indian Dancers Family Club **453**

Talent Roster of Outstanding Minority Transfer Students from
   Two-Year Colleges **4421**
Tales of the Muscogee **2083**
Tales of Wesakachak **3344**
Talking Drum Publications **1578**
Tallahassee Urban League **3598**
Tallcree First Nation **2629**
Tampa-Hillsborough Urban League **3601**
Tampa/St. Petersburg Minority Business Development
   Center **4073**
Tanadgusix Corp. **2448**
Tanakteuk First Nation **2669**
Tanana Chiefs Conference **431**
   Head Start Program **2427**
Tanana; Native Village of **2329**
Tanana River Rat **2512**
Tanning; Indian Hide **3326**
Tantaquidgeon Indian Museum **873**
Taos Day School **1254**
Taos Pueblo **244**, **2084**
   Head Start Program **1111**
Tatitlek; Native Village of **2330**
Tayagungin Tribe of Sand Point; Qagun **2307**
Taylor Museum for Southwestern Studies **1050**
Tazlina; Native Village of **2209**
Te-Moak Tribe of Western Shoshone Indians **206**
Teacher Recruitment; Minority • U.S. Department of Education
   • Office of Postsecondary Education **3959**
Teacher Training and Recruitment; Native Hawaiian Curriculum
   Development, • U.S. Department of Education • Office of
   Elementary and Secondary Education **2533**
Teacher Training, and Recruitment Program; Alaska Native
   Educational Planning, Curriculum Development, • U.S.
   Department of Education • Office of Elementary and
   Secondary Education, **2365**
Teachers Education Program; Indian Science **3482**
TechForce Scholarships; NACME **4338**
Technical College; Indian Vocational Training - United Tribes •
   U.S. Department of the Interior • Bureau of Indian
   Affairs **3999**
Teecnospos Boarding School **1197**
Tekakwitha Conference National Center **3505**
Tekakwitha Fine Arts Center **998**
Tekakwitha League; Blessed Kateri **389**
Tekakwitha; Musee Kateri **3232**
Tekakwitha; National Shrine of the Blessed Kateri **954**
Telecommunications; Native American Public **3479**
   Library **706**
Television; Native Voices Public **422**
Telida Village **2331**
Teller; Native Village of **2333**
Telling Our Story **3345**
Temagami First Nation **2925**
Temiskaming First Nation **3078**
Temple Mound Museum **881**
Temple Mound Museum; Indian **879**
   Library **660**
Tenants Union; St. Paul **3687**
Tennessee Attorney General's Office • Civil Rights and Claims
   Division **4237**
Tennessee Economic and Community Development Department
   • Minority Business Enterprise Division **4238**
Tennessee Health Department • Minority Health Office **4239**
Tennessee Human Rights Commission **4240**
Tennessee Personnel Department • Employee Development
   and Equal Employment Opportunity Division **4241**
Tesuque Day School **1255**
Tesuque Pueblo **242**
Tetlin; Native Village of **2334**
Texas; Alabama- Coushatta Tribe of **320**
   Indian Museum **1002**
Texas Association of Minority Business Enterprises **3796**
Texas Civil Liberties Union **3797**
Texas Higher Education Coordinating Board • Access and
   Equity Division **4256**
Texas Indian Bar Association **522**
Texas; Kickapoo Tribe of **318**
Texas Transportation Department • Civil Rights Division **4257**
Thames First Nation; Chippewas of the **2987**
Thames First Nation (Moravian Town); Delaware of the **3031**
Thames First Nation; Oneidas of the **3026**

That One Good Spirit—An Indian Christmas Story **2085**
The Four Directions 1532
Theodore Jamerson Elementary School **1267**
Theodore Roosevelt School **1198**
Theological Seminary; St. Herman's **2416**
    Library **2389**
Thessalon First Nation **3032**
They Never Asked Our Fathers **2513**
They Promised to Take Our Land **2086**
Theytus Books Ltd. **3280**
Third World Organizing; Center for **4294**
Thlopthlocco Tribal Town **279**
Thomas Fellowship Program; Julius A. 3389
Thomas Gilcrease Institute of American History and Art •
    Library **757**
Thomas Leonard Ebbing 1500
Those Who Sing Together **2087**
Three Affiliated Tribes • Head Start Program **1118**
Three Affiliated Tribes Business Council **260**
Three Rivers American Indian Center; Council of **512**
Thunder Bay Art Gallery **3227, 3281**
Thunder Spirit Lodge **480**
Thunder Warrior **2088**
Thunderbird American Indian Dancers **3506**
Thunderbird Publications **3282**
Thunderchild First Nation **3160**
Tidewater Regional Minority Purchasing Council **3809**
Timbisha-Sha Western Shoshone Tribe **52**
A Time to Be Brave **2089**
Times Mirror Minority Editorial Training Program **4348**
Tiospa Zina Tribal School **1298**
Tipi First Nation; Dakota **2888**
Tiyospaya American Indian Student Organization **428**
Tla-o-qui-aht First Nation **2829**
Tlatlasikwala Band **2670**
Tl'azt'en Nation **2724**
Tlingit First Nation; Taku River **2676**
Tlingit and Haida Central Council • Head Start Program **2428**
Tlingit and Haida Tribe of Alaska; Central Council of **2224**
Tlowitsis-Mumtagila Band **2667**
Tobacco Plains First Nation **2728**
Today **4450**
TOE Missouri Tribe • Head Start Program **1130**
Togiak; Traditional Village of **2335**
Tohaali Community School **1256**
To'Hajiilee-He **1257**
Tohono Chul Park • Library **758**
Tohono O'Odham High School **1199**
Tohono O'Odham Nation **15**
    Head Start Program **1074**
Tolba Menahan; Inter- Tribal Council of **473**
Tomorrow's Yesterday **2090**
Tonawanda Tribe **246**
Tongass Historical Museum **2407**
    Library **2391**
Tonkawa Tribe **291**
Tonto National Monument **850**
Tony Begay Memorial Award 1468
Toosey Indian Band **2806**
Tootinaowaziibeeng **2895**
Topeka Human Relations Office **4100**
Toquaht Band **2830**
Torres-Martinez Tribe **124**
Totem Heritage Center **759, 2408**
Totem Pole **2091**
Totem Pole (Canada); Richard's **3340**
Totem is the Raven; Our **2009**
Toth; Peter Wolf **1560**
Town Creek Indian Mound State Historic Site **964**
Track of the Moonbeast **2092**
Trade Center; North American Native American Indian
    Information and **3490**
Trade and Information Center; North American Indian **3469**
Trade; Minorities International Network for **3441**
Trade Workers of New Jersey; Minority Contractors and
    Coalition of **3704**
Traders Directory; American Indian and Alaska Native **1595,**
2451
Trading Post; Canyon de Chelly and Hubbell **1770**
Trading Post National Historic Site; Hubbell **843**
Traditional Indian Alliance **438**

Traditional Indian Council of Arizona; United **439**
Traditional Village of Togiak **2335**
Traditions for Tomorrow **3507**
Trail of Broken Treaties **2093**
Trailside Nature Museum • Westchester County Department of
    Parks, Recreation and Conservation **818**
Training Center; American Indian Rehabilitation Research and •
    Northern Arizona University **1042**
Training Center; Native American Research and • University of
    Arizona **1056**
Training for Indian Managers; Management Institute: 409
Training and Research Center; National Indian **417, 1039**
Transfer Students from Two-Year Colleges; Talent Roster of
    Outstanding Minority **4421**
Traveler's Guide; Indian America: A **1613, 3290**
Traveler's Guide; North American Indian Landmarks—A **1621,**
3296
The Treasure: Indian Heritage **2094**
Treaties; Ad Hoc Committee on the Human Rights and
    Genocide **3352**
Treaties Made, Treaties Broken **2095**
Treaty of 1868 Series; The **2096**
Treaty Council; International Indian **3426**
Treaty Four; Waywayseecappo First Nation **2906**
Treaty Rights or Civil Rights **2097**
Treaty Support Group; Racine **3828**
Treccani **4395**
Trees Co. Press **1579**
Trent University • Native Studies Program **3256**
Trexler II Memorial Library; Scott Andrew • Historical Society;
    Lehigh County **678**
Tri-County Urban League **3628**
The Trial of Leonard Peltier **2098**
Tribal Chairman's Association; National **3470**
Tribal Colleges Education Equity Grants • U.S. Department of
    Agriculture • Cooperative State Research, Education and
    Extension Service, **3948**
Tribal Colleges Endowment Program
    Higher Education Programs • U.S. Department of
        Agriculture • Cooperative State Research, Education and
        Extension Service **3950**
    U.S. Department of Agriculture • Cooperative State
        Research, Education and Extension Service **3949**
Tribal Council; Algonquian Confederacy Quinnipiac **449**
Tribal Council of California; Inter- **444**
Tribal Council; Mashpee Wampanoag Indian **472**
Tribal Council of Michigan; Inter- **476**
Tribal Council of Tolba Menahan; Inter- **473**
Tribal Courts • U.S. Department of the Interior • Bureau of
    Indian Affairs **4009**
Tribal Directory; Arizona Commission of Indian Affairs— **1598**
Tribal Directory; First Nations **3289**
Tribal Environmental Council; National **3471**
Tribal Film Commissions **382**
Tribal Government Program; Consolidated • U.S. Department of
    the Interior • Bureau of Indian Affairs **3979**
Tribal Government Services Division • U.S. Department of the
    Interior • Bureau of Indian Affairs • Office of Tribal
    Services **1052**
Tribal Governments; Aid to • U.S. Department of the Interior •
    Bureau of Indian Affairs **3974**
Tribal Governments; Violence Against Women Discretionary
    Grants for Indian • U.S. Department of Justice • Office of
    Justice Programs **4023**
Tribal Indian Ceremonial Association; Inter- **404**
Tribal Relations; Commission on State- **3358**
Tribal Schools; Association of Community **3366**
Tribal Schools; Association of Contract **3366**
Tribal Self-Governance • U.S. Department of the Interior •
    Bureau of Indian Affairs **4010**
Tribal Self-Governance Grants • U.S. Department of the Interior
    • Bureau of Indian Affairs **4011**
Tribal Sovereignty Program **425**
Tribal Unity Museum; Maine **907**
Tribal Voice **2143**
Tribally Controlled Community College Endowments • U.S.
    Department of the Interior • Bureau of Indian Affairs **4012**
Tribally Controlled Community Colleges and Universities;
    Assistance to • U.S. Department of the Interior • Bureau of
    Indian Affairs **3976**
Tribes; Council of Energy Resource **3390**

Tribes; Federally Recognized **2134**
Tribes Foundation; Five Civilized **396**
Tribes Foundation; United Indians of All **527**
Tribes Gaming Association; United South and Eastern **450**
Tribes; United South and Eastern **519**
Tribes; United Southeastern **429**
Tribune; The Atlanta **4425**
Trinidad Rancheria **127**
Trinity College • Watkinson Library **760**
Trowbridge Research Library; Harry M. • Historical Society and
Museum; Wyandotte County **823**
True People of the Western Hemisphere **381**
Trust for Native American Cultures and Crafts **1580**
Trustees of Reservations **910**
Tsa-La-Gi Page; Raven's **2142**
Tsawataineuk Indian Band **2747**
Tsawout Indian Band **2809**
Tsawwassen First Nation **2714**
Tse'ii'ahi' Community School **1258**
Tseycum Indian Band **2817**
Tsuu T'Ina Nation **2658**
Tuba City Boarding School **1200**
Tucker Elementary School **1220**
Tucson Urban League **3523**
Tuition Waiver; Michigan Indian **1438**
Tukiki and His Search for a Merry Christmas **2514**
Tulalip Tribe **336**
Tule River Reservation **102**
Tulsa Human Rights Office **4212**
Tulsa Indian Club **507**
Tulsa Minority Business Development Center **4213**
Tuluksak Native Community **2336**
Tumor Registry; New Mexico • University of New
Mexico **1061**
Tundra Times **2463**
Tunica-Biloxi Tribe of Louisiana **159**
Tuntutuliak; Native Village of **2337**
Tununak; Native Village of **2338**
Tununeremiut: The People of Tununak **2515**
Tuolumne Rancheria **128**
Turtle Mountain Band of Chippewa • Head Start
Program **1119**
Turtle Mountain Chippewa Heritage Center **967**
Turtle Mountain Community College **1333**
Turtle Mountain Elementary and Middle School **1268**
Turtle Mountain High School **1269**
Turtle Mountain Tribe **257**
Turtle Shells **2099**
Tusayan Ruin and Museum **851**
Tuscarora Tribe **249**
Tuzigoot National Monument **852**
Twenty Nine Palms **99**
Twin Buttes Day School **1270**
Twin Hills Village **2339**
Two Eagle River School **1223**
Two Worlds **2100**
Two-Year Colleges; Talent Roster of Outstanding Minority
Transfer Students from **4421**
Tyonek; Native Village of **2340**
Tzeachten Indian Band **2812**
Uashat Mak Mani-Utenam First Nation **3087**
Uchucklesant Band **2790**
Ucluelet Band **2831**
Ugashik Village **2157**
Ulkatcho Indian Band **2672**
Ulmer Native American Scholarships; Mark **1436**
Ultimate Reality and Meaning; Institute for Encyclopedia of
Human Ideas on **3416**
Umatilla Indian Reservation; Confederated Tribes of the **300**
U'Mista Cultural Centre **3216**
Umkumiut Native Village **2275**
Umpqua Indians; Cow Creek Band of **301**
Umunhon; Ni'bthaska of the **1991**
Unalaska; Qawalangin Tribe of **2341**
Unami Nation; Ani-Stohini/ **326**
The Uncertain Future **2101**
Underrepresented Minority Investigators Award in Asthma and
Allergy **4349**
Union Bar Indian Band **2737**
Union Institute
Native American Studies Doctorate Program **1404**

Native American Studies Program **1385**
Unitah and Ouray Tribe **323**
United Indian Development Association **409**
United Indians of All Tribes Foundation **527, 3508**
United Indians of Virginia **526**
United Minority Coalition **3517**
United National Indian Tribal Youth **3509**
United Native Americans **3510**
United Scholarship Service for American Indian Students **384**
United Sioux Tribes Development Corporation; Indian Job
Placement • U.S. Department of the Interior • Bureau of
Indian Affairs **3991**
United Sioux Tribes of South Dakota Development
Corporation **516**
United South and Eastern Tribes **429, 519**
United South and Eastern Tribes Gaming Association **450**
United Southeastern Tribes **429**
U.S. Bureau of Indian Affairs Scholarship Grant **1452, 2441**
U.S. Commission on Civil Rights **3832**
Office of Civil Rights Evaluation **3833**
U.S. Congress
Congressional Empowerment Caucus **3834**
U.S. House of Representatives
Congressional Human Rights Caucus **3835**
Congressional Native American Caucus **529**
U.S. Department of Agriculture
Cooperative State Research, Education, and Extension
Service
Higher Education and Multicultural Scholars Program
(Minority Scholars Program) **3947**
Tribal Colleges Education Equity Grants **550, 2363,
3948**
Tribal Colleges Endowment Program **3949**
Tribal Colleges Endowment Program • Higher
Education Programs **3950**
Farm Service Agency • Indian Tribes and Tribal
Corporation Loans **551, 2364**
Food, Nutrition and Consumer Services • Office of Civil
Rights **3836**
Food Safety • Civil Rights Staff **3837**
Natural Resources and Environment • Civil Rights
Staff **3838**
Office of Civil Rights Enforcement **3839**
U.S. Department of Commerce
Bureau of the Census • Equal Employment Opportunity
Office **3840**
Minority Business Development Agency **3841**
American Indian Program **552**
Minority Business Development Centers **3951**
Minority Business Resource Development **3952**
Minority Business Resource Development (Public and
Private) **3953**
National Institute of Standards and Technology • Civil
Rights Office **3842**
Office of Civil Rights **3843**
Patent and Trademark Office • Office of Civil
Rights **3844**
U.S. Department of Defense
Acquisition and Technology • Office of Small and
Disadvantaged Business Utilization **3845**
Department of the Air Force
Manpower, Reserve Affairs, Installations, and
Environment • Equal Opportunity Office **3846**
Small and Disadvantaged Business Utilization **3847**
Department of the Army
Chief of Staff of the Army • Office of Equal
Employment Opportunity **3848**
Chief of Staff of the Army • Office of Small and
Disadvantaged Business Utilization **3849**
Equal Employment Opportunity Compliance and
Complaints Review Agency **3850**
Equal Opportunity Agency **3851**
Department of the Navy
Civil Personnel Policy/Equal Employment Opportunity
Office **3852**
Small and Disadvantaged Business Utilization
Office **3853**
Personnel and Readiness • Equal Opportunity
Office **3854**
U.S. Department of Education
Office of the Assistant Secretary for Civil Rights **3855**

U.S. Department of Education   (continued)
  Office of Assistant Secretary for Educational Research and Improvement • Eisenhower Regional Mathematics and Science Education Consortia **3954**
  Office of the Assistant Secretary for Elementary and Secondary Education
      Office of Indian Education **530**
      School Improvement Programs • Native Hawaiian Family-Based Education Centers **2531**
  Office of Assistant Secretary for Postsecondary Education
      Minority Science Improvement **3955**
      TRIO—Upward Bound **3956**
  Office of Elementary and Secondary Education,
      Alaska Native Educational Planning, Curriculum Development, Teacher Training, and Recruitment Program **2365**
      Alaska Native Home Based Education for Preschool Children (Alaska Native Education) **2366**
      Alaska Native Student Enrichment Program (Alaska Native Education) **2367**
      Desegregation Assistance, Civil Rights Training, and Advisory Service **3957**
      Indian Education —Grants to Local Educational Agencies **553, 2368**
      Magnet Schools Assistance in Desegregating Districts **3958**
      Native Hawaiian Community-Based Education Learning Center **2532**
      Native Hawaiian Curriculum Development, Teacher Training and Recruitment **2533**
      Native Hawaiian Gifted and Talented **2534**
  Office of Hearings and Appeals • Civil Rights Reviewing Authority **3856**
  Office of Postsecondary Education • Minority Teacher Recruitment **3959**
  Office of Special Education and Rehabilitative Services • Native Hawaiian Special Education **2535**
  Office of Vocational and Adult Education
      Native Hawaiian Vocational Education **2536**
      Vocational Education—Indian Setaside **554, 2537**
U.S. Department of Education - Office of Educational Research and Improvement (OERI) **4477**
U.S. Department of Energy
  Office of Economic Impact and Diversity
      Office of Civil Rights **3857**
      Office of Small and Disadvantaged Business Utilization **3858**
  Office of Minority Economic Impact • Management and Technical Assistance for Minority Business Enterprise **3960**
U.S. Department of Health and Human Services
  Administration on Aging • American Indian, Alaskan Native, & Native Hawaiian Programs • Special Programs for the Aging, Title VI—Part B Grants to Native Hawaiians **555, 2369, 2538**
  Administration for Children and Families
      Administration for Native Americans **531**
      EEO/Civil Rights and Special Initiatives Staff **3859**
      Tribal Work Grants (Grants for Indian Tribes that Received JOBS Funds) **556, 2370**
  Equal Employment Opportunity Programs Group **3860**
  Health Care Financing Administration • Equal Employment Opportunity Staff **3861**
  Health Resources and Services Administration
      Native Hawaiian Health Systems **2539**
      Scholarships for Health Professions Students from Disadvantaged Backgrounds **3961**
  Indian Health Service
      Health Management Development Program **557, 2371**
      Health Professions Preparatory Scholarship Program for Indians **558, 2372**
      Health Professions Scholarship Program **559, 2373**
      Indian Health Service Loan Repayment **560**
      Indian Health Service Research **561, 2374**
      Office of Planning, Evaluation, and Legislation • Division of Program Statistics **1051, 2146**
  Indian Health Services
      Health Professions Recruitment Program for Indians **562, 2375**

      Research and Demonstration Projects for Indian Health **563, 2376**
  National Institutes of Health
      Minority Access to Research Careers (MARC) **3962**
      Minority Biomedical Research Support **3963**
  Office for Civil Rights **3862**
  Office of the General Counsel
      Civil Rights Division **3863**
      Public Health Division • Office of the Indian Health Service Bureau Chief **532**
  Office of Public Health and Science
      Bureau of Primary Health Care • Office of Minority and Women's Health **3864**
      Food and Drug Administration • Industry and Small Business Liaison Staff **3865**
      Food and Drug Administration • Office of Equal Employment Opportunity and Civil Rights **3866**
      Health Resources and Services Administration • Office of Equal Opportunity and Civil Rights **3867**
      Indian Health Service **533**
      Indian Health Service • Office of Tribal Self-Governance **534**
      Indian Health Services • Office of Tribal Activities **535**
      National Cancer Institute • Equal Employment Opportunity Office **3868**
      National Institutes of Health • Minority Programs Office **3869**
      National Institutes of Health • Office of Equal Opportunity **3870**
      Office of Deputy Assistant Secretary for Minority Health **3871**
      Office of Minority Health **3872**
      Office of Minority Health • Family and Community Violence Prevention Program (Family Life Centers) **3964**
      Office of Minority Health • Minority Community Health Coalition Demonstration **3965**
      Research Grants Division • Employment Opportunity Specialist **3873**
  Office of the Secretary • Civil Rights Compliance Activities **3966**
  Office of Small and Disadvantaged Business Utilization **3874**
U.S. Department of Housing and Urban Development
  Assistant Secretary for Fair Housing and Equal Opportunity **3875**
      Equal Opportunity in Housing **3967**
      Fair Housing Assistance Program—State and Local **3968**
      Non-Discrimination in the Community Development Block Grant Program **3969**
      Non-Discrimination in Federally Assisted Programs **3970**
  Assistant Secretary for Public and Indian Housing Department
      Office of Native American Programs **536**
      Office of Public and Indian Housing Comptroller **537**
  Civil Rights and Litigation
      Office of Assisted Housing and Community Development **3876**
      Office of Litigation and Fair Housing Enforcement **3877**
      Office of Program Enforcement **3878**
  Office of Departmental Equal Employment Opportunity **3879**
  Office of Native American Programs • Public and Indian Housing • Public and Indian Housing - Indian Loan Guarantee Program (Loan Guarantees for Indian Housing) **3971**
  Office of Small and Disadvantaged Business Utilization **3880**
  Public and Indian Housing **564, 2377**
  Public and Indian Housing—Comprehensive Improvement Assistance Program **565**
U.S. Department of the Interior
  Board of Indian Appeals **538**
  Bureau of Indian Affairs
      Administrative Cost Grants for Indian Schools **3972**
      Agriculture on Indian Lands **3973**
      Aid to Tribal Governments **3974**

U.S. Department of the Interior (continued)

Alaskan Indian Allotments and Subsistence Preference - Alaska National Interest Lands Conservation Act 2378
Assistance for Indian Children with Severe Disabilities 3975
Assistance to Tribally Controlled Community Colleges and Universities 3976
Attorney Fees - Indian Rights 3977
Bureau of Indian Affairs Facilities - Operations and Maintenance 3978
Consolidated Tribal Government Program 3979
Construction and Repair of Indian Detention Facilities 3980
Endangered Species on Indian Lands 3981
Environmental Quality Services - Indian Programs 3982
Equal Employment Opportunity Staff 3881
Fish, Wildlife, and Parks Programs on Indian Lands 3983
Forestry on Indian Lands 3984
Higher Education Grant Program 566, 2379
Indian Adult Education 3985
Indian Child and Family Education (FACE) 3986
Indian Child Welfare Act—Title II Grants 567
Indian Community Fire Protection 3987
Indian Economic Development 3988
Indian Education—Assistance to Schools 568
Indian Education Facilities, Operations, and Maintenance • Office of Indian Education Programs 3989
Indian Employment Assistance 569
Indian Gaming Management Staff 539
Indian Graduate Student Scholarships (Special Higher Education Scholarships) 3990
Indian Housing Assistance 570
Indian Job Placement - United Sioux Tribes Development Corporation 3991
Indian Law Enforcement 3992
Indian Loans—Economic Development 571, 2380
Indian Post Secondary Schools (Haskell and SIPI) 3993
Indian Rights Protection 3994
Indian School Equalization Program (ISEP) 3995
Indian Schools - Student Transportation 3996
Indian Self-Determination Contract Support 3997
Indian Social Services—Child Welfare Assistance 572, 2381, 3998
Indian Social Services—General Assistance 573
Indian Vocational Training - United Tribes Technical College 3999
Irrigation Operations and Maintenance on Indian Lands • Office of Trust Responsibilities 4000
Litigation Support for Indian Rights 4001
Minerals and Mining on Indian Lands 4002
Navajo-Hopi Indian Settlement Program 574
Office of American Indian Trust 540
Office of Indian Education Programs 541
Office of Tribal Services 542
Office of Tribal Services • Tribal Government Services Division 1052
Office of Trust Responsibilities 543
Real Estate Programs - Indian Lands 2382, 4003
Replacement and Repair of Indian Schools 4004
Road Maintenance - Indian Roads 4005
Safety of Dams on Indian Lands 4006
Services to Indian Children, Elderly and Families 4007
Southwestern Indian Polytechnic Institute • Library 761
Structural Fire Protection - Bureau of Indian Affairs Facilities (Fire Protection) 4008
Tribal Courts 4009
Tribal Self-Governance 4010
Tribal Self-Governance Grants 4011
Tribally Controlled Community College Endowments 4012
Unresolved Indian Hunting and Fishing Rights 4013
Unresolved Indian Rights Issues 4014
Waste Management - Indian Lands 4015

Indian Arts and Crafts Board 762
Indian Arts and Crafts Development 575, 2383
Law Branch Library 763
Museum 876, 2411
National Park Service
Canyon De Chelly National Monument • Library 764
De Soto National Memorial • Library 765
Fort Laramie National Historic Site • Library 766
Fort Larned National Historic Site • Library 767
Glacier National Park • George C. Ruhle Library 768
Grand Portage National Monument • Library 769
Haleakala National Park • Library 2550
Hawaii Volcanoes National Park • Library 2551
Hopewell Culture National Historical Park 974
Hopewell Culture National Historical Park • Library 770
Intermountain Cultural Resource Center • Library 771
Jefferson National Expansion Memorial • Library and Archives 772
Little Bighorn Battlefield National Monument • White Swan Library 773
Natchez Trace Parkway • Library & Visitor Center 774
Navajo National Monument • Library 775
Ocmulgee National Monument Library 776
Olympic National Park • Visitor Center - Library 777
Pipestone National Monument • Library & Archives 778
Point Reyes National Seashore • Library 779
Pu'uhonua o Honaunau National Historical Park • Library 2552
Scotts Bluff National Monument • Library 780
Sitka National Historical Park • Library 781
Natural Resources Library 782
Office for Equal Opportunity 3882
Office of Small and Disadvantaged Business Utilization 3883
Office of the Solicitor • Indian Affairs Division 544
U.S. Department of Justice
Civil Rights Division
Criminal Section • Civil Rights Prosecution 4016
Desegregation of Public Education 4017
Educational Opportunities Section 3884
Employment Litigation Section 3885
Equal Employment Opportunity 4018
Fair Housing and Equal Credit Opportunity 4019
Housing and Civil Enforcement Section 3886
Office of Complaint Adjudication 3887
Protection of Voting Rights 4020
Special Litigation Section 3888
Voting Section 3889
Community Relations Service 4021
Drug Enforcement Agency • Equal Employment Opportunity Staff 3890
Environment and Natural Resources Branch Library 783
Federal Bureau of Investigation • Indian Country Investigations. 4022
Immigration and Naturalization Service • Office of Equal Employment Opportunity • Discrimination Complaints Branch 3891
Office of Justice Programs
American Indian and Alaska Native Program 545, 2362
Office for Civil Rights 3892
Violence Against Women Discretionary Grants for Indian Tribal Governments 4023
Office for Victims of Crime • Office of Justice Programs • Children's Justice Act for Native American Indian Tribes 576
U.S. Department of Labor
Civil Rights Center 3893
Employment Standards Administration • Non-Discrimination and Affirmative Action by Federal Contractors and Federally Assisted Construction Contractors 4024
Employment and Training Administration • Native American Employment and Training Programs 577, 2384, 2540
Office of Small Business and Minority Affairs 3894
Office of the Solicitor • Civil Rights Division 3895

Index

U.S. Department of State • Equal Employment Opportunity and Civil Rights Office **3896**
U.S. Department of Transportation
  Federal Aviation Administration • Office of the Assistant Administrator for Civil Rights **3897**
  Federal Highway Administration • Office of Civil Rights **3898**
  Federal Transit Administration • Office of Civil Rights **3899**
  National Highway Traffic Safety Administration • Office of Civil Rights **3900**
  Office of Civil Rights **3901**
  Office of Small and Disadvantaged Business Utilization **3902**
  Research and Special Programs Administration • Office of Civil Rights **3903**
  U.S. Coast Guard • Office of Civil Rights **3904**
U.S. Department of the Treasury
  Internal Revenue Service
    Equal Employment Opportunity and Diversity Division **3905**
    Equal Opportunity and Organizational Management Division **3906**
  Office of Small Business Programs **3907**
  U.S. Customs Service • Equal Opportunity Office **3908**
U.S. Department of Veterans Affairs
  Center for Minority Veterans **3909**
  Equal Employment Opportunity Office **3910**
  Office of Small and Disadvantaged Business Utilization **3911**
U.S. Environmental Protection Agency
  Office of Civil Rights **3912**
  Office of Small and Disadvantaged Business Utilization **3913**
U.S. Equal Employment Opportunity Commission **3914**
  Employment Discrimination - Equal Pay Act **4025**
  Employment Discrimination—Private Bar Program **4026**
  Employment Discrimination Project Contracts - Indian Tribes **4027**
  Employment Discrimination—State and Local Fair Practices Agency Contracts **4028**
  Employment Discrimination—Title VII of the Civil Rights Act of 1964 **4029**
U.S. Federal Communications Commission • Office of Workplace Diversity **3915**
U.S. Federal Deposit Insurance Corporation • Office of Equal Opportunity **3916**
U.S. Federal Maritime Commission • Office of Equal Employment Opportunity **3917**
U.S. General Accounting Office • Office of Affirmative Action/Civil Rights Office **3918**
U.S. General Services Administration
  Office of Equal Employment Opportunity **3919**
  Office of Small and Disadvantaged Business Utilization **3920**
U.S. Indian Arts and Crafts Board **546**
U.S. Information Agency • Office of Civil Rights **3921**
U.S. International Development Cooperation Agency
  Agency for International Development
    Office of Equal Employment Opportunity **3922**
    Office of Small and Disadvantaged Business Utilization • Minority Resource Center **3923**
U.S. Legal Services Corporation • Office of Administration, Human Resources and Equal Opportunity **3924**
U.S. Library of Congress • American Folklife Center **784**
U.S. Merit Systems Protection Board • Office of Equal Employment Opportunity **3925**
U.S. National Aeronautics and Space Administration
  Office of Equal Opportunity Programs
    Affirmative Employment and Diversity Policy Division **3926**
    Discrimination Complaints Division **3927**
    Minority University Research and Education Division **3928**
U.S. National Archives and Records Administration
  National Archives - Pacific Region **4290**
  National Archives - Southwest Region **4291**
  Still Picture Branch **4292**
U.S. National Indian Gaming Commission **547**

U.S. National Science Foundation
  Design, Manufacture and Industrial Innovation Division
    Office of Small Business Research and Development • Office of Small and Disadvantaged Business Utilization **3929**
    Small Business Innovation Research Programs **3930**
    Small Business Technology Transfer Program **3931**
  Directorate for Education and Human Resources •
    Graduate Education Division • Graduate and Minority Graduate Fellowships Programs **3932**
  Human Resource Development Division • Alliance for Minority Participation Program **3933**
  Office of Equal Opportunity **3934**
U.S. Nuclear Regulatory Commission • Office of Small Business/Civil Rights **3935**
U.S. Office of Personnel Management • Office of Human Resources and Equal Employment Opportunity • Equal Employment Opportunity Division **3936**
U.S. Peace Corps
  American Diversity Program **3937**
  Volunteer Recruitment and Selection • Minority Recruitment **3938**
U.S. Postal Service • Diversity Development Office **3939**
U.S. Small Business Administration
  Business Loans for 8(A) Program Participants **4030**
  Management and Technical Assistance for Socially and Economically Disadvantaged Businesses (7(J) Development Assistant Program) **4031**
  Microloan Demonstration Program **4032**
  Minority Business Development (Section 8(a) Program) **4033**
  Office of Equal Employment Opportunity and Civil Rights Compliance **3940**
  Office of Minority Enterprise Development **3941**
  Office of Minority Small Business and Capital Ownership Development • Management and Technical Assistance for Socially and Economically Disadvantaged Business **4034**
  Office of Native American Affairs **548**
  Office of Small Business Development Centers **3942**
U.S. Smithsonian Institution
  Center for Museum Studies • American Indian Museum Studies Program **549**
  Museum of the American Indian **959, 2413**
  National Anthropological Archives **785**
  National Museum of American History • Cultural History Division • American Indian Program **877**
  National Museum of the American Indian **1581, 2449**
    Research Branch • Cultural Resources Department **1053, 2417**
  Office of Equal Employment and Minority Affairs **3943**
U.S. Social Security Administration • Office of Civil Rights and Equal Opportunity **3944**
United Traditional Indian Council of Arizona **439**
United Tribes Technical College **1334**
United Tribes Technical College; Indian Vocational Training - • U.S. Department of the Interior • Bureau of Indian Affairs **3999**
Unity Network **3509**
Universities; Assistance to Tribally Controlled Community Colleges and • U.S. Department of the Interior • Bureau of Indian Affairs **3976**
University of Alaska, Anchorage • Institute for Circumpolar Health Studies **2418, 2612**
University of Alaska, Fairbanks
  Alaska Native Language Center **2419**
    Research Library **2392**
  Alaska Native Studies, Inupiaq Eskimo Studies, and Yupik Eskimo Studies Programs **2429**
  Alaska and Polar Regions Department **2393**
  Alaskan Native Studies Program **2430**
University at Albany, State University of New York • Institute for Archaeological Studies **1054**
University of Arizona
  Arizona State Museum **1055**
  College of Arts and Sciences • American Indian Studies Program **1405**
  College of Law Library **786**
  Native American Research and Training Center **1056**
University of Arizona Press • University of Arizona **1582**

University of California, Berkeley
    Ethnic Studies Graduate Program **1406**
    Ethnic Studies Library **787**
    Native American Studies Program **1386**
University of California, Davis
    Michael and Margaret B. Harrison Western Research
        Center **1057**
    Native American Studies Program **1387**
    Western Research Center **788**
University of California, Los Angeles
    American Indian Studies Center **1058, 1583**
        Library **789**
    College of Letters and Science • American Indian Studies
        Program **1407**
    Department of Art History • Visual Resource Collection &
        Services **790**
University of Cincinnati • Archives and Rare Books
    Department **791**
University College of Cape Breton **3251**
    Beaton Institute **3243**
University of Colorado • National Center for American Indian
    and Alaska Native Mental Health Research **1060, 2420**
University of Colorado at Boulder
    Center for Studies of Ethnicity and Race in
        America **4299**
    Center for the Study of Native Languages of the Plains
        and Southwest **1059**
University of Florida • Samuel Proctor Oral History Program •
    Library **792**
University of Guelph • Institute for Environmental Policy **4300**
University of Hawaii
    Special Collections
        Archives and Manuscripts **2553**
        Hawaiian Collection **2554**
University of Hawaii at Hilo • Hawaiian Studies Program **2581**
University of Hawaii at Honolulu • School of Public Health •
    American Indian and Alaska Native Support Program **1408,
    2431**
University of Hawaii at Manoa • Hawaiian Studies
    Program **2582**
University of Hawaii Press • University of Hawaii **2600**
University of Idaho Press **1584**
The University of Iowa **1388**
University of Lethbridge • Native Studies Program **3252**
University of Maryland at College Park • Casey Journalism
    Center for Children and Families **4301**
University of Massachusetts • Horace Mann Bond Center for
    Equal Education **4396**
University of Miami • Lowe Art Museum **882**
University of Minnesota • Law Library **793**
University of Minnesota, Twin Cities Campus • Native American
    Studies Program **1389**
University of Missouri—Kansas City • Snyder Collection of
    Americana **794**
University of Montana • School of Law • Law Library **795**
University of Montana Occasional Papers in Linguistics **1585**
University of Nebraska—Lincoln
    Great Plains Art Collection **796**
    Native American Studies Program **1390**
University of New Brunswick • Micmac-Maliseet Institute **3283**
University of New Mexico
    Bainbridge Bunting Memorial Slide Library **797**
    Center for Southwest Research **798**
    Institute for Native American Development **1586**
    New Mexico Tumor Registry **1061**
    School of Law • Library **799**
University of North Carolina at Chapel Hill • Kathrine R.
    Everett Law Library **800**
University of North Carolina at Pembroke • Native American
    Resource Center **1062**
University of North Dakota
    Indian Studies Department **1391**
    School of Medicine • Indians into Medicine Program **1409**
    UND Center for Rural Health **1063**
University of Oklahoma **1392**
    Law Library **801**
    Western History Collections **802**
University of Oklahoma Press • University of Oklahoma **1587**
University of the Pacific • Holt-Atherton Department of Special
    Collections **803**

University of Pennsylvania • The University Museum of
    Archaeology/Anthropology • Museum Library **804**
University of Regina
    Interdisciplinary Studies Program **3257**
    Native Studies Program **3253**
University of Rochester • Government Documents and
    Microtext Center **805**
University of Saskatchewan
    Native Law Centre **3244**
    Native Studies Department **3254**
University of Science and Arts of Oklahoma • Native American
    Studies Program **1393**
University of South Dakota
    Governmental Research Library **806**
    I.D. Weeks Library • Special Collections Department **807**
    Institute of American Indian Studies **1064**
    McKusick Law Library **808**
    Social Science Research Institute **1065**
    W.H. Over State Museum **1066**
University of South Dakota—Bulletin **1689**
University of South Dakota Press • University of South
    Dakota **1588**
University of Tennessee at Knoxville • University Archives and
    Special Collections **809**
University of Toronto • Native Studies Program **3255**
University of Tulsa
    College of Law • Library **810**
    McFarlin Library • Special Collections **811**
University of Utah
    American West Center **1067**
    Special Collections Department **812**
University of Washington • Native American Studies
    Program **1394**
University of Western Ontario • Centre for Research and
    Teaching of Canadian Native Languages **3245**
University of Wisconsin, Milwaukee **1395**
University of Wyoming • Anthropology Museum **1017**
Unresolved Indian Hunting and Fishing Rights • U.S.
    Department of the Interior • Bureau of Indian Affairs **4013**
Unresolved Indian Rights Issues • U.S. Department of the
    Interior • Bureau of Indian Affairs **4014**
Upper Lake Rancheria **106**
Upper Nicola Indian Band **2772**
Upper Similkameen Indian Band **2745**
Upper Sioux Community **180**
Upper Skagit Tribe **342**
Upstate New York Regional Minority **3715**
Urban Ethnic Affairs; National Center for **4386**
Urban Indian Council; National **3472**
Urban Indians **2102**
Urban League of the Albany Area **3710**
Urban League of Arkansas **3525**
Urban League; Atlanta **3609**
Urban League; Austin Area **3792**
Urban League; Baltimore **3657**
Urban League; Bay Area **3544**
Urban League; Birmingham **3513**
Urban League of Broward County **3590**
Urban League; Buffalo **3714**
Urban League of Champaign County **3621**
Urban League; Charlotte-Mecklenburg **3742**
Urban League; Chicago **3625**
Urban League; Columbia **3781**
Urban League; Columbus **3612, 3755**
Urban League; Dallas **3800**
Urban League; Dayton **3756**
Urban League; Detroit **3670**
Urban League of Eastern Massachusetts **3664**
Urban League; Essex County **3707**
Urban League Executives; Council of **3669**
Urban League of Flint Housing Center **3674**
Urban League; Ft. Wayne **3630**
Urban League; Grand Rapids **3675**
Urban League of Greater Chattanooga **3785**
Urban League of Greater Cincinnati **3752**
Urban League of Greater Cleveland **3753**
Urban League of Greater Jackson **3689**
Urban League; Greater Lansing **3676**
Urban League of Greater Madison **3823**
Urban League of Greater Miami **3594**
Urban League of Greater Muskegon **3677**

Urban League of Greater New Haven 3576
Urban League of Greater New Orleans 3652
Urban League of Greater Oklahoma City 3767
Urban League of Greater Richmond 3813
Urban League; Greater Riverside Area 3549
Urban League of Hampton Roads 3810
Urban League; Houston Area 3803
Urban League; Indianapolis 3634
Urban League of Kansas City 3693
Urban League; Knoxville Area 3786
Urban League of Lancaster County 3772
Urban League of Lexington-Fayette County 3646
Urban League of Long Island 3717
Urban League; Lorain County 3757
Urban League; Louisville 3648
Urban League; Madison County 3619
Urban League; Marion Area 3635
Urban League; Metro Columbus 3613
Urban League of Metropolitan Denver 3570
Urban League; Metropolitan Orlando 3596
Urban League of Metropolitan St. Louis 3696
Urban League of Metropolitan Seattle 3819
Urban League; Milwaukee 3826
Urban League; Nashville 3789
Urban League of Nebraska 3700
Urban League of Onondaga County 3737
Urban League; Orange County 3530
Urban League of Palm Beach County 3603, 3604
Urban League of the Pikes Peak Region 3564
Urban League; Pinellas County 3597
Urban League; Pontiac Area 3678
Urban League; Quad County 3620
Urban League of Racine and Kenosha 3829
Urban League of Rhode Island 3779
Urban League of Rochester 3735
Urban League; Sacramento 3551
Urban League; San Diego 3553
Urban League; Santa Clara Valley 3558
Urban League; Seattle 3818
Urban League of South Bend and St. Joseph County 3636
Urban League of Southwestern Connecticut 3577
Urban League; Tacoma 3820
Urban League; Tallahassee 3598
Urban League; Tri-County 3628
Urban League; Tucson 3523
Urban League of the Upstate, Inc. 3782
Urban League; Washington 3585
Urban League; Wichita 3643
Urban League; Winston-Salem 3748
Urban League; Youngstown Area 3763
USET Scholarships 1453
Utah Community and Economic Development Department •
  Indian Affairs Division 598
Utah History • Information Center 813
Utah Industrial Commission • Anti-Discrimination Division 4259
Utah; Paiute Indian Tribe of 321
Ute Indian Cultural Center; Southern 448, 869
Ute Indian Museum 870
Ute Indian Tribe • Head Start Program 1139
Ute Mountain Tribal Library and Archive 814
Ute Mountain Tribal Park 871
Ute Mountain Ute 139
Ute Mountain Ute Tribe • Head Start Program 1078
Ute Tribe; Southern 138
Ute Tribe; Ute Mountain • Head Start Program 1078
Ute; Ute Mountain 139
UUACTION Alert Legislative Network 4451
Vacation Guide; Montana 4414
Vacation Guide; New Mexico 4418
Van Pelt Special Fund for Indian Scholarships; Adolph 1410
Vaughan Library/LRC; John • Special Collections and Archives
  • Northeastern Oklahoma State University 714
Venetie; Native Village of 2342
Vermont Human Services Agency • Economic Opportunity
  Office 4260
Veterans for Human Rights of Greater New York 3731
Video Arts; Film/ 3396
Viejas Tribe 25
Viger; Malecites of 3074
Village of Alakanuk 2151
Village of Anaktuvuk Pass 2156

Village of Aniak 2161
Village of Atmautluak 2165
Village of Chefornak 2175
Village of Clark's Point 2186
Village of Eagle 2194
Village of Kalskag 2228
Village of Kaltag 2229
Village of Kanatak 2158
Village of Kotlik 2250
Village of Lower Kalskag 2258
Village of Old Harbor 2286
Village of Red Devil 2303
Village of Sleetmute 2318
Village of Stoney River 2326
Village of Wainwright 2343
Vine Deloria, Jr.; A Conversation with 1788
Violence Against Women Discretionary Grants for Indian Tribal
  Governments • U.S. Department of Justice • Office of Justice
  Programs 4023
Violence and Extremism; Institute for Prevention and Control
  of 3498
violence; The Prejudice Institute/ Center for the Applied Study
  of Ethno 3498
Violence Prevention Program (Family Life Centers); Family and
  Community • U.S. Department of Health and Human Services
  • Office of Public Health and Science • Office of Minority
  Health 3964
Virgin Islands Minority Business Development Center 4261
Virginia Commerce and Trade Office • Employment
  Commission • Equal Employment Office 4265
Virginia Health and Human Resources Office • Public Health
  Programs • Minority Health Office 4266
Virginia Human Rights Council 4267
Virginia Minority Business Enterprises Department 4268
Virginia Regional Minority Supplier Development Council 3814
Virginia Transportation Office • Administration Department •
  Equal Employment Opportunity Division 4269
Visual Arts; Association for Native Development in the
  Performing and 3171
Visual Arts; Directory of People of Color in the 4404
Vocational Education; Native Hawaiian • U.S. Department of
  Education • Office of Vocational and Adult Education 2536
Vocational Training; Hopi Tribe Adult 1428
Vocational Training - United Tribes Technical College; Indian •
  U.S. Department of the Interior • Bureau of Indian
  Affairs 3999
Voices for Human Rights; Latah-Nez Perce 457
Voter Registration Education Project; Southwest 3503
Voting Section • U.S. Department of Justice • Civil Rights
  Division 3889
Vowell Indian Band; Glen 2733
Vuntut Gwitch'in First Nation 3170
W. K. Kellogg Foundation Fellowships in Community
  Medicine 4350
Wabasseemoong Independent Nation (Islington) 3043
Wabauskang First Nation 2949
Wabigoon Lake First Nation 2947
Wahgoshig First Nation 2981
Wahnapitae First Nation 2934
Wahpeton Dakota Nation 3147
Wahpeton Indian Boarding School 1271
Wahpeton Sioux Tribe; Sisseton- 315
Wahta Mohawks 2924
Waiau Elementary School 2580
Wainwright; Village of 2343
The Wake 2103
Wales; Native Village of 2344
Walk Across America and Europe 3398
Walker River Paiute Tribe 218
Walker Wildlife and Indian Artifacts Museum 920
Walking with Grandfather 2104
Walking in a Sacred Manner 2105
Walnut Canyon National Monument 853
Walpole Island; Ojibways of 3038
Walter P. Stewart Consultant Ltd. 3264
Wampanoag Tribe of Gay Head 165
Wampanoag Tribe; Mashpee 166
Wapekeka First Nation 2921
War Dead Memorial; Native American 528
War Lake First Nation 2872
Ward Hill Press 4397

Warm Springs Reservation; Confederated Tribes of the **303**
Head Start Program **1132**
Warpaint and Wigs **2106**
Warriors **2107**
Wars—Communique; Order of the Indian **1677**
Wasagamack First Nation **2905**
Wasauksing First Nation **3000**
WASG-AM **1709**
Washagamis Bay First Nation **2970**
Washington Human Rights Commission **4272**
Washington Minority Business Development Center **4066**
Washington State Capital Museum • Library and Photo
Archives **815**
Washington State Student Financial Aid Programs American
Indian Endowed Scholarship **1454**
Washington State University **1396**
Native American Studies Program **1397**
Washington State University Press • Washington State
University **4398**
Washington Urban League **3585**
Washoe County Law Library **816**
Waskaganish Band **3090**
Waskaganish; Cree Nation of **3089**
Waste Management - Indian Lands • U.S. Department of the
Interior • Bureau of Indian Affairs **4015**
Waste Management Library; Environmental Restoration/ •
Yakama Indian Nation **825**
Waswanipi; Cree Nation of **3091**
Waswanipi First Nation **3092**
Water Is So Clear That a Blind Man Could See **2108**
Waterhen First Nation **2896**
Waterhen Lake First Nation **3162**
Watkinson Library • Trinity College **760**
Watson and Dwyer Publishing Ltd. **3284**
Wauzhushk Onigum First Nation (Rat Portage) **2971**
Wawatay News **3308**
Way of Our Fathers **2109**
Waywayseecappo First Nation Treaty Four **2906**
We Are One: A Series **2110**
We Are a River Flowing **2111**
(We Someone, The Hopi); Itam Hakim Hopiit **1902**
A Weave of Time **2112**
Weaving; The Art of Navajo **1748**
The WEB **1690**
Webber Resource Center: Native Cultures of the Americas •
Field Museum **642**
Webequi First Nation **3041**
The Wedding of Palo **2516**
Weeks Library; I.D. • Special Collections Department •
University of South Dakota **807**
Wellbeing; Bendheim-Thomas Center for Child • Princeton
University • Woodrow Wilson School of Public and
International Affairs **4298**
Wellesley College • Margaret Clapp Library • Special
Collections **817**
Wells Band of the Te-Moak Tribe of Western Shoshone
Indians **219**
Wemindji; Cree Nation of **3093**
Wemindji First Nation **3094**
Wendat First Nation; Huronne- **3088**
Werner Publications **1589**
Wesakachak; Tales of **3344**
(Wesley); Stoney Tribal Administration First Nation **2649**
West Bay First Nation **3042**
West Center; American • University of Utah **1067**
West; Institute of the Northamerican **3417**
West Moberly Indian Band **2775**
West Palm Beach Minority Business Development
Center **4074**
West Virginia Human Rights Commission **3822, 4273**
West Virginia Minority and Small Business Development
Agency **4274**
Westbank Indian Band **2660**
Westchester County Department of Parks, Recreation and
Conservation • Trailside Nature Museum **818**
Western Art; Eiteljorg Museum of American Indian and **897**
Western Carolina University • Hunter Library • Special
Collections **819**
Western History Collections • University of Oklahoma **802**
Western Research Center; Michael and Margaret B. Harrison •
University of California, Davis **1057**

Western Studies; Center for • Augustana College **610, 1482**
Westernlore Press **1590**
Westside Fair Housing Council **3539**
Weymontachie First Nation **3095**
W.H. Over State Museum • University of South Dakota **1066**
Whapmagoostui; Cree Nation of **3096**
Whapmagoostui First Nation **3097**
What Color Is Skin **4471**
What Is an American, Part 2 **2113**
Wheelwright Museum of the American Indian **947**
Mary Cabot Wheelwright Research Library **820**
Wheelwright Research Library; Mary Cabot • Wheelwright
Museum of the American Indian **820**
Where the Buffaloes Begin **2114**
Whispering Pines Indian Band **2743**
Whispering Wind **1641**
Whispering Wind Magazine **1591**
White Apache **2115**
White Bear First Nation **3109**
White Deerskin Dance; Hupa Indian **1870**
White Earth Band of Chippewa • Head Start Program **1092**
White Earth (Chippewa) **187**
White Horse Day School **1299**
White Justice **3346**
White Man's Image; In the **1878**
White Man's Way **2116**
White Mountain Apache Tribe **20**
Head Start Program **1075**
White Mountain Archaeological Center **854**
White Mountain; Native Village of **2346**
White River First Nation First Nation **3167**
White Roots of Peace **3399**
White Shield School **1272**
White Swan Library • U.S. Department of the Interior •
National Park Service • Little Bighorn Battlefield National
Monument **773**
Whitecap Dakota/Sioux First Nation (Moose Woods) **3153**
Whitefish Bay First Nation **3001**
Whitefish Lake First Nation **2992**
Whitefish Lake First Nation (Atikameg) **2614**
Whitefish Lake First Nation (Goodfish) **2633**
Whitefish River First Nation **2929**
Whitesand First Nation **2922**
Whitman College • Myron Eells Library of Northwest
History **821**
Who Discovered America **2117**
Who's Who in Indian Relics **1628**
Wichita State University **1398**
Wichita Tribe **264**
Wichita Urban League **3643**
Wide Ruins Boarding School **1201**
Wikweminkong Unceded First Nation **3045**
Wildlife Commission; Great Lakes Indian Fish and **3405**
Wildlife Committee; Great Lakes Indian, Fish and **3827**
Wildlife and Indian Artifacts Museum; Walker **920**
Wildlife, and Parks Programs on Indian Lands; Fish, • U.S.
Department of the Interior • Bureau of Indian Affairs **3983**
Will Rogers Library **822**
William and Charlotte Cadbury Award and Franklin C. McClean
Award **4351**
William J. Mellor Collection **717**
William and Mary Ashby Day Care Center **3707**
Williams Lake Indian Band **2841**
Williamsburg/Brooklyn Minority Business Development
Center **3713, 4185**
Wilson School of Public and International Affairs; Woodrow •
Bendheim-Thomas Center for Child Wellbeing • Princeton
University **4298**
Wingate High School **1259**
Winnebago Business Committee; Wisconsin • Head Start
Program **1158**
Winnebago Indians; The History and Problems of **1854**
Winnebago; Minorities in Agriculture: The **1935**
(Winnebago); Nebraska Indian Community College **1326**
Winnebago Tribe **200**
Winnebago Tribe of Nebraska • Head Start Program **1101**
Winnemucca Colony **122**
Winnipeg Art Gallery **3285**
Winston-Salem Urban League **3748**
Winter on an Indian Reservation **2118**
Winterville Indian Mounds **922**

Wisconsin Health and Social Services Department • Affirmative Action and Civil Rights Office **4276**
Wisconsin; Menominee Indian Tribe of **359**
Wisconsin Winnebago Business Committee • Head Start Program **1158**
Witchekan Lake First Nation **3157**
Wizard Publications **2601**
Wolinak First Nation **3048**
Women of All Red Nations 395, **3511**
Women of All Red Nations; Dakota **395**
Women Alliance; Austin Minority/ **3793**
Women; AT & T Bell Laboratories Summer Research Program for Minorities and **4309**
Women Business Enterprises Office; Minority and • Economic Development Department; Boston **4115**
Women in Business; National Association of Minority **3455**
Women for Business and Political Development; Alliance of Minority **3354**
Women; Club of Indian **458**
Women of Color; National Institute for **3465**
Women Discretionary Grants for Indian Tribal Governments; Violence Against • U.S. Department of Justice • Office of Justice Programs **4023**
Women Health Education Resource Center; Native American 3474
Women for Human Rights and Dignity Development Corp. **3716**
Women; Panel of American **3494**
(Women for Racial and Economic Equality); WREE **4400**
Women Within Two Cultures **3347**
Women's Association; North American Indian **3489**
Women's Economic Alternatives; Center for **3740**
Women's Network; Indigenous **3414**
Wonder View Press **2602**
Wood Mountain First Nation **3165**
Woodard Award; M. L. 1468
Wooden Box: Made by Steaming and Bending **2119**
Woodenlegs Memorial Library; Dr. John • Dull Knife Memorial College **638**
Woodfords Community Council **90**
Woodland Cree First Nation **2618**
Woodland Indian Cultural Education Centre **3228**
Woodland Indians of Early America **2120**
Woodlands Before the White Man Came; Had You Lived Then: Life in the **1845**
Woodrow Wilson School of Public and International Affairs • Bendheim-Thomas Center for Child Wellbeing • Princeton University **4298**
Woods People Intertribal Native American Village **469**
Woolaroc Museum • Library • Phillips Foundation, Inc.; The Frank **648**
Woonspe (Education and the Sioux) **2121**
Worcester Minority Business Council **3666**
Workers of New Jersey; Minority Contractors and Coalition of Trade **3704**
World Citizens **4399**
World Emergency Relief **3512**
World Eskimo Art **2517**
World Eskimo-Indian Olympics **2354**
World in Our Eyes **2122**
Worthington Human Relations Council **3762**
The Wounded Knee Affair **2123**
Wounded Knee School District **1300**
Wrangell Cooperative Association **2347**
Wrangell Museum **2409**
WREE (Women for Racial and Economic Equality) **4400**
Writers; Freedom 3362
WRN-FM **3312**
Wunnumin Lake First Nation **3046**
Wupatki National Monument **855**
Wuskwi Sipihk First Nation **2849**
Wyandotte **294**
Wyandotte County Historical Society and Museum • Harry M. Trowbridge Research Library **823**
Wyoming State Library **824**
Yakama Indian Nation • Environmental Restoration/Waste Management Library **825**
Yakama Nation Library **826**
Yakima Nation Cultural Center **1013**
Yakima Tribe **350**
  Head Start Program **1152**

Yakima Valley Museum and Historical Association • Archives **827**
Yakima Valley Regional Library • Reference Department • Click Relander Collection **828**
Yakutat; Native Village of **2348**
Yakweakwioose Indian Band **2813**
Yale First Nation **2738**
Yale University Press 4376
Yankton Sioux Tribe **312**
Yaqui Tribal Council; Pascua • Head Start Program **1072**
Yaqui Tribe; Pascua **19**
Yavapai-Apache; Camp Verde **2**
Yavapai-Apache Community Council **3**
Yavapai-Apache Visitor Activity Center **856**
Yavapai-Prescott Tribal Library **829**
Yavapai-Prescott Tribe **11**
Yelland; CLA Scholarship for Minority Students in Memory of Edna **4312**
Yellowquill First Nation **3166**
Yerington Paiute Tribe **221**
Yesterday, Today: The Netsilik Eskimo **2518**
Yokotch of Mariposa; Chukchansi **89**
Yomba Shoshone Tribe **201**
Yonkers Minority Business Association **3739**
York Factory First Nation **2907**
You Are on Indian Land **2124, 3348**
You Can't Grow Potatoes Up There! **2519**
Young Memorial Scholarships; Jimmy A. **4327**
Youngstown Area Urban League **3763**
Youth AIDS Prevention Project (YAPP) 3707
Youth of America; Indian **398**
Youth Council; National Indian **418**
Youth at Risk; National Consortium on Alternatives for **3460**
Youth; Running Strong for American Indian **424**
Youth; United National Indian Tribal **3509**
Ysleta del Sur Pueblo **319**
Yuchi Indian Tribe 1469
Yuchi Tribal Organization 1469
Yukon Human Rights Commission **3945**
Yukon Human Rights Panel of Adjudicators **3946**
Yukon Indians; Council for **3267**
Yukon Territory Office of Aboriginal Language Services **3191**
Yurok Tribe **59**
Zia Day School **1260**
Zia Pueblo **238**
Zuni Cultural Arts Council **491**
Zuni Heritage and Historic Preservation Office **948**
  Library **830**
Zuni Higher Education Scholarships **1455**
Zuni Pueblo **245**
Zuni Pueblos • Head Start Program **1113**